Vancouver

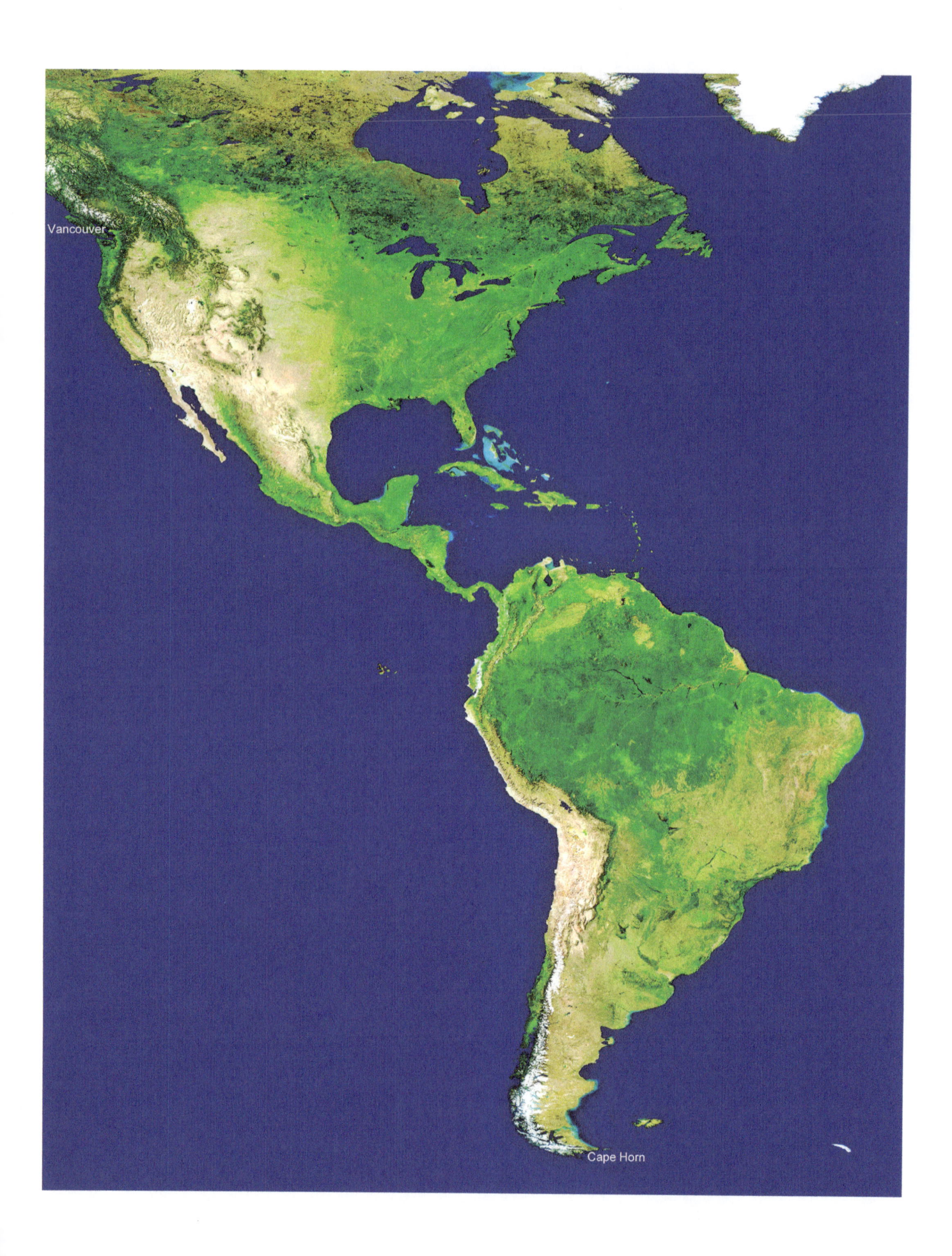

Cape Horn

SEQUITUR

to Cape Horn in Comfort and Style

Michael Walsh

SEQUITUR
to Cape Horn in Comfort and Style

Copyright © 2013 by Michael Walsh

Cover by: Edi Gelin & Michael Walsh

All rights reserved. No part of this book may be reproduced in any form by any electronic or mechanical means including photocopying, recording, or information storage and retrieval without permission in writing from the author.

ISBN: 978-0-9919556-0-2

Published by Zonder Zorg Press

www.zonderzorg.ca
michael@zonderzorg.ca

Printed in the United States of America
on Sustainable Forestry Initiative® (SFI®) Certified Sourcing papers.

Table of Contents

1. Beginnings: Dreams into Reality	7
2. Shakedown Cruise	14
3. Moving Aboard - Final Preparations	21
4. Heading South From Vancouver	24
5. Enjoying the Sea of Cortez	33
6. The Mainland Coast of the Sea of Cortez	71
7. To Isla Isabel	91
8. Along the Mexican Riviera	106
9. To the Galapagos	145
10. Passage to Peru	168
11. Limping to Lima	178
12. Back to Vancouver for a Break	187
13. Return to Peru	193
14. A Visit to Machu Picchu	234
15. Preparing to Leave Peru	273
16. Southward to Chile	281
17. To Arequipa, Titicaca and La Paz	301
18. Southward From Iquique	326
19. Passage to Valparaiso	340
20. Tsunamis Past and Present	374
21. To Valdivia for Repairs	403
22. Back in Vancouver Again	445
23. Return to Puerto Montt	451
24. To Isla Chiloe	477
25. Across Boca del Guafo	488
26. Across the Dreaded Golfo de Penas	506
27. Southward into the Furious Fifties	523
28. Magellan Straits to Tierra del Fuego	537
29. Onward to Puerto Williams	548
30. Repair to Papers and Equipment	565
31. To Cape Horn	582
32. To the Falklands	594
33. North From the Falklands	608
34. The South Coast of Brazil	616
35. The Long Brazilian Coast	625
36. Escape From Brazil	642
37. Through the Caribbean	649
38. Refit and Reorganization	669

This book is dedicated to Edi, without whom most of the superb adventures described herein would not have happened.

> Not all those who wander are lost.
> - *J.R.R. Tolkien*

> When you come to a fork in the road, take it.
> - *Yogi Berra*

> Two roads diverged in a wood, and I,
> I took the one less traveled by
> - *Robert Frost*

> Because it's there.
> - *George Mallory*

> Voyaging belongs to seamen,
> and to the wanderers of the world who cannot, or will not, fit in.
> - *Sterling Hayden*

Photo Acknowledgements:
The vast majority of the illustrations in this book are edited from the nearly 300,000 photos that Edi and I shot along the way. A few of the photos are of selected pages from published guidebooks, and their sources are given in the accompanying text. The maps have been edited from ones found on the internet, mostly in Wikimedia Commons, where they are listed as being in the public domain.

1. Beginnings: Dreams into Reality

This story has roots that extend back into the mid-1960s while I was messing about in my first sailboat. I was in the Royal Canadian Air Force at the time and was serving with Search and Rescue in Comox, on Vancouver Island. For twenty-five dollars I had bought a somewhat derelict 16-foot cedar lapstrake rowboat with a rotten transom.

Over the winter I had removed the rot and, based loosely on pictures in books from the local library, I converted the remains into a 14-foot leeboard yawl with canvas sails on lumberyard spars and fittings and rigging from the hardware store. With an arch-supported canvas cover over the forepeak, a food sack and a sleeping bag, I explored along the coast and up through Desolation Sound. I dreamed of someday sailing over the horizon to even wilder places. I dreamed of Patagonia and Cape Horn.

However, before I realized those dreams, the spectacular mountains on both sides of the Strait of Georgia distracted me from sailing. My spirit of adventure was instead quenched by exploratory and expeditionary mountaineering. Over the next fifteen years my exploratory urges were to take me to hundreds of summits, including over six dozen first-ascents on four continents. I spent some time seconded from the Air Force to the National Ski Team training in biathlon for the Grenoble Olympics. I didn't make the cut and went back to Comox, from where I was soon posted to France. I discovered wine and fine dining.

The after-effects from a 1967 broken neck caused me to lose some of the fine control in my arms and hands, and this ended my flying career. I transferred to the Royal Canadian Navy, trained as a Bridge Watchkeeping Officer and was granted a Certificate of Service as Master. I served in a variety of ships, including four of the old steam destroyers on Canada's west coast. Among my many voyages were six Pacific and six equator crossings. My last few years in the Navy were spent in the training system, including designing and implementing leadership programs for junior officers.

In 1981 I resigned my commission and moved to Vancouver, where I bought a 48-foot ketch, moved aboard and began slowly preparing to sail off over the horizon. To feed both me and the fit-out, I established myself in the wine industry, initially as a consultant. I met a woman and we married. I became a wine and food writer and a wine educator and then expanded into wine importing.

During this time, I also rekindled my boyhood hobby of coin collecting and developed my interest into an extremely successful one-man company.

Fast-forward through a number of boats to the end of April 2006, when I realized that a quarter century had passed since my retirement from the Navy and that I still wanted to sail off over the edge of the earth. I told my wife I wanted to sell the canal boat in France, sell the motor yacht in Vancouver and buy another sailboat. I wanted to sail off before I became too old to do so.

She had never been comfortable sailing too far from land, she still wasn't and she didn't want to go. We talked seriously, then we drew-up a friendly separation agreement. (An uncontested divorce was later granted.) While we searched for a house for her to buy, I began researching sailboats.

My initial research followed the old mindset of buying and refitting a used boat that was on the traditionalists' list of *"suitable offshore sailboats"*. I had been through this search process several times over the years. Looking back at the previous occasions I realized that as the searches had continued, I had gradually lowered my expectations and slowly accepted more compromises. The process seems to have been:
- search until I find an acceptable set of compromises;
- ignore or underestimate the boat's shortcomings;
- make the purchase; and
- spend great gobs of time repairing and modifying.

This time though, the more I looked, the more I realized the folly of accepting old design concepts, such as long overhangs, weak bows and sterns, tiny cockpits and cramped accommodations, which seemed to me to have evolved primarily from the limitations of bending wood. Many of the shapes imposed by wooden boatbuilding had been carried forward into fibreglass construction, and half a century later, boats that still have these limitations are considered *"suitable offshore sailboats"*

Tired of old, I began thinking of buying a new boat. After months of analyzing the broad variety of new boats, I finally settled on a cutter-rigged sloop with a hollow-cheeked, rather plumb bow, a broad, squat stern with an open transom, a fin keel and a balanced spade rudder. This new boat with its very long relative waterline length and huge cockpit seems to be the antithesis of the old ideas of offshore boats with their long overhangs, weak sterns, tiny cockpits and full keels with barn-door rudders.

The boat I chose, the Hunter 49 is the culmination of Glenn Henderson's eight-year redesign of the entire Hunter keelboat fleet. The 49 had been designed primarily for offshore passage-making and even at 15 metres length, it is easily single-handed.

The construction is solid fibreglass below the waterline, with balsa cored topsides and a cored deck. From the keel root forward, there are layers of Kevlar in the lay-up to add to the hull's strength. An interior fibreglass grid bonded to the hull provides further strength. There are broad, deep bilges with ample room to keep the machinery, the tanks and the batteries below waterline, while still providing a few cubic metres of stowage space for such heavy items as tools and spares beneath the cabin soles. All of this low weight contributes significantly to the stability provided by the 5,087 kilogram external lead keel and the 2.13 metre draft.

The prototype had been put through abusive sea trial testing by Steve Pettengill, who with his ocean racing records and Around-the-World Race experience is well qualified. He sea-trials all the new Hunter designs, repeatedly crashing the boats into stone jetties, and at full speed and under full sail in strong winds, he sails them up onto sandy beaches. He then spends weeks offshore in the nastiest conditions he can find to assess livability and to try to break things. The thinking is that if the new design can withstand Pettengill's abuse, it will likely handle a loving owner's occasional bumbling and also the odd nasty that Mother Nature can serve-up. If the boat doesn't take kindly to Pettengill's abuse, Henderson and his team go back to their drawing boards.

The prototype successfully passed, and the production line was just being setup when at the end of June, 2006 I placed the order. Although I could have had hull #6, my stipulation upon ordering was that I wanted no earlier than hull #20. I figured that producing a dozen-and-a-half boats would allow them time to setup the line, workout any bugs and to do some fine-tuning and tweaking. It would also allow for changes from crew feedback as the prototype, hull #1 did its tour up the East Coast.

I'm glad I waited; during the summer they added a tall rig option, taking the mast to 21 metres, and since I wasn't concerned with low bridges, I went for it. Down below, a couple of the more obvious changes were the higher and more ergonomically placed hand rails down the companionway stairs, and a change from teak to cherry for the interior cabinetry.

Construction on my boat began at the end of October and I visited the Hunter plant in Alachua, Florida in November 2006 and January 2007 to watch the progress and to fine-tune my requirements and options. She was hull #20.

I have been a boat owner since 1964, and until this current purchase, all of my boats had been used. Many of them were much more used than others, and several I would qualify as abused. I was looking forward to starting without someone else's idea of what works.

The boat was completed the last week of January, loaded on a flatbed and convoyed with up to three escort vehicles the nearly 6,000 kilometres from Florida, up Interstate-75, across Interstate-10 and up Interstate-5, arriving in Vancouver before dawn on the 5th of February.

As the working day began, I was down at Granville Island to watch her offloading from the trailer. With her keel attached, she would have been too high for the roads, so the keel was shipped on a pallet on the trailer.

The 5087 kilogram keel was offloaded, stood-up and she was gently settled onto it. It was bonded to the stub and the keel bolts were torqued.

The fit out then continued in earnest. Part of my purchase agreement had been to allow the boat to be displayed in the Victoria Floating Boat Show 20-22 April, and the dealer was working full-bore and without interruption toward having the boat ready for that date. It was to their great advantage to have the boat display well, and I thought that this would also be of benefit to me.

The mast was stepped and rigged, the boom was slung into place and attached. The bottom was barrier-coated and painted with anti-fouling. She was beginning to look like a seafaring lady, and she needed a name.

I had for months been running through lists of names, adding a few and deleting others. In Canada each registered ship must have a unique name; not only uniquely spelled, but also for unambiguous radio communications, uniquely pronounced. I did not want a Roman numeral affixed to the name, such as: Seabreeze XVIII or Carpe Diem XXVII, or whatever count those over-popular names were up to.

I finally settled on *Sequitur*. It is not a word in the English language, but *non sequitur* is. Non sequitur is a Latin phrase meaning: it does not follow; illogical, nonsensical, not following logically from what has preceded; an illogical conclusion. So I thought that Sequitur followed logically from what had preceded. Sequitur was for me a logical conclusion.

Before her arrival I had reserved the name with Ship Registry, and in the days following her arrival I had engaged an Appointed Tonnage Measurer to visit the boat in the yard. He collected his $450 fee and then waved his magic wand, uttered some official inanities and left, saying he would report the measurements to Ship Registry. In due course Sequitur was entered into the Canadian registry and I added her name to the transom and carved her Official Number and her Gross and Net Tonnage data as prescribed.

The fitting-out continued with the crew of Specialty Yacht Services slowly piecing together the complexities of the new boat. Once I had decided to order the Hunter 49, my next step had been to wade through the long list of standard equipment and options and to decide what I wanted. For ease of handling and for sailing performance, among the things I ordered were:
- the deep keel;
- the tall rig;
- the vertical battened in-mast furling;
- the self-tacking furling staysail;
- the asymmetrical cruising spinnaker;
- one electrical self-tailing winch in the cockpit;
- and for safety, the spare rudder system.

For interior creature comfort and convenience, among the options I ordered were:
- the three cabin layout with the workshop-office option in the starboard aft;
- the leather interior upholstery;
- the Splendide washer-dryer;
- the Quiet Flush electric heads; and
- the second top-loading freezer and second fridge.

When the had boat arrived in Vancouver I began adding or upgrading a number of other things, including:
- a Raymarine E-Series chart plotter with an E120 in the cockpit and an E80 at the nav station;
- a Raymarine 2 kilowatt radar dome on a Waltz swivel mast mount;
- a SeaCAS AIS SafePassage 100 receiver;
- a Rozendal Luneberg Tri-Lens radar reflector;
- a Raymarine 7002 autopilot with remote controller;
- a 40kg Rocna with 100m of 9.5mm hi-test chain as primary anchor;
- demoting the 20kg Delta with 15m of 9.5mm hi-test chain and 80m of nylon to secondary anchor;
- a Walker Bay FTD-310 Hypalon dinghy;
- a Torqeedo Travel 801 rechargeable lithium-ion electric outboard;
- a set of customized Ocean Marine davits;
- a custom dodger and bimini with matching pedestal and dinghy/davit covers;
- a 1225 Amp-hour house bank of 6v flooded cell batteries with Water Miser caps;
- a Fischer-Panda 4 kilowatt DC generator with a starting battery and switching to charge all three battery banks;
- a pair of Racor primary fuel filters with isolation switching to replace the single Racor;
- an Espar hydronic interior heating system; and
- forty-two folding nylon/glass-fibre MastSteps to the top of the mast.

I could have had the canvas work, the generator, davits and the electronics installed at the factory in Florida, but I had decided to have them installed in Vancouver to give me more control over their design and placement. There was still much to do as the Boat Show date approached and the yard crew scrambled toward getting Sequitur ready.

We were still waiting for a piece for the mast, and although the rig was stable without it, the engineers at the factory recommended against sailing. So midweek in wonderful sailing conditions we motored the 70 nautical miles across Georgia Strait and through the Gulf Islands to Victoria's Inner Harbour to setup in front of the Empress Hotel for the boat show. On the Monday following the boat show we motored back to Vancouver and the work on Sequitur's fit-out continued.

By late June the basic fit-out was complete, and although there was still some installation work left to be done, I took possession of Sequitur on the 4th of July 2007. I then spent the summer, autumn and winter shaking her down and single-handing her in fair weather and foul.

I enjoyed many quiet places, where I was able to relax and work on cataloging my upcoming auction. I still had commitments to assemble, catalogue and conduct two more sales in Toronto: February and October 2008.

The February Torex Auction was a resounding success, and after I had finished mopping-up the invoicing, collecting, packaging and shipping, I went back to enjoying Sequitur and getting to know her.

She is a large boat, 15 metres in length (listed as 49'-11" by Hunter) with a beam of 4.5 metres. With her headroom of just over 2 metres, she has a huge interior volume. The master suite is forward, with a semi-walk-around queen-size bed and separate heads and shower compartments. There are two cabins aft, the one on the port side with a semi-en-suite heads and shower. In the starboard cabin, I had specified a workbench rather than the standard settee, figuring it would save the usual marring and soiling of the galley counters or the dining table from the overhauling or repairing of equipment and greasy machinery.

Forward of this cabin is the galley, a space that is very important to me. I pride myself as a good cook, and among my many lives, I was a wine and food writer and I did some instructing in a culinary school. I found Sequitur's galley a joy to work in, with its large L-shaped layout and an island across from the stove. The island houses two top-loading freezers and provides additional work space. It also provides excellent bracing for cooking while underway in rough conditions.

The strong fiddles around the Corian countertops not only keep things in place, but also provide excellent handholds. Set into the transverse counter are two fridges and a deep, double sink. The extractor hood, the small overhead hatch and the two opening ports above the gimballed stove provide excellent ventilation when the adjacent companionway hatch is closed. The four cupboards, seven drawers and full length eye-level shelf provide more storage than I could find use for.

Across from the galley is the navigation station with a forward-facing, high-backed arm chair.

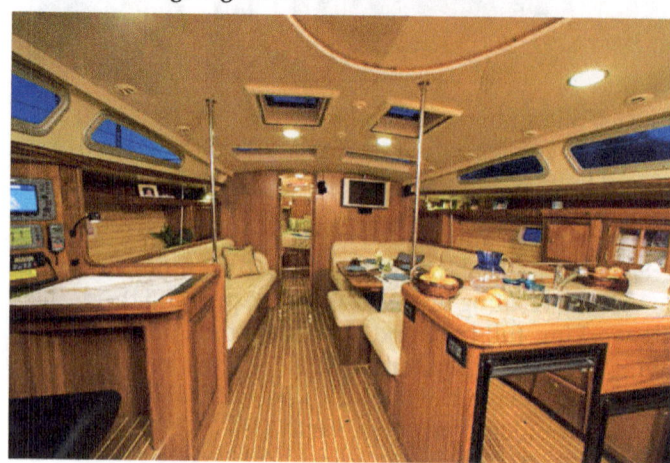

The interior offers a wonderful feeling of space, yet with all the openness, there is nowhere in the boat without a choice of secure handholds to enable safe and easy movement through the boat, even in heavy weather.

Up top, the cockpit has a large T-shaped layout with twin wheels, a walk-through transom and dedicated tether points. There are six locking cockpit lockers, two locking transom lockers and comfortable cushioned seating for up to twelve. The cockpit settees are long enough to lay down on and the central drop-leaf Corian table can easily dine six. For protection from the elements, I had installed a dodger and a bimini with roll-up or removable transparent side and rear curtains, making the cockpit easily convertible to many configurations from open to totally enclosed.

The jib, the staysail and the main are all roller-furling, and all the halyards, in-hauls, out-hauls and sheets are led aft into the cockpit. There is no need to leave the cockpit to set, adjust, reef or douse these sails. Solo sailing is simple.

Joining me onboard was my fourteen-year-old miniature poodle, Chianti. She and I had long since realized that something was missing in Sequitur. At the end of September 2007, a year-and-a-bit after my ex-wife and I had decided to separate, I began seriously searching for a companion who shared my dream of sailing off. I posted on a couple of Internet sites that focus on crew looking for boats and boats looking for crew:

> *"I am healthy, physically fit and very young for my 63 years. I retired as a Canadian Naval Officer in 1981 after eighteen years of service and have spent the past quarter century creating and running entrepreneurial businesses. Now it's time to play!*
>
> *In June 2006 I ordered a new 50-foot sailboat with all the modern conveniences and creature comforts. I took delivery of her in July 2007 and since then I have been getting to know her and how she handles a wide variety of conditions from calm to stormy.*
>
> *My intention is to sail off over the horizon, with no needs, no itinerary and no schedule. By the summer of 2009, I will have wound-down my last company, sold my Vancouver house, bought some holding property for later and moved aboard in preparation for heading out. Sequitur is fully capable of being single handed; however, I would prefer to share my adventures with a like-minded woman.*
>
> *Openness, honesty and kindness are essential. An exploratory nature and a thirst for adventure are very important, as is the physical ability to satisfy that thirst.*
>
> *I am looking for a companion, a friend and a soul mate."*

Without doubt, the most important criterion in offshore voyaging is a competent, cooperative and compatible crew. Without this, the best equipped and most seaworthy vessel is likely to have difficulty as conditions change, and one of the constants of life at sea is change. Competent crew can take a minimally equipped and barely capable vessel to the ends of the earth.

After six months of communicating with the many respondents and flying, driving and sailing to meet over a dozen of them, on the 30th of April I received an email from a woman named Edi.

At the end of April, while scanning through lists of boats seeking crew, Edi had come across a Canadian boat in Vancouver and she decided to contact Sequitur and her skipper. A flurry of emails ensued.

Among the things I learned was that Edi had been born in the Netherlands, that she was raised in South Africa, and that she speaks Dutch, Afrikaans and English. When she was sixteen, the family had moved back to the Netherlands, and two years later, at the age of eighteen she had emigrated to Canada on her own.

She had landed in Toronto in 1965 with $70 and an eagerness to explore her independence. She initially worked on an assembly line, then quickly found a work as a bank teller. Later she joined Canadian Pacific Airlines as an airport agent. There she met Peter, who was also an agent for the airline. They married and soon thereafter, transferred to Vancouver and they both continued to work while raising their daughters, Amy and Genevieve.

They had made very frequent use of their staff passes to travel with the children, exploring dozens of countries on six continents with such destinations as South Africa, Morocco, Iceland, Easter Island, China, Nepal, Peru, Chile, Ecuador, Turkey, Australia and New Zealand and on such adventures as bicycling through Japan, England and the Loire, Rhone and Midi regions of France.

Edi had returned to school for a three year course, graduating from Capilano College as a Graphic Designer/Illustrator. Peter's early death from cancer left Edi with two adolescent daughters to raise on her own.

After her daughters had finished high school and had left home to go on to university, she bought a house near the water on Vancouver Island, where she had the time to explore her artistic talents. She is an accomplished clay artist, creating among other things, exquisitely expressive and wonderfully glazed Budas and faces.

Extensive sea kayaking and some sailing with friends kindled in her a love of the sea, and this combined with her broad travel experience, spawned a desire for more sailing adventures. To expand her horizons, in mid-April she bought a one-month placement of the following profile on a British website looking for a boat:

> *"A gentle artist who has traveled the world extensively and has visited 80 countries is looking for a kind skipper to teach her the ropes. I have spent three and a half months on a catamaran in the Caribbean and have sailed in monohulls off Vancouver Island.*
>
> *I am courteous, kind and considerate, a non smoker and limited drinker. I'm looking for the same in a skipper. My passions are laughing, warm weather, bare feet, a bathing suit and the sea."*

I was interested in meeting, but Edi was leaving a few days later for two weeks on a boat in Mexico and was also planning to join a boat in Trinidad in early June. We continued the email contact, and after her return three weeks later from Mexico, Edi and I met in Vancouver.

We immediately felt a wonderful compatibility, we sensed a synergy as we dawdled over lunch at the False Creek Yacht Club. We organized to meet again on the weekend at Snug Cove on Bowen Island. I was at the time the Commander of the Vancouver Power and Sail Squadron, and the Squadron was having a rendezvous in Snug Cove; I needed to be there. I thought that it would be a wonderful venue for Edi and me to continue to get to know each other.

After Edi headed back to her home on Vancouver Island, I immediately began outfitting Sequitur's aft en-suite cabin for her. Although the boat came with fitted bedding, I thought the weave was a bit too coarse. I bought some finer sheets and pillow cases, new pillows, a duvet and cover and some fine new towels. I wanted her to be comfortable, not just with the boat, but also with me.

At the time, Sequitur's permanent mooring was at the Union Steamship Company Marina in Snug Cove, so the location of the rendezvous was a very familiar and comfortable place for me. I had also been an instructor, the Training Officer and the Commander of the Vancouver Squadron, so I knew and was very comfortable with the people at the Rendezvous.

For Edi it would be a strange format in a strange place with strange people. I was amazed and delighted with how well Edi adapted to the situation and very easily interacted with the group. She appeared comfortable and confident.

Not so immediately comfortable, possibly, was Chianti. In the beginning, she kept staring at Edi, trying to sort-out who this strange woman was, and what she was doing aboard. Soon, however they were getting along like old friends.

After the weekend rendezvous, Edi went back to Vancouver Island and I was very busy with work for the Canadian Numismatic Association. I was the current President, and we were preparing for the annual convention. The convention was to be in Ottawa in July, in conjunction with the centennial celebrations of the Royal Canadian Mint.

In the late winter we had been advised that Her Majesty, the Queen had granted us the privilege to use Royal with our association's name. I was deeply immersed in the tangle of legalities and internal politics that were involved in changing our constitution to allow changing the name to the Royal Canadian Numismatic Association.

A week after Edi had left, I emailed her and asked if she would care to join Chianti and me for a few days of sailing. I had to go to Lasqueti Island to visit with the Lasqueti Mint, which I was having design and strike my presidential medal for the convention. I had chosen to portray Sequitur on the obverse of the medal and Ray, the die engraver was having difficulty with the design. I also had to drop-off the silver and gold bullion to be used for the striking.

Edi accepted the invitation, and we sailed our bullion-laden vessel across the Straits to Silva Bay, where we spent a night on the False Creek Yacht Club's outstation float. The following day we sailed northward and secured to Ray's private mooring ball in a tiny bay off his private island just off Lasqueti. We had a wonderful evening and dinner with Ray and the Mint Master, Tolling and their wives.

Among the delicious things they served us was a great loaf of bread. Edi asked how it had been made, and we were introduced to the New York Times no-knead bread recipe. Later Edi was to tweak and evolve the recipe through increasingly delicious changes, until we finally had what we call Sequitur bread.

After we had returned Sequitur to Snug Cove, Edi headed back to her home in Craig Bay and I went to mine in Vancouver. A week later we sailed out across the Straits to spend a week cruising the Gulf Islands.

We had superb weather and wonderful sailing. Edi and I were getting along so splendidly that by the third night's anchorage, we had decided it made no sense to continue wearing-out two sets of bedding.

At the beginning of June Edi flew to Trinidad to join a boat, respecting an earlier commitment. With her was Isabelle from Montreal, with whom she had twice previously jointly crewed in the Caribbean. They had serious incompatibilities with their new skipper and felt unsafe. They bailed-out early in Venezuela and cobbled-together flights back to Canada.

Edi joined me on the numismatic circuit, with trips to Toronto for the June Torex, to Ottawa for the CNA Convention and to Saint John to confirm arrangements and sign contracts for the 2010 RCNA Convention. We went to Ottawa again, this time as guest of the Royal Canadian Mint for their lavish hundredth birthday celebrations.

During the last week of October 2008 I conducted my last auction. The three day sale in Toronto was again conducted simultaneously live and online, as had been all of my auctions since I had pioneered the format a decade previously. The market was at a peak, just before hesitating and collapsing on the heels of mortgage fiasco in the United States. My timing had been impeccable; the auction exceeded my previous Canadian record for the highest total price ever realized in a numismatic auction.

I spent all of November and well into December invoicing the mail and online bidders, receiving payments, packaging and mailing lots and paying consignors. When this was done, I began winding-down my twenty-one year-old company.

During this time Edi made several trips back and forth between our two homes, bringing to Vancouver things she wanted to sell. With great success, she listed them online on Craig's List, along with most of my furniture and other unwanted things. Both Edi and I were preparing our houses for sale.

Earlier we had jointly bought a wonderful top floor, corner loft in a century-old building, which is a registered historical site. However, its conversion from industrial to residential was not going to be completed until May 2009. This fit well with our schedule. If both of our houses sold before the completion of the loft, we could put the keepers among our furniture and effects into temporary storage and move aboard Sequitur.

We both listed our houses for sale. Edi also listed her car for sale, thinking because of its high price it would be a slow sell. Surprisingly, response to the Craig's List ad was strong and it quickly sold at her asking price. We were down to one car.

Through the remainder of the winter and the spring we continued with the fit-out and downsizing. Finally in late June 2009 Edi and I were ready to go sailing. We wanted to confirm that Sequitur was also ready.

2. Shakedown Cruise

We headed out from Vancouver in late June on a two and a half week shakedown cruise. The purpose of the trip was to test all of our systems and ourselves for extended cruising. We left Vancouver's False Creek on Monday 29 June and motored out into English Bay, where we set sail and tacked our way out in 20 to 25 knots of westerly winds and against the flooding tide. As we rounded the bell buoy, the winds started easing and we had a pleasant broad reach down the Straits of Georgia, which gave us an opportunity to continue practicing with the whisker pole and to try various preventer setups. In the late afternoon, just north of Active Pass, the winds finally died.

After five hours of sailing the batteries were still showing 100%. Not bad considering we were running both freezers and both fridges, the auto pilot, the chart plotters, the radar, the forward-looking sonar, the VHF, we spent some time on the SSB, and for lunch we ran the inverter to power the panini grill and to make tea. It looks like the 1225 amp-hour battery bank is happy with the 522 Watt solar array.

The Sooke Harbour House was named *"One of the five best Country Inns in the world"* in 2000 by Gourmet Magazine and second best hotel in North America. As well, it was called the *"sixth best small hotel in North America"* by Travel and Leisure Magazine. The restaurant's wine list had been awarded Wine Spectator's Grand Award for having one of the best wine lists in the world and it had received a Platinum Award from the Vancouver Playhouse Wine List competition in 2008. Our shakedown training for the day was gourmet dining ashore.

Frederique and Sinclair Philip have owned Sooke Harbour House since 1979, and in the days when I was a wine importer, Sinclair was a very good client. He is a proponent of seasonal, regional and whenever possible, organic foods. His menus focus on local fish and shellfish as well as on a wide variety of organic herbs, vegetables, salad greens and edible flowers from the restaurant's year round gardens. Local foragers supply wild mushrooms, wild seaweed and berries.

Sinclair wanted to see our new boat, and he offered to drive us to dinner and back. When he arrived onboard, he was so impressed with Sequitur that he did an extended tour, then phoned one of his friends, who is midway through building a sailboat, to tell him to come take a look also. This whole process took so long that Sinclair had to phone the restaurant a couple of times to tell then that: *"Table 6 is not late. They are with me and the delay is my fault; we will all be there shortly."*

We motored through Active Pass and across to Ganges on Saltspring Island, where we spent the next two nights on our yacht club's outstation. We had planned to sail onward on the 30th, but there was absolutely no wind, so we practiced shopping, storing the pantry, lazing about and playing visiting cruiser. We managed to pass this part of the shakedown without any problem.

The 1st of July, Canada Day was sunny and calm, and since we had dinner reservations at the Sooke Harbour House that evening, we decided to head out. We motored the whole day to Sooke, where we went alongside at the Sooke Harbour Marina. After we had secured and had taken the dog ashore, we cleaned and dressed-up in anticipation of dinner.

Among the things Sooke Harbour House is famous for is its gastronomic adventure, a surprise multi-course tasting menu chosen daily from the best available from their gardens, the sea and the local farmers. We chose this as well as the accompanying wine pairings, which began with glasses of Champagne. Seven courses and seven wines later, around midnight, Sinclair emerged from the kitchen and sat with us for the better part of an hour over port and wonderful conversation. He then drove us back to Sequitur. Without doubt, our day's shakedown evolutions were a huge success.

Thursday the 2nd of July dawned clear and calm. We motored out of Sooke Harbour and into a slight breeze in the Straits of Juan de Fuca. We ghosted along for about three hours in seven or eight knots of breeze, making four to five knots, then around noon the wind died. We motored for the rest of the day, out the Straits and into Barkley Sound and then into Bamfield Inlet, where we anchored for the night. The AutoAnchor in the cockpit let-out the anchor properly, but failed to count the rode deployed, and I had to redeploy and then count from the bow. Other than this, our shakedown evolutions for this day, which included the anchoring, the launching of the dinghy, the mounting the motor and taking the dog ashore, were accomplished without further hitch.

Friday the 3rd was another clear and calm day. After taking the dog ashore and back, and having breakfast, we took the dinghy, Non Sequitur around the inlet and landed to explore the boardwalks. Back on board and ready to depart, the anchor came up 180° out of alignment, so while Edi motored out of the Inlet, I worked on getting the 40kg Rocna into its place. Eventually, I secured a line around the roll bar and used it to assist the windlass in the recovery. I thought of adding a swivel between the anchor and the chain, but I need to do some more research to be sure that this wouldn't be adding a weak link to the system. While stowing the gear, I moved the anchor snubber stowage from the rope locker aft to the hooks in the sail locker, a much more convenient and readily accessible location.

We motored in glassy seas across Imperial Eagle Channel and through the Broken Group to a secluded anchorage on the north side of Walsh Island. This is a spectacular area, and I hadn't been here since the late '70s when as a naval officer I conducted leadership training programs here for junior officers. The area seems totally unchanged in the thirty years since; except for more boaters, it is still pristine wilderness.

Since the water in the anchorage was so clean, I decided it was a good time to test the new Spectra Newport II watermaker to see how it performed. We had set it to auto-flush every five days since we commissioned it mid-June, and because of the water quality in False Creek, we hadn't run it through a make cycle. We had about 50 litres of water remaining in the tanks, so I set the watermaker to run for seven hours, calculating it should net us about 440 litres of new water after the automatic back-flush. Unexpectedly, after its startup cycle, it gave a *Salinity Probe Failed* alarm and shut down.

I hauled-out the manual, and after a troubleshooting session, I determined the procedure to follow to do an override and run the system on manual. However, considering the warning: *"Note: this is a temporary repair that will destroy the probe cable. After several days in this mode you may have to remove the connector, strip and spread the wires and replace in the water."*, I decided to leave it for the installer to sort-out after our return to Vancouver. In retrospect, I should have carried-on with the manual override procedure as a real-time shakedown evolution. Nonetheless, at least I learned the theory of what to do.

Saturday the 4th of July was another clear and calm morning. After the dog walk and breakfast, the anchor came in much easier using the line I had left attached to the anchor's tandem eye. We motored in glassy calm waters toward Ucluelet and into a fog bank. This was a great opportunity to test the automatic fog signal on our Icom 604; it worked wonderfully, and sure was easier than manually sounding a signal. We also took advantage of the opportunity to practice our radar navigation, and since the approach to Ucluelet was through narrow, rock-strewn channels between islands, with several commercial and pleasure fishermen sharing the waters with us, it was a good practice.

The fog cleared just inside the entrance to Ucluelet Harbour, and we went alongside the fuel dock to practice topping-up the 840 litre fuel tanks and to practice paying for the diesel. We also topped-up the water tanks, calculating that the 527 litres should be plenty for the rest of the trip.

Around noon, we nestled in among five other boats from the Bluewater Cruising Association (BCA), alongside in the Ucluelet Small Boat Harbour. There was another BCA boat at anchor just outside the marina, making a total of seven that had come here for the annual BCA Vancouver Island Cruising Experience (VICE). The purpose of the VICE is to assemble off the west coast of Vancouver Island and sail west into the Pacific for three days, then turn around and head back in. The intention is to give the skippers and crew a real-time look at how they and their boats handle an offshore experience.

We had begun organizing in mid-January, and as many as eighteen boats played with the idea of participating. By the end of January, there were a dozen boats planning to sail out from Ucluelet in the first good weather window after the 5th of July. Boats joined and left the list, so here we were, in Ucluelet on the 4th of July, and the five-day gribs looked good. The seven boats were: Aquatherapy, a Beneteau 432; Borboleta, a Beneteau First 405; Pamdemonium, a Caliber 38; Sea Reach, a Spencer 42, Sequitur, a Hunter 49; Tahnoo, a Spencer 1330; and Way She Goes II, a Maple Leaf 45.

We spent much of the rest of the day checking-over the boat and replenishing the fridges with fresh fruits, vegetables, cheeses and meats. Before we left Vancouver, we had laid in a good supply of dried fruit, nuts, salami and other calorie-rich snack items. Also, before leaving Vancouver, I had spent much of a day cooking batches of pork barley stew, chicken and rice, and cream of asparagus and winter vegetable soup. These we had put into one litre Lock-and-Lock containers and frozen, providing us with eight quick-serve comfort-food dinners for offshore.

I tested the EPIRB battery, tested the Iridium satellite phone and downloaded grib files. Our newly installed Icom 802, AT-140 tuner and Pactor usb2-3 modem were still having teething problems, and we have to reroute the coaxial cable from the tuner to the antenna. Voice transmission and reception were spotty, but at least we were able to send and receive emails.

The group met on the float between the boats at 1800 and discussed departure time, route, communications and other details of the trip. Back in April or May, the group had decided on using as our destination Cobb Seamount, which rises to about 25 metres from the surface and lies some 250 miles WSW of Ucluelet. This extinct volcano, we reasoned, would be preferable to an arbitrary latitude and longitude.

The necessary details, such as departure time, and communications nets and minimum and maximum speeds under sail and power were discussed and decided upon cleanly and simply. We thought the meeting was over, but it suddenly took off onto tangents, discussing alternate destinations, Plan B, Plan B-2, Plan B-2 mod 1….

By the time it got to Plan C, we had decided to leave the camel designing to others, and we went below to file a trip plan with the Coast Guard and to start preparing dinner.

> *Over the years I have seen many would-be cruisers befuddle themselves with over-planning. Many spend years theorizing and devising contingency plans, then tweaking and refining them. They gradually become so concerned with their long lists of What Ifs that they scare themselves out of adventuring beyond the known. Often, when they do finally head out on their own, at the first unpredicted happening that was not covered in their long lists, they turn tail and run.*
>
> *I think that this contributes to the current huge popularity of the organized cruising rallies, such as the Pacific Puddle Jump and the trans-Atlantic ARC, each of which annually attracts more than 200 boats, and the shorter Baja Haha with over 100 participating boats. Mass sailings such as these are ideal for those who are uncomfortable with thoughts of doing the passage on their own.*

After a round of photos, the group of seven departed Ucluelet as planned at 1100 on Sunday the 5th and ran into fog shortly after the harbour entrance. We set sail off Amphitrite Point and headed off on a course of 240° in light northwesterly winds, making five to six knots. Sequitur was soon at the head of the fleet, and we communicated our AIS and radar contacts to the other boats as we crossed the shipping lanes off the entrances to the Straits of Juan de Fuca.

It was sloppy going; the winds were light, without sufficient pressure to steadily fill the sails in the westerly Pacific swell meeting the continental shelf and being combined with cross seas from a weather system off to the northwest. The winds slowly eased through the afternoon, and we were down to a bit above three knots. I was about to rig a preventer on the main to stop the boom from slamming, when the wrong combination of lull, swell and gust centred the boom then slammed it back out, blowing a shackle on the traveler. After I had jury-rigged the traveler with a piece of spectra, I made a note to myself to buy a few spares of each shackle, block and small fitting aboard.

With the wind light and variable, and with the continuing sloppy seas, we decided to flash-up and motor-sail. Because the group had decided on a speed of five knots under power, we motored along at a very quiet 1350 rpm. By the time of our 1800 VHF radio net, the remaining six boats were scattered across about fifteen miles and were now off the continental shelf and into a somewhat easier sea, though still quite sloppy. One of the fleet had decided it was too rough for them and they turned back to Ucluelet.

Around 2000, I went below to heat-up the pork barley stew that had been defrosting in the sink since mid-afternoon. It was not fully defrosted, and needed about fifteen minutes of slow heating and forking apart in a pot on the stove to be ready. The stove hit its 30° gimbal stops rather frequently, showing how sloppy it was, but even with this, our motion was quite comfortable.

The half litre bowls of thick stew and a big thermos of tea made the perfect meal; it was great warm comfort food. The shakedown lesson here was to take the evening's meal out of the freezer by noon and put it in the sink to defrost.

While Edi went below to bed, I took the watch from 2100 to 0200. I was very comfortable, laid back along the cockpit cushions, propped by pillows and covered with a thick fleece blanket. I had the chart-plotter screen swivelled so I could easily see it and monitor the split screen with chart, radar and AIS overlay. I used a solar-charged LED reading light and lost myself in a book. The wind came up after midnight and I shutdown the engine and setup on a broad starboard reach with staysail and the two-thirds of the main rolled out.

I woke Edi for her watch at 0200, and once she was on deck and comfortable with the situation, I went below to bed, and came back on deck at 0700, fresh and ready for another day. Fifteen minutes later Edi had brought up a breakfast of vanilla yogurt, toasted bagels, cream cheese and fresh coffee.

By the time of our fleet's 0800 radio net, we were fed, relaxed and very comfortable. I had rolled-out the full main, the jib and the staysail and we were moving along at about eight knots close-hauled on a starboard tack. It surprised us; therefore, that several in the fleet were uncomfortable with their ability to handle the conditions, and wanted to turn back. I told them we were very relaxed and at ease with the boat and the conditions, and that we would continue on to Cobb Seamount as planned. Pamdemonium echoed our desire to carry on. The rest of the fleet eventually decided to continue until early afternoon, and then discuss turning back in a 1400 radio net.

In the early afternoon, Pamdemonium announced that their forestay had parted, and that they had just completed jury-rigging an emergency forestay with halyards. The rig was stable for motoring, but they could not risk raising sails, and they considered it prudent to turn back. I offered my condolences and then waited for about fifteen minutes for some of the remainder of the fleet to volunteer to accompany the Pamdemonium back in.

Finally, after no response from the fleet, I told them that since none had offered to accompany Pamdemonium back to land, Sequitur would abandon the trip to Cobb and escort her. Almost immediately all the other boats decided to head back to Ucluelet. Since Pamdemonium would now have a good escort, I told them that Sequitur would carry on to Cobb Seamount, and that anyone who wished could join us.

Sequitur continued southwest, while the rest of the fleet turned around and headed northeast.

The swell continued at four to five metres with two to three metre seas, and the winds backed through west forcing us about 15° south of the rhumb line to Cobb, then 30o and eventually 40°. We kept a comfortable starboard tack and I took a long nap on the port side cockpit couch, while Edi stood watch. By 2000, the dinner had thawed, and it was easy work for me to heat the homemade chicken with rice and vegetables. There is nothing like a big bowl of hot delicious comfort food to add to a sense of security.

On Monday night, I again took the watch from 2100 to 0200, while Edi slept below, then I went to bed until 0700.

We have found that in the temperate zones, from mid-spring to mid-autumn, this rotation is ideal for a boat with only two watchkeepers, in that it gives one a sunset and twilight and the other a twilight and sunrise; the dark hours are shared, and they go quickly. Naps or bunk time between chores and watches during the day keep both watchkeepers fresh, alert and relaxed. The longer hours of darkness in the cooler seasons and in tropics make this rotation a bit less perfect, but still quite workable.

Shortly before 1400 on Tuesday the 7th, as we were nearing Cobb, the seas began to build, and become more erratic. We were pounding into waves more frequently, and with more force. After one particularly violent smash into the oncoming sea, we could hear a regular sharp banging. A quick look below to check for an unlatched cabin or locker door found nothing. The bang persisted, and we could feel it shaking the hull. The anchor had come loose. Our 40 kg Rocna had sheared its retaining pin and broken its lashings, and was now dangling over the end of the anchor roller and smashing into the bow. Good thing the bow, from the keel stub forward, has layers of Kevlar in its lay-up.

I quickly turned the boat downwind, put on my inflatable harness and tethered my way forward on the jacklines. I eased-out about five metres of chain with the windlass and let the anchor trail in the water beneath the hull. Then I went back to the cockpit and organized Edi with the spinnaker halyard and the power winch, and went forward again. I dipped the end of the halyard around the anchor chain and clipped it back onto itself, then walked it back, allowing the loop to slide down to the anchor. With Edi on the winch button and me holding the halyard outboard, we winched the Rocna onboard. Rather than lashing it on deck, I chose to place it shank-down into the chain locker, where it settled very securely. I then lashed it in place, and we turned and resumed our course to Cobb Seamount.

Around 1630 we began seeing flocks of seabirds, predominantly fork-tailed storm-petrels and Leach's Storm-Petrels, both in the air and on the water and there were dozens of Blackfooted Albatross cruising on the air currents. We had arrived at Cobb Seamount. We assumed that the shallow waters were teeming with fish and this attracted the birds.

After being off soundings for a couple of days in depths of 2500 to 3000 metres, the depth sounder was again reporting depths. In the swell, we were getting readings of 80 to 85 metres, then a quick rise to 24 and 19.5 metres, then back down to readings in the 80s. We had sailed over the summit.

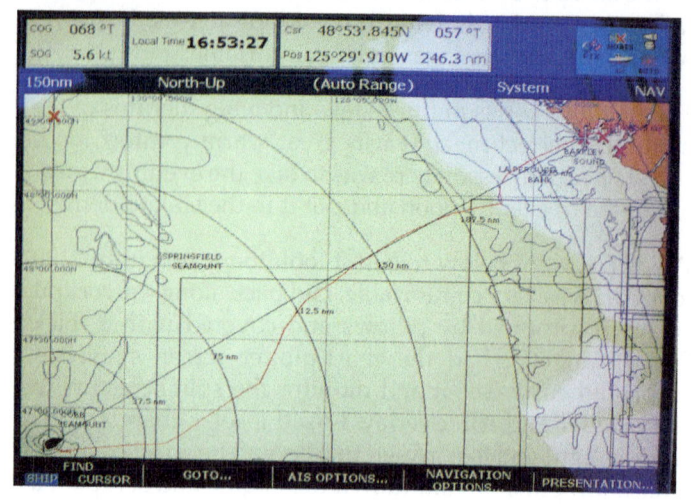

We fell off onto a much more comfortable downwind run, with the wind and the seas on our port quarter and began our return to Ucluelet. We were making about five-and-a-half knots, and with about 250 miles to go, this speed would take us about 46 hours to cover the distance and give us an arrival at the entrance to Ucluelet Harbour around 1500 on Thursday. An average of six-and-a-half knots would give us an arrival around 0800 on Thursday. This looked like a good safe window for making our landfall.

Edi had been taking her showers in the forenoon while I was on watch, and I had been showering in the late afternoon or early evening. While it wasn't really uncomfortable in the sloppy seas of the past couple of days, our current downwind course certainly made showering easier, and I enjoyed a much longer one than usual.

The motion was very comfortable, and I could have very easily prepared a meal from scratch. We had fresh boneless chicken breasts, beef tenderloin, red snapper fillets and pork tenderloin in the fridge, and among the vegetables in the crisper were asparagus, crimini mushrooms, red, orange, yellow and green peppers, celery, carrots, green beans and broccoli. We had a good stock of fresh ginger, garlic, shallots and onions. However, I had taken a Lock-and-Lock of homemade cream of asparagus soup from the freezer around noon, and by the time we had settled in to the downwind course, it was already nearly thawed. So I thawed some jumbo prawns in tap water, removed their tails and warmed them in hot water from the tap, added a knob of butter and some fresh tarragon to the heated soup and ladled it over the hot prawns in the bowl. Delicious, simple and very filling.

On the third night, I again stood an easy and relaxing watch from 2100 to 0200 while Edi slept, and I was fresh and eagerly back on deck by 0700. We were then making a steady seven-and-a-half knots; if this held, we would be making landfall around 0500 on Thursday, shortly before sunrise.

Wednesday was an uneventful, relaxing day with steady, but diminishing winds from the port quarter. Highlights were Edi's wonderful lunch sandwiches of sliced garlic-roasted pork loin, artichoke hearts, sun-dried tomatoes, Moroccan olives and blue cheese on pumpkin seed bread. We lazed in the cockpit, read, alternated watches and napped. By mid afternoon, the winds had almost completely died, and the seas had become glassy. I flashed-up the engine, rolled in the sails and set our speed for a dawn landfall.

We decided to do a load of laundry to tryout the washer-drier while underway, but could not get it to work. The yard was supposed to have set it up to work off the inverter, but after some troubleshooting, it became apparent that they had not yet hooked it up. Our laundry would have to wait until we are hooked-up to shore power.

On Wednesday night, I prepared tarragon chicken breast with gnocchi in a crimini, shallot and chardonnay sauce and a platter of asparagus with mayonnaise. I again stood watch from 2100 until 0200, and around midnight, we began meeting shipping heading in and out of the Straits. I had good radar and AIS plots and a strong radar paint of the Vancouver Island mountains to hand over to Edi when she relieved me.

I left her with the landfall, and went below to bed for a refreshing sleep and then came back on deck at 0530 to watch a spectacular sunrise.

Shortly before 0800 on Thursday the 9th we secured alongside in the Ucluelet Small Craft Harbour, where we spent a couple of days. Edi kept the washer-drier in our workshop/pantry busy while I overhauled the anchor and remounted it, then went to the chandlers and bought some fittings to repair the traveller, hauled the mattress out of the fore cabin and onto deck to rinse out the salt water and dry it in the sun. The starboard deck hatch there had leaked in the boarding seas and it needed to have its dogs tightened and its gasket wiped with vaseline.

We left Ucluelet midday on Saturday, heading northward into Pipestem Inlet to rendezvous with Aquatherapy and Borboleta and anchor for the night in a small bay near the mouth of Cascade Creek. We ran into fog in the harbour entrance, so we motored in the glassy seas and practiced our fog navigation for an hour or so until we ran out of the north side of the bank.

We anchored near a tiny island that was steep-to and an ideal place to land the dinghy and walk the dog. The intertidal area here is carpeted with oysters, but the red tide was in season, so we didn't harvest any. In the mid afternoon, Borboleta arrived and anchored, and then an hour or so later, Aquatherapy arrived and rafted on Borboleta. We did a rotating happy hour with the three boats.

Sunday the 12th was still calm, so we motored through the Broken Group, across Imperial Eagle Channel and around Pachena Point into the Straits of Juan de Fuca. It continued near windless, so we motored in the Straits, arriving in Port Renfrew in the early evening, just as the wind started. By the time we reached the anchorage at the head of the inlet, the wind was blowing about twenty knots directly up the inlet. I remember this place from my Navy days as being nearly always windy, with little protection from the prevailing westerly winds.

We tucked into the protection behind the stubby old abandoned breakwater, looked around the anchorage with the forward looking sonar and anchored in two metres of water. We were out of the wind and chop, and the tides until noon the next day would give us a minimum of just over half a metre under the keel. I kept the chartplotter on very large scale with the anchor as waypoint and a split screen showing the bottom. When I brought the dog back from her midnight visit ashore, the tide was rising and the track on the chartplotter showed a consistent pattern centred on the anchor's waypoint. We slept very soundly.

Monday the 13th of July was another clear and calm morning. We weighed and headed out before just before 0800, and were soon back out into the Straits with no wind and glassy seas. As we motored along, Edi brought the bagel toaster up to the cockpit and served a delightful breakfast. In the late morning, we rolled out the sails to catch a wind that had come up, but it soon died and we continued motoring. We motored through Race Passage against a strong ebb and pointed for Victoria's Inner Harbour, where we secured alongside for the night in front of the Empress.

Tuesday was another hot, sunny and calm day, and the lack of wind forced us to motor all the way from Victoria to Ganges, where we spent the night on the False Creek Yacht Club outstation. Wednesday morning we had a fine sail out of Ganges Harbour, through Captain Passage and out into Trincomali Channel, where the winds died. We motored up Trincomali, through Porlier Pass, across the Straits of Georgia and into English Bay, arriving home at the False Creek Yacht Club mid-afternoon.

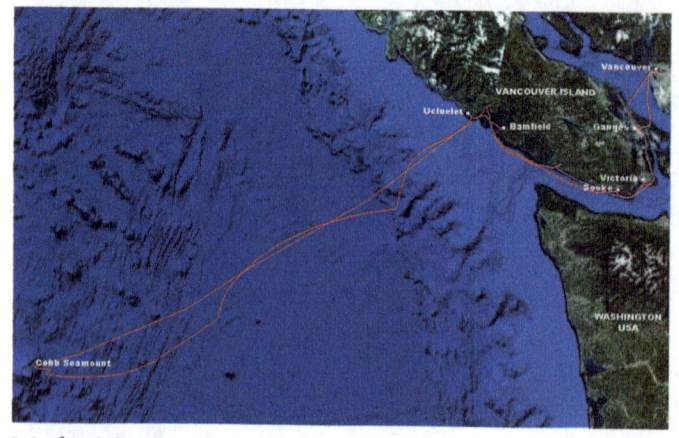

We had been out for seventeen days, had covered 940 nautical miles, including five days on the open Pacific and had only a short list of arisings from Sequitur's shakedown cruise. It certainly would have been better had we been able to sail more on the passages to and from the West Coast, but we were grateful for the 840 litres of diesel tankage and for the very economical fuel consumption.

3. Moving Aboard - Final Preparations

On 22 August I gave up possession of my house; it had sold two weeks previously. We were now officially living aboard Sequitur.

Edi and I had flown back to Vancouver earlier in the week from the Royal Canadian Numismatic Association convention, where I handed-over my President's gavel and relinquished the last of my official responsibilities. We then spent the week sorting, selling on Craigslist, trashing, packing and moving the keepers to the boat and to the storage locker.

Edi then went over to her house on Vancouver Island to continue with the sorting, selling, trashing, packing and moving, while I continued to sort, organize, juggle and stow onboard. Her house had not yet sold (a couple of weeks previously she turned-down an offer of 90% of ask) but it was priced well and we thought that it should sell soon.

Then we busied ourselves with the final bits of preparation for sailing off over the horizon.

Complicating our departure arrangements was the completion of our pied-à-terre in Vancouver. Over a year previously we had bought a new loft in a century-old industrial building in South East False Creek. It had initially been scheduled for occupancy in May 2009. A city hall strike delayed building permits and therefore, the beginning of the construction, thus delaying completion until August. We thought this would be no problem; August fit nicely with everything else.

However; the huge demand for construction on the Vancouver 2010 Winter Olympics projects caused the August date to migrate to October, forcing us to move our furniture and belongings to storage for a couple of months. It was a real juggling act moving over four decades of stuff from two houses totalling 500 square metres, into an 80 square metre loft and a boat. Having to do it through temporary storage certainly added to the complexity.

Jimmy Cornell's *World Cruising Routes* suggests the recommended timing for the passage from BC to California is between May and October. The preferred timing is during the warmer and more stable conditions in July and August. We could have delayed our sail-away until after moving into the loft, but not wanting to be caught by further delays causing us to have to transit the Washington, Oregon, northern California coast after mid-October, we were sticking to our original mid-September departure date. The plan became to fly back to Vancouver from California to take possession of the loft and move our stuff from storage. By that time, the hurricane season should be winding down, and we could safely continue south. So we planned to head out on the 13th of September, three weeks after our move aboard.

To keep us busy, there were still a few things to tweak on Sequitur. The watermaker was awaiting a new salinity probe, we still had to fine-tune the SSB antenna setup, we still had a problem getting the Raymarine AIS transceiver to talk to the Raymarine E Series system and we were awaiting the modifications to the cockpit canvas made necessary by the addition of the solar array arch. Then there was the final bit of spares and stores to assemble and stow.

On the 1st of September we received news that our new loft would not be ready for us until the 26th of September. This changed things considerably, and it no longer made sense to sail on the 13th of September, only to have to fly back from California two weeks later to take possession and move our things out of storage. We decided to delay our departure until the end of September.

Even with the further delayed departure, things seemed to have fallen into place very well; we had been able to secure a sublease for a prime moorage slip at the False Creek Yacht Club until the end of September, the storage locker period ran until the 29th and we gave the necessary fourteen-day notice of termination of contract.

Although we would have preferred the more stable August and September weather, early October would do. Besides, leaving later like this would mean that we wouldn't have such a long delay in California while waiting for the end of the hurricane season before being able to safely continue southward.

The day after Labour Day we moved Sequitur back over to Granville Island for a few final bits of work. On 10 September La Fabrica installed the last of the cockpit canvas, completing the full enclosure. We had delayed its completion until after the solar and wind arch was installed, and now we have a wonderful sun room with an additional 20 square metres or so of living space.

The new AIS transceiver was finally talking to the rest of the system, and we kept the old AIS receiver installed. It is available with the flip of a toggle switch, if needed. The new Raymarine Class B transceiver, with its antenna installed 21 metres up the mast, has a much greater range than the old SeaCas receive-only unit.

Work on resolving the installation of the watermaker made great strides; the problem was discovered to be a faulty membrane. It was removed and a replacement membrane was on order.

We were still working on getting the Splendide washer-dryer to work off the inverter. Even though the Xantrex 2500 inverter puts out 2500 Watts and the Splendide has a maximum absorbed power of 1300 Watts, it still wouldn't start. The power lights came on, but it did not initiate its cycle. The specs of the machine said the startup surge should be well under the inverter's max surge of 62.5 Amps at 120 volts, so we began thinking that the black box in the machine doesn't like the modified sine wave from the Xantrex 2500. Among the alternatives was to install a pure sine wave inverter to feed clean power to the washer-dryer, so we investigated this route in consultation with Splendide.

I ran a new coaxial cable from the AT-140 tuner to the antenna and waited for the radio expert to come to the boat to check over the SSB setup. We paused from time to time to relax and enjoy Vancouver.

We are blessed to live in one of the finest cities in the world, the boating around here is some of the most spectacular on the planet, Canada has often been called the best country in the world in which to live, we have a very comfortable life here, and yet here we were, preparing to sail away from it all.

We walked across the Granville Bridge to survey the scene and to shoot some photos of Sequitur alongside the False Creek Yacht Club. I was in awe of the spectacular scene from the bridge: Granville Island, False Creek, English Bay, the North Shore Mountains, the architecture and vibrancy of the city. The place is alive: the kayakers, canoeists, boaters, and shuttle ferries in the Creek, the buskers playing to the crowds of shoppers and tourists milling about the Granville Market, the walkers, joggers, skaters and cyclists on the sea walls.

I recalled the puzzled looks we received while on our canal boat in France. We often heard questions like: *"You're from Vancouver, so why do you come over **here** to go boating?"* As the days counted down toward departure, I found I was asking myself similar questions. I reminded myself the drive to explore new places, the desire for new adventures, had always led me from the comforts I knew.

One thing that eased our departure was having the loft in False Creek to return to from time to time and eventually when we tire of exploring way out there. It was comforting to have such a wonderful city to come home to.

As we walked across the bridge, we spotted a fascinating weathervane on a rooftop just up Howe Street from Sequitur's slip at the yacht club. It was a sculpture of a horseman dressed in medieval costume riding a horse backwards while engrossed in a book. We were captivated by the image, and told ourselves we must look-up the background on it. Finally, after many blind Google alleys, I found reference to it:

"Riding high among the rooftops in Vancouver is an unusual sight that awaits the casual viewer looking upward from street to sky; a 58 inch-high bright copper sculpture of a historical-looking figure riding a lively horse with a ringleted mane, reading a book while sitting backwards. The figure faces the direction of the wind as indicated by the four directionals and the tipped arrow upon which it rests.

"Closer investigation reveals this to be Rodney Graham's Weathervane sculpture, which depicts the artist dressed as the sixteenth Century humanist and classical scholar, Erasmus. Absorbed in the solitary activity of reading, the figure is lost in thought and contemplation, not having to worry about where he is going or what lies ahead but, as Rodney Graham puts it, is able to 'ponder on horseback' moving forward but also looking backward, to the past.

"Rodney Graham based the weathervane on a contemporary anecdote which claimed that Erasmus wrote his most well-known work, The Praise of Folly, on horseback during a journey from Italy to England circa 1510."

No wonder the image fascinated us; we were about to sail off on a folly, more absorbed in the process and in the voyage than we were in minutely directing its time and direction. We were confident in Sequitur's ability to take us safely where conditions and circumstances dictate, and in the process, she would lead us to many wondrous places and adventures.

On 29 September we said farewell to our miniature poodle, Chianti, my faithful companion for sixteen years. Chianti fell off the boat onto the float as we were heading-out on our afternoon walk, and she could not get up. I nursed her for a while onboard, then placed her in a shoulder bag and took the AquaBus across to Granville Island and hurried up to the Animal Emergency Clinic.

The vet's assessment was that there appeared to be some spinal damage, and while this might be treatable, with her advanced age.... The tears welled in my eyes. As the doctor continued to talk and I continued to blubber, it became clear that the best thing for Chianti was to say farewell.

Edi and I will miss her excitement, her eagerness, her energy and her dedication and affection. We'll miss her smile; I've never seen a dog smile before. Chianti had a wonderful life, and she will be with us in spirit as we sail out.

4. Heading South From Vancouver

At 1100 on Thursday the 1st of October, we slipped from the float at the False Creek Yacht Club and headed out, beginning our cruise on a bleak day, in a cool drizzle with no wind to help us along. Our son-in-law, Bram braved the drizzle and walked out to the middle of the Granville Bridge to shoot this photo of our departure, and as we motored out under the Burrard Bridge, Edi released thirteen helium-filled balloons.

We motored in still airs and fog out of English Bay, passing the bell buoy at 1202 and turned left to begin our southings, the first of what we anticipate to be many. Winds remained very light the whole day, so we continued to motor, transiting Porlier Pass at low water slack at 1530. By the time we had secured alongside the False Creek Yacht Club float in Ganges at 1805, the skies had cleared.

Friday dawned clear and it had warmed nicely by the time we left Ganges at 1055. There was virtually no wind, so we motored again, all the way to Sooke, arriving at 1805 to find the marina full. We were invited by David Carswell to secure alongside his large sports fishing boat, The Rig. The three onboard had just returned from a day of fishing, having quickly caught their limit of salmon and spending the remainder of the day doing catch and release. We chatted and sipped wine as David cleaned the catch, and he gave us a lovely filleted spring.

Edi and I then walked over to the Sooke Harbour House for dinner. We ordered the seven-course Gastronomic Adventure and a bottle of Veuve Clicquot to celebrate our departure from Canada and the beginning of our adventures. By the time we had finished our superb dinner, we were the last diners in the restaurant. We walked back to the boat in the moonlight.

We slipped from alongside The Rig at the Sooke Harbour Marina at 0750 and headed out in clear skies, calm seas and not a breath of wind. As we motored across the Strait of Juan de Fuca, Edi brought up the bagel toaster and we enjoyed breakfast in the cockpit. At 0955 we crossed into the US and at 1110 we secured alongside the Customs float in Port Angeles. We were quickly cleared and for US$19, were issued a Cruising Permit.

We moved to the fuel dock and took on 725.8 litres of diesel for US$502.36. Then we moved over to the guest float and walked about a mile up to the Safeway and bought fresh provisions for our passage to San Francisco. I hanked the US flag to our starboard halyard; we were ready to go.

We slipped from the guest float in the Port Angeles Boat Haven at 1505 on Saturday, the 3rd of October and set off for San Francisco. We caught the tail-end of the flood, then washed out the Straits on a strong ebb, rounding Flattery at 2147 under a full moon and clear skies.

We headed south west to clear the continental shelf and find strengthening northerly winds. We sailed southward in following seas and winds, which were generally 20-25 knots from the north and northwest. By mid afternoon on the 6th, we had crossed the latitude of the Oregon-California border, and we were about 100 miles north west of Cape Mendocino. The winds were up to 35 knots, the swell was in the 4-5 metre range and we were surfing off every second or third wave. In the evening, the winds were up over 40 with spikes above 45, and the seas were 5-6 metres and continued thus through the night. We kept watching the boat speed gauge as it went from the mid-5 knot range to up in the 12 and 13 knot area as each wave passed under us. We saw several surfs in the 14 knot range, and the fastest we saw was a 15.3 knot spike.

Throughout the blow, the skies remained clear and with the bright sun and full moon, we were very comfortable. It was not a storm; it was simply a funnelling of winds down the inside of the huge high stationed off the coast from northern Vancouver Island down past the tip of Baja. It seems we passed through the throat of a venturi.

During the trip we continued our breakfast routine of bagel toaster in the cockpit for bagels and cream cheese with capers and lox, dishes of yogurt and mugs of freshly brewed coffee. Our lunches alternated between hot paninis and arrays of cheese and crackers with fresh fruit, olives, artichoke hearts, nuts and so on. We made water to ensure the watermaker worked in rough weather and we even ran a couple of loads of laundry through the washer/dryer.

We maintained a course that kept the seas just slightly off the port quarter and the auto pilot was able to hold us with only two broaches in the 36 hours or so of the worst of the blow. Our speed made good was in the 8.5 knot range for much of Tuesday and through Wednesday morning. Wednesday afternoon, the winds started abating, and the seas eased so that we could start bending our course back toward the coast.

At 0305 on Thursday morning, exactly four and a half days from our departure of Port Angeles, were at the entrance to the traffic separation lanes off San Francisco, and we were in the lee of the land and protected from the northerly winds. Edi made a wonderful Ghirardelli hot chocolate to sip as we dawdled north eastward into Drake's bay to kill time waiting for daylight and a tide change to make our transit under the Golden Gate. We motored into Sausalito Harbor and secured to a mooring ball at the Sausalito Yacht Club, a free reciprocal of the Bluewater Cruising Association.

After a week of free mooring on a buoy at the Sausalito Yacht Club, we slipped and motored the four miles across San Francisco Bay to a slip at Pier 39. This is a great location from which to explore the city: it is half a kilometre from Fisherman's Wharf, just a tad further to the Italian District around North Beach and less than a kilometre from Chinatown.

The weather forecast was for a strong storm to begin overnight and last through Tuesday and into Wednesday. We quickly went up to the Safeway a few blocks from the boat and stocked-up on fresh provisions, so we wouldn't have to venture out in the predicted blustery rains. True to the forecast, we got back aboard just as the rain started, and through the evening we watched the barometer plunge down into the low 990s and listened as the winds kicked-up and howled through the rigging.

For two days we bounced around in the storm on J Float at Pier 39 with the 40 to 50 mile and hour winds with gusts to 60 of the past couple of days, it was rough. When I was out in the driving rain adjusting lines during the height of the storm on Monday night, I noticed that one of our fenders had unfastened itself and drifted away. I replaced it with a spare.

On Tuesday morning as we scurried through the storm to the lounge to do wifi stuff, Edi spotted the errant fender floating among the sea lions. It was still blowing too much to even think of recovering it then. During a lull in the storm on Tuesday afternoon, we launched the dinghy and zipped over among the hundreds of sea lions.

Edi managed to snag the fender on the first attempt, and we quickly retreated back to Sequitur.

After the storm had abated, it was still rough: the breakwater does not protect the floats on the west side of the pier from the wake of passing ferries and all the go-fast-boats. When I was checking-in at the marina office on Monday, I saw that the east side of the pier is much better protected from the surge by a long breakwater. I had asked if there might be a slip available on that side, and Theta, the marina manager said she might have one coming-up. A couple of days after the storm Theta phoned to tell us a slip on the east side had opened-up. It was only a 50 foot slip, so we would have to take the dinghy down and put it on deck so we could fit in.

We flashed-up and moved around to F-6, a much quieter slip, away from the surge and away from the constant noise and pungent aroma of the sea lions. We settled in to a much more pleasant spot, and our wifi antenna was able to pickup the free marina signal.

In my Navy days, we would store ship before departing on an extended cruise. All department heads would submit their lists of requirements, orders would be placed and trucks would arrive on the jetty. Transferring the stores onboard and below to their respective storerooms was quickly accomplished with a simple pipe: "*Clear lower decks of Leading Seamen and below to the jetty; Store Ship*".

Edi and I stored ship a little differently for a week and a half in San Francisco. We began by discussing what we needed to stock-up on. In this, we considered things such as staple items and favourite delicacies that we might not find, or not find as conveniently or not find as well priced further along. Some of our buying decisions were also based on the ease now of bringing items aboard, compared to doing the same thing by dinghy in an anchorage. Also influencing our decisions was an awareness that as we travel we will be finding many new items and adopting them into our diets.

Before we left Vancouver, we had laid in six dozen rolls of toilet paper, over a year's supply of rooibos tea, ten 1 kilo tins of coffee, 30 kilos of basmati rice, over a year's supply of Japanese rice crackers, three 4.5 litre tins of Italian artichoke hearts, three 1 litre jars of capers, and so on. Because of US Customs, we had left things like nuts, seeds and dried fruit until California.

In San Francisco we began planning our shopping by Googling sources online and planning routes on foot and by transit to buy and lug stuff back to the boat. Our first shopping expedition was out to a store in Inner Richmond, south of the Presidio. It was touted online in blogs and forums as having a great selection of Lock & Lock containers. We were not disappointed, and came back loaded with hard-to-find large sizes. These are wonderful containers and a real boon to cruising boaters.

Our next destination was Costco, a 30 or 40 minute bus ride from Pier 39. We made two trips and stocked-up on sun-dried tomatoes, more artichoke hearts, more capers, dried apricots and apples and cranberries, pecans, almonds, mixed nuts and a two-year supply of garbage bags for the galley. Safeway had a nice sale on pasta, so we struck pasta off our list with a fifteen pound purchase of rotini to double-up our existing assorted stock. We also topped-up our stock of toilet paper to over a hundred rolls.

We've also made three forays into Chinatown, where we picked-up large quantities of light soy sauce, oyster-flavoured sauce, sesame oil, sesame seeds, rice flour and other things to keep our wok going for many months. We have not yet found a good source here for bulk Moroccan olives, gnocchi and lox, so we will likely bring quantities back from our trip to Vancouver next week.

We had managed to fill only a small portion of our storage space, and we still had easy-to-access lockers empty, or nearly so. Our freezers still had six ready-to eat offshore meals from the batches we made before leaving Vancouver, and before we leave San Francisco, we intend topping them up with bags of frozen shrimp and scallops from Costco.

On Wednesday the 28th of October we flew back to Vancouver to take possession of our loft. By mid afternoon we were in a hotel a SkyTrain stop away from our new loft. We love the new Canada Line from the airport; particularly the fact that the Olympic Village station it is only a block and a half walk from our front door. We walked from the hotel to our mailbox and picked-up a month's worth of mail, and then over to the bank to sign papers and to ensure everything was in place.

On Thursday morning we sat in the food court in City Square, across the street from the hotel, enjoying the free wifi and getting caught-up on our cyber worlds. In the afternoon, we did our prepossession walk-through of the loft, and then took the SkyTrain to the airport to continue our flight from San Francisco to Nanaimo. We were in the departure lounge when we were informed that Nanaimo was fogged-in and the flight was cancelled. By this time, there was not sufficient time to take the SkyTrain and Blue Bus to Horseshoe Bay to catch the last ferry at 1900. So instead of transit fare to Horseshoe Bay, we paid $60 for a taxi to Tsawwassen to catch the Duke Point ferry.

The Duke Point Ferry lands some twenty kilometres south of Nanaimo, in the middle of nowhere, with no public transit facilities, no rental car agents. After we tracked-down and phoned a shuttle service and learned that they could take us to Parksville for $70, Edi phoned her friend Joan. When we walked off the ferry, Joan was there to meet us, and she very kindly offered us her car for the next couple of days. We dropped Joan at her house and by the time we got to Edi's it was well past midnight.

Friday morning Edi had an appointment for eye surgery in Nanaimo, and while she was there, I organized a rental car for the next few days, and then we reserved a U-Haul truck for Tuesday and Wednesday for our move of Edi's stuff to Vancouver. When Edi had finished with her day surgery, we returned Joan's car and then went home to continue packing and organizing.

Saturday and Sunday saw us continuing to pack and organize, then on Monday morning we drove to Nanaimo, left the rental car in the short-term parking lot and took the ferry to Horseshoe Bay, the Blue Bus downtown and the Canada Line to our lawyer's office at the Oakridge stop. We signed the completion documents and headed back to Parksville. One of the advantages of being a senior in BC is that my total round-trip fare from Nanaimo to Oakridge was $5.00, compared to Edi's non-senior fare of $34.50.

On Tuesday, by way of one last load at the dump, we drove to Nanaimo to drop-off the rental car and to pickup the rental truck. In the evening we paused to welcome Joan and Hanna for a farewell dinner. After a wonderful few hours of relaxing and sharing with friends, we went back to truck loading until 0200, when we finally fell into bed.

We were up five hours later to continue with the loading, having determined that we needed to leave around 0900 to comfortably make the 1030 ferry. We used every last bit of space in the truck, with the mattress and box spring just squeezing into the space left for them at the rear of the load and serving as the final load cushion. We locked-up Edi's now empty house and drove off to the ferry at 0905.

Possession of the loft was set for noon on Wednesday the 4th of November, and we had organized to pickup the keys at 1300 and to have the elevator reserved for our move-in for the rest of the afternoon.

We arrived half a minute past 1300 and began to unload, working nonstop until 1730 when we had moved everything up to the loft except for the kiln, clay roller and other such things destined for the storage locker. We decided to do the last bit of unloading the next day. We started unpacking, sorting and organizing.

On Thursday morning I measured the door of the storage locker and then the minimum width of the kiln, and saw that we had two millimetres to spare. That was the easy part; wrestling the 150 kilogram, awkwardly shaped kiln out of the truck, down the car ramp to the parkade, up the elevator to the next level, down the hall and into the storage area and finally into our locker was a bit of a task.

We finished the unloading, and while Edi went for her post-surgery examination, I returned the truck to U-Haul. We spent most of the rest of Thursday and Friday unpacking and arranging. By late afternoon on Friday we had dug out a usable kitchen and dining room from the mess, and we were ready to prepare a celebratory meal. We went shopping.

The new kitchen is the finest I have ever had the privilege of using. Its superb quality appliances are perfectly placed and everything works sensibly and flows wonderfully. It was a joy to prepare dry-seared rare beef tenderloin with béarnaise sauce accompanied by a crimini, shallot and garlic Marsala sauce over fresh gnocchi and a side of asparagus spears with mayonnaise. From the cellar, we had a bottle of 2002 Masi Amarone Costasera.

Our new loft is wonderful. It is a very tasteful restoration of an early twentieth century industrial building, located in a great area of what is often called the finest city in the world. Ours is a top floor corner unit, so we have exposed thick brick walls, exposed Douglas fir ceilings with huge beams. These and the concrete floors contrast superbly with the ultramodern European design of the kitchen and bathroom.

We were up early on Saturday morning to continue the unpacking and organizing until noon. We had made the loft habitable, but still requiring a week or so of unpacking, arranging and fine-tuning to make it fully comfortable. This would all have to wait; we had some sailing to do.

We locked-up, walked over to the SkyTrain station and rode to the airport. Like clockwork, we cleared through Customs, boarded our flight to San Francisco, got a shuttle to Pier 39 and rolled our luggage to Sequitur, arriving without a hitch just before 1800. The boat was as we had left it; secure and comfortable.

We slipped from F float at Pier 39 at 1130 on Friday the 13th of November under clear skies and in still airs. We were assisted by a 4 knot ebb as we motored under the Golden Gate at noon. Before we reached Point Lobos, the winds had come-up from the northwest and we hauled-out all three sails and continued southwestward on a beam reach, making a good 7.5 to 8 knots.

We were surprised by the earliness of the sunset at 1659; it was almost exactly two hours earlier than we had experienced on our trip from Vancouver to San Francisco five weeks earlier. An hour of this, of course was accounted for by the change back to Standard Time, and the other hour was due to the sun's autumnal progression southward along its ecliptic. With the sunset came a decreasing wind, and by 2100 it was down to 5 or 6 knots and with our course now southeast, it was directly in our stern and our sails were slatting. We flashed-up and motor-sailed through the night.

Midmorning on Saturday the winds again picked-up, and we sailed to the entrance into Morro Bay in 18 to 22 knots of northerly wind. The staysail furling gear decided to jam as we were rolling-in the sails, so I went to the foredeck and as Edi eased the halyard from the cockpit, I hauled the sail down in the old-fashioned way.

The seas were kicked-up by the winds, and we ran into some heavy swells as we approached the breakwaters at the entrance to Morro Bay, but with our 9 knots we powered through and into the relative calm behind Morro Rock. We secured to a mooring ball in front of the Morro Bay Yacht Club at 1405 after a pleasant 190-mile passage. We spent a couple of days relaxing and replenishing our fresh produce.

We slipped from the Morro Bay Yacht Club mooring ball at 1010 on Wednesday the 18th of November and headed out of the harbour at high water slack, timing our departure to increase our chances of finding a smooth transition into the predicted 3 to 4 metre swell. The gribs had shown a deep depression well off the Washington-Oregon coast with winds in the 50 to 60 knot range, and NOAA's sea state predictions were for the storm-generated swell to extend down the California coast to past Point Conception. Predicted winds were NW 20 to 25 knots for the first day of our passage southeastward to Ensenada and then decreasing as we moved south. The swells were also predicted to decrease as we moved south.

We crossed the bar with no difficulty and set sail to the southwest in 10-15 knot NE winds and 3 metre swell. Once clear of Point Buchon, we bent our course to the south to clear Point Arguello, and watched as the winds backed toward the north and increased to 20 to 25 knots. The swell was now in the 4 to 5 metre range from the northwest, and there were 2-3 metre wind-generated waves from the north-northeast causing a rather confused sea.

As we sailed along, a very determined booby kept attempting to land on Sequitur. First it tried to hang onto the lower spreader, but with the rolling and pitching of the boat and the smooth surface of the spreader, it could not hold on for more than a minute or two. Then it decided to try for the roll bar of the Rocna anchor.

After dozens of near misses, it finally landed and showed its incredible balance as it remained perched there for a couple of hours. As the winds increased after sunset to beyond 30, and as the seas became more confused, our passenger finally lost its perch as solid water came over the bow and washed it away. Over the next couple of hours it continued to try to regain its perch, flashing in the navigation lights, but never again managing to spend more than a few seconds on the perch.

Wednesday's sunset found us 5.7 miles WNW of Point Arguello in 30-35 knot northerly winds and confused seas of 6-7 metres. By the time we had rounded Point Conception at 1955, the winds were up to over 40 knots, so we headed around Government Point and into Cojo Bay in the dark to look for the three mooring buoys shown on the chart. As we tiptoed around in the gale, we found that all three buoys were occupied by commercial vessels, so we headed toward the beach to find an anchorage.

We dropped the anchor in 10 metres of water, but it did not hold; fortunately the wind was offshore, and we were being blown back away from the beach. As we drifted back out and I hauled in the anchor, I noticed we were in thick kelp and then suddenly out of it. The anchor came up as one big ball of kelp; no wonder it did not hold. I cleared the kelp off the anchor and we motored back in slowly to again find the edge of the kelp, then stopped and drifted back in the gale, dropping the Rocna just clear of the kelp. This time it held.

I veered 75 metres of chain in the 11 metres of water, put on the snubbers and continued to monitor the chart plotter to see that we remained within 75 metres of the anchor's waypoint. As we were enjoying dinner, the winds had increased to 45 knots with stronger gusts, but the radar and chartplotter showed we were well set.

Thursday morning dawned clear with 3-5 knot northerly winds and near glassy seas. The ships had vacated the moorings and all that were left in the bay besides us were another sailboat at anchor and a couple of power boats investigating a sloop and a ketch that were washed-up on the rocks at the foot of the cliffs to the northwest of us.

Seeing that we could offer no assistance, at 0920 we weighed and headed out under power in near still airs and glassy seas. What a difference in weather from the previous day. We continued along the coast to Santa Barbara, where we stopped and took on 175 gallons, about 660 litres of diesel. As we left Santa Barbara at 1640, the winds had increased to 7-8 knots on the port beam, so we sailed for an hour until the wind had backed to our stern and dropped to below 4 knots.

We motored through the night passing between Los Angeles and Santa Catalina and we continued to motor all day Friday in mostly clear skies and near glassy seas. At 1351 we crossed into Mexican waters and struck the US colours and hoisted our quarantine flag. At 2320 we came to 40 metres of chain on the Rocna in 9.5 metres of water just in toward the beach from the entrance to Ensenada's harbour.

Saturday morning, the 21st was again clear and calm, and at 0925 we weighed and slowly motored into the harbour, where at 1000 we secured to a float in the Marina Ensenada. After hooking up shore power and ensuring Sequitur was secure, we took our papers and walked the ten minutes or so over to the Central Integral de Servicios to clear in. An hour-and-a-quarter later, after shuttling back-and-forth across the hall to three of the offices (the fourth office, the Capitan de Porto is closed on weekends), and paying various fees and a requested bribe, we were granted a temporary entry clearance.

We would need to return to the office on Monday morning to complete the process with the Capitan de Porto. Back onboard, we struck the quarantine flag and hoisted the Mexican courtesy flag.

Directly across the float from us were fellow members of the Bluewater Cruising Association, Tony and Pat with their home-built wooden schooner, Forbes & Cameron. They had arrived a week or so previously, and Tony had his workshop setup on the floats, and was in the process of overhauling the main gaff.

On Sunday Edi and I walked part way, and then took a bus the rest of the way to Costco to top-up our pantry, cellar, freezers and fridges. Among the great buys were a kilo of portobello mushrooms for 51 Pesos (about $4.10), some Argentinean Malbec for 42 Pesos (about $3.35), 4 kilos of boneless and skinless chicken breasts at 76 Pesos/kilo (about $6.10/kilo).

On Monday morning we walked over to Starbucks to have a coffee, check our emails and add a post to our blog. From here we'll walk over to the Central Integral de Servicios to complete our clearance in with the Capitan de Porto, and immediately clear out with him, since our intention is to head out from Ensenada by noon, bound for Bahia de Tortugas, about 275 miles down the coast. The gribs show 5 to 10 knot W and NW winds for the next five days, and since our planned course is generally SE, we would have light following winds for the trip. We knew we would likely do a lot of motoring.

At 1015 on Monday the 23rd we walked over to the CIS to clear in and out with the Port Captain. The process took the better part of three-quarters of an hour, and seemed to involve the training of one of the four uniformed staff behind the counter. He was quite apparently running through his first ever attempt at a computer keyboard, and later, his first venture into the complexities of a credit card terminal as he took our 306 Peso fee. That fee took our clearance total to 1490.33 Pesos, which converts to about $120 Canadian.

By 1130, we had arrived back onboard Sequitur, and had began preparing for departure. I topped-up the water tanks while Edi secured below decks for sea. At 1205 we slipped from the float in Marina Ensenada and headed out under power, clearing the harbour entrance at 1220 and setting course of 235 at 6.5 knots into a southwest breeze of 3 to 5 knots, which was barely able to raise a ripple on the sea. Forty minutes later we developed a substantial vibration, and I immediately shifted the transmission to neutral.

As we slowly drifted forward, a great mass of kelp wafted out from under the stern; we had apparently motored through a raft of it. I put the engine astern for a few seconds, then paused as fronds floated to the surface. Using the boathook, assisted by occasional forward and astern thrusts of the engine, I cleared the mass, and within five minutes we were again motoring without vibration into a near glassy calm sea.

At 1344 we rounded Cabo Punta Banda and set course 180 to clear Punta Santo Tomas. We were by this time in a long slow 1 to 2 metre northwest swell with barely a breeze. At 1530 we rounded Punta Santo Tomas and altered to 160 in glassy seas on the slow swell, and we continued to motor under clear skies.

Our noon position on Tuesday the 24th had us just north of 29° North and 116° West, and there were now a few ripples on the sea. By 1300, a 6 to 7 knot westerly breeze had developed, and we hauled out the sails and glided along at 3 to 4 knots. By sunset the breeze had veered to near north and had subsided to around 4 knots. We flashed-up the engine and motor-sailed for a while until the slatting sails told us to haul them in.

Our midnight position placed us at 45 miles WNW of the entrance to Bahia de Tortugas, and a course of 120 would keep us well clear of any navigational hazards and 6 knots would have us approaching the entrance to the Bay after sunrise. I had an easy watch to turnover to Edi when she came up at 0200.

When I again took over the watch at 0700, the sun had been up for a quarter hour or so and we were about 9 miles WSW of the entrance to Bahia de Tortugas. With our course of 075, the NE wind of 6 to 7 knots was directly on our nose. Over the next hour or so, the winds piped up to 25 to 30 knots and remained directly on our bow as we motored into the bay through short, steep two-metre wind waves, which occasionally washed over the bows, and deposited small squid on the decks.

At 0855 I roused Edi from her sleep and at 0901 we came to 40 metres of chain on the Rocna anchor in 7.5 metres of water 3 cables off the pier of Puerto San Bartolome in Bahia de Tortugas. The winds were now a rather steady 15 to 18 knots from the NNW, exactly the winds we were looking for the past couple of days during our passage down from Ensenada.

Edi brought up the bagel toaster and we enjoyed bagels and cream cheese with capers and lox and a large thermos of fresh coffee. We were entertained by the fishermen setting and retrieving their nets, and being very closely supervised by hundreds of pelicans and dozens of sea lions.

We then lazed around in the cockpit in 25 degree weather until the sunset's sudden chill chased us down into the salon to continue our general inactivity.

The next day, Thursday the 26th, we continued our serious lazing until mid-afternoon, when we lowered the dinghy and motored over to the float at the end of the pier. We walked up through a very dusty, and obviously very poor town. Every block or so there was a small store, stocked mostly with packaged drinks and snacks. A few of them had small bins of root vegetables and a cooler with some sad-looking green vegetables. As we circled back toward the water, we ran across a farmacia, the writing on the wall of which told us, among other things, that it offered internet connection. The young chap behind the counter answered our question with, "18 pesos per hour."

Friday we put in much of a day seriously lazing about, punctuated by my pushing a few buttons to make another 180 litres of water to compensate our longish showers and for Edi having pushed a few buttons the previous day to program the washer-dryer through its cycle. In the middle of the afternoon we dinghied ashore and walked up to the farmacia to log onto the internet to do emails, to check the weather and to post another entry to our blog.

Our intention was to leave early the following morning and continue southward, possibly stopping in Bahia de Balenas, a day or so along the coast, or if conditions were suitable, continuing on to Bahia Magdelana another day or so further along.

We sailed off the anchor at 0820 on Saturday the 28th, setting a southward course to clear Entrance Rock and exit Bahia de Tortugas in NW winds of 10 to 12 knots with gusts to 15. Noon found us sailing on a SSE course in 12-14 knot NW winds making about 4.5 knots in the 2 to 3 metre NW swell. By sunset the winds had strengthened to 15-18 knots and we shortened to staysail and a partly rolled-in main for the night. The winds increased through the night.

At sunrise on Sunday the winds were 25 to 30 knots from the west and we sailing southeastward about 16 miles west of Punta Abreojos in rather confused seas on a large westerly swell. With the bands of cirrus coming from the west, and the looks of a coming storm, we decided to head into an anchorage around the point. At 1035 we came to 30 metres of chain on the Rocna in 6.8 metres of water in the lee of the point in Bahia de Balenas and protected from the growing storm.

We relaxed the remainder of the day and then on Monday we played chef. Edi baked bread while I made a pot of cream of asparagus soup from the snipped ends of the last dozen or so bunches of asparagus we had enjoyed. The soup was to put in the fridge for our next night passage meal, and the bread was to augment the nearly depleted supply in the freezers.

On Tuesday the 1st of December, we weighed and proceeded to sea under clear skies and a 7 to 9 knot easterly breeze. We sailed through the day and into the night in light winds, making between 3 and 5 knots south eastward along the coast of the Baja Peninsula.

Sunrise on the 2nd found us 18 miles northwest of Cabo San Lazaro, still sailing along in a light northerly breeze. Once we had rounded the cape at 1130, the winds died and we flashed-up and motored toward an anchorage. At 1310 we came to 40 metres of chain on the Rocna on a fine sand bottom in 8 metres of water in Bahia Santa Maria in the lee of Pico San Lazaro.

At 0710 on Thursday the 3rd, we weighed and motor-sailed southeasterly along the coast in a 6 to 7 knot northeasterly breeze, standing off the land far enough to get a steady breeze. With turns for 7 knots assisted by the breeze on the beam and a south-setting current, we were making just over 10 knots.

At 0905 we tacked to the east to round Punta Magdalena, and a while later, as we turned northward into Bahia Magdalena the wind came onto our nose. We hauled in sails and continued under power northward toward Puerto San Carlos. An hour later we spotted a sailboat heading southward out of the bay, and as it passed, we recognized it as Pamdemonium, whom we had last seen off the British Columbia coast in July on our way from Ucluelet to Cobb Sea Mount.

We chatted with Pamela and Dennis on VHF for a few minutes and they told us of free wifi available at anchor off a tiny community on the shore of the Man of War anchorage. We carried on past the Man of War anchorage and followed the buoyed channel up to Puerto San Carlos. As we passed between each of the dozen or so pairs of lateral buoys marking the current channel in the constantly drifting sands of the bay, we placed a waypoint on the plotter midway between them, effectively marking the mid channel for our return. Because the buoys are frequently moved, the charts cannot be expected to be up-to-date.

Puerto San Carlos was a huge disappointment; there appeared to be nothing but a dilapidated commercial pier with loading facilities, and no sign of anything of use to a visiting pleasure craft. There were no channels marked through the sand flats, where by far the most common soundings were less than 2 metres. There were several wrecks washed up on banks and beaches, but nothing that looked the least bit like a marina, let alone a safe anchorage.

We turned around and retraced our zigzag through the channel, much more easily now with the mid-channel marks on our chartplotter. At 1544 we came to 35 metres of chain on the Rocna anchor in 7 metres of water 750 feet off the beach in front of Puerto Magdalena in Man of War anchorage. A quarter hour later, the Capitan de Puerto came to the boat to collect a copy of our Crew List and to have us enter our details in his register. A little later, at sunset, the electrical generators somewhere in the little hamlet on the beach were switched on, and with the electricity came a very strong wifi signal.

Edi prepared another couple of loaves of New York Times bread to let rise overnight, one of them with Moroccan olives and sun-dried tomatoes, and the other with chopped walnuts and cranberries. We would have fresh bread to take us around the tip of the Baja peninsula and into the Sea of Cortez.

We weighed in Man of War at 0540 on the 4th of December and motored southward in light airs and calm seas. By the time Edi had finished baking the two loaves of bread at 0955, there were hints of some winds, and a while later we were ghosting along at about 4 knots on a beam reach in a 6 to 8 knot breeze.

Mid afternoon the breeze died and the seas became glassy, so we motored along through the afternoon and into the dusk in still airs. About half an hour after sunset we ran into steep wind waves on our port bow, and within a few minutes the winds had come up to 15 knots and we reached along at 7 to 8 knots, crossing the Tropic of Cancer shortly before midnight. Through the night the winds increased to 25-30 knots and backed to just abaft our beam, leaving very sloppy seas. We made good speed, and by sunrise we were about 60 miles from Cabo San Lucas.

By mid morning, the wind had veered to the east and onto our nose, and it had decreased to about 5 knots. We flashed-up and motored the rest of the way to Cabo San Lucas, arriving at the fuel dock in the port at 1420. We took on 752 litres of diesel and enquired about the cost of overnight moorage. Yikes! US$180 per night. The port is a man-made harbour, with no room to expand, and the huge demand for moorage from the very large charter fishing fleet contributes the very high prices.

At 1522 we came to 30 metres of chain on the Rocna anchor in 9 metres of water on a sand bottom outside the port and in front of the beach-side hotels and resorts. Half an hour later we were in our dinghy and on our way back into the port to buy some steak and fresh vegetables for dinner, returning to Sequitur at the end of the short dusk.

On Sunday morning, we dinghied back into the port and took a bus to Costco to begin our restocking. We bought eight thick pieces of beef tenderloin, eight thick pork tenderloin chops, three thick ham steaks, half a smoked turkey, a pork loin roast, a dozen-and-a-half bagels, four heavy loaves of bread, eight huge portobellos, three kilos of criminis, a dozen bottles of wine, a kilo of butter, eight packages of cream cheese, a dozen red, yellow and orange peppers, a couple of dozen tomatoes and so on. Thank goodness we had brought with us many cloth and mesh bags and the folding cart.

We took a taxi back to the dinghy dock and juggled the load back out to Sequitur. After stowing everything, we still had considerable room in the fridges and the freezers. Tomorrow we intend heading in to the CCC supermarket, where there is a broader selection of fresh vegetables and fruit.

Of the twelve sailboats in the anchorage, we have identified three others from Vancouver: Magenta, Pamdemonium and Zeeba, and we were looking forward to heading ashore with some of them for dinner in the evening.

We were lying at anchor about a hundred metres off the beach, in front of a near-solid wall of hotels and resorts, the waters around us churned up by a steady buzz of passing jet-skis, water taxis and para-sail boats. We were sniping a free wifi connection with our USB antenna.

In the evening's early dusk we headed in to the dinghy dock for a rendezvous with Julius & Margaret of Zeeba and Larry & Kim of Magenta. They already knew Cabo since they had been here a few days. Magenta had left Vancouver in mid-August, and Zeeba sailed on 21 September.

Larry talked with the bartender in a bar kiosk at the side of the dock and after he had received a recommendation for a good authentic Mexican restaurant, we walked through the town to the Maria Corona. We all enjoyed excellent meals, Edi and I opting for the Catch of the Day, which was mahi-mahi deliciously done in a foil papillote with peppers and herbs. This followed wonderfully the guacamole that was done for us table-side. Including the appetizers, three Coronas and the tip, the meal came to about $35 for the two of us.

This was the first meal that Edi and I had eaten ashore since Sooke Harbour House the evening before we left Canada, and it was the first socializing we have done with other boaters since leaving Vancouver. I think it is a great testament to our compatibility that we had forgotten that we miss the company of others.

5. Enjoying the Sea of Cortez

Cabo San Lucas is a high-priced tourist mecca, crowded, bustling and noisy. We had used it to restock our fridges, freezers and pantry, and with no other reason to remain it was time to move on.

At 0710 on the 10th of December I took the dinghy in to the port to buy fishing licenses while Edi prepared Sequitur for heading out. In answer to our questions a couple of days previous, we had been told that fishing licenses were sold only at a stand on the quayside near the Coast Guard station, and on a subsequent visit there, we were told they were sold only between 0600 and 1000. So I was heading in to attempt again to become a legal fisherman.

I tied-up and walked up to the stand, which was guarded by two machine-gun-toting soldiers, and asked to but licenses for Edi and me and for the boat. The agent asked whether we wanted one day or three, and when I replied we wanted licenses for several months, he told us we had to go to the office in the centre of town, which didn't open until 1000. So I went back out to Sequitur empty-handed.

After a leisurely breakfast, we weighed at 0844 and headed northeast out of Bahia de San Lucas in light airs and clear skies with a few scattered cumulus. By 0930, as we cleared the bay, the wind had established itself from the north at about 12 to 14 knots, so we rolled out the main and jib and sailed on a nice reach at about 7.5 to 8 knots. Through the early afternoon the wind veered to the northeast and increased to around 20 knots, directly on our nose for our course into Bahia Frailes, and the seas had become short and steep. We decided to motor into the weather the rest of the way, rather than tacking back and forth across the steep chop.

We took advantage of the engine's running to make water and do a couple of loads of laundry, and at 1615 we came to 30 metres on the Rocna in 8.5 metres of water a couple of hundred metres off the beach in Bahia Frailes. The headland diverted the wind, which was by this time northerly about 10 or 12 knots.

This is a remote and rather unpopulated area at the end of a dirt road with some fish camps along the beach. There is mention in the guidebook of a hotel and a bar and recently a few new houses taking advantage of the beautiful scenery. From somewhere here, our wifi antenna picked up a free connection.

After a leisurely breakfast in the cockpit we weighed at 0930 and headed out around Cabo Los Frailes under power to find the wind. Once we had cleared the protection of headland we were in the 1 to 2 metre short, steep seas generated by 20 knot NNW winds. Since our course was initially to the north, then to the NNW, this meant we would be beating our way upwind.

We rolled out the staysail and began hauling out the main, but it jammed in the mast. This was the first time I have had problems with it in the two-and-a-half years I have been sailing Sequitur. We examined our options: with other choices available, it was too rough to comfortably climb the mast the 3 or 4 metres required to fix the jam, we could motor back into the anchorage and clear the jam, or we could carry on to Bahia de Los Muertos under power.

If we turned back, the delay would mean a late night arrival in Bahia de Los Muertos, which is the next safe haven up the coast. If we motored, it would give us an opportunity to top-up the batteries and we would be able to power directly into the seas rather than tacking back and forth across them. We opted to continue on under power.

In the early afternoon the winds were up over 30 knots with gusts above 35 and the seas were a 1 to 2 metre short chop on a steep 2 to 3 metre swell. Every hundredth wave or so we took some heavy pounding, with solid water over the bows, and the motion was quite tiring. Otherwise it was a very pleasant day, with bright clear skies.

At 1650 we came to 25 metres of chain on the Rocna in 6.2 metres of water on a fine sand bottom in Bahia de Los Muertos. We relaxed for the rest of the afternoon, and in the evening enjoyed a wonderful dinner of rare beef tenderloin with béarnaise sauce and gnocchi in a sauté of diced portobello mushrooms, garlic, white onion, tomato and white wine, accompanied by fine green beans amandine.

After breakfast the next morning we cleared the jam in the main sail, then we spent until the early afternoon cleaning.

I started on the outside and Edi worked on the interior. While we have kept the boat relatively tidy and clean, this was the first opportunity that we have had to thoroughly clean the entire boat since we left.

This evening we took the dinghy ashore to a small float and walked the hundred metres or so to Restaurant 1535 for dinner. This is a rather modern facility, which is mainly a 20 metre by 20 metre steep-pitched thatched hip roof supported on wonderfully twisted mangrove posts and exposed pole trusses. It is open at three sides and the fourth side is the bar, kitchen and service area. Solid tables and comfortable chairs are set on a floor of large tiles, and the place has a pleasant feeling.

We shared a huge serving of nachos, enough in fact, to make a whole meal. Then our main course arrived. We each had a delicious dorado sautéed in garlic and butter accompanied by rice and greens. It was a wonderful meal in a fine setting, and including three beers and the tip, the evening came to CA$45.

The following morning, the 13th we took the dinghy ashore after breakfast and walked along the beach on the west side of the bay. The sand is very fine, and this made it easy walking along the wetted edge, having the small waves rinse our sandals from time to time. Along the way we paused to watch a fisherman throwing a net from a panga a short distance off the beach.

We very quickly covered the two kilometres to the resort developments in the south west part of the bay. As we slowly explored, we saw a golf course, a horse riding ring, a spectacular private dining room, outdoor lounges, an open-air hilltop chapel, reflecting pools, and we were taken by the tasteful style and quality of it all. There are amenities of a quality to please all but the most jaded resort goers.

We walked back along the beach past the fishing pangas hauled-up above the tide line and used a couple of them to frame this view of Sequitur in the anchorage, near the centre of the shot.

After our four-and-a-half kilometre walk, we returned onboard to relax for the rest of the day in the coolness the boat's cabin, which stayed at 25 and below all day, while the cockpit thermometer read just over 30º.

At 0745 on Monday the 14th we weighed and motored out of Ensenada de Los Muertos to find the wind and head up through the Canal de Cerralvo. The guidebook says: *"From November to March, winds typically blow from the north, down the Sea of Cortez. With the restriction of the channel by Isla Cerralvo to the east and the Baja Peninsula to the west, winds tend to funnel through the channel, bringing with it, wind driven waves. With adverse currents, strong winds and steep waves, Cerralvo Channel can become very challenging, so plan accordingly."*

We rounded Punta Perico still looking for the wind, but finding only still airs and glassy seas. Around Punta Arena de la Ventana and into the narrows, there was still no wind and the seas were still glassy and we continued to motor. It being Monday, and having the motor on and making plenty of electricity, it made sense to do some laundry and, while we were at it, make some water.

The day remained still and calm, and by the time we had transited Canal de San Lorenzo at 1345, Edi had run the third load of washing through the machine and cleared our backlog. At 1400 the watermaker completed its sixth hour, and had produced another 400 litres of fresh water. At 1418 we came to 25 metres on the Rocna in 6.5 metres of water on a fine sand bottom in Puerto Balandra, just as a breeze was beginning to ripple the waters. So much for the dreaded Canal de Cerralvo!

We had decided to save electricity and do the wash cycle only on the machine, and in the anchorage the wind made for perfect laundry drying conditions. Edi strung out the three loads and within an hour it was all dry. Through the afternoon the wind increased, until by sunset it was blowing down off the slopes above the beach to the northeast at about 15 knots. We were well anchored and comfortable. Comfortable, that is until early evening when a northwest swell started to build and the northeast wind kept the bows pointing upwind and kept the swell on the beam. As the swell built, so did the rolling and we spent our most uncomfortable anchorage of the trip.

At sunrise on Tuesday morning, after a long night of rolling and lurching, we looked out to the weather outside the anchorage to see steep white-capped seas, whipped-up by what appeared to be 20 to 25 knot winds. Punta Tecolote had protected us from the brunt of the weather; however, it could not prevent the rolling swell from entering the anchorage. Our intention had been to take the dinghy ashore this morning and walk along the beach to a road that went a couple of miles across the headland to Playa Tecolote. There are some cantinas and small restaurants along the beach where we could get some fresh fish tacos for lunch.

With the weather as it was, we thought we'd have breakfast and see if conditions improved. It was another clear and warm day, and we were hoping the winds would abate and seas subside a bit. The winds continued and sloppy seas remained, so at 1000 we weighed anchor and headed off in search of a better anchorage.

At 1000 on Tuesday the 15th we weighed in a very sloppy Puerto Balandra and headed off in search of a better anchorage. Our goal was Caleta Lobos, 2 miles south along the coast. As soon as we left the protection of Punta Tecolote, we were in 25 knot winds with short, steep seas running against an ebbing tide. As we approached Caleta Lobos and looked in, we could see that it would likely be uncomfortable in these conditions. We decided to continue on to La Paz; the entrance to the port was only another 5 miles along.

Forty-five minutes later we were wending our way along the 4.5 mile narrow buoyed channel leading past the offshore shoals and into La Paz harbour. At 1150 we came to 20 metres of chain on the Rocna anchor on a fine sand bottom off the Marina Don Jose. The anchorage was quite crowded; we counted eighty-four other pleasure craft in an area a mile long and half a mile wide, so finding a convenient spot was a tad difficult. We ended up settling for a spot about half a mile from the dinghy dock in Marina de La Paz.

After lunch we took the dinghy ashore and walked the mile or so to the CCC for groceries, and on the way back we stopped in a small office to buy our fishing licenses. Now we don't risk having the boat seized for fishing illegally. Even although we have not yet fished, just having the gear aboard without a license is illegal.

Back onboard with our groceries stowed, we were hailed just at dusk by two Armada sailors in a small panga, who informed us in Spanish (which we are just barely starting to try to learn) that we were in a restricted anchorage reserved for the Armada. After getting the approximate delineation of the area, which is not marked on the charts, nor the guide, nor indicated by any buoys, beacons or other markings, we flashed-up, turned on our navigation lights, weighed anchor and weaved our way through the crowded anchorage to find a space. We relocated to about two cables off the entrance to Marina de La Paz, and would now have a shorter dinghy run ashore.

On Wednesday, while Edi and I were enjoying a lazy morning in bed, there was a rapping on the hull. We disengaged and I went to investigate its source: A neighbouring boater had stopped by to inform us we were swinging out into the channel, and that the Armada would probably come along and tell us to move. To preempt the Armada, we decided to move the boat again. We moved closer to the Marina de La Paz breakwater, and tucked-in between it and a couple of ketches, Hadar of Palm City,

Florida and Fantasia of Honolulu, Hawaii. We were then only a cable away from the marina entrance.

The tidal current runs about 2 knots in the harbour as large volumes of water move in and out through the narrow entrance. The prevailing wind blows across the trend of the current, and boats at anchor swing to their own interpretation of the rhythm of the winds and currents, performing what has over the years been dubbed the "La Paz Waltz". For our debut, our dance card had us doing the three-step before we started the waltz.

This morning at 0930 we weighed and motored the cable or so over to the outside float of Marina de La Paz and secured alongside. Yesterday we had decided that at less than $40 per night, it made sense to lay alongside for a couple of days to make it easier to stock-up. For the following three weeks or more, we anticipate being away from anything larger than a few tiny fishing communities.

We hadn't been alongside, other than to refuel, since the two days we spent in Ensenada nearly four weeks previously, and it would be good to top-up the batteries with shore power, good to top-up the water tanks with a dockside hose, good to take long showers without the guilt of water usage, good to run the washer and the dryer without thoughts of power consumption, good to go ashore without the dinghy.

Being alongside makes many things more convenient. Shortly after we had arrived alongside, I took our two empty propane tanks up to the front of the marina office and had them refilled for just over $12. On Mondays, Wednesdays and Fridays a local fellow carts them away and a couple of hours brings them back full.

The previous two days we had walked from the marina into the old town along the malecon, and along the way we paused to admire the bronze sculptures which grace its length. The most intriguing is one of an old man in a paper boat gazing longingly out to sea.

On its pedestal is a plaque with the artist's poem, which translates to:

I have a boat of paper...
It is made from a page
where I wrote my dreams.
It has no anchors nor ropes.
I want to sail in it,
through the seven seas;
in the eighth, where I know, it will
come ashore in the port I long for.
... Has anyone seen the light
shining from its lighthouse?

In the afternoon Edi and walked the mile or so over to the CCC supermarket and hauled back two large cartons full of groceries on our little luggage cart. Among our better purchases were 4.5 kilos of fresh basa fillets at less than $5.50 a kilo; we had thoroughly enjoyed the ones we had bought a couple of days previously. We had also enjoyed the superb tomatoes, so we bought another couple of kilos for just under a dollar.

Back onboard, the basa fillets were zip-locked in pairs in the freezers and the fridges were crammed to their gunnels with fresh produce.

On the 20th of December we prepared to continue north. Our thoughts were to spend a few weeks exploring the anchorages between La Paz and Loreto, starting with a week or so visiting the exquisite little anchorages on Isla Espiritu Santo less than 20 miles north of La Paz. There, on the Island of the Holy Spirit we will figured that we would surely find Sequitur a more comfortable place to spend this Christmas Eve than we had found for her the previous year.

The previous Christmas Eve I had waded my way through the half metre of still-falling snow to Sequitur's berth in Snug Cove on Bowen Island. The photo serves as a reminder of one of the reasons we have sailed south.

However, the weather is only one of the reasons. On Saturday as we sat having lunch in the cockpit in 27 degree weather with a pleasant cooling breeze coming over the combings, I had observed how our diet has been changing. Instead of paninis appropriate to a cooler climate, Edi had prepared quesadillas and served them with delicious guacamole and fresh tomato salsa that she had made.

We both love exploring foods and different tastes, and our preferences have always been to prepare food from fresh ingredients, rather than to open packages. The supermarkets here are full of row upon row of the same standard packaged and processed foods that we ignore at home. However, the fresh produce shelves, dairy cases and meat and seafood counters offer many new things to try, and we were anticipating that as we moved through new areas on our voyage, we would find many more items being added to our diet.

After a leisurely breakfast on Sunday morning, we attended to the last few details before getting underway. I topped-up the water tanks and squared away up top while Edi stowed and secured below. Then ready to go, we walked up the floats with our bag of garbage for the bin, and our gate key to return to the marina office so we could get back our 400 peso deposit.

The garbage bin was open, but I had forgotten how Catholic Mexico is; the marina office was closed on Sundays. The nearby diving gear shop was open (it must be owned by pagans), and we popped in to it for one more attempt to find ear plugs for snorkeling. No luck, but they did confirm that the marina remained closed all day on Sundays.

As we were walking back to the gate and resigning ourselves to staying another day in the Marina de La Paz, we were hailed from their bicycles by Michael & Gloria Hanssmann of Paikea Mist. They had left Vancouver in August and after spending time in southern California, had come down the Baja coast from San Diego with the Baja Haha at the end of October. They had just returned to La Paz the previous day from a few weeks of exploration up the coast to Loreto, and were preparing to continue south along the mainland coast of Mexico to Puerto Vallarta to await the start of the Pacific Puddle Jump.

As we stood chatting with them by the marina office, Gloria noticed that a man had just opened the office door and gone in. I saw a fellow putting up some Christmas decorations on the door, so I went over to see if he could help us with the key return. He was apparently the manager or owner, and after some fumbling in his staff's files, he found our 400 pesos deposit stapled to a slip, and exchanged it for the key. We were now free to go.

We continued to chat with Michael & Gloria, listening to tales of their explorations up the coast, getting tips and ideas on places to see and generally catching-up on four months of adventures. Finally, after what must have been closer to two hours than one, we tore ourselves away and at 1310 slipped and headed out the buoyed channel.

The skies were totally blue and there was a very light northerly breeze. Since our intended destination was to the north, we motored, and at 1550 we came to 20 metres on the Rocna anchor in 4.8 metres of water on a fine sand bottom in Bahia San Gabriel on Isla Espiritu Santo (Holy Spirit Island). We were the only boat in three-quarter by half mile bay; we nestled into eastern corner of it, a couple of cables off an abandoned pearl fishery.

For over four centuries, pearls were harvested in the La Paz area of the Sea of Cortez, and with more efficient modern harvesting came the decline and eventual collapse of stocks. Now pearls come from the cultured farming process, but with the Isla Espiritu Santo chain having in 2003 been made into a National Marine Park, commercial activities here have been stopped.

On Monday morning we swam off the transom platform and tried out our new snorkel gear, then we sunbathed until it became too hot on deck and we went below to continue lazing about through the heat of the day. Mid-afternoon, when the sun had slanted to a better angle, we took the dinghy ashore to explore the ruins of the pearl fishery.

The major structure of the ruins was a series of dry-masonry walled canals, three metres or so wide, with the wall tops standing a metre or so above high water and their bases a couple of metres below. Canals at each end of the complex let sea water into the maze as the tides rose, and the water flowed through the parallel zigzag of the canals nurturing the oysters. Inland from the maze are some old building foundations, low walls, middens and a long ridge of the calcareous remains of oyster shells.

We had climbed the slopes above the ruins for an overview, and since we were already a third of the way up the ridge, we decided to continue to the top. We scrambled up through broken volcanic blocks, much of it quite porous, and through a sparse, but wonderful selection of cacti, succulents and low shrubs. Even with our sandals, the climb to the ridge top was quite straight forward, and the view from the top was well worth the effort.

The broad, undulating arid ridge top was composed of mostly large slabs of flat, shattered rock, still laying in place, and it was very easy to wend our way through and among the scattering of small succulents, cacti and stunted shrubs. We walked across to the cliff tops overlooking Ensenada Dispensa to watch the eagles soaring in the updrafts, and below the pelicans in their seemingly reckless dives for fish in the shoals.

On our return, we walked along the ridge toward the head of bays and descended through the broken blocks and slabs to the edge of the mangrove growth adjacent to the oyster farm. The sandals were not quite the proper footgear for the descent, and we promised ourselves that the next time we went ashore with even the hint of a chance of a hike, we would bring proper shoes.

We arrived back onboard in time pour ourselves snifters of brandy and settle-in in the cockpit watching a spectacular sunset. The 'mare's tails' or 'elephant tusks' among the clouds foretold the coming of increasing westerly winds overnight. These localized winds, called Coromuels in the La Paz area and Elefantes further north, would blow directly into our southwest-facing anchorage in Bahia San Gabriel, and the waves they generated would give us some pitching. We were securely anchored on the 40 kilogram Rocna on a fine sand bottom.

On Monday evening, we enjoyed a delicious dinner of butter sautéed basa fillets with a rice and black bean salad spiked with Moroccan olives, Spanish onions, roma tomatoes, celery, green, red, orange and yellow peppers, artichoke hearts and cilantro.

By mid evening the wind had picked-up, and we spent the night pitching at anchor as the Coromuel winds blew into the anchorage. The motion wasn't unpleasant; however, the sound of the anchor snubber lines creaking over the gunnels was a bit loud from our bed in the forecabin.

We slept-in on Tuesday morning to compensate. After a late breakfast of toasted bagels with smoked salmon cream cheese and capers and a pot of fresh coffee, we relaxed. Then at 1220 we weighed and headed out of Bahia San Gabriel and turned northward along the west coast of Isla Espiritu Santo past Punta Catedral and into Puerto Ballena. At 1310 we came to 16 metres of chain on the Rocna anchor in 3.5 metres of water on a sand bottom in Ensenada Gallo. This is the centre of three small bays that make-up Puerto Ballena.

After lunch we took the dinghy over to a white sand beach about 3 cables to the south and pulled it above high water line. At the near end of the crescent-shaped beach are cliffs of a conglomerate structure, with large and small rocks of varying composition and origin, which had in some past cataclysmic event been randomly cemented together, and are now being eroded by the seas into wondrous formations.

We started up the ridge, scrambling over bands of conglomerate rock alternating with areas of igneous slabs and shattered blocks and strata of eroded soft reddish porous rock. We threaded our way up past scattered succulents and cacti, scrub bushes and wisps of grass, all of them seeming to struggle for a few drops of water in this desert environment. As we climbed, the steepness of the slope decreased, and we were soon on the crest of a pleasant broad ridge that led us easily higher.

We paused to admire the views back out at Sequitur at anchor in the bay below us, and to watch the eagles gliding in the updrafts searching for their next meal. We saw rabbit droppings and many small burrows in the thin soil of the ridge, but we spotted no lunch for the eagles, nor did we see them have any success.

When we reached the summit, we decided to continue along the ridge that led southward and joined onto the spur that descended westward past the other end of the beach on which we had landed the dinghy. This gave us a lovely circuit, with a whole new selection of views, including those from the cliff tops looking down into Ensenada Gallina.

We found a good route down, avoiding the cliffs near the bottom by trending to the right as we neared the beach. Along the beach we walked through coarse sand, which appeared to be composed mainly of shell and coral fragments.

We arrived back onboard as the winds were beginning to pick-up from the west. We did an inventory of our fresh produce to check its condition and to help in menu planning for the following few days. We were down to two servings of the fresh green beans we had bought on the 6th in Cabo San Lucas, and we and were down to two large portobellos from that shopping. We still had fresh green, red, yellow and orange peppers to last a week or so, and plenty of tomatoes and some zucchini among the more perishable items, plus a good stock of celery, onions, and garlic. In the freezers we still had five or six dinners each of beef tenderloin, pork tenderloin chops, boneless and skinless chicken breasts, basa fillets and ham steaks, and there was half a smoked turkey in one of the fridges. We knew that we would survive rather well before we needed resort to opening cans.

A while later, after a spectacular sunset, the winds were up into the 20 knot range. We spent the evening gently pitching at anchor and enjoying a dinner of beef tenderloin with béarnaise sauce, portobello mushrooms, steamed new potatoes and steamed green beans with slivered almonds in brown butter.

The westerly winds continued through the night and on past noon on Wednesday, when they began subsiding. It was partly cloudy, with blue patches alternating with bands of altocumulus, pretending to be loosely gathered cotton balls. The midday temperature was 25° when I trimmed my beard in the breeze of the cockpit and Edi gave me my Christmas haircut.

Mid afternoon we took the dinghy over to the headland to the north and landed on the rocky beach. Huge blocks of pink stone, many four metres and more in height, lay scattered near the beach where they had landed at the base of the rubble slopes after their descent from the steep cliffs above. These blocks have fracture planes oriented at right angles, looking huge tossed dice.

When I had examined the ridge from the boat in the morning through binoculars, I had seen feasible routes to its top through a break in the cliffs half a kilometre or so to the east toward the head of the bay. I had also seen a ledge system that appeared to lead up to a jumble of blocks that ran up to a breach in the cliff face, and this seemed to offer a short way to the top directly above the boat.

We worked our way up through large and small blocks and across a couple of conglomerate strata toward the base of the cliffs. As we climbed, we had aimed toward the short route I that had seen to determine whether it was feasible.

When we arrived at the base of the cliffs, we threaded ourselves up a chimney behind a huge detached block and under a chockstone in its centre.

Beyond this, and across an airy ledge, another chimney led to a scramble across block tops to a final chimney that led to a gentler scramble to the cliff top. On the broad ridge-top we paused to catch our breath and to drink-in the spectacular view back down at Sequitur laying at anchor in Ensenada Gallo.

By this time it was 1600; there was only another hour-and-a-half before sunset, and we needed to get off the ridge and back to the dinghy. It would not be prudent to attempt to down-climb the route we had come up, so we had to find an easier way off the ridge.

We walked across the broad ridge top for a superb view down into Ensenada de la Raza, which had a sailboat at anchor in its centre. As we threaded our way through the rich desert garden along the tabletop flatness of the ridge, surrounded by amazing seascapes, we were increasingly thankful for being sufficiently fit and healthy to be doing this.

We ambled along the ridge, enjoying the setting as we looked for the breach in the cliffs and the route down. Beside us, out over the cliffs, the eagles were soaring in the updrafts and below, on the surface of the bay, dozens of pelicans were in a feeding frenzy among the fish in the shoals at the head of the bay. They were diving so frequently that it seemed as if they were conducting a dive training session.

We found a shallow gully breaking through the cliffs and took it down to the blocks at their foot, scrambled over and through them and then followed ledges across to a gentler rubble slope and diagonally down it past the base of the cliffs up which we had climbed. The major route finding chore from this point was to avoid the spines and thorns on nearly every plant. We regained the beach and walked along it back to the dinghy. We arrived back onboard about a quarter hour before sunset.

We had thoroughly enjoyed our afternoon's outing; the climb of the cliffs was particularly exhilarating. We remained at anchor in Ensenada Gallo again on Wednesday night, and again the winds came up after sunset. As predicted by the gribs; however, they had veered to the north, and we had a gentler motion overnight, protected by the headland to the north.

At 1010 on Thursday we weighed, headed out of Ensenada Gallo and turned northward to pass between the northern headland of the ensenada and Isla Gallo, which lays a quarter mile off. A couple of headlands further along, we altered in to Ensenada de La Ballena to see what the anchorage was like. We liked what we saw, and at 1105 came to 14 metres on the Rocna anchor in 3.5 metres of water about a cable off the white sand beach at the bay's head and half a cable off the cliffs standing directly out of the water to the north. The water was so clear we could see bottom.

We were nicely tucked in, protected from the north and northeast winds, which had been forecast. The skies were clear, the temperature was just passing through 25° on its way to the midday norm of 27° or 28° and it was Christmas Eve.

We thought back on our previous Christmas Eve, when I had taken the water taxi to Snug Cove on Bowen Island to dig Sequitur out from under the half metre of snow that had thus far accumulated in an ongoing storm.

The environment here is but one of the many dramatic changes we have experienced in the past year. I had wound-down a company I had started in 1987, I had passed on my Power & Sail Squadron Commander's gavel and my gavel as President of the Royal Canadian Numismatic Association, we had moved out of our houses and I had sold mine, we had moved aboard Sequitur and had become nomads, we had sold our cars and for the first time since 1960 I was car-less. The biggest loss of the year was our little poodle, Chianti, who died a few weeks short of sixteen years old, and two days before our leaving Vancouver. Through all these changes, Edi and I watched with delight as our rather new relationship deepened and flourished.

But here we were, in Ensenada de La Ballena anchored in pale green waters under deep blue skies with a light breeze cooling the sun's heat. We decided to take a picnic lunch and find a place on the cliff top to relax and enjoy it.

We took the dinghy to the near end of the white sand beach, from where we followed a natural route up a draw where the beach met the cliffs and we were soon scrambling over the last few blocks to the ridge top.

The top was very flat, and being mostly solid rock, it was quite barren, with the desert vegetation holding on only in those few pockets and cracks where over the millennia sufficient soil had gathered to provide a nurturing environment.

On the north side, the ridge is separated from the next headland by a deep ravine, down which runs a stream bed. Dry now, it showed all the evidence of being a very active, bubbling stream during the brief periods of summer rains. The rocks in it were well polished by the waters of many summer rainstorms, and the play of colours left on the rocks easily tricked our eyes into seeing reflecting pools of clear water and streams still flowing over small cascades. It was a wonderful mirage.

We meandered down the gently sloping slab to its end, and then back along the cliff tops looking for a nice natural picnic bench overlooking the bay. The pink stone here has a honeycombed or sponge-like structure, which in exposed areas appears to have been wind-sculptured into even more intricate designs.

Below, the seas had eroded great hollows and overhangs, so we exercised caution lest the stone was waiting for only our additional weight to finish its slow process of going to sea. Edi had made some wonderful paninis, cored and wedged some apples and filled our thermoses with hot tea, so we sat on a wonderfully sculpted slab of pink stone, enjoying our lunch and counting our blessings.

We awoke on Christmas Day gently bobbing at anchor in Ensenada de La Ballena. Midmorning we sat down to a delicious breakfast of toasted sesame bagels with cream cheese, smoked salmon and capers. Then shortly after noon we weighed and headed out of the ensenada to continue our way northward along the west side of Isla Espiritu Santo.

Our destination was El Mezteno, a tiny anchorage just big enough for one boat, and the last one on Espititu Santo. As we passed the mouth of Ensenada del Candeloro, the bay between last night's Ensenada de La Ballena and tonight's El Mezteno, we saw a sloop and a catamaran filling the small two-boat anchorage there. They were the third and fourth boats we had seen at anchor since we left La Paz, and we talked of how crowded the area was becoming, and hoped that El Mezteno would be empty.

As we rounded the headland and could see past the cliffs and into the narrow gut, we were relieved to see that El Mezteno was empty. This is a wonderful little place; a three-quarter mile cut between cliffs and just over a cable wide at its throat, with a small white sand beach at its head across which a v-shaped valley leads up eastward then bends and disappears northward around the cliff-topped slopes.

We came to 18 metres of chain on the Rocna anchor in 4.5 metres of water on a sand bottom about 2 cables off the beach and little more than half a cable off the cliffs on either side. The water is very clear here, and the bottom is plainly visible through the 5.5 metres at high tide. What a spectacular setting in which to spend Christmas Day!

With the sea so clear, we made water for four hours and the net 250 litres brought our gauge back up from half tank to the full mark. For an hour and a bit in the afternoon we sorted-out and rearranged the food staples in the lockers beneath the dinette and reorganized the drawers and cupboards in the pantry, replenishing as we went the smaller containers in the galley cupboard beside the stove.

We are gradually finding the proper places for things.

Edi started another couple of loaves of bread; one a Friesian clove cheese and garlic with fresh basil, the other a sun-dried tomato, Moroccan olive and fresh basil, using the New York Times no-knead recipe introduced to us by Ray Lipovsky on one of Sequitur's visits to the Lasqueti Mint. This amazingly simple recipe, easily Googled on the net, is ideal for making wonderful artisan loaves at sea or at anchor.

We relaxed, read and soaked-in the wonderful setting, and then in the evening, after another spectacular sunset, we went below to enjoy Christmas dinner.

I prepared turkey and served it with a portobello gravy, couscous and fresh asparagus spears with mayonnaise and we thoroughly enjoyed our remote Christmas dinner with a bottle of Segura Viudas Cava. We topped-off our evening with many squares of extra dark chocolate.

The night was completely calm, with not a breath of wind to disturb the water's surface, and from overhead, the half moon and star-filled sky lit the canyon walls of our cozy little anchorage. What a wonderful cathedral in which to spend Christmas.

We laid-in for a while on Boxing Day, not the least concerned at missing the jam of lineups at the blowout sales. On reflection, we haven't been to a Boxing Day sale for many years, so it was easy for us to be missing another scramble and crush session at the stores. A few scattered cumulus accented an otherwise blue sky, and the still airs left the waters mirrored as we lounged in the cockpit enjoying our breakfast in the 23 degree warmth of midmorning.

Around midday we baked the two loaves that Edi had mixed-up the previous day, and when they were sufficiently cooled, she prepared a picnic of sliced fresh-baked bread, sliced leftover turkey, blue cheese and artichoke hearts. This we loaded into the backpack with thermoses of cold water and we took the dinghy ashore to the white sand beach at the head of the bay.

There is a trail marker just in from the beach, which describes the route up the valley to the outlook over Caleta Partida as being: *"6 miles long, 4.5 hours duration"* and of *"high difficulty."* We had only a little over three hours left before sunset, so we decided to take a short-cut.

We angled up the boulder slopes toward the cliffs and found a route through huge blocks, around a soaring buttress, up a shallow gully and the chimney at its back, and in an hour we were on the top.

A pleasant ten minute's walk across the undulating slabs of the ridge top took us to an overlook down into Caleta Partida, which separates Isla Espiritu Santo from Isla Partida.

This narrow channel is less than a metre deep at low tide as it zigzags between low spits that thrust out from each island. There were nine boats at anchor in the caleta, all tucked up into the northern side, probably in an attempt to get some protection from the winds that notoriously howl through the gap, funnelling and magnifying the winter's prevailing northerlies.

With a couple of hours remaining until sunset, we needed to find a route off the ridge, which continued to the east, narrowing as it went, and becoming a complex of huge slabs separated by crevices a metre or so across and often two and three metres deep. This was rimmed on the south by a line of cliffs that appeared to continue unbroken for a mile or more. We backtracked and searched along the rim for a suitable chimney system to enable us to break through the cliffs. Down one chimney and around an airy ledge, we found easier going in big broken blocks that led us in half an hour to the trail in the dry river bed of the valley bottom.

Nearly an hour later, we arrived back at the dinghy on the beach, having scrambled through the overgrown, boulder-strewn shallow canyon of the river bed, through which the trail led. Many of the boulders choking the canyon were room-sized and bigger, some the size of small houses. In retrospect, it would have easier to have followed the rubble slopes and small rock faces above.

We sat on the beach enjoying a late lunch, for which we had worked-up a good appetite. As we ate, we were entertained by the antics of the pelicans diving for needlefish in the shallows. The sun was low in the western sky, so we waited for nice sunset shots, which didn't come; the setting and composition were correct, but the sky was too clear to offer any drama to the event.

We arrived back onboard in the dusk and relaxed until late evening, when I made a six-egg frittata with leftover turkey, green onions, garlic, red, yellow and orange peppers, tomatoes and tarragon. It had been a wonderful Boxing Day.

And on the seventh day we rested. It was Sunday, a week since we had left La Paz to explore Isla Espiritu Santo, and we were so filled with awe for this enchanted place that we needed to take a day off to let it all soak in. That, and to allow time for our bodies to recharge from the bursts of rather intense exercise we have had ashore. This was spa day; sunbathing on deck, manicures and pedicures, and other body work.

After another delicious dinner of garlic-butter sautéed basa fillets, we enjoyed another calm night at anchor in El Mezteno, we slept-in again, and after another midmorning breakfast of bagels with cream cheese, smoked salmon and capers and mugs of coffee, we decided to break the blissful monotony and move on.

We weighed shortly before 1100 on Monday the 28th and motored out of El Mezteno in seas as flat as plate glass, making water as we went to take advantage of the electricity from the engine's alternator. As we rounded Punta Mezteno, the point forming the north side of the anchorage, we had a view eastward into Caleta Partida and saw eight or ten boats at anchor there in the rather open roadstead, exposed to the winds funnelling through the gap separating Isla Espiritu Santo and Isla Partida; it was not our choice of anchorage.

Instead, we had decided to see if El Cardoncito, a narrow slit between the cliffs just outside Caleta Partida was empty. Unfortunately, as we looked northward a mile into El Cardoncito, there appeared to be a large schooner anchored in the middle of it, so we resigned ourselves to heading into the much larger Ensenada el Cardonal immediately to its north.

As we continued northward, it became increasingly obvious that the schooner was at anchor on some diving and snorkeling rocks just outside the entrance to El Cardoncito, and the anchorage was empty. We slowly nosed our way into the canyon. The cliffs standing directly out of the water on both sides meant there was likely deep water right up to them, and we continued down the middle until the water began shoaling near the beach. At 1120 we came to 21 metres on the Rocna in 7 metres of water.

This is a delightful little spot, with porous red rock cliffs standing twenty to forty metres vertically along both sides before lying back to gentler slopes, which are dotted with succulents, bushes and cacti to the 150 metre high ridge lines. The porous rock looks like sponge candy, with frequent larger voids, many three metres and more in size which in our imaginations are fairytale cave dwellings. The cliffs are less than half-a-cable on each hand, and there is a small white sand beach at the head of the bay, less than a cable-and-a-half forward.

Although the sun had slanted in through the hatches into our cabin first thing in the morning, by the time we had gotten out of bed, it was overcast. As the morning progressed, the skies darkened, and a couple of hours after we had entered the anchorage, it began raining. This was the first rain Sequitur has seen since a two-day rainstorm that welcomed us to San Francisco two-and-a-half months previously, and she was quite salty.

took the dinghy for a slow two-hour circuit along the base of the cliffs lining both sides of the anchorage. Along the way, we paused to watch a twenty-four legged starfish clinging to the rocks, a brightly coloured crab climbing from the water and many pelicans perched on the ledges.

We waited for the boat to be well wetted, and then stripping-off our clothes and grabbing mop and cloths, we went out to help the rain wash the salt from the boat. The rain continued for a couple of hours, and then stopped for a while, but the low dark clouds persisted, and it rained off and on until shortly before sunset. During one of the lulls in the rain a curious seagull landed on the dinghy, which was still hoisted in the davits, and stood there watching us and posing patiently for the camera.

The gull came back on Tuesday morning and sat waiting for us, so Edi got some leftover couscous with shrimp, and tossed bits into the water. The gull quickly scooted for the scraps of food as they were tossed, and when other gulls came close, it very aggressively defended its territory. This was its boat; time had been invested in wooing the boaters, effort had been put into posing for a photo shoot, no gull-come-lately was going to usurp its place.

We breakfasted in the cockpit, watching as the sun heated the rocks, converting Monday's rains into fluffy cumulus, which quickly dissipated as they rose. At about 1100 we

We also examined close-up the wondrous rock formations; here lining this anchorage are some of the most fantastic rocks we have ever seen. We saw frothy pink icing flowing over marshmallow pillars, a jumble of pauper's swollen bare shins and feet sticking out below tattered hems, stacks of pale red sponge candy, fairytale cliff cities; our minds strained trying to find ways to describe the formations.

We pondered the cataclysmic events that would have caused the huge variety of structure among the clearly defined strata that is so evident throughout the anchorages here in Isla Espiritu Santo and Isla Partida. It is obvious that there was a long series of volcanic eruption of widely differing types. Adding to the complexity of the formations is the general tilt of the strata, here dipping ten or fifteen degrees to the west, and thereby making accessible the diversity of exposure along the east-west tending inlets of the islands.

We returned onboard from our circuit to have lunch. Then mid-afternoon we took the dinghy to the sandy beach at the head of the inlet and landed it at low tide. The beach here is nearly flat, so hauling the dinghy to the high water line was not practical. Instead, we landed near the rocks that form the southern margin of the beach, and hauled the dinghy a short distance across the sand before we took the painter around the natural bollard of a rock.

Water from the rain was still running across the sand from the arroyo, which at this time of year is usually dry. We ascended a broad gully filled with large broken rocks and when it became too choked with vegetation, we moved out onto the more open terrain of the spur to its left.

We continued to upward through bands of sponge rock, and in one, we fancied we were visiting the local mail box to see if there was anything for us.

From sunny perches on the rocks we were being watched by a variety of lizards. The smaller ones were rather timid and quickly scooted off, while others, about 40 centimetres from snout to tail tip, were more curious and boldly watched us from a metre or two away.

Once we had reached the top of the line of cliffs, we circled back along the southern rim of the precipice to a spot overlooking Sequitur at anchor. This vantage point gave us a clear impression on how narrow the anchorage is and how well-protected it is from anything but a southwest wind. From our stance on the cliffs we paused to survey the incredible terrain through which we were wandering; this is truly an enchanted area.

By the time we had picked-out a route down through the lines of cliffs and walked along the rocks at the water's edge, back to the dinghy, the tide had come in sufficiently to float it. We pulled the dinghy over to a rock, and hopped-in. A few poles with the oars, and some weight shifting had us over the shallows and heading back out to Sequitur.

Back onboard, we hoisted the dinghy on the davits in preparation for the next morning's departure. When we came back up into the cockpit a while later to watch the sunset, our curious little seagull was again on its perch on the dinghy. It posed for a photo session in the sunset, adding yet another special moment to our wondrous time in this enchanted place.

On Wednesday the 30th we decided to sail north to San Francisco to bring-in the New Year. Isla San Francisco is a small island, less than two miles by two miles that lies some 20 miles north of our anchorage on Isla Partida, and about 5 miles off the coast of the Baja Peninsula.

Shortly before 1100 we weighed and headed under power out of El Cardoncito and turned northward past the frothy pink rock decorations of the point. Isla San Francisco lay to the north-northwest and the winds were from the north at 8 to 10 knots, so we hoisted sails and started reaching our way up into a short choppy sea under clear, blue skies with the temperature in the mid 20s.

By midday the winds had increased to the 18 knot range, and we shortened in to staysail and half a main. The steep waves were now large enough that every sixth or seventh washed over the bows, so to get a better angle into the seas, we motor-sailed the rest of the way. By the time we reached the lee of Isla San Francisco, the winds were in the 25 knot area, and spume was whipping off the crests.

At 1425 we came to 24 metres of chain on the Rocna anchor in 6 metres of water in the western lobe of the southern anchorage on Isla San Francisco. The wind continued to blow strongly from the north, but the water around Sequitur was rather calm, and the sandy bottom clearly visible. We were well sheltered from the waves by a narrow crescent of land, which was just a cable or so to the north of us. The land there; however, is only a few metres high, and the northerly winds blow unimpeded over it.

Isla San Francisco is now a part of the National Park system, and we were delighted to see such beautiful sites as this and Islas Espiritu Santo and Partida protected and preserved for future generations.

The anchorage we were in appears to be part of an ancient volcanic caldera, the southwestern half of which is now open to the sea. The northeastern quadrant is rimmed by a pale beige sand beach, which forms a crescent nearly a mile long. It is a spectacular setting with the muted reddish colours of the rocks accentuated by the greens of the desert vegetation and set-off by the blues and pale greens of the sea. There are no facilities, and so far it is a rather unspoiled wilderness.

On the western side of the anchorage is a hill 200 metres high, and we could have tucked-in under its slopes in an attempt to lessen the howling of the wind in the rigging, but we wanted the wind; our wind generator loves it. In some of the gusts we saw over 30 amps flowing into the batteries.

We are delighted with the Eclectic Energy D400, a virtually silent British machine that is little known in North America, where lower performing US-made models seem to dominate the magazine advertising, the test reports and therefore the market. Our D400 sits quietly adding charge to the house bank, and when the batteries are full, the energy is diverted to the hot water tank.

Shortly after our arrival we were entertained by synchronized swimmers. A flock of small birds gathered very tightly on the water, all facing the same direction.

Then as if on cue, they all dived under the water within a second of each other. These birds were much more attractive than the human synchronized swimmers we see in competitions; they had no ugly nose clips, nor did they have the bald-headed look imparted by bathing caps.

The birds resurfaced a minute or so later, most within a few seconds of each other, and still in a rather tight formation. The few stragglers were probably those that managed to find, catch and eat something while underwater. The group quickly reestablished formation and a minute or so later, reenacted the routine. This they continued for the hour or more that we watched, slowly progressing across the anchorage.

The wind continued strong for the rest of the day and through the night, mostly in the 25 knot range, with frequent gusts over 35. Fortunately, the wind was still coming from the north, and since we were only a cable off the beach, there was only a very short fetch for the wind to generate waves. We lazed and wrote and read for the rest of the day.

On Thursday the wind was still in the mid-30s, so we spent all day New Year's Eve onboard, doing chores and relaxing. Edi totally reorganized the food storage; our staples are now grouped together in logical order, and the ready-use items are now all close at hand. We had initially stocked our pantry as load after load came onboard from our buying sprees in Vancouver and San Francisco. Although we had tried to stow the food items in an orderly fashion, it generally was stowed where space was available, and eventually there was little logic to its placement. Now, Martha Stewart would be proud.

Among the things we knew we had onboard somewhere, but had not yet tracked-down were two 4.3 litre cans of artichoke hearts and 128 rolls of toilet paper. These are sufficiently large that we knew they would eventually show-up.

For our New Year's Eve dinner we enjoyed beef tenderloin and béarnaise sauce, butter-caramelized white onion rings and garlic and steamed new potatoes, and from the cellar we chose a bottle of the 2007 J Lohr Los Osos Merlot. As seems to be our mutual preference, we allowed the New Year to come-in on its own. We went to bed at 2245 and were lulled in an out of sleep by the creaking of the anchor snubbers straining to the 35 and 40 knot gusts.

The winds were still strong on New Year's Day; blowing a sustained 25 knots with gusts well into the mid-30s. After lunch we launched the dinghy and motored over to the beach for a walk along its crescent. Near the southern end we left the beach and headed up the slopes to the ridge-line, which forms the eastern margin to our anchorage. We scrambled along the crest in the strong crosswind to a rocky summit, where we paused to take-in the view.

We retraced our route along the narrow crest of the ridge and descended the slopes back to the beach. As we walked along the white crescent, we dawdled here and there to select some nicely coloured or well-shaped seashells. These we dropped in the dinghy on our way past, as we continued on to the far end of the beach for a scramble up the slopes and a view in the opposite direction.

We returned onboard and spent the remainder of the afternoon relaxing and listening to the wind howl through the rigging. In the evening we enjoyed a dinner of diced pork tenderloin wokked in garlic and ginger with white onions, celery, broccoli, zucchini, red, orange and green peppers and roma tomatoes, all tossed with al dente rotini, laced with oyster-flavour sauce and sprinkled with freshly toasted sesame seeds. It is amazing what can come out of the galley two weeks away from our last shopping. We are; however, getting low on fresh produce, and need to do some shopping soon.

By the time we had finished dinner on Friday evening, the wind had begun to subside, and it was down to around 20 knots when we went to bed. We had decided that we would continue north early in the morning, taking advantage of the last couple of hours of the flood tide, and expecting again the lower winds we had been seeing in the mornings.

Our destination was San Evaristo, a tiny community on the Baja Peninsula, some nine miles to the north-northwest. The guidebook mentions that there are about twenty full-time families living there, and that there is a school, a water desalination plant and a tienda. It was the tienda that interested us; we were hopeful that we would find it open and at the end of the festive week, still with some fresh produce to replenish our nearly depleted supply.

After breakfast on Saturday the 2nd we weighed. It was 0830, and the tide was still flooding northward for another couple of hours, which would give us a slight boost along. More importantly, leaving early meant that we wouldn't be encountering wind waves that here seem to be steepened by an ebbing tide. As we left the anchorage on Isla San Francisco, and lost the lee of the island, we ran full blast into 25 knot north-northwest winds. The course to San Evaristo was 315°, directly into the wind, and we didn't fancy a three or four hour beat into steepening seas. We motored, and took advantage of the engine's running to make water and heat it for our day's shower. One of the things that is becoming obvious to us here is that the first half of a Sea of Cortez cruise is upwind.

At 1020 we came to 35 metres on the Rocna anchor in 10 metres of water in the northern lobe of the anchorage at San Evaristo, tucked-in beneath the cliffs to the east and less than half a cable off the beach. Once we were confident of our anchor's set, we launched the dinghy and motored ashore, hauling the dinghy up the beach beside the desalination plant.

A hundred-metre walk took us to the tienda, and we entered through the open door to find no one. We called *"Hola!"* a few times, to no response, so we began selecting produce and putting it on the counter. Among two large mesh bags of white onions, I dug around until I had found four onions with firm ends and no rot. From the bin of potatoes I selected the seven problem-free examples, and we picked the three good cucumbers from the box. The garlic was easier; it was all in choice condition, as were the golden and the red delicious apples. We selected fifteen large eggs from a large box, and there being no fresh mushrooms, we settled for three cans, and finally we added a large can of refried beans.

Eventually, Edi's calling attracted someone's attention outside, and a pair of women came in, took-up station behind the counter and while one weighed the produce on a rusty old balance scale, the other jotted figures on a scrap of paper. They each did some calculations, compared notes and announced the total of 219 pesos. Our shopping spree had cost us $17.95.

Back onboard with the produce washed and stowed, we had lunch, entertained by the pelicans and blue footed boobies diving for fish near the cliffs. At one point, there was such frenzy that it appeared to be raining birds. The frenzy attracted some fishermen in a panga; they quickly motored over to the scene and used a throw net to catch some of the small fish.

We had finally run-out of bagels, so in the evening, Edi prepared four loaves of bread to rise overnight: a blue cheese, garlic and basil; a cranberry and pecan; a Moroccan olive, sun-dried tomato and basil; and a raisin.

On Sunday morning we dinghied ashore to a tiny rock and gravel beach that is wedged-in between the cliffs to the north of us. We landed at high tide and secured the painter around a huge conglomerate boulder that had been recently shed by the cliffs. A small arroyo led us nicely up from the beach to beyond the line of cliffs, and we were soon moving up the cactus and agave dotted slopes toward the ridge-top.

Once on the top of the ridge, we followed its crest along to the northward and over a couple of minor summits, from which we enjoyed views into downtown San Evaristo.

We crossed a windy col, open to the full blast of the northerly winds, and ascended to the summit of Cerro San Isidro. From there we had wonderful views back down at Sequitur, and of the surrounding waters and the off lying islands of San Jose and San Francisco.

Below us to the west was a complex of salt ponds, to which we had intended hiking from the village; however, the wonderful overview from the slopes of Cerro San Isidro made that hike unnecessary. The low beaches that form the northern margins of the salt ponds are open to the full brunt of the prevailing northerly winds; these would do wonders in speeding the evaporation. Through the small canal at the western end of the beach, it appears to be a simple matter to replenish the salt water.

To get a better view of the salt ponds, and to take a look down on the rooftops of San Evaristo, we moved out along the spur that runs southward from the peak. As we meandered, we admired the tenacity of the desert environment. This ridge, with winds that howl across it at 25 and 30 knots for most of the near-rainless winter, has only tiny, shallow pockets of soil. But from those pockets grow a diverse selection of cacti, succulents, bushes and grasses. We saw a young cactus, less than half a metre high growing, it seemed, directly out of the rocks. As harsh as its environment seemed to us, it appeared to be thriving, and was in bloom.

This was the first day on which we had not seen eagles soaring along the cliff tops; it was probably too windy for them. Even the pelicans seemed to be grounded because of the heavy winds. Nor did we see any of the lizards we usually encounter on our hikes. Grasshoppers were the only wildlife we saw. These were rather large, eight centimetres or so in length, and they frequently flew into us as we passed, being apparently unaccustomed to finding anything moving on the ridge. We thought of the possibility of augmenting our food supply, but after racking our brains to remember recipes for grasshoppers, we decided to give them a pass.

We returned onboard from our two-and-a-half hour hike, had lunch and then relaxed. The winds continued strong for the rest of the day, generally in the 25 knot range, with from time to time, sudden bursts that from the howl in the rigging sounded to be approaching 40. I came to the conclusion that the salt pans are here in San Evaristo because of the consistently high winds.

In the late afternoon and early evening we baked the four loaves of bread that Edi had started the previous day. While the oven was hot, I barded a loin roast of pork with garlic and baked it and a couple of potatoes as the basis of the evening's dinner, and to provide cold cuts for the rest of the week.

We had decided to get up early on Monday morning and continue northward with the flooding tide and in the usually lighter winds early in the day. We enjoyed a wonderful breakfast of fresh-baked raisin bread with cream cheese and mugs of coffee. I recalled that during my time in the Navy in the 60s, 70 and early 80s, raisin bread had been called *"officer bread"*. As officers, we had been expected to augment the ship's rations with the purchase of non-issue items. While each wardroom had its own particular list of items, the wardroom of every ship in which I served had raisin bread for breakfast toast, and the stewards called it officer bread.

So, after our breakfast of officer bread, we weighed at 0800 and under power we headed out of the anchorage at San Evaristo. The wind was north-northwest 25 knots and our course was again directly into it. As we cleared the top end of Canal de San Jose, an hour-and-a-half later, and left its funnelling influence, the winds eased to just under 20 knots. However within an hour they were back up to the midday norm of nearer to 30 knots, and the seas had built to rather steep two and three metre breakers.

Shortly after noon, we rounded Roca Negra, and bent our course to the northwest to gain the lee of the point forming the northern end of Bahia San Carlos. We were heading into our intended anchorage at Tambobiche, running diagonally across the breaking seas, when a particularly heavy wave bounced our secondary anchor, a 20 kilogram Delta, out of its chocks on the pulpit. At 1220, we found ourselves unintentionally anchored in 11 metres of water on 20 metres chain and 60 metres of nylon rode on the Delta.

We were about a quarter mile off a lee shore in strong winds and rather large seas that were occasionally breaking. We were anchored, but not at all well-positioned. I didn't want to compromise the quick availability of our primary anchor, the Rocna, by decoupling it from the windlass, so we had to recover the Delta by hand.

Eventually, I managed to hand in sufficient of the 3/4-inch nylon rode to lead back to the power winch in the cockpit. With Edi on the bow pointing the anchor, I juggled the helm, the engine and the power winch until the anchor was finally aweigh. With Edi back at the helm and me on the foredeck, I handed in the remainder of the chain and secured the Delta. At 1250 we came to 24 metres on the Rocna in 4 metres of water in the lee of the point in Tambobiche. While Edi prepared lunch, I overhauled the Delta's rode back down into its locker from the cockpit and decks, and then I made sure the anchor was securely lashed in place.

After lunch, we took the dinghy a half mile along the beach, landed through the surf and walked toward Tambobiche, a tiny community 26 miles up the Baja coast from San Evaristo. Tambobiche's glory days were in the 1800s and early 1900s, when it was one of the centres of the pearl fishing industry. The beach here is now used by the locals as a road between the village and their panga anchorage at the north end of the bay, and we walked along the beach until the tire tracks turned inland. We followed them and then a dusty mud road past simple stick fences, ramshackle palapas and shacks to Casa Grande.

Casa Grande was built at the turn of the century by a local pearl fisherman, who had a dream to live in a fine house. He financed his dream, so the story goes, with the proceeds of the sale of a rare five karat green pearl he had found. Some keep on dreaming, holding on tightly to their pearls, while others trade-in pearls to turn dreams to reality.

The house must have been an anomaly when it was built; today it certainly is, even in its advanced state of decay, it is the only structure of any substance in the area. The roof and the floors are gone, as is any interior woodwork there may have been.

The only wood remaining are a few roof rafters, fragments of a couple of second floor joists, and the stubs of veranda roof rafters at the front and the back. The nearly intact stuccoed and plastered masonry walls are half a metre thick, and they appear capable of standing for another century and more.

Back onboard, we sun-dried from our hot showers as we lazed in the cockpit, sipping snifters of brandy and listening on the stereo to our friend Andrew Dawes on violin with the Chamber Players of Canada performing Schubert's Octet for Winds and Strings. Our backdrop was the play of light from the afternoon sun on the peaks and ridges of the Sierra de la Giganta to our south and the west as we gently bobbed in our well-protected anchorage.

At 0750 on Tuesday, after a breakfast of officer bread with cream cheese and coffee, we weighed and headed out of the anchorage at Tambobiche in still airs under skies clear to the north and east, but filled with cirrus, cirrocumulus and cirrostratus to the south and west. As we lost the lee of the point there was still no wind, and as we turned northward we were bucking into steep 2 metre residual seas from the previous day's blow.

Within half an hour the winds began to blow from directly on our nose. They gradually increased in strength, and by 0930 they were in the 20 to 25 knot range and the seas were building above 2 metres. This followed well the pattern we had been seeing thus far in the Sea of Cortez.

There are wonderfully coloured rocks all along the Baja coast, and their variety continued to surprise us. A few miles north of our anchorage off Tambobiche we passed beneath cliffs showing a dozen and more differently coloured strata. It appeared to us to be the results of at least a dozen volcanic flows, each with a different composition. We saw greens, pinks, ambers and rusty reds

During our four hours of motoring, we ran three loads of laundry through the machine and made another 130 litres of water. At 1105 we came to 35 metres of chain on the Rocna anchor in 10 metres of water in the northern lobe of Bahia Agua Verde.

We were nicely tucked-in and protected from the swell by the bulk of Punta San Pasquel half a cable to our east, while half a cable to our west and two cables to our south was high land. To our north less than half a cable away is a low sandy isthmus, which joins Punta San Pasquel to the mainland. The beach there is used by the local fisherman to land their catch and haul-out their pangas.

Edi hung out the laundry to dry on the lifelines; it makes no sense to use battery electricity to dry it when there is a nice gentle breeze and a good warm sun. I launched and rigged the dinghy and we motored the mile or so to the village of Agua Verde. Our route took us just outside the surf line along the beach, where the two-metre waves were breaking, as we looked for a safe place to land.

Past the end of the sandy beach there is a line of cliffs, and just offshore from a steep point stands Pyramid Rock, a large isolated rock, which gives protection to a tiny rock and gravel beach. We landed there beside two pangas and hauled the dinghy up onto the narrow gravel strand. There we secured it to some crude wooden railings, which were being used by the fisherman to secure their boats.

From there we found a narrow strip of hardpan and rubble that ran along the foot of the cliffs just above the surf line. This easily lead us into a wonderful beach-side oasis of date palms, in which the village was sited. We walked along the winding, dusty mud street past a few chickens and dozens of goats, most of which were seeking shade beneath the palms and acacias.

We had been told of the locally produced goat cheese, and we were seeing its source. We continued along looking for the tienda, and questioned a man on its location. He walked with us for a distance to point-out the way, and told us in our rudimentary understanding of Spanish that he was the person who made the goat cheese that was for sale in the tienda.

As we approached, a woman emerged from a nearby house and went over to unlock the door of the tienda for us. The typically limited stock was quite neatly arranged on shelves, and along one side was a bush carpenter's version of an icebox. In the icebox were some nice green peppers, somewhat flattish and pointed. We asked whether they were hot, and the woman assured us they were *"no picante"*, so we selected eight, and thus we were introduced to poblanos. . We also found a good-looking bag of carrots, a wonderful big bunch of cilantro and among the large bin, the one good tomato.

We tasted the two varieties of goat cheese in the icebox, and while neither bore any resemblance to the wonderful wild quality to which I had become accustomed in France and in British Columbia, we had her cut a kilo-and-a-half off a loaf. The cheese was rather bland and still quite wet, but we gambled on the possibility that with some aging, it would improve.

As we walked back along the beach toward the dinghy, we were entertained by the pelicans diving in the shallows.

From what we have been able to observe, they approach the water vertically, and then just above it, rotate onto their backs and haul-in their wings as they splash down, their lower bill in position to scoop.

We launched the dinghy through the small waves in the protection of Pyramid Rock and motored back across the swell line, past Sequitur to the beach where the fishermen land their catch.

There we asked a couple of men there whether we could buy some fish, and were told they had none to sell; it had already been trucked away. Back onboard, we spent a restful the Twelfth Night of Christmas in a very calm and peaceful anchorage.

After an early breakfast on the 6th of January, we weighed at 0810 and headed out in still airs and glassy seas on a gentle half-metre swell. The skies were totally clear, and even the haze we had seen at the horizons the last few days was gone. We motored northward along the Baja coast of the Sea of Cortez, making water as we went, and at 1150 we came to a mooring ball in Puerto Escondido, in front of the Singlar Marina.

The inner basin at Puerto Escondido is a wonderfully protected harbour that can accommodate over 150 boats. Except for a 60 metre wide entrance channel, it is completely encircled by land, and is used by many boaters as a hurricane hole during the summer storm season. Lying immediately adjacent to the inner harbour is a small circular anchorage called The Ellipse, which can hold another fifteen or twenty boats, and outside the entrance channel is The Waiting Room, another protected anchorage, which can hold another few dozen boats at anchor.

With such fine harbour, it was natural for someone to develop a marina facility. In the mid-70s a marina was built in the Ellipse, but there was no power or water to the floats until 1982. Then in the mid-80s, a joint venture between the Mexican Government and a French investment group began the development of a resort hotel, golf course, condominium and marina complex. The float docks in the Ellipse were removed, destroyed, and never replaced. After a reported 20 million dollars were spent on building inlets and canals, installing an access road, a street grid, electricity and waterworks, work on the development abruptly ceased. Other than the infrastructure, the only remnant from the development is a Trailer and RV park halfway along the two kilometre access road to Highway Number 1.

In the late 90s, the Mexican Government listed Puerto Escondido in the first phase (2000-2006) of its Escalar Nautica plan under the list of Nuevos Centros Nauticos. About 2003, the quasi-governmental company, Singlar began the development of new facilities with some 40 million pesos. There are now new mooring floats, a fuel dock, dry storage facilities, a laundry, showers, a restaurant, a small tienda, a potable water supply, a wifi antenna and over 100 mooring buoys in the inner harbour. The plan is to complete the marina development, then begin selling building lots.

After lunch we took the dinghy the short distance to the marina floats to check-out the facilities. They are clean, modern and well laid-out. I paid 28 pesos for wireless internet access, and we spent an hour or so getting caught-up on two-and-a-half weeks of emails. I enquired about the mooring rates, and was told a mooring ball would cost us the Canadian equivalent of about $15 per day or $65 per week, and that anchorage in the harbour was at the same rate.

The mooring we had tied to was reserved for an arrival later in the day, so we decided against moving to another buoy, and when we finished with our emails, went back out to Sequitur and moved her to an anchorage in The Waiting Room.

There were about three dozen boats at anchor in The Waiting Room, and with the depth generally around 20 metres, and even with only 3:1 scope, a lot of swinging room is needed. We found a spot to drop the Rocna in 8 metres of water on a small ledge close in to the beach. I veered 24 metres including the 10 metres of nylon snubber, and the gentle northwest breeze put Sequitur beyond the edge of the ledge with 20 metres showing on the depth sounder. Our scope was short enough that our stern would swing clear of the shallows if the wind shifted.

After we had anchored, we dinghied back to the marina, and sat in the lounge for three hours or so, enjoying the internet access, and chatting with other boaters. There were five dozen or so boats at anchor and on moorings, most of them rather permanently, and a few, like us, on the way through.

We needed to but fresh produce, and the guidebook recommends the town of Loreto, twenty-five kilometres up the highway. I asked about transportation into town, and learned from one couple of flagging-down buses that go by several times a day on the highway a couple of kilometres away. Another option mentioned was hitchhiking, another was asking for a shared ride on the 0800 VHF net. One fellow suggested hiring a taxi for the day at $70, but then he added that it made a lot more sense to have Pedro arrange a rental car at $40 per day, all inclusive.

Pedro sounded like the answer. He operates the restaurant and the tienda in the new marina development. He also provides a strong secure connection wifi antenna aimed out across The Ellipse and The Waiting Room anchorages. We took our computers upstairs to the Porto Bello Restaurant and had Pedro subscribe them for a week of wifi service. We then had him book a car for us for shortly before noon on Friday, and we signed-up for his Friday evening filet mignon dinner at 100 pesos per plate.

On Friday morning the men from Hertz arrived with our nearly new air-conditioned Dodge Attitude, and after a signing ceremony on the trunk lid, we drove off to Loreto. About two-thirds of the way along is the golf resort and condo development of Nopolo. Already rather extensive, the existing resort is the beginning of a fifteen-year, three-billion-dollar development that will see 6,000 homes on 3200 hectares of land along the coast.

In Loreto we stopped to check-out El Pescador, the first of three recommended grocery stores. Then we drove to Fruteria to check it out, and since we had the car parked in the shade, we walked to ISSSTE, the third store on our list. Having compared them all, and decided on our choice, we went exploring in the old town on foot.

With a current population of around 10,000, Loreto is the oldest Spanish city on the Baja Peninsula. It was founded by Jesuit missionaries in 1697, and it was the capital of Las Californias from its founding until 1777.

There are many old buildings in the historic centre, and one of them particularly caught our attention. Kitty-corner from the city hall stands a solid-looking, dignified dusky-pink building, now converted into Hotel Posada de los Flores. As we walked into the lobby, we were immediately struck by the architecture and the wonderful play of light coming down from glass bottomed swimming pool, which forms the roof over the central portion of the lobby. The choice of colours, the quality of the finish, the appointments and the accents, all contribute to a very tastefully decorated interior.

We visited the Mision Nuestra Senora de Loreto, which was founded in 1752, and to me, the rather tacky Christmas decorations, which were still up well past the Twelfth Day, detracted from the charm of the interior.

From the church we walked along the rows of small merchants lining both sides of a narrow shopping street. The street, which is shaded by pairs of trees pruned and clipped into ox yoke shaped arches spanning the thoroughfare, is obviously oriented to the tourist. Most of the shops carried gaily coloured pottery, or brightly coloured weavings, or sterling silver trinkets, or tacky T-shirts, or a combination of all.

We stopped at a small taqueria for lunch, and as we sat on the patio waiting for our fish tacos to be prepared, a woman from a nearby table heard us speaking English, and came over to ask directions to the beach. She and her husband are fellow Canadians, recently retired and driving south from Vernon British Columbia; they had stopped in Loreto for lunch. We asked them to join us at the table and we had some delightful company as we all ate.

After lunch we went back to the main purpose of our trip to Loreto. We walked back to the ISSSTE to buy some bottles of well-priced Chilean Sauvignon Blanc, and then we recovered our car from the shade in front of the Fruteria. Fruteria is listed as specializing in excellent fresh produce, but they must have had a serious change in management since the guide was written. Their limited selection seemed to us to be mostly culls that were wilted, withered, blemished or otherwise beyond their best-before date.

We drove to El Pescador and found parking on the shaded north side of the building. This smallish supermarket has an adequate selection of produce, and with careful selection we were able to bag a good quantity of acceptable green peppers, poblanos, roma tomatoes, potatoes, carrots, white onions, Spanish onions, green onions, zucchini, avocados, bananas and apples.

There was an adequate selection of both packaged and unpackaged meats, as well as frozen, and we bought a couple of kilogram packages of frozen boneless and skinless chicken breasts. We had expected to find a great selection of fish in a place named El Pescador; we were wrong. There was not one piece of fresh fish to be had, and we bought the only package of frozen fish in the case. We also picked out one of the three packages of frozen shrimp. We asked where we could find fresh fish, but received no coherent replies.

On our way back to Puerto Escondido we stopped at the Mini Super in Nopolo. It was a bright, clean and modern facility, with nicely laid-out wide aisles, and complete with refrigerated deli and produce cases. However, the cases were powered-down and empty, and the shelves were stocked mostly with snacks, drinks and convenience foods.

We moved on, and next stopped at the small tienda at the RV park on the access road to the marina. It had superior produce to that which we had seen in Loreto, not quite as broad a variety, but what was there was fresher and more select. We topped-up our earlier purchases.

We ferried the load back out to Sequitur and unpackaged, repackaged, washed or cleaned as appropriate, and stowed our purchases in fridges, freezers, lockers, cupboards and drawers. Then we motored back to the dinghy dock and walked up to the restaurant for the steak dinner, arriving at a fashionable ten minutes after the appointed hour.

There were already about thirty people seated when we arrived, and we were signalled by a couple sitting at a four-top to join them. Lisa & John Caruso of Seattle are anchored in their Wauquaiez Pretorian, Andiamo just beyond us in The Waiting Room. They spend half the year cruising down here and the other half living aboard their other boat in Seattle and cruising the Pacific Northwest.

We enjoyed a delightful evening with them as Pedro, his family and his staff prepared and served a delicious filet mignon dinner. Our steaks were perfectly done; the chef hit rare on the nose, and they were surprisingly big, considering the dinner was only 100 Pesos, which was $8.06 Canadian at the prevailing rate. With dinner, Edi and I shared a marvellously complex and well-structured 2004 Anakena Ona Chilean Syrah, which with tip, brought our evening's total to a few cents over $58.

We declared make and mend on both Saturday and Sunday. During my years in the Navy, *"make and mend"* was called *"makers"*, and meant an afternoon off, while remaining onboard and available if required. The term derives from the Royal Navy in the days of sail and oaken ships, when the sailors would from time to time be relieved of their off-watch routine to make and mend their uniforms, which were not then supplied by the Navy.

Our make and mend had more to do with tending to the repair and maintenance of Sequitur. On Saturday, after some manual interpretation, I overcame a *"salinity probe failed"* alarm on the watermaker, and we made another four hours of water. Edi rearranged the pantry and storeroom, and found the missing toilet paper and twenty kilos of basmati rice, among other things of which we had lost track. She did not; however, find the missing 8.6 litres of artichoke hearts.

On Sunday Edi ran a couple of loads of laundry through the machine and hung them out to dry in the pleasant breeze and 25 degree afternoon sun. I troubleshot the new Magnum inverter-charger, trying to determine why it thinks the house bank is full when the trusty old LinkPro monitor told me it is only 78.5% charged. Finally, after running through a series of tests, I realized that it was simply that the LinkPro needed resynchronizing. Duh!

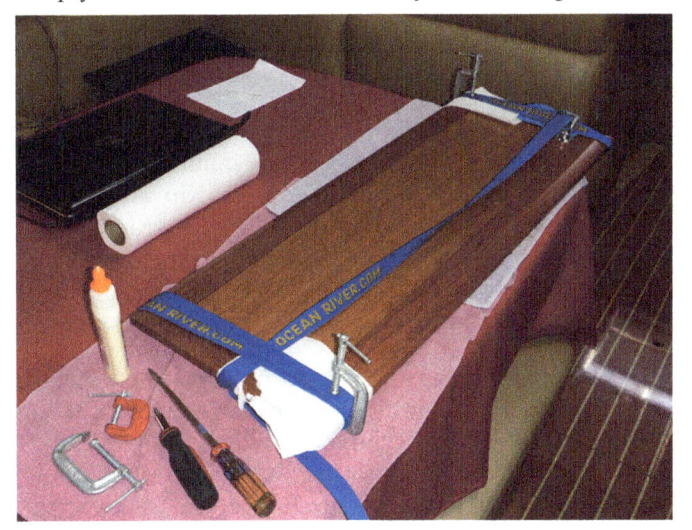

A bit less klutzily, I re-glued a locker door from the sea cabin. It appears it had been left unlocked, and last week's heavy seas had popped it open and slammed it around an adjacent edge, levering apart three of its corner joints.

After breakfast on Monday morning we took the dinghy the short distance across to the rocky beach at the base of the ridge to the north of us and secured its painter to a large rock. Then we climbed through the scrub and cacti to the top of the ridge, and scrambled along it to the summit overlooking Puerto Escondido, and then out ridge spurs to shoot some pictures. After a couple of hours of scrambling up and down a circuitous route, we arrived back at the rocky beach a couple of hundred metres away from the dinghy, where we were met by Kip in his dinghy. Kip and Mary are anchored a short distance away from Sequitur, and he had come over to offer us a ride back to our dinghy, and to invite us over to their boat for sundowners.

We had met him a couple of days earlier after he responded to a swap & trade announcement I had made on the morning VHF net, and had come over to Sequitur to negotiate and pick-up our Xantrex 2500 inverter, made spare when we had installed the Magnum 2800. Later that day we had entertained Kip and Mary in the cockpit.

Kip and Mary are fellow British Columbians, and they are anchored in Angelos, a short distance away from us here in The Waiting Room in Puerto Escondido. Kip kindly ferried us to our dinghy and assisted as we re-launched it.

Back onboard, Edi and I showered away the dust and sweat from the hike, had lunch and relaxed in heat of the afternoon. Then as the sun dipped toward the peaks of Sierra Gigantua, Edi whipped-up an artichoke dip and arranged it with a small platter of rice crackers and we dinghied across to Angelos.

Like us, Kip and Mary are sixty-something and retired. They live in Parksville, on Vancouver Island for half the year, and drive down here to live aboard their sailboat from mid-autumn to mid-spring. We enjoyed their hospitality and shared stories and wine and garlic sautéed escargots and wine and the company of others passing in dinghies and wine, and the evening flew by delightfully. We learned a lot about the local community; Kip has been coming here for many years, and has done much volunteering.

The next day, Tuesday was devoted to rest and relaxation onboard, sprinkled with a bit of maintenance. On Wednesday we accepted an offer from Kip and Mary to ride into Loreto with them as they did errands and shopping; this would allow us to gain from their local knowledge and experience. They even promised us we would find fresh fish.

After Kip dropped Mary off to spend a few hours at a spa with some of her girlfriends, he drove us to a house near the western edge of the town, where posted on the gate was a small sign indicating fish was available for purchase. Through the gate, standing on the walkway to the front door, was a simple table with a balance scale on it. We watched while a couple of men ahead of us each bought small bags of freshly filleted fish. Each had made his needs known to the fisherman, who then went around to into the garden, took fish from one of the coolers there and cleaned and filleted it to order on a small table.

When our turn came, I asked for prices, and was told 50 peso per kilo. So we ordered two kilos of yellowtail tuna fillets and two kilos of sierra fillets. The fisherman whooped with delight, and telling us this would take a while to prepare, suggested we might wish to do other errands and come back in half an hour or so.

We drove to another corner of town, where Kip needed to tend to some cell phone business, and before he went into the shop, he pointed us down the street to a house half a block away. On its gate was a small sign indicating it sold shellfish, and we walked through, into the courtyard to find a young boy playing at a table. His mother soon emerged from behind the curtain wall that partitions the outdoor kitchen from the rest of the courtyard. There were portable coolers sitting in the shade on the ground along the wall, and she lifted their lids to show us frozen bags of prawns of various grade and size and frozen bags of jumbo and small scallops. We bought a kilogram bag of each of the jumbo scallops, the small scallops and the big prawns for a total of 360 pesos, about $29 Canadian.

We rejoined Kip and he then took us to a few mercados to look at their selections of produce and grocery items. We did find and buy some baking powder and baking soda, but we searched again without success for fresh ginger root. Since we still had nearly full fridges and pantry from last Friday's shopping, the produce we saw did not enthuse us, so we bought none in Loreto, thinking to look again in on the selection at the tienda in Tripui, next to the port.

I'm not certain whether Vancouverites are still the largest per-capita consumer of mushrooms; maybe since Edi and I sailed out they've slipped a notch. We love mushrooms, and have not yet been able to wean ourselves from them, but we won't pay the 85 pesos being asked for an 8 ounce shrink-wrapped pack of so-so quality common whites at El Pescadero. To appease our craving; however, we bought six large and eight smaller tetra-packs of button mushrooms. These should serve us well in omelets, sauces and stir-fries.

On our way back to the port, we stopped at the restaurant in Tripui for lunch. We arrived at 1250 to discover that the place didn't open until 1300, so Kip sweet-talked the woman in the related resort office next door to unlock the restaurant and serve us some beer while we waited for the staff to come in. Like clockwork the staff arrived at 1300 and we ordered fish tacos. The servings were huge; three tacos each, and each with two large pieces of fish, and this followed bowls of soup, which came after a large platter of nachos and salsa. With five beer, the lunch for three came to just under $34 Canadian.

We shared a delightful hour and a half dining and chatting in the peaceful setting of the restaurant patio, which overlooks tastefully landscaped gardens and a swimming pool. After lunch we went the short distance across to the small tienda, and bought more roma tomatoes, green peppers, celery and broccoli to top-up our fridges.

Back onboard, we divided the fish and shellfish into twenty, two-serving packets and stacked them in the freezers. Our two freezers were again filled to their maximum capacity. Our fridges were also topped-up, with very little wiggle room. We were also very full from the lunch; so full that a dish of yogurt mid-evening was all we needed to eat.

Our intention last week had been to leave early morning on Friday the 15th to continue our journey northward. However, I had seen on Sunday that the gribs were indicating a strong wind storm later in the week. By Tuesday, the gribs convinced me that there would be 25 to 30 knot winds here and a bit stronger to the north on Thursday and Friday. It made sense to stay here until the system passed over on Saturday.

Thursday by midmorning, the winds had come up from the northwest into the mid-20 knot range, and probably because of the landform, there were rather frequent, sudden and variable gusts to the mid-30s from the west through the north.

The depth of water in The Waiting Room is generally around 20 metres, except for close in to the beach, or on a small 6 to 8 metre deep ledge near the entrance to the inner port. When we had anchored here the previous week, I had dropped the Rocna near the southeast edge the ledge in 8 metres of water, and had let out 24 metres of chain, including the 10 metres of the nylon snubbers. This gave us a 3:1 scope, and the gentle northwest breeze had blown Sequitur out beyond the edge of the ledge and into 20 metres on the depth sounder.

We had seen from the ridges above the anchorage how we were anchored right at the edge of the ledge. The paler water covering the shallow ledge was easily seen about 20 metres forward of our bows. As the winds built on Thursday morning, I decided it prudent to let out more chain to give us a better scope. I started the engine, then went forward and shortened-in to release the snubbers so I could then let out more chain. When I had the chain in to the snubber attachments at about 14 metres, a powerful gust popped the anchor out of the bottom and we started drifting downwind. We must have been right on the edge of the ledge, because the anchor didn't bounce or drag at all; it probably just swung down clear of the bottom as we moved southeast into the deeper water.

There was plenty of room astern of us; there were no boats in the way and the rocky beach downwind was a bit over two cables away. The engine was running in case it was needed, so I simply waited until the wind had pushed us to a good spot, and then veered another 50 metres of chain. The Rocna bit-in immediately and, after applying the snubbers, we settled in on 75 metres of chain in 20 metres of water.

The winds continued strong through the day, though they eased a bit in the evening. For Thursday's dinner we enjoyed panko-crusted jumbo scallops sautéed in butter and accompanied by basmati rice with tarragon and a butter-sweat of julienned white onions, green peppers, poblanos, zucchini, garlic and blanched carrots. Surprisingly good for its $8 price was the bottle of LA Cetto 2008 Chardonnay from the Valle de Guadalupe, up near the top of the Baja.

The winds blew through the night, and we were entertained in our berth by the creaking and straining of the snubbers working in the chocks. By midmorning on Friday, the hot sun on the peaks and ridges had again begun mixing air currents with the ongoing winds to add blustery, multi-directional gusts to the anchorage. The latest gribs showed the winds easing overnight, so we continued planning to head north early the following morning towards or to Caleta San Juanico.

During the afternoon on Friday the blustery winds had begun to diminish, and by evening the gusts were gone and a gentle breeze had replaced the strong winds of the previous two days. The latest gribs confirmed that the wind storm was near its end, and further validated our decision to head north on Saturday.

We enjoyed a dinner of scallops in ginger and garlic, wokked together with white onion, celery, carrot, broccoli, poblano, zucchini, green pepper, and roma tomato, all tossed with al dente rotini in oyster-flavour sauce and freshly toasted sesame seeds. We used the last of our ginger root. If we had we realized how difficult it is to find here, we would have laid-in much more. We made a note that the next time we see it, we would stock-up.

While we were finishing our breakfast on Saturday the 16th, we bade our farewells on the 0800 VHF net, and then I went up top to begin shortening-in while Edi squared away below. Just before the anchor broke-out, Kip motored over in his dinghy to bid us a personal farewell; we really enjoyed the time we had spent with him and Mary.

At 0820 we weighed and motored out of The Waiting Room at Puerto Escondido in a very light breeze, with near glassy seas and skies clear, but for wisps of cirrus at the horizon. Our ten days here was a longer stop than in any place except San Francisco, California. We realized that we had needed the time to rest and recover from all the physical activity we had undertaken during our two-and-a-half weeks in Espiritu Santo, Partida and other wonderful anchorages we had visited since we left La Paz.

As we rounded Punta Coyote and shaped our course northward toward Caleta San Juanico, we met 8 to 10 knot winds and half-metre seas from the north, so we motored into the wind, making water as we went.

I had expected larger seas to be leftover from the last two day's blows, but found instead that Loreto Bay seemed to be protected by Isla Coronados on its north and Isla Carmen on its east. We were in rather gentle conditions, so Edi pulled out some wool and began knitting me a pair of socks. After three hours of smooth going, once we had passed over the shallows between Isla Coronados and Punta Baja, we were punching through two metre seas.

At 1410 we came to 20 metres on the Rocna in 4.5 metres of water at low tide in Caleta San Juanico. We were nicely tucked-in, sitting between two rock formations that stand near-vertically thirty or so metres out of the water, and we were protected by them from both the swell and the wind.

The formation half a cable to our west was a large block of conglomerate rock, considerably taller than it is broad. Its top is covered with cacti, and it is connected to the beach at low water by a rocky isthmus, which is barely awash at high tide.

Half a cable to our east is a group of thin, spire-like rocks about thirty metres high, and on their cliff ledges and spire tops are eagle's nests. Perched on top of the slimmest spire is a nest somewhat larger than the rocky summit. Particularly when viewed from our anchorage, the spire appears to be wearing a slightly oversized Cossack hat.

We launched the dinghy and took a circuit around the anchorage to shoot some pictures. The rocks to the east of us appear to be the remnants from the erosion of some vertically tilted strata, and there are some rather improbable formations. The strata making-up the slimmest spire have a gentle undulating curve, and the spire is so thin that in places we could see right through it.

62

As we were passing under the spire, one of its residents returned to the nest, and I captured a shot of it on its final approach. I would think these eagles feel safe in their aerie; I cannot imagine how a predator would approach.

Back onboard we relaxed, and in the evening enjoyed our first sampling of the yellowfin tuna we had bought in Loreto. I seared the thick fillets, then let them finish in a bit of butter and served them with basmati rice and a julienne of fresh vegetables. Accompanying this was a 2008 Clos San Jose Sauvignon Blanc from Valle del Maule, Chile we had bought on our first trip to Loreto; even its cheap price could not justify its quality.

On Sunday morning we took the dinghy ashore to the shrine on the beach a cable-and-a-half north of our anchor. At the edge of the beach is a tree, and hanging on it and laying beneath it is a broad selection of mementos, ranging from the simple Kilroy-was-here type scrawls on stones, shells and pieces of wood, through notes in bottles, banners and bone carvings to a primitive-art wooden rendition of a dog. From the mementos we saw, this place looks to have been used by cruisers for decades to mark their passing through, and sometimes to honour the memory of departed friends.

When we had seen in the guidebook mention of the Cruisers' Shrine, we thought this would be an appropriate place to honour our departed poodle, Chianti. I wrote her name on the breast of one of her favourite toys, a stuffed frog and we hung it in a protected spot near the trunk of the tree.

We headed out from the shrine to do a circuit of the northern and western parts of the Caleta, and once we had left the lee of the rocks, we were steep, sloppy seas. Earlier in the morning there had been bands of cirrostratus and cirrocumulus decorating the sky and foretelling a change in the weather, and now the northerlies of the past few days had veered around to the east and were blowing unimpeded into the bay. There were breaking waves along the beach as we approached it, so we cut short our explorations and headed back to Sequitur. Back onboard, we were nicely protected from both the waves and the winds by the rocky spires to our east.

We spent the rest of the day relaxing in our snug little anchorage, and in the evening we enjoyed tarragon chicken breasts with steamed new potatoes and a julienne of fresh vegetables, accompanied by a 2006 Las Moras Cabernet Sauvignon / Shiraz from San Juan, Argentina.

After another very peaceful night at anchor in Caleta San Juanico, we had a leisurely breakfast and then weighed at 0930. Our course to clear Punta San Basilio took us directly through the two largest islands in the bay, at least according to the data from the official Mexican nautical charts. We have long heard of the inaccuracy of the charts here, and Caleta San Juanico is an excellent demonstration.

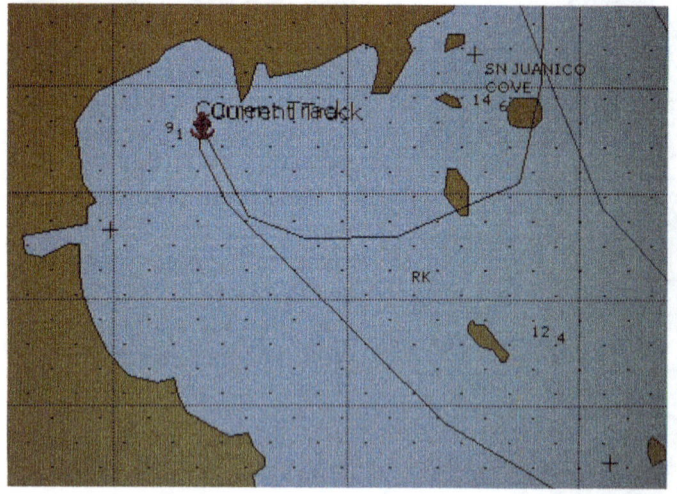

Many of the charts here are based on hydrographic surveys done over a century ago, and often the details that exist on them are rather sketchy. It appears to me that in smaller bays, particularly those with no commercial activity, there was no reason for the government to expend funds on detailed charting. Soundings are sparse and details such as islets, prominent exposed rocks and shoals may not be charted. If they are charted, they are often in the wrong place, of the wrong size or shape, or they may not actually exist. This is why our exit track took us directly through the two islands; the charted islands were not misplaced, they didn't exist.

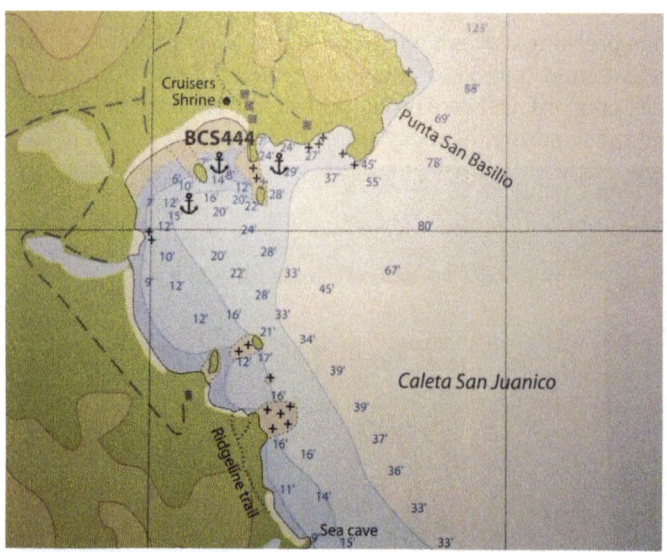

Compare the data from the previous official chart with that on this unofficial chartlet from *A Cruisers Guidebook to the Sea of Cortez* by Shawn Breeding and Heather Bansmer, both showing the same area of Caleta San Juanico. On the official chart there are three soundings in the entire bay and there is a random sprinkling of islets and rocks, which do not exist.

On the unofficial chartlet, there are very useful lines of soundings, bottom contours and accurately placed islets, shoals and rocks. Our anchorage was the one marked BCS 444 on the chartlet.

Once we had bumped our way across the non-existent islands and turned Punta San Basilio, we set our course due north to clear Punta Pulpito. There wasn't a breath of wind, the seas were glassy, and the skies were clear except for a fog bank dipped far over the northeastern horizon.

We motored at 2250 rpm making 7.7 knots, doing a load of laundry, making 68 litres of water per hour and adding electricity to the batteries. An hour-and-a-quarter later, as we were turning northeast around Punta Pulpito, a slight ripple came up and the anemometer bounced around in the southeast sector at 2 to 3 knots. By early afternoon the winds astern were in the 5 to 6 knot range, good for laundry drying, but still not enough to fill the sails on a run.

We motored into Bahia Concepción and worked our way southward in still airs and glassy seas. We headed down the centre of the two mile wide narrows, watching the depth sounder show extensive uncharted 5 metre shoals in areas of 10 and 20 metre contours.

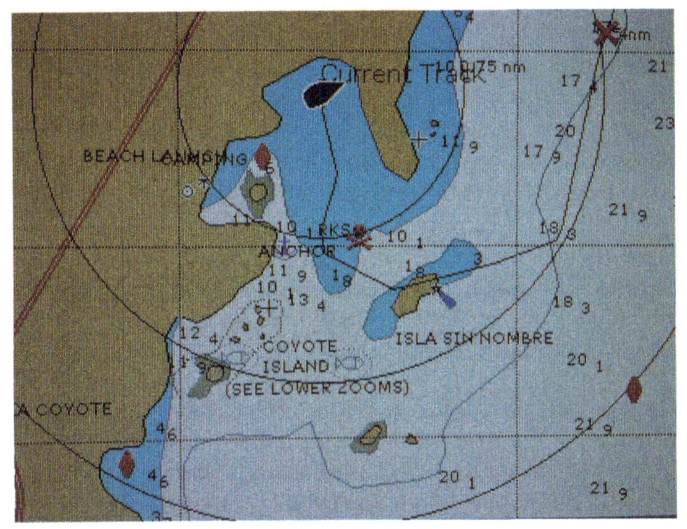

Before we entered Bahia Coyote, I had placed five waypoints from the Guidebook onto the chartplotter. Three of these were anchorages, one was an uncharted patch of rocks and one was an entry waypoint. On the chartplotter display above, the entry waypoint is the red diamond in lower right, and the Guidebook shows good water from it to the red diamond marking the anchorage in the lower left. On the chartplotter, which is based on the Mexican charts, there are two islands in the way.

Comparing this unofficial chartlet from the Guidebook to the official chart was very confusing, and to add to the discomfort, the sun was low and directly in our intended approach, its glare reflected from the calm water. I turned on the radar and did a split screen; one with radar alone and the other an overlay. The radar picture gave a very reassuring indication of the lay of the land, and confirmed the accuracy of Shawn and Heather's Guidebook.

Isla Sin Nombre, which is shown on the official chart, is likely without name because it doesn't exist. We proved this by motoring directly over its image on the chartplotter, while being careful to avoid the very obvious uncharted rocky patch, which I had indicated with skull and crossbones. We could have picked our way in to the bay without the chartlet from the Guidebook, creeping in with Edi on the bows looking for uncharted shoals and rocks and sorting-out the mis-charted islands with the aid of radar and eye. However, the chartlet allowed us to much more easily, confidently and safely enter.

At 1648 we came to 30 metres on the Rocna in 7.5 metres of water in Playa Santispac in Bahia Coyote, in Bahia Concepción. Our view was of Dogpatch.

We were overlooking RV and trailer-park slums. The entire beach immediately to the north of us was lined wall-to-wall with all size and quality of mobile gear: mega-rigs with pop-out sides, converted buses both modern and ancient, pickup campers, semi-permanent lean-tos, tents, and as we later found-out, the barren and dusty ground was littered with dog droppings.

One of the reasons we had decided to anchor here was that the Guidebook had reference to Ana's Restaurant serving fresh seafood dishes. The restaurant was on the beach, and after we had anchored, we could just pick it out through the screen of RVs, camper rigs and trailers that nearly blocked it from view.

Update:
In the summer of 2010 Shawn and Heather published a complimentary guide: Pacific Mexico: A Cruiser's Guidebook. This new volume is the most up to date and comprehensive guide of anchorages and harbours of the Pacific mainland coast of Mexico. Together with their Sea of Cortez guide, they offer sailors safe navigation in notoriously poorly charted waters.

More recently, based on their two best selling guidebooks, they have published electronic versions of their detailed charts for the iPad, iPhone, Mac and PC. These two chart sets pick up what the official government charts leave out and cover the most popular cruising areas of the Sea of Cortez and the mainland coast down as far as Bahias de Huatulco.

While the sun was setting, we took the dinghy the two cables or so to the beach, and hauled it up the sand to just beyond the line of dog droppings, which marked the high water line. We picked our way through the row of campers and walked across the dusty parking lot to the restaurant.

The exterior of the restaurant blended well with its slum environment, while on the inside, the plastic lawn furniture was appropriately draped with plastic tablecloths, and fit-in with the rest of the interior decor. The fake brickwork and mirrored posts added to the effect.

The place was rather empty when we arrived, so we picked a table next to the windows. However, when we sat down and saw the view out on the RVs, we changed sides to face into the room. On the recommendation of the waiter, we ordered the garlic fish, which he said was very fresh.

Shortly after we had ordered, the restaurant began filling with what seemed to us to be desperately lonely couples looking again for entertainment and seeking solace in their newly met fellow campers. As they waddled in (there were very few fit ones), they cobbled together random tables in groups of ten or a dozen or more and made much noise shouting greetings across the room in poor renditions of Spanish.

Our fish arrived as stiff and hard as salt cod. We tried to imagine how it would have been prepared to render it like this. Possibilities were that it had been fried until it was depleted of its moisture, or it may have been deep-fried, then stored and then later zapped in the microwave just for us. However it was done, it was the worst prepared fish either of could remember having had. A ball-capped fellow, introduced as the owner, fielded our complaint. He was obviously from the United States and we suspected that Ana had sold her restaurant to him since Heather and Shawn had included it in the Guidebook.

We returned onboard and relaxed in the stillness as Sequitur lay gently at her anchor. The quietness of the night; however, was punctuated by the sounds of the truck drivers using their Jake brakes to slow for the curves along Mexico Highway 1, which winds its way past the western edge of the anchorage. We decided to move on in the morning.

At 0905 on Tuesday the 19th we weighed and proceeded out of Bahia Coyote through glassy-calm seas, still airs and clear skies. The exit was easier than was the entry; the tide was higher and we simply went back up our track on the chartplotter, knowing it was safe water.

We motored at 2250 rpm, making water, doing another load of laundry and topping off the batteries. I did my weekly routine check of the electrolyte levels in the twelve cells of the two starter batteries and the thirty cells of the ten batteries that make-up our 1225 amp-hour house bank. When I had the house bank installed, I had bought Water Misers to use as cell caps, and these have proven to be a very wise choice. They certainly slow the consumption of water; in the more than two-and-a-half years since I installed them, I have used just over five litres of distilled water to service the house bank and the two starter batteries. On this visit to the batteries, I needed to add a small squirt into only two of the forty-two cells, the first I had needed to add in three weeks.

When we left the mouth of Bahia Concepción, I opted for the slightly longer passage around the Islas Santa Ines, rather than transiting the pass between them and Punta Chivato. While the Mexican charts show no hazards in the nearly three mile wide passage, both the Guidebook and Sailing Directions indicate that: *"passages should not be attempted without local knowledge"*. Similarly, we opted prudently to take the slightly longer passage around Isla San Marcos, rather than heading through Craig Channel.

At 1535 we came to 15 metres on the Rocna in 5 metres of water in the harbour of Santa Rosalia. Our swinging circle took Sequitur's stern within 40 metres of the end of a panga pier to our south and sterns of the boats alongside the floats in Marina Santa Rosalia to our west. The port here is an artificial harbour framed-in by a 500 metre breakwater on the east and a 320 metre breakwater on the south. The port, like much else here, is a remnant of the area's past as a company town for a French copper mining enterprise.

A century and a half ago, copper was discovered in the hills around Santa Rosalia, claims were staked and mining began. In 1885 a French company, Compagnie du Boleo purchased many of the claims and began mining and smelting copper on a grand scale. Much of the timber for the plant's construction was brought in from British Columbia, and heavy machinery came from Europe. By the turn of the century, over 100,000 tonnes of copper had been produced. The breakwaters of the port were completed in the early 20s using blocks of slag from the smelters.

The French turned-over the mines and the facilities to a Mexican company in the mid-1950s and shortly thereafter, the mines began running out of copper. With no more ore, the smelting plant was officially closed in 1986. The vast complex of the plant runs for a quarter mile or more along the shores next to the harbour and its buildings extend up into the hills inland. The buildings and machinery lie unused and in varying stages of decay.

We relaxed onboard for the rest of the afternoon, and in the evening we enjoyed a delicious dinner of prawns sautéed in butter with garlic, served on a bed of basmati rice and a butter-sweated julienne of carrot, poblano, green pepper, zucchini and white onion, garnished by sliced roma tomato in basil.

On Wednesday morning we launched Non Sequitur and dinghied the short distance to a float in the marina and then walked into the centre of town It is now over fifty years since the French pulled-out, and their influence is all but gone. There is a large old bakery, which sells bread that it claims to be baguettes; however, our purchase for the day's lunch had us thinking that the old French recipes had been re-translated too many times over the past half century.

The architecture has a French colonial look, and there is one church that is decidedly French. According to the bronze plaque on its front, the church was designed in 1884 by Gustave Eiffel, constructed in 1887 and displayed at the Paris Exposition of 1889 next to the Eiffel Tower. It was later disassembled and stored in Brussels until it was shipped to Santa Rosalia, where it was re-erected between 1895 and 1897.

The old town sits in a rather flat-bottomed valley no more than two hundred metres wide, which runs inland between steep hills. The main shopping area is in the first dozen or so blocks along the three central streets of the six that run up the valley for somewhat less than a kilometre. We walked up and down the streets looking in the shops, satisfying our curiosity and searching for fresh produce. There are many small businesses here, some of them no more than a three-seat taqueria cobbled onto the front wall of a house.

We finally found a sidewalk stall selling good quality fresh produce. It was little more than posts and beams held together by plastic tarps, and the produce was displayed still in its shipping cartons. We selected some avocados, oranges, bananas, poblanos, tomatillos, roma tomatoes, and a nice big cauliflower for a total of 69 pesos.

When we arrived back at the entrance gate to the Marina Santa Rosalia, whose floats we had used as our dinghy dock, there was a pelican standing guard. After a convivial chat and some posing for photos, it dived on a fish in the water below.

We returned onboard for lunch and then relaxed in the coolness of the salon for the rest of the afternoon, listening to the strangeness of rain on the decks. With only a few hours of rain on Sequitur's decks since mid-October, we had almost forgotten the sound.

We decided to walk back to Sequitur by way of the upper roads, to get views over the old ore processing facilities and the smelter. Among the abandoned and decaying works, there are pieces of equipment, some of them showing some signs of attempted preservation. Half way along, it began to drizzle, signalling the system passage foretold by Tuesday evening's clouds.

On Wednesday evening we dined on basa filets pan-fried in butter and garlic accompanied by steamed cauliflower and poblano and sautéed russet potato coins, all of which went wonderfully with the 2008 LA Cetto Chardonnay.

We decided to leave Baja California after a visit of just over two months. We had crossed into Mexican waters on the afternoon of 20 November, and had anchored off the beach in Ensenada later that night. We had then spent half a month making our way down the Pacific coast of the Baja, exploring four anchorages along the way to Cabo San Lucas. A further month-and-a-half thoroughly enjoying the southern half of the Sea of Cortez side of the Baja Peninsula, had brought us to Santa Rosalia.

The next good anchorage up coast from Santa Rosalia is Bahia San Francisquito, 78 miles and more than a degree further north. We had already rebounded four-and-a-half degrees northward since we had left Cabo San Lucas, and had noticed the progressively cooler and less stable climate. We had a wonderful time in Baja, but it was time to move on; there was much more to see and experience.

The crossing to Bahia San Carlos, on the mainland is only 74 miles to the east-northeast, and we decided to leave early on Friday morning, the 22nd of January. The gribs showed a stabilizing trend and forecast 15 knot WSW winds for the crossing, which should give us winds directly astern, and allow for a good 10 to 12 hour passage.

After breakfast on Thursday, we took the dinghy the short distance to the floats of Marina Santa Rosalia, and headed off on our last walking tour in the Baja. First we walked out to the end of the eastern breakwater, examining the slag blocks from which it had been constructed. It appears that for the above-water portion, molten slag was poured into forms approximately three by four metres in size and a metre deep to form large blocks. These stand one atop the other five high to form a rather even wall on the harbour side, and a concrete road five or six metres wide runs along the top of the wall. The seaward side is riprap.

As we were walking back from the end of the breakwater, we spotted a pelican, which had just caught a large fish, and was having difficulty swallowing it. We watched for a few minutes as it tried to work it down its gullet. While it was trying to swallow the fish, the pelican was being closely watched, and sometimes harassed by the rest of the flock. We finally wandered on, not knowing if it ever did get the fish down. I suspect that the pelican was a direct descendant of the one that had inspired the limerick often attributed to Ogden Nash, but written in 1910 by Dixon Lanier Merritt:

A wonderful bird is the pelican,
His mouth can hold more than his belly can,
He can hold in his beak,
Enough food for a week.
I'm damned if I know how the hell he can!

We walked back past the remnants and ruins of the copper processing plants, pausing to examine old machinery, including this steam shovel and steam crane.

The maker's plaques on the crane showed it had a 10 ton capacity at 19 feet and was manufactured by the Brown Hoisting and Conveying Machine Company of Cleveland, Ohio. Later, in researching the data from the plaque, I found that the company operated under that name from 1880 to 1893, when it changed its name. This piece then would likely be one of the original purchases by the French for the mines.

We continued on through the town and climbed a long winding set of steps that led us to the south side upper town, called Mesa Mexico (the hill community on the north side of town is called Mesa Francia). We worked our up along the streets to the cemetery on the ridge top.

The grave plots seemed to be randomly scattered, with no pattern to their placement, as if the thinking was: *"Here's a good place for papa"*. Many of the older graves were unmarked piles of stones, while some looked to have been later identified and dressed-up.

We walked back down past the shanty town that sprawled along a gully on the slopes of the cemetery and made our way through lanes and alleys to the upper town. Along the way we met a young girl with a tiny chihuahua wearing earrings, and had to take a photo.

We followed the road that cuts down and around the hill into the centre of the old town, and at its bottom, we admired what must be one of the town's original buildings.

Beside it, partly hidden by an abandoned car is an old adit, closed off by a grid door. I climbed over the hood of the car to look through the grid to see that the shaft had been used in recent years as a garbage receptacle.

We returned to Sequitur after our four-hour circuit and relaxed for the remainder of the day. After a delicious pork stir-fry, we went to bed relatively early, since our intention was to get up early the next morning to head across to the mainland in preparation for continuing south.

We had thoroughly enjoyed our two months on the Baja. We had seen and experienced a wide variety, during which time we stretched our muscles, but mostly, we did some very serious relaxing. We had many fond memories of our time on the Peninsula, particularly from the two magical weeks we had spent in Islas Espiritu Santo and Partida.

70

6. The Mainland Coast of the Sea of Cortez

At 0715 on Friday the 22nd of January we weighed and proceeded out of the harbour in Santa Rosalia. Edi steered Sequitur through the narrow gap between the breakwaters, while I cleared a small rug, a tangle of wire and a caking of bottom muck off the Rocna and secured it for sea.

It had rained again overnight, and we motored out under an overcast of nimbostratus, reminiscent of Vancouver this time of year. It was a bleak, cool morning, and for the first time in two months, we put on fleece and foul weather jackets. The winds had been in the 30 to 35 knot range the last couple of days, and we were prepared for the residual 2 to 3 metre northwesterly swell. As we left the land's influence, the winds settled in around 10 knots from the west-southwest.

Our destination was San Carlos, 74 miles across the Sea of Cortez on the Mexican mainland. The wind was directly in our stern, but not strong enough to give us the 7 knots we needed to make a daylight crossing and arrive in San Carlos before dark, so I put revolutions on the engine for 7 knots. The swell was running onto our port quarter, giving us a rather sloppy motion, so we pulled out the sails to add some stability and a small boost. We surged and slowed and surfed and wallowed with the rhythms of the swells as they carried us along and we watched the log bounce back and forth between 5.5 and 11 knots.

Mid afternoon, the sun began to break its way through the clouds, but by the time we arrived at the entrance to San Carlos at 1630, it had long since disappeared in dark clouds building to the west. We had averaged 8 knots on the crossing, assisted a bit by the light following winds, but mostly by the push of the swell.

The first thing we noticed as we entered Bahia San Carlos was the number of boats at anchor and on mooring balls. There were many dozens of them.

The next thing we noticed was a sailboat washed up on the shore, then another, and another, and another. Within a couple of hundred metres there were four sailboats, quite apparently freshly washed ashore. We later learned there had been winds up into the mid-fifty knot range earlier in the day.

We took a circuit around the bay, looking for a place to anchor, but found them quite scarce; any spaces not currently occupied by boats were occupied by private mooring balls. Eventually, at 1720 we came to 21 metres on the Rocna in 6 metres of water in the southwestern lobe of the bay. The boats freshly dragged ashore just a cable or so away from us helped ensure we carefully and securely anchored.

It had been a tiring crossing. The uneven motion of the sloppy seas and the damp cold wore us down more than usual, possibly because we had gotten up earlier than normal. We had a big vegetable omelet for dinner and went to bed early at 2300.

It rained very heavily overnight and on into Saturday morning, so we remained onboard relaxing and puttering until mid afternoon, when the showers stopped and the sun began peeking through the clouds. We launched the dinghy and took a circuit along the western shore looking at the boats aground. Two of them, a ketch and a sloop were well-found and apparently loved, while two others without rigs looked to have been derelict unfulfilled dreams.

There were also the fresh remains some runabouts, three or four of them, but hard to tell from the scattered pieces. As we were looking at the last of the boats on the western shore, we spotted another washed-up sloop in the northeastern part of the bay.

As we approached, we saw that there was an attempt in progress to haul her off the rocks. There was a line two-thirds of the way up her mast, which led to an anchored Vessel Assist launch, which had apparently already flopped the boat from her port side on the rocks, to her starboard side to seaward. We sat in the dinghy thirty or so metres away, watching as a diver and a crew in a runabout secured lines to the boat.

Then, as the launch hauled on the line on the mast, the powerful outboard of the runabout hauled on a line on the sloop's stern, and Dream Catcher slid easily and gently into the deeper water.

We continued on our slow circuit and headed into Marina San Carlos, and eventually found the dinghy dock. As we were landing, we saw two men standing on the float looking expectantly. One offered a hand landing, and Edi asked, jokingly, if they were waiting for their ship to come in. They said yes, just as we all saw the Vessel Assist launch bringing Dream Catcher around the end of the finger and in toward the float.

I told Dream Catcher's owner that I had shot a video and several dozen photos of the re-launching, and gave him our card so he could contact us. We explored the marina complex, its attendant shops and the businesses in the surrounding area, and then went back out to Sequitur. In the evening Edi made up four loaves of bread to rise overnight.

After Edi punched-down the bread on Sunday morning, we took the dinghy to the marina and headed off in search for a place to have breakfast. The first place in the marina building was way too casual for me, and being so close to the boats, it was too expensive. We passed on another spot in the shops along the marina side, and then around the corner, we rejected a pompous-looking place with a breakfast buffet.

We left the marina complex and crossed the street to climb the stairs to a promising-looking place, but were immediately blasted back out the door by a live quartet playing very loud breakfast music. We walked along to Club de Capitanes to find a bleary-eyed fellow telling us he had just arrived and was not yet setup.

We finally settled on a rather tacky looking place called Tequilas, whose interior was decorated with an improbable jumble of faded fishing photos, framed magazine or calendar clippings of Italian city scenes and some failed attempts at primitive art. We had our first ham and eggs breakfast in many months. Two good sized slices of ham, two eggs, hash browns that tasted more like McCains than fresh, and two triangles of toast with coffee and refills came to just under $7.00 each, including the tip.

After breakfast we caught a bus into Guaymas, a city about 25 kilometres south. The half-hour ride cost 12 pesos, just under a dollar and we got off as the bus turned inland from the waterfront near Monumento al Pescador.

We walked the short distance over to the new Singlar marina, and found the office closed, though the sign on the door showed it to be open 0900 to 1700 seven days a week. It is a new facility, having been completed less than three years ago, and we had wanted to enquire about moorage. There appeared to be several vacancies among the two dozen or so slips. We also saw that there is a good anchorage adjacent to the facility, but we could see no dinghy dock, nor any easily usable landing place anywhere nearby.

In a block and two in from the port we walked past many failed businesses and abandoned buildings. In a couple of places there were up-wellings of grey water from obviously broken sewer lines, and the streets for several blocks were running and puddled with pungent water. This corner of the city is obviously not the current prosperous one, though the architecture and quality of construction of the derelict buildings spoke to us of a much better time, of a time when this area would have been rather upscale.

We walked along to the eighteenth century church, Iglesia de San Fernando. Through broken windows, we could see that the roof had collapsed, and was being repaired. We heard the muffled drone of an amplified voice and saw a priest with a microphone pressed too closely to his mouth, conducting Mass in the gardens beside the church.

In front of the church is a park, the centrepiece of which is an ornate cast iron gazebo reputed to have been built in the late 1800s by Gustave Eiffel.

We walked back to the corner where the bus had dropped us, and waited for the next one back to San Carlos. On the way back, we noted the locations of the Soriana and Casa Ley supermarkets, which we need to visit to restock our larders in the following few days.

Back onboard we baked the four loaves of bread one at a time. Either our cast iron Dutch oven is too large or our galley oven is too small for baking more than one at a time, so we have developed a routine:

- Heat oven and covered pot to 450;
- put first loaf in covered pot for 30 minutes;
- remove lid and bake another 20 minutes;
- dump loaf onto cooling rack
- put next loaf in covered pot;
- repeat baking process;
- slice piece from freshly baked loaf and sample;
- repeat process until all loaves baked; and
- delay dinner; we've eaten four slices of bread.

At 1115 on Tuesday the 26th we weighed and headed over to the fuel float at the entrance to Marina San Carlos, where we took on 669 litres of diesel to top-up our tanks. While we were there, we also filled our nearly empty water tanks. We hadn't been running the watermaker in Bahia San Carlos because the water in the anchorage was so dirty. The fuelling took only 20 minutes, but the water ran so slowly through the water hose, that we needed an additional half hour to fill the water tanks. At 1215 we slipped and proceeded out of Bahia San Carlos and shaped our course southward for Guaymas.

The winds were from the southeast at about 5 knots and the seas lightly rippled on a slow northwest half metre swell. The skies were clear to the south and the east, but covered with cirrus and cirrostratus in the other quadrants. We motored across the mouth of Bahia San Francisco and then passed close under the fantastic rock formations that run from Cabo Arco to Cabo Haro.

By 1430 we had turned Cabo Haro and had found the transit leading into Guaymas harbour. Running along the transit in safe water put us about 2 cables to the east on the chart and running over the spit of Isla de Pajaros. The next transit across to the wharf face showed the chart to be skewed about a cable to the south. With our chart now re-gridded 2 cables west and 1 cable north, we continued into the harbour toward the Singlar Marina, which was too new to be shown on the chart. Our faithful and trustworthy *Cruisers Guidebook to the Sea of Cortez* showed the marina, so we knew where to look, and since we had visited the marina the previous Sunday, we knew what it looked like.

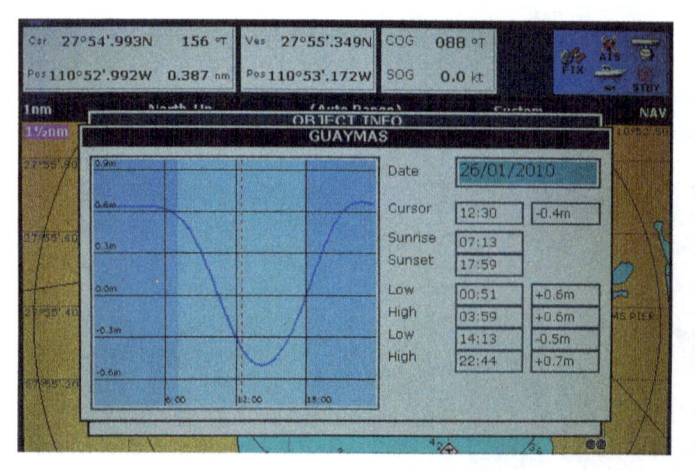

I called Singlar on VHF and asked for a slip assignment, and we were given slip A-9, which is the last one before the end of the south side of the float. The tables showed a minus 0.5 metre tide at 1413. It was then an hour past the low, and with the tide rising at 0.1 metre per hour, I saw that there would be a little over 2.5 metres of water in the slip. Sequitur draws 2.2 metres, so we should be okay.

We slowly made our way toward the slip, watching the depth sounder nudge closer and closer to 2.2 metres, and then we slowed to a stop on the soft bottom. We were still a good three cables from the slip. I backed off the bank and tried an approach a little further to the west. This got us a cable closer before we found another shoal. A fellow from the marina office was now on the float, and he indicated we should go back out and try an approach from the east, close along the wharf face. The water was good as we passed along the face, but we again slid to a stop as we passed its end. I again backed off and then tried an approach a few metres further off the wharf and this time we made it to about 30 metres off the slip.

Our intention had been to go stern-in and starboard side to the finger, and here we were now, properly positioned and poised to reverse into the slip, but we were aground. We had three options: the first was to put out the anchor and sit waiting for the tide to rise; the second was to back off the shoal and head out to slightly deeper water and anchor; and the third was to put the engine astern and slowly plough a furrow through the soft bottom and into the marina slip. I chose the third option.

Sequitur backs very well; I can normally thread her easily astern through any narrow or winding passage in a marina. However, with her keel in the ooze of the bottom, she behaved more like an old-fashioned full-keeled sailboat, and she went where she wished. After a few bursts astern, we eventually settled in at 1545 with our starboard side about 3 metres off the finger and our stern about a metre and a half short of the float. We passed lines to the marina staff, and I made the leap from the stern to the float to help them secure to the cleats and stag-horns on the floats.

Over the next couple of hours, as the tide slowly rose, I adjusted the lines, and just before sunset, our fenders made contact with the float and we were finally secured alongside.

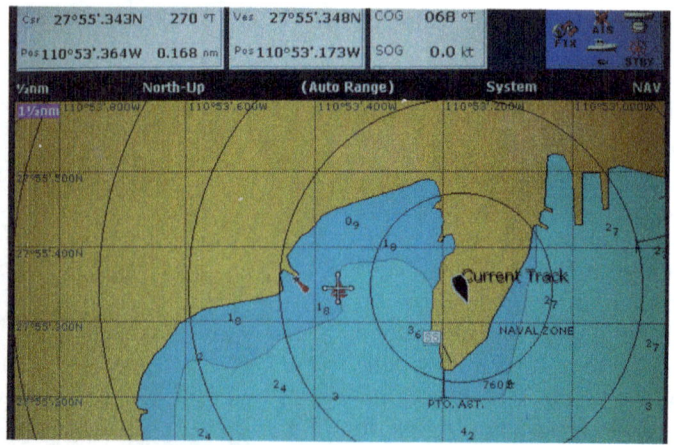

On the chart and the chart plotter, our GPS fixes put us near the centre of the land on Punta de Lastre, about a cable and three-quarters to the east. Even although we were aground, I knew we were definitely not that far onto the putty. I don't mind running aground on a soft bottom with a negative tide that is just turning to flood. In fact, if I had my choice that is the only way I would run aground.

74

We were later told by marina staff that the half metre of torrential rain from Hurricane Jimena the previous September had collapsed the retaining wall on the malecon next to the marina, and that the mud and silt that had washed down from the hills and through the streets of the city, washed out into the marina basin, under the slips and beyond. The marina is still trying to get dredging organized to restore depths on its approaches and under its floats.

By the time we finally secured alongside, the marina office had closed for the day, so I checked-in on Wednesday morning. We took moorage for a week for the equivalent of just under $130 Canadian, less than $19 per day for a 60 foot slip, including electricity, water and wifi. This is a bit cheaper than the US$180 per day we were quoted in Cabo San Lucas in early December. The week here would allow us to restock the fridges, freezers and pantry, allow us to do some long overdue maintenance, and give us the opportunity to wander around in a good-sized Mexican coastal city that hasn't been distorted or spoiled for the sake of tourism.

In the early afternoon we walked along the malecon for a kilometre or so, and then headed in through a street market, which had begun thinning-out and packing-up. The stalls left were mostly portable garage sales. As we walked, we saw damage still not repaired from September's hurricane. There had been extensive damage throughout the town, including the destruction of the domed roof above the altar of Iglesia de San Fernando. We had seen that on out Sunday's walkabout.

Much of the damage wasn't from winds, but rather from the torrential rains. Flash floods had washed mud down out of the surrounding hills, had cut new watercourses through the streets and had flowed into properties. Apparently, some newly paved streets were destroyed, and there is still much evidence of mud lying in the side streets, though some of these appear never to have been paved. We saw so many previously abandoned and derelict buildings through the city that it was difficult to discern the fresh damage from the decay and neglect.

We took a rather indirect route through obviously impoverished neighbourhoods and back out to the Soriana supermarket. There was a great selection of fresh fruit and vegetables and seafood, so we had no difficulty loading our shopping cart. We wheeled our heavily laden luggage cart back by a much more direct 1.9 kilometre route.

Thursday was maintenance day. I had arranged with Omar, the local diesel mechanic to come down to Sequitur mid-afternoon and assist me with routine maintenance on the Yanmar. We changed the oil and filter and made sure everything was in order. I did some troubleshooting and fine tuning on the Magnum 2800 inverter-charger, trying to get it to recognize shore power a little sooner, rather than inverting the top 15% or so off the batteries before going into a bulk charge phase. I was still trying to track-down the source of a fresh water puddle in a compartment beneath the pantry sole. Maybe mañana.

On Friday we relaxed in the luxury of having unlimited electricity, water and wifi, and of being able to go ashore without having to use the dinghy. After long showers, a late breakfast and some internet browsing, we went ashore and walked along the malecon to its end in search of fresh seafood.

In response to our question on Thursday afternoon, Omar had told us that there were seafood stalls along the street past the end of the malecon, but that it was a very long walk. When we told him we had walked over to the Soriana and back the other day, he changed his mind, and said the fish stalls were quite close. We found them after a very pleasant walk of just short of two kilometres that took us past the end of the formal waterfront and into a less tamed setting.

There were three stalls, one beside a fish processing plant on the water, and two across the road beneath a line of low bluffs. We crossed the road and compared the wares in the cases, and we easily settled on the stall to the right.

Not only was there a better selection, but there was a lineup of customers, one of whom had just parked her Mercedes SUV in front; the other stall had no customers. Over the years, we have had good results using the *if-it-is-full-of-locals* method as an indication of quality.

We saw what looked like jumbo scallops, but oblong rather than round, about five by seven centimetres in size and three centimetres thick. Through our non-Spanish and the non-English of the two staff, we asked what they were, and were told scallops. Although the shape and the surrounding white cowl told us they were different to our accustomed scallops, we bought a kilogram for 250 pesos.

On our way out to the fish stalls we had paused to watch a pelican trying to swallow a fish, which was quite apparently too large for its gullet. On our way back to Sequitur, the pelican was still trying to down the fish, so we stopped again to watch. We were not the only audience; there were determined gulls and other pelicans waiting for a chance at the catch. We pondered the bird's plight and were thankful that humans have found a more graceful and enjoyable way to eat.

We headed in through some of the business streets on our way back, stopping to look at the produce selection in one small supermarket, and quickly striking it off our list. Kitty corner from it was Especias Naturales de Mexico, a bulk foods store.

Inside we found a bin of slivered almonds, and I weighed-out a half kilo of them so I will no longer have to hand sliver or julienne whole almonds for my amandines. Edi found a bin of sliced dried ginger, and while not as nice as fresh, we would again have that special tang back in our wok.

Down the street we found a liquor store with a rather good selection of wine, and we picked a couple of inexpensive bottles to see if their contents warrant adding more to Sequitur's cellar.

For Friday evening's dinner, I experimented with the 'scallops'. They were very dense, almost the texture of abalone, but not the shape. I seared them in a dry, very hot pan, then added a bit of butter and julienned garlic and sautéed them for a while longer. This was served with basmati rice and steamed broccoli with a garnish of sliced tomato and tomatillo. With dinner we drank Chambrule Brut, a classic method bubbly from Baja, whose major positive characteristic turned out to be its low price. The 'scallops' had the delicacy and flavour of scallops, but their texture was a bit tougher and stringier.

I spent considerable time on Saturday morning Googling around on the net, trying without success to find out what our 'scallops' were, and how to best cook them. I finally concluded, that whatever there are, I would prepare the next batch as if they were abalone; sliced, pounded, panko coated and very quickly sautéed in butter.

Mid afternoon we finally got serious about tracking down the source of a tiny seep of fresh water into the compartment beneath the pantry sole. I had long suspected that it had something to do with the washer-dryer installed in a cupboard there, but had not thus far found the water's source. To eliminate other possibilities, we dug out the contents of the starboard aft compartment, beneath what used to be the queen-sized bed platform. There is no liner, just the inside of the hull, and it was totally dry, with no evidence of there ever having been moisture there.

The washer-dryer occupies a cupboard in the bulkhead between the pantry and the sea cabin, with the user access through cabinet doors on the pantry side and access to the back-end stuff behind panels in the cabinet in the sea cabin. I removed the panel and found all hose connections tight, with no evidence of any previous leaks. What I saw next really surprised me; there was a dryer vent duct leading out of the back of the machine. This was supposed to be a ventless dryer, so why the vent ducting? It led aft, into the compartment beneath the bed platform, but where did it go from there?

Next we lifted the queen-sized mattress and the starboard forward access cover to the compartment beneath the bed platform. The duct led into the compartment and terminated in an empty lint trap box, which simply lay on the bottom of the compartment. Surrounding it, and on every surface in the compartment was lint, and in the lower front end of the compartment there was a wet pad of lint. Stains on the compartment bottom spoke of there having been at times puddles of various sizes. The hot, moist exhaust from the dryer had no place to go but to condense and run forward, down the slope of the hull and accumulate in a growing pad of lint.

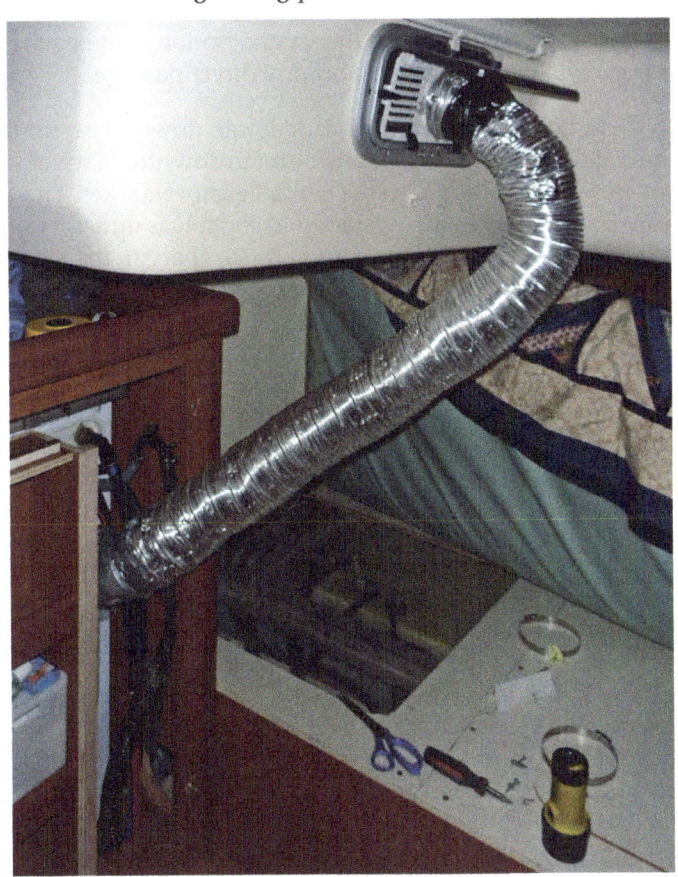

I removed the ducting and cleaned the lint from the compartment, then I setup a temporary vent out through the small Bomar portlight into the cockpit, and Edi started a load of laundry to tryout the machine. With the vent now led outside, the pantry and sea cabin no longer got humid during the dry cycle. I hauled out the user's manuals that had come with the machine to find we had one of each; one for the ventless model, and one for the vented.

It looks like the wrong model was ordered or had been received by the factory, or the installer was not supervised and left the vent flopping in the space and forgot about it or didn't report it. The space spans the width of the boat, and its after portion accommodates the main diesel tank. The port side houses the isolation transformers for the 120v and the 240v shore power connections. The last time I looked in there, we hadn't yet run the washer-dryer, and there would have been no telltale lint, and I would probably have glanced past the metal vent duct, dismissing it as being part of the diesel furnace ducting.

I then read through the manual for the Splendide 2000S vented model and searched online for its installation sheet to gather ideas on designing a proper vent for Sequitur's laundry. One of the problems, of course, is the watertight integrity of the boat, and a prudent mariner should always think carefully before cutting any hole through the hull, particularly an 11cm diameter hole. Sequitur's two aft cabins already sport five 13cm by 30cm holes through the hull, which are sealed by opening Bomar portlights. Two of these lead into the cockpit, directly above the washer/dryer.

Until I could design and install a more permanent vent, I duct taped a portlight-sized flange to the end of the duct and attached it to the frame of the opened portlight and secured it in place with the existing dogs.

With the prospect of such a huge project, we decided to start resting-up. We spent the evening relaxing and browsing the Internet, interrupted only by a delicious dinner of garlic butter sautéed basa fillets. In celebration of Saturday night, there was loud music blasting from various venues ashore, according to Edi, but one of the few benefits of being nearly deaf is that I heard very little but the thump, thump, thump of the base notes.

As we were busily lazing around on the Internet, we heard the first emergency vehicle sirens we've heard during our two-and-a-half months in Mexico. Half an hour later we heard more; this time I popped my head up into the cockpit to see what was going on. The Guaymas Bomberos were slowly driving by on the malecon just off Sequitur's quarter. The very modern pump truck had its sirens wailing, horns honking, lights flashing and was loaded to capacity with delighted children. Every half hour for the next several hours, they repeated the treat with more excited children.

For the previous few days, the midway for the annual Guaymas Carnival has been setting-up on the malecon directly astern of our slip in the Singlar marina. There were already a few small rides there when we arrived on Tuesday, but the major ones came in and began setting-up on Saturday. Experience tells me that the hoots, hollers and screams from the rides will drown-out the music that has been blasting late into the night.

With the noisemakers setting-up so close to us, this is an appropriate time to complete our preparations for the continuation of our journey. After several days of maintenance and repairs, relaxing and restocking, we were ready to head south to Mazatlan.

This next leg of our journey would entail our first overnight passage since we had arrived in Cabo San Lucas in early December. We had been a thoroughly spoiled by all the wonderful anchorages on the Baja side, with nearly always a choice of places within a few hours.

There are several popular ways to do the passage from Guaymas/San Carlos to Mazatlan, one being to cross back over the Baja side of the Sea of Cortez and hop down that coast to Las Frailes then cross the Sea again to Mazatlan. This entails two or more overnight passages, several day hops, and a total of over 550 miles. A second option is to do an overnight hop 190 miles down the coast to Topolobampo and another similar length hop from there to Mazatlan. A third option is to head out on a nonstop 375 mile passage, directly to Mazatlan, which in good conditions and with an early morning start, could entail only two overnights.

If we hadn't so thoroughly covered the Baja coast on our way up, we might have decided on heading back over to fill in some of the gaps. So we crossed off the first option. We have heard that Hurricane Jimena last September rearranged the bars in the entrance to Topolobampo and throughout the harbour, and that channels are not yet properly marked. Navigation there seems to be rather hit-and-miss. So we crossed off the second option, and began preparing to do the three or four day direct passage.

On Monday afternoon we headed into town past the carnival site and over to Serdan, the main downtown street, and we walked along it to the Santa Fe supermarket. The fresh produce there was outstanding, and it was difficult to restrain ourselves; we have only so much space in the two fridges. The roma tomatoes were in excellent condition and at 4.99 pesos (about 40 cents) a kilo, they were a real steal, as were the oranges for the same price. We bought them and broccoli, green beans, green peppers, chayote, avocados, and some wonderful baby zucchini, among other things. After we crammed our new purchases into the fridges and the pantry, we baked the four loaves of bread Edi had started on Sunday evening. The freezers are now stuffed to bursting with the addition of four new sliced loaves.

Monday evening I prepared the third and final batch of the 'scallops' that feel and taste more like abalone. Each of these I sliced into three steaks, lightly pounded them, then quickly sautéed in garlic and butter, and served them with a mushroom and shrimp gnocchi and grilled baby zucchini. We preferred these to the panko coated ones I had done on Sunday evening.

On Tuesday Edi continued to run loads through the washer-dryer, until there was nothing else we could find to wash. Much of Tuesday afternoon was spent cleaning Sequitur, with Edi working below and me up top. I spent a couple of hours with soap and brush and hose removing salt and dust and bird droppings.

I also scrubbed Sequitur's waterline free of marine growth and noted that next time we haul-out to do the bottom, we need to redraw the waterline upwards. We are down by the stern, with our current boot-topping being at the waterline aft and only about four centimetres clear of it forward. Without anti fouling protection, we had accumulated a line of weeds along the after half of the hull.

It looked like we could add another two hundred metres of anchor chain forward. With our immersion rate at 332 kilos per centimetre, this additional 460 kilograms in the bow will have a net effect of sinking us another 1.4 centimetres. But with the centre of buoyancy about two-thirds of the way aft, the actual effect should be to raise our stern a just short of a centimetre while lowering the bow nearly three centimetres. Even with this we would still be down very slightly by the stern, and our boot-topping would still be too low. We need to move it up four or five centimetres.

In the early evening, shortly after the screams and music began emanating from carnival grounds, it started raining. It rained more and more heavily as the evening went on, putting a very effective damper on the noise, and we enjoyed a quiet dinner of tarragon chicken breasts with basmati rice and a sauté of carrots, baby zucchini and chayote. I cooked two extra breasts and four extra portions of rice to set aside in the fridge for quick and easy meals at sea.

It rained heavily most of Tuesday night. The forecast had shown a major frontal system moving across the entire Baja, the Sea of Cortez and the Mexican Riviera on Tuesday and Wednesday, leaving light southerly winds in its wake. The winds were predicted to veer during the night on Wednesday to light westerly, then northwesterly. We decided to wait another day before departing, hoping that we would find some winds abaft the beam to move us southward.

It was still lightly raining on Wednesday afternoon as headed out on a walk around town. Edi continued her search for size 0 knotting needles, again without luck; it seems people don't do fine knitting in this part of Mexico. We worked our way along to Soriana, where we bought more cheese, cream cheese and butter. We also got nearly two kilos of boneless and skinless chicken fillets at 52 pesos the kilo and a little over a kilo and a half of basa fillets at 68 pesos. I was pleased they were bulk and fresh so that I'd be able to package them into two-serving bags and let them shape themselves into the available nooks and crannies in the freezers.

On the way back we paused on the main street to watch a couple of men doing a rather major cooling system repair on a truck at curbside. They had the radiator out, as well as the water pump, and there were a couple of fans and other sundry pieces lying about. It occurred to me that they would make good boaters, being able to tackle any repair job wherever and whenever needed.

Thursday the 4th of February dawned clear and calm, at least that's what we assumed must have happened. By the time we got up around 0900, it was a glorious, clear and warm morning, and a welcome change from the past few days. After showers, breakfast, dish-washing and all other water uses we could think of, I topped-up the water tanks. With over 525 litres in the tanks, we'll be able to give the watermaker a break on our passage to Mazatlan.

While I was checking the weather maps, gribs and forecasts, I saw that Puerto Vallarta had been hit by extreme winds on Tuesday night and Wednesday morning. Hurricane force winds in the 70 knot range caused about half of the two dozen boats at anchor in the La Cruz anchorage in Banderas Bay to drag. Fortunately, from the reports I read, no boats were lost and most of the damage was relatively minor. Those winds would have been during the same time we were experiencing our very heavy rains, and were likely part of the same system. We were thankful that we were on the edge of it.

With that system gone, the forecasts for the next few days looked rather calm in the Sea of Cortez. Winds were predicted to be from the northerly sector, from northeast through northwest in the 5 to 15 knot range, and seas were expected to be a metre or less. It looked like we could expect a rather gentle, slow passage the 375 miles to Mazatlan.

I walked up to the marina office to begin the exit formalities. The Marina Singlar is one of the Nuevos Centros Nauticos, a network of new transient marine facilities being setup by the Mexican government under its Escalar Nautica program. The buildings and the facilities are identical to those we saw in Puerto Escondido. I had seen online that they had a new marina in Mazatlan, so while I was in the office, I enquired about pricing and availability. I was told that moorage prices are the same at all Singlar marinas; this would mean the price would be less than a quarter of the prevailing rate of the other marinas in Mazatlan. There was one sufficiently large slip available, so I booked it.

We do not want to get into the habit of staying at marinas, but at less than $18 per day alongside, including electricity, water and wifi, it is difficult to justify the alternative of using diesel oil to generate electricity, of running the watermaker in an anchorage, of taking the dinghy ashore, of lugging computers to cafes and paying for wifi.

In the marina office, the official wheels turned slowly, and finally after the better part of an hour, I was told that the exit clearance papers would be ready in twenty or thirty minutes. I went back to Sequitur to help Edi in preparing the boat to head to sea. An hour later, I went back up to the office to pick-up the exit papers, only to be told they would be ready in another fifteen minutes. Just over half an hour later they were completed, stamped and signed.

At 1250, with the tide having just turned to flood, we slipped from alongside and headed out of the marina. Low tide had been very slightly above a zero tide, and it was more than half a metre higher than the negative tide that had allowed us to repeatedly find bottom on our arrival. On our way out we wouldn't have to plough a furrow through the bottom; nonetheless, we tiptoed slowly across the face of the wharf before turning south close along the moored shrimp boats, some of which looked to be well past their best-before-date. I knew they drew more than Sequitur, so I assumed the water near them was safe for us. We made it out into the channel without touching bottom.

There are two clearly visible transits that lead ships in and out of the harbour, the inner one consists of two white panels in the hills above Guaymas, and the outer one is a pair of very prominent red and white boards, one on an island and the other ashore. On our way in last week we easily found the outer transit, but had difficulty locating the inner one because of the errors in the chart with its variably skewed horizontal datum. Because it coincides with the corner of the commercial wharves, we easily located the transit on our way out, and as we followed it, we watched with amusement as our chartplotter ran our track on the wrong side of lateral buoys and over shoals. The outer transit ran us across the point of Isla Pajaros on the chartplotter, whose charts are based on the official Mexican charts.

At 1345 we cleared the fairway buoy marking the entrance to Guaymas harbour and hauled out the sails in 10 to 12 knot southwest winds, and set off on a course of 165° making 6 to 6.5 knots. As we lazed in the cockpit lunching on hot paninis, we realized that this was the first pleasant sailing we have had since we had arrived in the Sea of Cortez on the 5th of December. Through the late afternoon, the winds gradually decreased, and by sunset they were down to 5 or 6 knots. We flashed-up and motor-sailed on a course of 165° to take us clear of Isla Lobos, where we would alter to 150° to clear Farallon San Ignacio.

At 1855, while motor-sailing along in the starry, but still moonless night, we were on a course that would take us a little over 8 miles west of Isla Lobos, and more than 4 miles clear of the shoals that extend out to its west. We were in charted depths of 500 to 600 metres and beyond the range of the depth sounder.

Then the depth sounder started reading, showing 90 metres then in quick succession, reading 15, 12, 10 and 8.5 metres. I quickly altered 90° to starboard, away from land and watched as the sounder showed us running slowly off the western edge of a shoal. After about a mile on the westerly course, I came back around to our southeasterly course and settled on 150° to make Farallon San Ignacio.

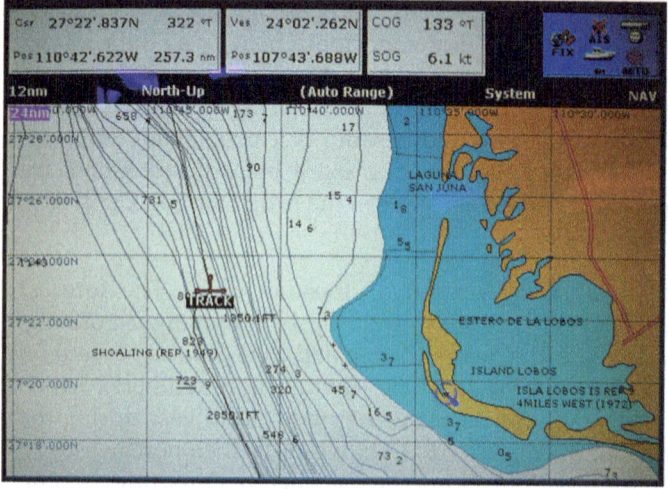

In examining the chart, out in the deeps to the west of Isla Lobos, I had seen a note "SHOALING (REP 1949)" with no position indicated. Also there is a note next to Isla Lobos to the effect that: "ISLA LOBOS IS REP 4 MILES WEST (1972)". This is valuable information, and it a serves as a very good lesson in the need to closely examine charts along the intended course before doing a passage. This is particularly true in Mexican waters, where the charts are notoriously in error.

This was a good lesson for me: examining the charts is good, but correctly responding to the information on them is even better. I clearly saw that I would need to add an even larger margin to compensate for Mexican charting errors. Even although I had allowed for the four mile offset, I hadn't allowed for the possibility of an even greater error in the position of the shoal, and I had cut the corner a little too finely.

We sailed into the night in following winds, mostly in the 10 to 15 knot range. Overnight the winds gradually veered to the north and began easing. By 0800 they were down to under 5 knots, so to keep the sails from slatting in the light swell, we flashed-up and motor-sailed at 1850 rpm.

For dinner I prepared a stir-fry of diced chicken breast fillets with garlic, ginger, celery, white onion, carrot, broccoli, green pepper, poblano, zucchini, and roma tomato tossed with al dente rotini in oyster-flavoured sauce and sprinkled with freshly toasted sesame seeds.

I took the first watch, from 2100 to 0200, during which time only one vessel came within AIS, radar or visual range. A half moon rose at 0018, so by the time I handed-over the watch to Edi, there was a good light along our course, and over a broad portion of the eastern and southern horizons.

The next turning point along our course was at Farallon San Ignacio, about a dozen miles off the coast at Topolobampo. The white, flat-topped rock, a quarter mile by half a mile in size, stands near vertically 140 metres out of the water and is steep-to all round except for a few detached rocks close in on the north. There were no concerns about shoaling here and the sheer cliffs make an excellent radar reflector. As we passed the rock, our radar and GPS both showed it to be about one mile east of its charted position. Thus is the variability of the charting along the Mexican coasts. Here the farallon is charted one mile too far west, while up the coast Isla Lobos is charted four miles to the east.

After light fickle winds for much of Friday, a 10 knot northwest breeze came-up mid-afternoon, so we shutdown the engine and sailed silently to the southeast at a little over 4 knots.

For dinner on Friday evening I prepared chicken fried rice using the two spare chicken breasts I had grilled in tarragon a few nights earlier and had put in the fridge for such an occasion. Garlic, ginger, white onion, carrot, celery, poblano, red pepper and zucchini were wokked in canola and sesame oil with a liberal dash of light soy, then the diced chicken was added and some of the extra basmati rice I had cooked earlier in the week. A quick toss of diced roma tomato and freshly toasted sesame seeds completed the easily prepared and delicious meal.

In the late afternoon on Saturday we were entertained by a large pod of dolphins playing in our bow waves, and we went forward to the bow to watch them frolic for about ten minutes.

For Saturday evening's dinner I prepared basa fillets sautéed in garlic and butter served with green beans amandine, grilled potato rounds and a garnish of sliced roma tomatoes with basil.

As we dined we were motor-sailing parallel to the coast north of Mazatlan and about 30 miles off and we were picking up weak and intermittent paints on the radar about 12 miles fine on our port bow. The targets were so intermittent that MARPA wasn't able to lock on to them until about 5 miles out. For the next few hours we passed about two miles clear of an elongated pack of erratically moving fishing boats working what I assumed was the edge of an undersea shelf, which was charted six miles too far east.

Our midnight GPS fix put us at 23° 26'375N, less than Sequitur's overall length north of the Tropic of Cancer. Since we left Guaymas on Thursday afternoon we had come four-and-a-half degrees south, and the previous couple of days we had enjoyed the warming. Two weeks previously when we had crossed from Santa Rosalia to Guaymas, we were dressed in layers, with fleece and foul weather jackets, socks and shoes. On this trip we started out with jeans and short sleeves with a fleece jacket at night. Here, the past couple of days had been shorts, tee shirt and bare feet with clothing optional through the middle of the day.

The crescent moon rose at 0155 on Sunday morning, just as Edi was coming on watch. I altered course to 090° to head directly in toward Mazatlan, which was then 30 miles to the east of us. This new course brought the 8 to 9 knot breeze forward onto our port beam and we shut down the engine and sailed at a comfortable 4 to 4.5 knots. This course and speed would take us in six or seven hours to the entrance to the marina, and give us a comfortable daylight arrival.

Before we had left Guaymas, I had printed an image from Google Earth of the Marina Mazatlan complex. This was much more useful to our navigation than was the representation on the latest Mexican charts. I had also placed on the chartplotter a waypoint marking the entrance to the marina, and this certainly made it easy as we headed in toward the line of beaches, rocks, condos and hotels looking for the gap between the buildings.

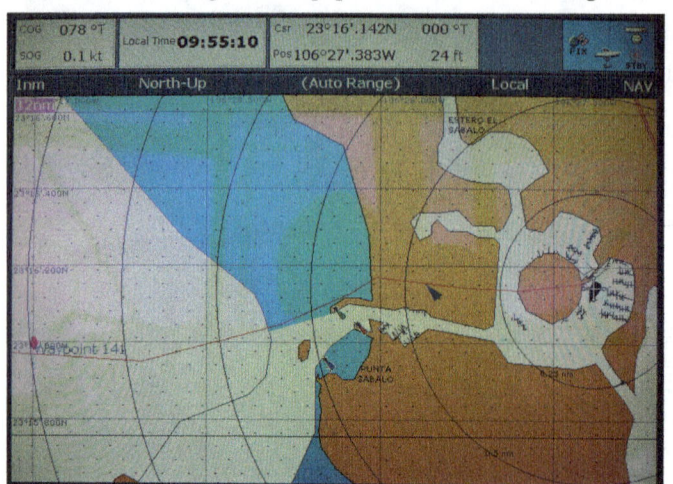

We arrived at the entrance waypoint shortly after 0900 and we slowly motored in guided by the well-placed channel buoys. At 0945 we secured alongside the float in the Singlar marina. On the chart plotter, our route had taken us the wrong side of the breakwater, up the beach and in through a few condos to the marina, then across the middle of its central island.

After settling-in and hooking up to shore power, we walked up to the marina office to check-in. We paid 1,476.54 Pesos for a week, about 211 Pesos per day, which is the equivalent of less than $18 Canadian. The online quote from Marina Mazatlan right next door to us showed that we were here at less than a quarter of the prevailing rate.

A better representation of our mooring position is from the satellite image of the area.

We spent the rest of Sunday lazing about. We slept-in on Monday and following a leisurely breakfast and some time on our computers, we went ashore to the marina office to sign our moorage contract. We had been told the previous day that it would be ready for us around 10 or 11 on Monday, so when we arrived in the office shortly before noon, we were asked to come back later in the day, or maybe the next day.

We walked out across the yard to look at some of the boats on the hard, and saw that Magenta had just been hauled-out. Then we saw her skipper, Larry across the yard and talked with him for a while; we had last seen him and his wife, Kim at dinner ashore in Cabo San Lucas in early December. They were hauled-out here to do some final work before heading to Polynesia and onward across the Pacific at the beginning of April.

Edi and I walked out of the marina complex and along the road to a convenient spot to flag-down a bus into downtown. The rather modern, air-conditioned bus with cushioned seats cost us 9 pesos each for the 25 minute ride into the heart of the old town, the Centro Historico. We got off at Mercado Pino Suarez, the century-old covered market which occupies an entire city block.

The first stalls we came to as we entered through the central doors were those of the butchers. There were ten or a dozen of them in close formation, plus another half dozen scattered among other stalls nearby. At most of the stalls butchers were busily working at joints, rendering beef, pork and goat carcasses down to more saleable pieces.

82

Some of the stalls specialized, such as beef only or goat only, while others carried a selection of meats. We stopped at one beef butcher who had tenderloin, and I asked him for four pieces, about five centimetres thick. He did a token amount of trimming, much less than I am accustomed to seeing, leaving intact much of the chain and the silverskin. The four steaks totalled three-quarters of a kilogram and cost 75 pesos, just over $6 Canadian. At home it would have been six to eight times as expensive, depending on where and when purchased.

In the aisles next to the line of butchers were chicken vendors and fish mongers, and further into the market were vegetable and fruit stands. We found one stand with fresh ginger and bought a large, multi-branched root to augment our supply of dried ginger. We bought fresh white mushrooms, the first nice mushrooms we've seen since the wonderful criminis and portobellos at the Costco in Cabo San Lucas.

From the market we walked through the streets of the historic district to the Basilica, the Cathedral of the Immaculate Conception. It is relatively new compared to most of the other large churches in Mexico, having been built from 1875 to 1899. The church is nicely set facing the Plaza Principal, a rather lush oasis of trees.

The interior of the cathedral is beautifully done, well-appointed and richly decorated without being gaudy or tacky. We both sensed a peaceful serenity and calmness immediately we entered. It appears very well cared for and well loved; as we were there, we saw several apparently volunteer parishioners circling and hovering in search of something to clean.

However fine the interior and the setting, the church itself has a rather plain exterior. It appears to have been constructed of concrete, or possibly whatever masonry had been used had later been stuccoed over. Whatever; it had then been painted with a very poorly rendered deception of mortar joints. Whoever did the painting really blew the alignment in several places. Maybe this is some of what I jokingly referred to as the "*Immaculate Deception*" when as a young teenager I began rebelling against my Catholic indoctrination.

We walked through the historic district looking at the mix of restored buildings, works in progress and derelict structures along the narrow streets. Most of the buildings are low, one to three story structures, many with an obvious European colonial influence. In Plaza Machado we stopped at a restaurant and sat on its patio overlooking the square. We each had two tacos, one fish and one shrimp, and washed them down with Tecates. The bill for the two beers and four tacos was 102 pesos, a few cents over $8, which is about the cost of a single beer in some Vancouver establishments.

We strolled back over to the covered market and waited for our Sabalo Centro bus back out to the marina. The bus route heads northward from the centre of the old town three-quarters of a kilometre to the water's edge, and then along the malecon past the nearly five-kilometre-long North Beach and Playa Camaron on the one side, and on the other side, rows of gaudy storefronts, tired and dated hotels, low-end condos and assorted derelicts, most of which seemed to speak of a better time a few decades ago.

At the northern end of this strip is an area of more recent development, called The Golden Zone. Our bus route then runs for four kilometres or so past more modern hotels and a bit better looking condominium developments, liberally sprinkled with Dairy Queens, Dominos, Burger Kings, McDonalds and other essentials of the US lifestyle. The bus then crosses a kilometre-long zone of vacant waterfront lands that are next to the recently developed marina complex, where we disembarked.

For dinner on Monday evening, I prepared two of the beef tenderloin steaks. The meat was not as marbled as I was accustomed to seeing, and it seemed much limper, slumping on the board as I trimmed some of the gristly chain and silver-skin from the steaks. My first impression was that the meat was freshly slaughtered, and had not been aged at all. I dry-fried it in a very hot pan for four minutes a side to give us our accustomed rare steaks, and served them with béarnaise sauce, gnocchi tossed in a butter sauté of mushrooms and garlic with a splash of chardonnay, and a side of green beans amandine.

The steak was tough, much tougher than I remember even a cheap cut of steak being in Canada. Besides being totally un-aged beef, they must also have had the cattle doing sit-ups; I cannot think of other ways to make such a lightly used muscle become so tough. I decided to use the remaining two steaks for a stir-fry.

On Tuesday we caught a bus to Walmart, which is located in a remote corner of the city, well away from the centre of town, and I think quite surprisingly, far from the thousands of US condo dwellers and most of the tourist accommodations. It was not at all busy, and as we wandered through the aisles, we kept getting the impression that it was suffering from a lack of business. There is a large fresh produce department, but the only thing there that tempted us was a large bin of well-priced mushrooms.

We took a bus back toward the marina and hopped off at the Soriana. The first impression we had as we walked in was of a thriving and prosperous business. The aisles were well stocked and full of shoppers. As we were browsing the displays, we kept seeing signs comparing Soriana's prices with those at Walmart. The fresh produce department was outstanding, and we bought a selection of mangoes, papayas, kiwis, bananas, oranges, apples, pears and plums.

Back onboard, I prepared a stir-fry using the remaining two beef tenderloin steaks from the central market. While the stir-fry was delicious, I cannot recall ever having had one with tougher beef. We decided that the un-aged Mexican beef falls well short of what we want and that we would wait until we got to Chile and Argentina before we tried beef again.

Just as it was getting light on Wednesday morning, I woke-up in a cold sweat, with a headache, nausea and sharp pains in the gut. After emptying myself into the head from all ends, I spent the rest of the day trying to recover, and Edi spent hers trying to nurse me back to health. I had very little appetite for anything, and even though I knew I needed to replenish fluids, I had no thirst, and had to force myself to drink. We couldn't figure out what had hit me. After napping, sleeping, dozing and otherwise laying around, I finally went to bed at 2100.

I woke on Thursday morning after a solid eleven hours of sleep much recovered, though feeling a bit weak and dehydrated. In the late morning we caught a bus to the Mega supermarket to check it out. This is another *everything* store, and would be considered huge even in the largest US and Canadian cities. Among other things, it has a bakery, a deli, a meat and a fish department, a huge fresh produce section, wide aisles of groceries, wine and liquor departments, a pharmacy, a clothing department, and major and small appliances.

We finally found affordable asparagus, and we hoped this was the sign of the beginning of its season here; we had missed it. We also found the first bagels we had seen in over two months, so we bought a dozen to try. I was still feeling a bit weak, so we returned to Sequitur and spent the rest of the day relaxing.

The Carnival in Mazatlan is the largest in Mexico, and the third largest in the Americas, after Rio de Janeiro and New Orleans. This week marks its 112th year and the festivities run for the six days leading up to Mardi Gras, literally, *"Fat Tuesday"*, the last day before Lent in the Catholic calendar. The tradition seems to have evolved into one of trying commit as many sins as possible, so that there will be plenty to repent during the forty days of fasting and deprivation of Lent.

Pancake Day is what I recall the day being called when as I was growing up in New Brunswick. It was a day when all the rich, fat and decadent foodstuffs, which wouldn't be used during Lent, were cleared from the pantry and larder. Traditionally cream, sugar, fat and eggs were combined into rich pancakes, which were then slathered with butter and saturated with the last of the maple syrup. This Tuesday Edi and I would have an easy chore; we have nothing to get rid of. We were totally out of foie gras and Beluga caviar, our shipment of tartufi bianchi had not made it from Alba, and other than our evening chocolate, for which we have each assumed a medicinal dispensation, we don't do dessert.

On Sunday afternoon we caught the bus in to the roadblocks in front of the Fiestaland Complex, at the beginning of the malecon. Fiestaland is commonly called Valentino's after one of the popular nightclubs in the Moorish styled waterfront complex that marks the transition from the malecon to the Golden Zone. The roadblock was there to divert traffic away from the parade route.

The Carnival parade was scheduled to begin at 1600, and when we arrived at 1530, there were already large crowds lining both sides of the four kilometre parade route from the fisherman's monument to Valentino's. As we walked along the malecon overlooking the beaches, we passed many hundreds, of chairs lined three and four deep along both sides of the street. These seemed to stretch the entire parade route, and they were being rented at 50 pesos each by entrepreneurs. They were empty.

We strolled along for half a kilometre or so, until the solid lines of chairs gave way to short spaces now filled with bring-it-yourself chairs and stools. Families were setup with patio chairs and tables, coolers of beer and sugar waters and bulging sacks of snack foods. Empty drink containers and food wrappers littered the area, reminding us of the days before drink container deposits and increased environmental awareness. We picked our way along through the litter and the jostling crowd into gradually less congested areas, until we finally spotted a vacant concrete sidewalk bench, commandeered it and settled in to enjoy the evolving scene.

As we sat there we saw the skies darken and threaten to rain on the parade. The average February rainfall in Mazatlan is 5mm, and they had already received well over that this month.

It did eventually rain lightly for a short while, and almost everyone seemed to ignore it and carry on with the party. Itinerant vendors of snack items, party decorations and body adornments noisily worked the crowds.

Then the parade came. It began with festooned beer trucks with scantily-clad bimbos bouncing to over-amplified thump-thump music. These were followed by another brewer's festooned trucks with scantily-clad bimbos bouncing to over-amplified thump-thump music and then another brand's festooned beer trucks with scantily-clad bimbos bouncing to over-amplified thump-thump music, and another brewer's trucks, and so on.

Eventually, after all the trucks from all the Mexican breweries had been exhausted, a disorganized, out-of-step and off-tune marching band strolled by.

The commercial section resumed with what seemed a dozen or more Bimbo floats. Bimbo is the largest bakery in Mexico, and the stores here are filled with their white-gooey-bread and packaged snack pastries. Their floats were variations on a central theme of cartoon characters mingling with scantily-clad bimbos bouncing to over-amplified thump-thump music.

This was followed by the royalty; an assortment of queens of this and that, most of whom appeared uncomfortable and awkward as they precariously perched on top of car roofs and truck cabs. We assumed that all the Mercedes and BMW convertibles were being used elsewhere.

Completing the royalty section was a flatbed trailer of drag queens.

Just before sunset, the last of the parade passed our spot, and we got up and followed it northward toward Valentino's. The crowds remained mostly in place, and presumably continued to party into the night. When we reached the barricades at Valentino's, we were just about the only ones heading north, and we countered a steady stream of people in the traffic-free street walking south toward the party. We continued north a few blocks to the traffic diversion and caught a bus back to the marina.

Instead of staying and partying, we had opted to have a quiet Valentine's Day dinner aboard. We enjoyed large fresh prawns sautéed in butter with minced mushrooms and garlic, accompanied by green beans amandine and steamed basmati rice, garnished with sliced tomatoes and tomatillos and complemented by a Chilean chardonnay. Somehow, we didn't at all miss the noisy crowd nor the heckling of the junk food street vendors.

On Monday we took the bus in to Valentino's and walked to Sam's Club for a look, but we found nothing there to tempt us. We walked further along to Home Depot to pickout half-a-dozen nuts and bolts from the self-serve bins. We found what we wanted, and a plastic bag to put them in, complete with a printed grid on its side to list the stock numbers and quantities. However, there were no pens to be found. We finally realized there weren't supposed to be any pens; we were supposed to wait for an employee to come by and try to identify the hardware and then to try to find the correct bins and then attempt to correctly do the listing for us. He eventually managed to list eight items for the six we had in the bag. This interesting twist on self-service added only fifteen minutes to the process, but it is still quite advanced compared to some other retail models we have seen in Mexico.

We walked across the street to the Soriana and selected another six bottles of wine to assist in replenishing Sequitur's cellar. We also picked-up some roma tomatoes, tomatillos, cilantro, green onions and avocados from the produce department, some delicious sliced ham from the deli and bagre fillets from the fish counter.

The weather continued unseasonably on Tuesday; cool, cloudy, rain showers and threatening to rain some more, reminding us of Vancouver this time of year. We decided to remain onboard, postponing our trip to the lighthouse until better weather, so we celebrated Mardi Gras by lazing about and getting fat, rather appropriate for Fat Tuesday.

It rained very heavily on Wednesday morning. It was a real tropical downpour, the type that lasts half an hour and then clears. Except this one continued to pour for more than an hour, before it slowed down to heavy rain for another long while, and then eased to light rain. It continued to rain on and off until mid-afternoon. So much for the 5mm total February rainfall statistic quoted by one source, or even the 12mm quoted by another!

We hunkered-down onboard and did some Internet shopping. Edi ordered some more books, and I ordered a replacement battery for my laptop. I also completed Sequitur's insurance renewal; it is amazing what we can do so easily now over the Internet. I asked for, received and reviewed quotes, read terms and fine print, decided on a broker and a policy, received an application to fill-out online, printed it, signed it, scanned it and emailed it back. From the time of making the decision to having insurance bound took less than twenty minutes, and this was while sitting on a boat in Mexico using a free wifi connection and dealing with a company on the east coast of the USA.

The solid overcast began to break a bit in the late afternoon. By the end of the day there were wonderful rippled cloud formations, which coloured to deep oranges and reds as the sun set.

On Thursday it was still cloudy, but at least it wasn't raining. The forecasts talked of a possibility of showers until mid-afternoon, then a clearing for the next few days. We gambled on the forecast being wrong, and didn't take an umbrella when we left Sequitur in the midmorning and caught the bus into the centre of Mazatlan. We stayed on the bus to the end of its run, along the commercial wharves, and we then walked along to the beginning of the trail up to El Faro.

Morro Calvario, Peru at 242 metres, Table Cape lighthouse in Tasmania at 180 metres and the lighthouse at Ancon, Peru at 172 metres to be higher than Mazatlan's El Faro. With this many so easily found, there must be many more that are higher.

While searching, I also found a claim that Sugar Pine Point on Lake Tahoe at 1,898 metres is the highest lighthouse, in elevation, in the world. This led me to think of navigation on Lake Titicaca; surely there are lighthouses there. The list of Peruvian lighthouses shows four. These range from 9 to 12 metres above water level, or 3821 to 3824 metres above sea level. I found reference to a lighthouse on the highest point of Isla del Sol, on the Bolivian side of the lake, which is given as 4096 metres. Sorry Lake Tahoe!

Whatever the height, we enjoyed the view back over the city, with the deep-sea ship harbour and small craft anchorage on the one side and the beaches along the malecon in the background on the other. The lighthouse sits atop Cerro Creston, which used to be called Isla Creston before the causeway was built to form the small craft anchorage and to add protection to the inner harbour.

After half a dozen switchbacks, the broad gravel trail gave way to concrete steps, which continued almost without interruption for 335 steps to the top. On the top of the hill is a very plain two-storey concrete building with a lighthouse tower growing out of its western end. The bland building is painted in Greek blue and white, or at least it was Greek to me.

Hanging by a wire on a nail pounded into the wall of the structure is a plaque, which declares the lighthouse to have *"una altura de 157 metros, sobre la marea alta media, y esta considerado como el faro natural mas alto del mundo"*, which translates as: *"a height of 157 metres above mean sea level, and is considered as the highest natural lighthouse in the world"*. I had elsewhere seen mention of it being the second highest, so I needed to find out which was correct.

After a bit of Googling, I found out that Mazatlan's boast might be a tad overwrought. From the limited searching I did, I found that the lighthouse at the top of Lover's Leap in Jamaica, at 530 metres is well over three times as high. The Gran Almirante Grau lighthouse in Peru, at 309 metres is nearly twice as high, as is the lighthouse on Deal Island, Australia at 305 metres. I also found Australia's Tasman Island lighthouse at 276 metres, Chacachacare lighthouse in Trinidad at 251 metres, the lighthouse at

There was a Carnival cruise ship alongside as well as a huge slab-sided vehicle transporter. As we headed back down the stairs and the trail, the transporter left its slip and headed out through the tight harbour entrance. The gap is quite narrow, and from our vantage point, it appeared even narrower than it is. For a while we almost expected to hear the screech and squeal of crushing steel plates as she slid through.

We walked across the causeway and caught the bus back into Plaza Machado, where we paused to enjoy fish tacos and Tecates under the trees on a patio facing the square. A short stroll past city hall and the cathedral took us to the market. There, we bought a kilo of large prawns and a big assortment of fresh fruit and vegetables, before catching the bus back out to the marina.

On Friday we relaxed onboard and did chores. Edi emptied our laundry hamper through the machine in preparation for our continuing south on Sunday. I gave notice to the marina office that we would be leaving, and asked them to prepare our departure papers and invoice for Sunday morning, figuring that this 48-hour notice should give them ample time. There is a Yanmar service agent in the marina, so I bought two 3.78 litre containers of lubricating oil for the engine and an oil filter to add to our spares.

On Friday evening we gave the ship's chef the night off, and we went out to dinner. We walked along to Fufo's Cantina, a waterside seafood restaurant in the Marina Mazatlan complex, and just 200 metres from Sequitur's slip at Singlar. However, the 200 metres was as the pelican flies; we had to go nearly four times that distance to get there because of the security fencing around the Singlar complex. Along the way we had a fine view back at Sequitur in the marina.

Sitting on the patio was a musician blowing a saxophone to the accompaniment of canned background music. He was playing oldies from the 50s and 60s, and when we arrived, there were half-a-dozen couples dining and listening to him. We both had a rather nice mahi-mahi stuffed with shrimp and crab in a creamy white wine sauce. This came with a plain scoop of mashed potatoes and some flavourful coconut-covered cubed beets that tasted like they had been cooked with pineapple. Our dinner for two, including three Coronas, nachos and salsa, a plate of garlic bread and a generous tip, came to 350 pesos, a bit over $28 Canadian.

The online forecasts at passageweather.com looked good again on Saturday morning when I checked. The winds were predicted to be northwest in the 10 to 15 knot area on Sunday afternoon and increasing slowly over the following couple of days to 15 to 25 knots. The seas were forecast to start out at under a metre from the west and then build to west 2 to 3 metres midweek. The grib files confirmed this, and we continued with our plans to head out on Sunday.

On Saturday afternoon we took the bus in to the beginning of the malecon, and then walked up to the Mega to top-up Sequitur's freezers, fridges and pantry in preparation for heading out. We found some fresh portobellos, and got half a dozen medium-sized ones, and we picked-out half a kilo of firm white mushrooms and a kilo-and-a-half of asparagus. A huge head of broccoli and another of cauliflower went into the cart, followed by some tomatillos, red peppers, a bunch of celery, six heads of garlic and some big carrots. These would nicely augment the produce we got at the market on Thursday.

While I was doing the vegetables, Edi was picking-out the fruit. She added a huge papaya, some limes, tangerines, mangoes, apples, kiwis and avocados to our growing booty. At home, brown eggs are more expensive than are white eggs, so we buy white eggs there. Here, on the other hand, it is the white that are the more expensive, so we picked-up a dozen browns for the equivalent of $2 Canadian. The label on their sturdy clear plastic container showed they were two days old, and that they still have four weeks before they do whatever it is that eggs do after a month.

In the bakery, we bought a couple of loaves of white bread and had it sliced, and we added a dozen bagels and some tortillas to the cart. Four bricks of cream cheese, half a kilo of butter, two kilos of yogurt and a kilo of Chihuahua cheese were added on our way through the dairy department. At the fish counter we chose six nice-looking supreme fillets, two for the evening's dinner and four for the freezer.

On our way to the checkout we picked-up a 32-roll bale of toilet paper, and then walked up the coffee aisle for a kilo of inexpensive Mexican grind. We have not been disappointed by any of the Mexican brands we have so far tried, in fact we now prefer it to the more expensive brands in the US and Canada. This time we chose one called Cafe Garat for 109 pesos the kilo.

For Saturday's dinner I sautéed the fresh supreme fillets with tomatillo slices in butter and julienned garlic, and served them with steamed basmati rice and asparagus with mayonnaise. The warmed tomatillo slices gave a wonderful light citrus counterpoise to the fish, and the combination harmonized deliciously with the unoaked Chilean chardonnay.

On Sunday morning with our bagels and cream cheese, we tasted the new coffee, and declared it very good and well worth buying again. After breakfast we did all the things that use water, before I topped-up the tanks. Even with taking daily long, hot showers, we have close to two week's supply aboard, so we'll be giving the watermaker a break again, and leaving it on auto-flush.

Our intention was to sail to Isla Isabel, about 90 miles south-southeast from Mazatlan. The island is a National Wildlife Preserve, situated about 15 miles off the Nayarit coast and some 70 miles north of Banderas Bay and Puerto Vallarta. Its volcanic origins and its unique bird life have at times caused it to be called the Galapagos of Mexico. Among the attractions are the nesting grounds of the frigatebirds and the blue-footed boobies. Our plans were to spend a few days there and then continue on to Puerto Vallarta.

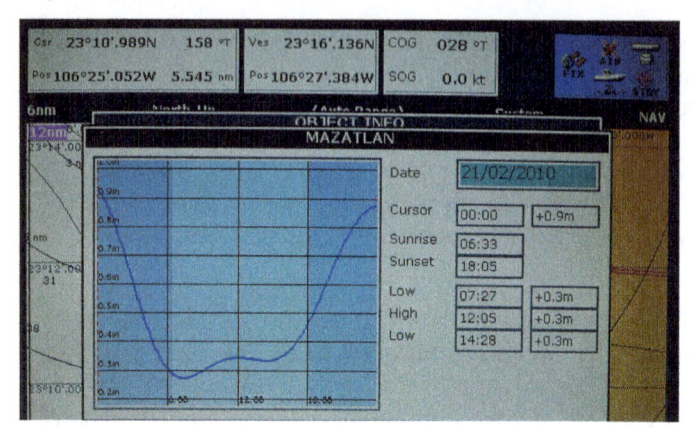

We anticipated departing around noon on the high tide. Technically it's a high tide, but it is actually little more than a slightly higher lobe of a seven-hour low tide of around 0.3 metres. Nonetheless, there should be sufficient water if we keep to mid-channel, and that should be easy, since there won't be any current running.

Shortly after 1100 on Sunday morning I walked up to the marina office to pay for the moorage and to pick-up our departure papers. When I had visited the office on Friday to announce our Sunday departure, Myriam had told me that there would be no problem, the office is open 0900 to 1700 on Sundays and that she would be there and she would have our papers ready. On my way up I had wondered if the papers would be ready, but it turned-out there was no immediate answer to my musings; the office was closed.

I went back to the boat and we continued to prepare Sequitur for sea. At 1215 I went back to the office to find it still closed. This time I had brought my camera, and I used the time and the trip to shoot some photos. I checked the office one more time on my way back to the boat, and Myriam had just arrived. She told me she was the only one in, and didn't have access to the files, so I would need to bring her our documents so she could fill-out the exit papers.

Finally, after three round-trips and a little over an hour and a half, we were cleared to go.

7. To Isla Isabel

At 1250 we slipped from the float and headed out through the narrow channel in slack water. Within a quarter hour we were motoring in open water and heading out to find some wind. At 1315 we rolled-out all three sails in a 10 knot westerly wind and set off southward on a beam reach, making 5.5 to 6 knots. Soon we were abeam Faro Mazatlan and then watching it move into our stern.

In the late afternoon Edi spotted a whale breaching over toward the eastern horizon, and then another and another. We watched as they moved past, a mile or so away.

I tried to shoot some photos, but at that distance, with the rolling and pitching of the boat while trying to anticipate where to be pointing the camera for the next whale to appear, and persuading the lens to focus on the whale and not on the nearest whitecap, most of them ended up a tad blurry.

The sunset at 1806 and found us with 2 metre westerly swells on our beam, and a breeze, which had gradually backed to the north and eased. We were slopping around in the 6-7 knot breeze from astern, and the autopilot decided to take a break. I flashed-up the engine and rolled-in the sails while Edi steered, and then I spent some time resetting Otto. We motored into the night, setting our speed at 5.3 knots to arrive off Isla Isabel at sunrise.

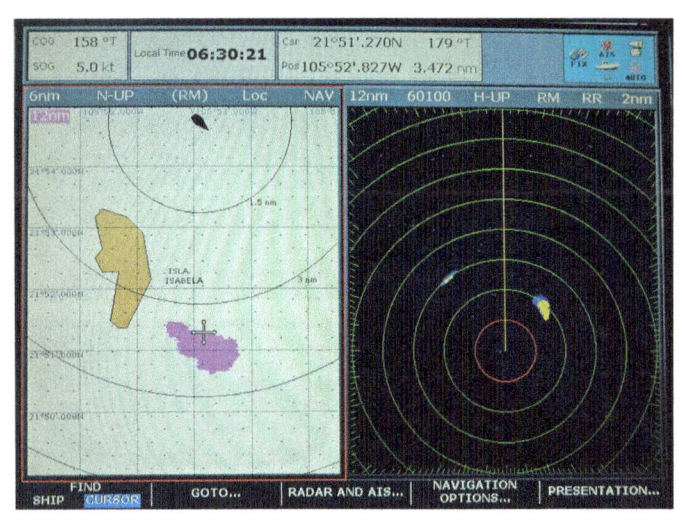

Following a refreshing sleep after my 2100 to 0200 watch, I was back on deck for sunrise at 0631. We were 3.5 miles north of Isla Isabel, according to the radar, and about 1.8 miles northeast of it according to the chartplotter.

Before we left Mazatlan, I had printed an image of Isla Isabel from Google Earth, and had marked on it the latitude and longitude of a small islet in the anchorage on the island's south side.

I placed a waypoint on the chartplotter corresponding to the position of the islet, and used it as a point of reference to tie the radar overlay to the Google Earth printout. This combination and a close eye on the depth sounder led us confidently and safely into the anchorage. At 0745 we came to 35 metres on the Rocna in 10 metres of water about a cable off the rocks to the west, north and east of us.

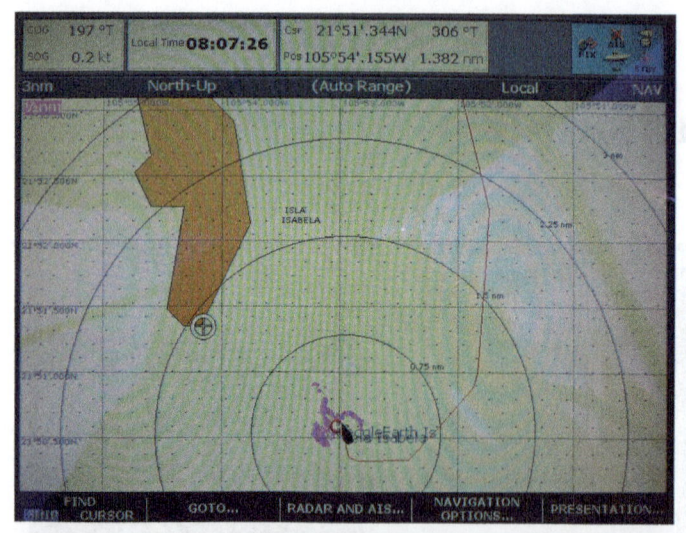

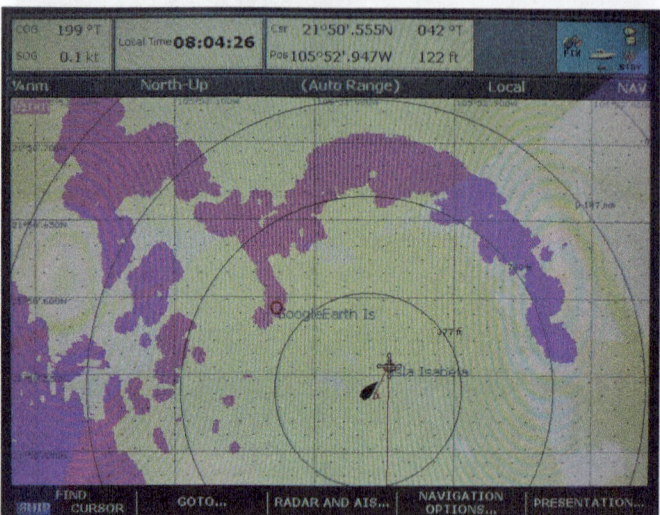

On the chartplotter's interpretation of the Mexican chart, we were 1.4 miles southeast of the anchorage, but according to the radar image, we were exactly the correct range and bearing from the Google Earth waypoint. Our eyes and our common sense easily confirmed this.

Edi had stood the 0200 to 0700 watch, so shortly after we had secured the snubbers, she went to bed to catch-up. We had a late breakfast, with the toaster in the cockpit and a basket of bagels and homemade raisin bread, some cream cheese and banana and a pot of fresh coffee. We spent the remainder of the day relaxing onboard. I did some reading and writing, and Edi continued on the pair of socks she is knitting for me.

When we were in New Brunswick last May visiting my family, my sister, Mary-Elizabeth had shown Edi some of the socks that she had knit. Edi was intrigued, and asked to be shown how to do them, and she received pages of handwritten instructions, expanded by detailed verbal explanations. Many months later, Edi decided it was time to start knitting, so she had dug out the instructions and some yarn and needles, and began deciphering the notes and trying to remember the verbal explanations.

After many false starts and some internet browsing for clarification on crucial points, she finally completed a sock just before we had left Mazatlan. On our arrival at Isla Isabel she was rounding the heel of the second one, clearly demonstrating that she has mastered the art. I would now have warm feet in Patagonia.

After breakfast on Tuesday morning we took Non Sequitur ashore, through the narrow entrance and into the little inner harbour, which is protected by the small islet next to our anchorage. We hauled the dinghy up on the coarse sand beach next to a line of fishing pangas and secured the painter to a jagged stag-horn of lava at the back of the beach.

The crescent beach is rimmed with fish camps, which support a very active fishery. There had been pangas coming and going through the daylight hours since we arrived in the anchorage.

We walked along the beach and across the short low-tide isthmus to the islet and climbed to its top through the roosting grounds of the resident boobies. They were not at all timid, and they remained in place, and apparently unperturbed as we passed within less then a metre of them.

From the top we looked down on a panga at the base of the cliffs. We had seen many others anchor in the same area since we arrived, without realizing why. This time our bird's eye view showed us what they were doing there. They were dressing their catch, either cleaning whole fish or cutting fillets off and throwing the remains to eagerly waiting pelicans.

Among the tufts of grass in the rocks that rimmed the cliff tops were nesting boobies, and we continued to be amazed at the lack of fear they demonstrated. We happened on a downy chick out on a stroll by itself, and it calmly watched us pass close by. Its mother seemed equally unconcerned.

To the east of us was a line of cliffs dropping vertically onto a coarse gravel and rubble beach, off which Sequitur was anchored. We retraced our route back down through the nesting grounds and across the narrow rocky isthmus. From here we headed up the narrow space between the low trees and the rim of the cliff

From the ridge top we looked down onto a lake in the ancient volcano crater on the one side, and on the other down the sheer cliffs onto the beach and out a cable or so to Sequitur. Across the island to the east lay a couple of offshore rock spires standing steeply out of the water. The sky above the island was filled with soaring frigatebirds, and the low bushes beside us were filled with their nests.

Their nests were at eye level, and we were able to look in on many young family groupings, which watched us with no apparent concern. In the nests were many rather recent hatchlings, which were still fluffy balls of down.

One little one looked almost as if it were dreaming of flying away.

We crossed the beach past the line of fish shacks, and at its western end we entered an extensive nesting area for frigatebirds and boobies. Nestled near its centre is a wildlife research facility.

The area was alive with frigatebirds. The males were either tending to their newborn chicks or they were courting the females with their distended red throated mating display. We had happened to arrive on Isla Isabel at the perfect

We slowly worked our way back down the edge of the ridge toward the beach, pausing along the way to observe the nesting birds. Some of the little ones were just starting to fledge and we saw the beginnings of wing feathers.

moment to witness both the courting and the nesting phases of their life cycle.

We were fascinated with the play of the courting ritual. This seemed to alternate between times when the female appeared to be totally disinterested in the posturing of the male, and times when the male feigned disinterest. Both the courting and the nesting takes place in the thick, low tangles of bushes that stand a few dozen metres inland from the beaches.

Near the beach, in the margin of coarse grasses is a booby nesting area. It was not unusual to find chicks wandering around on their own, seeming totally unconcerned about our presence.

Also in the grasses were iguanas. The ones we saw ranged up to 60 or 65 centimetres in length, and although rather tame, they seemed a bit more wary than were the boobies and frigatebirds. I spotted a large one, well over half a metre long, that was slowly walking across a slab.

It spotted me, stopped and went into a let-me-make-myself-look-bigger posture. It remained in varying degrees of erection for several minutes as we watched it.

We then visited the research facility, which at first appeared to be abandoned and no longer in use. I looked through a window into one room, which appeared to be a combination of office, kitchen, dining room and storage room. The stack of dirty dishes on the table didn't have a very thick growth of mould on them, indicating, I thought, that someone had been there within the past week or so. Overall, the place was in a very poor state of repair, apparently without maintenance, repairs or cleaning for many years.

We strolled back through the nesting trees of the frigatebirds to continue our wondrous observations. One small grouping I fancied was the boys sitting around, boasting and showing-off. Overhead there was a steady circulation of frigatebirds coming and going between the nesting trees and their fishing grounds in the bay. We were delighted with the tameness of the birds, which seemed almost to welcome our presence. It was as if we were entertaining them as much as they were us.

We walked back along the crescent beach past a couple of fishermen preparing their nets for their next trip. We stopped to ask if we could buy some fish and were directed to a shack at the eastern end of the line. The two men there pointed us to the fifth shack along the line, and the two men in that one told us to try the third one back along. We eventually tired of shack hopping and returned to Non Sequitur.

On our way back out to Sequitur, we stopped at a panga anchored off the inner harbour's entrance. The two men in it were taking fillets off their catch, one holding the tail and the other using the knife. We indicated that we wanted to buy some.

Gathered closely around the panga were pelicans and gulls, waiting for the fillet-less carcasses to be tossed. We had to be careful as we bobbed up and down next to the panga, that their low-tech rebar anchors didn't puncture our inflatable's tubes.

Once the last fillet had been removed, they were all skinned. The pelicans, knowing the routine, remained on station and ready to receive. While the one man skinned, the other dug into a tub and hauled out a supermarket bag full of supermarket bags, and selected one.

I indicated we wanted four fillets, but they put their entire stack of freshly processed fillets into the bag. I asked for *"la cuenta"*, the cost, and was told it was free with their blessings to us. Blessing them in return, I dug into my pocket and pulled-out two 50 pesos notes and they excitedly accepted them.

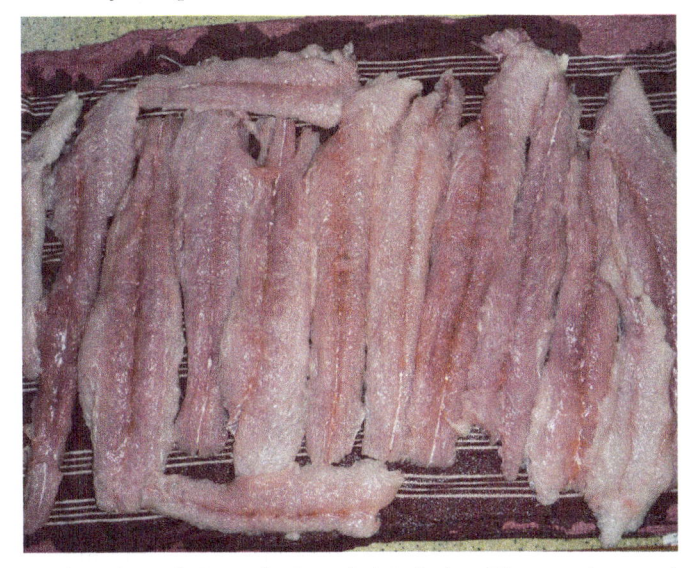

Back onboard, I washed and dried the fillets and sorted them into six meals. Five pairs of large fillets were for the freezer and one serving of four smaller pieces was for the evening's dinner. The fourteen fillets weighed a total of about four kilos.

In the evening I quickly sautéed the four smaller fillets in butter and a julienne of garlic and served them with tarragon basmati rice and asparagus with mayonnaise, accompanied by Concha y Toro Espumoso Brut. The asparagus and the rice were delicious. The fish was oily, and not at all firm, reminiscent of low-grade tuna scraps tinned in oil. It had a mushy texture, even though it was quickly cooked. We tried to think of some way to prepare it to advantage, but short of battering it and deep-frying, or making fishcakes, we could think of nothing.

The wine had a wonderfully active and persistent mousse, but that was one of its few positive attributes. It had very subdued fruit, a hard acidic edge and a bitter finish. We have been trying to find a good bubbly to replace our nearly depleted stock of Segura Viudas, which at around $17 a bottle in Vancouver, was our favourite Cava. We had stocked-up heavily with it when we found it at $6.50 at Albertson's in Moro Bay. We would have to keep on looking; the Concha y Toro Brut cannot justify its price at 115 Pesos, about $9.50. It could barely justify a price of even half that.

The weather continued clear and warm, with a fresh breeze blowing through the anchorage and keeping comfortable the temperature, which hovered in the mid-to-upper 20s. On Wednesday for lunch Edi made some tomato salsa and guacamole, and added a dish of refried beans, and we lazed in the cockpit dipping nachos, sipping cold Tecate and drinking-in the wonder of the place. We continued to be the only boat in the anchorage.

With the clear sky and our southerly latitude, our solar panels were really paying back. I had installed six 87 Watt Kyocera panels, for a total of 522 Watts above the awnings at the after end of the cockpit. I had toyed with the less expensive route of putting in fewer, but larger panels, but the dramatic drop in a panel's output with even the slightest shading on it, convinced me to take the more panel route. They are managed by a BlueSky Solar Boost MPPT controller, which gives our panel array a theoretical maximum output of 30.7 Amps, and I have seen the gauge show the output as high as 29.6 Amps. We can have partial shading on two panels and still see over 20 Amps.

Mid-afternoon on Wednesday we took Non Sequitur ashore to the beach at the base of the cliffs to our north. We had looked down on this beach from the cliffs the previous day, and I had seen a plausible dinghy route through the off-lying rocks.

We timed the surge of the swell and its occasional series of breakers, and made it safely through the rocks to the coarse sand beach. The tide was rising, so later on we would have an easier launch through the rocks. We hauled the dinghy up the sand bank and secured its painter to a slab of lava.

We skirted the base of the cliffs, hopping from rock to rock and weaving between fallen blocks, watching the colourful crabs scurry out of our way. In a few minutes we were at the southeast point of the island, marked by a low arch. The low tide had exposed an isthmus connecting the point to a small islet, and we walked across it.

It was quite windy, and the islet was a rather barren, windswept rock composed mostly of conglomerate and porous lava. As we were climbing a low face up from the beach, I heard a screeching, and saw a red-billed tropicbird fly out of a nearby pocket in the rock. I quietly and carefully searched, and found three others nearby, one of which eagerly posed for me.

Further up the slope toward the sparsely vegetated top, we paused to watch a pale green footed, pink-billed brown booby patiently supervising its downy chick's basic flying training. The young one's wing feathers were beginning to develop, and the bird appeared to be going through the fundamentals of wing control.

A brown booby with huge pale green feet welcomed us to the top of the rock. We continued to be amazed at the tameness of these birds. They acknowledged our presence, and as long as we moved quietly and gently, they watched us with curiosity, but with no apparent concern.

We left a pink-footed booby watching over Sequitur, and then we headed down off the rock and back across the tidal isthmus, which was now considerably narrowed by the quickly rising tide.

We climbed from the beach up the low cliff and walked northward along the east coast of Isla Isabel. Along the cliff tops was a narrow band, five to ten metres wide of rock and tufts of coarse grass between the cliffs and a dense thicket of low trees. In the tree tops were many hundreds of frigatebirds.

On the rocks, in the grassy strip and under the margin of the trees were boobies. Here we spotted our first blue-footed boobies. We had been fascinated with boobies since we had one land and ride for a couple of hours on the rollbar of our Rocna anchor as we weathered gale-force winds off California's Cape Conception in mid-November. That hitchhiker had been a brown booby, with pale yellow-green feet, and in this photo, its cousin seems as fascinated as we are by the blue-footed booby.

As we walked along, in many places it was difficult not to come close to the nesting boobies; there were often half a dozen and more, spaced within a metre or two of each other. Also, we had to be careful not to step on untended eggs. We saw a rather casual attitude to incubating, with the boobies stepping back to look at their egg from time-to-time, and some wandering off for a while, and then coming back.

101

At many of the nests, both the male and the female were present, and we watched as they spelled each other off with the sitting during. The incubation period is six weeks, so while one sits the other guards. There were several solo incubators, and we assumed that the partner had headed out to sea to dive on some fish. Some of these appeared bored with the duty and got up to wander. We could almost hear this one saying: *"OK, you kids be good, I've got to get away from this booby hatch for a bit."*

We have often watched the boobies rather clumsy takeoffs from the water, and lately have seen their difficulty in getting airborne from level ground. This is likely why they roost in wind-swept areas and near steep drop-offs. We saw many perched right on the cliff edge.

We watched two brown boobies beginning a mating ritual. We got the impression that the male's paltry offering of nesting material didn't meet with the lady's approval. She began preening and fluffing feathers, and after a while she walked away and abandoned her suitor.

The females are larger than the males, they have a longer tail and their feet are a deeper blue. Both were equally curious and seemed as fascinated with us as we were with them.

We then interacted with a very curious little blue-foot. It kept a constant inquisitive eye contact as it ran through a wonderful range of fascinating poses for us as we walked slowly past. The booby showed no timidity, even as we moved to within less than a metre.

A pair of blue-foots bade us farewell as we headed out of the nesting area.

The tide had risen to cover the isthmus and to block the passage around the point. We crawled through the tunnel, which was still barely above the water level, and we made it around the point without having to get our feet wet.

The tide was rapidly rising, and we needed to get back around the base of the cliffs at the island's south point, so we retraced our route. Along the way we met a brown booby with yellow feet and a pink beak.

As we reached the point, we saw on the rocks above the surf a pink-footed booby with a blue beak.

We arrived back at the dinghy and sat for fifteen or twenty minutes watching and analyzing the swell and the surf. About every minute and a half, a series of swells came in, with ten or a dozen of them cresting over a metre high and breaking. The troughs between the breakers allowed us to plot in our minds where the rocks were, and to plan a route out to deeper water. I consistently counted to forty-five during the lulls between the sets of swells.

We turned Non Sequitur's bow to seaward and into the water. We then stood beside her and crouched to see the advancing swells and to brace against their crashing surf. At the appropriate moment, at what I hoped was the beginning of a lull, I signalled Edi to climb in, then I shoved off and hopped in over the transom, dropped the motor and scooted out between the rocks and into deeper water. It went more smoothly than I had imagined, and in a couple of minutes we were back aboard Sequitur.

We had spent an idyllic three days on Isla Isabel, and our two short excursions ashore had given us a wonderful insight into the life cycles of the seabirds that nest here. It amazed us that the birds allowed us to spend this time so intimately among them, invading their privacy and their security during their mating, their nesting and their rearing of young chicks. It is such a vulnerable time for them, and through it all we continued to feel welcomed by them. Isla Isabel gave us experiences we will long cherish.

Our experiences ashore were sublime; however, like foie gras, or caviar or tartufi bianchi, a small amount fully satisfies. Adding more tends only to lessen the sublimity of the enjoyment. When we arrived back onboard Sequitur on Wednesday afternoon, we were so full from our experiences ashore that it would be easy to leave in the morning.

The predicted 35-knot northwest winds came up in the late afternoon and the wind funnelled over the low spit to our northwest and through the anchorage. Fortunately, the island protected us from the swell and the wind generated waves.

Shortly before sunset a sailboat anchored next to us, then a bit later, three large fishing trawlers anchored astern of us. The place was getting crowded, further signalling us that it was time to leave.

105

8. Along the Mexican Riviera

We weighed at 0620 on Thursday the 25th of February and motored out of anchorage on the south side of Isla Isabel. The winds had abated overnight, as predicted by the gribs; however, instead of the 15 knot northwest wind predicted, we found ourselves with only 3 or 4 knots. We motored into the sunrise under clear skies, with a few accent cumulus near the horizons.

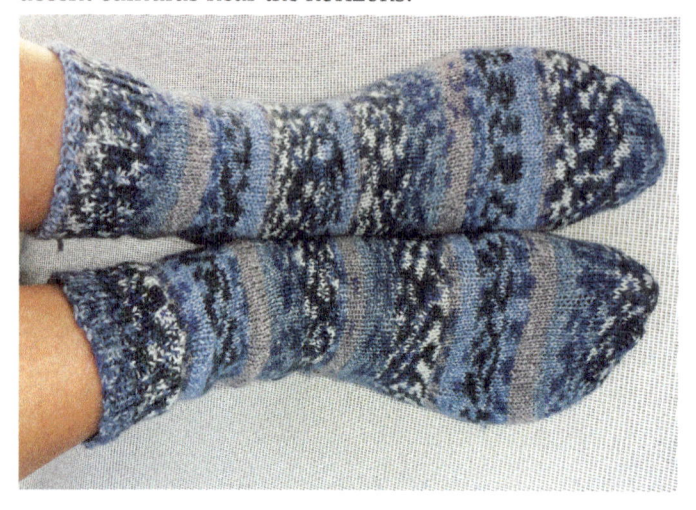

Mid-afternoon, just before we arrived off Punta de Mita, Edi finished knitting the second sock. I tried on the pair, and somehow, couldn't help but think of blue-footed boobies. Immediately after the modeling session, Edi unravelled the first sock, rewound the ball of yarn and started knitting it again. She had started the socks at different ends of their yarn skeins, and the patterns didn't match. Amazing patience and persistence!

At 1516 we rounded Punta de Mita and entered Banderas Bay. This large bay is some 15 by 15 nautical miles in size, is lined with beaches and is home to an exponentially growing number of condominium and resort developments. We headed along the north side of the bay to La Cruz, and at 1748 came to 22.5 metres of chain on the Rocna off the entrance to the new Marina Riviera Nayarit. We were nestled in among some thirty other boats riding to their anchors in this popular place.

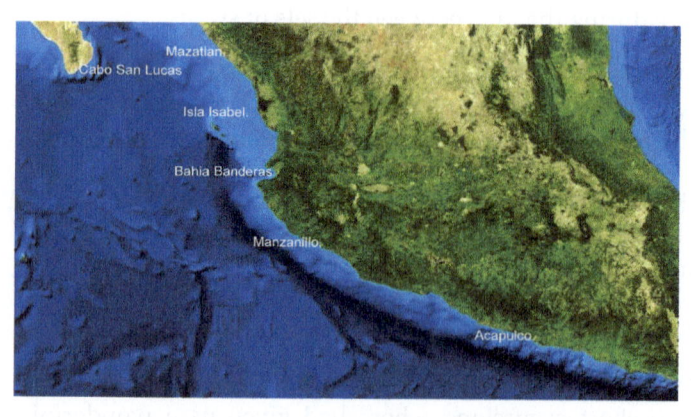

We were in the beginning of what is referred to by cruising sailors as the Mexican Riviera. The community of La Cruz was founded in the 1930s to support the mango orchards and other agricultural enterprises in the area. It remained a sleepy little farming and fishing village until quite recently. In 2008, a full-facility marina was opened with 340 slips accommodating boats from 10 to 120 metres, and in the marina's literature, it fancies itself as the best marina in Mexico.

On Saturday morning we took Non Sequitur into the marina and secured her to the dinghy dock. The access gate from the dock was locked, so we took the easy bypass around the elaborate security structure, and walked through the fresh fish market. The marina had built a very modern market for the local fishermen, complete with tiled booths, running water, refrigerated lockers and for clients to wash-up, hand basins with running water. About a third of the stalls were in use, and I can see this becoming a very popular market, both for the shore-side residents and the boaters.

We walked up through the village to the road to Puerto Vallarta, arriving just as the bus pulled-up. We hopped on, and for 15 Pesos each, we rode the 27 kilometres into Puerto Vallarta. The bus was nearly full, and as it continued to be flagged down every one or two hundred metres, it was very soon crammed. The trip took a little over an hour including a stop to refuel along the way.

We got off in the centre of town and walked to Costco to check-out its wares. With only four or five weeks left before our planned departure from North America, we need to start focusing on stocking-up for some long sea passages and for many months away from known or predictable sources of supply. The food selection at the new Puerto Vallarta Costco was all that we had hoped, and better. We headed back to La Cruz and to Sequitur contented with our findings that we would be easily able to replenish our pantry and cupboards.

After breakfast on Sunday we headed ashore to walk the beaches along to Bucerias, a town some six kilometres northeast of La Cruz. As we were heading into the marina, the Mexican Armada was coming out. There had been an increasing military presence here the past day or two, preparing for this morning's arrival of Mexican President Calderon at the marina to officially open the Mexico Cup Regatta.

We quickly left the marina and headed along the beach, past several pairs of machine-gun toting soldiers sweltering in their full battle gear complete with camouflaged armoured vests. The wiser ones were lurking under the trees, seeking some shade. As we passed the last of the armed soldiers, their attention went to the arrival of the helicopter carrying the President. With the soldiers now so preoccupied, we could carry on with our non-conforming activities, and we boldly walked away from the centre of everyone's attention.

The sand was fine and firm, and we walked easily in bare feet carrying our sandals. As we passed Sequitur out in the anchorage, the offshore breeze was pushing in a swell that broke on the shoals as one-and-a-half to two metre high surf.

The beaches are lined with condos, hotels and resorts, one after another, almost without interruption. Many of them are walled-off and secluded from the beach, almost as if it wasn't there.

Others have nicely incorporated the beach into their design.

In several places along the way we paused to watch the seabirds. Here, one sandpiper stands guard while the others rest on one leg.

After an enjoyable six kilometre walk, we arrived at a nonstop line of beach-side restaurants, each with its own variation of palapa roofs, and palm leaf table umbrellas.

We had arrived in Bucerias. Most of the restaurants had un-cushioned patio chairs and brash hawkers trying to lure clients. We selected a place with no hawkers, and took a beach-side table with comfortably upholstered chairs, just in the shade under a palapa roof.

We ordered fish tacos, chicken quesadillas and Coronas, and sat enjoying the passing scene. People were wading close to shore, others were further out trying to jump the breakers as they came in. Some horses rode past.

Itinerant vendors came by the tables trying to sell all kinds of things we didn't want. A woman came by balancing a tray of fruit juices on her head and sold some to a nearby table, the occupants of which seemed to buy something from nearly everyone, including buying from one vendor an absolutely butt-ugly carved wooden duck dish.

One had a stack of hats on his head, a clutch of plastic beach buckets hanging off his shoulder and an assortment of colourful cloth in his hands. His wares were too tacky even for the buyers of the duck dish.

A beautiful young girl, dressed in a traditional outfit was selling woven bags. She seemed to be preteen. We wondered whether she is a young entrepreneur, or that she is forced to work; we suspected the latter.

After lunch we wandered through the narrow streets and lanes that run just in from the beaches. These were lined cheek-by-jowl with small shop fronts, stalls, tables and pickup truck beds offering a broad variety of tourist souvenirs and kitsch. At least here, the souvenirs are still made in Mexico, not in China. A good number of vendors had locally made items mixed in with the general tourist spam, and some of them appeared to be stocked with only locally produced stuff.

108

At one stall, which was temporarily setup under the trees beside a pungent grey water ditch, the wares were a naive attempt at primitive art.

Above the hubbub on the streets were the homes of the locals. Many of the balconies here were nicely decorated, indicating to us a local pride and a relative prosperity.

We walked through the centre of town to the arterial road, and then along it until I stubbed my toe on a piece of rebar protruding up out of the sidewalk. Walking on the sidewalks in Mexico is much more hazardous than is climbing and scrambling around in the wilderness. There are unmarked open manholes in many places, gaping potholes, steps where they are not expected, no steps where there ought to be some, incongruous discontinuities in level, and as I found out, exposed rebar.

A few weeks previously in Guaymas, Edi had stuffed her leg down to above her knee into an uncovered electrical inspection hole in the middle of the malecon. The rebar had ripped my toenail off, and it was too painful for me to walk all the way back to La Cruz, so we flagged-down a bus to take us back.

On our walk from the bus stop down through the village to the marina, we stopped at a tienda and bought half-a-dozen eggs for less than 75 cents. Our lunch had been quite filling, and an omelet seemed appropriate for dinner.

On Monday afternoon we took the bus into Puerto Vallarta and walked around the Marina Vallarta complex. This area of hotels, shopping arcades, restaurants and bars surrounds a 450-slip marina, and looks more prosperous than many we have seen in Mexico; the vacancy rate appears to be less than 25%. A large new shopping centre is nearing completion, immediately next to the existing development.

It was mid-afternoon, but the marina office was closed. The sign on its door told us it was open from 0900 to 1400 and then from 1600 to 1900. An hour's stroll looking at the marina, the shops and at restaurant menus brought us back to the marina office at 1610, in sufficient time for us to wait only another ten minutes for it to open. We enquired about slip availability and rates. There are slips available and the rate of US$1.00 per foot including water and electricity is not bad, particularly with the continuing collapse of the US dollar. We decided this would be a convenient place to spend a couple of days while we stock-up.

Edi had accepted an offer on her house on Vancouver Island, and the deal was closing, so she decided to fly back to Canada to make sure everything fell properly into place. Thankfully, the Olympics were over; our loft is next to Vancouver's Olympic Village, and had she gone a week or two earlier, getting around would have been nearly impossible. She planned to spend a few days there and to run many errands.

There would be over five months of mail in the box, and to augment that stack, I had ordered some parts for Sequitur and a new battery for my computer. Edi had ordered another bunch of books from Amazon and she needed to buy a new battery for her computer. We had also been compiling a list of foods to buy that we cannot reasonably get down here, such as BC smoked salmon, Japanese rice crackers, extra-dark chocolate and real cheese that doesn't feel and taste like plastic.

We took the bus from La Cruz, which is in the state of Nayarit, down the twenty or so kilometres to the airport in Puerto Vallarta, which is in the state of Jalisco. We discovered that there is a time zone change between the states of Nayrit and Jalisco, the boundary between which is less than two kilometres north of the airport. This discovery took us quite a while; unbelievably, there are no clocks in the airport. There are no clocks in the ticketing area, nor any in the check-in area, nor in the departure lounges. There are no current time indications on any of the screens showing departures and arrivals.

Somehow we didn't clue-in to the lack of lineup at the check-in counter, nor to the early boarding announcements nor to other subtle clues. We thought we were early, so we dawdled in the lounge before the security screening. Finally well before the boarding time, according to our watches, Edi went through security.

Because Edi had a standby seat, and even although there were many seats open on the flight, instead of leaving the airport, I went back to check-in to see if I could confirm that she had been boarded. The agent told me she had arrived at the gate too late and was not allowed on. It was then that I discovered the time zone change.

I went out to the arrivals area and waited to welcome her back. She was delighted and relieved to see me there waiting for her. We bussed back to La Cruz, and the next day repeated the process with adjusted watches.

Back onboard Sequitur after successfully getting Edi on her flight, I decided to start making some water; our water tanks were getting low. I quickly discovered that the water in the anchorage off the beach in La Cruz is full of sediment. This entire corner of Banderas Bay is quite shallow, and the prevailing winds keep a rather steady surf breaking on the beaches and shoals along its northern side, churning-up sediment, which very quickly clogged the pre-filters on our watermaker. I got just under an hour on a recycled pair, so I replaced them with new filters, and these lasted only an hour and a half. Having made less than two-and-a-half hours of water since topping-up in Mazatlan on the 21st of February, the tanks were getting low. It was time to move.

At 0945 on Thursday the 4th of March I weighed and then headed southeast toward Puerto Vallarta. It was near calm, with the 2 to 3 knot airs barely rippling the surface of slow westerly swells. There were bands of cirrus making their way across from the west, foretelling a change in the weather.

It was easy to find the entrance to the port, I simply headed toward the cruise ship that was alongside. Easy, that is once I had distinguished the ship from yet another condo block. The entrance was narrow, but well-marked with buoys, and the chart was perfectly gridded to the actual lay of the land.

The entrance was straight forward for me, but apparently not for others. What appeared to be a catamaran and a sloop lay on the bottom just inside the entrance buoys.

Once inside the small harbour, I turned and ran slowly northward up a long, narrow passage between boats on both sides, which were secured to a wide variety of piers, wharves and floats. There were some haul-out and repair facilities, and some moorage for pangas and the low-end charter trade. There was also a Dogpatch-like collection of live-aboards, many of which appeared to be well beyond their best-before dates.

I called Marina Vallarta several times on VHF, but they apparently weren't monitoring, so I secured temporarily to the T-end of E float, and walked up to the office to arrange for a slip. Then I moved Sequitur along a couple of rows to G float, headed down the alley and backed into a five-and-a-half metre wide slip, which took her with half-a-metre to spare on each side. The floats are wood-faced concrete with robust cleats well spaced and well fastened. My overall impression is of a clean, well-equipped and well-maintained marina. I connected to shore power and filled the water tanks.

Standing guard over the marina are large iguanas, like this fellow, which is close to a metre in length. Of course Puerto Vallarta was made famous by the iguana. In 1963 when *The Night of the Iguana* was being filmed in this area, the star of the movie, Richard Burton was having a torrid and very public affair with Elizabeth Taylor. The couple attracted large numbers of paparazzi to Puerto Vallarta, made international headlines and this soon made the sleepy little town of Puerto Vallarta world-famous. A real estate boom began and has continued with few interruptions. It has for the last several years been the fastest developing tourist area in Mexico.

Surrounding the marina is a broad malecon onto which open many restaurant patios and bars, plus the standard mix of shops offering such things as souvenirs, jewellery and women's clothing. But added to the mix here are many fishing charter operators, resort timeshare hucksters, real estate agencies and condominium sales offices. Above the shops are stacks of condominiums.

I settled-in to a routine of working on maintenance items onboard, taking strolls ashore and feeling somewhat at a loss without Edi to share my days.

Among the projects on my list while alongside in Puerto Vallarta was to clean-out the bilges. This is never a pleasant task, and it is one I had been putting off for quite a while, but with Edi away to Vancouver, this was a good time to attack it. The bottom of Sequitur's main bilge is about 1.1 metres below the level of the cabin sole, and it is into here that all her other bilges drain.

Condensation from the fridges and freezers eventually ends-up here, as does any condensation on the inside of the hull, as well as the inevitable spillage of grey water when cleaning the filters in the shower sump pumps. In addition, there is a bit of unavoidable spillage when cleaning the sea water strainers for the engine and generator cooling water intakes, and there is always a small amount let in when popping out the speed and log transducer to clean it of barnacles. All this water makes its way to the lowest point of the bilge.

Nobody has yet designed a sump pump that will remove the last bit of water and leave a totally dry bilge; there is always a flow-back. Also, the float switch for the pump needs a certain depth of water to keep the pump on, and once the water level is no longer able to keep the switch on, the pump stops. What I am saying is that there will always be a shallow pool of water at the bottom of the bilge. This would not be so bad if the water were fresh and clean, but there is some sea water, and the microorganisms in sea water very rapidly decompose into a sewer-like stench.

A more pleasant task was installing eyebrows above the opening portlights in the cabin sides. Because the sides of the cabin slope in, and because the portlights open inward, if they are open when it rains, it rains into the galley, the pantry and the after head. I had found some covers online last September, a week before we left Vancouver, and the order arrived the day before we sailed out. The box had sat in my to-do locker since then. We can now leave the six portlights open for ventilation and ignore the falling rain.

Among the reasons Edi had gone to Vancouver was to pick-up a starter relay for the generator. For one reason or another, its arrival was delayed, and Edi extended her stay until it arrived. She filled her waiting time by shopping for things to bring with her on her return flight. She picked-up the relay on Thursday afternoon and listed herself as standby on Thursday night's redeye to Montreal and on a connection to Puerto Vallarta from there early Friday morning.

She juggled a 55-kilogram train of luggage onto the Sky Train, made her flight to Montreal and after an early morning dash through the terminal from her late arrival, made her standby connection to Puerto Vallarta. I walked over to the terminal from the marina and met her as she came out through Customs. We haggled-down a taxi rate and piled in for the short ride to the marina.

Among the things Edi had packed in her luggage were four beef tenderloin steaks from our favourite butcher. She had sealed these in a Lock-and-Lock container and they made it through Customs without a hitch. We thoroughly enjoyed one pair for dinner on Friday evening topped with béarnaise sauce and accompanied by gnocchi in a Portobello mushroom sauce and steamed asparagus with mayonnaise. With it we had a bottle of 2006 Los Vascos Cabernet Sauvignon from Chile to see if it merited adding to our list of purchases for Sequitur's cellar. The steaks were superb, but the wine didn't make the cut.

We spent most of Saturday shopping. First we took a bus to Walmart to buy a case of wine, a kilogram loaf of butter, three kilos of yogurt, three kilos of coffee, many cans of soup and tetra-packs of various things, such as salsa verde, sliced mushrooms and heavy cream.

After lunch we took a bus to the Mega downtown to look at it and to transfer to another bus to take us to Costco. After 5750 Pesos, they let us out with a wonderful selection, which included such things as four kilos of boneless and skinless chicken breasts, a kilo of jumbo scallops, a kilo of jumbo prawns, four litres of artichoke hearts, two litres of sun-dried tomatoes, two kilos of crimini mushrooms, two kilos of asparagus, a dozen red, yellow and orange peppers, two dozen bagels, large blocks of gorgonzola, gruyere, brie and aged cheddar, three dozen cans of Tecate and some bottles of Champagne Veuve Clicquot.

We carefully packed our Costco haul into four large boxes and five large nylon and canvas bags, and then negotiated a taxi ride back to the marina for 60 pesos. After we had loaded it all aboard, unpacked it and sorted it into the fridges, freezers, pantry and storage lockers, in the early evening we took a bus into the downtown Mega to top-up our stock of fresh fruit and vegetables. We were back aboard shortly before 2100 after an all-day shopping spree that cost us 7,675 Pesos, about $625.

On Sunday we played tourist. We enjoyed a leisurely breakfast in the cockpit, with toasted bagels, cream cheese, smoked wild BC salmon and capers, washed down with cups of hot coffee. We took a bus downtown to the hotel district and then walked along the malecon. There are many wonderfully whimsical sculptures along here, such as this one of the stone-eating man turning to stone. It looks like you are what you eat.

This fellow was selling grilled lobster tails and was armed with a holster filled with your choice of sauce.

Another interesting one is *In Search of Reason*, with its two pillow-headed children ascending a ladder to the sky.

We continued along as the broad malecon narrowed as it entered the beach area. The beaches then began to sprout a profusion of umbrellas, both cloth and thatched.

Under some of these, entrepreneurial cooks have setup temporary kitchens that produce a wide variety of fare for the beach set. Much of the fare is grilled skewers of what-have-you, which are then toted around the beach by vendors.

As we walked further along, there was a traditionally dressed mariachi group serenading a small gathering under the straw umbrellas.

Toward the end of the built-up section of the beach we paused for an hour or so at a table at a beach-side restaurant. We enjoyed a couple of Coronas as we watched the passing scene. As pleasant the time was, we both realized an hour was about all we could take of this sort of thing; we are not the type to sit around in a bar, nor to laze about on the beach. We have other things to do with our lives.

Back onboard Sequitur, we refreshed ourselves with some fresh blackberries and papaya with yogurt. Then we spent some time reorganizing the fridges and freezers. We managed to fit almost everything in, leaving out only a dozen large coloured peppers, which were so fresh, they would do well for the day or two it takes to liberate space in one of the fridges.

Then we walked back through the old town to the main plaza and the Cathedral of Our Lady of Guadeloupe.

Sunday evening's dinner was a celebration of Edi having sold her house, a celebration of our now being untethered from our old worlds, and a celebration of our being free to go and do as we please. For dinner I prepared tarragon chicken, and served it with basmati rice, crimini mushrooms in a cream and sauvignon blanc sauce and steamed asparagus with mayonnaise. To assist with our celebrations, we opened a bottle of Champagne Veuve Clicquot.

With our fridges, freezers and pantry again full, our intention was to leave midday on Monday the 15th and continue south. So after Monday's breakfast I walked up to the marina office, timing my arrival for 0920, allowing ample time for the office staff to have arrived after their 0900 scheduled opening. The office was not yet open, though the sign on the door said 0900, so I went back to the boat to continue preparing her for sea.

The interior is much less elaborate than many of those we had seen in Mexico. We continued walking northward, back to where we could catch a bus to the Soriana. The route we chose was a bit off the tourist track, and our surroundings were quite obviously of a different economic category. We bought a few poblanos and some cilantro at Soriana to top-off our pantry, and then caught a bus back to the marina. Its route went through some rather impoverished areas, not slums, but not far above. Even in an apparently prosperous place like Puerto Vallarta, Mexico's widespread poverty is very obvious. Once we take a few steps away from the thin veneer of tourist and snowbird developments along the beaches, the hills with views and other fashionable areas, and move through and beyond their layer of supporting infrastructure, the picture is not so pretty.

I finished topping-off the water tanks, puttered for a while and then shortly after 1000, I went back to the office to pay our mooring bill and to return the gate key. The office was still closed. Back at G float I met Izequiel, one of the marina's security attendants, and asked him about the office being closed. He told me, *"Is closed for holiday"*. *"What holiday?"* I asked. *"Holiday of 15 March"*, he replied.

Great! So here we were stuck in Puerto Vallarta for another day. Or not! I had left Sequitur's credit card details with the office manager, Adrianna when I checked-in, so I asked Izequiel if I could leave our key with him and give him a note for Adriana. He handed me his book and I wrote in it a detailed note to the marina authorizing them to charge us up to Monday morning. I then gave Izequiel the key and we were ready to go.

113

At 1053 we slipped and headed out of the marina and passed through the harbour entrance at 1112. In a hazy overcast, a light fog and still airs, we motored west southwesterly at 7.5 knots to clear Banderas Bay. The sky continued overcast and the visibility remained at 2 to 3 miles in thin fog as we rounded Punta Chimo and bent our course southwest at 1400. An hour later as we rounded Cabo Corrientes and turned south, the haze cleared, but the overcast remained, as did the near calm airs.

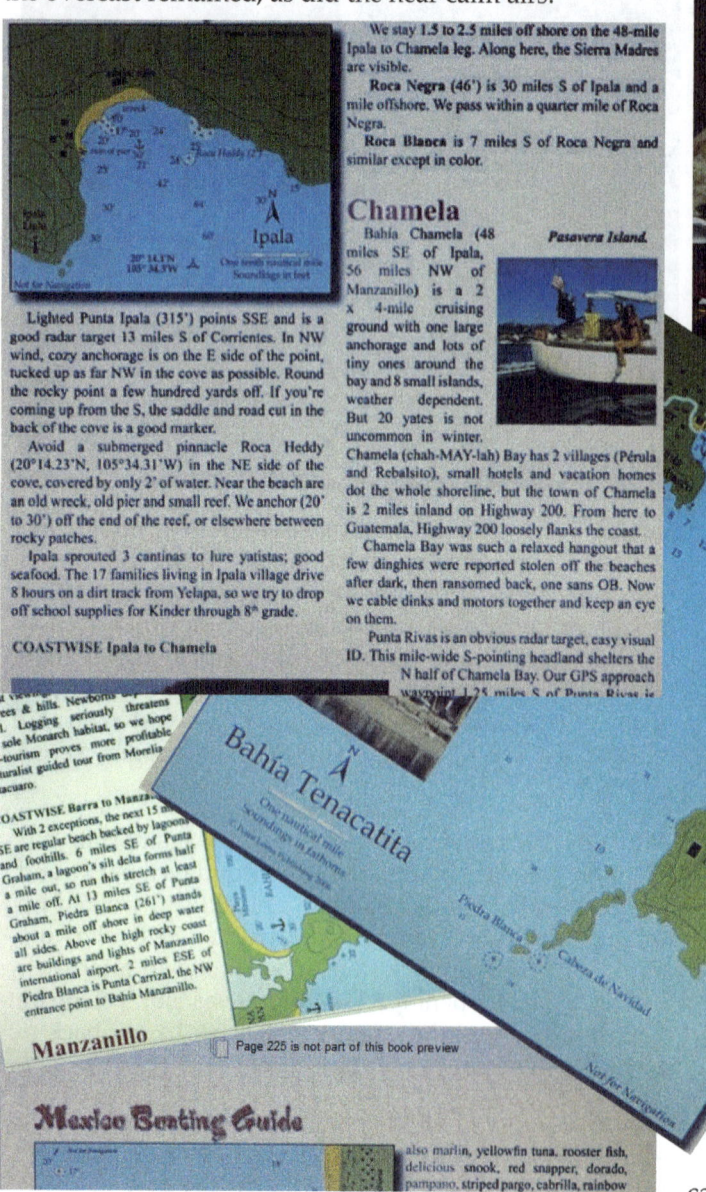

While we were in Puerto Vallarta I had searched in vain for navigational guidebooks for the coast to the south. There were none in Spanish, let alone in English. Online I found a listing on Amazon for a book titled *Mexican Boating Guide* by Captain Pat Rains, but it was not available for shipment. There was a *"Look Inside"* preview, and with some searching, I was able to find pages for almost every anchorage we might need on our way along the coast.

At 1715 we came to 30 metres on the Rocna in 10 metres of water off the beach in Bahia Ipala. Other than the fishing pangas moored along the beach, we were the only boat in the bay. It was not the calmest of anchorages. Even although there was land protecting us from everything but the south, somehow the westerly swell managed to refract around the point and, I think it also reflected off the rocks to our east. We rolled and pitched, not uncomfortably, but rather annoyingly.

For dinner I sautéed basa fillets in butter with crimini mushrooms and garlic and served them with basmati rice and fine green beans amandine with a garnish of roma tomatoes and basil. We continued our celebration of freedom with Champagne Veuve Clicquot.

The village of Ipala is reported to have seventeen families and three restaurants for the boating tourists. For some reason, the idea of going ashore here did not appeal to us, so at 0930 on Tuesday morning, we weighed and continued southward. The skies were clear overhead and to the west and north, while the other two sectors carried the remnants of the passing system. There was just sufficient breeze to occasionally ripple the surface of the 1.5 to 2 metre swell, so we again motored.

At 1646 we came to 35 metres on the Rocna in 11.5 metres of water in Bahia Chamila. With us in the glassy waters of the anchorage were seven other sailboats and a cruising trawler. We relaxed to the rhythm of the slow swell and in the evening had a wonderful omelet of ham, criminis, white onions, garlic, pablanos, red and yellow peppers and Chihuahua cheese served with butter-grilled yellow potato rounds.

On Wednesday morning we arose late and had a leisurely breakfast in the cockpit. The trawler and three of the

114

sailboats had weighed and departed, so we were now five sailboats in the anchorage. The wind had come up overnight, and the glassy surface of the slow 1.5 to 2 metre swell had been replaced by a choppy short-period wind wave on top of the swell, and the surf was more seriously breaking on the beaches to our north.

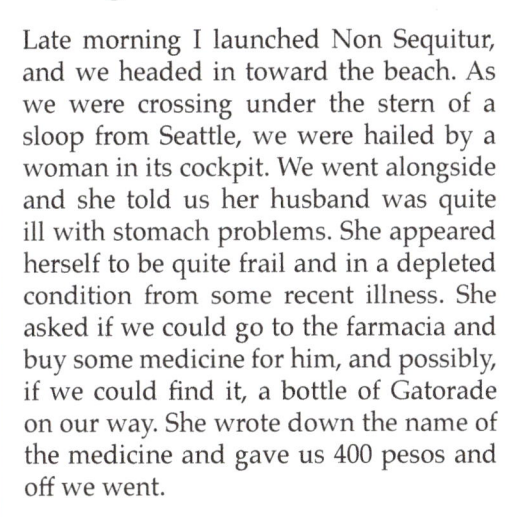

Late morning I launched Non Sequitur, and we headed in toward the beach. As we were crossing under the stern of a sloop from Seattle, we were hailed by a woman in its cockpit. We went alongside and she told us her husband was quite ill with stomach problems. She appeared herself to be quite frail and in a depleted condition from some recent illness. She asked if we could go to the farmacia and buy some medicine for him, and possibly, if we could find it, a bottle of Gatorade on our way. She wrote down the name of the medicine and gave us 400 pesos and off we went.

We landed through the surf without much difficulty, other than a wave catching Edi and getting the seat of her pants wet. We walked a couple of blocks away from the beach along unpaved streets to a paved road that parallelled the coast. There in a small tienda, we asked for directions to the farmacia and were told seven blocks along and on the left. In a diving shop in the next block we asked again for directions, and got the same story; we long ago learned to ask more than one source.

On our way to and from the farmacia we passed many colourfully decorated small businesses and homes. Some rather ramshackle places, like this curiosity shop, were well disguised with a profusion of blooming trees, shrubs and potted plants.

The farmacia was where it was supposed to be and it had the required medicine in stock, both patented and generic. At one-third of the price, we took the generic. Finding Gatorade should be easy; in Mexico, from huge supermarket down to tiny tienda, we have seen a larger variety and stock of fizzy sugar-water in the stores than we have seen anywhere else on the planet. This country seems totally hypnotized by the marketing of the big sugar-water manufacturers.

We walked into a small tienda, and there in the cooler was Gatorade in many flavours and two different sizes.

Back at Non Sequitur on the beach, we watched the surf, trying to find a pattern in it. As we were analyzing the waves, an elderly man was taking a young boy out for a ride in a makeshift carriage. In the sand, the dolly's balloon tires were much more practical than would be regular pram wheels.

We finally figured that we had sorted-out a pattern in the waves, and we launched Non Sequitur out into the tail-end of a train of breakers and I started rowing into water deep enough to drop the motor and scoot out. We were almost clear when the port-side oarlock popped out and the pin disappeared into the water. In our scramble to convert from rowing to paddling, the next train of breakers arrived, and we got caught-up in it.

Back on the beach, I popped the drain plug to let out the forty or fifty litres of water that the breakers had deposited in the dinghy. Fortunately, I had had the foresight to put my wallet, camera and the medicine in one of the dinghy's watertight lockers before we launched. I also remembered to replace the drain plug after the dinghy had finished draining. We reorganized, reanalyzed and headed out again. This time we made it.

We dropped-off the medicine and Gatorade at the Seattle sloop on our way back to Sequitur. Back onboard, we showered and Edi prepared some delicious chicken quesadillas, which we enjoyed as we relaxed in cockpit in the cooling breeze. The wind was blowing south-southwest about 16 to 18 knots, and would have been marvellous for our past two days' passages. On the previous day's passage, it would have given us a broad reach at 8 knots and better for almost the entire route. This day it simply complicated our dinghy ride ashore.

On Wednesday evening we enjoyed jumbo scallops sautéed in butter with criminis, garlic, white onion, poblanos and red and yellow peppers. This was served with basmati rice, roma tomatoes with basil and fresh asparagus with mayonnaise, and it was accompanied by a Concha y Toro Sauvignon Blanc from Chile. It was a wonderful dinner.

With the good sailing wind, we decided that we would continue southward in the morning, thinking of stopping at Careyes if the protection looked good. But with the swell now around from the southwest, the small anchorage would probably be a bit rough, and if so, we would carry on to Tenacatita Bay. There we could find better protection, as well as our friends Tolling and Kay from Lasqueti Island.

At 0923 on Thursday the 18th of March we weighed and motored out of Bahia Chamila. The winds had died overnight and the decks were wet with dew. There was not a breath of wind, so the seas were glassy, and there was a haze or light fog reducing visibility to 4 or 5 miles, just over our horizon. Overhead and to the north and west were scattered altocumulus, and there were more compact alto stratus in the other two quarters.

The swell continued to back a bit, and it was now from the southwest. This would mean a 1.5 to 2 metre swell directly into the anchorage at Careyes, so we motored on past its entrance and carried on toward Bahia Tenacatita. The chart appeared to be out a mile or so, skewed to the south west. I turned on the radar and navigated into Bahia Tenacatita with the aid of the radar overlay on the chart.

The popular anchorage is in the northwest corner of the bay, but two things directed us away from there. First, we were going to be seeing Tolling and Kay, who live the winter in La Manzanilla, which is some three miles away at the opposite end of the bay. The supporting reason was that with the swell now from the southwest, it would roll directly into the northern anchorage.

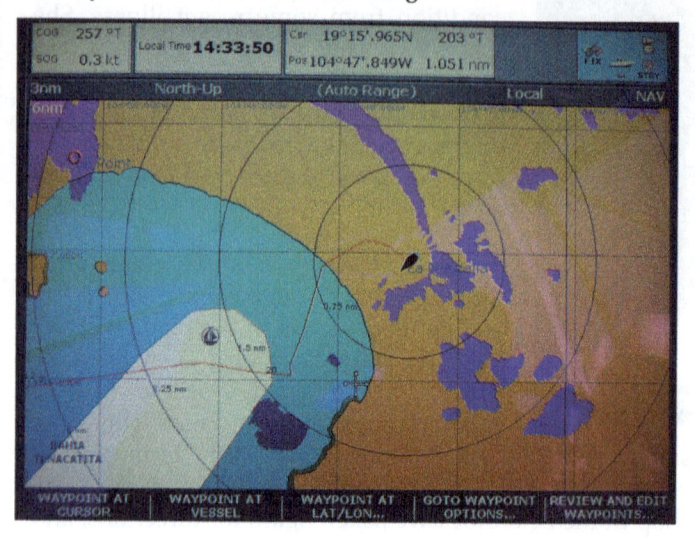

At 1422 we came to 25 metres on the Rocna in 6 metres of water about a cable off the beach in front of the centre of La Manzanilla. The chartplotter showed us to be 023° - 1.05 miles from our actual anchorage, and about half-a-mile inland, but the gentle motion of the boat told us we were still in the water.

I quickly found a free wifi signal to snipe with Sequitur's antenna. I sent an email to Tolling & Kay announcing our arrival. Then we relaxed in the cockpit, watching the passing scene, which included a horse being ridden in the surf just off our stern.

Then Tolling appeared on our boarding ladder. He had swum out to say hello, after he had tired of hollering to us without response from the beach. We sat and chatted in the cockpit and got caught-up on some of each other's happenings since both we and they had headed south from British Columbia last October. We also organized our spending some time ashore with him and Kay the next day. Then Tolling slipped back into the water and swam back to the beach.

We relaxed for the rest of the day, and in the evening enjoyed a delicious dinner of large prawns quickly tossed in a butter sauté of criminis, garlic, white onions, poblanos and red and yellow peppers, served with basmati rice and fine green beans amandine.

On Friday morning I launched Non Sequitur and we let go the painter to head in toward the beach. The motor wouldn't work. For the past couple of years we have been using a Torqeedo 801 with a rechargeable lithium-ion battery, and it had served us well. The beauty of it is that we need to carry no gasoline onboard. I had become lax in my care of the outboard, and had been leaving it in the bottom of the dinghy hauled up on its davits. I knew that the salt air corroded the electrical contacts, but had been using a wire brush to clean them the few times previously that the motor refused to turn. However, this time that remedy didn't work.

I had still not found a suitable replacement nor had I devised any jury-rigged solution for our missing oarlock pin, but I decided to head in to the beach using the oars as paddles. We made it through the surf easily enough, though right at the end a late breaker skewed us a bit and washed over the side tube, wetting us somewhat.

Once we had hauled the dinghy up to the high water line and secured it to a ring, we stepped through the line of palm trees and walked over to the market to meet Tolling and Kay. We wandered around the market with them, and Edi bought three DVDs from one booth. Then we went to Martin's Restaurant, a local favourite, with its palapa dining room perched up a flight of stairs and overlooking the bay. Even although Edi and I had eaten breakfast aboard Sequitur, we decided at 1130 to have another here.

We sat enjoying the company and I got caught-up on things numismatic in general and with the Lasqueti Mint in particular. I had commissioned the Lasqueti Mint to strike my Canadian Numismatic Association Presidential medals in 2008, and had sailed Sequitur to Lasqueti Island to strike the last few with Tolling.

The medals were struck in .999 silver on a century-old drop hammer press, using dies designed and hand cut by Tolling's partner, Ray. The obverse design was a rendering of Sequitur under sail. We also struck a few in .9999 gold, including some pure Mammoth Tusk Klondike gold. I had been so pleased with the result that I commissioned Lasqueti Mint to strike my 2009 Royal Canadian Numismatic Association Presidential medals. Again, Edi and I visited Lasqueti Island in Sequitur and picked-up the medals.

After a prolonged brunch, we walked through the market and then through the town to a mangrove swamp on its northern edge, where we watched the crocodiles. Fortunately, they were behind a chain-link fence, although it was in poor repair with many crocodile-sized holes through it.

In another section of the swamp, Tolling and I walked in to the edge of a lagoon and watched an ibis seemingly tempting fate near the jaws of some rather large crocodiles.

We walked back along the beach to Non Sequitur and bade Tolling and Kay farewell before heading back out to Sequitur. As we were paddling out, we got caught in a particularly large breaker and we both washed overboard. The dinghy remained upright and near at hand, so we climbed back in and continued paddling back out to Sequitur. Back onboard, I realized that I had lost a bit more than my pride; I wasn't seeing that clearly, and finally realized that my glasses had been washed off my face, and had disappeared.

Back onboard Sequitur, I dug out a spare pair of glasses, overhauled the motor and got it working. Then I stowed the motor in a cockpit locker, away from the salt air, where I should have been keeping it. I still need to find a pin for the oarlock.

Our intention was to leave on Saturday morning and continue southward, likely stopping in Manzanillo for a day or two before doing an overnight onward to Zihuatanejo.

At 0923 on Saturday the 20th we weighed and proceeded under power out of our anchorage off the beach in La Manzanilla. There was absolutely no wind - true still airs - and the seas were glassy. Neither was there any trace of the swell that we had experienced launching the dinghy on Friday. As we motored out of Bahia de Tenacatita, we saw some humpback whales swim past.

Among my ongoing projects was getting the Fischer-Panda generator working. I had changed the starter relay with the new one Edi had brought back with her from Vancouver, but still had no luck in getting the machine to start. In her wisdom, Edi had picked-up a second new relay while she was there, and my next step was to replace the fuel pump relay with it; I have deduced that they both use the same type. This was on my list for our next anchorage.

As we were exiting Tenacatita Bay, I noted that the alternator seemed to be undercharging. The meters showed that it was making only about 30 amps at 2250 rpm, less than half of what I normally see at that engine speed and a low battery. I had checked the belt while we were in La Manzanilla, and it had been properly tight. Fortunately as we rounded the point at the south of Tenacatita and shaped our course to the southeast, a breeze came up from the west at 6 to 8 knots. I hauled out the sails and shutdown the engine and we sailed along at 3.5 to 4 knots.

As we sailed a large pod of dolphins crossed our track, and some of them joined us for a while to play in our bow waves.

The alternator's belt was tight, but its sides were a bit glazed, and there was some black dust on the alternator case, indicating the belt was quickly wearing. Oh goodie! Another project for me to work on. I'll have to change the belt when we anchor, but beyond that, I need to determine why the belt was wearing so quickly.

In the mid-afternoon the winds became fickle and decreased to 3 to 4 knots, mostly from astern, so I flashed-up and we motored in toward Bahia de Manzanillo. As we neared the anchorage, the alternator began acting erratically, and eventually its output dropped to zero.

At 1613 we came to 24 metres on the Rocna in 9.5 metres of water off the marina in Las Hadas. We anchored at a short scope of just over 2.5 to 1 because of the lack of swinging room in the tight crowd of boats in the anchorage.

After we anchored and after I had given the engine a bit of time to cool down so that working in the engine compartment in the 33 degree weather was a bit more bearable, I changed the alternator belt with a new spare.

I flashed-up to test it, and saw that the output was still under specifications, but at least it was producing some electricity to help in topping-up the batteries. When I checked it again a quarter hour later, the meter showed that the alternator was no longer charging. I shut down, and decided to let things be for the night.

On Sunday morning I checked the alternator belt; it was properly tight and showed no evidence of slippage. On running, it had an initial low output, then nothing. I guess its 100 amp rating is quite undersized to be able to continuously supply the huge demand I have put on it since the Fischer-Panda generator ceased to work, and I have probably cooked it.

Just to let it know that I was still thinking of it, I worked on the Fischer-Panda for a while. I replaced the fuel pump relay, bled the fuel system, cleaned the air filter and ran the machine through a few start cycles. Other than my learning a bit more about it, I accomplished little.

We were sitting safely in a wonderful anchorage, and needed to take advantage of it, so I put down my tools, cleaned-up and launched the dinghy. I tested the motor, which had worked well after I had worked on it the previous evening in La Manzanilla. Now it decided to be petulant, and ran intermittently, and then ceased to run at all. I left the motor onboard and rowed us into the marina using the hoops of the dinghy's carrying handles as oarlocks. Of course, it was upwind, and yes it was awkward and ungainly, but we eventually got there.

We walked along the private malecon of the Las Hadas complex, which appears to be a combination of resort hotel and condominiums. The architecture is an interesting mix of Moorish, Spanish and modern pueblo, and the grounds are tastefully landscaped and very well maintained.

Our walk took us to the huge grounds of the All-Suite, All Inclusive Barcelo Karmina Palace Deluxe Hotel. It makes me tired just to say the name of this pompous resort, which according to its literature is of Mayan-style architecture: *"The ancient Mayan culture resonates throughout the royal grounds of the resort as a mark of respect for one of the most advanced ancient civilizations in history."*

We found it very odd to see all the Chinese statuary through the grounds as well as sculptures of Asian elephants in a Burmese or Thai style. Maybe there's more to the Mayan culture than most think.

We walked through the resort grounds, through the hotel lobby and out the road beside the golf course to the main road. There we caught a bus in toward Manzanillo, which took us past some superstores, such as Mega, Walmart and Office Depot. We got off at the Soriana and went in to enjoy the air-conditioning and to buy some fresh fruit and vegetables.

From the front of the store we caught a bus, which took us up the narrow winding road along the cliffs of Santiago peninsula, and we walked down through the Las Hadas complex to the marina.

Back onboard, I was again faced with an unwelcome situation. Our water tanks were getting low, and we had insufficient battery remaining to run the watermaker. I still hadn't persuaded the generator to work, our engine-driven alternator had packed it in, the sun was sinking behind the hills so the solar panels were done working for the day, and there was no breeze to run the wind generator. We spent the evening onboard rationing both water and electricity use.

With a hacksaw, a file and some emery cloth I converted a stainless steel bolt from the spares bin into a new pin for the dinghy's oarlock, and managed after some prying and wedging to pop it into place. I hoped that the difficulty I had in forcing it into place might mean it would be as difficult to come out again. It had come out when we bottomed in a trough just as I had the oar down deeply for a powerful thrust. The oar bottomed on the sand and the weight and momentum of the dinghy had done the rest.

On Monday morning our house battery was at 53% and slowly charging as the sun climbed higher. With the nearly flat battery and with the water now down to about 5%, we needed to go alongside and connect to shore power and to fill-up with water. I rowed the dinghy ashore into the marina, an amazingly easier task with the two functioning oarlocks.

We went to the marina office to enquire about moorage. The office was closed; it was just past 1000, and the sign said the office opened at 0900. Apparently we were too early. Edi watched as a boater from a dinghy walked with his computer bag into Freda's Marina Cafe, next to the marina office. She looked in and saw laptop users at the tables. We had brought our computers ashore with us, and we decided to have breakfast at Freda's.

I sent an email reporting on my progress on the generator to James, the Service Manager at Fischer-Panda, and asking him for the next step. I also sent an email to Brad at First Yacht Services in North Vancouver, thanking him for his advice and assistance, and telling him of our problem with the Balmar alternator. Then I started browsing to find information on possible replacements for the alternator.

After a very long breakfast, mostly spent on the Internet, we went back to the marina office and found it open. We arranged to bring Sequitur in at 1600. The marina is all Mediterranean moorage, and the mooring ball for our assigned slip had disappeared, so we would have to drop the anchor and back in on it. We went back out to the boat in the anchorage, where I found that the wifi signal from Freda's was just usable, though a bit intermittent using the antenna.

At 1550 we weighed and headed into the marina and dropped the Rocna about 30 metres in front of the slip and backed in to the 6-metre wide slot between two powerboats taking care not to foul our propeller on their mooring lines.

After we were tenuously moored, a swimmer with a snorkel dived on the mooring and eventually found and recovered the line from it. We secured our bow to it and readjusted our stern lines, then I plugged into shore power and filled the water tanks.

Sequitur's wifi antenna worked quite well here to pick-up Freda's connection. I received replies to my emails from both James at Fischer-Panda and Brad at First Yacht Services. James gave me some instructions, which I found a bit complicated, and I tried to decipher them using the Fischer-Panda manual. This proved to be even more confusing; the manual appears to have been translated from the original German through Japanese and Hindi, before arriving at an approximation of English. Brad's suggestion seemed much more straightforward: Remove the cover from the air filter and spray in some DW40 while initiating the start cycle. This made sense to me, but I decided to put down my tools and manual for the day, and to go at it again in the morning.

For dinner on Monday evening we walked along the waterfront to Los Delfines Restaurant. This is a rather large and elegant palapa standing directly out of the water at the western edge of the anchorage.

We were shown to a waterside table and were told they were having a steak festival, which included a choice of various cuts of steak, or a half chicken or grilled dorado fillet, plus a soup bar and a salad bar for 280 Pesos including service. We looked at the soup and salad bars and decided to go for it.

We started with bowls of delicious lobster bisque and then at the salad bar we chose from such things as smoked salmon, marinated beef strips, pecans and a variety of cheeses and a diverse selection of fresh vegetables. We both had the grilled dorado, and I found mine a bit overdone and tough, though very tasty. The wine list's pricing appeared to have a 300% mark-up at the top-end and nearly twice that at the bottom-end, which started at about 600 Pesos. At close to $50 for a low-quality supermarket wine, we opted for beer. We ordered Corona, and it came so cold that the foam froze as it was poured. We finished with crepes tatin served with vanilla ice cream.

Throughout dinner we watched the fish swimming in the surging water along the rocky shore beneath our table, and we copied other diners in tossing bread crumbs into the water to attract the fish. As the evening darkened, the restaurant's waterside spotlights attracted even more fish.

On Tuesday morning, I decided to start with Brad's suggestion, and spray WD40 into the Fischer-Panda's air intake. I unbolted the cover and gave a short spray as the engine started cranking. It gave promising sounds on the first starting attempt, so I repeated the process, and the generator started and ran smoothly. I kept it running while I reinstalled the air intake cover and buttoned-up the sound-insulating case. Thanks Brad!

The next task was to see what I could do to replace the alternator. Brad, whose advice on the Fischer-Panda had been spot-on, had suggested I look at a Balmar 95-210 on an AltMount adaptor. I looked at both the Balmar and the AltMount websites to get more information, and then emailed them with questions.

Wanting to ensure that I didn't miss a simple, near-at-hand solution, I asked the marina manager if he knew of any local sources for alternators. He told me the local expert was Electrico El Toques in Santiago. We took a taxi into Santiago for 40 Pesos, and were dropped-off in front of El Toques, which was a street-front workshop, little more than the width of its roll-up door. The largest alternator he had was 100 amps, the size of our current one, which we have found to be much too small.

We caught a bus back, and decided to continue past the exit to Las Hadas and go to the Mega. While we cooled-off in the air-conditioning I found some fresh shallots, the first we have seen since Moro Bay, California in mid-November, and at only 30 Pesos a kilo, I stocked-up. We also picked-up some fresh tomatoes, tomatillos, cilantro, avocados, bananas, mangoes and a big papaya. We had the foresight to bring our backpacks and one of our insulated bags, so packing the produce back to Las Hadas on the bus was easy.

Because of my rather intermittent and slow sniped wifi connection from Freda's, and Edi's inability to pick-up the signal at all with her computer, we took our computers up to Freda's and ordered couple of Tecates and a dish of guacamole. The dish of nuts that came with the beer, and the guacamole and its corn chips were so filling that we didn't need any dinner. For less than $10 we had a huge guacamole with lots of tostados, a large dish of nuts and two beer, plus secure high-speed internet connections.

On Wednesday morning I started the Fischer-Panda again, just to make sure it was fixed. It started easily the first attempt and ran smoothly, so I let it run and come up to temperature before I shut it down. Next on my list was to resolve the problem with the outboard motor. In my Internet searching, I couldn't find any outboard dealers in the area, other than Mercury, and I long ago learned to avoid that brand. I asked the marina manager if he knew of any, and was told of the possibility of some used ones. He said he would enquire and let me know on Thursday.

Meanwhile, I was going back-and-forth by email with Craig at AltMount, Rich at Balmar and Eddie in the Service Department at Hunter, looking for the best solution for our alternator problem. While waiting for replies, we decided to take the bus into Manzanillo's historic downtown. We discovered a drab, dull and lacklustre place. The church looked more like a warehouse than anything, and we saw very few attractive buildings.

We walked to the waterfront and along to the Armada base. Standing there facing the ships and the base was a bronze statue of a navy helmsman. He had disproportionately short legs and his facial features were very northern European, Germanic or Scandinavian, rather than the expected Spanish or native Mexican features. We could find no explanation.

We retraced our steps through the old town to the square and caught the bus back. Because we needed to transfer to the bus to take us to Las Hadas, we decided to do this at the Walmart and to use the opportunity to check it out. We found some 2008 Gran Tarapaca Chilean Merlot on special, discounted 29 Pesos to 90 Pesos and bought a couple of bottles. We also bought a kilo and a half of basa fillets among other things.

For dinner on Wednesday evening I sautéed the basa in butter with crimini mushrooms, shallots and garlic and added thin tomatillo slices as I cooked the second sides. This was served with basmati rice and asparagus with mayonnaise and accompanied by a wonderful 50 Peso Riesling Qualitatswein from the Rheinpfalz.

On Thursday morning I switched off the shore power and turned on the inverter so that I could monitor Sequitur's electrical system. Next I attacked the outboard motor, and after near fully disassembling it, I found a corroded contact in the throttle switch. Some jiggling and a liberal application of contact spray got it working again. I reassembled the motor and it still worked. With that problem solved, I was down to only the alternator issue to resolve.

Through the day I monitored the state of charge of Sequitur's house bank. It wandered back and forth between 99% and 100% as we used the coffee maker, the toaster, the kettle, our computers and various other AC and DC loads. Once the sun went behind the ridge above us around 1700, and with no wind and no shore power, the charge in the house bank started dropping as we continued our liberal use of electricity.

By 2200 the battery was down to 91%, so I flashed-up the Fischer-Panda and watched as it did a short bulk charge run at 170 to 180 amps, then tailed off to a float charge at around 75 amps. I ran it until the batteries were back up to 93% and shut it down, satisfied that it was performing properly. I switched on the shore power to continue the charging a bit more quietly.

On Friday afternoon, the 26th of March we left our slip in Marina Las Hadas, and moved back out to the anchorage. I had spent a lot of time during the previous four days investigating a possible replacement for our engine's alternator, and finally mid-afternoon I placed an order. We then decided we may as well wait in the anchorage for arrival of the new alternators, the mounting kits and their attendant bits and pieces.

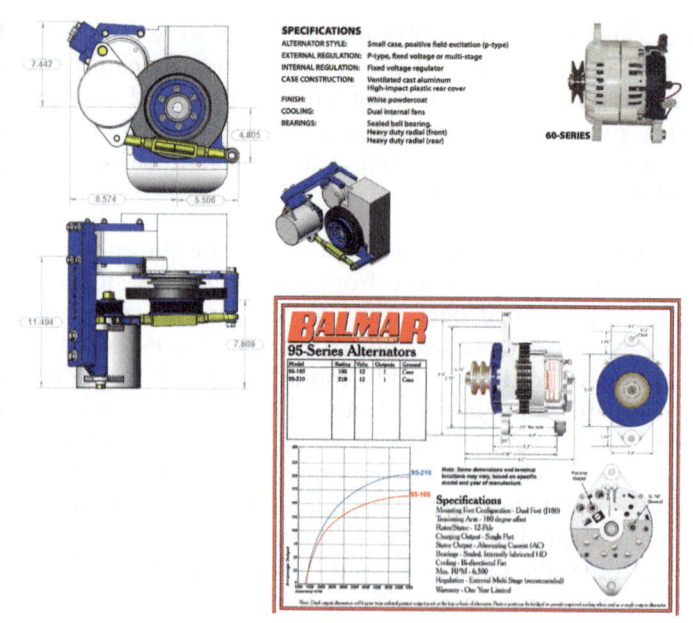

After exchanging nearly four dozen emails with Craig at AltMount, Rich at Balmar, Brad at First Yacht Services and Eddie at Hunter, and after further online investigations from their replies, I had finally settled on a twin alternator setup from AltMount with a peak output totalling 330 amps. The setup will allow us to switch between a Balmar 60-120 amp and a Balmar 95-210 amp alternator, or to combine both for 330 amps. This will offer many different charging possibilities. The setup can also provide an already installed spare alternator in case of the demise of one of the pair, and it can, if necessary easily replace the Fischer-Panda generator if it decides to cop-out again.

The mounting kits and adaptors were coming from AltMount in San Francisco, and the package went out by FedEx on Friday afternoon. The alternators, regulators and sensors were being drop-shipped from Balmar in Seattle, and would go out from there by FedEx on Monday. Arrival in Las Hadas was estimated as Wednesday for the first package, and Friday or Monday for the second. We hoped that the *"Canadian Vessel-in-Transit"* designation on the Customs declarations convinces the Mexicans to forgo duties and taxes without too much of a fight.

We were in an extremely pleasant and comfortable anchorage, just half a cable off the marina entrance, well-protected from most adverse weather that may come-up, and surrounded by lovely scenery in all directions. Just out of sight beyond the pretty scenery to our east is a great selection of big-box stores, which are a pleasant half-hour walk or a 6 Peso bus ride away. If we needed to be waiting for parts, this was about as fine a place as we could think of to be doing it. Besides, we had found a strong and steady free wifi connection to snipe.

With the installation of the new alternator setup, there is a possibility that I will have to move the Fischer-Panda generator forward a centimetre or two. In the exchange of emails with AltMount, Craig told me that the installed 95-210 extended 11 inches (27.94cm) forward of the faceplate on the Yanmar 4JH4 engine.

We have just 26.3cm from the faceplate of our 4JH4 to the after side of the case of the Fischer-Panda. Fortunately, the Fischer-Panda has a space of more than fifteen centimetres available on its forward side, and none of the connections in and out of the generator preclude my moving it a few centimetres. While I don't anticipate this being a difficult task, it is just one more thing to have to do. However, in later reviewing the dimensioned drawings of the setup, I saw that the alternator extends 11.494 inches (29.2cm) from the undersides of the bolt caps on the engine faceplate. I remeasured from that position, and found that we have just shy of 31cm, and may not have to move the generator.

We relaxed onboard Friday evening and all of Saturday and Sunday, as I unwound from the tension of the past week. On Friday evening I had come down with a flue of some sort, and it developed on Saturday. On Sunday it seemed to be abating when Edi came down with it. We hoped we won't pass it back-and-forth to each other and we simultaneously got over it. We both did our income tax returns on Sunday, and we will have to find a post office here to mail them back. While we were in an admin mode, I also renewed online Sequitur's Radio Station License.

I flashed-up and ran the generator a couple of times, just to make sure that it was repaired, and then began a routine of using it on bulk charge to maintain our house bank in the 70% to 80% range, where it more readily accepts a charge. Our solar panels continue to give us output in the 25 to 29.5 amp range for about six hours through the middle of the day, and lesser amounts in the early morning and late afternoon. We seem to be getting 200 to 220 amps a day from them. I also switched the Espar furnace to its hot-water-heating-only setting so we could maintain our accustomed level of comfort.

Among our neighbours in the anchorage off Las Hadas were Shawn Breeding and Heather Bansmer in Om Shanti, their 1976 Westsail 32. They are the authors of *Sea of Cortez: A Cruiser's Guidebook*, which many now refer to as the bible. We found their guide extremely useful during our two months on the Baja coast of the Sea. It allowed us to cruise confidently and to easily and safely enter some wonderful anchorages, which we might otherwise have ignored as being too risky.

As we made our way down the Mainland coast of Mexico, we often wished there was a guide as detailed and as accurate as theirs. Well, a little bit too late for us, but Shawn and Heather were down here doing final research for their upcoming guide to the mainland coast. They were just wrapping-up their season here and preparing to store their boat and head back to the Pacific Northwest for the summer. Although we spent very little time with them, we were so familiar with them through their Guide, that as they motored out of the anchorage on their way to haul-out, we felt the pang of seeing old friends leaving.

> Shawn and Heather's new guide: *Pacific Mexico, A Cruiser's Guidebook* was published later in 2010.

While we relaxed onboard, I watched online the progress of the FedEx shipment as it made its way from Mountain View, California, through Memphis, Tennessee to Guadalajara, Mexico, where at 0930 on Monday it was marked *"Available for Clearance"*. At 1434 it ground to a halt, and was designated as 'Clearance Delay'. Using Skype I phoned FedEx on their toll-free US number, and spoke with one International Shipping Agent, who didn't sound like he understood what I wanted and I perceived that he wouldn't do anything for us. I phoned again and got a more understanding agent; she sounded much more promising and said she would pass our email address on to the Guadalajara office.

And then on Tuesday morning Jesus intervened; we received an email from him in the FedEx office in Guadalajara. He informed us that the package was being held because, besides the machine parts, it contains a syringe and a tube with unknown gels. I emailed him back explaining that the gels were Tef-Gel and LocTite, necessary for the installation of the machinery, and attached a PDF of the installation photos and instructions from AltMount, showing and explaining the use of the offending gels. I suggested he remove and discard the offending gels, and forward the remainder of the package.

Late on Tuesday morning I received a reply from Jesus. He offered two options: The first is to have them remove the gel and release the rest of items with a real value. The second is to hire our own Broker Agent to release the shipment under our importer license. I replied, thanking him for his quick attention to this situation, and asking that he remove the offending gels and forward the remainder of the contents of the shipment to us.

I also attached a PDF of our *Anuada Mexico - Administracion General de Anuanas Permiso de Importacion Temporal de Embarcacion - Importador*, and suggested that he was aware that this certificate covers the boat, its machinery, equipment and contents, plus the duty-free and tax-free importation of any additional parts, machinery and equipment that are necessary from time-to-time for the repair and maintenance of the vessel during the ten-year term of the certificate. I told him that the shipment they are holding is covered under this Importador certificate. And then we waited.

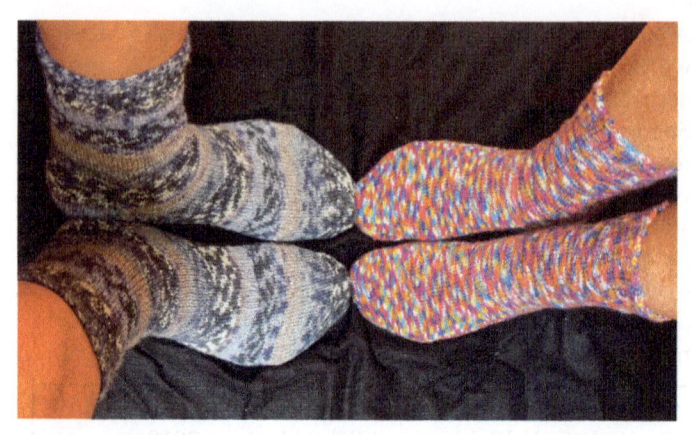

While we were waiting, Edi completed re-knitting my second sock, which she had unravelled as we entered Banderas Bay in late February. The reason it took her so long was that she decided to knit herself a pair at the same time, so she knit three socks simultaneously. Well not quite simultaneously, she finished three cuffs, and then did three legs, three heel-roundings, three feet and finally three toes. You'll notice that the patterns now lineup on my pair.

We continued to wait for a reply or for some change in the online tracking status of the package through the remainder of the day, and its status remained as *"Clearance Delay"* when we went to bed on Tuesday night. On Wednesday morning, the online status was unchanged, so I resent my last email to Jesus, suggesting that he might not have received it, and asking for an update.

I very quickly received a reply from Jesus, who told me he was *"...waiting the confirmation by my supervisor to confirm how the clearance process must be followed."* He continued: *"The last time when FedEx tried to release a shipment like this same case, this process took us more than one month because this must be done to the Customs Administration directly"*. Jesus went on to say: *"My supervisor told me that this process must be done by your own Broker Agent because we can hold the shipment no more than 5 days and this process will take us several days otherwise this shipment could be sent back. As an option, we can release the shipment under a simplify summary in which you would have to pay duty and tax of around US$95.00 and this process will take us from one to two days."*

I asked Jesus for a list of brokers, and received a link to a site listing contact information for the brokers serving the Guadalajara Airport. Of the fifty-seven brokers on the list, four showed websites, two of which worked, and five showed email addresses. I sent an email to the five, attaching the email correspondence between me and FedEx, and requesting assistance in clearing the package, and asking for rates and time estimate. Three of the emails bounced. The two that seem to have made it through were to the companies with working websites, meaning large companies, and we're probably lost somewhere in their head office under a stack of Panamax container ships. And then we waited.

In the meantime, the second package, the one with the alternators, regulators and sensors was making its way toward us from Seattle. On Wednesday morning the online tracking showed it had arrived in Memphis, Tennessee. We pondered its fate on arrival in Guadalajara, and then we waited.

Late on Wednesday morning, when we had not yet received any response from the brokers, I emailed Jesus, requesting that he release the shipment and charge the fees to my FedEx account number. He very quickly responded, confirming the clearance process: *"1. The gel (syringes) will be sent back to origin country, billing return freight to the sender's account number. 2. The rest of items will be released under simplify summary in which the taxes will be charged to your FedEx account."*

In my correspondence with Jesus, Edi and I had decided it would be best to not mention the second package, which if all goes well, will be arriving in Guadalajara on Thursday morning, We figured there was no sense complicating things. And then we waited.

Then at 1611 on Wednesday the FedEx online tracking site showed that the package was again designated *in transit* in Guadalajara, marked *"paperwork available"*. This sounded very promising. Then a little over an hour later, at 1718 the site showed the package as *"int'l shipment release"*. Jesus of FedEx seemed to have pulled some strings for us.

Three minutes later, at 1721 the second shipment, with the alternators, regulators and sensors from Seattle, was recorded as *"at dest sort facility"* in Guadalajara. We were on a roll. I triggered the FedEx automatic email notifications and waited.

On Thursday morning, the FedEx online tracking showed both shipments still in Guadalajara. There was no change in the status of the San Francisco package; however, the package from Seattle had been promoted to *"In transit - Package available for clearance"*. Then at 1244 on Thursday the Seattle shipment had its status changed to *"Clearance delay"*. I emailed Jesus and again asked for his intercession. Then we waited.

I lowered the dinghy from its davits and we went ashore for the first time in six days. I popped into the marina office to tell the manager that two FedEx packages might be coming for us sometime in the next week or so. Then we went to the marine supply shop, La Casa del Pescador to see if they had any LocTite or Tef-Gel for our alternator installation. No luck there, but it is just a small marina-side outlet for the main store in Santiago, and we will try there later.

In the meantime, we negotiated a 40 Peso taxi fare (down from the asked 50) to the Walmart and I looked there for LocTite and Tef-Gel or comparable products, again without luck. The main purpose of our trip; however, was to buy some fresh fruit and produce. We selected some very good looking tomatoes, tomatillos, red, yellow and orange peppers, mushrooms, carrots, oranges, mangoes, bananas and apples. We also got a kilo-and-a-bit of medium sized prawns for a bit under $7 and bought a very large calamari steak, just over a kilo in weight for 8.7 Pesos, about 72 cents Canadian.

When we arrived back onboard I took advantage of the free wifi connection to use Skype to phone my father in New Brunswick and wish him a happy ninety-sixth birthday. Both he and my ninety-two-year-old mother are in good health and are looking forward to the warming weather of spring. Dad told me my brother Peter had called from his sailboat in the Bahamas the day before.

For diner on Thursday evening I decided to cook some of the calamari steak, and since I've never cooked any before, I researched online for recipes. I find it much easier to experiment with new ingredients when they are inexpensive, and here with the cost per serving about 18 cents, the price of failure is rather minor.

One thing I saw repeated with every recipe and set of cooking instructions was that calamari needs to be cooked for either a few minutes, or a few hours; anything in between is tough. I decided on a hybrid of the various recipes, and came up with:

- Using a sharp knife, score each side of the steaks in a two or three centimetre diagonal pattern and place a sliver of garlic into each slit.
- Coat the pieces with olive oil, add salt and pepper and cover with Panko, pressing to adhere to the calamari. Let stand about 20 minutes.
- Heat olive oil in a heavy pan on medium heat, add calamari and cook for about three minutes per side, until golden brown.
- Serve with thinly sliced tomatillos.

One thing I reinforced in my mind again was that even on high, the marine propane stove does not get hot enough to properly sear panko. Also, the calamari was rather salty on its own, and didn't need any additional salt. I had prepared three pieces, one thick, one medium and one thin. After cooking, the thickest piece was the most tender, and the thinnest was the toughest, with its thinnest end quite rubbery, demonstrating the results of overcooking.

I think my next version of calamari steaks will be with them diced into cubes and quickly tossed in a hot wok with sesame oil, garlic and ginger, and then set aside until the end to be added back in when the vegetables are done.

Before we went to bed on Thursday night, I checked the FedEx site again to find no change in the status of the two packages. Both were still in Guadalajara, so we went to bed waiting to see what Friday would bring. But the Friday before Easter, Good Friday is a holiday in Mexico, meaning we shouldn't hold out much hope for any action.

We awoke on Good Friday to find that there had been no change online in the status of either of the packages. The first was still shown in Guadalajara marked *"int'l shipment release"*, while the second was also in Guadalajara marked *"Clearance delay"*. There was no reply from Jesus to my Thursday afternoon email, so I resent the email, suggesting he might not have received it. Then remembering that it was Good Friday, I thought that Jesus might be otherwise occupied, so we waited.

This was the middle weekend of the two-week Mexican Easter school break. There were lots of kids on the water, some being dragged around on inflatable toys behind speedboats, some water-skiing, some learning how, some razzing around on jet-skis, but the one thing they all had in common was that they did it while zigzagging through the boats at anchor, rather than a bit further out where there was so much more room and where they would not disturb anyone. They seemed to have adopted very well the callous attitude of their seniors, who have been razzing through the anchorage every day since we've been here.

There were also many overloaded boats on the water. There seems to be a very casual attitude to boating regulations here and even less enforcement. Some boats had so many it was difficult to count them as the came and went from inside, but it was not unusual to see two dozen on the seven or eight metre boat.

In the late afternoon on Friday I changed the pre-filters on the watermaker, and ran it while I ran the generator. In two hours I took the battery from 62% to 79%, but the pre-filters on the watermaker clogged in an hour and a quarter in the churned-up water of the anchorage. After the 25 litre membrane back-flush, we managed to net about 50 litres, a bit under a tenth of our tank capacity.

For dinner on Friday evening I prepared a stir-fry of cubed calamari steak, garlic, ginger, mushrooms, white onion, green beans, carrots, poblano, tomatillo, red, yellow and orange peppers and roma tomato, flavoured with a bit of sesame oil, a dash of oyster-flavoured sauce and a sprinkling of freshly toasted sesame seeds. I used neither salt nor soy sauce, and yet the calamari still ended-up way too salty. I guess it is the nature of the beast; it probably needs long soaking in milk or suchlike to leach-out the salt. We pushed aside most of the calamari and enjoyed a wonderful vegetable stir-fry.

We spent Saturday acting as one of the course pylons as jet-skis, speedboats and water-skiers raced around in the anchorage. The long Easter weekend seemed to bring-out large numbers of seemingly inexperienced boaters, many of whom ventured no further from the marinas than the anchorage, and then spent hours going in zigzags and circles among the boats.

Since we had dined the previous two evenings on the results my experimentation with the large calamari steaks, we decided we owed ourselves a treat. I dug some large scallops out of the freezer and sautéed then in butter with white mushrooms, shallots and garlic, with a splash of sauvignon blanc at the finish. With this we had basmati rice steamed with tarragon, roma tomatoes with a sprinkle of basil and plates of asparagus with mayonnaise, and we accompanied it with a 2009 Palo Alto Sauvignon Blanc from Chile.

On Sunday the speedsters through the anchorage continued until late in the afternoon, and then there was a pause for a while, until the evening shift took over. I again ran the watermaker, but this time its pre-filters clogged in only 31 minutes and shutdown the machine. This was a wasted effort; about 30 litres of water made and 25 of it used for the membrane back-flush, netting only 5 litres. I guess all the two-cycle engines buzzing around in the anchorage all day long has left a large amount of oil in the water, and this very quickly clogged the filters. The colours on the water may not all have been from the sunset.

On Monday morning the FedEx tracking site showed no change from last Thursday; both packages were still in Guadalajara and there was no email reply from Jesus. Then at 0931 I received a reply from Jesus, telling me the first package was out of the Customs area and its fate was no longer in his control. He advised me to call the FedEx Mexican 1-800 number for assistance. I tried, but a problem with Skype is that it defaults 1-800 numbers to the US or Canada, and calling it gives a *"number-not-listed"* kind of response. I tried all sorts of ways to make Skype call it as a Mexican number, but none of them worked.

In his email, Jesus also told me that his colleague, Fernando was working on the clearance of the second package. I called the US 1-800 number for the US FedEx call centre and spoke with an understanding woman in International Shipping who told me the first package had just been moved to the destination sorting area. She confirmed that the second package was still awaiting Customs clearance.

Then I received an email from Fernando with three documents attached. One was the commercial invoice from Balmar, the second was a personal use declaration and the third was a declaration of value. Of course, these last two were in Spanish and needed to be completed and signed. I copied the text from the forms to the Google Translate site and using the results as a guide, filled-out the Word document forms, printed, signed and scanned them to PDF and emailed them back to Fernando, asking him to confirm their receipt, and to inform me if anything else was required. And then we waited.

Meanwhile, at 1129 the status of first package had been changed to *"At FedEx destination facility"*, though it was still shown as being in Guadalajara. I assumed Manzanillo was a local delivery from Guadalajara, though at about 250 kilometres by road, this seems a bit far. But then, this is Mexico where the volume of FedEx packages is likely nowhere near what we see at home. Knowing one package was getting close, we waited.

And then at 1819 I received an automated tracking update, informing me that: *"FedEx attempted, but was unable to complete delivery of the following shipment"*, and gave the tracking number for the first package, the one from San Francisco that had cleared Customs on Wednesday afternoon and had sat for the Easter weekend in Guadalajara.

The email went on to say: *"Unable to deliver shipment, returned to shipper. No action is required. The package is being returned to the shipper"*. There was a new tracking number, which showed it in its way to San Francisco. How delightful!

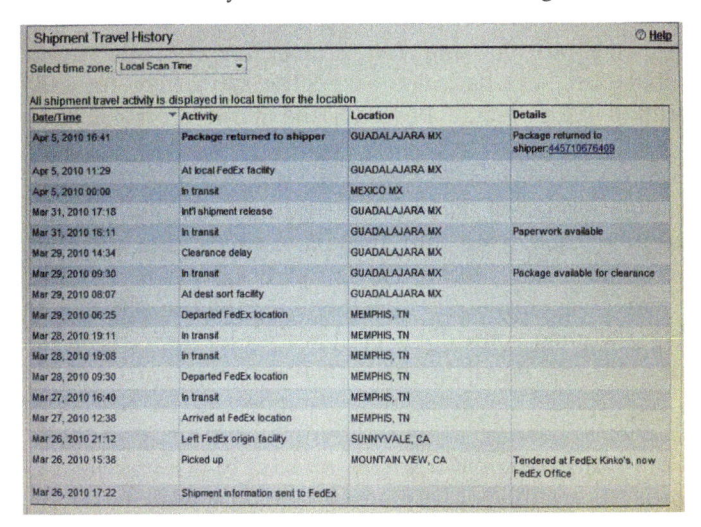

Date/Time	Activity	Location	Details
Apr 5, 2010 16:41	Package returned to shipper	GUADALAJARA MX	Package returned to shipper:445710676409
Apr 5, 2010 11:29	At local FedEx facility	GUADALAJARA MX	
Apr 5, 2010 00:00	In transit	MEXICO MX	
Mar 31, 2010 17:18	Int'l shipment release	GUADALAJARA MX	
Mar 31, 2010 16:11	In transit	GUADALAJARA MX	Paperwork available
Mar 29, 2010 14:34	Clearance delay	GUADALAJARA MX	
Mar 29, 2010 09:30	In transit	GUADALAJARA MX	Package available for clearance
Mar 29, 2010 08:07	At dest sort facility	GUADALAJARA MX	
Mar 29, 2010 06:25	Departed FedEx location	MEMPHIS, TN	
Mar 28, 2010 19:11	In transit	MEMPHIS, TN	
Mar 28, 2010 19:08	In transit	MEMPHIS, TN	
Mar 28, 2010 09:30	Departed FedEx location	MEMPHIS, TN	
Mar 27, 2010 16:40	In transit	MEMPHIS, TN	
Mar 27, 2010 12:38	Arrived at FedEx location	MEMPHIS, TN	
Mar 26, 2010 21:12	Left FedEx origin facility	SUNNYVALE, CA	
Mar 26, 2010 15:38	Picked up	MOUNTAIN VIEW, CA	Tendered at FedEx Kinko's, now FedEx Office
Mar 26, 2010 17:22	Shipment information sent to FedEx		

I quickly phoned the US FedEx office on Skype, and was put through to an International Agent who barely spoke English. I redialled a couple more times before the roulette wheel brought around someone who spoke English as a first language. She put me on to her supervisor, who efficiently took charge of the situation, sorted-out that it was probably the *"offending gels"*, the Tef-Gel and the LocTite that were being returned, not the whole shipment.

He also dug into the file on the shipment from Seattle, which was hung-up in Customs. He reviewed its email file and called Fernando's phone and left a message for him to respond to my last email. Within minutes, while still on the phone to the FedEx supervisor, I received an email from Fernando: *"Regards, pls put over blank numero de factura "S/N" and sent this wt the other format pls NOM letter"*. The supervisor and I sorted-out the email to mean that I should replace the Invoice Number with *"S/N"* on the Declaration of Value and send it again with the Personal Use Declaration. The supervisor told me he would keep a close watch on both of the shipments for us. I redid the form, printed, signed, scanned and emailed it back to Fernando, asking for an acknowledgement and asking him to tell me if anything else was required. And then we waited.

On Tuesday morning there was little change to the online status of the shipments. The first package was still shown as *"Package returned to sender"*, the second was still *Clearance delay"* but the third was shown as *"On FedEx vehicle for delivery"*. We hoped the third package was only the offending gels. Then midmorning, after the third package was delivered, in San Francisco, the first had a new entry inserted at 0000 on 6 March: *"At local FedEx facility, Mexico, MX"*. This was similar to the entry inserted on Monday, just before the *"returned to sender* comment*"*.

At 1112 I received an email from Fernando acknowledging my previous evening's email, saying, *"thks in process"*. Then at 1530 I received the following in an email from Fernando: *"Saludos,..anexo pedimento de la guia 412396323580, con impuestos por $ 3539.00 pesos, favor de depositar a la cta concentradora 5209 Banamex suc 4255 a nombre de Federal Express Holdings De Mexico Y CIA SNC De CV, referencia RODSCGDL51 si va a ser trasnferencia la clave es 002180425500052093.Gracias. (MAS GASTOS ADMVOS, ESTOS SE CONOCERAN CON EXACTITUD, YA LIBERADA Y FACTURADA LA GUIA) y enviarme la ficha por favor a la brevedad. Gracias"*.

I ran it through the Google Translator to see that it was payment instructions for me to settle the import fees and taxes on the package with a direct deposit at the bank. At 1605 I emailed back asking him to charge it to my FedEx account, telling him that is what Jesus had done the previous week with the first package. At 1812 he emailed me back saying he couldn't, and that I had to pay at the bank. It looked like we'd have go ashore to find a branch of Banamex.

Meanwhile, between the online package watching and emailing, I made water. We had been rationing the past few days, but now our water gauge had reached the beginning of the empty zone. I put in a cleaned pair of pre-filters and the machine ran for an hour and 17 minutes before the filters shut it down. I closely monitored the gauges and kept track of the output, recording the litres per hour, the salinity, the pump pressure and the pre-filter status. We made 67 litres on the first set of pre-filters. I changed them with a second set of cleaned filters, and this pair lasted only 33 minutes, making us 34.3 litres before shutting-down the machine. The third set ran for an hour and 46 minutes and produced 109.4 litres. The fourth run was with this last pair of filters, rinsed off. They lasted 28 minutes and produced another 26.7 litres. The fifth run was with the filters from the first run, rinsed and bleached in the sun for about 3.5 hours. They lasted 16 minutes and produced 13.8 litres. The sixth and final run for the day was the filters from the second run, rinsed and bleached in the sun for about 3 hours. They lasted 20 minutes and gave us 16.9 litres. So in 5.5 hours including the downtime to change filters, we made 268.1 litres of water, which after the membrane back-flush, netted us 243.1 litres, which is just shy of half of our tank capacity.

With all the notes and meter readings that I recorded, I should be able to better understand the watermaker. I do know that I need to find a suitable soft brush to clean the pre-filters better; the literature on the machine talks of rinsing the filters in water and using a soft brush to clean them. With care they can last through many dozens of uses. For the past three weeks I had been trying to buy replacement pre-filters to augment our existing supply of five sets, but have not received replies to my emails to two different agents in Mexico, so I again sent emails to the agents in San Carlos and Puerto Vallarta. With our recent experiences of bringing things in from the States, I am somewhat hesitant in using that route again, so we waited.

At 2021 I received an automatic tracking update email from FedEx, indicating the first package had been delivered. I had seen no change to its status on my visit to the tracking site a few minutes earlier. I quickly looked again, and saw a new entry for 1710: *"Delivered"* and the location *"Manzanillo, MX"*. It looked like the package was delivered to the marina in the afternoon, and signed for by Ruben, the Gerente de Marina. Great, this would give us another thing to do ashore on Wednesday, besides going to the bank, the post office and the marine shop La Casa del Pescador, and of course, going to the supermarket for fresh produce and looking for a brush to clean the watermaker filters.

Late on Wednesday morning we took Non Sequitur ashore for the second time in the twelve days that we have been waiting in the anchorage at Las Hadas. We secured it to the dinghy dock in the marina and walked up to the marina office to pick-up the package FedEx had delivered on Tuesday evening. The office was closed; we were too early, it was only 1120, and the sign said the office opened at 0900.

As we walked past Freda's Café, we saw Ruben inside having breakfast, so we spoke with him briefly, confirming the arrival of the FedEx package and telling him we would stop by on our way back from shopping and errands. We asked him for the location of the closest post office. He didn't know, and a discussion sprung-up in the restaurant among staff and regulars. They eventually agreed there was none in Santiago, and they told us we would have to go into downtown Manzanillo.

On our way up from the water we walked through the lobby of Las Hadas Resort and at the front desk asked where there was a post office. We were told of one in Santaigo next to the medical centre. Again, we proved the value of asking more than one source. Then at the taxi stand the waiting drivers discussed and confirmed the location of the post office in Santiago, and off we went for 40 pesos. As we rode, I kept an eye out for a branch of Banamex so I could make the direct deposit to FedEx for the second package. I saw none, and as we were getting out of the cab, I asked the driver. He told us there was one at the Centre Commercial.

Other than the two employees behind the counter, we were the only people in the post office. This certainly gave some strength to the argument that Mexicans do not trust their post office.

We committed our income tax returns and some other envelopes to their hands, hoping there is truth in the other side of the argument, that the post office has come a long way from the days that inspired the distrust. To hedge our bets, I took photos of the envelopes, more to dupe the staff into thinking we had evidence of the transaction.

We were still looking for Tef-Gel for the alternator installation, so I had also asked the cab driver for the location of La Casa del Pescador, the marine store. He had given us rough directions of a couple of blocks back and then in a few blocks. We walked back a couple of blocks to a ferreteria and asked in our rudimentary Spanish for directions and were told two blocks back and then in three and a half blocks. We found El Casa was exactly where it was supposed to be. It was staffed completely by young women, some not yet out of their teens, and mostly without any knowledge of things mechanical. We could find no Tef-Gel, nor any Duralac, and because of their non-experience, the discussing and thinking and analyzing and substituting thing did not happen. I did buy, somewhat in desperation a tube of Permatex anaerobic gasket maker.

We walked back down to the main street and caught a bus along to the Centre Commercial, where we located the branch of Banamex. There was a ticket dispenser by the door, with buttons for various transaction types. We were directed to push the first one and received a number. In the centre of the air-conditioned lobby were rows of comfortably upholstered chairs, probably two dozen of them, with people occupying them as they waited for their number to come-up on the electronic board. The six tellers cycled through the clients quickly, and our number soon lit-up. I had printed-out Fernando's emailed instructions and handed the sheet to the teller, and she keyed away at the computer, took my money and gave me a stamped receipt. It was a very comfortable and efficient operation.

We walked through the mall to the Mega supermarket and picked from a wonderful selection of fresh fruit and vegetables. We walked out with our two large cooler bags stuffed full and overflowing into three additional doubled supermarket bags; it was too much to juggle aboard the bus, so we flagged-down a taxi. We arrived back at the marina at 1430 to find the marina office closed. Of course it would be; the sign by its door said it was open from 0900 to 1800. Since we needed to have lunch anyway, we decided to have it at Freda's, next to the marina office and wait for Ruben.

The equivalent of $15 bought us a couple of Tecates with a bowl of nuts and a huge panini each. The paninis were so large that I had to finish Edi's. After a slow, relaxing time over lunch we walked next door to find the office still closed, so we loaded our groceries into the dinghy and went back out to Sequitur in the anchorage.

At 1543 I emailed Fernando giving him the Banamex branch address, the reference number and the time and amount of the deposit to the FedEx account, and I attached a PDF of the receipt. An hour later he replied to me with: *"Would you be so kind to sent me this payment by this way, bcs i need this to clare pls"*. I ran the text of my previous email through Google Translator and sent him back: *"He depositado los 3.539 pesos en la cuenta FexEx como usted instruido en 1300:14 hoy en el Banco Nacional de México en 944 sucursales Playa Salahla, Manzanillo, Ref: RODSCGDL51. Por favor, me informen lo más pronto que el paquete se borra."*, again with the Banamex receipt as a PDF attachment. A few minutes later he replied: *"Thks very much, in process"*. We thought that we might see the second package within a week.

Edi and I took Non Sequitur back into the marina shortly after 1700 to see if we could pick-up the first FedEx package, but when we arrived, the marina office was closed. Two marina employees were sitting outside on the bench, and they said Rubin should be along shortly. To fill the waiting time, we strolled along the short malecon, passing through the restaurants that spilled out across it to the water's edge, and we continued on to the breakwater that protects the southern side of the marina.

Then following a short wait back at the office, Ruben finally arrived and we picked-up the package. After I told him that another package might be coming from FedEx on Thursday or Friday, we went back out to the anchorage.

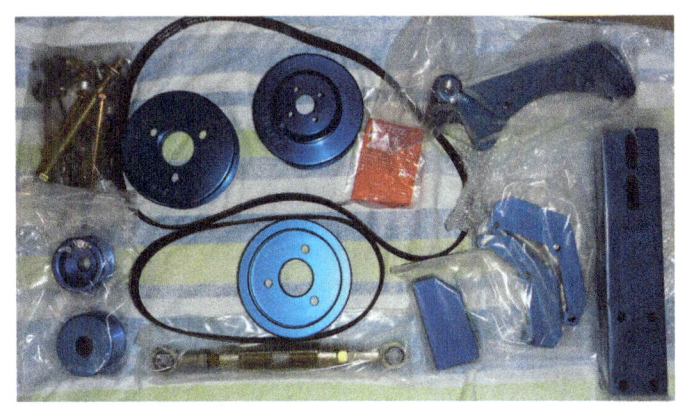

I opened the package and did an inventory, comparing the contents to the enclosed full-colour photo-inventories of the kits. The Tef-Gel was missing, but the offending LocTite was still there. Missing instead of the LocTite were all four of the smaller hex-socket cap screws from serpentine kit and all three of the small hex-socket cap screws from second alternator kit. I emailed Craig at AltMount, with a copy to Jesus of FedEx, asking him to confirm that the cap screws were in the package when it left his facility. I also asked him if the cap screws somehow ended-up being sent back to him with the Tef-Gel.

It seemed strange that similar rather attractive little pieces are missing from each kit, and with the package sitting around opened for over a week in Guadalajara, I really didn't really know what to think. The cap screws are not expensive, but without their exact specifications, I would be unable to replace them here. Even with their exact specifications, I doubted that I could find them anywhere around here. We would probably need to have them shipped in from the States and go through the Mexican Customs bureaucratic nonsense again.

It was beginning to look like it would have been less expensive, and certainly much quicker and much less frustrating to have Balmar ship the alternators to AltMount, and then for me to fly to San Francisco and pick-up the kits and alternators and fly back. But then we would have missed another lesson in third-world petty bureaucracy. And so we went to bed on Wednesday night wondering not only about the clearance of the delayed second package, but also about the missing pieces from the first package.

On Thursday morning there was no change to the online status of the package, there was no email from Fernando, there was no reply from Jesus, and it was still a bit early to expect a reply from Craig in California, a couple of time zones to the west. Neither was there any response to the emails I had sent to the watermaker dealers in Puerto Vallarta, San Carlos and Tijuana. And so we waited in a communications desert.

At 1130 I ran some text through Google Translator and sent it in an email to Fernando: *"No veo ningún cambio en línea con el estado del paquete. Podría usted por favor dígame lo que está sucediendo; no queremos tener que esperar aquí para otro fin de semana. Estamos en necesidad desesperada de las partes para que podamos reparar nuestro barco y continuar nuestro viaje. Por favor hacer todo lo que usted puede apresurar este proceso."* To be sure of the translation, I had run the Spanish text back through in the opposite direction and got: *"I see no change in line with the state of the package. Could you please tell me what is going on, do not want to have to wait here for another weekend. We are in desperate need of the parties so that we can repair our boat and continue our journey. Please do everything you can speed this process."* I was amazed at the closeness of the re-translation.

At 1240 I received the following from Fernando: *"Saludos, le informo que de hecho como el corte de liberacion es a las 14.00 hrs no se pudo liberary ayer, en proceso para liberar hoy, gracias"*, which translated to: *"Greetings, I inform you that in fact as the court of liberation is at 1400 hrs liberary failed yesterday in process for release today, thanks"*.

As we waited for the court of liberation to convene, we had visions of Hogarth's 1758 painting, The Bench with its panel of bored and disinterested presiding judges.

At 1336 the online tracking changed to *"In transit"* again for the first time in over a week, with the note *"Paperwork available"*. I have learned that this means the clearance documentation has been completed and is ready for the Customs officers to play bureaucrat with. At least something was happening.

At 1710 I received from Craig a reply to my email reporting the missing cap screws. He confirmed that the seven missing cap screws had been sent back. I was relieved to see that there had not been any pilferage from the package. OK, but now what? Since it would be much easier for him to deal with FedEx from California than it would be for me from Mexico, I asked him if he would contact FedEx and try to sort-out the mess. I suggested that since it was a FedEx error, they should expedite the shipment of the cap screws back to me, including pre-clearance through Customs at their expense.

Then at 1747, I received an automatic tracking update informing me that the status of the package had been changed to *"Int'l shipment release"*. It seems the bewigged judges had acted fairly. I hope this means the package will be delivered on Friday.

On Friday morning there was no change to the online tracking of the package, nor were there any replies to our emails on the botched first shipment or on the watermaker filters. I did; however, receive a PDF of the Sequitur's insurance declaration, which I printed and put in our ship's papers binder. Now we won't have to show the expired declaration, hoping the date won't be noticed.

While we were waiting for developments on the FedEx front, I again looked at the gribs and weather forecasts for the following five days. It appeared there would be 10 to 15 knot following winds from the northwest from noon on Saturday, backing to the west at 20 knots on Sunday. This looked like a pleasant breeze for sailing, though with the predicted 1 to 2 metre southwest swell on our beam, we'd probably roll a bit. All we needed was the delivery of the FedEx package.

When by 1130, there was still no change at FedEx. I phoned the US 1-800 number and spoke with a very sympathetic international shipping agent. I told her we had seen no change in the status of the package since its clearance the previous afternoon, and was wondering what was happening. She looked into the file and told me there was a note that indicated 24-hour delivery. She was not sure what that meant.

At 1204 the online tracking changed to: *"At local FedEx Facility"* in Guadalajara. It had taken eighteen hours for the package to make it across the room. We were hopeful that it would move more quickly for the remainder of its trip. After a light lunch of yogurt with fresh papaya, mangoes, oranges and strawberries, we took Non Sequitur into the marina and walked over to the office to speak with Ruben. He surprised us by being there, although he said he would soon be leaving. We installed ourselves at a table in the window at Freda's, with an unobstructed view up the road that leads down to the marina, so that we could see everyone approaching. And there we waited.

We ordered a couple of Tecates to show some support to the cafe, and setup our computers to help occupy our time as we waited. There was sporadic walk-by traffic, mostly people heading to their boats, but some of the passersby had the possible appearance of couriers, and I followed each to see where they headed around the corner. I questioned one with a clipboard, who had tried the marina office door, and Edi questioned another who appeared to be looking for a boat. The package was addressed to Canadian Yacht Sequitur c/o Marina Las Hadas, so we had to hedge all bets and follow all leads.

At around 1500, the online tracking site showed the inserted comment *"in transit Mexico, MX"* and it was time-stamped *"0000"*. This is similar to the sequence of events before the delivery of the first package, so we continued our vigil at Freda's with renewed hope and a large dish of fresh guacamole and tostados.

At 1536 I received a reply from Craig at AltMount concerning my request that he contact FedEx. He wrote: *"FedEx can't do anything. They said is the customs controls it and they never know what is going to go through. The list changes daily and sometimes that does not matter. Mexico is the worst they said. It was not their agent that held it back, it was the customs."* He continued: *"I don't know what to do for bolts now"*. I replied asking for exact specifications of the missing cap screws, and then we continued to wait.

At 1637 I received a reply from Craig on the technical specifications of the cap screws, with some suggestions on alternates if we cannot find the exact match. He also suggested Duralac DTD369B, a chromate containing jointing compound designed to inhibit electrolytic decomposition between dissimilar metals, as a substitute for the Tef-Gel. I had already found Duralac in my Internet search, and had looked unsuccessfully ashore on a couple of occasions. I emailed him with my thanks, and we continued our FedEx vigil at Freda's.

While we were waiting, Edi finished knitting a second pair of socks for me. She seems to have mastered the art; she knit this pair in a little over a week. Mind you, sitting around as hostages to the petty bureaucrats in Mexican Customs does provide an ample amount of spare time. At the rate she is knitting we'll each have a dozen pair of new woollen socks by the time we reach Tierra del Fuego. We waited for the FedEx delivery until 2000, and then packed up the knitting and computers and took the dinghy back out to the anchorage.

There was no further change to the online tracking data before we went to bed on Friday night. On Saturday morning I could not access any free wifi connection in the anchorage, so we had no updates until we sat down for breakfast at Freda's. Once online there, and seeing nothing new from FedEx, I called their US 1-800 number and asked for an international shipping agent. He told me the package had gone out on Friday for delivery, but when I told him we had sat waiting at the delivery point until 2000, he suggested the package may merely have moved to the hands of a contracted local courier, and he told me they do not do Saturday delivery. I asked for contact information for the local courier, but he could find none. He did initiate a detailed trace with email updates to me.

Acting on the long ago learned lesson that it is necessary to ask more than one source, I called again, and this time the wheel stopped at a pleasant agent who dug a bit deeper into the file and found that the package had left the Guadalajara facility on Friday afternoon. She suggested it may have moved to a facility closer to the destination. She did not think that they did Saturday deliveries.

A third call to FedEx connected me to another helpful international agent. I asked for contact information for the local courier, and she gave me their Guadalajara office phone number. She also said the courier's pick-up agreement at 1204 on Friday was for a 24-hour delivery, and that meant delivery by the end of the business day on Friday or on Saturday morning. In my response to my question on Saturday delivery, she said that many of the contracted couriers do. I called the number she had given me but after twenty rings without an answer, I assumed the office in Guadalajara was closed.

On our way up to Freda's we had stopped in at the marina office, which was open, surprisingly, since it was less than an hour after the posted opening time. I had spoken with Rubin, who confirmed that he has regularly received FedEx packages on Saturdays. So we have two votes for Saturday delivery and two votes against. We sat in the window at Freda's waiting for the confirming vote to roll down the road.

Many people came by the window, many of them carrying, pushing or pulling loads. Some were restaurant supplies, but most were provisions for the boats heading out from the marina. Unfortunately, there was not a FedEx courier among them. It was a decidedly slow day for couriers, and at 1500 we closed our branch office at Freda's and headed back out to Sequitur in the anchorage. On our way past the marina office we stopped in to tell Ruben we were leaving, and he said he would be there for another couple of hours.

We went to bed Saturday night still waiting for any change in the online status of the package and for update emails from FedEx. On Sunday morning there were still no emails and the status was unchanged. We already knew that the delivery did not happen within the agreed 24 hours, and now we confirmed that even when translated into Mexican and multiplied by the mañana factor, it had not arrived.

Our water tanks were again getting low; the gauge was indicating a bit above the upper end of the empty mark. It had been five days since we had made water and had brought our tanks to half full. I had hoped that by this time both FedEx packages would have arrived, and that we would be underway in water with less churned-up sediment, in waters more kind to the pre-filters. But here we sat, still in the anchorage at Las Hadas, and we needed water.

With the automatic five-day-interval membrane back-flush scheduled for mid-afternoon, it made sense to tie-in a watermaking session and save the additional 25 litres. I hauled-out the new brush we had bought to assist in cleaning the pre-filters, and I dry-brushed a pair that had been rinsed and left sitting in the sun since they had clogged after a run of only at 33 minutes the on their run a five days previously. I marked these set A and installed them in the machine. We got an hour and 14 minutes at high speed, giving us 83.7 litres of fresh water before the machine automatically switched to low speed to add life to the filters. It continued to run for 48 more minutes giving us an additional 43.3 litres on low speed, for a total of 127 litres on the filters. It looks like the little brush works.

I am delighted that we had been able to fit the watermaker into such an easily accessed location; it is under the bed in the fore cabin, and the triple-articulated spring-filled mattress easily folds out of the way. I exchanged the filters with another pair, named set B that I had brushed, but these were considerably blackened by what appears to be oil contamination. They lasted only 15 minutes at 72 litres per hour before causing the machine to switch to slow speed, and then they ran for an additional 23 minutes in the 55 litre/hour range before shutting-down. They produced a total of 51.2 litres. A third pair, set C was brushed and inserted, and these lasted 30 minutes on high speed and 23 minutes on low for a total production of 56.8 litres.

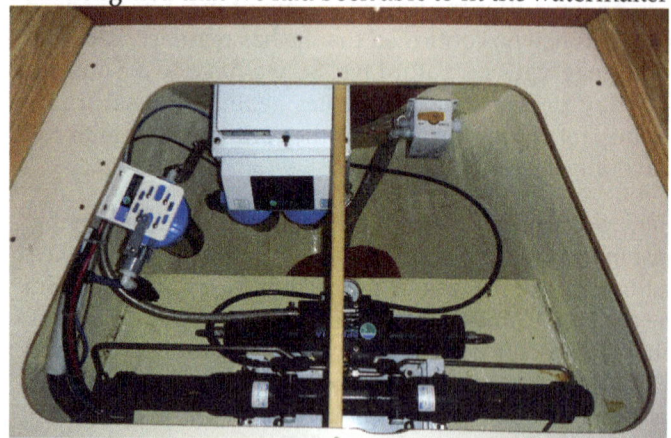

Our fourth pair of used filters, set D is really black from oil contamination, so I bypassed it and rinsed and wet-brushed set A, which had given over two hours on the first run. This time it lasted only 41 minutes, 16.5 of them on high speed, for a total of 38.4 litres. I don't know if the reduced performance is from not allowing the filter to sun dry before brushing, or whether it has to do with a greater sedimentation in the water from the higher wind. The anchorage was quite calm on the first run, but a bit choppy with large surf for the second.

I rinsed all the filters and laid them out in the sun in the cockpit to dry, turning them every fifteen or twenty minutes. After a couple of hours of drying, though it wasn't yet fully dry, I brushed set B, installed it and ran the machine again. It made only 5 minutes on high speed and another 12 on low for a total of 14.7 litres. I decided to call it quits for the day, ran the back-flush and we contented ourselves with a net production of 263 litres of fresh water, followed immediately by two longish hot showers, and a sun-drying in the cockpit next to the filters.

We went to bed on Sunday night with no emails from FedEx and no changes to the online status of the package. Monday morning we dinghied ashore to have breakfast and to setup our FedEx vigil at Freda's, only to find it closed when we arrived at 0850. We assumed then that it would open at 0900, so we sat under an umbrella at an outside table and waited. When 0900 came and went and then 1000 and 1100, we started thinking about a noon opening. The bartender happened by shortly after 1100 and when asked, told us it was the end of the high season now, and they are closed on Mondays.

Around noon, we were getting a tad hungry and thirsty. I saw that Ruben was in the marina office so I went over and in response to my question, he told me he would be there until 1400. In response to my other question, he told me the hotel had the only restaurant open on Mondays. We left him in charge of the FedEx vigil and we walked along to the hotel, arriving at 1215 to find the restaurant shutting down. It closed for lunch. How novel!

We were told that Las Delfines, further along the beach was open from 1230. We shared a plate of shrimp tacos and one of dorado tacos and three bottles of Corona and spent a relaxing hour and a bit as the only customers in an upscale hundred-seat waterfront restaurant. This is the place we had dined three weeks previously, the day after we had arrived in Las Hadas. Three weeks already! While it is a pleasant place, three weeks was way beyond the time we would have allotted to it had we not been held hostage by the petty bureaucrats in Mexican Customs.

We walked back over to Freda's tables, and Edi setup her knitting station while I went to the marina office to tell Ruben we were back. When I walked in, I saw the FedEx box sitting on a chair by the window. Ruben said it had arrived only a couple of minutes previously. He also said he had to pay the courier 92.80 Pesos for it. I reimbursed him and he gave me the factura, which outlined the charge, calling it *"Gastos Administrativos"*, which I translated to mean *"Bribe"*.

We took the package back out to Sequitur and started preparing to head out. Our next port along the coast is Zihuatanejo, 200 nautical miles away, a 30 to 36-hour passage in the forecast 10 to 15 knot winds. Our plan was to do an early start and arrive late the following afternoon. It was then nearly 1430, too late to leave unless we wanted to face a night arrival in an unknown anchorage using questionable Mexican charts. As much as we wanted to get away, prudence spoke more loudly and we decided to spend one more night in the anchorage.

We went ashore and walked along the waterfront, through the grounds of the Mayan styled resort, which prides itself as being decorated in artifacts of the Mayan culture. We admired all the Asian statuary, but could see very little Mayan.

We made our way to the southern side of the grounds and had the guard unlock and open the gate so we could climb down a set of rough stone steps to wade across a narrow tidal inlet and gain access to the beach.

The beach is very steep and has surf that builds in the last ten or fifteen metres and then quickly crashes in a sand-churning froth. We walked along the beach looking back over the surf at Sequitur and a dozen-and-a-half other boats at anchor off Las Hadas. Less than a kilometre along we cut in from the beach and walked a couple of blocks up a street that ran between Walmart and Mega.

Our fresh fruit and vegetables were nearly depleted, and we could stand a restock for the four of five days we would spend getting to Acapulco. We went into Mega and bought a selection of fresh produce, including papaya, mangoes, Anjou pears, oranges, kiwis, mushrooms, roma tomatoes, tomatillos, zucchini, broccoli, cauliflower, white onions and shallots. We also got six large skinless and boneless chicken breasts for just under $4 per kilo. The chicken and all the produce fit into our two insulated bags, and the eggs, bags of tostados and small items fit in a nylon boat bag. We couldn't get the taxi to lower his fare below 45 Pesos, so we walked across the street and caught a bus back to Las Hadas for 6 Pesos each.

Back onboard, I raised the dinghy on its davits and lashed it for sea, and we completed our preparations for leaving. At times we felt like captives here, hostages to the foibles of the petty bureaucrats in Mexican Customs. Now we were finally able to escape.

At 0752 on Tuesday the 13th of April we weighed and headed out from Las Hadas. We had decided to get up early and leave just after sunrise. Edi had put on a pot of coffee a squared-away below while I had readied for sea up top. It was a hazy morning with a slight ripple on the sea from very light airs as we motored out of Bahia de Manzanillo.

The haze turned-out to be the huge pall of smoke coming from the stacks of the oil-fired electrical generating plants that power Manzanillo and the surrounding area. Its pollution coverage appears likely to be as broad as its electrical coverage. We saw a further reason why our watermaker pre-filters clogged so quickly.

We also discovered why we were unable to see the twin volcanoes, 4330 metre Nevado de Colima and 3860 metre Volcan de Colima less than 90 kilometres inland. Besides fouling its own nest the emissions from the power plant drift inland and hang as smog over the city of Colima in the once pristine valley at the base of the volcanoes. The smog hides the volcanoes from view, not only from Colima, but from the coast and to seaward.

When I had shortened-in the anchor chain, the first three metres or so below the waterline were coated in a thick fur of mud, as were the nylon snubbers where they had been in the water. The remainder of the rode and the anchor came up relatively clean, but the upper layer of water had really dirtied the chain and the snubbers. Sequitur's decks were also dirty, with a dark brown, oily dust.

We were running low on diesel, having not refuelled since January, and having had to run the main engine to top-up the batteries, rather than the much less hungry generator. Although there was a fuel dock in the marina at Las Hadas, we had decided not to refuel there. The fuelling facility was being used as moorage by ten or a dozen power boats, lying back from buoys and anchors and Mediterranean-moored to the dock, blocking all access to the pumps. We didn't relish the hassle of having them leave to make room for our fuelling. Besides, with the preponderance of boats using the marina being gasoline-guzzling small powerboats, with very few diesels, we wondered about the condition of the diesel oil we would get there.

We needed to sail as much as was possible and conserve fuel. The air started moving a bit as we rounded Roca Vela and bent out course to the southeast, so at 0859 I hauled out the main and the jib, shut down the engine and we wafted along on a port tack at 3.5 to 4 knots in a 6 to 8 knot easterly breeze. An hour or so later as we watched the Holland America cruise ship Maasdam pass 9 miles to our southwest, I called them on VHF. They immediately responded and confirmed that we showed clearly on their AIS and we painted well on their radar. There was no need to do a radio check; that was accomplished by their instant and clear response. Four things done with one easy call, besides the three electronic checks, we also had the satisfying feeling that we are very visible to passing ships.

The breeze slowly veered, and by noon it was southwest, just abaft the beam and still around 6 to 8 knots. We had tacked and were ghosting along at about 3 to 4 knots. We continued thus through the remainder of the day and into the darkness of the New Moon night. Around 0300 on Wednesday morning the winds became fickle and combined with a sloppy cross-sea, so I flashed-up, furled the sails and we motored until sunrise, when I again hauled-out the three sails. The breeze had continued to veer and in the early daylight it crossed our stern to the port quarter. We jibed and moved along at about 3 knots.

Midmorning I went to the foredeck to haul the asymmetrical spinnaker up from the sail locker, unpack it and sort it out. This was the first time we have had conditions in which to fly the spinnaker this trip.

The fact was that I had never before flown a spinnaker, not just this spinnaker, but any spinnaker. This likely allowed a tad of inertia to assist my judgement of when it might be of use.

I did a slow and deliberate layout and analysis, and tried to remember details from the how-to video I had viewed two years previously when the spinnaker arrived from North Sails. I guess a combination of memory and logic came through, because we easily managed to rig, hoist and deploy the spinnaker on the first attempt. I had furled the jib before un-socking the spinnaker, and after deployment, rolled in the main. We moved along at 2.5 to 3 knots in the 5 to 6 knot breeze over our port quarter.

Our next port along the coast was Zihuatanejo, a 200 nautical mile run from Las Hadas, a 30 to 36-hour passage in the forecast 10 to 15 knot winds. But to this point we had seen winds at half the forecast strengths, and our thoughts of an arrival in the afternoon of the second day had long since passed.

As we sailed, we started passing sea turtles, easily made visible by the sun glinting off their backs a hundred metres and more ahead in the rather calm seas. Most passed at fifty and more metres from Sequitur, but a few were within twenty metres. A metre-long one passed almost within touching distance down the port side.

We saw a couple dozen of them in half an hour, all heading west, and we wondered how large this group was, whether it was a group or just a collection of individuals, where the turtles were going, whether they were going anywhere or just going west for a while. Three of the turtles we watched had birds riding on their shells. We thought this might be a symbiotic relationship, with the turtle being groomed of parasitic creatures and the bird feeding.

The wind continued backing and by late afternoon on Wednesday it was from the west at 5 to 6 knots and we lazed eastward at around 3 knots under spinnaker alone, with the Hydrovane keeping us on the best downwind course. At 2005 the sun set to find us with a four-hour run of 085 degrees, 12.7 miles, just shy of 3.2 knots.

By sunrise, the spinnaker spent more time hanging like wet laundry than it did filled and pulling. We were still moving along at a bit over a knot in the 2 to 3 knot puffs. By 1000, with still 32 miles to Zihuatanejo, I socked the spinnaker, flashed-up the engine and we motored at 1750 rpm, making 6 knots.

At 1533 we came to 23 metres on the Rocna in 7.8 metres of water in Bahia de Zihuatanejo, having covered 230 miles to make the 200 mile passage, and having sailed all but 10 hours of the 55 hour trip in winds of 8 knots and less. We had decided to stop here to refuel, thinking it might be prudent before continuing on to Acapulco. We spent the remainder of the day relaxing onboard.

On Friday morning we launched Non Sequitur and headed over to the Pemex fuelling pier to arrange for our fuelling. There were many small boats secured to the concrete pier, and the closer we approached the more obvious it became that the fuel dock had been abandoned.

The pumps were still in place, but they were stripped of their hoses and were looking forlorn. We went then to the pier leading to the Port Captain's office, only to find the office closed. I spoke with a couple of young local men, who said they could refuel by ferrying tanks to us in their water-taxi. I asked where they would buy the fuel, and was told up the inlet beside the pier.

We took the dinghy under footbridge and up the small inlet. It was a fetid, brown-water drainage rimmed with fishing pangas and small runabouts and leading into what appeared as squatters habitations at the edge of really desperate slums. Actually, from the flotsam on the surface of the lagoon, and from its aroma, brown-water was a bit too kind a description. If the diesel fuel came from here, we wanted nothing to do with it. We decided to continue south first thing the next morning.

At 0747 on Saturday, just as the sun was rising, we weighed and proceeded out of Bahia de Zihuatanejo under clear skies and still airs through the glassy-calm seas. Half an hour later, as we rounded Roca Negra we found a 5 to 6 knot easterly, likely the remains of the overnight land breeze. We un-socked the spinnaker and lolled along at 2.5 to 3 knots with Hydra steering us southward. We needed to make some southings to reach Acapulco, and decided we may as well take them now as they were offered.

The breeze veered and abated, and by 1015 the spinnaker was spending more time hanging limp than it was filled. We motored to the southeast until 1245, when there was sufficient sea breeze to have the spinnaker pull us along on a starboard tack at 2.5 knots. Through the remainder of the afternoon the breeze pushed us 18 miles southeast and in the early evening it veered to the northwest and increased to 8 to 10 knots. We continued at about half the wind speed.

At midnight we were making a good 5.5 knots to the south east in northwest winds of 10 to 12 knots. The wind veered slowly and by 0500 it had taken us to Acapulco's latitude. We jibed to steer east on a port tack and continued toward our destination at 5.5 to 6.5 knots in the northwest winds of 11 to 13 knots. At sunrise the winds had veered to a bit east of north, so we dowsed the spinnaker and rolled out the jib and main to continue eastward on a close reach. By midmorning the winds had eased and had come more onto our nose, so we flashed-up, rolled-in and motored into Acapulco Bay.

The anchorage was full of mooring balls, most of them occupied, and the areas without mooring balls were in depths of 25 and more metres. There were some small spaces among the mooring balls, but they were also in water 20 to 25 metres deep, and there was insufficient swinging room for even a short scope. We slowly motored through the anchorage, up one row and down the next, then over to a likely spot only to find a small previously unseen float. We were heading back to the outer and deeper edge of the anchorage to drop our Rocna, when we were approached by a man in a small skiff, who introduced himself as Hugo.

At 1210, after some quick negotiations he passed our line through the eye of his mooring ball, we secured to it and then passed him 700 Pesos for a two-day stay. We were just off the centre of the anchorage, and a close dinghy run to the piers and facilities of Club de Yates de Acapulco. We spent the remainder of Sunday onboard relaxing and cleaning. While I scrubbed above decks, Edi cleaned and organized below.

We sat on the mooring ball in Acapulco and relaxed from our passage. Among the emails in my inbox, once we hooked-up to a free wifi signal, was a reply from Club de Yates de Acapulco on my request a few days earlier for availability and cost of moorage. They confirmed availability and quoted US$3.50 per foot per day plus 15% tax, plus electricity plus water. That is just over US$229 per day not including power and water, more than ten times what we had paid in Guaymas and Mazatlan.

On Monday morning we launched Non Sequitur and headed in to the Pemex fuel pier at Club de Yates de Acapulco. There was no dinghy landing area, and the concrete pier was elevated a metre and a half above water, so while Edi held us alongside a piling I scrambled up onto the pier top to speak with the pump attendant. He indicated that we needed to go first to the yacht club office to apply for fuelling.

We motored between rows of Med-moored yachts to a ladder, which was the dinghy landing. We were assisted there by an annoyingly overzealous man who to us seemed to see only the possibility of dollars. Eventually he directed us to the office, which he said we must visit first, but insisted we come to him afterwards for all of our needs.

Other than Mary behind her desk, there was only one other person in the office, and he was sitting at Mary's desk waiting for her to finish on the phone. Eventually he was dealt with, and we replaced him in the two seats at Mary's desk while she went back to the phone. After some fifteen or twenty minutes, Mary had finished a series of phone calls, went outside for a meeting, and then turned her attention to us. We asked her the procedure for fuelling and learned we could go alongside the pier and then walk up to her office to apply for fuel and water.

In response to our question, she confirmed that for US$75 she could arrange an agent to handle our out-clearance from Mexico. She also told us it was US$35 per day to land a dinghy in the marina and leave the club facilities. This, she explained was for the gate pass needed to exit and reenter the compound. We had thought of having brunch ashore, so in reply to a question on dining facilities, she told us the club restaurant was for members only. I mentioned we were reciprocal members from the Bluewater Cruising Association. She looked it up on her computer and confirmed, saying; however, that we would need our membership card, which I had left onboard.

Edi and I decided to head back out to Sequitur to eat and to rethink our direction. We managed to ignore the shouts of the steadily approaching annoyingly overzealous fellow as we scrambled down the ladder and escaped in Non Sequitur before he had managed to coax his sixty-odd-year-old body back in from a pier and across the seawall to the dinghy ladder. We motored out to his continuing insistence that he could help us with all our needs.

As we were finishing lunch Hugo, the mooring ball owner knocked on our hull and hollered *"Hola"*. He had brought Alfredo, a friend who spoke a bit more English than did he. We talked of local transportation options and learned about the local buses and routes. We discussed fuelling options, and he suggested they ferry it out using an 80 litre portable tank and syphon the fuel into Sequitur's tanks. Buying it from a shore station would save the 15% alongside facility surcharge from the yacht club fuel pier, or the 12% surcharge at the other fuelling dock. Paying cash would also save the 15% sales tax. All he would want was 10%. However, when I mentioned we needed about 800 litres, the thoughts of ferrying that much seemed to cause him to lose interest in the project. I asked him of the other marine fuel dock, and he pointed it out.

He also told us we could land a dinghy at the old marina by the lighthouse, but that it was under repair, and landing was awkward. Their charge was 80 pesos per day for landing. Mid-afternoon Edi and I took Non Sequitur to the old marina to find new concrete floats moored as rafts waiting to replace near-totally decayed floats that were randomly held in place by the few steel pilings that hadn't yet rusted through and collapsed. I nosed the dinghy onto the riprap wall and we landed. Alfredo was there to take the painter and he rafted across with it in an old inflatable tied between shore and one of the new floats some five or six metres offshore. There he secured the painter.

We walked to the office to pay for the landing facilities, but the manager had no change for our 500 Peso note. He said we could pay on our way back. He told us the marina had new owners and was in the beginning stages of being revived. The marina/hotel complex was in a superb location and its good bones showed that it was once of high quality, but it was readily apparent that it last rubbed shoulders with any semblance of quality a decade and more ago.

We walked out through a construction site that looked more derelict than new, and up past the only construction worker in sight; he was tamping soil with a gas-powered tamper. The site gate consisted of a chain stretched two-thirds of the way across a mud road and a guard in a hut. At the rate of current progress, the project should be completed in a decade or so.

We caught a yellow bus for 6 Pesos each, and rode along the bustling, business-lined waterside road past attractive public beaches to Parque Papagayo. We walked through the shade of the trees in the zoological gardens, past ponds of birds and enclosures of small animals and past such incongruous attempts at history as a full-sized fibreglass naive rendition of the un-rigged hull of what we assumed was meant to look like an old Spanish galleon.

Out the other side of the park we spotted Home Depot, exactly where Google Earth had shown it to be. We left the 33 degree weather and entered the air-conditioned relief of the store. Our first mission was to attempt to find replacements for the seven cap screws that Mexican Customs had erroneously returned to San Francisco. Being US-centric, of course Home Depot had mostly American hardware, though there was a small section with drawer bins with metric fasteners. The contents were completely jumbled and in desperate need of sorting.

After nearly an hour of going through each of the bins in all the drawers, I had found no socket-head cap screws of the proper size, but I did find some hex-head cap screws. After going through to the bottom of absolutely every bin, I managed to find every one of the 8mm x 35mm hex-head cap screws they contained. The two 2-packs will replace the three missing 8mm pieces. To replace the four missing 6mm x 16mm pieces, I eventually settled on the only package of two 6mm by 20mm in the bins and one of only two packages of 6mm x 25mm, which I will have to cut down to length. I bought some additional hack saw blades.

We walked back along the street to the end of the park and then down toward the water to the Soriana supermarket. There we bought just over 3 kilos of chicken breast fillets at just under $4 per kilo, and a couple kilos of frozen cooked and peeled medium-large shrimp for less than $8 per kilo. We found wonderful fruit and vegetables and left the check-out with our two large cooler bags stuffed full. The bus stop was right in front of the door, and the air-conditioned yellow bus arrived within a minute to take us to the entrance to the marina. The marina manager still had no change for the 500 Peso note I pretended was the smallest I had. He said mañana, so we recovered our dinghy and left.

On Tuesday morning, as we were halfway through our yogurt with fresh oranges and mangoes, Hugo and Alfred pulled alongside in their runabout. We chatted and they offered to take me over to the commercial fuelling wharf, so off we went.

At anchor to the west of us was a Panamax cruise ship from the Norwegian Cruise Line and alongside the wharf was her sister the Norwegian Star. On our way to the fuelling facility we passed under the bows of Jesus Boat, a somewhat less impressive cruiser.

At the wharf I spoke with the pump operator and confirmed diesel and facility prices, discussed approach and mooring procedures and confirmed that water was freely and easily available. We then went back to Sequitur, and after I had finished my yogurt and fruit, I hoisted Non Sequitur onto her davits.

At 1100 we slipped from the mooring and headed over to the fuelling wharf. The Pemex facility is at the root end of the cruise ship centre, in the corner made by the wharf face and the steel pylons of the adjacent small craft marina floats. We needed to drop our anchor and back into the corner, securing with a line from the port quarter to a bollard on the wharf and with one from the starboard quarter to a cleat on the float. We easily settled into position and the hose handler came aboard to fill the tanks. We also were passed a water hose to fill our water tanks.

As the diesel tanks were filling, I took careful note of the tank gauge readings and the pump's litre count. We put 508 litres into the main tank, which holds 568 litres, so with the needle at the top of the empty mark there remained 60 litres in the main tank. Into the auxiliary tank we pumped an additional 227 litres, bringing its gauge from just below the bottom of the empty markings to the top of the full. The specifications show the size of this tank at 272 litres, so there remained 45 litres in it. The total for the 735.13 litres came to 7144.08 Pesos, including the 12% mooring charge and the 2% credit card fee.

At 1220 with our diesel and water tanks full, we let go the lines from the quarters and I shortened-in the anchor chain to haul us away from the wharf and the float, and then we weighed, and leaving the anchor a-cock-bill we headed out to find an anchorage.

At 1240 we came to 70 metres on the Rocna in 22 metres of water a quarter mile south of the cruise ship terminal and a cable clear of the shoaling around the isolated rocks, Las Dos Piedras off the point to our west. We secured and had lunch.

The pump attendant had confirmed that we could come back in and use the float as a dinghy dock, so after lunch we re-launched Non Sequitur, grabbed our two insulated bags and headed back in.

Once ashore again, we walked along the malecon past the cruise ship terminal, weaving our way through the pale pink cruise ship crowd as it waddled along. We crossed the broad, busy boulevard to the offices of the Capitan de Puerto, arriving at 1530 to find that the office closed at 1500. We moved the visit to our mañana list and crossed the boulevard again to catch a 5 Peso bus eastward to the other end of the city and to Walmart.

Among the great buys we found there was white or brown eggs at one Peso per egg, less than $1 Canadian per dozen. Edi picked-out two-and-a-half kilos of oranges at 3.9 Pesos the kilo, totalling about 80 cents Canadian. We also added a wonderful big bunch of cilantro, which cost the equivalent of 24 cents.

Firm, blemish-free white potatoes were 8.9 Pesos a kilo, but the winner of the day had to be the roma tomatoes at less than 50 cents a kilo. The continuing crowds around the frequently replenished bins told us this was an unusually good buy.

We picked-up some coloured markers so Edi can make our courtesy flags for Ecuador and Peru, both of which have coats of arms as part of their designs. We also replenished our supply of Lamasil, the toenail rot cream for 46 Pesos off-the-shelf. Our last supply came through a doctor's appointment in Vancouver and a prescription for exactly the same product at $48 for an identically sized tube.

On Wednesday morning we packed our folio of ship's papers into our shopping bags and took the dinghy over to the marina at the fuel dock. We went into the office to pay the 150 Peso landing fee and then walked along the malecon to the offices of the Port Captain. We were ushered into a third-floor, air-conditioned corner office overlooking the water to meet the Port Captain, a young woman in her mid-to-late-twenties, most likely a political appointee, who appeared to us to be in way over her head. She needed to constantly ask for assistance and advice from much older and very subservient staff.

She passed on to her staff for photocopying our passports, entry visas, ship registry document, crew list, vessel importation certificate and our exit documentation from previous Mexican ports. The documents were soon returned to us along with an Acapulco arrival document. I asked when the exit zarpe would be ready for our pick-up, and she told us Friday afternoon. We said we wanted to leave first thing on Friday morning, and would like to have the zarpe on Thursday afternoon. As simply as we tried to convey to her that we wanted to leave Mexico early on Friday morning when the winds were good for sailing, she didn't seem to comprehend that the winds or even the weather could play any role in timing our departure. She finally relented and told us the zarpe would be ready on Friday morning. I said we would be there when they opened at 0800, but she countered with 1000.

While we were sitting in the Port Captain's office waiting for her to return from one of her consultations, Edi spotted a plaque on her wall with a familiar looking name on it. There above a calendar was the only plaque on the wall, and it was from HMCS Qu'Appelle, a Canadian destroyer in which I was a Bridge Watchkeeping Officer and the Assistant Navigating Officer in the early 1970s. I told this to the Port Captain and asked if I could take a photo of her and the plaque, which would have been presented many years before on a visit by Qu'Appelle to Acapulco.

HMCS Qu'Appelle was in the squadron of ships in which I visited the South Pacific islands, New Zealand and Australia in 1969, while I was in HMCS St Croix participating in the Captain Cook bicentennial celebrations. I had joined Qu'Appelle in 1970, and in 1972 we again crossed the Pacific through Polynesia to New Zealand and Australia, and I have fond memories of my times in her. She was decommissioned in 1992.

We thanked the Port Captain for her kind services and told her we would see her early on Friday morning. When we left the building we caught a westbound bus along the waterfront boulevard, intending to go to the marine hardware store we were told was across from the entrance to the Club de Yates. After that we were planning to find our way to Costco. As we passed the marina where our dinghy was secured, the bus turned inland. We decided that we might as well go along for the ride, using it as a tour bus; a bargain at 5 Pesos.

The bus ran through thickening pedestrian, car and bus traffic in a street that was frequently blocked or narrowed by double-parked cars. Within a block of the facade of show along the malecon, we were in a slum, and the further in we went the slummier it became. After a few blocks, the bus route bent eastward and after a quarter hour or so, we spotted a Home Depot sign high above the scene a few blocks ahead. Beside us we recognized Parque Papagayo, and realized we were parallelling the coast a couple of blocks in from the downtown strip.

The bus then began climbing eastward into the hills as the coast curved around to the south. We knew that Costco was supposed to be in the next valley along from downtown, so we stayed aboard as the bus climbed through increasingly desperate housing and then went through a three kilometre long tunnel. We descended into a broad valley and got off the bus in front of a Soriana and across from a Mega. We asked for directions to Costco, but nobody knew of it, not even the aggressive taxi drivers. It seemed we were in the wrong valley.

We jay-walked across the broad road with its three medians separating service lanes from divided through-traffic lanes, and there we waited for a returning bus. We asked several bus drivers if they went to Costco, but were met with blank expressions. We were really in the wrong valley. Eventually a driver nodded, so we boarded and rode along as he bypassed the tunnel and wound his way up the steep road leading over the pass above the tunnel. We were definitely in the low-cost section of town.

Every available space was being used either for housing or for business. A cooling fan repair shop looked to be less than a metre in depth, and was using the entire sliver of space between a building's front wall and the sidewalk.

140

A key cutter and a typewriter repair shop were crammed into tiny ramshackle buildings, probably no more than four square metres in size and plunked onto a residential driveway verge. We tried to think of anyone we knew who still used a typewriter, let alone wanted to repair one.

We changed buses shortly after we had started down from the summit of the pass. This new bus took us back down to Parque Papagayo and to Home Depot, where we got off. We went in to use their air-conditioning as a reprieve from the 33 degree day, and to picked-up a cold bottle of water. After we had quenched our thirst, I went to a check-out to pay for it while Edi got a very detailed briefing over maps on how to get to Costco. We thanked the floor manager for his help and headed back out into the heat.

We walked past the park and back down to the main downtown strip, where we flagged a yellow-fendered collectivo labelled Colosio as instructed. For 12 Pesos each the collective taxi took us on a fifteen kilometre ride up a road winding through upscale residences and past the entrances to gated communities that spilled over the hillsides and cliffs above the southern rim of Acapulco Bay. We continued for fifteen kilometres up over a pass and then down onto a flat coastal plain and along it to Costco.

It was 1430 and we ordered a pizza from the Costco food windows and sat on the patio eating away at it until we were full. Their only pizza size was just shy of half a metre in diameter, a tad much for us at lunch, so Edi had the counter attendant foil-wrap the remaining slices.

This is the first Costco to disappoint us this trip. The store was not at all busy; the aisles were clear and easy to negotiate and at the checkouts there were no lineups. Missing was the wonderful selection of fresh vegetables, the crimini mushrooms, the portobellos, the fine green beans, the asparagus, the red, yellow and orange peppers. And it was not only the vegetable selection that was mundane; there were no specialty fruit. It was not at all like the range of specialty produce that all of our previous Costco visits had caused us to expect here. The fresh bakery churned-out mostly sweet stuffs; there were no bagels, no English muffins, no nice breads.

We did pick-up some hard salami, some thick ham steaks, some boneless and skinless chicken thighs and a good selection of cheeses. We also replenished our stocks of nuts, artichoke hearts, sun-dried tomatoes and Mexican coffee. Among the other things we bought were a huge bale of paper towels and a collapsible hand cart to help us carry it all. The wine selection did not inspire us to buy any, though we did buy some Torres 10-year-old brandy to augment our depleting stock. We were the only customers at the check-out, and we couldn't help thinking that the Costco expansion department had blown this site selection.

We loaded our purchases into our two cooler bags and three other boat bags and pushed the shopping cart out to the street edge of the parking lot. There I flagged a yellow-fendered collectivo and we loaded our purchases into the trunk and hopped in. A couple of minutes of slow driving netted the remaining two passengers, and off we sped back over the pass and down into the centre of town. We rode to the end of the taxi's run, when it turned at the corner by the Port Captain' office. We loaded our booty onto the two wheelies, our old luggage carrier and the new one, and walked along on the shady side of the street the four blocks to the marina. Just before the crosswalk, as we passed the open front of a farmacia, Edi spotted stacks of bottled water. I asked the clerk for the price per dozen of the 1.5 litre size, and we bought two twelve-packs for 96 pesos and reorganized our loads.

We loaded the dinghy and ferried our purchases out to Sequitur in the anchorage, unloaded, stowed and relaxed. In the evening we enjoyed the remainder of the pizza washed-down with chilled Argentinean Cabernet.

On Thursday morning I hauled four packages of sierra fillets out of the freezer and after they had thawed, boiled them in a quarter litre of water and then added a half litre of chicken stock from a tetra-pack and a half litre of white rice. To this simmering pot I added a diced small white onion, a diced large carrot, a diced large cauliflower stem and after tasting, some salt. After half an hour I added the cauliflower tops and some chopped zucchini and poblano, and the pot yielded four one litre Lock-and-Lock containers of passage dinners for the freezer.

After lunch two Mexicans in a runabout knocked on the hull and asked whether we needed any work done or any supplies. I asked if they could find Spectra watermaker filters, and the one fellow said he could. I showed him one as an example and wrote out the part numbers for him. I also asked whether he could find some Tef-Gel and some LocTite, and added them to the written list I gave him. We agreed to meet at 0930 Friday on the float at the marina.

At 1400 we went ashore to the marina by the fuel dock and paid the 150 Pesos dinghy landing fee. I offered a Canadian twenty and was given 240 Pesos for it. We walked around the western lobe of the bay, which was thick with small boats. After nearly two kilometres we arrived at the entrance gate of the Club de Yates, where we had been told there was a marine supply store.

We asked the guard where it was, and in reply he let us through the gate and indicated the first door on the left. He monitored to ensure we went into the shop and not into the marina. The shop was more oriented to boating knickknacks than it was to marine supplies, and prices were double to quadruple those at we see at home, even at our highest priced store, WestMarine. They had never heard of Tef-Gel. We were shown to the shop next door, which had an even less appropriate stock mix. We were monitored to the gate and locked back through.

We asked some locals if there were any ferreterias in the area, and were directed up a side street and around a corner. A quick glance inside told us it made no sense enquiring, so we snaked our way back down to the malecon.

As we went we passed an itinerant fish stall on the margin between sand and sidewalk next to moored and beached pangas. Much of the fish on display looked a long way from fresh, so we passed.

We caught a bus and rode back along the waterside boulevard. Unfortunately we had hopped on one of the buses whose driver prides himself with the loudest music and deepest bass in the city. With fingers in our ears, we endured it until we were past the Port Captain's office, then we got off to walk the remaining half dozen blocks to the Mega supermarket. Its thin selection of produce was mostly seconds and culls, and this very quickly told us we were still too close to the slums.

We continued walking along the malecon and after several blocks we arrived at Bodegas Aurrero, another supermarket. Its produce also screamed at its location in the cheaper end of town, so on we went.

Over the years we have repeatedly observed that the supermarkets in the poorer areas have poorly stocked fresh produce departments. They have instead shelves that are crammed with comparatively expensive packaged convenience foods, such as Krap Dinner, Hamburger Helper, Spam and the like. The aisles in these stores were are piled high with potato chips, snacks and huge containers of variously flavoured fizzy sugar waters.

We flagged a collectivo and rode the remaining five-and-a-half kilometres to Walmart for the equivalent of less than $2. Because it is in a more upscale area of the city, the selection of produce was extensive, diverse and in excellent condition.

Edi picked out a couple of large papayas, one slightly greener to last a bit longer, plus some avocados in varying stages, mostly green. She also found some fresh strawberries at an excellent price. I added some fresh Portobellos and some firm white mushrooms, plus red peppers and poblanos. We also bought two dozen frozen bagels and a big block of Chihuahua cheese.

We browsed the wine selection, but could see nothing to entice us. Besides, the Blue Nun had left the wine department and was last spotted eyeing the cucumbers.

Outside Walmart we were accosted by hoards of taxi drivers, but we shook them off and went to the bus stop to wait for a yellow, air-conditioned and tinted-windowed bus. For less than fifty cents each we rode in comfortably upholstered seats with quiet music for the nine kilometres back to the marina.

After some cramming and juggling, we managed to fit most of our perishable purchases into the fridges and freezers. We were again stocked-up for independent cruising, and were ready to head out to the Galapagos Friday morning, if the Port Captain comes through on her promise of a zarpe at 1000.

The winds were predicted to be light and variable the first three days out, but a building depression south of Panama on Tuesday and Wednesday should give us 15 to 20 knot south westerly winds and a beam reach for the middle half and hopefully more of our 1200-mile passage.

At 0920 on Friday morning we took Non Sequitur over to the floats at the marina and went inside to pay the 150 Pesos for our landing. The fellow who was supposed to get pricing on the watermaker pre-filters and Tef-Gel was not around. We left the marina at 0945 and walked along to the offices of the Port Captain, hoping that she had come through on her promise of Wednesday afternoon to have our zarpe ready for us at 1000 Friday.

We were a couple of minutes early, but were ushered in and given seats in front of Antonio, a fifty-something man who spoke no English. After some rudimentary communications, in which he mentioned *"migracion"* and *"aeropuerto"* and *"una hora"*, he started slowly hunting his way around a computer keyboard. In just under half an hour of replacing old screen data with our data, he managed to get a document to the printing stage, printed three copies and handed one to me to check the data for accuracy. It was the zarpe.

Once I had confirmed to him that the data were correct, he started the painfully slow process with another form, which he managed to complete and print in only twenty minutes and handed me a copy to proofread. This form was the Direction de Supervision, listing our departure from our previous Mexican port, our arrival in Acapulco, our departure from Acapulco and our next destination port, including Sequitur's ship registry number, port of registry, gross tonnage, net tonnage and crew list. I confirmed to him that this form also had the correct data, so he began to hunt-and-peck at a third form.

The third form was the Zarpe Internacional, which appeared to be simply a landscape-format rendition of the data from the portrait-format zarpe, which was missing only the crew list and the signature block for the ship's captain. This form had taken him another twenty minutes to complete and print, and after I had confirmed the data were correctly entered, he combined the three new documents with Wednesday's photocopies of our passports, entry visas, ship registry document, crew list, vessel importation certificate and our exit documentation from previous Mexican ports. He then shuffled the papers into three stacks and checked them a couple of times before he decided to commit a staple to each bundle.

Antonio took the stack of papers, which was over a centimetre thick now, and disappeared into the Port Captain's office for signatures. He emerged and sat down to admire his handiwork, and after a look of dismay, pulled out the first bottle of whiteout I have seen in nearly two decades. He had serial-numbered the Zarpe and Zarpe Internacional as 033. He painted-over the last 3s and in their places, with a ballpoint he wrote-in 4s, changing the serial numbers to 034.

He again sat back and admired his handiwork, and mentioned *"migracion"* and *"aeropuerto"* and *"una hora"*, adding this time *"lejos"*. I had earlier gathered that an immigration officer was coming from the airport in an hour. I now learned his lateness was because of the distance from the airport. Finally after an hour and three quarters, Roberto, el Delegado Regional arrived from Migracion. Antonio cleared off his desk, sat Roberto in his chair and placed the stack of papers in front of him.

The Delegado began a perfunctory scanning of the papers, and then must have realized we were not agents, but boaters clearing ourselves. He slowed-down to a thorough reading of each document, and then had Antonio recopy our passports with less contrast so the photos showed better. In just under half an hour Roberto managed to read the file, apply his signature to a dozen and more places and wear-down his rubber stamp some more. We shook his hand and thanked him for his fine services, and off he went.

But we were not done yet. I now needed to pay the exit fees of 306 Pesos. Antonio went back to his keyboard and after three unsuccessful attempts, managed to print two copies of an invoice. We left Edi at his desk with our files while Antonio and I headed down the stairs, stopping after three flights to retrace our route back up to the office. He corrected an error, photocopied the result and off we went again down the stairs.

This time we made it down to the main level, and then out onto the street where we walked along to an afterthought of a building, which was plunked on the lawn of the main building. He indicated to me the front door, and he went in the back and called me up to a wicket and asked for my credit card. We then spent almost half an hour as the fellow at the computer behind the wicket tried to learn how to use the payment terminal.

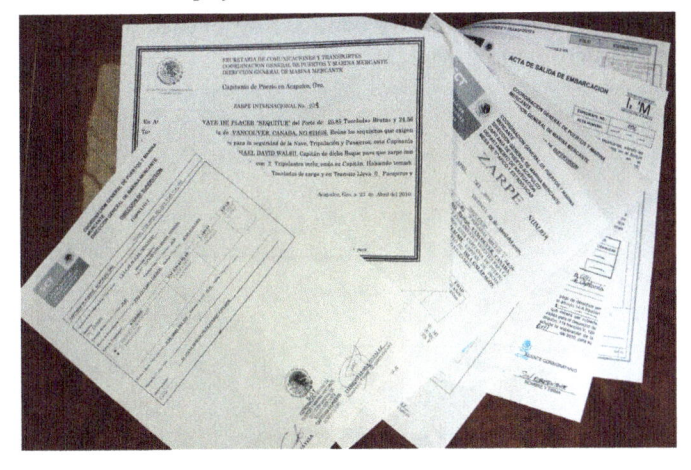

Finally paid and receipted, I followed Antonio back up to his office, where he practiced his rubber-stamping and flourished signature technique. Somehow, he seemed much more adept at this than with a computer and printer. We were finally issued with our zarpes and many other pieces of paper shortly before 1300. We thanked Antonio for his services, and attempted to do the same with the Port Captain, but we were told she was out to lunch, and as we had seen throughout the long morning, so were most of her staff.

We were delighted that we had managed to get our zarpes issued without having to resort to surrendering our passports and ship's papers to an unknown agent, paying US$75 and waiting two or three days. Weary and hungry, we walked back toward the marina. I had 157.70 Pesos left in my pocket, the last of the supply of Mexican currency we had bought in September in Vancouver. We decided to stop for lunch in the marina restaurant and use it up. We left the restaurant an hour later with 20 Centavos, recovered the dinghy and headed back out to Sequitur, free and ready to leave Mexico.

As if on cue, a female frigatebird took off from the masthead of a neighbouring boat and headed southward out of the anchorage.

As we were unshipping the motor and getting ready to hoist the dinghy, Capitan Alberto, the fellow who was getting pricing on the watermaker pre-filters motored-up with two friends. He said he had found filters, and showed me a written quote from a swimming pool filter supply house at 216 Pesos each, and that he would charge me 250 each to go and get them, saying it would take an hour-and-a-half. He assured me he had checked that the Spectra filter part numbers were on the list of compatible replacements. I told him we wanted four of each the 5 and the 20 micron and gave him CA$200.

Shortly before 1600 Capitan Alberto returned with only four 5 micron filters, saying they had no 20s in stock. He gave me back a hundred and wished us a safe trip.

Because of the lateness in the day, and to give the winds a chance to build a bit more, Edi and I decided to postpone our departure until first thing on Saturday morning.

As a receipt, I suggested I take a photo of him and the money.

144

9. To the Galapagos

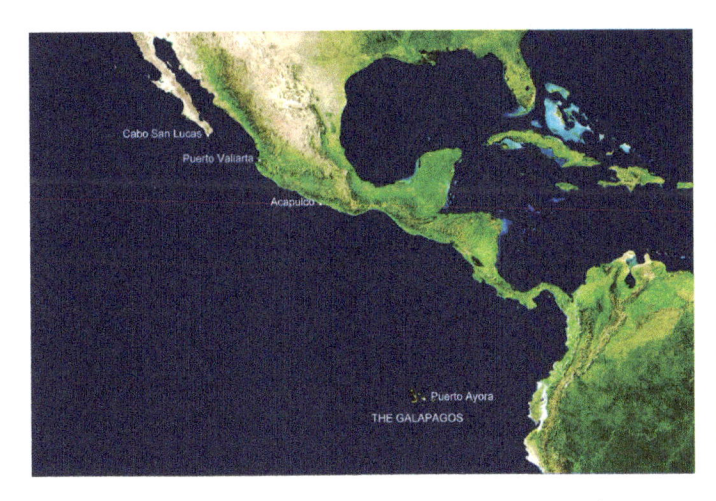

At 0824 on Saturday the 24th of April we weighed and headed out of the bay under power through glassy seas and still airs. At 0900 we were abeam Punta Brujas and bent our course to 150° to make Puerto Ayora on Isla Santa Cruz in the Galapagos 1196 nautical miles over the horizon. We thought that the passage would take us twelve to fifteen days, depending on how easily we made it through the doldrums. We had full fuel tanks, full water and a well-functioning watermaker, our fridges, freezers and pantry were filled to overflowing. We were set for a sixty-day passage if required.

We continued to motor at 5 knots through glassy seas with the occasional ripple until shortly before noon when a southwest breeze had started blowing at 4 to 5 knots. We hoisted the asymmetrical spinnaker and ghosted along steered by the Hydrovane as the breeze filled.

By mid-afternoon we were making 4.5 knots in 8 to 9 knots of breeze, and we had passed out of Mexican waters and hauled-down the courtesy flag we had flown for just over five months. It was near the end of its useful life.

The breeze backed slightly, and at 1600 we rolled-out the main, dowsed the spinnaker and rolled-out the jib. This moved us along at 5.5 to 6 knots on a close reach in a south-south west 9 to 10 knot breeze. We carried these sails through the night, slowly dropping in speed to under 3 knots as the breeze eased.

About 0300, an hour into Edi's 0200 to 0700 watch, a brown booby landed on the starboard lower spreader and remained perched there through the rest of the night. He was still there when I relieved Edi at 0700, but it flew away as the sun rose at 0722. A brown booby had hitchhiked a long night ride with us on our final passage into Mexico, and here at the beginning of our passage out of Mexico, another brown booby does the same thing. These are the only two avian hitchhikers that Sequitur has had at sea.

Half an hour after sunrise while Edi slept, I un-socked the spinnaker in the lee of the jib, and then rolled-in the jib and the main and we continued on at 2.5 to 3 knots in a 5 to 6 knot beam breeze steered by Hydra. Our noon position put us with a run of 88.1 miles for 24 hours of sailing in breezes generally in the 6 to 8 knot range, and never over 10 knots. The total distance for the passage to this point from Acapulco was 109.1 miles.

Through Sunday afternoon we continued sailing in a 7 to 8 knot southwest breeze and averaging 4.3 knots straight down the rhumb line. The skies were mostly clear, with only a few scattered cumulus and the breeze was warm. Overnight the breeze picked-up slightly and we moved along at slightly above 5 knots for a while.

On Monday morning, after Edi arose from her post watch nap, we enjoyed a very relaxing midmorning breakfast in the cockpit of toasted bagels, cream cheese, capers and smoked wild BC salmon with cups of fresh coffee.

Our second day's noon position put us 140 miles off the south coast of Mexico with a noon to noon run of 103.1 miles and a course made good of 150°, straight down our rhumb line to the Galapagos. The total for the passage was 212.2, a respectable run for the light breeze, but a bit slower than we would have liked.

The breeze continued to veer and by 1230 it had crossed the stern, so we jibed from the 160° we had been steering to 140°. By 1400 the breeze had become fickle at 2 to 4 knots and by 1530 we were becalmed. After flopping about in glassy calm for half an hour, we finally flashed-up the engine, snuffed the spinnaker and motored at 1600 rpm for an hour, until we found the beginnings of a south west breeze. There we shutdown and un-socked the spinnaker and sailed at 2 to 3 knots on a course of 150° steered by Hydra.

Sunset found us still ghosting along at 3.5 knots in a 6 to 7 knot breeze, which was finally beginning to strengthen. We slowly gained speed under the light of a near-full moon as the breeze built into a 10 to 12 knot wind. Shortly before midnight we crossed the latitude of the sun as it snuck past on the other side of the earth on its way to bring summer to the northern hemisphere. The sun would now remain north of us as we continue southward, and I need to adjust my internal compass settings of noon and sun and south and north.

We sailed at 7 to 8 knots on a beam reach in 12 to 14 knot southwest wind with Hydra easily keeping us on our course and on our rhumb line. Then at 0147 the spinnaker's tack shackle parted. I let fly the sheet and went forward to haul down the sock to snuff it, but found adverse winds making it awkward. I went back to the cockpit and flashed-up the engine and after I did my usual check for lines in the water, put the engine in forward at idle to turn to a more favourable relative wind for working-in the spinnaker.

Back on the foredeck with the more friendly flailing of the spinnaker, I dowsed it and while I was clearing away the sheets and lashing the socked spinnaker to the mast, a bight of the starboard sheet dipped into the water, and before I could do anything, the propeller found it and wound the engine to a stop. The engine was still in gear, and I could not shift it to neutral to try to unwind the mess.

I pulled-out the main and hove-to while I finished squaring-away the spinnaker. Then with the jib rolled out, I wore around to a course of 150 and at 0250 we continued along at 4 to 5 knots in an easing 8 to 10 knot southwest breeze. We decided to continue on, waiting for the next daylight calm so that Edi can snorkel down to the screw and attempt to unsnarl the mess.

Sunrise on Tuesday the 27th found us in southwest 7 to 8 knot breezes making 4.5 knots down our rhumb line. There appeared no calm in sight, and the seas were a bit too choppy for Edi to dive on the tangle, so we continued on. On Monday I had strung six watermaker filters on a line to dry in the sun, after they had soaked since Zihuatenajo in a covered bucket of fresh water. I now dry-brushed a pair and put them in the machine to begin making water. We made 236 litres in 3.5 hours, during which time I ran the generator and Edi started the first of three loads of laundry.

The breeze continued to veer and slowly pushed us southward. Our noon position put us 201.1 off the south coast of Mexico, having made 84.8 miles noon to noon and a total of 296.7 miles thus far on this passage.

At 1420 Edi finished the third load of laundry, and I shut down the generator with the battery bank at 96%. Before the sun lost its effect, the solar panels had brought the battery charge to 100%. We decided to hang the laundry out to dry rather than consume battery to dry it.

The light breeze continued to veer forcing us on courses progressively further south, so at 1712 we jibed to a course of 140° and moved along at 3 knots in a northerly breeze of 6 to 7 knots. The breeze became fickle and eased, and then at 1950, shortly after sunset we were totally becalmed.

We drifted with the south-setting current making good 8.9 miles due south between sunset and 0200, when a 2 knot northerly breeze assisted me in slowly wearing ship's head around from west to east and I handed the watch to Edi with us ghosting along under main and jib steering east and with the current, making about 2 knots to the southeast. When I relieved Edi at 0700, we had made 9.1 miles at 185° since midnight.

The sun rose at 0714 with us becalmed again and drifting south under skies mostly covered with stratocumulus. By 0950 a slight breeze from the northwest allowed our sails to add a small easting component to our southerly drift, and by 1040 we had picked up speed to 3 knots. Edi arose from her post watch nap, I started the generator and watermaker and Edi put in another load of laundry and made breakfast for us to enjoy in the cockpit. The generator runs so silently that it is just barely audible in the cockpit, and we often forget it is on.

Our noon position on 28 April showed we had made good 57.9 miles at 182° from the previous noon, for a total made good thus far of 347.6 miles at 153°, leaving 854 miles to go on a course of 149°.

At 1215 Edi started a second load of laundry for the day and half an hour later I shut down the watermaker, having made 138 litres in two hours and bringing the tank gauge to the upper part of the full mark. I then began overhauling the spinnaker, changing the tangled sheet for a spare one and replacing the parted shackle.

With the second load of laundry washed and hung-out to dry, we watched the dolphins frolic in the bow waves for a while. In the lee of the jib I un-socked the spinnaker, while Edi tended its sheet from the cockpit. At 1357 we then rolled-in the jib and main and set Hydra to steer eastward on a broad reach in the 2 to 5 knot intermittent northerly puffs. Our 1800 position showed we had made 9.77 miles at 140° since noon.

For dinner I made a double batch, one half to enjoy hot and the remainder to put in a Lock-and-Lock and in the fridge as a cold pasta salad for Thursday evening.

I toasted some sesame seeds in the wok as I cleaned and chopped vegetables, then setting them aside I wokked two large diced garlic cloves, diced fresh ginger and sliced white mushrooms in vegetable oil with a dash of sesame oil, and then added white onions, broccoli stems and carrots. Then after I had added rotini to a pot of boiling water, I added to the wok some diced ham steak, chopped broccoli florets, poblanos, red peppers and tomatillos, and when this was nicely heated through, I added a few dashes of light soy sauce, a few splashes of water and a shake or two of rice flour to make a nice sauce, to which I added a big dab of oyster-flavour sauce. I turned off the heat under the wok, added the hot, drained pasta, the toasted sesame seeds and a couple of diced roma tomatoes and tossed.

Part way through enjoying this delicious dinner we paused to watch a spectacular sunset, which was filling much of the western sky with golds, oranges and magentas. We hoped there was enough red sky to be 'a sailor's delight', and bring us some winds.

After dinner we jibed the spinnaker in 2 to 3 knots of breeze, and our midnight position showed we were averaging 1.7 knots southward. At 0015 we were becalmed and remained so until 0615, when a ripple grew into a westerly 2 to 3 knot breeze then slowly increased to 4 to 5 knots by sunrise at 0717, when it was pushing us along at 2.5 to 3 knots.

Shortly after sunrise I flashed-up the generator, started the watermaker and Edi put in the first of two loads of laundry. With the three loads the previous day, we have nearly emptied the laundry hamper, overstuffed with a backlog from our weeks of poor watermaking. In three hours we made another 206.6 litres of water, bringing the tanks back up near the upper end of the full mark. At 1030 we shutdown the generator, which brought the battery bank to 92%, while running our watermaker, washer-dryer, coffee maker and toaster. The solar panels and wind generator took over and by early afternoon had brought the 1225 amp-hour battery to 100%.

Our noon position showed a distance made good from the previous noon of 61.47 miles on a course made good of 158°. Not very good, but considering we were totally becalmed for 6 hours, and for the rest of the period we saw no breeze over 5 knots, not all that bad. About one-third of our movement was thanks to the south-going current. Our distance run thus far is 416.37 miles and we were 809.4 miles from Academy Bay, Isla Santa Cruz in the Galapagos.

In the late morning the breeze had begun backing to the southwest and by 1230 it was in the 7 to 8 knot range, moving us along at around 4 knots on a course of 145° under spinnaker alone, and steered by the Hydrovane. We were finally moving again, and at 1308 we sailed onto our first South American chart.

A few blue-footed boobies flew by, and for a while they played with the air currents around Sequitur, then they headed off to continue their fishing.

We started the afternoon on a beam reach, gradually changing through broad reach to run as the breeze veered again to the northwest and filled to around 10 knots. Our 1800 fix showed us making good just over 4.5 knots for the afternoon, and by sunset at 1942 we were moving in the 5 knot range, ringed by towering cumulus all around the horizons. The metre-high seas were becoming confused, likely from a couple of systems merging, and combining with the 2 to 3 metre southwest swell.

As the near-full waxing moon rose at 2115, we were moving along in a 10 to 12 knot west-northwest wind, still on a starboard tack under spinnaker alone and steered by Hydra. The wind's veering had caused me to keep adjusting Hydra to keep us on our course to the Galapagos, but now we were at the limit on this tack, and Hydra began nudging our course up a tad to keep the sail from jibing. I had wanted to sail 5 degrees below the rhumb line course of 150° to make up some of the eastings we had lost our last couple of low wind days. With the west-setting current through the Galapagos, I wanted to make landfall from the northeast.

Through the night we continued under the bright moon at 4.5 to 5 knots on a wind-dictated course mostly a tad above 155°. The sun rose at 0711 to show towering cumulus and altostratus at the eastern through southern horizons. The wind had recently backed to northwest and Hydra was again steering 150° and a bit below.

Shortly after sunrise I noticed that a young booby had decided to come along for the ride; it had found a perch on the lower spreader. A while later I flashed-up the generator, started the watermaker and when Edi arose from her post watch sleep, she put in the first of two loads of laundry to finally clear our backlog. In three hours we made another 208.5 litres of water, bringing the total for the trip so far to 10.5 hours and 789 litres. This is all on filter set B, which the condition gauge shows to still have many hours of production left before needing cleaning. The last in time I used this filter set was in the anchorage at Las Hadas, when it gave us only 17 minutes and 14.7 litres before clogging and shutting-down the machine. Its previous run to that was also in Las Hadas: 48 minutes and 51.2 litres. This certainly speaks loudly for the foul water in Las Hadas.

While the machinery purred quietly below we enjoyed breakfast in the cockpit. Edi had made some fruit compote by using a hand blender to macerate dried apricots and dried cranberries into thick pastes. These went wonderfully with cream cheese on our toasted bagels and baguettes. The compotes were simple and delicious, and without all the added sugar and whatever else found is in commercial preserves, I am sure much better for us.

The 30th of April is a significant day for me. After eighteen years of service I resigned my commission as a Canadian naval officer on 30 April 1981. My intention at the time was to buy a boat, fit it out and sail off over the horizon. Another significant 30 April for me was in 2006, when I told my ex-wife that a quarter century had passed and I still wanted to sail off. That conversation led to our separation and divorce and to my ordering a new boat that spring. The third significant 30 April was in 2008, when Edi sent me an email in response to my online ad looking for crew.

Our noon to noon run was 114 miles on a course of 155°, just five miles shy of the total of our two previous day's runs. Our total runs on this passage were now 530.4 miles and we were 610 miles from our landfall in the Galapagos. By the end of day we expected to be at our halfway point, and we were hopeful that we had our slow days behind us.

At 1400 I refreshed the spinnaker tack strop. Our 1700 position showed us moving along at 4.5 knots on a course made good of 150°. The temperature had dropped to 31.2° from 34° in the early afternoon.

The setting sun served as a backdrop for our dinner of giant scallops sautéed in butter with portobellos, shallots and garlic, served with steamed basmati rice, garnished with roma tomato slices with basil and accompanied by plates of steamed asparagus with mayonnaise.

As we relaxed over dinner, the western skies became increasingly spectacular.

By 0200 the wind had backed to south at 8 to 10 knots and we continued on a course of 130 at 4.5 knots under spinnaker and Hydrovane. At 0502 we were overtaken by a rain squall with variable winds in the 12 to 15 knot range. We altered course to north of east to run out the top side of the storm cell, which was plainly visible on radar. After the cell passed, we altered back to our southeast course and followed the storm

The sun rose at 0710 to show 9/10 overcast, mostly nimbostratus and cumulonimbus. At 0716, with the Guatemalan coast at 425 miles away our closest point of land, we passed within a cable of an unlit fishing vessel, 15 metres or so in length. The boat made absolutely no paint whatsoever on our radar, no matter how we tuned it, nor did it have an AIS transmitter. Rather scary! I was so preoccupied scanning the horizon for companion boats and tweaking the radar to try to pick it up, that I forgot to shoot photos.

Midmorning we finished a two-hour generator and watermaking run, leaving the tanks midway up the full mark and the battery indicating 89%. Our course made good from sunrise was 120° at 4.65 knots under spinnaker. We were being overtaken by a series of towering cumulus storm cells, so we doused the spinnaker and rolled out the main and jib to continue along on a course of 120° at about 4 knots continuing blustery and variable winds, mostly from the southwest and 5 to 15 knots.

Our noon position showed a course made good of 132° with 95.13 miles run from noon to noon and a total of 625.13 in daily runs. We were 593 miles at 153° from Acapulco and had 519 miles on a bearing of 149° to run to our landfall in the Galapagos.

We were overtaken by the first storm cell at 1210, just after we had rolled in the jib and hauled out the staysail and shortened the main to about quarter of its area. I quickly zipped-up the cockpit enclosure, and for the next six hours we battled nonstop in a seemingly endless series of towering cumulonimbus storm cells with torrential rain and twistingly variable winds. The variability was too much for the Hydrovane to handle, and I hand steered through most of the afternoon with very few breaks.

The winds in the cells were generally in the 25 to 35 knot range, and the maximum I saw on the gauge was 41 knots. We ran downwind, keeping the storms and the 3-metre short, steep wind-generated waves in our stern as much as we were able. Throughout the storms we remained dry and warm in our cockpit cocoon.

Shortly after 1800 the last of the line of cells moved on to the east of us and we were left steering east in steep, confused seas and a dying wind. At 1900 we jibed to 150° and half an hour later we were becalmed in sloppy seas. We drifted to the southeast through the night with the staysail and reefed main hauled tight in an attempt to stabilize the roll.

As it began to lighten at 0649 I hauled-out the full main and the jib and we began to move to the east-southeast close-hauled on a starboard tack into a freshening southeast breeze. As the sun rose I watched the remnants of a storm moving away to the north east and thin altocumulus and altostratus coming in from the south and west.

When we had lowered the spinnaker and stowed it in the sail locker before the storms hit, I had noticed considerable chafe at the top of the halyard. As the new day lightened, I cut away the chafed end and retied the pelican hook to the new end, and then wrapped the vulnerable section in fibreglass tape as a chafe guard. I left the spinnaker stowed, satisfied with the way the main and jib were pulling us along. Besides, re-hoisting it is an easier job for two, and Edi was below enjoying her post-watch sleep.

At 0755 I started the generator and watermaker. The filter set had completed 15 hours and produced 1029 litres, and still had life left when I shut it down with full water tanks at 0925. This is the same filter set which had given us only 17 minutes in Las Hadas.

When Edi arose she prepared breakfast and brought it up to the cockpit. We enjoyed toasted bagels with cream cheese, capers and cold-smoked wild BC salmon, washed down with a thermos of coffee.

Before she had brought up our breakfast, she had put a load of laundry in the machine, and when it finished, I shutdown the generator with the battery at 98% before she started the second load. On completion of the second load, the battery was at 96%, having had about 15 amps input from the solar array in the overcast skies and feeding the freezers and fridges and the chartplotter, instruments and radar. The Splendide is a very efficient machine.

Our eighth noon position put us with 60.26 miles made from the previous noon, with the total of our daily runs at 685.39. We were 649.5 miles at 151° degrees from Acapulco with 461 miles at 151° to our landfall in the Galapagos. Our closest land was the south coast of Guatemala 438 miles to the northeast.

At 1215 in a southeast breeze of 7 to 8 knots, we hoisted the spinnaker, un-socked it in the lee of the jib, rolled-in the jib and moved along on a course of 105° at 5 knots powered by the spinnaker, the staysail and the main and steered by Hydra. The breeze started gradually dying, and by 1320 we were becalmed. This was the first time since I tangled the sheet in the propeller that we have been becalmed in the daylight in relatively calm seas. I rigged safety lines while Edi put on her flippers, mask and snorkel and slipped into the water to take a look at the situation.

Sequitur was surging up and down in the slow swell and light cross chop left over from the previous day's storms, and Edi got a few scrapes from the barnacles on the Hydrovane rudder - we'll have to add anti-fouling paint to it next time we have a chance - and she was slapped and banged around by the bottom of the hull a few times. She reported one loop around a propeller blade and a twist around the shaft.

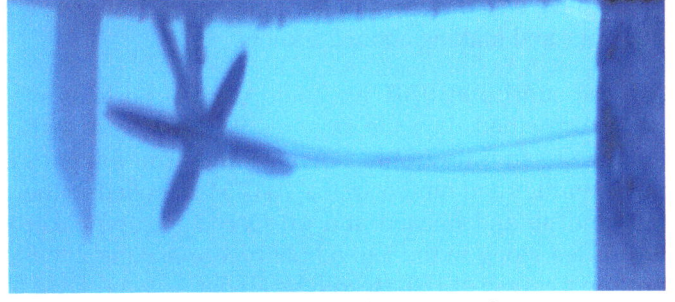

She took a camera down and shot some photos for me to analyze, and then she went back down with a boathook to try to pull the line free. After several attempts and a boathook donation to Neptune, she went back down with a knife, and later with another boathook, and then with the knife again.

While we were sitting becalmed, a line of towering cumulonimbus was marching down on us from the west. Finally at 1520, with the fouled lines cut as short as she could manage in the increasing surge, Edi came back onboard. I then flashed-up the engine and gingerly slip it in and out of ahead and astern a few times. Things seemed to turn okay without any weird sounds. I put our stern to the approaching storm cells and began motoring away to the southeast as they approached.

Shortly, the relative winds increased to between 10 and 15 knots from astern and I used the Hydrovane to steer us away on our best course. As we motored at 2000rpm, I tracked the storm cells on a radar overlay and plotted our best way through their advance. This went on until 1911, when we were finally clear of the last of the cumulonimbus towers. We hauled-out the main and jib and shutdown the engine. We sailed along to the southeast in the dying winds, making about 2.5 knots.

151

At sunset the sky was 8/10 overcast mostly with altostratus studded with cumulonimbus towering over the horizons. Shortly before 2100 we tacked to follow the veering breeze, which was now from the south, and we sailed to the southeast on a close reach. The breeze continued to veer and abate through the night, so we bent our course around to our destination course of 150°, and then gradually moved the wind around toward our beam. By dawn we were on a beam reach in a southwest breeze of 5 knots, and making about 2.5 knots.

With the sunrise at 0707 we could see the portents of another unsettled day; the sky was 9/10 overcast with altocumulus and altostratus showing through the few gaps in the cumulus and nimbostratus. At 0754 we rolled-in the main and jib and hoisted and un-socked the spinnaker and wafted along in the 5 to 6 knot breeze making 2 to 3 knots on a course of 150° steered by Hydra.

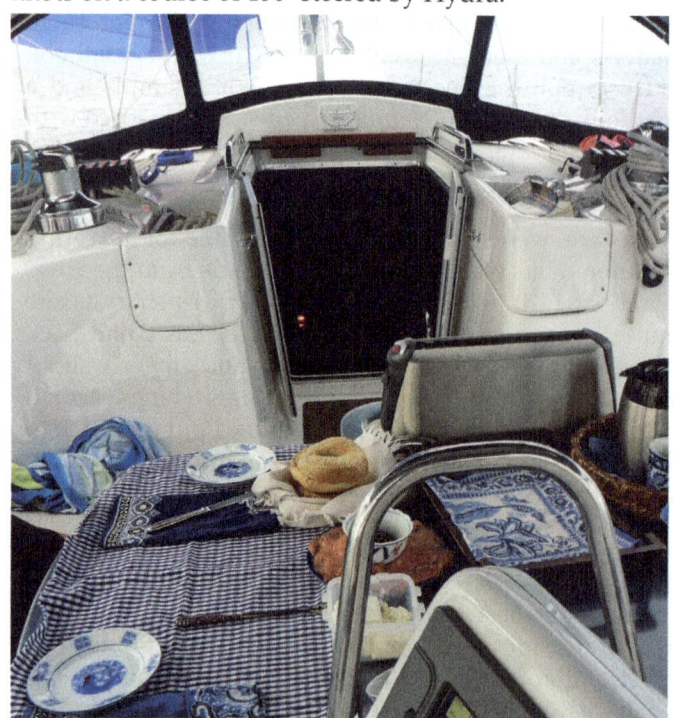

While we enjoyed another wonderful breakfast of toasted bagels with cream cheese, capers and smoked wild BC salmon and mugs of fresh coffee, I ran the generator and watermaker to bring the house battery back to 95% and the water tanks to full. Our worst set of filters from Las Hadas, the set that had given us 17 minutes there, had now given us 17 hours, and was ending each day in better condition than on the previous.

Shortly before noon another series of towering cumulus was rapidly marching across the horizon toward our starboard quarter, so we dowsed the spinnaker, but left it hoisted and rigged and lashed on the foredeck. We rolled out the jib and were pushed along the side of a passing storm cell using its localized 15 to 20 knot winds.

Our noon position showed us to have made 60.37 miles from the previous noon for a total of 745.76 in daily runs. We were now 708 miles from Acapulco on a bearing of 150° and our landfall in the Galapagos was 153° - 404 miles.

We continued to dodge storm cells until they had passed, and at 1315 we again un-socked the spinnaker and rolled-in the other sails, and set Hydra to steer us on a course of 150°. We moved along very pleasantly through the afternoon making 3.7 knots in the 6 to 8 knot westerly breeze. In the late afternoon, the first ship we had seen in a few days, Cepheus Leader, a near Panamax freighter bound for Japan passed at 14.5 miles down our port side. She was out of sight over the horizon, but thanks to our AIS transponder, we could watch her pass electronically, as she could watch us.

Our 1600 fix showed that we had made good an average of 3.48 knots since noon on a course of 145°. During dinner, as we were passing yet another storm cell, its wind reached further out than I had expected, and caught our spinnaker. While Edi steered, I let fly the sheet and went forward to haul-down the snuffing sock, but there was too much flailing and force in the by now 25 to 30 knot wind. I went back to the cockpit and lowered the halyard, laying the spinnaker in the water off our port bow.

Forty minutes later as we lay a-hull under bare poles in 30 knot winds and rain, I had socked the spinnaker in the water, un-fouled the port sheet (which had decided to do a wrap around the keel), hauled the sail aboard, unrigged it and stowed it in the sail locker. Then, making sure all lines were clear of the water, I flashed-up and we motored to clear ourselves from the storm cells. We continued with dinner, which was still nicely on the plates, thanks to Edi having taken them below and putting them on the stove-top and unlocking the gimbal. After dinner we shutdown the engine and ghosted along under sail in the 4 to 5 knot breeze, which by midnight had died.

We slopped and drifted through the night, until at 0537 with absolutely no wind, I decided to flash-up and motor. Sunrise at 0702 showed us glassy-calm seas, without a ripple to disturb the slow progress of the long swells. The sky was 9/10 covered with cirrus showing through the few gaps in the lower stratus, stratocumulus and stratus-fractus, and there were towers of cumulonimbus over the horizons.

Most of the time we had at least one booby riding on the bow, either on the Rocna anchor roll bar or on its shank or the shank of the Delta. An aggressive rider would fight-off all additional riders often for well over an hour before one managed to land. Then they would both fight-off other contenders for the roosts until a third made it on, and join in the defence, and so on. At one point we saw five boobies perched on the bow.

It is not an easy thing to land on a small target like this, with the boat slowly yawing from side to side and bobbing up and down, while moving forward and all of this motion changing the relative speed, direction and turbulence. We were fascinated watching the persistence of these boobies making many dozens of attempts to time a perfect landing, only to be fended off by boobies already there.

We made another 3 hours and 20 minutes of water, filling the tanks to overflowing after liberal showers and filling a dozen 1.5 litre water bottles for the fridge doors. The batteries were all up to 100%, and we continued to motor at 2000 rpm and making good 6.3 knots through the glassy seas.

Our noon position on 04 May put us 789.5 miles from Acapulco on a bearing of 151°, with 322.5 miles on a course of 154° to Isla Pinta, our landfall in the Galapagos. We had run 81.6 miles since the previous noon.

We continued to motor at 2000 rpm in glassy seas and dead calm airs, making an average of 6.28 knots through the afternoon and into the evening. Along the way we passed many giant tortoises swimming on the surface.

On several of these, boobies had found rides.

153

As the sun was setting there was a parade of cumulonimbus just over the western and southern horizons. It appeared to be marching along on a slowly converging course to ours, and we spent much of the night dodging the cells, which painted very clearly on our radar.

We used every point of the compass at one time or another and often passed within half-a-mile and felt the cold surge from the localized downpours and winds, but we managed to avoid being hit.

The sun rose for us with no fanfare or colour behind a solid wall of towering cumulus that formed the eastern margin of our totally overcast sky. Row upon row of cumulonimbus seemed to act as pillars supporting nimbostratus, and in most directions downpours were streaking from the cloud bottoms and trailing bits of stratus-fractus were looking for space to reform.

We spent the morning plotting relative velocities and weaving our way through the storm cells, and somehow managed to get hit only once by a downpour and twisting winds. To console ourselves, we took obscenely long showers as I again filled the tanks to overflowing with the watermaker.

Our noon position showed that we had made good 137.5 miles on a course of 153° since the previous noon. We were 151° - 926.9 miles from Acapulco and we have 185 miles on a course of 154° to make our landfall of Isla Pinta.

At 1215 we finally came clear of the line of storm cells that we had been working our way through for the previous sixteen hours since it began crossing our path. We were still motoring because it made much easier our task of weaving among the cells and their constantly changing, and often very strong winds close-in and the areas of near-calm between the cells.

As we cleared away from the influences of the last of the storm cells and motored south-southeast into the tower-free waters, we were heading straight into a 6 to 7 knot breeze, which seemed to be blowing directly from the Galapagos. Our options were to slowly tack our way upwind, or to continue motoring. We chose the latter. I setup the Hydrovane to steer us within 5° of dead upwind and we relaxed for the first time in a few days.

The wind continued to blow from the south southeast through the afternoon and we continued to motor into it and its generated waves as the skies became near-totally overcast with stratus, stratocumulus, nimbostratus and cumulonimbus. The few gaps in the lower clouds were filled by the bands of cirrus and cirrocumulus. Toward sunset the nimbostratus had dumped most of their weight and were trailing off as stratus-fractus, allowing gaps of blue sky to emerge. Towering cumulus still accented the horizons. The temperature at sunset was 31.2° and the barometer was at 1011 and slowly rising.

Hydra steered us through the night as we continued to motor directly into the wind, gradually having to crab port as we entered a west-setting current. By sunrise we were crabbing 10 degrees to maintain our course. Shortly after 0800 we entered a line of storm cells about 5 miles deep and experienced torrential downpours, steep and confused seas and 15 to 30 knot winds during much of the 44 minutes of our transit, most of which was hand steered. We passed out the other side and into gradually dissipating steep and confused seas.

Our noon position on our twelfth day place us emerging from the doldrums with a day's run of 114.2 miles and the total of our daily runs is now 1079.06 miles from Acapulco. The most northerly of the Galapagos, Isla Darwin is 272° 32.85 miles away, and I suppose that now we are into their latitudes and beginning to thread our course through them, we are officially in the Galapagos, though we still have a couple of days to go to our anchorage.

Through the early afternoon the sky cleared to fair-weather cumulus with streaked layers of alto cumulus and cirrocumulus above. The barometer had slowly risen from 1011 to 1013 over the past six hours. The wind continued from the south-southeast at 14 to 18 knots and the seas remained short and steep from encountering the opposing swell. We continued to motor into the wind and the waves, and we had increased our crabbing to a little over 15 degrees to stem the current.

As the sun rose at 0656 we could see Isla Pinta 7.5 miles to our east. Pinta is the most northerly of the main group of the Galapagos, so we had now truly arrived. The sky was half obscured, mostly with dissipating nimbostratus and stratus-fractus in the east and some altocumulus toward the eastern and western horizons.

At 0808 we hauled-out the staysail, half the jib and half the main and trimmed close hauled on a port tack making just under 6 knots into the 15 to 18 knot southerly wind and crabbing nearly 30 degrees in the 2 to 3 knot northwest flowing current. We netted between 4 and 5 knots along our intended course for the rest of the morning.

Our noon position put us 16.23 miles north of the equator, about 20 miles to the northeast of the top of Isla Isabela, the largest of the Galapagos islands. Our noon to noon run was 84.87miles and we had totalled 1163.93 in daily runs to come the 1123 miles from Acapulco. Puerto Ayoro, our intended anchorage was still nearly a day away.

We continued sailing to the southwest until at 1630 we ran out of water as we approached Isla Isabela. With the wind becoming fickle and the current coming straight up our intended course, we decided to motor down through the islands. We rolled-in the sails and motored to the southeast between Isla Isabel and Islas San Salvador and Santa Cruz.

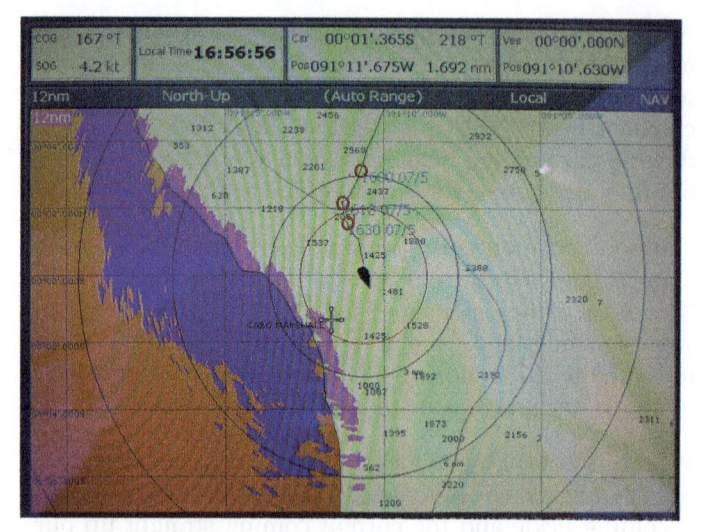

At 1657 we crossed the equator in longitude 91 10.630W, 1.7 miles northeast of Cabo Marshall on Isla Isabela. Since both Edi and I have previously crossed the equator by boat, this being my seventh crossing, King Neptune needed no special formalities from us.

We motored through the night against the current into the prevailing southerly wind with Hydra steering very nicely. The moon was in the final few days of its cycle and didn't rise until a couple of hours before dawn. I stood watch through to 0240 when we finally emerged from the fickle winds and currents between the islands and I was able to set Hydra on a dependable course to keep us away from land, and handed the watch over to Edi and laid down on the cockpit settee for a nap.

We arrived at the entrance to Bahia Academy at 0825 on 08 May, and after weaving our way through the dozens of vessels at anchor there, we finally found a spot to anchor. Our feathering propeller was stuck in forward, likely with the remnants of a sheet around it and preventing it from feathering and reversing, so we had to do the anchoring using the wind and current. At 0858 we came to 18 metres on the Rocna in 5.2 metres of water half a cable off the surf breaking over the reef off Puerto Ayora, the Galapagos.

We assembled the Fortress 37, shackled it to 10 metres of 9.5mm chain at the end of a 19mm nylon rode. I secured the rode at 13 metres to a stern cleat, then let out 12 metres on the bow anchor, dropped the Fortress over the stern and shortened-in the bow anchor rode back to its 18 metres and thereby secured the stern to keep our bows into the southeasterly waves that are a common feature of this anchorage. Also, with so many boats in this tight anchorage, nearly everyone lies to bow and stern anchors to prevent swinging and to allow close spacing.

We hoisted the quarantine flag, which Edi had made on the passage. She had also stitched together an Ecuadorian flag, but its hoisting would have to wait until we clear customs and we are officially in the Galapagos.

Once Sequitur had settled in on her anchors and we had shutdown the engine, we relaxed. For the first time in two weeks we no longer needed to navigate, we could relax our weather eye a bit and our only concern with watchkeeping was our usual anchor watch for the first while as we gradually gained confidence in our anchor placement.

We were anchored a bit close to a reef between us and the shore, but with the very crowded anchorage and our lack of control of the propeller, moving would be awkward. I decided re-anchoring could wait until after we had a diver clear the tangle on the propeller and the shaft and we had his report on the condition and freedom of movement of the feathering propeller blades.

We needed to organize our clearance into the Galapagos, to find a diver, to arrange refuelling, to have our empty propane tanks refilled, to find an electrician, to find a marine hardware store and to find fresh produce. At 1120 we hailed a passing water taxi and for 60 cents each we went ashore to downtown Puerto Ayora. A short walk along the malecon took us to the offices of the Armada and the Capitan de Puerto. Inside the Capitania we found no one available at that time who spoke English, and we were asked to come back in an hour.

We walked through the town past many cafes and restaurants until we saw one that attracted us. We sat in its gravelled patio at a table overlooking the passing scene as we enjoyed a late breakfast. Back at the Capitania we met in a small office with an official who told us we needed to have a permit to come to the Galapagos.

We told him we had come directly from Acapulco, Mexico, and we could find no permit office there, nor could we locate any on the ocean on our way across. He then asked us who our agent was, to which we replied we had none, and asked if he could find us one. He confirmed that one had been called and was on the way over, and then he added that we must also book a tour to one of the other islands, and asked us which tour we wanted him to book for us. Fortunately, before this bribe attempt had a chance to further unfold, the agent that he had called arrived and took over.

Javier is young fellow, still in his early twenties, who has spent most of his life in the Galapagos. We chatted briefly, and then left the Capitania with him to be driven across town to his office. He works for Johnny Romero from a small modern office of three, possibly four people. We gave Javier our passports, ship registry certificate and our zarpe from Mexico, and he told us we would be visited by a fumigation officer to examine the boat for infestations, and that in two or three days, if all is well with his inspection and our papers, we should be cleared in.

I explained our mechanical and electrical problems and asked him to organize a diver to come out and untangle our propeller, and for mechanic with electrical experience to assist me with the installation of the new alternators and to troubleshoot the generator, which had failed to start for several days. I also had him arrange propane tank refilling and a fuel barge to top-up our diesel tanks. We also asked Javier for the location of a good marine hardware store, and supermarket and of the beat restaurant.

We walked back through the town checking-out the hardware stores, and found them better stocked with marine supplies than those we had found in Mexico. We stopped in at the supermarket, which was directly opposite the water taxi landing. We perused its offerings and after picking-up a few items, we caught the water taxi back out to Sequitur.

The Ecuadorian currency is tied to the US dollar, and the country uses US paper money instead of printing its own, and US coins circulate freely here, alongside the Ecuadorian coins. I was fascinated by how heavily used the Sacajawea dollar is here, while in its ten years of existence it has failed miserably to circulate in the US, imitating the fate of the Susan B Anthony dollar a quarter century previously.

We spent all day Sunday aboard Sequitur, relaxing and baking bread. Saturday evening Edi had started six loaves of New York Times no-knead bread; we had finally ran out of bagels. She prepared two raisin loaves and one each of diced dried apricots, sun-dried tomato with basil, flor de calabaza with pumpkin seed, and cranberry with pecans.

The baking takes 50 minutes per loaf and our oven holds only one of the big round loves at a time, so it was a five-hour process to bake them off. When they were all done, and Edi was slicing them to cool before freezing, we sampled at least one slice of each with cream cheese. Then because we had been so bad, we sent ourselves to bed without dinner.

Late morning on Monday Javier arrived with a diver, who dressed and went down for a look. He shortly came back up and asked for his knife, and less than a minute later reported the tangle was now all cut away and the propeller was free. I had asked him to try to feather and un-feather the propeller into both forward and reverse, and he reported that it moved freely in both directions.

157

I then had him swim clear but with a view of the propeller as I ran the engine and shifted from forward to neutral to reverse and back. He reported the propeller started in forward and continued to turn forward only, never stopping.

After the diver had gone, I emptied-out the contents of the port side cockpit locker and tinkered with the engine transmission shift mechanisms, which appear to have been stressed and pulled out of position. I eventually managed to shift the transmission into neutral. I then flashed-up and ran the engine to start topping-up the battery, which had drained down to 62% over the past couple of mostly overcast and windless days. The alternator was putting-out about 35 amps at 4000 rpm (the engine's 2000 rpm), which is less than half its rated output, but at least it was producing something. After an hour-and-a-half, the engine overheated; it had lost its raw water feed. I shut down and started troubleshooting.

Then, at 1420 the Fumigation Officer arrived with his black satchel and came below into the galley and pantry. He poked around for a while, then took out of his bag a large syringe and poked it into back upper corners above the stove, in the backs of the cupboards, the insides of drawers and other places he thought likely. After looking and probing and injecting for a few minutes, he broke out in a broad smile and said OK. We had passed!

At 1640 Carlos and his crew arrived in the small canopied boat, which served as his fuel barge. In it were eight black 18-US-gallon plastic drums, a small Yamaha generator and an electrical pump being fed by a short hose ending in a wand with suction fitting. On the outlet end of the pump was a longer hose that ended in a gate valve and nozzle.

I organized fenders and secured the barge alongside, and then we began pumping the contents of the eight drums. Shortly after beginning the eighth drum, Sequitur's main tank reached its full mark, and we started on the auxiliary tank, taking it to about a quarter full.

Carlos told me he had delivered 140 gallons, so it appears he allowed for a half gallon not being picked-up by the system from each drum. I told him we needed three more drums, and he replied that he is organized and paid by the agent, and that I needed to go through the agent.

While the fuelling was in progress, Wilmer, the mechanic arrived. He spoke absolutely no English, so it took me a while to communicate with him what the situation was and what I wanted done. I got him started on removing the old Balmar 100 alternator, whose windings looked rather scorched, and while it was off, changing the raw water impeller, the access to which is much simplified by the removal of the alternator. I then got Wilmer started on installing the new Balmar 120 alternator and the mounting brackets for the Balmar 210.

At 1730 Javier arrived with an electrician, who went over the alternator installation with Wilmer and me, assisted by Javier's translation. Leaving the mechanic and the electrician below, Javier and the water taxi driver weighed Sequitur's stern anchor, attached a tow line to our bow and then as I weighed the Rocna, towed us out to an empty space near the centre of the anchorage, and there we came to 21 metres on the Rocna in 7 metres of water. Javier and the water taxi then set our Fortress 37 about 35 metres off the stern. I paid the water taxi $10.

158

Our new anchorage was in the middle of the fleet of tour boats that conduct sightseeing trips around the islands. Because of the regulations, these boats were all Ecuadorian, and likely because of their monopoly on the tour trade, they were mostly derelict or at best, very poorly maintained. Scattered among these were sailboats from around the world, which like us were restricted to anchoring in our port of entry.

The Ecuadorian bureaucratic tangle surrounding visiting yachts is a constantly moving morass of regulations. Yachts that arrive from foreign destinations without a cruising permit, called an *"autographo"* are allowed to spend up to twenty days in the Galapagos, but are restricted to their port of entry and are not allowed to travel to any other ports. Autographos for an additional one to five ports can take six to eight weeks to be processed, they cost $500 and upward, depending on the agent used and they are limited to only a few per month, so most cruisers ignore them. Foreign yachts that stop first in one of the ports of mainland Ecuador often cannot obtain a zarpe to the Galapagos Islands and they instead ask for their departure permit to be issued for a further destination, such as the Marquesas. They then make an *"emergency"* stop in one of the designated ports of entry in Galapagos.

Anyone aboard a visiting yacht wanting to visit the other anchorages or islands of the Galapagos is required to book passage on an Ecuadorian boat. From the selection of tour vessels we saw around us, we considered ourselves fortunate; we could see the quality and condition of what was being booked. Unfortunate are those thousands of foreign visitors who annually arrive by air or by ship with their pre-booked tours on these derelicts.

Many of the tour boats around us were sitting in slicks of oil, which we could see oozing through their planking seams and pouring out in the steady flow from their bilge pumps. We watched as garbage was thrown overboard into the bay and we saw a steady flotilla of jetsam moving past us in the surge of the anchorage. There was a petroleum sheen on the water, and we knew that our watermaker filters would very quickly clog. Our preconceptions on the pristine environment of the Galapagos were very quickly and erased.

Javier, Wilmer and the electrician went ashore at 1925. It had been a long and tiring day, and I didn't feel like cooking, so we radioed for a water taxi and went ashore for dinner. We looked at many places as we walked along the main street to its business end and then turned back to one with a sidewalk patio that had caught our eye. Edi ordered a fish burger and I ordered a grilled chicken breast. Edi's dinner arrived with some good looking hand-cut French fries, while mine came with a somewhat overdone sliced baked potato. My grilled breast was so thin that the chicken would have had trouble filling a triple-A cup.

On Tuesday morning the battery was down 53% and the day was lightly overcast. At 1110 a water taxi carrying three Armada officers in their white uniforms stopped by Sequitur as they conducted an inventory of boats in the anchorage. They asked the time of our arrival and I told them, adding several pieces of information: Naugala was our agent, the Fumigation Officer had come by and we were awaiting our clearance. They left satisfied.

At 1500 Wilmer arrived and continued working on the alternator installation. The fuel barge came alongside at 1555 and we took on all but 2 gallons in the three 18-gallon drums, filling our auxiliary tank. We now have 840 litres of diesel onboard again. At 1620 the electrician came aboard, conferred with Wilmer and went over the Balmar wiring diagrams. At 1635 Javier stopped-by to tell us we were now officially cleared into the Galapagos and Ecuador. I hauled down the quarantine flag and hoisted the Ecuadorian courtesy flag. At 1745 the electrician and the mechanic left.

At 1930 on Tuesday evening we took a water taxi over to Angermeyer Point for dinner in a restaurant housed in what was painter Karl Angermeyer's home. In 1937 he had left Hamburg, Germany, fleeing from the Nazi regime along with his brothers. After a long and adventurous journey he finally settled in the Galapagos, where he and his wife Marga lived in intimate contact with the wild, natural world. They built their house on one of the most beautiful settings in the Galapagos, and recently the house has been converted into a sixty-seat restaurant spread over a central dining room, a seaside terrace and an open-air garden.

The restaurant is accessible only from the sea, and the water taxi landed us on a float, which was simply a decked-over dory which is connected by a narrow wooden walkway articulated from the edge of the restaurant's garden. As the twilight was descending we were shown to a table on the rail overlooking the water. Beside us and just offshore was a 50 or 60 metre three-mast barkentine, and beyond her was Sequitur, somewhere out among the many dozens of anchored vessels, both commercial and pleasure, sail and power, small and large, and very modern to near-derelict. Weaving through the anchored fleet were water taxis, ship's tenders, freight lighters and dinghies. The scene was pulsing with life, yet it was placid and serene; the place was magical. Edi was moved to tears.

We shared a delicious tuna ceviche-carpaccio crossover. Then we each had an amazing pesto mahi-mahi, which was two thick slabs of fish sandwiching a layer of fresh basil leaves and napped with pesto. It was served with steamed baby potatoes and an assortment of fresh vegetables. With it we enjoyed a simple bottle of Chilean Chardonnay. We then each had the house sampler plate of three desserts with homemade ice cream.

Back onboard Sequitur, we went to bed with the battery at 46%, and since it was a windless night, we had no way to charge it until the sun came up in the morning. We hoped the freezers and fridges held until then.

We arose on Wednesday to a windless and totally overcast day. The battery was at 37% and the tops of the freezers were sweating. I made coffee by boiling water on the gas range and pouring it through the filter of our automatic electric coffeemaker, in the old-fashioned Melita filter manner. Not wanting to open the fridges or freezers, we delayed breakfast.

Javier and Wilmer arrived onboard at 0915, and by 1040 the alternator installation was complete, and we were ready to start the engine. The cooling water was circulating properly, so I ran the engine up to 1850 rpm and watched in relief as the new Balmar 120 supplied us with 100 to 105 amps. We monitored the engine temperature closely, not wanting a repeat of Monday's overheating episode. At 1050 the water stopped coming out the exhaust and the within a couple of minutes the engine temperature gauge had risen from 70 to 74 degrees. I shutdown.

I had thoroughly cleaned the raw water strainer on Monday afternoon, so we didn't suspect it. Wilmer suggested a clog in the raw water intake line, and Javier said he could get a diver with a roto-rooter type of device to try to clear it. Javier and Wilmer left shortly after 1100, and I set to work looking for the clog. The first thing I found was a fish in the raw water strainer bowl.

As I was removing it, I thought of how it would have gotten there, and began suspecting that the flailing line caught around the propeller may have destroyed or knocked off the bronze grill cover on the raw water intake. I closed the ball valve on the raw water intake through-hull, loosened the two hose clamps and removed the hose. Then I slowly opened the ball valve on the through-hull, which is nearly a metre below waterline. There should have been a metre-high fountain of water, but no water came in.

160

I closed the valve and quickly looked for something I could use as a probe. The first appropriate thing I saw was a spare hacksaw blade. With one exploratory thrust through the opened valve the probe immediately started a gusher. I quickly withdrew it and closed the valve.

With everything reconnected and the fish removed from the strainer, I re-flashed the engine and monitored the cooling system very closely as I ran the engine at 1850 rpm. Then at 1240 the raw water stopped circulating and the temperature again began to rise. I shutdown and again removed the hose from the raw water through-hull. This time there was an unrestricted flow of water immediately I cracked the valve.

I suspected the raw water intake suction had pulled a fish to the intake and held it there until the engine stopped, when the suction would have ceased and the fish freed to swim away. I re-flashed the engine and watched as the cooling water circulated properly. Now with the ongoing risk of sucking-in another fish, we need to keep a constant eye on the temperature gauge and an ear closely tuned to the sound of the exhaust. Any interruption in the flow of cooling water gives a distinctive hollow sound to the exhaust, and of course causes the temperature needle and digital readout to climb.

At a couple of minutes before 1300 the house bank finally reached 50%, the official level of a dead battery. Then half an hour later the engine's temperature again rose, so I shut down. There was another fish in the raw water strainer. I removed it and re-flashed only to find no cooling water flow, so I shutdown again and went through the process of probing the thru-hull. This time there was a fish stuck there. Within a few minutes we were up and charging again. I ran the engine until 1700, catching two more fish and bringing the battery back up to 74%. We ran the inverter in the evening for the computers, to make tea and to recharge some portable batteries.

On Thursday morning after running the inverter for coffee and toast and the computers, the battery was down to 57%. We let the solar panels maintain and slowly trickle a charge into the house bank until the clouds began weakening the sun's efforts. At 1530, with the battery at 58%, I flashed-up the engine and ran it at 1850 rpm for just short of three hours, catching only two fish in the process of bringing the house bank up to 74%.

Friday morning was heavily overcast and by 0830 the battery was back down to 60% after maintaining the fridges and freezers overnight, as well as powering the evening's interior lighting and running the inverter for such things as our computers and the tea kettle. At 0940, after the inverter had consumed another 3% powering our computers, the coffeemaker and the toaster, I flashed-up the engine and watched with satisfaction as the alternator put 95 to 100 amps into the system.

At the same time I also started the watermaker and ran it for an hour-and-a-half, netting about 75 litres. The water in the anchorage was rather murky, with a film of oil on its surface. The same set of pre-filters we had used so well on our passage from Acapulco began to clog a quite quickly, so I shutdown the machine shortly after the filters had kicked the system into its slow-speed mode and did a back-flush.

There were heavy rain showers on Friday afternoon and into the evening, with drizzle in between, and on Saturday morning it was still heavily overcast. With the battery at 57%, I flashed-up the engine and the watermaker while we had breakfast in the cockpit with an eye on the temperature gauge and an ear on the tune of the exhaust. We made another 64 litres of water as the filters gave us another 68 minutes of life before they clogged and shut-down the machine. Doing a back-flush of the filters and membrane would consume 25 litres of this, so I decided to forgo the procedure and remember to change the filters and do another run the following day.

By the time we shut-down the engine at 1040, it had brought the battery back up to 68%, and had caught only one fish in the process. By then the sun was burning through the clouds sufficiently strongly, so we left the batteries to care of the solar panels.

At 1300 we called a water taxi on the VHF and went ashore. I had brought with me the burned-out bulb from the port running light. I knew we have spares aboard, but I had not yet locate them, and besides, it makes sense to replace rather than to deplete spares. We went into the marine hardware shop across from the landing, and the clerk told us we needed to go to Bodega Blanco for such a thing. She said it was *"very far away, at the other end of town and required a taxi ride"*.

We walked across town to Bodega Blanco to find they had a close match for the bulb, but with opposed rather than staggered pins. We browsed their marine hardware stocks, but could find nothing that we needed, so we left empty-handed.

We continued along from there to the gates of the Galapagos National Park. Since the Park covers 97% of the archipelago, effectively the gates might be considered to be those of the city of Puerto Ayora, rather than of the National Park. With a population approaching 15,000, Puerto Ayora is the largest community in the Galapagos, and it is surrounded by the Park.

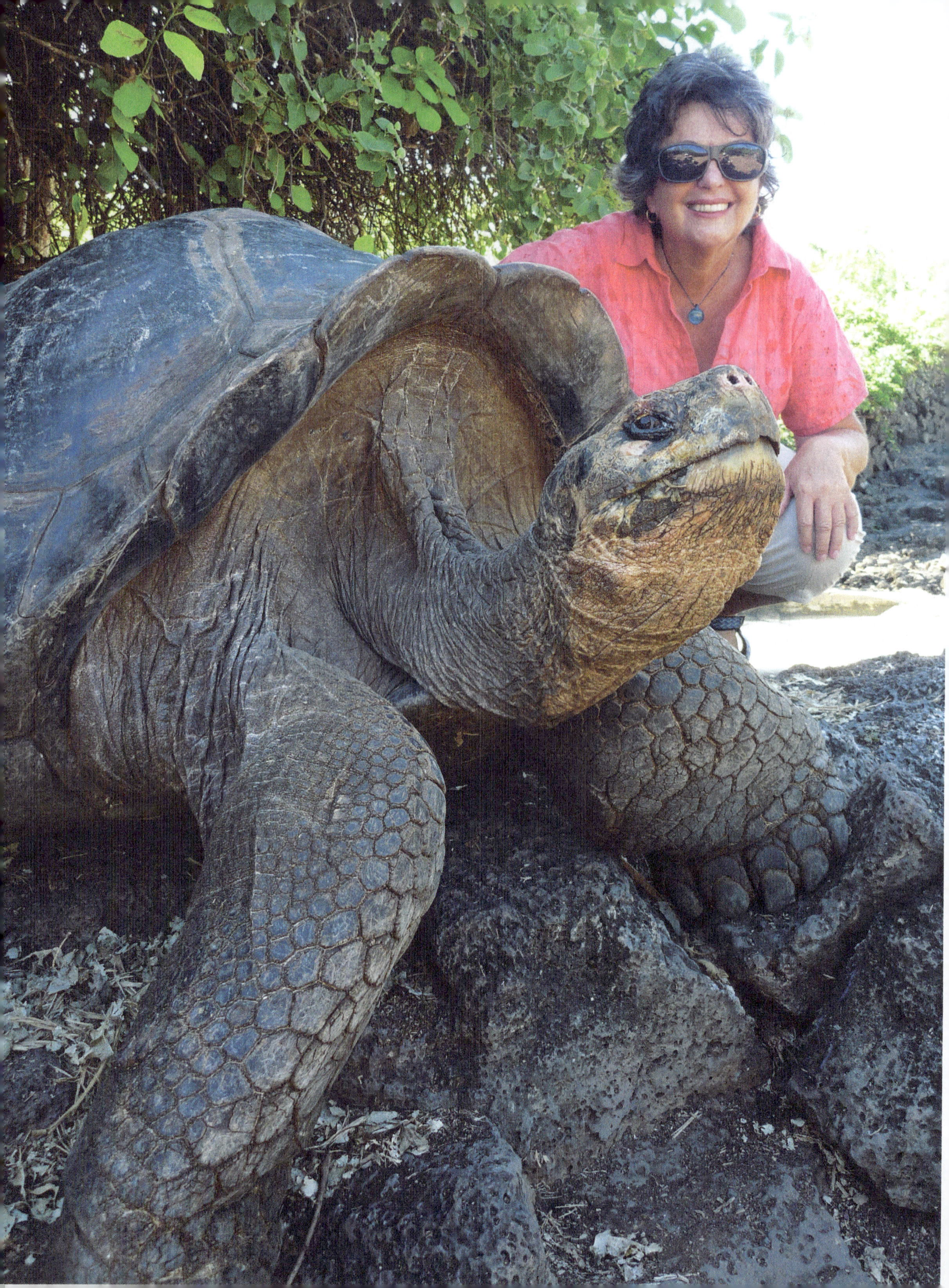

We looked around the grounds, and quite disappointed with their dilapidated state and unkempt appearance, we decided to head back. On our way into town we paused to look at the Japanese restaurant and sushi bar at the Red Mangrove Inn. This upscale inn sits on the water in the fringes of a mangrove swamp. It exudes a wonderful, gentle calmness.

We walked into the grounds of the Darwin Research Station and followed signs to the giant sea tortoises. We paused for a while and there to chat with a few of them.

The seaside patio was alive with iguanas, and a pair of seals formed the guard at the entrance to a tasteful little gazebo, which stood on pilings out of the water at the edge of the restaurant's patio. The place was so inviting we decided to have some sushi and beer. We were told that, unfortunately, that the sushi chef did not start until 1830, so we decided to come back another day.

We walked back through town, taking a couple of back alleys to see the place from a different perspective, and stopping at the supermarket for a few things before arriving back onboard in the late afternoon. In our absence, the house battery had fed the fridges and freezers and had in turn been fed by the solar panels, and had come up 2% to 70%.

As we arrived onboard I had noted that Sequitur's stern was skewed to starboard and the stern line was a bit slack. It appears that while we were ashore a passing vessel may have caught our stern line and moved the anchor. I shortened-in the line and our skew grew to over 30 degrees off the lone of the swell, and we rolled and slopped around. We needed to reset the anchor, but it was getting dark, so I let it be for the night.

At one point, we also watched the start of the tortoise production line. It seemed a very slow process, with a thrust and a great moaning grunt from him every fifteen or twenty seconds, while she lay passively.

Sunday morning we again ran the engine through breakfast, and coaxed another 45 litres from the watermaker's pre-filters before they shut it down. We also ran a load of laundry through the washer and Edi hung it out to dry on a clothesline that I had rigged between a shroud and the solar array arch. Four hours of engine running netted only one fish, but powered the computers, the coffeemaker, the toaster, the watermaker and the washer-dryer, and brought the battery up to 75%.

At 1245 we hailed a passing water taxi and I asked what he would charge to help reset our stern anchor, and we agreed on $5. I secured the stern anchor's rode at 25 metres to a stern cleat and then hopped aboard the little craft to direct the driver as I handed-in the line, then the chain and finally the anchor. The Fortress anchor is great in sand and mud, as long as there is no appreciable change in the direction of pull on it, so it serves well as a stern anchor, as long as there is a steady one-direction pull. If the rode is slack, and the boat swings, changing the angle of pull, it will almost certainly pop the anchor out of the bottom.

I directed the taxi driver to manoeuvre his boat in such a way to pull Sequitur directly back from her bow anchor and perpendicular to the swell, paying-out little by little the line and then the chain, until I was holding the Fortress 37 over the bows of the taxi as we continued to move slowly back. Just as Sequitur paused before beginning to spring forward on the weight of her bow anchor chain, I dropped the stern anchor and had the driver deliver me back onboard Sequitur, where I tightened-in the stern line about 3 metres. We were then riding pointed into the swell with a nice catenary to the stern line.

Mid afternoon on Sunday we hailed a taxi and had it take us over to Angermeyer Point, from where we walked along the broad trails to Finch Bay and its luxury hotel. From there we followed the beach and then a narrow track over a ridge and down the other side past some old salt ponds and beyond over a porous lava flow, which was naturally shattered into convenient building-block-sized pieces. After a little over half a kilometre we came to a site called Las Grietas, a narrow canyon cleft through the lava formations and filled at its bottom with deep clear water. This was the local swimming hole and it also served as the bravado place for the local boys starting to feel and exercise their testosterone.

After we watched the boys dare each other from higher and higher perches, we made our way back across the lava to the beach and from there back along the paths to the taxi landing. We ferried into town and slowly wandered through the streets.

It being Sunday, most of the businesses were closed, except for the bars, restaurants, tour booking offices, barber shops, internet offices, stationery stores, farmacias, souvenir shops, art galleries, convenience stores, produce shops, and other essential services. In fact, the only shops closed were the ones we wanted: the shoemakers to mend a broken strap on my sandal and the hardware stores to find a stitching awl to repair the mainsail clew.

We walked the back streets toward the northern end of the town and at 1745, shortly before sunset we arrived at the Red Mangrove Inn. We walked in and sat at a restaurant table on the patio over the water. The sushi chef wasn't due to begin for another three-quarters of an hour, and we remained relaxing there undisturbed watching the scene to seaward, the birds, the clouds and the setting sun.

When we saw the appropriate level of activity behind the sushi bar, I signalled a waiter to bring us menus. We ordered a couple of beers, and to test the sushi chef, we had decided to try a couple of rolls. The California roll and the tortuga roll arrived beautifully presented and were delicious enough to order a repeat, which we did. The four delicious rolls, three refreshingly cold beers and two wonderfully relaxing hours in this delightfully peaceful setting had cost us only $51 including taxes and tip.

On Monday morning we ran the engine to charge the house battery, and after breakfasting in the cockpit, I continued to monitor it while Edi took a taxi ashore to an internet office and to run some errands. She took my sandals to a cobbler who for $2.50 stitched-up the broken strap, and then without being asked, reinforced the stitching on all the other straps. Edi arrived back onboard in the early afternoon after having checked-out the morning activity and produce selection at the community market, and having located and bought some thick, sturdy darning needles and a couple of muffin tins.

While Edi was gone I continued to generate electricity and ran the watermaker again. I also called Javier on the VHF and he confirmed that the electrical switch for which we had been waiting had arrived from the mainland on Sunday, and that he was organizing the mechanic and electrician to come out and complete the second alternator installation. Mid-afternoon, a water taxi carrying two Armada officers came by doing an inventory of the vessels in the anchorage, and stopping to question the unfamiliar ones.

Shortly after the Armada had left, Anne-Margaretha, a steel ketch of twenty-two metres from Haarlem arrived and anchored next to us. In the process she passed sufficiently close to us that her skipper and I easily discussed the lay and scope of Sequitur's anchors. Onboard we counted ten people, and she had the appearance to us of being a charter vessel. Curious, I looked her up online to find she was on leg ten of a voyage that had taken her from the Netherlands early the previous September, southward to Antarctica and then northwest, passing Cape Horn at the beginning of March and arriving here in the Galapagos earlier this month. She was scheduled to head through Panama and be back in the Netherlands in August.

We were at a crossroads in the Pacific. In the week or so that we have been here, we have watched as sloops, ketches and catamarans from Australia, New Zealand, France, Norway, the Netherlands and the United States have arrived and left. Most of them had arrived from Polynesia and were heading to Panama or had come from Panama and were on their way to Polynesia. Far fewer sailboats arrive here from the north or south and even fewer leave heading in those directions. This day we saw a very rare arrival from Antarctica and Cape Horn.

Tuesday morning Javier came by in a water taxi to tell us the switch that had arrived was the wrong one, and they would have to reorder. I told him to not bother, and to cancel the installation of the second alternator. With the 120 Balmar working well, we can make do until we reach the mainland.

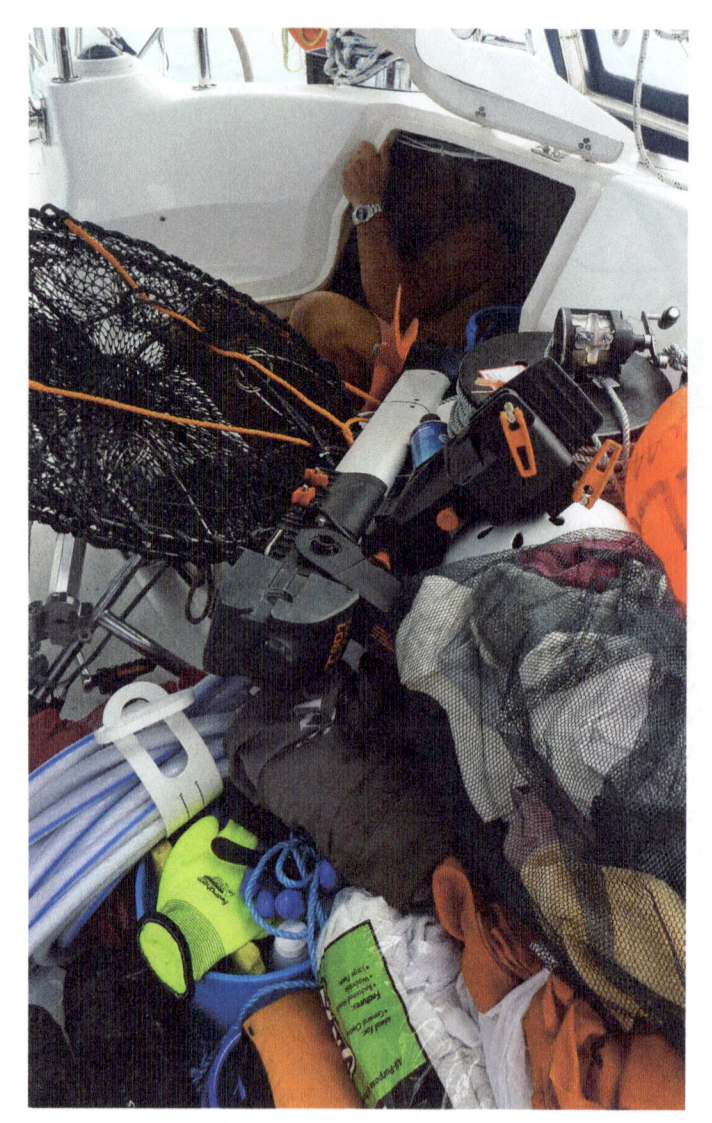

Our focus then went to preparing to leave the Galapagos on Wednesday. I tested the transmission in forward and reverse a few times to ensure my last week's temporary fix was holding, and for added confirmation, I again dived into the port cockpit locker to watch the levers working as Edi moved them. We then reloaded the locker.

At 1400 we hailed a water taxi and went ashore and walked through town to the Naugala office to get our invoice. We then stopped in at Bodega Blanca, the marine hardware store to buy some spare shackles to augment our diminishing supply. From there we walked the back streets across town to the market to pick-up some fresh fruit and vegetables and to the supermarket for a two litre container of yogurt.

Then after dropping-off the purchases aboard Sequitur, we picked-up more bank cards so we could raid the machines on our way back over to the Naugala office. We paid our invoice, retrieved our passports, ship registry certificate and our zarpe from the Galapagos to Callao, Peru.

Our invoice included port fees, anchoring fees, fuelling permit fees, police fees, inbound immigration fees, quarantine fees, fumigation fees, National Park fees, outbound immigration fees, zarpe fees and the fees for the compulsory agent to handle all of this for us. In addition, the invoice had the costs of the diver, the fuelling team and its water taxi, the electrician and the mechanic, plus in each case, the agent's surcharge on these costs plus an administration fee. There were over $1000 in fees on top of the charges for cost of the work and the supplies.

As disappointed as we were with the official and unofficial usury, we were more disappointed with the filthy waters in the anchorage and with the rather obvious blind eye being turned by the officials at every level to the blatant pollution by the Ecuadorian tour boats.

To leave with a better taste in our mouths and to fortify ourselves for the voyage, in the evening we hailed a water taxi and headed again to the Angermeyer Point Restaurant for a farewell dinner. We enjoyed a splendid dinner as we discussed the next leg of voyage.

Callao is just over 1000 nautical miles to the southeast of the Galapagos, and the prevailing winds at this time of year are from the southeast. The 180-hour forecast showed a 10 to 15 knot southeast wind for the entire period, with a little more southerly component near the coast. It looked like it would be best to start out on a port tack, heading southward and trying to make any bit of easting that is offered, or at worst trying not to lose any. Then after six or eight days, a starboard tack should give us a close reach toward Callao across the northbound Humboldt Current. This would mean sailing some 1400 miles and depending on the winds, might take ten to fifteen days.

After a wonderfully relaxing evening enjoying dinner and reminiscences of where we had been and a look at where we were going, we had the desk call a water taxi for a ride back out to Sequitur.

The following morning, while Edi was below preparing Sequitur for sea, I was up top finishing repairing the stitching on the mainsail clew cringle strops, which I had begun the previous morning. I was using a heavy darning needle, some waxed whipping twine and a pair of vice-grips to push and pull the needle. It was heavy work, which is why I had left it undone, but with fresher fingers I had it completed in little over an hour.

Once the sail repaired, I hoisted and secured the dinghy in her davits, and I shortened-in the rode on the stern anchor to allow the surge in the anchorage to loosen the Fortress' bite on the bottom. As I had hoped, the anchor worked free and I was able to hand it in rather easily.

By the time the dinghy was secured, Edi had finished the securing of everything below, so we flashed-up the engine and at 1115 on Wednesday the 19th of May we weighed and proceeded out of Puerto Ayora bound for Peru.

10. Passage to Peru

As we motored out of Academy Bay, the southerly swell was already up to 3 to 4 metres and it had been forecast to increase to 4 to 5 metres over the next day. This was the result of a 955 low in the Southern Ocean that was dissipating northward. The swell was then predicted to remain high for a couple of days before slowly decreasing to the 3 metre range. The sky was mostly clear, with a fringe of cumulus at the horizons and over the islands, and the barometer was steady at 1014. As we cleared the influence of the island, we were left with a light southerly breeze, so we continued motoring.

At 1440, with the southerly breeze at 7-8 knots, we set the main and jib on a starboard tack, shutdown the engine and set off down the rhumb line at 3 knots.

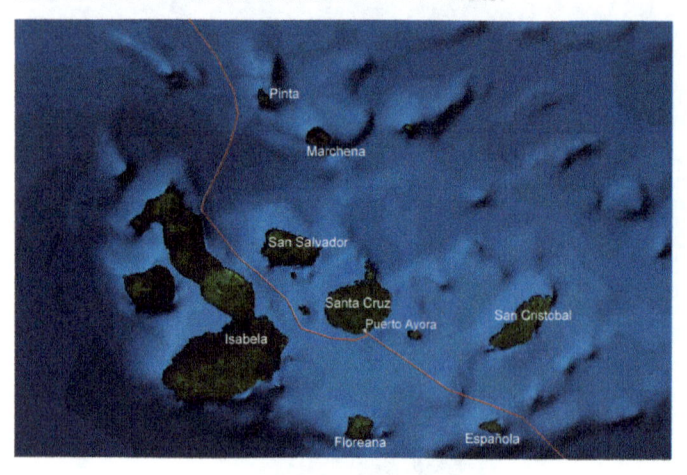

At 2030 we were back into variable winds influenced by the proximity of islands, and these were compounded by the varying currents over shoals and around islands. We flashed-up and motor-sailed until we were finally clear of Isla Española, the last of the Galapagos, and back out into the open South Pacific.

Shortly before sunrise on Thursday we shutdown and sailed. Midmorning, after we had put Isla Española twelve miles back, we struck the Ecuadorian courtesy flag.

Every morning in the tropics, when conditions permit, I take a stroll around the decks to remove the overnight collection of flying fish. If not removed, they quickly begin smelling.

The southerly wind had filled to 12 to 15 knots, and we continued close-hauled down the rhumb line for a couple of hours, making 2 to 2.5 knots into the northwest-setting current and keeping the 4 to 5 metre swell and the building wind waves on our starboard bow. Then as the wind began backing to the southeast, we were forced increasingly to the east, until the Humboldt Current was sweeping us well north of east. We tacked to try the other side, only to find we were beating directly into the 4 to 5 metre swell, which was now confused by wind waves, and the Humboldt was sweeping us too far westward.

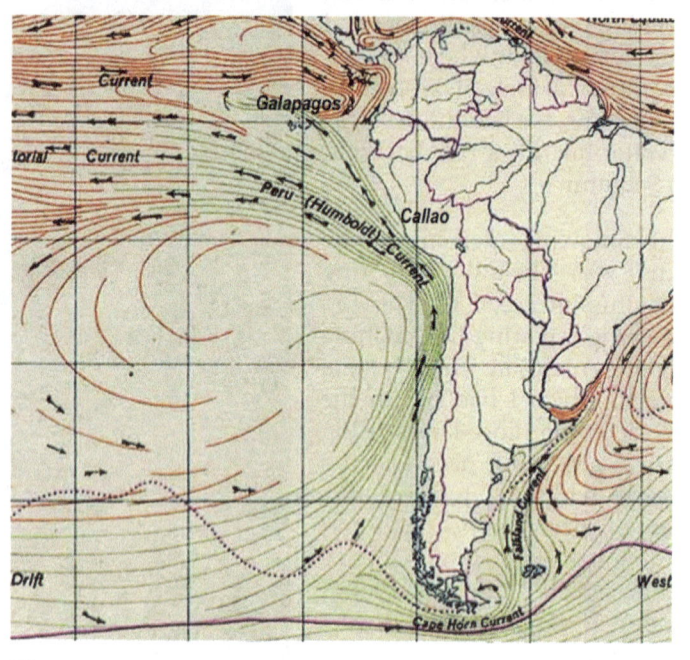

The Humboldt Current sweeps northward off the South American coast, and then it bends to the westward as it nears the Equator. In El Niño years, the Current is greatly diminished, and in some cases, reverses itself and flows slowly southward. The current El Niño cycle was earlier forecast to extend into the summer of 2010; however, I had seen a few mentions of the cycle ending earlier, and I suspected the Current was again running north. I could find no reports on the current state of the Humboldt Current.

Our only viable option was to flash-up and motor directly into the wind and current.

While rolling-in the jib, it jammed. I put on my harness and tethered my way to the bow to try to find out what was amiss, but in the dark with the bows pitching into the seas and swell compounded by some 20 knots of wind over the decks, it was difficult to sort-out. I decided the best bet at the moment was to lower the jib and lash it to the lifelines, which we did.

I left a quarter of the main sail out to serve as a stabilizing fin and we set the Hydrovane to steer our course to the southeast, directly toward Callao. The wind strengthened, and for a while it blew in the 20 to 25 knot range, but then settled in at 15 to 20. With her engine turning at 1800 rpm, Sequitur makes 6.5 knots, but now into the current, the wind and the seas, our hourly runs were in the 2 to 3 mile range. Our first day's run had been 76.6 miles, the second day's was 71.7 miles, the third, 73.8 and the fourth a mere 57.4 miles.

On the second day Edi baked a couple of dozen carrot and raisin muffins, and now that we were again in clean water, I made three hours of water and began a routine of making an hour and a half or two hours of water each morning, to bring the tanks back up to their full marks. The new Balmar alternator was working well, and our batteries were at 100%.

All was well except for the conditions we were in. We were bashing into a 4 to 5 metre southerly swell crossed by 2 to 3 metre southeasterly wind waves and motoring directly into 15 to 25 knot winds and against a 2.5 to 3 knot ocean current. Sequitur is normally a very stable boat in a seaway, but this combination of wind, wave and swell had us rolling and pitching uncomfortably. To compound matters, the weather was mostly overcast with heavy mist and occasional rain showers.

By Sunday afternoon, day five of our passage, we began thinking of alternate plans. If we continued on as we were, bashing into the wind, the seas and the current, we would run out of fuel before reaching Peru. We knew that whatever we did, if we wanted to get to Peru, we needed to get across the Humboldt. We could sail as close to the eastward as the wind would allow and let the current sweep us northward to the Ecuadorian coast. Alternatively, we could motor and motorsail across as quickly as possible by steering a course that would track us east to the northern coast of Peru, but we might not have sufficient fuel for this. Another option would be to continue motoring southeastward until we reached a point from which we could set a starboard tack and sail close-hauled across to the Peruvian coast at Ensenada Bayovar or Bahia de Paita. We chose the latter.

We continued motoring into the wind, seas and current, taking any eastings we could as we bashed our way toward 5° South, trying to balance keeping the engine at an economical speed while still making headway. We clawed and bashed southeastward at 2.2 to 2.5 miles per hour through Sunday and into Monday morning, when the hourly runs began creeping up: 2.65, 2.87, 2.97, and then at 0100 on Tuesday morning we finally got an hour's run of 3.015 miles, our first above 3 knots in several days.

The hourly runs steadily increased, and at 1100 on Tuesday, in latitude 04° 40' South, we had our first hour above 4 knots. I hauled-out the staysail and a third of the main and we turned eastward to motorsail just below the edge of the luff on the starboard tack.

In the early afternoon I went forward to sort-out and re-hoisted the jib. I had resolved its furling problem to it having picked-up the spinnaker halyard, which I had carelessly left with too much of a dip in it, and the jib had tried to wrap it while furling.

At 0200 on Wednesday the 26th we were finally back up to over 5 knots, with an hour's run of 5.052 miles. At 0645 on Wednesday morning we set the jib, staysail and main out full, shutdown the engine and continued to the east at 4.5 knots on a starboard tack in a 9 to 12 knot southeast breeze. The sky was mostly overcast with light cumulus beneath a broad layer of stratocumulus, the barometer was steady at 1018 and the temperature was 21.8.

We were then within 200 miles of the coast of Peru, and we were required to report to Tramar at 0800 and 2000 each day, giving reports of our position, course, speed, destination and ETA. We received no response to any of our twice-daily contact attempts, each of which included at least three calls.

By late on Wednesday afternoon the wind was down to 5-6 knots and we were down to about 2. Shortly before sunset we rolled-in the jib, hardened the staysail, and shortened-in and hardened the main and motorsailed. Our fuel was getting down; I had transferred half the contents of the auxiliary tank to the main tank, which was now showing one quarter full. This, I calculated to be about 275 litres remaining, which should be good for 55 hours of motoring at 1600 rpm. For the remainder of the day we consistently made hourly runs in the upper 4-knot and lower 5-knot range.

Shortly after midnight, when eighty miles off the coast of Peru we rather suddenly ran into a fog bank and completely out of wind. My first indication of the loss of the wind was when Hydra started steering us erratically. There was no swell, no wind waves, just flat water and fog. We were definitely out of the Humboldt Current.

I rolled-in the sails and we continued motoring east. Now with the relative wind from our motion alone, particularly since it was made turbulent as it passed over the boat, Hydra could not maintain a course. Compounding this was Otto, our Raymarine autopilot continued to suffer from *"Drive Stopped"* errors, and would not hold a course. We had to hand steer.

It was glassy calm, very damp and rather cold. To keep warm I had to put on fleece long underwear bottoms, a fleece jacket, some socks and a medium weight foul-weather jacket with the hood up. This was the first time in months that I had worn clothing at sea for other than entering or leaving port. We also buttoned and zipped-up the entire cockpit enclosure. It was a cold night, particularly considering we were within 5 degrees of the equator, and at sea level.

With the lightening of dawn came the view of the inside of a fog bank, with visibility less than half a cable. By 0815 a combination of the sun's heat and a building east-southeast breeze dispersed the fog, revealing a sky almost totally overcast with thin stratus. As the day warmed, we were able to peel off some layers of clothing and the strengthening breeze allowed me to set-up the Hydrovane to again steer our course. We relaxed from hand steering.

Shortly after noon, while some 20 miles from the port of Paita, we began meeting small wooden fishing boats, which didn't paint on radar until 2 to 3 miles away, and even then intermittently. At first there were a few close by, then a dozen and before long we were in the midst of several dozens of them.

As we picked our way through the fleet and in toward Paita, there was a steady stream of little boats coming out around the headland. There were hundreds of them, chugging to sea in the middle of the afternoon.

We hoisted the quarantine flag as we crossed the 12-mile line and worked our way into Bahia de Paita against the steady stream of fishing boats coming out.

At 1620 we came to 24 metres on the Rocna in 8 metres of water a cable or so away from the outer end of several huge raft-ups of fishing boats.

With all the boats that had streamed out past us during the previous few hours, it amazed us that there were still hundreds left. We reported our arrival to Tramar, the Capitan de Puerto and the Guardia Costera on the VHF, all with no response, and by the time we shut down and secured, it was so late in the afternoon that we decided to remain onboard until morning, and to begin our clearing-in formalities then.

There were many hundreds of small wooden boats, some open and some with tiny cabins. Most appeared to have half-a-dozen or more crew aboard, and on most of the boats, they appeared to be living aboard, with very little or no shelter and no facilities. The water in the harbour was full of flotsam and jetsam. We watched as people threw their garbage into the water, and at one point saw a pair of cheeks hung over the side. Who needs a bucket?

At 0900 on Friday the 28th we left Sequitur in the anchorage and took the dinghy through the moored fishing fleet to the pier to find out how and where to begin the formalities. On the way in we had to weave between all the flotsam, which included empty oil cans, empty drink containers, discarded oily rags, dozens of plastic bags. The harbour easily made its way to the top of our list as the filthiest we had ever seen, just above Puerto Ayora, Galapagos.

We arrived at the pier and secured our dinghy to the float on its east side, and then we walked along the long pier to its head, where we saw the Oficiana de Tourisme. We went in and asked where we could find the Capitania de Puerto and whether they knew the check-in procedure. A couple of phone calls were made and we were asked to come back at 1300 for an appointment with someone who could help us.

We hadn't yet had breakfast; we had brought our computers ashore with us with the intention of finding an internet cafe. We asked for the location of some, but no one in the office was familiar with the concept of internet cafes, but we were told that there were many internet shops in the centre of town, off to our left. We asked where we could find a restaurant for breakfast, and were directed to the west side of town, to our right.

We headed off, stopping at an ATM outside a bank. There was a lineup of eight or ten people for the two machines, so we joined it. We were quickly promoted up the line all the way to the front. The PIN view guards were broken off to afford a better view; it appears that most, if not all the people in the lineup were criminals-in-waiting, watching for an opportunity. We withdrew some Peruvian Soles at an exchange rate of about 2.7 to the Canadian dollar, and then we continued on our way in search of a place to have breakfast.

After zigging and zagging and crisscrossing the western side of town without seeing any sign of any restaurants, we eventually back-tracked to the centre of town, passing again the pink fire hall and what we called *"the Leaning Tower of Paita"*. Shortly beyond there we began seeing internet shops and restaurants, The restaurants were all very basic, and most had no customers. Using our rule of local patronage, we entered one that had a few people in it, but we soon saw that the people in it were not diners, but local women comparing their shopping finds with the staff. None of the staff took any interest in us.

We went back to a place we had seen earlier that had two of its dozen or so tables occupied. From the menu we ordered the most expensive breakfast: grilled fish, two pieces of bread, juice and coffee. The juice that arrived was unidentifiable, and Edi couldn't get beyond the first sip of hers and I couldn't finish mine. The coffee was a cup of tepid water and a small cruet of mate syrup, there was a basket with four bread rolls placed on the table and we were served plates with a tiny piece of grilled fish, no more than 8 x 5 x 1 centimetres in size, accompanied by a thin slice of tomato on a few scrawny greens. This was the deluxe breakfast for 5 Soles, about $1.85.Canadian. The meal easily surpassed the previous worst we had ever had, and it was apparently their finest offering. The restaurant fully deserves our four-thumbs-down award. We would have gladly have paid much more for a proper breakfast, but we could find none available in Paita.

We went off to select an internet booth. The first few we tried could not comprehend the concept of our having our own computers, and they were unable to accommodate our wish to plug-in to their connection. Nowhere could we find any shop with wifi, and finally we settled on balancing my computer on a keyboard drawer and having the proprietor root around behind the station's computer to dig out the ethernet cable for me to plug into my laptop. By the time we had done our emails, and I had downloaded the 180-hour wind and sea state charts, it was time to head back to our 1300 appointment.

Back in the Tourist Office we were met by a small delegation, and with them we walked over to City Hall and were escorted past the guards and up the stairs to meet with the assistant to the Mayor, Ricardo Griva. He spoke rather good English, and from him we learned that the delegation accompanying us was composed of Tourist Office employees who were trying to learn what to do with visiting boaters. It seemed we were the first sailboat to visit in a long time.

Once Roberto was apprised of our need to clear into Peru with Migracion, Aduana, Capitan de Puerto and whoever else wanted a piece of the bureaucratic action, he took us across the city's central square to the Capitania. There he arranged a meeting with the Capitan de Puerto, who told us we needed to go to the Autoridad Portuaria Nacional. Roberto escorted us through another square and along the narrow streets for ten or twelve blocks to the APN, and introduced us to the Jefe de Oficina, Luis Antonio Bodero Coelho.

Luis spoke no English, but had a passable command of French, so we communicated in French. He told us we needed an agent to do our clearing-in process, and he called one for us. He also told us that Customs wanted us to leave town immediately we cleared in, because we had not informed them in advance of our arrival. I told him we had tried without response to contact the Tramar and Guardia Costera daily at 0800 and 2000 since our crossing into the 200-mile zone of Peru. Luis intervened for us on the telephone with the Customs bureaucrat; there was a very heated, agitated and loud interchange. Finally, at the end of a long shouting match and after calling the fellow an *"idioto"*, he hung-up in disgust.

We had told Luis that the purpose of our visit to Paita was to refuel, and we asked him for his recommendation of a fuelling facility. He called Roberto Guzman Amayo, the manager of the fuel barge, Chata Tamy, and within twenty minutes Roberto arrived. He spoke excellent English and told us his diesel cost 10.80 Soles per US gallon, which converts to about $1.05 Canadian per litre. We discovered his barge was moored only a couple of cables from Sequitur in the anchorage, and we arranged to refuel the next afternoon. They took only cash, so we would need to raid the bank machines with our collection of cards to get sufficient to pay.

Liliana Huancayo, the driving force behind the clearance agency, Port Logistics arrived and was introduced to us. She outlined to us the process we must follow to be cleared-in, and went over the details of its cost, which was US$983. This was for port fees, Customs fees, Immigration fees, sanitation fees, her fees and fees to whomever else had managed to find a way to extort money from visiting boaters. These had to be paid in US dollars, cash only. We had seen earlier in the day that the bank machines dispense your choice of Soles or US dollars, but with low daily limits on our cards, we needed to do a counter transaction.

Liliana flagged a motocab, a small motorcycle with a rickshaw carriage as its rear end, and we squeezed in to be bounced, joggled and shimmied through the crowded streets to the local branch of Scotia Bank. Inside, we finally persuaded a teller to get a supervisor to get an accountant to process a US$1,000 withdrawal. We squeezed into another motocab and were jostled up the hill to Liliana's office, which is the front room of her house.

She sat at her computer, juggled two cell phones, a land line and a walkie-talkie as she filled and printed forms. An hour or so into this process, an Immigration officer arrived and from his canvas bag brought out blank forms, rubber stamps and ink pads. He stamped forms he had filled-out by hand, including visas, plus forms Liliana gave him, and who knows what all. Then he left.

Next came the official from the Ministerio de Salud, and he and Liliana had a long discussion, after which he began filling-out multi-copy forms from two pads in his binder. When he had completed the forms, but before he signed and stamped them, Liliana asked me for the $983 and from it paid the sanitation officer for his pretending to visit our boat and conduct an agricultural, pest, vermin and health inspection of it. He pocketed, signed, stamped, smiled and left.

Liliana then generated and printed another bunch of forms, and we piled into a motocab and hurtled down the hill, back to the APN office. By this time it was nearly 1730, and we sat waiting as a uniformed official hunted-and-pecked his way through an online form, inputting data from our Ship Registry certificate, our Radio Station License, our passports and from the forms that Liliana had given him. When he had finally completed the online form, he hit *"clear"* instead of *"print"*. It was 1830, and the receptionist and file clerk were waiting to leave as the official began again completing the online form. He told the women they could shutdown the office and go home.

Just short of 1900, when he had again completed the form, he tried to print it only to realize that the office intranet had been shutdown. The staff was gone and he didn't know how to turn the system back on. We were asked to come back the next day.

Liliana's husband, Santiago escorted us back down to the waterfront and out the pier, where we were introduced to a boatman, and were told he would taxi us out to Sequitur and bring us back in the morning. We told him we had a dinghy secured to the float at the end of the pier, and to illustrate our limited Spanish, we walked over to the edge to look down on the dinghy and point it out to him. The dinghy wasn't there.

We did a thorough search, in case someone had moved it out of the way, but found no trace of it. We asked some of the boaters and standers-by if they had seen it and Santiago asked around, all with no positive results. As we headed back in the pier and walked along to the Capitania to report the theft, Santiago called Liliana by cell phone, and she met us at the guarded gates. We were given access, trading our driver's licenses for passes, and shortly were received by a young Coast Guard lieutenant with very good English. I had him note the theft of the dinghy and its motor, and he agreed to my suggestion that I return in the morning with a detailed written report.

We walked back to the pier with Liliana and Santiago and as we went, reorganized the next day. We were taxied back out to Sequitur, arriving shortly after 2100 drained of energy and with our moods tainted by the events of the day. Added to that, we were thirsty and hungry, having had nothing to eat or drink except for the pitiful little breakfast so many hours before. We were disappointed by the lack of facilities for visitors, saddened by atmosphere of crime in the town, and although there were some bright lights, overall we were disgusted by the official incompetence and corruption.

Back onboard, I prepared tarragon chicken with basmati rice and butter-sweated carrots, onions and poblanos and we made our way through a bottle of Bolger Petit Syrah and snifters of Torres brandy, trying to replenish our bodies and drain our disappointments. I then sat down at the computer and started to write a report on the theft of the dinghy and motor.

On Saturday morning I finished writing the report, complete with inserted photos of the dinghy and its motor. I printed three copies and we went up to the cockpit to have breakfast and to wait for our boat to the pier. Daylight showed us that Sequitur had been stripped of various deck accessories. These were most likely taken while we were ashore on Friday. Among the things missing were the life ring, the automatic lifebuoy light, the boat hooks and the universal deck tool handle. Fortunately, the life-raft, the stern line reel, the sail sheets and the second and third anchors were still in place.

Thirty-five minutes after it was due, the workboat arrived, and the skipper wound us through the filthy harbour past the polluting boats.

We passed ongoing repairs, some of which looked like late attempts to stave-off dereliction.

After the skipper picked-up a giant squid from a fishing boat, he deposited us at the foot of a ladder at the end of the pier, and we walked to the head, where we were to meet Liliana. While Edi waited there, I headed to the Capitania to tender the report, and was told they would compose an official letter to attach to it, which would take half an hour. I could wait or come back, so I headed back over to the pier to join Edi in waiting for Liliana's 1000 rendezvous with us.

Shortly after 1100, with still no Liliana, we went back over to the Capitania to pick-up my copy of the official signed and stamped letter and attached report.

We then walked over to the APN office to see whether the form from the previous afternoon and evening had finally been printed. The uniformed minion phoned Liliana for us, and shortly Santiago arrived and with him we jostled up the hill in a motocab to Liliana's office, where she was in the throes of creating even more paperwork for our file. As we waited, Liliana's son, Felix came out to the office from the back of the house, and was introduced to us.

Felix is twenty-three years old and is part-way through an engineering degree in computer science at the University in Piura, fifty or so kilometres inland from Paita. At the same time, he is teaching IT programs. His English is limited, but we were able to carry-on a very pleasant discussion with him while Liliana worked at the computer. He is a highly enthusiastic and spirited young man, with a gentle soul; it was refreshing to meet him.

The previous day we had told Liliana that we needed to buy fresh produce, and she said she would take us to the local market. So, after she had finished her latest paperwork, Edi and I piled into a motocab with her and we were off on another race through the streets. We bounced up a street lined with nonstop rows of ramshackle market stalls for what seemed half a kilometre, and then we turned into a narrow lane lined with slightly less flimsy stalls and corrugated tin roofs. We passed a couple of obvious entrances, and stopped at a third.

Liliana told us to sling our backpacks around to the front and hold them tightly as she led us into the market. She took us past many fruit stalls without stopping or even slowing, and then presented us at the front of a very fine selection. With the assistance of her translation, the stall owner dug out firm, slightly green produce from under the tables and we had soon built a substantial pile of avocados, mangoes, kiwis, mandarins, miniature bananas and a big papaya, The total came to 11 Soles, about $4.

Liliana then led us through the passages to another 'building' that appeared to be mostly vegetable stalls. We bypassed dozens of good looking ones before she brought us to a halt in front of her favourite. Again she engaged the owner to assist us in picking-out a nice selection, including carrots, tomatoes, green and red peppers, peas in the pod and a couple of varieties of small new potatoes. He threw in a couple of small red peppers, and when I asked him if they were *"caliente"*, he nodded, but indicated not excessively so.

We loaded ourselves and our produce into a motocab and trundled back down the hill, and across and up to Liliana's office, where we picked-up some documents and bounced our way back down to the APN office. Liliana took the now finally printed form from the previous afternoon and evening's episode and sat at an office computer apparently to generate and print yet another document from it. This was duly signed and stamped.

With this we took a motocab back up the hill to the office and sat chatting with Felix while Liliana punched away at the computer, causing it to generate even more paper. Then with Felix and me in one and Liliana and Edi in another motocab, we chicaned our way back down the hill to the centre of town, and stopped in front of a bank so Edi and I could use our cards again to extract sufficient additional Soles to pay for the fuel. Again, there was a lineup in front of the two machines, and again we were quickly promoted by the robbers-in-waiting up the line to near its head.

With our stash of Soles secured, we hopped back into the waiting cabs and went to the head of the pier. Liliana and Felix accompanied us as we walked out the pier, and for the workboat ride out to Sequitur, so we invited them aboard for a visit. While the workboat waited, we shared coffee and a small platter of cheeses and sliced salami.

When I asked Liliana if we were now free to leave, she said no, there was still more paper; we still needed our zarpe. It would be brought out to us only after we had finished fuelling. It seems the belligerent Customs official wanted to ensure that we did in fact need fuel. Apparently, he was still miffed by our arriving in Paita unannounced, even although we had called to both Tramar and to the Guardia Costera twice daily, as required since we entered the 200-mile zone. It seems it was our fault that they had not replied to any of our VHF and SSB radio calls.

Liliana and Felix took the workboat back in to the pier and Edi and I prepared Sequitur for sea. At 1522 we weighed and motored the two cables or so over to the fuel barge Tamy to refuel. The anchor came up fouled with several pieces of line, a piece of net, a length of rubber hose and clumps of seaweed. I left the anchor a-cock-bill as we slowly stemmed the 18 knot wind and ebbing tide and approached Tamy while timing her swing on her mooring. Tamy is only 7 or 8 metres in length, and since our diesel fills are both on the starboard side aft, we secured with half our length beyond the fuel barge, and with our mooring lines straining in the wind we twisted Tamy on her mooring. This seemed of no concern to the barge operator.

We took on 184.6 US gallons (698 litres) of diesel for 1994 Soles and then at 1610 slipped our lines and went back over to the anchorage to await the arrival of our zarpe. While we were letting go the anchor, as we put the transmission astern the engine quit. I attempted to restart it, but it would not cooperate. The wind was strong enough to give us sufficient sternway, so using the wind we came to 25 metres on the Rocna in 8.4 metres of water.

Once I was satisfied of the security of our anchorage, I began to troubleshoot the engine problem. There was no electricity to the keyed start switch. I tried the batteries. The multi-meter showed that both the engine and the generator start batteries were well-charged, and that their selection and combining switches worked. There was current to the starter. I was in the throes of digging into the wiring behind the start switch when a workboat arrived with Liliana and a couple of uniformed men with the zarpe.

I told Liliana we couldn't start the engine, and we unable to leave until we could resolve the problem. I continued to troubleshoot for nearly an hour without much progress. I needed assistance and told Liliana I needed an electrician. By this time it was nearly 1900, and she phoned to organize one for the next morning, Sunday. Then she, the two uniforms and the unsigned zarpe left in the workboat.

At 0820 on Sunday morning Liliana arrived in a workboat with an electrician and his assistant, and I quickly introduced the situation to them. They began a systematic run through the cables and wiring harnesses, and by 1140 had tracked-down a loose connection behind the main distribution panel, restored it and I was able to restarted the engine. We then tested the systems a couple of times to ensure all was well.

I then went ashore in the workboat with the Liliana and the electricians so that I could do yet another run on the bank card to pay for the work. Liliana led us to a bank machine, where there was the usual milling group of criminals-in-waiting, and I withdrew some more US dollars. At Liliana's direction, I paid the electrician's agent or manager US140 for the more than three hours of work plus travel time on a Sunday morning. The electrician was a very skilled and diligent worker, and by North American standards, I considered his fee to be a bargain, the only bargain we had seen here.

We were met at the bank machine by Liliana's son Felix, and the three of us climbed into a motocab and bounced up the streets to a bakery. On Saturday I had mentioned to Felix that it was Edi's birthday; he had ordered a cake, and we were there to pick it up. While Liliana went off to generate more paper, Felix and I, with cake box in hand took a motocab back down to the waterfront, clambered down the ladder to the workboat and headed back out to Sequitur.

Edi and Felix and I spent a delightful hour and more chatting, sharing much more than just the coffee and cake. Felix is such a lively spirit, but we fear that with his openness and enthusiasm, and his rather apparent innocence, he will quickly be taken advantage of. We suggested he needs to travel outside of Peru, that he needs to gain a different perspective of the world. A few months in London, for instance, to polish his English would do wonders for his education. His eyes lit-up at these suggestions; possibly a seed has been planted.

At 1310 Liliana arrived with two uniformed men, and after a brief signing session, we were issued our zarpe. We were now free to leave Paita and continue on to Callao. Free that is, once I had paid the workboat owner for his water taxi service. He asked for US$240, and I enquired at how he had come to such a figure. A long discussion ensued and I eventually gave him $98. We bade farewell to Liliana and Felix, and turned to preparing Sequitur for the 500-mile passage to Callao.

We had arrived in Paita enchanted by the aliveness, the vibrancy and the colour of the fishing fleet. Enchanted by the hustle and bustle of the community of hundreds of boats rafted together in lines of a dozen, two dozen or more, row upon row, each boat with its crew of six or eight cleaning themselves and their boat from the trip just ended, or preparing for the one to shortly come. We left seeing dens of thieves and offices of organized extortionists hiding behind their bureaucratic positions.

The city of Paita has a population of 55,000 or 60,000, but as far as we could see, we were the only foreign visitors in town; we were certainly the only visiting sailboat. The lack of visitors is most likely because there are no facilities for outsiders, and that there are no facilities is likely an extension of the city's uninviting atmosphere. We felt preyed-upon, we felt used, we felt that we were seen only as owners of money to extort and of goods and equipment to steal. The history of Paita shows that in the seventeenth and eighteenth centuries it was a favourite haven for pirates, and to us they have not yet left.

At 1345 on Sunday the 30th of May we weighed. I watched the Rocna come up with a huge tangle of discarded lines and nets, which I cut away. As we engaged the transmission to begin motoring out of Bahia de Paita I thought for a while we were aground. The propeller was turning, but we were making no progress. The depth gauge showed we were in about 9 metres of water, and we were moving up and down in the slow swell, so we couldn't be aground. I finally concluded we must have run over the slowly sinking mass of lines and nets that I had cut free from the anchor, and we had somehow snagged them, and they were attached to junk on the sea bed.

I shifted to neutral and paused, hoping to let things fall off. Then I shifted astern to hopefully unwind a bit, then neutral again and forward through a few cycles until we began making a bit of headway. It felt like we were still dragging stuff, but as compromised as we were, the thought of remaining in Paita among the filth and corruption was worse than the thought of heading out on a 500-mile passage somewhat disabled.

11. Limping to Lima

The boat sailed as if we were towing a drogue. I rolled in the sails and we motored southward making 2 knots over the ground. We needed to clear Punta Foca, and then transit the broad mouth of Ensenada de Sechura and round its southerly point, Punta Tur some 50 miles south before we could shape a course directly toward Callao, the seaport of Lima.

At 2000 we contacted Costera Paita on VHF to tender our mandatory twice-daily report, making three attempts with no response. As the wind continued backing, I hauled out the staysail and a piece of the main and we picked-up a bit of speed, making good about 3.5 knots motorsailing. The moon rose at 2102 and lit the horizons. Fortunately, its light showed no fishing boats. We assumed that they do not go fishing on Sundays.

At 1350 I reported our departure to Tramar and Costera Paita, with no response. By 1430 we had worked our way out into a southerly breeze blowing around the headland, and I rolled out the main and jib, shutdown the engine and we sailed westward at about 4.5 knots to clear the point and to stand off the coast a safe distance before bending our course to the southeast toward Callao.

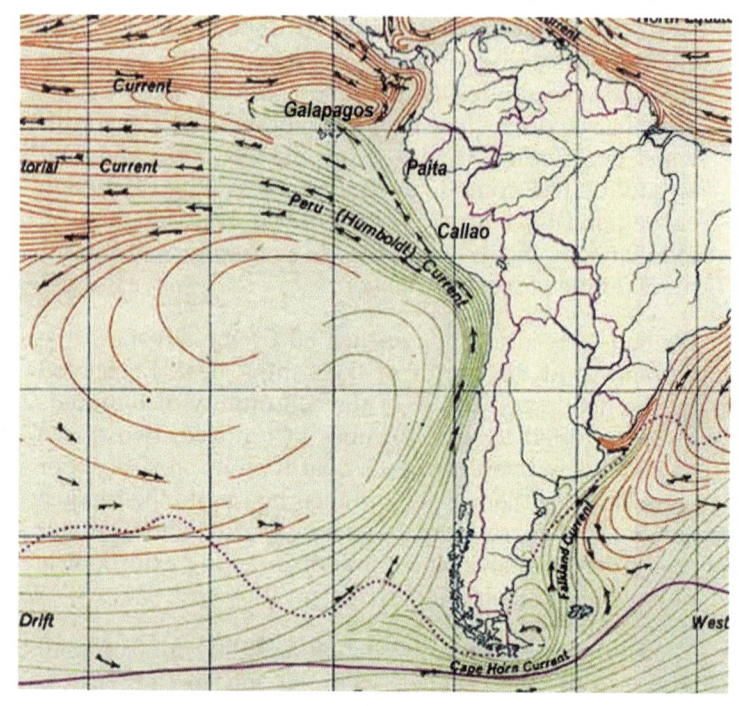

At 1653 Costera Paita contacted us on VHF and asked for our ETD from Paita. I told them we had already departed at 1345, and added that we had reported that fact to them at 1350, 1355, 1430 and 1500, all without response from them. They did not respond to this information.

At 1803 we tacked and came close-hauled into the 12 to 15 knot southerly wind to make good 110° at about 4.5 knots as we were skewed eastward by the Humboldt Current. The wind continued to back and we gradually found ourselves with a northerly component to our track and we were too quickly closing the coast. We tried the port tack, but the wind and current conspired to set us too far to the west, and it threw-in a slight northerly component. We could not sail any southings against the Humboldt Current.

At 2125 Costera Paita contacted us on VHF and asked for our position, course, speed and ETA Callao. They deal almost entirely with large commercial shipping, and they had difficulty comprehending an ETA of over a week for the trip. They had difficulty understanding that we were sailing and were at the mercy of the winds and the currents.

On Monday morning as we were beating into an 18 to 20 knot wind, I noticed that the port after foot of the solar array arch had worked its mounting bolts loose, and there was a gap between its pad and the hull. It appears that the yard in Vancouver had simply screwed it in place, rather than using bolts, nuts and backing plates. This is just one more reason for our growing disenchantment with the quality of the work done on Sequitur's fit-out.

I eased our course, and just before the screws pulled out, I lashed the arch down to the stern cleat using a length of spectra. This stabilized the arch and eased our minds a bit.

We continued to motor-sail between south and south-southwest as the winds and currents dictated, making good 3 to 4 knots. By noon on Monday we had made 84.67 miles over the ground, and had made 52 miles toward Callao. At 0900 on Tuesday we were contacted on VHF by Jim and Linda in an Outbound 46 out of San Francisco, who had been watching us on their AIS receiver. They were about three miles to the north of us, en route from La Libertad, Ecuador to Callao.

We could eyeball them, but their boat did not paint on our radar. We chatted on the radio for a quarter hour, and then over the next few hours watched as they slowly overtook us, passing within a couple of cables down our starboard side and then sailed off over the horizon to the south. Even at two cables range they only intermittently painted on our radar. We were later to find out that they refused to carry an AIS transmitter or a radar reflector, thinking it dangerous for them to be seen by other boats.

Our second day's run was 65.24 miles made good and we had made another 45.5 miles toward Callao. Our third day's scores were 67.83 made good and 33.5 toward Callao. The fourth day they were 88.14 made good and 62 toward Callao. On the afternoon of the fifth day Edi baked three loaves of bread, and the next morning she made a wonderful omelet, which she served with a fresh tomato salsa, toast and coffee.

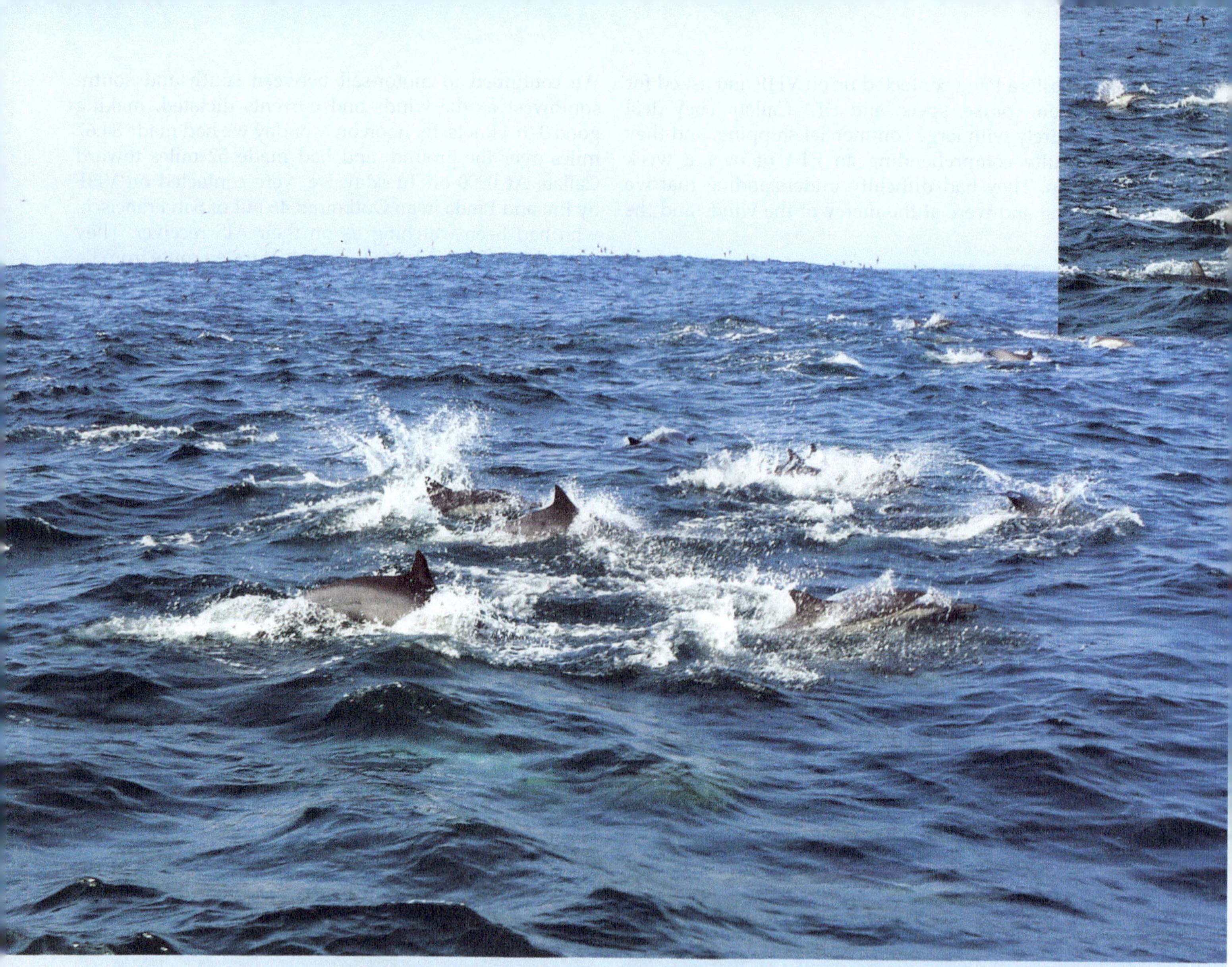

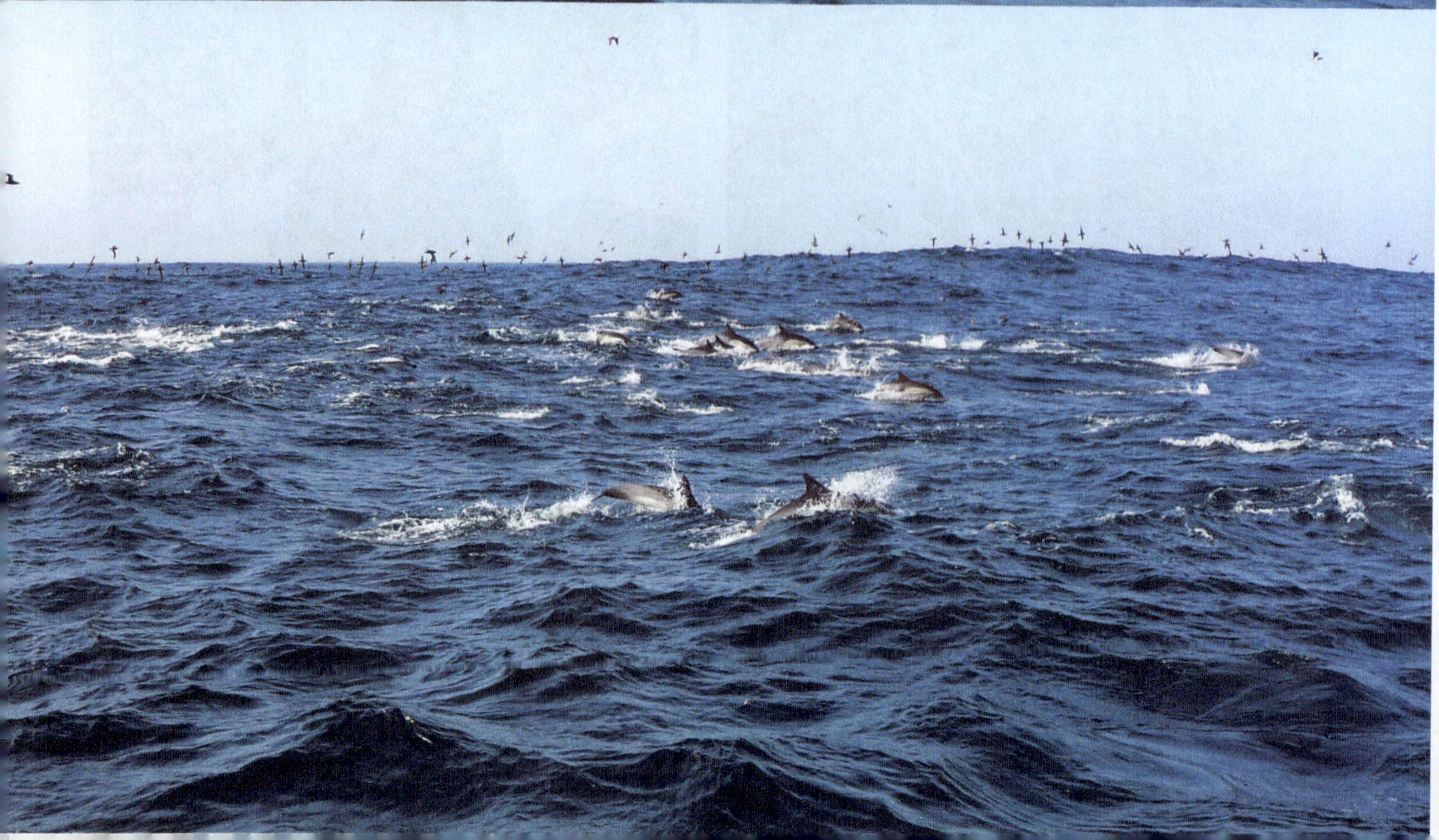

I made water for an hour or so each day to slowly bring our tanks up to the full mark and to keep the membrane fresh. We continued to attempt reports to Tramar and Guardia Costera at 0800 and 2000 each day, but received no response to our three or four calls at each report time.

Noon on Friday the 4th, our fifth day found us with a day's run made good of 96.11 miles and another 64.5 miles closer to Callao. Saturday, our sixth day gave us 79.03 over the ground and 56.5 miles closer to Callao. On Friday morning we had seen whales swim past, hundreds of dolphins and thousands of pelicans. The pelicans came cruising by in a series of squadrons of fifty to a hundred, and seemed to just keep on coming like the playing of a continuous loop video.

On Saturday afternoon we watched the dolphins do a fish ball-up close off our port side. While squadrons of pelicans and boobies provided air cover, the dolphins swam and leaped in coordination to encircle a buffet of fresh fish for all to feed on.

Sunday at noon we were another 64 miles closer to Callao, and at noon on Monday, after eight days and another 63 miles toward Callao, we were left with only 49 miles to go. Shortly after noon, the wind completely died and the Hydrovane lost its input, so still being without the main autopilot, we had to begin hand steering.

At 1415 I used our satellite phone to call Jaime Ackermann at the Yacht Club Peruano in Callao and gave him an ETA of 0200 on Tuesday morning. He told us they were in the process of installing additional moorings, but had none available for us for a few days. He asked us to anchor at the edge of the mooring field.

At 1532, after a few false ripples, a very slight breeze came-up, only 2 or 3 knots, but sufficient to allow Hydra to takeover the steering from us. At 1925, as we reached the 20-mile line from Callao, we called Tramar on VHF and they responded, asking for our ship name, then when we gave it, we received no further communication from them. At 2000 we called both Tramar and Costera Callao three times each, with no response.

As we entered the harbour of Callao, the light pollution from the city of Callao, refracted and reflected by the low overcast gave very clear illumination, making much easier our approach through the very crowded anchorage.

At 0146 on Tuesday the 8th of June we came to 25 metres on the Rocna in 10 metres of water at the outer edge of the mooring field of the Yacht Club Peruano in La Punta, Callao. As we approached the anchorage, we were shadowed by a workboat, and immediately we had secured, it came alongside. There was one man on board, and he requested we contact Tramar on VHF channel 68. We did so with no response. Over the next ten minutes we tried four more times before receiving a reply. Finally with someone on the other end of the radio, we gave our ship's particulars.

At 0205, satisfied, the workboat departed to allow us to secure for the night. It had been a long passage from Paita. It had taken us eight-and-a-half days, bucking directly into both the wind and the Humboldt Current and dragging a collection of nets and lines in our undercarriage; we were tired. After we had again checked on the security of our anchor set, shutdown the systems and locked-up, we fell into bed.

We slept until nearly 1100. We were having coffee and I was about to contact Jaime Ackermann on VHF to organize our arrival and stay at the Yacht Club Peruano, when Jaime arrived off our stern in a launch. We invited him aboard and shared our tales of Paita and our passage down the coast, complete with the lack of response to our communications. He understood it all; he said pleasure boaters should never go into Paita, and our radio contact experiences were true to pattern. We arranged to meet with him in his office mid-afternoon to do the formalities.

Mid-afternoon we called a launch on VHF and were picked-up from Sequitur and deposited at the yacht club float. Jaime met us and showed us around the facilities on the pier and introduced us to Chef Frano in the tastefully appointed dining room, which is marvellously situated with floor-to-ceiling windows looking out from the end of the pier.

We followed Jaime to his office and after he had reviewed our papers, he told us that, even although it had cost us more than four times the appropriate rate, we had not been cleared into Peru by Paita. We still needed to clear-in, and to do so we needed an agent. Because of the abuse we had received in Paita, he said he would do the clearance himself, he would act as our agent, and his fee was a beer. We liked his price. We gave him our papers and walked with him to the bank machine to withdraw some Soles to pay the 550 for the necessary sanitation inspection, and an additional 46 Soles for the Customs/Immigration fee.

We walked back out the pier, where Chef Frano welcomed us into the restaurant and showed us to a corner table. We discussed his menu with him. Edi had a craving for scallops, and he suggested he broil some for us with Parmesan cheese. We asked him what next and he said he would prepare a ceviche and then follow it with a lomo saltado, a sautéed beef tenderloin dish. We selected a bottle of Chilean chardonnay and had a splendid meal, with Frano commuting back and forth between the kitchen and our table, and providing a very personal service. We still had a tad of room left after the lomo saltado, and he recommended a causa rellena with crab, and off he went to prepare it.

While he was in the kitchen, Jim and Linda walked into the dining room. They are the couple aboard the Outbound 46 with whom we had spoken on the radio on our way south from Paita. We talked briefly with them and as our final dish arrived, we agreed to chat later and they went off to their table.

After a fully satisfying dinner, and wonderful conversations with Frano, we went into the lounge to flash-up our laptops and get the password to log into the Club's wifi connection. Jim and Linda joined us after their dinner, but the facilities on the pier were being closed for the evening, so we all headed down to the float to catch a launch back out to our boats. Jim and Linda were on their way to visit with Herb and Bev in The Lady J, and we stopped there on our way to Sequitur. Herb and Bev asked if we would like to join them, so we stopped there.

Herb and Bev are in an Ocean Trader trawler, and they had arrived with it from Florida in July 2006, and they have been moored at Yacht Club Peruano ever since. We spent a few delightful hours listening to them tell of their adventures coming down the coast, of traveling inland and of living in La Punta, Callao.

Of the stories Herb and Bev had of their journey, the most interesting and germane to us was of their experiences in Paita on their arrival in Peru in 2005. It was so bizarre that we later had Herb write it down for us.

It started about 300 miles off of the coast of Ecuador, right about even with the Peruvian, Ecuadorian border. We hit a net which completely wrapped itself around both our rudders. It was at night, and our speed reduced slightly for a few seconds as our props cut through it. The rpms went back to normal so I thought we were okay. I knew we were trailing some of the net as I could see it, but since we were on auto pilot and following a straight course I was unaware of the damage to out steering system until the next morning when I went to alter course. We have mechanical steering and the cable tighteners had both stripped out. I could steer with the emergency tiller, but I could not see where I was going as the emergency tiller is in the lazarette, so I steered with Bev on the bridge shouting directions to me. The closest port was Pita so we made for it.

When we got close we radioed the Coast Guard station and advised them of our problem an asked for assistance in coming into port. They sent a small patrol boat to tow us in, and they tied us up to the naval base dock there. I had new tighteners custom made an installed, and we were ready to go however, during overnight at 0230 we were boarded by pirates who had tied a panga up to the outboard side of our boat. I heard them on the cabin deck, opened the hatch saw them, shouted to Bev, "bring me my pistolos". There were two pirates on the boat and one in the panga; the two on the boat jumped into the panga, and they made their getaway. They had been trying to get into our electronics, but didn't; however they did get about a hundred dollars worth of equipment.

This brings me to the second part of the story: In Piata there are two competing authorities, the Naval base commander, and the Port Captain. The guard on the dock was attached to the Port Captain, but the dock belonged to the Armada base. The Armada commander was a nice fellow, while the Captain of the Port was an Asshole. The commander had the guard arrested, and he was scheduled to be court martialed. He was probably in cahoots with the pirates, however we never learned the outcome.

The Captain was also told to reimburse us for the value of the items stolen, about $100. The Captain was furious, and he immediately told me that he was fining us $25,000 dollars for entering the Port of Pita without his permission, even though he was the one who dispatched the tow boat which had brought us in. I demanded a hearing, and a full blown hearing was convened the next morning The panel was made up of three officers from the Port Captain's office, three from the Naval base and a seventh from the city of Pita. We were found innocent.

After a wonderful evening of stories, camaraderie, wine and fruit tarts, we called a launch and Edi and I headed back to Sequitur.

We slept-in until 1030 on Wednesday, and then I got up to tend to generating some electricity and making some water. When we had arrived and anchored, I could not get the transmission to shift out of gear. I now needed to get it into neutral so we can run the engine and start replenishing the house battery. I cleared-out space in the port settee locker and crawled in to jiggle and juggle the transmission linkage, but could not get it into neutral. Finally, I went down into the engine compartment and shifted the lever there.

I flashed-up the engine and started recharging the batteries, and at the same time, ran the watermaker. The water in the anchorage is murky, and the filter set that had done so well on the passage down from Paita went from 82% to a clogged-up shutdown in only 40 minutes and gave us 38 litres of water. However, making water daily or every two days, keeps us from having to back-flush the membrane with 25 litres of water, so we were ahead of the game. The filters refresh themselves between uses; the next day we got 30 minutes and another 28 litres, and then a further 10 minutes and 9.7 litres the following day.

In the mid afternoon we went ashore to meet with Jaime and to sign some papers, and then went off to explore the area. La Punta is very much an upscale neighbourhood, a waterfront area of Callao, a suburb of Lima. The streets are lined with a delightful mix of colonial mini-mansions and townhouses interspersed with modern. Many of the homes appear very well cared for, but there are many in need of attention, some nearing derelict.

We found a little market with produce stalls less than two blocks from the Yacht Club gates, and we selected one particularly inviting stall. We bought two bunches of asparagus, and when I picked-up a package of nice-looking button mushrooms from the counter, the woman put up a finger and went to the fridge and brought-out an even nicer and fresher package. She told us she would have some better asparagus the next day, and we asked her to put three bundles aside for us. A couple of blocks further along we found the bakery we had been told about, and we bought the best bread we have had since San Francisco.

Jaime came out to Sequitur late on Wednesday afternoon to officially welcome us to Peru; he had completed our entry for us, and had our stamped passports and 183-day visas. He said he had had a bit of a verbal battle with the official, who had wanted to give us only three months. Jaime insisted on six months, and he eventually won. I gladly paid him his fee of a beer, in fact I doubled it as we sat sipping tins of Tecate and chatting.

For dinner on Wednesday evening I prepared the last of our jumbo scallops and some of our remaining prawns. I sautéed the prawns in butter, garlic shallots and mushrooms to just short of done, then removed the prawns, and in the hot pan seared the scallops and plated them. The prawns went back in with diced roma tomatoes and a splash of Riesling for a final toss. This was served with steamed basmati rice and fresh Peruvian asparagus with mayonnaise and accompanied by the rest of the bottle of Rheinpfalz Riesling.

With the murky water in the anchorage making it poor for watermaking, running the washer-dryer onboard made no sense. On Thursday afternoon we bundled-up a large collection of laundry and took a launch ashore, where we walked along to the recommended lavanderia. This is housed in a wonderful old colonial house with a huge corner veranda. The charge is 4 Soles per kilo, and we were told it would be ready for pick-up at 1800 the next day.

We stopped to buy some more bread at the bakery and to pick-up our bundles of asparagus from the vegetable stall. With these in hand we walked along the malecon eastward, past the end of the fashionable district and into a less savoury neighbourhood. It was daylight and there was a lot of traffic, so we kept walking. Our intention was to visit the Marina Club facilities to see if they would be able to haul Sequitur and whether they were capable of doing the work we required.

After a couple of kilometres, we finally arrived and were asked to wait for a few minutes while the manager came back. A short while later Roberto Rios Garcia-Rosell, Gerante de Operaciones welcomed us with his Spanish-English dictionary in hand, and escorted us into his office. I told him we wanted to haul-out Sequitur in September, after we had returned from the summer in Vancouver. I asked about his access to qualified Yanmar mechanics, Raymarine techs and someone familiar with Fischer-Panda, all of which he appeared confident he could provide. He asked me to email him a detailed list of the work we needed done, and he would review it and get back to me. I asked for a tour of the yard and a look at the travel lift.

While we were in the yard we spoke briefly with Herb, who had just had The Lady J hauled and was waiting for a ladder so he could climb down. We invited him and Bev over to Sequitur for dinner on the weekend; we needed to do some freezer emptying before flying to Vancouver. He knew they had something planned Saturday or Sunday, but wasn't sure which. He would check with Bev and let us know. I told him we were also inviting Jim and Linda, and when he said they were meeting them later in the day, I suggested he confirm the date with Bev and invite Jim and Linda for us: 1700 Saturday or Sunday.

We took a bus back to the Yacht Club for half a Sole each. Out on the pier we watched for a while as Serge Jandaud, of Toulouse, France prepared his ocean rowboat, Clinique Pasteur Toulouse for departure on the 12th of June to row solo across the Pacific to Australia. We spoke with him briefly on the pier and learned he had rowed solo across the Atlantic in 2006. For his current 8000 nautical mile passage, he is estimating 6 to 10 months.

On Thursday evening Herb had radioed us to confirm Saturday evening, so when Bev arrived at 1700, we were ready. Herb was still aboard The Lady J in the yard, overseeing workers and would be along shortly. Another launch soon dropped-off Jim and Linda, and after a while Herb arrived. We sat chatting, sipping wine and nibbling cheeses and salami from a board Edi had prepared.

Around 1800 I began cooking. I sautéed our remaining seventeen boneless and skinless chicken breasts in butter and garlic and set them on a platter in the oven while I finished a huge wok of ginger, garlic, red onions, white onions, carrots, broccoli, cauliflower, asparagus and tomatoes, finished-off with soy and a picante tomato salsa and a liberal sprinkling of freshly toasted sesame seeds. With this and the platter of chicken breasts, we served a large bowl of steamed basmati rice and more bottles of wine.

We had a delightful evening, some six hours of swapping tales, sharing experiences and gaining information on this area and others. Around 2300 a launch was called and very shortly our guests were gone without Edi and I having to use one of our favourite quotes from Lin Pardey: *"Why don't we go to bed so these good people will have an excuse to go home?"* It was a splendid evening.

On Sunday afternoon we went ashore and caught a collectivo to the mercado, where we found the stalls rather deserted, being so late in the day. We caught a bus going to Avenida de la Marina and continued on to Plaza San Miguel. This is a huge, modern shopping centre, full of the same mix of upscale brand-name shops and boutiques that we would find any major North American shopping mall.

Early on Monday afternoon, as we were preparing to head ashore, Edi spotted a large fire in a ship some three miles or so north of us in the anchorage. There were twin billows of dense black smoke, one forward and one amidships, which looked like they were coming from bunker oil fires. It continued to burn black for a good quarter hour after she had spotted it, then the smoke began fading to dark grey and then progressively paler grey as water seemed to be bringing the fires under control. The ship continued to smoke alternately grey and black for another half hour, and was still smoking when we took the launch ashore.

We met briefly with Jaime and asked him for the timing of the installation of a mooring for Sequitur. He told us he had ordered chain and was expecting it to arrive this week, but could not narrow it down any closer. We again told him we were trying to schedule our flight back to Vancouver, and we needed Sequitur securely on a mooring in the Yacht Club's field before we went. We also reminded him, as we had discussed the previous week, that we wanted him to hire a tripulante for us to visit and clean Sequitur twice a week and to provide security while we were gone.

From Jaime's office we walked along the malecon, where we ran into Bev who was out walking with her parrot, Lorenza. Bev was looking for the sail loft of Steve Wagner, a sailmaker, repairer and canvas worker. We chatted and walked along with her until she headed into a boatyard she thought was the right place. Edi and I continued on to Panarello, the panaderia, where we bought a loaf and a dozen biscotti.

Callao is the location of the Peruvian Naval headquarters, in the anchorage are various frigates, destroyers and support ships, and on the shores of La Punta we saw the Naval Academy, the Naval Warfare School and other Navy-related establishments. In the late afternoon a couple of sloops from the Escuela Naval, each bristling with a crew of a dozen, sailed past under spinnaker.

Large crew are not unusual here; a ten or twelve-metre boat often heads out with ten or twelve or more onboard. We were fascinated with the fact that here in Peru the owners usually do not operate their own boats. They have hired crew. After their crew have prepared the boat for sea, the owners arrive onboard with their guests, very smartly dressed, often in suit-and-tie. They then sit with their guests in the cockpit while the crew sail the boat and serve them food and drinks. After the outing, the boat is brought to a mooring close to the Yacht Club from where the owner and guests are landed by launch, while the crew take the boat back out to its mooring to cleanup and secure it. This seems strange to us, but it appears normal here.

Just before noon on Tuesday we took the launch ashore, with the intention of taking a bus to Miraflores to explore that reputedly upscale district. As we passed Jaime's office, he came out and told us he would have a mooring ready for us to move to a bit later in the afternoon. He had also organized with Jullio, one of the launch operators, to regularly clean and keep a watch on Sequitur while we're gone.

Jaime was going to arrange a launch to come out and guide us to the mooring and to assist with our move, so we went back out to Sequitur to prepare for the move and to start getting her ready for our absence. We shuffled and packed and waited onboard through the afternoon without any sign of a launch and without hearing anything further from Jaime.

In the evening I cooked-up the last of our frozen raw peeled prawns in butter in the big wok with crimini mushrooms, garlic, white and red onions and served them with basmati rice and grilled zucchini slices. Even after seconds, there were leftovers.

After breakfast on Wednesday morning we took the launch ashore and walked up the pier to Jaime's office. His office was locked, and the woman at the reception counter, with her lack of English and our extremely limited Spanish, told us he was away for the day; he would be back mañana. We managed to communicate our need to move Sequitur to a mooring that Jaime had arranged for us. She was familiar with the situation, and she gave us a slip of paper with the name of the buoy on it, and indicated to us that a workboat would move us.

We took a launch back out into the mooring field to look at the buoy, and satisfied, we continued along to Sequitur and as we were being dropped-off, asked the launch skipper to let the workboat crew know that we were ready for the move.

At 1300 the workboat arrived and I passed the crew a line from the bow. Four minutes later our anchor was aweigh and stowed and we were being slowly towed through the moored boats. At 1315 we secured to a buoy with twin 25mm nylon strops, one on each of our bow cleats. The mooring is just off the main fairway that runs through the field to the Club pier, and it is very close to the guard barge. We felt very secure there.

We took a launch ashore to do some banking and to arrange for a taxi to take us to the airport at 2300. We have standby bookings on a fully booked Lima-Toronto flight departing at 0145 on Thursday morning; hopefully there will be some no-shows. On the way back to Sequitur, we stopped at the Club's very well-appointed and spotlessly clean washrooms on the pier, and we indulged in our first unlimited showers in many months.

Back onboard we continued to organize for our departure, dismounting the easily removable items and stowing them below, lest someone else remove them for us. Mid-evening I prepared a dinner based on the leftover prawns from the previous evening and using as much of the remaining perishables as made sense. We then cleaned-out and shut down the one fridge and one freezer we still had operating; we had over the week consolidated contents and shutdown the others. We closed the last of the through-hulls and called for a launch, giving to the boatman the leftover frozen food.

There was a strange feeling as we slowly motored away from Sequitur. She had been our very comfortable home for ten months and she had given us so many experiences. Over the previous eight-and-a-half months she brought us safely down the west coast of North America, across to the Galapagos and then onward to Peru, nearly a quarter of the way around the world. We knew she was a bit tired and in need of a refit. As we pulled away we watched her sitting placid and uncomplaining at her mooring, waiting for our return.

12. Back to Vancouver for a Break

At the float of the Yacht Club we were met by a night attendant who helped us with our luggage, loading the pieces into a couple of carts he had ready. He then escorted us up the pier, pushing one of the carts. After we had settled in at the guard post, the guard opened the gate and motioned for the taxi to come into the compound and closed the gate behind it.

We loaded our luggage into the trunk and got into the taxi. The driver told us to lock our doors and keep our windows up. A few blocks away from the security of the Yacht Club compound and away the obvious police and private guard presence of La Punta, we were passing through a neighbourhood that quickly illustrated why we had been told to keep our windows up. After a couple of kilometres of rough neighbourhood, we passed into a safer-looking area, and in less than half-an-hour we arrived at the airport.

The departures area was controlled-access, with a security roadblock filtering cars through. Nonetheless, we still felt uneasy unloading our luggage and manoeuvring it into the check-in area. At the counter we were processed and then told to wait three-quarters of an hour until the cutoff time to see if our standby reservations would yield seats. We sat and watched as more and more people entered the terminal, and we tried to will them away from our flight's check-in.

Thankfully, we were finally confirmed; it was approaching 0100 and it would have been awkward heading back to La Punta and getting a launch back out to Sequitur on her mooring and bringing her back to life from her hibernation. Our connection in Toronto went smoothly and we arrived in Vancouver in the late afternoon, picked-up a rental car and drove to our new Vancouver home, a loft in a new restoration of a century-old industrial building.

We squeezed into the loft, threading our way along the alleys we had left between the piles of furniture and stacks of boxes and bins. We had had very little time to unpack and arrange when we had moved it in the previous November upon taking possession. Now we were tired and hungry from our twenty hours of traveling, and the place was a mess.

We pushed some things around, unpacked, made comfortable the bedroom and bathroom and while Edi hacked out a clearing in which to dine, I drove over to iSushi to pick-up an order of our five favourite rolls. With the wonderful sushi and a chilled bottle of Cava, we unwound and celebrated our return to Vancouver.

We had booked the rental car for four days, so we focused that time on making full use of it, with trips to the big boxes, such as Home Depot, Ikea, Walmart and Costco, plus visits to our favourite Greek deli, Chinese vegetable shop and other far-flung places. We bought storage shelves, lighting fixtures, building material and paint, and I played electrician and carpenter while Edi played painter and decorator. Also, with all the stacks of boxes and bins seeming to be constantly in the wrong place for the next step or process, we both played mover many times; it seems many items needed to be moved a dozen times and more.

It would have been convenient to use our large balcony as a sorting area, but the pigeon proofing installed by the builder was ineffective. A new nest had been built and the balcony was covered in guano, in places up to 5 centimetres deep. There were also the skeletal remains of a pigeon in the center of the balcony. We were waiting for the people from Pest Control, who had installed the pigeon proofing, to come and sanitize; until then, it was deemed an healthy place.

Our furniture that was destined for the patio was downstairs in the storage locker, blocking the space needed for bins we wanted to store there, which were blocking loft space preventing us from hanging the art, which was wrapped in padded covers and blocking access to cupboards, which were filled with still-packed boxes that needed sorting on the balcony. And so it went.

Through the sorting and discarding and arranging and building and modifying, we did manage to get our internet, cable television and telephone hooked-up. The loft had been pre-wired during the construction and everything including the high-speed modem and wireless router were pre-installed, waiting only for activation. With their pre-wiring, the phone company was offering telephone, high-definition TV and high-speed internet totally free for one year, with no hookup charges, no contract, no commitment. We even recovered my telephone number, which after over twenty years I had given-up in August when we moved aboard Sequitur.

We also managed to cook and eat some deliciously civilized meals, made easy by the very close and easy access to three major supermarkets all brimming with eclectic selections and obviously competing with each other for the loyalty of the growing population of this upscale new neighbourhood.

While I was unpacking the few cases that were left over from my former three thousand bottle wine cellar, I ran into a set of tasting samples of vintage Armagnac from the 1960s and 70s. These were leftover from my wine importing days, and had been used to sort-out which vintages to import. Edi and I continue to enjoy a sip of old Armagnac after dinner, the 1961, '64 and '65 being particularly fine.

Rather gradually we made the loft comfortable, but it took longer than we had anticipated, and we are not yet finished. We were worn-out, and had not realized how tired we were. For several months we had been near-constantly busy, and had not taken more than a few hours at a time to relax since we were forced to do so by Mexican Customs in early April as they held us hostage with FedEx packages.

In Vancouver we were enjoying the wonderful summer weather, while Callao, Peru experiences its normal cool, glum winter. The weather gadget on my computer shows the early afternoon conditions in Callao as overcast and 18 Celsius, which is very standard for this time of year down there. During our time there we had not seen much but overcast skies and temperatures in the mid-to-upper teens.

We were very fortunate to have connected with Gonzalo Ravago, a member of the Peruvian Yacht Club and a fellow member of the Seven Seas Cruising Association. He had noticed that Sequitur wasn't being cared for. There was no bird protection and the boat was covered with guano. Jaime had apparently dropped the ball, failing to organize the crew to care for Sequitur as he had promised.

Gonzalo had taken the initiative to find our email address and to contact us. He sent photos and a suggestion that he organize a crew to clean Sequitur, to care for her and to provide her with some security while we are gone. Since then he regularly kept us informed on her status and sent photographs. He was also very responsive to our questions on the availability of goods and services and on arrangements for our haul-out when we return to Peru.

188

We spent the middle two weeks of July in New Brunswick, attending the annual convention of the Royal Canadian Numismatic Association in Saint John, and visiting with my family in the Moncton and Shediac area. My mother's memory has deteriorated rapidly in the fourteen months since we had last visited. By the previous summer, at the age of ninety-two she was no longer able to cook and maintain the house on her own, and she and dad finally moved out of their house. Mom is now in a senior care facility, and Dad is living with family friends.

We visited with Mom in the senior's home, where she appeared very happy and relaxed, though it was sad to see she had regressed to the mental age of a young child. Her memory had slipped so far that during the time we sat and talked with her, I am not sure she ever did place me as her son, though she did treat us as if she knew us.

Dad had suffered a mild heart attack in the spring, we assume in his attempt to cover for Mom's deteriorating condition, and he spent a few days in hospital. As a result of this, he finally had his driver's license revoked, but at the age of 96, I suppose it was about time. He is still a voracious reader and he still reads without glasses.

My brother, Peter and his wife, Linda have decided that after a decade-and-a-half of boating in the Bahamas and the Caribbean for five or six months every winter, they would to call it quits. While we were in New Brunswick, Peter left for Florida to sail their Cape Dory 30 back to Shediac.

We spent five days at the RCNA Convention in Saint John, primarily socializing, but I was also attending to some political responsibilities as the Immediate Past President. It was wonderful to spend time again with so many old friends.

On our drive back from Saint John, we took a circuitous route through Fundy National Park and Albert County. The tide was out in the Bay of Fundy as we drove through Alma, and we paused to shoot some photos of the fishing boats alongside the wharf in the estuary of the Upper Salmon River (now also known as the Alma River). Not far from here are the world's highest tides, with a range of 17 metres at the peak of the spring cycle. Mooring and anchoring are an adventure in this area.

On our return to Vancouver, we again set to work unpacking, sorting and arranging our belongings in the loft. In the storage room I installed shelving on two walls up to the three-metre-high ceilings. We installed new lighting fixtures in the entry hall and in the kitchen and hung a new chandelier above the dining table. Slowly we caused some order to emerge from the chaos, and we gradually became more comfortable in our surroundings.

During all of out sorting and arranging, we were also busy assembling a rather large pile of boat things to take with us back to Peru. There were still many items that we had ordered that had not yet arrived, and with only two and a half weeks remaining before we head south, we hoped they will all arrive soon.

One of the major things on our list was a replacement for our stolen Walker Bay dinghy. Walker Bay does not have a distributor in Peru, so we would have to try to ship a new dinghy in ourselves. Fortunately, Walker Bay's Head Office is in Vancouver, and only a five-minute walk from our loft. Because it was for export, and because the Sales Manager sympathized with our dingy theft in Peru, I was able to negotiate a very good price FOB the showroom. When I looked into shipping, the best quote was $985 plus crating and local trucking. The best crating quote came in at $385, so with trucking to the crating company and then from there to the freight forwarder, we were looking at something over $1500. The Sales Manager then suggested he get quotes for shipping to Peru directly from their factory in Mexico. This came in at a price that surprised even him: US$1300

Meanwhile, we were trying to arrange through the Peruvian Consulate in Vancouver a letter to ease our passage through Customs with replacements of items that were stolen from Sequitur in Paita as we cleared into Peru, as well as for repair and maintenance items for Sequitur as a yacht-in-transit. After three weeks, they have still not replied to our repeated phone calls and emails. At the same time I was emailing back-and-forth with Gonzalo in Peru, having him find out how we can best clear these items through Customs. He told us his agent had informed him that we would have to pay a minimum of US$1162 duty, taxes and fees on the dinghy, with a remote possibility that we might be able to eventually get it reimbursed after we left Peru. So here we were at US$2462 on top of the cost of the dinghy, so a total of about $6000 Canadian.

I agreed with Gonzalo's suggestion that he help us shop around for a dinghy when we return to Peru. We won't find anything as good as the Walker Bay, simply because nothing else even comes close to its quality and features. However, we hoped we would be able to find something new or used that will do for a while. Who knows, if word of our search for a good used inflatable spreads widely enough, we might even find our old one.

Over the past weeks we had been slowly gathering a pile of things to take back to Peru for Sequitur. Among the things we had in hand were:

- ten sets of pre-filters, two charcoal filters and a set of cleaning and storage chemicals for the watermaker;
- three boathook heads, for which we will find shafts in Peru;
- three locking pins for the Hydrovane, one to replace a broken one on the rudder and two as spares;
- a set of Wheel-a-Weigh dinghy wheels to ease beaching and launching our new dinghy when we get one;
- four new bulbs for the navigation lights to add to the depleting spares bin;
- one roll of spinnaker repair tape and two rolls of heavy-duty Dacron sail repair tape;
- a heavy-duty stitching awl;
- a bronze grill for the raw water intake so we won't catch more fish when running the engine at anchor;
- an assortment of stainless steel clevises, shackles and snap-links to replenish and add to the spares bin;
- a new cockpit light assembly to replace the existing malfunctioning one;
- a new dog for the transom door to replace the one that someone decided he needed more than we did;
- three replacement knobs for the galley stove, hopefully not as brittle a plastic as the ones I keep breaking;
- a zinc and maintenance kit for the Variprop feathering propeller;
- a batch of Spotless Stainless to clean the rust streaks and spots from Sequitur's stainless;
- another spare winch handle, we haven't lost one overboard yet, so an additional spare will likely mean we won't;
- a Rogue Wave ECB 5010 wifi antenna to boost our internet sniping ability;
- a D-Link wireless N router to convert Sequitur into a wifi hotspot;
- Tef-Gel, LocTite, individual Crazy Glue ampoules and other such items that are common here but are unobtainable there; and
- a large stack of new books to read.

We also had several things on order, but not yet arrived and things we had not yet picked up:

- four new relays and two new glow plugs for the Fischer-Panda generator to see if we can get it working easily and cheaply;
- a new head assembly, piston, piston ring set and gasket set for the Fischer-Panda generator to see if we can get it working if the cheap fix doesn't work;
- replacements for our depleted stock of fuel and oil filters and water pump impellers;

We also need to replace the sail cover for the Hydrovane. The nylon had deteriorated in the tropical sun, and by the time we had arrived in the Galapagos, it was starting to rip and fall apart. We kept repairing the new rips with duct tape, and by our arrival in Lima, there was almost as much tape as bare nylon. Replacement covers are $117 directly from Hydrovane's head office here in Vancouver. However, thinking that we could do a bit better by making our own, we removed the fabric from the frame and brought it back with us from Peru to use as a pattern.

Before we left Vancouver last year, Edi had given her old Husqvarna sewing machine to her daughter, Amy, thinking we would find a good replacement along the way. We didn't, and so far on our trip, Edi has been hand sewing everything, including our table cloths, napkins and courtesy flags.

One of the first things we bought when we returned to Vancouver was a new Brother XL-3510 sewing machine with a convertible free arm and flat bed, on sale at London Drugs. She tried it out by making linen kimonos for us, and she fell in love with the machine immediately.

Edi's next project was the Hydrovane sail covers. For $60 we bought enough rip-stop nylon and heavy cordura to make three replacements, and using the tattered remnants as a pattern, she quickly stitched-together a new cover. I bought a grommet kit and an additional bag of grommets for a total of $5.00 and inserted fourteen of them to complete the new sail cover. We packaged the leftovers to make-up the remaining two covers aboard Sequitur. Our outlay for the three new covers was $140 for the sewing machine, $60 for the fabric, $5 for the grommets and kit and less than $1 for the thread, for a total of $206. For this we got three covers, which would have cost us $351 to buy, so in effect, the sewing machine and grommet kit were free.

As a registered vessel, Sequitur is required to be marked with her name and port of registry on her stern with letters at least 10cm in height. There is no requirement for pleasure craft to have their names displayed anywhere else, and for various reasons, I chose not to place her name on her sides. However, in many anchorages we have seen situations where a more visible name would be useful, and we have been toying with the idea of putting Sequitur's name on her sides.

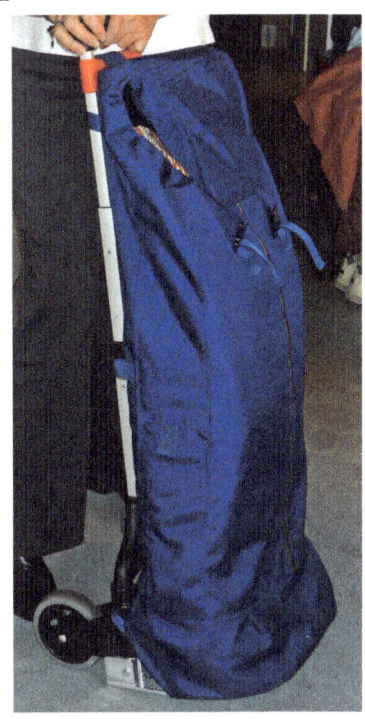

Edi came-up with the idea of putting Sequitur's name on the Hydrovane sail. A brilliant idea, I thought, so we commissioned four copies of Sequitur's name in white outdoor vinyl from Seaside Signs, who provided very quick and professional service. We'll apply these to both sides of two of the sails, and leave the third sail blank to keep our incognito options open.

Another sewing project was to design and make a bag for our MagnaCart folding wheelie. The new Brother stitched through up to nine layers of heavy coated cordura nylon with ease. Edi was delighted with the machine and we questioned the need to pay five times as much for a portable Sailrite, the cruisers' standard.

Edi is expecting her first grandchild, and I suppose, by default I am finally to become a grandfather. On the last Monday in August we had Edi's very pregnant daughter, Amy and the expectant father, Bram over for dinner, along with Bram's mother Els and his aunt Hennie, who were visiting from the Netherlands. We had a delightful evening of sharing with an expanding family. A few days later we had Edi's daughters, Amy and Genevieve and their fellows, Bram and Gregor for dinner to celebrate a pair of birthdays, Amy's 30th and my 66th.

With five days until departure, we began to focus seriously on our return to Sequitur. The last of the parts for the Fischer-Panda generator arrived on Monday, so on Tuesday morning I took the sky train and bus across to the Lynwood Marina on the North Shore and picked them up.

On Wednesday afternoon the replacement splines for the Lewmar Mamba autopilot arrived, and we were down to only one more shipment to arrive. The dog for the transom locker door was stuck in transit, so Sarah had them send another by overnight courier to hedge our bets.

With almost everything assembled, we began packing on Wednesday morning. Our checked baggage allowance in first class is three pieces each, not over 32 kilograms per piece. This should be much more than we require, but the trick is to distribute the weight and the volume, the delicate and the dense, the perishable and the robust into our three large cases.

On Thursday afternoon I picked-up the last bits from Granville Island, and realized that the autopilot drive splines were more complex than I had imagined. Lewmar doesn't sell the separate pieces, and they instead disassembled a burned-out drive motor and sent me the end plate with its gears and female splines, and for the male splines, they sent a used angle drive. There was no charge for the parts, only for the shipping.

The additional weight and bulk meant we needed a fourth case, so I walked up the street and bought one, and by 1830 we had finished packing. We had three bags weighing between 69 and 70 pounds on our bathroom scale and one at 62 pounds. We were hopeful that our scale is accurate and the three heavy ones would make it under the 32 kilograms limit on the check-in scale at the airport.

We had invited Amy and Bram over for dinner on our last evening in Vancouver, and they were due to arrive at 1900. We quickly cleaned-up ourselves and the loft, and as I was putting away the vacuum cleaner and Edi was finishing the last of the tidying, the entry phone rang. We enjoyed a pleasant and relaxing evening with the expectant parents.

The next morning the alarm clock worked, and got us out of bed at 0400. We shutdown the loft and were out the front door shortly after 0430 and pulling our luggage train toward the SkyTrain, on our way back to Sequitur in Peru.

13. Return to Peru

Our flight to Toronto was leaving at 0700 on Friday 17 September, and for our safe arrival with all eight pieces of our luggage aboard Sequitur in La Punta, we were depending on a long sequence of events to come-off near-flawlessly. The luggage train we had imagined worked well, and we had no difficulty getting all eight pieces, weighing somewhat over 160 kilograms (350 pounds) down the elevator and onto the street. It pulled easily, Edi with three pieces and me with five.

We easily made our way down the two elevators to the station platform, arriving seven minutes before the first train to the airport. There was no problem getting all eight pieces onto the train and off again at the airport, and we easily made our way to the executive class check-in. I had used some of my frequent flier points to book first class tickets to Lima and I still had my *Elite* Status.

The check-in scales proved our bathroom scales correct and the bags were weighed as 31.9, 31.9, 31.6 and 28.2 kilograms. Because of the amount of machinery parts and other metal in the luggage, we had decided it best to have it security pre-screened to prevent it being rejected. Baggage pre-screening went easily, as did security, and we were able to spend a bit of time in the Maple Leaf Lounge relaxing with coffee and muffins.

Our flight arrived on time in Toronto and we easily made our way along to the international area and relaxed with some pasta and wine in the Maple Leaf Lounge. We went down to the gate at boarding time, and after a few minutes, it was announced that the aircraft was unserviceable, and that a replacement would have to be brought over from the domestic side. We went back up to the lounge for the fifty-five minute delay. The flight boarded and departed with no further complications.

One of the few shortcomings of the new executive class configuration is that we are isolated from each other. Among the pluses is the full lie-down bed, and both Edi and I got four hours of solid sleep between meals, assisted by a few glasses of Champagne and Zinfandel.

The pilot made-up some time en route, but we still arrived half an hour late at 2330. Being in the first row, we were among the first off the plane, and with only one ahead of us in line at Immigration there was no delay. Once we mentioned we were returning to our boat in La Punta, we were granted a six-month visa.

We arrived at the designated conveyor in the baggage hall as the last pieces from an Atlanta flight were being picked-up. Shortly our flight's baggage started out, and we were delighted to see one of our bags trundling along near the front of the pack. The priority tag works even here in Lima!

But then, maybe it doesn't; we watched and waited for our other three checked pieces as the rest of the baggage rolled by for almost half an hour. Finally, when the crowd had thinned to only those with priority baggage, the last container was unloaded. The good news is that all of our baggage had arrived intact.

The bad news is that we were now even later. To ensure that we have a secure ride to La Punta, Gonzalo had organized a taxi to be at the airport to meet us, and he sent us a copy of the sign the driver will be holding. He would be outside waiting, but we still had to clear Customs.

We breezed through Customs and out into the arrivals waiting area and immediately saw the sign, prominent among the dozens being displayed. Gonzalo was with the driver and he motioned us outside to a meeting area, where we finally met this man who has been so very helpful to us. We loaded our bags into the taxi, which was a new and spotless van, and with Gonzalo leading the way in his car, we drove to La Punta.

It was 0115 when we arrived at the Yacht Club, and there were three tripulantes with carts waiting for us. They had been arranged by Gonzalo, and they and Gonzalo helped us off-load the baggage from the taxi and trundle it down the wharf to the waiting launch. Sequitur looked good as we approached, much cleaner now than when we had left her in June. Gonzalo and the tripulantes helped unload the baggage into the cockpit, and we thanked them and bade them good night.

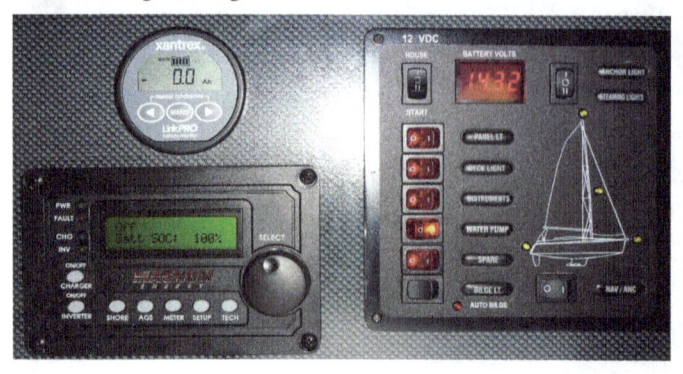

We unlocked Sequitur and went below to see how well she had fared during our absence. I switched on the lights and took a look at the instruments to check on the battery state. It showed 100%, with the house bank at 14.32 volts; our system had done well. I turned on one of the fridges and Edi and I stuffed a duvet into a clean cover and we went to bed and we were rocked gently to sleep. Home again.

We slept until 1030 on Saturday and then had a relaxing breakfast of Safeway sesame bagels, Victoria cream cheese and steaming coffee from fresh-ground Starbucks beans. We were delighted that we had had the foresight to bring the first couple of day's food with us. While Edi cleaned and tidied, I unpacked our 160 kilograms of luggage and we started the slow process of finding appropriate places to stow all the stuff. Happily, everything had made the trip without any damage, including all the machine parts, the electronic parts and our new sewing machine.

We slept-in again on Sunday, and it was nearly 1100 by the time we were out of bed and having breakfast. The weather was again overcast and cool, which we have learned is the norm for this time of year. From June to December, the temperature ranges from nighttime lows of 15 degrees to daytime highs of 20, and it is almost always overcast. We were only 12 degrees south of the equator, and with the first day of spring occurring this week, one would think it would be much warmer; however, air above the cold Humboldt Current interacts with the hot dry air over the coastal plains and creates a low overcast over the coast, insulating it from the sun. Rain is rare here, the annual precipitation in Callao being less than one centimetre.

Late on Sunday afternoon we took the launch to the yacht club pier and sat in the restaurant enjoying a long, slow dinner of dishes recommended by Chef Frano: ceviche, escabeche, arroz con pollo e lomo saltado. Because we were planning to go shopping for produce the next day, we asked Frano for his recommendations on places to go. He immediately said we needed to go to Minka Market in central Callao. He then suggested he take us there in the morning, so we organized to meet in the restaurant's bar at 1030.

The Minka Market is a huge complex of inter-linked buildings occupying about 12 hectares of land. We parked in the southeastern corner of the complex and walked into the first building, which was occupied by some three dozen butcheries and poultry stands. We decided not to do our meat shopping until after we had done our produce purchases.

Next we wandered through the fruit building, which boasts over sixty stands with fruit from the Peruvian coast, mountains and jungles. Frano helped us identify many of the fruits with which we were unfamiliar, and we loaded our cooler bags with new things to try.

In the vegetable halls, the more than ninety stalls are sorted by variety: greens, roots and tubers and so on. Frano again was a great resource, explaining the selection, the qualities, and the preparation of new-to-us items. We loaded our bags further.

Frano explained the merits of some of the many dozens of varieties of potato on display in the tuber section, and we picked-out a few of each of five of them.

Shortly before noon, we went to one of the stall-like restaurants in one corner of the market complex for chicharron, a traditional Peruvian breakfast of braised pork belly chunks, sliced sweet potato and red onion, which we loaded from a platter onto crusty rolls. From lunch we had Frano take us to his favourite poultry seller, where we bought eight large boneless and skinless chicken breasts. From there he took us to his favourite wine seller, where we selected half a dozen bottles to begin restocking our wine cellar.

We decided to leave the more than one hundred grocery stores and the fifty plus seafood stalls to another day, and we drove back to the Yacht Club, and thanking Frano for the wonderful experience he had given us, we caught a launch back out to Sequitur to stow our day's purchases. Dinner was fresh grilled chicken breasts with asparagus and some wonderful mashed potatoes

On Tuesday after a breakfast of fresh strawberries and cream cheese on bagels, we cleaned and puttered. I worked on trying to get the Fischer-Panda started, but after several variations and attempts and a couple of frustrating hours, I gave-up. I did have some success; however, in installing the new light in the cockpit, in replacing the stolen dog on the transom locker door and in installing the new wifi antenna and the new router and setting-up a secure wireless zone onboard Sequitur. The new wifi antenna was taking the signal from the Yacht Club and boosting it from an intermittent one or two bar to a steady three or four bar reception.

We slept-in again on Wednesday morning, and after breakfast we took a launch ashore and caught a collectivo along to the Marina Club and met with Ricardo to discuss hauling Sequitur next week. The next Wednesday looked good, but he said he might be able to fit us in on Monday. He told us he needed a copy of our ship's papers, so when we returned to the boat, we emailed PDFs of them to him from my computer, where they are already stored.

We walked across the street and to the corner to await a bus to take us to Minka. Many dozens of buses and collectivos went by in the next several minutes, but we saw none going to the Minka Market. A taxi stopped to offer us a ride; the driver wanted 6 Soles to Minka, but I said no and turned away. He then offered to take us for 5 Soles, only 2 Soles more than the bus. The taxi was clean, so we got in and rode comfortably to the market.

We wandered in and out of several of the more than a hundred grocery stores that are here. Many of them are small and have limited selection of stock, while others are quite specialized, with expensive imported goods. There are also several the size of a medium supermarket, and some of these are stocked more like a Costco, with bulk packaging.

We strolled again through the produce sections, amazed again at the range of items on display. We walked through the complex to the seafood building, which is separated from the main market by a wide margin, presumably because of the smell. By the time we arrived there it was well past noon, and only half-a-dozen fishmongers were still set-up. Those who remained were very low on stock.

We went out into the bus plaza next to the market and asked directions for a bus that would take us to Wong Supermarket in the Plaza San Miguel. When we arrived at Wong, we went upstairs to the mezzanine buffet al peso (buffet by weight), which has a large selection of hot and cold, savoury and sweet Peruvian dishes. We loaded our plates with a selection and slid them onto the weigh scale next to the cashier, where we were charged 17.90 Soles per kilogram, about $2.95 per pound. Our delicious and filling lunch for two came to $4.65.

After lunch we went down to the supermarket floor and continued our process of restocking Sequitur's fridges, freezers, lockers and pantry. We had brought the MagnaCart and its new zippered bag, and it easily swallowed bottles of wine, jugs of yogurt, blocks of cheese and one of our big cooler bags filled with a large variety of produce and some fish. Topped off with loaves of bread, including a baguette, and other light stuff, it was simple to pack, and it carried the load wonderfully onto and off the bus, into the launch and aboard Sequitur. Edi's design and sewing skills again proved themselves.

On Wednesday night at 2209 spring officially arrived in Peru; the sun had crossed the equator on its way south. On 26 October, it was scheduled to cross our latitude in La Punta on its way south. We were hopeful that Sequitur's refit would go smoothly and we would be able to follow closely in the sun's wake.

Late on Friday morning we took a launch to the club pier and to the restaurant to have lunch with Gonzalo and his wife Magdala to help him celebrate his birthday. Also joining them were Herb and Bev of The Lady J of Florida, Peter and Paula of Pacific Blue from Tilburg, Netherlands and Steven and Kimberly and their son Cullem of Odyle out of Half Moon Bay, California. We shared a splendid lunch, enjoying fine food, delicious Piscos and wonderful camaraderie with new friends through the afternoon and into the early evening.

The Seven Seas Cruising Association had just announced that Gonzalo is this year's winner of the Bateman Cruising Station-of-the-Year Award. From my limited dealings with Gonzalo so far, if he had not just won this award, I would have nominated him for it. He has been and continues to be a very valuable resource for cruising sailors in Peru.

We caught-up on news from Herb and Bev, who had arrived in La Punta in their Ocean Trader trawler from Florida in July 2006, and had remained here since, travelling inland and out. They had recently returned from a break in the Bahamas, and while they were there, they bought a canal-front condominium with moorage. They were planning to cruise The Lady J north from Callao early the next year to transit the Panama Canal and make their way across the Caribbean to their new cruising base.

Peter and Paula of Pacific Blue arrived in La Punta in year five of their cruise that has so far taken their Breehorn 44 from The Netherlands, down the east coast of South America, around Cape Horn and for a year and a half exploring Tierra del Fuego and Patagonia. They were hauled-out in the club yard and are awaiting re-launch before heading off to The Galapagos. Edi and Paula had a wonderful opportunity to practice their Dutch, and I picked Peter's brain for tidbits of information and gems of wisdom gained on their many months of cruising around the bottom of the continent.

Steven and Kimberly and their 14-year-old son Cullem had left the San Francisco area in October 2009 in Odyle, their Skookum ketch, and they cruised down the Mexican and Central American coast and then along the Ecuadorian and Peruvian coast, recently arriving in La Punta. From here they intend crossing the Pacific by way of Polynesia.

On Saturday we cleaned-out and rearranged the pantry and the two largest of the six cockpit lockers. Among other things, I reorganized the Jordan series drogue into a more suitable bag, which we had brought from Vancouver. I marked the bridles with tape to indicate the start of their attachment points on the stern cleats, so that it is quick and easy to rig when needed. The entire drogue system is now flaked into one compact bag, stowed in a cockpit locker and ready to deploy.

On Sunday we went ashore to find a convenient supermarket to buy a few things. We met Bev, who was on her way to the Vea supermarket, so we tagged along with her, catching a bus there for 50 Soles each. We completed our shopping and met-up with Bev, who had bought a dozen two-and-a-half-litre bottles of water, and needed to take a cab back, so we shared the 6 Soles fare with her.

One of the reasons we had needed to go shopping was to get some things for the potluck barbecue Frano was putting-on on the upper deck of the club restaurant. We had a wonderful evening, sharing with new friends recently met, and meeting still more cruisers. Among the additional cruisers we met at the barbecue were Pamela of Precious Metal from British Columbia, Max and Sandy of Volo from Australia and Doug and Jill of Companera from Alaska. Precious Metal was planning to sail westward through Polynesia, while Volo and Companera were heading south to Patagonia, as is Sequitur. We had a great evening, and had another opportunity to spend time with Gonzalo and Magdala.

On Monday we puttered, and then went ashore to take measurements of the club's 20-ton travel lift to see if it could accommodate Sequitur. As we arrived, Peter and Paula were in the process of re-launching Pacific Blue. Their intention was to leave on Tuesday, if they could get their zarpe by then.

From its listed dimensions and capacity, I calculated that the travel lift should be able to haul Sequitur. We spoke with Jaime Ackermann and asked him to confirm the measurements of the lift. I gave him Sequitur's critical dimensions and told him to book a haul-out for us if he saw that we can fit.

We had run out of oyster flavoured sauce the last time I did a stir-fry. We had seen small bottles of it in supermarkets since, but we considered it too expensive, and thought that we could do better. Our goal was to find Lima's Chinatown, so after breakfast on Tuesday we took a launch ashore and caught a van into central Lima for 3 Soles each.

After some fifteen or sixteen kilometres, we were let off at Plaza 2 Mayo and told to head across the circle and follow Nicolas De Pierola. We followed this modern street, which for the first two blocks or so is lined with musical instrument stores; I've never seen so many windows full of saxophones. After walking about a kilometre, we came to Plaza San Martin, where we asked the concierge at Hotel Bolivar for directions to Chinatown.

He pointed us to Jiron de La Union, a pedestrian mall. Walking along this mall, we sensed that we could have been in any upscale district in any old-world city on the planet. There were many wonderful facades from modern back through art deco, art nouveau, rococo and churrigueresco.

One building particularly caught our eye. Photographia Central, the photography studio of Frenchman Eugene Courret, founded in 1863 has an art nouveau façade with neo-rococó balconies inspired by a Paris house.

We continued along to Plaza de Armas, across which stands Palacio De Gobierno, the Government Palace, which is also known as the House of Pizzaro. We were in the Historic Centre of Lima, which since 1988 has been designated a UNESCO World Heritage Site.

To our left was Palacio Municipal, the Municipal Palace of Lima, or City Hall.

Behind us was a line of buildings with the typical balconies seen here in central Lima. These balconies were fashionable in the seventeenth century and it is reported that some 1600 of these ornate structures survive in Lima. The municipal government has initiated a programme in which individuals and companies can adopt a balcony to restore and maintain. We saw many wonderful examples on our walk.

We next walked along Huallaga, past the Basilica Cathedral of Lima, which was begun in 1535 by Francisco Pizarro laying the first stone. The first version was completed in 1538, and since then it has seen many additions, reconstructions and renovations.

We continued along for a few blocks and saw the shops gradually change to Chinese. We passed through the gates into Chinatown proper, and stopped at a simple restaurant for lunch.

We were thirsty from our walking, so we decided it was time to try an Inca Kola. We had read that this is the only national soft drink anywhere in the world that locally outsells Coca Cola. McDonald's forced Coca-Cola to allow Inca Kola to be sold in its Peruvian locales, the only country in the world where Coca-Cola agreed to such an exception to its arrangement with McDonald's. In a reversal of the standard arrangement, Inca Kola is the official bottler of Coca Cola in Peru.

I hadn't had a soft drink since my last Fanta orange while on a climbing expedition in the Hindu Kush of Afghanistan in 1975, where it was deemed one of the few drinks safe from dysentery. Somehow the sanitation of our surroundings prompted us to order an Inca Kola. It tasted very much like the very sweet cream soda of our youth, half-a-century and more ago. Here it is found on the tables of every class, from the wealthy to the poor. Our huge lunch, more than the two of us could eat, came to 20 Soles, about $7.30, including the giant Inca Kola.

After lunch we wandered through the rabbit warren of markets and we found plastic one-litre jugs of oyster-flavour sauce for 10 soles each. We bought two, and then crossed the street to the Mercado Municipal.

This is a very large, multi-floored market with hundreds of stalls segregated into type of wares sold. It was mid-afternoon, midweek and it was crowded and bustling.

There were aisles of fruit stands and rows of olive and cheese displays. We tasted a dried black olive, trying to find a replacement for the wonderful Moroccans we brought with us from the Parthenon Deli in Vancouver. It was bitter and a bit rancid; fortunately we still have a kilo or so left of the good ones.

There was a row of stalls dedicated to goat meat, most with milk-fed kid carcasses out on display.

We were fascinated by the casual approach to dining we saw in the market. There are aisles of counter-fronted open kitchens serving a steady flow of diners on stools. The food appears to be good honest home cooking from simple kitchens, some of them little more than a couple of metres wide.

We retraced our steps back along to the Plaza De Armas and along Jiron de La Union to Eglesia de La Virgen de La Merced, which was constructed in the eighteenth century in a churrigueresco style. As we were admiring the ornate façade from across the narrow street, the front doors were swung open. We took it as a sign for us to go in for a look.

The interior is richly decorated in a combination of churrigueresco and more modern styles, with extensive carved wood and masonry, and copious use of gilding.

Most of the side altars are more impressive than many of the main altars in other churches, and there is an obvious wealth indicated here.

We walked back through Plaza San Martin and along Nicolas De Pierola to Plaza 2 Mayo, where we caught a bus back to La Punta for 2 Soles each. From the yacht club pier we caught a launch back out to Sequitur; our mission to pick up some inexpensive oyster-flavoured sauce had been a success.

After breakfast on Wednesday the 29th we took a launch ashore from Sequitur to the Yacht Club Peruano, with the intention of going to Miraflores for a look around. At the bus stop we read the multiple place names on the frequently passing buses, looking for a mention of Miraflores. We saw none, so we figured we'd need to take a ride somewhere and then connect. We asked a couple of bus conductors how to get to Miraflores, and their replies were that they didn't go there. We decided to take a van to central Lima and work our way out from there.

Lima has a population of around nine million and it is linked by a public transit system with over 650 routes served by buses, microbuses, and combis operated by over 450 private companies. The system is very obviously unorganized and it appears to be unregulated by the local government. Miraflores is an upscale suburb, standing on a line of cliffs above the Pacific on the southwest side of metropolitan Lima, some eighteen kilometres along the coast southeast of La Punta.

There was a steady flux of passengers in and out of our very crowded van on the fifty-minute trip to Plaza 2 Mayo in central Lima. As soon as passengers vacated seats, the conductor would chant the destinations and heckle fresh passengers aboard. We were seldom less than full; at times there were passengers standing crouched in the low-roofed van, waiting for a seat. For most of the ride, we were twelve to fifteen in a converted nine-passenger van. Our fare was 1.2 Soles each.

From Plaza 2 Mayo, we walked east along Nicolas De Pierola four blocks until we came to Wilson, a major cross street leading off to the south, toward the coast, and we spotted a bus with a Miraflores sign among its half dozen destination placards. This small bus was much more roomy and comfortable than was the van, and the fare for the fifteen or so kilometre, forty minute ride was another 1.2 Soles each.

We headed out on a sightseeing exploration on foot and walked along Bolognesi, past the Canadian Embassy on our way to the malecon above the cliffs overlooking the ocean. There was a falcon soaring in the updrafts and we watched it for a while as it interacted with the falconer.

Along the cliff tops is a broad park with paved cycle and walking paths leading past well-manicured lawns and flower gardens. We followed the walkway northward, toward El Faro Miraflores, the lighthouse. Through the haze we could see the peninsula of La Punta forming the northwestern horizon.

We continued on past the lighthouse, passing an unbroken line of luxury high-rise condominiums. Most of these were very modern with wonderfully creative architecture, and by the quality, we could have been in West Vancouver, or along Vancouver's Coal Harbour or False Creek, or in any other world-class waterfront community.

We left the cliff-top park and walked back into the built-up area to find a street with buses heading northward toward Callao and La Punta. We eventually hopped into a crowded van with La Marina and Callao among its displayed destinations. The asked fare was 1 Sole each. After nearly half an hour we unfolded ourselves from the van in front of the Wong supermarket on La Marina in San Miguel, and shortly boarded a small bus tagged La Punta, which for 50 Centimos each took us to the Yacht Club. Our triangular route had taken us over 50 kilometres for a total of 3.9 Soles each, about $1.40.

On Thursday, we went ashore to do a careful measurement of the Yacht Club's travel lift, and determined the actual clearance under the crossbar is 5.48 metres, not the 5.9 metres that we had been told. My measurements of Sequitur show that she needs a minimum of 5.8 metres under the crossbar. Jaime suggested that they could hoist Sequitur and do the bottom work while she hangs there in the slings, and that they have staging that easily slides under the boat for the workers.

To me this seemed an excellent solution, and I asked him to proceed with organizing this as soon as possible. It appeared to be very good timing for this; the pier is being rebuilt in sections to replace corroded ironwork beneath its concrete roadway. The demolition, the installation of new steel work and the pouring of new concrete made it very complicated for the travel lift to negotiate temporary steel girders that span the construction site gap. Because of this, tying-up the lift by our hanging in it for our work will be of very little, if any inconvenience.

Friday the 1st of October was the beginning of our second year on this cruise; it is hard to believe it had already been a year since we left Vancouver. We went ashore and talked again with Jaime to reiterate our desire to be hauled-out as soon as he could organize it. We then went wandering, and in the late afternoon we stopped at the Yacht Club restaurant on the pier and sat on the upper deck in the sun enjoying broiled scallops and Peruvian Pilsner.

The scallops whetted our appetites sufficiently that we ordered a couple of plates of lomo saltado. We find it amusing, that here we are in the home of the potato, with over 200 species and 4000 varieties, and we discover variety 4001. The fries that came with our lomo soltado are McCain's frozen. McCain's started in my home province of New Brunswick over half a century ago and they are the world's largest producer of frozen french fries. They processes one million pounds of potato products each hour with 55 factories in 12 countries on six continents, and they sell one-third of the world's frozen potatoes to more than 110 countries.

As we were eating, the travel lift was slowly juggled out of the yard through the clutch of boats tied-up by the construction. As this was going on, workers arranged steel I-beam assemblies to temporarily span the demolished portion of the pier.

Just as we were finished our meal, the travel lift made it over the temporary span, and was left on the pier overnight, to continue the launching process in the morning.

On Saturday we talked with Jaime, and he said they should be able to haul Sequitur on Monday or Tuesday. We had hoped it would be sooner; we'd been back onboard from our Vancouver trip for over two weeks and since we're not making water in the anchorage, our water tanks were getting down to the empty mark. We had been waiting to fill the tanks until we were at the pier.

On Sunday afternoon we took a minibus to Plaza San Miguel to search for water jugs or jerry cans to use to bring water out to Sequitur from the pier. We explored Sodimac, a Canadian Tire-type big-box store, and at one point we had three clerks engaged in trying to determine exactly what we were looking for. Eventually we were sent upstairs to their sister store, Tottus, another big-box, this one a combination of supermarket, clothing and house wares stores. We struck-out on jerry cans, but I did find some deeply discounted polar fleece. I bought a very nice zip-pocketed vest, a similar jacket and a zip neck pullover for the equivalent of $6.25 each.

We walked along La Marina and then across to the Maestro, a Home Depot-type big-box store, where we eventually found 18.9-litre jerry cans, and bought two at 54.90 Soles, just under $20 each. The buses were very crowded, it being the municipal and district election day, and we crammed our way onto a minibus back to La Punta. We were among the few onboard without purple-stained fingers from the polls, but seeing the profusion of candidates on banners, posters and placards, and the apparent dozens of political parties in the race, we were likely the least confused in the bus.

We filled our new jerry cans on the pier and started the process of refilling our water tanks. If we ferry the pair of jugs each day, we'll stay ahead of our consumption, and gradually top-up the tanks. The jerry cans are very well designed, with a breather built into the spout, and the can's shape is perfectly suited to our filler holes, so that the filling process is hands-free once started.

Early on Monday morning we caught a launch to the pier to go to the Makro with Frano. We had seen him on Sunday afternoon, and he had told us he was taking Jill of Companera and Sandy of Volo shopping, and he invited us along with them. Makro is a members-only store, somewhat like Costco, and Frano offered to use his card for us. We replenished some of our staples, and we bought some things to try to determine whether larger quantities of them were warranted.

On the way past the Yacht Club office, I stopped in to speak with Jaime about our haul-out, He said it could be Tuesday, but would probably be Wednesday before they would be able to do it.

On Tuesday, while on our jaunt ashore for water, we stopped in to see Jaime, and learned that he was away for the day, so it looked like Wednesday for haul-out, at earliest. We then went to the small market around the corner on Bolognesi and bought some yams and a large bunch of asparagus, which was now coming into season. We also bought a kilo of eggs, which here, as in Mexico are brown, unless you want to pay a premium for white ones.

We find that we are using more eggs these days, often as omelet or a frittata in the evening. We seldom have eggs for breakfast; though, preferring instead to have bagels and cream cheese with our coffee. And speaking of coffee, the Peruvian Cafetal Selecto, which we had bought the previous day at Macro, we found to be as good as our current Starbucks House Blend.

We had finally run out of bagels, and so far we had not been able to find any in Peru. So taking matters in hand, on Tuesday afternoon Edi made a small batch to see how Sequitur's galley would fare.

It was a bit cool, so the yeast may not have been working to its best advantage; however, the finished product turned-out splendidly. We sampled our first one while it was still piping hot. Even ignoring the Edi factor, both in flavour and in texture, I preferred it to Vancouver's famous favourite, Siegel's.

Wednesday morning we sat down to a delicious breakfast of toasted home-made bagels, Peruvian queso crema and steaming cups of our newly discovered Peruvian coffee.

After breakfast I went ashore to get water and to talk with Jaime about our haul-out. He told me that it now looks like it won't be possible until early the next week. I told him that the level of fuel in our tank was below the inlet level for the Espar heater, so we have no heat or hot water onboard, and that we had been waiting until after haul-out to fill-up. Also the fuel level is below the intake for the generator, and without fuel we cannot try it to see if my attempts at repairs have been effective or not. Jaime said he would arrange a yard boat to tow us over to the fuel dock in the next day or so.

On Wednesday evening we had chicken breasts sautéed in butter and tarragon, accompanied by basmati rice and steamed asparagus with mayonnaise. With it we enjoyed a bottle of Riccadonna President Brut, which I hadn't had since the early 80s when I used to market it.

The weather continued to be cool and humid, the temperature ranging from lows of 16 or 17 to highs of 19 or 20, and there was a near constant overcast, which the sun sometimes managed to burn through for a short while in the mid-afternoon. We were only 12 degrees off the equator and the sun was nearly directly overhead, so even with the overcast, our solar panels still managed to put-out 12 to 18 amps at midday.

The overcast here is generated by the cool moist air over the north-flowing Humboldt Current meeting the hot dry air over the coast. The time of sunrise is currently getting earlier by about half a minute per day in Lima, and the length of day is increasing at the same rate. The time of sunset stays the same from mid-August through mid-October. For those two months, it sets at 1804 every day. Often the sun will break out below the cloud bank a minute or two before it sets, and we enjoy a very brief bit of sunshine.

On Thursday we went ashore by launch to catch a bus to San Miguel to do some produce and grocery shopping. On the way by the office, we spoke with Jaime about our haul-out, and to try to arrange a workboat to take us in to the pier to take on some diesel. He said the haul-out looked likely for Monday, and he told us he could organize the workboat immediately. We cancelled our plans to go shopping.

Jaime told us that the fuelling process requires us to go to the second floor of the Yacht Club and pay for the quantity we want, and keep the voucher to show at the pump. He would arrange a workboat to meet us at Sequitur. We walked along to the small foreign exchange office on the corner and exchanged some US Dollars for Soles. The margin between the buy and sell rates was one of the tightest I have seen: buy at 2.71 and sell at 2.76, a margin of just over 1.8%.

We went to the Club and paid for 30 US gallons of diesel at 12.5 Soles, which is $4.50 Canadian per US gallon, or slightly less than $1.20 Canadian per litre. The 30 gallons should bring the level of fuel in the main tank above the intake for the Espar furnace and the Fischer-Panda generator. This would mean heat and hot water and electricity, and would be an enormous improvement to our creature comforts. We told Jaime we had the fuel voucher and that we were heading back out to Sequitur to wait for the workboat. He said he would send one out shortly.

About an hour and a half later, a workboat arrived and I passed them a line and then let go from the mooring. The little boat pulled us through the mooring field and over to the end of the pier. There was an offshore breeze of 10 to 12 knots, and I used Sequitur's rudder to track closely behind the workboat. As we approached the pier end, I turned hard to port and tossed a line to the attendant as our stern swept past.

The workboat picked-up the strop from the mooring and I went forward to secure to the mooring. It was a simple operation that had us balanced between stern line to the pier and a bow line to a mooring.

I passed another line to the pier to haul across the fuelling nozzle, and we took on 30 US gallons of diesel. While the diesel was slowly pumping, I brought across the water hose and began filling the tanks. We figured we might as well top them right up; with the sliding schedule our haul-out has seen so far, we could only guess how long it might be before we are actually hauled. We will likely have depleted much of the additional 500 kilograms of water before then.

We were securely back on our mooring at 1735, just four and a half hours from speaking with Jaime. I switched on the Espar furnace, and after a failed start, I figured that it needed a longer priming from having run out of fuel. I tried it again, and it flashed-up and ran. We had heat and hot water again. I tried the Fischer-Panda a couple of times without success. At least now it has its fuel intake in the diesel, and with fuel, I figured that I should be able sort it out, working from the simple fixes to the more complex. But it was late, and that will need to wait for another day.

I cranked-up the thermostat to take the chill out of our bones, and to begin the slow process of taking the chill and the humidity out of the boat. During her many weeks of sitting in temperatures in the mid to upper teens with the humidity in the upper 80% range, she was damp.

On Friday we took a launch ashore to go to Wong in Plaza San Miguel. On the way by the office we talked with Jaime about our haul-out, and it looks like Monday is still on; although, he hinted for the first time that we might not be allowed to paint our bottom while hanging over the water.

We caught a minibus to San Miguel, and along the way, we passed some itinerant restaurants set-up on the sidewalks. There is a very different street-food culture here, as compared to back home. Here, diners sit and have a bowl of soup, a dish of stew or a plate of chicheron from the sidewalk vendors. At home the diners walk as they wolf-down a sidewalk hot dog or as they chaw from a bag of whatever from McDonalds, etc.

At Wong we bought another half-dozen bottles of wine plus a dozen-and-a-half cans of various legumes, both to sample and to continue with the restocking of Sequitur's cellar and larder. We also bought cornmeal, flour, yeast, small cans of milk and other things for baking. From the in-store bakery, we bought half-a-dozen potato buns; we are still trying to find bread here that is not sweetened. Like we saw in Mexico, the Peruvians seem to love sweet pastries, and this sweet craving apparently spills over into their bread. Edi's custom-made bag was filled to near capacity as we left Wong, but it handled the fifty-or-so kilograms wonderfully.

Back onboard Sequitur, while Edi catalogued and stowed our purchases, I prepared a rice and black bean salad with diced chicken breast, sliced Moroccan olives, artichoke hearts, cilantro, green onions, green peas, and what-have-you. The salad was for an impromptu potluck dinner for the visiting cruisers on the upper deck of the Club facilities on the pier.

In the early evening the crews from Companera, Odyle, Precious Metal, Sequitur, The Lady J and Volo assembled, and then we were joined by SSCA Cruising Station hosts, Gonzalo and Magdala. After an hour-and-a-half of quiet conversation and delightful sharing food with fellow cruisers, a couple of people started to make some noise from a machine in the corner and attempted to induce us to dance. Most of us moved away and tried to carry on with our conversations, though there were two or three who gyrated in a seeming attempt to convince themselves they were younger than reality showed.

We said our farewells to Jill and Doug of Companera, who were heading south early the next morning. They had been promised that their zarpe would be ready at first light. A young couple, newlywed school teachers who are taking a yearlong sabbatical-honeymoon, had joined Companera for the next legs of their cruise.

The 8th of October is Navy Day, a national holiday in Peru. It commemorates both the Battle of Angamos in 1879 and the anniversary of the creation of the Peruvian Navy in 1821. Rear Admiral Miguel Grau Seminario, who died in Battle of Angamos, is one of Peru's greatest heroes, and in 2000 he was recognized as the *"Peruvian of the Millennium"* by popular vote. Three Peruvian Navy cruisers have been named for Grau: the first launched in 1906 by Vickers, the second, ex-HMS Newfoundland, acquired in 1959 from Britain and the current one, ex-HNLMS De Ruyter, acquired from the Netherlands in 1973.

BAP Almirante Grau is the flagship of the Peruvian Navy, Callao is her home port, and she was lying to anchor just out from our mooring. She was dressed overall for Navy Day, and on this evening she was fully lit.

Companera motored past our stern at 0840 on Saturday morning, so it appears their zarpe had come through as promised.

Early on Saturday afternoon we went ashore and with Bev and Herb, and we took a taxi to Minka for some shopping. Edi and I bought a great selection of fresh fruit and vegetables, including some wonderful asparagus and a couple of varieties of potato. We also picked-up two kilos of boneless and skinless chicken breasts from the stand to which Frano had previously taken us. The quality had been superb; tender and delicious, and we wanted more. After our shopping, and precisely sixty minutes after we had agreed to meet in an hour, the four of us arrived at the designated rendezvous.

We had lunch in the restaurant section of the market complex, in a place called Miami Chicken. Edi, Bev and I each had the Peruvian equivalent of chicken Cordon Bleu. The servings were very large, and they each came with a salad and a huge heap of French fries. Of course, being in Peru, one would expect the potatoes to be superb. They were not; they were wet and mushy, like having been moulded from mashed potatoes, and they were bland as if from instant. They had very obviously chosen the wrong potato type, or they were using a McCain's wannabe. Herb had a big serving of skewers of beef heart with his heap of fries. Edi's and my lunch totalled S/48, about $17 including two beer.

After lunch we walked along Argentina the two blocks to Maestro. Herb needed some trim for The Lady J, and we needed some netting to keep the birds off Sequitur's solar panels and stern structures. A very eager eighteen-year-old Renzo was delighted to practice his English with us and to show-off his linguistic skills in front of his fellow workers. With his ebullient manner, he searched the store for us and helped us find and buy three metres of four-metre-wide netting. We also bought another two jerry cans, identical to the ones we had bought the previous week. Herb bought some of the netting also, and he found the trim he wanted. Renzo followed us outside and flagged a cab. The first one wanted s/10; we waved it on. We flagged one and he asked S/8, so we walked to one that had pulled-up behind it. The third driver asked S/6, so we offered S/5 and he agreed.

I paid Frano and we headed back out to our boats in the anchorage. Immediately we arrived back on board, Edi and I rigged the netting over the stern. That done, we set to stowing our purchases.

When we arrived at the Club, I had picked-up from Frano the jumbo prawns we had earlier ordered through him from his seafood supplier. Onboard I opened the package to find a neatly packed five-pound box of carefully selected and matched 15cm prawn tails. I was delighted. I broke the contents down into eight-prawn packages and froze them. Four prawns like these will be a good-sized serving for each of us. I also packaged the chicken breasts in pairs and froze them, and we now had the beginning of a stock in our first freezer.

On Saturday evening we dined on butter-sautéed trout with olive oil roasted yam chips and steamed asparagus with lime mayonnaise. With this we enjoyed Riccadonna Brut.

On Sunday afternoon, while Edi started another batch of bread, I went ashore to the Club to meet with Gonzalo, and we sat on the upper deck. Among other things, we discussed the delays we have been experiencing with our haul-out, and now the likelihood that we won't be able to paint the bottom while in the slings. We talked of the essential things I needed done on the haul-out, and from this, Gonzalo suggested we use a diver to clear the suspected tangle on the propeller, check its proper functioning and check the condition of the zincs. He recommended Juan Gomez, and as we were talking, he spotted Juan trying to make his way ashore from his punt over the raft of dinghies. Gonzalo's 6-year-old son, Gonzalito took their dinghy across and picked-up Juan.

With the assistance of Gonzalo's translation, I hired Juan to come out to Sequitur on Monday morning to clean our bottom, clear the propeller and change its zinc if necessary, all for S/150, about $54.

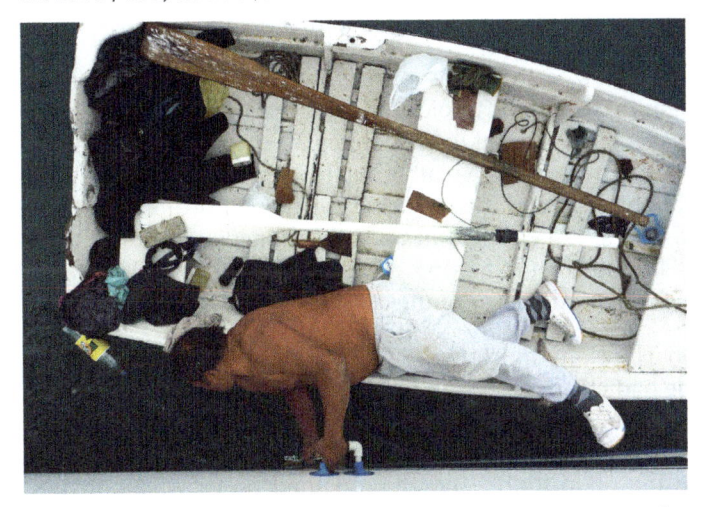

We were awakened at 0820 on Monday morning by the sounds of the hull being cleaned. Sprawled-out on the gunnels of his little punt, Juan worked his way around our waterline, hand scrubbing the 'beard' off the hull. It took him just short of an hour to do this, and then he left to do the same on The Lady J, which is moored a short row away from us.

An hour later he was back and dressing into his diving suit. He free-dived, and in a minute or so came up with a great mass of tangled line and net that he had freed from Sequitur's screw. He asked for a knife, so I rigged a line to a serrated boat knife, and down he went again.

After a couple of surfaces for breath, he came up with a five-metre length of 2.5 centimetre diameter line. He had allowed the remainder of the tangle to slowly sink to the bottom. It was now easy to understand Sequitur's compromised performance on our way out of Paita and down the Peruvian coast.

I then had Juan check the functioning of the VariProp propeller by hand feathering it from its forward stop to its astern stop, and he reported it was smooth and easy. I next showed him the new zinc, which fastens onto the after end of the propeller hub, and had him check the condition of the one currently installed. He resurfaced reporting that there was no zinc, so I assumed that it had been totally eaten away by galvanic action. I rigged a hex wrench on a line and sent him down with it to undo the three caps-crews in preparation for installing the new zinc. He came back up reporting that the screws were also missing. This I couldn't attribute to galvanic action; there had to be another cause.

Juan then carried-on with his free-diving to do a complete cleaning of Sequitur's bottom, and I pondered and mused. We had last had the zincs changed during our haul-out by Specialty Yachts on Granville Island in Vancouver in March-April 2009. As at the previous zinc change in the spring of 2008, the propeller zinc showed very little evident erosion from its year of use, probably no more than 20% of the volume, and with no apparent porosity, and again as previously, we had kept the old one as a spare. Unless we had been in an area with stray current, I could not see our current zinc eroding totally in eighteen months, when its predecessor had lost only 20% in a year.

The stray current idea looses steam when I consider that our bottom cleaner reported good zincs in Puerto Vallarta in March, and the diver we engaged in the Galapagos had reported good zincs in May. In neither case; though, do I now recall whether I had asked specifically about the propeller hub zinc, and the underwater photos of our propeller before we arrived in the Galapagos do not show the zinc.

The missing caps-crews caused me to think that they had vibrated loose, unscrewed and had fallen out, taking with them the zinc. The VariProp instructions for the installation of the zinc states: *"First, insert all three zinc-cone screws loosely, then tighten securely in succession. Use LOCTITE low (pink) and observe the little washers. They prevent the grease from squeezing out of the hub during operation. Be sure to clean the screws and screw-holes from any grease before applying the Loctite."* I did not directly supervise the work in 2009, so I had no way of knowing, other than by the increasingly poor reputation of the installer, that this procedure was followed.

Juan finished his bottom cleaning at 1210, and I very happily paid him the S/150. He certainly had earned it, having spent nearly three hours working on our bottom. On top of that, he had to row his punt the half mile out from the pier and half mile back.

To lighten things up a bit, we spent Thanksgiving afternoon baking. Edi had prepared a double batch of bagels and five loaves of New York Times no-knead bread. This time, she made the bagels by the poke-a-hole method, rather than the join-a-roll method, and with the Espar working and heat again in Sequitur, the bagels and the bread rose wonderfully.

We spent just over five hours boiling and baking, and we were delighted with the results. Sixteen large sesame bagels, two loaves of raisin bread, two loaves of cranberry and pecan and one of dried apricot. We now had breakfast baking for the next few weeks.

For Thanksgiving dinner we had jumbo prawns sautéed in butter, garlic and shallots, accompanied by basmati rice, asparagus with mayonnaise and sliced roma tomatoes with basil. The 2008 Valdivieso Sauvignon Blanc from Chile's Valle Central fell short of our expectations, even at only $8.16, and it is not a repeat buy.

On Tuesday we puttered on board. Among other things, I tried unsuccessfully to track-down online the specifications for the missing caps-crews and washers to fasten the zinc to the propeller. I had received no reply from my email to Specialty Yachts in Vancouver, so I emailed the VariProp distributor in Toronto. Their quick reply prompted me to order the screws and washers directly from them.

On Wednesday morning, Edi received an email from her pregnant daughter, Amy saying that her water had broken, and she was on her way to the hospital for delivery. Edi immediately booked a midnight flight to Vancouver via Toronto. She then went off with the other cruising ladies on a pre-planned lunch and shopping excursion in Miraflores. While they were gone, Herb and I took a cab to Minka and walked a short block to a zinc caster. We each ordered two streamlined shaft zincs, and the caster said they would be delivered to La Punta the next day.

Edi organized the driver of one of the taxis that had taken them to Miraflores to pick us up at the Yacht Club at 2230. The taxi was there at the appointed hour, and we negotiated a fare to the airport, a wait for up to an hour to confirm Edi's standby seat, and then to drive me, hopefully alone back to La Punta. Edi checked-in and was immediately confirmed to Toronto, with standby onward to Vancouver. I arrived back onboard a few minutes to midnight.

On Thursday morning I received an email from Edi that she had cleared through Customs in Toronto, but couldn't make the gate in time to get the 1000 to Vancouver. An hour-and-a-half later she emailed that she was confirmed on the noon flight, and that she had no news about the baby. She said that grandma might just win the race to Vancouver.

Amy's due date was Halloween, and Edi had assumed that since both of her daughters, Amy and Genevieve had been over-term, Amy would also be late, a week or two into November. Edi had been planning to fly to Vancouver the first week of November, but Mother and Mother Nature seemed to outfox Grandma.

At 0115 on Friday morning I received an email from Edi reporting her safe arrival in Vancouver, her quick SkyTrain ride to the loft, dropping her luggage and hopping back on the SkyTrain, then the SeaBus and then a bus to Lions Gate Hospital in North Vancouver, arriving in time have a quick chat with Amy just prior to her being wheeled in to deliver.

Grandma had beaten the baby by only 20 minutes. Edi sent an email: *"Little Annelies Marise is so gorgeous and has little dimples on her cheeks, has dark hair and is very pretty. Grandmother, mother and baby are doing fine."*

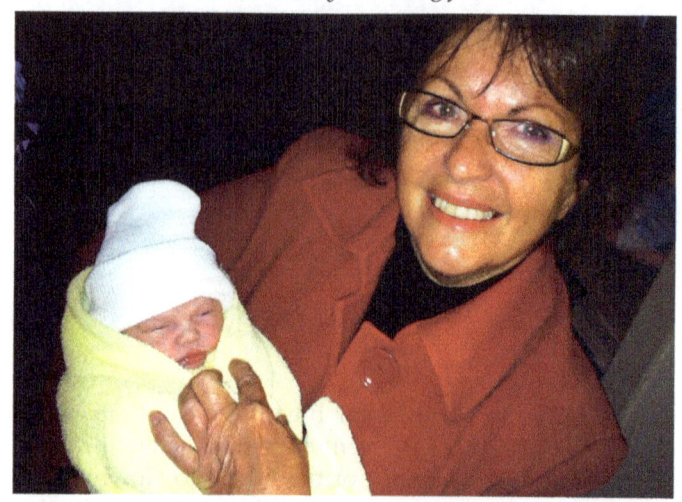

Later on Friday morning Bram, the proud father, emailed me photos from his iPhone and said the baby *"came into the world at 2828 grams"*.

208

With Edi back in Vancouver taking an immersion course at Grandmother Boot-Camp, I was left on my own aboard Sequitur. It was a strange transition; living aboard a cruising sailboat with someone is a very close thing, and it demands near-total interdependence. Ideally, there is no need to seek solitude, and even if there were, it would be a difficult thing to find. Therefore, to suddenly find myself alone was strange and somewhat disorienting.

Edi would not be back until midnight on the 29th; she had had a 35-year-old dental bridge come loose the week before she flew to Vancouver, so this was an ideal time to have it replaced. Her dentist said it would be completed on the 27th, so Edi booked the next flight after that, Friday the 29th. This would give her ample time to play grandma, and to gather-together the things we need to be brought back to Peru.

The only advantage that I could see to Edi's absence was that I could open-up all the engineering spaces and leave them open for days-at-a-time, while I worked on routine maintenance, doing some repairs and trying to resolve some problems. Even at over 15 metres in length, Sequitur is a small space, and to gain access to her systems, many hatches, panels and other structures need to be removed. We all know how much easier it is to troubleshoot and work on things when we don't have to put tools away and get everything back into place every few hours.

On Thursday I began a systematic analysis trying to find the reason, or reasons why the Fischer-Panda generator would not work. Interspersed with this, and to relieve my frustration with getting nowhere, was my search for 000 American Wire Gauge, or its equivalent 95 mm^2 tinned wire to connect the new 210 amp Balmar alternator to the house battery. By the end of the day on Saturday, I had totally run out of ideas on the generator, and had totally struck-out on the 000 gauge.

On Monday morning, while running the engine at 1800 rpm to recharge the house bank, I smelled a hint of cooking alternator winding insulation. The alternator was beginning to overheat, so I shutdown the engine. This was just another prompt that I really need to get both the generator running and the new 210 Balmar hooked-up and online, or at least one of them. I ran the generator through a few more unsuccessful start cycles, monitoring the drain on its start battery with a multi-meter as I did so. For the first time, it was reading below 12 volts, and not recovering. I didn't want to use the engine starting battery to try to start the generator, lest it be cycled too far down to start the engine.

The need for finding some 000 gauge wire really grew in importance; without it I couldn't hook-up the alternator. I renewed my search. Callao has a population of over a million, and is a suburb of Lima with its eight million people. It is the busiest port on the west coast of South America, with a huge commercial shipping traffic. It is the home port of the Peruvian Navy, it is the base of a very large fishing fleet and it has a large pleasure yacht fleet. I would have thought with all the boats and ships, there would surely be a supply of common marine goods, such as tinned wire. I found out that this is not so; they do have non-tinned, standard automotive battery cabling, but not tinned.

Why tinned? The salt air in the marine environment very quickly corrodes uncoated copper wire. By tin coating the strands, not only is the corrosion delayed by a factor of ten, but it also provides enhanced conductivity. I could get un-tinned 000 wire in Callao for a bit over $40 per metre, and for the eight metres we needed, that is nearly $325 on a temporary fix that will fail in a couple of years. Less-than-roll amounts of tinned 000 wire costs a little over $50 per metre in Vancouver, so for 25% more money, we get ten times the life expectancy as well as better conductivity. Nonetheless, I needed to get something working to charge our batteries.

After the engine and 120 Balmar had cooled sufficiently, I examined and tightened all the electrical connections, and flashed-up the engine. I ran it at 1150 rpm, and I watched as it put 75 amps into our house battery. I closely monitored the alternator's temperature and kept a keen nose for the first hint of scorching varnish. Everything remained normal, and I slowly brought the battery back up to above 85%. After I shutdown the engine, I used the multi-meter to check all ten batteries in the house bank, and all showed similar charges. I then went to the two

209

starting batteries, and while the engine cranking battery showed a good charge, the generator cranking battery was low. I noted that I needed to monitor it closely over the next while, and see of it is holding a charge.

On Tuesday morning I made launch runs ashore to get jugs of water to add to Sequitur's tanks. I was just about to call the launch for a trip ashore to Maestro and Minka, when I heard Bev call one. I quickly radioed her to have the launch swing by and pick me up on their way past. They were also on their way to Maestro and Minka, so we shared a cab. I looked for 000 wire at Maestro without success, but I did buy a couple of gallons of battery water. Its a quite a bit cheaper by the gallon, compared to the quart price at the gas station down the street from the Club, but not enough to cover the bus rides unless buying three or more gallons.

After we had all finished at Maestro, we walked on to Minka for some food shopping. Among other things, I bought a kilo of freshly shucked choclo en granos, giant corn nibblets, a kilo of tiny new potatoes, a kilo of wonderful mangoes, half a kilo of gorgeous fresh strawberries and a nice hand of bananas. I also picked-up a 2-kilo bag of boneless and skinless chicken breasts from the good shop for and a selection of S/13 to S/16 bottles of wines to try.

Meanwhile, Edi was back in Vancouver cooking-up a storm and feeding the new parents. According to her email, she prepared *"a roast beef dinner, complete with smashed potatoes, 2 litres of gravy, green beans amandine and carrots julienne"*. She had also baked, and she loaded the dinner and a dozen potato dinner rolls, some blueberry muffins and some raisin bread onto our wheeled cart and rolled it up the street to Bram and Amy's. Edi had invited her other daughter, Genevieve and boyfriend Gregor, and they dined as an extended family. Bram's parents were due to arrive from the Netherlands the following day.

Edi is using some of her time to run a *"test kitchen"* to try various baking recipes that can work aboard. She adapted a crusty potato bread recipe into dinner rolls, and baked them on a silicone cookie sheet. She reported having impressed everyone at the dinner table with the fresh crusty buns. She also made what she described as *"the best Nanaimo bar I have had, a great recipe for a potluck with no baking involved"*. She did banana bread, carrot cake squares with cream cheese frosting and carrot muffins.

Onboard Sequitur, I spent much of Wednesday the 20th tracing the wire runs to and from the various batteries, regulators, distribution panels, solar panels, wind generator, diesel generator and alternator, and I also spent some time troubleshooting the Fischer-Panda. I checked the electrolyte levels in all the batteries, and topped-up as necessary. The WaterMiser caps are working wonderfully; the batteries consume so very little water when compared to my previous experience. While I was checking the generator start battery, I saw that it had lost more charge; it was now below 11 volts, and it looked as if it had developed a small internal short, and that I needed to replace it. I began researching replacement batteries, and looking unsuccessfully online for sources in Callao and Lima.

Meanwhile, with all the mental and physical work I was doing onboard, I was eating more like a trencherman, than a gentleman sailor. For dinner, I prepared grilled chicken breast with mushrooms garlic and shallots, served with boiled comote Jonathan and boiled choclo en granos.

While preparing dinner on Wednesday evening, the Espar furnace stopped, and I guessed that I had discovered the level of fuel in the tank required for the Espar to work. It got quite chilly onboard, so I spent a large amount of time on Thursday commuting back and forth getting diesel fuel. Two jerry cans wheel very nicely on our MagnaCart the four blocks from the gas station on the corner. It is more convenient, and a bit less expensive to buy fuel there than it is at the Club's pier.

Pouring from a jerry can into Sequitur's tanks is best done through the auxiliary tank's filler on the starboard side deck, where it is flat and spacious. The other diesel filler is on the starboard corner of the transom, and while it is wonderfully easy to use when fuelling from a barge or a float, it would be awkward if done from a jug on a mooring or at anchor. The transfer pump then takes it to the main tank, which supplies engine, generator and furnace. I was pleased to find that the Espar furnace re-flashed after I had turned-up the thermostat. Sequitur began to warm again.

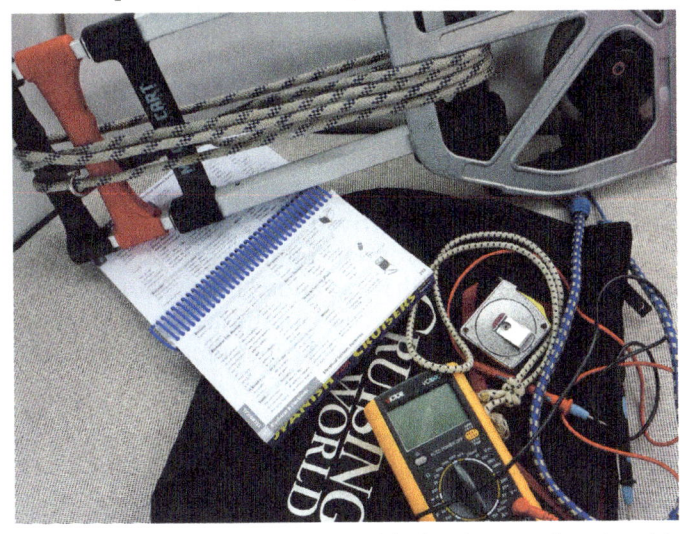

After lunch on Friday I assembled a battery buying kit and took a launch ashore to see what I could find. In the kit were multi-meter, tape measure, lashing line, bungee cords, Spanish for Cruisers bookmarked to the battery section, a boat bag and our Magna heavy-duty wheeled cart. In my pocket was a sheet of paper with the old battery dimensions, the dimensions of the battery box and the specs from the battery label. I took a bus to San Miguel and walked to Maestro, the Peruvian equivalent of a cross between Home Depot and Canadian Tire.

They didn't have what I was looking for, a heavy-duty truck battery, preferably a series 31. However, they did tell me that the Maestro over on Argentina had heavier batteries. By the time we had worked our way through the translations in Spanish for Cruisers it was getting late, so I bought two more jerry cans and then went across to Wong to buy some groceries.

Midmorning on Saturday I set out again with my battery buying kit. This time I took a taxi to the Maestro on Argentina, since there is no direct bus to there from La Punta. I very quickly found a suitable battery, a Delkor 31-900 heavy-duty truck battery, and it was charged to 12.59 volts. This is a series 31 with 900 cold cranking amps, and is exactly the same dimensions as the old battery it is to replace. A nice thing about it is that everything printed on its packing box is in unilingual English; I could easily learn far more about it by reading the box than I would in questioning a fully fluent-in-English store clerk.

I bought it and loaded its 26 kilograms onto the Magna Cart and negotiated a S/5 taxi fare back to La Punta. I loaded it into the launch and we went out to Sequitur. Unfortunately, just as I was slinging the heavy beast from the launch, a wake caused the launch to lurch, and the battery fell into the water. It sank like lead. Then having satisfied Neptune,

Poseidon, Davy Jones and whoever else needed a bribe, I spent another couple of hours on a launch-taxi-buy-taxi-launch trip. This one I managed to get onboard. With the new battery finally installed, I got back to troubleshooting the generator and trying to solve its riddle.

I spent Sunday morning and early afternoon ferrying water out to Sequitur, continuing to replenish her tanks. I then went over to the bakery to buy half-a-dozen pita for S/1.5 and to the mercado to buy a couple of ripe avocados for S/2. These were to prepare some avocado and cream cheese wedges for an impromptu cruiser's book exchange and finger-food potluck on the upper deck at the pier.

Back onboard from the festivities, I began tracking-down shipments that hadn't yet made it to Vancouver, trying to locate things we still needed, and supplying Edi with a shopping list of things to pick up for her trip back to Peru. After bashing around the marine retailers in Vancouver, Edi had located a 50-foot roll of 000 tinned wire for $350. A problem was that it was in Victoria, but the shop would bring it in for her to pick up on Thursday, the day before her flight back to Peru. Since the entire 50-foot roll weighs over 15 kilograms, and we need only 8 metres, or 25 feet of it at the moment, I told Edi to have it cut in half, and Edi can decide when she is packing whether there is space and weight availability to fit both pieces into the luggage.

As I was preparing dinner on Monday night, the stove went out. I quickly changed the propane tank and continued cooking. We now had two empty and two full tanks. I needed to learn where to get the empties refilled.

On Tuesday the 26th of October, the sun crossed our latitude and continued its way south. This is the first time the sun has been to the south of us since six months previously when we were on the third day of our passage from Acapulco to the Galapagos. Also on Tuesday, through many emails and Skype calls, I managed to track-down a source for cabinet latches that we needed to replace a broken one and to serve as spare. I arranged for the parts to be FedExed to Vancouver, but by the time the order was prepared in Florida, it had missed the last FedEx pick up. It would have to go out on Wednesday afternoon, with the hope that it breezes through Customs and makes it to our mail receiver on Thursday.

I made fuel and water runs on Wednesday morning and early afternoon, and in the mid-afternoon, I met with the only South American member of the Royal Canadian Numismatic Association. I had received a Christmas card from Richard in 2008, while I was the Association's President, and I kept it aboard as a reminder to look him up when I arrived in Lima. We spent a delightful afternoon and early evening discussing coins, collecting and many other things. He invited me to the next meeting of the Associacion Numismatica del Peru the following Wednesday.

On Thursday I again made runs ashore to get jerry cans of water, and on one trip the launch stopped at Precious Metal to pick-up Pamela on the way in. Pamela had just had her boat cleaned, and was very pleased with the results. I asked her who she had used, and she pointed to the launch driver, and said, *"His two brothers."* I organized with the skipper to have his brothers clean Sequitur on Friday, and he said they would be there at 0700.

At 0645 Friday morning there was a knock on the hull. The tripulantes arrived and began to organize their cleaning. After a quick survey, they took their dinghy ashore to get water, and came back with an assorted collection of tubs, drums and buckets. They began by undoing all the anti-bird lines and streamers to make it easier to get around on deck, and then they turned to cleaning the cockpit canvas.

After three hours they had removed much of the guano.

I had been concerned by the non-arrival of a package repair parts for the Lewmar engine/transmission controls. The package had been sent on the 8th of October by Royal Mail International Air Mail Signed-For service from Plymouth. The package had already consumed twenty days of their ten-day estimate, so I had emailed the shippers on Thursday, asking that they follow-up with Royal Mail. On Friday morning I received their forwarded reply from the Peruvian Postal Administration: *"EL ENVIO LLEGO AL PERU PROVENIENTE DE GRAN BRETA'A EL ENVIO FUE DESPACHADO EL 26/10/2010 DEL CCPL A LA ADMINISTRACION POSTAL DEL CALLAO. EL ENVIO FUE DESPACHADO EL 26/10/2010 DEL CCPL A LA ADMINISTRACION POSTAL DEL CALLAO."*

With it was their Babblefish translation: THE SHIPMENT I ARRIVE AT THE ORIGINATING PERU OF GREAT BRITAIN THE SHIPMENT WAS DISPATCHED THE 26/10/2010 OF THE CCPL TO THE POSTAL ADMINISTRATION OF THE PEBBLE THE SHIPMENT WAS DISPATCHED THE 26/10/2010 OF THE CCPL TO THE POSTAL ADMINISTRATION OF THE PEBBLE.

I decided to run it through the Google Translator, and got a slightly better version of it, though still confusing: *"Delivery is TO PERU FROM GREAT BRITAIN the shipment is CCPL THE 26/10/2010 THE POSTAL ADMINISTRATION TO CALLAO. The shipment is CCPL THE 26/10/2010 TO THE POSTAL ADMINISTRATION OF CALLAO".*

I was relieved to see it had arrived in Callao. Now, all being normal, after all the appropriate minions and bureaucrats have taken their time with it and added their fees, I figured that I should see it and an invoice for the taxes, duties, fees and bribes in a week or so. Then I could repair the broken transmission linkage.

One thing that is plainly obvious is that there is never a lack of things to do on a cruising sailboat; one certainly doesn't get bored. Time seems to slip past very quickly, even with the loneliness of being temporarily a solo sailor, the sixteen days of Edi's absence have flown by. Her flight was scheduled to arrive in Peru late evening, and I had organized a taxi to take me to meet her and bring her back to Sequitur.

When by 0900 I had received no email from Edi saying she had arrived safely at YVR, I assumed that she must have been very rushed getting all the luggage to the airport, checked-in and pre-screened because of its high metal content, that she had no spare time before boarding her 0700 flight to Toronto. By 0900, I would have received an email telling me she had missed the flight.

Her flight was scheduled to arrive in Toronto at 1423, and the connecting flight was departing for Lima at 1610 from the other end of the terminal. We had had plenty of time the previous month with the same connection, so I figured that she should have time to email me from the lounge. I sat waiting for her to tell me she was confirmed on the Lima flight; if all went well, I figured I would hear from her around 1500 Toronto time, which is 1400 La Punta time. After watching more than two weeks zip by in a flash, the last few hours seemed to drag by in ultra slow-motion.

At 1515 Edi sent an email from the lounge in Toronto, saying she was waiting to be confirmed on the flight to Lima. We crossed all of our fingers. A while later I received an email from her saying she had her seat confirmed onward to Lima.

After she had enjoyed Champagne and dinner, she was able to get a good sleep in the bed-seat in the First Class cabin. Shortly after midnight on Saturday the 30th, she arrived through Customs relaxed and rested and with all of her luggage intact. At 0105 we were back onboard Sequitur in the anchorage off La Punta and we were unpacked and in bed by 0130.

Less than five hours later we were up and enjoying coffee and biscotti in our new Villeroy & Boch settings, which were among the things Edi had brought back with her from Vancouver.

Everything about the winery oozed charm; the architecture, the vegetation, the accent pieces, the whole setting were all very tasteful and harmonious.

We were up at this very hour preparing to catch a launch ashore to join two other couples in a couple of taxis for the hour-or-so drive to Miraflores to rendezvous with Gonzalo. From there we were driven south along the coast some 300 kilometres to Ica, where we were introduced to Rafael Picasso Salinas, Director of Bodegas Vista Alegre.

Rafael and Gonzalo had gone to school together, and they had maintained a very close friendship over the years. Rafael's vineyards and winery had been established by his family in 1857; they are located just outside Ica and near the Nazca Lines.

Rafael led us on a wonderful tour of the facilities of the winery and the Pisco distillery, beginning with the experimental vineyard plots. Here, as in any progressive winery, new varieties and clones are planted to assess their suitability to the climate and soils. The vineyards here are in a desert environment, and they depend on irrigation. Vista Alegre uses a computer-controlled drip irrigation system.

Rafael led us through an old barrel room filled with no-longer-used botti. The maker's plaques indicated they were of Yugoslavian oak and made in Veneto. They are very similar to the Amarone and Valpolicella botti of the Lago di Garda region, and likely came from there a couple of generations or more ago through the family's ties with Italy.

Rafael then led us to their current barrel aging cellar, and I was very pleased to see that Vista Alegre is using small new oak barrels to age its better reds. I saw American oak as well as French barrels from Radoux, Demptos and Nadalie, and all those I saw were medium toast.

We spent some time looking at the wonderful copper of the Pisco distillery, and Rafael explained its use to the group. I have always enjoyed the gracefulness of the swan's necks above the pot stills.

We walked among the condensers and the serpentine cooling coils.

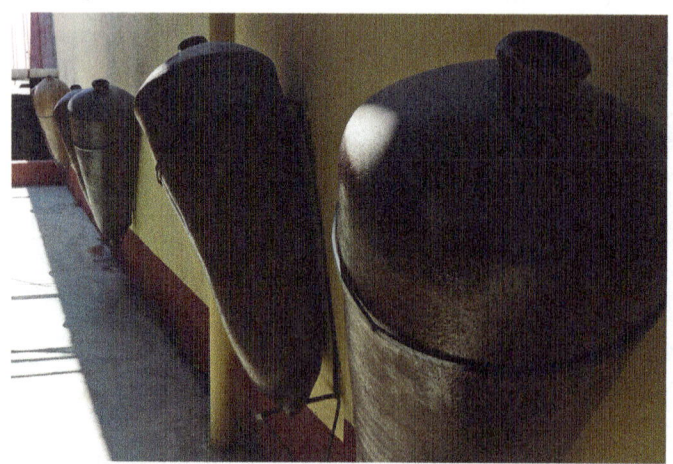

There is an old-world charm to the architecture and the decor in the distillery, and this is added to by some ancient Pisco ceramic urns decoratively mounted on the distillery walls and in the gardens, other urns serve as decorative accents.

We walked up a driveway and through an archway at the back of the compound and out into the vineyards.

A large plot of newly planted vines seemed to stretch all the way back to the foothills of the Andes.

Rafael invited us into his home, and into other private areas of the complex. He told us of the confiscation of the vast majority of the family's vineyard lands by the government in 1970, and of the family's long struggle to continue.

On the walls of one reception room was a collection of ancient burial bags and cloths that had been found on the property over the years. Rafael's wife had had these restored and mounted for display. Some were only fragments, many of which were reported to be over a thousand years old.

Some were remarkably well-preserved, like this purse.

The Nazca culture had flourished from the second to the ninth century in the Ica Valley near the family's winery and also in the valley of the Rio Grande de Nazca. The culture had been heavily influenced by the preceding Paracas culture, which was known for its extremely complex textiles. The culture is most famous these days for having produced the nearby Nazca Lines.

It is remarkable to see how well these fabrics have survived the centuries; I am assuming that the very arid climate, with little or no measurable rainfall is a huge factor.

We then went to the tasting room, where Rafael poured samples of his wines for us to taste. We worked our way through a range, with some very pleasant lighter wines, and then we got to his flagship wines.

The high quality of his Picasso Chardonnay surprised us, but then we were totally bowled-over by the 2007 Picasso Tempranillo. This is a wonderfully complex wine with a captivating nose of cassis, blackberries and underlying layers of leather and oak. On the palate are bright cassis and blackberry flavours that carry through into a long, clean finish. The tannins are firm, but well integrated and promise good aging potential. The overall impression is of elegance.

We bought a case. Several other members of the group also bought cases of the wines they enjoyed. We were then led through some gardens to a bar at the side of a swimming pool, where there was a splendid buffet laid-out. Rafael introduced us to his brother Alfredo, who oversees the technical aspects of the winery and distillery. Alfredo and I engaged in wine talk as we nibbled and drank. He introduced me to their Senorial, a Muscat Alexandria which I found remarkably similar to a fine Frontignan or Rivesaltes, and it went wonderfully with the pate de foie gras. Rafael saw my obvious enjoyment, and presented me with a bottle.

We then drove across to the other side of Ica, to Las Dunas, a small luxury hotel owned by the family. It is sited at the base of some huge sand dunes and near the airstrip from which flights over the Nazca Lines take off. We were led into the dining room to a poolside table, and Edi and I sat next to Rafael and his son Jaime at one end of the long table. There was a splendid buffet laid-out, with a large selection of hot and cold foods, with many Peruvian specialties. Onto my plate I managed to place a little bit of everything, not wanting to miss a taste experience.

We went back to our table and continued our lively conversation, and our attempt to empty a seemingly bottomless source of Picasso Tempranillo. The rest of the group left the table to go sand-boarding on the dunes, leaving Rafael and Jaime and Edi and me on our own.

We talked of eighteen-year-old Jaime's fifteen-year bout with brain cancer, of his wonderful spirit and of his having far exceeded his early life expectation. Rafael and Jaime were on their way to California the following week for follow-up on treatments at Stanford, where he continues to amaze the doctors.

The Picasso Tempranillo flowed endlessly into our glasses, at least at our end of the table, and we enjoyed an animated and broad-ranging conversation. Rafael asked if I wanted some lomo soltado, and seeing my enthusiasm, he took me to a cooking station where a chef prepared some as we watched.

The sand-boarding crowd rejoined us, and after postres and coffees we made our farewells and piled into the van for our return drive to La Punta. We were back aboard Sequitur at 2340 after an extremely full day.

We slept-in on Sunday and had a late-morning breakfast of toasted freshly-imported bagels with Peruvian Queso Crema and Peruvian coffee. In the early afternoon I sorted through all the things Edi had brought back in her luggage. In addition to biscotti and bagels, there were many kilos of our favourite 72% dark chocolate, a few kilos of asiago cheese, bags of dried fruit and several other edible niceties not available here. To feed the sewing machine, Edi had brought in several metres of cordura nylon, ultra suede and other locally unobtainable materials.

There was also 15 metres of 000 tinned wire, weighting 16 kilograms, eight cable terminals, four screw-post battery terminals and four Racor fuel filters that Edi had tracked-down with the friendly assistance of Peter Johnston at River Marine. Peter had gone out of his way to provide her with quick and accurate service at very low prices. This is such a refreshing change from the high prices, the lack of service, the lack of concern, the long order delays and the other frustrations we had with the two major marine retailers in Vancouver. We now had most of the pieces that I need to install the second alternator.

Early on Sunday afternoon, as we were puttering about onboard, Gonzalo and Magdala hailed us from their sailboat, Tatita. They were bringing our case of Picasso Tempranillo out to Sequitur. It was a very special delivery by very special friends of a very special wine from a very special day.

On Monday morning as I was heading out the gate with the garbage, the guard in the caseta called me over to tell me that a package had arrived for Sequitur. The spare assembly and the repair kit for the Lewmar engine control had finally arrived after three weeks in the mail. Taking-up almost the entire back of the package was a Customs declaration in Spanish printed in huge font on letter-sized paper. The Google translation that I had sent the shipper seems to have worked as I had hoped it would; the package had made it through Customs without duties and taxes. The declaration read the Spanish equivalent of: *"Repair parts for Canadian sailboat in transit. Parts will not remain in Peru. No value for Customs."*

My next hope was that I would be able to examine the new mechanism and determine what was amiss with the broken one. To this point, I had not been able to locate repair sheets, engineering drawings, or any other piece of guidance to help me. By ordering the whole new mechanism and the repair kit, I was hoping that I would be able to easily spot the problem and use some of the repair kit to fix it, leaving us with a new spare. If not, then I would swap the old mechanism with the new and be left with a broken spare and a repair kit to try set it right.

I donned my spelunking kit and tunnelled into the dark and cramped spaces aft of the port cockpit settee locker, managing to gash my head only once on a protruding bolt end. The space is so cramped that it is very difficult to get a proper look at the mechanism. After more than an hour of repeatedly twisting body joints, scraping skin, craning neck and seemingly extending eyeballs beyond their sockets, I had done sufficient examining, comparing, thinking, reexamining, re-comparing and rethinking, to finally figure out what was wrong with the mechanism.

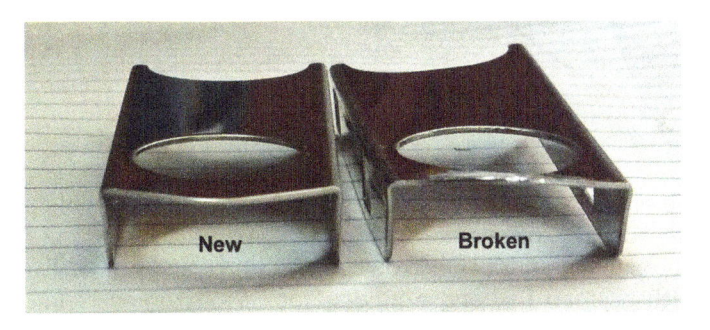

I determined that the stainless clip had bent and sprung off two of the four retaining lugs, and it was no longer holding the sheath of the shift cable. This allowed the sheath to move with the cable and rendered the transmission linkage ineffective. I replaced the clip after only forty-five minutes of manoeuvring my body and teaching my left elbow how to bend backwards and my fingers to grow a couple of centimetres and develop double articulated joints. I ran the engine and tested the transmission. We again had mobility. For the first time since we had left Paita in early June, I could shift forward and astern without having to go down to the engine space and push or pull the transmission lever.

On Monday afternoon we went ashore by launch and caught a taxi to Maestro on Argentina to look for, among other things, some spacers that I needed to continue with the installation of the alternator. We found the proper ones and we also bought a telescoping pole, designed for paint rollers. We had been looking for boathook handles to attach to the three boathook ends we had brought from Vancouver, and this was the best we had seen in the many times we had been out searching. We had no luck; however, in finding metric hardware, and we need to keep searching for some stainless 6mm lock washers. We walked along the two blocks to Minka and had lunch in a small chifa, before we bought some fresh fruit and vegetables and a kilo of eggs.

On Tuesday we took a bus along La Marina to San Miguel and went shopping at Sodimac and Tottus. Among other things, I bought a 100 Watt soldering gun so that I can solder the connectors to the ends of the 000 wire. I could not find any large gauge crimpers, and will need to keep looking.

We also bought some groceries and fresh produce, and picked-out a nice-looking fillet of perico. In the evening I prepared the fish in a brown butter sauce and served it with basmati rice and a julienne of carrots, onions and red and green peppers, garnished with roma tomatoes. The accompanying Gato Negro Sauvignon Blanc did not justify its price.

On Wednesday I went into the starboard transom locker to begin the process of repairing the autopilot. My analysis of the symptoms had concluded that the drive motor had not been properly installed by the yard in Vancouver during our fit-out. We had begun receiving intermittent *Lost Drive* error messages on the autopilot screen in late December, while we were at Isla Espiritu Santo in the Sea of Cortez.

As the problem worsened through January, and after I had eliminated electronic causes, I had discovered that the drive motor was hanging at the ends of its mounting bolts. It had apparently been hung there with the lead portion of its splines mated, but it had not been tightened up into place to fully engage the splines. I immediately tightened the drive motor up into its proper place, and the autopilot began working again. The damage had been done; however, and within two months the *Lost Drive* error began to recur with each new spell of heavy seas. By spring, the autopilot had ceased to function even in the calmest of seas.

Now it was time to see if my analysis had been correct. I dismounted the drive and shot a series of photos, some with grease still in place and some with the grease wiped away to reveal the damage and some of an undamaged unit. The Service Manager at Specialty Yachts in Vancouver, the yard that had done our fit-out, arranged to have Lewmar send some used parts for me to use to try to do a repair. In comparing the splines on the installed drive with those on the used, but undamaged drive, it is obvious that my analysis was correct. There are two distinct levels of wear; the first up to the point to which the loose splines would have reached, and the second the remainder of the splines that would have been engaged after the drive had been properly tightened home.

I could not easily get my head into position to see the male splines, so I manoeuvred the camera into position and shot some photos. Thankfully, the male splines appeared to be made of harder steel, and they showed only minor damage, some rounding and flattening at their ends. I need now to locate a heavy-duty 8mm hex wrench so that I can disassemble the drive motor and replace the end unit and its damaged splines with the spare. Then I will see if I can mount those replaced female splines onto the existing male splines without having to do any machining. If I can, it will save me all the work of removing and replacing the T bevel drive.

Late on Wednesday afternoon I went ashore and met Richard, and with him drove to Miraflores for the weekly meeting of Sociadad Numismatica del Peru. I was warmly received by the group as a Past President of the Royal Canadian Numismatic Association, and I told the small gathering that Richard is our only member in South America, and that I couldn't pass through Lima without a visit to them.

I had a delightful evening, discussing some of the different aspects of coin grading between our two countries, learning about the fascination of collecting Peruvian coppers and a myriad other numismatic topics. There were thirteen of us at the meeting, and during a break, I was presented with an extremely fine example of the 1925 Sole as a memento of my visit.

After much discussion, some trading and a small auction, ten of us drove across town to a private club above the cliffs in Miraflores, and there we sat in a private gaming room playing a round of dudo, a local dice game. About half an hour into the game a waiter came in with menus and took our dinner orders, and we continued rolling dice for another half hour or so. By the time we had finished the game, and had made our way up to the dining room, our dinners were ready. This is the regular weekly routine of the society, and I found it very civilized when compared to the monthly meeting routine of most Canadian coin clubs. Richard drove me back to La Punta, and I was back aboard Sequitur shortly after 0100.

On Thursday Edi and I continued with little projects aimed at getting Sequitur ready for continuing south. Edi tried-out the new Brother sewing machine for the first time onboard, as she made-up ultra suede covers for some of the cockpit throw cushions. The machine is rated at 70 Watts, so it was a very minor draw on the battery, never demanding as much as 5 amps while I watched the gauge. Mid-afternoon we made a run ashore to the pier to get water, and while we were there we paused for some ceviche and cervesa on the upper deck.

On Friday morning we went ashore and walked the three kilometres or so to an area we had been told has many marine hardware stores. We crisscrossed the area, we asked for directions, and all we could find were suppliers of commercial fishing supplies and very heavy marine goods. No one we asked knew of any source for stainless steel hardware or pleasure yacht supplies. We then walked back to Callao's version of 2nd of May Avenue and caught a bus headed to La Marina.

We got off at Plaza San Miguel and walked across to Maestro, where the only metric hex wrenches we could find came as half of a 26-piece set of US and metric. We bought it, plus an articulated mirror on an extendable wand and an assortment of nuts, bolts and washers. We then continued across to Wong, where we bought another eight kilos of flour and half a dozen bottles of wine in our continuing process of restocking Sequitur. For our current consumption we also bought some pork loin and some fresh produce, including portobello mushrooms, plus an assortment of cheeses and some breads.

On Sunday morning we made a run ashore to get water, and then shortly before noon we took the launch ashore again to meet Gonzalo. He had kindly offered to drive us around to try to find a replacement for our stolen dinghy. We drove the twenty-or-so kilometres to Miraflores, and stopped at Aquasport. We are looking for an inflatable in the 3.0 to 3.5 metre range, and they had only one in stock of that size, a Korean-built no-name. It looked well-built; but unfortunately, it was made of PVC, not Hypalon.

We learned that Aquasport manufactures a line of inflatables locally with imported materials, including Hypalon. Among the sizes they build is a 3.3 metre, which is available as either a fibreglass hulled RIB or as a slatted aluminum-floored roll-up. Their delivery time from order is two weeks. With Gonzalo's assistance, we had the Corporate Sales Consultant, Melissa Cuadros Montalvo write-up a quote for both models, the RIB at US$4,500 and the roll-up at US$2,200.

We then drove to the Regatta Club in Chorrillos. This is a very large and modern private sports club, founded in 1875, and Gonzalo had arranged to meet a fellow there who had some used inflatables, but we couldn't locate him. After making a phone call, Gonzalo said he would arrive around 1500, and suggested we have lunch while waiting.

Gonzalo asked if we liked Japanese, and from our enthusiastic response, he took us to Itamae, a Japanese fusion restaurant on the beachfront within the club compound. We started with some superb ahi sashimi, followed by an assortment of wonderfully creative rolls and finished with a platter of shellfish and vegetables. We spent an hour sharing broad-ranging conversation and outstanding food. Gonzalo would not allow us to pay for the lunch, lamely insisting that since we were not members, we could not pay.

On our way back to meet the fellow with the used dinghies, we passed some Inca terns, beautiful medium-sized birds with red feet and red beaks and distinctive white moustaches. Their range is restricted to where the Humboldt Current meets the coasts of Peru and Chile, and these were the first examples we had seen.

The fellow with the dinghies had not shown-up, so after Gonzalo had made another phone call, we piled into his car and chased back up the cliffs and into Miraflores to the fellow's boatyard. What he had were not suitable; either too large or too used. Gonzalo drove us back to La Punta, and then had to drive all the way back to Miraflores and rush to get ready for a family wedding in the early evening. We continue to receive such outstanding hospitality here in Peru.

We were still in our bathrobes after a very late breakfast on Sunday the 7th, when there was a knock on the hull. Eugenio Olivera of sailboat Mardulce had arrived in a bright red dinghy with Jorge Luis Montero, the Commercial Manager of Aquadventures. We had told Eugenio, as we shared the launch ashore with him on Friday, that we were looking for a new dinghy and motor to replace the ones which had been stolen in Paita. He had told us he had a friend.... We had told him we were busy on Saturday.... He had said Sunday, and here he was.

I quickly dressed and welcomed Eugenio plus Luis and his lady friend, Milagro onboard. We discussed the Sea Rider dinghy, and we were told it was built in Korea by a company from the Netherlands. It is made from a composite polyurethane fabric named Akron, which is a relatively new European material with an ultraviolet and abrasion resistance between that of Hypalon and PVC. We talked technical details for a while, and then Luis and I went for a spin around the mooring field.

The dinghy he had brought to Sequitur was a 3.8 metre folding aluminum floored model with an inflatable keel, and it was fitted with a Tohatsu 18-hp two-stroke engine. With the two of us onboard, it very quickly got up on plane and was very stable running at 15 to 18 knots. Back onboard, we talked more and shared email addresses so we could continue the discussion.

After Luis and party had left, I took my newly acquired heavy-duty 6mm hex wrench into the starboard transom locker and dismantled the end of the autopilot drive motor. I then replaced the end-piece, with its gears and damaged splines, with the spare end piece from Lewmar. I was working on the drive motor in the transom locker, rather than out in a more spacious place, so that I didn't have to undo all the electrical connections on it. My next hope was that the somewhat flattened and rounded ends of the male splines would fit into the replacement female splines. To my relief, a bit of delicate alignment and a few heavy thumps with a fist sent the splines home. In theory, we now have our electrical autopilot working again. Confirmation will need to await a sea trial.

While I was repairing the autopilot, Edi had set-up our sewing machine in the cockpit, and was designing and sewing together a cover for our Hydrovane.

On Monday morning Luis sent me an email with much additional technical information and some links to sites with more. We emailed back-and-forth a couple of times, adding greatly to my confidence both in his product and in him, and I learned everything I needed to know to make a well-informed purchase decision.

Luis is also the distributor for Tohatsu outboards, which is the brand that my research in Vancouver over the summer had pointed to as my first choice engine. They are the first builder of small gasoline engines in Japan as well as the first Japanese builders of outboards motors. Their new production facility has the capacity for 200,000 units per year, and they currently manufacture motors under the Tohatsu brand, as well as for Mercury, Nissan and others.

On Monday evening I emailed Luis, requesting a quote on a 3.6-metre dinghy and an 18-hp Tohatsu 2-stroke motor. He emailed me a formal quote, and with his reply he told me that he is buying a new 4.0 metre RIB and a 30hp engine, and that he was going to be putting into storage his current 18hp engine. He added, *"... there is the possibility to sell my current in use motor, next week will perform its first 300 hour general maintenance to have it in form for this summer"* I told him we were interested in the used motor, and asked him for a price. He asked when we could come with him to see the dinghies, and I said whenever it was convenient with him.

For dinner on Monday evening we enjoyed tarragon chicken with a butter sauté of mini portobellos, shallots and garlic, accompanied by mashed potatoes, fine green beans amandine and sliced roma tomatoes. The 2009 Las Moras Reserve Chardonnay complimented very nicely.

On Tuesday morning Luis called us on VHF and said he was in La Punta and could take me to see the dinghies. I called a launch and went ashore to meet him, and we drove through the extremely heavy traffic past the port and airport to a residential area. He introduced me to Percy Estrada Rojas, his technical expert who, according to the certificates on the wall, has been for over fifteen years a trained repair and maintenance technician for Zodiac inflatables and liferafts.

Luis and Percy showed me an inflated and assembled 3.6-metre model, and I was pleased to see the capacity plate on the transom indicated that it was CE certified and conformed to the ISO9001 standards. It is constructed with Akron PE, a composite polyurethane fabric certified to have high resistance to abrasion, pollution and UV. The fabric was developed in Germany for use in professional and rescue craft, and is being used by the US Coast Guard and the Royal Navy, among others. It was designed as a better alternative to costly Hypalon fabrics.

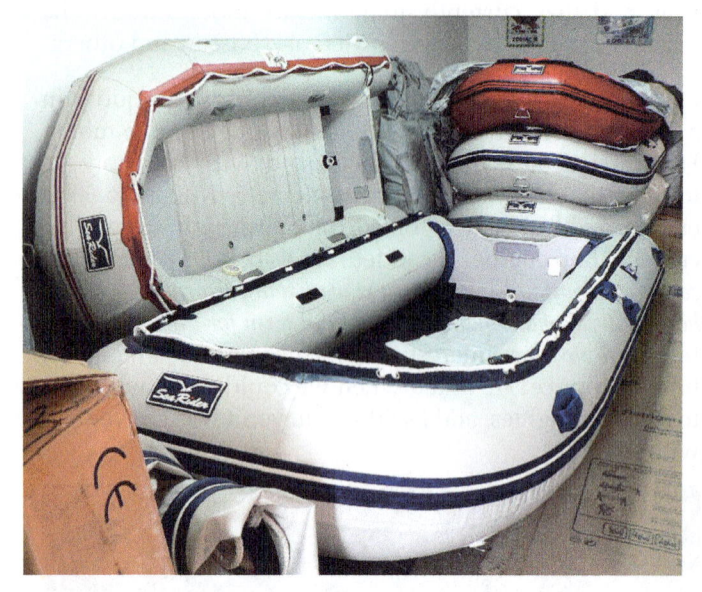

The boat looked very-well built and solid. I was told that the fabric is 1.2mm thick, rather than the industry standard of 1.0mm or less for this size boat. At 3.6 metres, the new dinghy is half-a-metre longer overall than our former Walker Bay 310, and I needed to confirm that it would easily fit onto our davits, on which the falls are 185cm apart. I measured the new dinghy's distance from its transom to its forward internal eye-pads as 200cm, and assessed that this small difference would present no problem. Its beam of 165cm is identical to that of the Walker Bay, and its weight of 68.5 kilograms is only 7.5 kilos heavier. The maximum load is 689 kilos compared to 620 kilos for the Walker Bay.

The Sea Rider 3.6 comes with two carrying bags for the rolled boat and the aluminum floor panels, a wooden bow seat with side hooks, an emergency patch kit, two aluminum oars, a bow bag, a fitted tube cover, a Scoprega dual high and low-pressure foot pump, a Ceredi big-dial pressure gauge and air valve adaptor, a can of 303 aerospace protector spray for the tubes and a complete installation course, including assembly and inflation procedures and overall care. For US$2,000 (which this week is CA$2,000), I thought it was a bargain.

I told Luis I would take the pale grey model with the blue trim, and I asked him to have the two forward eye-pad attachments reinforced so that we can use them as hoisting points. I also asked him to include a spare drain plug and a spare oarlock assembly.

On Tuesday afternoon Edi baked. She prepared a couple of loaves of potato bread, using the extra mashed potatoes I had made on Monday evening. While the loaves rose, she started on three different batches of biscotti: a slivered almond, an apricot and almond and a hazelnut and almond.

Baking is always a bit of a trick with a small gas oven in a boat's galley, but the three loaves rose and baked very well, and she found them easy to slice for their second baking.

By early evening we had six dozen biscotti. Edi then turned to the potato bread loaves.

The dough had risen wonderfully in the stable confines of the microwave oven. While Edi was back in Vancouver for the birth of her granddaughter the previous month, she had experimented with bread recipes, and this potato bread one was her favourite.

Finding good bread here in Peru, similar to our experience in Mexico; is very difficult. It is mostly too sweet or too tough. We had a baguette the previous week that nearly ripped our teeth out as we tried to bite-off, then tear-off a piece to eat. Edi's loaves had no chance to rest before we had sliced-off slabs to sample. Wonderful! Tender! Delicious!

On Wednesday morning, as the launch approached to take me ashore on a diesel run, I saw Steve Wagner in its bow. He handed me a rolled-up bundle, and I put it in the cockpit and boarded the launch. Steve had delivered the front centre panel of our dodger, into which he had fitted a replacement the window. While we had been away in Vancouver, the tripulantes had been too aggressive in their cleaning efforts, and had fogged it into near opacity.

Steve is widely reputed as the only sail-maker on the Pacific coast of South America, and couple of weeks previously we had walked with him from his sail loft to his tiny marine shop in the Mercado, and looked at his selection of plastic sheeting. He had a small piece of material identical to that which needed replacing. We would be able to see forward again from our cockpit.

On Wednesday afternoon, Edi and I took a bus to San Miguel and got off at Wong. The previous week we had taken advantage of a wine sale, offering 40% discount on many labels, and we had put a good dent into replenishing Sequitur's cellar. We had returned to continue the process. We picked-up an additional sixteen bottles, including half-a-dozen Freixinet Cordon Negro Cava at S/32.13, about $11.50 per bottle.

While we were there we also bought a 2.5 kilogram bonita tuna, and watched as the fishmonger cleaned it and cut it into the two-inch steaks we had requested. For $10.85 we had three pair of steaks for grilling and the end pieces for a fish stew.

On Thursday morning, Luis emailed with a quote on his used 18hp Tohatsu. He also told me that he needed to modify the transom of the dinghy by adding 2.5cm to the top of it so that the motor would be at its perfect depth. He added: *"We raise transoms all the time, will need to cut middle strake, open it a bit, drill 3 holes to place wooden stuckos and raise the transom with fiberglass, let it dry, sand a bit, re paint, and screw both front/rear engine plates to a higher transom position than before"*. I told him to proceed.

Also on Thursday morning we received an email from Gonzalo telling us that our wine order for three additional cases of Rafael Picasso's wines would be delivered to his house during the day, and that he could deliver it to us on the weekend. He forwarded the banking particulars for our direct deposit to Bodegas Vista Alegre's account. We had found the wines so outstanding that we couldn't leave without buying more. Unlike my experience with much of the rest of the wine world, the prices from the winery here are considerably less expensive than they are in the supermarkets. In other places, the prices at the winery are higher than in the supermarkets, since the producers do not want to undercut their distribution chain.

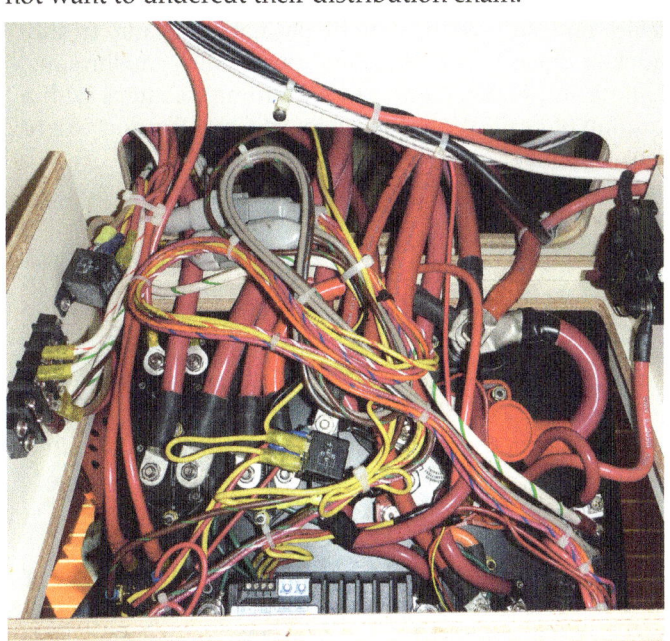

I opened-up the back of the main 12-volt distribution panel and examined the plate of spaghetti, trying to make sense of it. Also I needed to plan my cable runs from the 210 amp alternator to the house bank, and to include the start batteries for the main engine and the generator. My simplest approach would be to connect to the same terminals as the generator, since its nominal rating is 280 amps with a continuous output of 220 amps, so quite similar to the 210 amps of the Balmar.

I began working on the cables, fitting the terminals onto the ends of the wire that Edi had hauled back from Vancouver in her luggage. I tried without success to replicate a crimper with the internal articulations of our bolt cutter. I saw I had to either find a proper crimper or take the wires ashore and use a heavy hammer and a punch with concrete slab as an anvil. I had to take the wires ashore anyway, to see if our 220 volt 100 amp soldering gun can generate enough heat in the terminal and wire to draw-in some solder.

On Thursday evening I seared a pair of fresh bonita tuna steaks and served them with basmati rice and freshly shucked peas with sautéed portobello mushrooms, shallots and garlic, garnished with roma tomatoes with a sprinkle of basil. With it we enjoyed Cava Cordon Negro from Freixinet.

Midmorning on Friday we grabbed a bus along La Marina, and after more than hour, we got off on Prado at Arequipa, north of Miraflores. We walked the 3.7 kilometres down to Angamos and along it into the suburb of Surquillo a tiny shop at 1019 called Pernoshow. We were told it had a broad selection of stainless steel hardware, including milimetricos, which we had thus far not been able to find in Peru. They had bins of open stock of what we wanted, and we walked away satisfied.

We walked west back along Angamos for two kilometres to Huaca Pucllana, the partly restored ruins of a pyramid thought to have been built by the Lima Culture about fourteen to nineteen hundred years ago. It was mid-afternoon and our breakfasts had long since worn-off, so we stopped at La Bodega de la Tratoria, an Italian-style restaurant near the entrance to the ruins. We ordered two personal-sized pizzas, a prosciutto and an Italian sausage, and they were both delicious.

For S/10 each we bought tickets for a guided tour of the ruins. We learned that excavation began on the site in 1981, after two-thirds of it had been destroyed and built-over as Lima expanded. The preserved lands include the entire pyramid and several surrounding plazas. The construction technique was layer upon layer of small adobe bricks, placed vertically like books on a shelf. The site is surrounded on all sides by the upscale homes of Miraflores.

The adobe bricks were made from local materials, and there were dioramas showing the method of brick making. The clay was mixed by foot, and the bricks were individually hand-formed, as indicated by the remaining finger marks. From the bleached, starched and ironed clothing the brick-makers were wearing, we gathered that the Lima Culture had a highly evolved laundry service.

The Lima Culture used the pyramid and its surrounding plazas for religious ceremonial purposes. Some fourteen hundred years ago the Lima Culture suffered internal crises and was overrun by the Wari Empire from Ayacucho to the southeast. The ceremonial uses of the site ceased, and it became a burial place for Wari elite.

There was also a display depicting a ceremony. We learned that the main ceremonies centred on remodelling the structures, having banquets of shark meat, breaking ceramic jars and sacrificing women and children. Pondering the these last activities, we thought it a good thing that the culture was overrun.

We finished the tour and walked back through residential areas and along the boulevard walkway up the centre of Arequipa to Prado, where we caught a bus to La Punta. We arrived back aboard Sequitur shortly after 1800, after an eight-hour excursion for stainless steel nuts, bolts and washers. Of this we spent two-and-a-half hours on buses for a total fare of S/6, and we walked a bit over eight kilometres. We were tired.

We have begun to focus more closely on repairs and maintenance on Sequitur and on other details in preparation for the continuation of our voyage south. There were still many things we need to do before we even think of picking a date for our departure from La Punta. High on our list is to travel inland to visit some of the Inca sites.

To help us with this, on Saturday morning we had taken some fresh biscotti over to Precious Metal to have with the coffee that Pamela had offered. She had organized a tour the previous week for a group of her friends from Canada and the US, and she had offered to share with us the contact information for the hotels in Cusco and Machu Picchu and other places where they had stayed. She also gave us the contact information for Pepe Lopez, her local travel agent.

Among other things, I learned that Pamela and I had lived within a few kilometres of each other from the late 80s to the early 00s; she in White Rock and me in Crescent Beach, British Columbia. We had many mutual friends.

Much of the remainder of Saturday we spent cleaning and repairing. I re-secured the port after foot of the solar panel arch, which had worked free during our buck of the Humboldt Current. The installers at Specialty Yachts in Vancouver had not used a backing plate there, and with the strain from the wind generator and SSB antenna, which are mounted above it, all four bolts had worked free. They had used normal nuts with no lock washers, and there was no evidence of any thread lock having been used. We had limped into Lima with some spare polyester line lashing the arch down to the stern cleat. At least now we have large pan washers, stainless lock washers, Loctite and pal-nuts to keep things in place until we can have backing plates fabricated.

On Sunday morning Jaime came out to Sequitur by launch to deliver the 6mm stainless lock washers he had told us the previous week that he could get for us that same day. I paid him the S/7.40, and didn't have the heart to tell him we had gone to Surquillo on Thursday to pick up some.

A little later on Sunday morning, Gonzalo called us on VHF to tell us he was sending his son out in the dinghy to deliver our three cases of wine. A couple of minutes later Gonzalito arrived off our stern and expertly manoeuvred the dinghy alongside the platform so that the tripulante could easily hand me the cases. It was a very fine display of boat-handling by the seven-year-old boy.

A short while later Gonzalo motored past our stern in Tatita, and we thanked him for organizing the purchase and delivery of the wines from Bodegas Vista Alegre. He invited us to join him at the club at 1700.

I took a launch ashore to get another two jerry cans of water, and on the way in we stopped at Magic Carpet Ride to pick up Dave. He had arrived in La Punta a couple of days previously from another leg of his cruise, which had started in Seattle eight or nine-years previously. As I was filling the water jugs, Luis motored by in his Sea Rider, and he came alongside the landing. I loaded the water containers into the dinghy and we motored out to Sequitur.

I had decided to take a shortcut and load the water directly onto the side deck next to the water fills, as I had been doing from the launch. This saves lugging the 20 kilogram jugs into the cockpit, then out of it and a dozen metres forward over and under all the anti-bird lines and nets. From the dinghy; however, the lift to the side deck is over shoulder height, and somewhat awkward from the bobbing platform. I didn't plan it well, and in the process, both the first jug and I fell into the water. Fortunately, we both floated. Also fortunately, my glasses stayed on my head, and the pocket that my camera was in was zipped-up, and the camera was waterproof.

In the late afternoon, shortly after Gonzalo sailed Tatita past our stern with his family aboard, we called a launch to take us ashore to the club. Gonzalo is such a wonderful assistance to us and to other visiting cruisers. Without him, our stay in Peru would have been very much less interesting, and our impression of the place very much diminished.

We sat on the upper deck of the club, enjoying wonderful conversation and camaraderie with Gonzalo and Magdala and their two children. With us was Pamela of Precious Metal, who is sailing north on Wednesday to the Galapagos and onward to the Mexican Riviera. An hour or so later we were joined by Kim, Steve and Cullem of Odyle. After two delightful hours, we headed back to Sequitur to continue with our preparations.

Among the jobs on my long list was repairing and remounting the aft shower door. The door had popped free of its retaining catch when Sequitur awkwardly fell off a wave in early January off the Baja coast. The twelve kilogram weight of the flopping articulated door had torn out the six screws along with six chunks of acrylic that had held the hinge strip to the edge of door. I had repaired the door the following week, but it had again come off its hinges in a doldrums storm on our Passage to the Galapagos.

I removed the door hinge plate and removed a screw from it to serve as a sample when we head out in search of some that are 6 or 7mm longer.

Edi completed a Christmas card for me to give to Richard to thank him for his kind and generous hospitality during my visit to the Associacion Numismatica del Peru. She had made a cut-out window to display one of my RCNA Presidential Medals as an ornament on a watercolour rendering of a festooned bough of holly.

On Sunday evening we enjoyed jumbo prawns sautéed in a concassé of mushrooms, shallots and garlic into which I had rolled some steamed mini potatoes, and served with fine green beans amandine and sliced roma tomatoes. The 2009 Concha y Toro Trio, a Chardonnay, Chenin and Pinot Blanc blend, complimented the dinner nicely.

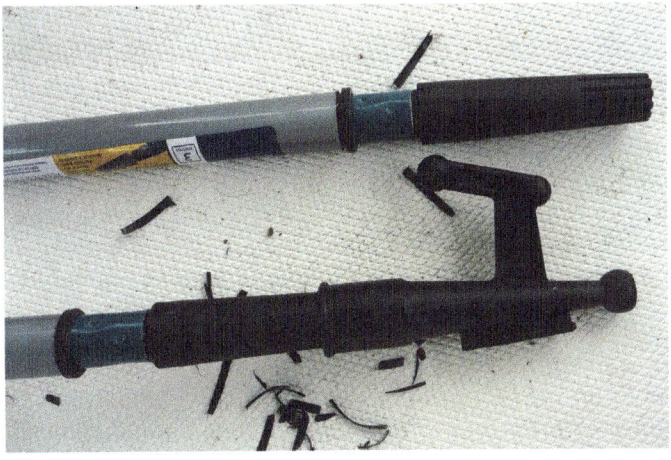

On Monday we negotiated a S/5 taxi and went to the Maestro on Argentina to pick up some screws for the shower door repair, and while we were there, we bought two more of the extendable handles that we had bought two weeks previously. I had whittled-down the tapered polyethylene splines on the business end of the handle and had installed and through-bolted onto it one of the three polyethylene boathook ends we had brought back from Vancouver. It had worked so well that I decided to use two more of the same model handle for the other two hooks. We will have the first new boathooks we have seen south of Puerto Vallarta, Mexico.

We added a few more things to our cart then checked-out from Maestro and walked across the street and up the block or so to Minka. For S/53 we bought three kilos of boneless and skinless chicken thighs and a tad over two kilos of boneless and skinless chicken breasts from our favourite shop. We then crossed the aisle to buy eggs; this time the chicken came before the egg.

The Cost of Eating Aboard Sequitur

Several readers of our blog had commented that from our dining photos, our food costs must be quite high, and some have asked how much we spend for our dinners. With this shopping trip to Minka I had again included prices. For S/3.5 we bought a kilo of eggs, which this time came to fifteen. The eggs here are so fresh that we keep them on the shelf, rather than in the fridge, and even thus, after two or three weeks, they are still fresher than supermarket eggs in Canada or the US. We added three fresh mangoes and two avocados for S/5, four very nice bunches of asparagus for S/10, two kilos of roma tomatoes for S/2, three kilos of mashing potatoes for S/7, a kilo of red peppers for S/4, two kilos of green peppers for S/6, a big head of celery for S/1 a half-kilo bag of shallots for S/1 and a quarter kilo of freshly peeled garlic for S/2.5.

Back onboard Sequitur, I divided the chicken into nine double servings of thighs and six double servings of breasts, giving an average cost of 63 cents a serving. To complete a typical chicken breast dinner, the cost would be 44 cents per serving for the asparagus, 47 cents for mushrooms, 10 cents for the potatoes, 6 cents for the tomato, 7 cents for the shallot, 6 cents for the garlic, 10 cents for the mayonnaise, and no more than 25 cents for butter and condiments. This is less than $2.20 per plate.

I wanted to compare the cost of our standard dinner with that of a *cheap* one, but since I have had neither Spam nor Kraft Dinner for well over forty years, I was out of touch with prices, and had to look them up on the net. I found 225 gram boxes of Kraft Dinner at between $1.49 and $1.89, and 340 gram cans of Spam at $2.35 each. Add to this the cost of the milk and butter necessary for preparing the pasta, plus a splurp of ketchup for the meat, and the cost per serving runs to more than our $2.20. Even without the cost advantage of our style of dining, we prefer Sequitur's current menu.

227

On Tuesday morning Edi made fresh blueberry muffins using some of the Costco dried blueberries she had brought in her luggage from Vancouver. They baked wonderfully in the silicone muffin tins, and we enjoyed some of them for breakfast with cream cheese and Peruvian coffee. The muffins were delicious; however, we found the blueberries too sweet. A check of the package showed glucose and fructose had been added in the processing. The next time we need to soak them in water to re-hydrate them and to try to remove some of the sugar. Maybe we could soak them in Pisco.

Later on Tuesday I continued with the process of mounting the terminals on the ends of the 000 gauge cable. On a launch ride ashore a day or so previously, I had asked Herb if he had a large gauge crimper that could accommodate 000 gauge, and he had told me he had made one from a retired bolt cutter. I called him on VHF and asked if I could borrow them, and because the launch service was so delayed with the South American J-24 championships taking place this week at the Club, he motored his dinghy over from The Lady J with the crimpers.

In short order I had crimped the four terminals, and had them ready for soldering, which would need to await a trip ashore where I can plug my gun into a 220 volt circuit.

I next turned to the remounting of the after shower door. The 12mm thick acrylic folding door had been attached to its hinge strip with 19mm long screws, and with the strip being a little over 12mm thick, there was less than 7mm of screw biting into the acrylic.

This time I crazy-glued the pieces back onto the door edge and drilled the holes 7mm deeper. I refastened the door to the hinge bar using 32mm long screws. We now have a door again on the after shower for the first time since May.

On Wednesday Edi and I took a launch ashore and caught a bus along La Marina and Prado to Arequipa. We walked south a dozen blocks to Santa Cruz, which we followed another seven blocks to Ovalo Gutierrez. The broad avenue was lined with upscale buildings housing a diverse selection of small businesses and corporate offices. Around the Oval were sited several fast-food franchises, and on our way past we took advantage of the McHead. Relieved, we continued around to Espinar to Deli France.

We had been told Deli France had some of the best bread in the region, and on the net I had seen reference to it having the second best bread in Peru. We examined their broad selection of French cheeses, pates, charcuterie and other delices français. They also have a small selection of French wines, from the Champagne, Alsace, Bourgogne and Bordeaux. For S/10.50 we bought a loaf of bread to try, and told ourselves we needed to return to stock-up.

We walked back the two blocks to Ovalo Gutierrez and went into the Wong supermarket there. Its front sections appear to be the renovated interiors of two fine old homes, and then beyond them, the store continues in more normal supermarket architecture. The Wong stores are very much upmarket compared to others we have seen in Peru. This Miraflores branch is yet a notch above the one we have been frequenting in Plaza San Miguel, with a decidedly more refined selection of goods.

On Thursday morning Edi headed ashore in the launch with Bev to go to the Gamarra Market, and I went in to the pier with them to fetch another two jugs of water. Back onboard, I opened-up the engineering spaces and began wiring the new 210 amp Balmar alternator. I had decided to tie the output from the alternator directly into the connections coming from the Fischer-Panda generator, after disconnecting the positive lead from the generator. My reasoning on doing it this way was that this should give me current flow into the systems in the same manner as would the generator, were it working.

After running the 000 cables and connecting them, I turned to sorting-out the wiring for the Balmar Max Charge MC-614 multistage regulator. The first four connections were easy enough to sort out: the blue wire from terminal 1 to the alternator's field terminal, the red wire from terminal 3 to the alternator's positive output, the black wire from terminal 4 to the alternator's ground and the white wire from terminal 12 to the alternator's stator output. That left me with the brown wire on terminal 2 and the separate red-wired fused pigtail.

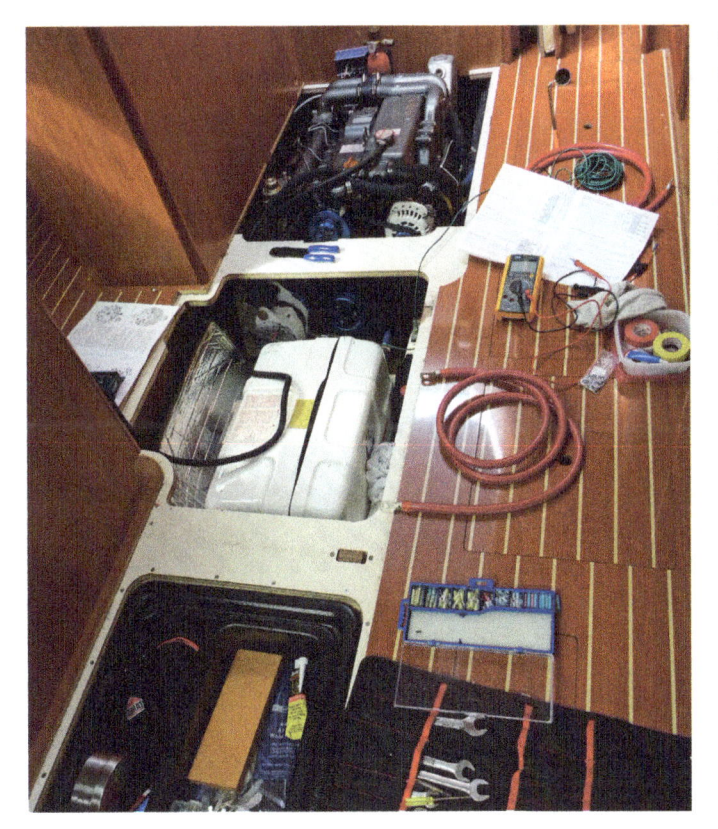

The brown wire needed to connect to the *on* side of the engine start switch. I traced some circuits and then cut the brown wire in the harness of the 120 Balmar and joined-in using a two-into-one butt connector. The fused pigtail is the for the positive battery sense wire. This needs to be connected to the positive side of the battery, preferably to the largest of the batteries being charged.

At 1225 amp-hours, our house bank is our largest battery, and it consists of ten 6-volt batteries. I chose the one which already had sensors attached, assuming previous installers had gotten it right. I ran the two recommended preflight tests with a multi-meter, and it passed them both. I then programmed the regulator to match our systems.

As I was doing the programming, Edi returned onboard from her shopping trip to Gamarra. It was late in the afternoon and I decided to close-up the spaces, cleanup the mess and continue the next day.

We started looking at travel arrangements to visit Cuzco and Machu Picchu. We were shocked to find that LAN Peru, the *"National Air Carrier"* of Peru charges triple fares for foreigners. Our flight from Lima to Cuzco return would cost us just over $1,200, but if we were Peruvian it would cost less than $400. Some further digging on the net revealed that bus fare from Lima to Cuzco return is in the $75 range, but the thought of a 21-hour bus ride was discomforting. We decided to shelve our planning for the evening.

On Friday morning I went ashore for two more jerry cans of diesel. The price was up again, which I had expected with the continuing collapse of the US dollar, to which oil prices are tied. I also filled and brought back two 20-litre jugs of water. The pier was very busy, teeming with competitors in the J-24 South American Championship being hosted by Yacht Club Peruano all this week.

Sharing the launch with me on my return trip were two crew members of the Uruguayan boat, Nomoyoc. We chatted briefly on the short ride to their boat, and I wished them well in their afternoon race. In the championship are entries from Argentina, Brazil, Chile, Peru, Puerto Rico and Uruguay. Puerto Rico's entry surprised me. While it is technically not part of any continent, when it is associated with a continent, it is North America.

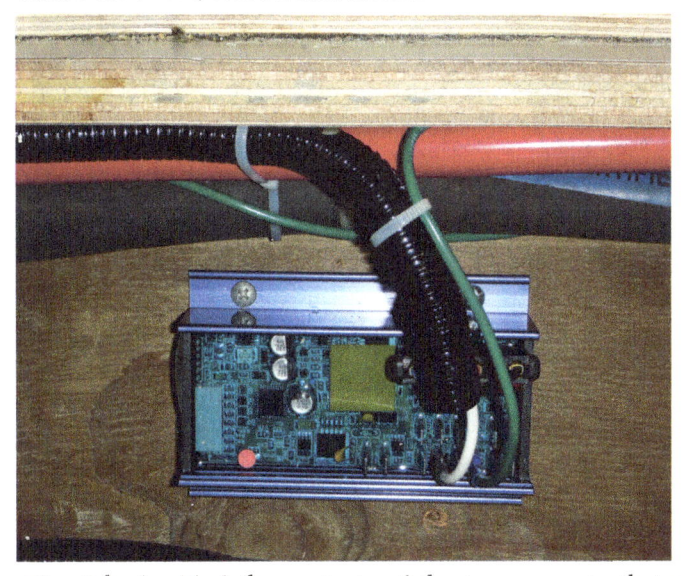

After I had added the contents of the jerry cans to their appropriate tanks, I returned to the alternator and regulator. I ran the tests again, and satisfied with my connections, I installed the regulator on the face of a longitudinal stringer in a conveniently accessible place just beneath the access lid to the generator compartment. I need only to install the drive belt to test the alternator, but I decided to leave the belt off until after I had run the engine the next morning for our usual hour or two of battery charging.

On Saturday the 20th of November I ran the engine without installing the drive belt for the Balmar 210 alternator. I had decided to hedge my bets and bring the house bank up to a higher state of charge before going live with my new alternator installation. This would provide a larger reserve of power should anything go wrong. I continued also to try to determine why the existing alternator has not been able to take the start batteries above 12.45 volts.

In the afternoon the final race of the J24 2010 South American Championships was held, and we watched from the cockpit. Hawky from Brazil won the Championship, followed by Peru's Scaramoush in second and Itau from Chile in third.

For dinner on Saturday evening I prepared bratwurst with parboiled then grilled comote accompanied by butter-sweated red and green peppers and quartered criminis. With it we enjoyed a Trivento Tribu 2009 Malbec from Argentina's Mendoza. It far surpassed the quality we had expected for its $7.09 cost, and it has been added to our buy list.

On Sunday morning I again ran the engine without belting the second alternator, bringing the bank back up from the depletions of the previous day and night and feeding breakfast's heavy demand from the coffee maker and toaster. After breakfast I again ran through all of my connections, and traced all the circuits. I also reread the installation manuals for the alternator and the regulator, and thumbed-through the appropriate sections of Nigel Calder's *Boatowner's Mechanical and Electrical Manual*.

By the time I had satisfied myself that everything was correctly done, Edi had prepared lunch. I welcomed the excuse to delay the inevitable. We sat down to some marvellous potato bunwiches of sliced leftover Bavarian bratwurst, Peruvian avocados, Danish blue from Costco in Vancouver, artichoke hearts from Costco in Acapulco and Moroccan olives from the Parthenon Deli in Kitsilano, accompanied by cups of South African Rooibos tea.

After our delicious international lunch, I could think of no more excuses to delay the trial of the new alternator. I put the belt on the pulleys and tensioned it with the convenient turnbuckle, then I flashed-up the engine and made the switches to all three batteries. Nothing exploded. There were no zapping arcs. There were no weird sounds or smells. The meters showed a charge of just over 80 amps at engine idle. I ran the engine up to a fast idle at 1100 rpm and watched as the ammeter climbed to over 150 amps. I smiled.

I ran the engine for an hour, closely monitoring the alternator, the cycling LEDs on the regulator and watched the ammeter, voltmeter and state-of-charge readings on the panel at the nav station. I also used the multi-meter to monitor the voltages of the house bank and of the two start batteries. For the first time since our generator quit, we were taking the start batteries above 12.45 volts. I watched as their charge rose over the hour to 12.9 volts, and confirmed that I had programmed the regulator properly.

230

For Sunday evening's dinner I put some skinless and boneless chicken thighs in the wok with a few drops of sesame oil and tore them into small pieces as they cooked. I set the chicken aside and into the juices and rendered fat in the wok, I added quartered criminis, diced ginger and garlic, sliced red onions and celery and later, some chunked red and green peppers. I built a sauce in the wok with a splash of light soy, a sprinkle of rice flour, a dab of oyster sauce and a slosh of boiling water from the pasta pot. I then added back in the chicken, added the hot rotini, sprinkled with freshly toasted sesame seeds and tossed. We made it a celebratory dinner in honour of my getting the second alternator working; we enjoyed glasses of Cava Freixinet Cordon Negro.

We continued the celebration with copas of Pisco Soldeica from Vista Alegre, accompanied by chunks of dark chocolate.

On Monday morning I again ran the engine at 1100 rpm to charge the house bank. The two battery monitors we have installed at the nav station are both showing erroneous State-of-Charge readings, resulting from the DC power having been switched off to safely connect the 000 cables to the system. The Xantrex LinkPro showed a flashing *"synchronize"*, indicating the bank needed to be brought to a fully charged state and then the LinkPro manually synchronized. The Magnum inverter remote showed *"Think'n"*, indicating that it still needed to sense the bank in a fully charged state before it could begin to calculate.

After an hour and a half of running, the charge ramped down from the 160 amp range to about 70 amps, as the regulator switched to the absorption phase. At two hours, with the battery accepting 13.5 volts, I shutdown the engine and watched the house bank settle to 12.65 volts, just shy of fully charged. I decided to leave it there for the day.

On Tuesday morning I ran the engine at 1600 rpm and watched as the alternators put 220 amps into the system, bulk charging for about 40 minutes, before ramping down to absorption. I watched as the toaster and coffee maker drew from the inverter and the regulator upped the charge rate to compensate. It appears we have the systems set-up and talking with each other nicely.

It was finally warm enough to have lunch outside in the cockpit, although we still needed the side curtains down. We enjoyed hot paninis.

As we lunched, we watched our neighbour, Herb working with two men trying again to fit a new awning above the fly-bridge of The Lady J. They had first begun working on it over two months previously, and the process seems to have taken-on a life of its own. We thought this might be the final fitting. However, later as I was waiting for a launch ashore, I noticed the awning was gone.

231

I have continued to keep in close communication by email with Luis on the purchase of the new dinghy and motor. Our inflation and orientation session, and the test run were originally scheduled for Tuesday, but by Monday it had slipped to Wednesday. Then on Tuesday evening, it slipped to Thursday morning.

On Wednesday morning I ran the engine at 1800 rpm and was pleased with how well the charging systems were operating. I spent some time looking further into travel arrangements for our trip to Cuzco and Machu Picchu. The previous week we had found that LAN Peru, charges triple fare for foreigners, and a flight from Lima to Cuzco return would cost us just over $1,200. We were left with the uncomfortable thoughts of a 21-hour bus ride. After further digging I found that Peruvian Airlines does not discriminate against foreigners, and we could fly to Cuzco for $169 each return. I started looking for the availability of accommodation to plan a time to travel. Fortunately, this is the beginning of the low season, making both availability and prices good.

Mid morning we took a launch ashore to catch a bus to Plaza San Miguel to, among other things look for a branch of Interbank, where I could find the easiest way to arrange payment to Luis for the dinghy and motor. On the launch ride in, we again spoke with Eugenio, who was shuttling between a couple of his boats. He had told us the previous day of Ricardo, a stainless steel fabricator, when we had enquired, and this morning he told us Ricardo was working on Madagascar in the Club boatyard. We looked for him, but nobody had seen him yet, but we were told he should be there soon.

We continued on to San Miguel, had a couple of frustrating meetings in a couple of banks, and then so that we didn't totally waste the trip, we picked-up a few things that we needed at Tottus and Sodimac. On our way back we again stopped in the Club's boatyard to see if Ricardo had arrived. I saw him, and we chatted briefly in his non-English and my non-Spanish, from which I gathered he was busy for another hour or two, and then could see me. A couple of hours later, while on a run ashore for water, I found him again in the boatyard, and showed him a drawing I had made of an outboard motor rack that I wanted built, and wanted him to give me a quote. We arranged for him to come out to Sequitur at 1000 on Thursday morning.

As we were waiting for a launch to take us back out to Sequitur, we watched two tour boats motor past the Club pier. On most days we have seen various types of these, from small three-to-four-person rowing punts to converted lifeboats. All seem to be filled to beyond safe capacity with tourists dressed in life jackets. They wend their way through the moored boats, which seem to be one of the highlights of the tour.

On Thursday morning we waited onboard for our meeting with Ricardo at 1000, and when by 1030 he hadn't arrived, we called a launch and went ashore. Edi went off in one direction on errands, and I went the other. I looked without luck for Ricardo in the yard, and then I continued on along the malecon for four blocks to the Club Universitario de Regatas to meet with Luis.

Luis ran through a short introductory course on the new Tohatsu 18hp two-stroke outboard, which he had mounted on the transom of his inflatable on its trailer on the pier. We did start and stop procedures, performed a fresh water flush, and covered the basic care and maintenance points. We unrolled the new Sea Rider 2.6 inflatable and I inspected the modifications that I had ordered. Everything was in order and the work looked very professional. Now that everything was ready for delivery, I delayed the acceptance until we had installed on Sequitur's stern a rack and locking arrangements for the outboard.

As I walked back to the pier, I again stopped at the boatyard to look for Ricardo, but still could not find him. In the mid-afternoon, Eugenio arrived off our stern in a launch, and with him was Jaime, another stainless fabricator. With Eugenio translating, we discussed my plans for the motor rack, took more measurements, and modified the plans. Jaime calculated a quote, and saying he was very busy with contracts at the moment, gave a completion date of not before 10 December. I told him we would be sailing toward Chile before then. He wouldn't budge on timing. We wouldn't delay our departure from Peru any longer. He relented. The completion was set for the beginning of December.

14. A Visit to Machu Picchu

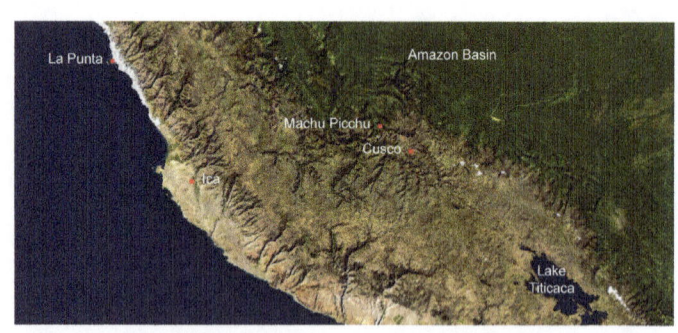

Both Edi and I knew that it would be a great pity to spend as much time in Peru as we have without visiting Cuzco, the Sacred Valley of the Incas and Machu Picchu. Machu Picchu sits at 2430 metres atop a steep-sided ridge on a loop of the Urubamba River in southeastern Peru, some 520 kilometres east of Lima, as the condor flies. To get there we needed to first travel to Cuzco, a city of nearly 400,000 people west of the Urubamba Valley at an elevation of 3360 metres in the Andes, with peaks reaching upwards of 6000 metres to its north and east.

In mid-November, as things were coming together in Sequitur and we were closing-in on our departure from Peru, got serious with the planning of our trip to Machu Picchu. We picked a date, and online I booked seats on Peruvian Airlines for 0930 on Friday the 26th of November, with return flights at 0940 on Friday the 3rd of December.

I had first begun planning a visit to Machu Picchu in 1969, as part of a climbing expedition to Peru's highest mountain, Huascaran in the late spring of 1970. However, events intervened; the Great Peruvian Earthquake of 13 May 1970, the most catastrophic natural disaster ever recorded in Peru, destabilized the northern wall of Mount Huascaran sending a kilometre-wide rock, ice and snow avalanche down on the towns of Yungay and Ranrahirca, burying them under 80 million cubic meters of rubble, killing 20,000, and leaving only 400 survivors. In total, the earthquake killed 75,000 to 80,000 people, with another 170,000 missing or injured and over 1,000,000 left homeless. The earthquake caused widespread infrastructure destruction and chaos in Peru in the weeks before we were due to arrive. We cancelled the 1970 expedition.

The 2010 expedition was down to the fine details when we asked Bev and Herb of The Lady J, our neighbour in the mooring field at La Punta, if we could use their taxi driver for our early morning trip to the airport. Bev phoned and booked a 0700 Friday pick up at the gate, but said it was not their usual driver; he was already booked. Instead, he was sending a good friend, Mirta in a green Hyundai.

There is always concern with taxis in Peru, particularly in the Callao area where we are. Two weeks previously, one of the visiting cruisers had been driven to a remote area and robbed at knife point of his passport and a large amount of cash, after having boarded an unknown taxi. On Thursday evening, on our way past the guardhouse, we booked a launch pick up at Sequitur for 0645.

The launch arrived about ten minutes early on Friday morning, and as the launch stood off our stern, we scrambled with the final details of preparing Sequitur for our week-long absence. We arrived at the gate early and nervously discussed alternate plans if the taxi appeared unsavoury. At precisely 0700 a youngish woman signalled us from the corner, and then half a minute later drove around the corner in a green Hyundai. We confirmed the S/30 for the trip to the airport, and off we went.

Mirta proved to be a wonderful driver, easily and skilfully weaving through the early morning crush of traffic. She appeared to know all the tricks, and calmly and smoothly manoeuvred through near-gridlock. At one point, as a taxi was trying to cut her off from the left, she gave the driver an 'evil eye' and he immediately backed off. We had a delightful ride to the airport with the only female taxi driver we have seen in this macho-dominated milieu. She helped us into our backpacks and sent us off in the proper direction, like a mother sending her kids to school.

Cuzco was declared a World Heritage Site by UNESCO in 1983, and its popularity as a tourist destination has exploded. It receives a million visitors a year, and its population has tripled in the past twenty years. The flood of tourists, most of whom come between June and September means that there is a huge supply of accommodation. Edi had travelled through Peru thirty-one years ago in 1979, and had visited Cuzco and Machu Picchu, among other wondrous places.

We were welcomed with cups of coca tea and shown to a very comfortable room. We figured that three days in Cuzco would give us time to explore and experience the city and the area, as well as to acclimatize to the high altitude. We were now 3360 metres above sea level (over 11,000 feet) and the air is much thinner than we have breathed the last many months at or very near sea level. The coca tea is to help us adapt to the high altitude and to diminish some of the symptoms of altitude sickness.

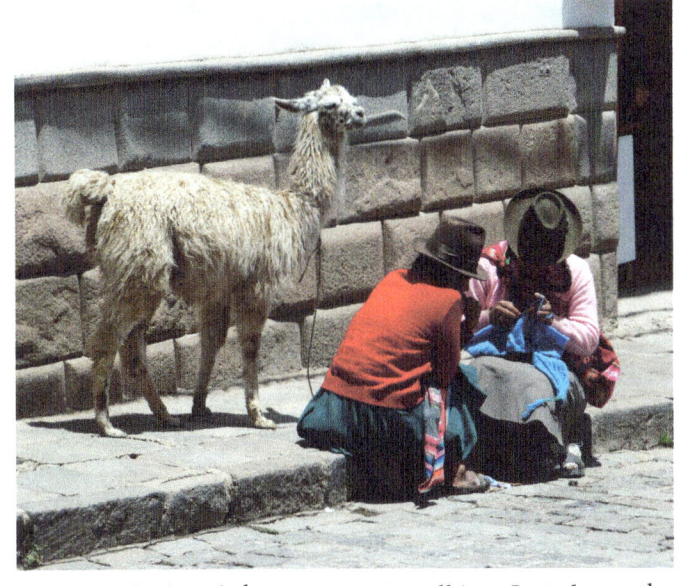

From her recall of the layout of Cuzco, we had picked an area to search for a hotel, and from online descriptions and reviews, we reserved three nights at the Rumi Punku, in a quiet street three blocks above Plaza de Armas toward San Blas. The hotel far exceeded our expectations. Its entrance is through a double jamb Inca doorway in an original Inca wall, which was once part of a sacred Inca temple, and it is one of only three in Cuzco belonging to a private house. It is an historic monument.

We unpacked and then went out walking. Just down the street from the hotel were two Inca women sitting on a curb resting, one of them knitting while their llama stood sedately on the sidewalk.

Through the doorway is an interior courtyard with balconies and hotel rooms overlooking it. The hotel began as a private colonial house, probably dating to the sixteenth or early seventeenth century, and in recent years has been converted into a very comfortable family owned-and-run hotel. The family continues to upgrade the property within the constraints of the INC (National Institute of Culture), and the hotel has recently been elevated to 3-star status. In the past few years they have taken-over the adjoining colonial house and have now wonderfully and quite seamlessly expanded their hotel into it.

A little further along, two very colourfully dressed young Inca women, one with a baby on her back and the other with a young lamb in her arms, were soliciting photos. For S/1 they posed while I shot pictures of them and Edi.

235

We continued our wanderings, poking into the shops that lined the streets. Some of the doorways led into courtyards crammed with small stalls and shops, most of them displaying a colourful mixture of the same merchandise. The repetition of merchandise from shop to shop amazed and disappointed us; much of the stuff was mass-produced, synthetic dyed and rather coarse. We saw very few examples of hand-crafted wares. As we passed each stall or shop, we were cajoled and heckled by shopkeepers touting their goods with amazing forcefulness. We wondered if they were aware that rather than attracting us, they were scaring us off.

We went back to the hotel and booked a half-day city tour in English, which began at 1400 and ran to 1830 for $15 each. At about 1340 we were picked-up at the hotel and escorted three blocks to the front of the cathedral, where we bought entrance tickets to it and its two conjoined churches for S/25. Sixteen of us were assembled and introduced to our guide, who began with a tour of the interiors of the three churches, which date to the early and mid-sixteenth century. These were lavishly decorated, with much gilding and a profusion of paintings, most of which are rather primitive in style, and in desperate need of restoration.

A common theme in the paintings was a fusion of the gods and idols of the pagan Inca beliefs with the gods and idols of the Catholic Church. The sun and moon were prominent. The Madonna was depicted in the shape of a tall mountain with a snake entwined around it.

She was often depicted with a bared and dripping nipple, or breastfeeding, as the Church played to the sentiments of the Incas. No photography is allowed in the churches, so I snuck a few without flash.

There is a painting of *The Last Supper* with a platter of the Inca delicacy, cuy, guinea pig laid in front of Christ. Again, the Church played to the Incas.

We next walked about four blocks to Coricancha, where at the entrance we paid S/10 each for admission to the site. Coricancha means *"Golden Courtyard"* in the Quechua language; it was originally named Inti Kancha, which means *"Temple of the Sun"*, and it is reputed to have been the most important temple in the Inca Empire. When the Spanish arrived in Cuzco in 1532, the floors and walls of the temple were covered with solid sheets of gold, and golden statues filled the courtyard. The gold was stripped from the temple to pay the ransom offered to the Spanish by Inca Atahualpa for his release.

The Spanish realized the significance of the site, and the Church being fearful of it, demolished much of it down to the foundations. On them they built the Cathedral of Santo Domingo, taking nearly a century to complete, and in the process, incorporating some of the older foundations and walls, and using the stones from the destroyed temple.

We then boarded a bus and were driven up into the hills on the north side of Cuzco to Saqsaywaman, pronounced very similar to *"sexy woman"*, where we bought entry passes for it and fifteen other Inca sites for S/130 each.

Saqsaywaman sits atop the hill at 3700 metres, immediately above the Saint Blas area of Cuzco, and it was built in the middle of the fifteenth century by the Inca emperor, Pachacutec. Some theories say that Cuzco was laid-out in the shape of a puma, and that the zigzag walls of Saqsaywaman represent its teeth.

There are three tiers of zigzag wall, the longest of which is about 400 metres, and they stand some six metres high. The blocks of stone used in the construction are some of the largest in any structure in the Americas, the largest being over 5 metres in height and weighing over 125 tonnes.

The construction is classic Inca dry masonry, with such precise fitting that in many places there is no space to insert even a sheet of paper between the huge stones. The remains represent only about 20 percent of the original structure, the Spanish having demolished much of the complex and used the blocks to build the religious and government buildings of Cuzco.

We walked through the ruins with running commentary by the guide as he propounded an Inca descendant's interpretation of the site. There are so many interpretations and theories of the Inca ruins and of the culture that created the impressive structures that we decided to just let the theories wash over us and to observe for ourselves without imposed or fixed ideas.

The bus had driven around to the far side of the site, and we re-boarded it and continued up to Pukapukara. On the slopes above the ruins sat an Inca woman surrounded by her display of both handmade and commercial wares as she spun wool.

We were guided through the ruins of Pukapukara, an imposing structure with panoramic views over the Cuzco Valley. Depending on the source of information, these were thought to have been a guard post, a stopping place for travellers, or possibly a hunting lodge.

The bus took us across the road and up a shallow valley a few hundred metres to the ruins of Tambomachay. Among the theories on this site, it was a storage centre, a water stop or the baths of an Inca water cult. Whatever; the masonry is superb and the water engineering is fascinating.

We were next driven to Q'enqo, whose name means zigzag. Here we saw a raised sacrificial altar, limestone caves and a tunnel with more altars hewed into the rock. There is an interesting semicircular wall of impeccable Inca masonry with nineteen niches, which were likely used as ceremonial seats around a central stage.

We were returned to Cuzco's main square, Plaza de Armas shortly before 1900, after very interesting tour, which we thought well worth the cost. We had not given ourselves time to acclimatize to the high altitude, and we certainly felt our lungs and hearts working overtime with the thin air. After our exertions of the day, our short four-block walk back up toward the hotel required a couple rest stops.

As we walked, the many restaurant touts cajoled and harassed us to dine in their mostly empty restaurants. We finally settled on a small place with white linen and a decent-looking menu. There were only two dozen or so seats in the place, five of which were occupied. The wine list was short and expensive, so we ordered a couple of cervesas. The menu was traditional Peruvian fare, and we both decided on the lomo soltado, the national dish of Peru, which is a dish of stir-fried beef tenderloin slices with onions and peppers, served with rice and French fries. The cervesas were cool and refreshing, but the tenderloin betrayed its namesake; we renamed it lomo so-tough-o.

On Saturday morning we enjoyed a very fine breakfast in the hotel dining room; a hot and cold buffet is included in the price of the room. Eggs were cooked to order and there was a warmer full of crisply done bacon. There were platters of ham and cheese, two types of fresh bread roll, croissants, sliced pound cake, an assortment of fresh fruit, cereals and yogurts. Pitchers contained freshly made juices: passion fruit, papaya, pineapple and orange, and there was a large vacuum urn of fresh coffee, and another of hot water for the selection of teas. We sat savouring some of nearly everything at the only window seat in the wonderful church-like ambiance of the dining room.

After breakfast we headed out to explore Cuzco. We walked up the steep narrow lanes above the hotel.

We followed even narrower lanes across the hill. Many of the buildings we saw were built using remains of Inca walls as foundations and in some cases, much or all of their walls.

We passed several small businesses casually set-up in the streets. Among these was an Inca woman sitting on the cobblestones with a very simple kitchen along the wall, while her three customers sat eating on the cobbles against the opposite wall.

239

One of the necessities of acclimatizing to high altitude is drinking plenty of fluids, regularly and in small quantities, not allowing oneself to become thirsty. We needed water, so we poked into a small tienda in which we saw bottles of water through the open door. To reach the tienda we had to pass through the living quarters, and in adjoining kitchen we saw an Inca woman with guinea pigs and a calico cat on the floor at her feet. The cat was a pet, but the cuy were for the pot. Cuy is one of the celebratory meats of the Incas. This is the creature we had seen in front of Christ the previous day in the painting of *The Last Supper*.

We came out overlooking Plaza San Blas, where there was a crafts market set-up. Again we were disappointed by the repetitious nature of the wares. Hand made merchandise was almost non-existent. In a couple of the small shops around the periphery of the square we found some hand crafted pieces, and in one of these I bought a nice hand woven shoulder bag.

We descended into the central part of the city and over toward the Mercado off Plaza San Pedro. Along the way were entrepreneurs of all ages plying their wares. The most precocious we saw were three children with two wheelbarrows of fruit. The youngest of these, a two or three-year-old, was really into her mangoes.

Inside the market itself, women were set-up casually sitting on the floor in the aisles surrounded by their small selections of goods.

A large portion of the covered marketplace was dedicated to casual open kitchens, with hundreds of diners sitting on stools two and three deep in front of the many dozens of very casual restaurants.

We passed many meat rendering booths, and wondered at the sanitation. Our decision not to buy any was very easy.

Back outside, we saw many more entrepreneurs vending produce from wheelbarrows in the streets. There is a very casual and fluid economy here.

We walked back through the city to our hotel, admiring along the way the simple beauty of the place.

At the same time that we had booked our city tour, we had also booked an all-day tour of the Sacred Valley for Sunday. The cost for the eight-and-a-half-hour tour was $25 each, plus $10 for an optional buffet lunch. At 0720 on Sunday we were picked-up at the hotel in a small bus, and shuttled to a rendezvous with a very comfortable larger highway bus. The bus eventually gathered about twenty of us and headed out of Cuzco.

The first stop was at the market in Q'orao. This was jam-packed with the same repetitious, garishly coloured and very ordinary wares we had already seen in Cuzco. The wholesalers and distributors of tourist trash have certainly done their jobs well; it is a pity that the retailers haven't. There was not an artisan to be seen.

At forty minutes into our thirty minute stop, a delinquent young couple was finally rounded-up and aboard the bus, and we continued on our way. We rounded a bend on our descent through a winding gorge, and stopped at a pull-off for a five-minute view over the Urubamba Valley. After the delinquent couple again kept us waiting, we continued down into the town of Pisac, at an elevation of 2970 metres.

241

In the middle of town we crossed the Urubamba River on a single Bailey bridge; the regular crossing had been washed away in the torrents of the previous February. We continued through town and then up into the hills past the amazing agricultural terraces of the Inca ruins.

The pass we had bought on Friday at Saqsaywaman allowed us into the site, and everyone aboard the bus also had admission tickets, except the delinquent couple. They decided to stay at the gate and wait for our return, which the guide told them would be in one hour. We were shown through some wonderful ruins of temples, baths and burial sites.

After drinking-in the superb views, we turned around and retraced our route. We paused to admire the superb masonry, and then followed the terraces back around to the bus. Everyone in the group somehow managed to arrive back onboard within minutes of each other; nonetheless, we arrived at the gate to pick up the delinquent couple almost half an hour late. I suspect there was something happening at a subconscious level here. They were happy to see us.

We drove back down into Pisac, which is a quiet town of 2000 people 33 kilometres northeast of Cuzco. On Sundays; however, according to all the guidebooks and online information sites, it comes alive with its market. The whole town is reported to convert into a street market which attracts traditionally dressed locals from the surrounding region, selling handicrafts and alpaca wool clothing as well as fruits, vegetables and meats.

It now appears that it is nothing more than a set-up for hawkers and vendors of all manner of souvenir trash. Other than a fabulous outdoor bread oven, we saw no artisans and little if anything handmade. We saw no produce market. It has become another place crowded with hopeful vendors duped by wholesalers and stuck with repetitious junk souvenirs. The only evidence that we could see of a purchase by our group was that the delinquent couple was sporting garish hats as they boarded the bus on time.

The guide then gave us half an hour to independently explore the area, pointing-out various options. We chose to follow a narrow trail and stairway leading across a sheer cliff, and through a tunnel piercing a rib on the face.

We drove down the valley to the town of Urubamba, and in the middle of town dropped-off the delinquent couple and some others who hadn't opted for the buffet lunch. We continued through town to a very restful place, Buffet Restaurant Muna, which is set in gardens at the edge of town.

There we enjoyed a splendid hot and cold buffet. We started with bowls of soup and carried on with a selection of cold items, including a delicious ceviche.

Then went back for the hot dishes. I sampled such things as roast guinea pig, pork cicherone, chicken in a wonderful yellow pepper sauce, plus a variety of potatoes and corn. Still having a bit of room, we went back for a sampler plate of four desserts, and some fresh, hot coffee. It was a splendid lunch for $10.

We arrived at the roadside just as the bus pulled-up, it having gone back into town to pick up the remainder of the group. We continued down the Urubamba Valley to Ollantaytambo at 2850 metres elevation. The town preserves much of its original Inca housing, streets and waterworks, and extending high up the steep hills behind it are magnificent agricultural terraces. Our passes again gave us entry.

At the top of the terraces sit an imposing fortress and temple, so with our not yet fully altitude-acclimatized bodies hampered with overstuffed bellies from our very recent lunch, we slowly made our way up the hundreds of steep, high stone steps.

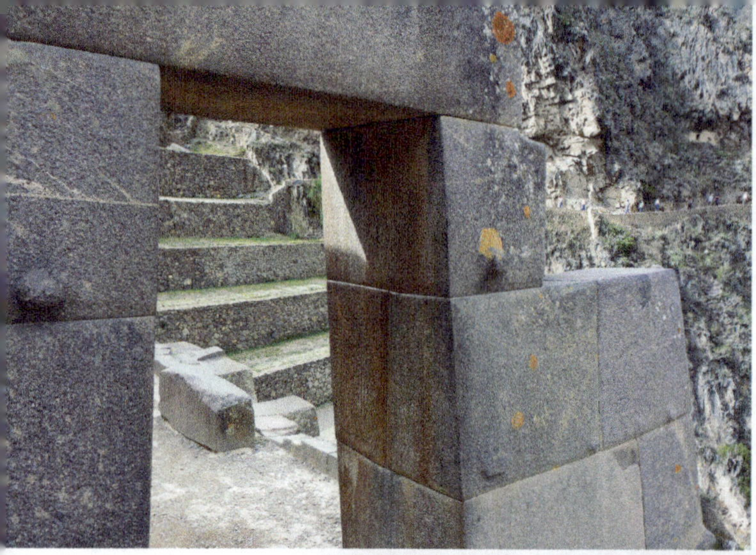
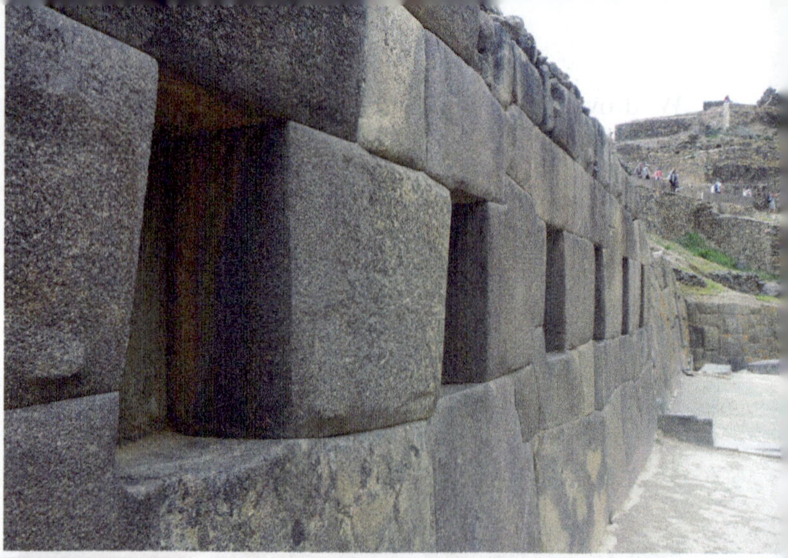
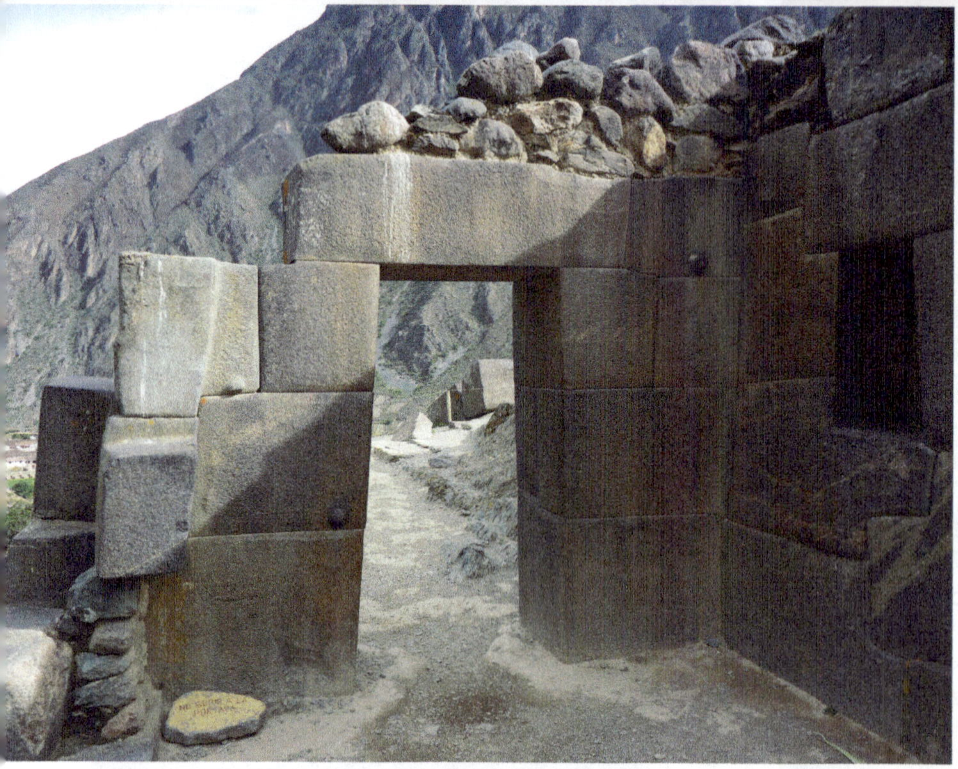
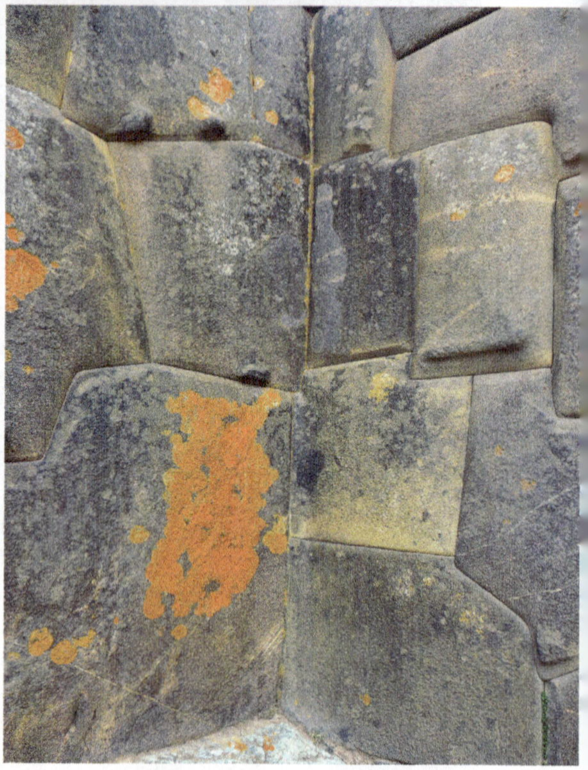
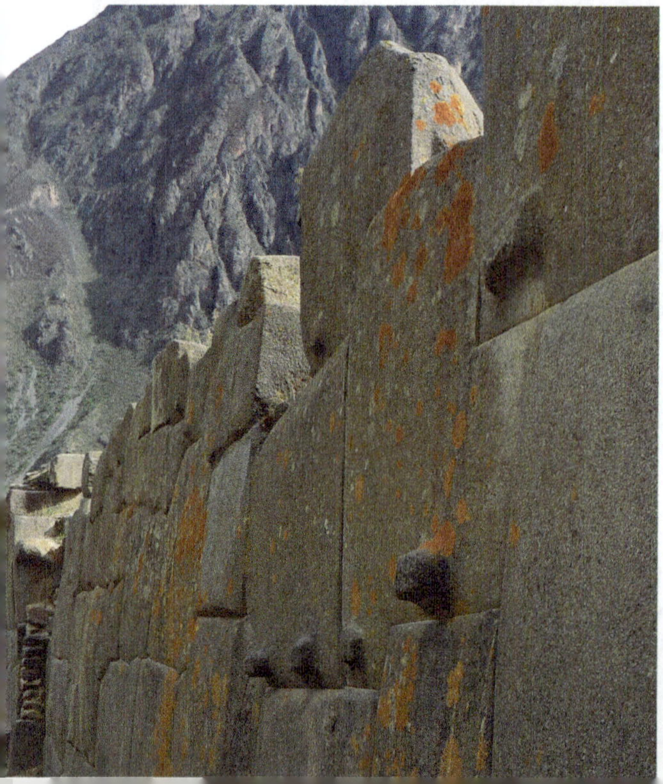
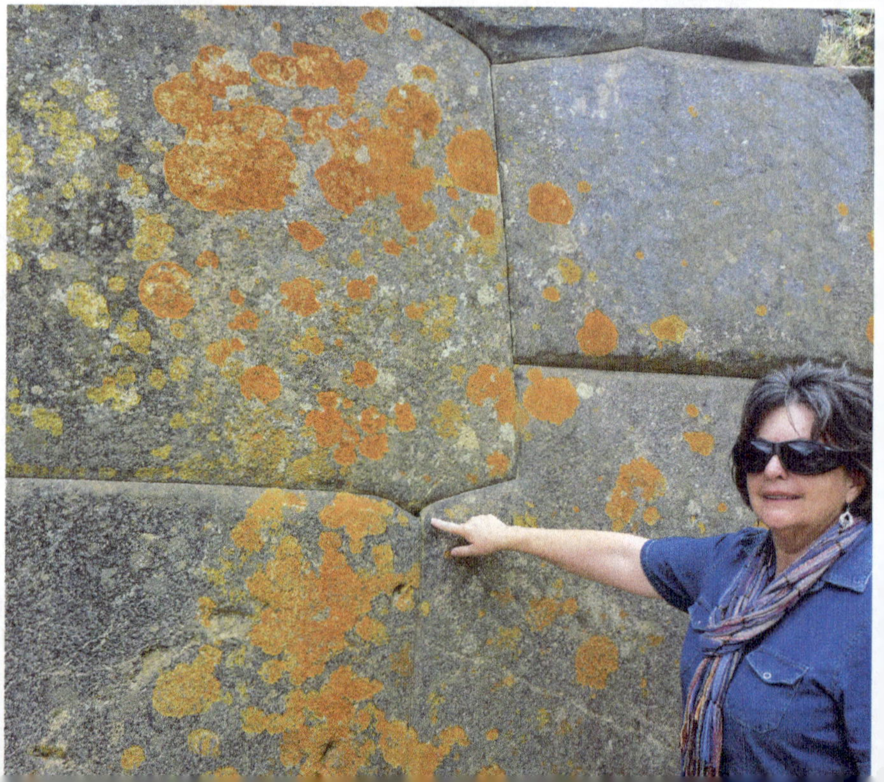

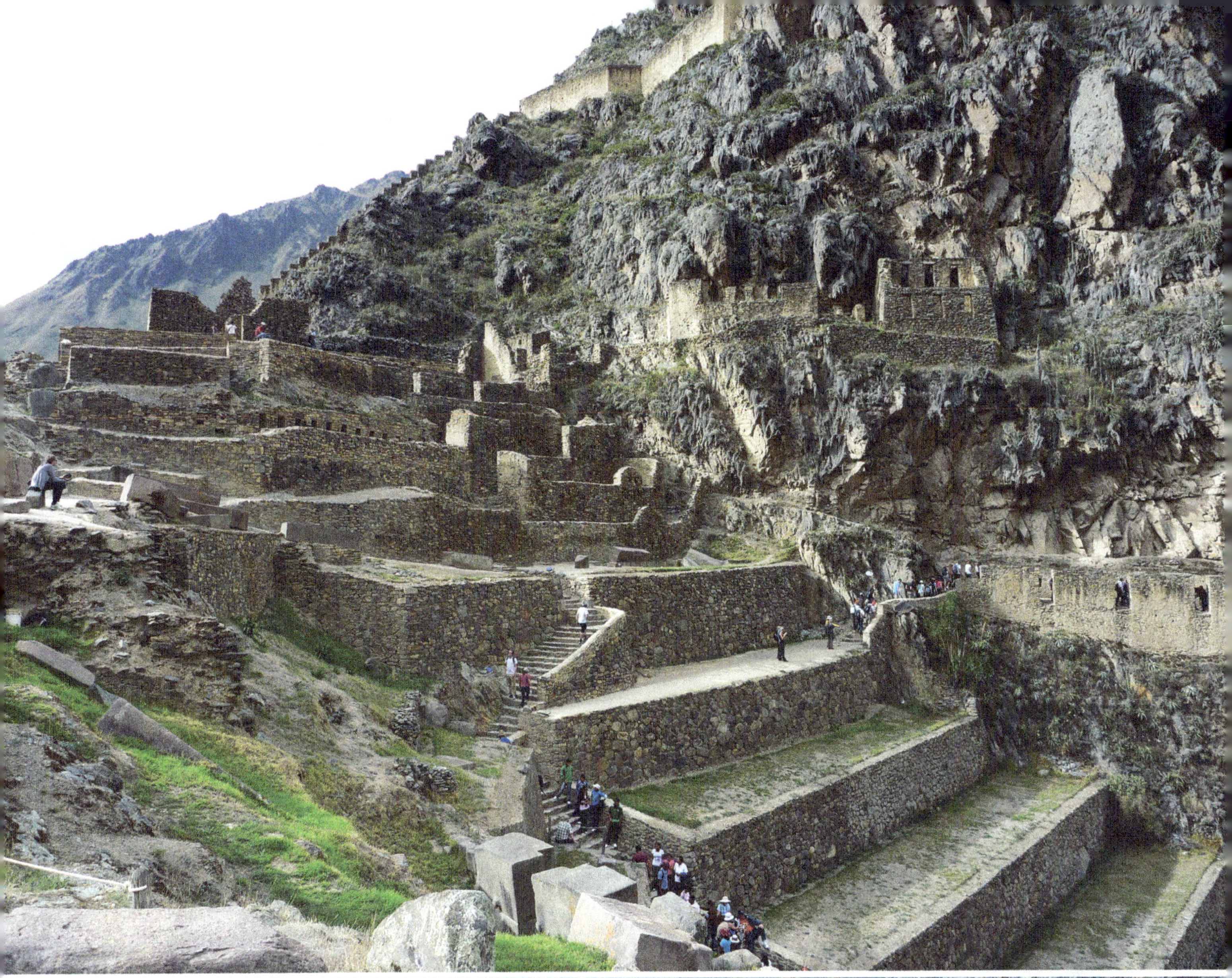
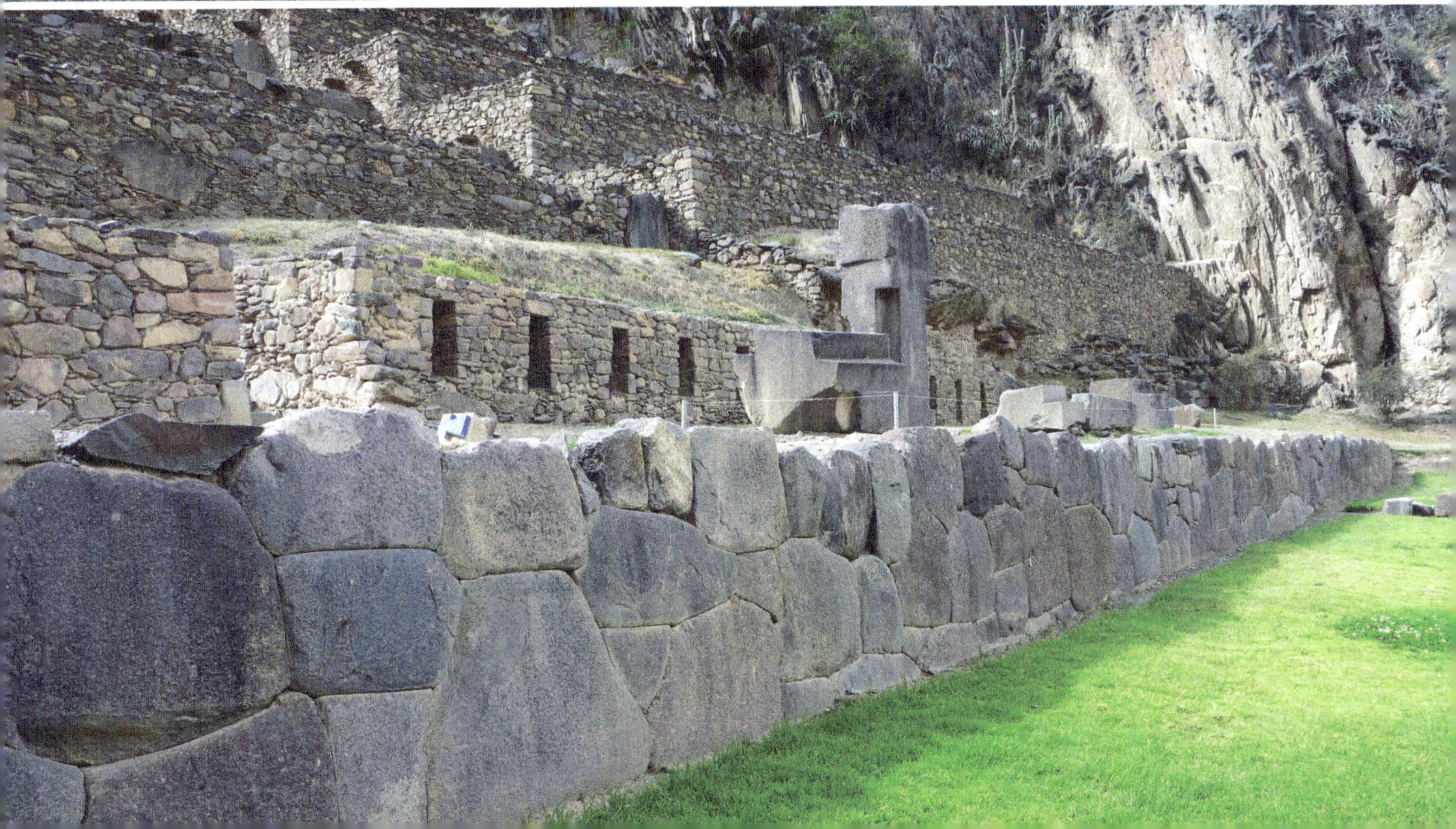

We were guided around the splendid architecture, which had so skillfully been wrested from the rock of the ridge top. The quality of the masonry continued to amaze us. Along one wall we saw a series of identically sized and proportioned trapezoidal niches in the wall, centred at head level. These dramatically amplified our voices when we stuck our heads in and spoke, or better yet, chanted.

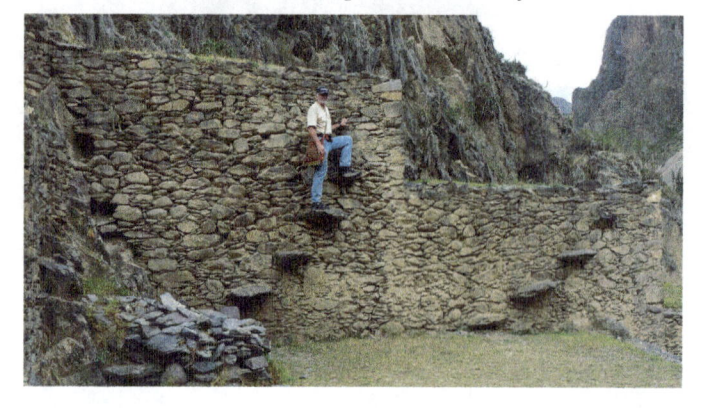

Back near the bottom of the site, I decided to try out the steps, which had been built into the terrace walls to give the Inca farmers easy access between terraces.

Back down in the town of Ollantaytambo we rejoined the delinquent couple in front of Inca Bucks. I wonder how long it will be before Starbucks brings suit, like they did against Haida Bucks in the Canada's Queen Charlottes.

We were bussed back up the valley to the town of Urubamba, where we turned west and headed up out of the Urubamba Valley. We arrived after half an hour in Chinchero at 3760 metres above sea level. Again our passes were punched and we walked through the gates and up the stepped street to a plaza at the summit of a hill. We had come to visit a colonial church built on Inca foundations. The interior is elaborately frescoed in floral designs, and there is an intricately carved altar. No photography is allowed inside the church, so we all paused in the doorway to shoot a few shots.

After touring the church, we headed down through a square that was quilted with displays of the same assortment of manufactured tourist stuff that we had been seeing everywhere else in the previous few days. We re-boarded the bus and drove back to Cuzco, arriving shortly after 1830. The tour was well worth its price for all except the delinquent couple, who simply had a long $25 bus ride to buy tourist hats they would have found cheaper in Cuzco.

In the evening we walked out and up the hill to Plaza San Blas to Restaurant Pachapapa for dinner. The guidebooks and online reviews rated this place as one of the better choices in town, and when we had asked at the hotel desk for a recommendation, it was their suggestion. The restaurant prides itself on serving Peruvian cuisine with African, European and Asian accents. We decided on an appetizer platter of a variety of potatoes and local cheeses, and we both ordered the beef tenderloin. The beef was served table-side from a clay pot in which it had been braised with vegetables. While it seemed a strange way to cook tenderloin, it demonstrated to us that even braised, the Peruvian tenderloin is still misnamed.

On Monday morning we got up at 0430 and were the only people in the dining room when it opened for breakfast at 0500. I had tried to check-out and settle our bill the on the previous evening, but the desk clerk had said the morning would be fine.

While Edi dished-up breakfast for us from the buffet, I went to the desk to settle the account, but the clerk told me to do it when we returned from Machu Picchu; we had arranged two more nights in this wonderful hotel on our return. Our prearranged taxi arrived on time at 0550 and drove us the half hour to the Poroy station.

When Edi had travelled from Cuzco to Machu Picchu in 1979, the train had been pulled by a steam locomotive, which had left from the San Pedro station near the centre of town and then slowly zigzagged, switching forwards and backwards for the better part of an hour up the very steep hillside to Poroy near the head of the Huarocondo Valley. These days, the routine is to take a taxi to Poroy for S/20 and save an hour and the additional train fare.

Seated across from us was Anna, a Russian woman in her twenties now living in New York and travelling on her own. Eight years previously she had come to marry an Italian, and after one year divorced. She told us she had decided a few days previously to come to Machu Picchu, and here she was.

We were served a very elegant and tasty breakfast, which the printed menu told us consisted of: *"Fresh Andean fruit salad; cape gooseberries, prickly pear, melon, kiwi and pineapple garnished with elderberry coulis. Andean smoked trout mini sandwich with arugula, light natural yogurt dressing and homemade anise bread. Swiss chard pie filled with bacon. Corn flour cookies covered with bitter chocolate stuffed with milk caramel."*

We relaxed in the very comfortable waiting room of the station and watched out the windows as the staff prepared for departure. We were soon boarded and settled very comfortably into leather seats in a VistaDome car of Peru Rail's early morning train to Aguas Calientes, a village at the base of Machu Picchu. Peru Rail is operated in a 50-50 partnership between the Orient Express and Peruvian businessmen, and the service has a definite European refinement.

We thoroughly enjoyed the three-hour ride, which took us down the Huarocondo Valley and canyon to the Urubamba River, and then down the river to Aguas Calientes. On the way we passed many Inca walls and terraces on the banks and slopes above the river.

We alighted from the train and walked through the adjoining covered market, which is the only route to the town. The hundreds of stalls were filled with the same assortment of mass-produced goods we had seen the previous few days. We braved the gauntlet of hecklers, cajolers and hawkers as we wove our way through the few hundred metres of aisles necessary to transit into the town itself.

From online descriptions and reviews, we had selected Hotel Presidente, which fronts on the railway tracks and backs on the river a block or so away from the central square. We had requested a view room, and were delighted with our third-floor balcony hanging out above the rapids of the Urubamba River. The roar of the river outside our room replicated the sound of surf on a beach in an anchorage, and soothed us.

We checked-in and then went on an exploratory walk around the town. The streets and lanes were lined cheek-by-jowl with restaurants and cafes; dozens of them, virtually all of them empty. We were heckled and harassed by menu-waving touts as we passed each restaurant, and scared away from daring to pause and read the menu, let alone to assess the place.

Based on our reading of printed and online reviews, we stopped in at Indio Feliz, which is tucked up a narrow lane off the main walking street up the hill from the central square. There were no touts, no hecklers, no waving menus; the place was busy. We were greeted by a charming and jovial Peruvian woman, Cannie who turned-out to be one of the owners. She and her husband Patrick Vogin, a French chef, had started the business twelve years previously. We were delighted and told her we would be back in the evening for dinner.

In the evening we were welcomed like long-time clients by Cannie, and shown to a large corner table. Everything on la carte looked tempting, but we opted for la menu, which at S/54 offered a choice of entrée, main and dessert from a large selection. Edi began with a French onion soup, which came with a large bowl of grated cheese and a side of sliced peppers. Cannie came over to talk with us, and we told her we were sailing around the world, and would shortly be continuing southward to Chile. She told us not to mention it to her husband; he is a sailor, and would never leave us alone if he found out.

Also to the table came a large basket of delicious fresh bread rolls and a huge earthenware dish of homemade butter. For my entrée I had chosen a quiche Lorraine, which came beautifully garnished and accompanied by sliced tomatoes with sauce Dijonnaise. It was the best quiche Lorraine I could remember having had since one in Nancy many years before.

Cannie must have told her husband about our sailing, because he soon came over to our table and told us of his boat in Tahiti, and of his Atlantic and Pacific crossings. He looked at our basket of bread and said there was a fresh batch in the oven ready in a few minutes, and that would send over a new basket.

Edi's choice of main was beef tenderloin in a pepper and carob sauce. It was accompanied by thickly sliced potato chips and an assortment of local vegetables. Finally a tender tenderloin!

My main course was grilled trout meunière, and it arrived piping hot, beautifully presented and accompanied by plates of fresh local vegetables and crisply fried potatoes.

For dessert Edi ordered an apple pie, while I ordered an orange one. Each came set in a sauce with a small scoop of homemade ice cream and a lovely fresh garnish. Like everything else we had been served here, they were delicious. The ambiance of the restaurant was wonderful, and there were huge bouquets and arrangements of fresh tropical flowers throughout.

As we were finishing our meals, Patrick came over and invited us to the bar. He told us that because we were sailors, he was offering us our choice of drink. We asked for Pisco puro. He had the bartender pour us glasses, but when the pour stopped at the normal level, Patrick took the bottle and filled our glasses to just short of their rims. The Pisco tasted familiar to us and we asked him about it. He showed us the bottle, which had a custom Indio Feliz label, and said they had it bottled for the restaurant by a distiller in Ica. We told him we knew Bodegas Vista Alegre there, and he said that was his source. What a delightful coincidence!

We were so fully satisfied with our evening at Indio Feliz that anything else would be anticlimactic, so we went to bed early. This had the added advantage of allowing us to be well-rested for our day on Machu Picchu. We had earlier in the day bought entrance tickets for the site as well as bus tickets for the 20-minute ride up the steep switchbacks to it.

Hiram Bingham is the first US citizen recorded to have visited and plundered Machu Picchu, and many in the US believe that he is the discoverer of it. However there are records of the site having been visited well before his 1911 so-called discovery. In 1867 Augusto Berns, a German had visited and plundered Machu Picchu, and there is evidence that J. M. von Hassel, a German engineer had visited the site even earlier. In addition, there are references to Machu Picchu on maps dating back to 1874. It looks like Hiram Bingham is just another Christopher Columbus, a man given way too much credit for simply following others' maps and routes and claiming discoveries.

In 1980, Machu Picchu received 145,566 visitors. By 2000, that figure had surpassed 420,000, and by 2008 it had doubled, reaching an all-time high of 858,211 for the year. The daily limit on visitors to Machu Picchu has now been set at 2500, although Peru's private tourism sector is fighting for 5000 per day, which would mean 1,825,000 per year, more than double the current levels.

We were here in the shoulder season, heading to low season, with expected visitors nowhere near the allowed limit. However, to have the opportunity to visit and photograph without crowds, we wanted to be up there early.

Machu Picchu sits on a steep ridge about 350 metres above the village of Aguas Calientes, which is also known as Machu Picchu Pueblo. While we were not the first westerners to visit the ruins, we wanted to be among the first to visit them this day. We were up at 0530, had a large breakfast from the hotel's included buffet, and were aboard a bus and heading up the hill shortly after 0600.

We were the first off the bus and through the gates, and we climbed immediately to the Hut of the Caretaker of the Funerary Rock, and then above it for the classic view over the ruins.

When we arrived, the mists were starting to rise from the valleys as the day began warming the moisture on the jungle vegetation below. We still had a clear view of Wayna Picchu, the sugarloaf peak rising some 300 metres above the far side of the ruins. I had fulfilled my half-century-long desire to stand here overlooking this fabled and awe-inspiring site. Edi had done what very few casual visitors do; after thirty-one years she had returned for a second visit.

I had first dreamed of visiting Machu Picchu in the late 1950s when my uncle Warren had shown me his April 1913 issue of the National Geographic. The issue was entirely dedicated to the *discovery* of these spectacular Inca ruins by Hiram Bingham. Bingham's 1911 photograph of an overview of the site was burned in my memory. After our 1970 expedition to Peru had fallen through, Machu Picchu faded in my mind, but when I met Edi in 2008 and learned she had visited the ruins in 1979, my interest resurfaced.

After drinking-in the wonder of the place and wallowing in the emotion of being there, we paused to photograph some of the llamas that were busily tending the terraced lawns.

As the mists rolled in, we started our descent into the main part of the ruins.

We came around a bend on a terrace, and there in front of us was a familiar face. Because we were so out-of-context, it took a few seconds to place the face, which belonged to Ken Garfinkle, a member of the Bluewater Cruising Association. We had last seen him in Vancouver Island's Barkley Sound in July of 2009, after we had completed our shakedown sail out Cobb Seamount and back.

After comparing notes of problems with boat fit-out, we continued on our separate ways. As we descended into the main ruins, the mists were beginning to obscure Wayna Picchu.

We made our way across the central plaza, giving the main part of the ruins a miss on our way past. We headed directly to the registration booth for the climb to Wayna Picchu at the far end of the site. Only 400 people are allowed to climb the peak each day, and we wanted to be among them.

I had read that there is a scramble during the high season, with people running from the buses to the booth to get into the line. Because it was nearing low season, we had been able to climb to Hut of the Caretaker of the Funerary Rock and explore that area before heading to the booth. We signed-in as number 66 and 67 and started along the trail to the peak as it continued to be enveloped in cloud.

252

We first had to descend into a narrow col, losing a bit short of 100 metres in the process. The summit of Wayna Picchu is at 2720 metres, about 300 metres above the main portion of the ruins. With the dip into the col, we now had nearly 400 metres to climb, which is reported to require an hour to an hour-and-a-half.

The trail is very well-made and in an excellent state of repair. Where it steepens, there are steps, many of which were built by the Inca.

Pausing along the way to smell the flowers gave us wonderful excuses to rest.

In one place steps were carved into a steep slab, which would otherwise have been difficult and dangerous to traverse. At the steep and exposed sections, heavy wire rope handrails, some 2cm in diameter are pinned to the rocks, and make the passage safer and easier.

After 25 minutes on the trail, we came to a sign indicating that the top was 25 minutes away. We were well ahead of the estimated time required. Not bad for a couple in their mid-sixties!

Shortly we emerged into an area of ancient Inca walls and other structures, and our pace slowed as we examined them in awe.

We were led higher through increasingly interesting ruins.

By this time we had lost all awareness of tiredness or any altitude problems.

Then high above us, we saw the remains of a house perched on the brink. Very steep steps led up to it past what appeared from below to be agricultural terraces. We continued up through increasingly interesting ruins.

Gradually we rose above awe inspiring views back down on ruins with the Urubamba River far below through the mists.

And still we climbed, completely absorbed in the magic of the place.

As the tunnel led into the rock, it narrowed and gained in height, but began to lean to the left.

We came around a bend and the way forward was through a very low tunnel, which required us to bend nearly double.

Then a set of steps partly carved in the rocks and partly laid, led us up and out of the tunnel and into the daylight.

The Incas had found an ingenious route past a very steep block. On top of it they had built agricultural terraces, making use of every bit of space possible.

We arrived at the summit and took a breather. Edi found a wonderful seat that had been carved into the surface of a large sloping rock.

We paused to look down on the main site of Machu Picchu and on down to the valley bottom.

I stood on the highest point drinking-in the serenity, sensing the sanctity of this Inca holy place.

The mists from the jungles below had mostly cleared, giving us spectacular views down on the ruins of Machu Picchu and the Urubamba River.

We headed down a very steep set of steps for a closer look at the ruins of an Inca house.

Its real estate listing might read: A solidly built older home with a bright, open plan with huge skylights and spectacular views over the valley.

We continued to be amazed by the quality of the Inca masonry, and by the geometric precision of the trapezoidal doors, windows and niches. These structures have withstood many earthquakes, which over the centuries have destroyed much else in Peru.

There was a wonderful view of the river valley through the window from inside the house.

We continued downward, and as we descended, the main site of Machu Picchu was emerging from the mists.

We continued down to the col and across it and started the climb back toward the main site. On the way up, we arrived at a fork in the trail, and decided to follow the route up Huchuy Picchu, the lesser peak between Wayna Picchu and Machu Picchu.

We continued down through awe-inspiring architecture, and seeking to see even more, we took an alternate route and scrambled down the steps on the terrace faces.

The way down is very steep, and we wondered about the Incas coming and going with heavy loads. There was no need for caution signs; the views of the route down screamed for it.

The way was steep, with high steps, narrow places and plenty of exposure. In one place the route led up a high-angle smooth slab with a rope to use as layback aid in walking up the slab.

The trail was less well made than the one up Wayna Picchu, but we had soon risen high enough to start getting views over Machu Picchu. We reached the summit and were rewarded with views back at Wayna Picchu in the one direction and down upon Machu Picchu in the other.

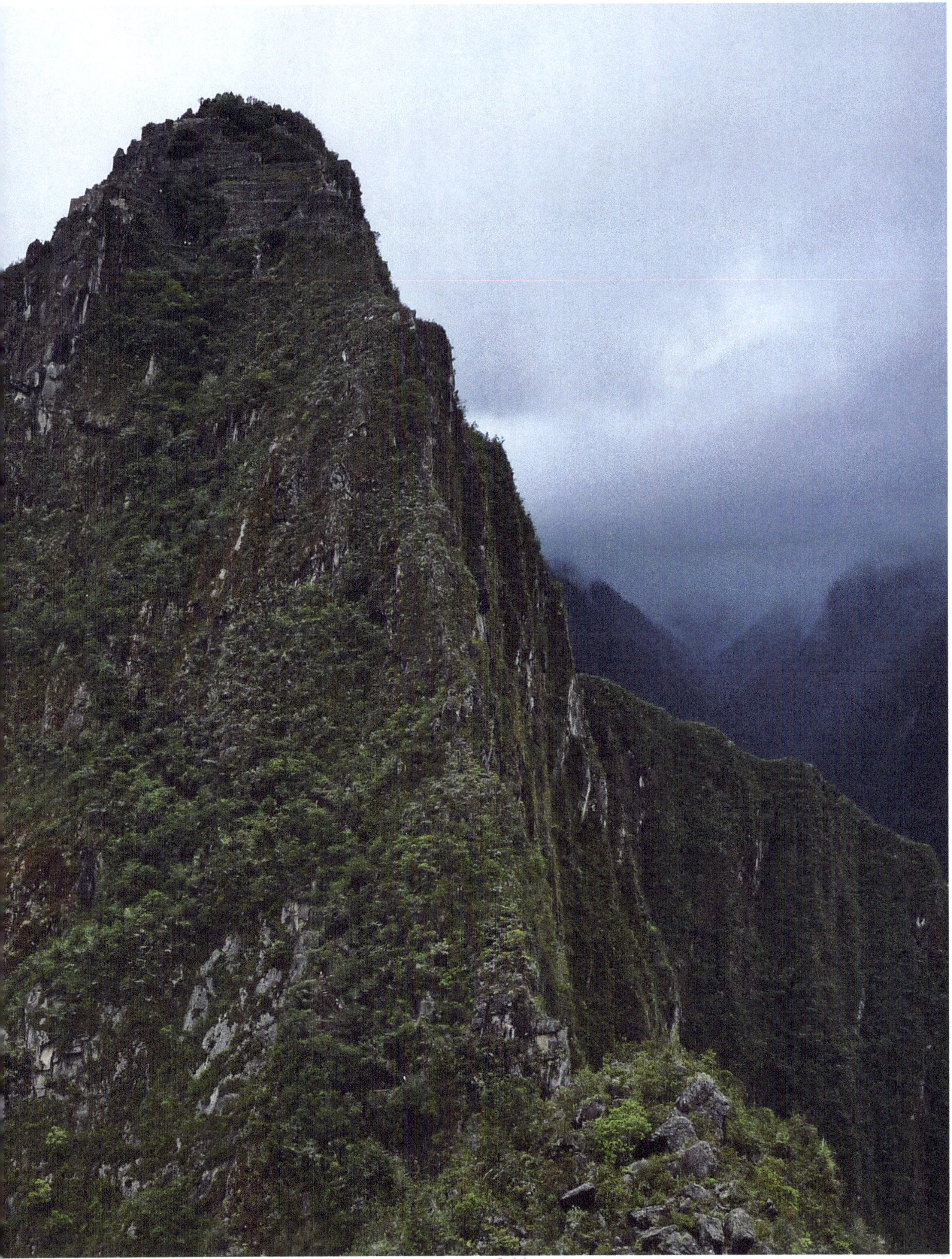

The mists had finished rising, and the clouds were thickening above the peaks, getting ready for their afternoon rain.

We looked past our toes and down to the Urubamba River some 600 metres below, and decided it was time to start heading down. We slowly worked our way through the main ruins, weaving a zigzag route leading gradually toward the exit.

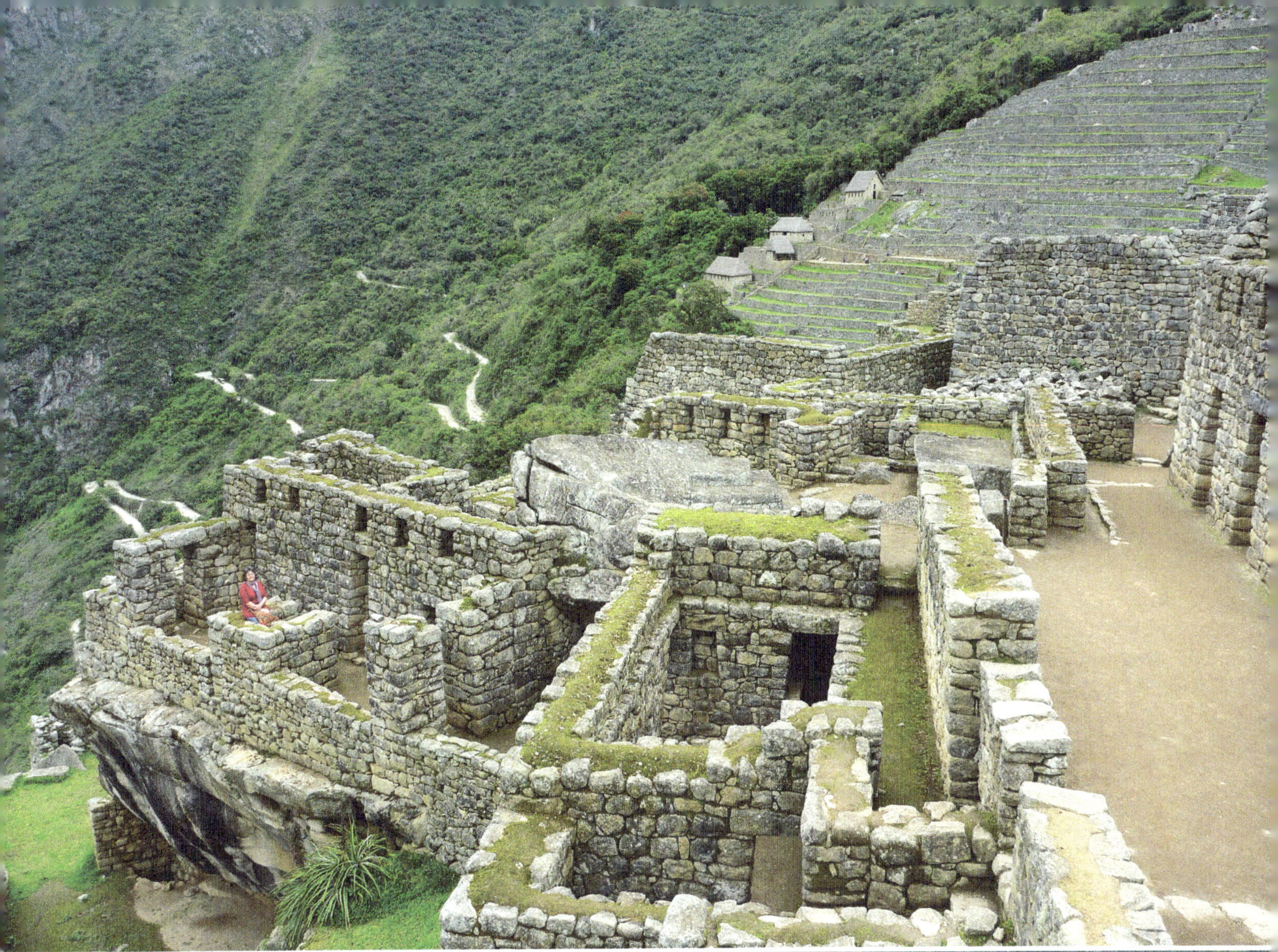

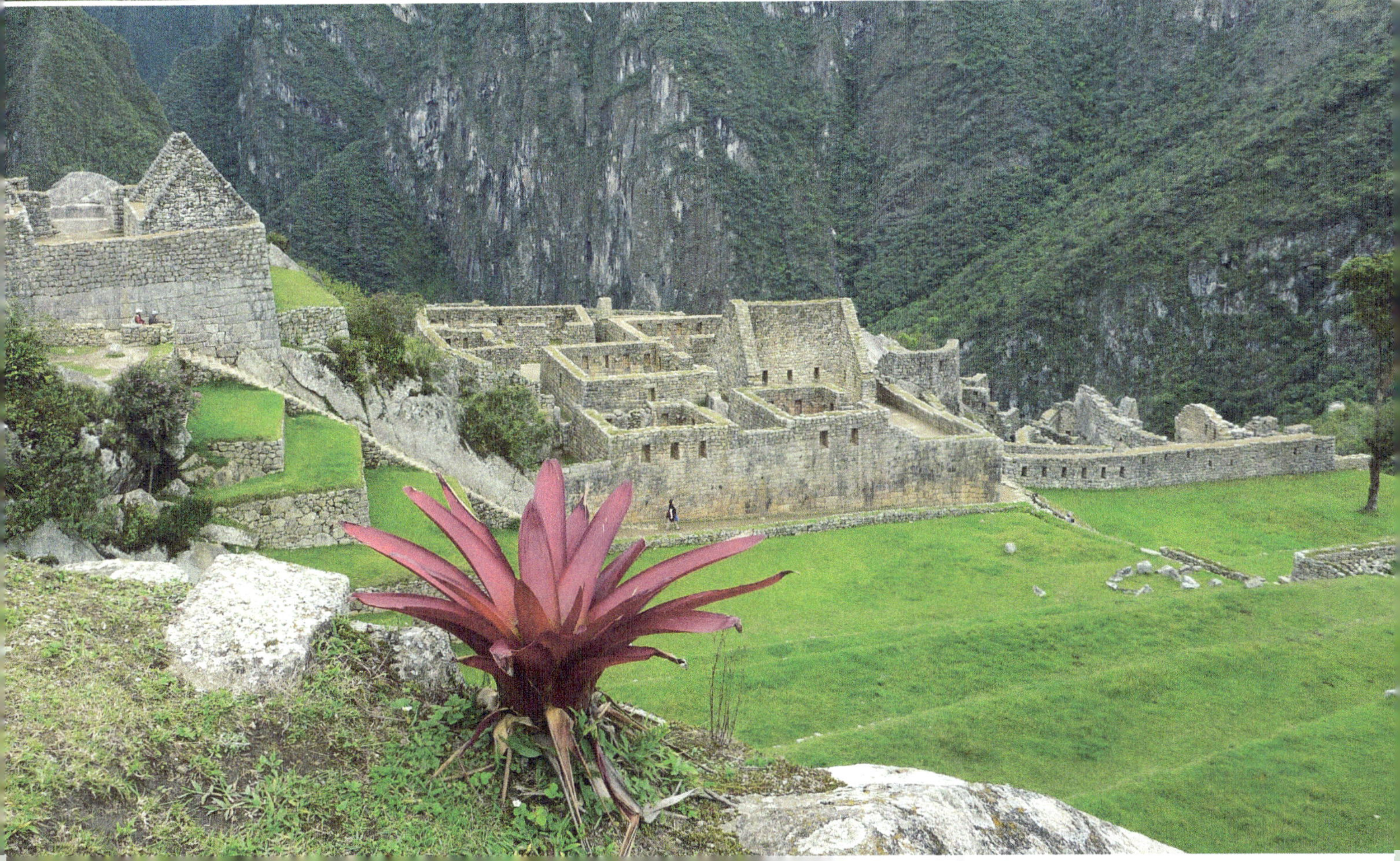

At every turn we saw amazing examples of the Inca masonry skills. The structures had been so well built that they have withstood many earthquakes over the centuries.

large blocks. Some of the stones are two metres and more in height and width.

Always looming above the ruins was the peak of Wayna Picchu. The mists has finished rising from the valleys, and the layer of cloud overhead was thickening and darkening.

We saw only two places where earthquakes had shifted some of the massive rocks. Both appeared to be from shifts in the bedrock, not from poor masonry. With Peru host to some of the most devastating earthquakes in history, we were amazed there wasn't more evidence of damage here.

The masonry varied from utilitarian using smaller stones, to masterfully crafted using precisely surfaced and fitted

We climbed to the Intihuatana, the Hitching Post of the Sun. This carved rock is believed to have been used by the Incas as an astronomical observatory, its precisely carved and aligned faces being used to lineup the celestial happenings.

We spotted below us a strikingly different structure; one made with white stones and having a curved wall. The Temple of the Sun served as a solar observatory, with its windows strategically placed to observe the astronomical events. Two windows are aligned to a stone altar in the center of the room to allow the sun's rays to signal the summer and winter solstices.

Below the Temple we examined a carefully carved cave called the Royal Tomb, which has step-shaped altars and in its walls, sacred niches.

As we continued toward the exit, we entered and examined some of the houses.

The Temple contains Machu Picchu's only curved wall and is reputed to have the site's finest stonework. We descended the wall to examine the superb dry masonry.

One of these had been fitted with a roof, which we surmised was replicating as closely as speculation allows the type of roof that might have been used by the Incas half a millennium ago, when Machu Picchu was inhabited.

We climbed up for a final overview.

Then we walked along an agricultural terrace to the entry gate, arriving there just as the rain began to fall. An empty bus had just pulled-up as we arrived in the loading area, and we boarded and sat in the back seats so that we wouldn't be bumped by all the packs as people boarded.

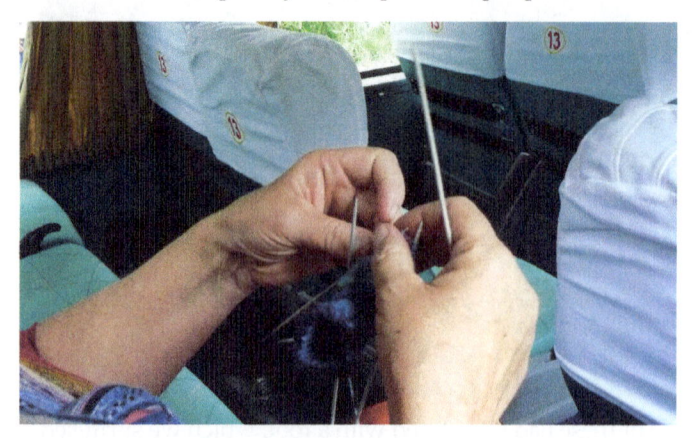

While we waited for the bus to load, Edi again took out her knitting and continued with a sock. Each time she wears it, she will be reminded of this fabulous day on Machu Picchu.

Our timing had been impeccable. We had spent just over eight hours wandering among the ruins, enjoying the splendour of the place while the weather cooperated with our every wish. The mists had waited for us to have an overview of the ruins before they began rising, then as we climbed Wayna Picchu, the cloud cover had blocked the sun, making our climb cooler and easier. On the summit of the peak, the mists had played a magical hide-and-seek game with the ruins, and through the afternoon the rains had waited until we had completed our explorations and had arrived back aboard the bus at the exit.

It was mid-afternoon by the time the bus had brought us back down from Machu Picchu and into the town of Aguas Calientes. We hadn't eaten since our breakfast nearly nine hours previously; we had obeyed the regulation that no food is allowed into the ruins.

Most others hadn't, and we saw people eating throughout the site, and were disgusted by the accompanying litter scattered all the way to the summits. Our climbs up beyond the Funerary Rock and back down, then up and down both Wayna Picchu and Huchuy Picchu had consumed all of our fuel, and we must have been running on adrenaline for several hours. We were hungry.

We freshened-up at the hotel and then went out in the rain to find a bite to eat. We had had such an excellent dinner at Indio Feliz the previous evening, and our hopes were high for another nice dining experience somewhere else in the town. We were badgered endlessly by menu-waving touts as we walked past empty and uninteresting restaurants.

We eventually settled on a small place with a handcrafted clay pizza oven in its back corner. All we wanted was a pizza and a cup of coffee; something to hold-off starvation until dinner. Steaming mugs arrived with contents somewhat reminiscent of coffee, and the house pizza came nicely thin-crusted, but lacking pizazz. The sauce was bland and the ingredients were sparse.

We wondered: With fresh ingredients so inexpensive why had they skimped on onions, peppers, tomatoes and other readily available local produce, why had they presented such a lacklustre meal? It is probably because most people come to Machu Picchu only once in their lives, the owner figured he didn't need to do anything to induce repeat business, not even to provide quality.

It continued to rain, so we took our filled, but unsatisfied bellies back to the hotel and napped. In the evening, we again walked out looking for a place to dine. We had read reviews raving about Chez Maggy: *"A longtime favourite and branch of the legendary Chez Maggy in Cusco is a good, relaxed place"*; and *"Chez Maggy is the only restaurant we went to twice ... Fantastic!"* It sounded good, so we decided to go.

We were cajoled, heckled and hassled at the entrance by a brash tout forcing a menu into our faces. I told the aggressor to back off; he was scaring us away from the place. I asked to be allowed to take our time reading the menu and to decide on our own whether we wanted to dine there. The menu read rather invitingly, and a nice selection of classic Italian pasta dishes caught our eye. We went in and picked a corner bench with our backs to the front stained-glass windows, and a view across the entire room. Ours was one of only three tables occupied.

The interior appears to be a confusion from attempting to imitate a 1960s hippie style using local Peruvian material. The same surly fellow who had accosted us at the entrance was our waiter, and from him we ordered cervesas and a guacamole appetizer followed by fettuccine puttanesca for Edi and a chicken cannelloni for me. Twenty minutes later, after the newly arrived couple at the table next to us was served their guacamole, I asked the waiter about ours. He went to the kitchen and returned with it.

Edi's pasta arrived shortly, but mine did not. After ten minutes, when my pasta had still not arrived, I walked up to the waiter at the kitchen servery and asked where my pasta was; I could see it plainly sitting there on the counter. A minute later he arrived at the table with my now tepid cannelloni. Our pastas were well past al dente, and the sauces were bland, thin and wet.

While we ate the sloppy pasta, an Inca couple, or one disguised as such, came in. He heated his drum head at the pizza oven, tuned it and they stood in a corner of the room and began making noise. The proprietor turned down the sound of the TV, which had been blaring a music show from above the bar. The uke, flute, drum and voice clamour continued for way too long, and eventually the TV was turned back up and the couple unsuccessfully polled the diners for money and attempted to sell their CDs.

Chez Maggy demonstrated to us many of the best ways for a restaurant to fail. However, it this remote corner of the world, flooded with nearly a million one-time-only visitors per year, they likely realized they need do very little to satisfy the hoards. The restaurant has been there since the 1970s, so their formula must be working. We went to bed sorely disappointed that we had not returned to Indio Feliz.

Our train back to Cuzco was scheduled for 1600 on Wednesday, so we had many hours to fill before we needed to be at the station. After an early breakfast on Wednesday morning we set-out on a walk down the river along the road to Machu Picchu. In one place, the sheer cliff dropped directly into the Urubamba, and to traverse it, a half tunnel had been wrested from face, offering a bed for a one-lane road.

Along the way we passed some modern Inca stone carvers, splitting granite blocks for the ongoing building boom that seems everywhere in Aguas Calientes.

We saw a wonderful example of the regular fracture planes of the local granite. This characteristic would have been of great assistance to the ancient Inca stonemasons.

Peru is reputed to have 20% of all the plant species on the planet and in the undergrowth along the sides of the road was a great variety of flowers. We met a local man on the road, and he went into the undergrowth and brought back an orchid, which he presented to Edi.

There were wonderful flowers everywhere, and we took time to admire a large variety of them.

There is no road to Aguas Calientes, and everything is brought into the community down the Urubamba Valley by rail. Except for buses to Machu Picchu and the park service trucks on the riverside road, there are no vehicles.

We walked back into town and as we passed the rail siding on the main street, we saw men laboriously carting building materials from a just-arrived freight car.

Above the river, the town is laid-out entirely with walking streets. Every thing is carried or pushed in a wonderful variety of wheelbarrows and one and two-wheeled carts.

Around midmorning it began raining, and for shelter we walked into the covered marketplace, which borders the train station and serves the only passage from train to town. Its hundreds of stalls filter money from the tourists as they arrive. On Monday afternoon we had searched the entire market, and I had found an attractive handmade alpaca shoulder bag, and we were still searching for a nice little candle holder for our dining table aboard Sequitur.

We found nothing to our liking, among the stalls in the marketplace, so we dodged the raindrops as much as we could, and made our way to Café Inkaterra, out along the river upstream of the town. It was wide open, but without a soul around, not even staff. We walked up the steps to the hotel and through its restful lobby to the dining room. It was a very tastefully decorated and peaceful place, but totally empty, except for one waiter folding napkins. We looked at the menu and decided that S/120 was more than we wanted to risk on the buffet lunch.

It was still raining heavily, so we walked back outside and along to a bench upholstered with reed cushions and set in the dry under the eaves. We sat watching the big rain drops glinting in an emerging sun, as they splashed on the jungle plants and flowers across the path. Edi continued with her sock knitting, and I continued reading *A Short Walk in the Hindu Kush*, Eric Newby's book, which I had meant to read thirty-five years earlier on my way to climb in Afghanistan's Hindu Kush. Retirement now gives us opportunity to do the things we have previously set aside.

Toward 1300, the rain had stopped, and the sun was more regularly breaking through the thickly scattered clouds. We decided to revisit Indio Feliz for our lunch, and we were welcomed as long-lost friends. My quiche Lorraine entrée on Monday evening had been so delicious, that we both decided to order a main course version of it for lunch. It came beautifully presented and accompanied by a large plate of sliced tomatoes, a bowl of sauce Dijonnaise, a basket of homemade bread rolls and a huge terracotta dish of homemade butter. Everything was delicious, including the huge steaming mugs of coffee.

I told Patrick that this was the best quiche Lorraine I have had since one in Nancy many years ago. His eyes lit-up and he grinned broadly; he said he was born in Nancy and his cooking was influenced by the cuisine of that region of France. I told him I had lived just north of there in 1966 and 67, when I was in the RCAF and serving with NATO. After lunch Patrick brought us huge snifters of Cognac to wish us fair winds on the continuation of Sequitur's voyage.

What a dramatic contrast there is between this restaurant and the others we experienced in Aguas Calientes. Indio Feliz is a true oasis in a culinary desert. They serve large portions of delicious food, the atmosphere is warm and welcoming, and the many staff members we saw were all jovial, cordial and very professional. On the three occasions we were there, the place was busy, while the other restaurants in town begged for customers.

We walked back to the hotel to retrieve our bags from storage, and again we were heckled as we passed each restaurant. Most were empty, or nearly so; the owners simply didn't understand.

There were many people sitting around, apparently waiting for the afternoon trains back to Ollantaytambo or Cuzco. By their looks and dress, they appeared to come from all over the world, and by their shape, one couple was most likely from the United States. They were certainly not fending-off imminent starvation with their ice cream cones.

We were harassed by stall-keepers as we made our way to the train station through the market and its repetitious selection of the same mass-produced tourist trash. Here again, the owners simply didn't understand.

Aboard the train, we settled-in across from a Japanese couple from Yokohama. Shortly after our 1600 departure, meal service began. Thankfully it was a light snack; we were still rather stuffed from our wonderful lunch. The menu read very invitingly, and because of our continuing thirst with the high altitude, we ordered cervesas, and were delighted to see that Peru Rail isn't gouging its captive audience; the cost was S/6 per bottle.

The snack was a very nicely presented assortment of regionally inspired tidbits and taste experiences.

While we ate, we enjoyed the passing scene out the windows as we re-ascended the Urubamba Valley. There were many Inca agricultural terraces on the river banks and the slopes above them.

We passed a suspension bridge, which led from a corral that appeared to be a staging area for the trail leading down the other side of the river.

We left the Rio Urubamba and entered the canyon of the Rio Huarocondo. Shortly after we began the ascent, the sun set and it quickly became dark. With no more entertainment from the passing scene through the windows, the staff offered us some of their own. A vividly dressed and masked wild man danced through the car in an apparently traditional Inca ritual.

And then the car hostess let her hair down and started modelling some superbly crafted baby alpaca clothing. Her male counterpart alternated with her, showing some wonderful outfits.

We were tempted into buying a couple of pieces each, when after the half-hour modelling session, they announced that the items were all available for purchase onboard. I chose two sweaters; one a wonderful coral red with cable knit patterns, the other with a patterned body and beige sleeves. There was no cellular connection for the credit card machine, so we had to wait until near the end of the trip to effect the payment.

The sweater that Edi wanted was too small, but the hostess said they could radio ahead to the station and have a larger one waiting there for our arrival. Someone else had already bought the scarf she wanted, so another was arranged for our arrival at the Poroy station. The fit was perfect, and Edi settled the account through a portable machine on the platform.

We were the last passengers to walk through the station and into the guarded compound outside its front, where we were approached by a taxi driver holding up his ID and license. Suspecting that we were his last prospects, we negotiated a very good fare down to Cuzco and to our hotel.

We were welcomed back at the Rumi Punku, where we needed no registration formalities; we were simply given a key, which let us into a huge room in the new section of the hotel, with a king bed and very large, modern bathroom. Our minds and souls were so filled with our adventures of the previous few days and our bellies were still filled with the wonderful food from Indio Feliz and the train, that we felt like nothing else but lying in bed with the BBC news looping on the TV. We quickly bored of it and fell asleep.

On Thursday morning we had a leisurely breakfast from the buffet, and then set out on foot to continue our exploration of Cuzco. We walked again up to Plaza San Blas, looking in all the shops along the way for an alpaca scarf to compliment my coral red sweater. Most of the scarves we saw were coarse and rather garish.

Along the way we enjoyed looking at the Inca walls, which are scattered through much of the city and incorporated into the newer buildings, many of which date to the beginnings of the Spanish colonial era half a millennium ago.

The exacting stone-cutting of the Incas fascinated us. Large blocks of half a meter, a metre and more in size were carved with their compound curves and angles matching the adjacent blocks with such precision that there is no room even a sheet of paper between stones weighing many tonnes each.

We worked our way down the narrow streets back toward the centre of town, passing along the way many traditionally dressed women, some leading llamas, others carrying loads on their backs, probably headed to the market to set-up.

As we neared the centre of town, in an area around the four and five star hotels, we found shops with finer baby alpaca scarves, but saw none that would complement my sweater. After nearly six hours of nosing around the stock of a hundred or more shops, we resigned ourselves to buying the scarf from Lima's Inca Market or a boutique in Miraflores when we get back down to the coast, or from the Peruvian shop on Vancouver's Granville Island when next we return to Canada.

We were hungry, and in desperation we had a bland and unexciting meal in one of the overpriced restaurants on the periphery of Place de Armas. The best we could say of it was that it filled the void.

We walked back to the hotel, passing along the way a seemingly endless supply tacky souvenir shops. Their only interest to us was that many of them were set-up in old buildings that still retained some of the magnificent Inca masonry.

Our Friday morning flight back down to the coast went smoothly, after a delay as the airline apparently amalgamated our partly filled 0940 flight with the next one at 1100. We easily found a licensed taxi within the Lima airport's security compound, and negotiated an uneventful S/25 ride to La Punta.

After a visit to the mercado for fresh produce for dinner and to the bakery for bread, we took a launch back out to Sequitur in the mooring field of the Yacht Club Peruano. All was well aboard, the solar panels had brought the batteries back up to 100% and the Bolaseca dehumidification crystals had worked well, and had kept the boat dry and fresh-smelling. It was great to be home.

Our heads and souls were still filled to overflowing with our experiences, and we couldn't stop thinking of the postulations in Gavin Menzies' book 1421: The Year China Discovered the World. So much of what we saw of the remains of the Inca Empire seemed to us to have had a Chinese influence in its conception and execution.

However, we needed to get our minds from the past and back into the present and onward; we needed to tie-up the loose ends and make our final departure arrangements. We had arrived in Peru in late May, and over six months later, we were ready to move on down the coast to Chile.

15. Preparing to Leave Peru

Many details needed attention. Among them, we had to take delivery of a new dinghy and motor, rescheduled for Saturday the 4th, but saw it migrate to the following week. We still needed to be lifted-out to clean the bottom, inspect it and change the zincs. Our more-than-a-dozen-times-delayed lift-out was finally scheduled by Jamie for Tuesday the 7th. Also on Tuesday, our stainless steel fabricator, another Jamie had promised to have the outboard engine bracket completed and installed on Sequitur's transom.

In between and around these, we needed to top-off our tanks with diesel and water. We needed to re-commission the watermaker, tune the standing rigging, overhaul the sails and the running rigging, change the engine oil and filter, change the three fuel filters, flash-up the second freezer and second fridge and start loading them with provisions for our passage south. All of these and many other tiny details needed attention.

On Tuesday morning the one Jamie delayed our lift-out until Thursday. I asked for a specific time, and he said early. I suggested 0800, and he said 0830, so I confirmed 0830 on Thursday the 9th of December with him.

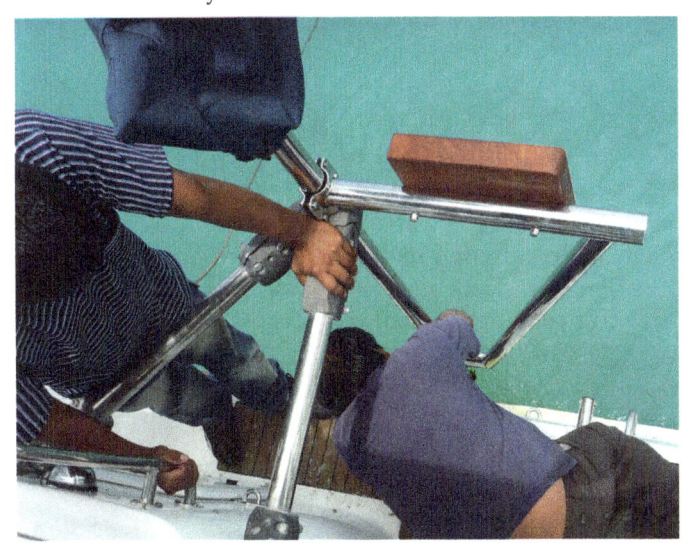

The other Jamie arrived as promised with the newly fabricated bracket for the new 18hp outboard engine. It fit perfectly, and other than his having mounted the clamp board on the wrong side, it was exactly as I had envisioned. The board was quickly and easily moved.

Wednesday was a national holiday in Peru, it was in celebration, from what I could gather, of the day that Mary finally got-up the courage to tell Joe she was pregnant. Luis had arranged with me to use the day for the dinghy and outboard motor commissioning. I took the launch ashore and walked along the malecon to his club.

We unpacked, unrolled, assembled and inflated the dinghy, and then we mounted and centred the motor and marked its position on the transom. One of the club tripulantes walked over to the gas station a block away to get four gallons (a tad over 15 litres) of gasoline in the fuel tank. Peru is one of the very few countries in the world still using some of the archaic US measurement system, the rest of the world having gone to the much less complicated metric system.

The dinghy was rolled out the pier, which was still rickety and not yet fully repaired from its damage in the tsunami from the Chilean earthquake earlier in the year. The tripulantes slung, swung and launched the dinghy, which we have decided to name Non Sequitur, in memory of the dinghy we had stolen in Paita as a part of our welcome to Peru in May.

Luis and I motored out to Sequitur in the mooring field, where we completed our transaction in the cockpit. We now have a dinghy and motor again for the first time in six and a half months.

We secured the dinghy and took the launch ashore in the early afternoon and caught a bus to San Miguel, where we picked-up some things at Maestro and then went across to Wong. We hadn't yet had lunch, and had decided to do the per-weight buffet. An indication of our fuel burn of the previous week was evident by the massive protein stacks on our plates as they were weighed through by the cashier.

We then went below to the supermarket and started the process of refilling Sequitur's pantry fridges and freezers. Among the things on our list was ground beef so we could prepare some pasta sauces and a chilly con carne. The standard grind was S/22 per kilo, so instead we opted for the huge shucked and cleaned scallops complete with attached roe for S/19 per kilo. Who needs ground residue of beef when scallops are less expensive? We bought all they had.

On Wednesday evening I woked-up a celebratory dinner to welcome our new dinghy. I toasted some sesame seeds in a dry wok as I cleaned and chopped the vegetables. Quartered champignons de Paris and mini portobellos, sliced oyster mushrooms, celery, white onion, scallions, pak choy and chunked red, green and yellow peppers and roma tomatoes were among the ingredients that went into the wok with a few drops of sesame oil in the last of our canola oil. When everything was nearly cooked, I tossed-in a couple of huge handfuls of scallops and tossed until they were just firm, then sprinkled on the toasted sesame and we were ready. Instead of breaking the bottle of bubbly over the bows of the dinghy, we had opted for a better use.

At 0750 on Thursday morning I lowered and launched the dinghy from the davits and took it to the newly installed dinghy dock. Its predecessor had been destroyed by the Tsunami; its replacement was less than a week old.

I had brought the dinghy ashore to clear our stern and enable Sequitur to enter the lift-out dock. Also, I wanted to ensure all was ready for our lift-out. The travel lift was not there!

I went looking for it. I walked along the pier past the crew which was continuing its demolition and reconstruction of the pier's roadbed, and there was a yawning gap in the travel lift's route to the haul-out dock.

I continued up the pier to the security gate and Jaime's office. He was not there, and the attendant told me he would be in mañana, the next day. I walked across to the work yard and saw the travel lift buried behind a clutch of boats and trailers and other impedimenta. This was not looking good for our scheduled lift-out in less than 15 minutes.

274

In my non-Spanish, I spoke and gesticulated with Godofredo Alvarez Rivera, one of the senior tripulantes, and told him of our scheduled lift-out. He replied in his non-English and gestures what I understood to be that he would organize it. Assured, I took a launch back out to Sequitur.

Toward 0930 a tripulante arrived onboard Sequitur, and pantomimed that we needed to lower the SSB antenna and topping lift. He thought the antenna was a backstay and he wanted to stabilize the mast before we unfastened it. I pointed-out our B&R rig and convinced him we had no backstay and a very stable rig. I released the SSB antenna and topping lift and allowed them to sag to the mast. At 0942 we slipped from the buoy and motored to the pier, backed into the dock and watched as slings were passed under our hull.

Shortly after 1000, Sequitur was lifted, and as our side decks came level with the dock sills we stepped ashore. Sequitur was out of the water for the first time in a year and a half.

The bottom had no encrustations, only the slime expected from sitting on a mooring in horribly polluted water for over six months.

A couple of tripulantes spelled each other off as they power-washed the bottom. I was delighted to see that the bottom paint was still good. We had last had the bottom done in March 2009 with Interlux Bottomkote, and it looked like it would last us until our projected haul-out in Puerto Montt, Chile in the southern autumn.

I could see that the zinc at the end of the propeller hub was gone, as were the two shaft zincs. We can only hope that they have been missing for only a short while, and that nothing has been eroded by electrolysis.

Once the bottom had been power-washed, I took my bag down onto the rolling platform under Sequitur, and had it rolled in to the propeller. I unscrewed the plug, screwed-in a nipple and greased the gears of the VariProp, then removed the nipple and replaced the plug. Next, I used Q-Tips and CRC contact cleaner to clean-out the threads in the end of the propeller hub. With LocTite on the caps-crew threads, I installed the hub zinc and torqued sufficiently to compress the lock washers to just closed. I then installed the two shaft zincs, again using LocTite on the caps-crew threads.

All of this was watched by a very interested tripulante, who proudly posed beside the completed work.

In the middle of this procedure, Gonzalo and Magdala arrived at the Club to say hello and to arrange a farewell with us. We had thought they had gone to New York, but they had cancelled the trip. I was dirty and distracted with the zincs, so I directed them up to the upper deck to make arrangements with Edi.

I inspected the bottom, and could see no sign of any electrolytic erosion on the propeller, the shaft, the struts, nor on the through-hulls. Everything looked fine, and we were ready to splash. While the bottom was being power-washed, I had walked up to the office and paid for 200 gallons of diesel. Now we were lowered to just above the water, and there we took the fuel. The main tank took 135.0

275

gallons, the gauge stopped at 192.75 when the auxiliary tank reached its fill, and I put the remaining 7.25 gallons into our two 5-gallon diesel jerry cans. It had been a very close calculation. We topped-off the water tanks, taking on about 480 litres.

At 1315 we were re-launched, and with two tripulantes onboard, we motored out into mooring to an electrical buoy near the centre. I allowed Augusto to take the helm and get us to the proper place. Within twenty minutes, with the assistance of launches they summoned by cell phone, the crew had hooked us up to moorings fore and aft, and had run our shore power cable to the outlet on the forward buoy.

The entire process, from preparation through lift-out, servicing and re-launch to re-mooring and connection to the electrical buoy had gone very smoothly. Jaime was nowhere to be seen.

In the central area of the Club's mooring field there is a wonderful network of mooring buoys with shore-power outlets, and some of these even have fresh water bibs. We were connected to a 110-volt, 30-amp outlet. Shortly after 1600 the breaker was made in the control barge, and we were on shore power for the first time in nine months.

In the late afternoon we caught a bus along La Marina and Prado to Arequipa, where we caught another bus to Parc Kennedy in central Miraflores. We nosed around in the shops, including in a couple of multi-merchant artisan complexes. They had mostly the same repetitious, mass-produced trappings we had seen in Cuzco, Pisac and Aguas Calientes the previous week. We bought nothing from them.

We walked over to Gonzalo and Magdala's home and spent a delightful time chatting, drinking bubbly and nibbling on hors d'oeuvres catered to us by seven-year-old Gonzalito. Leaving the young one with the maid, Gonzalo then drove us over to their favourite restaurant, Rafael.

Among the wonderful dishes that came to the table was the largest serving of foie gras that I had seen since the Alsace, when I sat in the kitchen of Domaine Weinbach drinking a range of Vendanges Tardives and Sélection de Grains Nobles from the property's Grand Cru vineyards. Colette, the owner of the domaine was at the stove searing foie gras, while her winemaker daughters Catherine and Laurence poured.

Another outstanding plate was the beautifully presented seared tuna that Edi had ordered. It captured the essence of chef-owner Rafael Osterling's cuisine, a fusion of Asian and Mediterranean styles with fresh Peruvian ingredients. At the end of the evening Rafael came out, and we spoke briefly.

We shared a widely rambling conversation throughout the dinner, and we thoroughly enjoyed the opportunity to give back a small bit of the wonderful hospitality that Gonzalo and Magdala have offered us these last few months. Gonzalo's driver took us very comfortably and safely back to La Punta.

As wonderful as such socializing is, we needed to turn to more mundane things if we wanted to make our scheduled departure. With shore power and full water tanks, Edi flashed-up the washing machine and ran several loads of things tired of repeated hand washing as well as a backlog of tea towels, serviettes and other niceties. We decided against using the dryer, and the cockpit became a drying room.

Edi mixed-up a triple batch of biscotti, plus some dough for a batch of bagels, a couple of loaves of crispy potato bread and two pizza crusts. These were all set aside to do their thing while we went ashore and caught a taxi to the Maestro on Argentina. We bought assorted hardware, including chain and padlocks for the dinghy and motor, and we also picked-up another six bags of Bolaseca dehumidification crystals.

We loaded our purchases into the bag on our wheelie and crossed the street to the Minka market. We bought four kilos of boneless and skinless chicken, two kilos each of eggs, local cheese, comotes, mashing potatoes, green beans, red peppers, ripe tomatoes, red onions and green mangoes. We added four bunches of asparagus, and a kilo each of riper mangoes, firmer tomatoes, hard avocados and a hand of ripe bananas for banana loaf. Other small purchases took our load to well over 40 kilos.

Everything stowed easily and we still had room leftover for our final shopping trip. We spent the remainder of the day baking, pausing for a while between bagels and biscotti to insert two large pizzas into the oven and then into our bellies.

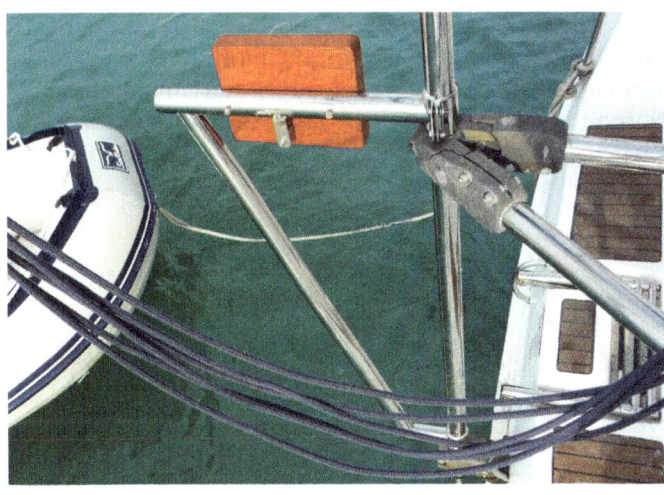

On Saturday I fine-tuned the new outboard engine bracket, adding bushings fabricated from the polypropylene of a yogurt bottle to the clasps. I also replaced the common nuts with nylock ones, so that I could set the correct grasp on the shaft and allow the bracket to swivel easily, but with some resistance.

I re-rigged the falls on the davits, which we had stowed for safekeeping when we arrived in June. With some bumbling as I taught myself how it could best work, I hoisted the motor off the dinghy and onto its new mount. I was delighted with how well the pieces all fit together once the dinghy was hoisted.

I had emailed and then later spoken with Jaime about our wish to sail away on Tuesday, asking him to contact the agent for us so that we could initiate the departure procedures. We waited onboard for the remainder of Saturday for agent to come.

On Sunday morning, as we continued to wait for the agent, I continued with pre-departure chores, including inspecting the Hydrovane and installing its rudder. I then set about re-commissioning the watermaker from its more than six month sleep.

The instruction manual for the Spectra Newport 400 Mk II is so well written, and in such clear language, and machine controls are so well conceived and executed, that it was a breeze to bring the watermaker back to life. I changed the charcoal filter and the 5-micron and 20 micron pre-filters, pushed some buttons, twisted a valve and the process began. The storage solution purge sequence ran smoothly, as did the ten-minute purge of initial product water, and within forty minutes we were ready to start making water. I closed the relief valve, pushed the Auto Run button and watched as the machine began delivering water at the rate if 68 litres per hour.

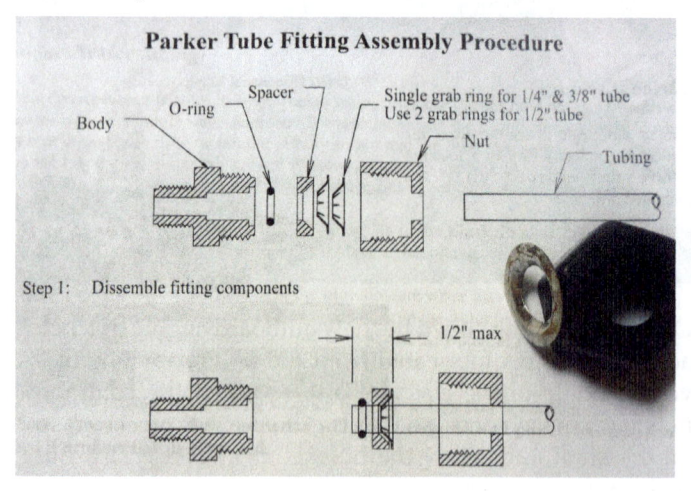

Then a pop, a whoosh and the sound of a rapidly turning pump broke my contented state. I quickly pushed the Stop button, and went forward to inspect the source of the commotion. The Parker tube fitting connecting the tubing from the pump module outlet to the Clark pump had failed. I undid the fitting to discover that only one grab ring had been used by the installer to connect the half inch tubing, instead of the two explicitly called for in the manual. My trust in the work done by Specialty Yachts, our fit-out yard in Vancouver, sunk to a new low. I would now have to thoroughly inspect every connection, and try to find a source for more grab rings.

I bent the tabs slightly on the single grab ring and reassembled the connection. Then using a rolling hitch on the tubing with monel locking wire, I secured the tubing in the connector. I re-flashed the watermaker and ran it for four hours, making 270 litres of water.

While the watermaker was doing its thing, we continued with other details of preparing Sequitur for the next leg of the voyage. In the mid-afternoon Gonzalo, Magdala and Gonzalito, tacked close aboard our stern a few times and we had a brief conversation. In the late afternoon Luis came by in his dinghy to say farewell, and he presented us with a large jar of white asparagus, which his uncle grows down the coast in Paracas.

We had given-up on the agent arriving, when near dusk there was a knock on the hull and Jorge Romero Gardella, the agent requested permission to board. We sat in the salon going over the procedure and digging out our ships papers, entry documents, passports, visas, immunization cards and other assorted papers, when there was another hail from alongside. Gonzalo, Magdala and Gonzalito had finished their sail and on their way ashore, they stopped by to give us a box of skin care products, including lots of sunscreen from his company, Yanbal International.

On Monday morning we continued with our preparations for departure. While Edi organized below, I put on my old mountaineering harness and went up the mast using the folding steps, and pushing a triple prussic knot up the spinnaker halyard as a safety. I was up the mast to reinstall the speaker for the foghorn and loudhailer, which had been installed by Vancouver's Specialty Yachts, and which had come crashing down to the deck during our passage to the Galapagos.

In the mid afternoon we took a bus to Plaza Vea to pick up last-minute items, and took a taxi back with our huge load. Edi found creative ways to stow the overflow of our fresh produce. The less perishable items were conveniently accessible on the shelf above the stove and galley counters.

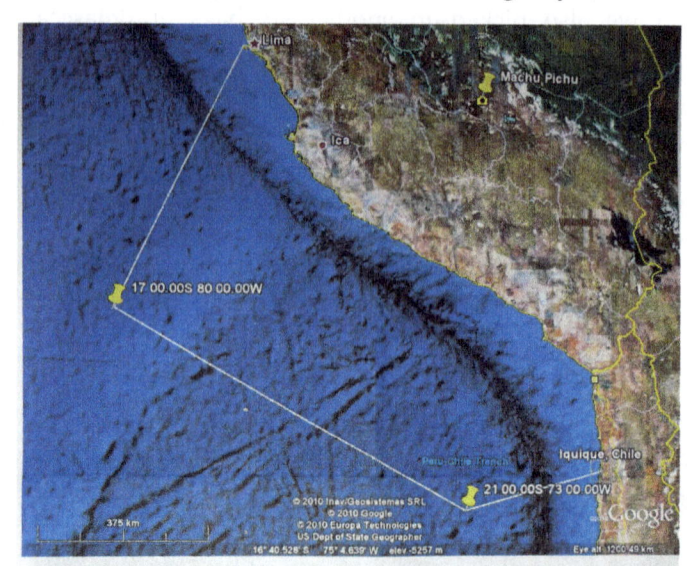

With the expected winds from the southeast, we intend sailing a course of 208° on the port tack until clear of Peruvian waters. We then intend making best use of wind, current and sea state to make for Iquique, Chile, while remaining clear of the 200-mile limit of Peru.
With an anticipated 10-15 knot wind, and the north-setting Humboldt current, we expect to make good 4 to 5 knots along our courses, which will give us an ETA Iquique 8 or 9 days after departure Callao.

While Edi stowed our purchases, I prepared a chartlet of our planned passage from Callao. The idiocy of the system in Peru is that they insist we provide an exact passage plan with courses and speeds, plus turning points and latitudes and longitudes with times at each, and an ETA at our final destination.

278

The narrow-minded people who devised the system obviously had no idea of sailing, nor of the unpredictability of courses-made-good with constantly changing weather and sea state. The minions who now administer the system perpetuate its asininity. I decided the best way to appease them was to offer them a routing that took us very quickly out beyond their 200 nautical mile limit, and then kept us beyond their claimed territory down the coast to our destination, Iquique, Chile. They have effectively forced us to skip the rest of Peru.

It is so sad that the incompetent bureaucrats who administer the system make it impractical for visiting yachts to safely and enjoyably cruise the coast. Instead, they force us flee the country and to tell other cruisers to avoid it.

I printed off the chartlet and caught a launch ashore to settle the invoices from the Yacht Club for our six-and-a-bit months moorage, our lift-out charges and fees for the launch services. I then met with Jorge, and we went up to the Club office to begin the paperwork.

In a little under an hour and a half, and with the help of Pamela, the office administrator, Jorge generated and I signed a stack of paper over two centimetres high. Among these was yet another Sanitario inspection, this one costing S/552 and bringing our total Sanitario charges in Peru to S/2650. I questioned the charges and received a very vague explanation.

On the way back out to Sequitur, we passed the Sanitario vessel on a mooring. I wondered if the charges imposed on us are to aid in the cleaning and restoration of the dilapidated and filthy vessel.

Our last three ports: Puerto Ayora in the Galapagos and Paita and Callao in Peru, are the three most polluted and filthy harbours we have ever experienced and I wondered whether we were being inspected to ensure that we don't carry away with us any of their filth.

I returned onboard to the wonderful aroma of banana loaf baking in the oven, and all seemed well again.

On Tuesday morning the 14th of December I was up at 0700 to complete our preparations for departure. Among other things, I went up the mast to remove the bird netting from the spreaders and the pig stick flying anti-bird streamers from the top of the mast. While I was up there I inspected the antennas and instruments and reinstalled the wind vane.

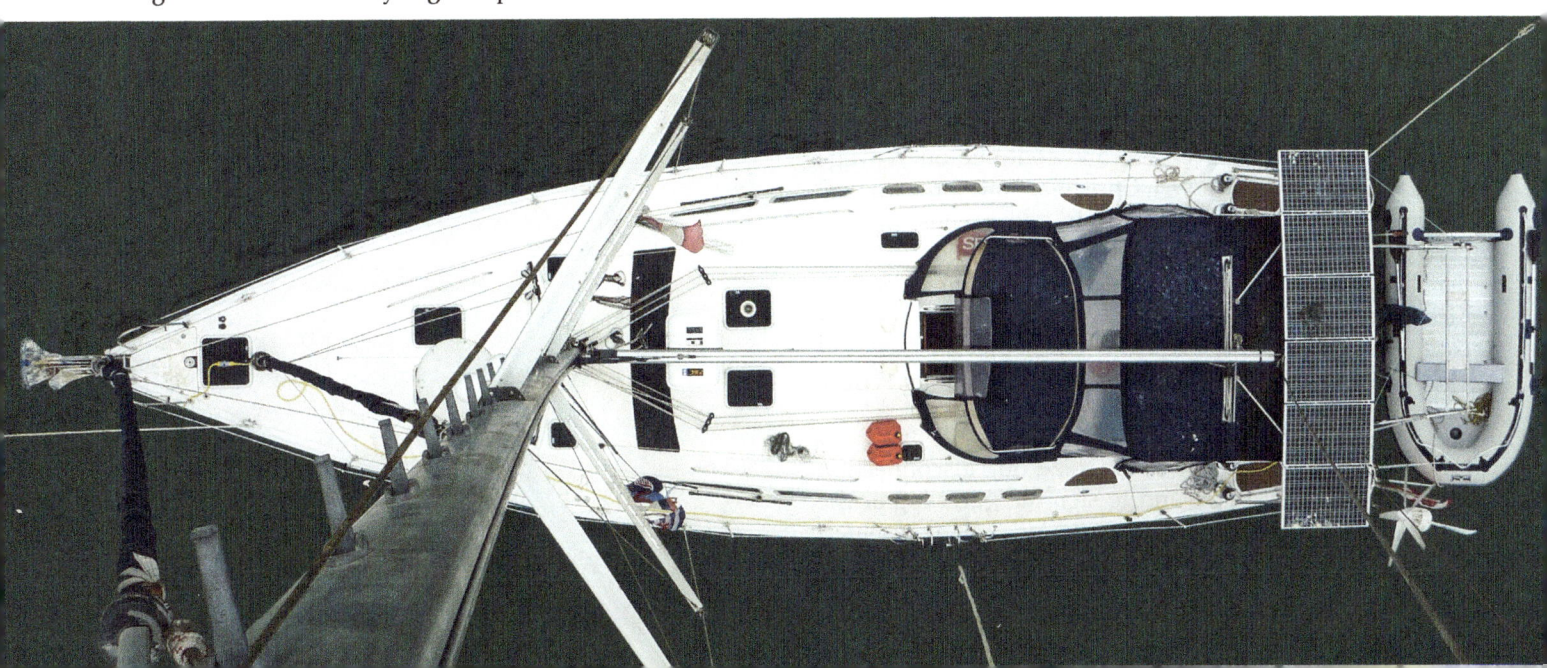

When he said that he had never had a visit to Sequitur, I asked him to come out with me then in the launch, as we waited for the work boat to come and undo the electrical connection and the fore-and-aft mooring buoys.

By the time I had finished and was back down, Edi had completed stowing and squaring-away below. She had devised so many wonderful ways to securing for sea, such as using cushions stuffed into the shelves and cupboards to keep things in place. By 1020 we were ready to depart, and we sat around waiting for Jorge to arrive with the Sanitario and Autoridado Portuaria Nacional people, who were due onboard at 1000.

At 1115 Jorge arrived onboard alone with the signed and stamped paperwork, including our zarpe, our permission to leave Peru. We were free to head to Chile.

With Frano looking so comfortable in the galley, we were tempted to Shanghai him as our chef for the passage to Chile. In the end, we didn't keep Frano; he went ashore with the launch that had come out to disconnect us.

As we prepared to leave Peru and continue our voyage southward, Edi had drawn a Christmas card for us to post on our blog and to send to family and friends. Shortly before noon on the 14th of December we sent and posted it with the following note: *"We send you our greetings for a Merry Christmas, and our wishes for a happy and prosperous New Year. Because of our anticipated sporadic internet connectivity over the next week or two as we sail from Peru to Chile, we are sending this card a bit early."*

I went ashore by launch to organize our disconnection from the electrical buoy, and to sign the guest log at the Yacht Club. While I was writing in the log, Frano presented me with a bottle of wine and wished us a bon voyage.

16. Southward to Chile

At 1315 a launch came out with a crew, and we were systematically detached from the electrical buoy and from our fore-and-aft mooring. We slowly motored out of Bahia de Callao while attempting to contact Tramar on VHF Ch 16 to announce our departure. Finally, at 1338 Tramar called us and asked for our ETD. I told them we had departed at 1315. The radio operator then asked for our destination and ETA, to which I replied we are a sailboat and depending on the winds, the current and the sea state, we could be in Iquique in seven to ten days. This was no good; the operator wanted a time and date. I told him I could give a range of dates. He insisted, so I reeled off a totally imaginary time including minutes and seconds. This apparently satisfied the idiotic bureaucracy.

At 1430 we rounded the northern cape of Isla San Lorenzo, altered course to the southwest and continued motoring, looking for the wind to help us on our way. We were still waiting for a breeze at 1830 as we watched our first pretty sunset in months. We had watched sun go down rather ingloriously throughout the spring in La Punta, with the low cloud cover hiding all but a hint of colour.

We called Tramar as required at 2000, and received the customary response: Absolute silence. What a farce this bureaucratic nonsense is; all vessels underway in Peruvian waters are required to report their positions twice daily, at 0800 and 2000. Not one of our many dozens of VHF and SSB calls in May and June were ever answered, and it appears that the office continues to maintain the same standard of service. They can watch Sequitur full time on AIS, so I have no idea why they need verbal reports.

The Peruvian system of dealing with foreign cruisers is so asinine and nonsensical that it causes us to very strongly recommend that cruisers avoid visiting Peru by boat. Had we known it would cost us nearly $1,000 in Sanitario fees to anchor in some of the most polluted water we have ever seen, we would have thought seriously. Had we known it would cost us fifteen hours in paperwork and nearly $1500 in fees, bribes and graft to enter the country, we would have thought even more seriously. Had we known of the culture of corruption and crime along the waterfronts that would see Sequitur stripped of her dinghy, motor and safety equipment, we might have considered visiting Peru by air from Ecuador or Chile. Visitors by air are automatically granted a six-month visa on entry and the total fees are $21.

Yet, had we not stopped at La Punta, we would have missed the hospitality of the Yacht Club Peruano. We would have missed meeting Gonzalo and Magdala, and enjoying their wonderful spirit, their hospitality and their dedication to cruising sailors. We would have missed meeting Frano and having him show us through Minka, Makro and introduce us to Peruvian cuisine in his restaurant on the Yacht Club pier. We would have missed the introduction to Rafael Picasso and our wonderful experiences with him at his winery and distillery in Ica. We would have missed the cheerfulness, kindness and generosity of Eugenio, who introduced us to Luis for a new dinghy and motor and to Jaime for new stainless steel. We would have missed the wonderful tripulantes at the Club, Godofredo, Agusto and Julio outstanding among them.

The facilities of the Yacht Club Peruano are good, with many dozens of mooring buoys in a 24-hour guarded roadstead. Our mooring fees for six months came to S/2103, and until 30 November, this included launch services. This was a reasonable charge. However, from 1 December a launch services fee of S/20 per day is being added to the mooring fee, nearly trebling it. There is a further S/20 per day fee for club services that was to have been introduced on 1 December, but has been deferred until later. When implemented, the cost for moorage on a ball in La Punta would be more expensive than that for a private slip in downtown Vancouver's False Creek with electricity and water in a secure marina with wonderful facilities in the heart of one of the greatest cities in the world, which is situated in of one of the finest cruising areas on the planet. We think that YCP might be a tad out of line with its new charges.

The wonderful people notwithstanding, the compelling thing in our minds and souls was that we needed to get Sequitur out of Peru. The governmental systems seem to do everything that they can to make visiting boaters feel unwelcome, uncomfortable and unwanted. That spirit is what spawned my official passage plan from La Punta to Iquique: Get out to the 200-mile limit as quickly as we could and stay at least 200 miles off as we parallelled the coast.

On Wednesday morning we were still motoring southeast directly into a 4 to 6 knot breeze and into the 2-knot Humboldt Current looking for the wind to strengthen, or veer or back to give us something usable. To lighten the mood, Edi served eggs Benedict for breakfast, and we began to settle into the rigours of being at sea again.

By noon, the wind had swung around to SSE 10 knots, so we pulled out the full main and jib, set the Hydrovane to steer our best course to the ESE and we took off at 4.5 to 5 knots. The sky was clear and we were enjoying some of our first blue skies in months. Winter and spring in La Punta are mostly overcast and very humid. Sequitur was now finally able to begin drying-out.

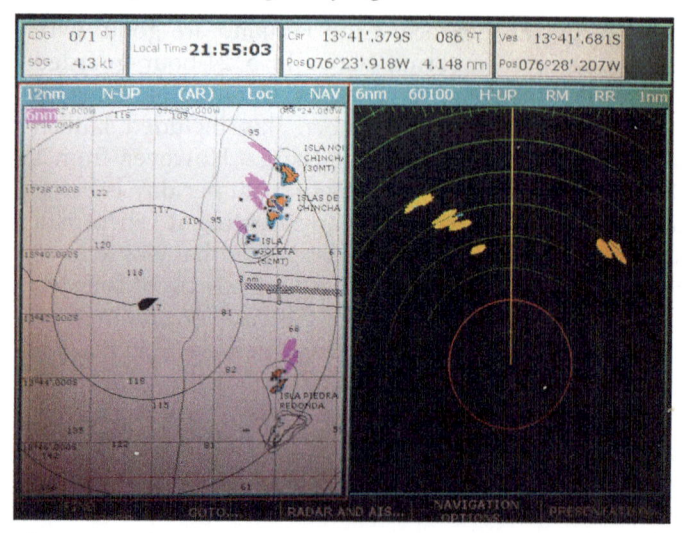

The winds had taken us back in toward the coast, and rather than stick to our artificial official passage plan, we continued where the winds took us. Sounds like sailing, doesn't it? Screw the bureaucrats; God seems to know what she is doing. At midnight we were off the entrance to Bahia de Paracas, and we continued on in.

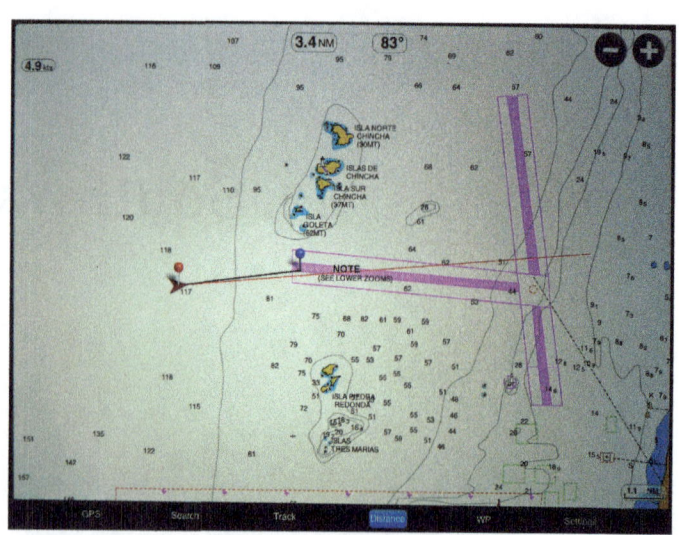

The Navionics Marine HD program in my iPad gave a wonderfully useful fourth look at the navigational situation as we passed through a group of unfamiliar islands and reefs in the middle of the night. It is a great supplement to the Raymarine chartplotter and Navionics charts. With its built-in GPS and charts, its quick and easy scalability makes a very convenient and highly portable addition to eyeball, radar and chartplotter.

At 0150 we came to 20 metres on the Rocna in 6 metres of water on a sand and mud bottom in Bahia de Paracas. We attempted to contact Tramar and Guardia Costera. No response. After a good night's sleep, a nice leisurely breakfast and some drying-out in the sun, at 1220 we weighed and proceeded out of the bay. We attempted to contact Tramar and Guardia Costera. No response.

An hour later we motored around the northeast point of Peninsula de Paracas and passed the famous Candelabro de Tres Brazos, which is often erroneously related to the Nazca Lines. The Candelabra is visible only from the sea, and in one report I read that it has been dated back about 2000 years.

As we watched the huge geosculpture move past, we imagined all kinds of scenarios that might have led to its design, placement and production. Why there? Who was meant to see it? What did it mean? While we answered none of the questions, we did strike another line off our list of *must see* sites. We motored through El Boqueron and out into the open Pacific and went looking for different wind.

There was a southeast 8 to 10 knot breeze as we headed out, and coupled with the Humboldt Current, the only use our sails could make of it would give us way too much westing on the one tack and take us onto the rocks on the other. We continued motoring, bending our course to the southeast as the headlands allowed, and as we went we ran the watermaker, producing 296 litres and bringing the tanks to their full marks.

At 2115 on Thursday evening, after we had finished making water and had wasted more energy on attempting to contact Tramar and Guardia Costera without response, there was a smell of scorching varnish. This could mean only one thing; an alternator was overheating. I shutdown the engine and we hauled out the jib and main.

The breeze had strengthened and was now SE 7-8 knots and moved us along at 3 to 4 knots to the south-southwest. As the influence of the Humboldt increased, and gave us too much westing, we tacked to the east slowly closing again on the southeast line of the coast. And thus we sailed through the night and into midmorning on Friday, as the winds slowly increased to around 16 knots and the resulting seas built.

We were in a very confused combination of steep southeasterly wind waves crossing a 2 to 3 metre westerly swell and being influenced by the sheer at the edge of the Humboldt Current. We hove-to to provide a comfortable motion for breakfast and watched as the current and wind combined to set us north-northwest at just over 2 knots. After breakfast, we set off again, endeavouring to remain in the band of relatively undisturbed water between the coast and the edge of the Humboldt.

At 0505 on Saturday morning, shortly after the eastern horizon had lightened to announce the pending sunrise, there was a loud bang, followed by the fluttering and flapping sound of a flogging sail. The clew cringle on the main had parted. I hauled-in the main and we continued along under jib alone. At 0800 I again went through the futile effort of attempting to contact Tramar and Guardia Costera.

The winds continued in the 15-knot range from the southeast, and this made Puerto San Nicolas a feasible port of refuge to come to anchor and repair the sail and investigate the alternator smell. As we approached the bay, the winds gradually increased and were by mid-afternoon in the 25 to 30 knot range. Under jib alone, I made five tacks through the bay and at 1519 we came to 50 metres on the Rocna in 12 metres of water on a mud and sand bottom. We were tucked in a corner under the huge complex of an industrial facility and its loading wharves, and still the wind howled over us. While the land was close enough to deny fetch for wind waves to build, it provided us no protection from the wind. The wind howled through the rigging and we saw gusts well into the 30s. I again went through the futile effort of attempting to contact Tramar and Guardia Costera.

An hour or so later an industrial barge with an un-muffled diesel came alongside and we were informed that this was a private facility and that we were not supposed to anchor here. I told the man we had sought refuge to do some repairs, and once done, we would be on our way again. He seemed satisfied with this, and the noisemaker departed back to the pier, leaving us with only the howling of the wind in the rigging.

On Sunday morning, after I had again gone through the futile effort of attempting to contact Tramar and Guardia Costera as required at 0800, I began repairing the clew. The webbing attaching the cringle to the sail had chafed and parted.

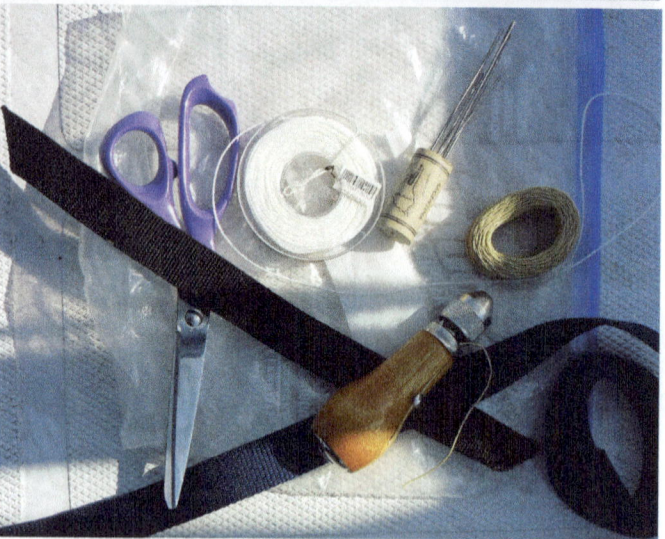

We dug-out one of our stitching awls, some waxed twine, nylon webbing and other items needed for the repair. The stitching awl I chose is one that since the late 1960s had been in my mountaineering repair kit.

It had been with me on expeditions up Mount Waddington, the culmination of British Columbia's Coast Range, on a solo grand-traverse of New Zealand's Mount Cook, on first-ascents in the Stikine Icecap on the Alaska border, on more first-ascents in the Hindu Kush of Afghanistan and on lots of playing in the French, Swiss and Italian Alps on such peaks as Mont Blanc, the Eiger, the Matterhorn and a new route on the Torre de Vajolet. The awl had repaired more than its share of boots, packs, gaiters and crampon straps and now it was put to work repairing a sail.

The wind had decreased somewhat overnight, but as the sun warmed the barren mountain slopes across the bay, the cool air was pulled in off the sea and soon the wind was up into the mid-20s again. I dressed in double layers of fleece to try to keep warm in the cool wind and started stitching double layers of webbing to reattach the cringle. Holding on with my thighs and flopping back-and-forth as the boat weather cocked in the wind and threw the sail from side to side, it took an hour and a half to stitch the first strap into place.

Out of the direct roar of the wind, I unwound a bit, and then began investigating the alternator smell. I could detect no odour on the new 210 amp unit, but there was a residual smell on the 120 amp. Since the drive belt on the 120 also drives the engine's fresh water pump, I couldn't simply take off the belt. Instead, I decided the best course of action was to disconnect the harness at the 120's regulator, and allow the 120 to spin without any exciting current.

While I was deep into the engineering spaces, I installed a temperature sensor between the 210 alternator and its regulator. Then I serviced the engine and ran it up to see that my remedy had worked. Everything checked-out well; the 120 was freewheeling and staying nicely cool, the 210 was putting in 140 amps at the engine's 1500 rpm, and the newly installed temperature sensor was reading a cool 68 degrees.

As I was running-up the engine, the un-muffled barge approached with four uniformed passengers and motioned it wanted to come alongside. I hauled three fenders out of the transom locker and ranged them along the starboard quarter. The barge was skilfully manoeuvred into place against the 25-knot wind and all four uniforms came onboard. They were from the Guardia Costera and wanted to see our papers and to find-out what we were doing there.

To give fuller access to the engine while I worked on it, I had removed our accommodation ladder down into the interior of the boat, and I had also removed the engine cover box. While Edi held the Coast Guard at bay in the after end of the cockpit, I scrambled down into the salon and got the dossier of ship's papers. I handed the spokesperson our passports and the file from our clearance out of La Punta. I told him we had put into San Nicolas to repair our mainsail and to do some engine and electrical repairs. The sail was now repaired and the engine was just being run-up to check the effectiveness of its repairs.

The uniformed minion dithered through the papers, trying to make sense of them; I doubt that anyone knows what they all mean. He finally asked if we had a photocopier onboard, to which I replied an honest "*no*", ignoring our scanner and printer that would provide copies. I told him if he wanted copies, the offices in Callao could provide them, adding that there are five and six copies of each document on file in the various offices there.

For nearly half an hour the three spare stooges stood there looking ridiculously awkward as their dithering and indecisive leader fumbled back and forth aimlessly through the papers, trying to look important. I told them that if my electrical repairs proved effective, our intention was to leave at first light in the morning, before the day's winds begin building, and then I added forcefully that I needed to get back to the repair and testing. Eventually it must have dawned on them that we weren't going to offer them any bribes or gifts, and they left.

I took a break, and after being revived with a breakfast of bagels and cream cheese with hot coffee, I went back at it. After another ninety minutes in the buffeting wind, the second strap was firmly stitched into place, and I took another break.

The third strop took only an hour and a quarter to stitch into place. The four and a quarter hours of tensed muscles from holding on against the wind and flailing sail had wearied me and given me aches in areas I have not had them in many years.

At 0535 on Monday the 20th we weighed and proceeded out of Bahia San Nicolas as the sun rose. Our visitors the previous day had been from the base in Puerto San Juan, ten miles down the coast, and they had told us to report our departure to them by VHF. We received no reply to our multiple attempts. There was an 8 to 10 knot breeze from the southeast, and this gradually built as we motored out and around the headland, where we hauled out the staysail and half the main. We sailed out to the south-south west to stand a safe distance off the land and at 0800 we again went through the useless exercise of calling the Guardia Costera.

Through the morning we sailed close-hauled on a port tack, making to the south-southwest at five knots, then in the early afternoon we tacked across the wind and current to make very slightly north of east at 4.5 knots. The sun set at 1830, and with it went much of the wind. We flashed-up and motored directly into the breeze with a piece of the main flattened as a stabilizing fin against the beam swells.

We had a craving for pizza, and knowing that delivery would be difficult, I made one. We enjoyed it off the cutting board in the cockpit with the light of the full moon adding to the ambiance.

Watchkeeping, navigating, napping, reading, cooking, eating and sleeping filled our days, interspersed with running the watermaker, running the washing machine and relaxing. I had noticed my muscle aches were not going away, and I had developed sore and swollen throat glands. Edi had the same sore throat, and then I developed severely inflamed gums and a few hours later, so did Edi. We were wheezing and congested and we had headaches.

We started to realize that we had been poisoned by the fine dust blown off the ore heaps by the high winds in Puerto San Nicolas. Sequitur was caked with a black sooty deposit. I must have breathed in huge quantities of the black dust as I sat stitching the sail, and it was now showing its effect. We began a routine of mouth rinsing with Perichlor, a chlorhexidine gluconate anti-gingivitis rinse, and slowly our inflamed gums eased. Ibuprophen relieved our headaches and lessened my body aches.

Shortly after 0500 on Thursday the 23rd, as we were motoring directly into a 10 to 12 knot southeast wind, the engine stalled. I suspected a clogged fuel filter, and rather than attempt to clear and restart the engine, I hauled out the jib and two-thirds of the main and set off to the eastward on a starboard tack. We were making poor progress, much less speed than expected and yawing and wallowing.

As the dawn came, I saw that we were trailing lines from our stern. Things now made sense; the stalled engine would be from our running over a line and wrapping it around the propeller, and the sluggish sailing would be from the trailing lines.

I tied a heavy galvanized chain hook to the end of a 13mm nylon line and used it to snag one of the trailing lines. There was too much pressure from the sails to pull a bight of the line aboard, so I rolled-in the sails and tried again after most of the way was off the boat. I brought 3 or 4 metres aboard using a sheet winch to assist, then tied-off the end and cut the line free.

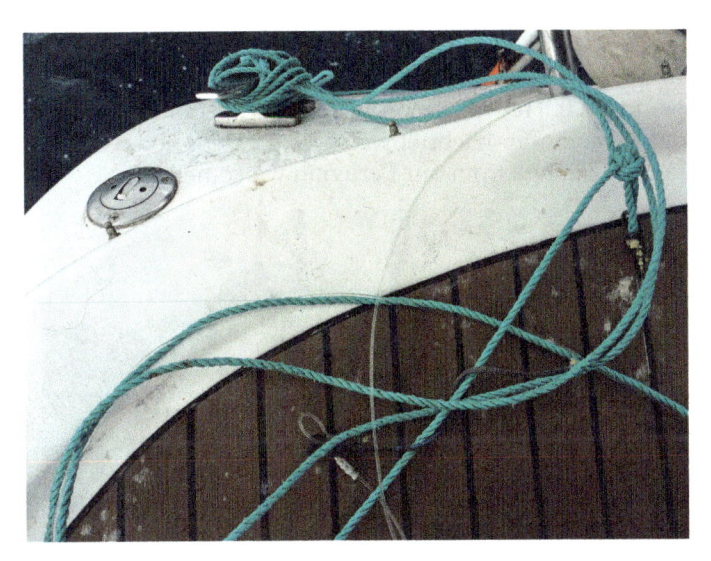

I had wanted to leave sufficient lengths of each of the lines so that it might be possible to work the tangle free from the prop. I repeated the process with the other trailing line and we soon had two ends secured to the transom cleat. I attempted without success to work the lines free of the propeller.

Thirty-two minutes after I had noticed the lines, we were free again, and I hauled-out all three sails and we set off east-southeast at about 4 knots. The winds continued favourably and we maintained hourly runs in the 4.5 to 5 knot range and course made good between 110 and 115 degrees. By 2200 we were just over 20 miles off the coast of Chile, and our course to Iquique was 160. The wind had started backing, and by the time we tacked, we were able to sail a course just a few degrees above south at about 3.5 knots into the current. This held and improved through the night, and by sunrise on Christmas Eve, we were making a course just a few degrees west of our rhumb line.

Edi prepared some delicious spring rolls, which we had with the last of our peanut sauce. At 1309, as we were eating, we received a *Merry Christmas* message on our chartplotter. It took me a minute or so to realize it had come from a passing ship, Industrial Century, on her way from Iquique to Balboa. It had been sent by DSC using his AIS to get our MMSI. I called him on VHF and returned the greeting. For land-bound text-messaging freaks, this is the sea equivalent. We chatted for a bit and then went on with our separate worlds.

Besides being a wonderful show of fellowship, this also confirmed again for us that our AIS and VHF were working. This was the first response we had had to our VHF transmissions since the idiotic exchange with Tramar as we were leaving Callao.

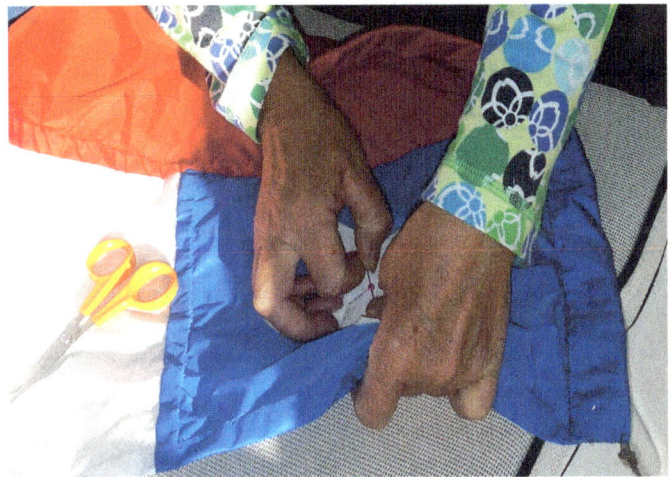

In anticipation of our arrival in Chile, Edi began stitching together a courtesy flag, and I dug-out our quarantine flag from the locker.

In the mid-afternoon we tacked and started making hourly runs above 6 knots for the first time in months. The wind was south-southeast 10 to 12 and we were tracking east-southeast. In the evening I ran the engine to charge the batteries and to make water. By 2000 the wind had veered to the south at 4 to 6 knots and we ghosted along toward Iquique 22 miles away.

By midnight we were 18 miles northwest of Iquique and the wind strengthened a bit and allowed us to continue slowly but directly toward our destination. At 0400 we were 5.4 miles from the port and moving toward it at about 3 knots. I thought that if the wind held we should be at anchor by 0600.

As we sailed into the harbour the wind decreased and nearly died. We ghosted along making the last 2 miles at 0.2 to 0.5 knots through near glassy seas and using the occasional puffs to move us. In the middle of this was a necessary tack to take us to our anchorage. Also, we had to thread our way in past many anchored fishing boats and mooring buoys. It was Christmas morning and the harbour was very quiet.

There were many very large jellyfish in the water, and some very playful seals. Fortunately, we didn't have to try to manoeuvre around these. At 0752 we came to 18 metres on the Rocna in 4 metres of water. I left the sails up for a while hoping to set the anchor, but there was insufficient wind to give much strain on the chain. I set the snubbers, rolled-in the sails and we were in Chile.

Sequitur was tucked in between the fishing fleet and the ships of the Armada de Chile. Within five minutes of arrival, a dinghy from the Yacht Club came out and asked us if we wished to go alongside in their marina. We told them we had picked-up a Peruvian fishing line with our propeller a couple of days previously, and we couldn't use the engine to manoeuvre alongside. We asked them to confirm with the Chilean authorities that we would remain comfortably at anchor under quarantine until after the holiday and the weekend.

Sequitur was filthy with the fallout from the fine dust that had blown off the ore heaps while we were in Puerto San Nicolas. We hauled-out the buckets and mops and began cleaning the black sooty deposit from the boat.

Mid-afternoon on Boxing Day an Armada inflatable came alongside, and a lieutenant in crisp whites asked permission to come aboard. We welcomed him into the cockpit while his boatmen remained in the launch. He told us that we will be visited by officers from Migracion, Sanidad, Aduana and the Armada the next morning around 1000. He was very courteous and spoke excellent English, and after his brief welcome, he departed. What a dramatic change from our Peruvian welcome!

Shortly after 1000 on Monday an Armada inflatable came alongside and we welcomed five officers onboard and seated them at the cockpit table. The health and sanitation officer inspected below for compliance with agricultural and sanitation regulations. We easily passed. After having paid over S/3000 for sanitario inspections in Peru without an inspector ever having visited Sequitur, this was a refreshing change. For just short of an hour the officers examined our papers and documents, and copied data from them, and through the entire process we carried-on a lively and jovial conversation. Without the conversation, the process would have likely taken only half as long, but both they and we were thoroughly enjoying the interchange.

The Sub-Lieutenant in charge of the party told us we were now officially cleared-in, but that we needed to go to the Harbour Master's office to complete the process and pay the appropriate fees. He pointed out the building as the yellow one near the floats of the yacht club, and then they departed. I struck the quarantine flag and hoisted the Chilean colours and we were officially in Chile, and without any hassle.

288

On our way in he pointed-out the locations of shoals and rocks to avoid and some leading marks to use in navigating the narrow, shallow channel into the marina. Passage for us was only possible at high tide, which would give us a quarter metre or so under the keel. The next daylight high tide was at 1532 on Tuesday, so I organized with the yacht club to come in then.

At 1523 on Tuesday we weighed and motored in toward the marina. I left the anchor a-cock-bill and stationed Edi on the foredeck to prepare to let-go the anchor on my signal. The intention was to drop the anchor, swing around and back-down on it to a Mediterranean mooring on the float with a 3-metre-long finger to our starboard.

We lowered the dinghy and mounted the motor, finding it much easier this time than it was on our first attempt. We headed in to the marina and secured to a very run-down float with sun-scorched plywood and rusted-out mooring cleats. We were welcomed by one of the men who had come out on Christmas morning to offer us moorage at the club floats. He showed us the intended slip, which was in better repair than the one where we had left the dinghy. I asked the depth and was told about 2 metres. In our laden state, we require 2.2 metres, to which he replied there were no rocks and it was a very soft bottom. I reminded him of our wrapped propeller and need of a diver. He said he would organize one.

We headed over to the office of Gobernacion Maritima, the harbour master and met again young Sub-Lieutenant, Victor Caceres who had done our clearance aboard. Very friendly staff copied data from our ship's papers and completed some forms, then told us to come back on Wednesday, adding that the paperwork would likely be back from Santiago on Tuesday, but in case it wasn't, why waste a trip. How refreshing!

It went perfectly. With the offset of the snubber attached to the anchor chain from a side cleat, our lead to the anchor was square to the stern and we nestled-in very comfortably balanced between stern lines, springs and anchor. We were in a slip designed for a very small boat; in fact, our neighbour across the finger was no more than seven metres in length, and she looked too big.

Back at the yacht club we were introduced to Abdul, the diver. He loaded his gear into the dinghy and we headed back out to Sequitur in the anchorage. In less than five minutes of free-diving Abdul had cut-away the fouling lines and inspected the propeller, insuring the blades feathered and un-feathered easily. I took him back to the yacht club floats and paid him 25,000 Pesos, about CA$52.

We headed ashore in search of fresh produce. We walked into a scene from the Old West; balloon-framed wooden buildings with false facades, ornate door and window frames, lavish trim and very aged bright paint.

Some of the buildings on the periphery of the old town seemed beyond hope of restoration, and were it not for the very arid climate, they would have rotted away many decades ago.

As we walked we imagined we were in Canadian Prairies of the 1880s, or possibly in some Hollywood cowboy and genocide movie set from the 1930s and 40s. We kept expecting a posse to gallop through.

And then we came to Plaza Prat, which at first looked like an architect's rendering. Ranged around its periphery were some very well-restored classic buildings in a combination of Georgian and Spanish Colonial architecture.

The theatre was particularly impressive, and appeared to have been recently restored.

Leading away to the south from the plaza is Boulevard Baquedano, which was the nitrate aristocrats flaunted their power and wealth with lavish homes. Built between 1820 and 1920, many of the imposing houses along the very broad boulevard were constructed of Douglas fir from British Columbia, Canada.

Covered observation decks seem to have been a standard feature of the homes, and many along the boulevard have been wonderfully restored and there is a very evident pride in the heritage.

Our Lonely Planet guide showed Supermercado Rossi about a kilometre away in the centre of the old town and we made our way over to it. We were sorely disappointed; it was without doubt the worst we have seen since the central Baja coast. The produce was dismal; there was a very limited and poor selection of low quality and culls at high prices. Our first impression was that we were in the slums, then we thought that there must be a huge fresh produce market nearby.

We bought some green peppers, tomatoes and a piece of beef loin plus a couple of bottles of very well priced Chilean wine and went back to Sequitur. For dinner I prepared a lomo soltado in memory of Peru.

Late morning on Wednesday the 29th we caught a collectivo to Zofri for 1000 Pesos, just over $2. Zofri is the largest zona franca, or duty-free zone in South America. It was set-up in 1975 and has grown to encompass over 240 hectares of shops and warehouses supplying consumers and distributors in northern Chile, southern Peru, Bolivia, Paraguay, Brazil and northern Argentina.

There are over 500 retail shops, with many of these being dollar-store-type outlets. There is also a very large section of upscale brand-name stores, consumer electronics outlets, major and minor appliance stores and a huge auto mall. We bought a digital clock for our master cabin, a strap wrench for Sequitur's oil and fuel filters and a large piece of pork tenderloin for our dinner.

As Edi was preparing pancakes for breakfast on Thursday morning, there was a knock on the hull. I answered it to learn that another boat was coming into the slip beside us, and that we needed to move our port bow line from the opposite finger. I moved the line to a steep lead aft and watched as Blue Dame, a Jeanneau 49 DS from Hallevisstrand, Sweden turned in front of us and ran aground five metres from our bows. Blue Dame's crew scrambled to let-go their anchor and get lines to the staff on the floats, and I checked clearance with our bow, and there was nothing else for us to do.

We sat in the cockpit eating pancakes with Grand Marnier and maple syrup. Blue Dame had come in at the moment of the lowest tide, the skipper having misread the tables. We figured that they should float free in three or four hours, and there was nothing anyone could do to assist.

After a wonderful breakfast with front-row seats on the action, we went ashore and walked around the waterfront to the street-side fish stalls. We chose the busiest fishmonger and picked a nice-looking mahi-mahi weighing just over 3.25 kilos.

We agreed when he suggested it be cut to pan-fry size, and watched as he quickly and expertly skinned, filleted, and butterflied the fish for us. The cost was 3900 Pesos, about $8.30 for four double servings plus a soup from the backbone.

We dropped the fish in one of Sequitur's fridges and caught a collectivo up into the hills on the eastern edge of the city. We were heading to Agro, the local market, which has hundreds of stalls and stands selling fruit and vegetables, meats, cheeses, groceries and general merchandise. It sprawls across an area of about six city blocks in a collection of buildings and shelters.

In the first produce building we came to we filled our cooler bag with lovely fresh fruit and vegetables and then explored the remainder of the huge complex. We could find only one bakery, and from it we bought half-a-dozen large rolls. We went back to the main street and tried to catch a collectivo back to the marina. For more than twenty minutes we tried, but kept getting *our* taxi commandeered by locals who knew the ropes. Since it was downhill, we decided to start walking. We could see the port about four or five kilometres away, and the slope was gentle. It was early afternoon without a cloud in the sky, the sun was only two degrees from our latitude, but it was surprisingly temperate, with the dry air and the cooling influence off the South Pacific.

After a couple of kilometres we came to a major cross-street, and a couple of blocks along it we saw a huge shopping centre with a Sodimac, which we recognized from Peru. In Sodimac we picked-up two 220v 32 amp electrical plugs so I can make-up adaptors for the Chilean shore power.

A block further along we found a huge Lider supermarket. Among other things we bought a kilo of butter, a kilo of mushrooms, assorted ham and salami and a dozen bottles of wine at ridiculously low prices compared to those we have seen so far. We also bought a bottle of Chilean Pisco to try.

Outside we joined the line waiting for a taxi, and in about ten minutes, it was our turn. We tried to describe our destination to the driver, but he couldn't comprehend *"Puerto"*, *"Marina"*, *"Club de Yates"*, *"Capitan de Puerto"*, *"Gobernacion Maritima"* nor any other name we could conceive to convey to him our where we wanted to go. He searched the crowd for someone who spoke better English, and she seemed as lost as he was. Lost, that is until I hauled-out my camera and showed them a photo of our destination. They both knew it immediately, and knew it as everything we had been calling it. It seems they didn't think any gringo would want to go there with groceries.

On Thursday evening we enjoyed some of the very fresh mahi-mahi butter-fried and accompanied by rice and a butter-sweat of a julienne of carrots, red and green peppers and small white onions. The mahi-mahi was pronounced well worthy of at least two more for the freezer.

After dinner we tried our three different Piscos: a Pisco Puro from Vista Alegre and a Pisco Mosto Verde Torontel Don Santiago, both from Peru. From Chile we had Alto de Carmen, an aged supermarket brand. Possibly because we love fine aged spirits such as Cognac, Armagnac, single malt, the aged Chilean Pisco won the round, though the Vista Alegre Soldica was close. All were superior to the harsh, raw spirits used in making Peru's favourite drink, Pisco sour.

We spent a quiet day on the 31st, taking a walk through the old parts of town and sitting aboard soaking in the scene. A group on Inca terns decided to pose for us on the pulpit of our neighbour's boat.

Our New Year's Eve was celebrated quietly on board with a diner of the last of our jumbo prawns, which we had bought through Frano in La Punta. We spent the evening reminiscing about all the wonderful experiences we had enjoyed during the past year, enjoying the stillness of our small space and thanking Whomever for our continuing good health. We are so blessed to be doing what we are doing; it would be wonderful if everyone could feel as fulfilled.

With Sequitur securely alongside on the float, Edi and I decided to do some exploring inland. As we were walking around in Plaza Prat on the afternoon of New Year's Eve, we had stopped to talk with a tour operator, Manuel Gonzalez who was just closing-down his shop-front for the day. We asked whether he offered tours to Santa Laura and Humberstone, and from his descriptions, we booked an all-day tour with him for Sunday the 2nd of January.

We were picked-up at 0830 on Sunday morning in front of the Yacht Club gate by Manuel, his wife, Sandra and his driver in a rather new 12-passenger Toyota bus. After stopping at a hotel to pick up a man from Santiago and then at another to pick up an ex-Chilean couple from Australia, we headed up the thousand-meter hillside above Iquique and into the Atacama Desert.

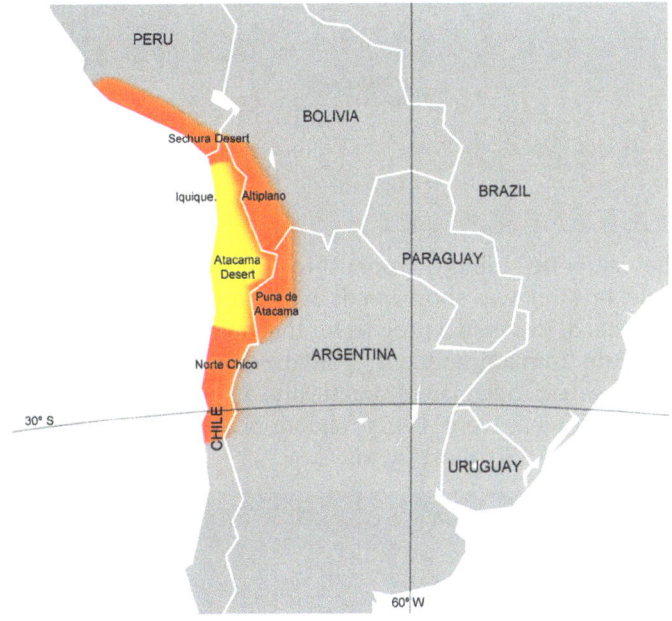

The Atacama Desert stretches for a thousand kilometres along the northern coast of Chile. It is known as the driest place on Earth, with many of its areas having received no measurable rainfall since record-keeping began. It is so arid that its mountains, which reach to nearly 6900 metres are completely glacier-free. To the north of it is the Peruvian Sechura Desert, and although a little less arid, it is considered by some geographers as a part of the Atacama. To the east lie the arid Altiplano of Bolivia and the Puna de Atacama of Argentina. These high barren plateaux are second in height only to the Tibetan Plateau of central Asia.

Areas of the Atacama are so dry and lifeless that NASA has been using them to test instrumentation in their Mars landers. In a series of tests in 2003 they duplicated tests that had been done on Mars in searching for signs of life, and found none. This is truly barren land.

The barren and desolate heart of this vast arid place is full of mineral wealth; large areas of the surface of the Atacama are covered with thick caked layers of salt-rich crust called caliches, and among the salt content is sodium nitrate, Chilean saltpetre. In the early 1800s came the discovery of what became the world's largest deposits of sodium nitrate, important in the production of fertilizer and high explosives. The deposits were in the unsettled northern areas of the Desert claimed by Bolivia, Peru and Chile.

As the wealth of the area became more evident through the mid-1800s, the dispute over the territory grew. Several boundary treaties and agreements between the three countries finally fell apart when, after half-a-dozen years, Chile discovered an 1873 secret defensive pact between Peru and Bolivia. In 1879 Chile declared war on Peru and Bolivia, starting The War of the Pacific. In 1883 Chile emerged the victor, annexing the two southern provinces of Peru and the entire Pacific portion of Bolivia, leaving that country landlocked and effectively castrated.

The saltpetre mining boom brought huge wealth to Chile, but this was short-lived; in the early 1900s German chemists discovered a process for the chemical production of nitrate from ammonia. By 1940 the demand for Chilean saltpetre had declined dramatically, and the mines and mining towns were being abandoned by the scores, leaving some 170 ghost towns.

We first stopped at Santa Laura, about 1000 metres in elevation some 50 kilometres east of Iquique. This had been established by the Guillermo Wendell Nitrate Extraction Company in 1872, when the region was still a part of Peru. The company prospered and quickly grew into a thriving town in the middle of desert, with British machinery and British-styled buildings.

The company faltered, and in 1902 was taken-over, and then in 1913 its production was halted to change to a new extraction process, in an attempt to increase its production. The Great Depression caused a slump in demand and the company went into near bankruptcy before being taken-over in 1934 by COSATAN, (Compania Salitrera de Tarapaca y Antofagasta).

The company went into rapid decline and the works were abandoned in 1960. After becoming a ghost town, it was declared a national monument in 1970 and opened to tourism. In 2005 it was declared a UNESCO World Heritage Site.

We wandered through the nitrate extraction plant, with its receiving hoppers, crushers, conveyors, compressors and huge steam engines.

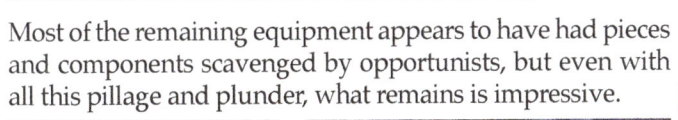

Most of the remaining equipment appears to have had pieces and components scavenged by opportunists, but even with all this pillage and plunder, what remains is impressive.

Also impressive are the massive British Columbia and Oregon Douglas fir posts and beams that had been used in the construction. In the arid desert environment these pieces, some over 30 x 30 centimetres in size, are wonderfully preserved after more than 140 years.

Outside the extraction plant is a century-old horse cart with wooden wheels that appear as sound and ready for use as they would have been the last time a horse was harnessed between its shafts.

Nearby, the headquarters building has been turned into a museum with dioramas in many of the rooms showing the typical furnishings and goods in use at the time of the site's prosperity.

We got back into the bus and were driven a kilometre or so eastward to Humberstone. Like Santa Laura, this site was also established by a British entrepreneur in 1872. James Thomas Humberstone established the Peru Nitrate Company, and named the site La Palma, which quickly grew to be one of the largest saltpetre extractors in the Atacama.

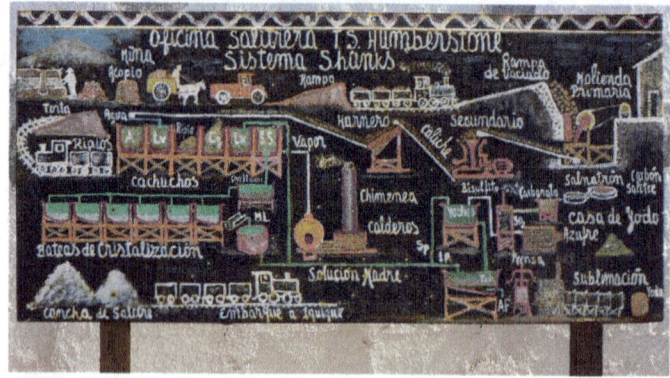

Near the entrance we looked at a rather primitive rendering of the flow of saltpetre from the desert through the processing plant and onward by train to the coast.

Like its neighbour Santa Laura, it approached bankruptcy and in 1934 La Palma was also acquired by COSATAN, who renamed the site Oficiana Santiago Humberstone in honour of its founder. The townsite reached its maximum population of 3700 in 1940 and then began a rapid decline until it was abandoned in 1960. With Santa Laura, in 2005 it was declared a UNESCO World Heritage Site.

Outstanding among the many well-preserved buildings is the theatre, which still retains most of its original interior. A lack of funding over the years has led to only the lower levels of the exterior having been painted, but again, the dry air has preserved the unprotected wood.

We were impressed with the bakery, which is a part of the community store. The huge stone bread ovens, the bread paddles, the receiving bins and the pile of fire wood all looked ready for the next batch. Throughout the site, the dioramas are well-done and show the way of life in this very remote corner of the world half-a-century and more ago.

Half-a-century after they were abandoned, most of the buildings remain in a remarkable state of preservation, due mostly to the extremely arid environment and also, I would think, to the remoteness from vandals.

A fascinating place in Humberstone is the iron swimming pool. The pool was riveted together like a nineteenth century ship's hull. It appears ready for filling, though a look at the filter room shows that the huge circulating pump and the steam engine to power it both need some repair.

Also on display is a passenger rail car that would have been crowded with more than eight people. From the size of the car, we assumed that passenger demand was light.

On display are some of the tiny, narrow-gauge locomotives that hauled the ore to the crushers and the finished product to the coast at Iquique.

Among the wonderfully organized displays was a two-room one depicting the mould-making shop for metal castings. Because of the extreme remoteness of the area, most machine pieces and many day-to-day items needed

298

to be fabricated locally. Ranged on the walls were wood carved forms that would have been used to make sand casts for all manner of items from huge gears, cams and pulleys to plumbing Ts, Ys and Us.

There was even a pair of moulds for a toilet bowl, and between them a cast iron toilet. I hope they had seats for them, because just the thought of sitting on an iron john gives me a pain in the butt.

There were displays of some of the typical kitchens found in the homes. We thought of remodelling Sequitur's galley to give it more of this rustic look, akin to some of the galleys we have seen in 'traditional offshore sailboats', but in the end we decided Sequitur's clean, efficient and modern galley does just fine.

We re-boarded the bus and drove a short kilometre to the Pan-American Highway, which we then followed southward through the Atacama Desert. Shortly we drove through an oasis town in which were growing huge tamarugo trees. These are one of the few trees that prosper in the near waterless environment of the Atacama. They have one or two deep taproots, which extend as much as 15 metres down into the ground to reach water, but they also have a dense surface mat of roots to capture moisture from overnight dew.

As would be expected in such a harsh environment, the trees are very slow growing. We examined the stump of a recent pruned branch on one tree, and on it saw rings so closely spaced that they would require a good magnifying glass to count.

The cashew-shaped and sized seed pods are edible and provided a valuable source of nutrition for the indigenous people, as well as food for the Spanish conquistadors as they crossed the Atacama in their conquest of South America.

We continued to the southeast to the oasis town of Pica, where we were taken to the local swimming hole. It is a natural crack in the rocks, which reached down to the water table, where the water is 40 degrees. The small pool was so overcrowded, and the water was so murky that we wondered about its health safety. We decided against going in.

Pica is a very lush oasis town of about 6300 people. Large mango, lemon and lime orchards fill much of the oasis not taken up by housing, and there are large plantations of bell peppers and tomatoes, among other crops. The population increased by nearly 50% between the 1992 and the 2002 census, and has been increasing at the same rate since. There is concern that with the rapid increase of water for domestic and agricultural uses, the aquifers will be quickly depleted.

Manuel then escorted us to Restaurant Don Emilio, a simple establishment a few blocks away. We sat down to an included-in-the-price lunch starting with a salad, followed by a choice of beef or chicken with the usual Peruvian accompaniment of both rice and potatoes. I asked Manuel about the Chileans using this practice of both starches together, and he reminded us that the people in the area were originally Peruvian, and they have kept their ways. Included in the price was a choice of beer or wine, and we finished with fruit, ice cream and coffee.

After lunch we went to a private swimming pool to relax. Edi and I didn't like the look of the water, and sat in the shade of an umbrella poolside while the others got dirty in the pool. Later, as we were visiting a church in the town, the man from Santiago received a cell phone call telling him of a magnitude 7.1 earthquake in the Valdivia area. We immediately thought of tsunami, and the huge devastation caused by the one the past February. We grew increasingly concerned about the safety of Sequitur sitting at the Yacht Club down in Iquique. In the open ocean, tsunamis travel at around 500 knots, and this means that if a tsunami had been generated by the quake, it could affect Iquique 2 hours and 20 minutes after the quake.

We expressed our concern and tried to get more information. The quake had occurred at 1720, so that meant a tsunami it generated would reach Sequitur at 1940. By then it was 1830, so it was impossible to make it back to Sequitur in time to do anything. The Santiago man got assurance that the short-duration quake was deep and inland, and that reports said there would be no tsunami.

As we drove into the desert across vast expanses of arid wasteland back toward Iquique, we couldn't stop thinking of the possibility of a devastating tsunami. We arrived back aboard Sequitur as the sun was setting, delighted and relieved to find her well and safe, and that there had been no tsunami from the earthquake.

It had been a wonderful day full of new insights of places dry and barren beyond imagination, places showing evidence of lost dreams, places lush and productive in the middle of vast wasteland and places in our minds full of fear and concern for Sequitur's safety. We were glad to be back aboard Sequitur, and will gladly take the dampness of the coast over the near-lifelessness of the Atacama.

17. To Arequipa, Titicaca and La Paz

With Sequitur safe and secure at the Club de Yates de Iquique, Edi and I began looking at travelling further inland. We wanted to visit Arequipa in southern Peru and Lake Titicaca on the Peru-Bolivia border, and while there continue on into Bolivia. Edi had been to both Arequipa and Titicaca in 1979, but had not visited Bolivia, and she wanted to tick-off her 81st country. It would be my 66th, an average of one per year.

On Monday morning, the 3rd of January we walked a kilometre northeast to the bus depot. Inside we saw twenty-or-so bus companies ranged in booths through the terminal, and except for their grubby, jumbled and dilapidated condition, looking much like car rental booths in first world airports. We asked about buses to La Paz, Bolivia, and were told to go to Calle Esmeralda, where we would find bus services to Bolivia.

After another kilometre and more of walking, we arrived in an area lined cheek-by-jowl with tiny and rather squalid bus company offices. No one seemed the least bit interested in offering us any information on their services, nor in selling us tickets to La Paz. We then started thinking of renting a car to do the trip.

Back on board, I booked online a rental car from Hertz for pick up on Wednesday morning. Then in the afternoon, we walked the kilometre or so south through the historic centre of the city to the Hertz office to confirm arrangements. The agent could find no sign of our reservation in her computer, not with reservation number nor account number nor name nor date. We then asked to make a new reservation, and part-way into the process we were told that we could not take the car into Peru or Bolivia; the auto-theft rate in those countries was way too high for them to take the risk.

We asked if other companies might have a different policy, and she told us that Europcar might. She gave us directions, and off we went half a kilometre eastward. Europcar's agent gave us the same high crime story, and said that as far as she knew, no rental companies allow cross-border travel into Peru.

We thought again of travelling by bus, so we walked the kilometre and a half back to the bus terminal. This time we asked about buses to Arequipa, and were directed to a company, Pullman Carmelita which sold us tickets for a four-and-a-half hour ride to Arica, a collectivo taxi ride through the border crossing and on into Tacna, Peru and then a connecting bus to Arequipa, all for 23,000 Pesos, about $46 each. We booked seats on the 0930 Wednesday departure, scheduled to arrive in Arequipa at 2100.

After an early breakfast on Wednesday, we slung our small daypacks and walked over to the bus terminal, arriving well in advance of the required half hour before the scheduled 0930 departure. At 0930 there was still no bus, and we were told it would shortly be along. Over the next few days we were to learn that late bus departures were the norm.

We finally got underway at 0945, and again we climbed the 1000 metres up from the coast and into the Atacama Desert.

For the next five-and-a-half hours of our four-and-a-half-hour leg to Arica we drove east to the Pan-American Highway and then north along it through the desert without any sign of water.

301

The valley bottoms were without rivers or streams, there was no sign of life off the road. After more than five hours, we passed a valley bottom with a spread-out community, which appeared nearly devoid of vegetation, but it must have had some source of water for its existence.

A bit further along, as we began descending toward the coast we saw a green-bottomed valley, and as we approached the coast and Arica there was gradually more evidence of water, and with it, shanty towns.

We arrived at the bus terminal in Arica at 1530, six hours after the scheduled departure of the announced four-and-a-half-hour trip. We would become accustomed to this non-Swiss timing as our trip progressed.

We asked at Pullman Carmelita's booth about our connections to Arequipa, and we were taken walking out of the terminal and along the streets to a collectivo compound. We were introduced to a driver, the agent gave him some money, and we were asked to sit and wait. After about ten minutes the driver escorted us to his taxi and we got in, keeping our packs with us, and declining his offer to put them in the trunk. Another ten minutes passed as three additional passengers were recruited and loaded. Our passports were taken and after a further fifteen minutes, the driver reappeared with them, complete with exit paperwork.

We drove northward 20 kilometres to the Chilean exit post and got out and into the line-up for exit formalities. Once processed, we walked through into no-man's-land while the taxi was driven past the gate. We drove through a very wide no-man's land to the Peruvian entry post, where we again got out and joined the line-up. Once we reached the head of the line, the processing was easy, and we were again granted 183-day visas to Peru at no cost.

When travelling by bus there was no entry fee, arriving by air we paid S/21 each to Migracion, and arriving by private boat we paid S/23 each for Migracion, plus an additional US$975 in Paita and then S/598 to arrive in La Punta and another S/598 to leave Peru. We were told that we had been as a special favour, granted 183-day visas in La Punta. The 183-day visas now appear to us as the standard, Edi and I having been automatically granted them when arriving by air and by bus. It appears the authorities think that bus travellers have no money, that air travellers have some spare cash to be extorted, and that owners of private yachts are wealthy and ripe for picking.

We walked through and put our packs on the belt of the x-ray screening machine, the screen of which was being *monitored* by a woman leaning against the far wall, totally immersed in her book, and oblivious to the passing scene. We re-boarded the taxi and were driven the remaining 30 kilometres to Tacna and to its bus terminal.

We found the booth for our connecting bus, Transportes Julio Cesar, and were told the bus would depart at 1645. We also were reminded of the two-hour time change between Chile and Peru. Our 1700 arrival was actually 1500 in Peru's time zone. We were now thankful for the nearly six hours on the bus; it was more comfortable on the bus than in the terminal.

As the time for our scheduled departure approached, we walked over to the departure gate and presented our tickets, only to be told we needed to purchase terminal-use boletas before departure. We were directed to the kiosk, where we paid S/1.20 each for the privilege of using a dirty and totally run-down terminal with no facilities.

With our newly purchased boletas, we were allowed to board and wait for the not-on-time departure. The antimacassars on the seats showed a recent ownership change; it looks like Julius Caesar is continuing to expand the Empire.

302

Finally we left and headed northward toward Arequipa. About an hour into this leg of the journey, the bus stopped at a police check, and everyone was ordered to disembark. The checked luggage bins were inspected, and officers boarded the bus to rummage through the passengers' effects. After more than twenty minutes of this paranoid police-state procedure, we finally re-boarded and continued northward. There were two more of these police checks along the way, demonstrating to us a lack of confidence of the previous police units by the next ones.

At 2345 Peruvian time (0145 Chilean time) we arrived at the Terrapuerto in Arequipa, a tad beyond the 2100 advertised arrival time, no matter which country's time we used. We walked through the terminal pausing to ask a security guard the proper taxi fare to Plaza de Armas. He told us no more than S/5. At the entrance we were met by a clutch of taxi drivers wagging their passes, and we chose one. He quoted S/5 to Plaza de Armas, so we followed him to his taxi.

I had chosen Sonesta Posada del Inca from our now two-year-old Lonely Planet guidebook. The hotel was on the main square and showed a high-season rate of $79 for a double, including breakfast. We arrived at the hotel to find the rack rate at US$240, but the clerk said we could have a room for $120 because of noise of the 24-hour hotel construction. We decided to look further.

The taxi driver was waiting for us at the door, and we re-boarded the cab. He drove us to a series of six hotels in an increasing radius from the Plaza until we finally found one with an available room.

Santa Teresa Park Hotel is a five-block walk from Plaza de Armas, and across the street from Monasterio Santa Teresa. The rate was S/90 per night, about $25 including breakfast. The lobby looked clean, the staff was tidy and well turned-out. It was just past midnight Peruvian time, past 0200 Chilean time; we were tired and road-weary. We took the room, paid the taxi driver an additional S/5 and went to bed.

On Thursday morning we slept-in a while, but managed to make it down to the dining room for breakfast before its scheduled completion. Our breakfasts were a couple of pieces of a dry, tough and rather tasteless Peruvian version of pita bread, two tiny balls of margarine, a small dish of extremely sweet jam, somewhat reminiscent of strawberries and small cruets of a bland-tasting thick maté-coffee and hot water to thin it out. Needless to say, we prefer Sequitur's breakfasts.

We walked across the street to look at Monasteria Santa Teresa, and then went strolling along the streets, which are lined with wonderful while stone buildings in a mix of colonial styles.

Many of the doorways we passed along the way were open, and glimpses through them and into the interiors and courtyards were marvellous.

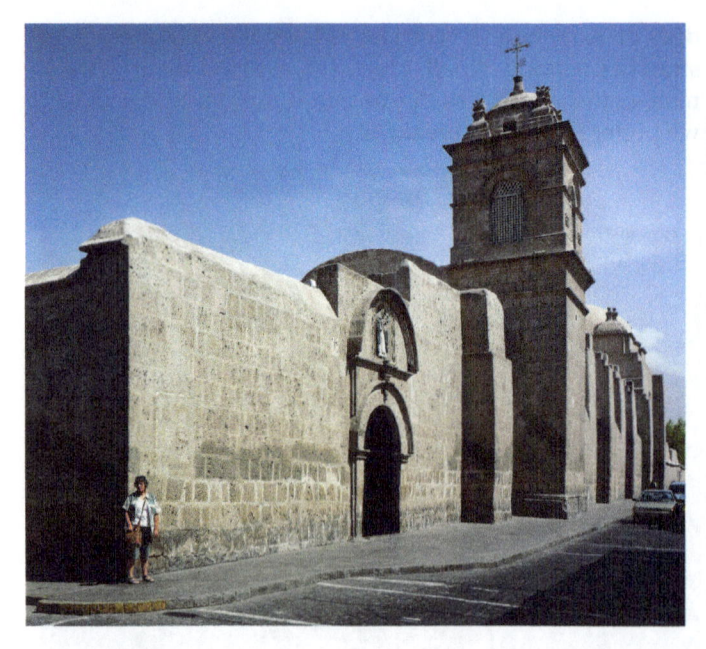

We shortly arrived outside the walls of Monasterio de Santa Catalina, the Santa Catalina Convent. The convent had been founded in 1579 by a wealthy Spanish widow, Dona Maria de Guzman, and it soon grew to occupy over 20 hectares of land in the centre of the city.

The tradition in upper-class Catholic families at the time was to send their second sons and second daughters into religious service. Widows at the time also traditionally went to a convent, and Dona Maria's main purpose for establishing the convent was to give her a place to live very comfortably, but she also wanted to provide a place for the wealthiest Spanish families to send their second daughters. They paid well for this, and dowries of 24,000 sliver coins, a huge amount in today's money, were not unusual.

Dona Maria set-up a luxury retreat to which the wealthy nuns brought with them fine china, silk curtains, rugs, fine clothing, and many of the other trappings of their former positions in life. To make things easier, they had one to four servants each. They brought-in musicians, they threw lavish parties, and in effect, they carried on with the lives to which they had been born and to which they were accustomed.

However, for lesser privileged daughters, being sent to a convent meant living in chaste poverty. In a cloistered convent, such as Santa Catalina, the nuns would be imprisoned for life and never see their families or the outside world again. In effect they were given a life sentence for a crime committed against them by the Church.

Their only contact with the outside was through the parlours, small holes in a wooden grill system half a metre thick, through which they could talk to the person on the other side. There were also segmented lazy-Susan devices in the wall through which items could be passed.

304

We saw a couple of private parlours, likely for the wealthier and more privileged prisoners, and also a communal one, probably for the non-privileged nuns. Seeing these, we could not stop thinking of the atrocities that the Church had perpetrated on the people in the name of religion.

I am being quite blunt and critical in my opinions here, but I believe I am qualified to be. I was raised a 'good' Catholic in a traditional family. I was a senior altar boy, I had been sexually molested by a priest and physically abused by several of the nuns who taught me in school. I had been indoctrinated and brainwashed and taught to lie to the priest at confession. I find it amazing that the nuns told us that every one sins and that we all must confess. To comply with their expectations and those of the priests, I had to make-up sins to rattle-off to the priest in the confessional. In hindsight, it appears I had a rather normal Catholic upbringing.

I vaguely remember my aunt, the second daughter heading off to the convent for her life sentence in a cloister in Japan. I watched a few years later as my uncle, the second son was ordained a priest. I remember after my grandmother's death how my uncle left the priesthood and my aunt kicked the habit and left her cloistered existence. With their mother dead, their external compulsions were gone, and they had no internal compulsion to continue in their roles as the hollow servants of God that they had long since realized they were playing. They each married, she too late to have a family, but he sired a son. What a waste of the primes of their lives!

We next looked at a more sumptuous parlour, which seemed to be for the wealthiest nuns. It probably also doubled as one of their party rooms.

We strolled through the Silent Patio, admiring the architecture and the play of light on its many facets. It is a very peaceful place, yet so full of energy.

We came to a men's washroom, which was easy to guess was a recent addition for the convenience of the tourists.

In 1871 the Pope had sent a very strict Dominican nun to reform the convent. She quickly sent all the wealthy nuns back to Spain and freed their servants and slaves. In 1970, after having sustained damage from two recent earthquakes, the Convent was forced by the mayor of Arequipa to modernize, to install running water and electricity and to open its doors to the public. Once housing over 450 people, one-third of them nuns and the rest servants and slaves, today there remain only about twenty living in the modernized northwest corner of the complex.

The architecture is impressive and made even more so by the play of the light on the shapes. We found it difficult to restrain ourselves from shooting photos. Every direction invites yet another few shots. The vaulted domes flanking the square are impressive, supported on the one side by massive stone pillars and on the other by off-white sillar stonework, some adorned with frescoes.

We entered the novitiates' cloister. Here the young teens, full of raging hormones and life would be ripped from their families and friends and forced into a world without men. They would have been force-fed daily religious brainwashing and indoctrination, forced to deny themselves, forced to live a lie and pretend they were chaste and pious. This is not saying that none among them was dedicated to the holy life, but with so many of them forced into this lifestyle by their families and the Church, I have to wonder how many really were true to the vows they were forced to make.

We entered some of the novitiates' cells, mostly rather plain and simple. In one we found a rather more luxurious simplicity, and assumed it must have been for a wealthier teen. In all of them we noted double beds with two pillows, a theme we would see repeated through much of the convent.

The novitiates' chapel was remarkable to me in that, while there were icons and idols of the Virgin Mary and other female saints, there was no image of Christ to be seen. It was as if the Church thought the young girls wouldn't be able to handle an image of a man in their frail state.

Then there were the sumptuous accommodations of the very wealthy nuns. These were bought and sold like condominium suites, and provided all the creature comforts available at the time, including servants' quarters, so they could be close at hand.

What remains of the old convent tells a very confusing story. It is a story of well-funded widows moving into a peaceful solitude, a story of wealthy dilettantes leading hedonistic and carefree lives, a story of young unwilling second daughters being sentenced to a life of seclusion and loneliness, a story of destitute women hoping to find shelter, protection and support.

Among the more intriguing places in the complex were the kitchens, many with beautiful domed ovens. In almost every cell we visited, except for the few very basic ones and those in the novitiates' cloister, there were kitchens.

We saw lovely private outdoor spaces with stairways leading to the interconnecting rooftops, by which the nuns would be able surreptitiously go visiting and to receive visitors. Most of the stairways had been clumsily closed-off or blocked, likely by the strict nun sent in 1871 by the Pope to shutdown the hedonistic goings-on in the convent.

Many of the kitchens would have been run by servants or slaves, but I would assume that many of the ovens also provided an outlet for the nun's reputed love of baked goods, and especially of pastries.

309

We were fascinated by the huge range of style and layout of kitchens throughout the convent. Many were rather simple affairs, while others were rather large and complex The simplest, ones appeared as places to heat tea water and prepare only basic items. The owners of these probably dined from the communal kitchen.

While most of the kitchens we saw were interior rooms with holes in domed roofs acting as chimneys, we saw some outside kitchens as well. These were likely used in the warmer months to prevent overheating the interior of the cells.

The vistas down the narrow streets of the 20-hectare *city-within-a-city* were beautiful in the bright sunlight.

The narrow lanes between the buildings had been named after the major cities in Spain: Cordova, Toledo, Granada, Sevilla and so on.

The streets invited us to follow them, leading us past the many cells, all of which we entered and explored.

At the northern end of the convent complex we came to the communal laundry, which was composed of half urns ranged along a water runnel with pebbles used to temporarily dam the water and divert it through narrow troughs into the tubs.

The range of furnishings from cell to cell showed a broad variety of taste and of apparent wealth or lack of it. It also showed us the level of comfort or discomfort the nuns had adopted.

Adjacent to the laundry is a lovely sun courtyard with stairs leading to the rooftops. Also in this area is an open-air communal bath for the servants and slaves, who were required to bathe before entering the cells to service their mistresses. We assume, possibly in error, that all the servants were female.

In some cells we saw a level of comfort that would have been unknown except among the very wealthy and privileged people, no matter where in the world at the time.

We looked at the nun's communal bath, which was a small swimming pool that would have held a metre or so of water.

It appears that vanity screens were added many years after the construction of the bathing room. These crude devices were likely the result of the strict Dominican nun sent in 1871 by the Pope to rid the convent of decadence. We imagined the new regime requiring the nuns to cower behind them to don bathing robes.

From what we saw, sanitation facilities were simple and sparse, mostly chamber pots, some of which were mounted in benches or in one case, a throne. We saw a very stylish British porcelain bed pan with instructions in a calligraphy script glazed into its interior.

We climbed onto the rooftop and looked out over the convent complex to the city beyond. We were struck by the near total lack of trees, which was brought to our attention by a very tall, lonely palm a block or so away.

Sister Ana de Los Angeles Montegudo lived in the convent until her death at 84 in 1686. She was beatified by Pope John-Paul II on his visit to Arequipa in 1985. Many of her personal effects are on display in the rooms of her cell.

We stopped to examine another room filled with her furnishings and effects, and I wondered what miracles the Church had invented for her to have performed to qualify for sainthood.

One charmingly basic cell had been lovingly painted with simple frescoes by a former resident.

We walked through the communal dining hall where the nuns would take turns reading the lives of the saints from a pulpit as the others dined.

A large cross-shaped art gallery is hung with many dozens of pieces of religious art, mostly from the seventeenth and eighteenth century Cusco School of painting, which was a fusion of the Spanish and the Inca cultures.

Outstanding to us among the paintings was this Madonna and Child. With our tour of the art gallery, we had completed the circuit of the convent. During our four-hour exploration, we had been passed by dozens of guided tours, other couples and some individuals, all of whom seemed in a race to *do* the convent. They all passed us so quickly that there was seldom more than a minute's wait to have our scene devoid of other people.

When we finally emerged from the convent in the early afternoon, we were overwhelmed by a sense of freedom. I thought of my aunt, Mary-Louise who had been compelled by tradition and family to enter a cloistered convent, and I sensed just a hint of the huge relief she must have felt in leaving.

We walked across the street and along to a small shop selling baby and royal alpaca goods. Here we very quickly found the scarf I had been looking for in Cuzco, Pisac, Aguas Calientes and Miraflores in early December. Here the alpaca goods seemed more original, and not the identical mass-produced ones we had seen from the huge wholesalers who supply the tourist markets with spam. We bought three beautiful scarves, one for my neck and two to serve as colourful table runners, one aboard Sequitur and one back in the loft in Vancouver.

With our purchases bagged, we asked the woman in the shop for her recommendation for lunch and she bubbled with enthusiasm as she described to us Restaurant Sol de Mayo. We were sold, and quickly walked the kilometre or so down to and across the river and on up the other side to the restaurant. It is a wonderfully peaceful place with inside, patio and courtyard tables. We chose a big table under an umbrella in the courtyard. The establishment specializes in camarone, river prawns. We shared an entrée of papas y queso and then splendid mains of prawns. Edi had hers with garlic and I had mine in butter, and with them we had 620s of cervesa Arequipana. It was one of the finest meals we had had in all of our time in Peru, ranking with those at Rafael in Miraflores and Indio Feliz in Aquas Calientes.

We walked back into town and to the Plaza de Armas, where we chose from the many dozens of tourist agencies around the periphery of the square. We booked seats for S/54 each to Puno on Lake Titicaca the following morning at 0700 on a Cruz del Sur bus. While with the agent, we asked her if there was a supermarket nearby, and she directed us to a huge Plaza Vea about four blocks along and beside the river.

We went back to the hotel to offload our scarves plus some Inca hats that we had also bought in our wanderings. The goods in the shops here are so much nicer and more individualistic than those we had seen in the shops elsewhere through Peru. Having refreshed, we headed out again and walked the four blocks back down to the far side of the Plaza de Armas. Nearly every shop along both sides of the street for the four blocks was selling eyeglasses. There are a hundred or more eyeglass shops; it is like Broadway and Willow in Vancouver times ten.

We turned and walked toward Plaza de Armas and paused to look at Iglesia de Santo Domingo. The exterior is in the excessively ornate Arequipan style, which appears to be derived from the churrigueresco style we had seen in central Lima.

The interior of the church is impressive. The delicate pastel shadings on massive stonework offer an understatement to the sumptuous gold leaf on the altars, pulpit and fittings.

The interplay of light and shadow with form and texture cause vistas in the church appear as if they were clippings from sixteenth or seventeenth century paintings

From the church we continued on to Plaza Vea and bought some sliced ham, sliced cheese, bread rolls and bottles of water for lunch on our next day's bus trip.

We arrived in the dining room on Friday morning at 0600, just as the buffet was being set-up. We realized then that our previous morning's breakfast had been served to us after the buffet had been cleared away. However, the buffet breakfast was of the same low quality, though there was more of it, not that this was of much merit. While we were at breakfast we used the knives and plates to assist us in making fresh sandwiches from the ingredients that we had kept overnight in the fridge in our room.

We checked-out and flagged a cab to the Terrapuerto for S/4. We checked-in and were directed to sit for a few minutes in the main lobby until the departure lounge opened. When the lounge opened, we were then told we needed to go back out to the kiosk and purchase departure passes. Having dutifully paid our S/2 each we sat in the very comfortable upholstered lounge furniture and talked with a young couple from Quebec City while we waited for the bus.

A few minutes after the scheduled departure time, the bus began loading, and we left the terminal only a little more than twenty minutes late. During the seven-and-a-half-hour trip, we passed many salty lakes as we climbed from Arequipa's 2350-metre elevation to over 4000 metres, and on many of the lakes along the way we saw pink flamingos, though they proved impossible to photograph through the windows of the bus bumping along the rough and winding road.

Shortly before 1500 we entered Puno and the bus wound its way down to the Terrapuerto near the shores of the lake. We walked through the terminal looking for a bus company that offered transportation to La Paz, Bolivia. From one booth we were directed to the far end of the complex. There we met a woman full of energy behind the counter in a booth that listed Bolivia among its destinations. We booked second-row seats for S/30 each and at the same time bought a tour to Titicaca's Uros floating islands later in the day for S/25 each.

We asked her about a hotel, and she put up a finger, dialled a number on her cell and booked a room for us for S/140, about $50 at the Punuypampa Inn, just off the Plaza de Armas. She took us to a taxi and she got into it with us to ensure that the driver didn't take us to his commission-making hotel.

We dropped our packs, freshened-up and went down to the lobby to await our pick up by Inka Tours at 1545. As predicted, it was late, but shortly after 1600 we were paged and we then loaded onto a bus already filled with over two dozen tourists. After one more stop for a couple of elderly women, we headed down to the lakeshore. There we were directed to an old and dilapidated passenger launch at the end of the pier.

Once we had all loaded, the boat was pushed off the pier and its engine started in forward gear. After about five minutes there were huge billows of smoke and steam pouring out of the engine compartment. One of the crew opened the lid and told the skipper to shutdown the engine. We drifted powerless on the highest navigable lake in the world as the crew went through what appeared to be a rather frequently performed routine. After three or four minutes we were making way again, and threading our way up a narrow channel between the reeds and some tiny low-lying clay islets.

Along the way we passed a woman rowing a punt into town while her husband lounged lazily in the bow, a seemingly normal behaviour that we have often seen among the indigenous Peruvian people.

As we neared the floating island designated for our tour, the skipper shut down the engine and we drifted in toward a space alongside. He flashed-up again a minute or so later for a few seconds with the engine in forward gear. I suspected that the boat's transmission was inoperable, and as the tour went on, this became very obvious.

The boat was hauled in to the island with its lines and secured to stakes, which had been driven into the reed matting. We stepped onto the island and were introduced to our hosts. A Uros man then explained and demonstrated with models the construction methods used in building the islands from lashed-together sawn blocks of root mass topped with cross plies of reeds.

Edi was amazed by the huge increase in the number of islands since her 1979 visit. As we snooped around, it became obvious that the people do not live on this island, and quite likely on none of them. To us it appears likely that they commute to work, do the tourist thing and then go home at the end of the day. The proliferation of islands was to serve the seemingly unregulated tour operators and their somewhat tacky tours.

While the others were absorbed with the Uros indigenous people babble, Edi and I watched as a man sewed together reeds into panels for the buildings.

After the spiel on tradition, which seemed to be glorified for the tourists, the displays of gaudy, aniline dyed, stencilled and spray-painted *"handicrafts"* were uncovered for us to wonder about; to wonder why there were no handmade items.

We were directed to board an ungainly reed and wood catamaran and were taken across to the next island, powered by an outboard on the rear while two of the Uros played at rowing from the bows. As we got off, we were told the charge was S/10 each for the ride.

We watched as other non-traditional reed boats were rowed, paddled or powered past. Beyond the boats and back toward Puno we saw the luxury hotel, Libertador Lago Titicaca on a private rocky island. When I asked about it, the guide told me it is used mostly by politicians; no one else can afford its high prices.

The island to which we were taken was filled with gift shops all loaded with tacky tourist spam. While we were in the islands, in just the small area near us we must have seen three or four dozen tour groups cycling through the routine. We thought that the Uros should add an E to their name; it was very obvious that their main focus is on gathering Euros and other currencies.

Our tour boat's engine was again convinced to start and it motored across to the island, where it bumbled alongside with its lack of transmission. We quickly loaded and departed. As we motored back in the increasing dusk, ominous black clouds rolled over the southern horizon, and soon there were huge displays of lightning, and shortly thereafter, rain. About a kilometre short of the pier the engine quit, and we were again adrift. This time, probably because it was dark and the crew had no light, it took nearly fifteen minutes to restart the engine.

As we approached the stubby, rickety pier, the wind was blowing, and the skipper's judgement was off as he swung the boat around and shutoff the engine to drift onto the landing. We missed it and the stern went drifting past two metres off the pier end. It was just too far to jump and the rope throw missed. They managed to get the engine going again, and we went around for another attempt. This time the skipper successfully bounced us off another boat's bow and crashed us into the pier side. As we quickly disembarked, I confirmed my observations with the crew; there were no life jackets onboard. I had also noted that none of the boats were showing any navigation lights. The tour operators are operating in an apparently totally unregulated and very dangerous manner.

Looming above us was the lighthouse, which at 3824 metres is the second highest in the world, second only to the one on top of Bolivia's Isla del Sol, which is listed as 4096 metres. We couldn't help thinking of the ridiculously hollow claims by Lake Tahoe, California that their Sugar Pine Point lighthouse at 1,898 metres is the highest in the world.

Our bus was waiting for us, and it took us back up the hill, and very fortunately our hotel was the first stop along the way. On the way through the lobby, we asked for a restaurant recommendation, and were told of La Casona and shown its menu.

The restaurant, just across Plaza de Armas is furnished in an early twentieth century style, with antiques ranged on shelves on the walls among the collection of old religious paintings. The white linen and the impeccably mannered waiters added to the relaxing atmosphere.

We decided to say farewell to Peru with our last lomo soltado. We started with copas of Pisco puro and nibbled on papas y queso as we watched a parade go by outside with its rattling and thumping drums, blaring brass and people doing a twisting zigzag dance along the street. After the parade had endured for nearly half an hour, we concluded that they must be going round-and-round the block; there can't be that many musicians and dancers in the city. We had a very nice dinner, and including the Piscos and cervesas, it came to S/68, less than $25 for two.

The following morning we had the included buffet breakfast in the hotel, and then at 0620 took a taxi down to the Terrapuerto for our 0700 bus; the departure was only fifteen minutes late. We wound along the shores of Lake Titicaca toward the Bolivian border through intensively used land. Every piece appeared cultivated, including terraces up the hills and ridges.

Frequently we passed local women dressed in the traditional garb, and it was pleasant to see the real thing, not the for-the-tourist versions.

Soon the buss arrived at a chain strung across the road. We were at the Peruvian exit post. We were told to get out and join a line-up for exit formalities and then to walk across the border where the bus would meet us. We made it to the wicket where we presented our passports and visa slips and were duly processed. We then followed the others up the hill and to the Bolivian side of no-man's-land and joined the lineup there.

We reached the wicket and were told we needed to go back to Peru to have our passports stamped. We followed the others back across the no-man's-land to the Peruvian post and tried to sort-out with them where we had to go. We finally got our stamps and walked back up the hill to the Bolivian side, where we again joined the line-up. We were granted 30-day visas and allowed to cross out of the no-man's-land and into Bolivia.

In about three hours we arrived in Yunguyo, the last Peruvian community before the border. After a quick spin through it to drop-off and pick up passengers, we continued on toward Bolivia.

Our first impression was of eggs. They seemed to be everywhere, stacked waist high in the booths and along the building sides.

There were more arriving by handcart. There was a brisk market in eggs; we watched as people stopped to pick up a few, a small bag full or a flat or two at a time.

After nearly an hour and a half, everyone had re-boarded the bus, which had driven through as we were being processed. We continued along the few kilometres to Copacabana, on the outskirts of which we stopped and waited for twenty minutes as the bus ahead of us was processed. Then it was our turn; a man came on board and announced to the passengers that there was a Bs1 fee to enter the town. He was greeted with jeers and protests as he worked his way through the bus collecting the town's toll. We had no Bolivian Soles, having decided we would need none until we arrived in La Paz. A young Brazilian woman in the seat ahead of us gave me a Bs5 piece, from which I paid the levy and gave her back the change.

The chain was lowered and the bus was allowed to continue on into the grubby little town. The bus terminal is the few streets around a small square, and there were dozens of buses filling every conceivable space. People milled about in the muddy streets lugging their bundles, bags and backpacks. The word chaos must have been coined here, and the word squalor came quickly to mind.

We were told to disembark and a Bolivian bus was pointed-out, which would take us the rest of the way to La Paz. Fortunately, having no luggage to recover from the hold, we quickly made our way over to the bus and prominently stationed ourselves next to its door and at the head of the growing lineup.

I had observed that there were no reserved seats on the Bolivian bus, and we wanted first choice. When finally the door opened, we took the two front lakeside seats and settled-in to watch the unfolding chaos outside. While we were waiting for the departure, I walked across to a sidewalk money changer and got rid of the last of our Peruvian Soles, trading them for Bolivian Soles. I repaid the Brazilian woman, who had taken the seats behind us.

After a long delay, we finally left Copacabana and were pleased to see there was no exit fee. After about thirty kilometres, we descended in the pouring rain to a small village at the edge of a narrow strait, Estrecho de Taquina. In the water we saw a congested and chaotic coming and going of all manner of boats, barges and lighters.

We were told to disembark and were directed across a muddy lot to a long line-up at a ticket booth. After having long since given-up on trying to dodge the large raindrops, we made it to the head of the line and we bought two heavily-used ferry tickets at Bs2 each. Quite wet by this time, we sloshed our way out a very rickety structure, which was pretending to be a pier and crammed ourselves into an already overloaded boat.

We could see no life jackets, nor could we see any lockers for them. The skipper started a big, noisy outboard, which was mounted in a well toward the stern, and off we went across the half-kilometre-wide straits.

We walked along the lakeshore and took-up a vantage point out of the rain under the overhangs of a building. From there we watched the parade of barges coming and going from four landing wharves, or for what passed as wharves.

As we approached the cobbled-together structure that passed for a pier on the other side, he turned the vessel around and backed in.

We watched as the barge carrying our bus got skewed on its approach. The crew used barge poles, straining muscles and many minutes to straighten it around. The barge made it in, the bus offloaded and then started re-claiming its passengers along the way. The entire straits-crossing process took nearly two hours.

While we were being transported across, our bus had joined a line-up of other buses, cars, vans and trucks, which were being conveyed across on outboard-driven barges.

In another two hours we were driving through the very gaudy architecture of the upper suburbs of La Paz. The city has a population of over 1.5 million, more than half of which has built on the hills and plateau up to 1000 metres above the old town. The new buildings are a mix of ugly, garish, gaudy and ridiculous.

Our bus drove down the hill and past the bus terminal to the loud protests of some passengers. After a couple of turns it pulled to a stop in front of an office. This apparently served as its terminal. It was 1730 and we had arrived.

We walked back up the street and across to the Terrapuerto, where inside we began looking for signs indicating service to Iquique. It was Saturday evening and it seemed that everyone had already booked overnight service to Arica and Iquique. None was available. We did manage to find a company, Trans Salvador with a four cancellations on their 0500 departure the Sunday morning, but only as far as Arica. Otherwise all we could find was for Monday. For Bs150 each, a little over $21 a ticket we booked two of the cancelled seats, which happened to be in the front-row.

We asked the clerk for a hotel recommendation, and she told us the Passport Hotel, up the stairs beside the terminal and across the upper street, was good. We thanked her, went outside and climbed the fifty-or-so steps up a retaining wall to the street above and looked in vain for the hotel. We did spot the Hotel Latino, which has a rather attractive façade on a corner a couple of blocks southward. They had a double room for Bs210, about $30, payment in advance. Edi asked if there is hot water and we were told yes. Being cautious, Edi asked to see the room before we paid, so the bellhop took us up the elevator to the fourth floor for a look. A quick inspection showed the room to be acceptable, so I went back down and paid.

It was shortly after 1800, and we had a 0500 bus to catch. We decided to eat early and go to bed. We asked at the desk for a restaurant recommendation in the area. She knew of none. We asked about a pizzeria. She didn't know of any, but she said there was a place up the street a couple of blocks where we could get a dinner. We went up to it to find it crowded with locals eating and a noisy party carrying on in an upper mezzanine. We were told there was no food for us.

We were at the end of the commercial part of the street, so we walked back down past the many sidewalk vendors of grease-balls and storefronts vending pre-cooked deep-fried chicken parts and cold potato fries. On our way along we spotted a tiny sign frosted into a window, indicating this was the elusive Passport Hotel. There was no other visible identification.

We had almost resigned ourselves to having a grease-ball dinner, when I sighted a chifa a couple of blocks away, across the Terrapuerto's lot. We went over to it and we each had a rather tasty polo y verdura, in which the chicken came with a mix of vegetables on rice and thick, spicy noodles. There was no cervesa, so we had bottles of water. Our total outlay was Bs50, just over $7.

Back in the hotel, we realized we should have done a much more thorough examination of the room. There was no flow from the hot water taps, there was no heat in the room, the toilet took five or more minutes to drain, the bed was lumpy and the pillows were wads of rags stuffed into cloth bags. We slept very poorly, and to relieve the discomfort, at 0400 we got out of bed, dressed and walked to the Terrapuerto. At least the wooden benches in the terminal weren't lumpy.

The terminal; however, was also cold, the roof leaked and it was full of people sleeping on the floor and on benches, some of them in sleeping bags, others wrapped in blankets. At 0445 the kiosk selling terminal use fees opened, and I bought our coupons, glad to pay to get out of La Paz. The bus pulled into its slot and began loading shortly after 0510, and at 0540 our 0500 bus departed. Twenty minutes into the trip, we were served a hot, sweet tea and a bag of small salty biscuits. These began warming us. The seats were very comfortable, and we were able to sleep for much of the four-hour trip to the border.

As we approached the Chilean border, we began passing a slowly crawling line of transport trucks. This went on for what seemed several kilometres. It appeared we were approaching an extremely inefficient crossing.

We stopped at the Bolivian exit point and remained on the bus for nearly half an hour waiting for our turn to offloaded and join the long line-up for processing. When we finally made it to the wicket, we saw two officials inside holding-up many hundreds of bus passengers, hundreds of trucks and dozens of cars. They must have felt very important to be able to do this.

We re-boarded the bus, and when the count was correct, the driver took us across a broad no-man's-land to the Chilean post. Here again we waited for our bus's turn to join another line-up. The Chilean post has numbered stations from #1 to #6, in the order they are to be visited, so after we had finished with #1, we walked across the road to #2. We were soon told it was not yet our turn, and that we had to wait on the bus until it was. When our bus's turn did arrive, we took our packs and went to #2 for Migracion. They took the forms we had completed on the bus, stamped them and our passports and sent us on to #3, Aduana. There we were told we had to have our luggage with us, but when we told them we had only our packs, they waved us through, giving us exoneration on posts #4 through #6.

We tried to re-board the bus, but were told to go to a waiting area of mud puddles, litter and a portable stand selling grease-balls sugar-water and other such items. As we waited, a small flock of Blackheaded Gulls very timidly scavenged for orts. The birds must be food for the locals; they were extremely wary.

After another half-hour wait, we were allowed to re-board the bus, thankful that it hadn't been raining. A little over two hours after we had arrived at the crossing, the last of the passengers had completed their processing and were back onboard.

We left and drove around some salty marshes bordering Lago Chungara. In the marshes we saw pink flamingos, and on the far side of the lake the 6350-metre snow-capped volcano, Parinacota.

I shot a few dozen photos out the sealed window of the moving bus trying to capture an adequate image of the flamingos, but with all the moving around and trying to keep my balance, the 4600-metre altitude made me a tad woozy.

As the view across Lago Chungara to Parinacota receded into the distance, we sank deeper into our near-fully reclining seats and went to sleep. We arrived at the Terrapuerto in Arica at 1530, and immediately did the rounds of the dozens of bus companies looking for the next available seats to Iquique. At the Pullman Cuevas y Gonzalez booth we found two front row seats on an 1830 departure for 7500 Pesos each. We bought them and then went to another booth to pay the terminal use fees.

We hadn't eaten since the small bag of crackers on the bus in the wee hours of the morning as we were leaving La Paz. We were hungry and very thirsty. We went upstairs to a crude bar and ordered a litre of cervesa to share, and then when we finally convinced the staff that we wanted to order food, menus were brought over to the table. After many failed attempts we finally attracted the attention of the bartender and ordered a couple of what the menu's sandwich section called Americanos.

What arrived was a thick slab of flatbread some 20 cm in diameter filled with sliced beef, a couple of fried eggs, avocados, tomatoes, mayonnaise, and seemingly whatever else was lying around. Each one looked to be enough to feed a family. When mine had disappeared from the plate, I realized how famished I had been. Edi finished all of hers but for the some of the top layer of bread. We were thankful that service was so slow and inattentive; it was more comfortable sitting in the sleazy bar than it would have been standing down in the overcrowded waiting room.

Our bus began boarding a little before 1830, and pulled out less than a quarter hour late. We slept almost the entire way back to Iquique, awakening for a police boarding and passport check in the middle of the trip and at a couple of stops to let off passengers. At 2300 the bus stopped in a dumpy commercial area of Iquique, backed-up through a set of barn doors. We were at the end of the run. We were in Iquique, but where we didn't know. We followed three men who seemed to know where they were going, as they boldly strode across the yard, opened a door in the gate and passed through to the street.

There was a waxing crescent moon low in the sky, and this I knew would be west. We walked westward along a well-lit street following at a distance the three men, until two turned south. We continued to trail the westbound one until he too turned left. We thought of finding a taxi, but saw none available, so we continued walking westward, toward what we knew would eventually be the ocean. After nearly a quarter hour we spotted far ahead a large lit-up Christmas tree in what appeared to be a plaza. Edi recognized it as the tree in Plaza Prat, so we continued another four or five blocks and came out into Plaza Prat. We then knew we were only five or six blocks from the Club de Yates.

At 2330 when we arrived at the Yacht Club there was nobody to open the gate for us, so we climbed over the two and a half meter wall, picked our way in the darkness to the float and to Sequitur. She was safe, secure, fresh-smelling and welcoming. It was so good to be home again.

We slept-in on Monday the 10th of January. When we awoke, we began thinking of continuing southward. We needed to restock our fridges with fresh produce and dairy goods, and lay-in a new supply of lunch and snack items. Also there was room in the freezer for more fish and another batch of bread. Our third propane bottle had expired on Boxing Day, and we were cooking on our last one; we needed to refill the three empties.

I finally got around to mounting the dinghy wheels. With Sequitur stern-to on the float, I was able to do the job standing on the float and working at waist-to-shoulder level. Part way into the measuring and remeasuring process, I concluded that the transom on our dinghy was thicker than Davis, the manufacturer of the Wheel-a-Weigh had counted on when it supplied the attaching bolts. The stainless steel bolts were too short. I searched through our stock of hardware and found none appropriate.

Next door to the Club de Yates is Marco, a huge luxury yacht-building company. We thought that if anyone in Iquique had quality stainless hardware, this company would. Since 1953 they have built over 650 vessels, and for many years their focus has been on luxury motor yachts up to 100 metres in length. I grabbed the too-short bolt and we walked over and asked if we could buy eight similar stainless bolts, but half an inch longer. We were introduced to Rosita Rivera, who spoke very good English, and she took us into the parts department, where the appropriate bolts in 316 stainless were quickly found. The longest part of the process was in their trying to figure-out what to charge us for them.

Finally, we were charged 2,500 Pesos, $5 for the eight. It was likely their smallest sale ever; they are currently building an 85-metre yacht, which will have one master suite and six double guest staterooms, and will take a crew of 24 to operate. It is for sale, but we decided not to ask the price.

I completed the wheel mounting, and we now have a dinghy equipped to land under power through the surf and onto the beach, and able to rather easily re-launch into the surf.

While I worked, I was entertained by a variety of shore birds, among them a Blackish Oystercatcher, striking with its red bill and eyes and its pale pink legs and feet.

We continued to puttered on board, doing odd jobs and recharging our internal batteries. Then on Tuesday we went shopping. We hailed a collectivo to Supermercado Lider for 2000 Pesos. There we roamed all the aisles, having the merchandise remind us what we needed, and allowing it from time to time to inspire us.

We then loaded our cart with fresh items. Among these were some superb oyster mushrooms at a stupidly low price, and finally some decent black olives. They were not as good as our favourite Moroccans from Parthenon in Vancouver, but they were head-and-shoulders above the rancid blacks we had tasted in Peru. We bought two kilos and Edi pitted them when we arrived back onboard.

The high tide we required to exit the marina was around 0300 and 1530 on Tuesday, 0400 and 1630 on Wednesday and 0500 and 1730 on Thursday. We decided to slip from the float on Wednesday's afternoon tide and lie to anchor overnight for an early Thursday departure. After breakfast on Wednesday I went to the Yacht Club office to settle our mooring account and to get details on refilling our propane tanks.

The Club Manager, Patricio Vargas gladly accepted our 187,500 Pesos ($375) for the fifteen days we had been alongside. He also introduced me to his wife, Graciela, a taxi driver who was to take me and the three empty propane tanks to the refilling depot and bring me back. She spoke virtually no English, so we shared a delightful pantomime interspersed with my few Spanish and her few English words. The three-quarter-hour trip cost 3,000 Pesos, $6.

In the late morning Edi and I took the wheelie and went to buy sparkling water. We find it so refreshing while sailing, and rotate a stock through the fridges. From a small supermarket we picked-up a six-pack of 2.5-litre and a twelve-pack of 625s. We wheeled them back past the street-side fish stalls and stopped at the fishmonger we had previously used. His eyes lit-up when he recognized us, and he hollered to his cohorts that his Canadians were back. We selected a 5-kilo male mahi-mahi, and the monger cleaned and filleted it for us.

On our way back to Sequitur, we stopped at the offices of the port authority to do the necessary paperwork to depart Iquique. We explained that we would be leaving the marina on the afternoon tide and anchoring in the bay overnight, for an early morning departure on Thursday.

The young Able Seaman clerk seemed a bit lost in how to process us, but a bright young bosun Leading Seaman helped him through the process. When the paper work had been generated, we were told that a boat would come to Sequitur in the anchorage at 0900 the next morning to issue our zarpe.

We topped-up our tanks with water from the marina floats, and then had a complex, but uneventful slip from our Med-mooring. We undid our chafing strops on the float cleats, looped the stern lines back onboard, eased them as we shortened-in the anchor cable and once the stern was clear of the finger, let go and hauled-in lines. As we were weighing, the anchor cable brought-up a welded-together grid of rebar with lines attached. It looked like an old, disused mooring anchor. I freed it and continued to weigh, and once the anchor was visible and free of fouling, Edi slowly motored Sequitur onto and along the transit that led us through the narrow, shallow channel. At 1648 we came to 20 metres on the Rocna in 6 metres of water, set the starboard snubber and shutdown.

I sorted the mahi-mahi into meal-sized freezer bags and stacked them into the freezer. I hauled-out the frozen backbones of our previous mahi-mahi and with the new backbone, some celery, onions, garlic, carrots and potatoes, among other things, made-up a large fish chowder. This was put into two one-litre Lock & Lock containers; one for the freezer and the other in the fridge for the first night's meal on our passage.

Thursday's 0900 came and went with no visit from the authorities; so did 1000. I radioed to find-out what was happening, and eventually received a reply that I needed to report to the office and pay the departure fees. Trying to gain some sympathy and save unlashing and launching the dinghy, and then slinging, lowering and mounting its motor, I explained that our dinghy and motor were secured for sea, and that it was a long and difficult process to use it to head in. I asked if they could send a launch to pick me up. They said their boats were busy at the moment, rescuing some surfers overcome in the unusually high seas, but that sometime around 1400 they could come and get me.

324

Toward 1530 I was picked-up and taken in to the offices of the Gobernacion Maritima. On the way in we passed one of the un-muffled workboats from the fishing fleet. The shrill roar of these workboats pierces the otherwise noisy clamour of the working waterfront, making it seem quietly peaceful in comparison.

The money-taking women were back on duty in the offices, and one of them explained to me that the seamen the previous day didn't know that foreign yachts had to pay an exit fee. She asked me for US47.41. I asked why she wanted US dollars, a currency which at the time was trying to demonstrate that it is one of the world's less stable. She mumbled something about foreign yachts and I lost track of her thoughts as she apparently did also.

I told her I had no US currency, and offered to pay in Chilean Pesos. She said the exchange rate was very unstable and she couldn't predict what value she would get for them. I told her the Chilean Peso is stable; it is the US dollar that is being jerked around. To save my walk across town to a money changer and pay their fees, I eventually persuaded her to take 25,000 Pesos.

By the time our zarpe had been issued, it was approaching 1700, and by the time I was motored back out to Sequitur, it was well past that hour. We decided to remain at anchor overnight and leave early the following morning.

18. Southward From Iquique

At 0809 on the 14th of January we weighed and proceeded under power out of Bahia de Iquique. We reported our departure to Port Control, and quickly received an acknowledgement. Once we had cleared the headlands and bent our course southward, the breeze strengthened, and at 0936 we hauled-out a full main, staysail and jib, and set-off on a port tack making 4 knots to the southwest in the 8 to 10 knot southerly breeze. The coast is very drab, with absolutely barren slopes leading up to the world's driest desert. We watched as small, low and fluffy cumulus formed a short distance offshore and quickly dissipated as they reached the land.

In the late afternoon the breeze had decreased to less than 5 knots and we were down to just over 2 knots, but with the northbound Humboldt Current, our southwesterly heading was being converted into a track much closer to west. We flashed-up and hauled-in all but a stabilizing blade of the main to help counter the 3-metre southwest swells, and we motored south. While the sun set as a flattened oval into a clear, haze-free horizon, we enjoyed the fresh mahi-mahi chowder for dinner. We motored through the night.

At 0711 on the 15th of January the sun crossed our latitude on its way north. When it rose four minutes later, it was as close to due east as I would likely ever witness at sea. The last time the sun had passed us going north was on the 27th of April on our third day out from Acapulco to the Galapagos. I thought that if things went according to our current plans, Sequitur would remain south of the sun for the next couple of years.

At 1110 on Saturday we again found some movement in the air, and we hauled-out the main and jib. As the breeze grew to south 10 to 12 knots, we sailed on a starboard tack back in toward the land, making 135 at about 5 knots. In the next five hours we made just over 30 miles, as the wind grew through the mid-afternoon, and then decreased. At 1620 we were ghosting along with the sails slatting as the winds died. We rolled-in the sails and began motoring.

Instead of turning south along the coast, we continued southeast. Ahead of us some 15 miles distant was the port of Tocopillo, and with the thoughts of another night of motoring, it was too inviting to resist. Between 1700 and 1705 I radioed Tocopillo Port Control three times to report our intention of anchoring-in-transit overnight, but received no response. I continued this every hour until our calls finally received a reply.

The sun went down at 2030, and 20 minutes later, with a large waxing gibbous moon over our shoulders, we came to 55 metres on the Rocna in 13 metres of water 3 cables off the crashing surf. There was a large surge in the anchorage, but Sequitur rode it well. I reported our arrival to Port Control, and we were welcomed to Tocopillo.

I prepared two heavily-loaded oven-sized pizzas and by 2130 we were eating our way through the first one with a bottle of 2009 Las Moras Malbec, as the second one baked. We started into the second pizza, and left the rest of it for the next day's lunch. We enjoyed a wonderful sleep, lulled by the surge in the anchorage.

326

At 1025 we weighed and proceeded under power in glassy-calm seas, on which every few minutes some small ripples falsely announced the coming of a breeze. The promised breeze never appeared, so we continued motoring in glassy seas through the remainder of the day and into the night, making an average of 3.5 knots into the Humboldt Current.

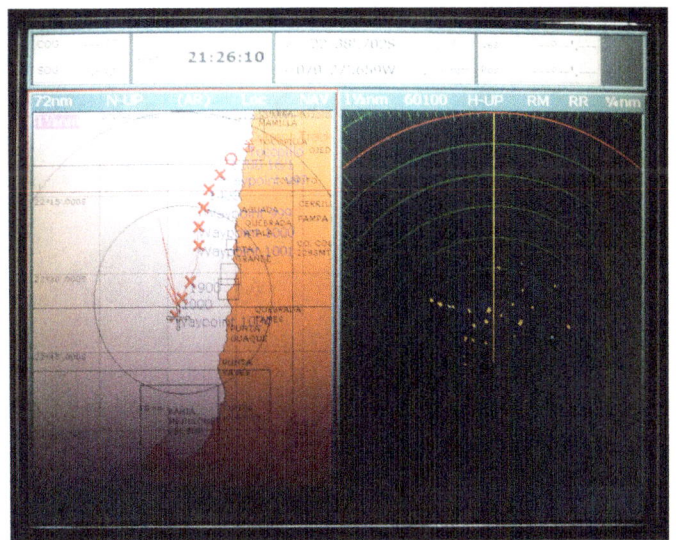

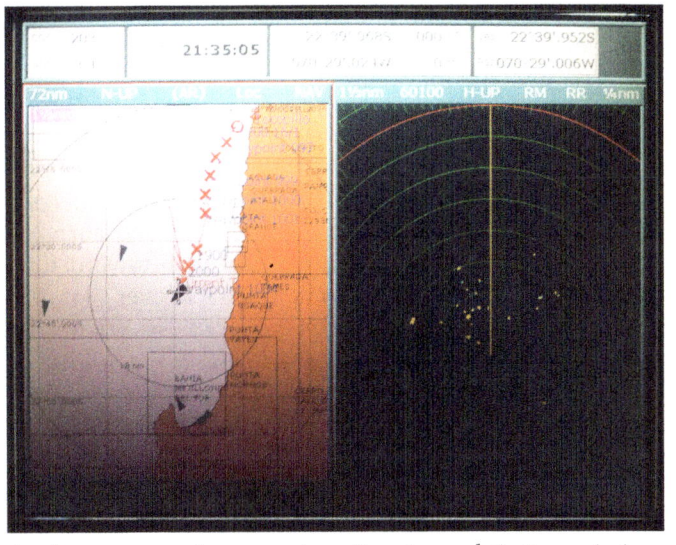

In the morning as I went on deck to prepare for weighing, I had a better view of our surroundings than we had had on our arrival in the dusk and moonlight. We were anchored next to some the very colourful boats of the local fishing fleet.

In the water all around Sequitur were many hundreds of large, multi-coloured jellyfish. The close-in scene was very pretty; however ashore it was not so picturesque.

An hour or so after sunset on Sunday, while I was below preparing to wok some prawns in ginger, garlic, oyster mushrooms, three colours of peppers, and other goodies, Edi reported the chart plotter was giving a *Lost Position Fix* error message, and that the ship's position was skewing across the chart. Then the ship's icon disappeared, as did the icons of the AIS contacts.

This continued intermittently for nearly an hour, and then it seemed to correct itself. This had happened previously a few times, the first time only a couple of months after I had taken delivery of Sequitur in 2007. I had reported this first incident to the installers of the system when I returned to Vancouver, and had been told it was only a *"general GPS system anomaly"*.

Tocopillo is a described as an ugly little city, whose main claim to fame are its huge thermo-electric plants, which generate electricity for the mining communities and mines far inland in the Atacama. Among these is Chuquicamata, one of the world's largest open-pit mines, which until recently was the world's largest single source of copper. The title is now held by Mina Escondida some 250 kilometres to the south, with an annual production of 570,000 tonnes.

On Sunday night I had my iPad with its Navionics program switched on, and its GPS showed no problem with keeping a fix, there was no *"general GPG system anomaly"*. I began suspecting more strongly that our infamous Vancouver installers had made an intermittently poor connection between the GPS antenna and the plotter.

Sunrise on Monday found us still motoring southward in near windless conditions, bucking against the current. At 1231 we crossed the Tropic of Capricorn, and Sequitur was finally out of the tropics after eleven months. A breeze was beginning to fill from the south, and by 1300 it was blowing 12 to 14 knots and building. I rolled-out two-thirds of the main and the whole jib and we took off at better than 6 knots close-hauled on the starboard tack, pointing about 20 degrees above Punta Tetas.

At 1400 we were 272 Faro Punta Tetas 1.3 miles making good a course of 133 the past hour. We appeared to be on a course to clear the crud off the point by 3 or 4 cables. Ten minutes later, a combination wind shift and current change around the point swung Sequitur in toward the point. We were 2 to 3 cables off and closing at over 6 knots. In 2 to 3 minutes we would be on the rocks. Not good!

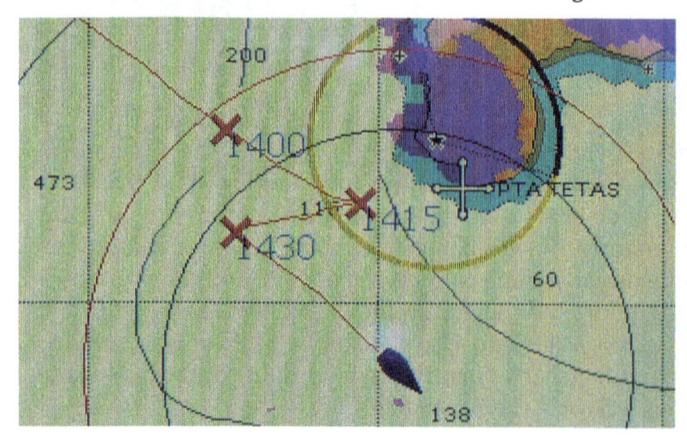

I quickly tacked a nice tight 90 degrees, but watched as the current took our track around nearly 180 degrees as we clawed off the point. I had been closely monitoring the slowly broadening clearing bearing on the lighthouse as we approached Punta Tetas, and was ready for evasive action if needed. The change of course in toward the rocks had come very suddenly, but within a minute we had tacked. I was glad that years of naval navigation training and experience had taught me to never be complacent. After 15 minutes we tacked back to our southeasterly course toward Antofagasta.

At 1515, when we were 12 miles off the port limits, I called Antofagasta Port Control and reported our position and ETA. At 1600 I eased the sails and came to a beam reach eastward to the port. This was the first time we have had the wind anywhere but on our bows in over eight months. We continued along on a beam reach and then a broad reach until 1805 when we rolled-in the sails and flashed-up the engine.

A dinghy approached Sequitur and the occupant motioned for us to follow him through the channel. We motored in his track as he led the way in a slightly winding unmarked channel, through the surf and past a breakwater into the marina of the Antofagasta Yacht Club and onto fore and aft moorings.

We were moored in a calm harbour just off the remains of the old pier originally built for the loading of saltpetre. The historic pier dates from the beginnings of the nitrate boom, but its claim to fame comes from having been used by the Chileans when they landed in February 1879 to capture the city, which was then the major seaport of Bolivia.

328

Once we had secured, Teo introduced himself and welcomed us to Antofagasta and to the Yacht Club. He gave us the lay of the land and the location of important facilities. The Yacht Club is in the heart of the historic downtown, and sits between two large and modern shopping malls, two and five blocks away.

On Tuesday morning I launched the dinghy, and in the early afternoon we rowed the 30 metres or so to the end of the closest Yacht Club float, and walked ashore to look for the administration office, so that we could register. We didn't find it, but in our search, we did find the Yacht Club Restaurant. The smells were overpowering, and we went in to see a very elegant dining room with no patrons, but many scurrying waiters.

We were taken to an outer room, which was crowded with diners ranged along the windows overlooking the marina. We had a superb lunch, starting with shared entrées of scallops in Parmigiano and prawns in garlic butter. For main course we each had fresh grouper grilled and smothered in a shellfish laden creamy wine sauce.

We asked our waiter for directions to the administration office and it was still closed for lunch when we arrived at its door. We walked out through the gates and along in the direction indicated to us for the offices of the Capitan de Puerto. Along the way we admired a slab-sided building that had been masterfully transformed with creative tromp l'oiel.

From life-like painted pigeons on illusions of balconies to images of external plumbing mingling with the real stuff, and a view down a non-existent street to clouds matching the real ones, it is a work of art that plays many tricks on the eyes.

We couldn't find the Port Captain's office, so instead we went shopping in the huge Tottus supermarket. Sequitur's pantry and fridges are full again, and we are in a very clean, peaceful and friendly port. We have decided to stay for a few days more.

On Tuesday we had gone ashore for a while, but as the day progressed, we felt less and less well. On Wednesday morning we were feeling quite ill, and by evening we were too ill to eat, and we went to bed on empty stomachs. My problem seemed to be a stomach flue of some kind, while Edi's was more in her sinuses and lungs. By Thursday afternoon we had decided that our previous week's nearly

60 hours in buses, bus terminals and other public transit modes, through what amounted to third-world squalor teeming with snotty-nosed children, we had contracted a variety of illnesses. They had slowly worn us down and our bodies were busily fighting their way back to health. We were very tired and slept 10 and 12 hours per night and had little energy for much during the days.

We lazed around onboard, not having the energy to row the 20 or 30 metres to the float. The Armada patrol vessel came through the anchorage a few times, mostly we suspected, to chase the teens off the old pier, which was closed because of its very dilapidated condition.

At least we had a strong wifi signal from the Yacht Club, and I spent many hours online, downloading the installation manuals and user manuals for some of our equipment. The installer in Vancouver had kept our hard copies, probably thinking he needed them more than we did. I also ran an email exchange with RayMarine, troubleshooting our autopilot, which had a problem not covered in the manuals.

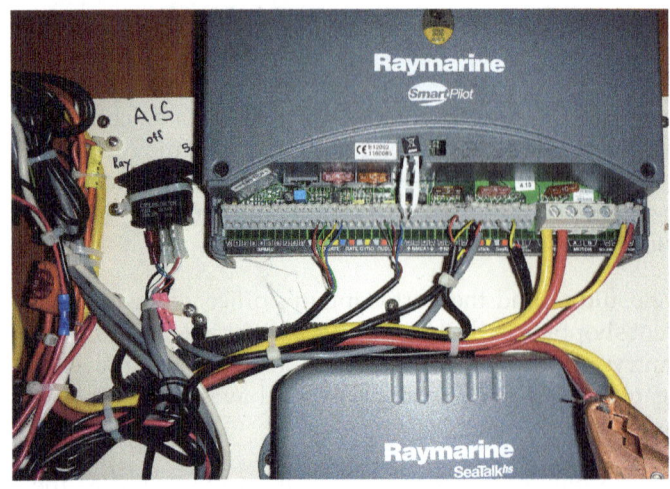

The procedure followed a routine: I received an email with the description of a test to run; I conduct the test and report results; then receive another set of instructions for the next test, and so on through most of Thursday and into Friday. By early Friday afternoon, I got Otto working again. The problem had been a poorly made connection between the course computer and the drive unit.

On Saturday I finally tracked-down a loose connection in the control unit of the second freezer, and got it working again. I had been intermittently troubleshooting it since September, when it refused to flash-up again when we returned from Vancouver to Sequitur in Peru. In the afternoon we were finally feeling well enough to head ashore again.

We walked northward past the old pier and along the malecon. There are fish and fresh produce markets a few hundred metres north of our mooring, but as we expected for a Saturday mid-afternoon, most stalls were closed. Starting a short distance north of the markets are beaches; these were very colourful scenes, overflowing with sunbathers, swimmers and paddlers.

Just off the waterfront is a huge Lider supermarket. It is nice to see that Antofagasta shows a respect for its heritage; standing in front of the modern supermarket and its two-story mall is the preserved century-old stone façade of an old brewery, Compania Cervecerias Unidas, Chile's leading beverage company.

We decided to go in and explore the supermarket to familiarize ourselves with its offerings and help with our restocking of Sequitur before we again head south. We had been amazed in Peru by the very poor selection of coffee for a country that was recently among the ten largest producers of coffee in the world. We had hoped to find a better selection in Chile.

Instead, we found over two dozen different types of Nescafe instant, and only three brands of real coffee, including a stupidly expensive Juan Valdez organic. We were thankful we had stocked-up on coffee as we saw good buys in California and Mexico along the way.

We earmarked a number of things to pick up on a later stocking-up visit. Then we walked back along the main waterfront boulevard past the old rail yards. These are no longer in use and are fenced-off and in the process of being restored.

Here and there along the way I shot photos through the fence rails of some nicely restored machinery, including this lovely portable steam power plant.

Locomotive 209 appears to have been well-restored, but I can find no information on it online, except for a listing of its existence, its classification as a 4-6-2T, and that it was built by the North British Locomotive Company in Glasgow and owned by Ferrocarril de Antofagasta a Bolivia.

We continued through the centre of the historic downtown, admiring the mix of Victorian and Georgian architecture, with here and there Italian influences and some decidedly Chinese elements.

We came to Plaza Colon and saw the longest park benches we have ever seen. Edi sat on one that stretched about 30 meters and declared that the bench was taken.

We continued up a three-block-long pedestrian mall, which was alive and bustling with Saturday afternoon strollers and shoppers. We headed west along a busy street to the plaza in front of Mercado Central.

Plaza Emilio Sotomayor celebrates the colonel who led the Chilean troops ashore along the pier on 14 February 1879 to take Antofagasta.

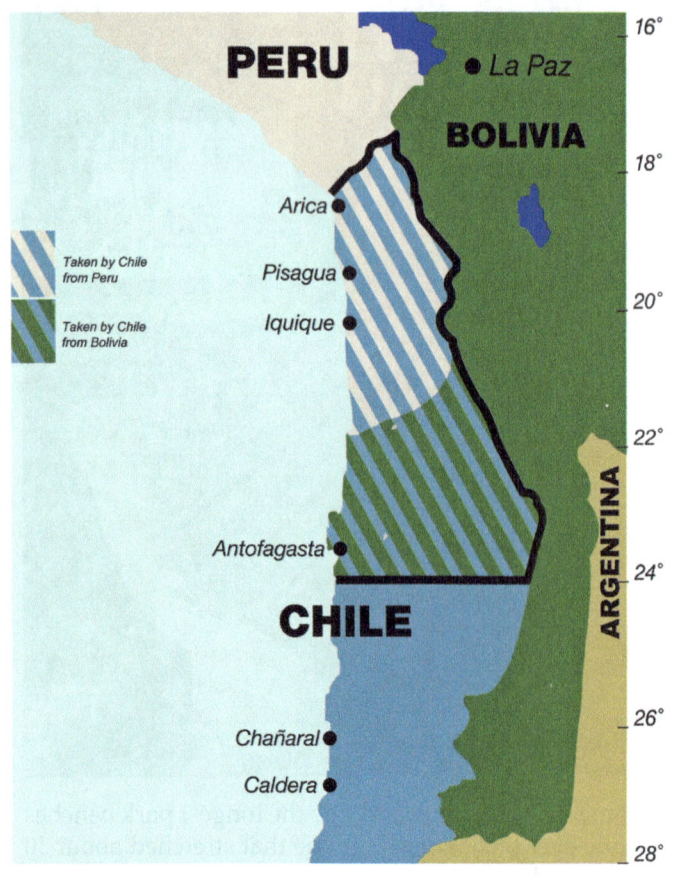

Chile declared war on Bolivia and Peru with the landing on the pier. The War of the Pacific lasted until 1883, with Chile emerging the victor. She annexed the two southern provinces of Peru and the entire Pacific portion of Bolivia.

There were stalls set-up in the plaza near the monument, but they were nearly all kitsch souvenirs. We explored inside the market to find a poor selection of mediocre produce. However, out the other side of the market we spotted a large supermarket. Inside we found wonderful fresh oyster mushrooms at $3 per kilo, and couldn't refuse them. We ended-up carrying three bags of groceries out of the store and back the kilometre and more to Sequitur.

Along the way back to the waterfront we passed a particularly interesting Moorish-styled building. Unfortunately, renovations and *"improvements"* of its bottom floor have spoiled the overall effect. We hope that the new lower façade is simply a temporary cover, which hasn't spoiled the original structure beneath it.

On Sunday our health was further improved, and we ventured out again, this time with our wheelie and its custom bag. We started at Sodimac, the local Home Depot-type store, only much larger. Among the things we needed was a large pump thermos for day-long hot tea while at sea.

As we had seen on our trip to nitrate ghost towns, the mineral wealth of the region fostered disputes over territorial boundaries. Treaties and agreements between Chile, Peru and Bolivia collapsed when Chile discovered a secret defensive pact between Peru and Bolivia..

I also needed to try to find some way to replicate the oarlocks for the dinghy. On my second rowing venture, the 20-30 metres from the float to Sequitur, the plastic pintle sheared and oar became a paddle. I had temporarily lashed the oar to the side rope to make a barely passable oarlock, but we needed something more permanent.

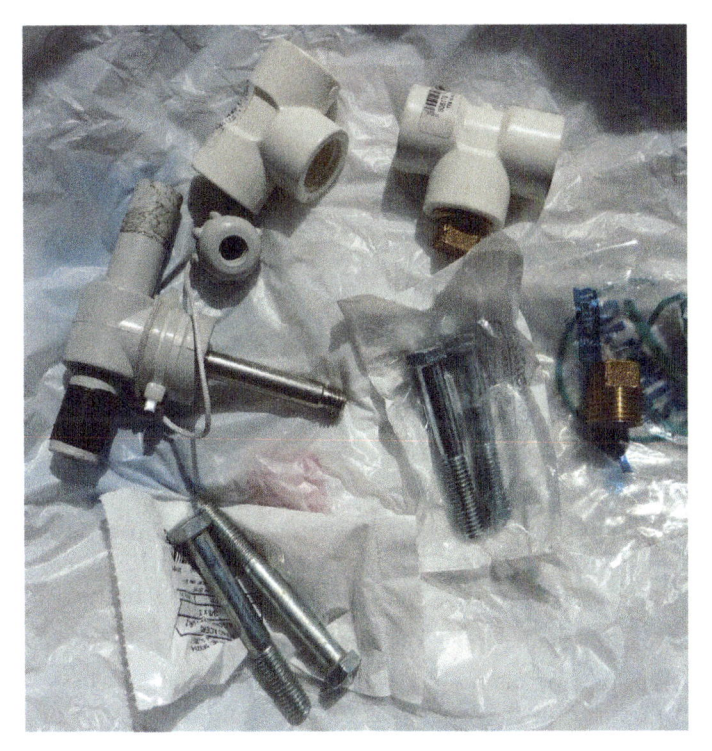

I had bought a spare oarlock from Luis, when I got the dinghy, but the breakage on my second use of the oars didn't portend well. We searched the plumbing aisles looking for appropriately shaped and sized pieces to cobble together into an oarlock. We eventually had a small team assembled assisting us: an English-speaking teen with no knowledge of hardware fittings, a woman who specialized in PVC and other plastic fittings and one who knew copper and bronze pieces. I'll need to do some cutting and drilling, but I think we will have a couple of more robust oarlocks when I finish.

On our way back we loaded a shopping cart with produce and groceries at the Tottus, and crammed much of it into the cooler bag and the wheelie bag and waddled back the two blocks to the Yacht Club and dinghied back out to Sequitur. Our lockers, pantry, fridges and one of the freezers were again nearly full, and we had started loading the second freezer.

Edi spent the afternoon making bagels, crusty potato rolls and bread to help fill the freezer while I spent time online trying to troubleshoot the problem with the Fischer-Panda generator.

In the evening I prepared the Peruvian national dish lomo soltado and served it with the usual accompaniment of rice, and even although we had seen McCain's in the freezer chest at Lider, we decided to forgo the French fries that normally are also on the plate. With dinner we had a superb bottle of 2007 Picasso Tempranillo, from the cases we had laid down in Sequitur's cellar.

On Monday we walked the four blocks to the Budget/Avis office and reserved a car for the next morning. Edi had insisted that we visit San Pedro de Atacama, and we had decided that renting a car would be the best way to do the nearly 1000 kilometre trip.

On Tuesday morning when we picked-up the car, we were introduced to a tiny new Chevrolet Spark with air conditioning and a crisp five-speed manual gearbox. The car was very well designed and laid-out, and we both immediately concluded that GM must have had the car designed and built in Japan; it was way beyond US standards. We headed up the long winding hill out of Antofagasta and into the Atacama Desert. In less than half an hour we joined the Pan-American Highway and followed it north for another hour or so before we turned onto the highway heading eastward to Argentina.

333

Powering the air conditioning in the searing heat of the desert and climbing the long, steep hills seemed a strain on the engine, particularly at 3500 metres in elevation. A few times we had to downshift to fourth, then to third, and when even third lugged, down into second gear. We later learned the car has a tiny 1.2 litre engine, and that it is meant as an around-town vehicle. Nonetheless, it served us well and comfortably across the Atacama and back, zipping along at 100 to 120 kph, except on the up-hills.

Once we had topped the hill and reached the desert, we began passing ruins of abandoned nitrate mining towns. There were small roadside signs naming the sites and their dates of operation. Most of the signs we were able to read as we whizzed by showed abandonment in the years following World War I.

The buildings in most of the townsites had been built of adobe, and they are still rather intact, likely because of the extreme dryness of this, the world's driest desert.

Even with all the abandonment, there is still a lot of mining going on in this area of the desert. We drove past many active sites, some of them huge. At one point we drove past an open-pit mine's overburden and tailings piles that stretched for 8 kilometres along the highway. They appeared to be between 50 and 100 metres high, and we couldn't see how far back they extended.

I had never thought of dump truck buckets wearing-out, but they must; we saw a replacement for one in a pull-off beside the highway. It appeared to be about 10 metres wide, and was wider than both lanes of the highway combined.

We stopped in Calama and parked under the shade of a large tree to have lunch, which was centred around a quarter of a quiche each, left over from the previous evening's dinner. We had chosen to stop in Calama because of the description in our Lonely Planet guide: *"How do we put this delicately? Hmmm, there's just no other words for it: Calama is a shithole."*

Calama's claim to fame is that it is the bedroom community and service and supply centre for one of the world's largest open-pit mines, Chuquicamata, which until recently was the world's largest single supplier of copper. Intrigued to see if Calama is worse than Paita, Peru, we had to visit. Our easy decision: Paita wins for worse.

After lunch we continued south-westward toward San Pedro de Atacama. Along the way we saw many mirages, as the desert morphed into lakes and marshes with inviting small islands. We could easily imagine the hot, thirsty prospectors chasing mirages across desert, looking for water.

We descended off one high ridge and into a broad, flat-bottomed valley, Valle de la Luna, the Valley of the Moon. NASA had conducted some of its Mars rover testing and experiments here, one of the driest parts of the driest desert on the planet.

We then drove the long winding hill up a steep ridge, Cordillera de la Sal, and then followed an equally long, steep and winding road down the other side to San Pedro.

As we arrived in the small town of 3200 people, we passed long adobe walls along the streets. Adobe was to be the main theme we would see as we explored the historic little oasis.

The town sits at 2440 metres in a huge basin, surrounded by spectacular scenery. Among these are Chile's largest salt flats, otherworldly rock formations, geysers, volcanoes, salt lakes, marshes and flamingos.

This was a pre-Columbian crossroad and Pedro Valdivia is reported to have visited it in 1540 on his way across the Atacama to colonize the Mapocho Valley. The early seventeenth church, Iglesia San Pedro fascinated us; its *new* adobe walls date to 1745.

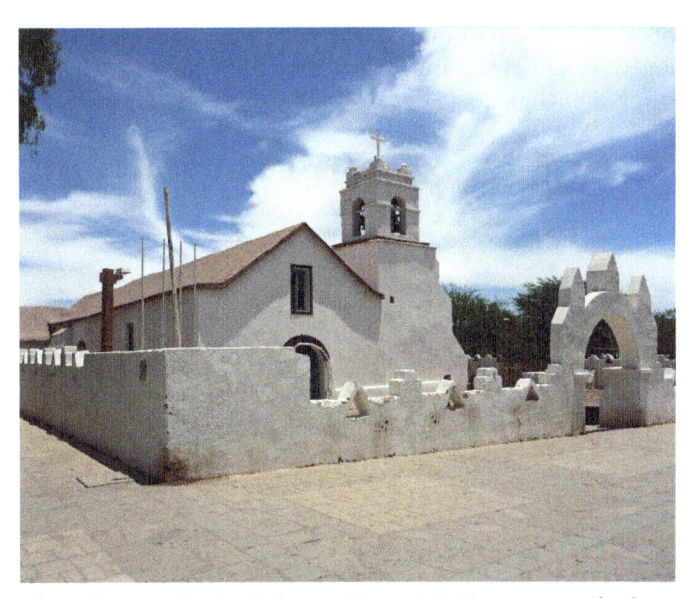

The whitewashed adobe walls and bell tower with their surrounding fence suggests a simple and serene place, yet it oozes energy.

Both Edi and I agreed that this is the nicest church we have visited on our cruise so far. The interior has hand-hewn floor boards, roof beams and ceiling slats, the walls are whitewashed and near-unadorned. Its stark simplicity exudes spirit, and we sensed a quiet peace laid-down by centuries of simple, genuine people.

The interior is also nicely plain and simple. Thankfully, nobody has been allowed to despoil the simplicity with gaudy, ornate trappings. We were intrigued with the ceiling, which is made of cardon, the local cactus wood.

The town is filled with young backpackers and adventurers; many hundreds of them. The low adobe buildings are crammed full with souvenir shops, internet cafes, restaurants, hotels and tour operators, yet the town retains a delightful charm.

There is a bell on display at the back of the church, on which is the casting date 1607. On the wall of the church near the entrance is a marble plaque indicating that mass was said here on the 5th of March 1557.

We found out after we had returned to Antofagasta that San Pedro has been declared a United Nations World Heritage Site. This would account for the lack of runaway commercial development. Our impression of the development of facilities for tourists is that they have as much as possible restored original buildings, and where not possible, replaced old with new replicas.

Everything we saw in San Pedro spoke of a local pride in the town. The streets were very clean, the buildings well maintained and they were attractively painted and decorated. In the shops we saw a completely new set of souvenirs; the knit goods, weavings, leather goods, pottery and jewellery were different to those we had seen in Peru. Unfortunately, the stock was repeated in nearly every store; they all use the same wholesalers, and there are few if any local goods.

We looked into the interiors of some of the restaurants as we passed them. They each had their own rustic charm and looked very inviting, but we were still full of quiche, and were not tempted to stop.

After a couple of hours browsing and exploring, we went back to the car, which had been baking in the near-vertical tropical sun. We were thankful for the air conditioning as we retraced our route back up the nearly 1000 metre climb over the Cordillera de la Sal, where we ground along at 30 to 35 kph in second gear on some of the long, steep grades.

The highways are well-engineered and in excellent condition, and we easily arrived back in Antofagasta just before sunset, parked the car in the security of the Yacht Club compound and made our way back out the rickety floats to our dinghy.

A 20-metre row brought us to Sequitur, where we enjoyed a leisurely dinner and reflected on the day. The car had cost 23,652 Pesos and the gasoline was 31,000, for a total of $109.30 for a wonderful excursion across the driest parts of the driest desert in the world to a charming little centuries-old oasis town, whose roots are lost in prehistory.

On Wednesday the 26th of January we slept in a while, and then began preparing for Sequitur's departure from Antofagasta. We had had a good break, we had recovered from the illnesses we had picked-up on our Chile-Peru-Bolivia-Chile bus trip, and we had seen the sights in and around Antofagasta. It was time to continue south.

The Club de Yates de Antofagasta is wonderfully sited at the edge of the nicely restored historic city centre, which is an alive and bustling area that still serves as the downtown. The Club seems to focus on social and family activities; it has a gymnasium, two swimming pools, a beach, a large restaurant, outdoor patios, barbecues and so on.

There is limited mooring tied off rickety floats, which undulate in the surge and jerk at the boats, which in turn jerk back. Our fore-and-aft mooring out in the basin seemed far preferable, and was very comfortable. We saw many more boats stored ashore in a large yard than we saw tentatively secured in the water at the floats. The club has a 34 tonne travel lift, that appears easily large enough to handle Sequitur, and we were curious about the rates for a haul-out. After several fruitless attempts, we gave-up asking.

After breakfast we dinghied to the float and walked along the malecon to Terminal Pesquero, a fresh fish market huddled in ramshackle buildings next to the fishing boat anchorage.

After a circuit to assess the quality of the wares and the mongers, we stopped at a booth that had some large chunks of great-looking albacore tuna. We had the monger slice off some 2.5cm thick, two-serving steaks. Further along we stopped to buy a couple of bags of large scallops with roe attached.

We then went across the parking lot to the next set of ramshackle buildings, which house a fresh produce market. We bought a selection of mostly greenish mangoes, some just barely green bananas, some firm small tomatoes and some small zucchini.

As we walked back to Sequitur with our booty, we paused to look again at the historic old nitrate pier. We were tempted to take a stroll out to its end; the climb over the barricade, the balance across the beams, the crawl under the plywood hoardings were not the deterrent. What kept us off was the memory of the seeing the Armada chasing kids off the pier and thoughts of two Canadian senior citizens sitting in a Chilean jail.

After lunch we walked southward along the main waterfront boulevard looking for the Capitan de Puerto so we could finally officially clear in, and then clear out. On our way we were passed by a train of flatcars laden with huge crude copper plates. Then in the port we saw dozens of mining truck tires over three metres in diameter.

We finally found the Port Captain's office and after some enquiries, we were directed to a desk at the end of the long room. There, a Petty Officer and two ratings worked away at trying to sort-out the clearance procedures for visiting foreign yachts. They get very few.

Finally, they were rescued by Petty Officer Zuniga, who introduced himself as Franco in rather good English. As I dealt with the technical details, Edi delved into the social. Franco had learned his English by watching Spanish subtitled television programs and movies. He seemed thirsty to practice speaking, and we shared a delightful half hour as the zarpe was prepared for our voyage from Antofagasta to Valparaiso with alternate ports of Taltal, Puerto Calderilla, Puerto Huasco, Bahia Tongoy and Los Vilos. Again we were amazed with the friendly, cheerful and helpful service offered by the Chilean maritime authorities. This is such a pleasant change from the process we endured in Mexico, Ecuador and Peru.

On our way back to Sequitur, we stopped in at the Tottus to finish our restocking of Sequitur. We bought a broad selection that included such items as wonderful oyster, portobello and button mushrooms, baby bak choy, pizza sauce in screw-valve bags, sliced smoked ham and six 2.5 litre bottles of sparkling water. Without our wheelie to tote the load, we really stretched our arms on the way back.

We stopped in at the Yacht Club office to announce our departure and to pay our bill for the use of the moorings and the Club facilities. The first three days are free, and then the rate is 10,000 Pesos per day, $20. We paid the manager 70,000 for our ten-day visit, effectively $14 per day in a snug, comfortable mooring. Again I asked about charges for haul-out and about what other services are available, but the managed said he had nothing to give me. It seems it is negotiable at the time of the service.

We rowed Non Sequitur back out to Sequitur using the lashed replacement for the broken starboard oarlock. On my chores list is the modification of the plumbing fittings we had bought at Sodimac. I was hopeful I could put together two sturdier oarlocks for Non Sequitur.

Onboard, we crammed fresh goods into the last few spaces in the fridges and freezers and loaded the baskets with fruit and vegetables that don't need cooling.

19. Passage to Valparaiso

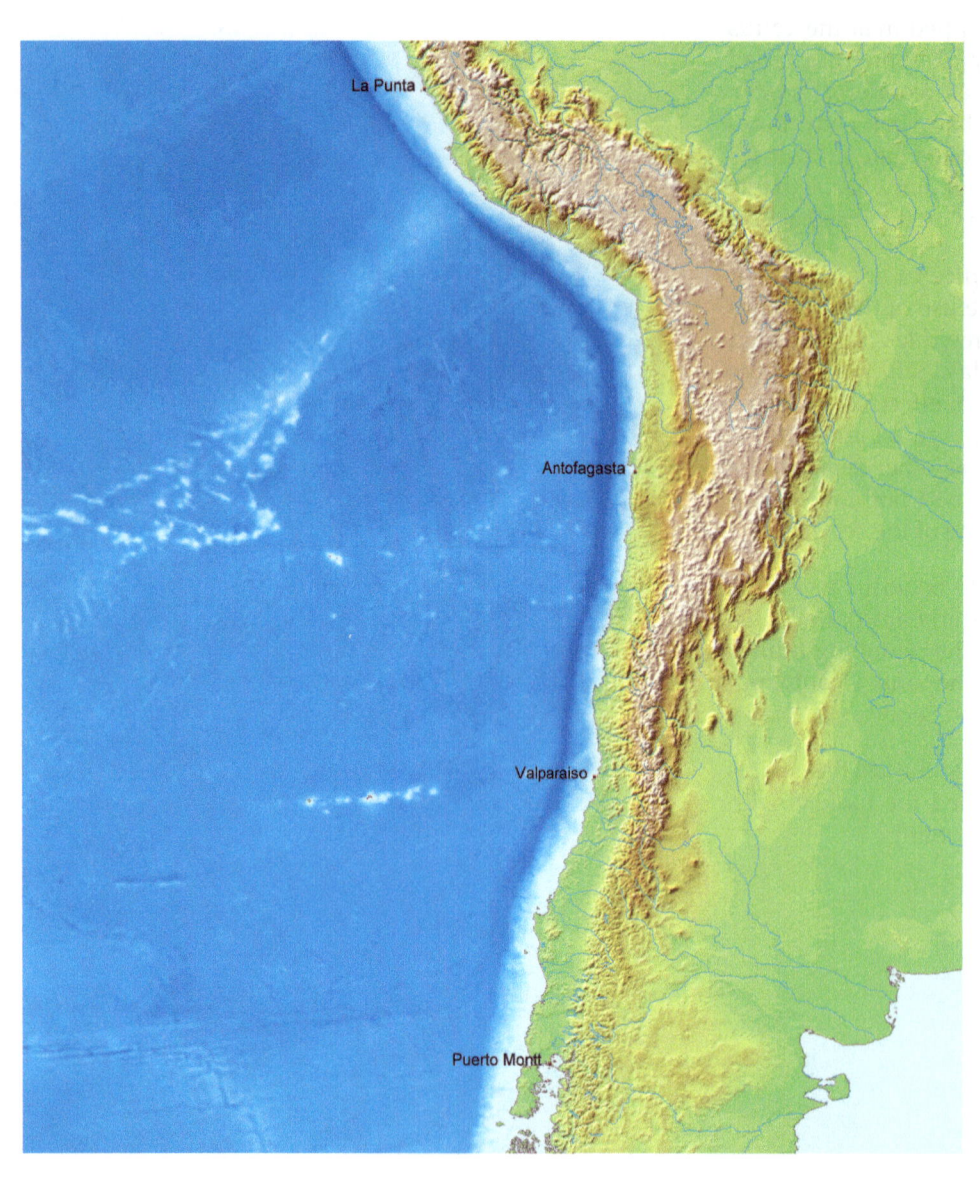

An hour and a quarter later the wind had come up SSW 6 to 7 knots, so we hauled out the sails and set off on a port tack making about 3 knots to the west. The wind backed and built slightly, so that by noon we were making hourly runs to the WSW of 4.5 knots and better.

We had left Antofagasta with totally empty water tanks; the surf through the entrance of the marina stirred-up such sediment that the watermaker's pre-filters clogged very quickly, and we had been making just enough to get by. While washing my hands after clearing the mooring lines and hoisting the dinghy, the water pump began had begun sucking dry, so I shut it off. Once we got out into clean and undisturbed water I flashed-up the watermaker, and in five hours we made 299.3 litres. The solar panels had maintained the battery through the five hours of watermaking, going from 63% to 60%, while also running the auto pilot, the chartplotter and other navigation instruments, as well as the fridges and freezers.

At 1915, as the wind died, we hauled-in the sails and motored at 1500 rpm. With the alternator again charging the batteries, I again ran the watermaker, and

Our passage to Valparaiso is a bit over 600 miles straight into the Humboldt Current and the prevailing winds. The weather gribs and online sites were showing 5 to 15 knot winds from the south and 2, 3 and 4 metre swells from the southwest. The possibilities of making much over 5 knots were very remote. We knew that it was going to be a slog, and we wanted to have plenty of fresh food.

On Thursday the 27th of January, after we had finished our emails, I rowed the dinghy forward to unfoul the line through the mooring strop, then rowed aft to untie from the other mooring. We hoisted and secured Non Sequitur, flashed-up the engine and at 0905 slipped and motored out into the surf coming through the marina entrance.

in three hours made another 208.4 litres. The output with the higher power of the alternator was nearly 70 litres per hour, compared to 50 litres per hour on battery only.

At 2302 we were contacted on VHF by a huge tanker northbound for Iquique. He was 15 miles south and had been monitoring us on his AIS, as we had him. We were on end-on, end-on collision courses and, noting our slow speed, he asked our intentions. I suggested we both alter 5 degrees starboard until our CPAs were 2 miles, and he agreed. It is nice to see again the effectiveness of our AIS transponder. It is so much more valuable than simply a receiver, and dramatically better than no AIS at all. We are amazed by sailors who refuse to install even a receiver.

Sunrise on Friday found us motoring in glassy calm seas making 3.3 to 3.6 knots bucking the Humboldt Current past a low, barren coastline. We had decided to remain closer in to the coast in hope of finding a reduced current, and possibly even a counter-current.

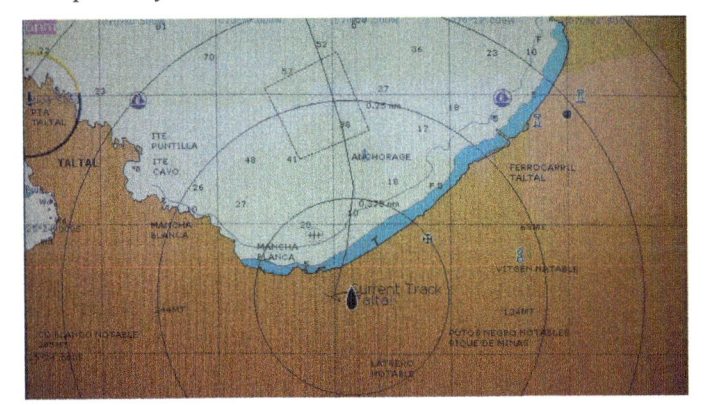

When the sun set at 2034 we were still motoring in windless conditions. At 2220 we came to 50 metres on the Rocna in 16.5 metres of water in Taltal. Our chart plotter showed us to be in the heart of downtown.

We had tiptoed into the anchorage in the dark with no moon and only the reflection of the few town lights across the water to illuminate our way. As I was setting the anchor, I noticed a small fishing boat moored about 20 metres off to starboard. Then I saw another and then several more within 30 metres; we were on the edge of the moored fishing fleet, none of them with anchor lights. I allowed my eyes to become accustomed to the scene, and then we weighed and moved 30 metres east to a clear space.

We had a very comfortable night's sleep, and in Saturday morning's light I was able to see the scattering of small wooden fishing boats around us in the anchorage.

After a leisurely breakfast we weighed at 0925 and motored out of the bay. As we went, the radar overlay showed the skew of the chart datum; the chart was gridded about 4 cables to the northeast. Sorting this out in the near absolute dark as we approached the previous evening had been entertaining.

At 1000 we hauled-out the main and jib and headed west on a port tack in a SSW 8 knot breeze. Forty minutes later the wind had nearly died, so we flashed up and motored to the southwest to clear Baisla Blanca. The wind totally died and we continued motoring into the afternoon in glassy seas on a 2 to 3 metre southwest swell. In the late afternoon the wind built to southerly 4 to 6 knots as we bucked into the northbound current.

Shortly after 1800 a fishing boat turned toward us and the crew all wildly waved, warning us away and indicating they had laid a long line or drift net across our path. We could see they were looking for it, and it seemed they weren't quite sure where it was. We followed their hand signals and turned away to the west-northwest, keeping a close lookout for floats and other signs of their gear. For three quarters of an hour the fishing boat ran zigzags to the south of us, parallelling our course and searching for its gear. Finally it found the western end, and their focus changed from shepherding us, to recovering their lines.

The sun set through a compact band of nimbostratus, the wind remained southerly 0 to 5 knots and the swell remained southwesterly at about 3 metres, so we continued motoring through the night and into the following afternoon, making 3 to 3.5 knots into the current. In the late morning we made another two hours of water and brought the tanks to full.

Finally tiring of motoring into the current in near windless conditions, at 1529 we came to 30 metres on the Rocna in 10 metres of water in Puerto Calderilla, about a cable off some cottages on the jagged basaltic rocks in a well-protected volcanic crater. It was time to take a break.

We slept in for a while on Monday morning, and for breakfast Edi prepared eggs Calderilla: poached Iquique eggs on sliced Antofagasta ham on homemade crusty potato buns with hollandaise sauce and sliced Antofagasta hydroponic tomatoes and cups of Peruvian coffee.

We lazed around in the warm sun and did a few small chores. For lunch Edi made some ground beef and rice filling and baked some empanadas, which she served with a fresh guacamole and some tostitas and rooibos tea.

In the evening I made a quiche using a pat-in butter crust from a recipe I hadn't used since the early 80s. The filling was Edam-type cheese, diced chorrizo sausage, diced onions, sliced oyster mushrooms, quartered mini button mushrooms four eggs and the rest of the 400ml tetra-pack of whipping cream not used in making the crust. It was rich!

With the quiche we had crisped potato rounds and a bottle of Valdivieso Brut. It was an eating day; we were hungry. It is amazing how much energy is consumed by the constant aerobic exercise in maintaining balance as Sequitur pitched and rolled in the 2 to 3 metre swells with no wind to fill the sails and dampen the motion.

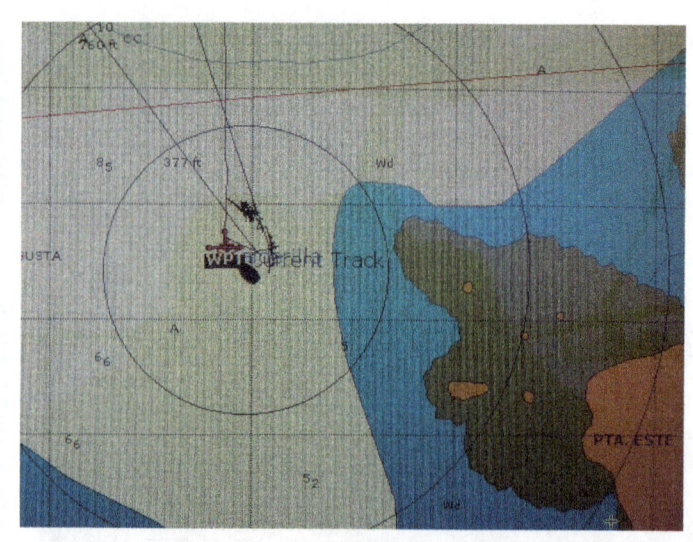

We slept in a bit on Tuesday the 1st of February, and then after breakfast we prepared to get underway again. The chartplotter showed a tight paint of Sequitur's track as she swung to anchor, showing its great assistance in keeping an anchor watch. With the anchor alarm set a short distance beyond the scope of the anchor rode, it sounds as soon as the anchor drags. We have not yet had the Rocna drag, unlike my experience with CQRs and Danforths, which seemed to drag every third or fourth anchorage.

At 1040 we weighed and proceeded out through the break in the rim of the ancient volcanic crater. We motored through glassy seas looking for wind. Shortly after 1100 we spotted a small pod of dolphins, the first we have seen since early June off the north coast of Peru.

Our noon position report included glassy calm seas on a 2 to 3 metre SW swell and 10/10 low stratus. We continued motoring into the Humboldt Current, making a little over 3 knots. Ten minutes later there was a small ripple on the water, and shortly thereafter, a southwest breeze had built to about 6 knots. We hauled out the sails and lolled along making good just slightly less than with the engine. Twenty minutes later the wind vanished and we were back to glassy seas. I hauled in the jib, tightened the main as a stabilizer and we motored.

342

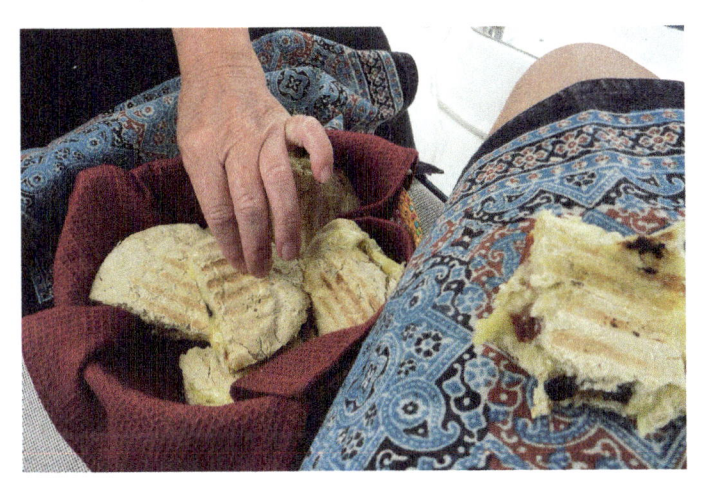

To cheer up the glum of the day, Edi prepared some hot paninis from fresh crusty potato rolls, Chilean butter cheese, Moroccan olives, California sun-dried tomatoes and Peruvian artichoke hearts. A delicious international lunch!

Through the afternoon the wind again a couple of times tricked me into deploying the sails for a few minutes. Then at 1742, as we were motoring in still airs, the autopilot gave a *Drive Stopped* error message, and switched off. I fumbled with the Hydrovane for half an hour, trying to get it to steer for us, but the only wind over its sail was from our own motion. We resorted to hand steering. At 1835, still with no wind, we decided to head into Bahia Salado to anchor for the night and in the morning to attempt to repair the autopilot. While we were still in clean seas, we made another 207 litres of water and brought the tanks back to full.

We tiptoed into Bahia Salado watching for anchored and moored vessels. As our eyes became accustomed to the scene, anchor lights and deck lights on boats became car and house lights ashore. We finally concluded there were no lit vessels in the bay; we needed only watch for unlit ones. Finally, at 2210 we came to 40 metres on the Rocna in 11.5 metres of water, secured the starboard snubber and shut down.

In the morning when I went on deck to survey the scene, I saw we were at the edge of the most densely packed field of buoys I have ever seen. There were many dozens of them, all trailing their pick up lines just waiting to snag a passing propeller. I looked across to the other side of the boat and saw less than 50 metres away another extensive, densely packed field of buoys. We had somehow managed to come into the bay in the black of a moonless and overcast night, and find the narrow lane between the two fields. They were not marked on the chart and they were unlit.

After breakfast I attacked the troubleshooting on the autopilot. Everything looked good at the course computer end, so I again went into the starboard transom locker. The rewiring I had done in Antofagasta still looked fine, so I checked our Vancouver the installer's other connections. Sure enough, I found another faulty connection. On this one the wire had been poorly stripped; there was a large tag of insulation remaining and the partly-bared wire had been then poorly crimped. No wonder it had failed. It must have been past teatime when the installer did this, and she had rushed to get it done. I redid the connection, tested the system and we again had Otto available for work.

For lunch Edi made some ground beef and rice filling and baked it into some empanadas, which she served with a fresh guacamole and some tostitas and cups of rooibos tea.

After lunch I went onto the foredeck and hauled the spinnaker out of the sail locker. I redid the tape repair on a tear near its tack and patched a tear in its snuffer. I then checked over the tack strop, shackles, cringles and sheets, and packed the snuffered chute back into the sail locker ranged and ready to deploy. We relaxed the rest of the day in the very peaceful anchorage.

At 1015 we weighed and picked our way past the hundreds of buoys littering the bay. We concluded they weren't mooring buoys, otherwise there was a huge fishing fleet missing. They were most likely a shellfish farm with suspended lines of cultured mussels or oysters. There are three isolated houses along the shoreline, and a compound of a dozen or so buildings, appearing to be a processing plant and housing site.

On Thursday morning I transferred the remaining fuel from the auxiliary tank to the main, bringing the tank gauge there up to a needle's width below the quarter mark. The main holds 580 litres, so we were down to less than 140 litres, having gone through a bit more than 700 litres since leaving La Punta. We also have one full and one half-full jerry can lashed on the foredeck, an additional 30 litres.

At 1936 we came to 30 metres on the Rocna in 9.5 metres of water, abeam the light on the small islet protecting the mouth of the inlet. The chart was quite inaccurate; its datum was skewed over a mile, some of the charted features were not a true reflection of reality, and marked soundings did not jive with our readings. I decided to anchor as we crossed our sounder's 10 metre line.

Shortly before noon we rounded Punta Cachos and bent our course to the southwest to clear the coast. There was a west-northwest wind of 5 to 6 knots, so I went forward to rig and hoist the spinnaker. By the time I had run the sheets, shackled-on the tack, attached the halyard to the head and hoisted the bundle, the wind was down to about 4 knots. I hoisted the snuffer and as the spinnaker filled, shut down the engine and rolled-out the main. We lolled along at 2 knots on a beam reach in a slowly dying breeze. After an hour and a quarter of praying for the breeze to fill, we finally snuffed the spinnaker tightened the main and flashed-up the engine.

As the sun went down beside the light on the islet, it cast a large reflection of itself in a multi-ringed halo against the thin cirrostratus. Sequitur rolled in the sloppy surge, but we were secure and happy to not be motoring into the current and swell.

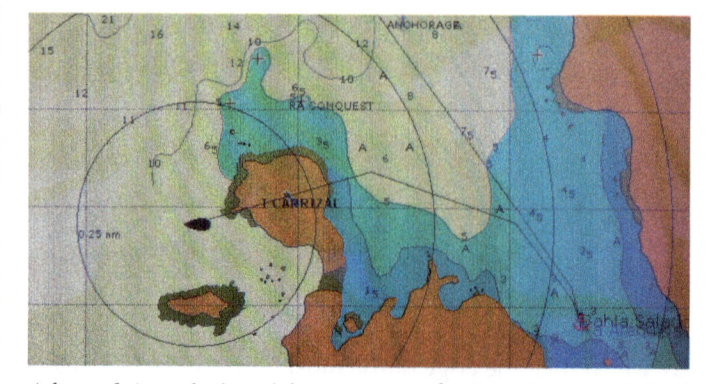

At 1450 we spotted the first albatross we had seen since our sail over the summit of Cobb Sea Mount in July 2008. The day continued windless, so instead of using our short supply of diesel motoring into the Humboldt Current, we decided to divert into Caleta Herradura de Carrizal, a small inlet I found on the chart. We made water on the way in to bring our tanks back to full.

After a leisurely breakfast, we weighed and proceeded at 0938. The sky was completely overcast with low stratus, the seas were lightly rippled from the 2 to 3 knot variable breezes that came and went, and there was a 3 metre southwest swell. We motored over the top of the small islet and right through the lighthouse on the chartplotter, reinforcing again the need to use basic navigation methods, prime among which are eyes and common sense.

344

As we rounded the headlands and turned southward, the wind again fixed itself directly on our nose at 6 to 8 knots, not quite strong enough to give us any southing against the Humboldt on either tack. We resigned ourselves to motoring into the wind and the building swell. I went forward to lash the socked spinnaker to the mast and shrouds to keep it from flailing in the sloppy going.

The swell built to 4 metres and we lolled along, somewhat stabilized by the fin of the hardened main, and making good hourly runs in the 3.5 to 3.8 mile range. With our diminishing fuel supply, we decided to head into Puerto Huasco, rather than motoring into the current.

We contacted Huasco Port Control and told them of our intentions. We were welcomed and told the lat and long of an anchorage to use. I plotted it, and found it to be within a few metres of the spot I had earlier picked-out. At 1630 we came to 30 metres on the Rocna in 8 metres of water half a cable from moored harbour tugs and fishing skiffs and about two cables off the Muelle de Pasajeros, the passenger wharf. I set the starboard snubber, shut down the engine and reported our arrival to Port Control.

We soon became a regular part of the boat tours that did a twenty-minute circuit from the muelle out past the lighthouse, then three or four metres off our side on their way to the tugs and then back through the fishing skiffs to the muelle. Every half hour, one or the other boat, loaded with a fresh batch of tourists motored past.

After lunch we launched Non Sequitur, mounted the motor and tried to start it. We hadn't run it since late December in Iquique, and I had thought it would take some time to get going. Disappointingly, it started on the first pull, and I have no story to tell of troubleshooting. We headed through the moored skiffs and in to the muelle. We landed, and after some discussion with one of the tour boat operators, had the dinghy towed by a man in a rowboat to a mooring buoy and secured.

We climbed the stairs from the passenger landing and walked in the pier to the shore and past a ragtag collection of flea market stalls, souvenir selections, dollar-store-type stalls and near the town end of the line, some produce sellers. We noted the low quality of much of the produce on our way by, and hoped we would find something better in town.

The town of 4500 people appears as a semi-abandoned ex-mining centre, which here and there shows signs of a revival. There is a well laid-out and manicured malecon in the centre of town, and we strolled along it past an equal mix of thriving and destitute businesses. We checked-out the produce markets as we passed them. The first one we came to was clean, neat and had fresh and healthy-looking stock, and then the next several small marts seemed to decrease in quality as we went.

We were looking for a source of diesel to replenish Sequitur's tanks, and some questioning directed us to the town's pump, a Copec service station along toward the lighthouse and a block above the waterfront. The diesel pump is across the lot from the gas bays, and we asked whether there was diesel available. The price, at 550 Pesos, or $1.10 per litre was better than anything we had seen since Chata Tamy in Paita at the end of May 2010.

We walked down the hill to the water's edge to look for a suitable dinghy landing, and found a rather crowded beach with swimmers, waders and sun dolls. I walked over to the lifeguard and after ten minutes of fumbling in my non-Spanish, made him understand we wanted to land our dinghy on the beach. He seemed very hesitant, but eventually, he said we could land over at the end near the rocks. Our thought was to dinghy four jerry cans ashore, fill them at the service station and head back out to Sequitur with another 80 litres of fuel. This would be much easier than using the muelle and trudging the kilometre each way to and from the service station.

On our walk back to Sequitur, we checked-out the produce sellers on the other side of the street, and found mostly old stock and culls and musty smells. We arrived back at the first one and it looked even better than we had remembered. We loaded a few bags and bought a two-and-a-half-dozen flat of eggs, and carried on.

We stopped at the office of the Capitan de Puerto and asked them for information on filling Sequitur with diesel. We were given the telephone number of the Copec dispatch office in Santiago and said we should call them to have them send an oil truck to meet us at the fisherman's wharf. We decided to walk over to the wharf to check-out its suitability, and asked directions. It was eight kilometres away; we decided not to walk over.

The Capitania is at the western end of the town, in an area that a century-and-more ago would have been the mining port's centre of prosperity. There are still a few of the old company offices and houses in good repair, but most are derelict or in ruins. One of the buildings which has survived is on a rocky hilltop with commanding views. From its appearance, it could have been headquarters, or a general manager's home.

Back onboard, I hauled-out the satellite phone and dialled the number we were given for the Copec dispatcher. As the tour boats circled us on their now routine track, I tried every combination of prefix: dialling code, area code, city code, but could not get a good number. I gave-up.

I unlashed the two jerry cans on the foredeck and added their contents to our main fuel tank. The needle moved up to about the three-sixteenth area of the gauge. The main tank holds 580 litres, so we have around 108 litres remaining. We had left La Punta with 870 litres in the main, auxiliary and jerry tanks, and had run the engine a total of 261 hours since then. Sequitur's fuel consumption has ranged from 2.8 to 3.0 litres per hour, so this also points to our having 100 to 120 litres remaining in the tank. I calculated that even if we have to motor the whole way into the current, we had sufficient fuel to get us to Coquimbo, which with its neighbouring communities, is a population centre of over 300,000. Surely there is convenient diesel there. We would feel much more comfortable, though if the wind gave some relief to the engine.

On Sunday we weighed and proceeded out of Bahia de Huasco in still airs and glassy seas beneath an unbroken canopy of low stratus. We motored out past the thermoelectric plants on the point and then bent our course to the southwest to clear the points further south.

As we passed the point, we watched a dory with two fishermen pitching in the surge and the breakers crashing on the jagged rocks. The fishing close-in must be great for them to risk being smashed onto the rocks or being swamped in the breakers and the surge of the swell.

As we were watching the fishermen, a whale surfaced and blew its misty breath. This is the first whale we have seen since our crossing from Mexico to the Galapagos.

The whale seemed to be imitating the exhaust plumes coming from the thermoelectric plants on the coast. As the whale breathed, its dorsal fin was just clearing the water, giving us a hint of its huge size. As the whale continued its breathing cycle, its back arched through the water with the dorsal fin emerging and following in a gentle curve.

We continued motoring in glassy seas with not a breath of wind, and we continued to consume our diminishing supply of diesel fuel.

In the late afternoon, as we were still motoring and depleting our fuel, we began to see small ripples on the water, which indicated the commencement of a breeze.

At 1746 Edi sighted a sailboat heading north closer in to the coast. It had only the main up and was most likely motor-sailing; there was still no wind. This is only the second sailboat we have seen at sea since leaving Mexico, the other being an Outbound 46 in early June 2010 south of Paita, Peru.

At 1940 with continued still airs, we altered course toward the coast, heading in to Ensenada Gaviota to anchor for the night and hope for wind in the morning. As we were motoring with the swell on our beam, we hauled-out the main to serve as a stabilizer.

The sun set as we were approaching Isla, and we were left with the faint illumination from a day-old moon low in the sky over our starboard quarter.

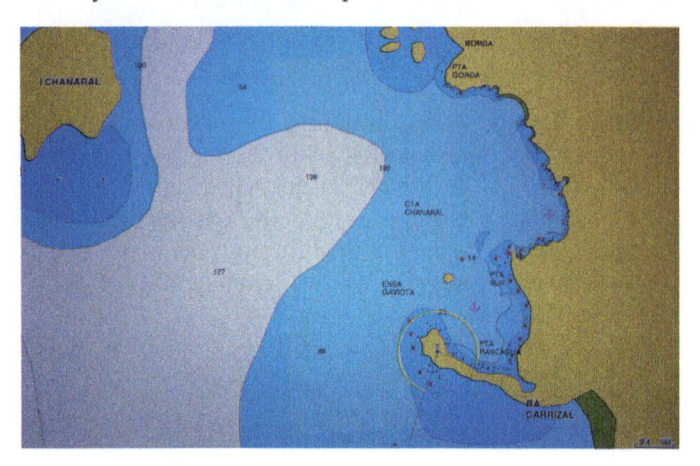

We tiptoed into the ensenada, searching in vain for the small islet in its mouth that is indicated on the chart. Neither our eyes nor the radar could pick it up. Fortunately, there is a lighthouse on the point, and we were able to use it and our radar overlay to safely enter the small bay and we closely monitored the depth sounder.

As we came to shoaling water I slowed to an idle and I watched the depth sounder. We crossed 12 metres and then 10 and 9 in about a cable's run, so I stopped and reversed back along our track to the 12-metre sounding and let go the Rocna there. A car ashore shone its lights on us and flashed them on and off. A few minutes later a small fishing skiff with two men came out and gesticulated wildly, indicating danger. They were in near-panic and we could not understand their fast-rattling Spanish. We first thought there were uncharted fish weirs or pens, and I searched the water in the direction they indicated with our million candlepower searchlight. I saw nothing.

Finally, I realized they were indicating it was very shallow where we were. I told them our sounders showed we were in 12 metres and that we had seen an even shoaling to 9 metres a cable in toward the beach. They insisted we were in dangerously shallow water, and trusting to their local knowledge, I followed their advice to weigh and move to a safer location. We followed them slowly toward the point, watching as the depth sounder indicated we were moving into gradually shoaling water. When it got to 7 metres, I let go the anchor again.

Again they did their near panic thing and persuaded me to weigh and follow them to a safe place. They took us closer to the point, to 6 metres and very close to an anchored fishing boat and indicated we should anchor there. To their chagrin, I moved away from the fishing boat to give us some swinging room, and at 2213 let go 35 metres on the Rocna in 11.5 metres of water, with the lighthouse bearing 220. After I had set the snubber, secured the foredeck and made my way back to the cockpit, the men in the skiff were still hovering around the stern of the boat. They appeared to be waiting for a gift of something. We both continued with our processes of securing Sequitur for the night, writing the ship's log, setting the anchor and depth alarms and generally making ourselves unavailable. They finally left.

The anchorage was very rolly with cross-reflections of the swell seeming to come from every direction. We were up at sunrise, and as we watched a pelican takeoff from the water, we weighed and took-off from the uncomfortable ensenada. The tide had just reached its low, a little over a metre lower than it had been when we had juggled anchor placements on arrival. With the lower water and the daylight, everything still looked good. The surge in the inlet showed no indication of isolated rocks or shoals where we had been on our way in, nor where we had first anchored.

We turned the point and motored southward in still airs and glassy seas watching the rising sun burn away the few tiny cumulus to leave totally a clear sky.

348

For breakfast, Edi prepared eggs Gaviota, crumbled Asiago cheese-topped poached eggs on microwaved diced smoked sausage on toasted sliced crusty potato rolls garnished with sliced tomatoes and served with fresh-ground coffee.

We were threading our way down through groups of small islands standing one to five miles off the coast and creating somewhat of a separate sea from the main body of the South Pacific. We supposed that this area would make a good feeding and breeding ground for the whales.

At 1020 a 5 to 6 knot breeze had come up, and I hauled out the main and went forward to unlash the spinnaker, re-rig it and then launch it close-hauled on the starboard tack.

At 0900 we were still motoring in glassy seas. At 1000 a few small patches of ripples were beginning to appear, and as we looked at these, hoping for wind, we watched a few dark blue whales swim past a cable or so off our starboard side. They were of the same type as we had seen on our departure from Huasco on Sunday. From the huge size, the colour, the hump forward of the blowhole, the breathing characteristics and the small dorsal fin, we identified them as a blue whales.

Satisfied that all was well on the foredeck, I made my way aft to trim the sails and shut down the engine. With the sails trimmed, we accelerated from just under 4 knots under power alone to a little over 5 knots with the assistance of the sails. I shut down the engine and watched as we slowed to 2.5 knots.

I played with sail trim for nearly half an hour, trying to coax a bit more speed out of Sequitur, but beating into the 5 to 6 knot wind and a slightly adverse current, 2.5 knots was all she could give us. I flashed-up the engine again and we motor-sailed with the main and spinnaker, making either side of 5 knots.

We ran with this configuration for nearly three hours to the south-southeast between the islands, but when we needed to alter to the south to keep off the coast, we put the wind directly on the nose. I snuffed the spinnaker, hardened the main, reversed the traveller and we continued motor-sailing, but with our speed reduced to the 3.8 knot range.

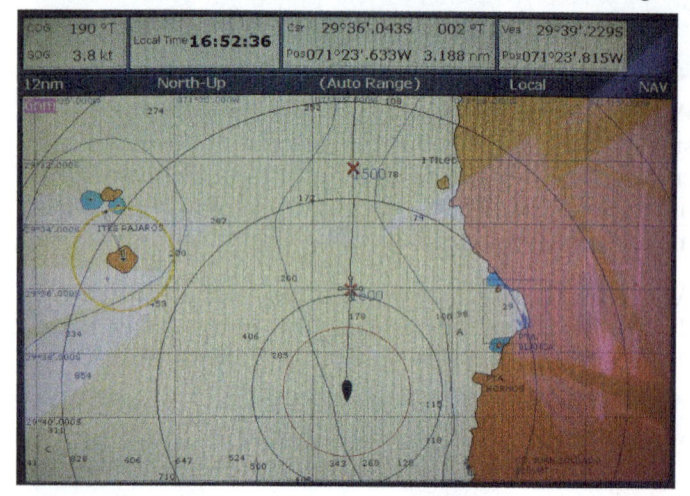

Shortly before 1700 we did a practice run past the Horn, passing with the Horn about 4 miles off our port side. For the geographically-challenged, this is not the famous Cabo de Hornos at the southern tip of the Americas, but the local Punta Hornos.

For dinner I prepared pan-grilled mahi-mahi with grilled zucchini and potato rounds, which we enjoyed in the cockpit as we motor-sailed southward into the current and wind, making 3.5 knots toward the Coquimbo suburb of Herradura de Guayacan.

As we finished dinner, the sun set at 2039. At 2226 with a thin crescent moon over our shoulders, we came to 30 metres on the Rocna in 9.5 metres of water 2 cables off the dinghy dock of the Yachting Club La Herradura, on the southern side of a mile-across circular bay.

We slept-in on Tuesday morning, and then in the early afternoon we launched the dinghy, mounted the motor and headed in to the Club. We secured Non Sequitur to the lee side of the float and walked in to the administration office to ask about obtaining diesel fuel. The woman in the office directed us to the local gas station about two kilometres along the road to Coquimbo.

As we walked along, we saw many new housing developments, completed condominium towers and terraces, rows of townhouses and half-a-dozen or more major new projects under construction. One new development we walked through appeared complete, but so far unoccupied. There seemed to be sales offices and show suites everywhere. The roads, sidewalks and other infrastructure had not kept pace with the developments; we resorted to dusty paths and make-do sidewalks for about a third of our two-kilometre walk.

We finally arrived at the gas station and saw their diesel pump and 5600 per litre price. There is a street directly across the boulevard, which leads the one block to the beach. This would afford easy access from our beached dinghy to and from the diesel pump. We continued along to the huge new supermarket, which takes-up the next block. The place is so new that on the GoogleEarth image dated 12 June 2010, the lot has been cleared and there are piles of construction material around a roughed-out perimeter foundation.

We did the rounds, checking their stock, and then picked up a few things we needed, plus a few we didn't, though not many; we hadn't brought our wheelie and it is two kilometres back to the Yachting Club. Among the indulgences were a couple of thick cuts of Paraguayan beef tenderloin, custom-cut for us by a butcher whose adequate English came from several months living in North Carolina a few years previously.

Back at the marina with our purchases and slightly longer arms, we asked the tripulantes on the pier where we could get diesel. One of them motioned me to follow him, so I laid down the groceries and he led me up to a gas pump. We had seen it earlier, but had believed the sign on it that indicated it was 95-octane gasoline. When I asked about the sign, he told me it was correct, it was gasoline, but he thought it should also work in a diesel. I decided to go no further with this fellow's technical expertise.

My further enquiries for marine fuelling facilities brought a mix of responses, ranging from there are none in Bahia La Herradura and there are none in the Coquimbo area, to a casual mention of a facility about ten miles south along the coast called (and my deafness comes into play here) Las Bacas, Cacas, Dacas, Gacas, Lacas, Pacas, or whatever.

Back onboard, after we had stowed our purchases, I checked the chart, and about ten miles south, as the albatross flies, is a marina named Las Tacas. I searched the Internet for it with no luck. It was listed in the World Port Index, but there were no data other than its name and location.

As we enjoyed a simple lunch of sliced baguette and cheese with cold beer we surveyed the beach across from the gas station to see what it would be like for a dinghy landing. It was end-to-end people, ten or a dozen deep and all through the water. This was on a Tuesday afternoon; what is a weekend afternoon like?

In the evening we enjoyed our first beef tenderloin in many months. I guess the move away from the tropics and back toward the temperate zone has brought a change in our natural dietary urges. I dry-fried the steaks three-and-a-half minutes per side in a hot pan, put them on the hot plates in the oven while I quickly sautéed the quartered mushrooms, shallots and garlic in the hot pan juices, added a large dollop of butter and later a liberal splash of Sauvignon Blanc while I plated the asparagus and added the gnocchi to its still-boiling pot of water. The gnocchi were then tossed in with the mushrooms, the asparagus received a squeeze of mayonnaise, the steaks were slathered with béarnaise sauce and the plates were garnished with tomato and basil. With it we had a superb bottle of Santa Carolina 2008 Gran Riserva Barrica Selection Cabernet Sauvignon. It was a wonderful welcome back to the 30s latitudes, though we were at only 29° 59', a mile shy of the 30s.

We slept-in again on Wednesday, and then spent the remainder of the day puttering and baking. Edi had started a couple of batches of New York Times bread on Tuesday, and it needed baking. Since we were going to have the oven on, and since we had just run-out, Edi had also made-up a batch of twenty-five bagels to raise, boil, garnish and then bake. It was early evening by the time the bagels and loaves of bread were out of the oven.

Since we had sampled the bagels and bread as they came out, we were not very hungry, so I quickly tossed together an egg dish for dinner. To some diced Italian salami searing in the wok I added two diced red potatoes, a diced onion, three minced garlic cloves and some chopped celery. When the potatoes had nearly cooked, I added diced red and green peppers, and a couple of minutes later, five beaten eggs, which cooked in a few seconds. It was a delicious Sequitur foo yeung.

We were up relatively early on Thursday, and for breakfast we enjoyed a sampling of our fresh raisin bread and cracked wheat bread plus bagels, both cracked wheat and sesame.

After breakfast we sliced the remainder of the baking, divided it into small freezer bags and stowed it in the freezers.

We had decided to rent a car to check-out Las Tacas to the south, to see if in fact they have a diesel fuelling facility, and if not, to shuttle our four jugs with diesel from the service station. We also wanted to do some shopping and tour the local area. Among other places, we wanted to visit La Serena, the second oldest city in Chile.

351

We took Non Sequitur over to the Club floats and walked along to the administration office, which also serves as the portal in and out of the Club. We asked the office manager where we could find a car rental company, and she gave the air of being too busy to help, though we couldn't see with what. Her young assistant took the initiative and looked-up the address and phone number for us. We asked if we could phone, and she dialled the number and enquired for us. The company had no cars available for the next few days. I asked about other companies, and the manager then berated the young assistant, apparently for being helpful to us.

We withdrew and reassessed our options. We decided to take a taxi over to the gas station to pick up our diesel fuel. I timidly asked the young assistant about a taxi, and asked if she could reserve one for us to arrive in thirty minutes. She phoned and ordered the cab. We went back out to Sequitur, picked-up the four jerry cans, the wheelie and bungee cords and dinghied back in to the Club, arriving at the gate five minutes before our taxi was due. We waited for fifteen minutes for it to not show-up, then thanked the office staff and told them we would walk.

We made our way along the streets of La Herradura, up the off-ramp from the boulevard and past the new condo developments, crossed the six-lane divided road and walked up to the diesel pumps. We finally got the attention of one of the attendants, they likely being unaccustomed to seeing a wheelie and four jerry cans pull up at the pumps. We had him put twenty litres in each of the four cans, paid him 44,966 Pesos and put our booty to the side to begin looking for a taxi.

I went into the pay station/store, which was full of beach-goers buying huge jugs of sugar-water and bags of salted grease. There was a long lineup at the one cash register, so I decided not to bother waiting to ask them to call a taxi. While Edi stood guard over our fuel, I went out to the six-lane boulevard and spent twenty minutes trying to flag a cab; they were all occupied. Edi and I then decided to take the fuel down to the beach, where she would watch it while I went and brought the dinghy over. We relayed the jerry cans two-by-two out of the service station, across to the median, across to the edge of the service road, and across it to the sidewalk leading down to the beach. As I approached the beach with the next relay, I saw a buoyed line stretching across the water some twenty metres out, no doubt to keep the many jet-ski drivers from harassing the bathers. I retreated to the service road.

Our next plan was for me to walk across and along to the supermarket and find a taxi there. I found none. I had a lot attendant call one and in six or seven minutes, it arrived. The driver spoke no English, so in my semblance of Spanish I told him we needed to pick up my señora on the camino lateral on the way to the Club de Yates. It was the first metered taxi we have been in since leaving Canada, and the fare for the two kilometres was 2700 Pesos, $5.40. Also new here is the noticeable shortage of taxis; we have been accustomed to a huge oversupply and extremely depressed and even then, negotiable prices.

The eighty litres of diesel brought the fuel gauge back up to the three-sixteenths area of the dial, where it had been when we left Huasco thirty hours of motoring earlier. I calculated we have enough fuel in the tank for about thirty-six hours of motoring, which into the Humboldt Current means about 135 miles. Valparaiso was 195 miles by sea from our anchorage in La Herradura, so that meant we needed some wind or some more fuel, preferably both.

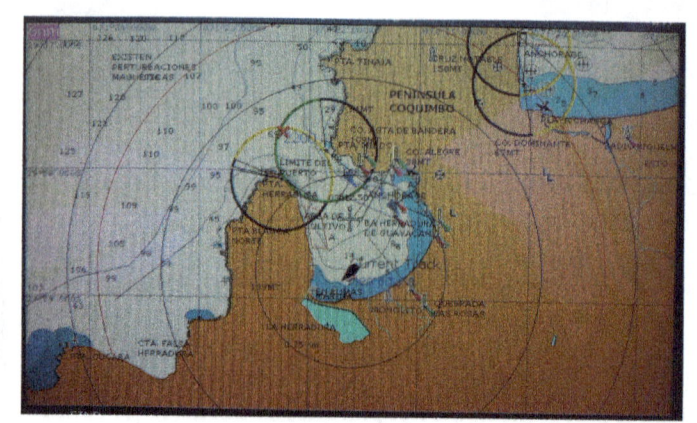

On Friday morning we hoisted the motor onto its mount, and then the dinghy on its davits, secured for sea, and at 0955 weighed and proceeded out of the bay. La Herradura is a circular harbour about a mile in diameter with a narrow, well marked entrance on its northwest and a broad band of 5 to 10 metre deep water on its south and east sides. It provided us with one of the most comfortable anchorages of our entire trip. With such a fine natural anchorage and a population of over 300,000 in the area, it amazes us there are such poor marina facilities.

We motored out of the bay and around the headlands to its south through still airs and glassy waters. These must be the conditions seen by those who first named this ocean the Pacific. Overhead sun was beginning to be felt through the low thin stratus.

As we came in VHF range of Las Tacas I radioed the marina to enquire about the availability of diesel. The woman on the other end of the radio said they had plenty; they would be ready for us when we arrive.

We organized lines and fenders, and shortly before 1300 entered the tiny marina and were directed to the small guest float. We were introduced to the yard manager, Victor who explained the float was not strong enough for us other than for a few minutes. He said fuelling was done in the haul-out slip, and I told him I wanted to survey it and Sequitur's route into it and back out. I had never before seen such a tightly-spaced marina.

The haul-out slip was lined with truck tire fenders, and my measurements showed there to be about 15 centimetres spare width for Sequitur. There is 3.5 metres of depth in the slip, but there is a shallow rock on the approach to it. Victor told me we had to pass very close to the boat on the corner as we turned in toward the slip; the rock lies 5 metres off its bows.

Victor put two yard hands aboard Sequitur to provide pilotage knowledge and to handle lines on the way into the slip. I threaded the narrow s-curve past Med-moored boat's anchors on the one side and boats on floats on the other with a metre or so to spare on each hand. Then turning the corner, threading the needle between a boat's bow and an unseen shallow rock, we slid into the slip with no room for our fenders.

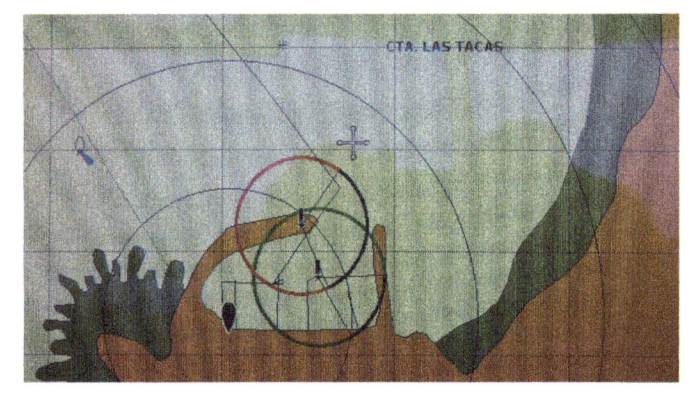

The chart is extremely accurate here; the chartplotter centred Sequitur precisely in the slip, and I had noted on the approach to the marina that the isolated rock awash is depicted in its actual position. We have observed that the

353

busier ports have accurate charting, properly gridded to GPS, while the less-used bays and anchorages have not been upgraded, and their charts are often a mile or two off and have charting features inconsistent with reality.

We took-on 721 litres of diesel, meaning that we had been down to 119 litres remaining. The marina does not take credit cards for fuel, so Victor had one of the marina crew drive me to an ATM on his motorcycle for the cash to pay the 432,600 Peso tab.

The next task was to figure-out how to back Sequitur out of the slip, turn her 17.5-metre overall length through 180 degrees in the 20 by 30 metre basin with shoals and rip-rap on the west and moored boat bows on the east and line her up to thread between the isolated shallow rock and boat bow on the corner.

Fortunately, Sequitur backs very well, and her stern walks to port with astern power. It went well, and surprisingly easily. There was sufficient room with Non Sequitur nearly brushing the shrouds of the boat astern to port for our Rocna to clear the mouth of the slip by about 2 metres. A short burst ahead with full starboard helm stopped our sternway, kicked the stern more quickly to port, gave a bit of forward motion and continued the boat's clockwise rotation. As the stern passed the mouth of the slip, a gentle touch of stern power with full port helm added to the clockwise spin, checked our forward motion and pulled our stern a metre or so into the slip. As the bows lined-up with the gap between the isolated rock and the moored boat bows, we began the sinuous threading through the narrow gaps past Med-moored boat's anchors on the one side and boats on floats on the other. We passed a quarter metre off the guest float and Victor, who had been onboard to guide us past the unseen bottom dangers, jumped off, gave us two thumps up and waved us a farewell.

It was the tightest manoeuvring I have ever had to do in my over four-and-a-half decades of boating. Normally when all goes well with mooring, berthing or anchoring, there is no one watching; the huge audiences are assembled only when everything goes wrong. As we left Las Tacas, Edi told me there were people lined along the marina, on condo balconies and in other vantage points watching and waiting for a cock-up. We were sorry to disappoint them.

We motored to southwest to clear the headlands and move offshore, and then turned south. The ocean was as glassy as I have ever seen, so glassy that the clouds reflected off its surface.

Occasionally a slight movement of air caused some minor ripples, and from time to time we saw scattered patches of ripples. Mostly though, there was not a breath of wind, so we continued motoring through the day.

Around midday we saw a slight ripple on the water, the first hints that the air was starting to move; however, the gentle rolling of the boat in the long swell gave more movement to the anemometer than did the occasional breath of breeze.

Through the early afternoon the ripple built in a breeze that nudged the needle all the way up to a shade over 2 knots. Unfortunately, this is way too little for the sails to do anything with, and even if it were sufficient, it was directly on our nose. Added to this, we were heading directly into the Humboldt Current, which from our SMG and RPM, I calculated at about 1.3 knots. We would need a wind of 10 knots or more for our tacks to give us a southing.

We must have used the wrong wind dance; the breeze disappeared and the ripples flattened back toward glassiness. As we continued motoring southward into the Current through the remainder of the day, the swell from the southwest had begun building and was approaching 2 metres.

For dinner I prepared a stir-fry with the tenderest pork we can recall having had. We had bought it from the English-speaking butcher in the supermarket in La Herradura.

Sunrise on Saturday brought a continuation of the glassy seas. When the reflection of the sun runs unbroken across miles of water, you know the ocean is calm. We continued motoring, pleased we had refuelled.

While we were motoring, the alternator was keeping the batteries at 100% and keeping us in hot water. Edi used these to do five loads of laundry on wash cycle only, and used the heat of the cockpit enclosure as our drying room. We ran the watermaker a total of 14 hours and made 875 litres of water, one and a third times the capacity of our tanks, which had been down to less than a quarter when we left La Herradura.

In the small hours of Sunday morning we were visited by a series of flights of birds, which played for a couple of hours in the slipstream off Sequitur's bows.

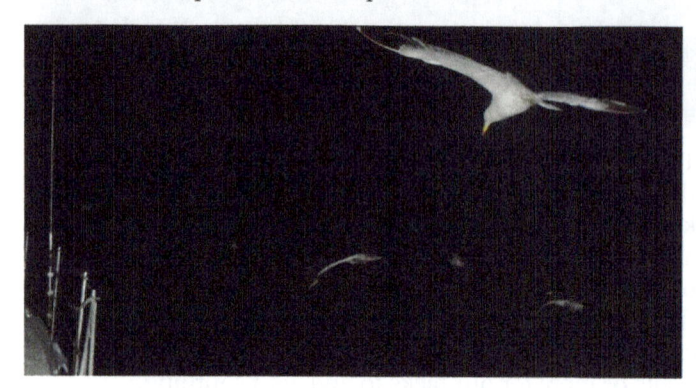

At first I thought they were boobies; they acted very much like the ones that we had fly escort for us in southern California and on our passage from Acapulco to the Galapagos. They were only ghostly images in the black of the night, illuminated only by the stars and the navigation light. For whatever reason, they all flew on our starboard side, with the navigation light giving them an eerie green tinge; none flew on the port side. Later, looking at the flash photos, I could see they were likely terns.

By sunrise a light breeze had come up from the south-southwest, and half an hour later it was blowing near 15 knots. I hauled out half of the main and the staysail and we beat into the wind and current close-hauled on the starboard tack making only a few degrees below our rhumb line to Valparaiso.

The wind built to over 20 knots and we were making better than 6 knots over the ground. An hour later the wind was back down to 6 to 8 knots and I flashed-up and we motor-sailed with the sails offering stability in the confused seas whipped-up by the hour of strong winds clashing with a southwest swell that had built to over 3 metres.

When Edi arose from her post-watch sleep, she brought breakfast up into the cockpit. We enjoyed toasted homemade breads with cream cheese and coffee as we watched Valparaiso grow on the horizon.

As we breakfasted the wind again filled, and by noon it was back up over 20 knots. We kept our sails up until we reached the lee of Punta Gruesa 2 cables before we anchored. After days of motoring in glassy seas and still airs, we finally had sailing winds just as we arrived at our destination.

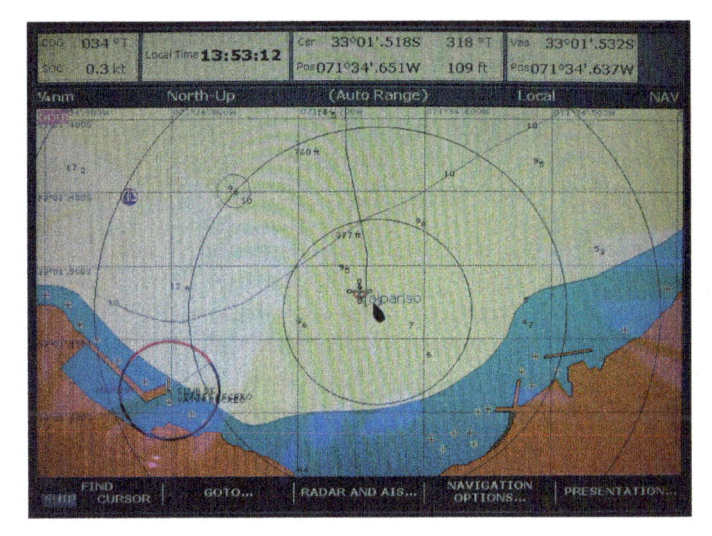

At 1342 on the 13th of February we came to 35 metres on the Rocna in 9 metres of water a cable off the rocks and just over a cable off the entrance to the Yacht Club de Chile. After I had set the anchor snubber, I reported our arrival to the Armada using the VHF, giving the beginning of March as our estimated time of departure. It was time for another break.

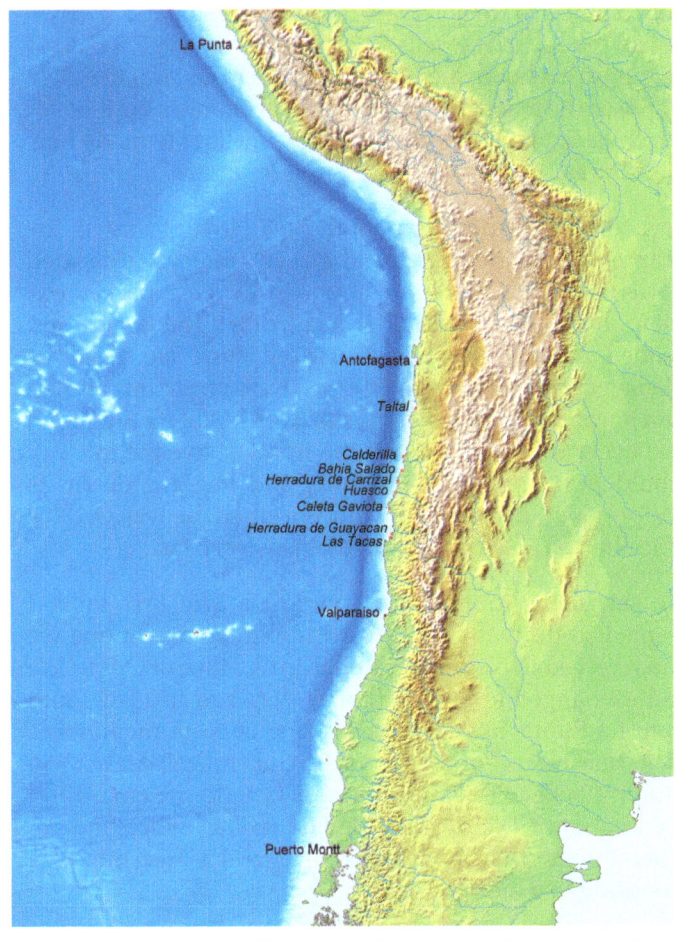

Our passage down the coast from Antofagasta against the Humboldt Current and through long calms had taken us two and a half weeks and seven anchorages. Our logs showed the passage had been 695.3 miles, that we were under way for a total of 199 hours and 19 minutes and that we had run the engine for 165 hours. Our average speed calculated to under 3 knots. Five of our seven anchorages had been made in the dark.

Midmorning on Valentine's Day, Ramon came out from the marina in the Club launch to welcome us and provide us with local information. In fluent English he informed us that the launch was available to us 24 hours per day, gave us the VHF channel monitored by the Club and said that the office and the restaurant were closed on Mondays. He then answered our questions about supermarkets and local transportation. He is a member of the club and he moors his forty-something-foot Beneteau here. He also works in the marina, but unfortunately, he was leaving the next morning for Santiago for a few days.

Shortly after Ramon left, we were visited by an agent from the Ministerio de Agricultura department of Servicio Agricola y Ganadero (SAG), who inspected our fridges and pantry and completed a form attesting to our cleanliness (at no charge, compared to Peru's S/550 fee). Chile is diligent in inspecting all traffic arriving from the north, because of the plant disease and insect infestation problems in the Peru and Bolivia border areas. Fortunately, they have the expanse of the Atacama to act as a natural buffer, but road and marine traffic is checked.

After lunch we called the launch and took our cooler bags ashore. Other than the launch operator, a few people working on boats in the yard and the gatehouse guard, the Club was abandoned. We walked out the gate and for half a kilometre or so along the bland retaining wall below the freeway.

This incredibly stupid transportation *"improvement"* cuts-off the waterfront from the rest of the city in much the same way that misguided planners had done in Seattle.

We eventually came to a rickety wooden staircase up the twenty-plus metre wall and onto the freeway and along to a buss pull-off. There we caught a bus for 330 Pesos each to the Baron stop, where we spotted the Jumbo supermarket. We replenished a few grocery items, loaded-up with fresh produce and had the butcher trim a piece of beef tenderloin and cut us four thick filet steaks.

On the way back, our bus stopped at the Recreo station, half a kilometre past the Yacht Club, and we had to lug our heavy bags over a kilometre back past the Club to the rickety stairs, and then back along beneath the ugly freeway wall the half kilometre to gatehouse. What a horrible mess the freeway has made of the waterfront! I think with great pleasure on the successful fights to prevent the same ghastly fate to Vancouver's waterfronts in the 1950s and 60s. How blessed Vancouver is to have escaped the legacy of bad planners.

When we took the launch back out to Sequitur, and after we had unloaded our purchases, I had Luis, the launch operator assist me in setting the 18 kilogram Fortress as a stern anchor to keep our bows pointed into the swell coming into the anchorage. We had spent a very rolly night with the wind and swell being at right angles to each other.

The major virtue of the Fortress is that it is light weight and easily disassembles for compact storage. Also, it is widely touted as being among the strongest holding of all anchors. Its great downfall; however, is that this is only if there is a steady pull in the same direction. With a wind or tide shift, it notoriously pops free, and often will not reset. Our employment of it as a stern anchor, opposing the pull of the Rocna, is one of its very few safe uses.

With Edi standing on Sequitur's bow pointing the lie of the bow anchor, Luis and I in the dinghy used the Fortress' rode to haul Sequitur back. Just before the tension became too much, I dropped the Fortress over the side and let the rebound on Sequitur's rode set the anchor. With its ten metres of chain and 40 metres of nylon it had plenty of scope to keep our stern set. Back onboard I tensioned the stern rode to ensure the anchor had set properly.

As the evening's breeze came up, we began rolling heavily. It appears the tide, swell and wind had conspired to pop the Fortress free, and its rode was slack. I hauled in some of the rode to reset the anchor, but as I was cooking dinner, it broke free again. Our rolling was the worse we have ever experienced in an anchorage, and after dinner two of our Stokes dinner plates slid off the counter into the sink and broke.

On Tuesday morning we called the launch to take us ashore. We wanted to explore downtown Valparaiso, to see the Victorian architecture, to ride the escalator cars up the escarpments, to visit the historic cemeteries. When after half an hour the launch had not arrived, we called again. Nearly half an hour later Luis arrived in the inflatable launch, and when we began to board, he said he could not take us ashore. He was told that we could not leave the boat. We were under arrest!

Boat arrest, house arrest, call it what you may, I wanted to know why. Luis had no answer but that the Club Manager told him to tell us we could not come ashore. He seemed as frustrated as we were. He mumbled something about authorities, police, paperwork and boat search, and he shrugged his shoulders and rolled his eyes. An hour later as I was preparing to launch the dinghy, reset the stern anchor and then head in to see the Manager, Luis came back out and said the Manager had asked him to bring me into the office with our ship's papers.

During my half-hour meeting with the Manager he continued to act surprised that I was able to show him each single document that he asked for, that all was in order and that he could find nothing to justify his having detained us. He offered no apology, he gave no explanation, he did nothing but continue to demonstrate his gross incompetence. Then he had the audacity to tell me he would charge us 7,500 Pesos per day to anchor in the open and rough roads near the Club. It appears he managed to get himself hired into a position for which he is totally unqualified. He somehow reminded me of La Punta.

Back onboard and disappointed at having wasted the heart of the day through the Manager's idiocy, we decided it was too late to head downtown. Instead, we packed our computers into out shoulder bags, called the launch and headed in to the clubhouse to use the wifi. I had asked the Manager for the code for the secure connection, and he said it was open; there was no password. When I suggested that every condo dweller on the slopes above the freeway would be using the connection, and bogging-down its performance, he was totally unconcerned; he was OK, the office had a cable connection that was very fast.

We sat in the lounge and connected. The first thing I wanted to do was check back through emails to one we had received in November from Kim & Steve of Odyle. We had exchanged a few notes after they had headed south from La Punta, and we recalled one of them mentioning their fine reception at the yacht club in Valparaiso. We couldn't believe it was at this one. I found the email, and it was about Club de Yates de Higuerillas, where among other things, they had received a week's free moorage alongside in a modern marina.

I immediately Googled Higuerillas, looked at an image of it on Google Earth and examined the chart of it in my iPad's Navionics program. We quickly finished our emails, packed-up our computers and went to the float to take the launch. On the way out to Sequitur, Luis asked if everything was now OK, and we told him that all was now absolutely perfect. We mentioned nothing else except that we were going to shift our anchorage a bit.

Back onboard, we quickly secured for sea, and in less than ten minutes we had weighted anchor and were motoring northward.

We headed a half mile or so off the coast, up past Vina del Mar and the seemingly endless development of upscale condos ranged on the slopes above the beaches to the north. Less than ninety minutes later we came to 30 metres on the Rocna in 9.5 metres of water off the entrance to the marina of the Club de Yates de Higuerillas. As I was setting the snubber, a launch came out from the marina to welcome us. They told us that the staff had now gone for the day, but that in the morning we could come inside to a float. They then advised us to use their mooring a short distance away, so we obliged, and they assisted our moving onto it.

In the evening we celebrated our escape from the Club de Yates de Chile with a butter sauté of Antofagasta scallops, Iquique camarone, oyster and portobello mushrooms, shallots and garlic, served with Peruvian rice and steamed broccoli, all of which was very nicely accompanied by a 2009 Anakena Sauvignon Blanc.

In the late morning a launch came out from the marina and put two tripulantes aboard. They told me that we would be going to a stern tie with fenders required only on the starboard side and that we needed a stern line from each quarter. To my question of anchor, they said we wouldn't be needing it.

We slipped the mooring and motored into the marina, then swung around 180 degrees and backed onto the end of a float. As we approached, the two tripulantes went to the bow and with boathooks they each picked-up a weighted line running from anchors on the marina bed. With these they hauled aboard moorings lines, which they cleated on each bow. A tripulante on the float had meanwhile taken the two stern lines I had thrown to him, and dropped their eyes over cleats there. We balanced the boat between the four lines, remaining about half a metre off the float. It was a very smooth and easy operation.

It was just past 1230, and a few days previously we had organized to meet Bev and Herb of The Lady Jay in Vina del Mar for lunch at 1330. We had been keeping a loose email connection with them since leaving La Punta, and they had asked several weeks previously whether we would be in Valparaiso mid-February; they were on a cruise ship from Rio around the Horn to Valparaiso, arriving 15 February. We went out the gate to the road and caught a blue bus into Vina del Mar. I had looked-up the address and looked at an online map of their hotel, but when we got off the bus in the centre of town, we could find no one who had heard of the hotel, nor of the streets that it is on or near. We tried to flag a taxi, but they were all full. Finally in a cell phone shop and found a clerk who told us the collectivo taxi number to catch, and where its closest stop is.

In the taxi was an English speaking man who helped us tell the driver where we wanted to go. We got out at the base of Cerro Castillo and walked up the hill, going into a hotel part way up to ask for directions. The woman had never heard of the hotel, even though, as we found out later it is only another block up the hill. It seemed to make sense to me that the website address of Avenue de la Marina it is down the hill and a block along to the river bank, so we went that way but again asking in hotels, could find no one who had heard of Hotel Little Castle. Finally in one hotel we found a woman who took us out the back entrance, through the parkade and onto a street, and there pointed us in the right direction. This led us to nowhere close and to no one who could help us.

By this time it was nearing 1500, and we were very late for our lunch meeting. We decided to walk back to a bus stop and catch a bus into Valparaiso. Then on a street corner we bumped into Bev and Herb. Bev had seen us out the window of their hotel a couple of blocks away, up on the hill, and they had come down to search for us as we had zigged and zagged through streets of the old part of town.

We wandered and talked, as we looked for a restaurant among the dozens on both sides of the main shopping street. All we saw were outlets for grease balls and other unhealthy fare, or they were dessert rooms. One of the things we continue to observe through Latin America is the overwhelming desire for deep-fried foods, greasy things and sweets. We eventually settled on a place offering pizza, and we shared a couple of the worse pizzas Edi and I recall ever having had; worse even than the niggardly thing we had eaten in Aguas Calientes when we had returned from climbing Wayna Picchu, Huchuy Picchu and Machu Picchu. The pizza notwithstanding, we shared a delightful hour and more over lunch, catching-up on each other's adventures since we had last been together in La Punta.

As Edi and I rode the bus back to Higuerillas, we reflected on the tenseness and disorientation we had each felt the past couple of days. As wonderful as it was meeting with Bev and Herb, we had felt ourselves under the duress of a schedule. This was so foreign to our experience of the past so many months that it had put us very much off centre; we had wandered aimlessly through the streets of Vina del Mar. We thought back on stories of boats having been lost because their skippers felt compelled to sail to a schedule, rather than to the prevailing conditions and a mariner's wisdom. We resolved again to try our best to keep away from hampering ourselves with a schedule.

On Thursday the 17th we took the red bus into Valparaiso, winding our way on the narrow coastal road past the stacks of condos above the beaches almost non-stop the fifteen or so kilometres from Higuerillas to Vina del Mar. We remained on board as the bus passed Valparaiso's downtown core and continued along the commercial waterfront.

The bus went to the eastern end of the city and then turned up into the hills, going through progressively poorer residential neighbourhoods. Over the crest of the hills in sites with commanding views out over the Pacific beaches to the south and west were some of the deepest slums. Finally, the bus came to its terminus in an area of depressing squalor. We were told to get off.

We quickly walked across the road and boarded the first bus in the line of those that had turned around, and almost immediately it departed. On the way back we had a view of the slums from the opposite angle. We got off several blocks after the bus had crested the hill, in an area of small stores and other businesses and of some moderate prosperity.

From there we headed down the hill toward Valparaiso's waterfront, looking for the famous old cemeteries. Along the way we asked a man walking his dog for directions to the cemeteries, and to reduce confusion we showed him our map. We hadn't been able to match any of the streets on the ground with those on the map.

He indicated a cemetery to the west and others to the east, so we concluded we were in the middle ground between the three, though we still could not place ourselves on the map. We could identify no points on which to take a fix. We continued down a road into a worsening slum, and coming around a bend, we saw two women, one with a large dog and the other with a golf club. They approached us and said we were in the wrong place. They told us to go back immediately. Here we will be beaten, robbed, stripped and left. Almost as prearranged, a bus came around the bend heading out of the slums and stopped beside us. We thanked the women and got on.

We paused in front of the headquarters of the Chilean Armada to admire its architecture.

Some of the buildings have rather seamlessly incorporated old with new.

We got off the bus in the heart of the downtown, and walked along admiring the grandeur of the old buildings. The streets are lined with glorious old buildings, many of them rather massive and most of them well preserved. They appeared to have been built as the headquarters of major banks and other prosperous enterprises. Many of them seemed to still be serving that role. There is a very obvious pride in the heritage of the old buildings, and we saw marvellous examples of the old being preserved as the city modernizes.

One of the features of Valparaiso we wanted to see is the ascensors, the sloping elevators which take people up and down the steep hillsides of the city. We found the entrance to the Reina Victoria, the oldest one, which had been built in 1883. We paid the 250 Pesos each and waited for the next car.

While the ride is nowhere near the length, the height nor the grandeur of the one up Hong Kong's Victoria Peak, it was a very interesting rise up through the buildings as the waterfront emerged and sank below us. We paused briefly to drink-in the view out over the downtown core to the commercial and naval shipyards and the cargo piers.

Through the gap between two houses we could see a cemetery two ridge-tops away. Because of the deep ravines, or gullies between the ridges there are no direct routes.

We plotted a plausible route to get us there, and that took us down a steep street into the ravine. As we walked we saw more and more graffiti on the walls. It appeared to us as if this is allowed, or even encouraged, since there is so much of it, and there seems no evidence of any attempt to remove it or to paint it over.

We were on a bit of a plateau, maybe best called a somewhat flattened ridge top. We walked down a slope to the edge of the ridge and were led around as the street bent to follow the edge. We sat on a wall enjoying the sandwiches Edi had made and looking out over the rooftops to the colourful houses on the next ridge.

We began seeing buildings with decorative paintings, and as we continued down the hill we saw that nearly every surface is decorated with varying degrees of art. Much of it is rather naïve and crude, but some of it is primitive. We saw no evidence of a budding Leonardo da Vinci or Rembrandt.

The further down we went, the more graffiti we saw. Some appeared political, but most was rather benign.

We started back up the next ridge, and paused on a set of steps which had been decorated with a mosaic of broken tiles.

The graffiti continued up the hill, offering visual relief to the rows of otherwise bland and dilapidated buildings. The further up we went, the more sparse became the wall painting, and the more run-down became the buildings.

The jumbled tangle of electrical wiring shows that many additions were made after the fact, and that underground runs are sorely needed.

The roadway became so steep that the sidewalk resorted to stairs every few metres, and the wall painting continued, even though the woodwork could have used the paint more.

We arrived at the first cemetery, which from its ridge-top situation has a commanding view out over the downtown and the harbour beyond. The guard let us through the gate and we began a slow wander past the mausoleums and crypts.

Many of these mini-temples are of impressive design and execution, and are very well cared for. Others appear to have been forgotten or ignored for many decades and they have fallen into sad states of repair.

We examined some of the tomb plaques in the mausoleum of the officers of the Armada de Chile. Among these is one for Rear Admiral Javier Molina who died in 1892, and would very likely have fought in the War of the Pacific 1879 to 1883 when Chile bested Peru and Bolivia.

One grave seemed obvious to us to belong to a florist, or at least, its occupant's descendants were florists. It was entirely covered with potted flowers, and surrounding it were planters full of well-tended plants.

In many of the mausoleums are altars, which are well-lit through stained glass windows and visible through intricate ironwork doors. Many of the structures in the cemetery would make far better homes than the shacks and squatters' huts we saw on our way.

We headed back down the hill toward the city core, passing an increasing array of wall art along the way.

We continued to be fascinated with the great numbers of wonderful old buildings from the eighteenth and nineteenth century of British and other European design. We learned later that UNESCO has declared the whole of old Valparaiso a World Heritage Site.

In many areas we saw scenes that seemed straight out of San Francisco's Haight-Ashbury or Toronto's Yorkville of the 1960s. However, in Valparaiso, the clock seems in many ways to have stood still since then.

On our way back through the centre to town we stopped at a bookstore to buy a current guide to the Chilean vineyards, and further down the street, we went into the Servicio Hidrografico y Oceanografico de la Armada de Chile (SHOC for short). We needed a chart atlas. In La Punta, the skipper of the Dutch yacht, Pacific Blue had given us his portfolio of charts for northern Chile, Puerto Montt to Arica. They were heading north and no longer needed them. We still needed the southern portfolio, from Puerto Mont to Cape Horn.

We bought a copy of the new 2009 edition of Pub 3042, Atlas Hidrografico de Chile, a tome 31cm by 44cm in size and 5cm thick, which includes all the 800 or so current Chilean nautical charts. It is printed in full colour in very high resolution that takes well to a powerful magnifying glass when required. The Atlas meets the requirement to have a portfolio of current paper charts on board.

We continued along to the Mercado to take a look. Although it was by this time late afternoon, the market was still quite active, with most of the stalls still open.

There were produce trucks still unloading fresh goods and there were many shoppers inside, though the selection of produce was obviously greatly diminished.

365

With so much produce laying around, the market was well populated with rodent control staff.

Some of these were less alert than others. We found nothing to tempt us in the market, so we continued on to the Jumbo supermarket, where we picked-up a few items, then boarded a red bus back to Higuerillas.

The Club de Yates de Higuerillas is a very active club, with owners often aboard their boats, many of the boats being taken out in the late afternoon for an evening sail, and over half the hundred or more boats being alive on the weekends. There is a peaceful and relaxing atmosphere on the floats; there are no motor yachts, and on most days we saw children playing in cockpits and on the floats.

The tots seemed intensely interested in something beneath the floats; they were peering and probing at something. We asked what had caught their interest, and they showed us a plastic bucket.

When we bent to look in, they all followed, and we saw mostly a reflection of the several faces in the water, which half filled the bucket.

A young chap reached into the bucket and somewhat timidly pulled-out by one of its long spines what appeared to be a shrimp. It is so refreshing to see the children fascinated with their natural surroundings, and not indoors glued to a TV, a computer or a game machine.

With Sequitur securely on a float in the marina, Edi and I decided to head into the vineyards to start replenishing our depleted wine cellar. On Monday morning, the 21st of February we took the blue bus into Vina del Mar and walked from midtown up and over Cerro Castillo, then down the other side and past Reloj de Flores, the floral clock toward the beaches.

Our destination was the lobby of the Sheraton Hotel, where our information told us there is a Europcar rental car office. We had attempted to book a car online, but we struck-out. A personal visit was needed. There were barricades along the street for hundreds of metres on either side of the hotel, and we had to walk over half a kilometre past the hotel and beyond Castillo Wulff before it was possible to cross the street and make our way back. As we neared the hotel entrance there was horrible wailing music and there were throngs of noisy fanatics jammed against the barricades with dozens of officious security guards all puffed-up and wired for sound. We walked boldly through the gamut of guards, smiling inside as we watched them part and then refill in our wake. Our *pretend-we-belong-here* ploy worked, and we were ushered into the hotel lobby.

At the Europcar desk Gaston greeted us in fluent English, and explained there was a music festival starting the next day, and the major TV network was airing its morning show in front of the hotel with many of the pop idols as guests. No wonder the fanatics! Thankfully the hotel lobby is insulated from street noise, and we were able to quietly reserve a car for Wednesday morning. Also, to satisfy our curiosity, we asked Gaston why we had always seen a crowd of people shooting photos of each other in front of the Reloj de Flores. He told us that it is one of very few attractions in the city.

On Tuesday we flagged-down a blue bus outside the Club de Yates, and I asked the driver if he went to the Reloj de Flores. To make sure he understood, I showed him the map and pointed to the pictorial representation of the floral clock. He confirmed that the bus would take us there.

We rode the twenty minutes or so along the coast and into the centre of Vina del Mar, but instead of getting off there as we had the previous day and walking westward the kilometre and a bit to the Sheraton, we stayed on the bus as it turned east, believing the driver's saying he would take us to Reloj de Flores across from the Sheraton. I kept waiting for the bus to make a right turn and commence its loop out to the coast, but we continued to wind up a valley into the hills to the east. I grew increasingly concerned, and after way too long, I went forward and asked the driver about our Reloj de Flores. He then said he didn't go there; we were on the wrong bus.

By this time we were several kilometres through slow traffic and up into the hills. We got off, walked across the street and caught the next bus back into the centre of Vina del Mar, got off and walked the kilometre and a bit to the Sheraton. We were an hour and a quarter late in picking-up the car, but it appeared no problem to Gaston.

We loaded our small daypack and shoulder bag into the car and drove off to the directions Gaston had given us to escape Vina del Mar and Valparaiso. The road and highway signs were great until we made our exit into Casablanca to look for our first wineries. Once we were off the main highway, we saw very few road signs, and our road map did not at all coincide with the winery maps in our Guia de Vinos de Chile. One of the very few signs we saw was directing us to the beaches southward along the coast.

367

After fruitlessly driving in several squared circles without any signs nor any indication of the existence of a wine industry, we gave-up on the Casablanca wine region and decided to head into the Maipo Valley. It was long past noon when we arrived in Melipilla, and we decided to have lunch there. The absolute lack of restaurants, or our inability to spot any, caused us to divert into the shaded underground parking lot of a large supermarket. While the sun roasted in the upper 30s outside, we relaxed in the cool cross-breeze with our fresh rolls, ham, cheese and a tregnum of sparkling water from supermarket upstairs.

The first concentration of vineyards and wineries eastward out of Melipilla is in the area called Isla de Maipo, so off we went. I had earmarked Terrapaca as one winery to visit, and we easily found it following a huge roadside tourist map and the winery's own ample signs. We arrived at the gate to be told by the guard that the winery was not receiving visitors today. Even after I had explained we had come all the way from Canada, he would not relent.

We drove off in search of other area wineries, including Santa Ema and Baron Philippe de Rothschild. We drove up and back many roads, but saw no more winery signs, nor could we find anyone to ask directions. On one road, we drove about eight kilometres of winding blacktop with no intersections or side roads, until it abruptly ended at a private gate. We retraced our route back the eight kilometres to its first intersection and there saw no evidence of a Sin Salida sign; no mention of it being a cul-de-sac, a dead end.

It was by this time late afternoon, and even had we found a winery, by then it would most likely have been closed for the day. We saw a sign indicating a way to Ruta 5 Sur, the Pan-American Highway, and we gave-up on the Maipo wine region. We worked our way across a network of small roads to Route 5 and headed south on it. The superb condition of the roadway and its mostly 120 kilometre per hour speed limits quickly took us past the exits to the Cachapoal Valley, the northern part of the Rapel wine region, and we continued on to San Fernando, where we exited and headed to Santa Cruz. We had decided that if we were going to keep striking-out, we may as well do it in the finest of the Chilean wine regions, the Rapel's Colchagua Valley.

We drove into the small city of Santa Cruz shortly before 1900 and stopped in the front of the Hotel Santa Cruz on Plaza de Armas and went in to see if we could have a room for the night. My online search had found the hotel highly recommended and I had decided the quoted rates of US$120 to $150, CA$117 to $146 worth the splurge, but I had been unable to book online. When at the front desk we found that the least expensive room they had available was 175,000 Pesos or about CA$340, we decided to ask the clerk for alternatives.

She told us of Hotel Casa de Campo, and we had remembered seeing it on the road shortly before the outskirts of Santa Cruz. She phoned the hotel to confirm they had a room for us, we thanked her, and back we went.

We were greeted warmly by the owner in a luxuriously rustic lobby, and he insisted we look at the room before committing.

We were shown to a very tastefully and comfortably appointed room with a king-size bed, cathedral ceiling and a loft. There was a huge walk-in shower in the ultramodern bathroom and the entire setting had a marvellous tranquillity about it.

A door led onto a broad, deep balcony overlooking a greensward and beyond it to vineyards, corn fields and gently rolling mountains. It was serene, we were delighted. We checked-in and unwound from our day's rather frustrating travels. The room including breakfast was 72,000 Pesos.

We asked the proprietor for his recommendation of a restaurant in the area with a great wine list and good food. He told us of El Candil, on the left across the bridge on the road to Lolol. We found the sign to Lolol, crossed the bridge and then spent a frustrating half hour and more on a maze of one-way streets, all of which seemed to go the wrong way. We decided to look for other restaurants, but noted we hadn't seen anything in our wanderings through Santa Cruz. Edi went into a pharmacy and asked, and came out as uninformed as before. We finally saw an appropriate-looking restaurant, but when we stopped to check it out, it was closed.

I suggested to Edi that Hotel Santa Cruz must have a good restaurant, so we went for a look. The menu looked good and I was delighted with the wine list. It is organized by producer, and is very well priced. We ordered a bottle of 2005 Hacienda Araucano Cabernet Sauvignon Reserva. For 9,000 Pesos (CA$17.50), it drank like a $75 bottle in a restaurant back home, and it went splendidly with our thick beef tenderloin.

I had ordered it because of its connection to the Lurton family of Bordeaux, which I knew very well from my years as a wine importer. They own several prominent chateaux making splendid wine, and had shown me superb hospitality on several of my trips to Bordeaux.

After a restful sleep in Casa de Campo's luxurious bed, we had a huge and superb breakfast in the dining room. Then we went off in search of Hacienda Araucano, which our Guia showed to be in Lolol. The computer savvy will wonder if this place is for real, or is merely for laughs, lol.

What isn't for laughs; though, is the evidence still of the huge destruction from the previous year's earthquake. We were told over 1600 of the houses in the commune were damaged, a very large percentage of them destroyed. As we drove through we saw the cleanup still in progress a year later.

The way to Araucano is well-marked, and we easily found the winery nestled in the foot of a ridge at the edge of its vineyards at the end of a few kilometres of gravel road.

The door to the winery was open, but we could see no reception office or tasting room, only a working winery with crates of white grapes being unloaded and dumped into the crusher/de-stemmer. It appeared that the harvest had begun. We watched for a while, and then walked around the exterior of the building looking for an entrance for visitors. We saw none and when we arrived back at the working entrance, we walked in and through the winery to a likely looking staircase on the back wall.

We were greeted at the small tasting bar, just outside the offices at the top of the stairs. I explained I knew personally the Lurton family in France, and had stayed at their Chateau Bonnet in Entre-Deux-Mers and toured and tasted at their several chateaux in Bordeaux. We wanted to taste and select some wines to add to our boat's cellar. She said that, unfortunately Francois Lurton had just left for the family's winery in Argentina's Mendoza, and that Gabriela Escobar, the person in charge of tastings and visitors was in an important meeting. Realizing however our seriousness and my family connection, she phoned Gabriela, explained the situation and passed the phone to me. She said she was tied-up until 1600, when she could see us. We talked further and she agreed she would receive us for a tasting at 1500.

It was just shy 1130, so we had some time to fill. We drove back toward Santa Cruz a few kilometres and turned in at the road to Vina Santa Cruz, which we had seen earlier on our way past. It is one of only two wineries in the small Lolol Valley, which has a microclimate with cooling marine influences, morning mists and a large daily temperature range, all superbly suited to bringing-out intense varietal characteristics in the grapes.

We were received by a rather smarmy and obsequious fellow who fawned over us with his obviously memorized and well-practiced lines, jokes and animations. The Santa Cruz winery is built on the California model of attracting tourists, with reception and tasting rooms capable of swallowing several bus loads at a bite. The sales room is filled with a broad selection of wine-related trinkets and winery-branded goods.

They have a funicular running up to the peak next to the winery, and on the peak are three indigenous *"villages"*, representing the three most important ethnicities of Chile: the Mapuche and the Aymara of the mainland and the Rapa Nui of Easter Island. I mentioned to our host that this is only the second winery cable car I had seen, and he said there are only three in the world, but he could not name them. I told him that I had several times been up the cable-car to Sterling in Napa, but that I did not know the third. Their price is 20,000 Pesos per person for tour, tasting and cable car ride to the native cultural dioramas.

The winery has 140 hectares of vineyards, 20 hectares of which are on terraced slopes. Carménère makes-up 41% of their plantation, Cabernet Sauvignon 33%, Syrah 19% and Merlot 14%. The remainder are in Malbec and Petit Verdot. Santa Cruz is in the enviable position of being able to select only the finest of their harvest and sell the remainder of the grapes. Then from the wines made with grapes that they keep, they select only the finest to put under their own label, selling the lesser quality to other wineries.

They mature their wines in French oak and it was fun to see again the familiar tonnelerie names branded into the butt ends. Santa Cruz makes three ranges of quality: Reserva and Gran Reserva, both of which they bottle under the Chaman label, and their Edicion Limitada, TuPu. These wines spend two years in new oak.

After he realized he could not sell us a tour or tasting, nor a T-shirt or hat, he shushed his lips and quietly snuck us down a flight of stairs to a small tasting set-up. He poured us a range of wines, and from our tasting, we bought a case of the 2007 Syrah Gran Reserva and two bottles of the 2007 TuPu, which is their top-end blend of Carménère, Cabernet Sauvignon, Malbec and Syrah.

With more time in hand before our rendezvous at Araucano, we drove back through the city of Santa Cruz and took the road toward Apalta. I wanted to see Casa Lapostolle, the property of the French company that, among other things, owns Grand Marnier. They had shown me superb hospitality in Paris in 1989, when I had organized a small-group wine and food tour of the Champagne, Alsace, Burgundy and Paris. They took the sixteen of us to a Michelin-starred restaurant for dinner and then to the Crazy Horse for a show and a bottle of Veuve Clicquot per couple.

The winery is carved six stories high into the side of a hill, and is an architectural masterpiece, though this is visible only from the inside. On the slopes and plain beneath the winery are their *"organic and biodynamic"* vineyards. The price for a tour and tasting is 20,000 Pesos per person, but since we had neither the time for the tour nor the desire to spend near $80 to see yet another tank room and barrel cellar, no matter the grandeur of the setting, we declined.

The person who received us in the small office appeared to be more a bean counter than an oenophile, and anyone who may have been sympathetic to our case was elsewhere and busy preparing for harvest. No matter my story, no matter our desire to buy wine, the clerk could not be induced to give us a tasting without the fees.

Knowing the wonderful reputation for quality that their wines enjoy, I asked for a half case of the Casa 2008 Cabernet Sauvignon and a half of the Casa 2008 Carmenere. Casa is their bottom-of-the-line label, and had we been allowed to taste, we would most likely have bought more, and probably up-label.

We still had time in hand, so we drove onward a bit further to the Montes winery. This winery's bottles consistently place among the top ten Chilean wines in tastings, and they have a well-deserved international following.

We were received by a young man rather fluent in English, and he offered us a fine range of wines to taste. We were impressed with the quality of the 2010 Limited Selection Leyda Vineyard Sauvignon Blanc. It was the first example of that grape in a long while in which we had found the typical Sancerre gooseberry and hints of cat pee characteristics with a tropical finish. We were tired of the grapefruit and hard acid we were finding in so many Chilean Sauvignon Blancs. At only $8.25 the bottle, we asked for two cases.

While the chap was getting the wine from the cellar for us, we did a short self-tour of the barrel cellar. Softly playing in the background was a marvellous recording of Gregorian chants giving the place a mystical atmosphere, which we will fondly remember with every bottle of Montes.

We drove back through Santa Cruz to Lolol and back in the dusty road to Hacienda Araucano. We were warmly received by Gabriela and we sat with her at a tasting bar on the loft overlooking the winery floor, where the Sauvignon Blanc was being crushed and de-stemmed and pumped into fermenting tanks. Gabriela told us the harvest had begun that morning and this was the first of their Sauvignon Blanc from Casablanca.

She told us the reason she couldn't receive us earlier was that she was in meetings arranging the reception of a large group of their importing agents from around the world the next week, during the annual Harvest Festival. She was with the catering chef, tasting him the wines so he could cook to them.

We were poured a wonderful range of wines, including library wine that she had earlier opened for the chef. These were long-since sold out, so we concentrated on the current offerings. We were most impressed with the 2008 Humo Blanco Pinot Noir.

I have had a great love affair with Pinot Noir since I first tasted it in a barrel sample of 1966 Clos de la Roche in Morey-St-Denis while travelling in the Burgundy in 1967. The grape is extremely fickle, and while it often makes a good wine, it rarely reaches the sublime quality I was first introduced to so many years ago.

I am not saying that the 2008 Humo Blanco Pinot Noir was a match for the Clos de la Roche, but it does have a wonderful Burgundian quality so rarely found outside that region. The morning mists of the Lolol Valley and the cooling effect from the Pacific less than 40 kilometres away, plus the intense heat and sun during the middle parts of the day provide an environment that seems to favour the Hacienda's Pinot Noir. The complexity of the deep, post-glacial alluvial soils add to the mix. We bought two cases of it.

We were also very impressed by the 2009 Humo Blanco Sauvignon Blanc, and its marvellous Sancerre qualities induced us to buy a case of it. Our tasting with Gabriela at

Hacienda Araucano wonderfully capped-off our experiences in the Chilean wine country. We had begun with a series of bumbles and had finished on a marvellously high note.

We drove back toward Sequitur, using signs to the coastal city of San Antonio as our guide through the maze of roads, but once in San Antonio, we could find no signs at all to Valparaiso, a city with a population of over 300,000 only 70 or so kilometres further northward along the coast. Eventually I remembered my driving in France in the 60s and 70s, in the days when all roads from a town led to Paris, and to nowhere else. We turned east to follow the signs to Santiago, and we were shortly rewarded with signs to a freeway back north-westward to Valparaiso.

We stopped at the supermarkets on the hill of Con Con, above Higuerillas and loaded-up with groceries and fresh produce. We arrived back onboard with a car full of booty at 2130.

With Sequitur's fridges, freezers, lockers and pantry again filled to capacity, we were ready to continue. So before heading into Vina del Mar to return the car on Thursday morning, I walked over to the marina office to with the ship's papers to commence the process of getting a zarpe for our departure on Friday morning.

The Yacht Club has been granted the privilege by the Armada to apply online for departure papers for its members and guests. This wonderful convenience meant we didn't have to go all the way into Valparaiso to the Capitan de Puerto and then wait there for the processing. The woman in the office told me to come back at 1700; the zarpe would be ready then.

After we had returned the car, Edi and I spent the remainder of the day preparing Sequitur for sea and baking. Edi made a couple loaves of banana bread and I made a quiche to put in the fridge for snacks and meals along the way. We were leaving on a 370 nautical mile passage offshore to Robinson Crusoe Island, and depending on the winds and currents, we could expect to be at sea for three to four days.

I went back over to the marina office at 1700 to find that the zarpe was not yet ready; the Armada had had a question, and we had been in town returning the car, and unavailable to be found to answer it. They wanted to know whether Sequitur was a coastal boat or an offshore one. I told her offshore, she relayed it. The Armada replied that the zarpe would be issued mañana.

20. Tsunamis Past and Present

We received our zarpe on Friday at 1115, and at 1145 we slipped from the float under a cloudless sky with a light breeze from the west-southwest. Our course to Robinson Crusoe was 263 degrees, so after we had cleared the marina and the headland, we motored into the breeze.

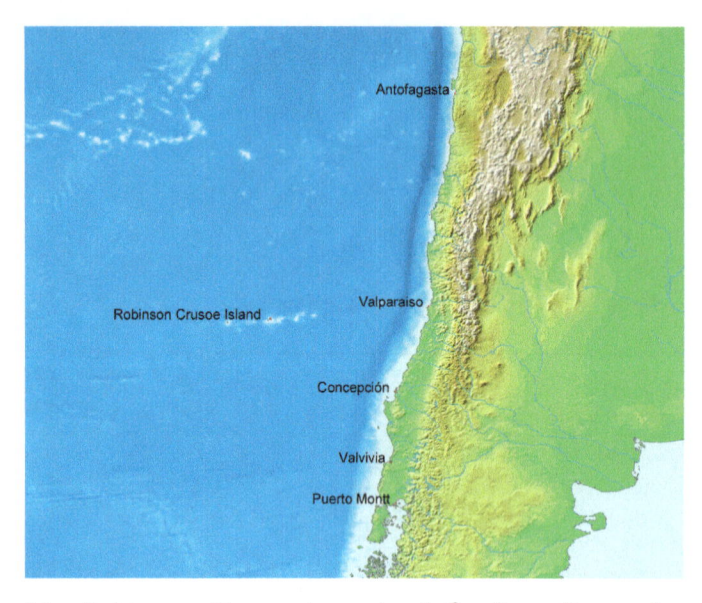

Isla Robinson Crusoe is part of the Juan Fernandez Archipelago, which was discovered in 1574 by Portuguese explored Juan Fernandez. He named the island Mas a Tierra, meaning closer to land, and named the furthest island Masafuera, meaning further away. Mas a Tierra gained fame through Alexander Selkirk, a Scottish mariner who, after a dispute with his captain, asked to be put ashore there in 1704. He spent four years and four months marooned there, and after his return to Scotland, he became somewhat of a celebrity. Daniel Defoe, inspired by his adventures and stories of survival, wrote the novel Robinson Crusoe. As a tourism move by the Chilean government in 1966, Mas a Tierra was renamed Isla Robinson Crusoe, and the furthest island, Masafuera was renamed Isla Alejandro Selkirk.

Once we had reported our departure to the Armada, and reached cleaner water, we flashed-up the watermaker. The needle on our tank gauge was bouncing on empty. The water on the floats was non-potable, and even had it been potable, we didn't want to add any to our tanks unless absolutely necessary. They are now completely chlorine-free, and we want to keep them that way.

The breeze remained light through the afternoon, and then in the early evening it began to back. At 1845, there was just sufficient breeze from the southwest to justify hauling-out the sails, so I shutdown the watermaker and the engine and we ghosted along at just over 3 knots in rather flat seas on a long 3 metre swell. By 2100 the breeze had decreased to the 3 or 4 knot range, so I flashed-up and we motor-sailed, making 5 to 5.5 knots through the night

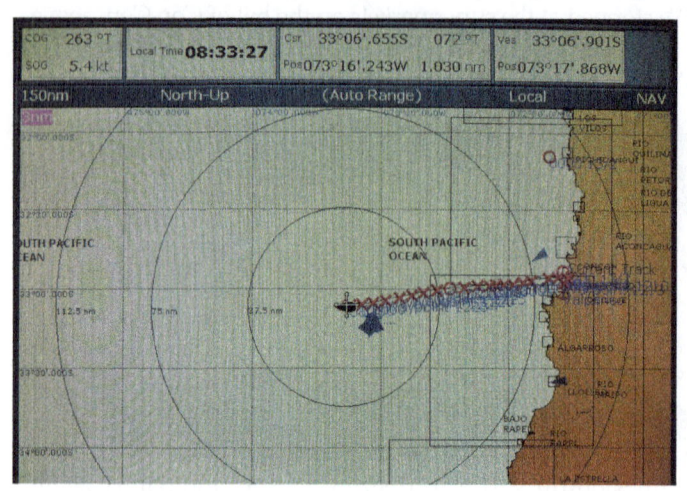

When I turned-over the watch to Edi at 0100, there was a group of AIS icons gathering about 25 miles away, fine on our port bow. At 0600 when I again took over the watch, they were about 6 miles south, and still in a tight knot. We could see their lights from time to time when both we and they simultaneously rose on swells. We assumed they were fishing boats. We continue to be delighted with our AIS transponder; we can often see ships out to 100 miles, and better yet, the ships can see us.

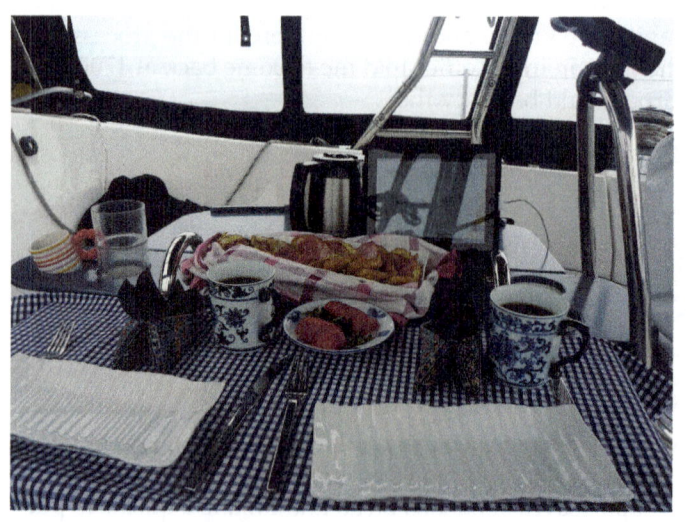

When Edi got up from her post-watch sleep, she prepared a wonderful breakfast of pain perdu à jambon with sliced roma tomatoes and chopped fresh basil and a pot of hot Peruvian coffee.

I flashed-up the watermaker and resumed filing the tanks as we continued motoring through still airs and glassy seas. With the engine running and heating the water we were making, Edi ran three loads of laundry through the machine.

At 1720 we hauled-out the main and jib and set off on the port tack in a 6 to 8 knot south-southwest breeze, making just above 3.5 knots. By 1900 with a strengthened breeze, I hauled-out the staysail and we were began making hourly runs in the 5-knot range. When the sun set rather ingloriously a couple of hours later, we were still making above 5 knots.

We continued this comfortable sail through the night, and when Edi arose from her post-watch sleep, she prepared a wonderful brunch of quesadillas stuffed with grated butter cheese, diced pepperoni, avocado, black olives and green peppers, accompanied by fresh Peruvian coffee.

By the late afternoon the wind had subsided to the 6 to 8 knot range from the southwest, and we flashed-up and motor-sailed through the sunset and into the night. At 2200 the wind had again picked-up to above 10 knots, and I shutdown the engine and adjusted the sails. We sailed through the remainder of my watch and into Edi's, until at 0400, when the winds nearly died, she awoke me so that I could harden the sails and set-up for motorsailing again.

We continued to motor-sail in light airs into the daylight, and in the midmorning we enjoyed a wonderful breakfast of toasted fresh bagels and other breads with cream cheese and hot Peruvian coffee. As we motor-sailed, we ran the watermaker.

We picked-up our landfall on Isla Robinson Crusoe shortly past noon, and we watched the island grow out of the sea ahead of us as we enjoyed freshly made beef empanadas with a delicious avocado and tomato salsa, washed down with hot rooibos tea.

As the island grew, the winds filled, and at 1630, with our water tanks full again, we shutdown the watermaker and engine and sailed close-hauled on the starboard tack in the 8 to 10 knot breeze. The land effect as we approached the island brought variable winds up to 20 knots from around the compass, so at 1810 we hauled in the sails and motored the last mile or so to the anchorage.

At 1858 on 28 February we came to 33 metres on the Rocna in 11 metres of water in Bahia Cumberland, Isla Robinson Crusoe. We reported our arrival to the Armada and relaxed.

We enjoyed a wonderful dinner of Paraguayan beef tenderloin with béarnaise sauce with Canadian gnocchi in a portobello and oyster mushroom and shallot cream sauce, grilled zucchini rounds and roma tomatoes with fresh basil. This was superbly accompanied by a bottle of Hacienda Araucano Humo Blanco Pinot Noir 2008. It was an absolutely splendid way to celebrate our arrival at this island we had both long dreamed of visiting.

The next morning we sat enjoying breakfast in the cockpit and drinking-in the scene ashore. The island is small, only 22 kilometres long by 7 kilometres wide, and it is extremely rugged, with steep-sided volcanic peaks and ridges reaching to 915 metres in elevation.

The water is a pale blue-green colour and it is wonderfully clear. We could see the bottom 11 metres down, and watch the fish swimming around Sequitur's hull and anchor rode.

We had arrived one year and one day after the devastating tsunami from the Bahia Concepción earthquake had hit the island. The scene from Sequitur's cockpit looked normal enough; if we hadn't been aware of the destruction ashore, we would have thought nothing amiss.

We launched Non Sequitur and mounted the motor on its transom with such ease it surprised us. The swivelling motor mount we designed and had fabricated in La Punta has been a wonderful device. The motor started with the first pull, and we headed in to the pier.

Securing there, we were amazed at the clarity of the water, which allowed us to see hundreds of fish swimming in and out of the shadows among pilings beneath the pier. We reflected that this was by far the clearest water we had seen in well over a year.

We walked up the pier into a scene of frenzied construction. There were piles of building material, there were scattered shipping containers and there was new framing in progress. The foreshore was a beehive of activity.

It appeared that the entire town had turned-out to work on the new construction. There were as many women as men in hardhats, most of whom (both men and women) looked very much out of place in this nature of work. It was certainly was a community effort.

An open fishing boat was offloading cleaned fish to a wheelbarrow on the pier. These were a large, dense-fleshed fish that looked somewhat like tuna, but when we enquired their name, we were told there were not tuna, but some other variety whose name eluded us.

There was an all-woman crew working at the landscaping of a large park at the foot of the pier.

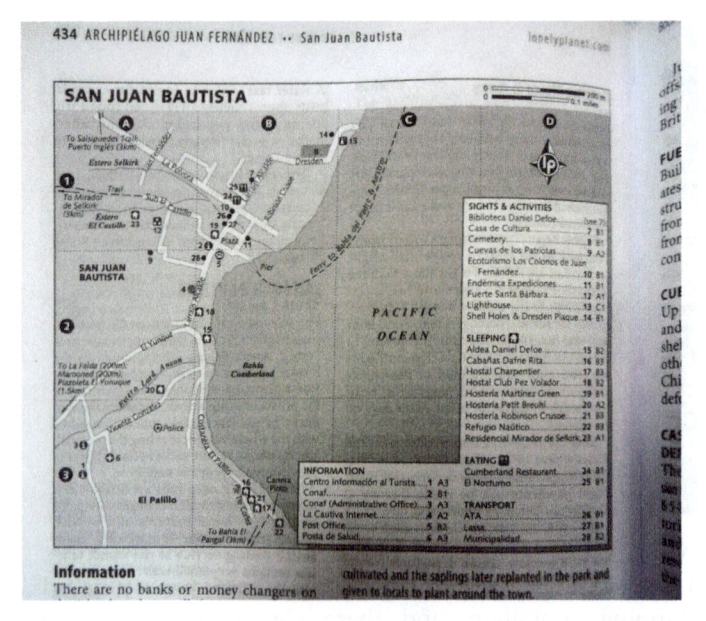

The map in our two-year-old Lonely Planet guidebook showed a dozen businesses along Larrain Alcalde, the main street in the Island's only town, San Juan Bautista. Among these were restaurants, accommodations, tour companies and other services for the tourists. What we saw when we arrived ashore was that the entire central business area had been destroyed and swept away by the tsunami.

The new park is in the location of the former downtown. It appears, and that the townspeople had decided to replace it with the park.

When we finally got an internet connection over a week later, I looked at Google Earth to see if its image predated the tsunami. It did, it was from August 2007, a year and a half before the inundation. We were amazed at the number of buildings there once were.

From what we saw, all the buildings along the waterfront were destroyed. The southwestern shoreline of Bahia Cumberland is a steep hillside, and here the second or third building away from the water was above the tsunami's reach. However, the main commercial centre was on the relatively flat land to the west and north of the pier,. Everything there was swept away.

We headed up through the town to the new post office. Correos de Chile had set-up a shipping container on a foundation slab vacated by the former building during the tsunami. Throughout the town we saw so many similar foundations; they were all that remained of the former buildings.

We climbed the gentle slope away from the water through what used to be downtown, and then up the steeper slope to the edge of the tsunami damage. A satellite dish about 15 metres above sea level was twisted and dented and still muddy from the devastating inundation.

We continued our exploration of the remains of the town, and as we crossed La Polvora, we saw a damaged, but re-erected tsunami evacuation route sign. From a SAG officer, we heard that there were seventeen deaths from the tsunami, and from another source, we read that there were seven killed and eleven missing.

Along the waterfront to the north of the pier, we walked through a nearly finished malecon with children's playground equipment and a wide assortment of adult exercise apparatus.

Further up the hill, in the base of an escarpment, we came to a group of dank caves. These were shelter for forty-two patriots exiled by the Spanish for four years after the 1814 Battle of Rancagua, during the fight for Chilean independence. The caves, Las Cuevas de Los Patriotas are now listed as a UNESCO World Heritage Site.

The gym equipment appeared to have just arrived; it was laying about still in its shipping wrap next to freshly poured mounting pads. To me this waterfront site is a much more pleasant placement for these exercise machines than in a stagnant room of a commercial gym.

We continued along through the cemetery, which was obviously much disrupted by the tsunami. Tombstones were askew, broken and scattered about. It will take a long time and much research to restore markers to their proper place.

On the point beyond the cemetery we saw the base of the former navigation light. Its foundation was canted at a twenty-odd degree angle, and the light tower had been removed from the base. Off the point were a few dozen Juan Fernando fur seals doing headstands and other equally humorous poses in the shallows. Nearby was the new light, still with the concrete forms in place.

In the volcanic rock of the cliffs adjacent to the light is a 15 to 20 centimetre diameter hole with a bullet lodged deep inside.

The German cruiser Dresden was the only survivor of the rout of Admiral von Spee's German Squadron by the Admiral Sturdee's British Squadron in the Battle of the Falkland Islands 8 December 1914. She had escaped to the southwest. HMS Kent and HMS Glasgow gave chase around Cape Horn and a long search ensued.

Finally on 14 March 1915, Dresden was found at anchor in Cumberland Bay and was engaged. Some of the British rounds which missed her lodged into the cliffs. Dresden was badly hit and she soon ran up a white flag. There are conflicting reports: some say Dresden sunk from the damage, others report the Germans fearing the capture of Dresden, scuttled their ship. There are many Germans buried in the nearby cemetery, though with the tsunami damage, we could find no German names.

We walked back to the pier and out toward its end. Along the way we passed a group on horseback heading off into the interior. Tourism activities here include trail rides and hiking on a network of trails in the mountains, plus snorkeling and scuba diving in pristine waters along the coast. Among the diving sites, of course, is the wreckage of Dresden in 60 metres of water. The site is also occasionally used by the Chilean Armada for diver training.

On 24 February 2006, Chilean and German divers found and recovered Dresden's bell. Chile presented the bell to the Museum of the German Armed Forces, Militärhistorisches Museum der Bundeswehr at Dresden in November 2008, one hundred years after the commissioning of the cruiser.

The owner of the boat told me he had some that he could sell us. I asked how much? He asked how many? I said four. He said 8,000 Pesos each. I asked how big? He said like so, placing his hands about 35 centimetres apart. I said two. He said 8,000 Pesos each. I said OK.

When they had finished unloading the fish, I got into his boat with his crewman and we motored out to an area full of small wooden crates near completely awash in the water. I then realized the nature of all the crates we had previously seen.

When we arrived at the end of the pier, there was an open fishing boat alongside, next to the set of stairs where our dinghy was moored. We watched as the crew hauled large fish, appearing to be 4 to 6 kilos each, from beneath the grates in the bottom of the boat. These were put into a large fibreglass bag, hung on a scale, the weight noted and the contents lugged up the stairs and dumped into the back of a pickup truck. There were easily more than a hundred fish offloaded from the boat.

At a pause in the action, I asked one of the fishermen whether they had any langosta. The Juan Fernandez spiny lobster is a delicacy in the finest restaurants of Paris, Madrid and Rome, but it has become a rather scarce item. Its harvest is now restricted to catching from small wooden boats without using nets.

He selected one of the crates, manoeuvred alongside it and he and his crewman struggled it up onto the gunwale. Between the slats I saw dozens of langosta in a writhing mass of legs and spiny feelers, many of which poked through the cracks.

They balanced the crate on the gunwale and a thwart and used a rusty claw hammer to pull double-headed nails to free a part of the lid. The skipper asked me to choose my two, but not being a spiny lobster expert, I asked him to pick what he thought were the two best. He seemed to take this as a compliment, and he dug around and carefully selected what I could easily see were the two largest in the crate.

Back aboard, I transferred the langosta into our largest pot, a little over 30cm in diameter and 40cm deep. Even with their tails tightly curled, it was a very tight squeeze to get them both in, and they both let me know that wanted very much to get out. I filled the pot with seawater and refreshed it a few times through the late afternoon and early evening.

They nailed the lid back on, re-floated the crate at its buoy and we headed back in to the pier with our catch in a plastic crate.

This is the first time I had been lobster fishing in over half a century. Among my childhood homes was Shediac, New Brunswick the self-named *"Lobster Capital of the World"*, and on a few occasions I had gone out on Shediac Bay to help pull traps.

The Juan Fernandez lobster is actually a very large crayfish, and not related to the Atlantic lobster. It has the reputation of being very succulent, almost sweet, and with a delicate texture. We put our catch into a small used carton from a stack on the pier, paid the skipper 16,000 Pesos, about $32, and we headed back out to Sequitur.

I had to tie the lid down to prevent our $32 from walking away. Each time I refreshed the water, our dinner guests were sprightly, and when it came time to heat the water in the pot, I transferred them back into the cardboard carton. They danced around in it celebrating their more spacious quarters.

The fishermen had told me to prepare them by boiling seawater for twenty minutes, so by the time the langosta were done, so were the butter-sweated red, yellow, orange and green peppers, the Peruvian rice, the sliced roma tomatoes with chopped fresh basil and the dish of melted butter. The langosta were so large that one was almost too much for the two of us, so I shelled one, and we enjoyed a splendid dinner accompanied by a superb 2010 Montes Leyda Vineyard Sauvignon Blanc. We deemed this to be one of the two or three finest meals of our entire cruise thus far.

The second langosta was shelled and put in the fridge, to be served the next evening warmed in an oyster mushroom, shallot, garlic and Sauvignon Blanc cream sauce over a bed of rice and complemented by more of the 2010 Montes Leyda Vineyard Sauvignon Blanc.

The skies quickly cleared, and in the late morning I took Non Sequitur ashore to find the offices of the Armada. Because of the near-complete destruction of the infrastructure and curtailing of most businesses, there were still no public internet services available on the island. We had decided to head back over to the continent, and for that we needed a zarpe from the Armada. Fortunately, the offices of the Capitan de Puerto were on a hilltop and they had been above the reach of the Tsunami.

I hadn't been able to get a grib on the SSB, and with no internet we had no current weather maps. I asked for a forecast and was shown a report indicating no disturbances and a steady 15 to 20 knot southerly wind for the following two days. This was very favourable for our crossing; our destination was Bahia Conception, the entrance to which lay on a bearing of 122°, and we could expect a three-day passage in comfortable winds broad on the starboard bow.

It rained overnight, and then well into the morning as we were enjoying breakfast, the sun began breaking through and creating a very low rainbow over the town of San Juan Bautista. It appeared that the entire townsite was the end of the rainbow. I managed somehow to catch a shot of it with our three pendants all flying clear: the False Creek Yacht Club, the Bluewater Cruising Association and the Seven Seas Cruising Association.

I received a zarpe for 1000 the following morning, Thursday the 3rd of March. On the way back through the former town centre, I passed a pair of new fibreglass boats named Robinson and Crusoe, which were sitting on a foundation slab. I assumed that they were replacements for ones destroyed.

We spent the remainder of the day relaxing and preparing for the three-day sail. Among other things, Edi baked three more loaves of bread, a raisin, a whole wheat and a cracked wheat. Our fridges and freezers were still well-stocked from Higuerillas, and we needed nothing from ashore. Even if we had, the two small tiendas we saw were both closed, and we assumed that the proprietors were likely among the work parties we had seen along the waterfront.

On Thursday morning as we were preparing to depart, we watched an Armada supply ship nudge its bow up to the beach, open its bow doors and begin discharging bundles and crates onto the foreshore. The cleanup from the tsunami had taken a very long time, and it appears that the reconstruction phase was now in full swing. It will be interesting to watch the progress over the next while as the little town rebounds from the disaster.

At 1025 we weighed and proceeded under power out of Bahia Cumberland, and continued to motor to clear the turbulent winds generated by the sun on the steep cliffs. The winds seemingly came from every point of the compass as we headed eastward to clear Punta Pescadores, where we could bend our course to the southeast for the crossing.

We were about two cables off the cliffs and beyond the 100 metre soundings when at very close range, dead ahead we spotted a pair of floats with a line between them. We could almost hear the tangling of the propeller. I quickly shifted to neutral and turned the helm hard a-port. The buoys slid down the starboard side.

We then spotted several other buoys nearby with lines streaming from them. I gingerly reengaged the transmission and we tiptoed out of the mine field.

Once we had cleared the island a few miles, we launched a message in a bottle, to see where, when and if it is retrieved and recognized. The note asked the finder to email details, but the chances of our receiving any information from it are infinitesimal.

At 1115 we hauled-out the staysail and half the main and headed off to the east on the starboard tack in southeast winds of 15 to 18 knots. The seas were confused heaps of water 2 and 3 metres high, which I assumed were from the wind waves meeting at right angles with the 3 metre southwest swell.

The confused seas continued into the afternoon, with short, steep chop up to 3 metres in height on top of the 3 metre swells.

Thankfully, the pressure of the 15 to 18 knot wind on the sails remained consistent and kept us from rolling around.

However, we slammed into many seas during the afternoon and on two occasions took a depth of green water over the bows, a rare occurrence in Sequitur. It was not comfortable going.

Through the early evening the wind built to the 25 to 30 knot range and continued an oscillating veering and backing through 60 and more degrees. I had set the autopilot to steer a wind angle, and our sinuous course somehow kept us close to our rhumb line for Bahia Concepción. Spindrift was blowing off the crests of the waves as we continued to pound into increasingly confused water and winds.

We were delighted with the cockpit enclosure, which allowed us to stay dry and warm with all the wild water flying around in the near gale conditions. To maintain our warmth we were bundled-up in three layers of fleece, and we were wearing our toques for the first time in a long while.

Toward sunset, the winds abated to a bit above 20 knots and the blown spume ceased. We continued to pound into the very short seas confused by the cross swell. With this windward pounding into the seas our progress was slowed, and our position at sunset showed that we had been moving along at just short of 5 knots. Somehow we had managed to remain very close to our rhumb line.

Overnight, the winds continued in the 20 to 25 knot area, and their direction ranged from easterly through southwesterly. I had never before seen such a rapid and repeated veering and backing in winds of such force as these. The seas remained very confused. The sunrise brought again the visual dimension to the flip-flop motion we were experiencing. Our 0800 position showed we had made good a shade over 36 miles from midnight, and that we were within a mile of our rhumb line.

The wind continued to twist around in the eastern through southwestern sector of the compass, and remained above 20 knots, often blowing the tops off the steep waves. I could not figure-out the weather system we were in; I had never before experienced anything like it, and I was as confused as was the sea.

Late in the afternoon of our second day of constant pounding around in confusing winds and confused seas, I sensed that we had re-entered the Humboldt Current, so I adjusted our course to compensate.

Through the second night the wind remained in the 18 to 22 knot range, but by this time it had more-or-less stabilized from the south-southeast. We continued close-hauled on the starboard tack in somewhat less lumpy seas in a long 3 to 4 metre southwest swell.

Through the third day we made hourly runs in the 5 to 6 knot range until the winds began easing after sunset. At 2300, with the wind down to under 10 knots, and our progress to windward and across the Humboldt Current down to under 3 knots, I flashed-up the engine and we motor-sailed.

Midmorning on Sunday, our fourth day out, we were again under sail when we began seeing fishing boats, and soon we were in the thick of them. Most of these small wooden vessels did not paint at all on radar until within half a mile, while others, presumably metal or fitted with proper radar reflectors, painted very well from a dozen and more miles.

Carla Belen closed very close on our port bow, continuing to motor toward us on a collision course and not displaying any indication of fishing. We were under sail, she was on our port bow, so we were the stand-on vessel on two counts, and she needed to give way. She finally stopped.

And then Edi and I simultaneously spotted a line from her bows running to a string of floats across our path; she lying to windward of a long drift net, and appeared to be working it in. I quickly tacked, and Sequitur just crossed the space between two floats as we swung around to starboard. For a brief while we waited for the tangle around the keel and rudder, but it did not come. We sailed clear.

We sailed to the southwest along the line of floats looking for the end of the gear, so that we could tack back and resume our course. Shortly before noon we made landfall on Punta Tumbes, the northern end of the peninsula that frames Bahia Concepción, and as the wind died, we flashed-up and motored.

On the way in we met many fishing boats heading out, and we were overtaken by several deeply-laden ones on their way in. Many of the inbound fishing boats we saw were loaded down to such a degree that their scuppers were awash.

On the way in to our intended anchorage, the chart indicated a wreck awash on a shoal well-marked with both light beacon and fairway buoy. The very obvious masts of wreck awash now add to the warning of the presence of the shoal. We moved into safe water, and at 1640 on Sunday, the 6th of March we came to 24 metres on the Rocna in 8 metres of water off the Armada base in Talcahuano. We were in Bahia Concepción, the epicentre of the February 2010 earthquake that had caused such widespread damage outright and with its huge resultant tsunami.

We had made a rough crossing from Isla Robinson Crusoe and were rather beaten-up, so after we had reported our arrival to the Armada, we decided to do nothing but relax and unwind.

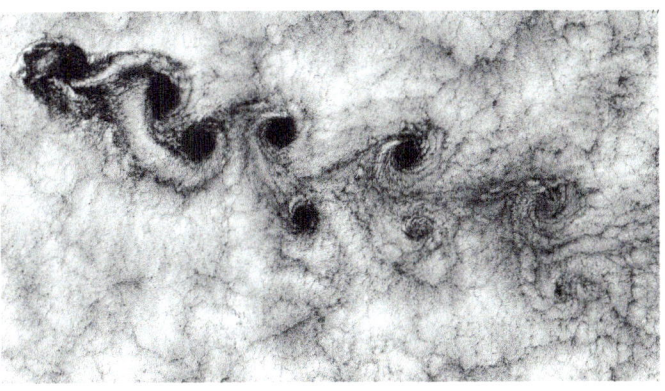

Days later while we were ashore and had finally found an internet connection, I was looking for images of Isla Robinson Crusoe prior to the tsunami. Among the images that came up in the search was one showing the von Kármán vortex street in the lee of the island. The cloud vortices off the Juan Fernandez Islands are used by Wikipedia as an illustration of this repeating pattern of swirling vortices caused by the unsteady separation of flow of a fluid around blunt bodies. This finally explained the very puzzling confused winds and seas on our passage.

Two cables to the east of us was Huascar, the 1864 ironclad battleship, a prize from the Peruvian Armada during the War of the Pacific. It had been used by the Chilean Armada until 1900, and it is now restored, preserved and maintained as a museum open to the public.

Five cables to the north of us was the Armada's major shipyard. Among the ships being refitted was Esmeralda, Chile's tall ship, which is used for training junior officers and seamen.

A couple of cables to the south was the entrance to the fishing port, and there was a very steady parade of empty fishing boats heading out. A few of them obeyed proper speeds going past our anchorage, but most of them seemed to delight in creating the largest wake possible.

Balancing the steady flow of outbound fishing craft was the deeply laden inbound flow.

As pretty as the scene was, there was still much evidence of the destruction caused by the February 2010 earthquake, which was centred very near Bahia Concepción. It was the sixth strongest earthquake ever recorded. A couple of miles to our east, across the fishing boat route we saw the upturned hull of a large freighter, which had been rolled up onto the shore by the quake's waves and the ensuing tsunami.

After breakfast on Monday we launched the dinghy, mounted the motor and headed in to the pier adjacent to the Armada offices. The pier was the grounded hulk of an old ship, which years ago had been filled with rocks and gravel to serve as Ponton Errazuriz, the landing for the ships' boats of the Armada. We were helped in securing the dinghy and in scrambling up the ladder by Christian, a young Armada seaman who is the engineer on a sleek, covered, high-speed Boeing RIB of some 6 or 7 metres length. We were assured it was OK to leave the dinghy there.

We were the only cruising yacht in the entire bay, and we quickly became a feature on the parades of tour boats. Less than an hour after our arrival we were visited by two young Armada ratings who asked to come onboard to inspect our papers. After they had boarded Sequitur, their launch continued out to a cruiser anchored in the roads. They seemed more interested in examining the fittings and layout than they were of looking at the papers; we suspected that they had come aboard only to see the boat. This was more-or-less confirmed when they flagged-down a passing tour boat for a ride back to the shore.

We walked through a foreshore that had been scrubbed bare of all but the strongest structures. What had managed to survive the magnitude 8.8 earthquake didn't fare well with the tsunami waves, which followed.

Most of the wreckage and rubble had been cleared away from the public areas, but more than a year later, there were still many private structures that appeared to have had little or no work. It is reported that 80% of the area's population was left homeless, and that the entire area moved 3 metres westward.

The destruction was so widespread that it was likely difficult to determine where to start. Everywhere we looked, we saw infrastructure being restored; roads were dug-up to repair water and sewer mains, temporary electrical lines appeared as cats-cradles, curbs and sidewalks were being rebuilt.

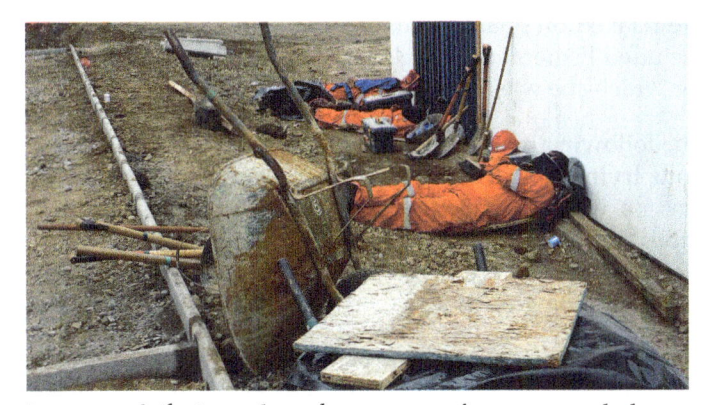

I assumed that workers have come from up and down Chile to assist with the restoration. There were large and small crews working throughout the town centre, not all of them resting.

We were intrigued with the creative approach to replacing the damaged infrastructure. For instance, the sidewalks were being laid in many different patterns, materials and colours. One fascinating stretch that had just been laid was a wonderful optical illusion that made the sidewalk appear so much like undulating waves that we had to slide our feet along to make sure it was flat.

We noted that there were modern high-rise buildings standing and apparently undamaged. We know from all the seismic upgrading and seismic engineering we have seen in Vancouver the past few decades, that properly engineered and constructed buildings will withstand major quakes.

We made our way along to the Santa Isabel supermarket, which was in a huge tent on a former parking lot in the centre of town. It was stifling hot inside; the exhaust heat from the freezer and refrigerator cases was heating the entire tent, and staff members were fanning themselves to keep from melting. The shelf stock was limited to basics, but we found the few things we needed. Outside on the sidewalks were many stalls with entrepreneurs selling items not available inside. We bought some wonderful tomatoes at 3 kilos for 1000 Pesos, about $2.

Back along the waterfront, next to the fishing port, the old fisherman's market had been re-roofed and some of its walls re-erected. It was a lively scene, with a broad variety of catch fresh from the boats. We bought a kilo of what looked like smelt, de-headed, split and scraped of gut, spine and ribs for 1000 Pesos.

On Wednesday we went ashore and caught a bus marked Nuevo Llocolon, which we were told would take us into the city of Concepción. After nearly half an hour of riding past what seemed a dozen or more universities, we wound our way through the centre of the city and started out its south side. Along the way we saw rather dramatic evidence of the earthquake.

Some destroyed buildings were still untouched more than a year after the quake. We were told that this toppled high-rise is tied-up in legal and insurance disputes.

The bus took us across the broad, shallow expanse of the Rio Bio Bio, giving us a passing view of the collapsed bridge upstream, where reconstruction was in full swing.

The bus continued south, and then turned east into increasingly depressed slums. When it seemed we were in the deepest possible squalor, the next turn brought an even lower level. We then made some sense of the bus name: Llocolon, very near the asshole. We reached the end of the line in a muddy bus loop, and we were told to get off. We very quickly dismounted and shouted down a bus that was just leaving the loop, paid the 350 Peso fare and relaxed for the ride back into Concepción.

The bus driver had assured us that he went to the Lider supermarket we had earlier passed near the Rio Bio Bio on our way from Talcahuano. We were let off nearly a kilometre's walk from the store, the closest the bus went on its return trip. We bought heavily, and on reflection, too heavily for the long walk back to the bus. We were weary after we had finally made it back aboard Sequitur.

We relaxed on board, watching the passing scene, which included Esmeralda doing sea trials on her engine repairs for which she was in the dockyard.

The following morning we went ashore and spent over an hour trying to track-down an internet connection. There was no wifi available and we finally found an internet shop that allowed us to plug in an ethernet cable, and we spent nearly two hours catching-up on two weeks of emails and blog postings.

We decided that the infrastructure damage was still too broad for us to enjoy staying in Talcahuano much longer, and we were thinking of moving up into Bahia Coliumo, a considerably more prosperous place a dozen or so miles to the northeast, and then after refreshing there, to carry on to Valdivia.

I began running the engine to bring the house battery back up, since the sun had been hiding much of the time, and our solar had not been able to keep-up and the house bank. It had fallen to 65%.

Edi kept busy by baking three loaves of bread and two dozen bagels.

In the early afternoon, on one of my regular instrument checks, I saw that the charge into the batteries had stopped. I opened the lid and checked the regulator read-out. There was no power to it. I opened the engine compartment to trace the wires, and found a small stream of water flowing from the raw water impeller. I shutdown the engine, closed the seacock and set to work to see if I could remedy the problems.

I assumed that the spraying seawater and vapour from its hitting the hot engine must have compromised the electrical connection at the alternator, which is located just above the leak. The stream of water appeared to be coming from beneath the supply hose clamp. My first thought was a cracked water hose.

I removed the clamp to discover a pinhole in the bronze pump casting. I opened our damage-control kit and selected a patching compound. I kneaded a gob of Stic-O-Steel Pow-R-Putty into the proper consistency and colour, applied it to the hole and waited for it to cook itself and set. It is supposed to begin hardening in two minutes, but more than half an hour later it had done little but crust-over. I tested it by opening the seacock, but did not hold, and the water squirted out again.

I kneaded a second type, Soldimix, which I had bought in Mexico. It required a heat light to set it, so I used Edi's hairdryer and some inverted amps to cook it for five minutes. It still needed at least two hours to cure.

Just as I was finishing with the hairdryer, an Armada launch pulled alongside, there was a knock on the hull and we were told to evacuate the anchorage. There was a tsunami alert, and we must be out to over 25 metres depth by 2000. It was then 1855. I told the Armada officer that we had no power, that the engine room was all torn apart, and that we would have to sail out. Fortunately, there was a light offshore breeze. Edi and I scrambled to prepare Sequitur for sea and for a tsunami.

Thankfully there was still sufficient amperage in the house bank to use the anchor windlass, so I hauled-out the staysail, weighed and then rolled-out the main and jib. At 1906 we sailed off the anchor and headed out into Bahia Concepción following the parade of Armada and commercial ships through the rain into deeper water toward the 25-metre line 4 miles out the shallow bay. On the way we passed reminders of a previous tsunami.

We turned on the VHF to Channel 16 and listened to the chatter. We had been keeping it off at anchor because the Chilean fishermen use Ch 16 as an around-the-clock chat-line, seemingly in bold defiance of the Armada's attempts to stop this dangerous abuse. After every announcement that the channel is for emergency and calling only, there is a round of catcalls, whistles and other stupidity.

There was an 8 knot southerly breeze, and we headed on a beam reach eastward to clear the shoal, and once past, we slowly ran downwind toward Thor, an ocean patrol cruiser being towed out by a pair of tugs. We had been told that if we needed assistance, the anchorage would be full of Armada ships. This was very encouraging.

As we sailed out, the skies began clearing and the rain slowed to a drizzle. We passed under the stern of Thor, which was being manoeuvred to her anchor by the tugs. She was being built for Iceland by the Armada yard in Talcahuano, and was near completion when seriously damaged by the 2010 tsunami. A year later she was again nearing completion, and here she was preparing for the 2011 tsunami.

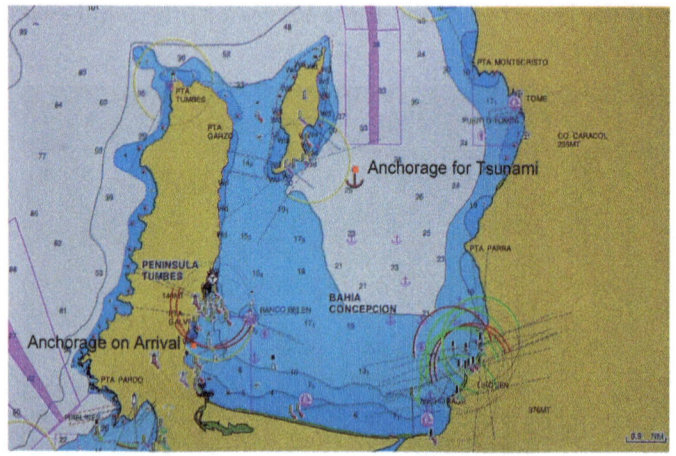

At 2002 we came to 100 metres on the Rocna in 25 metres of water with Isla Quiriquina as a breakwater.

A double rainbow came out and seemed to be pointing-out favoured anchorages a bit further north, but we decided to stay put. We watched in clearing skies as other vessels settled-in around us.

The sun set with a couple of dozen large ships anchored in a mile-and-a-half circle and more arriving. Sequitur was by far the smallest vessel in the emergency anchorage, and the only pleasure craft. There were no fishing boats; most of them had motored out to sea to fish, and the remainder likely decided to let disaster relief replace their vessels if destroyed. This area is the hotbed of Chilean socialism.

Among the Armada vessels was a diesel submarine, which continued to motor around in large circles through the evening. We never did see it anchor, and I questioned whether it could.

I reported our anchorage position to Talcahuano Port Control, and then prepared a 5-egg oyster mushroom, diced salami, green and red pepper, red onion and tomato omelet. We enjoyed dinner without wine in an eerie calmness. Our policy is no alcohol at sea, and none in a tenuous anchorage.

At 2135 there was an announcement on VHF Channel 16 that the tsunami was expected from 0025 and onwards. Comfortable in our anchorage and with our preparations, we went to bed around 2300. While I slept soundly, sometime after 0230 Edi awoke and began hearing excited radio chatter as the tsunami was reported coming down the coast. At about 0300 she felt Sequitur drop and then rebound and continue to move up and down for a while. I normally sleep very soundly, and Edi had decided there was no need to poke me awake. I missed the tsunami.

On Saturday morning we were told that the tsunami watch was being maintained because of continuing aftershocks, and we were advised to remain in the anchorage. We watched as Esmeralda motored back and fourth past us, probably continuing to perform sea trials from her engine work in the yard.

Esmeralda was joined by a medium patrol boat that is configured very much like a frigate, and her small size made Esmeralda look much larger.

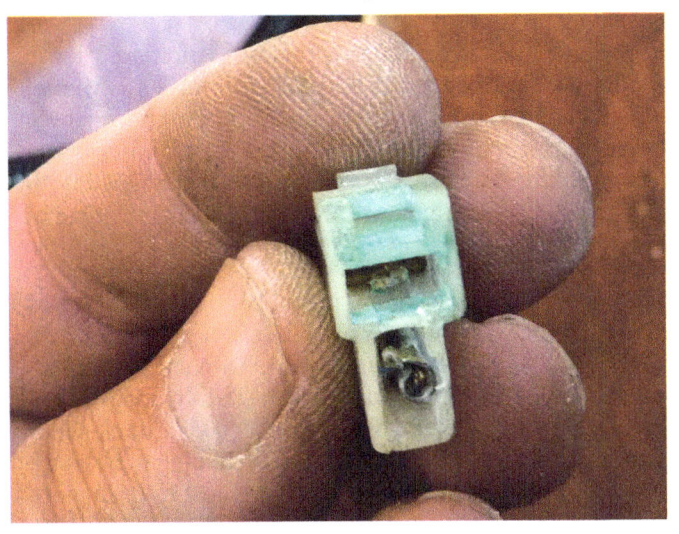

I opened-up the engine compartment and began again tracking-down the wiring problem. The putty patch had set hard, and it held when I opened the seacock for the engine's raw water intake. I found a corroded connection from the regulator to the ignition wire.

After I had removed the faulty connector and rewired the circuit, I ran a diagnostic test on the regulator, and it checked-out. I then turned the start key and got nothing but a click. It sounded like a stuck solenoid on the starter. The starter is buried rather deeply down the port side of the engine, and I fumbled around trying to get my hands and some tools into the cramped confines.

It was 1320, the house battery was down to 52% and the sky was still partly cloudy. As if in answer to my plea, the clouds moved off and we enjoyed clear skies for the remainder of the day. I continued head-down in the engineering spaces, and by 1900 the solar panels had brought the house bank back up to 59%. We went into electrical conservation mode. Among other things, we switched-off the VHF; the fishermen were playing music on it, having their dogs bark into the mike, putting their kids on air. At one point a kid hollered *"tsunami, tsunami, tsunami"* into the mike.

To make the best of a tough situation, I prepared lomo soltado and we enjoyed it with a bottle of 2005 Miguel Torres Gran Reserva Cabernet Sauvignon. After dinner we relaxed with copas of Sol de Ica Pisco Puro and cubes of French 72% dark chocolate. We went to bed at 2300 with the battery at 56%. Maybe we should have shared some of our 72% with it.

At 0815 on Sunday the battery was at 53%, and the sky was 6/10 with cumulus. By noon with skies still partly overcast, the battery had come up to 54%. The tsunami watch was over and we decided to head back in to Talcahuano. We had 100 metres of 10mm chain down with a 40 kilogram anchor on its end. This was too much to think of hauling in by hand, so I used the windlass, which consumed just over 28 amp-hours and brought the battery down to 52%. We were 2% away from an officially dead battery.

We had decided to move to an anchorage off the entrance to the Club de Yates in Caleta Manzano, just north of the Armada dockyard. We sailed off the anchor in a southerly wind of 12 to 14 knots, and had a pleasant sail for half an hour, until the winds became fluky in the lee of the land. As we repeatedly tacked and wafted our way in, we had difficulty resolving the land features with the chart; there were isolated rocks where there should have been a breakwater with a light at its end. We finally spotted the beacon at the end of the line of rocks, and decided that the breakwater had been destroyed by the 2010 tsunami. The rocks were the remnants.

On one of the rocks was a sailboat of about 10 metres length, dry and canted at 35 or 40 degrees onto its starboard side. It had apparently been washed there in the latest tsunami. Three men and a motor launch were working on trying to re-float the boat.

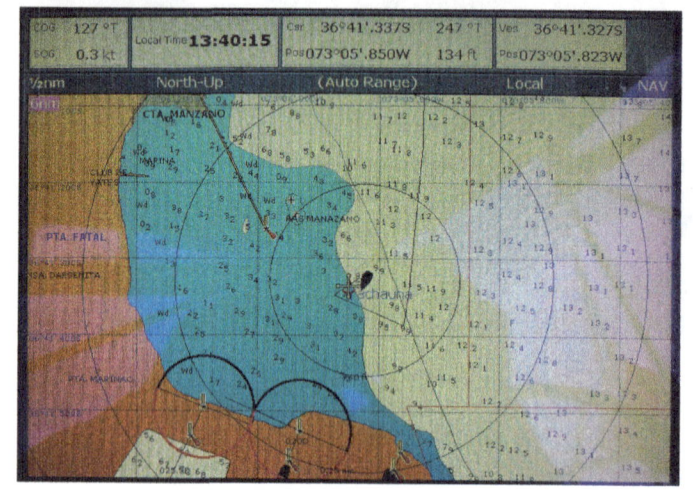

We sailed in to very gradually shoaling waters, and when I saw the sounder find the 10-metre line, I turned to starboard into the now westerly breeze, and leaving the jib aback, dropped anchor as we hove-to. At 1328 we came to 30 metres on the Rocna in 9.8 metres of water.

After I had reported our new anchorage position to Talcahuano Port Control, and we had eaten lunch, we launched the dinghy and mounted its motor. As we motored slowly past the stranded boat, we could see that the men had rigged lifting strops around the hull fore and aft, and that they had some heavy webbing tensioned with come-alongs on the adjacent rock, hoping to stabilize and prevent pounding with the rising tide, which was by this time near its crest.

It appeared to us that they need a crane barge to lift the boat off; even at high tide it was too high out of the water to be pulled off. Realizing that we could do nothing to assist, we continued on our way in to the marina.

We secured Non Sequitur to a new section of float, and as we looked back out to the marina entrance, we could see how much of the breakwater had been destroyed by the 2010 tsunami. The new float we were on was connected to the shore by a rickety patchwork of wooden floats and planks.

Ashore, the tangle of wreckage that still lines the water more than a year after the earthquake and its tsunami, speaks volumes to the huge destruction that occurred. Our own personal smaller tsunami likely added little to the mess. With so much else to do of much higher priority, little if anything has been done to restore the yacht club.

Other than lines of damaged boats on stands and on the ground, there remains little else ashore to indicate this was once an active yacht club; the clubhouse and associated buildings are gone. We walked out onto the road and headed along it through the Armada dockyard.

Along the way we came to the stern of an old submarine, which according to the nearby brass plaque, was an H-Class from the first fleet of Chilean submarines, dating to 1917. It had been recovered from the bottom of the Bay in 1989.

As we were looking at display, I recalled the story about the British Columbia Government early in WWI clandestinely buying two submarines that had been built in Seattle for the Chilean Armada, but not yet delivered to them. I surmised that H-6 is a sister-boat to those.

We continued along past the elegant, but still under repair dockyard headquarters. It sits on high ground, above the tsunami line, but it did not escape damage from the earthquake.

We then arrived at Huascar, the 1864 ironclad warship captured from Peru in October 1879 in the Battle of Angamos during the War of the Pacific. Until we had been vacated for the tsunami alert, we had been anchored just off her starboard side, and we had finally come to visit.

Huascar is moored about 50 metres off the end of a pier, and transportation to and from her is by way of a foot ferry strung between two lines and hauled back and forth by two Armada seamen. We boarded the ferry and were asked for our tickets. We told them we had none, and they asked how we had gotten through the dockyard gate. We explained we were from a Canadian sailing yacht and had anchored at off the Club de Yates and walked down through the dockyard. They seemed a tad puzzled by this apparent breach of security, and they seemed ready to press further when more visitors arrived. They tended to the new arrivals, and probably finding that easier, ignored us and concentrated on still others as they arrived.

They paid us no further attention. Then with what they deemed a good load of passengers, they slipped the lines from the pier and began to haul the ferry across. We thanked them for their kind services as we disembarked to climb the accommodation ladder to Huascar. They grinned.

One of the first things I saw once aboard the ship might be considered by some with twisted humour as a pratfall. The brass plaque indicates the place where Arturo Pratt was killed on 21 May 1879 after he had bravely boarded Huascar from Esmeralda, his command in the Battle of

Iquique during the first weeks of the War of the Pacific. His refusal to surrender his ship to the overwhelming force of the Peruvian Armada that morning, his defiant spirit and his bravery inspired the Chileans to fight on and to eventually win the War.

A bit further along is the plaque marking the death a few months later on 8 October 1879 of the Peruvian Admiral Grau, who had been using Huascar as his flagship since the start of hostilities. The Chilean Armada captured Huascar on that day in the battle of Angamos, and the ship remained in Chilean Armada service until 1900. There seems to be a street named after Grau in every community in Peru, and one named after Pratt in every one in Chile.

From reading a nearby plaque, I gathered that Huascar lost not only the Fleet Admiral that day in Angamos, but also the ship's Captain, two First Lieutenants and a Second Lieutenant. With such a swath cut through the top end of the ships company, I assumed the lower decks fared no better, and it is little wonder the Chileans took Huascar as their prize.

We looked around the upper decks, and I was intrigued by the huge size of the main gun turret. It is 7 metres in diameter, about two-thirds of the beam of the ship, and it base is on rollers on a ring one deck down. It can be rotated through 360 degrees by 16 men working cranks below decks.

The gun could swung through a full circle in fifteen minutes.

Just aft of the gun turret below decks is the most defensive combat helm, even more protected than the fortified combat helm on the upper deck. The ship was built with five watertight compartments, each isolated by heavy iron bulkheads fitted with geared iron doors.

In the forecastle, forward of the gun turret is the seamen's mess, with its bench seats, trestle tables and slung hammocks. Aft of the gun through a watertight bulkhead is the engine room with its huge steam engine in a pit in its centre. Along the sides are the junior officer's cabins.

Aft of the engine room, through a watertight bulkhead is the wardroom, a large space, elegantly furnished and decorated, where the officers dined and relaxed. The space brought back very strong memories of my various wardrooms in the old steam destroyers of Royal Canadian Navy in the 1960s and early 70s.

It is richly appointed with fine cabinetry in a variety of woods, some of them finely burled. Running athwart-ships and along the after bulkhead are upholstered settees, which I assumed served to seat the officers during meetings.

Outboard of the wardroom are officer's cabins, a few of which have portlights, which had been let through the iron armour, appearing to be 20 or more centimetres thick. A translucent glob of glass appears to have been poured in to fill the hole.

Across the wardroom flats aft is the admiral's cabin, which fills the entire stern space.

Leading forward off the starboard side of the salon is the admiral's sleeping cabin, which has beautifully burled panelling on the bulkheads and in the fitted cabinetry. We were amazed with the splendid state of preservation of this historic ship, and were delighted by the freedom we had to wander around in it and explore.

Above the Admiral's quarters, on the after end of the main deck is a deckhouse in which is located the Captain's cabin. This is another richly appointed space with fine cabinetry.

Outside its door is the main conning position of the ship, with large double wheels, compass binnacle and voice tubes to the engine room. In the after end of the covered helm position is a stern-chaser gun.

There is a very fine model of Huascar displayed in the wardroom, which gives an overview of the vessel. Among other papers on view is a copy of the original contract, specification and builders certificate, which had been compiled by the World Ship Trust and presented to the Chilean Armada.

Throughout our self-guided tour we were enthralled by this wonderfully restored and maintained piece of Chilean and World heritage. We salute the Armada for its foresight in preserving this historic ship, and in its generosity in so superbly displaying it to the public.

We took the foot ferry back across to the pier, and followed the small group out through the dockyard gate. Our original intention for coming ashore was to go to the offices of Gobernacion Maritima and ask someone there where we could get a marine electrician to look at Sequitur's damaged wiring.

We were introduced to Sub-Lieutenant Juan Leiva, who was Duty Officer. He was a recent graduate of the naval academy and had just spent a year training aboard Esmeralda, he told us in rather fluent English.

Juan explained that the widespread damage in the entire area from the earthquake and tsunami meant that there were few if any services available. He said he could do nothing for us now, late on a Sunday afternoon, but he told us the Armada could supply us an engineer on Monday morning. He emphasized that this was not standard policy, but because of the ongoing lack of services, it could be authorized. We thanked him for his and the Armada's generosity, and told him we would radio Port Control in the morning when we were ready.

We walked back to the gate, pausing on the way past to shoot a photo of the brass plaque marking the height of the 18-metre tsunami. It was mounted above my head-level on the outside wall of the gatehouse. We then headed in through the walkway, but were stopped and asked for our passes.

I explained to the Duty Petty Officer that we had just walked out from our Canadian sailing yacht, which we had left at anchor at the Club de Yates in Caleta Manzano. He spoke virtually no English, and apparently understood even less, so in my very limited Spanish I tried to explain the situation. I told him we had just been with the Duty Officer, and pantomimed that he should call him. One of the things I remember from my Canadian Navy days is that weekend duty watch personnel can be very unfamiliar with many aspects of their temporary post. The standard rotation would likely have them cycle through a position such as gatehouse watch once in a blue moon. He dug through drawers and files, clipboards and sheaves of paper looking for a list of phone numbers. Then evening colours intervened.

I stood to attention beside him as he officiated in the flag-lowering ceremony, as would any properly-trained naval officer, no matter from which country. This seemed to earn some respect, but not admission through the gate. I suggested Edi and I walk back over to Gobernacion Maritima and have the Duty Officer phone him. He was relieved at this.

We met the Duty Officer just leaving the building, apparently on his way to do evening rounds, and he quickly came back in with us and told the desk Petty Officer to phone the gate for us. As we approached the gate again, the Base Naval bus pulled-up, and the gate Petty Officer indicated for us to board. MPs came onboard to check the passengers' IDs, and one remained onboard, apparently to guard us and ensure we went nowhere but back out to our yacht.

For two kilometres through the dockyard, back along the route we had earlier walked, the young MP stared at us, certain we were foreign spies here to blow-up the Armada base. We got off at the Club de Yates, where a prominent sign indicates that the buildings next along the road are the Munitions Depot. The MP got off with us and stood there watching while we walked out the float, boarded Non Sequitur and motored out of the marina. He was still there as we climbed back aboard Sequitur.

The battery was at 54%; it had come up only 2% in the thin overcast of the afternoon. When we went to bed it was down to 51%, and I toyed with the idea of shutting down the fridges and freezers. Thoughts of all the fine food stored there prevailed, and I left them on, pleased we hadn't defrosted in a long while. I was up early on Monday morning, very concerned at the battery having sunk to 45%. The early solar energy was just beginning to flow into the system, and after breakfast when I was head down in the engine compartment, I remembered an old trick from the horrid American cars of the 50s and 60s. I gave the starter solenoid a bang with a hammer, and tried the engine. It started.

I ran it at 2000 rpm, and for 5 hours I watched as the combined efforts of the solar panels, the wind generator and the alternator added a net of over 550 amp-hours to the batteries. By 1400 the charging system was comfortably in its absorption phase and the house bank was above 90%. I shutdown the engine, and we hopped into the dinghy to go ashore.

We headed around the eastern end of the dockyard complex, along the breakwater and past the huge graving dock. Thor, Esmeralda and the other refitting ships had come back in from their tsunami alert anchorages, and were again alongside.

We had decided we had seen enough of the Bahia Concepción area and we were ready to head to Valdivia. For this we needed a zarpe. We secured Non Sequitur to a bollard on Muelle Errazuriz, just along from Huascar, and we walked into the Gobernacion Maritima building, where we were directed to the zarpe counter. There were two ships ahead of us, so we waited for half-an-hour or so until it was our turn.

While we were waiting, we spoke with Sub-Lieutenant Juan Leiva, with whom we had dealt the previous afternoon. We told him that we had rectified the electrical problems, and that we didn't require his engineers. We thanked him for his kindness in offering them, and told him we were asking for a zarpe to Valdivia for 1000 the next day.

When our zarpe was nearly completed, requiring only an official signature, we were asked when our last safety inspection had been. We had not been given one when we arrived in Chile in December, nor had we been offered one since. We had no idea one was required. The Jefe del Departemento de Operaciones was sent for, who happened to be our young Sub-Lieutenant Juan Leiva. We discussed the situation. He maintained we needed an inspection. I told him the boat was to the north of the dockyard, and that I could bring it down and anchor on their doorstep the next morning to make it easier for the inspector. He appreciated this and told us the inspector would bring the zarpe out in the morning.

When we went to bed at 2300, the battery was at 81%, and in the morning it was at 73%. I flashed-up, and at 0912 we weighed and proceeded in to our 1000 rendezvous anchorage next to Huascar. Edi had breakfast ready as we came to 20 metres on the Rocna in 6 metres of water at 0945 less than a cable off Huascar.

As we finished breakfast, the inspector and an assistant came aboard, checked our fire extinguishers, surprised to see we had 8 and that all were current. He found that the liferaft still has just over a year before it is due for inspection, he noted that the EPIRB, though none is required, still has a couple of years before a battery change, and so it went.

Then we got to the emergency signals. All except the orange smoke were 2 or 3 months expired. I had overlooked them; the boat and all its kit were commissioned less than three years previously. It appears our fit-out yard in Vancouver, Specialty Yachts had saved a few cents and supplied us with part-expired emergency signals.

To explain the situation, I told the inspector we had been unable to find any replacements, and with the disaster here in Bahia Concepción, it was unlikely we would. I suggested we would refresh our kits in Valdivia. He pondered, he wavered, and then said he would check by phone with the Capitania de Puerto.

He got an OK, he gave us the zarpe, and he and his assistant left. We were free to continue south.

21. To Valdivia for Repairs

We received the zarpe at 1040 on Tuesday the 15th of March. Within six minutes we had flashed-up, weighed and were motoring northward.

As we entered the narrows between Isla Quiriquina and Peninsula Tumbes, approaching a drying reef that extends nearly halfway across the mile-wide strait, we met an incoming tsunami. Fortunately, this one was a fishing boat, rather than a destructive wave. It would not have been a good place to meet a real tsunami.

Our noon position had us motoring north-westward near the mouth of the bay in a variable breeze of 2 to 5 knots under skies half-filled with cumulus. Fifteen minutes later we altered to 270 to head across the top of Peninsula Tumbes and its off-lying reef, Quiebra Olas. Extending over the horizon to the north were many dozens of fishing boats working their gear, so we squeezed between them and the reef.

It had rained heavily overnight, so I set-to draining the water from the dinghy before lashing it for sea. I pulled its plug and lowered its stern to a steep angle and it was nearly drained when a small open fishing boat motored-up and offered to sell us fish. I declined their offer, and continued securing Sequitur for sea.

We bent our course to the southwest to cross the Golfo de Arauco and continued motoring at 1500 rpm in a 4 to 5 breeze from the east-northeast. The western half of the sky was completely overcast and we were heading directly into the 3-metre swell. We continued to see large, dense mats of seaweed floating on the water, and we kept a close lookout for these as we motored, not wanting to foul our propeller or clog out raw water intake.

Finally the wind began to build, and at 1550 we hauled out all three sails and headed off on the port tack in an 8 to 10 knot breeze from the south-southwest. With the current, this gave us a bit more westing than we wanted, but at least we were sailing again. The wind gradually strengthened and veered, and by 1800 it was back to its standard of coming directly from where we wanted to go. I flashed-up the engine, rolled in the jib and staysail, shortened and hardened the main and we motor-sailed directly into the 20-knot wind, its fresh waves and the swell. We were back to our standard conditions.

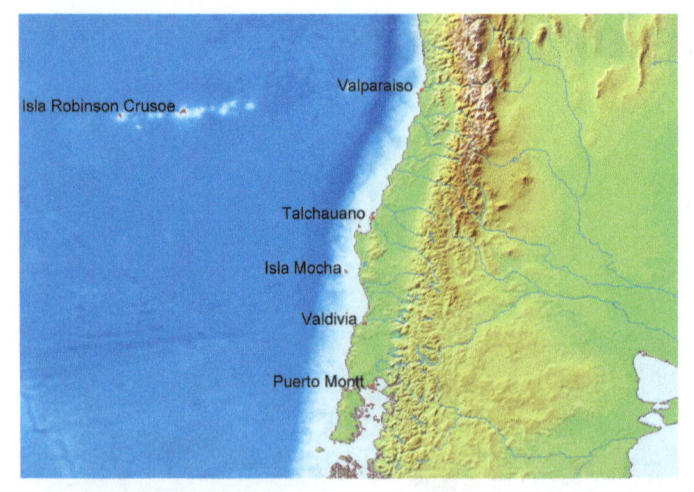

At midnight we were finally sufficiently clear of Isla Santa Maria and the headlands framing the western side of Golfo de Auroco to come to a southerly heading. Clearing the land brought us more fully into the Humboldt Current, and our progress was slowed to the mid-2 knot range. I turned the watch over to Edi at 0100, having made good 2.602 miles at 193 degrees during the past hour. When I took over again at 0600, we had progressed another 13.43 miles, a bit shy of 2.7 knots.

At sunrise, a few minutes before 0800 on Wednesday the 16th, we were still motoring south, directly into the wind, which at this time was blowing 15 to 18 knots. The reefed main was acting as a stabilizer against the roll from the 3 metre southwest swell, and the sky was clear, except for a fringe at the western horizon.

Our 0900 fix showed we had made 3.987 miles the previous hour, and a look at the chart showed a 1-knot north-south tidal flow. I looked at the tide tables and saw that we were in the beginning of an ebb.

As if to celebrate this welcome news, pods of dolphins came and played off Sequitur's starboard side. Most were Dusky Dolphins.

A few were Southern Right Whale Dolphins. There were hundreds of them, and the seemed to be on their way from the north-northwest and heading south-southeast. With their black and white markings and their prominent dorsal fins, the Dusky Dolphins looked very much like miniature Orcas, Killer Whales.

By noon the wind had died to a 3 to 4 knot breeze and we were motoring along at 1500 rpm, making close to 5.5 knots on a course of 170 under clear skies in the southerly ebb. I had flashed-up the watermaker at 1100, and at 1500 shut it down and put it on auto-flush, having netted 240 litres.

We were now 38 degrees south, and our gradual move away from the equator and the waning of summer combined to make it cooler. We had earlier rolled down the side curtains, and then the stern ones. Then it was time to install the quarter panels and completely button-up the cockpit.

Around sunset, when we were about 15 miles northeast of Isla Mocha, we were hit by rain squalls. We were delighted the cockpit was fully zipped-up. The torrential downpours, were whipped by 25-and-more-knot winds, which seemed to come from every direction in turn.

Isla Mocha is the small offshore island on which Miles and Beryl Smeeton and John Guzwell made landfall in 1957 after sailing 1300 miles under jury-rig for 34 days following the pitchpoling and dismasting of their ketch Tsu Hang 1100 miles west-northwest of Cape Horn. We had both earlier read *Once Is Enough*, Smeeton's book on the adventure, and we were now reading Guzwell's *Trekka Round the World*, describing his experiences in Tsu Hang.

The previous evening we had passed the port of Coronel, where Tzu Hang had finally landed in 1957, and from where a few days later they were towed by a very helpful Armada to the dockyard in Talcahuano, where we had just been. It was wonderful seeing these places while reading of these long-ago adventures by these three fellow British Columbians.

The rain squalls came and went, and as sunset approached, we saw rather ominous storm cells over the western horizon, and hoped they would pass clear to the north of us.

At sunset, the sky to the west was looking a bit friendlier, and when I went below to switch-on the navigation lights, I noticed the battery was down to 72%, and there was a 22 amp outflow on the metre.

I quickly checked the alternator's regulator, and found it tested OK, but it seemed somehow unable to make the alternator work. Was the fault in the alternator? Was its wiring harness at the engine compromised by the seawater leak a few days before, and now dud? I had stupidly run the watermaker without monitoring the battery state and it appeared that the four hours of 28 amp draw, added to the ongoing draws of the autopilot, instruments, chartplotter, fridges and freezers had taken their toll.

By this time, the wind had died, and we continued to motor southward on the tail end of the ebb, making 4.4 knots. At midnight our progress was down to 3.6 knots as we headed into the flooding tide, and the battery was down to 63%. I had left the radar off to conserve power, and with the addition of the navigation lights we were consuming 24 amps. We had found the Chilean charts of the area to be accurate, our AIS showed any larger vessels and the wooden fishing boats didn't show-up on radar anyway.

When I turned over to Edi at 0100, we were making 3.5 knots, and when I resumed the watch at 0600, our speed over the ground was down to 3.1 knots and the house bank was at 54%. Sunrise at 0800 brought a 9/10 overcast of stratocumulus and a southerly 10-knot wind. With the wind in its standard-to-us on-the-nose position and with the adverse current, we could make no reasonable headway toward Valdivia under sail. With the depleted battery, and with no promise for a reprieve from the solar panels in the overcast sky, I thought it best to continue motoring southward into the wind.

I spent a few hours reading manuals, referring to Nigel Calder and head-down in the engine spaces trying to resolve the charging problem. I changed the regulator with a spare, but found no remedy. I put the leads of the multi-meter on every conceivable combination of contacts looking for amps, volts and ohms. I got nowhere.

We were 58 miles from a safe anchorage in the mouth of the Valdivia River. I figured that with the tide turning to ebb, if we have the same south-going current as up the coast, we could make 5 knots and better at 1500 rpm. I didn't want to run the engine any faster, since we were low on fuel, and beyond 1500 the consumption curve begins to rise too steeply. At 4.5 knots average, we could make the anchorage in the last of the dusk.

By 0900 the wind had veered and increased to a little over 20 knots. This gave us a 20 degree angle between the wind and our destination, so I had hauled-out the staysail and half the main and we motor-sailed. Our hour's run was 3.78 miles. It remained mostly overcast through the morning with 6/10 and 7/10 cumulus and stratocumulus. The solar panels were just able to kept-up with the consumption.

We seemed to be again in adverse currents; our progress was slowed to runs of 3.32, 3.16 and 3.31 miles to noon, when we had made it to within 45 miles of our proposed anchorage. Through the early afternoon, the wind rather quickly abated, and by 1500 we were in light airs and I had hauled-in the staysail to keep it from slatting. The sky had cleared and our solar panels were slowly adding amps to the bank. The tide turned and our hourly runs climbed gradually from 3.58 at 1500 through 3.62 and 3.92 and then at 1800, to 4.17. We were 24 miles from anchorage.

At 1900 were another 4.51 miles closer, and at 2000 we had gained another 4.77 miles. We had less than 13 miles to go as the sun set and I continued hand steering to save power; there was no wind for the Hydrovane. Shortly after the 2010 sunset the winds quickly piped-up to over 20 knots, and began whipping-up steep waves. We began rolling and pitching, and as I was adjusting the main and rolling-out the staysail to take advantage of the wind, the engine died. The fuel pump must have sucked air from the much-depleted fuel tank during a heavy roll.

I let it be, since we had a good sailing wind, which appeared able to bring us easily into Bahia Corral in the mouth of the Rio Valdivia and to anchor. We were making nearly 7 knots when the chartplotter began to flicker on and off, so I shut it down. I also switched-off the instruments, and we had an exciting sail in a now nearly clear sky lit by the near-full moon over our shoulder. Within an hour the wind had veered quickly and had fallen to around 5 knots. We ghosted along, letting the wind dictate our course, and slowly closed the land.

I hauled-out our Chilean chart atlas, and used the Navionics charts in my iPad with its built-in GPS to take fixes and to navigate. However, I had foolishly allowed its battery to get too low earlier by reading an iBook, and hadn't recharged it. Its battery was at 4%, so I used it only intermittently.

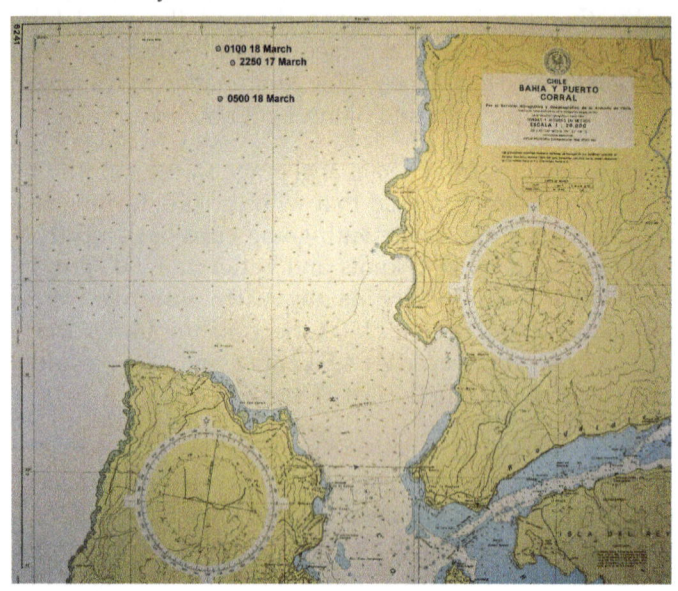

At 2250, when our fix showed we were 4.5 miles from the entrance of the river, the wind completely died. We sat with slatting sails until I finally gave-up and hauled them in at 2335. I told Edi to go to bed, and I took my last fix on the iPad before its battery state shut it down. I flashed-up a portable Garmin Etrex, took a fix and started a track. When at 0100 the Garmin showed we had drifted about 2 cables to the northwest, I confirmed my visual fixes, and relaxed a bit more. We were slowly drifting away from the land, which lay to the east and to the south of us. The closest shoal water was now 2.1 miles to the east.

About half an hour later the wind began stirring and before long there was a gentle breeze from the south. I hauled-out the main and staysail, and tacked back and forth across the wind as the ebb flowed out of the bay to counter our progress. At 0500, when my fix showed we had netted less than half a mile toward the anchorage in four hours of sailing, I hauled-in the sails, and we lay a-hull as I took a nap on the cockpit settee.

At 0805 I hauled-out the main and staysail and again began tacking in toward Bahia Corral in very light airs. At noon, we were 1.7 miles from the Limite del Puerto line and we were finally making some headway into a strengthening breeze. The tide was due to turn to ebb in an hour, and the draining of the Rio Valdivia would need some power to stem. I had read in the pilot: Pub 125, Sailing Directions (En route) West Coast of South America that: *"Due to the limited manoeuvring room and swift currents here, entrance is restricted to daylight only; entrance and departure are prohibited on an ebb current."*

Fortunately, the breeze grew into a light wind and we began making better progress. The skies had been clear all day thus far, and the solar panels were adding over 25 amps into the system. I turned on the instruments so that I had a better measure of the wind, and to monitor the depth of water as I tacked close to shore to make better progress in some eddies. At 1400 we were stemming the ebb abeam the port of Corral, very slowly crossing the ferry lanes with their frequent traffic. For several minutes we sat beside a buoy, losing a few metres, gaining them back, plus a couple, and then slipping back again, until the wind increased a knot or so and we gradually crept forward out of the lanes and then beyond the coming and going fishing boats at their offloading port.

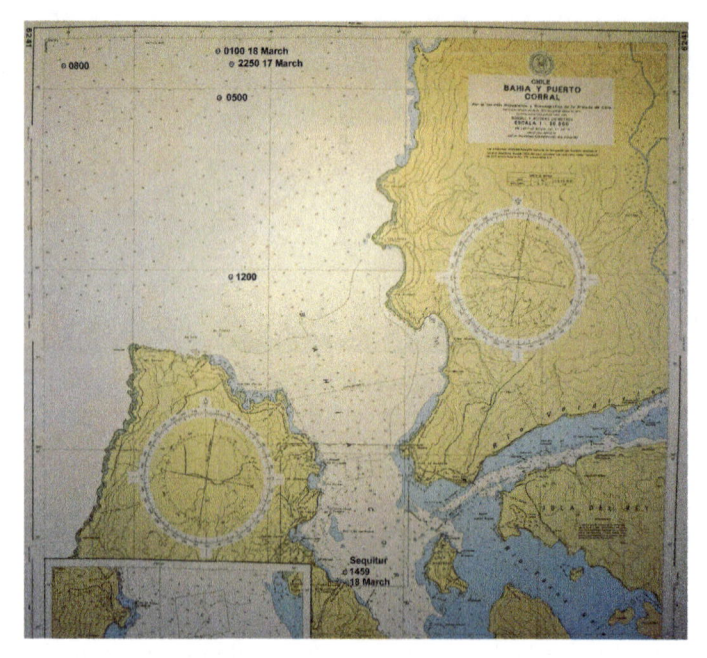

At 1459 we came to 30 metres on the Rocna in 9.9 metres of water beneath a jagged cliff just beyond the fishing port. The last 6 cables had taken us 59 minutes. The house battery was at 49%, officially depleted. I was depleted also, having laid down for only 3 hours in the past 33.

Using one of our portable VHFs, I called Corral Port Control and reported our arrival from Talcahuano to Valdivia, gave our anchorage position and informed them of our need of a tow upriver to the Alwoplast boatyard for repairs. A little short of an hour later, Corral Port Control called and gave us the phone number of Alwoplast. I dialled it on our satellite phone, and received a recorded message in Spanish. It was late on Friday afternoon, so I gave-up.

I made some attempts at resolving the alternator problem and tried unsuccessfully to start the engine. Fortunately the sky remained clear, and by the time the sun had ceased its work with the solar panels, the house bank was up to 51%. In the evening I made a chicken thigh stir-fry and we enjoyed it with 2008 Carmen Cabernet Sauvignon.

On Sunday morning the battery gauge read 46% as we launched the dinghy and mounted its motor. We had decided to head upriver to Alwoplast to see if we could initiate some assistance.

At 1040 we headed up on the end of the flood with a stiff downriver breeze blowing steep waves against the current. We passed a good reminder of the proper side of a green lateral beacon. The wreck awash marked the shoal even better than did the beacon.

We secured Non Sequitur to a float in front of the Alwoplast buildings and went looking for someone. The office was closed, and in one of the large boat sheds we spoke with a man who said the facility was closed on weekends. He suggested we try the Club de Yates de Valdivia next door.

We quickly scooted the dinghy over to a Club float and stepped onto the pier to meet a Canadian and an Oregonian. Each was a single-hander, and each had arrived during the previous week or so.

Tim, the Oregonian had sailed his Valiant 37 directly from New Zealand to visit a friend.

Brock, the Canadian had come in his Westsail 32 non-stop from Prince Rupert, British Columbia. He was heading to Halifax.

We explained our need of a tow, and by this time a couple of men who worked for the Club had arrived on the pier. One of them spoke a little English, and with our amalgamated scraps of language, we soon had him on his cell phone organizing a tow. 50,000 Pesos was proposed, I countered with 40,000, and within half an hour a narrow wooden dory arrived and Edi and I were being motored across the river.

We headed over to a small homestead sitting on the riverbank in the protection of a low, tree-covered island. It was a concoction of makeshift everything, and had we been told it was a set for a hillbilly movie, we would have believed it. Rodriguez first took us to a dilapidated launch that had a 20 degree list to starboard; we were told that it had a stronger engine. Fortunately its battery was too flat to start the engine. We then went alongside a more modern cuddy-cabin runabout with a 50 horsepower outboard.

The engine started, the boat was bailed-out and at 1415 we headed downstream, while the Rodriguez syphoned fuel from a spare tank to the main. The boat ran well and we gained confidence as we went. The tide had by this time begun to ebb, and there was a stiff crosswind as we motored.

Along the way we passed a large fish farm near the riverbank. Alongside it was a ferry barge with a truck and trailer. Their mounted tanks were being loaded with fish through a hose. We later saw a larger ferry with two truck rigs approaching.

We arrived at Sequitur, and I quickly arranged two of our 25-metre, 19mm mooring lines into a towing bridle. There was a strong onshore wind, and we were anchored less than half a cable from the shoals.

I passed the bridle ends and once they were secured to the launch, I signalled to Rodriguez to haul us forward toward the anchor to reduce the load as I weighed. I used the windlass to bring in the 30 metres of rode, and as soon as I saw the anchor, I gave the signal and at 1525 we were under tow. The battery was at 49% and slowly charging with the solar panels and wind generator.

We started slowly upriver against the ebb and across a stiff wind. As we went, a sailboat approached from our starboard beam and passed under our stern. Then it came about and passed up our starboard side and cut across our path so closely that the towboat had to alter to avoid colliding with it.

408

For several minutes Klipper of Valdivia compromised our way, until its skipper either realized the position he was putting us in, or he tired of doing it. Whatever the case, it was a very poor demonstration of his understanding the Rules and a great demonstration of his poor seamanship.

Rodriguez seemed to know the river well; he chose a meandering route up the 5.4 mile run to the Club de Yates, taking advantage of a combination of wind shadows, counter eddies and deep channels close to the riverbanks. I had switched on the instruments to monitor the rudder position and the depth sounder as I steered to follow the movements of our tug, and the least depth I saw was one shoal close to the bank at 3.2 metres.

The launch stemmed the current and expertly hauled Sequitur into a slip, and at 1758 we were securely balanced between quarter lines and bow lines. The tow had taken just over two and a half hours, and we had employed Rodriguez and his assistant and their boats for just shy of four hours. I felt that the 40,000 pesos I had negotiated down to was too little for this, so I paid the originally quoted 50,000. For the equivalent of about $100 we had received amazingly professional service. That amount wouldn't even cover the premium on breakdown insurance back home, let alone cover the deductible.

However hesitatingly, awkwardly and ingloriously she had done so, Sequitur had finally arrived in Valdivia on Saturday the 18th of March. We had a nearly dead battery bank, a generator that refused to start and two non-functioning alternators.

As a band-aid, I hauled-out our shore-power cables and various adaptors and began to rig a connection to the electricity on the pier. I pieced-together a line with a Chilean plug on one end and a 125/250v-50 amp socket on the other and connected Sequitur to the shore-power. The breaker popped.

This made no sense to me; the socket leads to an isolation transformer designed to take from 100 to 250 volts. The multi-metre showed 220 volts arriving at the socket, and my understanding is that the isolation transformer doesn't care about polarity.

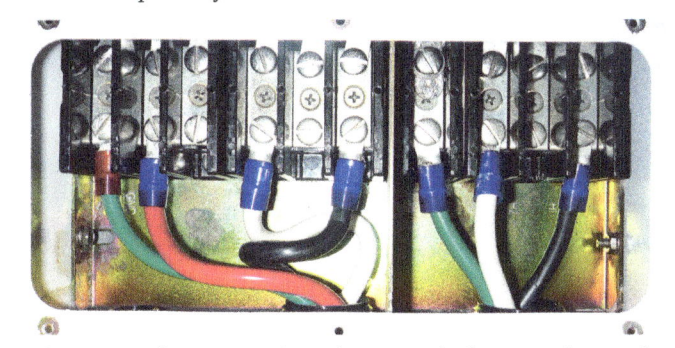

I dug out the manual and opened the panel on the transformer and tried to make sense of things. The wiring and the wiring diagram agreed with each other, and in theory, things should have worked. I added this to our lengthening list of needed repairs.

I cobbled-together another set of adaptors and tried the shore power to Sequitur's 125/250v-30 amp inlet. The breaker popped. My understanding of a transformer is that power comes into a coil, excites it and creates a load by transferring the power by induction across a gap to an adjacent coil. If there is not an adjacent coil to take the power, then it is a short circuit and the current pops the breaker. What I was seeing appeared that there was no adjacent coil to which the current could transfer.

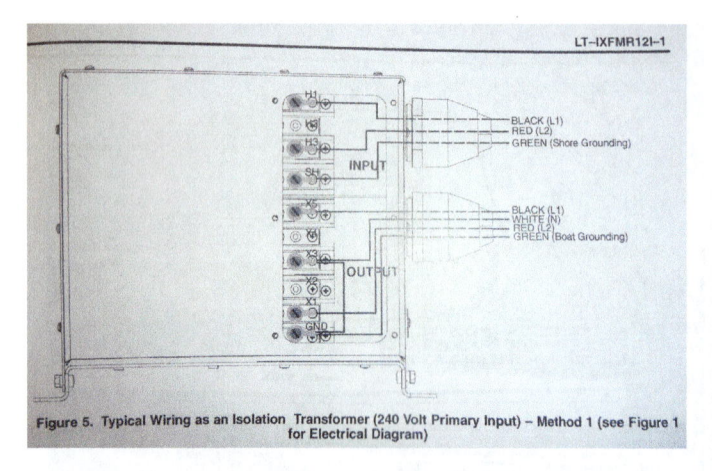

Figure 5. Typical Wiring as an Isolation Transformer (240 Volt Primary Input) – Method 1 (see Figure 1 for Electrical Diagram)

I delved deeper into Sequitur's wiring and her wiring diagrams, I studied the manuals for the two isolation transformers and Nigel Calder's *Boatowner's Electrical and Mechanical Manual*. Meanwhile, the gauges on the panel indicated that the sun had quit work for the day. The battery was at 51%, and amps were flowing out.

On Sunday morning, with the battery at 47%, we took the 20 bus into Valdivia and transferred to the 9 bus, which took us to Sodimac. Inside we found a 550 Watt Black & Decker Smart Battery Charger, with an automatic three-stage charging system. We also picked-up a 25-metre extension cord, some plug adaptors, a coil of wire and an assortment of electrical connectors.

We took a taxi to Supermercado Lider and picked-up some fresh produce. Then with our heavy loads we walked a kilometre or so to the river and along it a couple of kilometres past the Club de Yates in-town marina to the bridge, where we caught the 20 bus back out the 8 kilometres or so to Sequitur. We had dramatically misjudged the distance from Lider to the bridge, but at least we got our exercise.

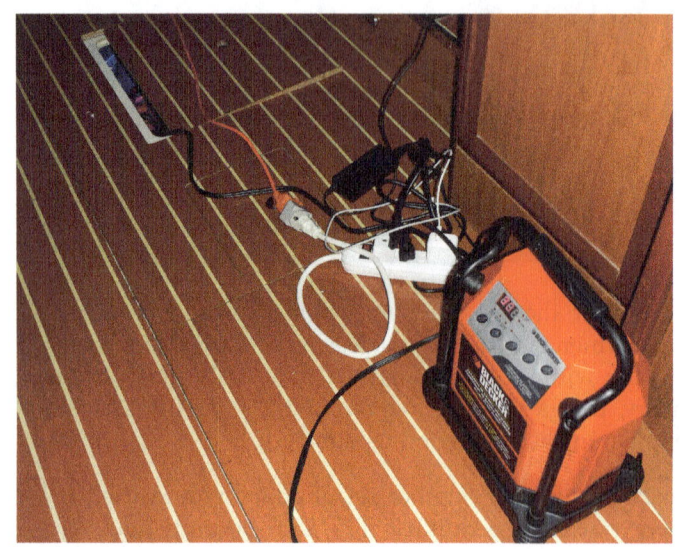

Back onboard I plugged the extension cord into the box on the pier and connected the charger to the house bank. I then plugged-in the charger, selected 'wet cell', poked the buttons to 30 amps and watched as our gauges seemed to give a nod of approval. I began by putting on a surface charge, bringing the voltage up to 14 volts, and then I continued with a deep charge. With no assistance from the sun or wind in the low overcast and rain during the next two days, the house bank gradually took a charge.

On Monday morning I walked over to Alwoplast, where they build large power and sail catamarans. I was impressed by the crisp, professional look of the offices, with Lloyds and ABYC certificates on the walls, and equally impressed by Ronald. I explained our situation and Sequitur's engine, alternator, generator and wiring problems to him and I asked if he could help. He said he was very busy with current work and wouldn't be able to do anything until the next day, and then only a bit. This was fine with me; I had at least stopped the bleeding and had set-up an intravenous. The patient was stable.

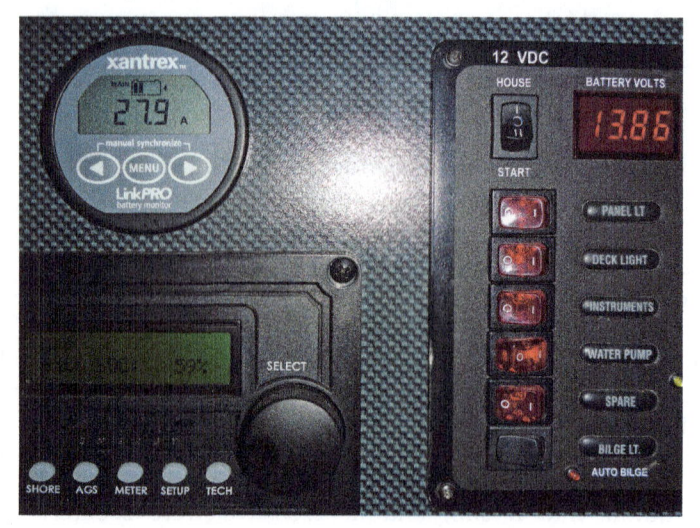

We went to bed on Monday with the house bank at 59%. There was a good positive amp flow and the voltage was reading 13.86, so I turned on the Espar to make some hot water, to add some heat to Sequitur's interior and to dry her out from the dankness of the recent weather. Even its tiny amp demand had been deemed excessive with the depleted battery, but now we were able to begin regaining comfort.

Mid-afternoon on Tuesday Ronald and Hector, one of his marine electricians came over to Sequitur, and I introduced them to the problems. For an hour they rooted-around in the transom locker, under the berth in the port-after cabin and in other spaces trying to resolve the isolation transformer and/or shore-power connection problem. Then Ronald needed to get back to running the business, so he left Hector to continue. He found a large resistance in the reverse Y adaptor that I was using to connect the shore power to the 50 amp inlet. Though I couldn't see how this was popping the circuit, I asked him to butcher the Y and make-up a simple inline 30 amp to 50 amp adaptor. He needed some parts, so he left for the day, with a promise to be back mañana.

As I was rooting around the 50 amp isolation transformer in the space under the berth, where it had been installed by Specialty Yachts, I discovered well-hidden below it a small double circuit breaker panel. It had tripped. Immediately the light went on in my head; these breakers served both the 30 amp isolation transformer in the transom locker and the new 50 amp one beneath the berth. With these breakers off, there was no load for the transformer coils and a short circuit resulted. I switched on the breakers.

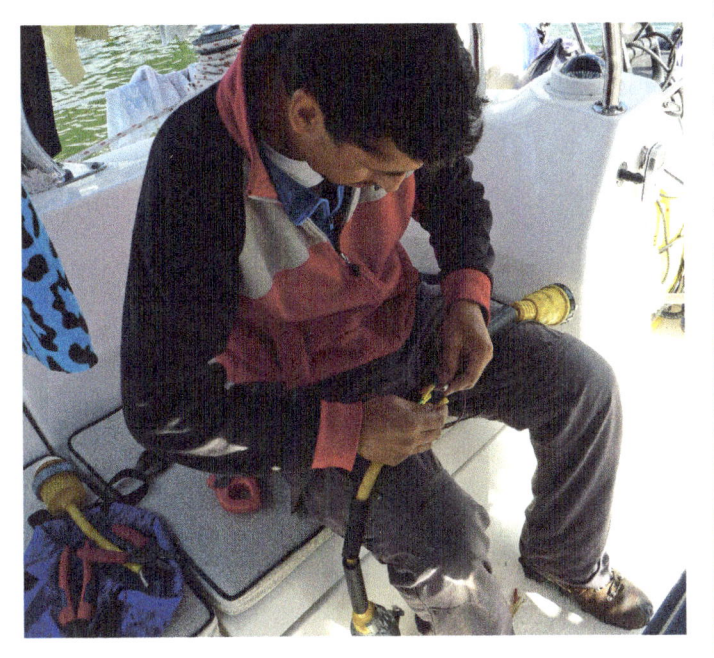

Our access ashore was by scrambling out over the anchors, timing the surge of the boat in the current, and hopping onto the top of the railing on the float, and then down onto the boards. This was impractical, so I rigged a line from Sequitur's quarter to a cleat on the finger and with a couple of shackles, and attached Non Sequitur to it. Coming and going then became a matter of climbing down into the dinghy and gliding it along the line for the 5 or 6 metre shuttle.

On Wednesday afternoon, when Hector had come back and completed the adaptor, I plugged-in the cord and we finally had proper shore power. I let Sequitur's system take-over from the Black & Decker, and we went to bed that night with the house bank at 82.5% and charging at a good rate.

Sequitur was secured bow-in in her slip, balanced between four lines. On her starboard side was a fixed steel pier of posts and beams, which gave us no possibility of using fenders. Because of eddies in the 2-knot tidal and river currents, and the nearly 2 metre tidal range, we needed to keep Sequitur off the pier. On her port bow was a narrow steel finger, low in the water with sharp edges and with no practical way of protecting Sequitur's hull from being damaged by it, so we secured her a metre or so off the finger.

On Wednesday afternoon we were visited by two Armada ratings. They came onboard to inspect our papers and then told us that we must report to the Capitania in Valdivia on the next day. On Thursday we took the 20 bus into town and walked along the malecon to the offices of the Port Captain. We presented ourselves and all of our papers, but they had no idea why we were there, and neither did we. After nearly an hour of their trying to figure things out, they finally told us all our papers were in order and there was no need for us to have come in.

We walked along the river to the Club de Yates Valdivia, got the access code for the wifi and spent a couple of hours getting an internet fix and catching-up on our emails and blog. Other than the security and maintenance staff, we were the only people in the place.

On the way back we stopped to look around the covered market along the riverbank near the bridge. Although it was late in the afternoon, most of the stalls were still occupied and there was a good selection of both produce and seafood available. We noted it for later, and continued back to Sequitur.

We arrived back onboard to find the house bank at 100% and on float charge. To save diesel oil, I switched on the electrical water heater and plugged in a couple of electrical heaters, and turned down the thermostat on the Espar furnace. Sequitur's electrical system was now off the critical list, but still on life support.

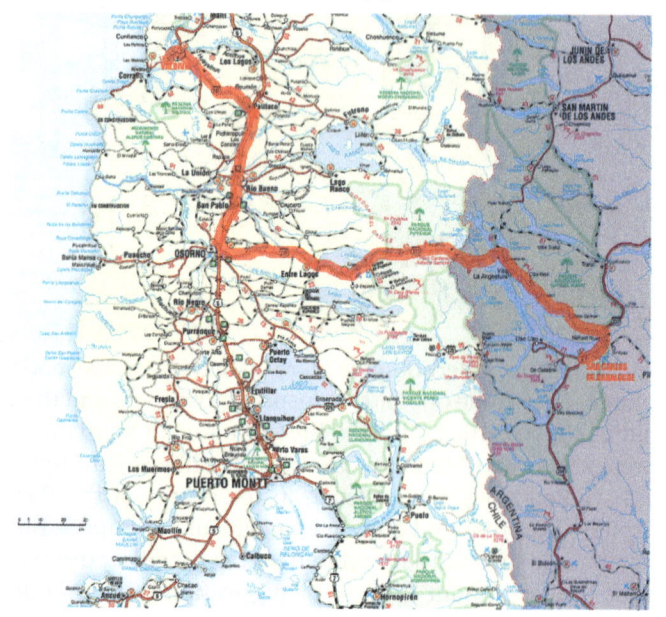

With the electrical system stabilized, we decided to rent a car and drive to Argentina to renew our Chilean visas. We had returned to Chile from our Arequipa, Lake Titicaca and Bolivia trip on 5 January, so our three-months were up on 5 April. Edi had fond memories of her visit to San Carlos de Bariloche in 1980, so we decided to head there.

We reserved a car from the Europcar office in town and on Thursday morning, the 31st of March we drove off to the south and east to Paso Cardenal. Again, as on our previous two road trips in Chile, we found that the locals must all know their way around, and that there was no need for directional road signs.

We did eventually find our way to the summit of the pass, in the middle of the widest no-man's-land we had ever seen. It is 31 kilometres between the Chilean Customs post and the Argentine one. It is a dozen kilometres wider than the one I remember between Iran and Afghanistan on my 1975 trip.

We stopped at the first community we came to, which was over 100 kilometres beyond the last Chilean one. Puerto Villa la Angostura is a town very much like Whistler, back home in British Columbia. It seems to be both a summer and a winter sports hub, with lakes, rivers, mountains and ski resorts. After hours of almost no traffic, we were in a crawling traffic jam. It was mid-afternoon, and we hadn't eaten since breakfast, so we stopped to look for a restaurant.

We looked at several places, none of which had interesting menus, and we finally settled for a place touting its authentic Patagonian cuisine and in which there were several tables of diners, normally a good sign. Being in Argentina, we thought we couldn't go wrong with beef tenderloin steaks with mushrooms. We were terribly mistaken; it was a horrible Teutonic rendition. We added a new entry to our list of worst meals.

We were getting deeper and deeper into German influence. Los Rios region around Valdivia, Los Lagos region to its south and the area we were heading into in Argentina were one of the favourite destinations for German emigrants. After WWII, San Carlos de Bariloche became one of the main hiding places for Nazis fleeing prosecution for war crimes. The countryside looks very much like Bavaria, the names on the billboards and businesses are heavily Germanic, the architecture is a blend of Schwarzwald, Bavarian and kitsch, and but for the Argentine license plates on the cars, we could as easily have been in Bavaria. We saw several businesses named Arrayan, or Arayan.

San Carlos de Bariloche sits on the southern edge of a large lake, which is part of a chain about 100 kilometres in length. It is in the eastern foothills of the Andes, and peaks rise up to a little over 2000 metres behind the city.

We found a very comfortable room in a new twelve-room hotel on the hill with a view over the historic centre of the city and the lake just below. We were still hungry after our very disappointing lunch, so we asked the desk clerk for a recommendation for dinner. He told us that a short walk away is a fine German restaurant.

We arrived at the door of Tarquino Parrilla-Restaurante, which is housed in an amalgam of massive posts and beams that are variously curved, carved, hewed and fitted into place. The place seems to be waiting for the arrival of Hansel & Gretel or maybe it is a leftover from a movie set for the Hobbit.

Edi had a goulash mit spatzle and I had a huge platter of Kalbsbries with accompanying sauces, and we enjoyed our delicious dinners with bottles of Warsteiner. Because Sequitur's cuisine is so wonderful, we seldom feel the urge to dine out; it seems that we do so only when forced to by a trip away. The restaurants we chose; therefore, have a tough standard to meet. This one just made the mark. With our bill came a discount coupon for chocolate in one of the city's many chocolate works; the area is famous for its chocolate. We asked the waitress for her recommendation, and she told us the one on the coupon wasn't her choice. She suggested Torres.

We were nearly out of chocolate aboard Sequitur, and we had been amazed at the utter lack of unadulterated chocolate we had thus far seen in South America. All that we had found listed sugar as its first ingredient, was heavily milked, and/or was full of various fruits, nuts or other distractions. Finding a 70% or 80% chocolate increasingly became our goal as our supply onboard dwindled. We had seen many specialty chocolate shops in Valdivia; in fact, the chocolate business is listed as one of that area's prime industries. Our visits to several of them found us nothing but chocolate-flavoured sugar and milk confections.

Back in our hotel room, we searched online for chocolate in the Bariloche area, we asked the desk clerk, and we went to bed dreaming of finally replenishing our chocolate cache. After the insipid coffee and the nearly inedible commercial bread and pastries of the continental breakfast in the hotel on Saturday morning, we checked-out and headed off to the Torres works.

We explained to the sales clerk what we were looking for, and she seemed apologetic as she offered us a taste of their least adulterated. It was sweet, waxy and mundane. It seems there is no demand for what they all call bitter, but what we think of as chocolate.

We headed back into the centre of town and down a hill that reminded us of San Francisco's Lombard Street. Bariloche's Dr John O'Connor is a similar steep, one-way, switchback two-block descent.

As we headed back toward the Chilean border, the sky cleared and we enjoyed marvellous views as we drove around the eastern and then across the northern shore of the large lake. The mountains of this region reminded me very much of those on Vancouver Island. They are about the same height, 2000 to 2200 metres, and have similar structure and vegetation.

The spires on one of the mountains look so similar to those in the Mackenzie Range, where I had made many pioneering ascents in the 1960s and 70s, that I thought I was back on the Island.

Clouds rolled in as we approached the summit of the pass, but not enough to fully obscure a steep peak that looks very much like some of my old haunts on Vancouver Island.

414

We checked-through the Chilean entry post and our passports were stamped for another three months. We were good until 1 July. When we had finally wound our way out of the mountains and back to the highway, we turned south. We had decided to visit Puerto Montt, the southern terminus of Pan-American Highway. Among other things, we wanted to survey the marine facilities and the grocery shopping for Sequitur's planned arrival.

Edi had seen signs for a Holiday Inn, and we spotted it very quickly as we arrived in the downtown. It occupies the top six floors of a new eleven-storey building on the waterfront, in the heart of the historic district. We drove into the secure parkade and took the elevator to the eleventh-floor lobby and checked in.

Once we had settled into our large ultramodern tenth-floor room with its marvellous view out over Seno Reloncavi, we began to think of dining options. We hadn't eaten since our midmorning bland and simple breakfast in the hotel in Bariloche, and it was already early evening. Knowing that we were one in three on dining on this trip, and not wanting another disappointment, we took the elevator down to the huge Supermercado Bigger, which is a part of the new complex.

There we bought a barbecued chicken, a baguette and a bottle of wine and took the elevator back up to our room, where we enjoyed a wonderfully relaxing dinner overlooking the sea.

After a very good breakfast in the hotel, we took the elevator down to the supermarket and filled a cart with all the heavy, bulky and awkward groceries we could think of needing in Sequitur. These would have been a chore to fetch by bus, but with the car, they presented no problem. We wheeled the cart down the moving ramp to the car in the parkade, and then took the elevator back up to our room to pack-up and check-out.

Thus far we had a limited our touring of Puerto Montt to rides up and down the elevators. It was time to explore the marinas. We drove out of the parkade and onto the waterfront road, Avenida Diego Portales, and followed it the six kilometres or so to Marina del Sur.

We arrived to find that the office is closed on weekends. Of the three main marinas here, this one is reputed to be the most exclusive and expensive.

We continued along half a kilometre to Marina Oxxean, where we spoke with the woman in the admin office. She told us that she would have a price list put together for Sequitur and emailed to us on Monday, when the manager returned. While we were out on the floats checking-out the facilities, we spotted Odyle, with Steve hanging from the mast. Actually, he was suspended in a bosun's chair varnishing the mizzen.

We had last seen Steve, Kim and Cullem in La Punta, Peru in November, when they had sailed south. They had just returned from exploring down as far as Laguna San Rafael, 320 nautical miles to the south. We stood on the floats chatting for half an hour, harvesting much personal knowledge of the area from them. Among other things, we learned that the travel lift at Oxxean was not working, but that there was a good one just down canal at Reloncavi, where they also have very good dry-storage facilities.

We bade Steve and Kim farewell and drove down to Club Nautico Reloncavi. The woman in the admin office poked Sequitur's dimensions into her computer and from the screen, prepared a list of charges for their various services. The fees seem very reasonable: 96,750 (less than $195) for a two-way haul-out, 21,500 per month dry storage, 43,000 per month for mooring on a float and 200 per kilowatt-hour for electricity. We went out to inspect the travel lift.

The second week of April we watched as the new cat was moved from one of the sheds, launched and had its mast stepped. This was a good sign that things were progressing.

Its plaque showed its capacity at 60,000 pounds, well able to handle Sequitur's weight. The crossbar height, though makes it a very tight fit, with only about 5 centimetres to spare. Adjacent to the travel lift is a very large dry storage area that appears to be well guarded. A walk of the floats showed them to be modern and well-maintained. We decided we would use the marina in June to haul-out Sequitur and store her while we take a break before continuing south.

We drove back up the Pan-American Highway the 160 kilometres to Paillaco, and then cross-country another 50 through Valdivia to the marina. Sequitur's batteries were still at 100%, the water tanks were full and once we had ferried our groceries aboard, so were the pantry, fridges and freezers. It was good to be home again.

For over a month we continued to wait for Alwoplast to fit us into their busy schedule, and begin rebuilding our electrical systems and to set right other things that our Vancouver yard had mucked-up on our fit-out.

Alwoplast is a very busy place; among other things, they custom-build 57-foot catamarans with a base price of US$1.6 million, and while we waited, they were in the final fit-out phase of their latest one, rushing to meet an end-April delivery date.

Alwoplast was founded in 1987 by a then 44-year-old Alex Wopper. He had built a 34-foot steel yacht and he and his wife sailed it from Germany, around Cape Horn and then spent six months exploring Patagonia. When they arrived in Valdivia, they decided to stop and set-up a boat-building business. Alex is now CEO of a company with 45 full-time employees and an international following. They are ABYC, Lloyds and ISO certified builders, and except for a few things like carbon-fibre masts and booms, they do almost all of their own fabrication. Besides building new yachts, they also run a small repair and maintenance service. I walked over to Alwoplast and spoke with Ronald Klingenberg, the Production Manager, just to let him know we were still eager to have his crew start on Sequitur.

While we were waiting to be scheduled in, we were also waiting for the end of daylight saving time. This had originally been scheduled for 13 March, but extended to 02 April so Chile could make better use of sunlight and increase energy savings. This was extended again, and at latest report DST was expected to end on 08 May. We hoped that Alwoplast would not take a lead from the Chilean government and start delaying.

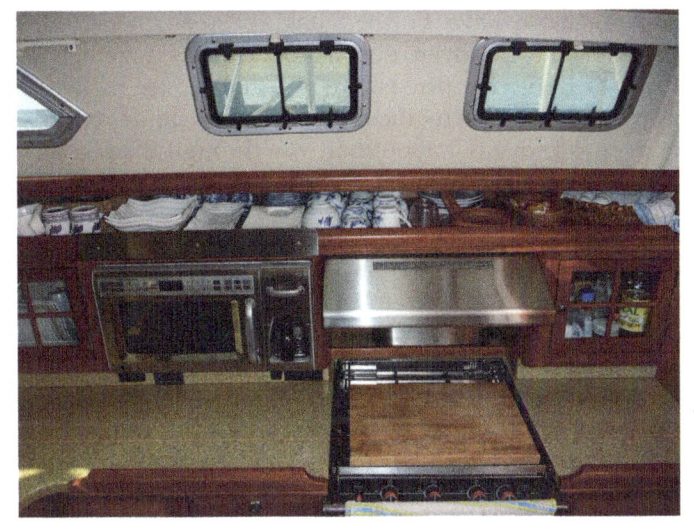

It is now well into autumn in Chile and the weather in Valdivia in the autumn and winter is mostly cloudy and rainy. As April has progressed, it has gradually become wetter, with only two or three days without rain per week. We have spent a lot of time cocooning, enjoying the comfort and dryness of Sequitur. Edi reorganized the pantry and cupboards and we read and relaxed and in the evenings watched movies on the flatscreen.

There were many types of shellfish, including several varieties of mussels and clams. For the mussels, the prices ranged from 500 Pesos per kilo for choritos, 667 per kilo for cholgas and 1000 per kilo for maltones. Not knowing the difference between them, we bought a kilo of the least expensive, the choritos. If we like them we could then move up the price scale on our next visit.

On the few days without rain we took the bus into Valdivia and went to the mall to get our online fix with its free wifi. One day we checked-out what appears to have originally been the municipal produce market, but is now the local souvenir and crafts market. Of the sixty or eighty merchants that are set-up in the three-floor building, virtually all of them carry the identical merchandise. The wholesalers seem to have done very well, and we saw very few shops that had anything but the manufactured kitsch everyone else had. There was nothing of interest to us.

On the riverside just below the so-called crafts market is the produce market. The side toward the water is lined with fishmongers, while on the town side are the fruit and vegetable stands.

Back onboard, I steamed the choritos in a bit of white wine, garlic, shallots, tomatoes, peppers and fresh parsley and served them with Peruvian rice and a dipping dish of melted butter. The little mussels were tender and succulent, and they went wonderfully with the 2009 Humo Blanco Sauvignon Blanc.

The next dry day we went back into town and bought a kilo of each of the maltones and the almejas for 2000 Soles. The maltones look like large PEI mussels, and the almejas are medium-sized hard-shell clams, much like the quahogs of my youth in Shediac Bay. Back onboard we steamed them a bit of white wine, garlic, shallots, celery, tomatoes and fresh parsley and served them with grilled comote rounds and a dipping dish of melted butter. The mussels were flaccid and bland and the clams were rubbery and rather tasteless. The wine seemed wasted on them.

While we were in the market we saw several stands with smoked salmon, and from the labels on the vacuum packs we saw that it was produced from farmed salmon in Puerto Montt. We selected a large fillet a bit over half a kilo for 2500 Pesos. The salmon turned-out to be hot-smoked, rather than cold; nonetheless, it did very well for our next four breakfasts with fresh bagels, cream cheese and capers.

Besides baking a couple of two-dozen batches of bagels, Edi regularly baked bread. She has gradually modified the New York Times no-knead bread recipe to suit Sequitur's galley and oven, and the results are delicious.

Edi runs the loaves through our bread slicer, Zip-Locks it and puts it in the aft freezer, so we have a wonderful supply of fresh sliced bread. The bagels are also pre-sliced and frozen, so our breakfast on most mornings is either toasted bagels or toasted fruit bread with cream cheese.

During the month we've been in Valdivia, Edi also made another two batches of biscotti. On the first batch, the propane tank ran out during the first bake, and the oven cooled before we noticed it. I changed the tank and we rescued the batch.

The biscotti are a marvellous accompaniment with our after-dinner Pisco. After four months of comparing Peruvian and Chilean Piscos, we have concluded that Pisco is definitely a Peruvian drink. We have not been able to find any Chilean version that comes close to the quality of our favourite Peruvian Pisco, Sol de Ica from Vista Alegre.

Often after we have finished baking bread, bagels or biscotti, while the oven is still hot, I throw together a couple of thin-crust pizzas. We're usually over halfway through the first one by the time the second comes out of the oven. We make it about halfway through the second and put the remainder in the fridge for lunch the next day.

Our supply of chocolate ran out, and we have found nothing comparable to our supply from Vancouver. We'll have to bring in four dozen bars when we return. We are also running low on our favourite after dinner drink, the Senorial Moscato. We should have bought much more of it when we were in La Punta; it is as good as most Vin Santi with biscotti at a tiny fraction of the price.

We finally got tired of lugging our computers to the mall and sitting next to the noisy games arcade to do out emails and get our internet fix. We researched the cell providers to see which one had the best coverage down through Patagonia, and we chose Entel. We were greeted in the office by Andrea, who spoke no English, but guided us quickly and easily through the various USB stick programs, then installed and launched the one we chose. We now have unlimited internet access for both our computers for less than $60 per month.

Our diesel was getting low, and the Espar furnace stopped working, most likely because its feed line draws from well above the bottom of the tank to prevent running the engine's supply dry. Through Marcello at the Club office, I ordered a barrel of diesel from a fuel distributor. It was delivered to the head of the pier, and Marcello and I rolled it out to Sequitur's slip, where we pumped into a bucket brigade of jerry cans. Ten fills emptied the 200 litre drum and brought Sequitur's tank up over the quarter mark.

We also had our three empty propane tanks refilled, rather expensively since it is not produced in Chile and it needs to be imported. Since we started our voyage we have refilled ten five-kilo tanks: two in La Paz, Mexico December 2009, two in the Galapagos in May 2010, three in Iquique in January and now three here. Our consumption has averaged about three kilograms per month.

As we continued to wait for Alwoplast to begin work on Sequitur, we continued to relax. With the cool, rainy days we remained onboard and cocooned inside. This was much easier with our new USB internet stick, and with our well-stocked fridges, freezers and pantry. We read, browsed and relaxed, and we ate well.

Some days brought torrential rains, dropping ten or more centimetres, and by the time the rains letup and we wanted to go ashore, the dinghy was half full of water. The first couple of times, I bailed-out by hand, then Edi asked why I didn't simply haul-up the dinghy on the spinnaker halyard. The bailing job was reduced from twenty minutes to five.

As the days became cooler and danker, we again had a craving for beef, so on one of our town trips we had the butcher at Unimarc cut four thick tenderloin fillets. The butcher's lack of skill, or possibly his attitude rendered rather poorly and sloppily trimmed medallions, with much remaining gristle, silverside and fat. The ones we had cut in Valparaiso were beautifully trimmed, but at less than a third of the price we pay back home, I guess we can't be too picky.

Not all of our breakfasts are bagels or toast; from time to time we crave eggs, and Edi serves-up something creative like eggs Benedict, pain perdu or just simply fried eggs on toast.

During the third week of April there was a three-day storm with a day of sustained northerly winds in the 25 to 30 knot range with very strong gusts into the upper 30s. We had a couple of days warning, and everyone in the marina rearranged their moorings. I doubled-up the quarter lines and the one on the port bow and tightened the springs. With the winds came torrential downpours, and on the third day, as it cleared, a 36-foot steel yacht came in from Easter Island.

I trimmed two of the steaks further, dry-fried them four minutes a side and served them smothered in béarnaise sauce with gnocchi in a mushroom, garlic, shallot and cream sauce accompanied by butter sweated carrot and zucchini fingers and sliced tomatoes with chopped fresh basil. With dinner we enjoyed a Chaman 2007 Syrah Gran Reserva. Even though the steak was a bit wild and stringy, dinner was splendid. With the two remaining steaks I made a lomo soltado a couple of days later.

Silas Crosby is from Comox, on Vancouver Island and was built from a bare hull by Dave, the skipper. He and his mid-20s niece, Meredith left Baja Mexico on 5 February and sailed a 6500 mile offshore route to Valdivia via the Galapagos and Easter Island in 59 days.

When the sky clears every few days and the sun finally comes out, particularly after a big storm, it is easy to understand why so many cultures through the ages have worshipped the sun. The riverside environment takes on an almost surreal aura, very serene and pastoral.

We spent a very quiet Easter cloistered inside in the rainy weather, and then on Easter Monday, which is not a holiday here, it cleared. After Edi had started the dough for a batch of bagels, we went to town to restock with fresh produce, wine and other staples.

Back onboard Edi continued working-up the bagel dough, and for the first time in weeks, it was warm enough in the cockpit to set the dough balls there to rise. Over the months, Edi has gradually tweaked her bagel recipe, the kneading process, the boiling time and the baking procedure. This time we ended-up with the largest, lightest and most wonderful bagels, and we couldn't wait for morning to sample them. We decided to substitute bagels for biscotti as our after-dinner treat.

Tuesday morning we had fresh bagels, lightly toasted and slathered with cream cheese, sprinkled with capers and layered with smoked salmon. Edi's recipe tweaking has really paid off; the bagels are better than those from our favourite Vancouver sources, and knowing Edi, the tweaking will continue.

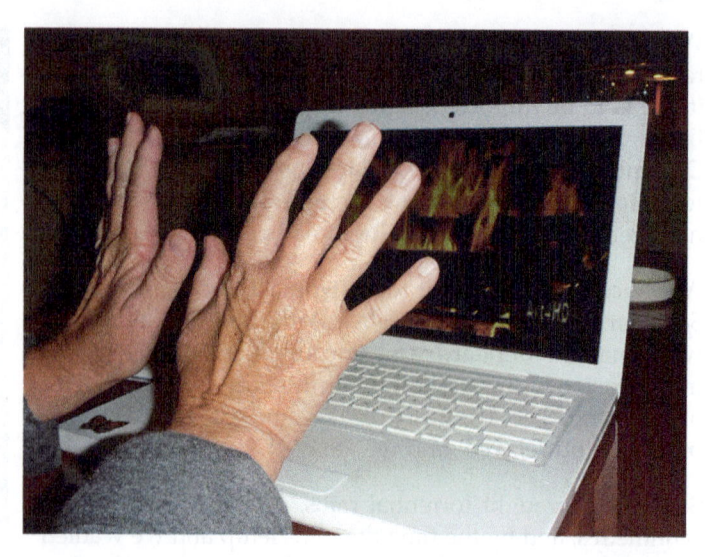

The Espar furnace would not start, and I suspected it was because the fuel level was too low for the pick up line. We bought a barrel of diesel, and after we had put the 200 litres into the tank, the furnace still refused to flash-up. I suspected that the furnace had attempted unsuccessfully to start too many times, and for safety had switched to what the manual called factory reset. We resorted to electrical heaters and Edi found a video of a fireplace to cosy-up to.

On the days it didn't rain, we watched the birds playing on the river next to Sequitur. A mix of cormorants, loons, pelicans and ducks seemed to have a daily ritual of floating down the river on the ebb, then taking-off and flying back up a few hundred metres, only to float back down again. The takeoff point was beside the boat and we watched hundreds of birds play conveyor belt.

Other bird entertainment was watching the loons carrying their chicks around on their backs. The loons never came close enough to Sequitur to allow me to shoot a really sharp picture, but some of the hand-held long telephotos turned-out adequately focused.

Then at the end of April the new catamaran, Pacific Eagle was launched. This was a good indication that Alwoplast was on schedule with its completion and we were a step closer to our turn with their technicians, mechanics and craftsmen. We loved the crisp efficiency we saw in the progress on the final fit-out of the cat, and wished that we had had a similar level of competence with Sequitur's fit-out.

The 30th of April was the 30th anniversary of my retiring from the navy, the fifth anniversary of my decision to separate from my ex-wife and buy a new sailboat, and the third anniversary of my meeting Edi on the internet. We celebrated the date with mahi-mahi grilled with basil and lemon and accompanied by a bottle of Undurraga Brut.

On our previous few trips to the supermarket we had found very inexpensively some huge bunches of fresh basil, and besides on the mahi-mahi, we enjoyed it chopped on tomatoes, accenting lunch sandwiches and incorporated into quiches. We continued taking advantage of the clear days to head into Valdivia to restock with fresh produce and to continue buying selections of wine to try to find a good-value red and wine to stock-up the cellar. We also continued to eat well.

As we slowly worked on depleting the stock in our freezers, we came-up with creative dishes. One day we fancied chicken Cordon Bleu, so I took-out a freezer bag with what I thought was a pair of chicken breasts. When it had thawed, it turned-out to be chicken fillets. Not to be deterred, I cobbled-together the strips around some ham and cheese slices, egged them and coated them with panko. With dinner we enjoyed a wonderful bottle of Carmen 2010 Margaux Cabernet Sauvignon. It was a well-balanced and nicely complex wine with flavours of cassis and blackberry and hints of vanilla and feel of tannin. It was the red we had been looking for, and at 1745 Pesos ($3.49) a bottle, a real steal. We realized we needed to quickly return to the supermarket to buy a substantial quantity before it disappeared from the shelves.

On the 4th of May Geoff and Linda and their dog Jessie arrived in their sloop, Curare after a 23-day passage from Easter Island. They are also members of the Bluewater Cruising association, and left Vancouver in the summer of 2007. There were now five North American boats at the marina, four of them Canadian. Sequitur is the only one that stopped in Peru on the way; the others having heard or read that it is better to avoid stopping there.

On one of our trips to town to deplete the supermarket shelves of Carmen Margaux, we bought another package of celery. Our previous one had lasted a month, and we anticipated this one would as well. The things are huge here, over 60cm long and more than 15cm in diameter, and they cost 525 Pesos, about $1.05. It was crisp, succulent and wonderfully flavoured, and even cut in half, it barely made it into the fridge.

While we were in the supermarket, we also found some fresh Peruvian asparagus, so we picked-up a few bundles, and then went looking for beef tenderloin. A rather sloppy butcher needed our coaxing and that of her fellow butcher to trim the fillet a bit better, and she was in a dither as she weighted and packaged the four medallions.

When I unwrapped the steaks that evening, I noted that the total weight was .994 kilos and the price was 2485 Pesos, just under $5.00. Then I looked more closely at the label and saw it had been coded as osso bucco. I decided not to take the tenderloin back to the supermarket to point-out the error, but instead dry-fried a pair of them and enjoyed them slathered with Béarnaise sauce and served with gnocchi in a mushroom, shallot and garlic cream sauce with a side of asparagus and mayonnaise. The Araucano Humo Blanco 2008 Pinot Noir complemented splendidly.

On one of our trips to town to buy another dozen Carmen Margaux, we saw a great-looking package of skinless and boneless chicken breasts in the meat cooler; however, it was not priced. We asked a staff member to find the price, but after about ten minutes and two additional employees, we were no further ahead. We decided to take it anyway, and headed to the check-out. The clerk couldn't find a price, so he sent a supervisor off to the meat department. Fifteen minutes later we were still waiting. We tried to offer a price for the package, but it appeared the clerk had no way of doing that. Eventually, I was taken to the meat department, where the meat manager tried to sell me a different package, but I insisted I preferred the look of unpriced brand. He went off and after some ten minutes or so, came back with a strip of barcode labels and stuck one on my package. The clerk scanned the barcode and watched as the package description came-up, but there was no price with it. He tried again; same result. He tried a third time and manually added the price on the barcode label; this time it worked. He punched the keys to total the sale, but the machine wouldn't allow it; there were two unpriced chicken packages that needed attention. He called a supervisor to use her code to void the two lines. Finally after more than half an hour and eight staff members, we had our chicken.

Back onboard Sequitur, I found four wonderful-looking breasts, and after freezing two, I prepared tarragon chicken and served it with steamed rice and more of our fresh asparagus. The chicken was tender and juicy, and well worth the wait. It went splendidly with the Carmen Margaux.

We continued to watch the activity aboard Pacific Eagle as the Alwoplast crew completed her fit-out. When we saw the new owners arrive and do a walkthrough, we knew we were getting nearer to heading over to Alwoplast. On the Friday the 6th we were delighted as we watched Pacific Eagle motor out of the marina on what we assumed was a sea trial.

It was blowing about 15 knots as they left, so we knew they would have good conditions. In the late afternoon they returned, and we could sense an upbeat spirit aboard the cat. Things really looked good for us when we saw the Australian colours hoisted on Saturday.

We went to town on Mothers' Day to buy more of the 2010 Carmen Margaux. There were only five bottles left on the shelf, and next to it with the identical barcode were bottles with a new label 2010 Carmen Classico Margaux. My many years of experience in the wine business told me this was likely also a blend change. We bought the last five bottles and two of the new label to see if the blend was the same.

Because the tenderloin was rather poorly trimmed and a bit tough, I had thinly sliced the remaining two steaks and put them in a marinade of soy, balsamic vinegar and lime juice for two days. With this I made a lomo soltado, and with it we tasted the two different labels of the Carmen Margaux. They were identical; we would continue laying-in a large stock.

Mid-afternoon on Monday the 9th Ronald came over from Alwoplast and told us they were ready for us to move over to their marina. Within a minute, I had flashed-up the engine and was unfastening the dinghy from alongside, while Ronald began undoing mooring lines. Within ten minutes we were secured alongside the end float at Alwoplast. Our seven and a half week wait was nearly over. Once we had secured, Ronald, the Operations Manager told us work would begin first thing the next morning.

Sure enough, shortly before 0900 on Tuesday, Ronald and Claudio, one of his stainless steel fabricators arrived onboard. Together we looked at various options to correct the mounting of the solar arch above Sequitur's cockpit.

On our passage from Paita to La Punta, Peru in June 2010, the port after mounting foot had come free, and the entire arch with its half kilowatt of solar panels and the wind generator were threatening to go overboard. If it went, it would have likely taken the cockpit awnings and other things with it. The yard in Vancouver that had installed the arch had neglected to install backing plates, apparently taking the easy route of fastening the arch directly to the fibreglass hull. Before we had left La Punta, I had installed large washers as a temporary backing, and they served the purpose well; however, a more substantial fix was required.

Claudio quickly went to work, first cutting an access hole through the liner of the cockpit locker to gain access to the space beneath the arch mounting. He then took measurements, prepared a sketch and headed off to his shop.

He was soon back with a mock-up, callipers and a scale drawing. After some more measuring and another trip to the metal shop, he was back doing a test fit. Things were looking good.

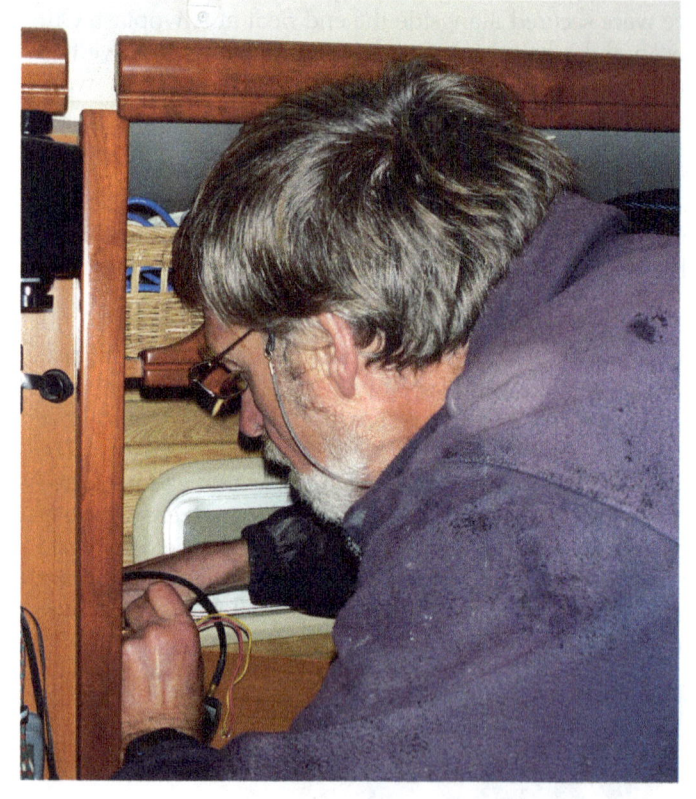

By early Wednesday afternoon, the solar arch mountings were properly backed and reinforced. The locker access holes had covers fitted and screwed in place, and the installation was finally as it should have been before we left the yard in Vancouver.

As work progressed on the outside, we busied ourselves inside. Edi tried a new bread recipe from her friend Helene in London. It is a no-knead method with no rising, simply mixed and poured into a pan and put in a cold oven as it heats to 375°F. This seemed to be a good use of a warming oven, but the rather flat loaf that resulted showed the gas oven likely heated much too quickly. Anyway, with the hot oven, we baked-off another batch of bagels. With a hot oven from the bagels, pizzas were not too far behind.

Meanwhile Ronald dived into the starboard transom space and began analyzing the problem with the Espar furnace. He is very familiar with Espar, having installed them on the boats they build at Alwoplast, and he was using the Espar diagnostic instrument. Because the wiring to our furnace from our control panel was of different colours to that specified in the manual, he had difficulty sorting it out. It appears the installers had used what wire they had, rather than going by the book and making it easy for future servicing. Eventually he got his instrument to respond, and he took the error codes to his office to interpret them. The igniter was showing a fault, and he contacted the Espar distributor in Santiago for a replacement.

On Thursday, all of Alwoplast's workers were busy with other projects. Edi spent most of the day diving into the lockers and digging-out the food stores, sorting them and redoing the inventory list in her computer. At times there were piles over half a metre high on the table and settee as she sorted.

By the end of the day she had repackaged, reorganized and rearranged the food lockers. Most of the bulk items were now out of their packages and into Lock-and-Lock containers and sorted into easy-to-find and easy to access places. She also began two lists: one consisting items to bring back with us from Vancouver, and the other of items to buy before we head south into Patagonia from Puerto Montt.

424

On Friday morning Ronald brought his engine expert, Arno and an assistant to Sequitur. The mechanics and I spent some time looking-over the Fischer-Panda generator, running it through its start cycles, checking the fuel flow and generally troubleshooting everything that I had thus far done. Because of the tight space around the generator in the boat, we determined that the best course was to uninstall the unit and have them tear it down in their shop.

The mechanics then dismounted the raw water impeller from the main engine. Because of the placement of the engine, this requires the removal of the 120-amp alternator and the port forward engine mount. The patch that I had applied in Bahia Concepción was still holding, but I told them to braze a proper repair on it, and also to order a new pump. The new one will be installed and the repaired one put in the spares bin.

We took advantage of the clear day on Saturday and went into town to the supermarket for groceries and another dozen bottles of wine. Sequitur's wine cellar is nearly restocked for the next season's cruising in the wilderness of Patagonia. We walked back through town and along the river, where the small cruise boats were coming and going with a few off-season tourists. The infrastructure along the riverfront shows that boat tours must be a thriving industry in high season.

We browsed our way through the riverside seafood and produce market. We saw no fish that tempted us, and among the produce, the only thing we found of interest were some nice fresh shallots. We searched in vain for more of the wonderfully huge branches of fresh basil. There had been none in the supermarket either, so it is back to dried basil.

On Sunday we dug the power washer out of the transom locker and Edi used it to blast the grime off the decks and canvas, and to clean the cockpit cushions. Meanwhile I worked at clearing the blockage in the vent to the forward holding tank. It appeared that some insects had decided to take-up residence in the vent at the through-hull, and had gradually completely blocked the opening. With no vent, the tank had become inoperable without undoing the deck pump-out cap, and we had moved our operations to the after head. Of course, the malingering through-hull was placed such that I needed arms a few centimetres longer and fitted with double-articulating fingers. Eventually I managed to remove the through-hull, clean it out and reinstall it, and we again have two operating heads.

On Monday morning, Ronald and his mechanic were back to attack the Fischer-Panda generator. We systematically went through a troubleshooting procedure, starting with the fuel system. The filter, pump, shutoff solenoid and injector were inspected and found functional; the engine was getting fuel. The glow plug showed the proper voltage on the start cycle; the fuel was being heated. The air intake was clear; the engine was getting air. The only thing left was the compression.

425

On Tuesday the mechanic brought in a compression tester, and found very low pressure. This pointed to a stuck valve, stuck piston ring, blown head gasket, a holed piston or a cracked head. Whatever, the generator definitely had to come out.

On Tuesday afternoon Alwoplast launched the prototype of a floating office. Like other things we have seen here, it is well-designed and expertly crafted. For its fitting-out, it was placed across from the new catamaran and next to one of the solar-powered water taxis the company builds.

On Wednesday morning Hector, the electrician came aboard to disconnect the electrical harnesses from the Generator, followed half-an-hour later by Ronald and an assistant, who rigged a sling and lifted the 80 kilogram machine up out of the bilge.

After some more rigging, the three of them manhandled the generator up the companionway ladder and into the cockpit, over onto the side deck and down onto the float. From there it was wheeled up to the sheds to await pick up by Arno, who will take it to his shop to tear-down.

We were left with an empty space forward of the engine, which will make it easier for Hector to sort-out and resolve the problems with the alternators and the engine wiring harness

The generator had just left when there was a commotion aboard Pacific Eagle, the newly completed Atlantic 57 catamaran. The cat was in the final stages of preparing to sail away, and the crew was assembled for farewell photos. Their destination is home port, Cairns, Australia, and they intend heading there via the Galapagos, Panama and Cape Town.

After several rounds of photos from both sides, the last line was slipped and Pacific Eagle gently eased away from the float and out through a thick mist into the slowly ebbing Valdivia River.

Alwoplast built its first Atlantic 57 catamaran in 2008, and Pacific Eagle is their seventh. They have now sold their eighth one and are well along on its fabrication. The boat is built to the design of Chris White of Annapolis, USA, and a page on his site: www.chriswhitedesigns.com speaks highly of Alwoplast.

Among those on the floats bidding bon voyage to Pacific Eagle was Alex Wopper, the founder and owner of Alwoplast. He looked like a proud father watching another of his children heading off to explore the world.

After the departure of the cat, Hector came back to Sequitur to dismount the two alternators from the engine and take them and the spare regulator up to the electrical shop to bench test. He left the inspection of the engine wiring harness until after he had sorted-out the alternators.

Mid-afternoon on Thursday Francisco, an Alwoplast shipwright came aboard to begin planning the installation of the dryer vent from the rear of the dryer into the cockpit. When I had ordered the boat, I had specified a ventless washer-dryer, but through some mix-up, a vented washer-dryer had been installed, and it wasn't until the end of January 2010 when we were in Guaymas, Mexico that we discovered this. We had been trying to track-down the source of a tiny seep of fresh water into the compartment beneath the pantry sole and the high humidity in the pantry and the sea cabin.

The washer-dryer occupies a cupboard in the bulkhead between the pantry and the sea cabin, with the user access through cabinet doors on the pantry side, and access to the back-end stuff behind panels in the cabinet in the sea cabin. I had removed the panel at the rear and found all hose connections tight, with no evidence of any previous leaks. What I saw next had really surprised me; there was a dryer vent duct leading out of the back of the machine. This was supposed to be a ventless dryer, so why the vent ducting? I had next dug out the user's manuals that came with the machine to find we had one of each; one for the ventless model, and one for the vented.

I had followed the ducting aft into the compartment beneath the bed platform to find that it led into that space and terminated in an empty lint trap box, which simply lay on the bottom of the compartment. Surrounding it, and on every surface in the compartment was lint, and in the lower front end of the compartment there was a wet pad of lint. Stains on the compartment bottom spoke of there having been at times puddles of various sizes. The hot, moist exhaust from the dryer had no place to go but to condense and run forward, down the slope of the hull and accumulate in a growing pad of lint.

It appears that the wrong model was ordered, or had been received by the factory, and whoever installed it was not supervised, and simply left the vent flopping in a blind space, and forgot about it, or otherwise didn't report it. The space spans the width of the boat, and its after portion accommodates the main diesel tank. The port side forward houses the isolation transformers for the 120v and the 240v shore power connections. The last time I had looked in there, we hadn't yet run the washer-dryer, and there would have been no telltale lint, and I would probably have glanced past the metal vent duct, dismissing it as being part of the bilge ducting.

I had then read through the manual for the Splendide 2000S vented model and searched online for its installation sheet to give me some ideas on designing a proper vent for Sequitur's laundry. One of the problems, of course, is the watertight integrity of the boat, and a prudent mariner should always think carefully before cutting any hole through the hull, particularly an 11cm diameter hole. Sequitur's two aft cabins already sport five 13cm by 30cm holes through the hull, which are sealed by opening Bomar portlights. Two of these lead into the cockpit, directly above the washer/dryer.

In Mexico that January I had removed the ducting and cleaned the lint from the compartment, then I set-up a temporary vent out through the small Bomar portlight into the cockpit, and we had run a load of laundry to try the machine. With the vent led outside, the pantry and the sea cabin no longer got humid during the dry cycle. It was not an elegant solution, but it served the purpose at the time, and I continued to rig the temporary vent through the portlight whenever we used the dryer.

Here in Valdivia with the expertise of Alwoplast at hand, we decided it was time install a permanent vent. We discussed routing, Francisco drew-up a plan and then went off to get the proper tools for the job that he had laid-out.

427

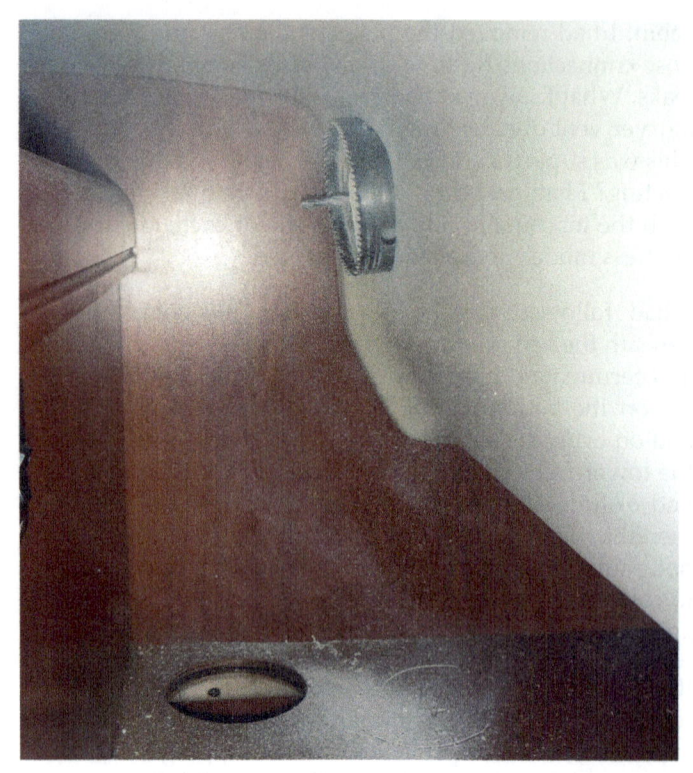

In not much over an hour we had an eleven centimetre diameter hole in the top of the cabinet, another above it out through the cabin liner and a third through into the cockpit. The design is to have the new vent run up the back of the machine, diagonally across its top, up the hole in the cabinet top and then out through a conduit to a flap-covered fitting at the forward end of the cockpit. Rather than beginning the next phase late in the afternoon, Francisco cleaned-up and left.

Midmorning Ronald and Arno arrived on board with pieces from the stripped-down generator engine. The head, valves and piston top were severely corroded, showing the engine had ingested salt water. Ronald suspected that the engine had drawn water in through the exhaust, and there is a possibility that exhaust water/gas separator was incorrectly installed. I dug into the spares locker and brought out a new cylinder head and valve assembly, a new piston and new piston rings. I did not have a new cylinder, but the corrosion on the inside of the existing one looked to be little more than surface only, and some light honing might restore it.

Shortly after 0800 on Friday morning Francisco was back onboard to continue with the vent installation. At the same time Claudio, the stainless steel fabricator setup his plasma welding machine on the bow and welded onto the pulpit a piece that he had fabricated to replace the one damaged when Sequitur's bow was rammed while alongside having work done at Specialty Yachts in Vancouver.

When Claudio had completed the restoration work on the pulpit, he began designing and fabricating a mount for the stern-light. By definition this navigation light must be white and be placed as nearly as practicable at the stern showing 67.5 degrees from right aft on each side of the vessel, and it must be visible two miles. The original placement was on the transom, to starboard of the centre walkthrough. With our additions of the Hydrovane and the outboard motor mount to Sequitur's stern, the light lost portions of its arc of visibility.

I had long been thinking of moving the light up to the after side of the solar panel arch, and with the expertise here at Alwoplast, I saw this as a great opportunity to get the job done. Shortly after Claudio had headed up to the shop with his measurements, Hector arrived to dismount the existing stern-light and begin fishing its wires from inside the transom locker up through a tube of the solar arch to the new location.

On Saturday we relaxed onboard waiting for the predicted earthquakes that would end the world. We postulated that Harold Camping's great Doomsday earthquake, which was occupying much online and print space and broadcast time, had a better chance of occurring here in Valdivia than anywhere else.

According to the US Geological Survey, the magnitude 9.5 Valdivia quake of 22 May 1960 was the largest ever recorded and the tsunamis it generated were up to 25 metres high. Recent seismic activity shows that Chile is still among the world's most earthquake-prone areas. Even although the several-day drizzle had turned to heavy downpour, we noted that Alwoplast had not yet begun building arks.

We did have one major shock; however, early in the morning I learned that my mother had passed away the previous day at the age of 93. She had a long and good life, and was in good health until into her ninety-first year when her mind began rapidly deteriorating. Although I had seen very little of her in recent years, she was never far from my mind and she continued to be a major force in my life. I will dearly miss her. Rest in Peace Mom.

I consoled myself with thoughts that extended voyaging dictates that communications and relationships with family and friends become less frequent. It is not that we wish a lesser contact, it is simply a function of the time and the distances involved. Our life energy is focused on where we are and on what we are doing, and because of this, we miss the intimacy and immediacy of the lives of those not with us. However; for our lives to evolve and for our aspirations and dreams to be realized, we all need to move on.

We awoke on Sunday the 22nd of May, the 51st anniversary of the Great Valdivia Earthquake, not at all surprised that the world did not end on Saturday as predicted. However, as predicted elsewhere, in the early afternoon the sun began burning through the overcast. We took advantage of this to catch a bus into Valdivia.

As we were preparing to leave Sequitur, an Alwoplast prototype water taxi was returning from a run on the river.

On Monday morning Hector was aboard early to complete the wiring on the newly repositioned stern-light. Once he had completed it, he began sorting-out the installation problems with the AutoAnchor, the cockpit-controlled windlass switch and rode counter. This was yet another item that has failed to work properly since it was installed by Specialty Yachts in Vancouver during our fit-out.

The sun broke through the overcast mid-afternoon on Monday, so I used the break in the rain to catch a bus into Valdivia. The Club de Yates had finally prepared an invoice for our seven-week stay at the marina. I got off midtown and raided a bank machine, then walked the kilometre-and-a-bit to the Club. An aluminum yacht of Maltese registry was in the basin refuelling from a truck, which was parked on the brink, and I had to wait for the Club Manager to finish with it. Our moorage charge for the fifty days came to 268,470 pesos, about 10.75 per day.

I stopped at the supermarket on the way back and found some fresh basil and oyster mushrooms, among other niceties. In the evening I prepared chicken breasts stuffed with ham, cheese and basil leaves. We enjoyed this Cordon Bleu et Vert with a butter-sweated julienne of onions, carrots, oyster mushrooms and red, green and yellow peppers.

On Tuesday Ronald and Hector arrived onboard with a complete troubleshooting guide printed-out from the AutoAnchor internet site. Our manual had not made it back onboard after the Vancouver installer used it for several days trying to sort-out why the system worked intermittently and was giving a seemingly random melange of error messages. With Ronald in the cockpit and Hector in the anchor well, they quickly sorted-out the error messages to a faulty connection at the windlass. This was properly re-wired and sealed, and the system finally works as intended.

Hector next set to work on the foghorn to see if he could get it working again. During a storm the foghorn-hailer speaker had come loose from the mounting that Specialty Yachts had installed on the mast. For a few hours it had swung around, dangling from its electrical wires, bashing itself against the mast until it had finally broken its tenuous tethers and crashed to the deck. Somehow, it had managed to remain onboard, and I had found it wedged in a corner a couple of days later. In our next anchorage I had taken it back up the mast, reconnected it to the wires and lashed it temporarily in place, but I could get no sound from it.

With Hector now up the mast with a multi-meter on the speaker wires, I switched on and activated the hailer, and he got a current. Fortunately, the wires hadn't been broken inside the mast, and for the first time I had a reason to appreciate the poor electrical connections used by our Vancouver installer; however, I could find no appreciation for shoddy speaker mounting. Hector reconnected the speaker, but we still could get no sound from it. He took it up to the shop to troubleshoot and attempt to repair.

On Wednesday while we were baking more bread, Francisco came aboard to finish the cabinetry work on the re-routed dryer vent. While he was in the sea cabin completing the job, he was treated to the aromas of a cranberry-pecan loaf and a dried apricot one. After he left Edi ran two loads through the full wash and dry cycles to celebrate our finally having a proper system.

On Thursday Hector came aboard with a repaired foghorn-hailer speaker. Not only had he overhauled its electrical circuitry, he had also rebuilt the shattered horn, fabricating new fibreglass pieces to replace the missing plastic bits. He went up the mast, connected the wires and we got a bright, clear voice through the hailer. He next test-fitted a newly fabricated horn mount and took it back to the shop to fine-tune. Shortly he was back to finish the installation.

All our minor work was now completed, and mid-afternoon on Thursday Ronald came aboard to give us an update on the procurement and shipping status of various parts that are needed to continue with work on the generator, the Espar furnace, the alternators and the engine. Pieces were in transit or shortly would be, and we expected to begin the rebuilding and the repairs on the major things within a week.

On Sunday the 29th of May we celebrated Edi's birthday quietly onboard Sequitur. The weather continued cold and very wet, but we were warmed by a birthday card from Annelies. We assumed that she had a bit of assistance in composing it on her iPad.

Work on Sequitur had ground to a halt as we waited for parts to arrive. As wonderful as the technicians and workers are here, they are severely hampered with parts procurement problems, being near the end of the world. We spent most of our time inside, hunkered-down and trying to stay warm. Thankfully, Sequitur continued to be a perfectly dry boat, with no leaky hatches, windows or portlights.

A week later, on Sunday the 5th of June the rain had stopped and the clearing sky prompted us to venture into town for grocery shopping. We returned under rather blue skies, just in time to wave bon voyage to Jonathan, the German catamaran that had just completed her repairs at Alwoplast. She was off to Tahiti on the continuation of her circumnavigation.

As Jonathan motored out, we saw that the sky had cleared sufficiently to afford us a view of the erupting Puyehue-Cordon Caulle volcano upriver to the southeast. Even at 130 kilometres distance, the 10,000 metre-high ash plume was impressive. Fortunately, the prevailing winds and local weather pattern mean that none of the ash would come anywhere near us.

On Monday night we were hit with 30-knot winds, violent gusts and torrential downpours, and the whole Valdivia area was hit by a power outage. We awoke on Tuesday morning to a cold cabin; the igniter for our Espar diesel furnace was still in transit from Germany, and without electricity, our electric heaters were useless.

Fortunately, the battery had been full when the outage began, and it was still at 96% after inverting power for our breakfast's coffeemaker and bagel toaster demand. Not knowing how long the power might be out, we decided against using the inverter to power the heaters, so we put on a few extra layers of clothing. Edi put on her fingerless gloves and began knitting me a pair.

By midmorning Ronald had hooked-up some temporary cables from the factory's emergency generator to the floats, and we had shore-power again. I turned on our heaters and blew the circuit. Ronald made-up and installed a heavier breaker, and we were again warming.

The regional power grid was on and off through the day and evening as the storm continued with severe gusts, heavy lightning, thunder and hail. The Alwoplast generator automatically switched-on a few seconds after each outage and we saw only tiny pauses in our power. To speed the cabin warming, we baked bagels and bread, and with the oven warmed, a quiche for dinner.

The next morning we read in the online news: An unusual storm bringing hurricane-force winds, heavy rain and hail had damaged more than 100 homes in a Chilean lake resort. Emergency officials were already dealing with a volcanic eruption in the region. Looking further I found that in Villarrica, 115km northeast of Sequitur, the winds blew at nearly 200 kph, the equivalent of a Category 3 hurricane, ripping off many roofs. Although there is no record of any previous tornadoes, Chile's meteorology centre said Tuesday's storm was a strange one that had some characteristics of a tornado. We were pleased it wasn't quite that windy at Alwoplast.

On Wednesday morning, the mechanics arrived with the cleaned and tested injectors for the engine. They reinstalled them, adjusted the valves, changed the oil and replaced the fuel and oil filters. The engine's 2000 hour routine maintenance was completed, and it was awaiting only the arrival of the new raw water pump to be ready to flash-up.

Late on Wednesday afternoon Ronald brought the new raw water pump onboard. He said that it had just arrived from the Yanmar distributor in Santiago, and that the mechanics would install it the next morning.

Sure enough, first thing Thursday morning, the one month anniversary of our arrival at Alwoplast, the mechanics were back onboard to install the pump and to remount the alternators. Then Hector arrived to reconnect the wiring and the engine was ready to start. I turned the key and there was silence. The starter did not turn. Was it a stuck solenoid? Was it something else?

Hector dived into the engine compartment and with the aid of a flashlight quickly found heavy corrosion on the starter's electrical contacts, most likely caused by the spray from the raw water pump leak. Unfortunately, the starter is buried under the supercharger, and the latter will need to come off to gain access. Hector went ashore to report this arising to Ronald and to get the mechanics back from town to remove supercharger.

Mid-afternoon the mechanics were back onboard to removed supercharger and the starter. There was heavy corrosion on the terminals, plus some on the casing, and Hector took it up to the shop to clean and overhaul.

As he was finishing, the mechanics arrived with the rebuilt Fischer-Panda generator and with the assistance of a couple of workers from the boatbuilding shop, manhandled it onboard. Once the generator was in the cockpit, they set to work reinstalling the turbocharger on the engine and ensuring that it was again ready to start. It flashed-up on the first turn and ran smoothly, quietly and smoke-free.

When we had installed the new Balmar 120 alternator in the Galapagos, we had used the existing Balmar regulator. I now suspect that it was the cause of the two burned-out alternators. I had ordered a pair of MC-614 Max Charge regulators from Balmar when we were in Las Hadas, Mexico, but had used only one of them, the one on the 210 amp unit. The second new regulator was still a spare, and I wanted to replace the old ARS-4 regulator on the 120 with it. Among other things, it has battery and alternator temperature sensors and associated damage-control programming.

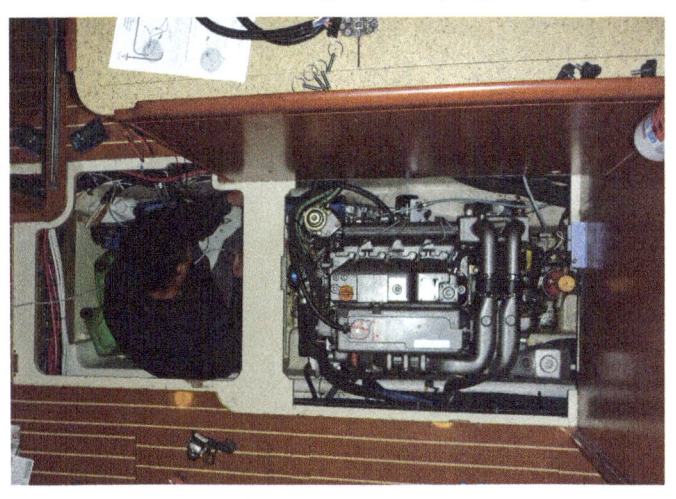

At 1725 Hector returned with a cleaned-up and bench-tested starter. Since it was already very late in the day, he told us he would be back to continue mañana.

Shortly before 0900 on Friday Hector arrived to continue. He installed the starter and then overhauled all the electrical connections in engine room. Shortly after 1000 Ronald came aboard with the new Balmar 120 alternator, which has just arrived from Seattle. Hector exchanged the freewheeling burned-out one with the new one and hooked it up to the regulator.

Hector and Ronald went to work sorting-out the wiring while I shut off the shore power and switched on the inverter with the electric heaters as a load. The 160 to 180 amp draw from the heaters soon had the battery nudging down, and in twenty minutes it was down below 96%. This gave capacity into which the alternators could charge, and allowed us to take some useful readings.

433

Satisfied, Ronald went back to his other duties, and Hector completed the installation and set-up of the new regulator and the temperature sensors. Everything was now ready for the installation of the generator, but by this time it was past quitting time, so we resigned ourselves to waiting until Monday.

To console ourselves, we enjoyed the dryness and relative warmth of Sequitur as the storm intensified outside. Our view out the cabin windows and across the Valdivia River hasn't changed much the past few days; however, the weather forecast looked promising, calling for light rain showers on Saturday and then a mix of sun and cloud for Sunday.

On Sunday the 12th of June there was a brief respite from the bleak weather, and we took advantage of it to catch a bus into town for some grocery shopping. We were into our thirteenth week in Valdivia and our sixth week at Alwoplast; most of Sequitur's repairs had been completed.

On Monday morning a team of four manhandled the Fischer Panda generator down from the cockpit and placed it in its compartment forward of the engine. Sadio, the mechanic reinstalled it on its mounts, re-plumbed the cooling water circuit, the water heater lines, the fuel lines and the exhaust. Then Hector began reconnecting the electrical harnesses as Ronald and I analyzed the cause of failure.

Ronald very quickly saw that the exhaust water-lock had been installed at the same height as the generator's engine exhaust. I referred to the very explicit and illustrated installation instructions for the Fischer-Panda in a Hunter 49 and saw that the water-lock had not been installed in the position called for.

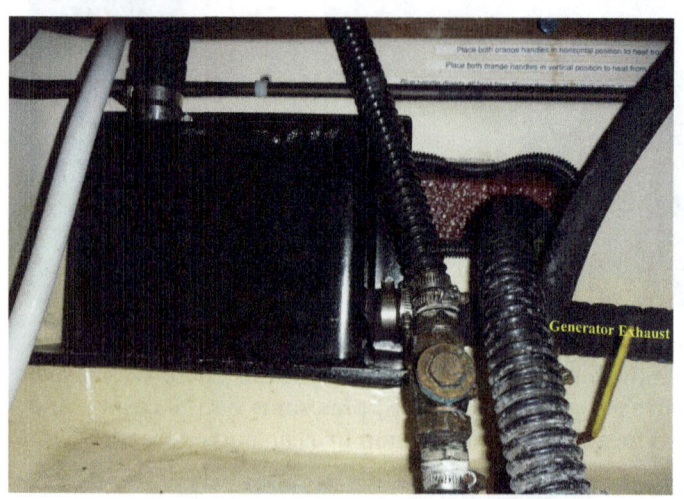

Instead of being placed at the bottom of the after bulkhead of the main bilge compartment, our water-lock had been mounted higher up on the forward starboard side of the compartment, with its inlet at the same level as the generator's exhaust. Its function as a water-lock was thereby defeated, and our generator's catastrophic failure appears to have been the result of another faulty installation by Specialty Yachts in Vancouver.

We determined the remedial action was to lower the placement of the exhaust water-lock in the main bilge compartment to the prescribed level. Sadio removed the water-lock and repositioned it 9.5 cm lower. This was clearly an improvement over the previous position. To hedge our bets, we also decided it was prudent to raise the level of the generator mounting. A plan was devised, measurements were taken and work was begun in the shop to manufacture new mounts to place the generator 13.5 cm higher. This would then place the exhaust outlet 23 cm higher than the inlet to the water-lock, and would prevent a recurrence of the ingestion of salt water in through the engine's exhaust.

Meanwhile, Hector had completed the electrical reconnections, and the generator was ready to flash-up. After we had de-aerated the fuel system, filled the cooling system and opened the raw water inlet, I switched on the power and pushed the start button. The engine started immediately, ran for two or three seconds and then shut down. After another two identical results, we re-bled the fuel system, but saw no improvement. We pored over the troubleshooting pages in manual, but it was getting late, so Ronald took manual home to study overnight.

On Tuesday morning Ronald disassembled the fuel solenoid and tested it to find it okay. He next checked the exhaust temperature sensor wiring, and refreshed its connections.

The generator started and ran. We switched the shore power off, switched the inverter and the heaters on and watched as the generator provided the required 180 amps. We continued to run it for about ten minutes, and then we shut it down and went back to shore power, satisfied that it was running again. Ronald then took precise measurements of the generator compartment and of the generator, and went to the shop to fine-tune the manufacture of the new mounts.

Later in the day, when Edi was preparing lunch, and the shore power was reading 88 volts, I decided to run the generator to provide more power for the panini maker. I switched off the shore power, flashed-up the generator and switched on the inverter. The generator ran smoothly, and the meter showed it was providing 95 amps at 13.8 volts into the system and allowing the inverter to supply us with the 1200 Watts demanded by the panini maker.

The four indicator lights on the remote panel continued to show green, as I monitored the panel and the gauges. Then, after running like this for about five minutes, all the lights on the panel suddenly went out and the generator quit. It looked like a blown fuse in the generator's control box. I decided to leave it to Ronald and Hector to sort-out.

On Wednesday morning, Hector came and quickly found in the terminal block for the remote control panel that F-1, the DC system's fuse had blown. He replaced it, and the remote panel lights came on again. We flashed-up the generator and it ran for a few seconds and blew the fuse again. Before Hector could begin to troubleshoot, Sadio and Julio came aboard with the new mounts to elevate the generator up to a better level above the water-lock.

They unbolted the generator from its mounts, disconnected the exhaust, fuel, raw water and water heating lines and lifted the unit, its wiring harnesses still connected, onto the galley sole.

Within an hour, the old mounts were relocated onto the tops of the new mount blocks, the blocks were bolted into place and the generator was installed into its new higher position. The exhaust was sloping down as it exits the generator engine, and continued its downward slope through the bulkhead to the water-lock. The height between the exhaust and the water-lock was 23 cm.

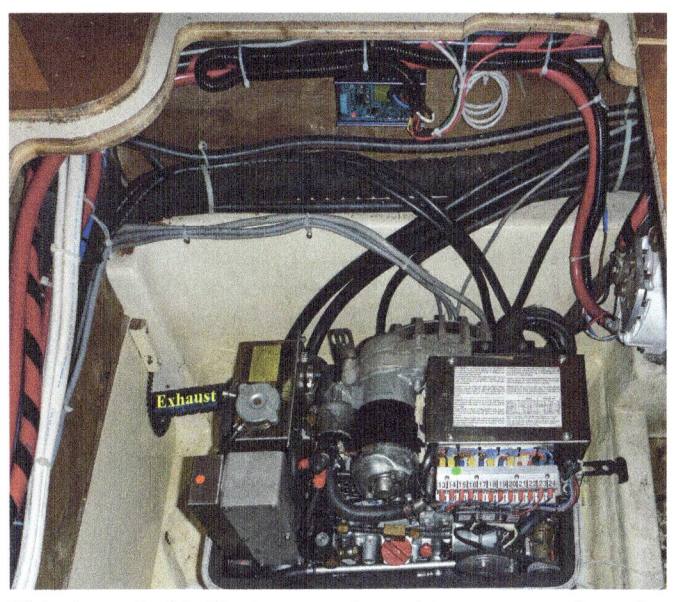

This is a decidedly improved position to one done by Specialty Yachts in Vancouver. Their installation, shown here, with its near-horizontal lead all the way from the exhaust to the water-lock inlet, allowed the ingestion of salt water into the engine and led to the engine's destruction.

We tracked-down the problem with the F-1 fuse; the manual calls for a 15-amp fuse, but a 10-amp fuse had been installed instead. With the proper fuse installed, the generator flashed-up and ran properly. I reinstalled the sound-insulation case and ran the generator for over an hour while applying various loads to it with the shore

435

power switched off. The generator easily handled the widely varying demands of the inverter as the electrical heaters' thermostats cycled them on and off.

While we had access to the professionals at Alwoplast, it was wise to clean up our list of outstanding items, and try to find places for some of the bits and pieces in our UFO (Unidentified Found Objects) bin. One of the most worrisome things was the door in the aft shower. We needed to install a lock on it to keep it from flying open in rough seas. It had ripped itself off its hinges and smashed one of the portlights during rough weather in the Sea of Cortez early the previous year. From the beginning, I have been using the forward shower, and Edi the after one, so I was not that familiar with it, other than having repaired the door and remounted it.

I examined the door to try to come up with ideas for a lock, and saw that, while the door was fitted with a latch, on the jamb where its corresponding lug should have been, there were only four screw holes, one of them filled with the stub of a broken-off screw.

When I told Edi we needed to get Alwoplast to manufacture a lug to fit the door's catch, she remembered a piece she had found in the vanity when she took-over the after head in 2008. We couldn't identify it at the time, so it had become the start of our UFO bin.

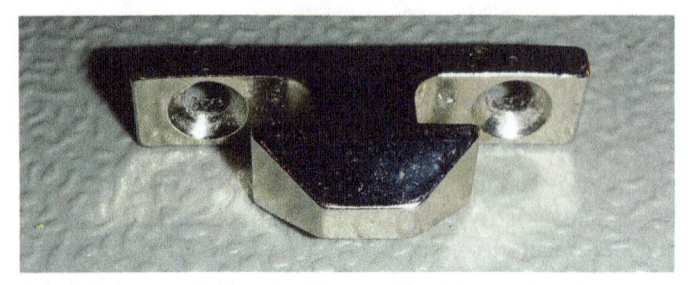

I dug it out, and saw that it was the missing lock lug.

It appeared that the original holes were drilled too low on the jamb, causing the lug to not engage with the jaws of the lock. With the reputation for incompetence that Specialty Yachts has earned in my mind, I pictured one of their crew being assigned to drill new holes and reposition the lug. A screw was over-torqued, the lug was stashed and the job was likely reported as being finished.

I confirmed that the new holes had been drilled at the proper height. All that was required was an easy-out or other such tool to remove the broken screw. I took the lug to Ronald and he quickly got proper screws from the well-organized bins in the parts room. He then spoke with Francisco, gave him the parts and within twenty minutes the stub of the broken-off screw had been backed out, the lug had been mounted and we finally had a lock on the shower door to keep it in place while at sea. We would no longer need to wedge the teak grid up against it when we prepare for sea.

The only thing remaining on our list of repairs was the Espar furnace. The glow plug was due in from Germany on Wednesday, and on Thursday afternoon Ronald told us it had just arrived in Santiago. It was being FedExed and should be here on Friday. We both expressed our hopes that it was the only problem with the furnace.

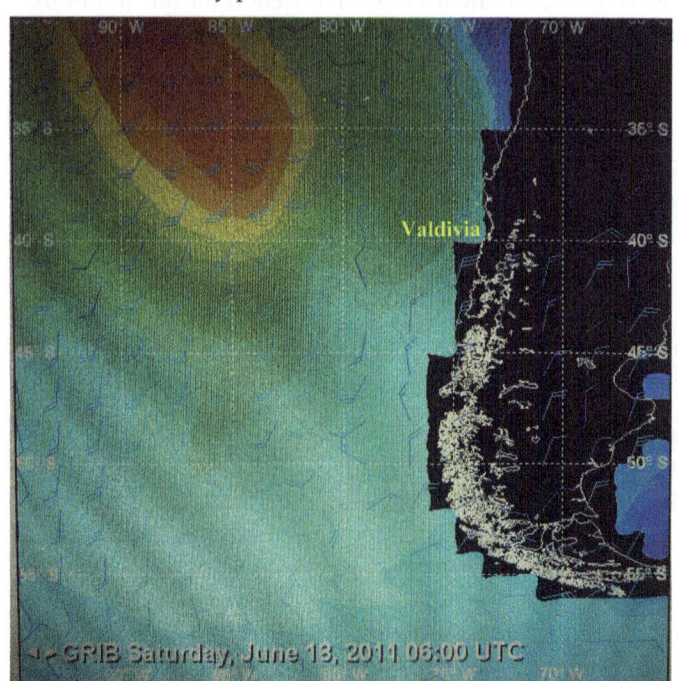

I began looking at online weather forecasts and downloading grib files to see if there was a window to allow us a safe and comfortable passage to Puerto Montt. There was a deep depression 250 miles west of us on Thursday, which was tracking eastward with 50-knot winds and 11-metre seas. It was forecast to turn to the northeast and by Saturday begin dissipating. The coast was expected to be hit by 30-knot northerly winds from Friday morning through midday Saturday.

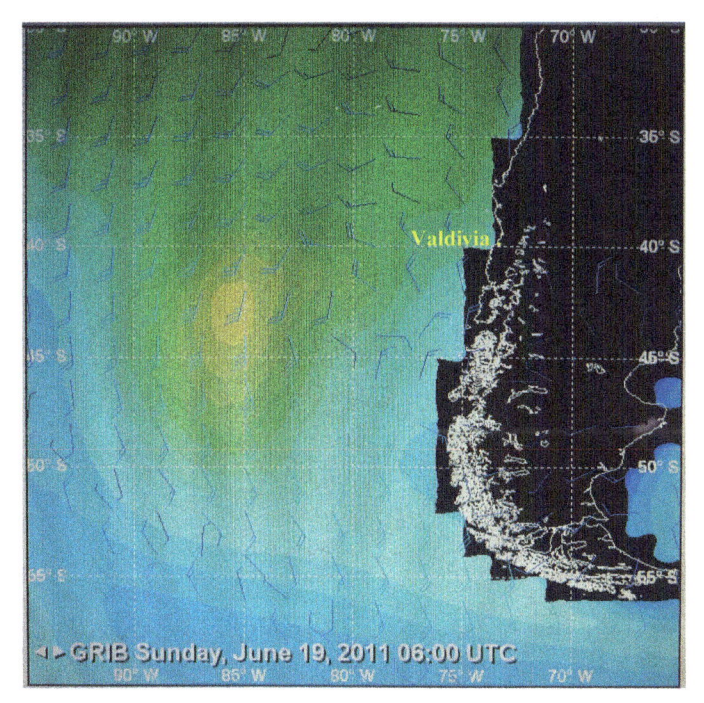

By early Sunday morning, the local winds were forecast to be in the 15 and 20 knot area and the swell in the 6-metre range. This appeared to be the beginning of a weather window suitable for our continuation southward.

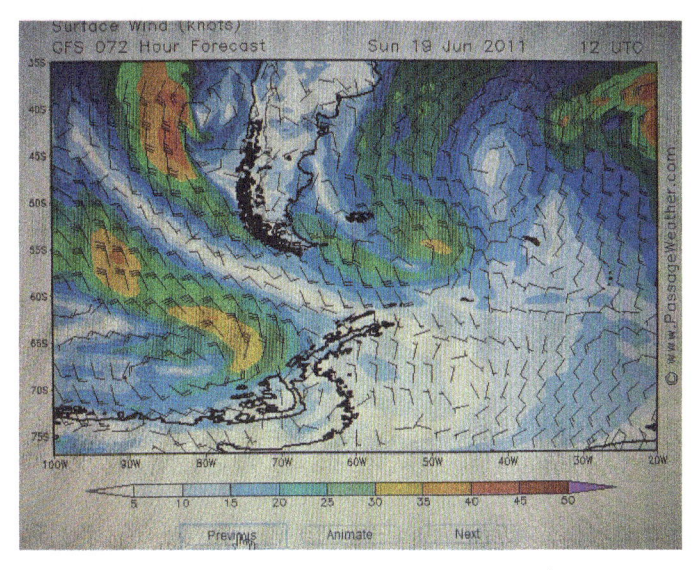

I looked at forecasts on PassageWeather, and they seemed to confirm what the grib files were showing. By Sunday morning, the winds offshore and to the south from Valdivia would be less than 20 knots.

The Monday morning forecast showed easterly winds in the 20-knot range. While three and four days is a bit long for accurate marine forecasts in this area, the general tendency of the current systems bodes well for a departure on Sunday. I asked Ronald to prepare an interim invoice for the materials, supplies and work done to date as well as for the moorage and electricity.

The invoice I was presented with was shocking. It was so different from the costs I had anticipated, that I had to reread it several times to make sure I was reading it correctly. Every time I studied it, I was floored by the amount being charged. I knew we had used many kilowatts of electricity, running our electrical heaters to try to keep Sequitur warm in the single-digit temperatures, and I was aware that electricity is very expensive in Chile. I was also aware that the cost of moorage on clean, modern floats in a well-run marina is not cheap. Procuring parts and importing them to this near-the-end-of-the-world place is also very expensive. Employing highly qualified, efficient and professional workers doesn't come cheaply.

What shocked and amazed me was that the invoice total was so dramatically below the amount I had anticipated paying for such excellence.

The cost of moorage was only 3000 pesos a day, about $6, but by far the largest contributor to the low invoice at Alwoplast was the labour charge. This is 11,700 Pesos (about $24) per hour, which, with the postal strike in progress in Canada, I was reminded is only a dollar more than Canada Post's starting wage for unskilled employees.

I am accustomed to much higher rates for boat work; even the shoddy, careless and inexperienced work we received from Specialty Yachts in Vancouver was invoiced at $75 per hour, and there the invoiced hours included their learning time, their coffee and tea breaks and their cell phone conversation breaks.

On Thursday evening, to celebrate many things, we had the last of the Iquique mahi-mahi from the freezer. With it we enjoyed basmati rice, a butter-sweat of mushrooms, red peppers and zucchini and a delicious bottle of Undurraga Brut. Among the things being celebrated was the elopement of Edi's daughter Amy. She and Bram had quietly snuck off to Niagara Falls with granddaughter Annelies and got married on Wednesday. Edi and I discussed whether we owe some cattle to our new in-laws in Holland.

On Friday morning Ronald reported that the FedEx parcel with the Espar glow plug would not arrive until Monday. I told him the weather window now looked good from Sunday afternoon through early Thursday, and that a Monday afternoon or Tuesday morning departure appeared best for us. We decided that regardless whether the Espar was repaired, we would leave on Tuesday at the latest.

On Friday afternoon the couple from Spirit of Africa, the catamaran astern of us returned from their sojourn in South Africa. We chatted with them on the float, and they invited us over for drinks in the early evening.

Rowland and Miki had arrived in Valdivia from Cape Horn and the channels the week after we had. Rowland's brother Peter had come back from South Africa with them for a couple of weeks, and the five of us spent a wonderful evening chatting.

We invited them over to Sequitur for pizzas and wine on Sunday evening. I prepared three oven-sized rectangular pizzas and we spent a wonderful four hours sharing notes on places they have been that we want to visit, and vice-versa. Rowland gave us some good pointers on shore lines in the Patagonian and Tierra del Fuego anchorages. Wherever possible, they used four lines, balancing the boat between them and making the anchor redundant, other than as an aid to backing into a protected slot.

We have three lines, two 100-metre polypropylene reels and an 80-metre nylon webbing on a Norwegian wheel, plus a 180-metre spool of 19mm nylon in case we needed a very deep anchorage. When I told him I had been thinking of getting another long piece of polypropylene in Puerto Montt, he suggested he could sell me two of his four lines; they would not likely need them as they are heading to Polynesia and onward.

On Monday morning, the first clear, sunny day in three weeks, Rowland dug out of his forward lockers two custom-made nylon stuff sacks with 80 and 100 metres of 19mm line. He offered them to me at a price I couldn't refuse.

Meanwhile, Ronald arrived aboard Sequitur with the just-arrived glow plug for the Espar furnace. It had been ordered nearly six weeks previously, and through an error in Germany, had been sent by regular mail rather than by courier.

Ronald clambered into the transom locker and went to work. We all kept our fingers crossed, hoping that the problem with the furnace was the glow plug, and only the glow plug.

At Ronald's request, I switched on the furnace and turned up the thermostat. The furnace began cycling and shortly, white smoke came out its exhaust. It had come back from the dead. It smoked heavily for a long while, as the excess diesel in the exhaust system slowly burned off.

I reported that there was no heat from the radiators, and Ronald found that the coolant wasn't circulating, so he uninstalled the furnace and took it to the shop to tear down. There was a seized impeller in the pump, so he overhauled it and rebuilt the furnace. Then he went back into the transom locker and reinstalled it. It flashed-up and ran properly this time, and for the first time in three months, we had proper heat aboard.

It was early afternoon by the time the furnace repairs were completed, and we saw a possibility of finally leaving Valdivia. We headed into town to the Armada offices to see if we could get a zarpe issued for an afternoon departure. After about two hours of very slow intranet connection, the petty officer managed to process our departure for Puerto Montt.

We had been just over three months in Valdivia, not by choice, but because of the need to repair failures to systems that had been installed by Specialty Yachts in Vancouver. We were ready to move on from Valdivia, and hopefully, also able to move on from the results of the deplorable work that had been done on Sequitur's fit-out.

It was shortly after 1500 when we arrived back aboard Sequitur, and we scrambled to ready her for sea. At 1530 we slipped from the float at Alwoplast and eased out into the ebbing river and headed downstream. After more than thirteen weeks, we were finally on our way again.

We enjoyed a very rare sunny day as we motored out toward the Pacific past idyllic scenery. Except for a few small wisps of cloud, the sky was blue, and the single-digit temperature reminded us we were less than a day from the beginning of winter.

We passed another reminder in the river. The mast of a long-ago shipwreck clearly showed the proper side to pass the green beacon. We decided to pass green to green, since we were leaving port.

The ebb assisted us all the way out the river, adding up to two knots to our speed until we reached the outer reaches of Bahia Corral at 1700. The wind was light and fickle around the headlands, so we continued to motor. The sun set at 1737 to begin the longest night of the year in the southern hemisphere, and the temperature dropped further. We had zipped-up the full cockpit enclosure, and remained comfortably warm with the Espar running below and an electric heater on in the cockpit.

By 2000 we had rounded Punta Gatera and had bent our course southward. We were now officially in the Roaring Forties, and we were motoring directly into the Humboldt Current and into an 8 to 10 knot wind. The swell was from the west-southwest at 5 to 6 metres, leftover from the recent storm. Through the night the wind built to the 20-knot range and the 3 to 4 metre seas it generated crossed uncomfortably with the swell.

The morning of the 21st the winds remained around 20 knots directly on our nose, and we continued to motor into confused seas, but we stayed dry and warm in our cocoon. At 1316, the official time of the solstice, the sun finally began heading south again. As we approached Golfo Coronados, we began to be slowed even further by the waters ebbing out of the Golfo de Ancud. We were down to 3.19 miles made good during our slowest hour, with the engine at 1800 rpm, enough for 6 knots. Then as the tide turned, we started speeding up again and by 1600 were above 6 knots. The winds began to abate in the early afternoon, and as entered the protection of Peninsula Lacui, they were down to under 5 knots.

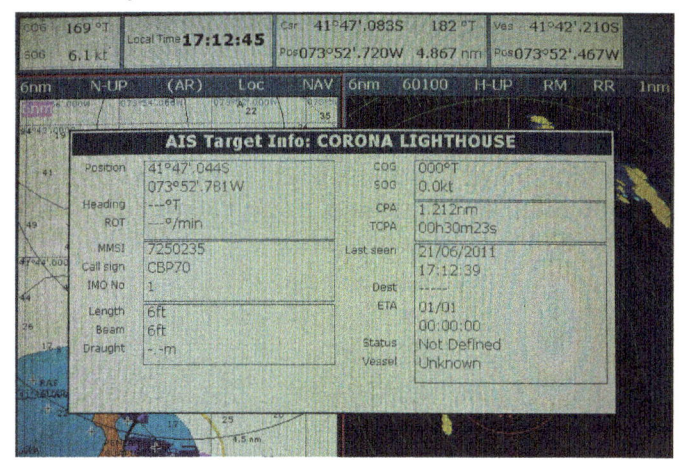

Because we had been slowed by the strong head winds and by the Humboldt, the tidal currents in Canal Chacao would be adverse, so we had decided to anchor for the night in the lee of Punta Coronas. As we approached the point, I saw that the AIS target I had been watching, and had thought was an anchored ship near the point, was actually the Punta Corona lighthouse. This is the first time I have seen an AIS transponder at a lighthouse. What a marvellous way to show the light from 50 or 75 miles away, and also to grid the chart to the GPS.

At 1730 the sun set to end the shortest day of the year. We were still about 3 miles from our intended anchorage, but fortunately, because of the latitude there is nearly an hour of twilight, even in this season.

At 1816 we came to 30 metres on the Rocna in 8 metres of water three cables south of Faro Corona, and just out of its illumination arc. As we were securing, the lighthouse keeper called on VHF to welcome us to Ancud and to ask for our arrival report.

The sun rose at 0821 as we watched a dozen or more fishing boats head out from Ancud. While Edi put on the coffee and made a 2.5 litre pot of tea in the pump thermos, I prepared Sequitur for sea. At 0848 we weighed and proceeded toward Canal Chacao, the narrows that separate Isla Chiloe from the mainland of Chile.

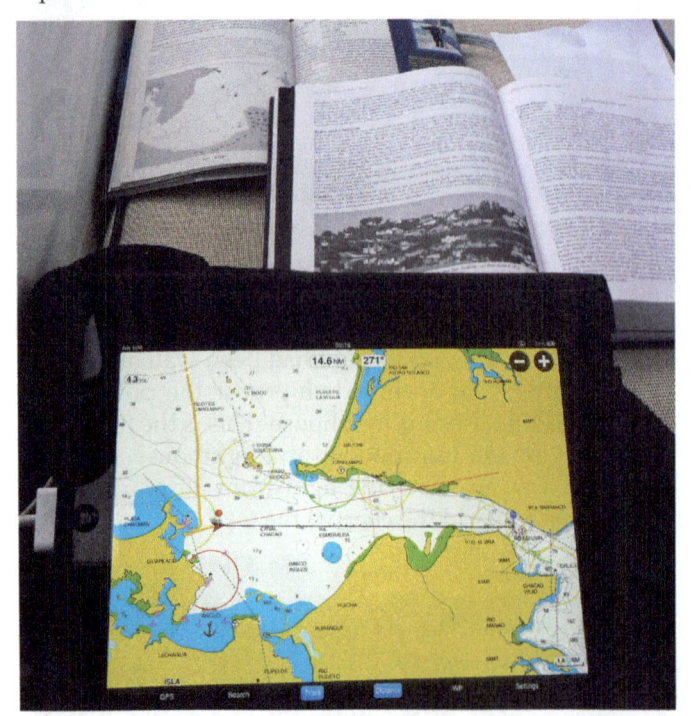

As we motored eastward toward Canal Chacao, we enjoyed a ham and eggs on toast with Peruvian coffee in the comfort of the enclosed cockpit. At 0953 I spotted our first penguin as it surfaced for breath off our port quarter. The sky was totally overcast with low stratus, there was no wind and the sea was glassy. As we progressed, our 2150 rpm speed increased from 4.5 knots at 0900 to 6.1 knots at 1100 and 7.7 knots at 1200 as we passed Roca Remolinos.

This nine-mile-long strait has a bad reputation, with currents up to nine knots, and in addition to tidal rips, whirlpools and overfalls, and there is a drying rock, Roca Remolinos in the middle of its narrowest point. From our anchorage it was ten miles to the start of the narrows, and sixteen to the narrowest point. I had timed it to leave three-and-a-half hours before the end of the ebb, working into a weakening counter-current and arriving in the narrows at the turn of the tide. The flood would then assist us all the way from Roca Remolinos to Puerto Montt.

We saw nothing but flat, calm water the entire passage through, with none of the rips, whirlpools and overfalls we are so accustomed to in British Columbia waters. The dreaded Canal Chacao was more peaceful than Vancouver's False Creek.

Just past Roca Remolinos, at the end of the narrows, the channel is crossed by a steady stream of ferries between the mainland and Isla Chiloe. We managed to slip through the gauntlet without having to alter course or speed.

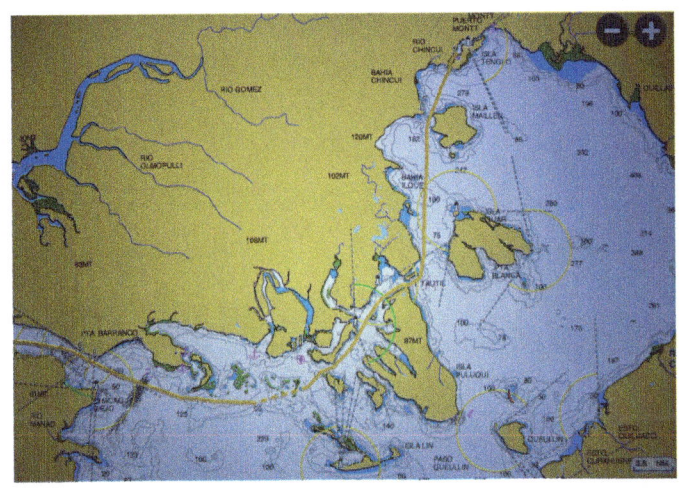

Because of the stories I had been hearing of the *"dangerous"* currents among the islands down here, I had initially planned to take the long way around to Puerto Montt. However, when I saw how benign the conditions are in reality, I decided to weave a more direct route through the islands. Instead of taking 52 miles, we made it in only 38, and at our 7-knot speed this cut two hours off our passage.

The waters were calm, the channels were well charted and well marked, and the passage was a joy. Along the way we saw many fish farms strung-out on buoys from the sloping gravel beaches. At many of these were floating sheds, workshops and camps.

The sun set at 1720 as we were approaching the southern entrance to Canal Tenglo, and half-an-hour later we were secured alongside on the inner face of the outer float at Club Nautico Reloncavi in Puerto Montt. Overnight, the weather window slammed shut, and the frontal system brought torrential rains and winds over 25 knots, but we were safe and snug, and finally in Puerto Montt with all systems working.

On Thursday morning it was still very windy, and the rain was blowing sideways as I walked up the floats to the office. I arrived shortly after 0900 to learn that the office didn't open until 1000, so I braved the gale and slanting rain and made my way back to Sequitur, where the Espar furnace was keeping us warm and cozy in the not-much-above-zero weather.

Shortly after 1000 I went back out into the storm and up the floats to visit the office. The women there spoke less English than I did Spanish, so through a halting and disjointed conversation, I learned they knew nothing about our haul-out, and that Alexandro, the office manager would be in at 1400.

Two more walks through the afternoon's pelting rain brought information from Alexandro that the Club has never before had so many boats hauled-out. The yard was overflowing into neighbouring areas, and while they could just fit us in, they had no stands, and were scrambling to fabricate some for the two boats ahead of us in the line. He said it was unlikely they could haul us until Monday, or even Tuesday. I explained our wish to head back to Canada as soon as we could, and he said he would do everything possible to speed the process.

By Thursday evening the storm clouds were retreating to the east, and the winds had abated. Friday morning was calm and mostly sunny, but it remained cold, and the Espar continued to keep us comfortable. Midmorning Alexandro informed us that they could haul us at 1000 on Saturday. There were no boats scheduled after us, and the travel-lift could then simply remain in place supporting Sequitur until the stands could be fabricated.

In the early afternoon the contents of our main fuel tank fell below the intake level for the furnace, and the furnace shut down. Since we were being hauled the next morning, I decided there was no need to do a jerry can bucket brigade from the gas station; there was still sufficient fuel in the tank to run the engine to motor over to the haul-out, and the Fischer-Panda generator could still be run to power the electrical heaters.

441

The crossbar on the travel-lift was just high enough to accommodate Sequitur, if we removed the wind generator and lowered its mast. Unfortunately, the mast had been constructed without the ability to be lowered. We saw this as a good opportunity to modify it to make it easier for the next times we are hauled.

When I began dismounting the wind generator, I found that the installer had saved a few cents and had left only about five extra centimetres of wire. The generator could not be lifted out of its mounting socket because of the tight wire. There were no quick disconnects installed, and I was left with no option but to cut the wires in the cockpit locker and to attach a fish line to them. This allowed me to pull the generator out of its socket, lay it on edges of the solar panels, cut the wires and attach another fish line. Had I installed the generator, I certainly would have done it differently to this Specialty Yachts *get-the-job-done* approach, which showed no concern about future use, care and maintenance. While I was in the locker, I found two more unidentified, unlabelled and unprotected wire ends; we'll have to track-down what Specialty Yachts foul-up this is.

After we had finished with the wind generator, we took a bus into town to the bus depot to begin organizing our return to Vancouver. For a total of 36,000 Pesos, we bought semi-cama tickets to Santiago on TurBus for their 2000 departure on Saturday night. Then we walked across the street to Supermercado Bigger to pick up a barbecued chicken for dinner; our fridges and freezers were nearly empty.

Back aboard in the early evening, we turned on the oven to 550 degrees to bake flat bread for Saturday's breakfast, olive focaccia for Saturday's lunch and pizzas for Saturday's dinner to serve as and sustenance on our trip to Santiago and wait for standby seats at the airport. The hot oven assisted in keeping Sequitur a bit warmer, though with the near freezing temperature and high humidity, it needed augmentation from the generator and electrical heaters. We had already shutdown a fridge and a freezer, and after the baking depleted the last of our vegetables, cheese and meat, and we shutdown the other two.

Shortly before 1000 on Saturday morning a yard worker came onboard to assist with our move to the haul-out slip. The slip is 5 metres wide and Sequitur's beam is 4.47 metres, so backing in to it would be a bit tricky, particularly since there are no floats or guides inside it, just widely spaced concrete pilings. On my first attempt, I misjudged the cross wind and the tidal eddies and arrived at the mouth a tad askew. I aborted the second attempt almost immediately it had begun, and on the third go we slipped flawlessly in.

As Sequitur was lifted, I monitored the gap between the bottom of the crossbar and the top of her boom while comparing it to the amount of keel still below the sill of the haul-out slip. There seemed to be more keel below the sill than space above the boom.

I had lowered the boom onto the top of the arches to gain more room. Finally, with the boom just brushing the crossbar, Sequitur was wheeled out over the hard with less than 5 centimetres to spare under her keel.

My first concern was the condition of the zincs. The one on the hub of the VariProp was almost completely eroded, with just a ring of crumbly metal remaining in place. The two shaft zincs were about half gone. All three of these zincs had been replaced in early December in La Punta, Peru, and the erosion seems to me to be excessive for less than seven months of use.

I wondered whether the mooring field in La Punta, Peru has a stray current problem. There are dozens of buoys there with 220 volt power outlets, and an extensive nexus of underwater electrical cabling to supply them. Our zincs had been eroded completely away when we were lifted there after five months on a mooring half a cable or so from the edge of the electrified buoys. When we went back in, we had sat connected to an electrical buoy for a week before we left for Chile. However, I cannot dismiss the thoughts that our rapid zinc erosion might be the result of yet another faulty installation by Specialty Yachts in Vancouver. This might explain our steady battery drain of 2.8 amps with all systems shut down.

Sequitur was very slowly moved through the crowded yard with her keel barely off the surface while crew walked ahead to remove pebbles and flatten irregularities in her path. The previous day we had seen no available space in the yard sufficiently large to accommodate Sequitur, but Alexandro had told us they could fit her in.

She was taken through the yard and into an adjoining property, which also appeared filled to capacity, and there shortly after noon, she was settled onto a thick plywood pad. Almost immediately, workers and a welder began fabricating a custom support system while Sequitur remained supported by the travel-lift. We returned onboard to continue preparing Sequitur for our absence and to pack for our trip.

One of the things I needed to do was pickle the watermaker. This is a very simple procedure, which is clearly laid-out in the Spectra manual, and involves removing a hose at its quick-disconnect fitting and clicking into place a service hose with its quick-disconnect fitting.

I was very pleased at the condition of the bottom. The anti-fouling paint had lasted very well during the 26 months since it had been applied, and we had only a small layer of slime, which came off easily with a power-washing.

443

The previous year in Peru, when I had done the storage procedure, I had discovered that the Specialty Yachts installer had not installed the quick-disconnect fitting, so I had to unscrew the hose clamp he had installed in its place, wriggle the hose off the barb, remove the other part of the fitting from the service hose and wriggle it onto the barb. I had then forgotten to buy a quick-disconnect fitting while we were in Vancouver, so I again had to do the procedure the awkward way. We hoped that the people at Specialty Yachts Service were enjoying our quick-disconnect fitting. I added a note to our things-to-do list while back to Vancouver: *"Buy a fitting so that the storage procedure will be as easy to perform as Spectra had intended."*

We spent the remainder of the afternoon organizing, cleaning and packing. Among the things we did was place containers with Bolseca dehydration crystals in the two showers, the three sinks and in a bucket in the pantry. We were hopeful that the nine kilograms of crystals would keep Sequitur's interior dry during the wet southern winter.

At 1840 the taxi we had ordered arrived under our stern ladder, and for 5,000 Pesos it took us to the central bus depot. The bus departed on time at 2000 and we laid back in the very comfortable reclining semi-cama (half-bed) seats for our 13.5-hour overnight trip to Santiago. From there an 8,000 Peso taxi took us to the airport, where we settled-in shortly before 1000 to wait to see if our standby reservations would yield seats on the 1830 Air Canada flight to Toronto. The flight showed full, but knowing there are nearly always no-shows, we crossed our fingers and waited.

We didn't make it, so we headed out to find a hotel for the night. We took a free shuttle to a nice four-star hotel five minutes from the airport, checked-in and weighed our options. We wanted if possible to avoid having to connect through the United States, with its over-the-top paranoid security, so Air Canada to Toronto was our only option. After being bumped again, and seeing that the next few day's flights from Santiago were heavily oversold, we decided to bailout and fly to Lima, Peru where the Wednesday night flight to Toronto showed some open seats.

We made it onto the flight from Lima, found connecting seats in Toronto and mid-afternoon on Thursday the 30th of June, we arrived back at our loft in Vancouver. We then began the slow readjustment to the change of scene and to realign our thinking from third world to first.

22. Back in Vancouver Again

Our thoughts were to spend the summer in Canada while winter spends its time in Chile. Our immediate goals were to warm-up and dry-out from more than three months of cold dank weather in Valdivia and northern Patagonia.

Back in Vancouver, while the rest of North America suffered through weeks of one of the hottest spells on record, we continued waiting for summer to arrive. While the news headlines from the other side of the Rockies were riddled with references to heat waves, deaths from heat and global warming, we sat in Vancouver watching the west coast weather change from rain to drizzle to rain showers to heavy overcast to a few hours of sun and then back to rain again. It remained cool, bordering on cold. I tried installing summer:

INSTALLING SUMMER.....
■■■■■■■■■■□□□□□□□□□□□□□□□□□□□□□□□□□ □□□□□ **30% DONE.**
Installation failed. 404 error: Season not found.

As we cooled our heels in the heart of what many call the finest city in the world and adjacent to some of the finest cruising waters on the planet, we questioned why we had decided to leave all of this to go boating. Since leaving Vancouver in October 2009, we had taken Sequitur over 9500 nautical miles, well over one-third of a circumnavigation. A large portion of our voyage had been heading into the wind, going against the current and being hampered by the results of the deplorable work that had been done with Sequitur's fit-out by Specialty Yachts.

On a fair day we walked along the shores of False Creek to Granville Island and past the boatyard used by Specialty Yachts. We could identify none of the boats in the nearly empty yard as being their projects. Their floats, for which we had previously waited weeks to be fitted-in for work, were nearly half empty. We counted twelve vacant slips, and we thought back to our double-rafting days there. Granted it is July and everyone is supposed to be out boating, but in 2007, 2008 and 2009, as Specialty bumbled-along with our fit-out and repairs, the yard and the floats were crowded to overflowing all summer long.

A few days later, taking advantage of another spell of sunshine, we took the SkyTrain downtown and walked along through Gastown to Chinatown. We were surprised to see that almost all the small Chinese greengrocers along Pender, Gore and Keefer had disappeared. Where there had formerly been dozens of wonderful little shops with great selections of fresh oriental greens like pak choy, gai lan and sui choy, as well as a broad selection of mainstream produce at very good prices. Gone also are many of the fresh fish mongers and small butchers. Now the shops are almost entirely given over to medicinal herbs, dried foods, and oriental packaged goods, with virtually no fresh selection. We surmised they lost their fresh market to all the new upscale and trendy supermarkets, like Whole Foods and Urban Fare that have sprung-up as Coal Harbour, Yaletown, Gastown, Tinseltown, Chinatown and the Olympic Village have gentrified all around them.

On our walk back around the head of False Creek and through Olympic Village we had a good look across the Creek at the progress on re-roofing BC Place Stadium. Gone is the old marshmallow-in-bondage roof, and nearly completed is the new standing-rib-roast roof. The old roof was air-supported through a system of huge pumps and access to the building was through airlocks. The new roof will be fully retractable and the spaces formerly occupied by air pumps and air locks will be liberated.

445

After a week or so of self-imposed quarantine to rid ourselves of any travel bugs we might have picked-up on our five-day commute from Puerto Montt, we walked over to visit with Bram, Amy and Annelies. The granddaughter was nine months old, full of spirit, crawling and starting to stand. It is time for Bram and Amy to start moving things higher up on the shelves and elsewhere.

Amy was enjoying her twelve months maternity leave and Bram had last year quit his job and began working from home. He is a software engineer and had worked as a games developer for a large Vancouver company before deciding to head out on his own; a bit scary with a new baby, but it comes with the marvellous benefit of fully participating in Annelies' early development.

Bram had been writing applications for the Apple iPad, iPod and iPhone platforms, and one of these, a game called *The Little Crane That Could* had over a million downloads in one month, and it was for a while the top downloaded game in Britain. He is delighted with the response.

I downloaded the app to my iPad and played with it for a while; it proved to be rather challenging. It employs a realistic physics simulation and offers full control over the crane, allowing you to rotate, elevate, bend, extend and grapple. The tasks and challenges that Bram has created are certainly not easy, and it is in no way a casual game. By the time I had worked my way through the tasks in the free level I was addicted, so like thousands of others, I anted-up my $3.99 for the premium version.

It rained and drizzled for much of the following week and from five days out, the weather forecast looked bleak for a scheduled Vancouver Power and Sail Squadron evening raft-up in False Creek. However, by the time we had assembled near the end of the Creek, the skies had mostly cleared and we had a delightful evening. We shared wonderful, lively conversation as we all tried to put a dent in the mosaic of potluck platters, dishes and bowls spread over two tables and a ledge. It was certainly more relaxed and civilized boating than we had experienced in a long while.

Vancouver is fortunate to have such a wonderful waterway as False Creek in the heart of the city. It is even more fortunate to have most of its long shoreline dedicated to a public access and parks. The central portion of this is the twenty-two kilometre long walking, jogging, cycling and inline skating path that twists non-stop from the downtown Convention Centre around Stanley Park, up and around False Creek and out to Kitsilano Beach.

Nearly a month after we had hauled Sequitur in Puerto Montt and headed back to Vancouver, we were still in awe at the cleanliness of the environment, the sense of security, the peacefulness and the comfort and the ease of life. We were still adjusting to having a constant and reliable supply of electricity, water, heat and cooking gas, of having a superb selection of shopping within a short walk, of not stumbling into holes in the sidewalks and of having clean, modern public transit.

Had we not spent so much of the previous two years making-do in the third world, these simple things would have been taken for granted, or even gone unobserved, as they likely are by most in Vancouver. With all the creature comforts we had here, we were not yet to the stage of yearning to head back to Patagonia, particularly since it was winter down there.

To contribute to our relaxing, we fine-tuned the decoration of our loft. Edi applied some oil to the century-old Douglas fir beams and ceiling, which gave them a great visual pop. We were amazed at the condition of these old timbers; they seemed as good as new and reminded us of the 140-year-old ones we had seen earlier in the year in the ghost towns of Chile's Atacama Desert.

446

While we were it, we also added some accent paint on the walls, rearranged the furniture and rehung the paintings. Our loft in an old industrial warehouse was becoming very homey.

In August we flew east to visit my family in New Brunswick, and to attend my nephew Andrew's wedding. Sarah, his bride won the battle of alma maters; they were married in the chapel of her Mount Alison University, rather than in his Saint Francis Xavier. It was the first church wedding that I had attended since 1959.

My father, now ninety-seven years young, is still grumbling at his driver's license having been taken away the previous year after he had a mild heart attack. One of the good results of his hospital visit then was that the doctor examined his eyes and told him he could give him vision in his blind eye. Dad was born with sight in only one eye, and he had spent more than ninety-six years that way. A simple cataract operation last year gave him binocular vision for the first time. He still reads without glasses.

While we were in the East, Edi and I took a day-drive down to Nova Scotia to visit Peggy's Cove and other communities in that area. We were delighted to see that the area has not been Disney-ized; it still retains its quaint charm. We also drove across the Confederation Bridge to Prince Edward Island and along to Charlottetown for a feed of steamed mussels and yam chips.

We flew back to Vancouver and continued to be awed with the way in which the city has developed, and is continuing to develop. It is such a resident-friendly and visitor-friendly city. With its criss-cross of pedestrian walkways and paths, its many streets that include dedicated bicycle lanes, its waterfront that is nearly all public and accessible, its profusion of parks and green spaces throughout, the city centre is one of the most habitable on the planet.

Vancouver is a very young city; she was celebrating her 125th birthday in 2011. It is great to see that the older buildings are being preserved and incorporated into new developments. A good example is the Hotel Georgia, to which a forty-eight story hotel and condo tower was added while fully retaining and restoring the original building.

One of the penthouses sold for over $18 million. Just down the street a 59th and 60th floor condo is going for $28 million. Vancouver continues to have a commercial and residential construction boom, while the rest of the world slows, slumps or implodes.

Further along down near the harbour, the Marine Building, completed in 1930, and for a while the tallest building in the British Commonwealth, is now surrounded by modern towers, some as much as three times as tall.

On one of our many walks through the city, we passed the downtown floatplane terminal. This always seemed a very normal facility to us, and as we walked past, four planes took-off and five landed. The frequency of the commuter and charter flights also seemed normal, until we realized that since we sailed south, we have seen no floatplanes; none at all!

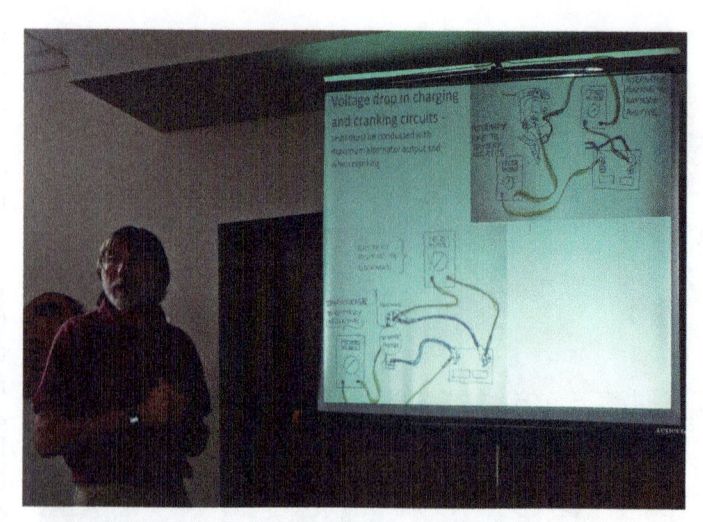

Mid-September the Bluewater Cruising Association organized a series of presentations in five western Canadian cities by Nigel Calder, the author of a major cruiser bible: *Boatowner's Mechanical and Electrical Manual*. We went to two of these in Vancouver, an excellent afternoon seminar on boat DC electrical systems, and a more general evening presentation entitled: *If It Ain't Broke, Just Wait*, a very appropriate boating title.

The following evening Edi and I gave a slide presentation to the Vancouver Power and Sail Squadron on the first two years of our cruise. We were slowly easing our way back into boating, meeting old friends from the BCA and VPS.

To keep my foot in the door to my former world as a wine importer, wine writer, wine educator and wine judge, we attended a number of wine tastings. At these we met many old friends, former wine clients and students, but the highlight was Luke Smith. He blames me and some superb Burgundy that I sold him for his having abandoned the corporate world, planted a vineyard and built a winery: Howling Bluff on the Okanagan's Naramata Bench. He is delighted with the move. So are we; his wine is superb.

Rather than offering my standard Sequitur calling card to wine producers and to my former colleagues in the wine business, I designed a new logo for a revamped wine-oriented Sequitur card.

We had planned our return to Sequitur in Patagonia for the third week of October so we could help granddaughter Annelies celebrate her first birthday on 14 October. Edi made a dress-up doll from a pattern she had saved for over thirty years from when she had made a similar doll for daughter, Amy. Annelies seemed to be a bit confused with the new kid in the house.

The other grandparents, Bram and Els had come from The Netherlands for the birthday and we had the extended family over for a big roast-beef-and-all-the-trimmings dinner. Edi had baked a birthday cake and we all officially welcomed Annelies into her second year.

With most of the family formalities concluded, we turned our full attention to our preparations for returning to Sequitur in Puerto Montt. When we were in Valparaiso, we had spoken in detail with SAG, the Chilean department responsible for, among other things, agriculture related importations. We learned that seeds and nuts were admissible only if salted and roasted, that dried fruit was permitted only if seedless, that dairy products were allowed only if pasteurized, and so on. We had found nuts and dried fruit in Chile, but at $35 and more per kilo, we had to find a Vancouver alternative.

We bought bulk raw hazelnuts, pecans and almonds, slow-roasted them in the oven, bagged them in heavy poly bags, sprinkled in a show of salt and dressed the packages with creative labels, including nutritional data, barcodes and local names. We weren't being deceitful; the nuts were roasted and salted. We simply needed an easy way to communicate this to Customs and SAG.

Through the summer we had been accumulating things to take back with us to Sequitur. Things which are unavailable, of poor quality, or way overpriced in Chile, like coffee beans, chocolate, and rice crackers, to name only a few. Also we gathered things like additional tools, replacements for items that had broken, and fresh spares to replace spares that had been used.

Two days before our scheduled flight, I began packing the accumulated piles into the four checked bags and four carryon bags we were allowed. Fortunately our flight was a few days before Air Canada's change from two 23k pieces of checked baggage per person to only one. Even so, there was no way we could get it all into the allowed eight pieces; we needed a ninth, and this would incur excess baggage charges of $225.

We were then faced with the problem of getting five pieces of checked baggage onto our LAN Chile connection from Santiago to Puerto Montt, which allows only two. We could have interlined the four pieces without much hassle, but the fifth was up in the air... or maybe not!

We decided to book a rental car and drive the 1000 kilometres to Puerto Montt. With the car reserved for three days, we cancelled the flight for a full refund of the $750 fare. The rental car at just under $500 with drop-off fees, plus gas, freeway tolls and hotel would total about the same as the connecting flight. The huge bonus was that we would have the car to use for running errands and to do our grocery shopping when we arrive in Puerto Montt.

On Tuesday evening, the day before our flight, we walked over to Amy and Bram's for a family get-together and farewell. Then we went back to the loft to continue our packing.

By late on Tuesday evening I had managed to juggle fragile and tough, bulky and small, heavy and light, soft and hard items into five suitcases; four of them at exactly 50.5 pounds and one excess bag at 70.5 pounds on our bathroom scale. This took full advantage of the 23 and 32 kilo weight limits. I hoped the airport's scale agreed. Our four carryon bags were limited to 10 kilos each, but they weighed a total of 75 kilos; way over weight, and this wasn't counting Edi's very heavy purse. Fortunately the pieces were dense, undersized, and inconspicuous. We hoped they would be ignored.

23. Return to Puerto Montt

On Wednesday morning the 19th of October we juggled our nine pieces of luggage aboard the Sky-Train, needing to jamb the door only for the last piece. The checked baggage weights were on-the-nose, and we breezed through the check-in process with our pre-printed boarding cards. Our carryon pieces looked innocent and were not weighed. Boarding in Toronto for the continuation to Chile went smoothly, and we were pleased to see all five checked pieces on the conveyor in Santiago at noon on Thursday.

All of our bags were x-rayed as we passed through the Customs screening, and agents asked to examine four of the pieces. We were able to easily explain the roasted and salted nuts, the many kilos of Asiago and other cheeses, but the smoothness of process suddenly stopped when one of the agents pulled-out a bag with four propeller shaft zincs. It took a while and another agent to finally relieve her mind that these unfamiliar objects were not contraband. We were released and wheeled our more than 200 kilos of loot to the rental car.

We had reserved a standard-sized sedan, but there was none available, so we were given a Nissan X-Trail, into which the baggage just fit in one layer with the seats folded down. We paused for the night in Los Angeles, about midway along our route to Puerto Montt. We arrived back at Sequitur in the yard at Club Nautico Reloncavi in Puerto Montt at 1630 on Friday the 21st.

We moved our bags aboard, unpacked and began the slow process of waking-up Sequitur from her winter slumber and getting her ready to carry us onward. To begin with we are camping onboard with few creature comforts; nonetheless, it was good to be home again.

The near-steady overcast, the single-digit temperatures and the copious rain disguised the fact that Spring was already a month old. We began the slow process of awakening Sequitur from her winter slumber and getting her ready to carry us southward.

The electricity in the yard and on the floats in the marina is dirty. I'm told variously that it has a bit of stray current in the neutral or in the ground. Whatever the cause, neither of our shore power connections would accept the electricity. I saw this as no great problem, we would simply plug our 30-Amp Black & Decker 3-phase battery charger, which we had bought at Sodimac in Valdivia. Oops; great problem! We had lent it out in Valdivia, and were just remembering that it had not been returned. Fortunately we still had the rental car from Santiago for another day and a half, so Sodimac was added to our Saturday's shopping circuit.

Sodimac was out of 30-Amp chargers, and we could find none at any other store, so we bought a 10-Amp one, which would do, but it would considerably cramp our style. With no source of cooling water, we could not run the generator while we're out of the water, so with a trickle of 10 Amps from the charger and the input from the solar panels in the glum weather, we would need to budget electrical consumption.

We stopped along the way to fill four jerry cans with 80 litres of diesel, and at Supermercado Jumbo we bought a huge load of heavy staples, including three ten-kilo bags of flour, two dozen beer, a replenishment of wine and other things that would be awkward by bus. Also, because we had emptied Sequitur's fridges, freezers and larder of all fresh goods before we had gone back to Vancouver, we bought a full supply of fresh setting-up-galley goods.

Wanting redundancy, I re-marked it in 10-metre lengths with coloured ties, using the rainbow sequence: red for 10, orange yellow, green, blue, then double red for 60, and so on. I also added a white tie at each 5-metre length.

Slowly the battery bank came up to the point where, after a couple of days, we could flash-up the Espar furnace to supply us with heat and hot water. Fortunately, my diagnosis of its failure to run when we had arrived in Puerto Mont had been correct; the diesel level was below the furnace intake. The next day we ran two loads of laundry through the washing machine, turned-on the large fridge and Edi set-up the sewing machine to do-up new cockpit cushion covers. Sequitur was beginning to feel like home again.

While Edi sorted, inventoried and reorganized the food stores, I overhauled the main and secondary anchors. The galvanizing on the 100 metres of chain on the Rocna was still very fresh, and I saw no need to end-to-end it yet. Our AutoAnchor cockpit control and rode counter had finally been put right after so many bumbling attempts by the fit-out yard in Vancouver. In Valdivia, Alwoplast had been easily able to correct the incompetent fit-out installation.

While we were in Vancouver, I was finally able to track-down a propeller shaft rope cutter that would fit onto our 38.1mm diameter shaft and into the 25.5mm gap between our VariProp and the strut bearing housing. R&D Marine in Hertfordshire, UK make a broad range from 316 stainless to fit most shaft and strut hub diameter combinations. They quoted £182 including express shipping to Vancouver. The cutter arrived with everything necessary for installation, including hex wrenches, LocTite and an 8mm drill bit to dimple the shaft for the setscrew. The instructions were in concise, un-translated English. Drilling the 3mm-deep dimple into our very hard stainless shaft required four full battery charges on our portable drill, but other than that, it was simple to install, and should save our hiring divers to untangle lines from the screw.

When we had stocked-up with food and spares in San Francisco and began seriously laying-in our wine cellar, Sequitur had settled into the water to the limits of her bottom's anti-fouling. The slightest ripple would wet the unprotected area of the hull and Sequitur regularly grew a beard. Now I wear a beard, but Sequitur is a lady, and a beard is unbecoming on her. We need to move the anti-fouling up, or as is commonly said among cruising sailors, raise the waterline.

452

The weather began to dry-out a bit during our second week back in Patagonia, so through Tideswell Marine Services, I arranged to have Sequitur's bottom done, including raising the waterline 8cm. David, the British owner talked two of his workers into spending Saturday cleaning and sanding the entire bottom and then applying a first coat of primer above the existing line. Then everything paused for Chile to celebrate Halloween. This is a national holiday, and the next day is also, so people can recover from their sugar overload. Officially they are observing All Saints Day and All Souls Day.

While we were employing Manuel Labour on the hull, Edi and I took advantage of the sunny day to bus along to the market in Angelmo. This is a long, rambling collection of buildings with a focus on a seafood and fresh produce market. Besides what arrives by truck, the Angelmo fish market is supplied by many small boats, which raft-up seven and eight deep along the pier.

Although most produce arrives by truck, some still arrives by horse and wagon.

There are small, impromptu merchants spread-out in a central courtyard, some with only a few items to sell, others with a broader selection.

Inside are more permanent stalls, offering a nice selection of fresh produce, artisanal cheeses, homemade preserves, honey and assorted condiments. Mixed-in with the produce stands are the fish mongers. Many of these offer fresh whole fish, and it appears that as the day progresses, the stock is gradually converted to fillets, steaks and other renderings.

There is also a large selection of shellfish at some of the stalls, but with the prevalence Red Tide and the danger of Paralytic Shellfish Poisoning, we have decided to restrict our shellfish to the certified canned variety for the present.

Behind most of the stalls were workers, young and old, busily adding value to the sea harvest by opening, cleaning and packaging a broad variety of seafood.

These were then displayed on sloping easels for the customers to easily browse. The attractive displays worked well; there was a steady stream of purchases, and the cleaners and packagers continued to replenish the displays.

By far the most common fish we saw were farmed Atlantic salmon, followed by merluza, which we learned is hake in English. We found some cold-smoked salmon, and bought a couple of 125-gram packages for 1000 Pesos each, which works-out to about $16 per kilo.

The next morning we enjoyed some superb lox on fresh baguette with cream cheese, capers and basil leaves. We told ourselves that we would need to buy much more of this before we head south.

We then walked along the half kilometre stretch of shops leading to it from central Puerto Montt. Most of the shops offer a boring selection of factory-made souvenir kitsch, identical to that in the shop next to it, and to the one beside that.

On Tuesday when we were trying to work out the logistics of buying 12 litres of bottom paint and some thinners, we met our neighbour across the lane. Roger is a retired banker with Coutts in the Strand, and he had just arrived back at his boat, El Vagabond. He and his wife have been wintering up in Los Rios Region, farm-sitting while friends travel. He had driven down to paint the bottom a week in advance of their moving from farm to boat. Within half an hour we were driving with him to buy bottom paint. Edi and I had brought our shopping bags and wheelie so we could be dropped-off at Supermercado Lider for another shopping spree on Roger's way back to the boats with his paint and ours.

We arrived at the paint store just as it was bolted shut for the 1300 to 1500 lunch break. With the paint store closed, we reorganized; Roger dropped us off at Lider and went off on other errands telling us he would pick us up again shortly before the paint store reopened. Ideal; we now had a ride back with all of our groceries, and we had an hour and forty minutes for a whirlwind shopping spree. When roger returned to the supermarket we had something over fifty kilograms of loot. Our fridges and freezers were beginning to fill again, as was the pantry.

On Thursday we made another bus trip to Mall Central and walked up the hill to Supermercado Jumbo. We returned with four overstuffed bags, the two cooler bags filled with nine one-kilo vacu-packs of pork loin and eight huge turkey thighs for the freezer, plus two huge wax-covered blocks of a local semi-mature cheese called Chanquito, five blocks of butter, five of cream cheese and on and on. It is a long process to stock-up for four months, especially by bus.

One of the few things useful to us that we found in the shops near the Angelmo were some very nice soft reed baskets. We bought a pile of them, thinking that because they breathe well, are rather pliable and have securable lids, they will be perfect bins for stowing potatoes, carrots, onions and other root-cellar items in our two well-below-waterline lockers beneath the forward cabin sole. They will also serve well as ready-use containers to further sort our frequently used clothing.

We are steadily crossing entries off our list of things to do before we continue southward. While Edi organized below, I busied myself with such things as unpacking, reassembling and re-inflating the dinghy, checking and overhauling the running rigging and continuing to rewire some of the poorly done electrical connections from our Vancouver fit-out.

On Saturday afternoon, the 5th of November one of David's workers began applying the first coat of anti-fouling paint to Sequitur's bottom. We are slowly getting closer to going into the water and we are pleased to see our pre-departure to-do list shrinking.

On Monday, the 7th of November David Tideswell told me that the new 38mm through-hulls had arrived from Santiago. Since I now had them in hand and they looked good, I decided to proceed with the disassembly of the existing overboard pumps from the holding tanks. I had delayed this task with the reasonable excuse that if we couldn't get proper fittings for the new pumps, it was folly to remove the existing system, no matter how poorly it performed. In reality, I knew that it was going to be a shitty job.

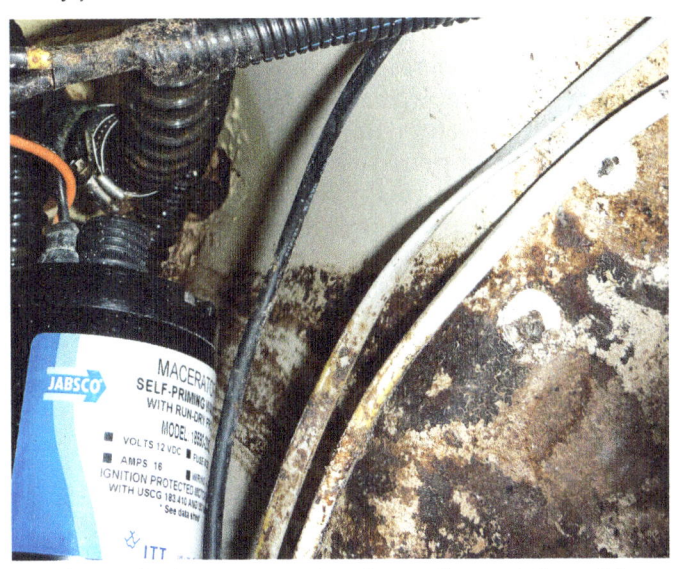

We have had poor service from the existing Jabsco macerator pumps from the beginning, with low pump volume, a slight seepage and its resultant odour. I had had Specialty Yachts Service change the one serving the forward head in late 2007 or early 2008 in Vancouver because of excessive seepage. Since then it had continued to seep whenever it was used, and I had gone through a lot of spray Lysol. The pump had not been used since before we had arrived in Puerto Montt in June, so the seeped effluent from the time of its last use had, thankfully, composted to a relatively benign mess.

The first thing I noted when I began to dismount the pump was the apparently standard-for-them shoddy electrical connections used by Specialty Yachts Service when they had replaced the pump. The crimp connectors were sloppily wrapped in tape with several gaps, allowing moisture onto the wires.

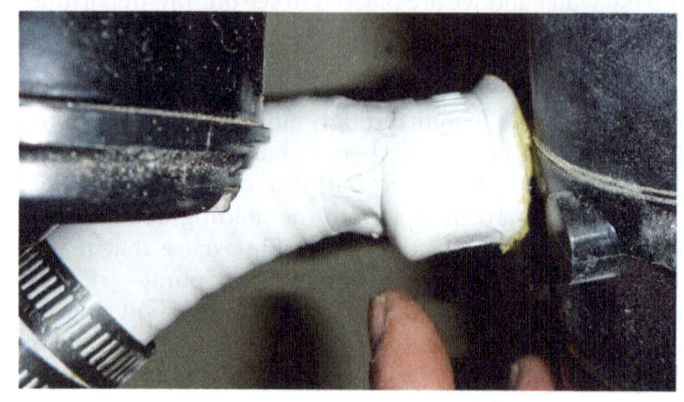

The next thing I noted was the hose clamps on the pump outlet. One of the clamps had missed the hose barb, and had been tightened down to restrict the outlet to about half of its diameter, greatly reducing its cross-sectional area. No wonder the pump strained so much during pump-out; its outlet was severely compromised.

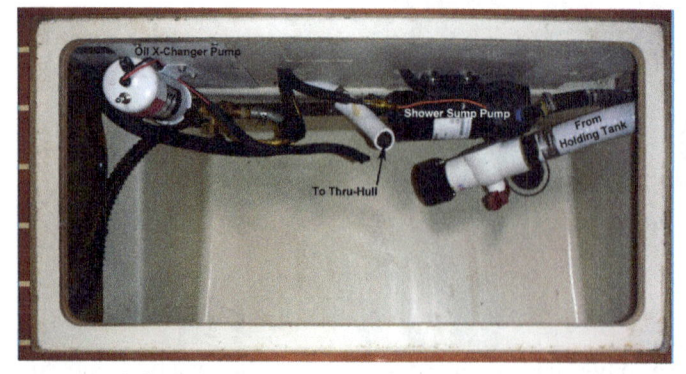

I removed the Jabsco pumps and cleaned-out the bilge areas in preparation for the installation of the new Whale Gulper BP2552B pumps, which we had bought at River Marine in Vancouver in July. They had strongly recommended these diaphragm-type pumps, rather than a macerator type. The thinking is that since the heads have their own macerator pumps, the contents of the holding tanks don't need the complication of further macerating at pump-out. A 38mm line from the tanks through the pumps and out the 38mm through-hulls will be very simple and efficient.

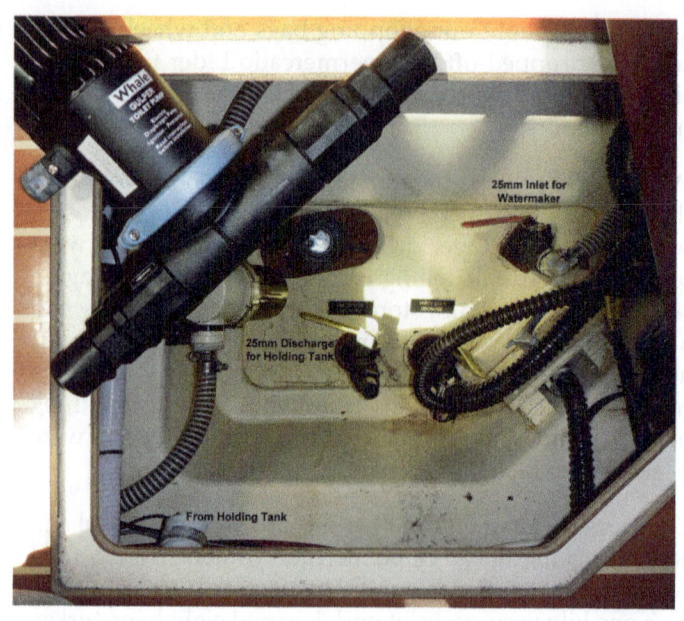

We needed to replace the existing 25.4mm through-hulls with the new 38mm ones. In the forward bilge, instead of replacing the old through-hull that had been used by the macerator, we decided to put the watermaker inlet line onto it. This would solve two problems: move the watermaker inlet upstream of the blackwater outlet and provide an easily flowing bend in the hose from the pump to the new 38mm through-hull.

In the after bilge, the Jabsco installation had been properly done, with shrink seals on the wiring and hose clamps properly in place. This was in line with what I have seen with virtually everything that was originally done at the Hunter factory. It would have been wonderful if this professional level of work had been continued by their authorized dealer in Vancouver, both during our initial fit-out and with subsequent installations and servicing.

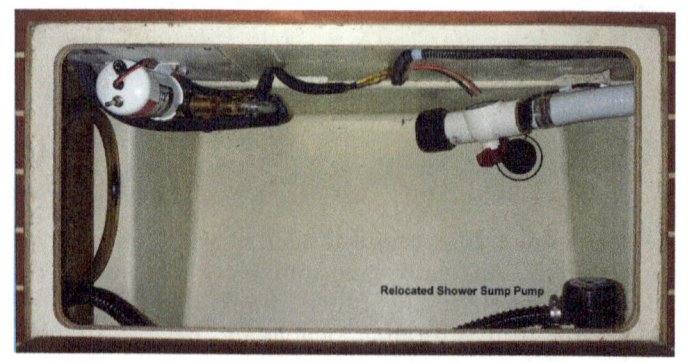

To make better room for the new pump, I needed to move the shower sump pump, which was mounted beneath the shutoff valve for the former macerator pump. I found a better placement for it, hanging from the locker top across from the bulkhead where it had originally been installed. This positioning makes cleaning the pump filter much simpler. In the original placement we needed to remove the contents of the bilge bin down to the 40cm level to get to the filter. In the new location, the filter is just beneath the lip of the 60cm deep by one metre by one metre storage space and it can be cleaned with little or no disruption of the stored contents.

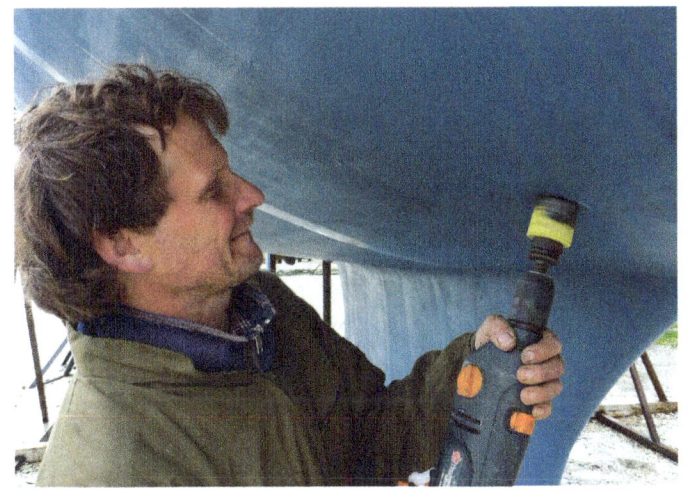

On Tuesday afternoon David and I removed the hose barb and elbow from the watermaker's through-hull and test-fit it to the former macerator through-hull to make sure the pieces mated before we committed to the plan. They were compatible, so we removed the former inlet through-hull for the watermaker and rebored the hole in Sequitur's bottom to 38mm. The hull is 20mm thick at that point, laid-up in layers of Kevlar and fibreglass.

We then moved to the main bilge and rebored the existing 25.4mm hole to 38mm. It is always daunting to drill holes in the bottom of a boat, particularly large ones like these. At one metre below waterline, the 38mm hole in the main bilge will admit slightly over 5 litres per second. At 50cm depth, the one in the forward bilge will admit just shy of 3.6. That's a total of over 500 litres per minute; a large amount of water.

The plug from the forward bilge showed the hull to be 32mm thick and the one from the hole in the main bilge showed a 20mm hull thickness.

With the holes bored, we began the process of properly closing them. We cleaned and epoxy-sealed the cut surfaces and cleaned the surfaces immediately around the holes to properly receive the bedding compound. The next day, after the epoxy had hardened, we used Sikaflex 291 Marine Sealant to bed the skin fittings, the backing disks and the threads of the ball valves. Once the compound had 'cooked', we again had a watertight hull.

The second coat of bottom paint was applied and the masking tape removed to reveal the raised waterline with an attractive symmetrical accent line. We were nearly ready to go back in the water, so on Thursday afternoon I ordered a fuel truck to come on Friday morning to fill Sequitur's tanks with diesel. I also requested the travel-lift to lift us off our stands on Friday afternoon so we could apply a first layer of paint to the stand pad patches.

457

The timing of the tides was perfect for this; we could hang in the slings until high water about 1500 on Saturday, allowing us to get two coats on the patches with proper drying times between.

On my way back from seeing Alexandro, the marina manager, with whom I had been making the fuelling and travel-lift arrangements, I spotted a southern lapwing with two new chicks. The spring hatch had begun.

As I approached, the hen gave a signal.

The two chicks headed beneath mother's wings.

I was left looking at a six-legged bird.

Our minds turned again to storing ship with cruising essentials. We had a very good, boat red, but had not found a good white. Our boat Merlot cost about $3.65 a bottle, so we figured $4.00 should find us a satisfactory white. With Thursday evening's dinner we tasted three wines at 1900 to 2000 Pesos, and while they all went well with the sautéed merluza fillets and brown basmati rice, the clear winner was the 2011 Carmen Insignia Chardonnay. We made a note to lay-in a stock of it.

On Friday morning at 1000, precisely as arranged, the fuel truck arrived at Sequitur in the yard. We took on 825 litres of diesel for 561,000 Pesos, about $1140. Shortly after we had completed refuelling, we paused for a few moments of silence in commemoration of Remembrance Day. Then a little while later we watched as 11:11:11 of 11-11-11 happened. Eleven minutes and eleven seconds past eleven o'clock on the 11th of November 2011.

We took a bus into town and walked on a sight-seeing jaunt through the main shopping streets to Plaza de Armas. With a population of 175,000 in the 2001 census and a current estimate of 230,000, Puerto Montt is a rapidly growing trade centre for the southern regions of Chile. Across from the Plaza is Iglesia Catedral, the oldest building in Puerto Montt, dating to the city's founding in 1853. In the restoration after the 1960 earthquake, its facade was rebuilt in wood. Although the church looks Greek to us, many of the other older buildings in the city have a Germanic look; most of the early settlers were from Germany.

We continued through the downtown and up the hill to Supermercado Jumbo, where we resumed our laying-in a four-month stock of groceries and supplies.

Our shopping lists are constantly being amended. It seems immediately items are crossed-off, new ones find their way on. On this trip we lugged back two cooler bags and two huge canvas bags, each weighing a little over ten kilos. There is no direct bus to or from Jumbo, so two bus fares are required; they do not know the concept of transfers here.

Then at 1600, again exactly as arranged, the travel-lift came and lifted Sequitur off her stands so we could paint the patches that had been under the pads. The stands had to be cut away, since they had been custom built and welded into place when we had been hauled-out. Immediately our bottom was clear of the pads, one of David's workers arrived to apply the first coat of anti-fouling paint to the missed patches and to the bottom of the keel. At 0800 on Saturday morning David applied a second coat to the patches and keel bottom, and a third coat to the leading edges of the bow and keel.

We knew it was time to put Sequitur back in the water when we found her plans for putting down roots. Maybe she had grown comfortable in the yard and wanted to stay, or maybe she was taking pity on us for having spent so much time living up in a tree-house, that she had decided to help-out with easier access.

Shortly before the crew went off for their two hour lunch at 1300, they came and moved Sequitur to the lip of the launching dock to be ready for high tide at 1500. I spent the next couple of hours checking and rechecking the through-hulls from both inside and out. Then I hoisted our Canadian colours and the Chilean courtesy flag. I also organized lines and fenders on the starboard side so that we would be ready to secure alongside the float after being launched.

459

At 1500 the crew returned, and within a few minutes Sequitur's keel was wet again. As she was lowered past the lip, I hopped aboard and checked the bilges. Everything looked fine, so I switched on the engine and was delighted when it started immediately, and ran as if it had not been idle for over four and a half months.

We motored the short distance around the ends of the floats and into the marina and secured starboard side to on the long floating finger coming off the access ramp. The entire process went very smoothly; the yacht club's yard crew are experienced and efficient professionals. Once we were secured, I checked the bilges again just for peace of mind. Then I decided to start the generator to top-up the battery bank. It failed to start on the first attempt, so I tried it again and it caught and ran smoothly. Edi and I began the final stages of preparing for the continuation of our voyage, the next portions of which are through rather remote regions of the planet.

From Puerto Montt, it is over 1200 nautical miles through the Patagonia Channels to Tierra del Fuego and Cape Horn. From there it a little over 400 miles to Stanley in the Falklands, another 800 miles in the Furious Fifties to South Georgia and then over 3000 miles to Cape Town, South Africa. Although the region is spectacularly beautiful, it is a harsh environment that is sparsely populated and has very few opportunities for supplies and services.

Before we leave Puerto Montt, Sequitur must be fully serviceable and tuned, and she needs to be stocked with food, fuel, supplies and spares for four months or longer. While some replenishment is available in Ushuaia, Argentina and Stanley, Falklands, it is rather expensive and it is unwise to depend on finding anything.

The first thing I needed to do was dig out the hose and wash nearly five months of winter dirt off Sequitur. As I was preparing to hose-down the cockpit, David arrived saying he had a couple of hours we could use to complete the installation of the new blackwater pumps.

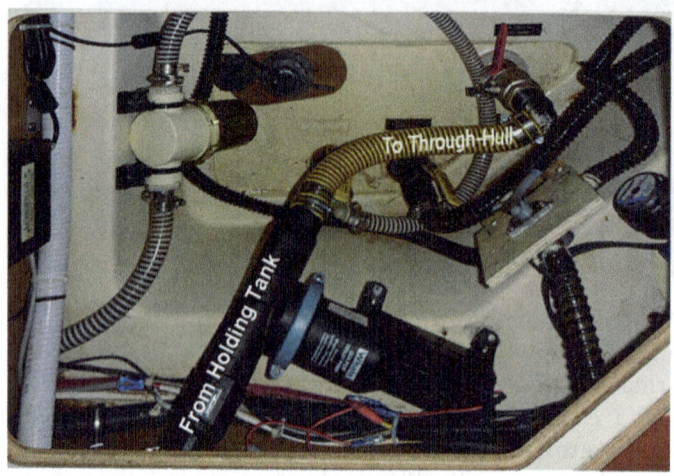

In total, to make the six connections in the new 38mm blackwater lines and the reconnection of the rerouted watermaker inlet, it took us three hours. All the hose barbs were installed with bedding compound, the hose ends were heated onto the barbs and double-clamped while still hot.

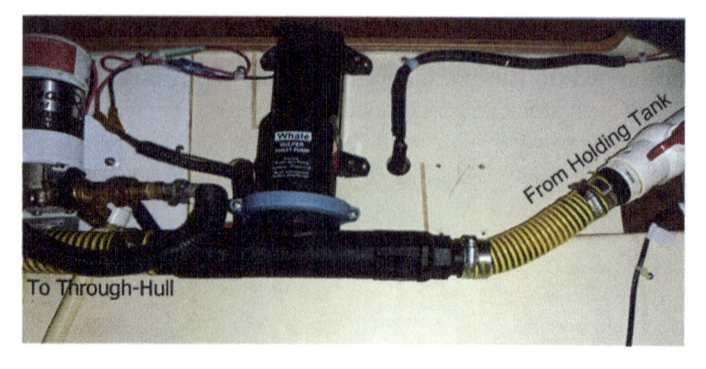

We tested the pumps, and were pleased with the results. We now have efficient and odourless blackwater plumbing. While many parts of the installation were straightforward and I could easily do them on my own, I was pleased to have David with his professional experience, his proper tools and his appropriate bedding compounds. When we had finally finished the installation, he admitted it was a two-man job.

We spent Sunday cleaning and rearranging. This is a much easier task in the water, with electricity from the generator and a hose bib on the float beside the boat. Edi ran four loads of laundry through the washer-dryer and got us caught-up again. I tidied-up the wiring runs from the new pumps and re-stowed the revamped bilge space.

460

On Monday we took a couple of buses up to Supermercado Lider to continue our stocking-up. For the trip back, we juggled sixty or seventy kilos of groceries and supplies aboard two buses. Heavy items in our bulging wheelie bag, the rest in two cooler bags and two canvas bags. A dozen bottles of 2011 Carmen Chardonnay and a half dozen bottles of Undurraga Brut were among the heavy items, as were two dozen cans of shrimp, the first we had seen since California. We love them for omelets, pizzas, quiches, sandwiches and for so many other dishes, and have searched in vain in every supermarket for two years. It is strange to us that none was available in Mexico, the Galapagos, Peru and until now, Chile.

We also purchased some fresh filete de blanquillo to try. I sautéed it in butter with shredded basil leaves and coarse-ground black pepper and served it with kokoro rice and a butter-sweat of julienned vegetables. The fish is wonderfully firm, nicely flaky and it has a deliciously delicate, non-fishy flavour. It is the least expensive fish in the market, and we assumed that it is unpopular here because it is non-mushy and it doesn't have heavy fishy flavour. Hooray! We'll buy much more. We have been amazed at the taste in fish in Latin America; we saw in Mexico and Peru, and now in Chile that the popular fish cooks as a soft, mushy mass and that it is very fishy in flavour. This is the antithesis of our preferences.

On Tuesday morning Edi prepared eggs Sequitur, her take-off on eggs Benedict, with sauce Alfredo, rather than Hollandaise. After breakfast, we continued to clean and organize. While Edi continued sewing covers for our cockpit cushions and pillows, I hauled-out our power-washer and sprayed-down the boat, starting in the cockpit, doing the inside and the out of the canopy, and eventually ending-up at the bow.

When Sequitur had been hauled in June, we had needed to cut the wind-generator mast so that she could fit in the travel-lift. The mast had been designed as a fixed unit, welded to the solar arch, and when it was installed by our fit-out yard in Vancouver, it had been wired so short that there was insufficient spare wire to lift the awkward 25-kilogram generator of its mount without cutting the wires at their first emergence from the steel work, down in a cockpit locker.

Through David Tideswell, I had contacted Juan Moya, a stainless fabricator and asked him to make a 40cm-long clamping sleeve to rejoin the severed mast. He assured us it would made from 416 stainless, and that would be ready on Monday.

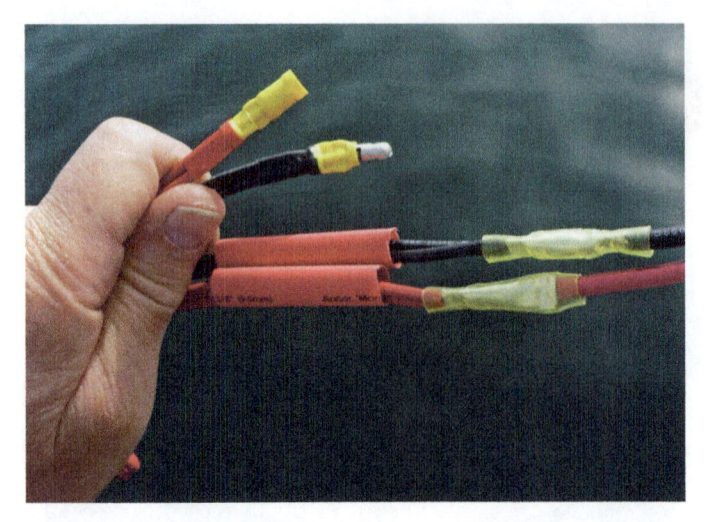

While I was waiting for the stainless fabrication, I spliced an additional metre of wire to the run, and put quick-disconnect fittings on the ends and sealed the connections with heat-shrink. Because I didn't have enough tinned 10AWG, and can find none in Chile, I used twinned lengths of tinned 14AWG to carry the current. I prepared the ends of the leads from the wind-generator with mating connectors, so that once the steel work was complete, the generator would be easy to remove from and to replace on the mast, and the mast would be easy to lower if required again for haul-out.

We had been trickle-charging the battery bank for three weeks, and still could not get the charge up. With the generator now running, I had thought the bank would soon fully charge and hold its charge. It didn't. It looked like a failed bank, and a more local one than the weekly financial crisis in the United States these days. I had contacted Gami, the local battery specialist store, and two techs came on Wednesday morning to isolate, load-test and capacity-test the ten batteries in the bank.

When I shut off the charger and the solar inputs and switched off the main switch for the techs to do the tests, the voltage had been at 14.05 and both battery monitors were showing the bank was 100% charged. The voltage began rapidly falling before the tests were even started. The batteries failed miserably; the worst one showed 22% capacity, the best only 47%. I thought of doing an equalization to try to get a bit more life out of the bank, but with the passages ahead of us, the sound decision was to replace the entire house bank.

I rode back to Gami with the techs, and we looked at options: They had four Trojan T-105 225Ah batteries in stock, and could get an additional six in a week or so. They also had six Bosch T-105-type 226Ah batteries in stock, and could get the remaining four by Thursday afternoon. Knowing how long a week or so is in Latin America, I opted for the Bosch batteries, once I was assured that the price includes delivery and installation. For the cost of a million and three-quarters, I had hoped that it did.

On Thursday, while we waited for Juan, the steel fabricator and the remote possibility that the battery installers would make it before Friday morning, I went up the mast. I had received notification that there was a recall on the forestay fittings on Seldén masts installed between 2004 and 2008 on various models of 12 to 16-metre sailboats: Arcona, Bavaria, Brouwer, Comet Pheonix, Dehler, Elan, Etap, Falcon, Finngulf, Hallberg Rassy, Hunter, Incistor, Maxi, Najad, NIC, Omega, Pronavia, Reflex, Saga, Salona, Southerly, Sweden Yacht and Van de Stadt. I needed to check the part numbers on ours to determine whether they are among the affected ones. As I reached the staysail attachment, I easily saw the part number on the fitting, and noted it was the recalled 517-914. It is so convenient to have the steps installed on the mast, making an excursion like this a simple one-person exercise.

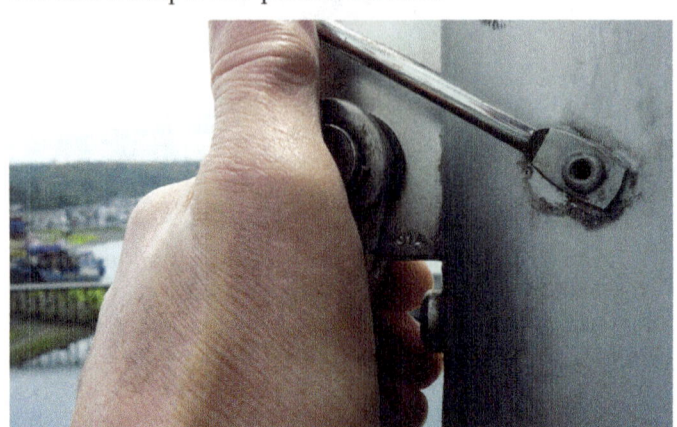

I continued up the mast to the forestay fitting, and confirmed that it also is the questionable one. While I was up the mast, I did a quick visual inspection of the standing rigging, and will do a more thorough one and any necessary tuning when I find a rigger to do the fitting replacements.

From the mast I had a nice view out over the surrounding area. I looked across the floats to the clubhouse and beyond it to the yard to see that over half of the boats had now been put back in the water after their seasonal haul-out or for repairs and maintenance. Like us, many are in the final stages of preparing to leave. Most here are from Europe, and are intending to continue on up the coast a bit before shaping their courses for such places as Isla Pascua, Pitcairn and Polynesia.

Among the non-Europeans in the marina with us at Reloncavi are Max and Sandy of the Australian sloop, Volo, whom we had met in La Punta, Peru the previous year. They had spent the winter here installing a new engine in their boat. Also among the sailors we had met in La Punta were Steve and Cullem of the ketch, Odyle. Steve's wife Kim had taken a job in the California when they had gone back to escape the southern winter. The job was too good to leave, so she had stayed behind, and Steve and son Cullem left the middle of November to sail Odyle back to California via Pascua, Polynesia and Hawaii.

We had spent the entire day Thursday aboard waiting in vain for the battery techs from Gami and for the steel fabricator. On Friday the 18th I went up to the marina office and had Alexandro call Gami to find out when they were coming. They said there was a shipping delay from Santiago, the batteries were arriving late morning, and they would be at the boat in the afternoon. At 1645 the techs from Gami arrived with new batteries and wheeled them in two cart loads down the floats to Sequitur.

We lugged the ten 28-kilogram batteries aboard, first to the side deck, then to the cockpit and finally down the accommodation ladder to the main salon. The techs carefully mapped-out the wiring diagram of the existing battery bank, so that they could put the complicated set-up back together in the same way with the new batteries.

I figured it made good sense to also shoot photos of the complex wiring scheme before anything was disconnected.

463

There was one cable with a lightly corroded lug, and I wanted to renew it. I had some 000AWG tinned cable and matching lugs left over from the rewiring I had done in twinning the engine alternators while we were in Callao, so we used some of these spares to make-up a new cable.

I removed the WaterMiser caps from the old batteries and put them onto the new batteries. Shortly after 1930 the installation was completed, and I switched on the 12 volt system, made the breakers for the solar panel input and parallel charge circuit and powered-up the charger. Everything looked good and the bank began taking a charge.

We lugged the old batteries up into the cockpit, then up onto the side deck and finally down onto the float. The techs from Gami were surprised, and I think rather disappointed when I told them they couldn't have the old batteries. It took me a while to communicate this to them in my sparse Spanish and their near total lack of English. I think they were looking forward to equalizing and restoring them and making some money; however, I had the other ideas.

On Saturday as we waited for the new bank to come up to full charge, Edi and I went back into town and walked up the hill to Jumbo for more groceries. Among the items we brought back were half a dozen bottles of our favourite Chilean bubbly: Undurraga Brut Royale, which was on sale. Also on sale was the new 2011 Chardonnay from Cono Sur, at two for 3750 Pesos, or about $3.75 per bottle, so we added four bottles of it to out booty.

As I was beginning to prepare dinner in the early evening, almost exactly 24 hours after the new house battery had been installed, it reached 100% charge. We were hopeful that with the new bank, the twinned high-output alternators and the repaired generator, our electrical problems were behind us.

We had finally gone through the first of three ten-kilo bags of basmati rice we had bought wholesale in August 2009 from the importer in Vancouver. So that we could have some with dinner, I opened the second bag.

With the basmati rice, I served filete de blanquillo sautéed with fresh basil, oyster mushrooms, garlic and shallots, accompanied by a butter-sweat of julienned carrots, onions and red and green peppers and garnished with sliced tomato and shredded basil. With dinner we tasted the new 2011 Cono Sur Chardonnay, and found it to be well-structured with delicious tropical flavours and a pleasantly long, clean finish. It is a steal at the price. We easily decided that we would buy much more.

Sunday was cold, windy and rainy. We spent the day onboard doing little things inside, and mostly relaxing. One of the little things Edi did was to freeze some fresh basil leaves. We currently have a wonderful, inexpensive source, and we have already put-up two litres of individual leaves in extra virgin olive oil. The frozen ones will augment and add variety to these.

Monday continued cold, windy and rainy, except that instead of just a boring steady rain, we had bouts of heavy downpour added to relieve the monotony. I received a reply from Seldén on the mast fittings. Because of the difficulty of our location and the time constraints, Tom Sharkey of Seldén USA said: *"I will be working with you directly to try to get the issue resolved in the most efficient and logical manner."* This is encouraging, since he has commissioned every prototype that Hunter has designed since 1998, and is very familiar with our rig.

For breakfast on Tuesday, Edi prepared some pain perdu au jambon from leftover baguettes, and we washed it down with delicious cups of Starbucks coffee. We had finished the last of our Peruvian coffee, and started into our first of many bags of Costco Blend beans, packaged by Starbucks. We had brought a large quantity with us on our return from Vancouver.

After breakfast, I went off to find David and to see whether we had missed the announcement of the retirement party for Juan Moya, the stainless fabricator. We assumed he retired; we haven't seen him since he promised more than two weeks previously to complete the job in a few days. David was not around, and one of his workers told me he was not yet back from Santiago, where he had gone on Friday morning.

A severe front came through midday, and seemed to stall over us. For much of the remainder of Tuesday a northerly wind howled through Canal Reloncavi and drove a heavy downpour near sideways. We hunkered-down, warm, cozy and dry inside Sequitur. Even if the steel fabricator had shown-up, the weather made it impossible to work on the project.

The storm brought yet another power failure; we've lost count now of how many we had seen here and in Valdivia. David told us of power spikes when the system is re-powered, citing a recent instance in which the power came back on at 440 or 880 volts on Isla Tenglo causing havoc. It is a good idea to disconnect the shore power cord immediately the power goes out here. With the power outages, the wifi from the clubhouse dies also, and sometimes takes a day or two to restore.

By Wednesday morning the storm had passed, and while the sky was still heavily overcast, it wasn't raining. Late morning, when neither David nor Juan could be found, Edi and I took off on another shopping trip to Jumbo. Our grocery supply for four months is now nearly complete, needing only the final shorter life-span items, which will be purchased the day before we head out. Edi reorganized the stowage again; we now have things nicely categorized into fourteen different lockers, and much easier to locate.

On late Wednesday afternoon I received an email from Tom at Seldén USA informing me he had just received a shipment of replacement forestay fittings from Sweden, and that a FedEx package was addressed to us and awaiting pick-up in his office. The last international FedEx took two weeks to reach us in Las Hadas, Mexico, so we were hoping that the Chilean system is less broken and corrupt.

On Thursday morning I finally tracked-down David and enquired of the steel fabricator. He told me he needed to contact him urgently, since he had a delinquent part for another boat as well. I also told David the old batteries were on the float, and that he was welcome to take them and see if he could equalize some more life out of them. He said he was rushing off to the LAN office to book a flight to London, his father had just passed away, but that he would contact Juan Moya and see to the batteries. A short while later, one of David's workers arrived with a cart and began hauling away the batteries. However; there was no sign of Juan.

465

We continued to organize. We have been living aboard for approaching two and a half years now, and things are pretty much stowed in their most logical and convenient locations; however, we continue to tweak. We still have some unused stowage space, for which we will eventually find a use.

On Friday morning Edi arranged a do-it-yourself platter for breakfast consisting of cream cheese, capers, cold-smoked salmon, basil leaves in olive oil and liberally peppered avocado slices to put onto split baguette chunks from the toaster. This, and the fresh-ground Starbucks coffee provided us with the energy and stimulation we needed for the tedious task of continuing to wait for the steel fabricator and for the FedEx package with the new mast fittings from Seldén. Since Thursday afternoon we have been unable to track the FedEx shipment online because of another wifi failure.

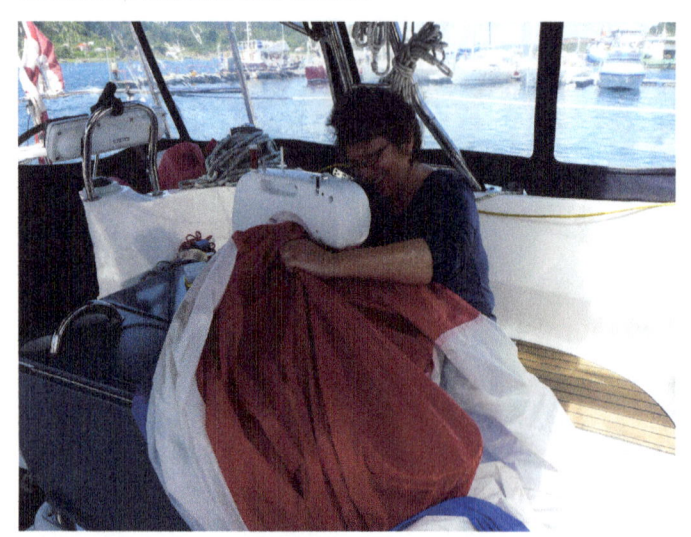

Saturday dawned clear. It was the first fully sunny morning in well over a week. After breakfast I hauled the spinnaker out of the sail locker and trailed it back into the cockpit so that Edi could repair a tear in it. It had torn near its tack on the point of a sprung spring-clip on the lifelines during our passage to the Galapagos. At the time, I had done a temporary repair with sail tape, which soon flapped free and needed to be re-enforced with duct tape. The duct tape held well, but it lacked the required aesthetics.

While we were working on the spinnaker, Alexandro, the Club Manager walked by on the float to check on the workers installing new finger floats on the floating pier. We asked about stainless fabricators, and he knew of none. We asked about the restoration of the wifi, and he told us the telephone company's system had exploded during the recent power outage and restoration. A replacement system is being couriered from the States, and will arrive when it does. We told him our FedEx package with the mast fittings had been shipped on Wednesday, and he told us that the two-day service sometimes arrives within a week, but it usually takes longer.

While Edi was repairing the spinnaker, I continued preparing Sequitur for sea. I mounted the sail on the Hydrovane wind-steering autopilot, secured the Ankorlina tape reel on the side of the pushpit and adjusted the barbecue on the stern rail. From the sail locker I hauled out the two stuff-bags each with 100 metres of floating line. I checked them over and re-stowed them, ready to secure our bow to rocks or trees ashore in the tight and windy anchorages of Patagonia and Tierra del Fuego.

I also hauled the two stern-line reels out of the port transom locker and mounted them on the stern rails. Each of these also has 100 metres of polypropylene. While the sun continued to shine, we kept at little chores outside, among them, re-connecting the HF antenna, which had been disconnected so we could fit into the travel-lift for haul-out.

As we worked outside, we were able to watch some of the causes of the frequent wakes that sweep through the marina. There is a rather steady marine traffic up and down Canal Reloncavi, the narrow 3.5-mile-long meandering strait that separates Isla Tenglo from the mainland and forms the busy working harbour of Puerto Montt.

Starting around 1730 on Saturday afternoon, a steady stream of heavily laden small boats headed down, their decks crammed with passengers. The most plausible explanation we could conger-up was that these were the people returning from a Saturday excursion to Mercado Angelmo, heading back down the coast to their isolation.

Since we had arrived on the float two weeks previously, we had been admiring the large catamaran moored in the slip across from us. We were initially attracted by the pleasing design and the finely crafted appearance, then we noticed the Alwoplast logo on the side of the house. For two and a half days we had watched as it busily prepared to go out, then late in the afternoon with a dozen-or-so people aboard, it motored away from its slip. Two hours later it came back in.

It still had its main up as it approached the slip. I assumed that the halyard had become stuck, since the skipper attempted to back into his slip with the sail still up. Fortunately there was only a light breeze, four or five knots blowing northward up the channel. Unfortunately it was blowing off the slip and it was a bit fickle, clocking randomly from southeast to southwest. The main was still rather tightly sheeted, rather than being let fly, and on the first approach the breeze veered and blew the cat to starboard.

On the second attempt, the breeze backed around to the southeast, the sail jibed and blew the cat off to port. The skipper made two more attempts while continuing to keep the main sheeted and drawing, and allowing the wind to skew the 55 or 60-foot catamaran off its approach line.

Finally, the skipper realized, or was told, that he still had his mainsail up. There were delegations of people to and from the mast as they tried to figure-out how to lower the sail. Eventually someone must have found the halyard, because the sail started coming down. A couple of conferences later, someone decided what was needed to bring it the rest of the way down. Then with only a few bumps, the cat was safely back in its slip.

It is a good thing we enjoyed the warm sunny Saturday, because Sunday dawned gloomy and drizzly. By midmorning; however, the drizzle had changed to rain, and this was being slanted by blustery northwest winds as another front came through. We cancelled our planned shopping trip and cocooned inside, practicing for the weather we will encounter as we head toward Tierra del Fuego.

With the high humidity here, we were very pleased with our decision to change our cotton sheets and pillow slips for bamboo ones. Besides their wonderful soft, silky texture, they are totally non absorptive and have an anti-mildew characteristic. Because they warm very quickly with body heat, they are great to slip between on a cold dank night. We also changed our cotton bath towels for bamboo, and love the way they wick-away water without saturating and then dry quickly.

On Monday morning the sun was back, this time interrupted by a scattering of light cumulus puffs. Not back; however, was the internet connection, so I could not I track the FedEx package with the forestay fitting. After breakfast I went ashore to the office to find some answers. I noted as I passed the catamaran that its mainsail was still in the same heap of disarray in which it had been left after its embarrassing dousing on Saturday.

In the office, Alexandro told me the FedEx package had not arrived. I gave him the tracking number, and he used his iPhone to do a tracking, finding out that it is estimated to arrive on Wednesday. He had no estimate on the restoration of the internet connection. I next went to David's shop to see if there was any news on Juan, the steel fabricator. The steel job had been promised for Monday, and since this was again a Monday, even though the third one now since the promise, we grabbed a sliver of hope that we might see Juan. I saw David as he was scrambling to tie-up loose ends before flying off to London for a couple of weeks. He had spoken with Juan, who had promised to be here later in the day.

While we waited for Juan, we watched the yard crew bring another two fingers for the floats. They have been steadily overhauling and refurbishing the old pieces ashore and floating them into place to reconfigure the marina slip layout. We anticipate that we will shortly need to move from our berth alongside the long finger; we are in the way of their progress.

As we were watching them delicately manoeuvre the two floating fingers, a large power cruiser nosed out of its slip and rapidly accelerated, seemingly hoping to create as large a wake as possible as it passed the workers in their tenuous positions. This is yet another demonstration of the widespread lack of wake awareness here, or a blatant disregard for its results.

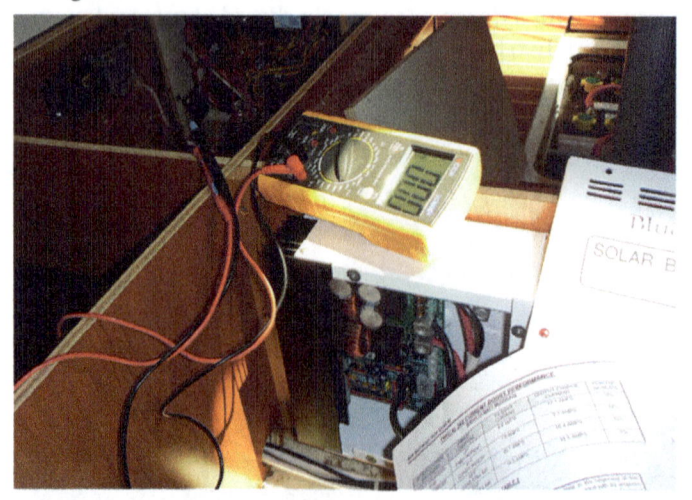

As we waited for Juan, I hauled-apart the main salon, trying to track-down why the solar panels have ceased to add their charge to the new battery bank. I had been poring through the BlueSky MPPT charge controller's manual for the past few days, searching for wisdom. I had redone all the connections on the new batteries, and had scrupulously matched the before-photos of the wiring with the current installation.

The troubleshooting pages in the manual had no entry for our combination of readings, and we had no internet connection to follow their advice of looking at their website for other issues. It came as little surprise that another Monday passed without any sign of Juan.

Tuesday dawned relatively clear with a stiff wind from the south driving cumulus past us and into a building stack of dark clouds against the mountains. The yard crew were back at work early, attaching the newly arrived fingers to the float. Just as we finished brunch, there was a knock on the hull; the crew were ready to move Sequitur. The wind was by this time well over 20 knots, so we did the prudent thing and squeezed forward to the last available metre of the float, rather than trying to manoeuvre against the wind onto one of the new fingers.

Once I had re-secured Sequitur in her new position, I went off in search of answers to a list of questions. As I approached the marina office, I saw a telephone company truck in the lot, an assortment of fresh wires on the roof and a new antenna. The office staff confirmed the wifi was about to be restored. All of my other questions could be answered online except: Where is Juan, the stainless steel fabricator?

The internet connection fix was a temporary and tenuous one that had been cobbled-together by the phone company from old parts while waiting for new equipment to arrive from the US. Nonetheless, by wandering around I was able to find some wifi signals sufficient to add an addition to the blog, to download a week of emails, to track the FedEx package and to contact BlueSky to further troubleshoot the solar controller.

The FedEx package with the forestay fitting replacement kit was showing online as being in Santiago, released from Customs and *"Tendered to authorized agent for final delivery"*. This boded well for its previously estimated Wednesday delivery; however, this is Latin America, and we have learned there is more than one meaning of mañana. We enjoyed a fine sunny day waiting for Juan, the stainless fabricator to not arrive.

As we waited, the wind continued strongly from the south. In the mid-afternoon Alexandro came down the float to tell us that the next finger installation was to be right through the middle of Sequitur, so we needed to move onto one of the new fingers, allowing the crew to continue on Thursday. The wind was forecast to abate in the evening, but by sunset it was still strong. We gambled on a calm early morning, and we won. Edi and I were up at 0630 and we easily warped Sequitur around in glassy-calm conditions.

With Sequitur now stern-to, we finally had easy access to and from the float through the transom doors. It was a level entry to our stern platform and it would have been wonderful during the previous couple of weeks in easing the loading aboard of all our supplies. Shortly after we had finished breakfast, the yard crew arrived and began installing the next finger.

469

While we waited for the then one day late FedEx package and the many weeks late steel fabricator to arrive, I hoisted the dinghy off the deck and down into the water using the spinnaker halyard and the electric sheet winch. I then cut off the chafe and refreshed the shackle attachment on the end of the spinnaker halyard.

Next I lifted the outboard engine off its mount, which was convenient now, immediately adjacent to the float and at waist level. I lugged it over to the dinghy, attached it to the transom, connected the fuel line, pumped the bulb and whispered a prayer to the outboard god. I pulled the cord and the engine started immediately. I was delighted; this was the first time we had run it since April in Valdivia.

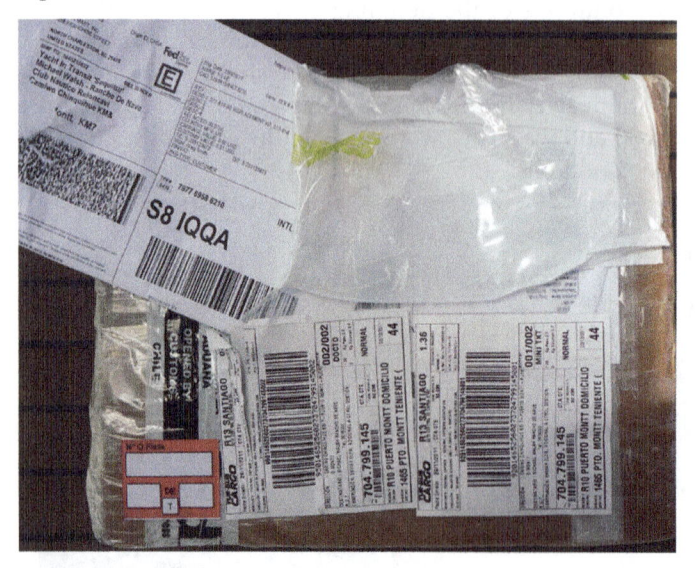

In the early afternoon, as I was puttering in the cockpit, one of the yard crew came by to tell me a package for Sequitur had just arrived at the gatehouse. As I was walking up the ramp to fetch the package, I stopped to chat with Max of the Australian sloop, Volo. I asked him about stainless steel fabricators, and he told me of one *"up the down street a few blocks from the junction with the up street, and then up a side street a bit. You can't miss it; the doors are normally open."* I asked him to translate up street and down street.

Armed with these wonderful directions, once I had picked-up the FedEx package and dropped it aboard, I grabbed the wind-generator mast tail and took a bus into town. By the time I had arrived at the end of the up and down streets, I had forgotten whether I needed to go up the up or the down. I walked up the up a few blocks, then down the down, all the while looking into the side streets for something that looked like a stainless steel shop's open doors. And there it was!

In my non-Spanish and the non-English of the foreman and a fabricator, hugely assisted by a dry-erasable board on the office wall, I communicated what I needed, specified the materials and the dimensions and was delighted when told it would be ready mañana. I asked; *"¿mañana mañana o mañana tarde?"* The fabricator said, *"tarde a cuatro"*, tomorrow afternoon at four. I was on a roll, and dared not ask the price.

I walked down the down to the main road and along it to the Mercado Angelmo. Along the way, I paused to take-in the working waterfront. At the potato wharf was the usual assortment of small craft dried-out at low tide. Further along there were two boats being rebuilt on the narrow strand between the high water line and the sea wall. Here the boat owners seem to get a few extra lives out of ancient wooden craft, where at home the boats would long since have been abandoned.

470

I walked around in the Mercado, closely examining all the fish in all the stalls. Mostly the fish were farmed salmon and merluza, and I saw some that looked like mackerel. At two of the stalls were some small diamond-shaped fish, like sole, but vertical rather than horizontal. I was told they were reineta. I bought one for 2000 Pesos and the fishmonger threw it to a colleague to clean, skin and fillet.

Back onboard, I opened the FedEx package from Seldén and examined its contents. Everything required for the fitting replacement was included, except the rivet gun. There were rivets, cap-screws, drill bit, thread lock, Torx bits, cotter pins, fishing line, fishing wire and washers. According to the detailed, illustrated instructions, the drill bit and rivets are required only if the halyard sheave box is the type riveted to the mast, rather than screwed.

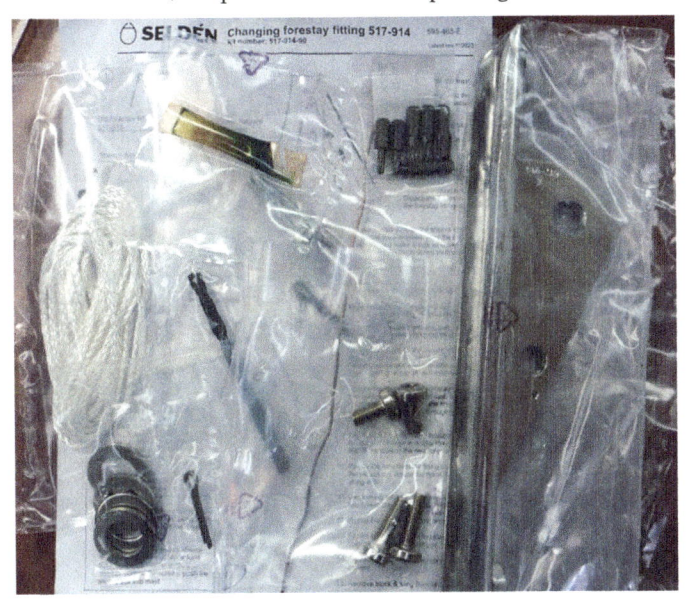

The instructions for the two types of screw-fitted sheave boxes looked easy. The ones for the riveted box were more complex, involving drilling, filing and riveting. With odds of two to one that we had the easier install, I went up the mast to see what we had. Of course, since Sequitur never chooses the easy path, she has the riveted sheave boxes in her mast.

Looking at the set-up on the mast, and reading the instructions, I could see that, if our sheave boxes had been the screw-in type, changing the forestay fitting would have been well within my ability to do. However, not having a rivet gun, let alone a 6.5mm one, and with no access to one, there is no way I can do this job on my own.

Tom had warned me of the possibility of needing a 6.5mm rivet gun, so before David had flown back to London last week to tend to family affairs following his father's death, he confirmed he had a proper rivet gun and was able and willing to do the job for us. Earlier, through Alexandro, I had spoken with a local Beneteau owner who does all the fit-out rigging and maintenance for the many Beneteaux here in Puerto Montt. He is scheduled back from a ten-day trip to Vina del Mar on Monday the 5th.

Thursday evening I prepared the filete de reineta to see whether it was worthy of a larger purchase. I lightly sautéed it in butter with basil leaves, and served it with tarragon-seasoned basmati rice and a butter-sweat of julienned carrots, onions and garlic. To hedge our bet, I accompanied it with a bottle of Undurraga Brut Royale. The hedge won; the fish had a mushy texture and a rather mundane taste. Fortunately, the wine was excellent, and I had bought only the one fish.

In the early afternoon on Friday Edi and I linked a couple of buses up to Supermercado Lider for another round of shopping, and hauled-back a full wheelie bag, and three other fully stuffed cloth sacks. After we had stowed everything, I took a bus to the bottom of the down street and walked up to the steel shop.

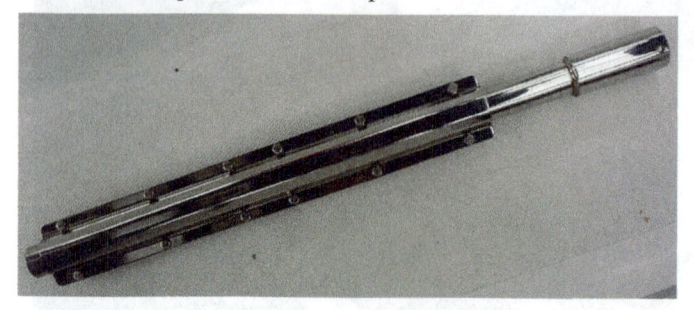

They had stuck to a textbook definition of mañana; the fabrication was complete, exactly as requested, crafted from 6mm 316, bent to fit the wind-generator mast while leaving a 1mm gap between the flanges on each side, drilled with twelve holes each fitted with 6mm stainless bolts, nuts and lock washers. The cost was 40,000 Pesos, slightly under $80.

The wind was howling out of the north as I used the new pieces to splint the severed mast tail back onto its stump. However; I left the job there for the day, as the wind was just too strong for me to comfortably and safely work in the somewhat precarious position required. I was surprised that Juan Moya, the delinquent steel fabricator did not show-up proudly bearing his four-week project.

At Lider we had found some wonderful asparagus, freshly arrived from Peru, so had I spent fifteen minutes or so selecting the six best bundles out of the two-hundred or more on display. Among many other things, we also bought another dozen-and-a-half filete de blanquillo, two dozen on-the-vine tomatoes and a large bouquet of fresh basil. Dinner was delicious.

On Saturday the wind continued in the mid-20-knot range from the north. For much of the day it steeply slanted the frequent rain showers, making remaining below a wonderful option. I continued to troubleshoot the BlueSky solar controller, but I had become rather frustrated with the email chain that had developed with BlueSky tech support during the week.

From the email conversation, it seemed as though I was dealing with a call centre in India or the Philippines, with an operator who simply asked questions off a list, and who seemed not absorb the meaning of the answers he received. In my initial email I had told him the answers to each of his subsequent questions. I found it totally unbelievable; it was as if I was living through a Monty Python skit. It was very frustrating, to say the least.

I read and reread the fourteen emails in the thread, trying to see if I had missed something. I pored-over the manual looking for something I may have misinterpreted. I became more frustrated.

To relieve the frustration, for Saturday evening's dinner I prepared tarragon chicken breasts with oyster mushrooms, shallots and garlic, served with fluffy basmati rice, garnished with sliced tomato with shredded fresh basil and accompanied by fresh Peruvian asparagus. This was wonderfully complemented by a 2011 Carmen Insigne Chardonnay, which drinks like a $15 bottle for only $3.75. While none of this fixed the Solar Boost, it did boost my spirits.

We slept-in on Sunday; the view up through the rain-splattered hatches above our bed did not encourage an early start. We did eventually get up, and Edi prepared a delicious brunch of ham and eggs with sauce béchamel and toasted baguette, but the day continued gloomy. Rain sprinkled from the low overcast each time I started outside to continue with the wind-generator installation, so we remained cocooned.

In the late afternoon the rain showers finally stopped, and a few blue patches began to appear. There was no wind, the water was glassy and I could find no excuse not to continue with the wind generator installation. I spent well over an hour on top of the solar panel arch, supporting and juggling the heavy generator while making and securing the electrical connections while trying not to step on the panels or to drop tools or the generator through their glass faces while maintaining balance from the wakes generated by a steady parade of boats passing by in the channel. Shortly after 1900 the job was complete.

After breakfast on Monday morning I went up to the marina office to speak with Alexandro on a few points, primarily about contacting the mast rigger, who was due back from his trip to Vina del Mar. He phoned the rigger and told him we now have illustrated instructions translated into Spanish. The rigger said he would be at Sequitur mañana. Oh, what a wonderful word the Latin Americans have! I dug deeper and learned it would be mañana tarde.

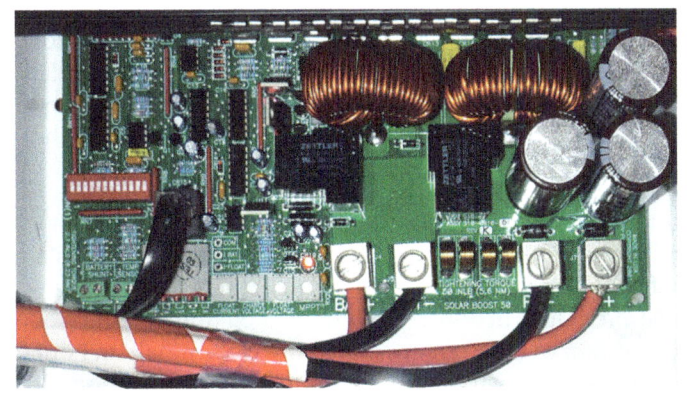

I read and reread the previous few day's email thread with BlueSky, looking for some lost meaning. I took another round of readings inside and outside the charge controller, and finding them identical to what I had initially sent, I sent off a rather heavy email, including all the present readings, and asked to be passed to a supervisor, not an offshore call-centre supervisor, but one back at headquarters in California. John replied, saying it was only him and Rick doing the tech support, and they were in the plant in California. He asked what I wanted to do now.

I asked him to call me on the satellite phone. A short while later John called and we talked for, according to the timer on the set, 18 minutes and 39 seconds, going round and round until we finally both agreed that the charge controller was not working. After we hung-up, I followed his advice and refreshed all the connections, which I had refreshed a few days previously in my initial troubleshooting. An hour later, with the same anomalous readings, I resolved that the controller was kaput. I bypassed it, and made the solar panels feed directly to the batteries. We will need to use the solar panel breaker, switching it on and off as our controller.

I went to bed still thinking of the solar controller, and laid awake for half an hour running through my mind the sequence of events during the installation of the new battery bank. One anomaly continued to pop up; the installer from Gami had needed to gain an extra couple of threads on two of the new, shorter battery posts. For one he had moved the temperature sensor for the Magnum inverter-charger to an adjacent battery. For the other, he had cut off two lugs from wires and spliced the wires together onto a single lug to fit onto a crowded post. What if one of the removed lugs had been a temperature sensor for the solar controller? Things began to make sense to me, and I relaxed and fell asleep.

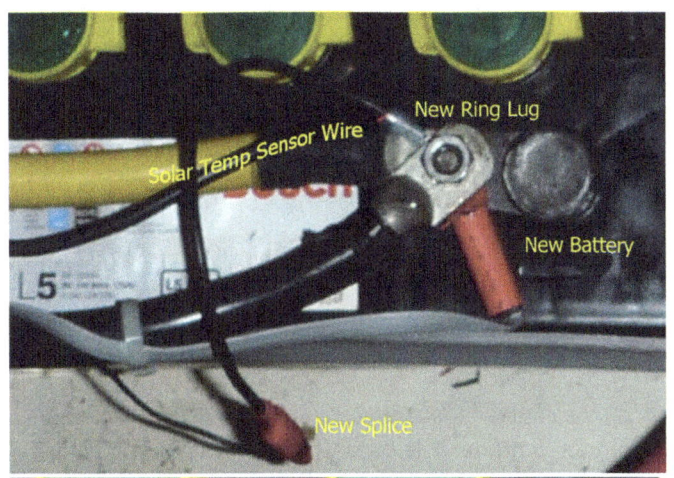

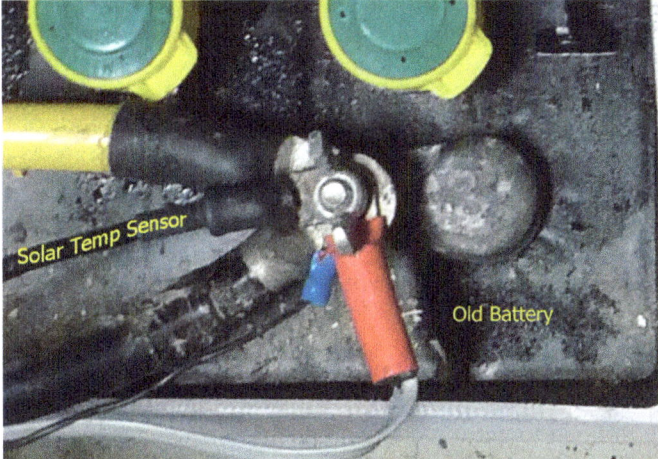

In the morning, my thinking was confirmed; the temperature sensor had apparently been mistaken for a common lug and had been discarded and replaced with a new ring lug and was sending a closed circuit signal to the controller.

So, I dug my way back in to the BlueSky Solar Boost box, removed its cover again and removed the leads from the terminals labelled TEMP SENSOR. I then dug down to the bypass wiring, disconnected it and led the solar panel wires back to the controller, then switched on the breakers and Voila! The MPPT Active LED began a slow blink. I adjusted the MPPT pot until it came on steady, indicating Bulk Charge. We again have a working solar controller. The next step is to adjust the Bulk, Acceptance and Float levels, and further fine-tune the settings.

We waited for the rigger, who the previous day had said he would be at Sequitur *"mañana tarde"*. By my experience, the afternoon starts not at noon, but at 1500, after the lunchtime siesta. When 1600, 1700 and 1800 had come and gone without the rigger, I spoke with Alexandro, who called the rigger and was told he would be at Sequitur *"mañana mañana"*, tomorrow morning.

For dinner I made a frittata with caramelized Spanish onions, crimini mushrooms, yellow and green peppers and shredded fresh basil, and served it with pan-fried red potato coins and sliced tomatoes.

We waited until 1300, officially well past the end of mañana mañana, then we went ashore, caught a bus to the Mall, and walked in search of the Hertz office. It was not where the Chilean Hertz brochure showed it to be. We found a Europcar office only to be told they had no cars available, so we asked them for directions to Hertz. We followed their directions and still we found nothing.

We asked in a service station with no luck, until we asked a young carabinero lieutenant, who had pulled in to refuel. He radioed to get directions, then told us he would drive us there. We got in and drove around several blocks with still no Hertz. He eventually dropped us at a small local car rental agency, where we rented a car for a day so that we could run a series of last-minute errands in preparation for heading out.

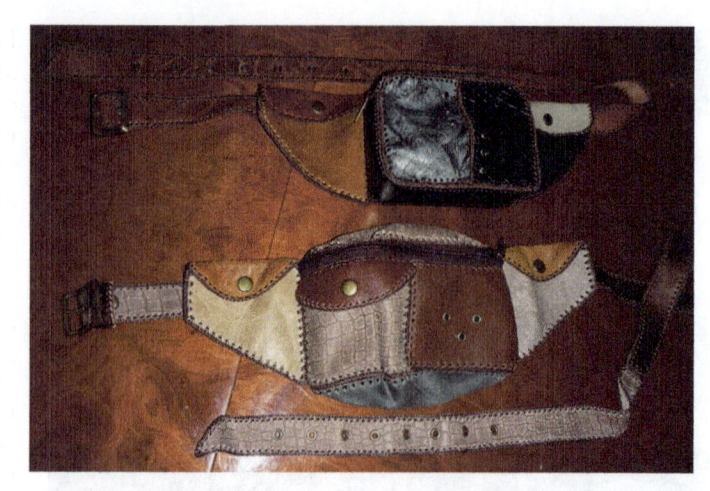

Our first errand was a trip to the airport to a little crafts shop, where we had seen some exquisitely hand-crafted leather goods when we had dropped-off the rental car from Santiago in October. We had searched in vain for similar belly packs throughout the shops in Puerto Montt and Angelmo. Fortunately, our favourites were still in the airport shop. It was a good lesson: *When you see something you really like, buy it; don't rely on finding it elsewhere.*

On our way back, we stopped at Sodimac to buy new fire extinguishers; Sequitur's were just at their expiry date. I also bought a three-metre length of galvanized 9mm chain to secure the dinghy and motor. We drove back to Sequitur for lunch and to see if the rigger might show-up. As I was chaining the dinghy and motor to the float, I was hailed by George, our delinquent rigger. He was working on a freshly re-rigged ketch down the float, and said he would be over to Sequitur shortly. While I waited, I carried on with chores, which included mounting the new fire extinguishers.

While continuing to wait, I emptied the contents of four jerry cans of diesel into the main tank, bringing it back to full. We had burnt 80 litres running the Espar furnace for heat and hot water for 45 days, plus we ran the generator for 16.3 hours. Adding the diesel to the tank was simple, with Sequitur stern-to on the float. I simply stood on the float and poured into the filler on the upper part of the starboard transom.

By the time I had finished my chores it was nearly 1830, and the rigger was still on the ketch. I walked over to talk with him, bringing with me the forestay fitting and the illustrated instructions, now translated into Spanish. I invited him over to our cockpit and we spent half an hour going over the instructions, examining the installation kit and taking a look at the mast from the foredeck. George said he would start mañana. I narrowed him down to 0930.

Edi and I then loaded six empty jerry cans into the trunk of the rental car and drove off to Supermercado Lider. Sequitur's fridges, freezers, wine cellar and pantry were now fully stocked. Nonetheless, we combed the aisles, allowing the stock on the shelves to prompt us on anything we may have missed. We filled a large shopping cart to near overflowing.

On our way back we stopped at a gas station and filled four cans with 20 litres each of diesel, plus two more with 20 litres each of gasoline for the outboard engine.

Among the things we bought were some winter squash, some heads of cauliflower and broccoli and a couple of hands of green bananas, some just beginning to yellow. By the time we had lugged everything aboard and stowed it, it was nearly 2200 and we were rather hungry from our lugging. For dinner I sautéed two fillets each of fresh blanquillo with basmati rice and asparagus spears.

At 0900 I went out onto the foredeck and spent twenty minutes arranging the rigging, lowering the jib and the staysail and generally preparing for the rigger. Then I went below for breakfast, knowing I would have plenty of time for it before George arrived. I was right; he arrived at 0950.

It took George a while to familiarize himself with the B&R rig and absorb its stability. Then I hoisted him aloft as he assisted with the mast steps along the way. He had quite a time breaking-free the Torx screws securing the forestay fitting, but eventually got them moving.

Shortly before noon he had the old fitting out and he came down to exchange it for the new one, to pickup the rivets and rivet gun, the new screws and the LocTite.

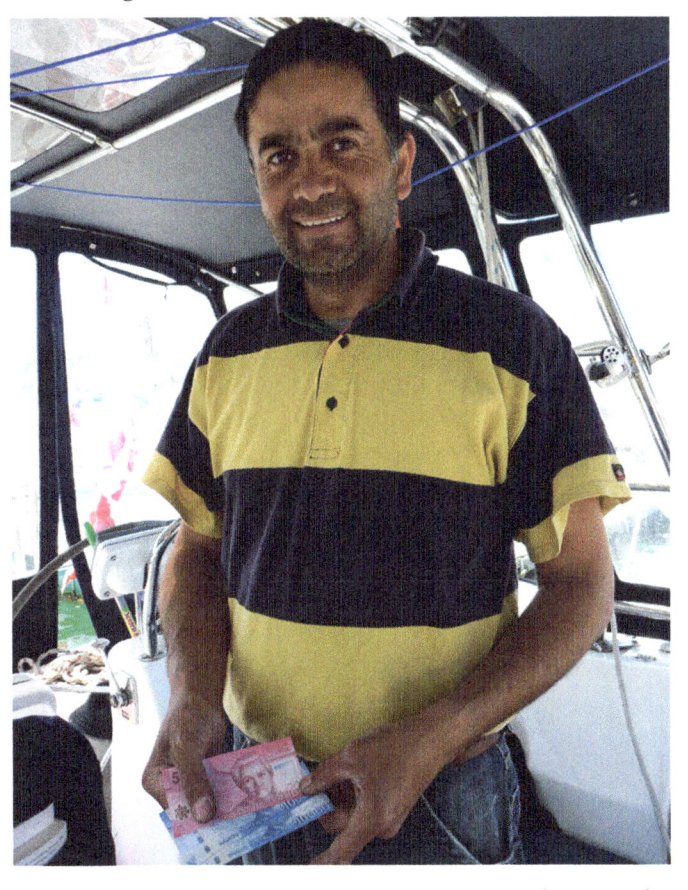

At 1320 George signalled to be lowered from the mast; he was done. I told him that I would re-tune the rig, re-hoist the sails and tidy-up. He had been at it for three and a half hours, plus half an hour the previous evening, plus whatever his travel time. I asked him how much, and was nearly floored when he told me 25,000, about $50. Riggers at home charge $75 and up an hour, and charge for their travel time, their cell phone time and their pee breaks. George has no receipt book or invoice pad, so I gave him cash and took a photo. We expected that Seldén wouldn't balk at my rigger expense reimbursement claim without a receipt.

475

Immediately George had left, we rushed ashore to return our rental car, due at 1400. On the way up the ramp we met Max of the Australian sloop Volo. He had just received their zarpe after three days with the Armada. We had our boat portfolio with us and were heading to the Armada office on our way back to ask for a zarpe for mañana.

In the Capitania when we arrived was Roger of the British ketch El Vagabond. He was there on his third visit and we chatted with him for half an hour as his zarpe was finally completed and issued. There was only one person in the office; it was another church holiday. When our turn came, we asked for a zarpe for that evening, figuring we'd be best to start there and work our way forward. It was likely Edi's smile that won it, but the young Petty Officer eventually relented, and within half an hour we had a zarpe for 0700 mañana, and it was issued all the way to Puerto William in the Beagle Channel.

We spent the remainder of the day squaring-away the rigging, hoisting the motor and dinghy, and generally preparing Sequitur for sea again. Southward From Puerto Montt

We were up early to continue with our preparations for sea. Sequitur had been either alongside or on the hard in Puerto Montt for nearly half a year, and there were many details to attend to in insuring she was ready again to proceed. After breakfast I left Edi with the final details as I walked up to the marina office to pay our fees for re-launch, mooring and electricity. We would have done this the previous afternoon, when we had returned with our zarpe, but it was another church holiday in Chile. The office had been closed as they celebrated the Feast of the Immaculate Deception.

The office was still closed when I arrived, so I waited for about ten minutes for Alexandro to arrive. A little over an hour later, after the marina crew had finally given-up on finding a key for the electrical box on the float and broke-into it to read our meter, I had our invoice completed and paid.

24. To Isla Chiloe

Edi had everything secured when I returned, so I flashed-up the engine, and at 1030 we slipped our lines and proceeded under power out of the marina and down the channel into Seno Reloncavi. We had enjoyed Puerto Montt. It is a rather pleasant city for the frontier town that it is, situated at the end of the road and on the edge of a vast wilderness that extends to Cape Horn. We used it well as our last opportunity for repairs, maintenance, spares and supplies. We were more than ready to leave, and we hoped Sequitur was also.

It was a clear and calm day as we motored out into the Sound. I called the Armada at Puerto Montt Radio on VHF Channel 16 to report our departure, as required. No response. I called again seven times, every two or three minutes we until finally received a reply.

By the time of our noon observations, a light breeze had come-up, 2 to 3 knots from the southeast. By 1230 it had increased to 4 to 5 knots, so I hauled-out the main and the jib and we motor-sailed on a port tack. By 1700 the wind had built to about 12 knots, and we had shut-down the engine and were making 4 to 5 knots in varying winds as we weaved our way past islands and around points, heading generally southwest.

Along the way, the foreshores and bays were filled with fish farms. In places, picturesque little rural communities had their previously wonderful pastoral settings marred by these modern factories. I suppose this is one of the many costs of progress.

As we crossed the 30-mile expanse of Golfo de Ancud, the wind came from the northwest at 16 to 18 knots, and we sailed for a while at hull speed of 8.9 knots on a beam reach. With the beam seas, the heel became a tad uncomfortable, so I rolled-in the jib and shortened the main, and we continued more comfortably with staysail and reefed main, making around 6.5 to 7 knots. It was great to be sailing again.

At 2000 I made the required call to the Armada, failing to receive any response from them on my three attempts.

At 2032 we rounded the western point of Isla Mechuque and rolled-in the sails to motor into the small Caleta Mechuque. A wonderful double rainbow from a quick rain shower pointed the way to the anchorage off the tiny, isolated hamlet.

We motored past the tiny outpost community of Mechuque and around a point. At 2109 we came to 45 metres of chain on the Rocna on a mud bottom in 9.9 meters of water in a very tight little bay. It was low tide, and with the level due to rise 5 meters overnight, our 4.5:1 scope would change to 3:1 as the tide rose.

We were in a very well-protected anchorage in calm weather, our batteries were at 100%, we had full water tanks from the marina with plenty of it hot from the day's running, we had a boat full of food and supplies and souls full of satisfaction that all was well.

Saturday morning looked glum up through the hatches from our bed, so we were not eager for an early start. We decided to stay at anchor for another day and hope for a break in the weather to go ashore for a look around.

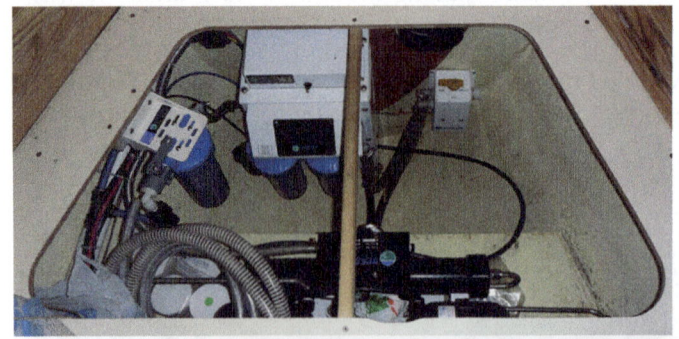

This was our first opportunity to use our new dinghy wheels, which we had brought back with us from Vancouver to La Punta the previous year and installed in Iquique in January. They worked wonderfully. I drove the bow onto the gravel beach, stepped out onto the dry, and then we rather easily rolled the dinghy up to the high water line with the motor still down.

The water in the anchorage was clean, so in the early afternoon I decided it was a good place and time to re-commissioned the watermaker. If there were problems we were still close enough to civilization to rectify them. I changed the charcoal filter and the pre-filters, ran the purge cycle and took a water sample. The salinity was < 100 ppm. Satisfied, I set it to auto-flush on a 120-hour cycle.

The little village of Mechuque is very rustic and pastoral. It appears that forestry was once important, but the big trees are now mostly gone. Fishing is important, and there are several fish farms along the coast. Also, the rebuilding and repairing of fishing boats appears to be a casual and rather primitive pastime, with boats scattered along the shore in various stages of life and death.

By the time I had finished with the watermaker and we had eaten lunch, the weather still looked iffy, but we decided to head ashore anyway. As we approached, a cow and a calf came down a trail and onto the beach and walked along it, followed by two dogs and a cow-herder and another cow. The beach was the trail from the pasture to the cowshed.

We walked up the one-lane brick road and across the one-lane bridge into the centre of the settlement. Along the way we passed an assortment of very Germanic-styled houses, mixed in with a 60s back-to-the-earth architecture that would go unnoticed on Saltspring or Lasqueti Island back home.

Everywhere we looked was a rustic scene of real life being scraped out of a harsh environment and shaped with no purpose other than to make do with what was available. Houses, workshops and outbuildings were erected on stilts overhanging the water to take advantage of the steep waterfront and the six meter tidal range.

A few doors up a side lane, sitting on a hillside overlooking the slough that cuts the community in two, sits an abandoned and deteriorating house that looks rather noble in comparison to its neighbours. We wondered whether its size made it too much to maintain.

In the middle of the community of a few dozen is the church, and across from it a medical clinic. Around the corner is the office of the Carabineros de Chile.

As we walked, we found several edges of the town, it being difficult to go more than a hundred meters in any direction without popping out one side or another. Dark clouds continued passing over and spitting the occasional shower on us as we wandered. However, we were fascinated with the beauty and genuine quaintness of the place, and carried on. After nearly two hours, we returned to the dinghy, easily re-launched it with its wheels and motored back out to Sequitur.

Sunday opened as a bleak and windy day. I called the Armada radio stations in the area with our mandatory 0800 position report, and received no response, which was not in the least surprising.

Just down the street, next to the new waiting room for the ferry, is the local grocery and general store. Small patches of paper taped in the window showed they had bread, potatoes, hen, chicken, chicken wings, turkey wings and sausage. Since we needed none of these, we decided not to go in.

Edi prepared a breakfast of pain perdu au jambon served with sliced tomatoes and chopped basil, and we enjoyed it with steaming fresh-ground Starbucks from our local source.

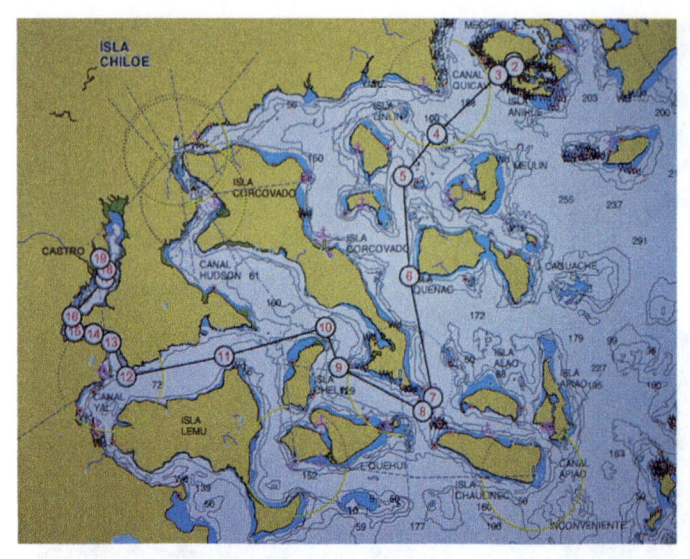

At 1008 we weighed and motored out of the caleta and into more open water so we could roll out some sails. Our destination for the day was Castro, about 50 miles away along a course woven between islands, rocks, reefs and shoals all washed with varying tidal currents. The wind was initially from the northwest at 6 to 8 knots, so we motor-sailed to maintain our desired 5 knot speed. As the day progressed and the winds and our course shifted, we sailed every point from close hauled to dead downwind.

It was not only headlands, rocks, reefs and shoals that we needed to avoid. Along the way much of the shoreline was lined with shellfish and salmon farms.

Some of these are modern and appeared well-maintained, while many others are rather dilapidated. The beaches are littered with washed-up detritus from the farms; old floats, tanks and general garbage. There does not appear to be much regulation on the farms, if there is even any at all. They are often placed in navigational channels, and in some cases take-up entire bays.

At 1850 we came to 50 meters of chain on the Rocna in 11 meters of water at low tide in front of the Armada station in Castro. With the tidal range of 6 meters, we were just shy of 3:1 scope. Once we were properly secured, I called Castro Radio, the Armada station on VHF to report our arrival, and received no response. Two further calls had similar results. Our several attempts to give our required 2000 report also failed to elicit any response from the Armada.

At 2115, just before sunset and just as we were finishing dinner, an inflatable with two Armada ratings arrived off our stern. They asked to see our zarpe. I handed it to them and they were soon satisfied that all was in order. I told them we had received no response from Castro Radio after many attempts. They questioned whether our radio was working, and I assured them it was, and told them of hearing many other unanswered calls to Castro Radio. I requested they call us on their portable. They had none, but said they would call in a few minutes, from their office. They did. We replied. They said goodnight.

We awoke to a bright, clear day with a light southerly breeze. After breakfast we launched the dinghy and headed ashore to explore Castro. We first putted along the shoreline to the northwest, looking at the long line of stilt-houses lining the waterfront. Many of these appeared to be well beyond their best-before dates; some are in the late stages of dilapidation. However; there is a new breath of life in the row, with two very modern and obviously upscale homes being built in the middle of the slum. We surmised that this will quickly spread along the row, transforming the little area into a better neighbourhood.

We headed back along the shore to the dinghy float below the Armada station, and secured Non Sequitur to a bollard. It being near low tide, the ramp was very steep, nearly 40 degrees. We wandered around in the base for a while, searching for the gate, so we could ask permission to moor at their float, as is suggested in the two cruising guides we have. Finally we were directed to the main gate, and we spoke with a rather stern Petty Officer, who told us it was forbidden for us to use their float.

For plan B, we took the dinghy over to a gravel beach, lowered the wheels and motored the bow up onto the dry. We rolled Non Sequitur about a dozen meters up and secured her painter to pier rail. I also looped a chain through the motor and dinghy eyes and around an upright iron I-beam, and secured the loop with a heavy padlock. Memories of our stolen dinghy and motor in Piata are still with us.

We walked along through the waterfront park, which is decorated with machines of a bygone era. There is a small, very narrow-gauge steam locomotive on display, rather nicely restored and maintained, which unfortunately seems to be a recurring target of local graffiti artists.

There are also several steam engines, both stationary and wheel-mounted. The region has a rich agricultural and forestry history, and these engines would have been a welcome replacement for both horse and human sweat.

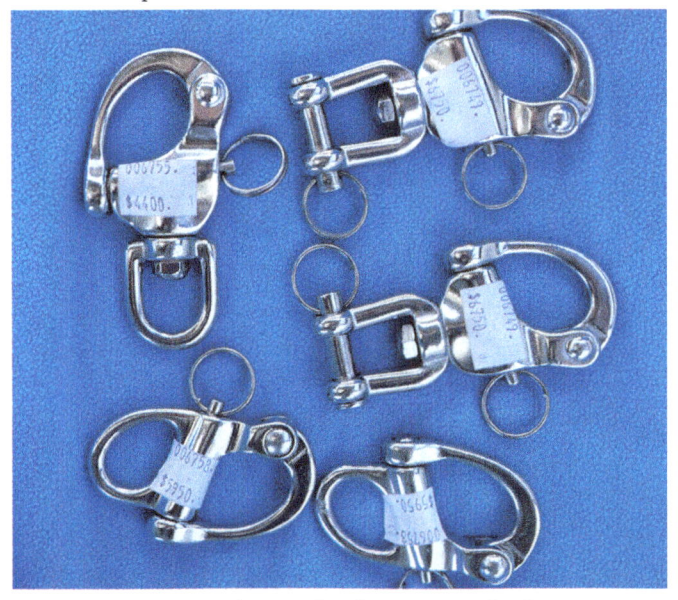

We spotted across the road a ferreteria, which seemed to specialize in marine hardware. As we were looking around inside, I spotted a chain of a dozen or so pelican hooks hanging from a post, and noted they were all stamped 316.

481

We needed two to make slinging our outboard engine to and from the dinghy easier. The basic swivel-eyed one I wanted with a 2cm bight was priced at 4400 Pesos, a bit less then $8.80, seemingly less than wholesale back home. When our ticket number came-up at the service counter, I asked for four more like it, and was told the chain was their entire stock. I picked-out the five 2cm bight hooks from the chain, and the clerk offered them all to us at 4400 each. The bargain improved.

We walked up the steep hill to the centre of town, which is sited on a plateau. Facing the Plaza de Armas is Iglesia San Francisco de Castro, which was completed in 1912 as a replacement for a church destroyed by fire, which had been a replacement for an even earlier fire-ravaged one.

The interior of the church is finished entirely with shellacked wood, which the signage proudly proclaims is the height of the local Chiloe artisan craftsmanship.

We walked back through the town to the eastern edge of the plateau to Hosteria de Castro having a cervesa each and enjoying the wifi connection. Immediately outside the window beside us was a huge araucaria tree with several pairs of nesting black-faced ibis.

After we had satisfied our birdwatching and internet cravings, we headed toward the northern brink of the plateau, where we found a staircase that descends the steep embankment to the waterfront.

The view down and to the north was of old and peaceful settings; but sprinkled across the skyline behind us were the cranes and derricks of new construction. Castro is the capitol of Isla de Chiloe and it has a population of about 35,000. It appears to be in a boom cycle, the city looks and feels prosperous and has an upbeat energy.

We descended the stairway and path and walked along to the dinghy to head back out to Sequitur to prepare her for departure the following morning. On our way along the waterfront we watched as a small ferry took-on fuel from a tank-truck on the wharf. Fuelling boats is very different in South America. So far we had pumped from a barrel on a pier, hauled jerry cans from a gas station, filled from a truck while hauled-out, filled in a travel-lift well, pumped from jugs in a water taxi and snaked a hose from shore while Med-moored. We were sure there would be more variety to come.

We spent the remainder of the afternoon and on into the evening reeving a new piece of thick elastic cord into the hem of the dinghy cover in our continuing attempt to modify the cover to fit the davits, and to make it easier to use. The previous week, Edi had made and reinforced holes through it to accept the tackle falls. Finally, just before sunset, we put the cover in place and hoisted the dinghy. Although it still needed a final adjustment with the dinghy hauled-out on a beach, it was ready for sea.

We were up early to bright sunshine on Tuesday morning, with a gentle breeze from the southeast. Edi prepared breakfast by melting slices of Asiago on ham in the sauté pan, then topping with eggs and covering the pan with a lid to baste. This she served on toasted split baguettes and garnished with sliced tomato and fresh basil leaves.

At 1022 we weighed and motored back down the inlet from Castro. It was nearly calm as we passed the many fish farms that line the shores and often extend well out into the channel. At one of these, a transport ship was pumping aboard a load of salmon to haul away for processing.

With all the shellfish we have seen here, both canned, smoked and fresh, we assumed we would be seeing shellfish farms. We passed many of these operations, which consist of suspending seeded lines beneath floats and waiting for the shellfish to mature clinging to the lines. It certainly makes for an easy harvest.

In the more remote areas, where commuting to and from the fish farm might be a bother, it appears that some prefer to live on the farm. On many of the fish farms there are rather comfortable-looking homes, but instead of picket fence and lawnmowers, there are mooring cleats and life raft launchers.

483

As we moved out of the channels, the winds picked-up and became more stabilized in their direction, so we rolled-out the staysail and half of the main and beat into the 15 to 18 knot southerly winds. As we tended southwest, we had wonderful views across Golfo de Corcovado to the mountains on the mainland, particularly the impressive Volcan Corcovado.

We headed up a narrow blind inlet that doglegs its way through wonderful pastoral settings, with black-necked swans paddling in the quiets, sheep grazing on the slopes and cattle in the rich grass along the banks. We continue to see settings that are so reminiscent of the Gulf Islands, Desolation Sound and other wonderful places back in British Columbia.

In the early evening we came to 35 metres on the Rocna on a mud bottom in 10.1 metres of water in front of a few houses and a church at the beginning of the shoaling about two miles up the inlet. The tide was just turning to ebb, and we would lose 5 metres of depth to the low.

Wednesday morning brought another clear day. While Edi prepared breakfast, I puttered in the cockpit doing a few chores, like drilling and bolting a sickle onto a long cane of bamboo to use as a kelp cutter. To make the scene even more idyllic, a couple of horses and a colt came down and grazed in the beachside meadow in front of the church.

Shortly after 1000 we weighed and headed back down the inlet on the tail-end of the ebb. We were about to pass around the stern of an anchored boat so as not to compromise his anchor line in the narrow channel, when a person onboard began frantically motioning for us to pass ahead.

We came within ten metres of a floating air hose before we noticed it. The boat had a diver down on a hooka, but flew no flag or signal to indicate the fact. We barely missed our first opportunity to test our new propeller line cutter.

We rolled-out the staysail and half the main and motor-sailed thirty degrees either side of the wind as we wound our way through the zig-zag-zig of Canal Tranqui against the beginning of the flood tide. Sequitur seems to attract wind on the nose.

The skies remained totally clear and we enjoyed another warm late spring day. The navigation was easy, but it was necessary to maintain a close lookout for shellfish farm buoys, which have a habit of appearing in the middle of the most convenient route through a passage or around a point. Nonetheless, we were able to relax and enjoy the wonderful countryside we were passing through. It certainly reminded us of the British Columbia coast.

The fish farms continued, and as they became more remote, their accommodations became more complex. We saw one with a floating four-story building, which we assumed contained not only workshops and offices, but also quarters and mess for the work crew.

Volcan Corcovado tended to hog the horizon to the east as we headed toward the southern end of Isla Chiloe. At one point, as we skirted a group of large orange buoys of a shellfish farm, Edi spotted a thick yellow line along Sequitur's side. It was a good 3cm in diameter and was attached to the two buoys we had just passed. I quickly shifted to neutral and we watched as we drifted past the 30 metres or so of floating hawser. It looked as if the mooring line for the buoys had recently parted, and for the second time of the day, we narrowly missed testing our new line cutter.

As we motor-sailed into the wind, we ran two loads of laundry through the washer and dryer, and we made three hours of water. At 1655 we came to 50 metres of chain on the Rocna in the middle of the fishing fleet off Puerto Quellon. We spotted a Copec and a Petrobras filling station on the waterfront street, one on either side of the fishing wharf.

485

After we had secured, I used the transfer pump to move fuel from the auxiliary tank to the main, and then poured the 80 litres from the four diesel jerry cans into the auxiliary tank, bringing it back near full. While the main tank is the most convenient to fill when we are moored stern-to on a float, the deck fill of the auxiliary tank is the easier to use the rest of the time. Our intention was to refill the jerry cans at a gas station ashore and top-up the auxiliary tank then refill the used cans, so that we are as close to our 920 litre capacity when we leave here, our last stop on Chiloe and our last opportunity for fuel without the usurious 50% to 75% surcharge reported down the coast.

All of this concentration on refuelling brought me to thinking of our own replenishment. For dinner I sautéed some filete de blanquillo with oyster mushrooms, shallots and garlic and served them with basmati rice, sliced tomato with shredded basil and a side of asparagus spears with mayonnaise. It all went splendidly with the 2011 Carmen Chardonnay.

For Thursday's breakfast Edi prepared a small platter of sliced avocados, tomatoes and basil leaves, and we enjoyed toasted split whole wheat baguettes slathered with cream cheese and topped from the platter. We were enjoying our fresh produce while it lasted, and we were counting on finding a bit more during our jaunt ashore for diesel.

In the late morning we launched Non Sequitur and motored in to the commercial wharf, where we were able to find a slot being vacated by another inflatable. While Edi sat and protected our property on the milling and crowded wharf end, I walked up to the Petrobras station, filled two jugs, lugged them back to the dinghy, took the two remaining empties back in the wharf, filled them and paid the 54,080 Pesos for the 80 litres.

The scene at the ends of the commercial and fishing wharves was very active and chaotic, with large and small vessels steadily coming and going and being variously loaded and unloaded. Back onboard, I added about 12 litres to top-off the auxiliary tank. Having no great desire to lug a jug ashore to top it up with an additional 12 litres, I stowed the remaining three full jugs and the part-used one. Sequitur now has a little over 900 litres of diesel in her various tanks.

After lunch we took Non Sequitur back to the wharf, intending to secure it with chain and heavy padlock. The wharf end was submerged by the high tide, and the remaining stub was overflowing with boats. We continued along to a beach and I drove the dinghy up onto the sand, delighted with the wheels. There was no secure point on which to chain it, so we left it to fate and walked into the town looking for a grocery store to buy some fresh produce.

Puerto Quellon is officially the end of Ruta 5, the Pan-American Highway. If we were to leave our loft in Vancouver, head six blocks east, turn left onto the beginning of Oak Street and, staying on the same road as it changes names southward, we would end-up in Puerto Quellon. Simple directions, really, but we had chosen chose a more complex route. We were truly at the end of the road, and this was our last opportunity to find selection and reasonable prices.

We found a rather smaller Bigger, and in it we selected fresh mushrooms, green peppers, broccoli, cauliflower, Fuji apples and a huge bouquet of fresh basil among other things. We took our booty wandering as we searched for a wifi connection. Back down on the waterfront we finally saw a wifi sign in the window of the bar/lounge of Hotel Tierra del Fuego. We went in, sat down and opened our computers to find a five-bar signal. We ordered a couple of cervesas and got the code. We couldn't connect. I told the barkeep, and he rebooted the system, then phoned the service provider. The internet was down on the entire island of Chiloe, but even without it, the 1000 Pesos each for the beer was a bargain.

We were delighted to find our dinghy and motor where we had left them, at the foot of a ramp down the seawall. The tide had reached its maximum flood, leaving us with a very simple relaunch. We headed back out to Sequitur to stow our purchases and to prepare to depart early on Friday morning to cross Boca del Guafo to the Archipelago de las Guaitecas.

25. Across Boca del Guafo

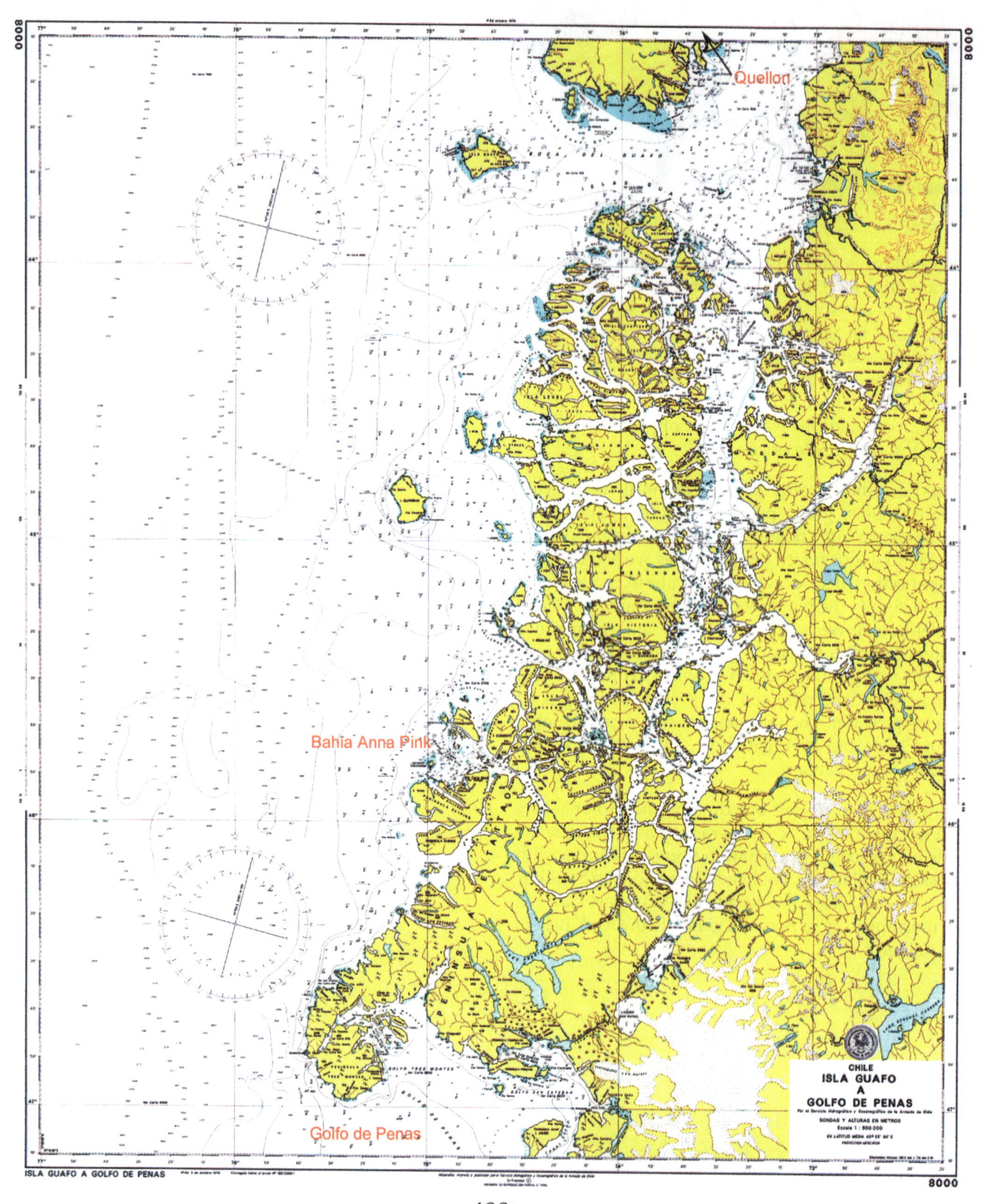

Our route onward required us to cross Boca del Guafo, a gap a little over twenty miles wide, which separates Isla Chiloe from the continuation of the chain of islands offshore the Chilean mainland. Through the gap pours a rather steady series of storms, which often adversely interacts with the local strong tidal currents. Once across the Guafo, we will be in relatively more quiet inside waters and will work our way down through the channels and out to Bahia Anna Pink. From there, the recommended route heads along the lee shores, around the peninsulas and across Gulfo de Penas to the continuation of the channels.

The Pilots, Sailing Directions and Navigator Guides all speak rather scarily of the dangers of crossing the Boca del Guafo and the Golfo Corcovado, with phrases such as: *"pretty hard, if not dangerous"*, and *"sea conditions very hazardous"*. They all emphasize correct timing for the crossing. We decided to follow the recommended procedure and leave Quellon on the high tide, which was at 0610 on Friday. We were awakened by the light of the sunrise coming through the cabin hatches, and at 0623 we weighed and headed out under power in calm seas and clear blue skies.

As we motored down the winding channels between the islands, and down to the bottom of Chiloe, Edi brought breakfast up into the cockpit in her customized serving basket, which she designed to clip onto the central handholds on the cockpit table. We now have a very convenient way to keep things secure and in place for cockpit dining at sea. We enjoyed a wonderful breakfast panini with sliced Tuscan ham, local cheese, tomatoes and fresh basil leaves. The Yacht Club Peruano cups and saucers reminded us of our La Punta friends Frano and Gonzalo; we toasted them.

There was a light breeze from the southeast, just sufficient to fill a stabilizing main and staysail as we motor-sailed across the dreaded gulf. We ran two loads of laundry through the machine and ran the watermaker for four hours, netting about 200 litres of fresh water. Shortly after 1400 we entered the Archipelago de las Guaitecas and half an hour later passed the village of Melinka.

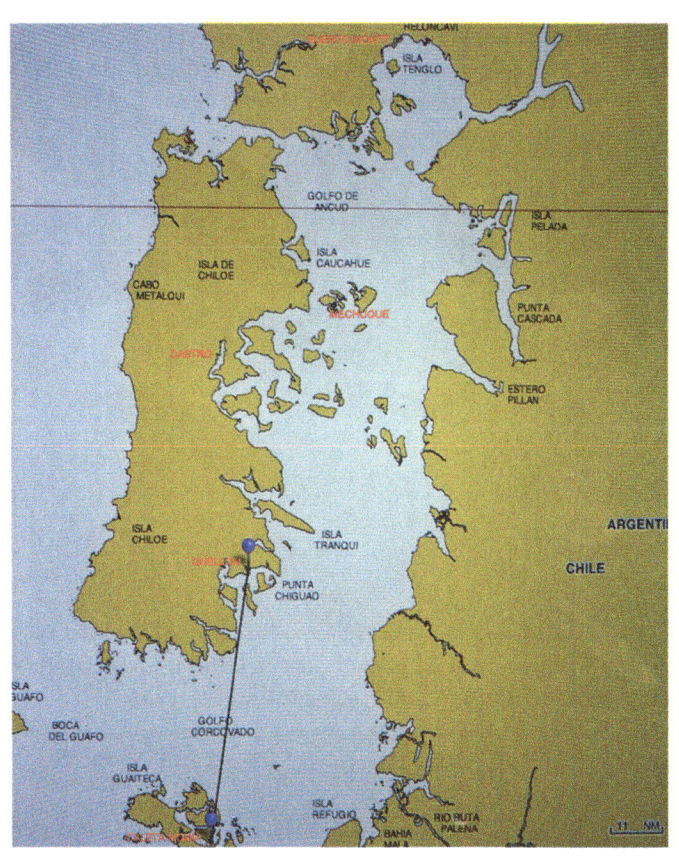

At 1529 we came to 45 metres on the Rocna in 11 metres of water on a mud bottom in Caleta Momia. The tide was very near low, and was due to rise about 2.5 metres to its high.

The area reminded us very much of the Broken Group in Barclay Sound, off the west coast of Vancouver Island. The charts; however, quickly brought us back to Chilean reality with their gross errors with the horizontal datum, the near complete lack of soundings, and the misplaced islands, coves and points. Our chartplotter showed us securely anchored two cables inland.

We arose early again on Saturday to take advantage of the tide. It was just coming to high as we weighed at 0700 and headed through the narrow uncharted passage to the southwest of our anchorage. The Guide says the narrows have a minimum depth of 5 metres, but as we motored slowly through, we found a patch of bottom with less than our 2.2

metre draft and we ground to a stop. I allowed the following current to swing our stern around about 90 degrees to port, and then backed off into deeper water and continued out.

Shortly we were in the charted channel and relaxing with pain perdu au jambon and fresh-ground Starbucks.

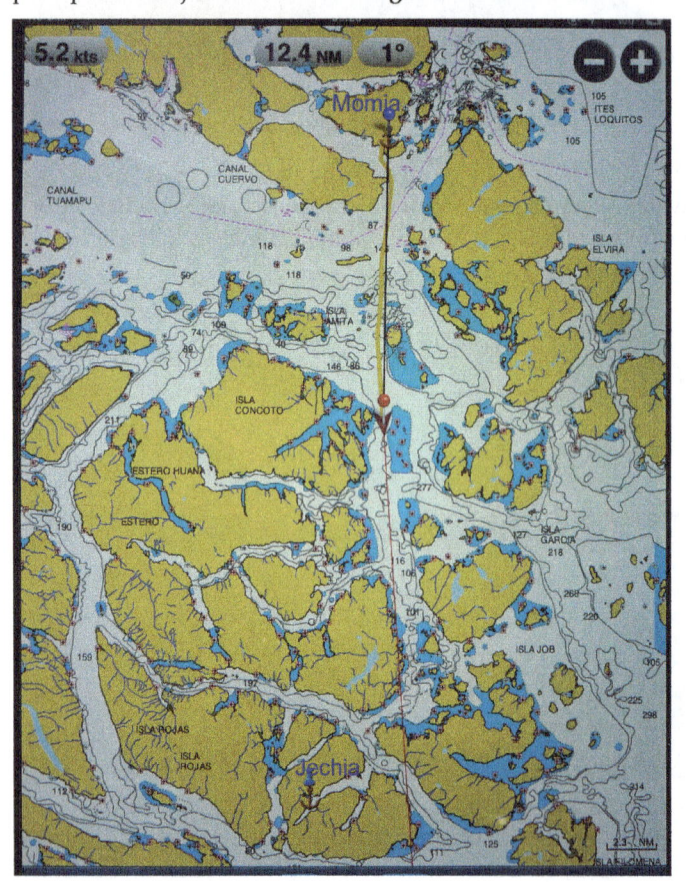

Our intended destination for the day was a rather new marina tucked in a cove near the end of a winding and forked inlet on Isla Jechia. To get there we would follow Canal Perez Norte southward. This rather straightforward passage is between four and eight cables wide, and it is bounded by a collection of large and small islands, islets and rocks, with no marked hazards in the channel. However, it is the unmarked ones that concerned us. There were some small freighters and fishing boats using it, so we gained confidence.

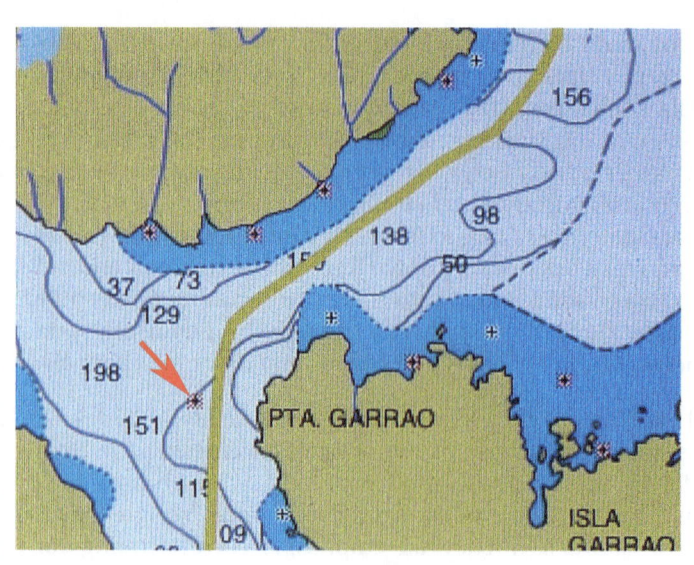

A bit disconcerting was the drying rock chart symbol on a 100-metre sounding line near mid-channel off Punta Garrao. I decided to give the charting anomaly more than a cable's berth on the way by, thinking it made no sense to go aground on a charted feature. Then we arrived at the entrance to Estero Chulle, which is labelled Area Sin Sondaje, which translates as Area Without Soundings. Our destination was up the uncharted inlet.

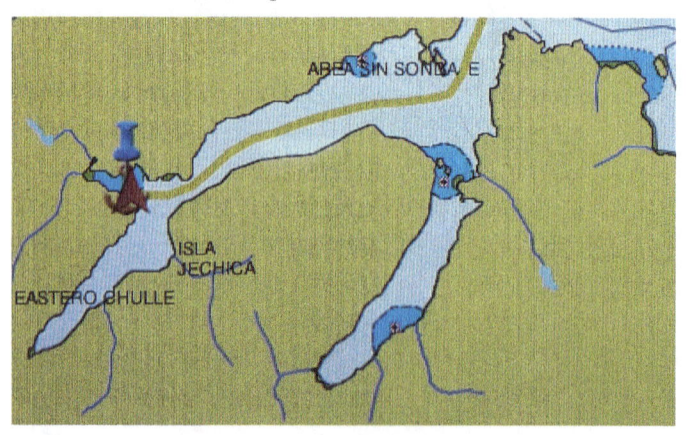

I figured that if someone took the bother to build a marina, they would also ensure that the waters leading to it were safe to navigate. We headed in through generally 40 to 50 metre depths, with only two under-10-metre surprises on the sounder. As we slowly motored past the end of the float, we spoke with two staff who had come down to assist us. We indicated we would anchor, and they said we could moor on the float. We asked how much, and to the $30 fee, we said we still preferred to anchor.

At 1257 we came to 32 metres on the Rocna in 8 metres of water just beyond the marina floats.

490

It had begun to rain lightly, and the wind began to gust in cycles, from calm to over 25 knots for a few minutes and then back to calm. We delayed our excursion ashore to check-out the marina facilities as we monitored the effects of the light williwaws on Sequitur's anchorage. We were so comfortable and content onboard that it was late afternoon before we thought again of visiting the marina, and we quickly dismissed the idea.

The place had an eerie feel about it, something we both sensed, but couldn't explain. In the late evening I created three pizzas, one and a half for dinner and the remainder for a couple of underway lunches.

We slept soundly until the brightness of a sunny morning came through the hatches and awoke us at 0620. It was glassy calm as I went forward to remove the snubber and prepare to weigh anchor.

The anchor came up clean, with no kelp to cut away for the first time since we left Puerto Montt. We slowly motored past the vacant marina with its clubhouse, restaurant, bar, three six-person guest cabins, separate accommodations and facilities for crew, and wondered if anyone has ever used it. We postulated that it was an upmarket wilderness destination for city folk, and possibly an itinerary stop for high-end motor-yacht package tours from the mainland. Whatever, it held no attraction for us.

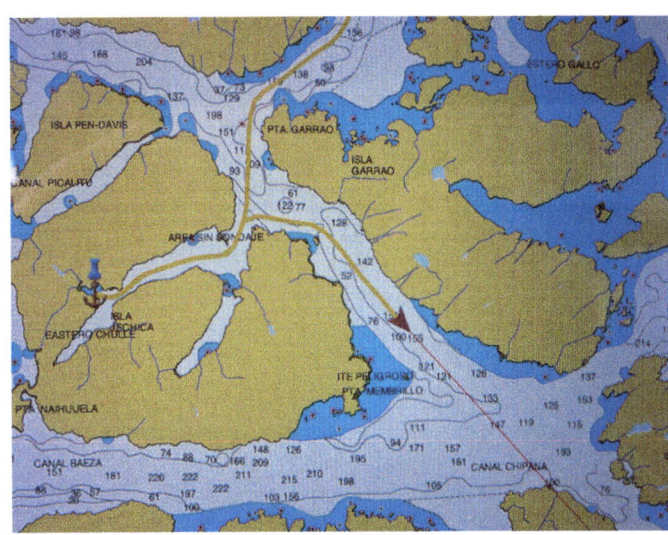

We retraced our inbound route on the chartplotter, knowing that if we hadn't found bottom on the way in, then we were not likely to on the way out. At 0751 we again arrived in soundings and turned to follow Canal Chipana out into Canal Moraleda. By midmorning the sky was completely overcast, and as we turned south in Moraleda, the 10 to 12 knot northerly wind had generated some rather large waves that were being steepened by the opposing tidal current.

I rolled-out the sails and we ran downwind bucking the ebbing current and slopping around in the steepened following waves. There was not enough wind for the intended course, so we used the engine to help us move against the current. We followed the western margin of the navigable channel, which is punctuated by marked and unmarked rocks, reefs and islets. We correctly guessed the name of the white rock islet; there is one such named on every section of every coast we've been on.

Shortly after 1600 we began slowly nudging our way into Puerto Americano. *Patagonia & Tierra del Fuego Nautical Guide* by Mariolina Rolfo and Giorgio Ardrizzi (which I call the Italian Guide) cautions: *"shoals outside the entrance... Depth in the channel is 3 to 4 metres; approach with care favouring the W side"*. Alberto Mantellero's *The First Yachtsman's Navigator Guide to the Chilean Patagonia*, (the Chilean Guide) says: *"Lots of shallow spots, follow recommended route in the sketch with someone on bow to spot rocks"*.

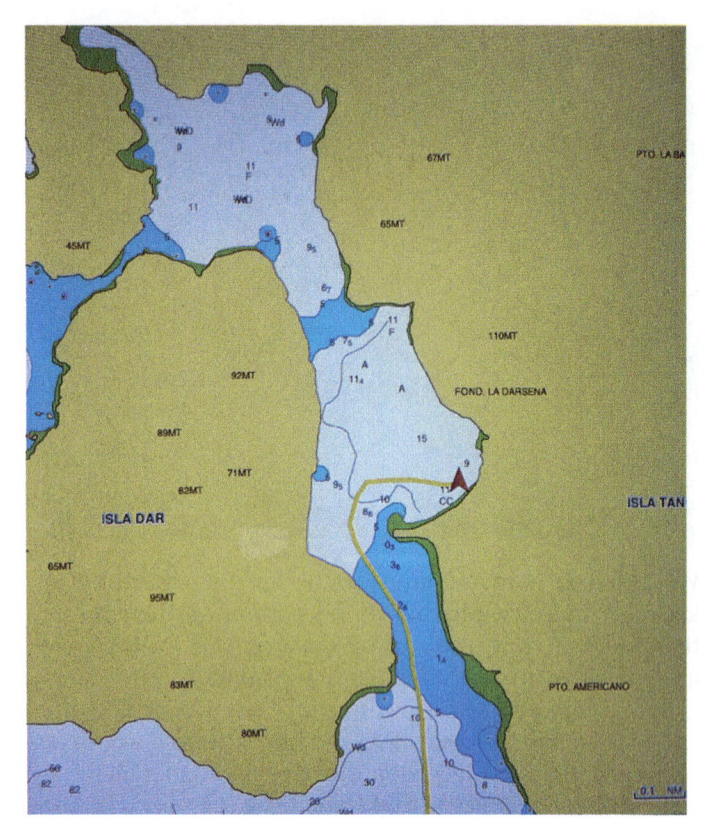

As is my preference, we were entering on a rising tide, which is convenient should we unexpectedly find bottom. We must have properly followed the directions, because our anchor was the first part of the boat to find bottom as we came to 33 metres in 9.9 metres of water in behind a grassy point in an anchorage basin aptly named Fondadero la Darsena, which translates as Anchorage Basin. It was 1625, and we had made 50.3 miles in about 9.5 hours.

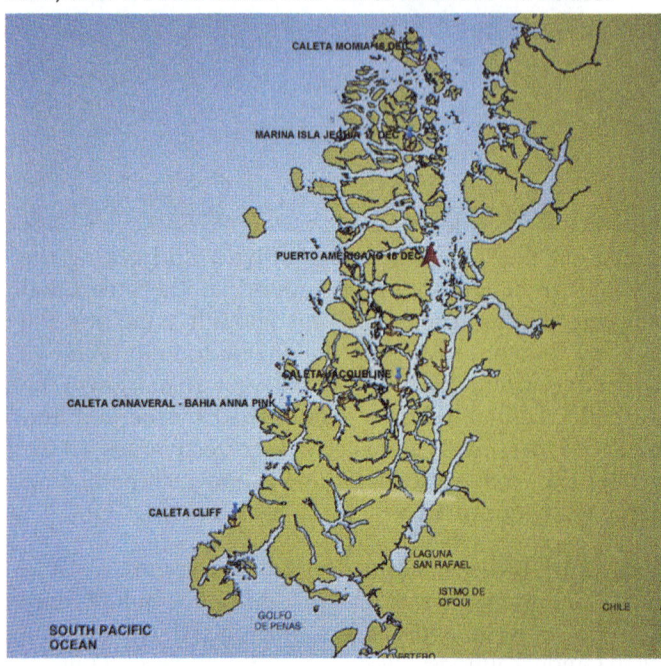

We had logged half a mile shy of 300 miles since leaving Puerto Montt; six days of traveling and three of replenishing and relaxing. We looked at the route ahead. The system of channels we were following southward ended in a cul de sac at Laguna San Rafael. To continue south, we needed to head westward to the open Pacific and make our way around the headlands there.

Theoretically, the next three legs of our voyage would be about 45 to 50 miles each, taking us to Bahía Anna Pink and along the lee shore to Caleta Cliff. Our intention was to then wait there for suitable weather to make the overnight crossing of Golfo de Penas, a leg of a little over 100 miles.

The barometer had been falling from 1020 at Sunday noon to 1017.2 when we anchored to 1014.5 when we went to bed. Monday morning was so glum that dawn's light didn't awaken us, and it was 0740 before I woke-up. The barometer was down to 1010.1 and the sky was an unpleasant mix of nimbostratus and stratus fractus. It was rather calm in the anchorage, and the scud was hanging on the ridge-tops, indicating little if any wind aloft and outside. Our route for the day was mostly through narrow channels, so having no wind was not a problem.

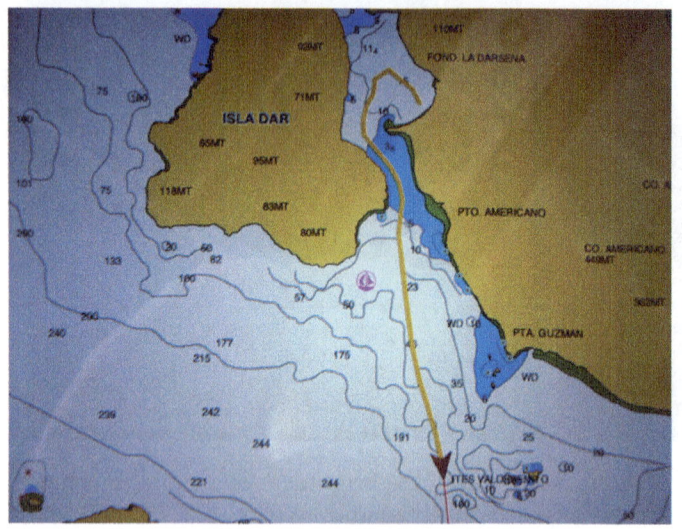

At 0832 we weighed and slowly picked our way out through the shallow narrows, successfully clearing them at 0850 and setting a southerly course as the rain began. Once we were clear of the lee of Isla Tangbac, we were again in sloppy following seas. The northerly wind was just 2 or 3 knots faster than our motoring progress, so sails would have done little but chafe.

However; the following wind did blow the increasingly persistent rain into the after end of the cockpit, so I inserted the quarter panels and rolled down the three rear panels and zipped-up the entire cockpit. We are delighted with the superbly crafted canvas work we had done in Vancouver by La Fabrica. It makes Sequitur comfortable in even the bleakest weather.

While I was buttoning-up the enclosure, Edi had gone below to the galley, and not long after I had finished, she brought breakfast up into the cockpit. While the toaster worked on split baguettes, we started into the fried sausage rounds with basted eggs and Béchamel sauce, sliced tomatoes with chopped basil and steaming cups of fresh-ground Starbucks coffee.

It continued to rain, and as the wind dropped, the clouds settled toward the water's surface and visibility lowered to about two miles. We remained snug and warm in the cockpit.

In the early afternoon, Edi reheated some of the extra pizza from Saturday night. We have found that though leftover pizza is delicious, the crust tends to soften while stored in the fridge. Reheating it in the microwave does nothing to address this, but a frying pan works wonderfully by crisping the crust bottom for a while, then putting the lid on to warm the top and retain the moisture. Wonderful!

At 1645 we came to 30 metres on the Rocna in 8.3 metres of water in Caleta Jacqueline, a beautiful little cove about a cable by a cable and a half in size. Our radar overlay confirmed the accuracy of the chart as we slowly motored into the area without soundings. The sketch in the Italian Guide has a line of soundings through the entrance, and we proved them accurate. The barometer had continued slowly falling, it was sitting at 1006.8 and the rain came more heavily.

A couple of hours later, the sun broke through and I watched as the cloud formation moved away to the east. The sunny patch proved to be quite small; over the ridge to the west came another band of glum, and it was soon raining more heavily than before. We were thankful that the sun's appearance hadn't seduced us ashore to explore the little cove.

Tuesday was another glum morning, with no appreciable light through the hatches to awaken us. We got up to a heavy rain at 0740, and began looking at options for the day. The barometer was at 1006.5, very slightly down. The clouds were scurrying past the tree tops around the anchorage, indicating high winds outside. Our intention had been to head to Caleta Canaveral in Bahía Anna Pink, about 46 miles away on the open Pacific coast. We decided to have breakfast.

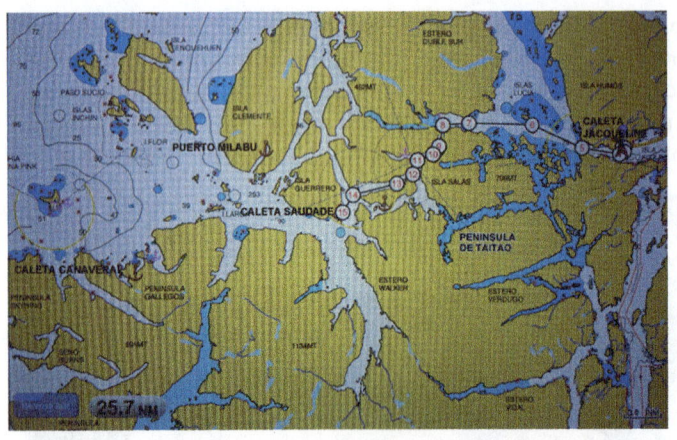

The rain was coming through in regular bands, with heavy downpour and high winds, then a lull, followed by more heavy rain and a lull. We could sit and wait-out the storm, or move closer to the coast. Caleta Saudade sounded like an ideal destination: *"a really tiny cove that affords hurricane-proof protection"*, according to the Italian Guide. It is about 20 miles short of Caleta Canaveral. If conditions improved along the way, we could carry on; if they deteriorated, there were alternates, or we could tuck our tails between our legs and cower back to Jacqueline.

We took advantage of the first lull after breakfast to weigh and head out of Jacqueline. The weather was benign as I removed the snubber, shortened-in and then weighed. But as we left the anchorage, the blue patch was quickly receding to the east, and being replaced by a nimbostratus.

Not long after we had motored out into Canal Chacabuco and turned west, the next band of rain hit. The winds blew down the inlet from the west-northwest at 20 to 25 knots, but we remained snug and dry.

During one of the lulls, we were overtaken by a robust-looking workboat, the type that services the salmon farms that fill the area. On its port bow was painted PTO RED II, and we wondered whether the other bow was named STBD GREEN I. This was to be the last boat we would see for more than a week.

As we were passing north of Islas Canquennes, we watched the approach of an ominously dark mass of cloud filling the entire western horizon and extending from sea level on up. Soon we were hit by a violent squall with sustained winds over 40 knots and gusts to 50. The radar image showed it to be less than a mile through, so we knew it would soon be over. We remained dry and comfortable.

The winds continued extremely variable, cycling regularly from a few minutes at 5 knots to a few at 35 knots and then back down. We entered Canal Pulluche shortly after the turn to ebb, and were nicely assisted along, making at best 8.4 knots with turns for 6. We had earlier been slowed by headwinds and the tail end of the flood to 3.2 knots with the same engine speed.

As we emerged from Pulluche there was more blue than cloud for the first time in a couple of days, but the wind continued to cycle up to 30 knots or so and back down. The weather looked too unsettled to continue on into Bahía Anna Pink, so we headed for Caleta Saudade.

At 1455 we came to 25 metres on the Rocna in 8.3 metres of water on a sand and shingle bottom. We launched Non Sequitur and I attached the lines from the two stern reels and rowed ashore. The tide was still sufficiently high for me to loop the lines around trees while standing in the dinghy. The branches were covered in mosses and other parasitic growths, and were very slimy. I reeled-off enough spare line to double the distance, and while Edi secured the lines on the reels, I pulled the dinghy back out to Sequitur.

We used the sheet winches to haul taut the lines, then I went forward and set a short snubber. Finally, I cranked-in the winches to nestle Sequitur nicely balanced in the northwest corner of the tiny cove about a boat's length from the trees. The wind whistled through the tree tops, but it was calm on deck.

To satisfy my curiosity, I climbed the mast to see at what level the wind began, and found it starting to blow as I reached the second spreaders. I had an opportunity while I was aloft to examine the anchorage. It appears to be about 60 metres wide and 100 metres deep, with a fringe of kelp extending some 20 metres or so out from the eastern side and one of about 10 metres on the west. The trees grow right to the steep rock shore, and in most places overhang and obscure the rocks. There is no beach, nor could I see any practicable place to land.

The barometer remained rather stable in a shallow low, and it rained in waves throughout the remainder of the day. While we enjoyed the very calm and comfortable anchorage, the wind howled and built whitecaps in the sound less than half a cable ahead of Sequitur's bow.

We looked at the various options for our onward route. Around the point from Caleta Saudade is the spout of a funnel, which directs the winds, swell and tides in from the open Pacific. Heading out through this leads into Bahía Anna Pink, which has the open ocean on its north and west sides. Caleta Canaveral is a well-protected inlet about halfway along the south side of the bay. Around Peninsula Skyring is Seno Pico-Paico, which is reputed to offer protection from all winds. Southwestward, on Peninsula de Taitap, Caleta Cliff and Caleta Suarez also are reported to offer all-round protection. Tucked around on the Golfo de Penas side of Peninsula de Taitap is Puerto Barroso, a good haven. In stable weather, none of this presents any problem.

Wednesday the 21st of December, the first day of summer didn't awaken us until nearly an hour and a half after sunrise. The barometer had remained nearly steady overnight; it was up 0.3 to 1007.8. When I poked my head out into the cockpit at 0730, there was a small sunny patch overhead, so while Edi put on the coffee, I drained the dinghy from the rains, hoisted it and secured it in its davits. By the time I had completed this, it was raining again. We quickly scrubbed plans for a post-departure breakfast in the cockpit, and we enjoyed a more leisurely one below to the sounds of the downpour on the decks.

Finally, at 0930 the weather cleared and we quickly hauled-in the starboard stern line and heaped it in the cockpit wing. It slid very easily off the tree. I started the port line, then left its retrieval with Edi and went forward to remove the snubber and shortened-in. When Sequitur was properly aligned, we weighed and Edi drove us out of the tiny hole. The mountains had fresh snow on them down to below the 400 metre line. Welcome to summer.

Our intention was to poke our nose out into Bahía Anna Pink and see what conditions were like. I figured that with the rather steady barometer, there shouldn't be any serious winds. As we motored directly into the 12 to 15 knot winds, we were in and out of rain showers as clumps of nimbostratus passed over.

By 1130 we had passed the last of the islands protecting us from the Pacific swell, and we took the occasional spray over the foredecks, but our full enclosure kept us dry.

Shortly before noon we were hit by a squall with winds of 45 knots and gusts well into the 50s. With it came torrential downpour. Within fifteen minutes it had passed and the sun broke through the tatters behind it.

Half an hour later we were engulfed in a severe hail storm that had hailstones bouncing into the cockpit through the line leads and other gaps that falling rain can't find. There was a quick chilling of the air in the minutes leading to the storm. Edi continued knitting, comfortable in her layers of fleece.

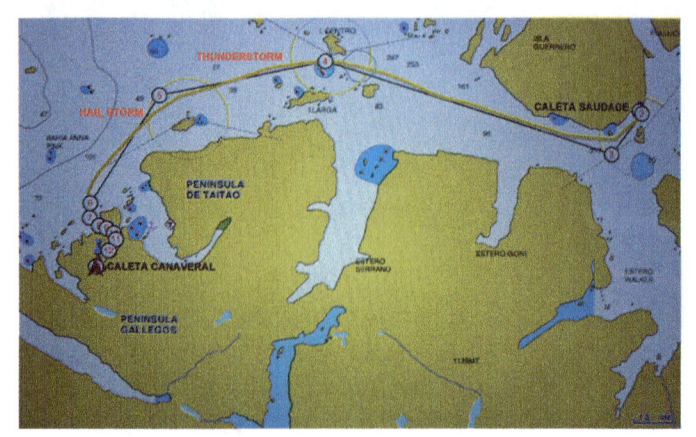

We decided to head into Caleta Canaveral and call it a day. We were less than 5 miles from its entrance. With the WNW wind, it was on a lee shore with the 2 to 3 metre swell being compounded and confused by wind and storm cell waves. Approaching it was easy; the low rock in the centre of the entrance was well-marked by breakers and easy to spot.

Immediately we had passed through the narrows, the water calmed. It was difficult to believe the placidity of our surroundings compared to those through which we had just travelled. We motored the mile to the head of the inlet and at 1402 we came to 32 metres on the Rocna in 10.2 metres of water at near high tide. We had made about 150 litres of water en route, and the tanks were nearly full, the batteries were at 100% and the barometer was slowly rising at 1010.1.

As we relaxed, we continued to be hit by a succession of severe stormlets of five to ten minutes duration with high winds and heavy rain. Within minutes of their passing it was clear and calm, with only the wetness of the decks and the canvas as evidence. The barometer continued to slowly climb; it was 1012.0 at midnight when we went to bed, and it was up to 1013.1 when I got up to a steady light rain at 0715.

It continued to rain after breakfast, so I sat and played some Daily Sudoku games on my iPad as a diversion from decision-making. As I worked through to the Diabolical level the barometer rose. At 1050 it was at 1016 and the rain had stopped. At 1100 we weighed and headed back up the inlet to the narrows.

It was nearly completely overcast, with some flashes of blue to the north and to the west and there was very little wind. As we motored through the gap and out into Bahía Anna Pink, the sea surface was barely rippled and there was a gentle, two-metre swell.

The hills along the coast appeared to be covered with smoldering fires; the evaporation from the previous days' rains was filling the sky with rapidly rising clouds. The few remaining patches of blue were soon obscured.

As we watched a large raft-up of gaviotas pass close down our starboard side, the rains began from an intense cell. We were soon hit with 45-knot winds, a torrential downpour and then hail. It looks like the birds had taken to the surface to sit-out the short storm. Sequitur carried-on through it with the staysail and a third of the main and some hand steering to keep her close-hauled. Again, hailstones found a way to bounce into the cockpit

After the cell's passage, the sky cleared overhead and we enjoyed the warmth of the summer sun. I started the watermaker and Edi put a load in the washer-dryer and we bounced around in the confusion of the post-squall seas meeting the swell, which was meeting the continental shelf. Edi carried-on with her knitting, while I played Captain.

We were hit by a second squall as we rounded Peninsula Skyring, this one equally intense, but without the hail. After it had passed on to the north, and we were again under blue skies, we watched a huge and growing cumulonimbus upwind. It was tracking north; we were heading south. If the pattern held, there were more building behind it.

We were fascinated with the patterns of foliage on the trees clinging to the windswept south-facing slopes of the sound. There is a wonderful interplay of greens that in some ways looks like an organized botanical display.

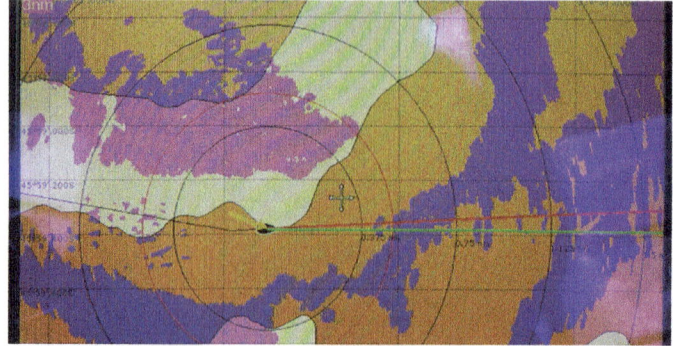

We decided to call it a day and divert into Seno Pico-Paico, an uncharted sound that corkscrews into the peninsula. I sheeted close-hauled on a port tack and with the swell on the starboard bow and our course slightly diverging from the coast to allow the storm to track up to the east of us. When the cell was passing our line, we tacked and surfed toward the mouth of the sound.

We reached the protection of the south arm of the sound before the next of the series of storm cells arrived. The next squall appeared to be half an hour away, so I figured we should be anchored before its arrival.

The approximate shape of the sound is on the chart, but there are no depth soundings, nor any other details. Its charted position is about 6 cables west-northwest of reality. Both the Italian and the Chilean Guides say it is deep, with no hazards. We used our eyeballs and radar to steer a mid-channel course.

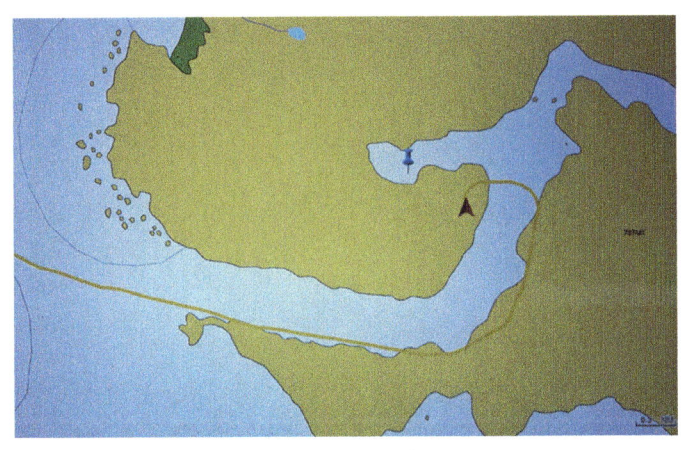

At 1659 we came to 45 metres on the Rocna in 14.5 metres of water in a beautifully calm cove. The chart-plotter and iPad had taken an overland route, offering a great example of why these marvellous devices are to be used as guidance and sources of information, but not necessarily accurate information.

The eye is the most important navigational device. Trust it, and use information from the compass, depth-sounder and radar to add to what you see. Filter this information through the pilots, sailing directions and guides and then interpret the charts with the resulting amalgam. After all of this, trust the eye, remembering that it is on the actual rocks and shoals that boats that run aground, not on the paper or electronic representations of them.

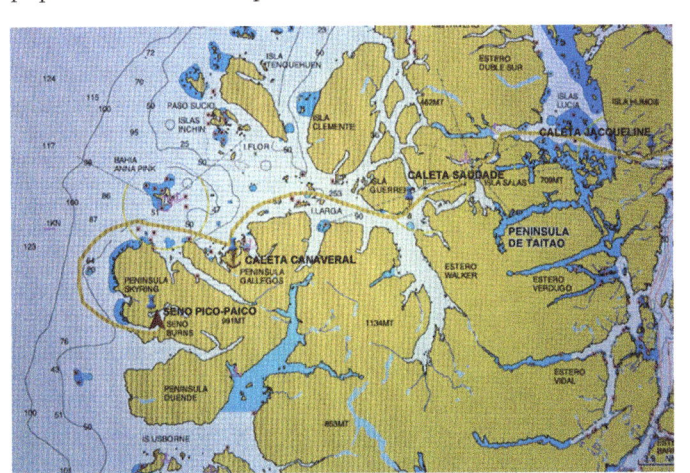

The barometer had continued to rise: 1017.5 at noon, 1020.5 when we anchored and 1025.2 when we went to bed at midnight. It was 1028.3 at 0750 when I got up to send our 0800 position report to the Armada.

Edi got up and put on the coffee while I shortened-in, and we weighed at 0832. I used Sequitur as a 15-metre-long cursor to retrace the track on the chart-plotter as Edi plied me with hot Starbucks and toasted baguettes slathered with cream cheese and black currant jam.

We were just finishing breakfast as we had our first look outside the inlet and began to feel the effects of the Pacific swell. Overhead a slow parade of low cumulus puffs was being pushed along by the southwest 10 to 12 knot surface winds and the water was beginning to chop. We cleared the sound at 0935, and set a course to pass between Punta James and Rocas Hellyer, and make Punta Pringle. We had decided to head for Caleta Suarez, with Caleta Cliff as a shorter alternate if conditions deteriorated.

As has been our experience thus far, the wind, swell and tide were on our nose. I hauled-out the staysail and half the main and we motor-sailed at 1750 rpm about 20 degrees off the wind, parallelling the coast. Tide, seas and current conspired to keep our speed in the 4 knot range until early afternoon, when the tide turned to ebb and we moved above 6 knots. The cumulus had moved off or dissipated, and we relaxed in the sunny cockpit. Edi continued her knitting.

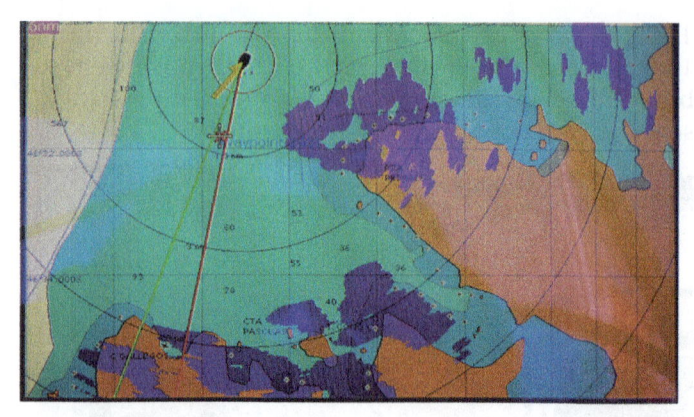

We had been heading for a waypoint from the Italian Guide that I had placed on the chart-plotter indicating a safe approach to Estero Cono. As we approached, I switched the radar to transmit and saw the chart was skewed about 1.2 miles to the southeast. A chart-plotter course to clear Punta Pringle to the west by a mile would have made for a very hard landing.

The Italian waypoint proved very accurate, and we continued on in with cautious confidence. The inlet we were looking for, Estero Cono is immediately to the south of an imposing conical peak. As we came around Punta Pringle, Monte Cono quickly identified itself.

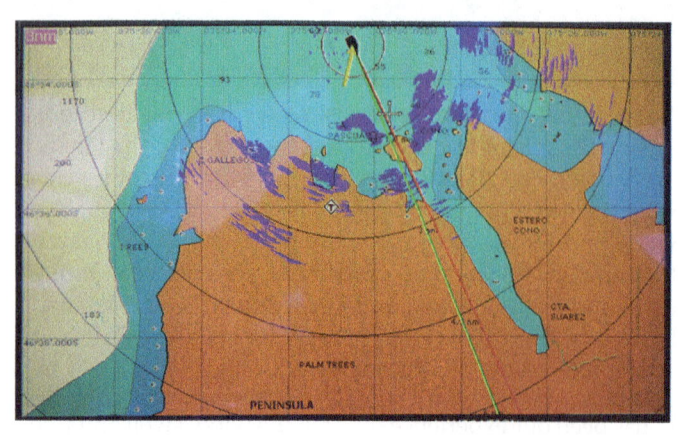

I pointed Sequitur toward the gap and watched as the ship's head cursor settled on the radar image of the passage between Isla Cono and Monte Cono, while the chart showed the overland route. We decided to ignore the chart image and followed our eyes. Once we had lost the wind in the lee of the island, I rolled in the sails and we motored into the calm of the inlet.

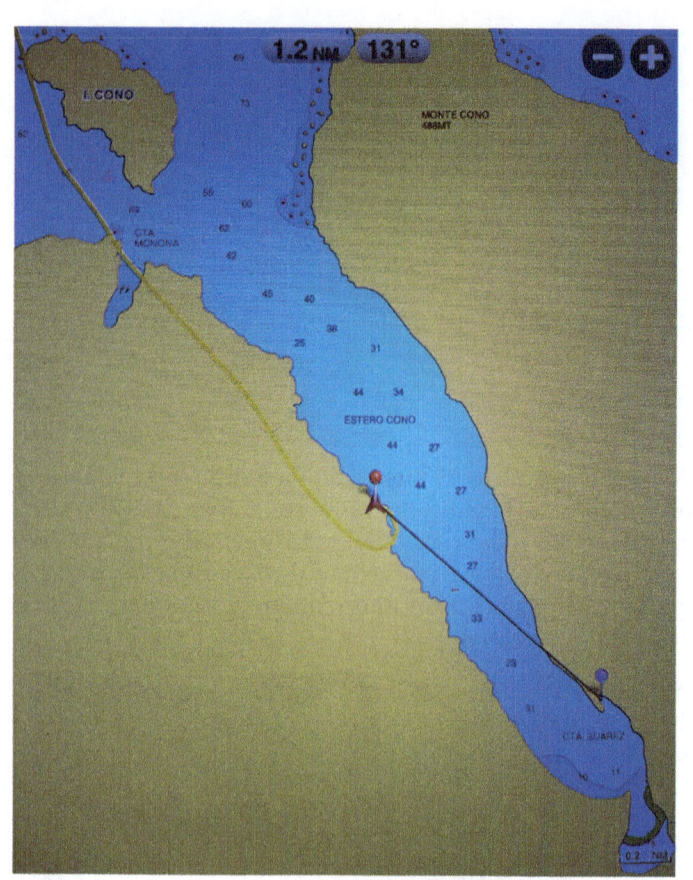

We confidently headed up Estero Cono with the radar showing us centred between the steep walls about two cables on either side, and the sounder confirming the chart soundings. We were reminded again to take care by a sunken wreck symbol off a small point about two miles in, as the inlet narrows. Half a mile further along we passed a narrow gravel peninsula and swung around its end and headed in through a gap less than a cable wide to Caleta Suarez.

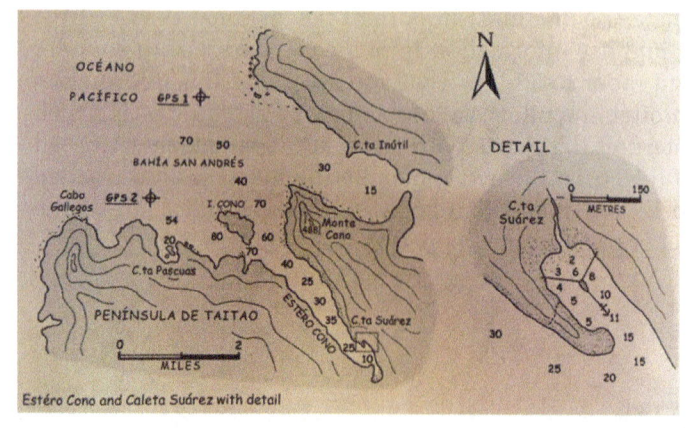

Estero Cono and Caleta Suárez with detail

In the Rolfo-Ardrizzi *Patagonia & Tierra del Fuego Nautical Guide* (the Italian Guide), there is a clear chartlet and a detailed sketch of Estero Cono and the tiny Caleta Suarez near its head. These and the written descriptions allowed us to confidently enter the rather tight slot with sloping gravel shores. At 1920 we came to 20 metres on the Rocna in 8.8 metres of water.

The anchorage is described in the Italian Guide as: "...*one of the safest and most beautiful coves in Patagonia. ...strategically*

500

located to ease the long bluewater passage between Bahía Anna Pink and the channels S of Golfo de Penas". The Guide goes on to say: *"Estero Cono is bordered by wide beaches, which makes it one of the few places in the Chilean channels where it is possible to enjoy a nice stroll on the sand".*

We celebrated the new moon with blanquillo sautéed with oyster mushrooms, shallots and garlic slivers, accompanied by basmati rice and Peruvian asparagus spears with mayonnaise. The 2011 Carmen Chardonnay complemented wonderfully.

We launched the dinghy and I rowed ashore trailing the line from the port stern reel. I looped it around a steel pin, which had been hammered into the top of an inverted tree trunk, which was deeply implanted into the gravel beach and strategically located in the centre of the head of the cove. Fishermen routinely use this anchorage as a refuge from storms, and their lines and moorage arrangements line the shore. I hauled through a doubling of line, and after Edi had secured the one end on a cleat, I pulled the dinghy and the other end of the line back out to Sequitur.

Saturday the 24th of December dawned bright and calm, the barometer had remained stable overnight, slightly above 1029.5 and there were wisps of cirrus overhead. It was so calm in the anchorage that, were it not for the gaviota flying upside-down in the lower left corner of the inverted photo, it would be difficult to tell reflection from reality. After I had sent our 0800 position report to the Armada, I rejoined Edi in bed for our first sleep-in in nearly two weeks.

We warped our stern line tight with a sheet winch as I veered another 10 metres of anchor cable. By 1935 we were secured. The sun and moon set within three minutes of each other, according to our data, very close to eclipse, but they were out of sight blocked by Monte Cono.

We finally arose midmorning to find our world right-side-up again. It continued glassy-calm as we enjoyed a leisurely breakfast in the cockpit.

After breakfast we dug the baskets out of the port bilge compartment in the forward cabin. In the baskets were our bulk stores of such things as salamis, cheeses, yogurt, olives, carrots, potatoes, onions, shallots, ginger and garlic. Edi washed the cheeses and I sorted the vegetables looking for bad ones. There was a bad carrot that had affected a few others, but otherwise, things were keeping well.

The previous evening Edi had started some loaves of Sequitur bread, and she bashed them down, gave them a quick knead and set them to rise again, before starting some baguettes. We decided to head ashore for a walk, so we left the vegetables airing, the cheese drying and the bread rising in the heat of the cockpit enclosure.

We rowed over to the eastern shore, beached the dinghy and began exploring. We walked out to the point and around it to head back out toward the ocean, looking for the sandy beaches described in the Italian Guide. While there are beaches, which are rare in this region, we think the translator got a bit fine with his word for gravel. On our way back we came upon a fire pit, which the fishermen had built with what looks like a piece from an old boiler as its central theme. Around it they had erected a crude shelter of plastic sheeting strung-up in the trees.

In front of the fire shelter are lines suspended from the overhanging tree limbs. Though they look like swings, these are used by the fishermen to attach their mooring lines. I couldn't resist taking a ride.

We found many plants in bloom, reminding us that although it is Christmas Eve, it is summer here. Not having a field guide to the flora, we had to content ourselves by calling them pretty little white flowers with pointed petals, and other such names.

There was one with oval white petals in sets of three, which looked to me a little like an apple blossom with some of its petals removed.

Then in the middle of a small daisy patch, I spotted some Dutch tulips, but when they started walking, I realized they were only Edi's sea boots. She had painted them with tulip designs to make them easier to find, and less likely someone would take them in error.

We did see a delicate pink flower like a downward pointing trumpet, which Edi later identified as the Lapageria rosea or Chilean Bellflower, locally called Copihue. It is the national flower of Chile.

Suddenly beside us was a splashing. In the shallow tidal pool a large salmon had apparently been waiting for the tide to rise when we disturbed it. It was well over half a metre long, As I was thinking of wading in to pickup some fish for dinner, it thrashed itself out of the shallows and swam away.

Edi recognized another as possibly a wild fuchsia.

We walked around the head of the caleta to a fresh water stream with a substantial flow coming down off Monte Cono. This is mentioned as a good source of drinking water in Mantellero's *Navigator Guide to the Chilean Patagonia*.

Back onboard from our jaunt ashore, we baked the two loaves of raisin bread, the officer bread of my years in the Navy. We then did the two fat baguettes, which during my canal boating years in France, were referred to as batards.

Our water tanks were down to below a quarter, and the house bank was at 67%. The water in the caleta was clean, and the weather was so calm that there was no sediment, so I started the watermaker and flashed-up the generator. This is only the second time we had run the Fischer-Panda since leaving Puerto Montt, and it started immediately and ran flawlessly. We ran the watermaker for five hours, then set it to auto-flush, netting about 320 litres of fresh water. During this time, the generator brought the bank up to 95%.

The barometer began a slow decline, settling to 1026 when we went to bed at 2300. On Christmas morning, when I arose to send the Armada our 0800 position report, the barometer was at 1025. There was an SMS on the sat phone from Amy, Bram and Annelies, exchanging Christmas greetings in reply to those we had sent before going to bed. I crawled back into bed to give Edi some assistance in sleeping-in.

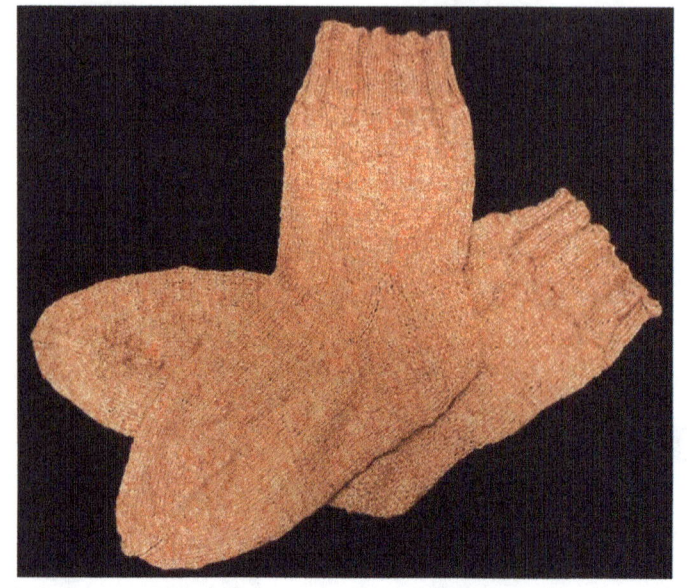

We eventually did get up. Long gone are the days of excitedly rising at the crack of dawn to see what Santa had put in the stockings. My stockings were empty, but they were there, a wonderful pair that Edi had just finished knitting from some fine linen yarn she had bought in Vancouver's China Town. My gift to Edi was my ongoing fulfillment of a promise to take her sailing in comfort and style to the remote corners of the world.

For breakfast we enjoyed toasted fresh officer bread and split batard with cream cheese and black currant jam. This was our third Christmas of the voyage. The first was in the idyllic setting of Isla Espiritu Santo in the Mexican Sea of Cortez and the second was arriving in Iquique, Chile after our passage from Peru.

We still had seven avocados remaining, and they were in remarkably fine condition. Our on-the-vine tomatoes had also held well, so Edi prepared a guacamole for lunch, which we enjoyed it with nacho chips and rooibos tea. It was not a traditional Christmas lunch, but by now we have learned that we are in many ways far from traditional.

However, from time to time we do follow tradition. For dinner I prepared turkey with a pecan and mushroom dressing and steamed potatoes all lapped with a thick pan gravy and accented with boat-made Chilean cranberry sauce and accompanied by a side of Peruvian asparagus with mayonnaise.

With it we enjoyed a bottle of Picasso Tempranillo from Sequitur's cellar. We fondly remembered buying the wine on our visit with Rafael in Ica, Peru and we thought of our friend Gonzalo who made that magical visit possible. With our after-dinner chocolate we opened our last bottle of Rafael's Vista Alegre Señorial, and toasted our Peruvian friends. It was a splendid Christmas.

26. Across the Dreaded Golfo de Penas

I again reviewed the information in our copy of *Patagonia & Tierra del Fuego Nautical Guide*. Among its stern warnings on Golfo de Penas, it has the following to say: *"This expanse of water, wisely respected by sailors of all times, must not be underestimated, but faced with the utmost care."* The Guide goes on to say: *"One of the characteristics of the gulf is the big SW swell raised by the polar and southern ocean storms. On meeting the shallower waters of the area, the waves tend to raise and lose their regularity. A light NW wind can create seas confused enough to pester the crew of a small yacht."* The Guide continues with a reminder to all sailors that: *"even large ships do not cross the gulf in bad weather."*

There is a further warning that states: *"The main requirement in the event of any problem is to be able to claw off this lee shore against its insidious current."* The Italian Guide later says: *"As a conclusion, keep in mind this first rule: bad weather in Golfo de Penas takes you onto shore."*

I had read accounts of sailors heading southward to the Patagonian Channels describing long waits for conditions suitable for a crossing of Boca del Guafo. There are blogs of boats waiting many days, some over a week for the conditions or the courage to head out through Bahía Anna Pink. There are many stories of sailors waiting for weeks for their proper conditions to attempt the crossing of Golfo de Penas.

We had found benign weather in our crossing of the Boca. Our multi-small-step approach had not too uncomfortably brought us out of Anna Pink to the edge of Golfo de Penas. Armed then with the wisdom of those who had gone before, we were poised after our Christmas break to head out.

I awoke at 0630 on Monday, and seeing the barometer had risen slightly overnight to 1024, we decided to head out early to attempt a daylight crossing of the Golfo de Penas. I raised and secured the dinghy while Edi secured for sea below. Then as I removed the snubber and shortened-in, Edi hauled in the stern line. The anchor came up foul with a piece of 3cm hawser that seemed attached to the bottom. With a boathook it was soon cleared, and the anchor was home and lashed by 0650.

It was glassy calm as we motored out into Estero Cono and headed back to the open Pacific. Edi went below and in a few minutes appeared with a thermos of fresh-ground Starbucks, the toaster and slices of Sequitur bread.

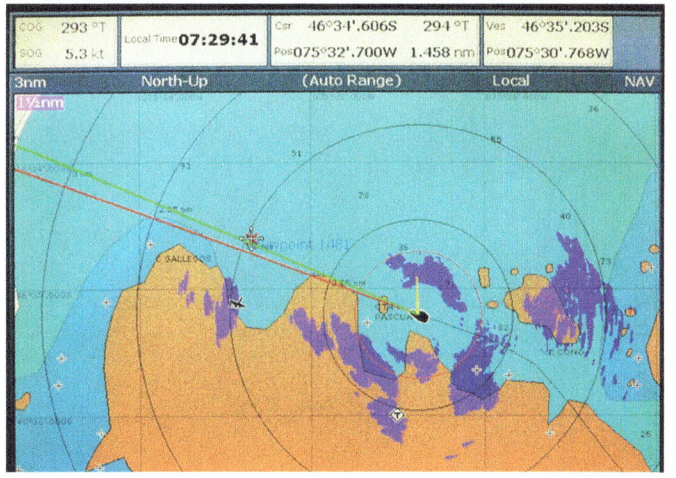

As I navigated and piloted, Edi toasted and spread, and we enjoyed breakfast on the run. I used a waypoint from the Italian guide to confirm my visual observations and the radar image, and we easily and confidently motored out among the islands in the mouth of the inlet.

It was completely overcast with low stratus, which sank as we went, and soon became fog. Visibility was generally 2 to 3 miles, and since our radar and AIS showed no contacts, I decided there was no need for the foghorn.

There was a light southwest breeze of about 6 knots, so I hauled-out the staysail and half the main and we motor-sailed close-hauled on the starboard tack in the gentle 2 metre ocean swell. As we went, we watched the gaviotas and albatross and saw a few whale spouts, but none close-by.

At 0800 we were still out of radio range with the closest manned lighthouse, so I sent our position report to Directemar by SMS on the sat phone. At 1045 as we approached Cabo Raper, I raised the lighthouse on VHF and gave a position and movements report. By this time, the tide had turned, and we were making 6.5 to 7 knots, the engine still being assisted by a light southeast breeze, which was now broader on the bow as we bent our course around the headland.

Shortly after noon Edi brought a basket of lunch up into the cockpit. I bit into a spring-roll, and was surprised and delighted to find it stuffed with turkey, dressing, gravy and cranberry sauce. It was a bit of a twist on my family's traditional Boxing Day lunch of Christmas turkey-dinner-leftover sandwiches. I commented that we were missing the traditional Boxing Day sales, but Edi reminded me we were on a Boxing Day sail, and that ours was much less crowded.

We saw no ships; we hadn't seen any in many days. As we crossed the near-glassy-calm Golfo de Penas, I ran the watermaker for four hours and brought the tanks back up to full.

Several times on the crossing we spotted the spouting of passing whales, but always they were too far away for us to catch a decent photo. As we approached Isla San Pedro a pod swam across our bows, and from the prominent shark-like fin and the breathing pattern, we easily identified them as fin whales, or common rorquals.

At 2000 I raised Faro San Pedro on the VHF and gave the Armada watchman our 2000 position report. Forty minutes later we entered Bahia San Pedro and at 2052 we hauled in the sails and motored between the shoals and rocks into our anchorage in Puerto Escondido. At 2125 we came to 32 metres on the Rocna in 11 metres of water in a tight, calm cranny.

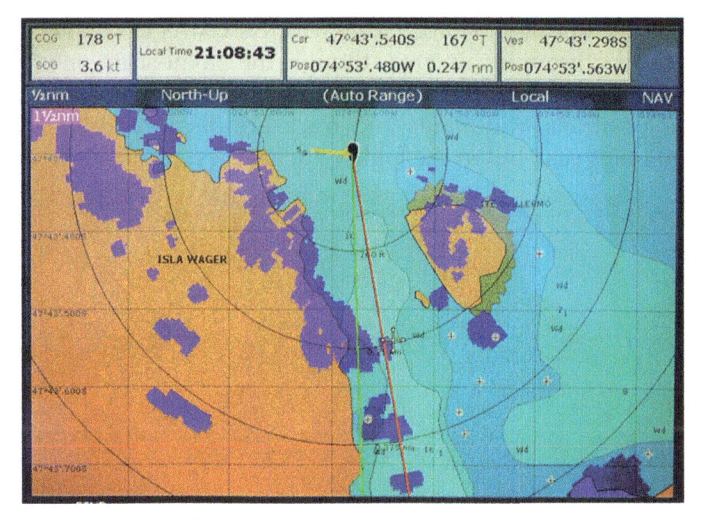

We were delighted with our Golfo de Penas crossing; it had been a very comfortable 90.6-mile daylight passage. Fortunately, all the scary paragraphs in the guides, the pilots, the books and the blogs were for us unfulfilled.

During our approach I had been up and down from cockpit to galley preparing some pizzas for dinner and heating the oven. The oven was hot when we secured the anchor, and the first two pizzas went in shortly thereafter. While extra pizzas for later lunches cooked, we started into a pair of salami, black olive, sun-dried tomato, red and green pepper, oyster mushroom, Spanish onion, slivered garlic, fresh basil, two cheese pizzas with some 2007 Picasso Tempranillo.

Tuesday I was up at 0735 to check the barometer and the sky. The pressure had remained stable overnight at 1024 and the sky was a glum, detail-less grey of low stratus. There was no wind and the sea was calm. I gave our 0800 report by VHF to the duty watch-keeper at Faro San Pedro, and we enjoyed a leisurely breakfast waiting for the tide in Canal Messier. At 0949 we weighed and slowly retraced our entry track back out of the anchorage, and once clear of Roca Plana, shaped a southeast course for the entrance to Messier.

Across the bay, two or three miles away was an ongoing series of whale spouts in groups of six, eight and ten at a time, then randomly across ninety degrees of the horizon. The spouts were like those from a steam calliope churning-out a rousing march. Only missing was the sound. My camera refused to focus on the whales, choosing instead to grab the gaviotas dotting the waters in the foreground.

We motored through a flock a mile or so deep, and watched as the birds struggled to get airborne, running frantically across the water for dozens of metres before finally succeeding.

We entered Canal Messier and motor-sailed southward, directly downwind as the flooding tide began to push us along. This was the first time in many, many months, we were going with the wind and the current. We met one ship, the first vessel we had seen in over a week.

The low overcast persisted until early afternoon, when the stratus began separating and allowing some blue to show.

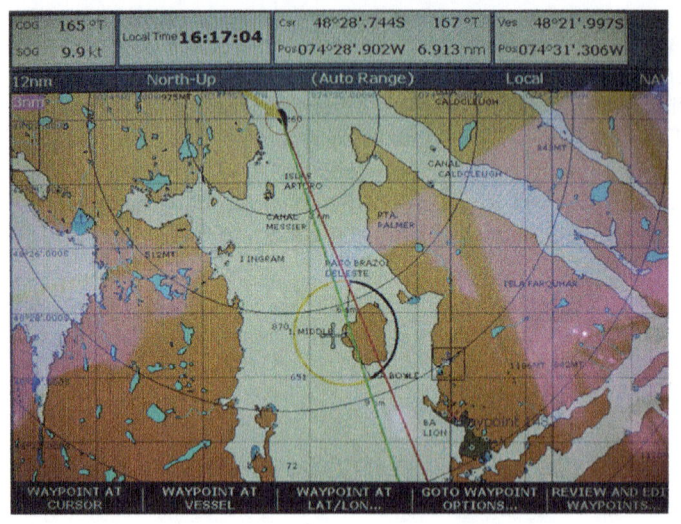

The wind picked-up into the low-to mid 20-knot range and conspired with the flooding tide to move Sequitur along at 8.5 to 9.5 knots, with the occasional surf over 10 knots. We were moving along so nicely that we had decided to continue past our intended anchorage and head to one of our two alternates, 13 and 22 miles further along.

The first of these, Caleta Connor is described in the Italian Guide as: *"...may become uncomfortable with strong winds from the N/NW. ...With winds from this direction, Caleta Morgane is a better choice."* With our winds from the north above 20 and the barometer falling, we opted for Morgane at 22 miles.

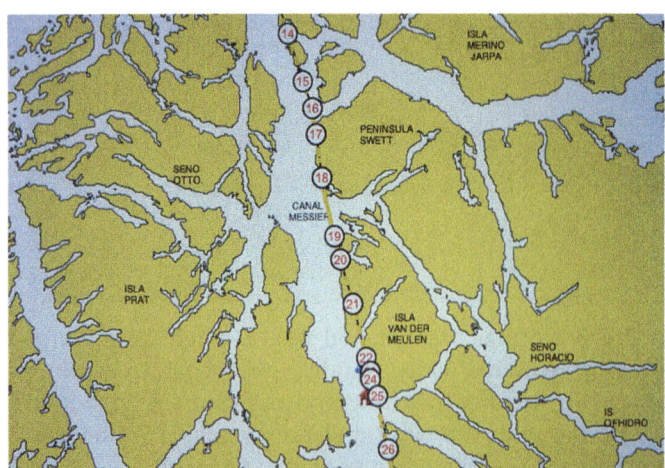

We were finding the large-scale nautical charts to be very accurate through this area, though the small-scale ones appear yet to have been re-jigged to GPS. At low zooms, our positions, waypoints and track are displaced about two miles east, but in the higher zooms they are accurate.

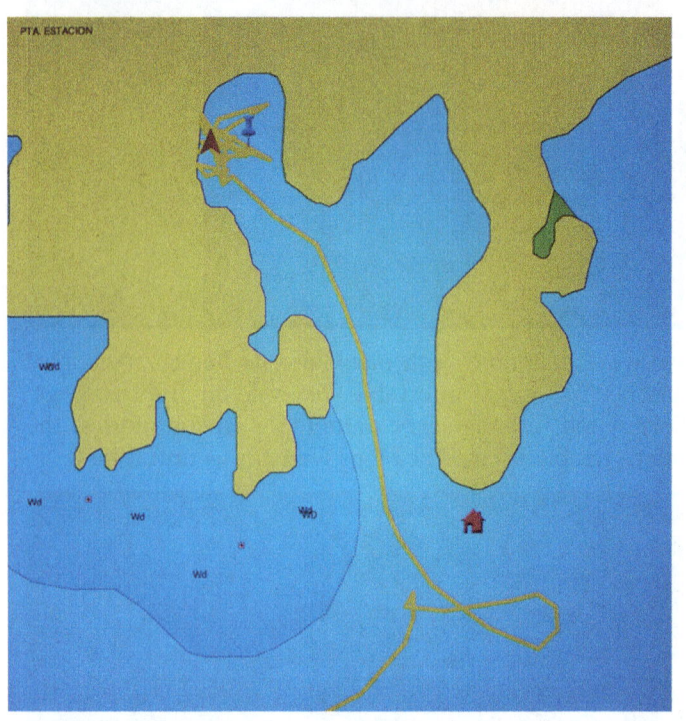

The wind was up into the mid-30s when we rounded the point in search of the entrance to Caleta Morgane. I did a dance at the entrance, remembering the wise advice during my naval officer training: *"When in doubt, stop the ship"*. After a reassessment and confirmation, we continued on into the uncharted cranny barely three times Sequitur's length in size. There were wind eddies from the storm outside as we manoeuvred the bow into an appropriate position to let-go the anchor.

Finally after a few backs and forths, we let go the Rocna and veered 15 metres of chain into 8 metres of water, just enough to hold us off the rocks while we launched the dinghy and got the first stern-line to a tree ashore. After the second stern line was attached, I veered another 5 metres and we settled in about 5 metres off the steep rocks of the shore astern. At 1951 we were well secured, and prepared for a spell of bad weather; the barometer had fallen 5 points since noon, from 1024 to 1019.

510

I donned my chef's toque and prepared tarragon chicken with a sauté of oyster and white mushrooms, shallots and slivered garlic and accompanied it with basmati rice and the last of our asparagus, and garnished by our second last tomato with shredded fresh basil. We enjoyed it with a bottle of 2007 J Lohr Los Osos Merlot from Sequitur's cellar.

I awoke with the first light of the sun coming through the cabin hatches shortly before 0600. The barometer had risen appreciably overnight, and was back up to 1023. Outside was clear and calm, with insufficient clouds to accent a photo. I prepared our SMS to the Armada and went back to bed for a while.

At a much more reasonable hour, we enjoyed breakfast in the cockpit with toasted split baguettes, cream cheese, capers, smoked salmon, fresh basil and cups of fresh-ground Starbucks.

After breakfast we did a few chores, but mostly dawdled and relaxed in the pleasantness of the sun. We were waiting for the proper tide to assist our day's passage. The weather was cooperating superbly, so we had decided to take the 30 mile round-trip detour up Seno Iceberg to the foot of the glacier. The barometer had continued rising; it was 1025.3 at 0800 when I had sent Directemar our morning position report.

I took a slow row around the tiny caleta and then hoisted and secured the dinghy while Edi squared-away below and prepared again for sea.

Some bands of cumulus were moving in from the southwest, along with a light 6 to 7 knot breeze when we weighed at 1000. At 1020 we crossed the line into a flow of pale green glacial till coming from the tidewater glacier at the head of seno.

At 1250 we reached the terminus of both the glacier and the sound.

In front of us was a wall of ice nearly 2 kilometres wide being fed by an ice-field that extends more than 300 kilometres north-south along the spine of South America. The vast Hielo Continental Sur is over 25 kilometres wide here, near its northern end.

I moved Sequitur through ice floes and bergy bits to within a cable or so of the face, which appears to stand close to 100 metres above the water. We heard the frequent grumble and crack of seracs collapsing in the icefall above the terminus, and watched a few new bergy bits being calved.

Accompanying us up the last few miles of the sound were many dozens of playful Blackchin Dolphins, and they continued to play with Sequitur as we dawdled in the ice-filled waters beneath the glacier snout.

Finally after half an hour of basking in the grandeur of the place and watching the dolphins frolic, we put Sequitur's stern toward the glacier and slowly picked our way back out through the scattering of ice. We had been blessed with superb weather for our diversion.

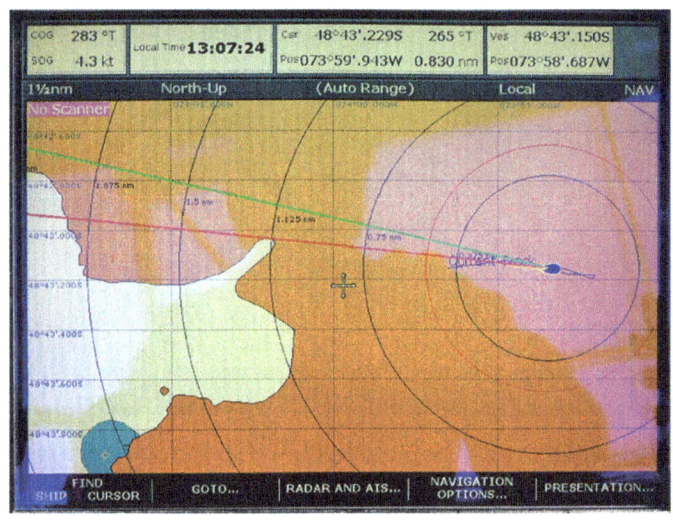

The chart on our Navionics card for the Raymarine chartplotter shows Seno Iceberg only crudely, with approximate landforms and no soundings. According to it, we had run Sequitur well aground at the head of the sound.

The Navionics app for the iPad is one year newer, and includes a new chart of Seno Iceberg, with many soundings, good bottom contour detail and a much more accurate shoreline detail. It is precisely keyed to the GPS. We are seeing much new charting in the Chilean waters, particularly those which are more frequently navigated, and even some, like Seno Iceberg, which have virtually no traffic, but deserve so much more.

As the glacier retreated behind us, Edi reheated some of the leftover pizza and we enjoyed a delicious lunch. Meanwhile, the day's second load of laundry was in the washer-dryer.

We saw no traffic, in fact we had seen only one ship in the previous ten days. Then, as we again entered Canal Messier and turned southward, we spotted a ship across the channel. It was not displaying its AIS, and as we came closer, I realized it was the wreck of the steamship Capitan Leonidas aground on Bajo Cotopaxi, a mid-channel shoal with only 4.9 metres of water over it. The shoal was named after the English steamship, which had awkwardly discovered the shoal in 1889.

513

At 1800 we came to 55 metres on the Rocna in 18 metres of water in the centre of a 150-metre basin in Caleta Sabauda.

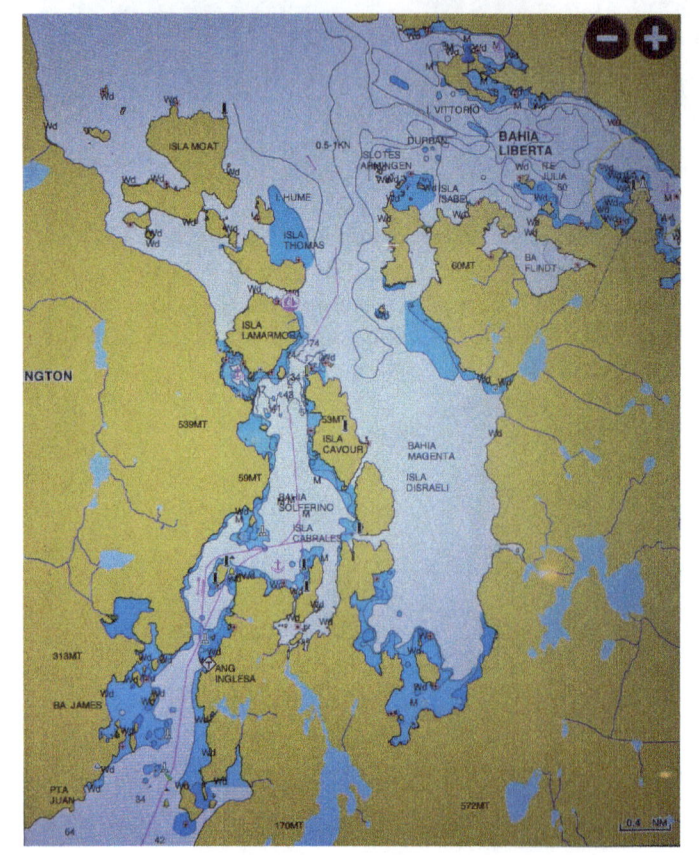

As required, I called Puerto Eden Radio to report our ETA at Isla Medio Canal, and then again as required at 10 minutes before arrival.

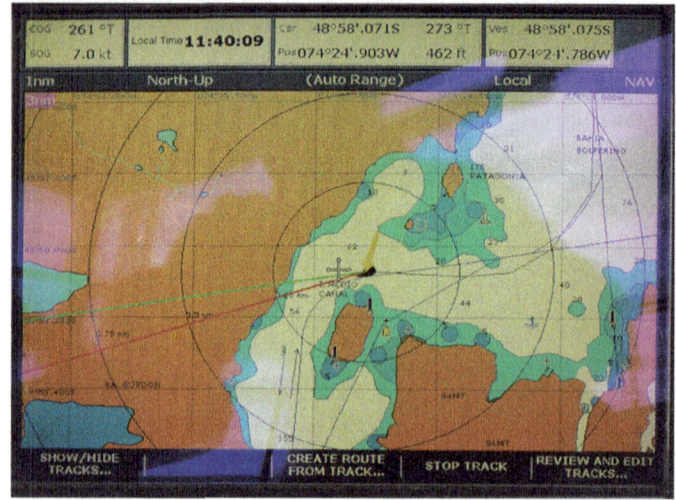

We passed through the most restricted sections of the pass almost exactly at low water, carrying our 7-knot speed, and we continued through the remainder of the narrows with the beginning of the flood.

We were less than 3 miles from the entrance to Angostura Inglesa, the notorious winding rock and shoal-strewn narrows with flood and ebb currents of 6 to 8 knots and short-duration slacks. Sounds very much like the British Columbia waters in which I have boated in since the mid-60s, only more gentle. In some BC narrows, the currents run at more than 16 knots.

On Thursday morning when I got up to send our position report to the Armada, the barometer was down slightly from the previous evening. We dawdled over breakfast and puttered aboard waiting for the tide, then at 1045 we weighed and picked our way through the islets, rocks and shoals and out of Caleta Sabauda and headed toward English Narrows under thickening cloud.

At 1355 on 29 December we came to 35 metres on the Rocna in 11 metres of water in front of downtown Puerto Eden, a village of 176 people. It had taken us 692 miles of winding channels and 16 anchorages to cover the 462 miles from Puerto Montt. We were 487 miles from Cape Horn, and our route there is slightly less sinuous. Our latitude was 49° 07' 39" South, almost the antipodean equal to Vancouver's latitude.

After we had reported our arrival to the Armada, we chatted for a bit with the person on the radio. We asked about a weather report, and he said he could bring us one later in the afternoon, after it had arrived from Punta Arenas. The barometer was continuing to fall, and an official forecast would be good to have.

After a quick snack we launched Non Sequitur and motored the short cable to the pier in front of the office of the Carabineros de Chile. We figured it was a safe place to leave the dinghy. Besides, with a population of only 176, everyone knows everyone else, and there's nowhere to hide.

There is a boardwalk which follows the coastline and connects the houses and workshops lining the waterfront. We decided to follow it first to the right, around the north side of the tiny bay and out to the point. Along the water's edge were many boats dried-out, some possibly for their last time.

A bit further along, However; we came to a major rebuild. Tornado was receiving a new stem, a new keel, and from all the cut pieces lying around, probably some new ribs and a re-planking. We have seen these major projects underway in crude conditions on beaches from Puerto Montt southward.

515

We arrived at the point and examined the new boat terminal, which is used by the weekly Navimag ferry between Puerto Montt and Puerto Natales. On its north side, the sunny and windy one, was an array of masts supporting solar panels and wind generators. The terminal was completed in the autumn of 2010 as an infrastructure enhancement project by the Chilean government.

We continued around the point and out into the suburbs following the winding boardwalk. We were back to our standard routine of heading directly into the wind, which continued to howl from the north.

In many ways the scene was how I remembered Bamfield on the west coast of Vancouver Island, back in the 1960s, before it became touristed. With the remoteness of this area, I think it will be a long time before Puerto Eden spoils itself with a prettying-up for visitors.

All along the shoreline are boats dried-out or hauled-out. Some appear very-well cared-for, while others seem to have long since lost all love. We were intrigued with the vivid colours, which even on the neglected boats was still rather bright, and would offer good visibility at sea.

We passed several piles of crab traps. We had learned that king crab is valued harvest, commonly caught in this area. We were eager to see if we could find some. There were few people about, and we wondered whether this was due to it being Christmas week, or simply because the tiny village has so few people.

Beside the boardwalk across from the church was a manger scene made-up with two-dimensional pasteboard cut-outs propped-up in an A-frame of fern fronds and evergreen boughs with some tinsel and a four-pointed star. The cast of characters was simple: a cow, a shepherd with lamb, a magus, a carpenter, a virgin and a baby; one of each.

I had brought our portable VHF with me, and as we were on our way back from the north end of the strung-out village, I received a call from the Armada. It was the person to whom we had reported on our approach and arrival at anchor. He had come to Sequitur, and seeing our dinghy ashore, called.

We coordinated a rendezvous, and shortly we met the Capitan de Puerto, Victor Flores Saavedra.

next day to use the wifi there. We thanked Victor for his kind assistance, and then we walked along to the left of the pier to Supermercado Eden.

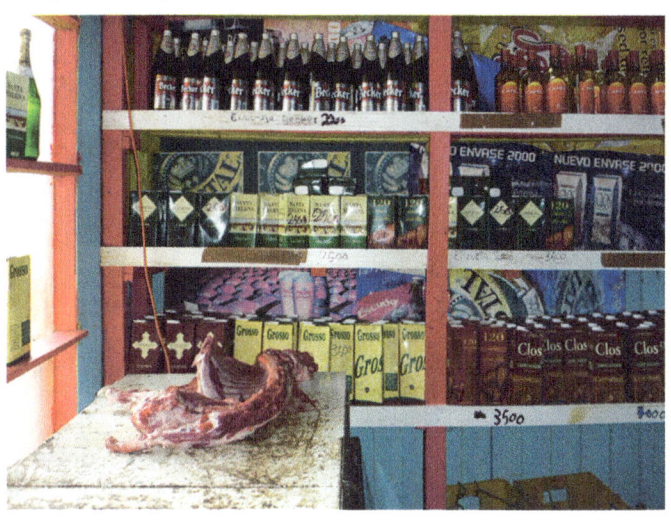

The stock in the meat department was a tad sparse, but the liquor department was a bit better, with a selection of four white wines and three reds, all in tetra-packs, plus one brand of beer and one of Pisco.

We told him we had read of a woman who bakes bread to order, and we were looking for her. Her husband is the village woodworker. His eyes lit-up, and he scooted us around a point to the north and up to a rickety wooden jetty. We walked up to the doors of a woodworking shed and sawmill. We were met there by a burly man, obviously a woodworker. I told him we wanted pan. He asked: *"¿cuántos?"* I replied: *"cuatro"* He asked: *"¿Kilos?"* I replied: *"Panes"* He said: *"bollos"* I said: *"Veinticuatro"* He said: *"mañana"* I said: *"gracias"*. I love these simple Spanish conversations; a great economy of words. I had ordered twenty-four buns for the next day.

As we headed back toward the Armada inflatable, I asked Victor about getting some centolla, the famous local king crab. He stopped and pointed back to where we had been. We walked back into the property and hailed the woodworker, and he hailed his wife. We negotiated for two kilos of shelled leg meat for the mañana., and confirmed with her the two dozen bread rolls.

We went back to the Armada inflatable, and Victor drove us around the point, into the bay and back to our dinghy on the Carabineros pier. We asked him about an internet connection, and he invited us over to the Capitania the

In the fresh produce section were a few onions, potatoes, apples and oranges, all of them in lesser condition than those aboard Sequitur. We did spot some eggs on the floor in a corner, and asked for 20. As the husband meticulously counted and re-counted the eggs, his wife calculated the price, eventually coming-up with 4000 Pesos, more than double what we had been paying Puerto Montt. However; even at $4.80 a dozen, the free-range brown eggs compare well with Vancouver prices.

The wind howled through the anchorage the remainder of Thursday, but with less than a cable's fetch, there were no waves. The barometer continued to drop; it was at 1011.5 at midnight, and was down to 1006.9 when we dinghied ashore shortly after noon on Friday. The previous day we had spotted the convenient large trash tip on the pier, and we brought our sixteen-day collection of recyclable and non-recyclable garbage with us to deposit.

We were met on the pier by the locals, who eagerly sniffed our garbage. The friendly pack of eight to a dozen motley mutts, with various additions and drop-offs along the way, eagerly came with us on a walk.

We checked-out the progress on the reincarnation of Tornado, and admired the craftsmanship that continues to give new lives to vessels that in other parts of the world would have long since been abandoned.

We arrived at the almacen and la señora eagerly unlocked the store and welcomed us in.

She pulled-out a colander of twenty-four rolls, and carefully counted them again into a bag. This almacen (small grocery store) is much better stocked and appears much more sanitary than the supermercado we had visited downtown the previous day. We asked about eggs, and she showed us some jumbo browns.

We asked for 30 of them, and she carefully loaded our Lock & Lock egg containers. One of the eggs was so large that I crushed its top when I clipped the lid into place. As we were counting eggs, a young lad came into the store with the king crab we had ordered. We gave the woman 21,000 for our purchases and she passed 9,000 on to the lad.

We closely examined the fresh produce in the bins and saw nothing to tempt us. It was rather thoroughly picked-over, with little but a few culls remaining. We were delighted that Sequitur's stock of produce had been lasting so well, though we had run out of asparagus and fresh tomatoes. Our escort of dogs was waiting politely outside the store, and led us back around the point and into the centre of the village.

In the bay with Sequitur was the French sloop Ilena; she had arrived six hours after us, using the high-water slack through the narrows. We had spoken briefly with Patricia and Philippe during our walk ashore in Mechuque on our second day out from Puerto Montt.

After a quick lunch, we re-boarded the dinghy and motored around the point to our south and across the next bay to the Armada station. Victor greeted us and showed us around the offices and gave us a desk to set-up our computers. The station is staffed by three Armada personnel, who stand 24-hour watches, one-in-three, and Victor was off watch. He generously allowed us to use the wifi to catch-up on over two weeks internet drought.

Saturday morning was again glum and rainy. The barometer was stable at 1011.2 when I got up at 0855. I started the Fischer-Panda and ran the watermaker for three hours, netting 190 litres of water and bringing the battery up to 86%. Edi started three varieties of biscotti; an almond, a hazelnut cranberry, and a chocolate pecan.

While Edi was slicing the loaves after their first of three bakings, there was a knock on the hull. Philippe had rowed over from Ilena to invite us over at the end of the afternoon. We finished the baking and relaxed onboard while it drizzled, rained and poured outside.

In a lull in the rain we motored Non Sequitur across to Ilena, and spent a delightful two-and-a-half hours with Patricia and Philippe. They opened a bottle of Champagne Laurent Perrier and we toasted to *"fair winds and following seas for the coming year"*. We shared tales of the routes and anchorages we had taken in getting here. They had started in La Rochelle and had sailed to Greenland, Newfoundland, Nova Scotia and then spent last Christmas and New Years in Annapolis. From there they went across to Senegal and Gambia, then back across to Martinique, through the Caribbean and Panama and around to La Punta, Peru. They had thought of stopping in Paita, but they had read my report on Noonsite describing our experiences with the corruption and crime there, and they gave it a miss. From La Punta, they looped out into the Pacific and back in at Valdivia, where they stopped at Alwoplast for some work.

Toward 2000, the wind came around to the southeast and increased. Both Ilena and Sequitur had anchored into a northerly wind, protected by the head of the bay. Now, with the wind blowing into the bay, there was a mile's fetch for the wind to generate some waves.

Ilena was bouncing around in the chop, and with 60 metres of chain out in 12 metres of water, she had swung very close to the shore of the tiny bay. Edi and I put on our foulies and prepared to head back to make that sure Sequitur was secure, while Philippe and Patricia scrambled to adjust their anchor.

As we were climbing down into our dinghy in a driving downpour, the Carabineros Captain came out into the anchorage in a large inflatable and asked us if we wished to raft alongside their boat on the pier. We declined, but Ilena accepted. We drove Non Sequitur directly into the 25-knot wind, heavy rain and steep chop back to Sequitur. The weather god was getting-in his last before our toast for *"fair winds and following seas for the coming year"* kicks-in.

Shortly after we had changed out of our wet clothes and into some dry, the winds began abating. By 2100 they were below 15 knots and the barometer was rising. We were rather full from all the nibblies aboard Ilena, so instead of dinner, around 2300 I heated some of the king crab, melted some butter and Edi sliced some home-made baguette. We opened a bottle of Undurraga Brut Royale and slowly and decadently we made our way toward the New Year. We still had a bit of bubbly remaining in our glasses for a midnight toast to 2012 with the accompaniment of two firecrackers ashore, one boat's red flare and a toot on Sequitur's fog horn.

The barometer had climbed to 1020 when I got up at 0830, and the sky had changed from low stratus to scattered cumulus. It was a bit after 1100 by the time we had finished breakfast and puttering about and made it ashore for a walk along the boardwalk. It was warm enough that we needed only two layers on the bottom and three on top. It was hard to believe that this is summer on the 49th parallel.

We walked to the end of the village, the end of the boardwalk, and then retraced our steps back along, watching as we went the arrival of the Navimag ferry on its weekly trip south. From the rise on the end of the point we watched it come to anchor, and we sat there on the steps fascinated with the buzz of activity around its stern.

A swarm of small boats jockeyed for position on the lowered tail ramp. New passengers were deposited aboard, a few dozen tourists were lightered ashore, and serious offloading of boxes, crates and drums to the small boats began.

We wanted fresh tomatoes, and we were gambling that our best bet was with the slab-sided boat heading north. We walked along the boardwalk, parallelling it, and watched it take-up its mooring where we had seen it on our way north, and where we had seen the skiff from the almacen pier moored as we were on our way back.

... and as the missing links in the cart tracks were put into place across the boardwalk.

We watched as cartons and crates were transferred to the skiff, and as the skiff motored through the shallows of the low tide to the almacen pier. Our tomatoes were looking better, that is if there were any in the load.

We watched as a half dozen men transferred the new stock of groceries up onto the pier,..

The cart was checked by a rope as it was rolled down the tracks to the pier. There it was loaded with the new stock and an old Briggs & Stratton was fired-up to run unclutched through two sets of reduction gearing to a makeshift rope gipsy. A young fellow tailed the line as the windlass hauled the heavily laden cart up the slope to the front the almacen.

We had our first look at the produce through the spaces between the slats of the crates, and were disappointed to see nothing but melons; boxes and boxes of melons. As boxes and crates were lugged into the store, we finally spotted what appeared to be tomatoes. We followed the box into the store and stood by it waiting for it to be opened.

Everyone seemed focused on the melons and the cherries, so we finally took the initiative and opened the single crate of tomatoes. We picked-out a fine assortment of nicely firm ones ranging from red through dark orange to yellow in colour. La señora weighed them and asked for 3500 Pesos for the 3.5 kilos. This we learned is how one buys fresh tomatoes in Puerto Eden. A short while later there would be nothing but culls.

In the evening we hosted Patricia and Philippe aboard for dinner. We sipped Montes Leyda Vineyard 2010 Sauvignon Blanc with cashews and almonds as I prepared a stir-fry of pork with ginger, garlic, Spanish onion, carrots, cauliflower, broccoli, red and green peppers, oyster mushrooms and tomato tossed with rotini and toasted sesame seeds. With this we enjoyed the Hacienda Araucano 2008 Valle de Lolol Pinot Noir.

We had a delightful evening, chatting and discussing a broad range of topics, most of them twice. Patricia speaks no English and Edi no French, so I translated the French for Edi and Philippe the English for Patricia. We told them our intention to continue south in the morning, but Patricia and Philippe told us they were remaining in Puerto Eden for another day or two, to take-on some diesel and to restock their fresh produce. Being a more traditional offshore design, Ilena has much less storage capacity than does Sequitur.

27. Southward into the Furious Fifties

I got up Monday morning, the 2nd of January at 0800 to a low overcast and light drizzle. The barometer had remained rather stable overnight, down just half a point to 1022.5. After breakfast, while Edi prepared Sequitur's interior for sea, I changed the pre-filters on the watermaker, then we both hoisted the engine off the dinghy and the dinghy onto its davits. At 0955 we weighed and headed out through Paso Sur and continued southward along Canal Messier.

Out in the channel the wind was from the north at 8 or 9 knots, so it was practically useless to us on our route southward. The clouds varied through the day from low stratus, to low stratocumulus to low stratus with stratus fractus, and the precipitation ranged from misty drizzle through to light sleet. According to the guides, we were travelling through spectacular country, but except for a fleeting glimpse of an icefall up an inlet, we saw little but low clouds and water and the thin stripe of land that separated them.

Edi went out at one point and towelled the sleet off the cockpit windows. It is hard to believe we were at the same distance from the equator as Vancouver, but in summer. The winter day in Vancouver was likely nicer than ours.

I ran the watermaker for 6.5 hours and filled the tanks, while Edi ran a load of laundry through the washer-drier. At 1415 we reached the end of Canal Messier and turned into Canal Wide, which we followed for three hours, before turning up Estero Gage, a narrow inlet on its western side, heading for the night's anchorage. About two miles up it we saw a shack and a shed along the water's edge, most likely a fishing camp. It is in a lovely setting, but very remote.

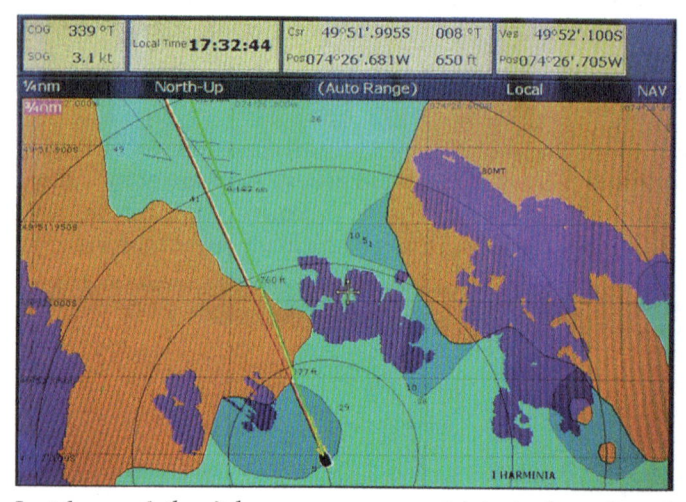

Just beyond the fish camp are some islets to thread, and then the inlet narrows. The further up the inlet we went, the less accurate was the chart. The chartplotter wanted to take us on an overland route, the paints on our radar gave an additional number of options. Thankfully, our mariners' eyes found the correct passage.

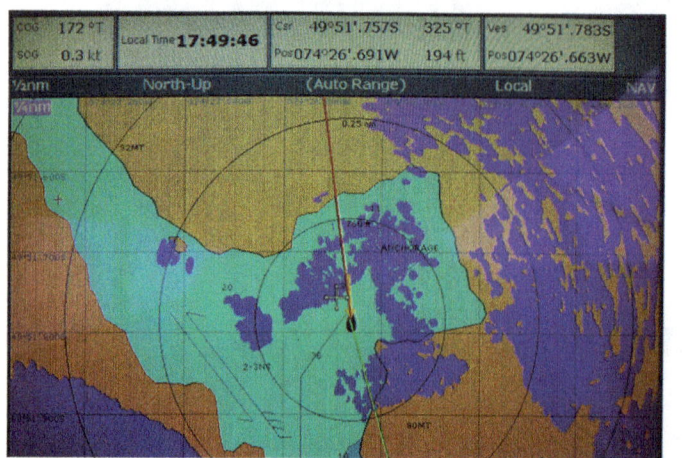

After the narrows the chart shows a rather square-shaped bay; however both the Italian Guide and our radar showed it to be one half the size with more pointed corners. Our eyes saw this version also, so we went with reality and came to 33 metres on the Rocna in 11 metres of water in a peaceful little bay about a quarter cable from the trees. Our anchor was positioned so that we could swing, but if the winds came up, we could run stern-lines to the north and east sides and warp Sequitur back into a tight, protected cranny.

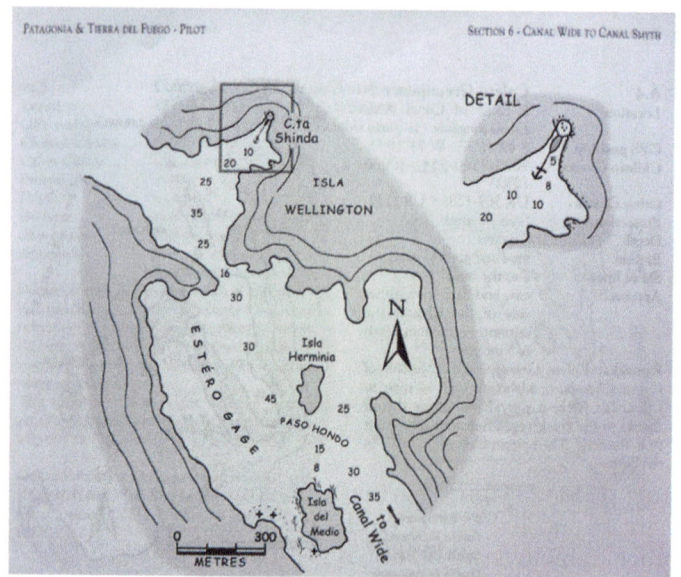

We love the detailed sketches in the Italian Guide. These appear to have been rendered from satellite images, likely GoogleEarth. With their excellent descriptions, the plans make anchoring in wonderful little places like Caleta Shinda much more easy.

In the evening I prepared centolla Shinda for dinner. I sautéed diced shallots and garlic in butter, added some small button mushrooms, some sauce Alfredo and then some Puerto Eden king crab to gently heat. I served this on a bed of basmati rice and garnished the plates with sliced Navimag tomatoes and Puerto Montt basil leaves in olive oil. The 2010 Montes Leyda Vineyard Sauvignon Blanc accompanied superbly.

The barometer remained stable overnight; it was at 1017.8 when I got up to send our 0800 position report by sat phone SMS to Directemar.

It was still completely overcast and was drizzling as I walked around on deck to find a good signal.

We dawdled over breakfast, and then at 1005 we weighed and headed down the inlet in a light drizzle. I had been waiting for the tide to turn to ebb to assist us on the passage, and for the faint possibility that it might stop raining. The tide did turn, but the rain persisted. Looking back up Estero Gage as we passed through the narrows, we could see potential for spectacular views, but the low clouds filled most of the scene.

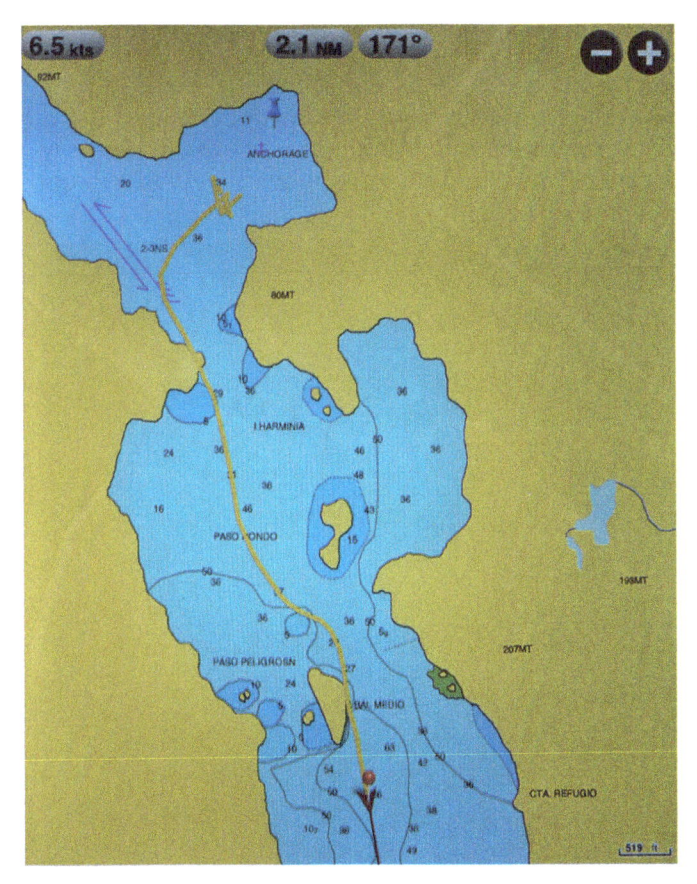

Once we were through the narrows I moved the engine up in speed and the beginning of the ebb assisted in moving us along the calm inlet. Again we see the charting errors, but since leaving the wonderful works of the Canadian Hydrographic Services, we have accepted this as the norm.

Our intention for the day was to continue down Canal Wide to Canal Concepción and then into Canal Inocentes to an anchorage an hour short of Angostura Guia, a narrows dependant on slack water for easy passage. I have found the Navionics app on the iPad a wonderful tool in planning passages. With the iPad's built-in GPS, it offers at a glance a handy range of information, including a course-made-good cursor, speed over the ground and dynamic distance measurement, to name a few. I had recently begun using the route planning function to plot from the destination back to the origin, and then using this as an ongoing glimpse of distance to go. As each waypoint is reached, I remove it and move the distance pin to the next one.

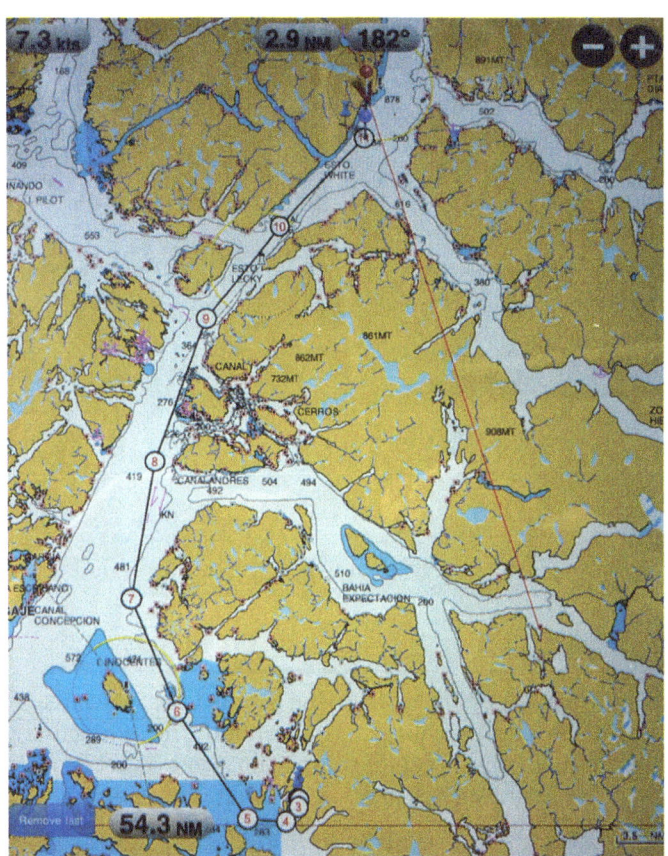

This screen shot shows that our distance to the planned anchorage is 54.3 + 2.9 miles, a total of 57.2 miles, and that we're making 7.3 knots.

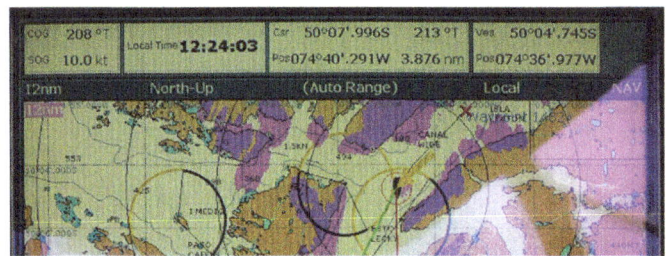

The clouds lowered and it continued to rain. Visibility was down to under three miles and our views were water and cloud with misty bits of land here and there. The wind strengthened to around 25 knots from the northeast and we jibed down the channel assisted by the ebb, making better than 8 knots, with surfs on the wind waves taking us frequently above 10.

We remained dry and comfortable in the cockpit, enjoying the Patagonian summer in our multiple layers of fleece, heavy jackets and toques. Edi had put on her knee-high neoprene kayaking boots to help keep her feet warm. She continued to knit.

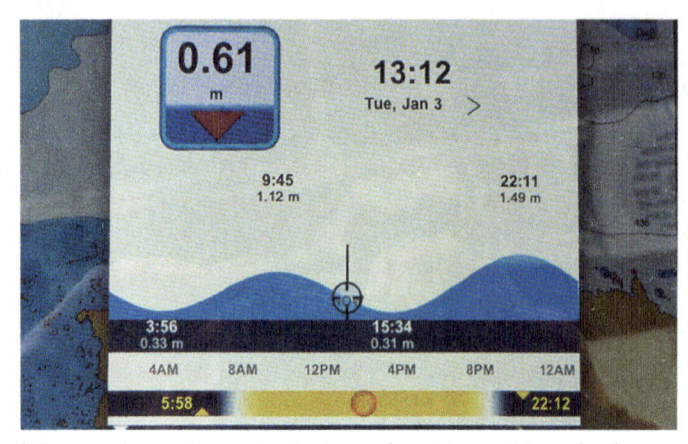

We were benefiting nicely from the ebbing tide, which was scheduled to continue until mid-afternoon. The interactive tidal tables in the Navionics program are a marvellous tool, offering at fingertip a graph of what is happening.

Edi went below and created a marvellous lunch of shrimp and water chestnut spring rolls, served with spicy peanut sauce and hot rooibos tea. We find that a broad variety of food, pleasingly presented adds so much pleasure to our days. We are definitely not the can-and-spoon-over-the-sink types.

We rode the last of the ebb down Canal Concepción, and as we turned into Canal Inocentes, we were pushed along by the beginning of the flood. The clouds lowered to very near the surface, and visibility was at times reduced to under a mile in drizzle or mist or fog, sometimes all three. An interesting aspect with the Chilean charting is that where surveying and sounding are considered incomplete, the area is tinted blue, regardless of the depth. I have the plotter and iPad both set to pale blue for 20 metres and less and dark blue for 5 metres and less. The Chilean chip and app default the incomplete areas as 5 metres and less.

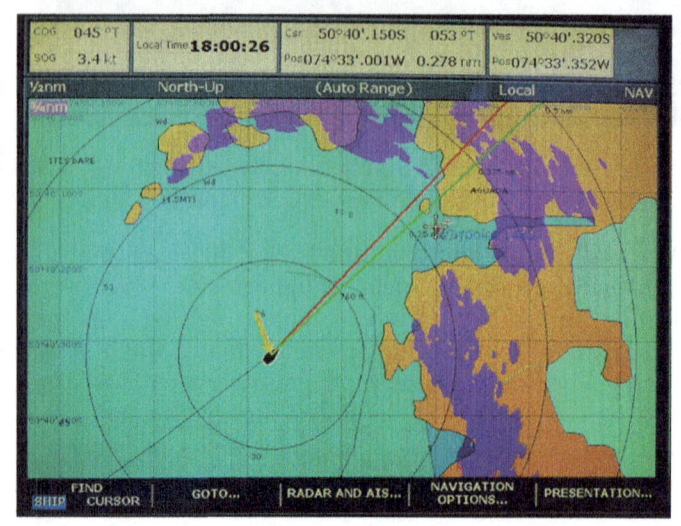

The wind was up over 35 knots from the northwest, directly in our stern as we sailed up Inocentes. We found the lee we were looking for under Islotes Long, and rolled in the sails a mile short of the entrance to Caleta Paroquet, and motored in a fluky 10 to 15 knot wind into its head.

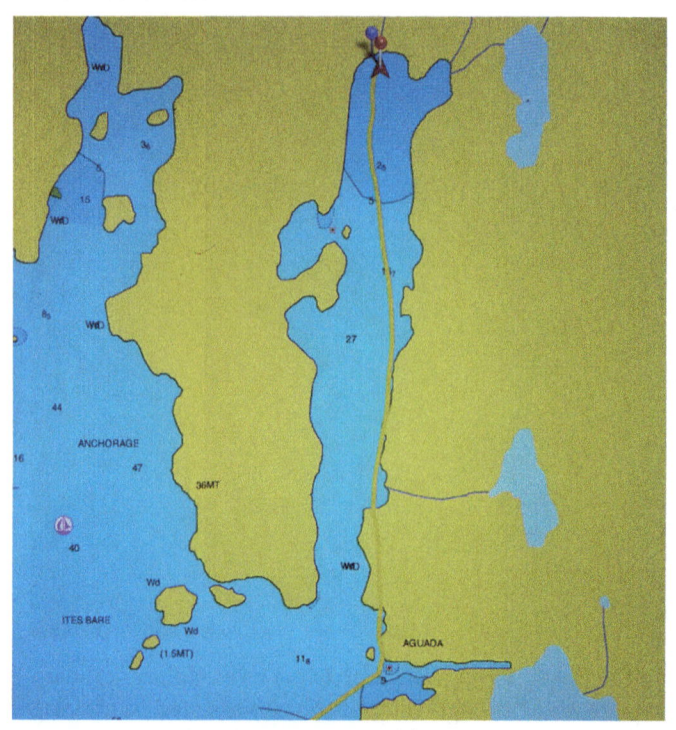

At 1910 we came to 20 metres on the Rocna in 10 metres of water, and by 1930 we had set two stern-lines ashore.

The water is very clear, and the steep shore is readily visible down several metres, so we confidently brought Sequitur within a few metres of the trees. There was almost no wind at the water's surface, so Sequitur sat patiently at her anchor waiting for me to set the lines around trees ashore. What should be an easy chore is complicated by the slimy rocks on the foreshore and the slippery wet coating of moss and fungus on everything beyond the water's edge. This is a very wet temperate rain forest.

I prepared a quiche for dinner, based primarily around some small choritos, like tender baby mussels, and we enjoyed it with a bottle of Undurraga Brut. This was partly because we felt like it and partly to celebrate having reached the Furious Fifties.

The barometer continued its slow and steady decline. It was at 1014.6 on Wednesday morning when I sent our position report to the Armada. The sky was full of low nimbostratus with a few tatters of stratus fractus and it was raining lightly.

We had a leisurely breakfast, I having calculated we needed to leave the anchorage at 0945 to make Angostura Guia at slack water. The stern lines came off easily and we weighed at 0947 and then headed out in a steady drizzle.

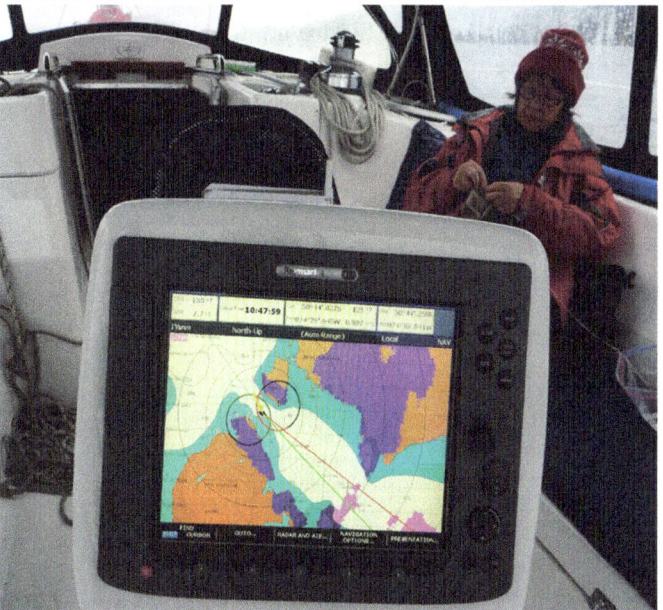

One hour later we passed through the tightest bit of the narrows with the beginning of the flood, and were making 7.7 knots with turns for 7. As we were half an hour from the narrows, we heard a Securite on the VHF. A northbound ship, the Colca was giving its mandatory report of its ETA at the narrows. I responded and gave our position and ETA. Northbound has priority and Colca requested a standard port-to-port passing.

A short while later, on a bend in the narrows we met Colca, only the second ship we have met in two weeks. With all the half-mile and mile-wide straight channels we have been in, it is amazing that chance happened to have us cross paths in some of the more restricted waters of the area. The Guia is only 1.5 cables wide.

In the early afternoon Edi heated the leftover quiche. Again we were reminded that we should always eat our quiche as leftovers; it seems to taste so much better the next day.

The wind blew strongly from the north-northwest and northwest through the afternoon, generally in the 25 to 30 knot area, with gusts above 35. The skies remained overcast, though with some occasional definition to the bottoms of the clouds.

At 1600 we were less than a mile from our intended anchorage in Caleta Damien and the winds had piped-up to above 35, and with the long fetch there were large waves with whitecaps and some blowing spume. We made the turn across wind and waves very close to the lee shore rocks of Isla Vancouver to get around the kelp-marked reef off the southeast point of Isla Whitby, and finally found lee from the howling northerly, which by this time was gusting well into the 40s.

There were wind eddies as we slowly motored into the narrow passage between Whitby and Vancouver Islands and positioned Sequitur at the mouth of a dimple in the shoreline, recommended in the Italian Guide as protection from all winds. At 1614 we dropped the anchor in 12 metres of water, veered 30 metres of chain and launched the dinghy to began setting stern lines.

By the time the dinghy was launched, the wind had blown Sequitur close to the rocks on the starboard quarter, so I took the port line ashore first, looped it around a tree and back to a sheet winch. We warped the boat away from the rocks off the starboard quarter, then I took the starboard line ashore. By the time I had rowed ashore, the wind had veered all the way around and was blowing Sequitur's port quarter near the rocks.

With Edi on the engine and helm following my hollered instructions, we kept her off the rocks as I struggled to set the starboard line. Finally, at 1844, exactly two and a half hours after dropping the anchor, we had warped Sequitur into a three-point-balance and shut-down the engine.

Throughout this exercise, the wind came variously from northeast through northwest, either side of our lie, and it varied from calm through 40 knots. It rained heavily, then stopped, then downpoured, then rained lightly, then paused before another cloudburst.

In the evening as my sauce Bolognese simmered, I ran the transfer pump to move about 250 litres of diesel from the auxiliary tank to the main. The barometer continued falling, reading 1007.0 when we anchored and 1006.3 when we went to bed at midnight. The rain persisted, varying from steady drizzle to heavy rain and back as waves of nimbo-whatevers passed over.

I was up at 0650 to the sounds of a wind shift. The winds were now out of the south, and I winched-in the port stern line to haul us away from the rocks. The barometer was at 1009.0. At 0800 when I sent our position report, it was up to 1009.7 and at 1000, after a delicious breakfast of smoked salmon, capers and cream cheese on toasted split baguettes with fresh-ground Starbucks, the barometer was at 1011.6.

The timing of the tides, and therefore the currents along our route meant there was no sense leaving until they had turned. We released the stern lines and weighed at 1055, and were lead out of the caleta by a pair of playful dolphins.

There was some definition to the cloud bottoms as we reentered Canal Sarmiento, and a few slivers of blue began appearing as we sailed south-southeast into a south-southwest wind of 10 to 12 knots.

As we continued down Canal Sarmiento, variously sailing and motor-sailing as the winds came and went, the barometer continued to rise; 1016.7 at noon, 1019.7 at 1600 and 1021.2 at 1800. This rapid change caused us to pass under a cloud atlas of skies.

I ran the water-maker for five hours and netted 310 litres after the back-flush. Edi used some of this, running two loads through the washer-dryer, but at the end of the run, our tanks were full. We have seen many sources of fresh water in streams in the anchorages, but we prefer to push buttons rather than doing the jug and dinghy routine.

In the early afternoon we enjoyed a simple lunch of rice crackers with salami, black olives and a variety of cheeses. Our Lock & Lock containers have kept the crackers amazingly crisp and fresh. The previous year the many dozens of packages were perfect after nine months.

As we nibbled, we were entertained by three very playful sea lion pups, which spent a good fifteen minutes jumping clear of the water as they parallelled our track. Eventually, they must have either tired from the exertion, or tired of waiting for Sequitur to join them in their frolic.

At 1650 we came to the end of Canal Sarmiento and turned east into Paso Farquhar. As we rounded Punta San Bartolame, the south tip of Isla Carrington, the mountains of Cordillera Sarmiento came into view.

They are not high compared to those with which we are accustomed in British Columbia. The highest in this range is only 2011 metres, more than 200 metres below the highest peak on Vancouver Island, and more than 2000 metres short of Mount Waddington across the Straits in British Columbia's Coast Range. The Patagonian peaks are spectacular, like many back home. However, as we looked at them, we thought that many sailors coming this way who have not been blessed with sailing and climbing along the coast of British Columbia, would most likely be much more impressed than we were.

We headed down Canal Union to the east of Isla Hunter to Paso Victoria and through it to the entrance to Caleta Victoria. There, we were met by an escort of dolphins, which led us in.

530

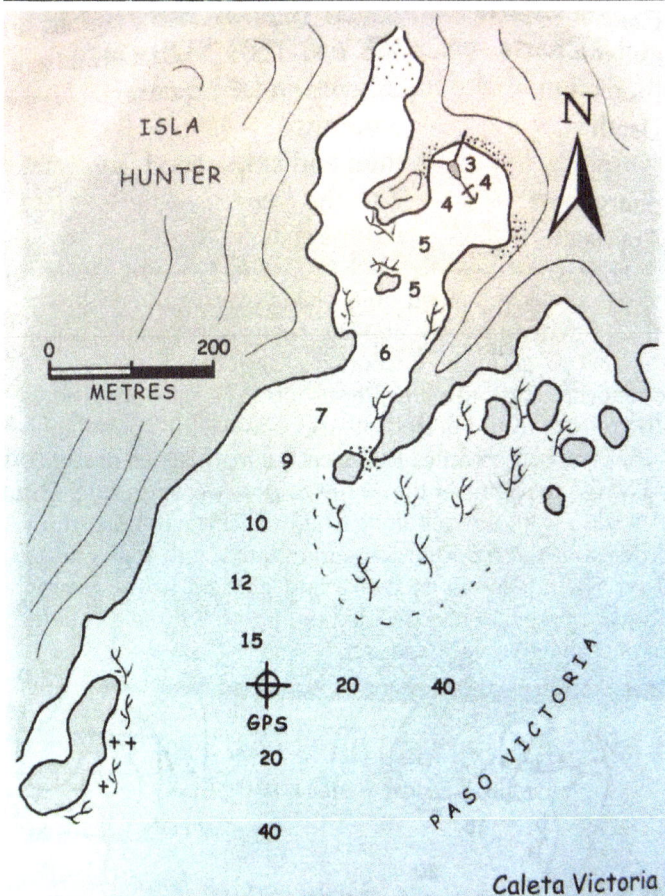

At 1954 we came to 12 metres on the Rocna in 3.6 metres of water and I went ashore to set a single stern line ashore around a tree at the top of a low cliff.

We picked our way in past tiny islets and visible rocks, and past patches of kelp marking unseen rocks. The sketch in Italian Guide shows the minimum depth through the entry passage is 5 metres and in the basin the depth is generally 4 metres with one 3 metre sounding.

Our Hunter was at anchor on Isla Hunter in the most beautiful anchorage we had thus far seen in Patagonia. The dolphins came over to welcome us. Our latitude was just a few seconds south of 52 South, and sunset is not until 2215, so after I had secured Sequitur's stern line, I took a short walkabout.

As I walked, I saw a rather freshly cut tree stump, and not far away I came upon the site of an impromptu lumber mill. It appears a visiting fisherman had used a chainsaw with a lumber jig to cut some planks, and left behind the slab-wood. The trees in this region are sparse and stunted, but even so, I supposed that they are a ready supply of boat building and repair material.

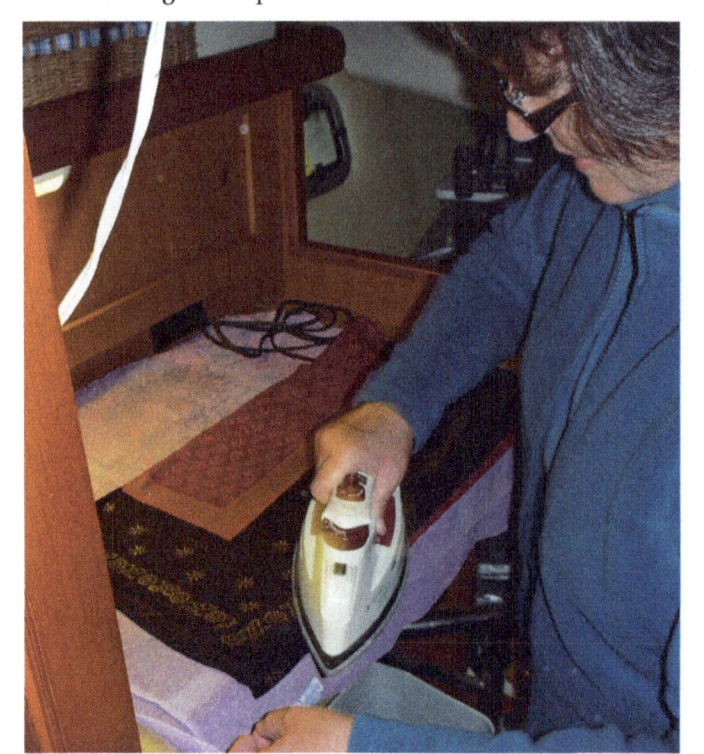

While I was ashore, Edi had decided to catch-up on her backlog of ironing. We have a wonderful assortment of tablecloths and serviettes aboard, which add so much to the enjoyment of our meals. She was still at it when I returned aboard to begin cooking dinner.

I sautéed filete de blanquillo in butter and served it with basmati rice and a butter-sweat of julienned carrots, onions and garlic, garnished by sliced tomatoes with basil leaves in olive oil. Sequitur's boat white, the 2011 Carmen Chardonnay continues to amaze us with its quality for only $3.75.

The barometer remained quite stable overnight, and it was at 1021.0 when I got up at 0720. There was a small fishing boat next to us in the anchorage. It appears to have set a stern anchor and put a bow line ashore. The NAT on its bows indicates it is from Puerto Natales, a town with a population of 18,000 about 65 miles to the east along a series of canals and across the spine of the Andes to its dry eastern side. The town is a few kilometres along a highway from the Argentine border and it is reported to be inundated with tour groups on whirlwind gawks at peaks and glaciers in the nearby national parks. We had decided to forgo the three-day side-trip and give the place a miss.

For breakfast Edi prepared basted eggs and served them lapped with an Alfredo sauce on split scones topped with basil leaves and garnished by sliced fresh tomatoes with a grind of sea salt. We enjoyed this with steaming cups of Starbucks coffee.

As we waited for the tides for our day's passage, we decided to take the dinghy ashore and go exploring. We were about to push off from Sequitur when we spotted a family of Cauquen Cabeza Colorada, Ruddy-Headed Geese, a male, a female and four chicks. Not wanting to disturb them, we waited as they made their way from the grass, across the gravel strand and into the water.

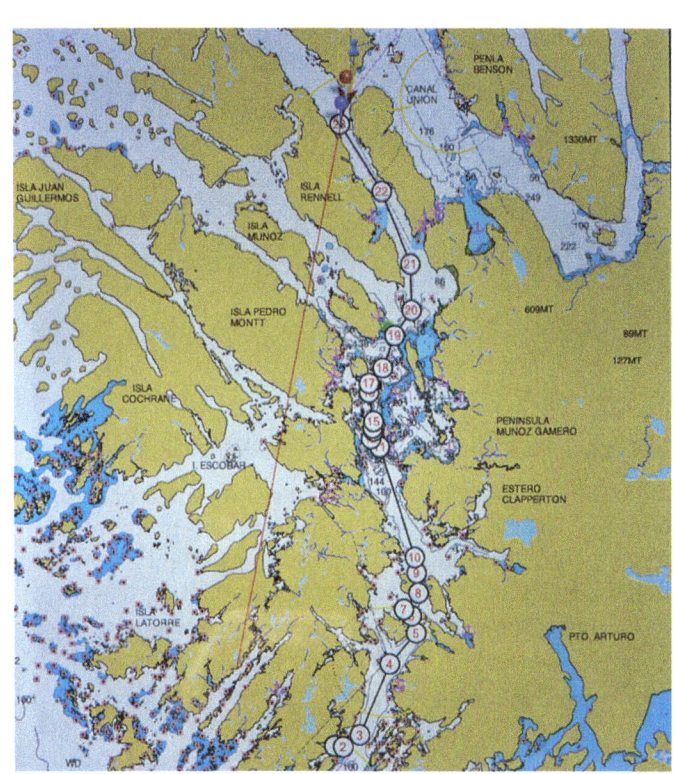

From the north, the tide floods in from the ocean and flows southward toward the pass. In the southern portion, the flood is northward from the Straits of Magellan. These two tides meet in the middle, so we had planned to head into the pass on the flood and to catch the change to ebb in the middle and ride it out toward the Straits.

Like our Christmas anchorage in Caleta Suarez, there are easily walkable beaches here. We took advantage of the rare opportunity to stretch our legs.

Our planned passage for the day was 48 miles long, through Canal Smyth to an anchorage within 4 miles of the Straits of Magellan. Along the way were two major bottlenecks of rocks, shoals and shallows. The first of these, Paso Summer is a doglegged narrows through an area of many shoals. The second, Paso Shoal is marked by rocks, islets and wrecks. The entire passage is very well charted and it navigation is assisted by lights, buoys and beacons.

We slipped our stern line off the tree and while Edi was reeling-in the line, I went forward to clear a bit of kelp on the anchor. At 0914 we headed out of Caleta Victoria in still airs and calm seas with a thin cirrostratus overcast. As we went, the high clouds were replaced with fluffy fair-weather cumulus. Monte Burney a 1512-metre volcano dominated the skyline to the south, then the east and then the north for the major portion of our passage as we motored through glassy waters.

Monte Burney looks like a 3000-metre mountain of British Columbia. In fact, all the hills and mountains in this region make me think that we are moving along at the 1500-metre level; the tree lines and glaciation are that far displaced.

As we approached the turn at the most narrow portion of Paso Shoal, we were overtaken by the Armada supply ship, Aquiles on her way south.

Our timing with the tides was impeccable. We enjoyed a small push to Paso Summer, transited it during the tail end of the flood and headed into Paso Shoal with the beginning of the ebb down the other side.

We had earlier communicated on VHF and had given our intentions through the narrows. She advised that she would pass down our port side, and we advised her we would remain to the starboard side of the navigable channel. Aquiles arrived at the turn of the narrows three minutes before Sequitur, and turned across our bows, posing wonderfully in front of the wreck of Santa Leonor, which in 1968 hadn't been as diligent with her navigation.

The wreck of Santa Leonor, a former US Navy transport, was attributed to a navigational error. Her hulk serves as a good reminder to navigators to be constantly aware of their position, their surroundings and most importantly, to their movements relative to those surroundings. Santa Leonor wrecked on a shoal apparently then still well marked by the 1904 wreck of the Islotes Adelaida.

As we motored southward along the continuation of Canal Smyth, we passed under a few more pages of the cloud catalogue. The rapidly changing sequence of clouds indicated to me that there was a weather change coming, and that it was a change for the worse. This was confirmed by the barometer, which had been steadily falling since my midnight reading of 1022.5. It had been 1020.0 when we weighed, and it was reading 1012.9 at 1650 as we approached the entrance to Caleta Profundo, our anchorage for the night.

It had remained rather windless as we wound our way among the rocks, shoals, islets and islands. As we went, I had run the watermaker for three hours, netting 220 litres after the back-flush, and Edi had put a load of laundry through the washer-dryer.

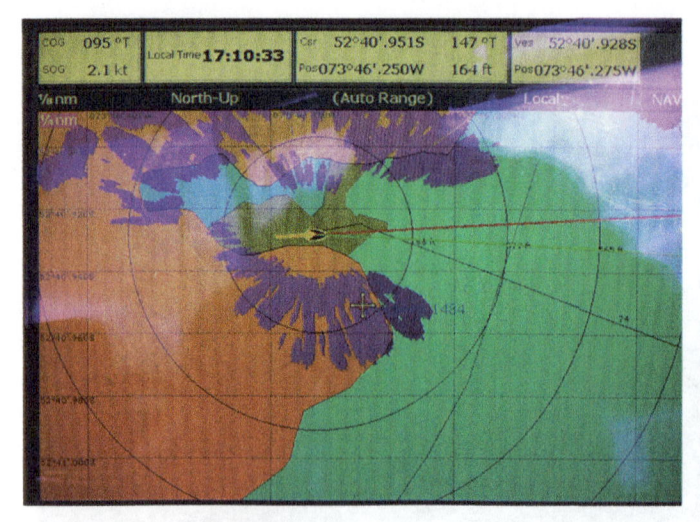

According to the guides, Puerto Profundo provides a selection of anchorages. I picked one recommended in the Italian Guide, but when we had entered, found that it was only a few metres wider than Sequitur's length. With the winds fickle and gusty, we decided not to bet Sequitur would remain mid-caleta as we got our lines ashore. The slot was so narrow that it took me several back-and-forths to turn around.

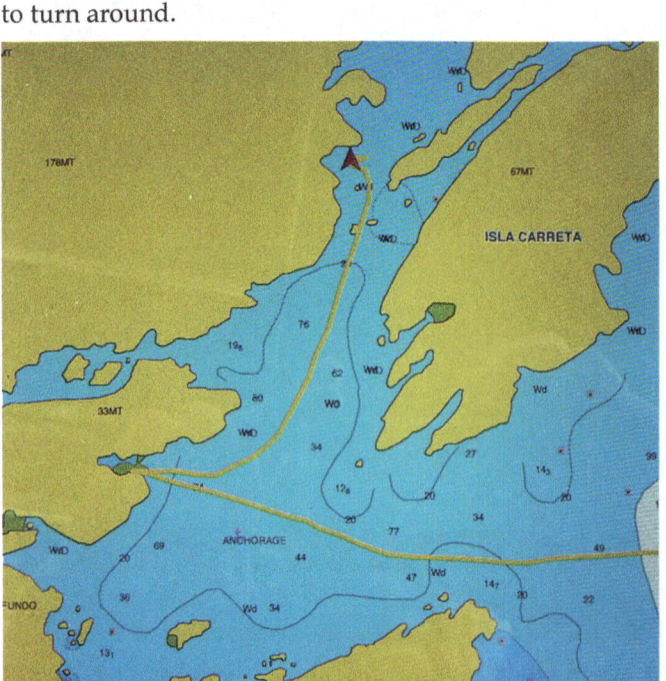

After dinner, while I was up top checking the stern-line and anchor, I paused to drink-in the colours in late-evening sky. It was past 2200 and sunset was still a quarter-hour away, followed by the long high-latitude twilight. The water was glassy in the anchorage, but there was a wind ripple out at the mouth of the bay.

We headed northward and threaded between some rocks and tiny islets, finding soundings of 10 metres and deeper in the 10 metre wide passes. The rocks and shorelines are very steep-to. Because kelp generally marks any unseen rocks and reefs, the pilotage is rather easy. Nonetheless, we move dead slow through areas like this, remembering the caution of one of my navigational instructors in the Navy: *"Never approach land faster than the speed at which you are willing to hit it"*.

At 1805 we shut-down the engine, having securely balanced Sequitur between 30 metres of snubbed chain and a single line around a stout tree ashore about 10 metres off our stern at the head of a tiny semicircular bay.

Our stern-tie was well-placed and Sequitur was protected from the north-westerly winds that I was expecting. The rapidly falling barometer indicated that we were seeing the end of the calm conditions of the previous two days, and I was hopeful that the approaching system was not too severe. Our next leg would be taking us out of Canal Smyth, around Isla Tamar and into the Straits of Magellan. We needed good conditions.

28. Magellan Straits to Tierra del Fuego

This area around the entrance of the Straits is notorious for the severity of its weather. *"Fifty-metre-high breakers on the rocks of the lighthouse"* and *"150-knot winds"* are among descriptions found. Nearby is Bahía Cuarenta Días, Forty Day Bay, which was named for the length of the wait of a ship for conditions suitable for it to take supplies to Faro Islotes Evangelistas.

Saturday morning there was a low overcast hanging over the anchorage and there was a light breeze. Outside in the main part of the caleta we could see a light chop, indicating some wind, but the hanging clouds meant there was not much. At 0932 we undid our stern lines, weighed and headed out into Canal Smyth. I called Faro Fairway on the VHF to report our movements and intentions.

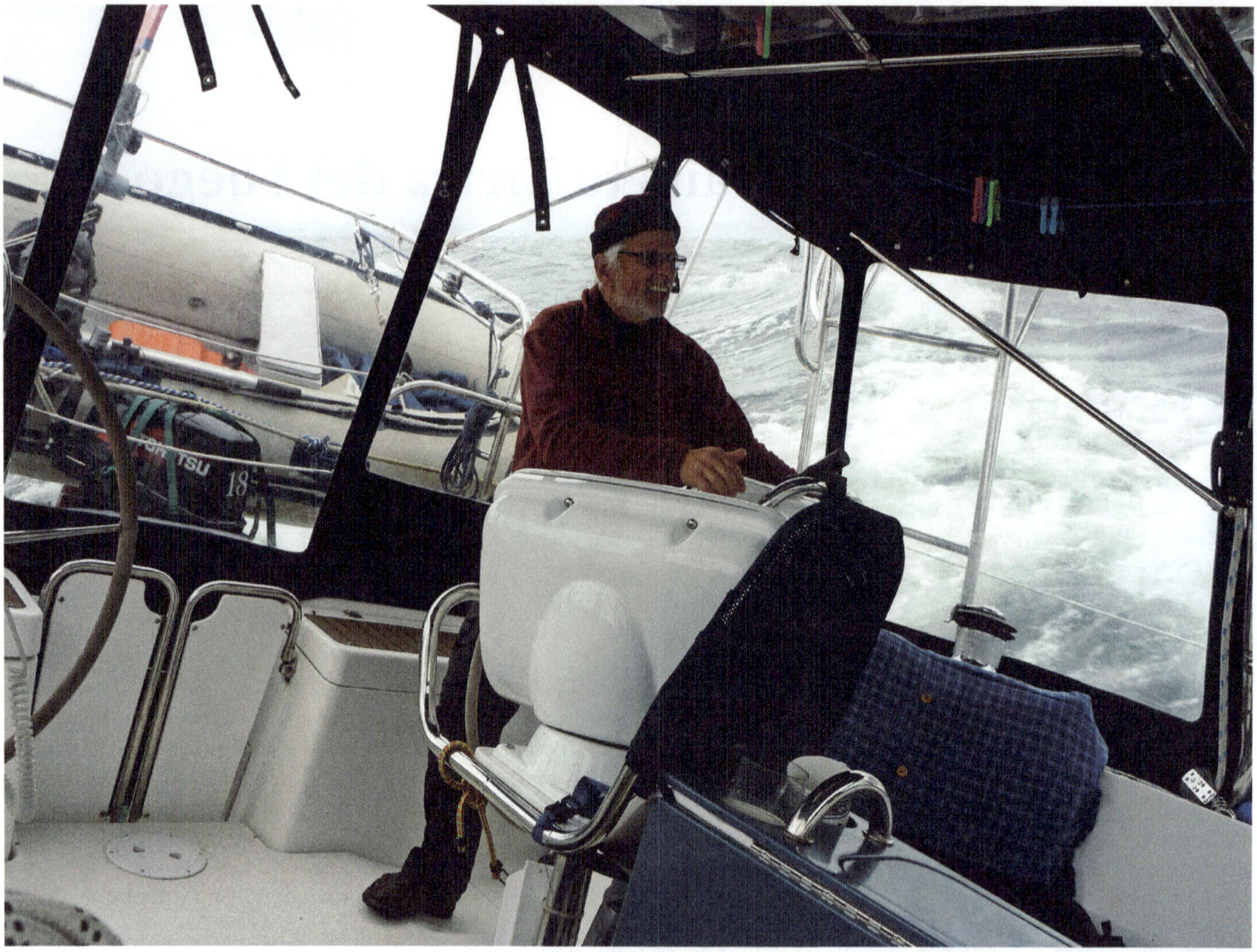
18

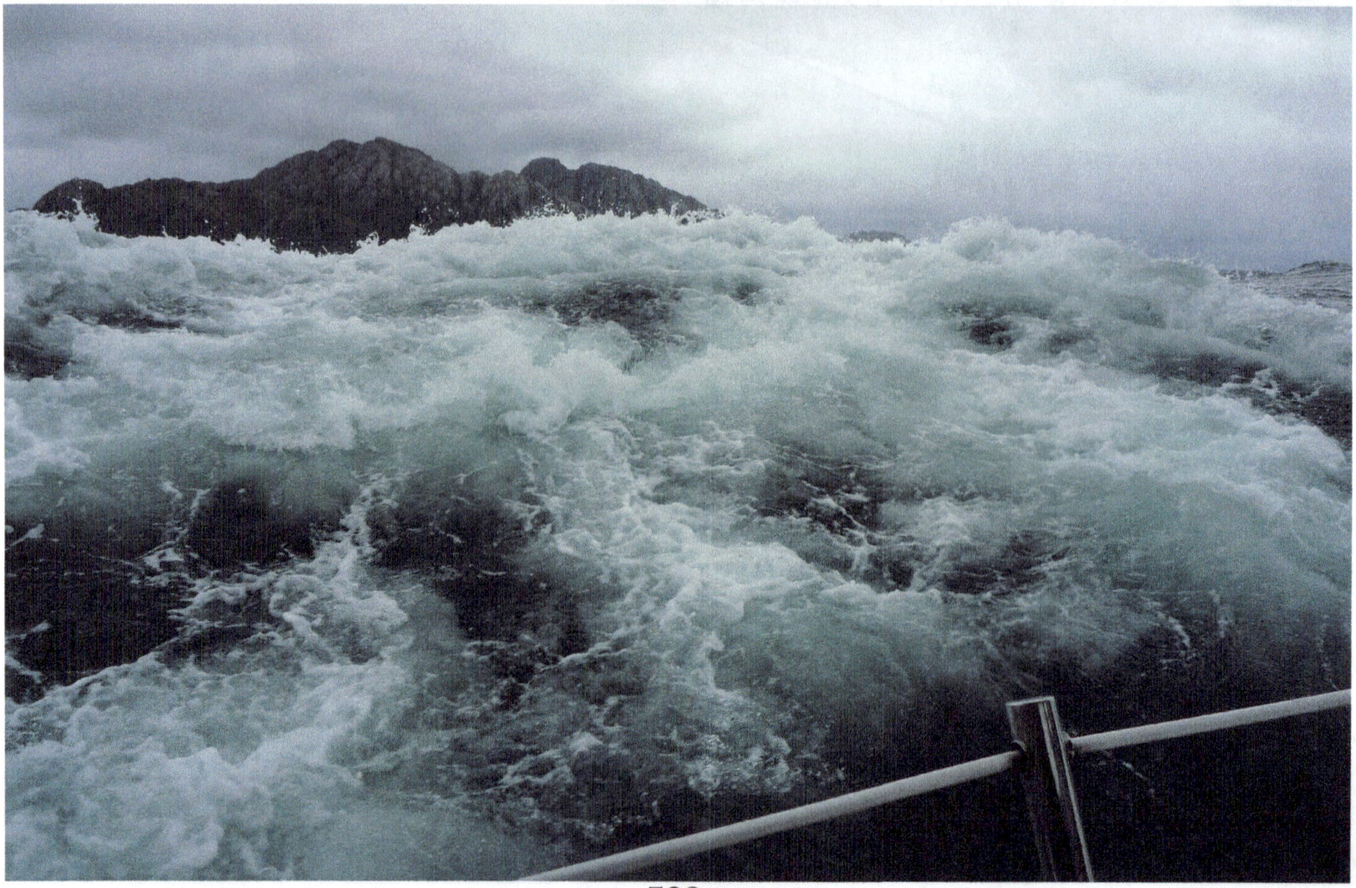

I hauled out the staysail and a third of the main and we sailed on a beam reach in a growing northwest wind as we headed out toward the Straits of Magellan. As we cleared the protection of Punta Henry, the winds increased to 20 knots and we were met by the swell coming in off the Pacific.

The winds built to 30 knots, and I would have loved to put both them and the swell in our stern; however, we first needed to round Isla Tamar. For nearly an hour I closely monitored the autopilot and slowly adjusted course to maintain a balance between safety and comfort.

I slowly worked around to a broad reach, putting the swell a little on our quarter. Our speed varied between 6 and 12 knots, depending on whether we climbing the back of a swell, or were surfing down its front.

Slowly Tamar fell abaft our beam and we were able to put more of the wind and swell behind us. Out in the Straits the conditions were rather more comfortable with both wind and swell in our stern. The winds moved above 30 and the barometer continued its downward trend, passing through 1007.0 at noon. At 1330, the 3-metre swell combining with the building wind waves persuaded us to seek shelter.

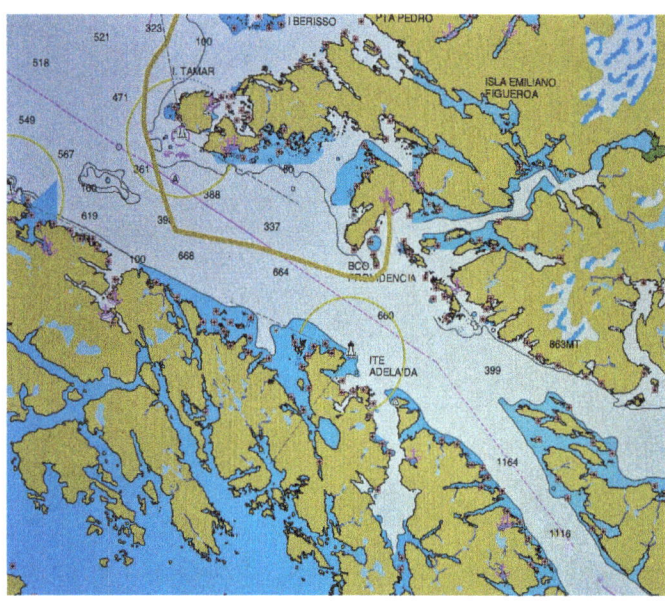

We jibed to port and headed eastward for lee around Isla Providencia. First we needed to clear Banco Providencia, a patch of crud extending 1.4 miles out from the island. Finally, at 1416 we found some lee and rolled-in the sails a mile from the entrance to Caleta Providencia.

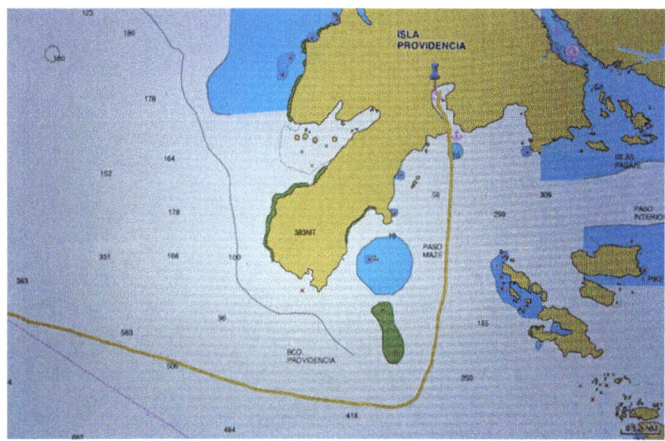

At 1526 we shut-down the engine, having secured Sequitur nicely balanced between 30 metres of chain in 18 metres of water and a line off each quarter around trees on the steep shore. Our stern was 5 metres off the rocks, and the after depth sounder indicated we had 3.8 metres beneath our rudder.

We decided to head out after breakfast and to continue as long as it was relatively comfortable. We enjoyed toasted split baguettes with cream cheese and black currant jam and cups of fresh-ground Starbucks, and at 0840 we weighed and motored out through glassy-calm waters.

As we have been doing these stern-ties, we have gradually refined our routine and our set-up. The largest improvement was following Edi's suggestion to move the line reels from the stern rails to around on the quarters. This makes them more convenient to the stern cleats, the sheet winches and provides a comfortable seat from which to reel-in the line on departure.

Our intention was to continue along the Straits for as long as the conditions allowed good progress, and then to seek the next available shelter. At 1000 our log recorded: Sky 10/10 altostratus, stratus, Wind 0-2, Swell ½ metre, Barometer 995.4 falling. We were very comfortably motoring at just over 6 knots. At 1100 the wind was on our nose at southeast 8-10, and the barometer was down slightly to 994.8. At noon the only change was the barometer falling to 993.5. At 1235 it began raining and 1320 the wind was up to over 20 knots directly on our nose, the barometer was at 991.3 and our speed was under 5 knots. We decided to duck into Caleta Playa Parda.

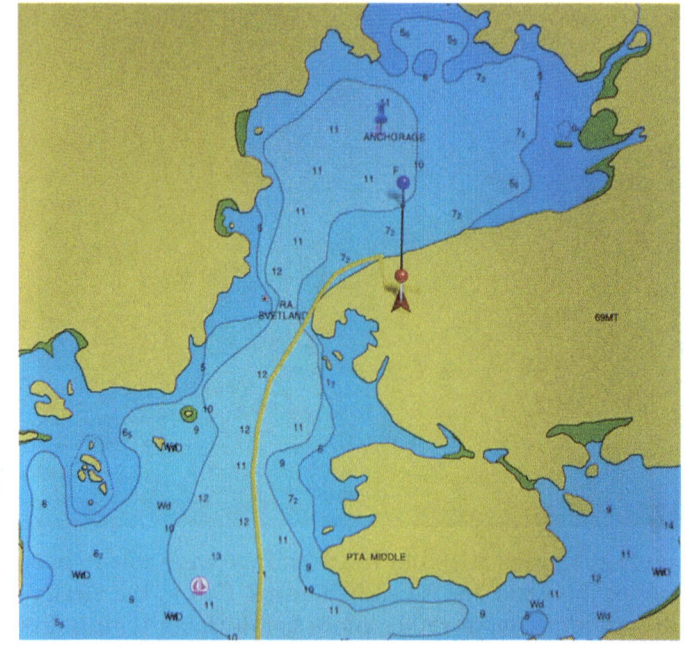

When I went outside for a look around on Sunday morning, the 8th of January, the water was a mirror. The sky was completely overcast with altostratus above patches of nimbostratus. The barometer had sunk to 999.5, down from midnight's 1004.2.

After I had established the chart error, we picked our way past the shoals outside the entrance and threaded through the 20-metre-wide channel into the basin. The caleta is well charted, except for the datum skew of about 0.8 cables north.

We easily located the lines hanging from the rocks on the south side of the basin, as mentioned in the Italian Guide. We motored in closely along the cliff face in 8 to 10 metres of water and examined the condition of the lines as best we could through the wind-driven rain, and then determined the most suitable spot to set the anchor.

At 1426 we came to 25 metres on the Rocna in 9.8 metres of water and then launched the dinghy. I took the port stern-line and rowed across the 20-knot northerly wind to the cliff face, and then along it to the most southerly of the lines. The line was rather fresh, and it appeared well set, so I threaded our stern-line through its eye and pulled through sufficient to double the distance to Sequitur.

I then had Edi secure her end of the line around the winch and using it I pulled the dinghy and line back to Sequitur. The wind came in gusts up to the mid-20s and then completely died, but the rain continued heavily. I was completely soaked by the time I had secured the end of the line around the stern cleat.

I repeated the process with the starboard line and then winched-in to balance Sequitur between the two lines and the anchor. At 1512, 46 minutes after we had set the anchor, we were securely moored, and I shut-down the engine. We were getting better at this, even in awful conditions.

We had settled-in with our stern about 3 metres off in a small indentation in the cliff face. Our stern sounder indicated 7.8 metres beneath the rudder, and the bow sounder showed 8.4 beneath the front of the keel. The barometer was at 989.2 and falling, it was raining heavily and the wind gusted in unpredictable cycles from calm to 30 knots. We were warm and cozy below.

I had tucked our stern in against the cliffs protecting us from the southerly winds that would signal the moving on of the low pressure system. The system instead continued to slowly deepen; the barometer was 985.6 when I checked the lines and went to bed at midnight.

As I picked our way between the rocks and shoals, Edi reeled-in the stern-lines.

I was up at 0625 with the light pouring in the hatches in our cabin. I poked my head out into the cockpit to check the stern-lines, and was invited on up by the absolute stillness of the morning. There was not a breath of wind, the water was glassy-calm, the barometer was stable at 985.5.

I grabbed my iPad and the Italian Guide and headed back to bed for a conference with the Admiral. My supposition was that we were nearing the middle of a very large low pressure system, and that we should enjoy a rather calm period until the barometer begins to rise. We decided to get up and leave immediately to take advantage of the calm, and to breakfast en route.

By 0730 we had cleared the kelp-marked shoals and rocks and were out in the main channel of the Straits of Magellan. The Straits are 2 miles wide at this point, they were glassy-calm and we were motoring along with a slight boost of the flooding tide making 7 knots with turns for 6.5.

At 1040 we entered Paso Tortuoso and began to feel the influence of the tides coming in from the southeast, and we were slowed to below 5 knots at the narrows. Then in the early afternoon we began to benefit from the ebb down the other side and moved back above 6 knots.

I hoisted and secured the dinghy while Edi put the coffee on and secured below. We let-go the stern-lines and weighed at 0710 and motored out through mirror-like waters.

We had begun seeing whales spouting when we entered the shallower and narrower waters of Paso Tortuoso and Paso Ingles.

A few of them kept Sequitur company for a while, and from their fin and breathing characteristics, I identified them as fin whales.

Later, while Edi was below preparing lunch, I heard a very large splash off our port quarter, and turned to see an area of greatly disturbed water. A whale had breached a dozen metres away. I quickly grabbed the camera and pointed it in the direction of my best guess of where next it might appear. I was rewarded a while later by a spectacular tail-stand with the mountains as a backdrop.

I called Edi up from the galley, and we both watched and waited for the next breach. She finally needed to get back down to the lunch she was cooking, and shortly after she went, I watched a marvellous arching leap.

My rewards continued as Edi brought up the lunch basket of hot quesadillas with blue cheese, sun-dried tomatoes, black olives, chicken and a Chilean version of Gouda. We watched whales all around Sequitur, but we saw no more leaps.

In the early afternoon a southeast breeze of 3 or 4 knots came up, but by 1400 it was glassy calm again. The barometer continued its slow decline; 983.8 at 1100, 982.2 at noon, 981.3 at 1500. The sky remained totally overcast.

At 1700 there were chips of blue appearing in the western horizon and the barometer was down to 979.8. I figured the centre of the low was approaching us and we were seeing its eye. The chips grew to a narrow band with heaps of clouds beyond it, and this gave more credence to my thoughts on the eye of the depression. It appeared we were in for a short period of calm, followed by a shift to southwest winds.

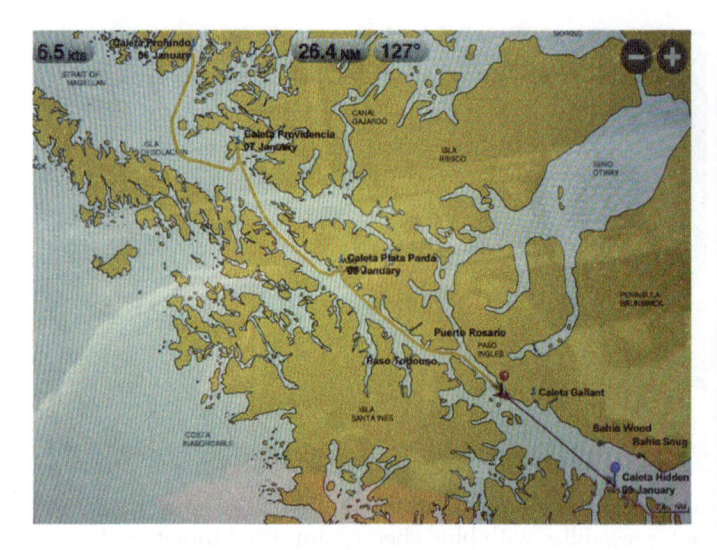

I had placed some symbols on the iPad to indicate locations of possible anchorages. In the calm conditions we had already passed the first of these, Puerto Rosario, and we had decided to press on to Caleta Hidden as long as conditions allowed.

As the afternoon progressed, the sun tried to burn through the altostratus, bit it didn't succeed. The barometer continued its downward trend, passing through 978.8 at 1800.

We easily found the entrance to Caleta Hidden, and threaded through the shallow narrows, with barely below-water rocks well-marked by kelp beds on our starboard side.

Close at hand on our port side was a mid-channel rock with a reef extending to the shore on the far side and rocks awash and kelp-marked submerged rocks on the near side. The navigable channel is about 10 metres wide and we found the least depth of 5 metres that was mentioned in the Italian Guide.

At 1857 we came to 30 metres of chain on the Rocna in 14 metres of water and launched the dinghy. I took two stern-lines ashore, looped them around stout trees and pulled them back aboard. I added a snubber to the anchor chain and veered another 5 metres while Edi hauled-in on the stern lines.

At 1918 we were nicely balanced between three points, and I shut-down the engine. We are getting better at this; only 21 minutes this time, but there were no contrary winds, nor was it raining. Within half an hour we were hit by torrential rain and swirling winds as a squall passed over, but we were well-secured, snug and dry; the furnace was on and the aromas of dinner were beginning to tease.

The barometer bottomed-out at 977.3 after dinner on Monday, and it was up to 982.3 when we went to bed at midnight. At 0745 on Tuesday morning it was up to 987 as Edi prepared breakfast.

Caleta Hidden was calm when we weighed at 0828 and picked our way back out through the narrows and into the Straits of Magellan. We were at the entrance to Canal Acwalisnan.

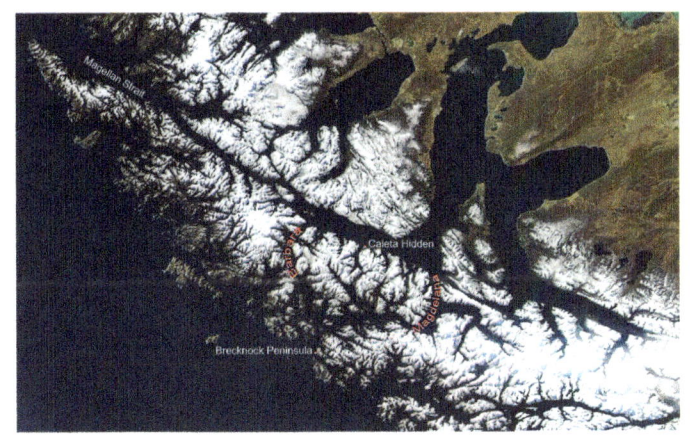

To get from the Straits of Magellan to the Beagle Channel there are three routes, from West to east they are: Canal Barbara, Canal Acwalisnan and Canal Magdalena. According to the Italian Guide: *"The Chilean Armada enforces rules very strictly in waters of the extreme south: only Canal Magdalena is an approved route, while navigation in the other two is prohibited."* In the Chilean Guide, we find: *"the only one authorized is Magdalena and the other two are prohibited"*. Both of these guides then go on to describe in detail the prohibited routes.

I again read our zarpe, which gives an overview of the routing we are to take: *"... Canal Smyth - Estrecho de Magallanes - Canal Brecknock ..."*. We were not told how to make passage south from the Straits of Magellan, so we chose the most direct route, Canal Acwalisnan, saving two days.

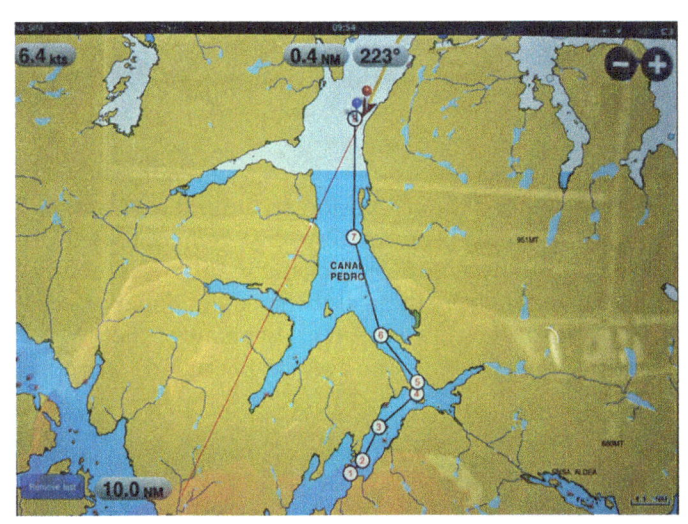

Likely the reason the Armada prohibits passage through Acwalisnan and has left it incompletely charted, is Paso O'Ryan in its middle. Here there is a least depth of 4 metres in the narrows constricted by rocks awash and hidden, and there are no aids to navigation. The flood tide can attain 8 knots, making it necessary to do the transit at slack water. Both Guides reported the tides were Bahia Woods plus 1 hour. Accordingly, our departure from Caleta Hidden was timed so that we would reach O'Ryan an hour after the turn of the tide.

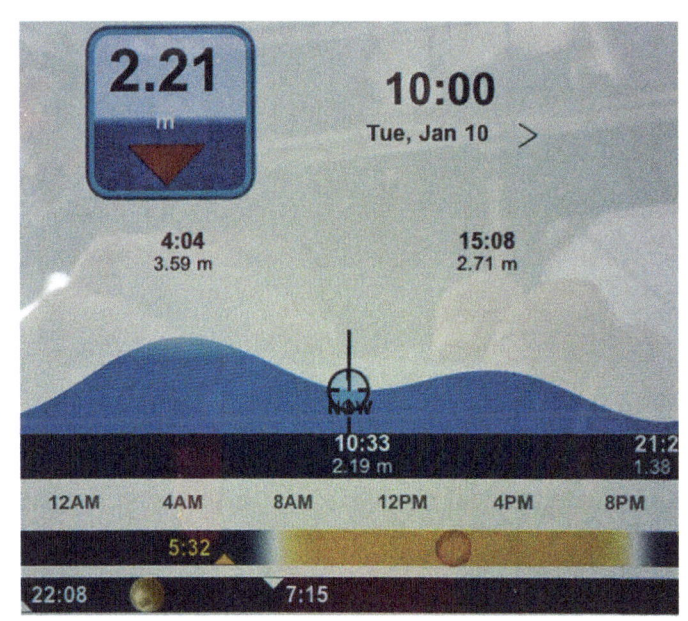

The tides were ideal for our passage, with an ebb to a rather high low at 1033 at Bahia Woods, 1133 at Paso O'Ryan, followed by a gentle flood to a rather low high. This meant we should experience minimal currents.

At 1100 we were 3.6 miles from the pass, making 6.6 knots and on schedule to be in the middle of the narrows within seconds of predicted slack water.

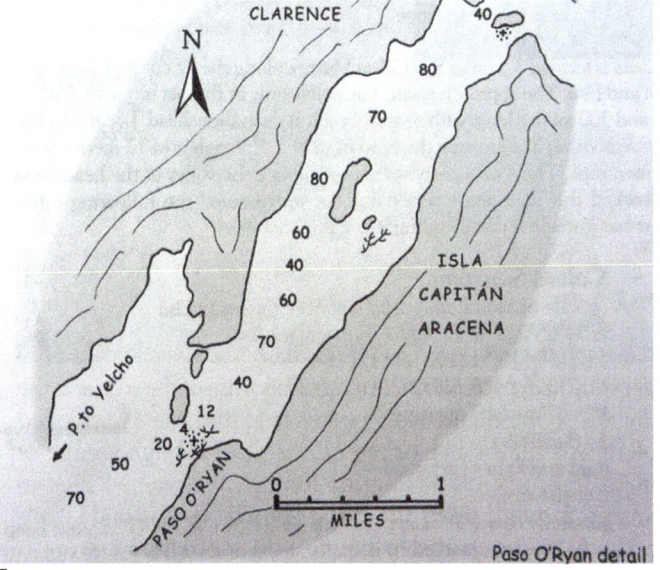

Paso O'Ryan detail

It was calm as crossed the summit of the pass and watched the sounder run rapidly up from over 30 metres depth to 20, 10, 6, 5 and then settle-in on 4 for a while, before racing back down to 20 and deeper, exactly as indicated in the detail on the chartlet in the Italian Guide. Paso O'Ryan was behind us.

Ahead of us was our first view of Tierra del Fuego. Ahead of also was the open Pacific, and we had to head into the wind, waves and swell down Canal Cockburn and expose ourselves to the open ocean to get around the western end of Isla Grande de Tierra del Fuego.

Edi brought up a basket of lunch and because of the seas and the rather frequent squalls, we clipped it onto the table. We enjoyed Italian salami, the beginning of our second huge wedge of asiago and some of the Puerto Montt cheese we had aged in our port forward hold, our root cellar. The cheese had taken-on a marvellous character, akin to a fine aged Gouda.

The barometer was slowly climbing; it was 991.8 at 1400 and 992.1 at 1500. The winds had come around from the northwest to the southwest, indicating the backside of the depression. They were blowing 25 to 30 knots, ripping crests off the whitecaps. The seas were 1 to 2 metres with 2 to 3 metre swells, so the conditions were rather benign for the area. At 1540 we put Punta Chasco abaft out beam.

At 1640 we entered Canal Ocasion and found lee from the seas and the winds. The squalls; however, continued to roar through with almost predictable regularity, seeming to come when we were in the tightest navigational places, nearing shoals, rocks or narrows. Fortunately, they were visible in advance both to the eye and the radar.

As we motored up the channel, I sensed overwhelmingly we were entering a flooded mountain cirque at 1500 metres in elevation, the tree-line and snow-line was that far displaced. At 1958 we secured with two bow lines and two stern lines ashore in Caleta Brecknock. The anchorage is notorious for its sudden and severe katabatic winds, called williwaws.

It had been another long day, eleven and a half hours of navigating through mostly uncharted or poorly charted waters.

Shortly after we had secured we dug three of the jerry cans of diesel out of the locker and I poured them through the deck fill into the auxiliary tank, which still had a bit in it. While I prepared dinner, I ran the transfer pump to move the contents of the auxiliary tank to the main tank, bringing it up to a needle's width above the quarter mark. This indicates about 180 litres remaining.

For dinner I sautéed some filete de blanquillo and served it with basmati rice with tarragon, a butter-sweat of julienned carrots, onions, green peppers and garlic and a garnish of sliced tomatoes with basil leaves in olive oil. To celebrate our arrival in Tierra del Fuego, we opened a bottle of Undurraga Brut. The skies opened-up to welcome us with a torrential downpour and the four lines ashore held Sequitur snugly against the williwaws.

29. Onward to Puerto Williams

A ridge that appears fifteen minutes away is topped in three or four. The next summit is made in a quarter of the estimate. Everything appears on a grand scale, but is in reality in miniature. From Sequitur's decks it appeared we were surrounded by soaring mountain walls. From the tops of those low rock bluffs, Sequitur looked large.

On Wednesday morning the barometer was up to 1005.2 from its midnight reading of 1000.1. After breakfast we took Non Sequitur ashore and went walking. We were amazed at how deceptive the distances are here.

548

Walking is pleasant on the ridge tops, but in the hollows and gullies there are many soft, squishy areas of wet-foot makers. We quickly learned to step on the tufts of grasses. After an exhilarating circuit, we were quickly back down to Sequitur.

Three minutes later we released the stern lines and hauled them in. We let-go the port bow line and hauled it in, and as I slowly backed out of the nook, Edi released and recovered the other bow line.

The wind was gusting to over 20 knots from all directions as I retrieved the anchor. Up with it came a large collection of kelp, which was easily cut away with the sickle-on-a-bamboo we had cobbled together.

The sky was a little over half filled with cumulus as we motored out of Caleta Brecknock and into Canal Ocasion. The barometer was very slowly climbing and the winds were fickle, coming from every direction and in all forces from 0 through 7. Edi prepared a breakfast of pain perdu with thinly-sliced salami and basil leaves, and we enjoyed it in the cockpit with fresh-ground Starbucks coffee

We were enjoying the southern summer weather; Edi was dressed in long underwear and fleece pants on the bottom and three layers of fleece plus her Gill offshore foul-weather jacket on top. Knee-high neoprene kayaking boots, hand-knitted woollen socks, woollen gloves and toque completed her outfit. We were so pleased that we have a fully enclosed cockpit, and need only these clothes to keep warm.

The charts are badly skewed in this area, with a variable datum shift, mostly between half and three-quarters of a mile. The land-forms depicted do not always reflect reality, and we have seen one substantial island missing from the chart. The squalls continued, and we were hit by one with 45-knot winds and an accompanying downpour as we entered Canal Brecknock.

The mountains appear to be of substantial height, in the 1800 to 2000 metre range, until the chart shows them to be only 500 metres or so high. Again we sensed we were sailing along at the 1500-metre level.

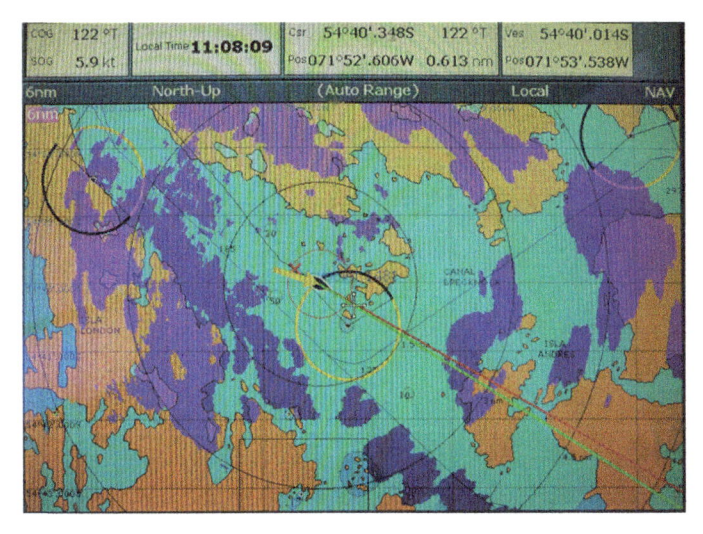

I found the radar very useful in relating the features we were seeing with the chart, as inaccurate as it is. Fortunately, the area is rather well marked with lights, beacons, and buoys, and these aided us in identifying our route as we picked our way among the islets and rocks.

In a lull between squalls, and once we were settled onto a longish leg, I went forward to bag the bow lines and stow them back down in the sail locker. The laid rope of these lines is less easy to handle than is the braided rope we have on the stern-line reels. It twists and kinks, but thankfully because it is so slippery, it rarely snarls.

We threaded our way for 56.8 miles through Canal Brecknock and Canal Ballenero to an anchorage in Caleton Silva. Along the way we were hit by seven squalls during the 10.5 hours of the passage and saw the skew in the chart datum vary from half a mile to well over a mile.

At 1940 we came to 35 metres on the Rocna in 8.8 metres of water toward the northern side of the small bay for more protection from the northerly winds. The datum was offset 1.2 miles northeast. This was our first anchorage in a long while without lines ashore; we were protected from the winds, the fetch and had room to swing. The barometer had peaked midmorning at 1005.5, and had then steadily declined, reading 999.6 when we anchored.

On Thursday morning the barometer was on its way up again, having climbed overnight to 1005.3 when we sat down for a breakfast of toasted split baguettes with cream cheese, smoked salmon, capers and basil leaves in olive oil.

The windlass appeared to have mangled itself internally. It is one of the Lewmar models with both gipsy and line drum, and while the windlass motor ran, but the gipsy and drum did not turn. I made sure the clutch was tightened and tried again. The burrr of the motor running was all that happened; it was all noise and no action. The hand crank refused to turn the gipsy and drum. I bent a chain hook onto the end of our starboard stern line, hooked the chain and ran the line back around the jib sheet winches and up to the power winch at the forward end of the cockpit.

A 14-metre pull, a snubber set at the bow, a reset of the chain hook, another 14-metre pull, another snubber set and the anchor was aweigh, but trailing.

Fortunately the wind was blowing us out of the caleta and into clear water past the reefs at its northerly point allowing us the time to do this exercise.

The winds were variable 10 to 35 knots from the west and northwest and there were a few chinks of blue showing in an otherwise darkly overcast sky of billowing nimbostratus. Squalls were frequent. By 1000 the barometer had started on its way back down again, passing through 1003.

Ahead lay the Beagle Channel, and over it were clear blue skies, offering distant glimpses of the snow-clad peaks along its shores. The mountains appeared to be 3000 to 4000 metres high, rather than the 1500 to 2500 metres they really are.

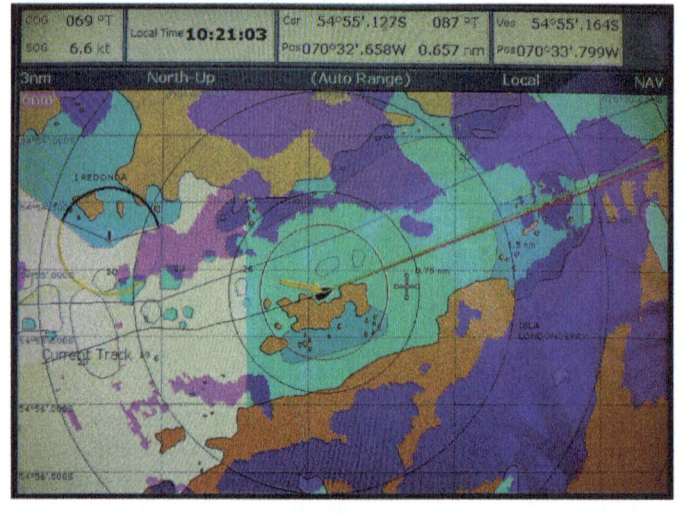

The charting is absurdly inaccurate for such a well-travelled route. We were met by two outbound coastal freighters as we made our way past Isla Darwin and into Brazo Nordeste del Canal Beagle.

552

The distant sky remained enticingly blue as we continued east, but our cover of clouds seemed to be moving in pace with us, along with the occasional squalls and rain showers. The barometer maintained its slow downward trend, passing through 1001.7 at noon.

Shortly after noon we were overtaken by the small cruise ship, Via Australis, one of a number which offer access for armchair travellers to this remote area, allowing them a passing view of the scenery from the comfort of their lounges. While their scenery is the same as ours, we get to feel its fabric.

The winds built through the early afternoon and the barometer continued its decline, 997.8 at 1500, 994.7 at 1600. The steep pressure drop brought northwest winds above 30 knots at 1600 and then at 1720 they passed 40 knots.

The mountains along the Beagle channel look so much like the scenes in which I played during my climbing days of the 60s, 70s and 80s. I saw vistas reminiscent of the Tiedeman and Tellot Glaciers on the way to climb Mount Waddington in British Columbia; of Alaska's North Baird Glacier up which I went three times chasing unclimbed peaks in the Stikine Icecap; of the Hindu Kush in northeast Afghanistan where I had chased other unclimbed summits; and of the Aiguilles above Chamonix, where I joyously played many times.

The only difference was that the mountains along the Beagle are truncated, cut-off at the knees, missing their bottom 1500 to 3000 metres. Either that or they are confused between feet and metres.

We poked Sequitur's nose in toward the foot of a tidewater glacier, but because of the reef on the lee shore and the winds in the mid-40s, we didn't go too close in.

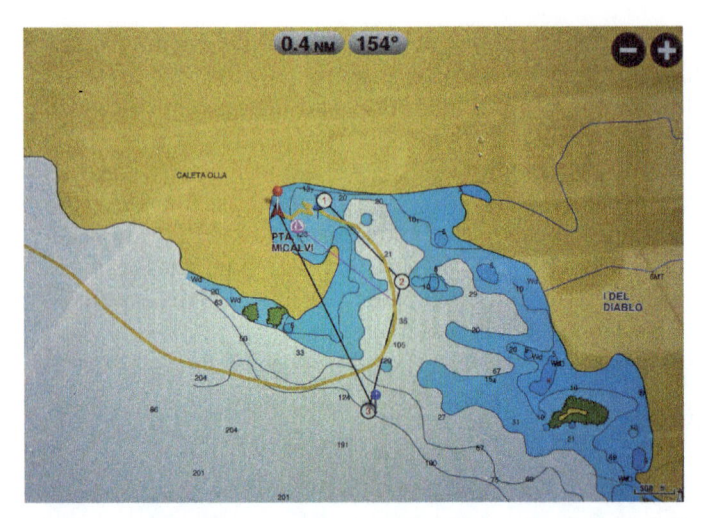

At 1810 we came to 65 metres on the Rocna in 15 metres of water and backed in toward the lee of a line of trees on the western side of Caleta Olla.

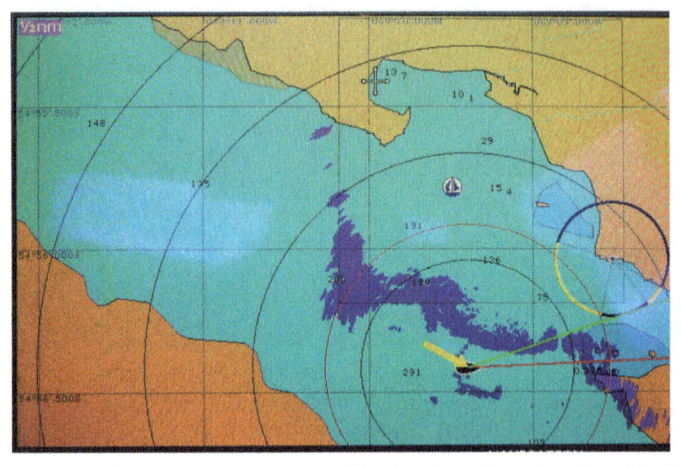

Again, the one-year-newer Navionics chart in the iPad showed a newly published chart of Caleta Olla. It is much more closely gridded to GPS than is the earlier version in the chart-plotter, which had us out in the middle of the Beagle Channel.

There were two boats, Antipode and Polar Wind, already at anchor and stern tied. Two men dinghied over from Antipode and offered to take our stern-lines ashore and tie them to trees. This made our mooring for the night so much easier, particularly with the offshore wind filtering through the trees.

We were 55 miles, just one day away from Puerto Williams, and we had logged 1255.6 miles since leaving Puerto Montt five weeks previously. Being only a day away from Puerto Williams, this anchorage is popular for the small charter operators on their view-the-glacier tours along the Beagle Channel. An hour after we had settled-in, a third charter boat, Lille d'Elle arrived, anchored and stern-tied next to us. This was the first time we had seen other sailboats since Puerto Eden, and only the second time in the month since Castro.

When I got up on Friday the 13th the barometer was up to 997.4 from its midnight reading of 994.6. I have always considered Friday the 13th as a lucky day. I was born on the 13th, and turned 13 on a Friday the 13th.

After breakfast I organized chain hooks and shackles on the foredeck in preparation for winching-in the Rocna. We then launched the dinghy and I went ashore in the light rain to release the stern-lines. There was little wind at water level, but our mast-top anemometer showed it was blowing northwest 20 with gusts to 25. At 1100 I let-go the stern-lines and pulled the dinghy back out to Sequitur.

While Edi reeled-in the port stern-line, I took the starboard one forward to rig it for shortening-in the 65 metres of chain we had out. At 1123 we began winching-in the chain in 12-metre hauls, then snubbing it, resetting the winch line and hauling again. By 1145 we had done four of these pulls and brought the chain to up-and-down, and the 25-knot westerly wind pulled the anchor clear of the bottom as we drifted into deeper water.

554

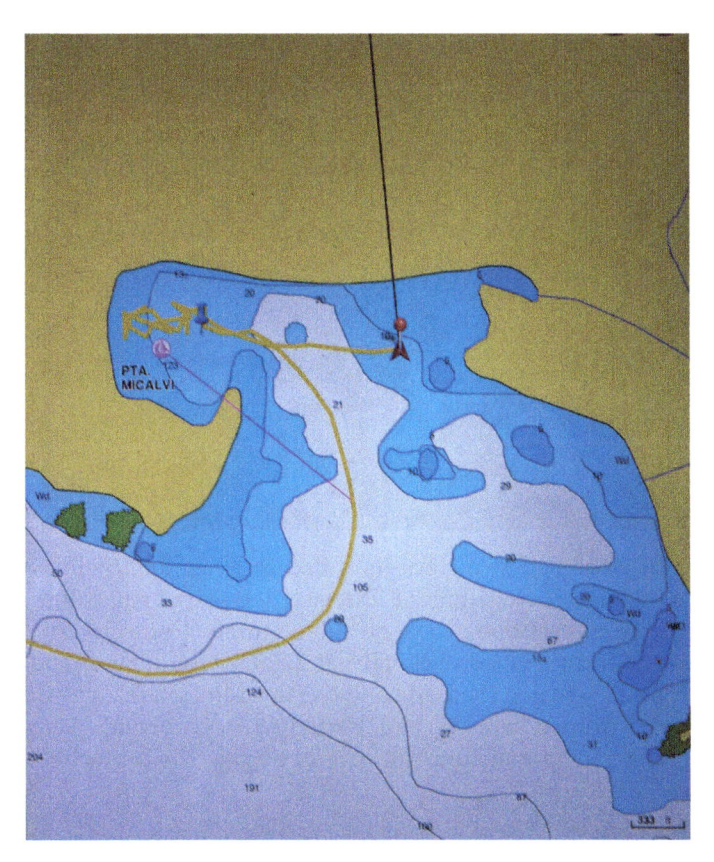

Sequitur was facing north, so I put the engine astern and turned the helm to port to back out past Punta Micalvi through the area of 20 metre and deeper soundings. We made no sternway; the wind continued blowing us, still facing north, straight east. I ran forward and veered the Rocna's chain to 22 metres as our keel touched bottom at 1154. The Rocna held the bow pointing north, while our keel nestled alongside an apparently soft shoal.

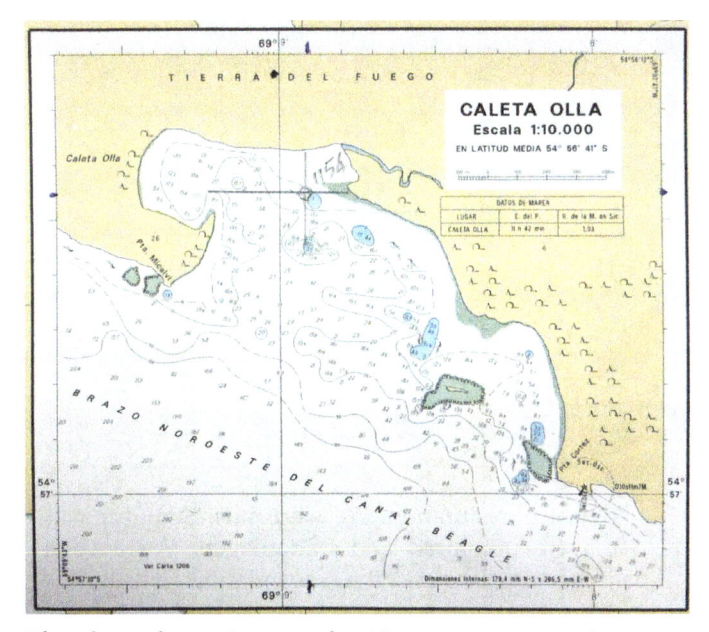

The chart showed us on the 10-metre contour, close to a 1-metre patch, the iPad showed us on the deeper side of the 10-metre contour, the chart-plotter showed us in the middle of the Beagle Channel and the depth sounder showed us in 2.0 metres of water. We decided to believe the depth sounder.

The wind pushed against Sequitur's port side and the Rocna held our bows pointing north. Had we a working windlass, I could have pulled Sequitur off, but with the wind building through 30 knots, I decided not to risk shortening scope while exposing our stern, and therefore, our rudder to the shoal.

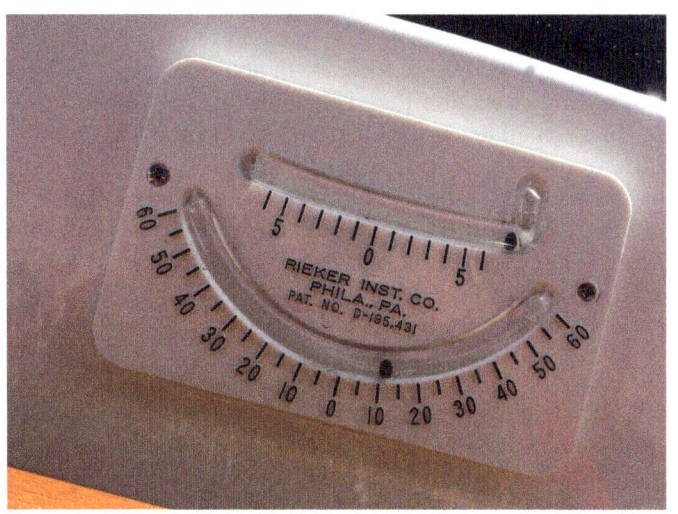

We took-on a 12° list to starboard.

I figured out why we had been unable to make sternway; the Lewmar transmission linkage had failed again. I had replaced it in La Punta in November 2010, after it had failed during our departure from Paita, Peru. This made our sticky situation even more sticky.

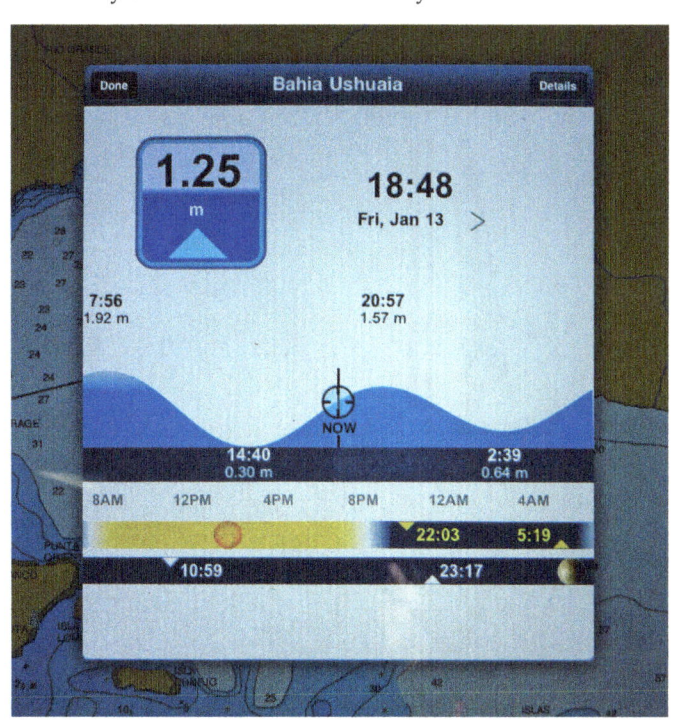

We were about mid-tide, on an ebb at 1154 when we ran aground. From predictions for Ushuaia 30 miles away, the level was 0.89 metres and it was predicted to drop to 0.30 metres at 1440. We had another 60 centimetres to fall. The next high was 1.57 metres at 2057. The predictions for Puerto Williams 25 miles further along were parallel and only 6 minutes later. I figured from this that Caleta Olla was 6 or 7 minutes earlier than Ushuaia.

I reported our situation to Alcamar Yamana, the Armada radio station for the area. I told them we were safe and in no immediate danger, and that we would most likely float free in the early evening. The skipper of Polar Wind, one of the other sailboats in the anchorage, discussed the situation, and he translated more precise details of our situation to the watch-keeper at Yamana.

Though the winds were forecast to abate in the evening, through the afternoon they continued to strengthen into the 40s with gusts above 50 knots. It was directly on our beam, and added a few degrees to our list, which never went beyond 15°. The shoal is apparently steep-sided; as the tide fell, Sequitur's keel seemed to simply slide down its face. The tide bottomed at 1430. The barometer was up a bit to 998.8. I watched wind gusts of 48, 51 and 54 on the gauge; there were stronger gusts when I wasn't watching.

We floated free at 1830, and I went forward and by hand shortened-in the chain by 3 metres to pull us into slightly deeper water. The winds were gradually abating as predicted, and were in the 20s, though there were still gusts into the upper 30s. At 2000 I began discussing plans for our extrication with the skipper of Polar Wind.

A quarter hour later four men came aboard from Polar Wind and Antipode and helped me organize the lines and to prepare the Rocna and its 100 metres of chain for jettisoning. We took the two polypropylene bow lines, joined them to make a 160-metre tow line. We tied a mooring line and a fender to the snubber on the anchor chain and undid its bitter end. When we saw Lille d'Elle leave her anchorage and head toward us, we fed the chain out of its locker and overboard.

We passed the tow line to Lille d'Elle by dinghy, and once it was secured and we began moving forward, we undid the anchor snubber and jettisoned the remaining chain with its attached snubber, mooring line and float.

At 2043 we had two stern-lines tied to trees, the towline was detached from Lille d'Elle, and the skipper and his mate from Antipode took our 20-kilogram Delta out 80 metres and dropped it. Finally, at 2058, we had balanced Sequitur between the Delta and the stern-lines, back a few metres from where we had started in the morning. We reported to Yamana our safe arrival back in the protected side of Caleta Olla.

We reflected on the events of the day and concluded that Friday the 13th was very lucky for us. The shoal had been soft and steep-sided, the Rocna had held us beam-on to the shoal, the wind was on the beam, we were with the first boats with which we had shared an anchorage in nearly two weeks, only the second in over a month, the skippers were professional. Had our engine transmission linkage and windlass conspired to fail together almost anywhere else during the previous month, it would have been much worse.

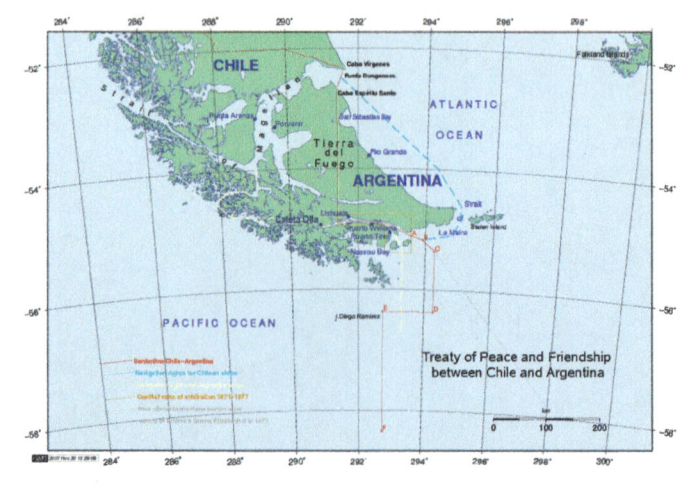

We looked at our situation. We were safe, Sequitur was safe, we were uninjured and undamaged. We needed to repair the windlass and the transmission linkage. We needed to recover the Rocna and its 100 metres of chain. The wind was predicted to be 25 to 30 through the day on Saturday, then strengthen overnight to the mid-40s. Puerto Williams was 55 miles downwind, 30 miles past Ushuaia, Argentina. Our zarpe was to Puerto Williams. There are strange politics, outstanding border disputes and there is much border posturing between Chile and Argentina.

There is a long-standing border dispute between Chile and Argentina, primarily concerning possession of Picton, Lennox and Nueva Islands and with the scope of the maritime jurisdiction associated with those islands. The dispute brought the countries to the brink of war in 1978.

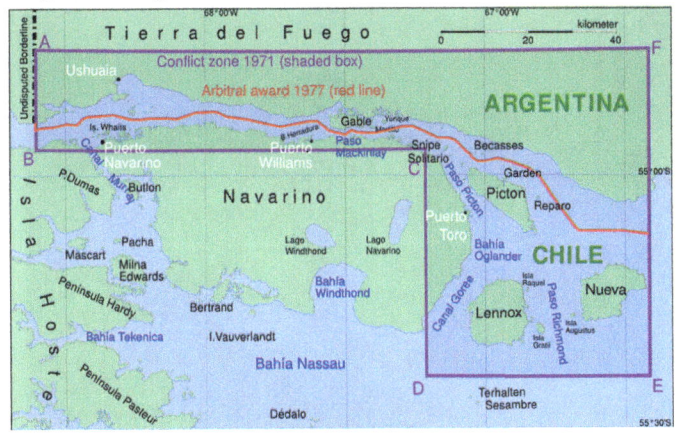

The conflict began in 1904 with the first official Argentine claims over these islands that had always been under Chilean control. The conflict passed through direct negotiations, then in 1971 the two countries agreed to submit the dispute to binding arbitration. In 1975 a binding international award confirmed the islands belonged to Chile. After refusing to abide by the decision, the Argentine junta pushed the controversy to the brink of war in 1978 in order to produce a maritime boundary consistent with Argentine claims.

In 1979 the dispute was submitted to the Vatican for papal mediation, and in 1984 the Chilean claims were again upheld. Although Argentina signed the 1984 Treaty officially recognizing the islands as Chilean territory, they still unofficially consider them as their own.

I asked the watch-keeper at Alcamar Yamana if we could proceed directly to Ushuaia, and received a very definite no. We must first go to Puerto Williams to clear-out through Immigration and the Armada.

I opened-up the access panels into the back of the engine and the transmission and then flashed-up the engine. With Edi watching over the stern, I went below and shifted the lever on the transmission upwards. The shaft turned, the boat moved slowly forward. I marked in the deck log: *"UP - FORWARD, DOWN - ASTERN"*. We had workable, if somewhat awkward power.

I was up at 0715 to see the barometer down overnight to 999.8, the sky full of low nimbostratus and the sprinkling of a light rain. We had breakfast and then prepared for the task ahead. I organized the assorted chain hooks, shackles, strops, lines and the spinnaker halyard. I flashed-up the engine and instructed Edi on the operation of the transmission lever, and tested it.

We launched the dinghy and I rowed ashore and untied the stern-lines, then Edi pulled me back out with one of them. We clipped the dinghy to the davit falls and hoisted it just off the water.

We then began shortening-in the rode on the Delta using the spinnaker halyard, hauling-in about 16 metres per set. At 0941, toward the end of our fourth set, the wind blew the anchor free and we drifted into deeper water trailing the Delta on 15 metres of chain. I had Edi shift the transmission into forward, and we slowly motored toward our fender marking the Rocna. A few minutes later I swung Sequitur around hard to port and had Edi shift to neutral and allowed our way and the wind to slowly carry us toward the fender. As we drifted, I went forward and waited to see the anchor chain indicate the Delta was skipping along the bottom. At what I deemed the appropriate moment, I veered sufficient rode to allow the anchor to bite, veered a bit more and snubbed it and watched the anchor set at 0948. The bow was in 7.5 metres of water, the stern in 4.8, and the marker above the snubber shackle was about 20 metres off our stern. I estimated we were directly over the Rocna.

We lowered the dinghy and I rowed it over to the marker with a stern-line from the reel, tied the stern-line to the mooring line on the fender and had Edi pull me back to Sequitur. At 0952 I was back onboard with the marker fender. Then up on the foredeck I hauled in as much of the mooring line as I could by hand before it came to the weight of the chain. With a prussic knot around the line, we used the spinnaker halyard to hoist the snubber and then a bight of the chain onto the deck. I shackled the end of another snubber to the chain and took turns on a cleat. We reset the spinnaker halyard, took-up the strain, removed the snubber and with Edi on the power winch button, we hoisted a 15-metre bight of chain.

On the next reset and hoist we had the Rocna aboard; we had been very close over it. We still had 80 metres of chain to recover, so we continued the slow and deliberate process, until at 1215 we finally shipped the bitter end.

I next took the starboard stern-line to a prussic knot on the Delta rode and we prepared to weigh with the power winch. We were lightly stuck in the soft bottom through a combination of falling tide and a slowly dragging Delta in the sustained 25-knot winds. Edi went below and shifted the transmission ahead and I tried to power Sequitur out of the muck. Edi came back up and worked the power winch while I did the throttle. We finally managed to pop the keel out and we burst ahead trailing the Delta into deeper water.

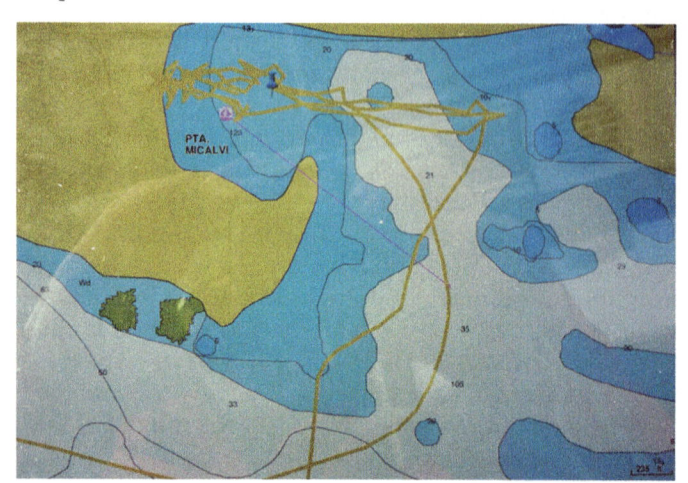

Sequitur's track on the iPad offered some interesting doodles of our time in Caleta Olla.

Once we had cleared the caleta and set course eastward along the Beagle, I went forward and began to sort-out the jumble of anchors, chain, lines and hardware. We attacked the trailing Delta first by looping a line around its chain and working the loop aft and up to a side cleat. Then the spinnaker halyard was put to use again to hoist the chain and the Delta aboard. We were motoring directly downwind, and with our 7 knots speed, the 25 knot winds were much more comfortable.

There was still much to do on the foredeck, but we were very weary from our exertions and rather hungry. I came back to the cockpit to get out of the wind and to relax for a bit, while Edi went below and prepared some pesto, shrimp, sun-dried tomato, black olive and cheese panini for lunch.

I had reported our anchor recovery and departure from Caleta Olla to Alcamar Yamana after we had settled-in on a safe course along the Beagle Channel. The watch-keeper told us that it had been arranged that we could stop at Puerto Navarino and do our out-clearance from there. He asked for an ETA, and I told him I was rather busy at the moment and that I would need to find Puerto Navarino on the charts and in the pilots, and that I would get back to him in 30 minutes.

After I found Puerto Navarino, directly across the channel from Ushuaia, I gave an ETA of 1800. I went back onto the foredeck and fed the Rocna's chain out around the bow roller and back down into its locker, then we used the spinnaker halyard to hoist the 40 kilo anchor around and into its place on the bow roller. Next I stowed the Delta and tidied-up the deck. All the while the following wind remained above 25 knots. Finally with clear decks, we hauled-out sails and we ran at 8 knots and more.

558

At 1731 we came to 40 metres on the Delta in 13 metres of water in front of the Alcamar house in Puerto Navarino. Like the other Alcamar posts, Navarino is manned by one Armada member who lives there with his family for a year. The Alcamar house in Navarino was built in 1928 as the administration centre for the region. It remained as such until the founding of Puerto Williams in 1951.

When we had settled-in on the anchor, we launched the dinghy, mounted its motor and headed ashore to meet the station watch-keeper. As we were motoring ashore in the dinghy, Edi was looking back at Sequitur, and saw the Rocna drop from its bow roller into the water. I had removed the securing line from it to launch the Delta, and I had forgotten to re-secure it. We turned around and I hurried onto the foredeck to see if I could stop all the chain from running out. I was too late; the locker was empty.

I got back into the dinghy and we carried-on ashore. The population of Puerto Navarino is seven. The Armada watch-keeper, Alamiro Villarroel, his wife Valeska and their son Vicente had just arrived in the post in December to begin their year. They plied us with coffee and cupcakes and we enjoyed a very pleasant visit. I left our zarpe, passports and visas with Alamiro, and we returned to Sequitur to begin recovering the Rocna and all its chain for the second time that day.

I didn't want to risk undoing the shackle from the bitt, so we needed a few short hauls with the spinnaker halyard to get enough chain on deck before we could hoist a full run up the mast. Each pull takes as much chain off the deck as it does from the water. The wind began building from the southwest as we worked, and after nearly two hours it was blowing above 30 knots.

We were in to just shy of 25 metres on the Rocna and the Delta had slowly dragged so that the Rocna was taking strain in the yaws to starboard. I decided to snub the chain to a midships cleat on the port side. The rocks to leeward were too close to think of veering more scope.

I was up every couple of hours through the night to ease the Delta's rode a few centimetres to freshen the chafe spot. The wind was well up into the 40s. At 0710 on Sunday morning the barometer was up steeply to 1004.5, and the winds continued to howl through the bay. The forecast was for decreasing winds in the evening. At 1400 they were still blowing in the 40s with the occasional gust above 50, and the barometer had risen to 1008. The Rocna held us; the rode on the Delta was slack except at the end of the yaws.

The winds began abating in the late afternoon, and at 1800 they were down to 10 to 12 knots and the barometer was up to 1009.8. Alamiro, the Armada watch-keeper called us on VHF and asked me to come to the office. He had the previous day asked for a written report of our grounding in Caleta Olla, and I had compiled a three-page report and put it onto a USB stick. I took with me a bag of things that Edi had assembled from the pantry that we had not yet found use for, and could not foresee any.

Alamiro and I did our business, and he told me that the zarpe would be ready on Tuesday afternoon. The weather forecast for Monday was for calm, with 5 to 10 knot winds in the late day and increasing slightly into Tuesday. Alamiro and Valeska invited me upstairs to their home for coffee. Before I left, Valeska had finished baking some bread and packaged-up three loaves and Alamiro added a bottle of wine. I went back out to Sequitur, and Edi and I enjoyed a delightfully casual dinner of fresh, hot bread and cheeses with 2009 Terra Andina Reserva Merlot-Syrah.

It was calm overnight, and on Monday morning the sea was a mirror. Sequitur had swung around and she was pointing toward the reef and rocks to the east, toward which her stern had been blown in the 40 and 50 knot winds of the previous day and a half. She was laying quietly to the Rocna. The Delta's rode was limp.

To our north, across the Beagle Channel was Ushuaia, Argentina. Closer, I estimated a little under 100 metres away, was an Armada mooring buoy. I had asked Alamiro about and he had said that since there was no Armada ship on it, it would be okay for us to use it temporarily

As I was organizing lines in preparation for attaching Sequitur to the buoy to make it safer to begin the long process of weighing, an Armada patrol vessel entered the bay and headed toward the buoy.

Fortunately, Alacalufe was on a patrol and just passing through, so I continued the preparations. I attached the end of the port stern-line to the dinghy and motored over to the buoy, looped the line through the eye of the buoy's strop and headed back toward Sequitur. I pulled the line taught and secured it to itself.

Back onboard Sequitur, using our sickle-on-a-bamboo, I began clearing some of the huge accumulation of kelp that had snarled around the rode of the Delta and the chain and snubber line of the Rocna.

With a sheet winch, I then warped our stern toward the buoy to bring the bow more closely over the Rocna. Then we began the multi-step process of weighing the Rocna using the spinnaker halyard:

- clip in,
- take-up the strain,
- undo the snubber,
- winch up 5 metres,
- cut away the kelp,
- winch up 5 metres,
- cut away the kelp,
- winch up 5 metres,
- set the snubber,
- ease the bight of chain down to deck,
- cut away the kelp,
- Repeat.

Shortly after 1300 the shank of the Rocna appeared through the kelp, and the task of kelp clearing became more serious.

Shortly before 1400 we had the Rocna on deck.

561

We took a breather for a quick lunch; the wind was coming up, and we didn't want to delay too long our move to the buoy.

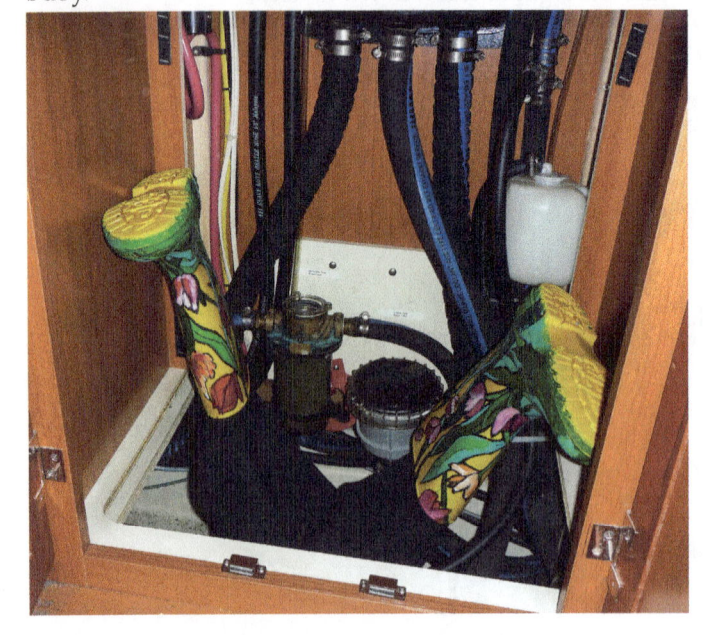

After our quick lunch, I rigged the starboard-stern-line to a prussic knot on the Delta's rode and ran it to the power winch in the cockpit. I started the engine and sent Edi below to hang down into the space beneath the port aft wet locker to have quick access the transmission shift lever, in case we needed to use the engine.

Up-top, I shortened-in the Delta, snubbed the rode with a prussic, re-set the stern-line, undid the snubber, shortened-in further, snubbed the rode with a prussic, re-set the stern-line, undid the snubber and hauled the Delta to the surface in a great tangle of kelp.

I then undid the starboard stern-line from the winch, turned-up the port stern-line, which was attached to the buoy and began warping Sequitur's stern across to the buoy. The wind was about 12 knots on our beam and blowing directly toward the rocks and reef. We were slowly making our way across to the buoy, slowed by the tangle of kelp. I twice had Edi shift the engine astern for a short while to quicken the pace.

Finally, at 1535 Sequitur's stern was within 20 metres of the buoy, and her bow had room to swing clear of the kelp-marked reef. I shut-down the engine and relieved Edi from her transmission lever duties. We then set to work at clearing the tangle of kelp on the Delta, Edi on the sickle-on-a-bamboo and me on the weed-hook-on-a-curtain-rod. We were so thankful that we had cobbled-together these tools.

With the kelp tangle cleared, I used the dinghy to run mooring lines from our side and bow cleats, and in a couple of steps, had the buoy's strop around our starboard bow cleat with a safety line through the strop's eye and across to the port bow cleat. It was a few minutes past 1600.

562

I took a short break and then went forward to sort-out the tangle of chain, lines, strops, snubbers and anchors on the foredeck. I was able to hand-in the Delta and settle it in its bow roller, and after I had re-stowed its rode in proper order for use, I attacked the Rocna's chain. Finally, at 1822, with the aid of the spinnaker halyard and Edi on the power winch button, I set the Rocna into its bow roller and lashed it in place.

I mixed a measure of oil into one of the jerry cans of gasoline on the foredeck, and refilled the dinghy's fuel tank. It was our first refilling since buying the dinghy and outboard in La Punta in December 2010. Alamiro had asked us to come back in with our ship's papers; the previous visit he had omitted asking us for our Customs documents.

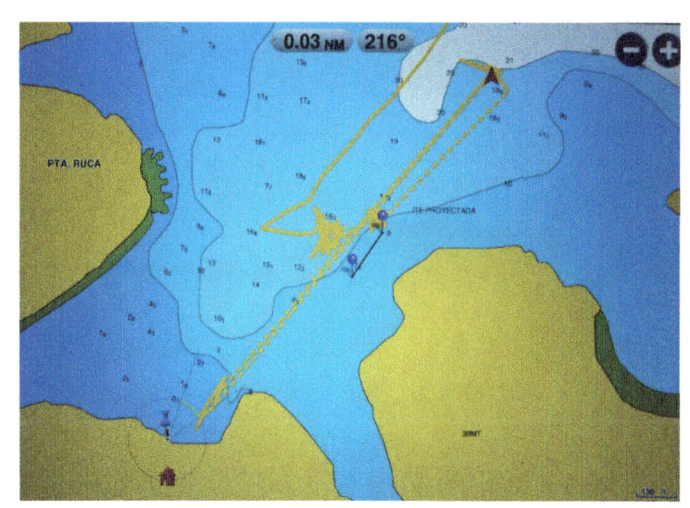

I had brought my iPad ashore with me, and its GPS confirmed my visual fix that had showed the chart skewed about 0.3 cables southwest.

When Alamiro finished his business with the other boat, I gave him our Customs documents. Then Valeska invited Edi and me upstairs for coffee and what looked exactly like an Italian panettone. It is a Christmas staple in most of South America.

When we arrived ashore, Alamiro was busy with a local fishing boat, so while we waited for him, we walked over to the point to read a plaque, which outlined the historical significance of the place.

We were back onboard by 2100, an hour before sunset, and watched the slow progression of high-latitude twilight. The skies leafed through a few more pages of the cloud catalogue for us, including lenticular, cirrostratus and a marvellous example of cirrocumulus mackerel.

Tuesday morning was again calm, and the water was near glassy. The barometer had dropped slightly overnight to 1006.4. I ran the generator and water-maker to bring the levels up and I ran the Espar furnace to heat the boat and make hot water, and we waited for a call from Alamiro that he had received our zarpe and was coming out to deliver it to us.

Alamiro called us on VHF at 1530 and said there was a problem with our papers, and asked me to come ashore to discuss options. I took Non Sequitur to the float and walked up to the Armada office. I was told there that Sequitur's Declaracion de Admision Temporal had expired, and that we had to go to Puerto Williams to renew it before a zarpe could be issued for us to leave Chile.

Frustrated and confused, I rushed back out to Sequitur and explained to Edi what I knew of the situation as we hoisted the motor off the dinghy and hoisted and secured the dinghy. I flashed-up the engine and sent Edi back down into the hole to shift the transmission, and at 1550 we slipped from the buoy and headed out of Puerto Navarino, bound for Puerto Williams.

30. Repair to Papers and Equipment

The wind in the Beagle Channel was initially in our stern at 10 knots, so it barely shaped the sails as we motor-sailed eastward along the Beagle Channel making 7.5 knots with the tide. I had reported our departure to Alamiro by VHF, and gave an ETA Puerto Williams of 2000. Along the way we met one sleek high-speed and two obviously cheaper catamarans whisking tourists back to Ushuaia from day-trips to view penguins and glaciers.

I ran the water-maker for 3 hours to bring the tanks up to better than half full. At 1850 the wind veered from light westerly to light east-northeast, and I adjusted the sails. Within ten minutes the wind had veered around to east, and increased to 15 knots. In less then a quarter hour it had gone from west at 10 knots to east at 15, directly on our nose. I rolled-in the sails.

By 1940, when we rounded the cardinal buoy marking the north end of Banco Herradura, the wind had backed to north-northeast and increased to 20 knots. I contacted Puerto Williams Radio to announced our approach and explained our compromised anchoring capability and our lack of proper engine control. I requested a mooring either alongside the Micalvi or on a buoy.

The Armada radio operator told us there was no space available at the Club Naval de Yates Micalvi, nor was there an available buoy. He told us we must anchor. I chose a spot out of the channel with the broadest belt of soundings between 5 and 10 metres, and when we found 7.5 metres on the sounder, with Sequitur slow ahead and stemming the wind, I went forward to hand-launch the Delta. Just before I let go, Edi called me back to tell me the Armada operator called and said, *"No, not there, further north"*. As we fell off and I manoeuvred back up into the wind, I again explained our compromised handling and anchoring capability to the Armada.

The Armada was watching Sequitur both visually, by radar and on AIS, so they knew exactly where we were. We slowly motored directly into the wind, which at 20 knots kept us barely moving forward at engine idle; this was good, as it gave me some control on our speed without having to banish Edi to the engine room to shift in and out of gear. A few minutes later, the Armada operator told us to anchor where we were. It looked safe, so at 2016 we came to 30 metres on the Delta in 8.8 metres of water, and I sent Edi below to shift the transmission to neutral. The wind pushed us back and we gently set the anchor on the mud bottom. Off our port bow was a pair of leading marks on the slope of the shore, and we were south of their transit line.

After we had shut-down the engine and settled-in, another Armada voice called us on the VHF. We were told we couldn't anchor there; we were in the airport runway approach. The transit markers that we saw off our bow mark the northern edge of the runway. We discussed our great difficulty in weighing and manoeuvring. Then the skipper of Polar Wind came on the radio, explaining he had seen us come in, and had rushed over to the Armada office, and would explain our compromised situation.

565

At 2124 the Puerto Williams Pilot called on the radio and informed us we must move to a buoy in the inner basin. I reiterated our difficulty in moving. The pilot said for $100 the pilot vessel could take us in. This seemed a good bargain for the service, and I told him to arrange it.

At 2142 the pilot boat arrived with its crew of three, plus four Armada personnel. The boat was quickly secured alongside, and under the direction of their petty officer, the three Armada ratings hauled-in the anchor rode as I pointed its lay to the skipper of the pilot vessel. At 2155 we secured to the buoy in the basin close to Micalvi. I gave the skipper 50,000 and thanked his crew and the Armada personnel. We had arrived in Puerto Williams.

The barometer had floated between 1005.8 and 1007.0 all day Tuesday and was at 1006.4 when I got up at 0845 on Wednesday. It was completely calm with a low stratus overhead. We were less than a cable from Micalvi, the Armada supply ship built in 1925 and after long service in the south, purposely run aground in 1962 to serve as a mooring pontoon and it subsequently became the most southerly yacht club in the world.

After breakfast we launched Non Sequitur and rowed over to the gravel strand next to Micalvi, and we walked along the gravel road to the offices of the Capitan de Puerto. There we were told to go to the Aduana, the Customs office. We followed the sketch map we were given and arrived at Aduana to find the office empty. We were told that the woman would be back in a while. We waited.

While we waited we met Martin, ground agent for some small cruise ships, including Via Australis, which we had seen a few days previously in the Beagle Channel. He speaks very fine English, and he kindly offered assistance. We asked where we could buy diesel, and he showed us on our map where the Copec station is. Then he offered to help us transport some to the boat with his truck.

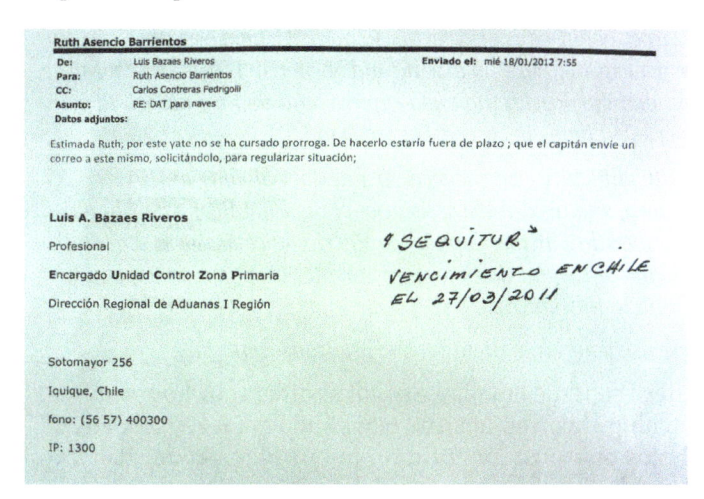

We had arrived in Puerto Williams with an empty auxiliary and nearly empty main fuel tank. The level was below the intake for both the Espar furnace and the generator, but thankfully, not for the engine.

The Aduana official did return in a while, as promised. With great flurry and gesticulation she showed us a copy of an email, blunting her finger as she pointed-out that Sequitur was illegally in Chile. She spoke no English, so our conversation was rather choppy and truncated. From it, I gathered that we must get down on our knees and write an email to Aduana in Iquique and offer contrition for our not having renewed Sequitur's Declaracion de Admision Temporal every three months, and beg that we not be given too many lashes for our grievous transgression. She said that in five days or a week, a decision will be made on our fate.

We met Martin outside the office, and he drove us back to the dinghy and we all went out to Sequitur. I loaded the four diesel jugs into the dinghy and Martin and I rushed back ashore, hoping to make the filling station before the 1300 shut-down for midday siesta. We made it with a couple of minutes to spare, and for 54,500 I had 80 litres of diesel pumped into our jerry cans. Martin then drove me and the fuel back to Micalvi, dramatically simplifying the process of getting fuel.

I poured the contents of the four jugs into the auxiliary tank and then transferred it all to the main, bringing the level there up to just a hair shy of the quarter mark. The main holds 150 US gallons, 568 litres, so the gauge indicated we had brought the level up to 130 or 140 litres, and that there would have been about 50 or 60 litres remaining when we arrived.

After fuelling both Sequitur and ourselves, we headed back ashore. This time we needed to get our passport visas renewed; it was 90 days since we had returned from Vancouver, and our visas were due to expire at midnight. We had hoped to have arrived in Ushuaia, Argentina before their expiry, and avoid the 110,000 Pesos internal renewal fees. The immigration officer was not in, so after waiting for over an hour, we finally collared a young fellow from another office along the corridor and an officer from the Policia de Investigaciones Control Migratorio, and asked if we could leave our passports in their care for processing, and we would pick them up the next day.

We went shopping for some fresh produce. Puerto Williams is a town of about 2000 people, and it is considered the southernmost town in the world. The vast majority of the population is Armada and government employees and their support structure. They have a government store and supermarket, which used to be available to visiting cruisers, but the few local merchants protested, and cruisers are now relegated to meagre selections of overpriced and over-the-hill goods.

We went into a tienda and found six good tomatoes among the many dozens in a large bin of mostly unpleasant-looking ones. There were some semi-fresh hockey pucks, the flat cylindrical things that pass as bread rolls, and we picked-out a dozen not-too-bad-looking ones. There were two 1 kilogram packets of pangasius fillets in the freezer, we gambled on one of them. Our bill came to 8330.

On our way to and from the Aduana and Migracion offices and the tienda, we had walked past the prow of the Armada ship, Yelcho, which in midwinter 1916 rescued Shackleton's crew off HMS Endurance on Elephant Island in the Antarctic. This time we paused to look.

We stopped at Micalvi on our way back; we had brought our computers with us in our backpacks, and we used the wifi in the lounge to catch-up, and for me to compose and send an email to Aduana in Iquique requesting special consideration for our expired Admision Temporal. I ran the Aduana email through Google Translate and got: *"Estimated Ruth, for this yacht has not extended course. To do so would be late, that the captain send an email to this one, request, to regularize situation;"* I think I got the gist of it. I composed and sent a reply:

"We were informed yesterday, 17 January that the Declaracion de Admision Temporal for our sailboat needed to be renewed. This was the first time since we arrived in Chile in December 2010 that we were told of this requirement to renew every 3 months. From January through December 2011 we were issued a zarpe in Iquique, in Antofagasta, in Valparaiso, in Juan Fernandez, in Talcahuano, in Valdivia, in Puerto Montt, and at none of these were we told of the need to renew the Declaration.

"We renewed our passport visas as we were told was required, we paid the required Servicio de Atencion a La Nave fees, and Senalizacion Maritima fees in both 2010 and 2011. We left Puerto Montt on 09 December 2011 with a zarpe to Puerto Williams, and even then, we were not informed that we needed to renew our Declaracion de Admision Temporal. We assumed all of our documentation was correct and in proper order.

"On 13 January in Caleta Olla, 50 nautical miles short of Puerto Williams, we experienced mechanical problems with the boat, in which our windlass broke, making anchoring and weighing anchor extremely difficult. At the same time the linkage to our transmission broke, and we lost the ability to use the engine. We were told the problems could not be repaired in Puerto Williams and that we needed to go to Ushuaia, Argentina for parts and repairs.

"We were told to go to from Caleta Olla to Puerto Navarino, where a zarpe would be issued for us to go to Ushuaia. With difficulty, we made it to Puerto Navarino and anchored. It was there we were told that our Declaration had expired, and that we needed to go to Puerto Williams to correct the problem.

"With difficulty, we made it to Puerto Williams at 2015 on 17 January, and needed the assistance of the Pilot Boat to safely moor. This morning at the Capitan de Puerto office we were sent to the Aduana office and there we were told to write you an explanation of our circumstances.

"We ask your kind attention and assistance with this."

After I sent the email, we spent another four hours online, catching-up on emails and news and I managed to load 260 photos and post an addition to our blog. About halfway through this, there was a call to Sequitur from the Capitan de Puerto on the club's VHF. I replied and was told our decision had come in from Iquique, and that a zarpe could now be issued.

I told the person at the Capitania that we would be in the following morning. So much for the five to seven day doom-and-gloom estimate of the Aduana officer.

We took our computers and our groceries back out to Sequitur and I sautéed the pangasius in butter with a julienne of garlic and shallots and served them with tarragon basmati rice, bottled white asparagus with mayonnaise and a garnish of Puerto Williams tomatoes with chopped basil leaves in olive oil. With dinner we enjoyed a superb bottle of Montes Leyda Vineyard 2010 Sauvignon Blanc.

For breakfast on Thursday morning Edi prepared basted eggs and sautéed sausage rounds on toasted hockey puck bread lapped with hollandaise sauce and garnished by sliced tomatoes with basil leaves and accompanied by fresh-ground Starbucks coffee.

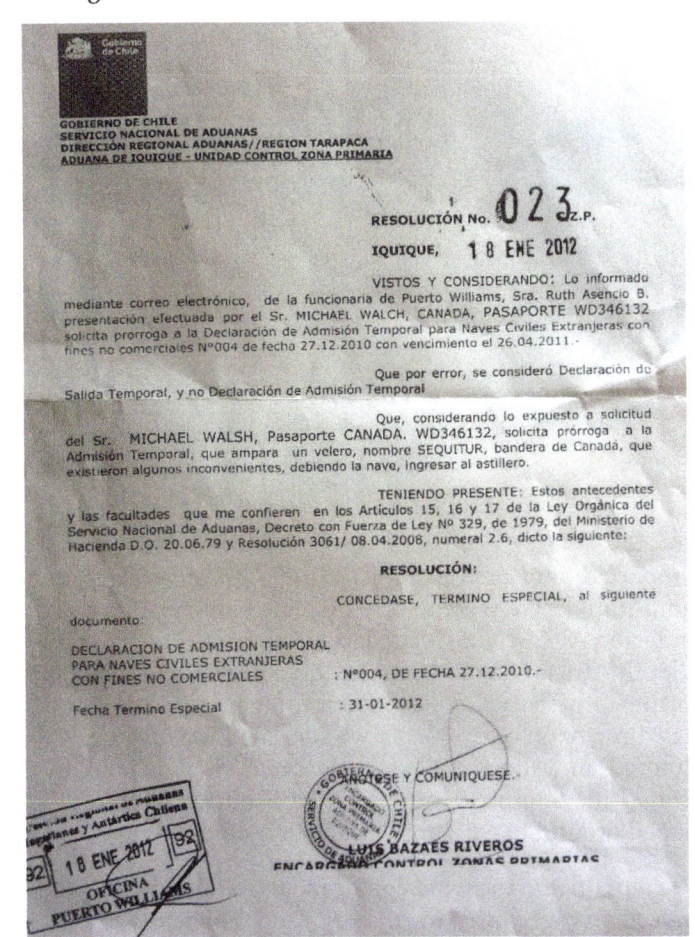

We walked over to the Capitania, and there were directed to the Aduana office. Ruth was in, and she presented us with the letter from the Aduana in Iquique, which translated as:

"VIEW AND CONSIDER: The information provided by e-mail, the officer in Puerto Williams, Ruth Asencio B. presentation by Mr. Michael Walch, Passport Canada WD346132 request an extension to the Temporary Admission Statement Foreign civilian ships for non-commercial N° 004 dated 27.12.2010 due on 26.04.2011.

By mistake, it was considered Temporary Output Statement, and Statement of Temporary Admission.

That, considering the above at the request of Mr. Michael Walsh, Passport Canada WD346132, request an extension to the Temporary Admission, which covers a sailboat, name SEQUITUR, the flag of Canada, that there were some problems, having the ship, enter the shipyard.

BEARING IN MIND: This background and powers conferred on me in Articles 15, 16 and 17 of the Organic Law of the National Customs Service, Decree-Law No. 329 of 1979, the Ministry of Finance DO 20.06.79 and Resolution 3061 / 04.08.2008, item 2.6, issue the following:

RESOLUTION:

GRANTED, special terms, the following document:

TEMPORARY ADMISSION STATEMENT WITH FOREIGN SHIPS FOR CIVIL NON-COMMERCIAL

Special Term Date: 31/01/2012".

Reading through this, it appears that the Aduana official in Iquique stretched the rules to near breaking to make them fit; nonetheless, we were absolved and free to go before the end of the month. We went upstairs to the Migracion office to find our visa extensions requiring only a trip to the bank to pay the 10,800 Pesos extension fees. A three-block walk to the bank, a payment, a stamped document, a walk back and a notation on our visas took little time, and we headed back to Sequitur for lunch before my 1500 appointment at the Capitania for the zarpe.

After lunch I went to the Capitania for my 1500 appointment. I arrived to find out that several others also had 1500 appointments; they group together the zarpe applicants, so that the Aduana and Policia officers could make only one trip to do their rubber-stamping. Within an hour, the four officials had typed, printed, written, signed, dated, stamped, copied and stapled enough paper that Sequitur was deemed fit and ready to leave Chile.

I went back to Micalvi and sat on the foredeck with my computer; Sequitur was just outside wifi range out on the buoy. I downloaded weather forecasts and grib files, and the conditions looked good for a midday departure on Friday. The winds were forecast to be strong overnight, but decrease to southwest 15-20 by noon.

On Friday morning, the slowly ebbing tide and the light wind were keeping Sequitur's stern pointed eastward, opposite to the direction we needed to head to exit the narrow inlet. I timed the yaws, and at the appropriate moment, sent Edi down into the hole to shift the engine into forward. At 1109 I slipped the mooring line and ran aft to the helm and we slowly turned and motored out through the narrows. Once we had left the protection of the harbour, we were in 20 to 25-knot winds.

Shortly before noon we rounded the cardinal buoy marking the end Banco Herradura and turned westward into steep 1.5 metre seas and winds of 25 to 30 knots. I rolled-out the staysail and a third of the main and we motor-sailed with the wind about 25 degrees off the port bow. At 1205 we crossed into Argentine waters, and an hour or so later, we were overtaken by an Armada patrol ship of about 25 metres length, pounding heavily into the steep seas.

The winds increased to 35 knots, the seas grew to over 2 metres and became more confused. The skies were mostly clear, with a scattering of cumulus over the mountains. I rolled-in the staysail and left a stabilizing fin on the main. We were being tossed around, but were warm and dry, protected by the full cockpit enclosure.

The winds continued in the mid-to-upper 30s, and clocked between west-southwest and west-northwest as we pounded into increasingly confused seas. In the pounding, the Rocna snapped its secondary lashings and hung a-cock-bill, bruising Sequitur's nose.

At 1700 we were at the entrance to Bahia Ushuaia, and

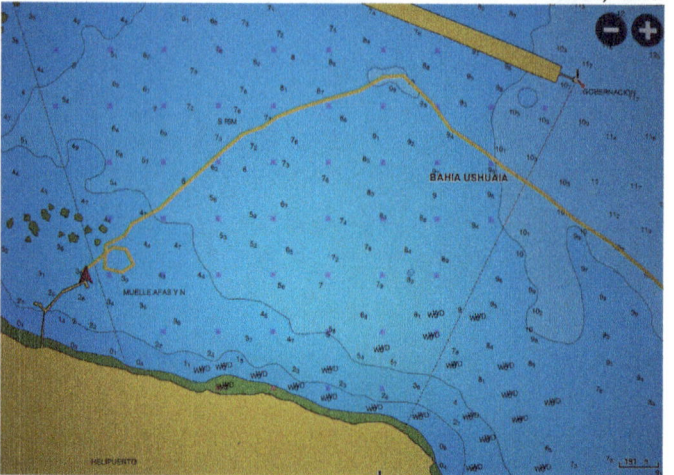

I reported our arrival to L3P, the Argentine Armada radio station. We were told to go alongside at AFASyN. I contacted AFASyN on VHF and we were told to raft onto a South African flagged boat on the north side of the pier. Fortunately, the wind was down to about 30 knots, and was directly on our nose, so we stemmed it as we slowly motored in. About half a cable out, when we finally spotted the South African flag, I let Sequitur fall-off and looped around to gain time for the lines and fenders.

We crept up into the wind again, and as we were just about centred on the South African boat, I sent Edi below to shift into neutral, while I went to the side deck and passed the breast line to the person on our host. I rushed forward and tossed the bow line to a burly man on the bow, just as I heard the rattle of the Variprop, indicating we had gone into neutral. We had arrived in Ushuaia.

The skipper of the South African boat was an extremely nervous person, and he very obviously did not want anyone rafted alongside him. He fussed and fumbled with lines and fenders as I told him Edi had grown-up in Pretoria, South Africa, and asked him where he was from. He said that neither he nor his boat had ever been to South Africa; it is a flag of convenience and he is from the USA. He continued to fuss with lines and fenders.

A uniformed person came aboard and checked our zarpe and passports, and told us we must go to the Prefectura Naval offices to clear in. We bundled-up in many layers of fleece, pulled our toques down over our ears, put on our heavy offshore foulies and headed out into the 30 to 35 knot winds and the 6 degree temperature of the summer day.

The most difficult aspect of the clearing-in process was the half hour walk in the cold, dusty wind. For the first time in over two years there were no fees to pay, nor were there any bribes, and we were quickly cleared and welcomed in a one-person, one office process with no redundant bureaucracy. It felt like Canada.

We asked the Armada rating who cleared us for directions to the closest supermercado. Five blocks later we found Argentinian beef and we had the butcher cut two 6cm-thick medallions. Among the other things that we found were fresh mushrooms and basil, and in the evening we enjoyed our first good steak since summer in Vancouver. With it we tried a couple of malbecs, starting our process of finding Argentine wines to add to Sequitur's cellar. Neither was a repeat.

The winds abated in the late evening, and were down to under 10 knots when we went to bed. I awoke in the middle of the night to the sounds of footsteps on deck and looked up through the hatches over the bed to see a boat had come alongside us and was tidying-up its lines. Quickly I saw that they were competent, needed no assistance, and I went back to sleep.

On Saturday morning I started working on disassembling the windlass to see if I could find the problem. I chatted with the skipper of the boat that had come in overnight. It was Christophe of Antipode, the fellow who had taken our stern lines when we had arrived in Caleta Olla, and who had come aboard and organized with me our tow off the Rocna on the following day, and had taken our Delta out and set it when we arrived back in the lee of the trees.

I continued working on the windlass, finally concluding that I needed to dismount it. While I worked, the skipper from the South African boat fidgeted with his lines and fenders, and then he came over and announced that he had asked to move to another spot, and that I needed to stand-by for the imminent move.

I had to empty the contents of the sail locker and climb down into it to remove the panel in its forward bulkhead to gain access to the wiring connections on the windlass motor. Also, this made it easier for me to get a wrench on the after two bolts attaching the windlass to the deck. Access to these was very tight, and each wrench turn gained half a hex, and the wrench needed to be flipped to gain the second half. I progressed at twelve wrench pulls per thread, each wrench set requiring fingertip manipulation. The space was too constricted for a socket. When I finally turned the nuts off the over-length bolts, it was nearly 1400; I took a break for lunch.

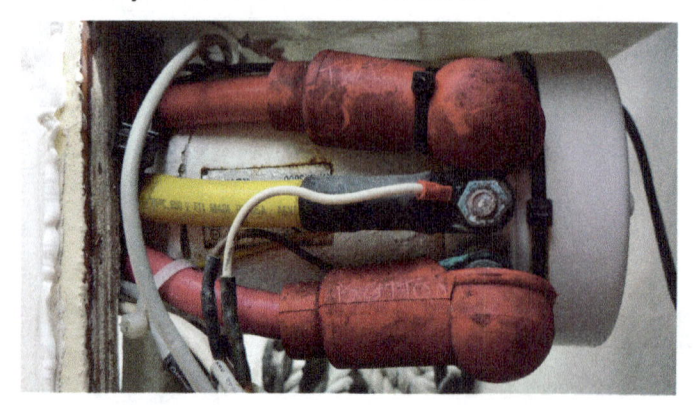

After lunch, before I removed the windlass wiring, I marked the terminal boots and took a series of photographs, so that correct reassembly would be easier. I then brought in the heavy guns; the lower cone was seized on the shaft, and required heating and much rubber mallet bashing to break free so that I could drop the shaft with the attached motor and gear-case down from the bolts beneath the deck.

Meanwhile, the skipper of South African boat was still fidgeting and fuming, impatiently waiting for one boat to leave and another to move so that he could make his move. I had earlier learned from the Russian who had helped on the bow when we had arrived, that South African boat's skipper had told the marina officials to send us away and to not allow us to come in out of the storm and raft on his boat.

Finally, after fussing and fretting all day, things were in place for the boat move. The skipper insisted because he was moving to the next space ahead, that he move out forward. I pointed-out that the wind was about 20 knots from dead ahead, and the only thing holding Sequitur and Antipode against the wind was our bow line to Paratii 2, the 30-metre aluminum schooner that was the inboard vessel of the raft. I told him he had to back out. He demanded to go forward. I turned and walked away.

Christophe, the skipper of Antipode was on deck on his boat by this time, and I spoke with him in French, the language we most easily shared. When I told him of the South African boat's insistence to move out forward, he rolled his eyes. We began to rig our lines for the canoe-hulled South African boat to move-out astern. We ran one of our polypropylene bow shore lines from our port stern cleat, outside everything, and around the South African boat's bow and back to a cleat on Paratii's starboard quarter.

The South African boat squirted out easily astern, and Sequitur with Antipode attached to her starboard side, swung slowly in on our bow line, aided by the polypropylene line to our stern cleat. A few minutes later our springs were set and our fenders adjusted, and we relaxed in the peacefulness of having no fussing and fidgeting alongside. I had the windlass out and decided to lay down the tools for the day.

The wind howled in the rigging on Sunday, blowing above 30 knots for most of the day. My fingers were cut, scraped, bruised, and hangnailed from the line, chain and tool handling of the previous week and a half, so I decided to take a day off. On Monday morning I attacked the engine control mechanism. I removed the port wheel and then the engine's electrical panel.

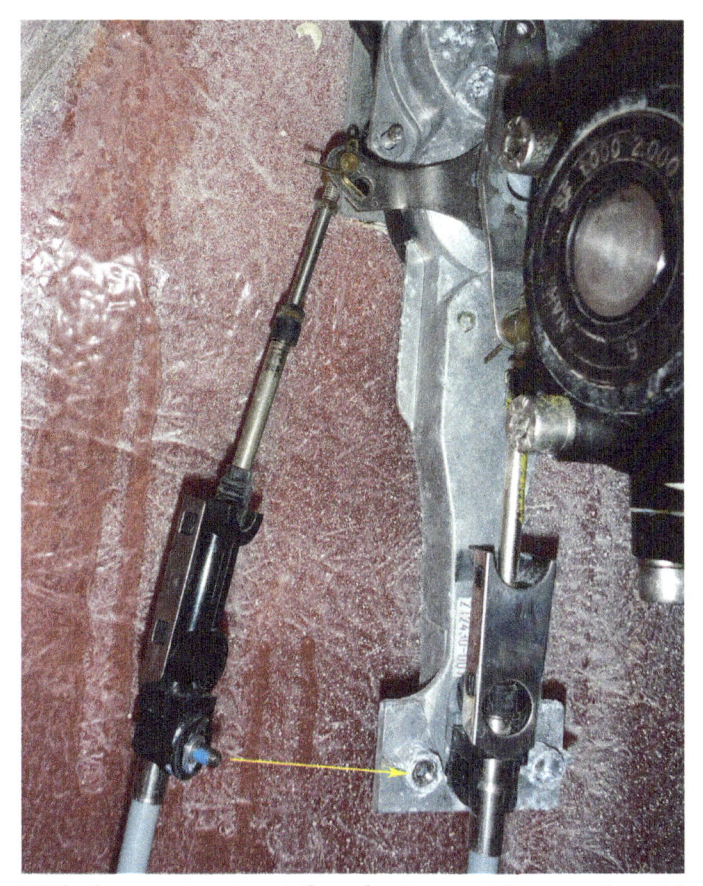

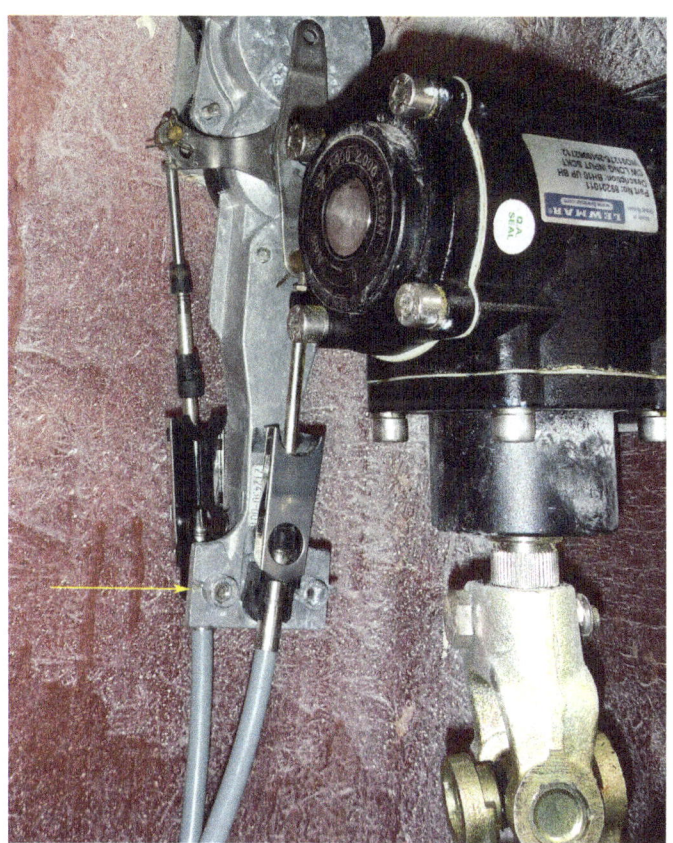

I dug the contents out of the port cockpit settee locker and tunnelled my way in. I dismounted the control mechanism, removed the snap-on cable-retaining cover, reattached the cable hub with a new screw and fresh LocTite, reinstalled the snap-on cover and remounted the mechanism to the bulkhead. With Edi hanging into the hole over the transmission, I tested the linkage. It worked correctly, and Edi was pleased to be relieved from her engine room duties.

With the panel out and the wheel out of the way, I could stick my arm in through the hole far enough to take some flash photos inside. After checking results and re-aiming the camera a few times, I finally got pictures showing the transmission linkage. I compared the photos with the mechanical drawings in the Lewmar repair kit, and quickly found the problem. The cap-screw that secures the cable sheath had backed out. I could see the undisturbed blue of LocTite on the threads, so it appears the cap-screw had been insufficiently tightened.

On Tuesday morning the skipper of Paratii 2 knocked on our hull and informed me that they had embarked their ten *"friends"* and were leaving within half an hour. There was nobody aboard Antipode, so Edi and I would have to do the move by ourselves. Paratii 2 is a 30-metre aluminum schooner owned by the Brazilian sailing adventurer and author, Amir Klink.

573

The wind was light from right ahead, or slightly on the starboard cheek, so I ran a line from our bow under Paratii's bow and to a bollard on the pier. Paratii sprung off and then let-go Sequitur's lines from her starboard side, and backed out. A few gentle tugs on Sequitur's bow line and a slow walk up the pier with it, assisted the wind in blowing Sequitur and Antipode across the gap to nestle onto the pier. Edi passed the stern line and in short order, we were settled-in and secured.

We were then directly alongside the pier. Directly ahead of us was the South African flagged boat, which had by then gathered a very large French-flagged commercial boat and a smaller German-flagged private yacht alongside. The skipper was near apoplectic with all the traffic back-and-forth across his decks.

For us, being alongside the pier meant that loading would be much easier, and we needed to do a lot of it. We walked into town looking for the closest car rental office that showed-up on GoogleMaps on my iPad. We followed the iPad's GPS, but there was no car rental office. We asked in a Peugeot sales office, and were directed north along Avenue Maipo to a car rental next to a Renault dealership. There was none there.

We went into the lobby of an upscale hotel and asked. The clerk made a phone call to confirm availability, and gave us a card with directions to Jumping Rental. There we waited for a fellow to arrive and drive us a few blocks to an office building and we followed him in and up the elevator. He filled-in a form, I signed it and we had a car for a day.

We drove back to Sequitur and loaded three propane bottles and four diesel jerry cans into the car and drove-off in search of propane. Two of our four propane bottles were empty and one still had a bit remaining, but prudence dictated we get it filled anyway. We have been averaging 41 days per bottle, so four full bottles should do us for five months or more. We had been given directions to Sartini Gas: *"across on the northeast extremity of the city near the roundabout; lots of tanks; you can't miss it."*

After a false stop at a truck depot that had Sartini Gas tanks out in front of its building, we found the real place. We have never seen such inexpensive propane fills. It cost 54 Pesos ($12.50 Canadian) for three 4.5-kilogram charges. Not each; for all three.

We drove back into the city and were informed by billboards, posters and bumper stickers that Ushuaia is the Capital of the Malvinas. We had thought that Stanley was. There is apparently a renewed claim by Argentina on the Falklands, South Georgia and a slice of Antarctica, and we had been informed of heavy fines, possibly boat confiscation if we took Sequitur there without Argentina's permission.

We stopped at a large supermarket and loaded a cart with all the heavy and awkward items we could imagine needing. We also found four large cauliflower heads, some fresh-looking zucchini, a couple dozen nice roma tomatoes and a few kilos of potatoes, onions and carrots. The produce selection is very slim, mostly root and other long storage items.

Continuing on our way back toward Sequitur, we stopped at a gas station to fill the jerry cans with diesel. The pump operator said they were allowed to do only two jerry cans at a time. He filled two and I followed him inside to pay. He poked a few keys on the computer, he winked, and we went back out to the car to fill the other two. The cost for 80 litres was 296 Pesos, $68.31 Canadian, about 85.4 cents a litre.

We continued on to Rombo Repuestos an importer/distributor of machinery, tools and equipment. We had been told that they might be of assistance with our windlass. I met Edgerdo, who speaks some English, and he told me they had no windlasses. He went on to tell me that bringing one in would take three or four weeks.

He motioned me to follow him, and we hopped into his truck and drove four blocks to Torneria Industrial Percara, where I was introduced to Jorge Percara. He said he was very busy with other projects, but Edgerdo persuaded him to strip-down the windlass gearbox and see if it was reparable. Jorge said he could start on it mañana la tarde, tomorrow afternoon.

I rejoined Edi, who had been patiently waiting in the car, and we drove back to AFASyN to unload our groceries, diesel and propane and wheel them out the pier to Sequitur.

On Monday evening the fuel level in our main tank had fallen below the intake for the Espar furnace, so we had no heat or hot water. The first thing I did after moving things aboard was to add the 80 litres of diesel to the tank, re-flash the Espar and restore our basic comforts. After we had refuelled and stowed the groceries, we went back to the car and went in search of the fish shop.

It seems people do not eat much seafood here; there is none fresh in the supermarkets, and the frozen selection is extremely basic and uninviting. We had been asking where the fish market is, and mostly came-up with blanks. However; two people had indicated a fish shop called La Costa five blocks up the hill from the water to the north of downtown.

We found it, but there was nothing fresh, only frozen. There were some slide-top freezers along the wall, and in them, besides the whole frozen salmon, hake and king crab, were small bags of shrimp, mussels, clams, scallops, crab and other shellfish, plus calamari and unidentified dark fish fillets. Nothing was labelled, and there were no prices on the bags. From the bored woman at the cash register I asked for prices, and was told the bags were 20 Pesos each. They appeared to be sized according to value.

In the display cases were trays and bags of frozen fish, and I disturbed the bored woman again to ask for the names of the various fish. With indifference, she rattled-off names that were completely unfamiliar. We forced ourselves beyond her attitude, and bought a large fillet of a white-fleshed fish, plus six bags of scallops. Her demeanour made us to wonder why she was there. For dinner, I sautéed the fish fillet with one from a small packet we had bought in the supermarket to see if either was worth stocking. Neither was.

For breakfast on Wednesday morning Edi basted some Puerto Eden eggs on sliced ham and served them lapped with hollandaise sauce and a sprinkling of Asiago on toasted split baguettes, and garnished the plates with sliced roma tomatoes and fresh basil leaves. With it we enjoyed our usual cups of fresh-ground Starbucks coffee.

After breakfast, Christophe knocked on our hull to tell us he was heading out within the quarter hour to Puerto Williams. For the past few years he has been taking friends out on sailing trips along the Beagle Channel and around the Horn from Ushuaia and Puerto Williams.

Christophe has a wealth of sailing experience; he entered his first solo round-the-world race, the 1990-91 BOC Challenge, and won it in 120 days. He entered his second solo round-the-world race, the 1994-95 BOC Challenge, and won it in 121 days. He entered his third solo round-the-world race, the non-stop 1996-97 Vendée Globe and won it in 105 days.

We again thanked him for his assistance in Caleta Olla, wished him bon voyage and cast him off.

We then loaded the four diesel jerry cans into the car and went off to refill them, after which we drove to Jorge Percara's shop to see if he had torn-down the windlass gearbox. We arrived at 1430, and he told us with a broad grin that he had meant at the other end of the afternoon. We dropped the diesel at Sequitur and then went downtown to return the rental car.

We stopped at a couple of supermarkets on our way back, looking for fresh produce. At one we found some fresh-looking broccoli and bought five large crowns. We also bought some firm avocados. We have seen no produce stands here, nor anything resembling a farmer's market. Neither have we heard of any. We walked back to Sequitur.

At 1745 we headed out to check on the windlass gearbox, following the gravel road around the south side of Bahia Encerrada and then along Fuegia Basket to Rombo, where we dropped-in to see Edgerdo. He phoned Jorge and encouraged, motioned us to follow him to his truck, and drove us the four blocks to the machine shop. Jorge greeted us with an impish smile and showed me the gears.

There was a sector of about 45° that had broken cogs, most stripped to below their roots. It was easy to understand why the windlass had ceased working. I asked him if he could repair it, and was pleased with his quick positive response, and with his proposal to braze on new material and cut new cogs.

576

I looked around his machine shop and saw he was well-equipped for the job. I asked him *"¿Cuando y Cuanto?"*, When and how much? He mentioned 2,000 Pesos, about $460, and then a discussion ensued with Edgerdo in the middle interpreting. Jorge pointed to all the big projects he had on the go, I pointed to the calendar and our need to get around the Horn and onward to South Africa. We settled on his starting on the gears on Monday and agreed on the 2000 Pesos. As we were leaving, he added *"tal vez antes"*, maybe sooner.

I was awakened on Thursday morning at 0745 by the sounds of wind howling in the rigging, and by an unfamiliar sound from the fenders. I quickly dressed and went out into a 45-knot north-easterly blowing Sequitur directly onto the side of the pier. The tide was very high, and our deck was about half a metre above the top of the pier. A couple of the fenders had popped out and they all needed to be readjusted lower. With Sequitur's side again protected, I went below and checked the tide chart. There was just half an hour and only a few centimetres to high tide, so I considered that the fenders would do.

The wind played games through the day:

- Northeast 30 with gusts to 45 at 0745;
- Southeast 5 with gusts to 8 at 0915;
- North 15 with gusts to 25 at 1015;
- Southwest 10 with gusts to 18 at 1400;
- South 20 with gusts to 40 at 1600;
- Southwest 35 with gusts to 45 at 1610;
- South 20 with gusts to 35 at 1900; and
- Calm at 2340 when we went to bed.

It varied from drizzle to downpour to sunny and back, and the barometer bounced around between the low 980s to the mid 990s. Except for my moving the fenders back up to the gunwales when the tide receded, we stayed inside.

After sleeping-in until 0915 on Friday morning, we had a leisurely breakfast and then popped out of our cocoon to a sunny and calm day. Two more boats had come in overnight and moored, one third-out astern of us and the other third-out across the pier. There were now six pretending-not-to-be-commercial 16 to 25-metre boats on the pier, and the place was teeming with *"friends"* disembarking luggage, backpacks, ski equipment, mountain bikes and other paraphernalia.

We had for the previous few years read repeatedly updated accounts in the cruising press and on internet pages, such as Noonsite, of Argentina's draconian treatment of innocent cruisers, with very heavy fines and penalties for reportedly impromptu transgressions of unknown regulations. Watching the scene in Caleta Olla, Puerto Williams, and now Ushuaia, we can now make some sense of the reports.

It appears to us that many foreign-flagged yachts are here conducting commercial cruises, while pretending to be cruisers on innocent passage with some friends. We have watched the boats arrive, disembark their friends, embark new sets of friends and head back out on a well-oiled schedule. We suspect that the scare stories published in the press and on the internet have been submitted by these pretending-not-to-be-commercial operators. We had received wonderful hospitality from the Argentine authorities, likely because they recognize us as legitimate cruisers.

Shortly before noon we walked into the centre of the city and up the hill to the La Costa. We had tried the scallops, and were back for more. We were relieved to see that the bored lady was not there; in her place behind the counter were two friendly and professional men, likely the owners. In the freezer cases were an apparent fresh stock of scallops and some large, plump shrimp. We picked-out six bags of each, paid the 240 Pesos, put them in our cooler bag and headed back to Sequitur. We had wonderful shellfish sufficient for twelve meals for two for the equivalent of $2.30 per plate.

On our way back we stopped at an ATM and withdrew 2000 Pesos, in preparation for paying Jorge for his work on the windlass. Back aboard we repacked the shrimp and scallops into stouter bags and topped-off the after freezer with them.

We were relaxing after lunch, when Edi spotted Edgerdo on the pier through the side lights. I quickly went up top to see him walking slowly along, looking closely at the boats. I hailed him, and he told me that he had come to tell us that Jorge had finished working on the windlass. As he drove me over to the shop, I hoped that finished meant successfully completed, rather than unable to continue and quit.

When we walked into the shop, the broad smile on Jorge's face told me he had been successful. Not only had he rebuilt and recut the stripped gear, he had also shaved-down the faces of and added a seal on the motor-to-gearbox joint, which had suffered from slight electrolysis. When I commented on his speedy work, he proudly pointed to his involute gear cutter. I happily counted-out the 2000 Pesos. On our way back to Sequitur, Edgerdo stopped at his store so I could buy some 80W90 oil to fill the gearbox, which Jorge had said was the only thing left to do.

By the time I arrived back onboard, it was nearly 1900, so I decided to wait until the morning to begin the re-installation.

Saturday morning after a delicious breakfast of toasted split baguettes slathered with cream cheese, sprinkled with capers, loaded with smoked salmon, garnished with basil leaves and washed-down with fresh-ground Starbucks coffee, I set to work on the windlass. I quickly noticed that the circlip and Delrin washer were missing from the bottom of the shaft. I assumed they had been left on Jorge's bench, but to save the 5 kilometre walk, I searched our spares, and could find no 20mm ID circlips.

I finally decided to walk over to the shop. On my way past the club office, I stopped in to pay our moorage bill. I said we would likely be ready to leave on Sunday, and I asked to pay for the eight days. Because it was our first visit to AFASyN, we were given three days free, the total was $158.

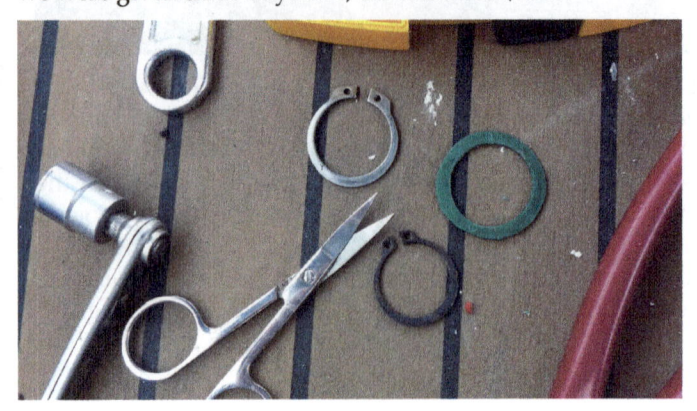

We could not find the missing pieces, and Jorge sent me over to Rombo Repuestos, from where I was given directions to Bolonera. There for 3 Pesos I bought two circlips, but they had no Delrin washers. Back onboard I fashioned a washer from a thick polypropylene bottle cap. I'm sure the windlass won't mind a green washer rather than the white one.

The outside diameter of the new circlip is too big to fit onto the shaft and then into the hole. Extrapolating from the very poor drawings and sketchy information provided in the Lewmar windlass literature, I gathered that the circlip's purpose is only to prevent the drive key from sliding out of the keyway. I used some Monel locking wire to do a double wrap in the circlip groove and cinched it to replicate the circlip's job. The roll of locking wire had been issued to me by the Royal Canadian Air Force in 1964 as part of my toolkit, and it has been in my mountaineering and sailing repair kit ever since I had moved up from Aero-Engine Technician to Pilot in 1968.

578

The remounting process took several hours, during which time there were heavy rain showers. From some of these I retreated to the warmth and dryness of the salon, from others I climbed down into the sail locker and closed the hatch to work at the nuts through the wiring access hole. It was late evening by the time I had finished the installation. I left the tidying-up until morning.

On Sunday morning Edi prepared pain perdu au jambon garnished with basil leaves, and served me a huge, hungry-man portion with sliced roma tomatoes and fresh-ground Starbucks coffee.

After breakfast I finished-up with the windlass installation and did a few other chores up top, while Edi prepared below for sea. Shortly before noon we walked the 2.5 kilometres across town to the Prefectura Naval to get our zarpe to Puerto Williams. Again we were delighted with the simple one-office process, with no fees and no hassle. After we signed a very heavily worded oath not to visit the Malvinas without Argentina's permission, our passports were stamped and we were granted our departure papers to Puerto Williams.

We took a route back that allowed us to stop at two supermarkets. At the first one there was a fresh bin of bulk crimini mushrooms, and I loaded a kilo and a bit into a bag. We also bought some big, fresh red and green peppers, some small zucchini and more roma tomatoes. At the second we found two more rather fresh cauliflower heads, and I loaded some more roma tomatoes into a bag to juggle at the check-out to get rid of the last of our Argentine money.

The AFASyN pier was overflowing with boats, rafted as many as five deep along both sides. Many of them were pretending not to be commercial operators, but there were a few actual cruisers, including Polonius, a small Polish sloop with eight men aboard, which had rafted along our starboard side Saturday evening, fresh from their Atlantic crossing. Also just arrived was the French sloop, Ilena with Patricia and Philippe, with whom we had shared Champagne and dinner in Puerto Eden at New Year's.

We quickly organized our lines for departure; Polonius had already moved, so it was a matter of getting a push on our bow so we could motor ahead out from tightly between rafts of three boats forward and four aft. At 1444 we slipped and headed out of Bahia Ushuaia, past Holland America's Veendam and four smaller cruise ships alongside the commercial wharves. The wind was variable, 0 to 4 knots and the sky was mostly covered with stratus, and cumulus.

At 1513, as we were motoring eastward the engine hesitated and slowed. I went below and switched from the starboard Racor filter to the port one. The engine picked-up its rhythm for a bit, but at 1542, as we were enjoying lunch in the cockpit, it slowed and died. I had intended changing the engine-mounted secondary fuel filter, but hadn't gotten around to it. It looked like my opportunity had arrived.

I rolled-out the staysail and half the main and we ghosted along in a 6 to 8 knot northeast breeze. I would have put out more sail, but there were a few squalls to the west that appeared to be tracking toward us. The fuel filter's awkward positioning is the main reason I had deferred changing it. I was interrupted in my task three times as squalls overtook us, and I needed to tend the helm and the sails. Leading up to, during and following the squalls, we made between 5.5 and 7.5 knots eastward toward Puerto Williams.

After the filter was changed, the engine started immediately and ran smoothly. I switched back to the starboard Racor, ran the engine for a few minutes to ensure all was well, then shut it down and we continued sailing in the 12 to 15 knot following wind. In the late afternoon the wind died and we began motoring again, reaching Puerto Williams and coming to anchor in the quarantine area at 2001. We launched the dinghy and motored it ashore to the Capitania, where we were welcomed and told to come back at 1000 the next morning to clear in. While we were there we applied for permission to use the Armada wharf to take-on about 700 litres of diesel at noon on Monday.

Back onboard, I tossed some scallops in a butter sauté of criminis, shallots and garlic and served them with basmati rice, julienned carrots and baby zucchini and sliced roma tomatoes. The 2011 Cono Sur Chardonnay again drank well beyond its price.

After breakfast on Monday morning we took the dinghy ashore from the anchorage and walked up the hill to the Capitania to clear in. This was an easy, but rather long one-office process, which required the payment of another 49,500 Pesos.

We dinghied back out to Sequitur, and had the opportunity to test the windlass for the first time. After I shortened-in to sit over the Rocna in the light swell to break it free, it came up easily, but covered in kelp. As Edi motored toward the Armada wharf, I cut away the kelp and stowed the anchor. The wind was westerly about 15 knots, so we easily stemmed it to and prepared to gently come alongside the wharf.

As we were approaching, Edi was ready to hop up onto the wharf with the bow line to place on a forward bollard. The closer we came to the wharf, the more obvious it was that the car tire fenders we had seen from afar were truck tires, then tractor tires and finally, massive mining truck tires.

Edi held us alongside with the engine as I scrambled up three metres or so using the tire lugs as a ladder. I took the breast line to a bollard, then we ran a long bow line and sat on it against the wind while we waited for the fuel truck.

We took-on 692 litres of diesel oil, bringing our tanks back up to 920 litres. I walked over to the Copec station to pay the 485,784 Pesos bill

We then motored along to Micalvi, where we rafted fourth out, alongside Land Fall, a US-flagged sloop. I counted nineteen foreign sailboats on Micalvi when we arrived, and within three hours there were two more.

The barometer had been below 1000 since Thursday morning, down to 985 that evening, up to 994 on Friday, back down to 978 on Saturday, and then remained quite stable in the 977 to 979 area through Sunday and Monday. We appeared again to be in the centre of a very large low.

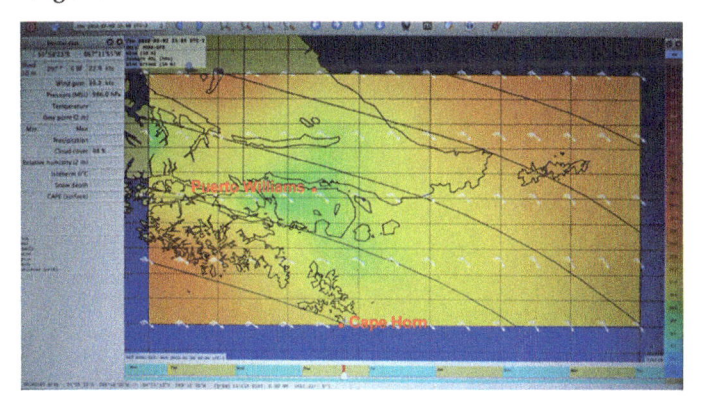

I downloaded grib files to try to make sense of the weather, and to look for a window for us to round Cape Horn. From the predictions on Monday afternoon, the first decent opportunity appeared to be midday on Thursday, when winds were forecast to be down to less than 25 with gusts under 40 knots.

We decided to look at new gribs midday on Tuesday, and if it still looked acceptable, to apply in the afternoon for a zarpe for an early Wednesday departure for the 90 mile trip down to the Horn. From there we would let the conditions dictate our onward route.

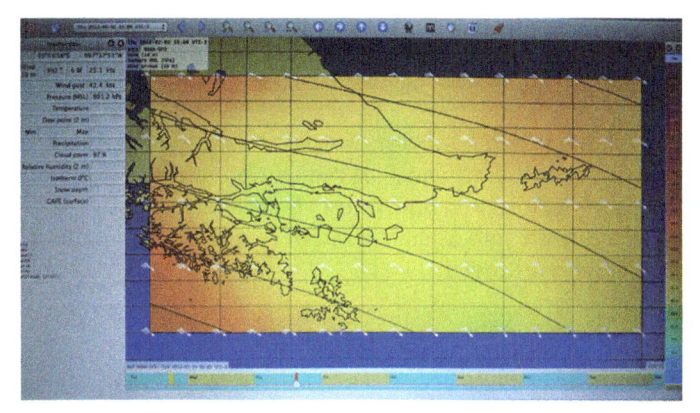

On Tuesday the predictions for Thursday looked quite similar, with slightly stronger winds, so in the early afternoon we dodged rain and hail squalls and walked over to the Capitania and applied for a zarpe to Cape Horn, departing early on Wednesday morning, the 1st of February. On Tuesday, the last day of January we were issued a zarpe from Puerto Williams to Cabo de Hornos, for departure early on Wednesday morning, the 1st of February. There appeared to be a weather window opening on Thursday morning and slamming shut on Friday afternoon. We had decided to head out in Wednesday's iffy weather to be in position when the window opened.

With our zarpe issued, we walked from the Capitania over to the almacen to see if there was anything worth buying. The vegetable selection was down to a few shrivelled potatoes, one mushy tomato, a few so-so carrots and a bin of rather decent onions. We took none. However, in the freezer was a large selection of one-kilo bags of skinless and boneless pangasius fillets. We had enjoyed the packet we had bought a couple of weeks previously, so we bought two more. We also bought a dozen hockey-puck bread rolls.

We spent much of the remainder of the afternoon enjoying the free wifi connection of the Club Naval de Yates Micalvi. In the evening I sautéed the fish fillets and served them with tarragon basmati rice and a butter sweat of julienned carrots, red and green peppers, shallots, garlic and quartered crimini mushrooms. The 2011 Carmen Chardonnay accompanied splendidly.

31. To Cape Horn

We were up shortly after 0700, and while Edi brewed a pot of coffee, I organized our lines to enable us to easily slip out from the nest of boats. Comings and goings the previous day had put us second out from Micalvi, with three commercial sailboats rafted outboard of us. At 0740 we slipped and headed eastward along the Beagle Channel in rather calm seas. The 6 to 8 knot northwest winds were insufficient to offer any push to our sails, so we motored. Above us were bundles of stratus and tatters of stratus fractus and above them, through the gaps, the sky was filled with altostratus. There was fresh snow on the hills down to about 300 metres; it was a cold midsummer

Edi took advantage of the smooth going to go below and prepare breakfast. She scrambled some eggs, which she added to ham and cheese on sliced hockey pucks and then browned them in a covered dry frying pan. Our Cape Horn version of eggs McMuffin went wonderfully with steaming cups of fresh-ground Starbucks from the thermos. She had used the tail-end of the bag of beans, leaving us with only two bags remaining. We have been averaging eighteen days per 907-gram bag, so in about five weeks we'll need to revert to our stock of Peruvian coffee.

The Beagle Channel east of Puerto Williams narrows and twists between islands that mark the separation between the tides flowing in from the east and from the west. We passed close to some isolated mid-channel rocks, and saw them thick with cormorants and penguins.

Further along, past Isla Snipe we passed another reminder to mariners of the difficulty of navigation in these waters. It appears a freighter had found a submerged rock and converted itself into a chart symbol to aid the navigation of those who followed.

Logos was a missionary ship loaded with bibles and Christian proselytizing literature to distribute to heathens around the world. She had left Ushuaia 04 January 1988, and at 2354 hours found a rocky shoal off Snipe Island.

We reported to the Armada watchkeeper at Alcamar Snipe, and a few miles further along, at Alcamar Toro. There are five of these one-family Armada outposts east of Puerto Williams, whose responsibility is to monitor and maintain radio contact with passing traffic. As we passed Puerto Toro, the most southerly village in the world, we saw one sailboat on the wharf.

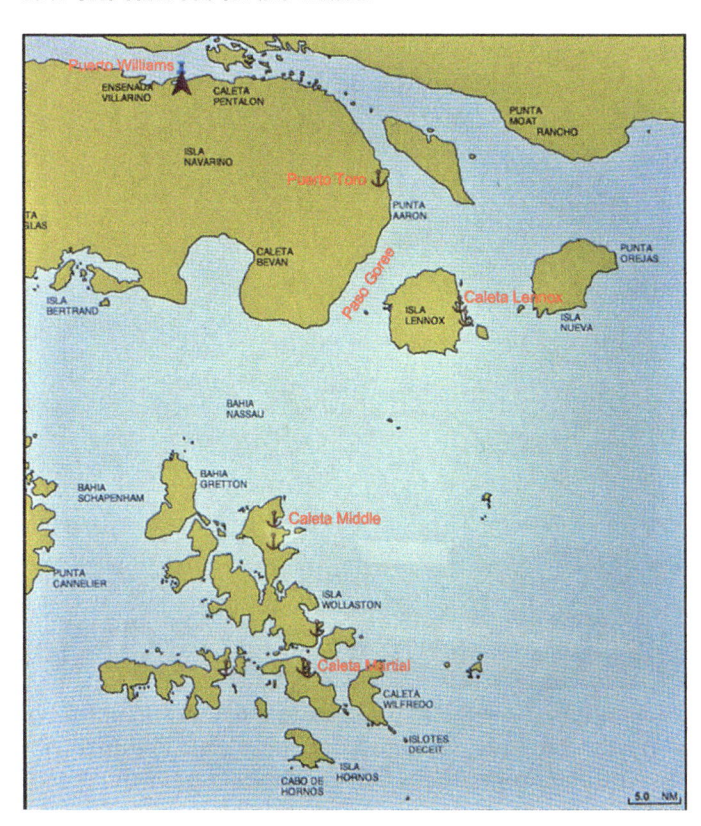

The weather was still rather benign, so we decided to continue southward. We told the Armada watchkeeper at Toro that we would head to through Paso Goree and cross Bahia Nassau to Caleta Middle, an anchorage on Isla Wolliston, or possibly continue to Caleta Martial on Isla Herschel. As we approached Punta Aaron, we were hit by 35-knot winds from the southwest funnelling up through Paso Goree from Bahia Nassau.

The Italian Guide says about Bahia Nassau: *"...crossing between Paso Goree and Isla Wollaston can prove very hard in heavy weather. Even large yachts may be forced to sail back and find shelter in Caleta Lennox. The long fetch and the violence of the wind can rapidly develop extremely violent conditions, so that navigation in the bay might become impossible..."* I considered this and thought of our beating directly to windward in deteriorating conditions for 28 miles before finding lee. I came 45° to port and as we reached across the top of Paso Goree to find some lee from Isla Lennox, I called Alcamar Toro and reported that we were diverting to anchor in Caleta Lennox.

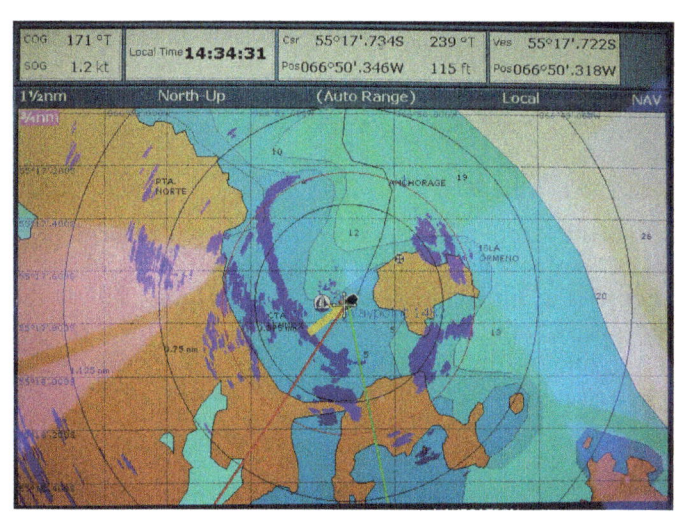

It took us nearly three hours sailing, motor-sailing and motoring to cover the 12 miles to Caleta Lennox, the final 4 miles of this into 45-knot winds and steep seas. At 1426 we came to 25 metres on the Rocna in 5.5 metres of water about 2 cables from the low isthmus and point forming the bay, directly in front of the Armada building. The land offered no protection from the wind, but because of the short fetch, the seas had little chance to build.

Already in the anchorage was Guapita, a French-flagged sloop of about 10 metres. We had seen it arrive in Puerto Eden just before we left in early January. I set a long snubber on the chain, and we cocooned below as the anemometer bounced around in the upper 40 and low 50 knot range and Sequitur yawed in the wind shifts, which I assumed were being generated by interaction with the islands at the point.

At 1840 the 19mm nylon snubber snapped in a particularly violent gust, which was likely well into the 60s. I had watched the anemometer from time-to-time, and had seen gusts as high as 57 knots; the shrieking of the rigging clearly told us this one was stronger. I pulled-on my offshore foulies and went forward to rig a new snubber.

An hour later, after I had organized gear and warmed-up, I went back out and added a second snubber to share the strain. Even with hi-tech underwear, three layers of fleece, insulated pants, offshore foulies, toque and gloves, I was quite chilled by the time I came back from my midsummer strolls to the foredeck.

For dinner I prepared a quick sauté of scallops, garlic, shallots, red and green peppers, roma tomatoes and crimini mushrooms and served it with basmati rice. For the first time in many weeks, we had no wine with dinner because of the tenuous nature of the anchorage. We decided not to undress, but rather to sleep fully clothed on the settees in the salon, ready for quick action if necessary. This was the first time we had used this prudent step since Sequitur left Vancouver.

I was awakened at 0430 by the stillness and the cessation of howling in the rigging; the wind had decreased dramatically. By 0520 the wind had died. We quickly got up, and prepared to leave. It took us about ten minutes to coax the Rocna out of the mud bottom, and at 0555 on Thursday morning, a few minutes after sunrise, we weighed and headed out of Caleta Lennox. Bahia Nassau had a light chop, the remnants of the storm, as we shaped course across it for Paso Mar del Sur.

As we motored across Bahia Nassau, the wind filled from the northwest, and we rolled-out some sail. The further we went, the longer the wind's fetch and larger the seas. By 0800 we had 18 to 22 knot winds on our starboard quarter, and we were making 7 knots. As we approached the islands, we met a small cruise ship heading north, and a short while later we had found the lee of Isla Freycinet. Our 1100 fix showed us about to enter Paso Mar del Sur.

At 1145 we were through the 4 cable wide pass, with its nearly 2 cable chart skew, and on our final leg to Cape Horn, at least to the Cape Horn that the tour operators visit. The Armada-manned lighthouse, the Cape Horn monument, the fair weather anchorage and the access stairs are all on the eastern point of Isla Hornos. Cape Horn is two miles west and nearly a mile further south.

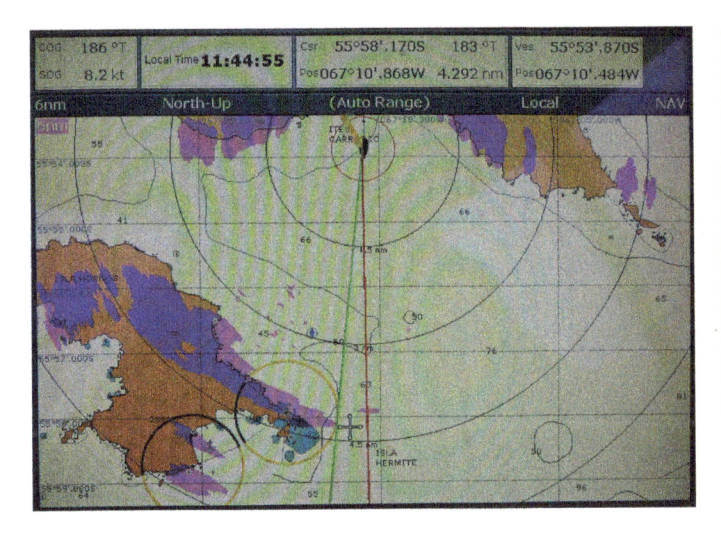

We continued past the tourist's Cape Horn and skirted well clear of the badly mis-charted reefs that mark the southeastern point of Isla Hornos.

As we went we came increasingly into the 4 metre westerly swell, which was rather like a gentle roller-coaster. Once we had put the reefs well abaft our beam, we turned and motor-sailed straight into the swell, making about 4.5 knots with turns for 8.5 and assisted by the 18 to 20 knot winds at 45° on the starboard bow.

The peak at Cape Horn is shown on the chart as being 425 metres high, and we watched as the bottom 70 or 80 metres of its face was obscured by the tops of the swells as Sequitur bottomed-out in the troughs.

We were sufficiently close-in that the height of the Cape gave us lee from the northwest wind. The sky had been completely obscured with low stratus, mist and light rain since we entered the islands. It was Groundhog Day, and there was no doubt that the little rodent would not have seen its shadow here. We pondered whether this meant that summer would soon come, or that it was over. The winter-like weather gave us no clues.

The slow roller-coaster ride westward took us over half an hour, which gave plenty of time to think of how long we had dreamed of doing the Horn, how long we had planned the voyage, how long it had taken us to prepare before actually starting out, how long it had taken us to get to this point. And there we were, about to round Cape Horn.

We continued along westward until we had clearly passed the most southerly point. We had rounded Cape Horn east to west.

We put a message in a bottle and launched it. The message was simple: 02 Feb 2012. Cape Horn. Michael & Edi. Yacht Sequitur. Email: yacht.sequitur@gmail.com.

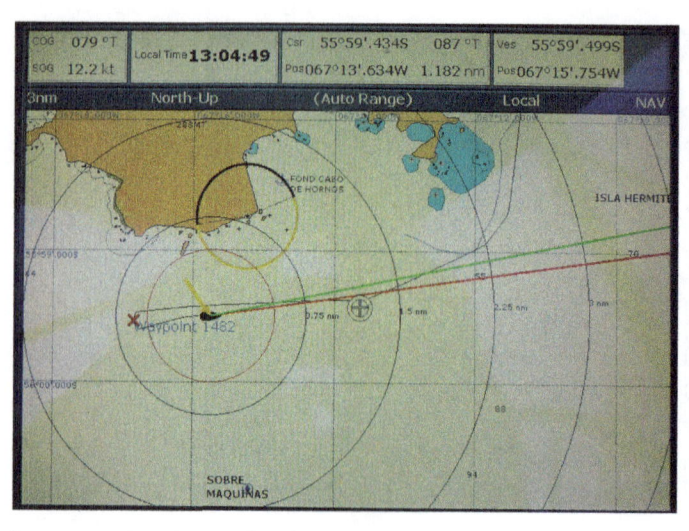

I put our 1300 fix on the chart-plotter as we turned through the trough of the swells and headed east. When we had settled-in on our easterly course and had done a west to east passage of the Cape, we were surfing into the upper 13-knot range.

The run back to the tourist version of the Cape was quick, and as we ran, we felt a huge relief at finally having completed this goal we had so long ago set for ourselves. By 1330 we had cleared the reefs off the east point, done our departure radio contact with the Armada watchkeeper at the lighthouse and were well on our northerly route into the wind and back to Paso Mar del Sur.

While we were in the lee of Isla Freycinet on our way through the pass, Edi went below and prepared a big platter of nachos with two cheeses, sliced black olives, diced roma tomatoes and with it we enjoyed steaming cups of rooibos tea. Once we had left the lee of the islands and were out into Bahia Nassau, we were into waves generated all day by the northerly winds.

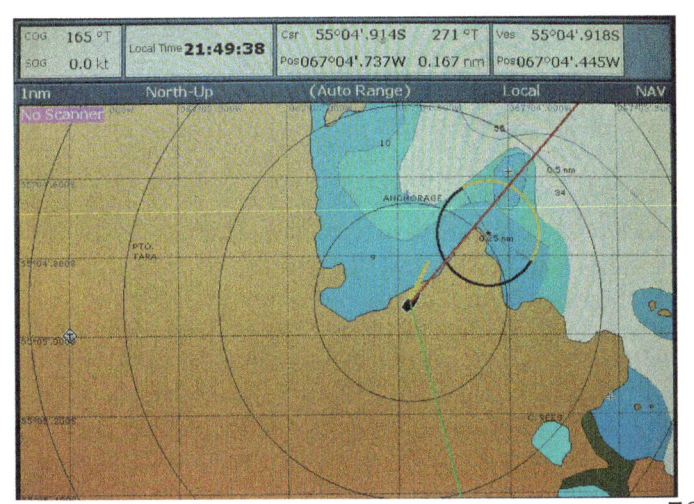

The 44-mile run across the Bahia to Puerto Toro took us until two minutes after sunset at 2129. There, we secured stern-in, starboard side to on a wonderful, modern wood and steel wharf in the most southerly village in the world. We reported our arrival to the Armada watchkeeper by VHF. We had made 110 miles during the day.

We were feeling a great mix of relief, weariness, elation, tiredness, satisfaction and pride. We needed to celebrate. After we had left the Horn I had put a bag each of prawns and scallops into the sink to thaw. I sautéed them in julienned shallots, garlic and red and green peppers and quartered criminis, added the lot to a hot Alfredo sauce and served it over al dente linguine. We celebrated with a bottle of Mumm Domaine.

During the night a German-flagged commercial sailboat had come in from Antarctica with a group of clients from Spain. We chatted with the tourists briefly on Friday morning as we organized our lines to slip and head out. Some of them offered to help us, but we long ago learned it is safer and easier to do it ourselves than to risk having overeager and inexperienced people take unpredictable initiative. We declined their assistance, saying we needed the practice. We easily and safely left Puerto Toro at 1045.

The weather was initially rather benign as we motored into a 10 to 12 knot wind under skies half-filled with cumulus. We passed again isolated rocks with penguin, cormorant and sea lion colonies. The Chilean-Argentine border runs through the Beagle Channel, and at times it is necessary to cross into Argentine waters for safe navigation. On one of these crossings, we were contacted on VHF by the Argentine Armada, requesting our intentions.

The weather deteriorated rapidly, and by the time we arrived back in Puerto Williams at 1612, the wind was blowing above 25 knots. We secured sixth out in a raft off Micalvi, alongside the French sloop Ilena, where Philippe and Patricia helped us with our lines.

Through the evening and the following morning several more boats came in to fill to overflowing the available space on Micalvi. Some had to anchor in the seno.

On Saturday morning our house bank was at 87%, which with the lack of solar input was ample to see us through until Monday afternoon or evening. All the electrical connections on Micalvi were in use, and there was a backlog of requests for any that became available, so unless the sun came out and stayed out, we would have to depend on the generator.

After dinner on Sunday evening, the battery was at 71%, and I decided to run the generator to bring it back into the upper 80s. I switched it to its start cycle and it failed to start. I tried again with the same results, and again, and again. It was late, so I deferred action until morning. I was out of bed and head-down into the Fischer-Panda by 0700 on Monday, with the house bank at 63%.

I checked the fuses, drained the water separator, changed the fuel filter, tested the fuel pump, bled the fuel lines and still no start. I changed the glow plug relay; still no start. I cleaned the air filter; still no start. I sprayed WD-40 into the air intake and got a kick or two, but no start. I waited a few minutes and tried it again; same results. Ten minutes later, at 0954, I tried it again and it started and ran perfectly. We brought the bank up to 87% and relaxed.

The snow had come down to within 200 metres of sea level, it was a cold, blustery and rainy midsummer day; we cocooned inside. As we relaxed and unwound, we reflected on where we were and where we had been. According to Wikipedia: *"Owing to the remoteness of the location and the hazards there, a rounding of Cape Horn is widely considered to be the yachting equivalent of climbing Mount Everest, and so many sailors seek it out for its own sake."*

Reflecting on our passage to this point, we saw clearly that it would have been much easier and simpler for us to have waited at anchor on the south side of Golfo de Penas for the appropriate weather window. From there we could have made a downwind and with-the-current three-day run to the Horn, round it and run with the wind and current northward into the Atlantic to north of 50°. That would have saved us six weeks and dozens of tenuous anchorages. We chose instead the more wild and scenic route.

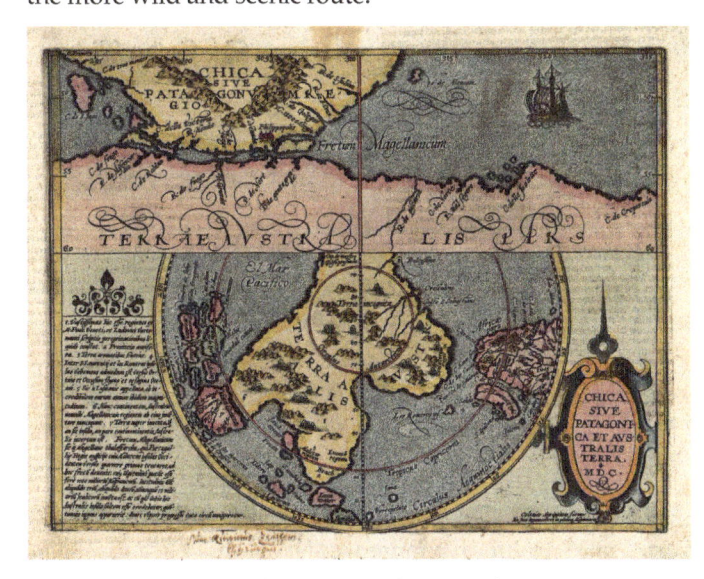

A 1600 map by Matthias Quad showed the contemporary view of the area now known as Cape Horn. The top map, in a flat projection, shows the Strait of Magellan dividing Patagonia from Terra Australis, or the unknown southern land. The bottom map shows Terra Australis on a polar projection, with four peninsulas. The peninsula facing Patagonia is the subject of the upper part of the map.

Looking into the discovery of the Cape, we found that in the early seventeenth century the Dutch East India Company had a monopoly on all Dutch trade with the Orient via the Cape of Good Hope and the Straits of Magellan, then the only known sea routes. Seeking an alternate route, Isaac Le Maire a prosperous Amsterdam merchant and Willem Schouten, a ship's master of the town of Hoorn formed a joint venture and received additional financial support from merchants of Hoorn. Two ships, the 360-ton Eendracht and the 110-ton Hoorn left Holland in June 1615. Hoorn was destroyed by fire while burning-off barnacles on the Argentine coast, and the expedition continued in Eendracht.

In late January 1616 Eendracht sailed southward of known land, and later recorded: *"In the evening 25 January 1616 the winde was South West, and that night wee went South with great waves or billowes out of the southwest, and very blew water, whereby wee judged, and held for certaine that ... it was the great South Sea, whereat we were exceeding glad to thinke that wee had discovered a way, which until that time, was unknowne to men, as afterward wee found it to be true. ... on 29 January 1616 we saw land againe lying north west and north northwest from us, which was the land that lay South from the straights of Magelan which reacheth Southward, all high hillie lande covered over with snow, ending with a sharpe point which wee called Kaap Hoorn."*

It is interesting to reflect that Kaap Hoorn was named after the Dutch town of Hoorn, not far from where Edi was born. It later had its name corrupted by the English to Cape Horn because of its shape, and in Chile it is known by and charted as Cabo de Hornos, which translates to Cape of Ovens.

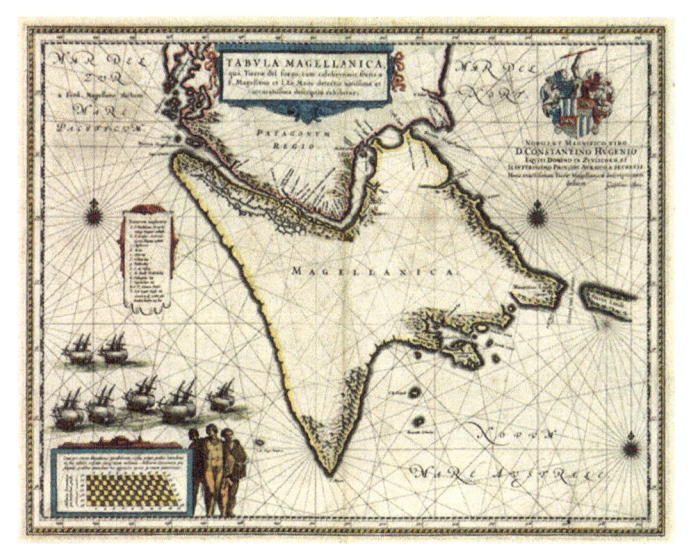

When it was discovered, the Horn was thought to be the southernmost point of Tierra del Fuego. The highly unpredictable violence of the area's weather and sea conditions made exploration difficult, and it wasn't until 1624 that it was realized that Kaap Hoorn was on a separate island. As late as 1635, new maps such as this one by Willem Blaeu of Amsterdam were depicting Kaap Hoorn as the southern tip of Magellanica, or Tierra del Fuego.

Nearly two centuries of use as a major shipping route, and hundreds of shipwrecks would pass before the discovery of Antarctica, only 400 miles across the Drake Passage from the Horn. A 1635 map by Jodocus Hondius of Amsterdam showed for the first time Kaap Hoorn on an island south of Tierra del Fuego. The map also showed for the first time the western portion of Tierra del Fuego broken-up into islands.

A sailor who had rounded the Horn was traditionally entitled to wear a gold loop earring in his left ear, the one which had faced the Horn on a typical east-about passage. He was also entitled to show-off a tattoo of a full-rigged ship and was allowed to dine with one foot on the table. Edi said absolutely not to the foot on the table, she didn't like the idea of a tattoo, but she thought that the earring might be OK.

We hauled-out our sophisticated surgical equipment for the piercing, which consisted of a sail stitching awl, a wine cork and a rubber mallet.

With rather quick work, I had a ring in my ear. To reduce the risk scaring the crew with the sight of blood, I wore my red jacket. To reduce the risk of infection and the possibility of pain, I resorted to a more modern technique: Photoshop.

As we had previously seen, there is still obvious tension between Chile and Argentina concerning their national boundaries. They very nearly went to war in 1978 over disputed possession of islands in the eastern entrance to the Beagle Channel. The dispute simmered, heated, cooled and heated again until the Treaty of Peace and Friendship of 1984. This drew the Beagle Channel boundaries and then extended them to seaward to divide their territorial seas and zones of economic interest. After some bends, the boundary runs south into Drake Passage along the meridian of Cape Horn. Chile's claim on a large wedge of Antarctica extends northward from the South Shetland Islands to the midpoint of Drake Passage, from where it runs west to the meridian of Cape Horn to intersect the 1984 line.

On our onward passage, once we exit the Beagle Channel, we intended standing 15 miles or so south of Isla Tierra del Fuego, and rather than transiting the Straits of Le Maire, we intended passing to the south of Isla de los Estados and around its eastern end. Descriptions in the pilots of strong tidal currents, up to 10 metre standing waves and dangerous overfalls in the Straits of Le Maire persuaded me to avoid that passage. Similarly, at the eastern end of los Estados, the confused seas, the tidal rips, the overfalls and the strong landward set make it prudent to be well to seaward there. We were looking for a two or three day fair weather window to get past Isla de los Estados and well out into the Atlantic to its northeast, where we could expect to find increasingly stable weather.

As we sat waiting for the weather, so did many others. On Sunday there were three rafts of six boats each along Micalvi's west side, blocking the channel at low tide. Her eastern side was chock-a-block with a mix of near-derelicts and other long-term moorage boats. Because there was no more room, there were several boats at anchor in the seno.

On Monday there was a major shuffle of boats, as several headed westward to begin their long treks up the canals toward Puerto Montt, and one, Polonius, the little Polish steel sloop with eight men aboard, which we had seen in Ushuaia, headed for Antarctica. The commercial operators appeared to be wrapping-up their season and preparing their boats for a long hibernation. The transient boats were down to seven, two French, two Belgique, a German, a New Zealander and a Canadian.

In the early afternoon on Tuesday we took a walk around the head of the seno and along an old logging road that follows the ridge. We found a trail down to the beach at the point opposite Micalvi and from there we walked the beach back around.

It was heavily overcast and a bit dark for midday, which is likely why we spotted a juvenile Garza Bruja, a Black-Crowned Night Heron wading in the shallows. It probably thought it was night.

Once we were back around the seno, we continued into the centre of town, walking through the Armada residential area to the almacen. The sad-looking carrots were still there, as were the overripe avocados and the two lemons, but there were some decently fresh tomatoes in the top bin and three new bags of potatoes on the floor. Our stock of tomatoes and potatoes was already more than adequate, so we were not tempted. We did; however, buy two more kilos of frozen pangasius fillets and two dozen more of the hockey puck rolls.

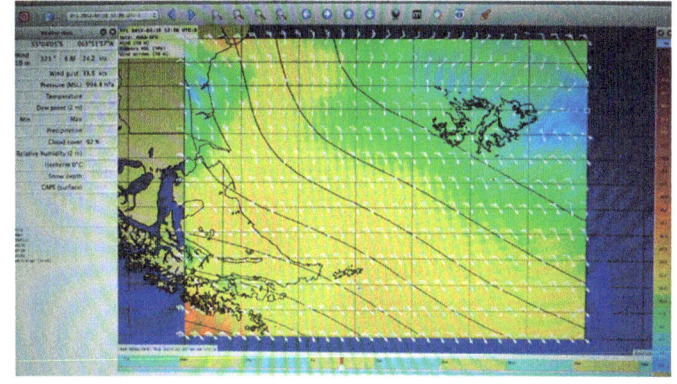

Tuesday morning's grib showed more positively the weather window we had been watching. The forecasts appeared to show some usable weather beginning early on Friday morning, that by maintaining 7.5 knots sailing and motor-sailing, should allow us to make the eastern point of Isla de los Estados by sunset. From there, 20 to 25 knot northwest and north-northwest winds should give us a fast reach, possibly a run toward the southern side of the Falklands.

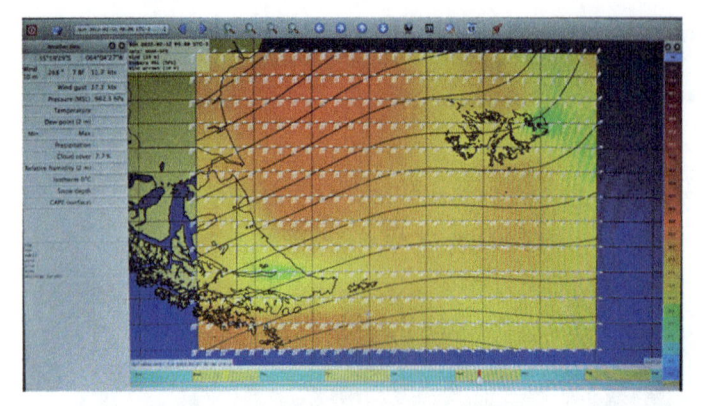

The winds were predicted to back to west on Sunday and gradually increase to 30 knots, allowing us to run around the eastern side of the Falklands and shape a more northerly course toward Cape Town. Of course, these are nothing but computer-generated predictions, and we were aware of the need to update and monitor them closely before applying for a zarpe.

The barometer had been fluctuating in a low range for days. It was 983.9 when we arrived back from the Horn, down to 974.2 on Saturday morning, up to 980.0 Sunday afternoon, up further to 986.6 Monday morning, back down to 977.0 Tuesday morning, quickly up to 990.1 Tuesday midnight and up further to 995.2 at Wednesday noon. During this period, the winds in the marina had blown from every quarter and from every Force, 0 through 8 with gusts into Force 9. It rained, the sun shone, it hailed, the stars came out, there were squalls and then totally blue skies and it snowed on the hills just above us. In the process, we observed Midsummer's Day in Puerto Williams.

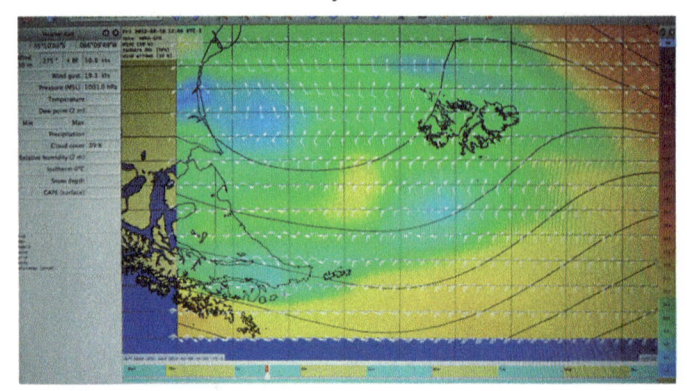

Wednesday afternoon's grib predicted an earlier easing of the northerly winds between Isla de los Estados and the Falklands, with the winds at 10 knots and below by noon on Friday as a high builds west of the Falklands.

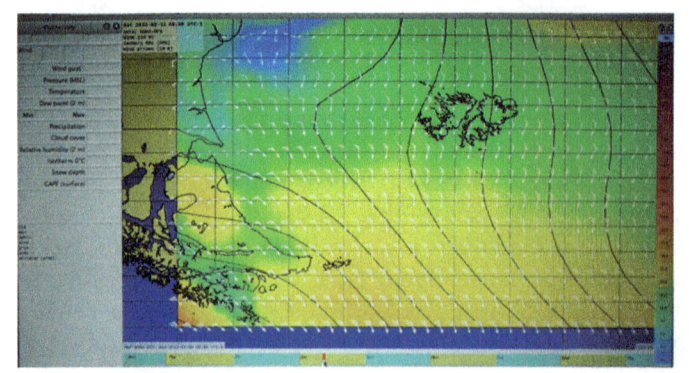

The high is then predicted to move rapidly east leaving to the south of its path, and on our proposed course, 20 to 25 knot northerly winds into Saturday. I figured that these conditions should allow us to make good speed eastward across to the south side of the Falklands. Again we reminded ourselves that these gribs offer machine-made predictions without human adjustments, so we use them as planning tools, always mindful of the rapidly changing and near unpredictable weather of this region.

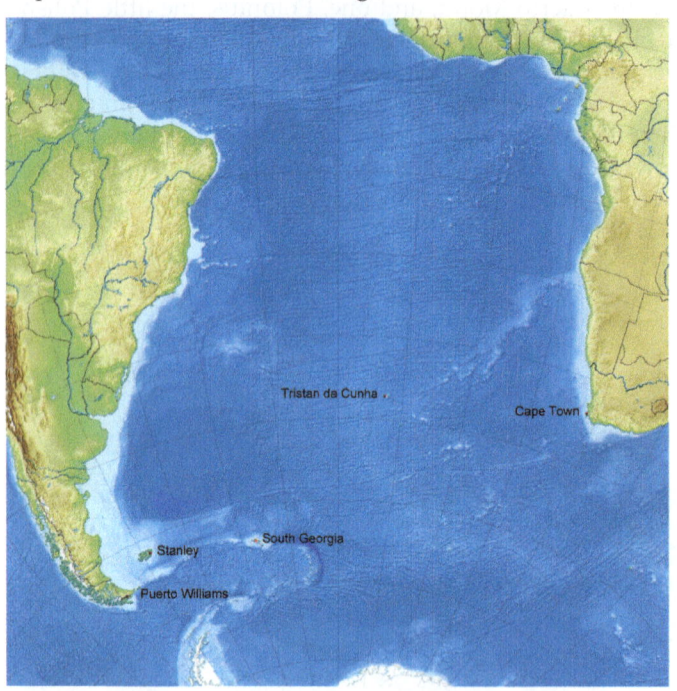

It is about 4400 miles from Puerto Williams to Cape Town. With following winds and currents for a major portion of the way, we could expect to make an average of better than 150 miles per day, so the passage might take 30 days. Mike Harker in his solo circumnavigation with his Hunter 49 made many 200-mile-days in crossing the South Pacific and the Indian Oceans, and he had a 1398-mile week. He averaged 157 miles per day for the complete circuit.

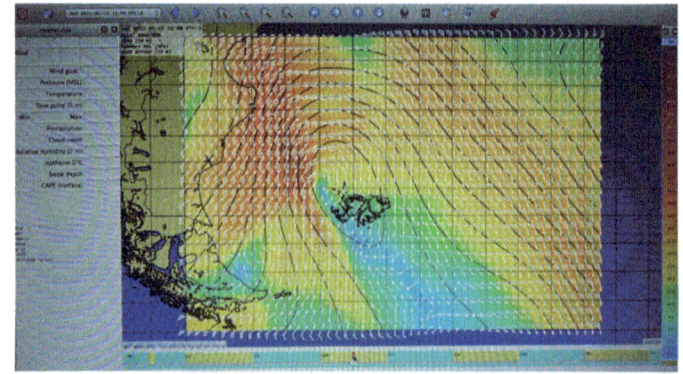

On Thursday morning, the 9th of February, the gribs showed a system with 45 and 50 knot winds building northwest of the Falklands midday on Sunday and then moving southeast to about where we would be with an early Friday departure. We re-examined the gribs and our options, and we quickly decided to apply for a zarpe to Cape Town for a 1500 departure, which would put us in the Falklands before the storm.

I had been unable to make my new MacBook Air work with our Iridium satellite phone through X-Gate to give us access to underway weather information. I had exchanged dozens of emails and spent much time on the sat phone discussing the problem with the techies at Global Marine Networks, and none of us could figure-out the problem. In theory, it works, but in practice for us, it did not. Once we leave port, we would have no access to weather information, and would need to continue relying on reading the skies and the barometer. With the notoriously unsettled weather in the region, and also the lateness in the season, we decided to forgo our planned visit to South Georgia.

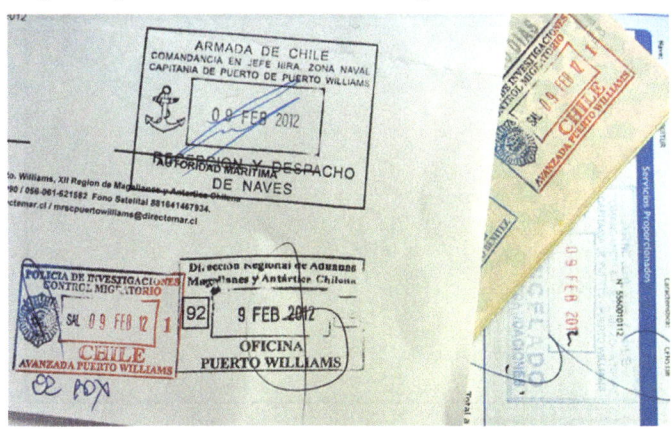

We prepared Sequitur for sea, and at 1330 headed over to the Capitan de Puerto to apply for a zarpe to Cape Town. The Armada personnel were quick and efficient in preparing the zarpe, the Customs officer quickly scanned and stamped our documents, the Migracion officer stamped our passports cheerfully and wished us safe navigation. This left only the civil servant plug-in-the works who does the financial part of the process. He dawdled, had tea, did useless things, read manuals, dug in files and tried to pretend he was busy. We have long ago learned that to push this type of person leads only to longer delays, and likely to a fine-tooth-comb treatment. We exercised our patience as he managed to stretch-out the process for over an hour and a half and finally came-up with an invoice for 49,500 Pesos, obviously disappointed he could find no other fees to charge us.

It was nearly 1600 by the time we got back to Micalvi and I went into the bar to find Miguel and pay for our moorage and electricity. We had spent two days alongside before heading to the Horn and another six waiting for a weather window to head north. The charges came to US$168, which I paid with our last 66,900 Chilean Pesos, our leftover 22 Argentine Pesos, and our last US$23. Other than a few coins, we were out of all American money, North, Central and South. It was a good time to head to another continent.

We were third-out in a raft of six in the middle of the three rafts on Micalvi's west side. Ahead of us was another raft of six, and the one astern had four boats. We were dead centre of the sixteen boats, with a cat's cradle of lines strung from each to counter the unpredictable wind shifts, the rachas and the williwaws. We needed the cooperation of seven other boats to dig ourselves out.

Before we had headed over for our zarpe, we had informed the skippers of the boats astern and the one outboard us of out departure intentions. The two additional boats outboard us had come in while we were uselessly delayed at the Capitania and their skippers were ashore doing paperwork. The boat directly astern of us, the New Zealand ketch, Victoria was ready to head to Puerto Toro to stage for a run to the Horn. They told us they would be leaving after tea. Finally at 1706 we slipped and headed out, a little over two hours later than we had planned.

32. To the Falklands

Our zarpe said Cape Town, but we were headed to the Falklands. The Argentine government is again turning-up the heat on their claims to the Malvinas (Falklands), and we needed to keep all mention of the Falklands from our communications. As we motor-sailed out the Beagle Channel, we religiously stayed in Chilean waters, taking a considerably longer route, and then we went out to clearly beyond the Argentine 12-mile Territorial Waters line before heading north of east along the south coasts of Isla Tierra del Fuego and Isla de los Estados.

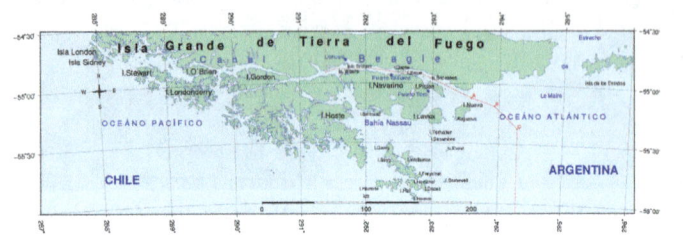

The sunset at 2122 had found us turning southeast around the northeast corner of Isla Picton. Four minutes later the full moon had theoretically risen in the overcast sky. The wind was southeast at 10 knots as we motored directly into it at 7 knots. It began raining. At 0600, shortly after sunrise on Friday morning it was still raining. The wind had gone around to our starboard quarter and was assisting us along a bit with its 10 knots. We continued motor-sailing into a cold, dank day. By midmorning the rain had stopped and the clouds had nearly all moved off to the east, or had dissipated.

It warmed rapidly in the cockpit, and by the time Edi had brought brunch up, I had stripped-off nine pieces of clothing, and was down to only two layers of fleece on top and insulated pants on the bottom, plus wool socks inside low shoes.

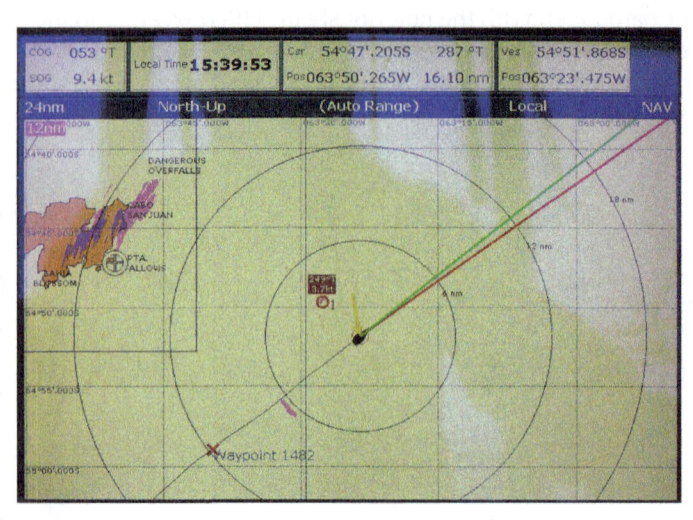

Friday noon we were 193° - 20.4 miles of the southeast cape of Isla de los Estados, the last piece of Argentina. We had made 132.3 miles in just under 19 hours, almost exactly 7 knots in adverse tides and winds. Through the middle of the day as we came to our CPA on Estados, we watched an Argentine patrol vessel shadowing us on its 12-mile limit. It parallelled us until apparently convinced we wouldn't enter their waters.

We were also being watched by hundreds of albatross soaring in the wind currents above the waves. These were mostly Black-browed and Royal, but also there were also many Wandering Albatross. We also saw dozens of Antarctic Fulmars, which braved very close to the boat.

We continued to monitor the sky and the barometer for changes that would signal the deepening of the depression northwest of the Falklands. On Friday the barometer rose above 1000 for the first time in over two weeks and made it to 1005.4 at 0700 on Saturday, before beginning a slowly undulating decline.

594

On Saturday afternoon Edi spotted a formation in the clouds, and we jokingly wondered whether it was our weather window.

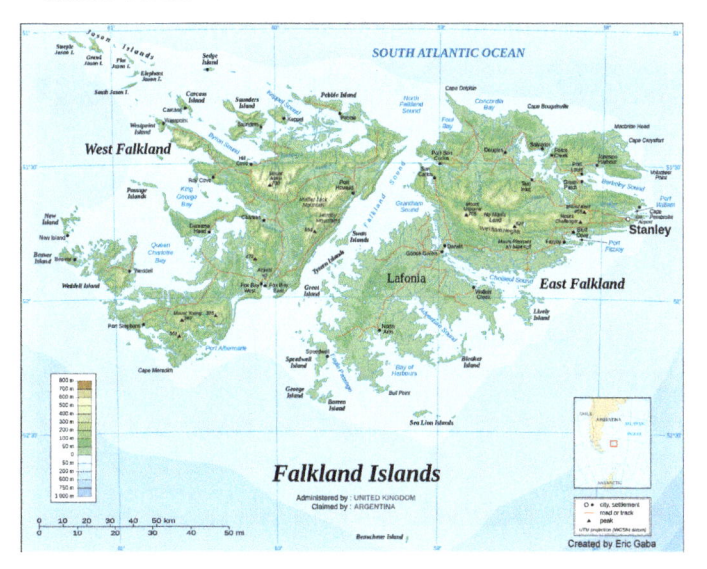

On Saturday afternoon the winds veered to northeast and increased to over 20 knots and our speed was down to 5.5 as we motored directly into it. At 1706 our 24-hour run was 154 miles, down from our first 24-hour run of 170.3. At 1945, as we were approaching Sea Lion Islands off the southwest corner of the Falklands, the engine died. I went below and switched the Racor primary filter from the port to the starboard one. I restarted the engine and we continued for another 10 minutes, then died again.

I rolled-out the staysail and half the main and sailed east-southeast. I went below to change to a fresh port filter, which took until 2209 in the sloppy and confused seas. We resumed our motoring northeastward, directly into the wind. We still had 75 miles to go to make Stanley. At 7.5 knots we would be there shortly after 0800 Sunday morning, well before the blow forecast for late afternoon. Our progress slowed as the tide turned and at midnight we were down to 4.5 knots at with turns for 8.

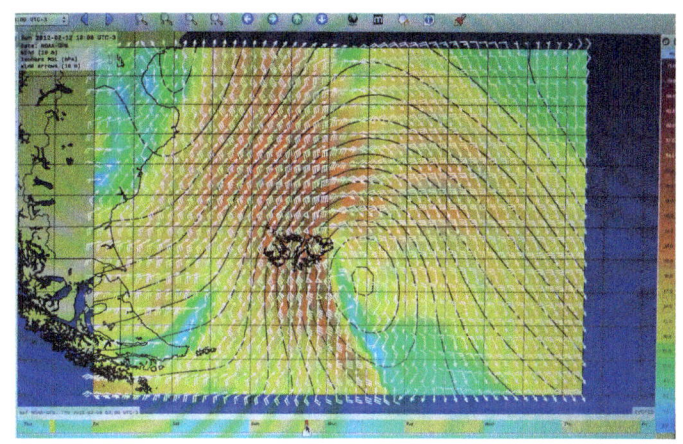

I still had the grib files from Thursday's download, so I looked again and at the cyclone that had been predicted to pass over Stanley at 1800 on Sunday. On my iPad I plotted a dozen-or-so anchorages along the coast, which would offer some protection from the predicted 50+ winds and we pressed on, making the best speed possible against the tide and wind.

At midnight the barometer was at 989.8, at 0700 Sunday it was down to 982.9 and further down to 979.1 at 0900, when the wind was northwest 18 to 22 and assisting us along a bit. At 1025 we were hit by a squall with gusts to 42 and heavy rain. At 1113 another more gentle squall passed over with winds to 33. At 1247 a more violent one hit us with 45 to 50 knot winds. I headed north toward Port Fitzroy.

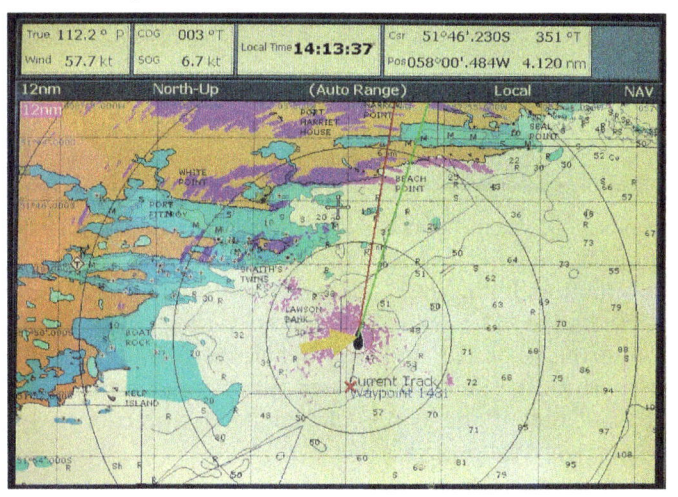

At 1413 we were about 4 miles from the entrance to Fitzroy when sustained winds over 50 knots and rapidly building seas made progress difficult. Thoughts of approaching an increasingly lee shore as the wind backed made me reexamine the situation. At 1430 I rolled-in the last hanky of the main and put our stern to the storm to run with it to seaward under power.

At 1440 I decided to turn southward into the troughs, shut-down the engine and lay a-hull under bare poles. I had pointed our bows south in case I needed to use the engine to gain some southings to clear Wolf Rocks to the east-northeast of us. I watched our drift on the cockpit chart-plotter and was pleased with its direction.

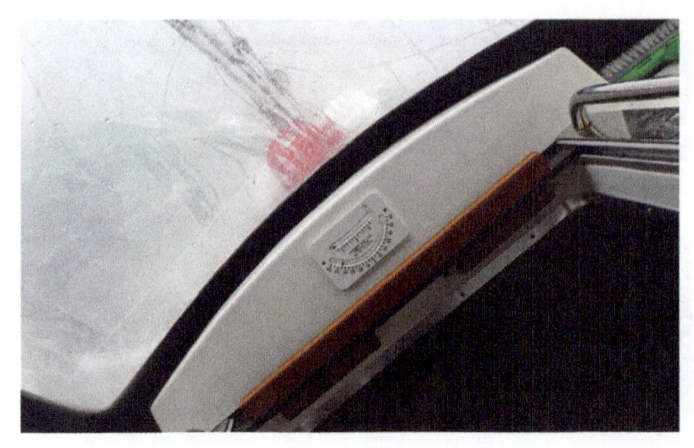

We also watched the inclinometer jam-up a couple of times against the stops at 60°, but never could get a camera in position to record more than 43°. We were hit by a few breaking waves, and Sequitur took them in stride. I thought of launching the Jordan series drogue, but realized that we were just fine without.

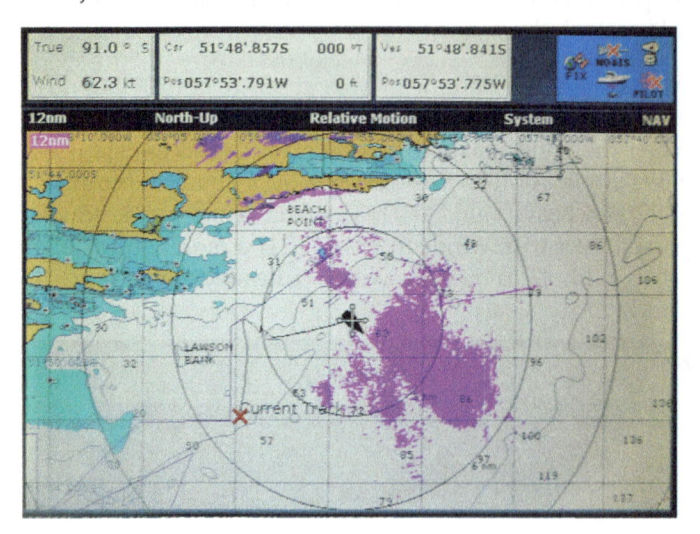

We went below and cocooned in the rather more peaceful salon. We called FishOps in Stanley on VHF and reported our situation, telling them we were comfortable, safe and in no danger. The watchkeeper told us they had been monitoring us on AIS and would maintain a watch. From the chart-plotter there I monitored our drift east-northeast, and saw that if the wind maintained its direction, we should clear Wolf Rocks.

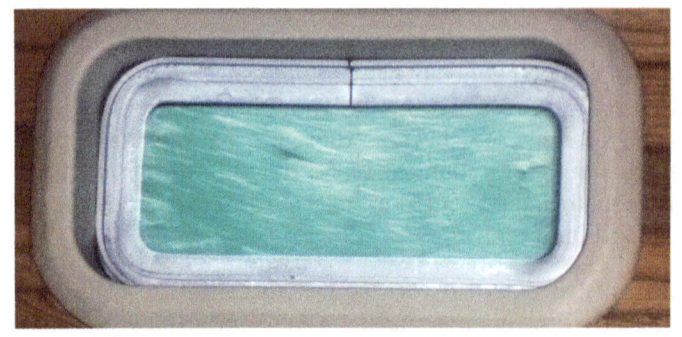

The port sidelight in the salon was looking bottom-ward a few times as breakers hit our starboard beam. Overhead, through the skylights and hatches we watched as great depths of green water sluiced over the decks. We remained dressed, with boots on and covered ourselves with duvets and napped.

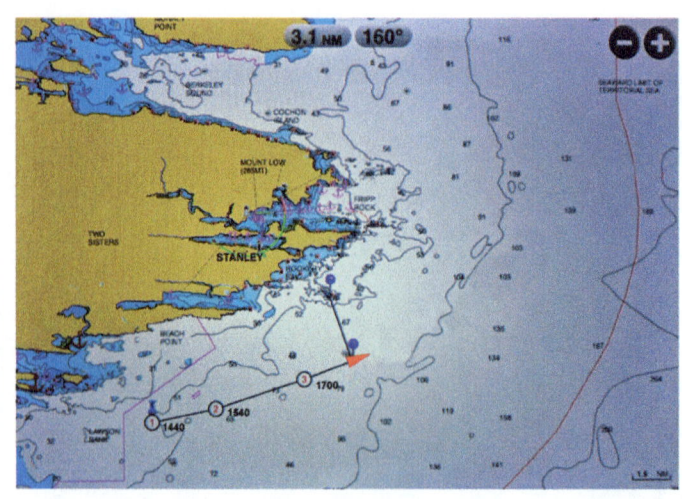

I set-up a plot on the iPad to track our drift, and we laid down on the main salon couches to relax and watch the storm happen. At least every half hour I awoke to monitor the situation on the iPad beside me on the settee, and to put on an hourly fix. At 1740 we drifted past Wolf Rock, clear by 3.1 miles and continued drifting to seaward. I told Edi that the next piece of land to the east of us was the west coast of Chile, a complete circumnavigation away. We relaxed further and slept more soundly.

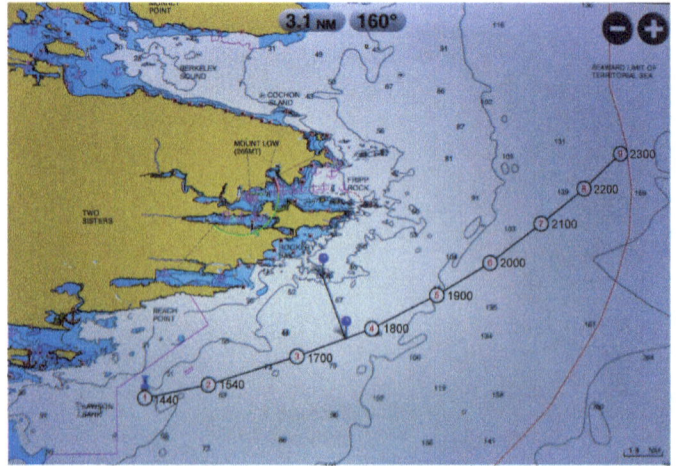

By 2200 the winds had abated to the low 40s and we were rather hungry, not having eaten since breakfast. As Sequitur rolled in the troughs, I juggled a Lock-and-Lock of frozen sauce Bolognese in the microwave to defrost, and then did the same with a Zip-Lock of basmati rice. Our usual routine is to make extra portions when we cook, and freeze them in one-meal batches for times when it is difficult to be more creative in the galley. This was one of those times. I heated the Bolognese in the wok as the stove gimbals hit the stops, added a can of sliced mushrooms, a can of black beans and finally the rice. We wedged ourselves into the couches and spooned comfort food from huge China Town rice bowls.

Re-energized by the hot food, we prepared to get underway again and see if we could make Stanley. At 2300 we flashed-up the Yanmar and began motoring westward, back toward the Falklands. We had drifted nearly 25 miles and had 19 miles to go to make it into Stanley Harbour. The seas were initially 4 to 5 metres and rather confused, and we were able to make 3.5 knots directly into them and into the 40-knot winds. By 0230 we had gained some lee from the high winds and seas and were in more manageable conditions.

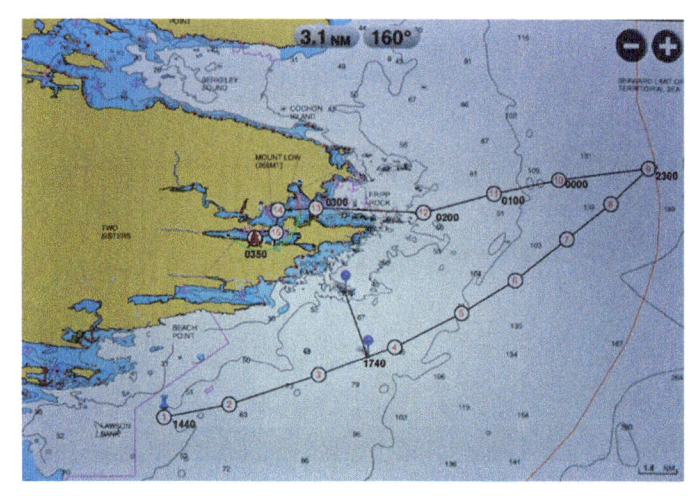

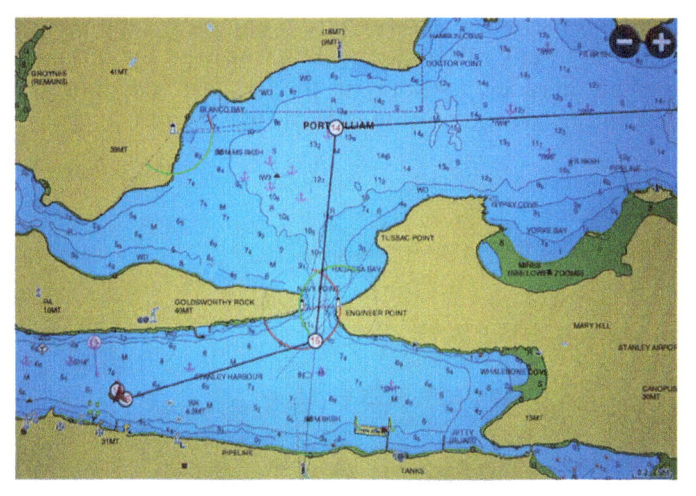

By 0300 we were in comparatively pleasant waters, we had found the Blanco Bay sector light and were on its line. We easily found the red transit lights through the narrows and then headed up-harbour into the 35 knot wind to a spot in front of the public wharf, where at 0340 on Monday the 13th we came to 35 metres on the Rocna in 8 metres of water. We went back below to our settees and went to sleep until nearly noon.

Near midday when we woke, it was still blowing a gale in the harbour, so I called Customs on VHF to tell them we would like to remain onboard with our quarantine flag hoisted, and to delay heading ashore to clear-in until the weather calmed on Tuesday. They had no problem with this.

As I was speaking with the Customs agent there was the loud bang of our anchor snubber snapping in an upper-40s gust. I went forward and rigged a new one and set another as a back-up for it. This is the second 19mm laid nylon snubber we have snapped; maybe ten metres does not provide sufficient stretch, maybe it was a bad batch of rope.

On Monday evening the winds were down to under 30, but the long fetch from the west made it rather bouncy in the anchorage. The Customs officer had told us that Tuesday would be busy with a dozen fishing boats and a cruise ship arriving in the morning, so when we took the dinghy ashore after breakfast, we decided to walk along the waterfront and up the hill to Customs, rather than trying to meet them on the jetty.

As we walked, we saw the cruise ship and fishing boats at anchor. We later learned that the fishing boats are Taiwanese squid jiggers, and that there are about 100 of them working the local waters.

Clearing-in was a simple process; for the first time in nearly two and a half years, we did the process in fluent English. As we chatted with the Customs officer, we learned he was a fifth generation Falklander, and that there were about 3300 residents of the Islands.

On our way back we wandered among the markers in the cemetery. In our quick scan, we saw stones engraved with dates back into the 1860s, though we know there must be older, since the Stanley was first settled in 1844 by the British when they moved the capital of the Falklands here from Port Louis.

Back in the centre of town, we walked past Jubilee Villas, row-houses built in 1887 to commemorate Queen Victoria's Golden Jubilee.

A short distance further west along the waterfront is Christ Church Cathedral. Built in 1892, it is the most southerly Anglican Cathedral in the world. The golden arches on its western lawns are not to mark a McDonalds grease depot; they are the jawbones of two blue whales, erected in 1933 to commemorate the centenary of British administration of the Falkland Islands.

Further along we saw the mizzen mast from the Great Britain, at one time the largest ship in the world. She had been launched in Bristol in 1843 and had arrived in Stanley storm-damaged in 1886, where she remained until she was returned to Bristol for restoration in 1970.

We learned that Stanley has been the final haven for many storm-damaged ships that managed to claw their way here, but were too severely damaged to continue. One of these is Jhelum, launched in Liverpool in 1849, she limped into Stanley severely damaged from rounding Cape Horn with a cargo of Chilean guano. She was used for storage for many decades, and only in the last few years began breaking-up, recently losing her bow in a storm.

Many of the damaged ships which couldn't continue were used as storage, some became the basis for wharves and jetties. The East Jetty, next along to the east of the Public Jetty is based on three hulks, only one of which is still visible, Egeria, a Canadian barque of 1066 tons built in 1859. She limped into Stanley severely damaged during an 1872 voyage from London to Callao, and was condemned and scuttled.

After our clearing-in procedures, and an orientation stroll, we headed back to the dinghy on the finger float. Next to that float, on the Public Jetty is a larger 30-metre float, which is used by passenger lighters from the cruise ships. We had learned that when there are no cruise ships in port, private yachts are permitted to use the float. The last lighter had just taken passengers back out to the cruise ship, so the float was available to us for a few days until the next ship arrived.

We went back out to Sequitur in the anchorage to prepare to come alongside the float. Back onboard, I went forward to begin shortening-in the anchor chain. The windlass motor whirred, but the gipsy did not turn. It appeared that the strain of snapping the snubbers in Isla Lennox and here in Stanley did-in the gear again. We spent a bit under two hours weighing the anchor with the spinnaker halyard. The last ten minutes of this was in motoring at up to 2800 rpm forward and astern with the anchor chain up-and-down, trying to break the Rocna out of the mud of the bottom. Finally, at 1950 we secured alongside the float.

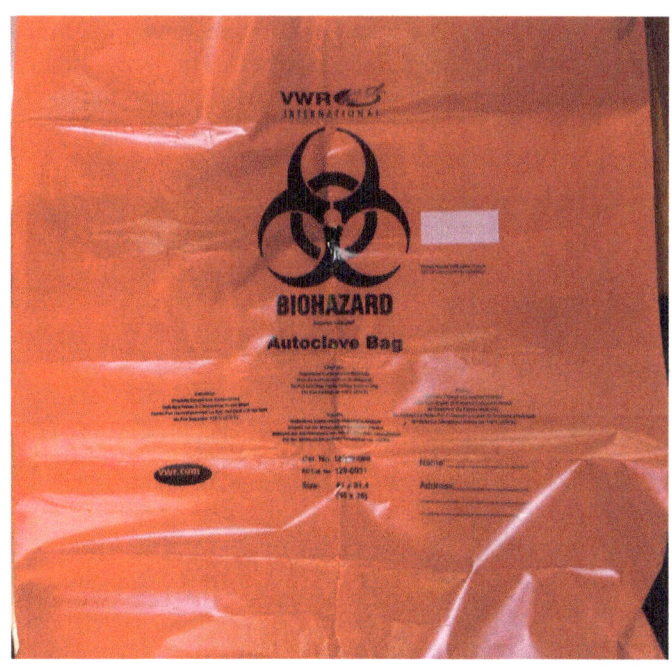

When we had cleared-in, we had been given a biohazard bag in which to place all of our non-Falklands organic garbage and any wrappings that had touched it. The Falklands are fortunate in being free of most serious plant and animal pests and diseases, and these bags make it simple for visiting yachts to handle their garbage.

After breakfast on Wednesday morning we started with cleaning-up from the heavy weather. Down below, we had sustained a broken bowl and a chipped candle holder. Up top the Hydrovane suffered a bent retaining pin and a sheared one. I hadn't removed the sail from the unit, and the hurricane-force gusts were a tad much for the pins.

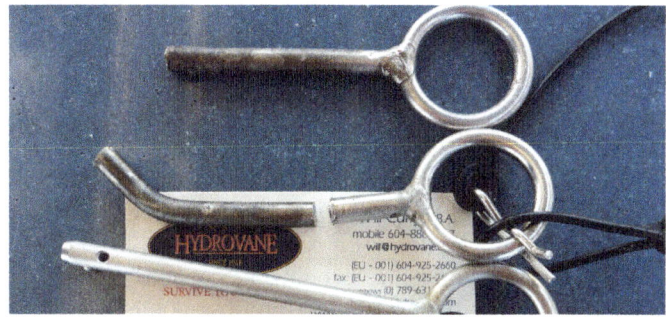

We abandoned the mess of chain on the deck until the next day, and went below. It was Valentine's Day. To celebrate, I sautéed Puerto Eden king crab in a julienne of Puerto Montt shallots and garlic and Ushuaia crimini mushrooms. This was served with Vancouver's Little India basmati rice, Ushuaia broccoli and Puerto Williams tomatoes. The Undurraga Brut Royal from Valle de Leyda accompanied splendidly.

Although the wind had bent the pin, I could not straighten it no matter what I tried. I needed to hacksaw it into pieces so I could remove it.

From the spares bins I brought-out two new pins and quickly replaced the damaged ones. The only other damage that I could find up top was that our foghorn speaker had been blown off its mount on the mast and had apparently disappeared overboard.

Among the things we had organized when we were ashore clearing-in on Tuesday was a delivery of diesel oil to the float. We were pleased and surprised to see that diesel, at the equivalent of $1.21 Canadian per litre, is about 15% less expensive in the Falklands than it is in Puerto Williams. We brought the tanks back up to full at 920 litres.

We went to the Falkland Islands Company's West Store, where among other things, we found very inexpensive meat and cheese. We bought a package of fresh local beef bangers to try. Wednesday evening I prepared a British grilled dinner, with bangers, courgettes, potato rounds and cherry tomatoes with fresh basil. The bangers were lean and delicious; we committed to buying at least six more packets.

We had also found wonderful back bacon at less than a third of the Vancouver price, and then saw it was even cheaper still, being offered at buy one, get one free. We bought eight packages. We also bought three packages of fresh basil and a couple dozen on-the-vine cherry tomatoes. The markets were all out of eggs, and there would be none until the next ship came in; however we still had a small stock onboard.

For breakfast on Thursday morning Edi prepared basted eggs with back bacon, English muffins, cherry tomatoes and fresh basil leaves.

On Wednesday we had spoken with Sybie, owner of the Pod Gift Shop next to the Visitor Welcome Centre just across from the Jetty where Sequitur was secured. She told us she had friends with laying hens, and she could have them save a few for us. We asked if three dozen would be possible, and she said in four or five days, yes.

After breakfast Edi washed and applied Vaseline to all the hatch and port-light gaskets. We had a few drops of water come in a forward one as breaking seas sluiced over the decks in the storms. I went along behind her and adjusted all the dogs. We hadn't done this in nearly three years, and have had no leaks until this storm.

Edi also repaired a loose corner grommet on the sun cover over the skylights in our cockpit canopy. It appears that several bouts of winds in the 50s and 60s were a tad much for it. The remainder of the canopy remained in fine condition, performing splendidly in keeping us warm, dry and protected during the storms.

A cruise ship was scheduled in on Friday morning; we had to be off the float by 0600. To avoid having to get up early Friday morning, on Thursday evening we headed back out into the anchorage, where we came to 38 metres on the Delta in 7.5 metres of water in front of the Cathedral. The winds later in the evening were up to 40 knots, but the anchor held well in the mud.

For dinner we had Falkland Islands spring lamb chops with basmati rice and a butter-sweat of julienned of carrots and red and green peppers, garnished by cherry tomatoes and shredded fresh basil. With it we enjoyed a bottle of Casa Lapostolle 2008 Rapel Valley Cabernet Sauvignon.

The gribs showed Friday to be rather calm through until late afternoon, so after breakfast we launched Non Sequitur and motored out through The Narrows and out Port William to Gypsy Cove. As we entered the cove, we were met by an escort of dolphins, which scooted within a few centimetres of the dinghy. They led and followed us all the way in to the beach, into water just deep enough for them to swim.

601

Our dinghy wheels made it easy for us to land on the fine sand beach, and to pull Non Sequitur above the next while's tide. There were a couple of flocks of Magellanic penguins on the beach, as well as many individuals and groups on the slopes above the beaches. They were a mix of sleek-feathered and very motley moulting birds.

After enjoying watching the antics of the penguins on the beach, we carefully picked our way up the slopes, being mindful to not step above the dens, which are dug up to two metres into the sandy soil.

I came across a pair striking similar poses. One was sleek and smooth-feathered, while the other was a seemingly non-ending moulting of down. The ground was so thickly coated that it appeared to be snow.

In the penguin's rookery and denning area was a pair of Magellan geese. The male struck a striding pose for me as I lingered, enjoying its gracefulness.

The female quietly rested on one leg, seeming unconcerned that I was only three metres away.

After a delightful hour and a half among the birds, we headed back down to the dinghy, launched it and motored back around the point, through The Narrows and into Stanley Harbour. Once past Engineer Point, we turned east to look at a couple more of the area's many shipwrecks.

The first was the steam tug Samson, which had worked the area for many years, towing, rescuing or salvaging ships in distress. She had broken her moorings in the great gale of 1945 and blew up onto the beach. She came to rest not far from the wreck of Lady Elizabeth, which she had rescued off Uraine Rock in 1913.

Lady Elizabeth, a 223-foot ironclad barque was launched in Sunderland, England in 1879. In 1889 she had brought bricks and cement to Stanley for the construction of Christ Church Cathedral. On a voyage from Vancouver to Mozambique in 1913, she was battered in a storm southwest of Cape Horn, losing four men and her deck cargo overboard. She limped into the Falklands, and on her approach into Stanley, struck Uraine Rock, putting a large hole in her hull and badly damaging her keel. The steam tug Samson later towed her into Stanley, where she was condemned and sold to the Falkland Islands Company. She was used as a storage facility until 1936, when she broke her moorings in a storm and washed up onto the beach at the eastern end of the harbour.

Back onboard Sequitur, we relaxed. The cruise ship had left, but there was another one scheduled to arrive in the early afternoon on Saturday and to depart by 1800. It made sense for us to remain at anchor on Friday night and then return to the float after it had gone.

On Saturday we watched Hanseatic come to anchor about two cables from us, and through the afternoon we felt the steep wake of the steady stream of lighters to and from the float.

As the Hanseatic's last lighter was hoisted aboard, we weighed using the cockpit power winch and then motored in to the float. In the anchorage with us had been the French sloop Guapita, with whom we had anchored in the storm in Caleta Lennox on our way to Cape Horn. She came in shortly after us and moored ahead of us on the float.

In Guapita were four young men aged 24 to 27, finished university and wandering for a bit before getting seriously into work. We invited them over for pizza on Sunday evening and spent a delightful few hours devouring four different pizzas that Edi had created from a wonderful list of ingredients that included artichoke hearts, sun-dried tomatoes, shrimp, red, green and yellow peppers, mushrooms, white onions, garlic, black olives, basil leaves, pesto, tomato sauce, sausage, ham, salami, gorgonzola, gouda, mozzarella, asiago and I can't remember what all.

Guapita is a 9.5-metre sloop that two of the lads had bought in the south of France and had sailed down the African coast to the Cape Verde Islands, crossed the Atlantic, the Caribbean and transited the Panama Canal to enter a race to the Galapagos. From the Galapagos they went to Juan Fernandez and Valdivia, where they picked-up the other two French lads through an Internet posting for the three-month trip down through the Chilean canals, around the Horn and up to Buenos Aires.

After we had seen them in Lennox, they had gone to the Horn and had done the compulsory return to Puerto Williams. From there they cleared out to Ushuaia and got a zarpe to Buenos Aires with permission to stop in Isla de los Estados. While they were at anchor in Estados, they were hit by the southern edge of the storm that had hit us, and they dragged onto the rocks and put two holes through their hull, fortunately above the waterline. They had done temporary patches and had taken the best winds available and had come to the Falklands for refuge. They will likely have a time explaining to the officials in Buenos Aires why they visited the Malvinas without Argentine permission.

During our short time in the Falklands we have seen an increasing display of signs, posters and flags to publicly pronounce that the Falklands are British. There are formal posters and decals that declare: "Falklands - British and Proud of it", "Falklands - British to the Core" and other such sentiments. In car windows are displayed impromptu banners and posters and there are Union Jacks flying from every available place.

On one Land Rover we saw a scribbled poster declaring: "How can we give back what was never theirs?"

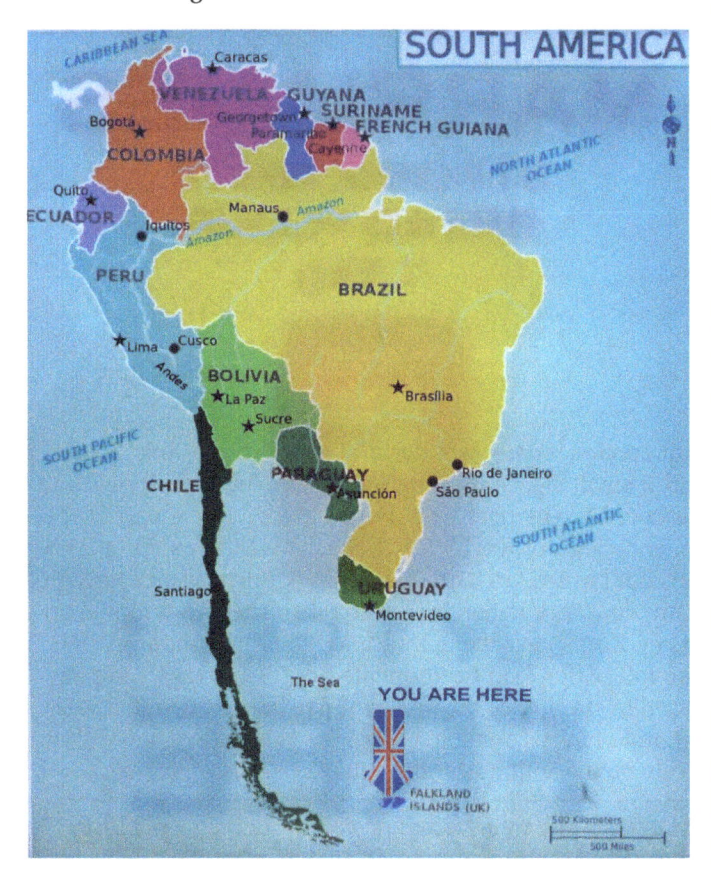

At the Seafish Chandlery Supermarket we saw a large poster outside the front doors with a redrawn map of South America that ignores the existence of Argentina.

On our way back from the supermarket we were passed by a long parade of horn-beeping vehicles festooned with British and Falklands colours, banners and posters. There was an air of British pride evident everywhere we went in Stanley, and there was an equally evident disdain for all things Argentine. The thirtieth anniversary of the Argentine invasion and occupation was only a few weeks away, and the mood in the Falklands was upbeat. However; everywhere there is amazement that Argentina has the audacity to even think of again turning-up the heat on their claim to these islands that were never theirs.

On Wednesday we walked up the hill and along to the west past the rows of cottages on Pioneer Row. These houses were built in 1849, many from kits shipped-in from England, and they were originally homes for the military pensioners who came to settle the Islands.

We continued along through a rain squall, back down to the waterfront and past Government House, the home and offices of the Governor of the Falkland Islands. The building originates from the 1840s, with extensions added by subsequent Governors. We assumed the 12-metre satellite dish is a recent addition.

Further along we came to a monument that serves as a memorial to the Battle of the Falklands on 08 December 1914, in which the British Squadron destroyed the German Squadron. We had previously seen the final fate of the German ship, Dresden, which had eluded the British ships here and was hunted-down and forced to scuttle months later at Isla Juan Fernandez, Chile.

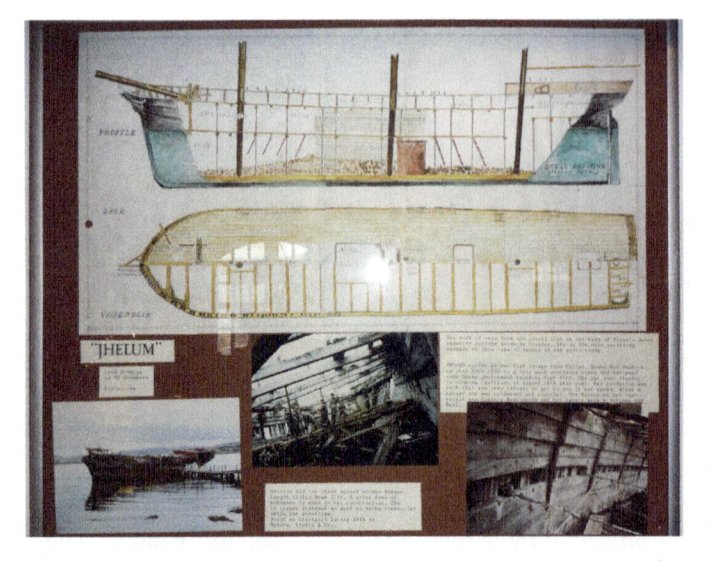

Through the continuing squalls, we walked along to the museum, where we were fascinated with the range and quality of the displays. There are many artefacts from the early settlement of the Falklands, and of much earlier visits by English explorers. There is also much background information on the many shipwrecks in the area.

Most fascinating to us among the displays is a well-laid-out capture of the events surrounding the Argentine invasion and occupation in 1982. There are Argentine proclamation letters, propaganda leaflets, and posters; there are scribbled notes from the starving young Argentine conscripts begging residents for food; there is a replica of one of the hundreds of squalid Argentine bunkers in which the conscripts defended their Military Dictator's stupidity. There are memorials to the British personnel and ships lost in the seventy-day occupation.

Edi spotted some wonderfully shaped old ink bottles, and a small sign indicating that examples were for sale at the counter. The note went on to say they were part of the general cargo of the John R Kelley, a wooden ship of 2364 tons built in 1883 in Bath, Maine, USA. She was on a voyage from New York to San Francisco when she was wrecked on Kelley Rocks near the entrance to Stanley Harbour in 1899. The ink bottles had been donated by the salvage company to sell in support of the museum. We bought two that were still full of ink as our souvenir of the Falklands. They will sit nicely on the antique windowsill of our Vancouver loft.

> Many months after we had posted to our blog a photo and some background information on the ink bottles, we were contacted by a woman who said: *"I have been researching the shipwreck of the John R Kelley in Port Stanley and was so excited to see your beautiful photos of the ink bottles and your identification of them. My grandmother was on the Kelly when it broke up in the outer harbor She was on board as a tutor for the Captain's daughter. They were taken into Port Stanley as a precaution and she spent three weeks there, before another ship came in without a Captain so they continued the trip to San Francisco. My mother had always said that the cargo was ink bottles but I had not been able to verify it."*

On our way back from the museum we saw the latest wreck on the shores of Stanley Harbour. Some unfortunate owner had his four-by-four vehicle demonstrate its off-road capability. It seems there was a parking brake failure and the vehicle rolled backwards down the hill of Holdfast Road from the museum, across Ross Road and over the embankment, just along from the wreck of the Jhelum.

Our pause in the Falklands allowed us to luxuriate in a wonderful little haven of First World quiet, polite, organized and predictable society. Except for our two trips back home to Vancouver, this was our first taste of sedately civilized society since we entered Latin America in November 2009. This is not to say that we find no charm in the Latin American ways, it is simply stating that we are accustomed to other ways.

With our onward direction in mind, we assessed Sequitur's condition. We have nothing but high praise for the Hunter 49, finding it a wonderfully sea-kindly vessel, very comfortable and secure in all weather through Force 12. However; the poor quality of the installation work done during the fit-out by Specialty Yachts in Vancouver continued to jeopardize our safety and to impair our enjoyment of this wonderful boat.

The Raymarine chart-plotter continued to malfunction, losing the radar scanner input, rebooting, going back to factory default and erasing all data and settings. This was happening randomly every few hours, seemingly the result of a particular, though still unidentified vibration. It had begun a few days south of Puerto Montt, after we had crossed the Boca de Guafo into the northern Patagonian channels. With this, we had lost the input from both of our AIS units, the Raymarine transceiver and the SeaCas receiver, so we could see no other vessels' AIS signatures. Fortunately though; our transceiver works, so we were visible to other vessels. I suspect some more of Specialty's poor connections are to blame, but thus far through my troubleshooting up the mast and down below behind the system's components, I had not been able to track-down the cause.

The Icom 802 SSB radio, the antenna and the tuner installation that we had done by Specialty performed very poorly from the beginning, and for over a year has ceased to work at all, so we have no access to weather information by voice nor through gribs by Sailmail, so we need to rely on the satellite phone. While we were in Vancouver, I changed over from a Microsoft-based computer to a new MacBook Air, and I had not yet been able to get the Iridium satellite phone to work with it, although the program is designed to work with Macs. So while we have hundreds of minutes on our Global Marine Networks account, I cannot use the XGate email, web browser or weather applications.

The thought of venturing out on a three or four week, 3500-mile crossing to Cape Town without ongoing access to current weather information, without dependable radar and without being able to receive AIS data, did not sit well with us. Additionally, with our anchor windlass broken again, approaching an unknown lee coast in unknown weather after a month's passage without convenient anchoring capability seemed imprudent if better options were available.

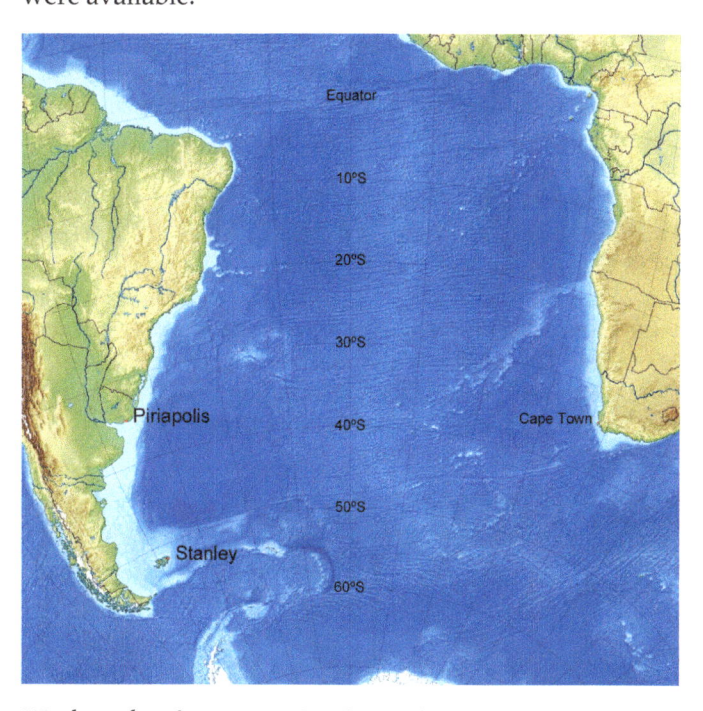

We thought of staying in Stanley and getting our electronics and windlass repaired; however, we were tired of many months in multiple layers of fleece, of wearing long underwear, of wearing double toques, of sleeping under two heavy duvets, all this with the Espar furnace turned up high. We were tired of the constant highly humid cold weather. We looked north, closer to the equator. Argentina was totally out of the question; we risked very heavy fines, even boat confiscation for having visiting the Malvinas without Argentine permission. We looked at heading to Piriapolis, Uruguay.

33. North From the Falklands

We had been watching the weather forecasts throughout our stay in the Falklands, trying to get a handle on the pattern of storms to the north. In reading various pilots and guides, I gathered that on the crossing northward, it is very difficult to miss being caught-up in a storm. Cyclones generate every two or three days from the interaction of the hot winds above the Argentine Pampas with the cold Antarctic waters flowing northward. These storms often arise very quickly and are difficult to accurately predict.

In referring to the passage between Tierra del Fuego and Rio de la Plata, one quote states: *"sailors should be ready to deal with at least a couple of cold fronts, with many hours spent hove-to, it being senseless, if not dangerous, to fight against the steep seas raised, even if close to the coast."* Another: *"The approach of a cold front usually brings a rotation of the wind from NW to SW and a considerable increase in its velocity. When this happens, it is far better to heave-to than to beat close-hauled into 40 or 50 knots of wind."* And another: *"The average front lasts around twelve hours, though southwesterlies raging three days are not uncommon."* Piriapolis is 1025 miles and slightly east of north from Stanley, and I calculated that including being hove-to for 12 to 24 hours, the passage should take us seven and a half to eight days.

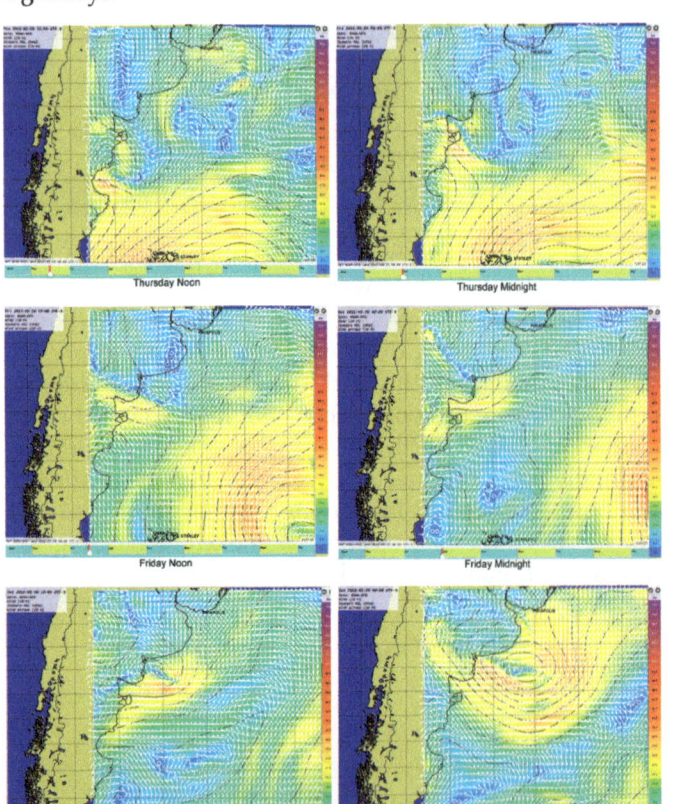

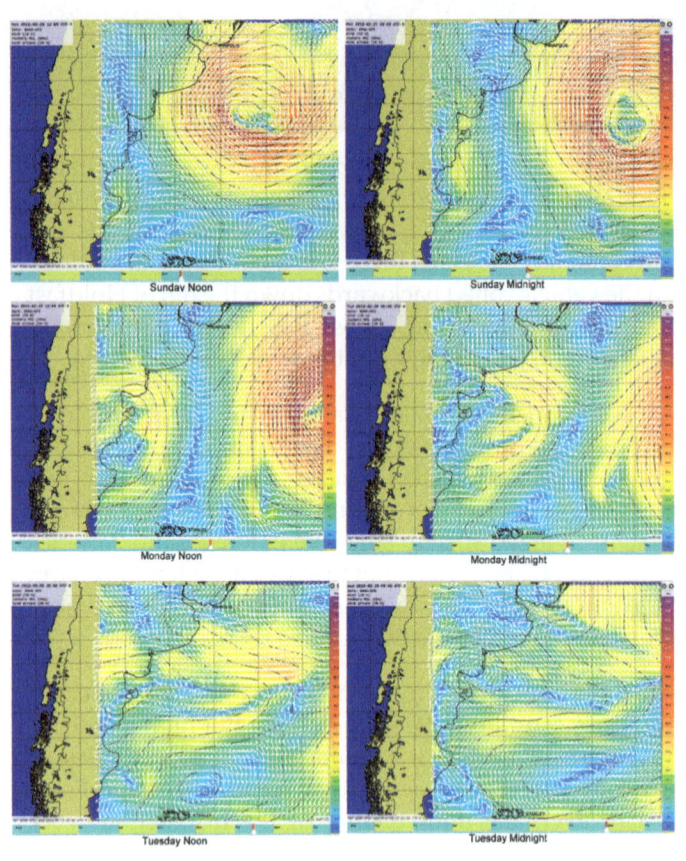

On Tuesday the 21st of February, the gribs showed a deep depression predicted to develop the following Saturday off the Argentine coast 500 and 600 miles north of the Falklands and to deepen further as it tracks eastward across our intended path. The gribs predicted winds over 70 knots on Sunday, and we wished to avoid being in them.

By Sunday midnight the storm's centre was predicted to have moved east of our proposed track, so we decided to wait until midday on Thursday to head out from Stanley to be in position to take advantage of the southerly winds on the backside of the hurricane strength storm.

We had no courtesy flag for Uruguay, so Edi took our now-useless Argentine flag and with a few creative snips and a few runs through the sewing machine, she converted it into a passable facsimile of the Uruguayan colours.

The winds had been predicted to be southwest 25 to 30 at midday on Thursday as we left Stanley, and we found this to be the case as we motored out through the narrows and set sail for a run out Port Williams and then northward past Mengeary and Volunteer Points. We were hit by a series of squalls with winds into the upper 40s, so we ran with about two-thirds of the staysail and a third of the main, making 6 to 7 knots.

Thursday midnight found us in west-southwest winds of 30 knots with gusts to the mid-40s and still making better than 6 knots with very short sail. At 0442 we crossed the 50th parallel of latitude, leaving the Furious Fifties and entering the Roaring Forties.

At noon on Friday the winds were down to 15 with gusts into the mid-20s. They had backed a bit and were approaching south-southwest. I rolled-out the remainder of the staysail and we continued northward at about 5.5 knots. I didn't want to get too far north too quickly, wanting to give the forecast depression time to pass ahead of us.

By late afternoon the wind had eased to 10 to 12 knots, still rather steady south-southeast. The barometer was 1017.5, the first time we have seen it above standard pressure in over five weeks. The sky began clearing. At midnight on Friday the wind had backed to the south and had decreased to 8-10. The barometer was up to 1020.0 and the clear sky showed-off most of its stars and a waxing moon.

By noon on Saturday the wind had backed to east-southeast and increased to 15-20 knots. The barometer continued a very slow climb, and was at 1020.3. The sky was completely overcast with a combination of altostratus, stratus and cumulus. The seas were becoming more confused with a 2-metre steep chop. At 1400 the barometer began falling, passing through 1018 at 1500, and an hour later it was 1016.7. At 1800 the glass read 1014.2 and at 2100 it was at 1009.9.

At 2140 we were hit by a squall with 45-knot winds. I turned Sequitur southwest, rolled-in all but a metre or so of the staysail and the main, went below and closed the hatch. I looked at the grib files in my computer, and plotted our position. The prediction showed that we should be in 15 to 20 knot southeasterly winds. As the northeast winds moved above 50 knots on the anemometer, I knew the storm had developed earlier and further to the south than had been predicted.

At midnight we continued to drift at about 2.5 knots on a course of 250° in front of 50-knot easterly winds. The barometer was at 1007.9. We were very comfortable as we slept on the salon couches. I awoke from time-to-time to reset the auto-rebooted chart-plotter and to check the radar for contacts.

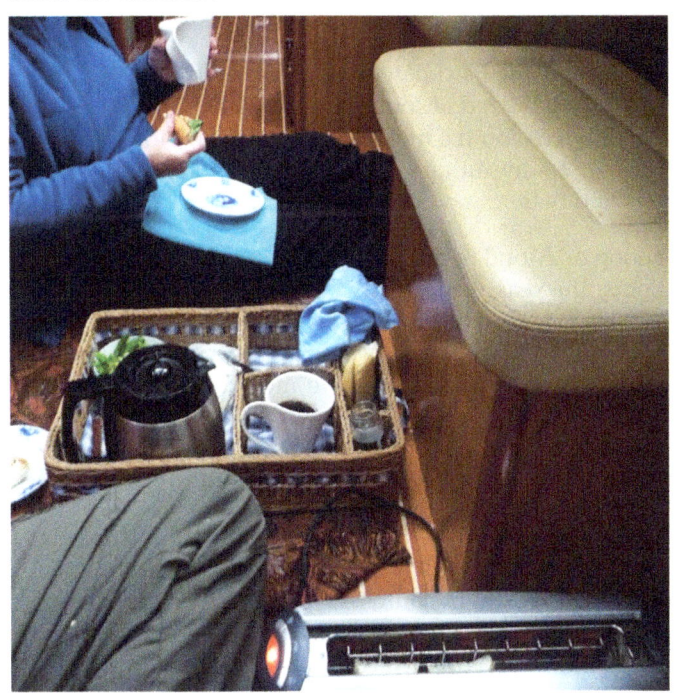

For breakfast we resorted to a tactic I had learned in my Navy days while crossing the Tasman Sea in a Force 12 blow. We sat on the sole and leaned against the lee couch to enjoy our smoked salmon and capers on cream cheese slathered toasted split baguettes. Edi had even managed to brew a fine thermos of Starbucks coffee as Sequitur weathered the storm.

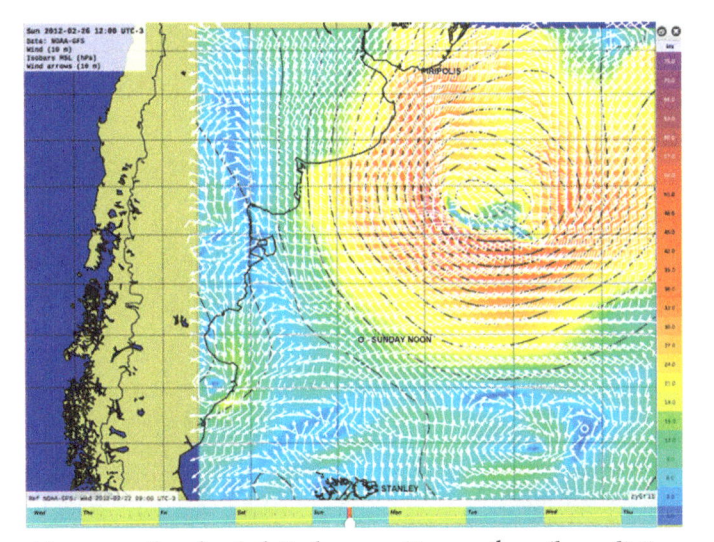

At noon on Sunday I plotted our position on the grib prediction for that time to gain an idea of the shape of the theoretical storm. It showed the system to the northeast of us moving eastward. Our drift had gradually swung to a course of 290° and had slowed to 2.2 knots. The winds had veered to south-southeast and were still in the upper 30s and mid 40s. Because the seas were up to over 5 metres, I decided to remain as we were for a while longer. The barometer was at 1002.0.

At 1710 on Sunday, with the wind around to south and down to 25-30 knots, and the seas to between 4 and 5 metres, I flashed-up the engine, rolled-out a tad more sail and turned north to run at 2100 rpm in front of the seas. We surfed at above 13 knots, then wallowed and surfed again. By 2000 were averaging 7.7 knots as the wind continued to veer and subside. The seas remained above 4 metres.

By midnight the barometer had rebounded to 1004.2, the wind had stabilized at south-southwest 20-25 and the seas were down to about 4 metres. We continued motor-sailing with half a staysail and a third of the main, making 7.5 knots and better.

At noon on Monday the winds were variable from calm to 5 knots, the seas were lightly rippled on a 1-metre swell. The barometer continued its slow climb and was at 1004.9 and the sky was nearly fully overcast with a few cumulus giving accent to the stratus. We motored with the sails hanging limp.

Through the afternoon the wind slowly filled from the east and then gradually backed, allowing us a pleasant broad reach. By midnight it was blowing from the northeast at 15 to 20 knots, and we were heading almost directly into it and into increasingly confused seas that were countering the northbound current. We motor-sailed, making 5.8 knots at 017°, directly toward Piriapolis.

Tuesday dawned with a very low overcast, which soon lowered to fog. Through the morning the visibility slowly decreased until by 1020 it was down to under 30 metres. I ran the watermaker with the filters that were nearly clogged from the glacial till in Beagle Channel. The automatic back-flush every 5 days over the past several weeks seems to have cleared them, and within four hours we had full water tanks.

Tuesday noon the sea was very lightly rippled from the variable 2 to 4 knot airs and there was a slow 1-metre swell. The barometer had remained in a gentle fluctuation between 1004 and 1005 since Monday. We motor-sailed directly toward the Uruguayan coast. At 1451 we crossed the line on the chart indicating the northern limit of sea ice; We were officially out of the iceberg zone.

The fog persisted through the day, with visibility varying from 25 to 100 metres. The wind continued just off the nose and increased to about 15 knots as we motor-sailed into it. An hour or so after sunset, the waxing moon gradually brightened, and the stars began to appear through the dissipating fog.

Wednesday morning the barometer finally broke out of its narrow range and rose through 1007 at 0800. After her post-watch sleep, Edi prepared a wonderful brunch of scrambled Falklands farm-fresh eggs, Falklands beef bangers, toasted Falklands split baguettes, Falklands roma tomatoes with Falklands basil and we washed it down with cups of fresh-ground Starbucks coffee from Costco in Vancouver. Because the seas were rather calm and there were neither ships nor land within our radar horizon, we enjoyed it below, in the comforts of the salon.

We began selectively unzipping and opening the panels in the cockpit enclosure to allow the breezes to start drying-out canvas and cushions. This was the first time they had been opened other than for access since the middle of December.

We had peeled-off our multi-layers of fleece, climbed out of our long underwear, doffed our insulated pants. Edi gathered-up the clothes we wouldn't be needing for a long time and ran a few loads through the washer-dryer. In the afternoon we took long hot showers and then, for the first time in well over a year, we allowed the sun and warm breeze in the cockpit to dry us. We had left the Roaring Forties.

Through the night the wind veered to south-southeast, but at 6 to 8 knots it barely kept the sails filled and offered little assistance to our motoring along about 40 miles off the Argentine coast. Thursday morning's brunch was rather European, with baguettes, cheese slices, ham, tomatoes and olives. We enjoyed it in single layers of clothing in the cockpit with the side curtains pulled back to offer a cooling breeze.

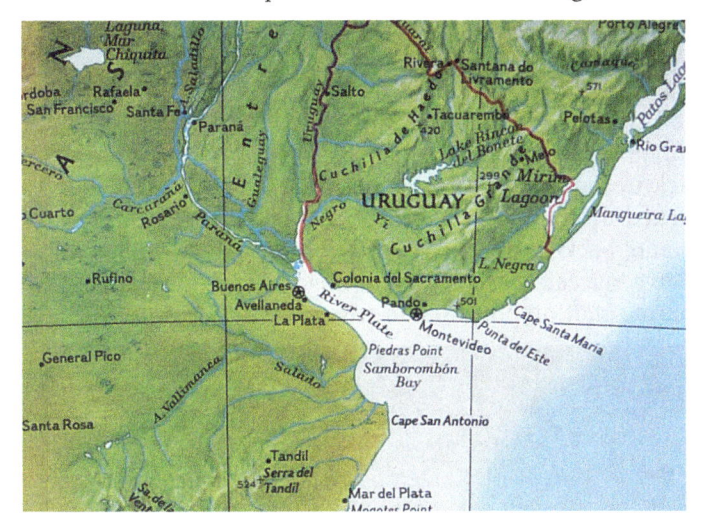

On Thursday afternoon we began crossing the broad mouth of Rio de la Plata. It is called the widest river in the world, touted to be 120 nautical miles wide at its mouth. However; a look at its geography shows it is simply a broad bay into which some rivers flow about 150 miles inland from the capes.

As we headed across the bay, I noticed we had picked-up a stowaway. A pigeon roosting on the main out-haul, likely blown to seaward in a storm and now catching a ride back in.

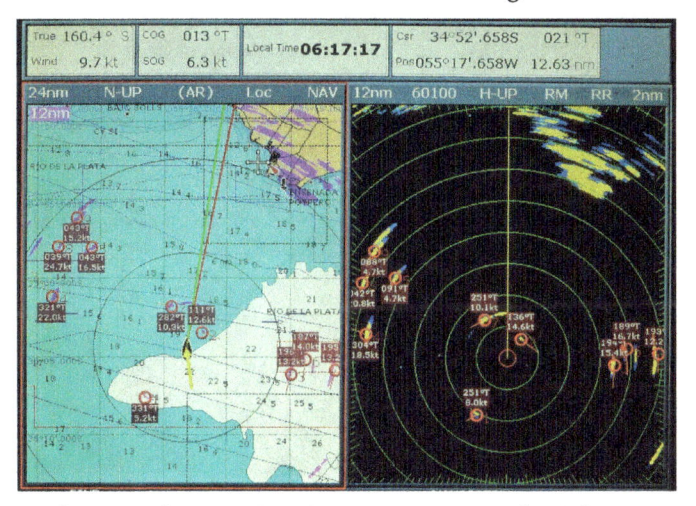

In the small hours of Friday, as we approached the main shipping lanes between the sea and Buenos Aires and Montevideo, we encountered an increasing number of radar contacts. Without either of our AIS receivers being picked-up by the chart-plotter, I had to rely on using the radar's MARPA tracking function. This can handle only 10 contacts at a time, and is limited on our system to 12 miles range, so I selected the 10 most dangerous targets.

At 0630, as we came in VHF range, I called Control Piriapolis Prefectura Radio, but received no response. I continued to call every quarter hour or so with the same results. Finally at 0836, as we were inside the breakwater and approaching a temporary tie-up on the haul-out dock, I received a response. Six minutes later, we secured alongside and were met by two Prefectura officials, who took our data and welcomed us to Uruguay. We were told to report to the Aduana, Migracion and Prefectura offices in the next few days. We liked the casual approach. We were tired. We went below and slept.

Our passage had taken us a little over seven and a half days, and we had been hit by only one cyclonic storm.

After a couple of hours nap, I went up to the marina office and checked-in. It is a modern marina with a huge work yard and a 50-or-more-ton travel-lift wide enough for most catamarans. It is owned and operated by the Ministry of Transport and Public Works through the National Hydrographic Department. We had fond memories of the wonderful facilities and services at the Mexican equivalents of this public marina complex, and we were looking forward to a similar experience here.

In the office was a huge woman with day-glow hair. She exuded an attitude that this was her own private domain and that we very privileged to be able to use the marina and to have her serve us. In her I saw the perfect caricature of a self-important, job-protected civil servant. After what she likely thought was the appropriate amount of ignoring of my presence in an otherwise vacant office, she finally stopped sucking her thumbs and called a fellow to come and show me to a mooring, so we could move off the temporary one.

The mooring I was shown was next to last along the breakwater. There are no floats, and the breakwater wall is about 2 metres high, done in a post and beam construction with two concrete beams, one at about half a metre up from the water and the other as the edge of a broad public walkway along the top. There is absolutely no security nor any privacy. There is a line of buoys about 5 or 6 metres apart and 30 metres out in the basin from the wall. There is plenty of space for floats and fingers in the basin; maybe they are planned for later. There were two mooring spaces open, the one closer in was too narrow.

The mooring buoys have no strops, simply a rusty iron fixed eye. I took the dinghy out and tied a loop of polypropylene through the eye so we had something to pick-up on the way by. We then motored Sequitur over, picked-up the loop, put one of our bow shore ties through it and backed in to the wall through the 6-metre gap between a catamaran and a 15-metre Argentine sloop. The marina staff do not assist in any way.

On Friday evening we celebrated our arrival in the sub-tropics; our first time in a warm, dry climate in over a year. I sautéed some Ushuaia scallops and prawns in butter with garlic, onions, button mushrooms and Falklands red and green peppers and served them with tarragoned basmati rice and a garnish of Falklands tomatoes and shredded basil. With dinner we enjoyed a bottle of Undurraga Brut Royale.

On Saturday morning we walked through the downtown to the fierra, the weekly market set-up in the fields at the northeastern corner of the city. We found repetitious stock from the same wholesalers on each stand. There was very little local, though we did find some very fresh fine green beans and bought a kilo. We had left without breakfast, so from a passionate little baker we bought a half-a-baguette-sized nuts and honey filled cross between a croissant and sticky-bun and munched on it as we walked back to the beach and the Hotel Argentino.

Hotel Argentino was built in 1930, likely at the height of the area's popularity, and the hotel is still the focal building of the city. Piriapolis was founded in 1890 and is now named after its founder, Francisco Piria. It had initially been named El Balneario del Porvenir, the Resort of the Future.

The city of 8830 permanent residents is a tired and dwindling beach resort with vacant buildings, vacant lots and failing businesses all along the once prime beachfront. The beachfront businesses are now mainly empty restaurants and cafes intermingled with tacky kitsch shops all with stock that looked to be from the same suppliers. We were not impressed.

We bought some fresh camarone from a stall across from the marina, and for dinner I sautéed them in butter with garlic, shallots, button mushrooms and red and green peppers. With them I served green beans amandine and a garnish of roma tomatoes and shredded basil. With it we thoroughly enjoyed a bottle of Montes 2010 Leyda Sauvignon Blanc.

On Sunday Edi kept the washer-dryer busy finishing the cleaning-up of our cold-weather clothing and washing the salt out of the cockpit cushion and pillow covers. I puttered with a list of blue jobs.

Monday, after a brunch of Falklands back bacon, crumpets and Sybie's friends farm eggs daubed with hollandaise sauce and garnished with tomatoes and basil, we headed off to Migracion with our papers from Aduana and the Prefectura to finish our check-in process.

We walked through town half an hour to the bus depot and bought tickets at about $2.60 each for Bus #1, the air-conditioned highway bus to Punta del Este. About 30 kilometres out of town we were dropped at the side of the highway at the exit to the airport. From there we made it across the divided roadway, up the access road, through the parking lots and into the terminal to find air-conditioned relief from the 35º day. Inside we tracked-down someone to get a Migracion officer to take us backwards through to the uncleared side of international arrivals and into an office, where we were processed for a 144 Pesos fee, about $7.30.

We walked back through the midday sun to the shade of a highway-side bus shelter, where we waited nearly an hour for the first bus to Piriapolis. This happened to be the number 8, a local seaside rattletrap at 26 Pesos, $1.30 each, which dropped us off half an hour later across from the marina. We had tried to have the Migracion officer clear us both in and out at the same time, but he said it was not allowed, so this nearly four hour process will need to be repeated when we clear-out.

Although there are a few fascinating old hotels and homes, mostly in Germanic and Italianate style, we had found no charm in either the geography nor the people of Piriapolis. Because the town is a beach-side resort and holiday destination, everything seems overpriced, this on top of Uruguay being one of the most expensive countries in Latin America. There is no chandler; the only shop even hinting at marine supplies has little more than fishing gear and boat toys. We would have to import parts to repair our windlass or a complete replacement. Nobody we had spoken with could recommend anyone to look at our Raymarine problems.

To make things even less attractive, the marina facilities are rather basic and very expensive. Many of the staff are rude and we sensed an air of contempt for 'Gringos'. We didn't seem welcome, and since there is no safe anchorage alternative, we had decided to move on. Online I had found a Lewmar dealer listed in Rio de Janeiro, Brazil, a little over a thousand miles along the coast from here.

On Thursday morning I enquired at the marina office about getting some diesel. Miss Dayglow punched the buttons on the office phone and thrust the handset at me. I spoke with the man who operates the fuel pumps in the marina yard, and learned he is not allowed to fuel foreign boats on the same day as contacted. This appears a way for the marina to extract an additional day of moorage. I organized fuelling for 0900 on Friday, telling him we would need about 700 litres to fill our tanks.

There are gasoline and diesel pumps alongside the wharf, the first we have seen in over two years. However, the marina rents the space alongside the pumps, so it is necessary to raft-up on the boat already there. To ensure we were in position to get our fuel, immediately the British sloop, Cutting Edge left the spot on Thursday morning, we moved Sequitur over to nest on the resident boat.

While I was in the dinghy organizing the bow line for our move off the mooring ball, I noticed three bolts missing on the chainplate holding the anchor roller to the bow. It appeared they had sheared from the strain in some of our anchorages. There were still four bolts holding things in place; however, I wanted to replace the missing ones before we headed out. I had none that would fit, so I went to the office, where Miss Dayglow called the yard supervisor, who called Julio, who came aboard to look at the job. He said no problem, he had stainless bolts, nuts and washers that would fit; it would take him less than an hour. He then said he had spare time now, but that he couldn't do the job until the next day because of the marina policy. I booked him for 0830.

After lunch we repeated the commute to Migracion at the airport. This time we caught a rattletrap bus both ways, and the process took just short of four hours. Piriapolis is certainly not a boater-friendly port.

On Thursday evening we had Phil and Julia of the sloop, Illawon aboard Sequitur for drinks and nibblies. They had built their steel boat in Toronto and sailed away in 1992 and they have been sailing around the world ever since. They were moored just astern of us at the fuel wharf. Among the things we learned from them is that Canadians require a visa prior to entering Brazil; it is the only country in the Americas with such a requirement. They told us that the closest Brazilian Embassy is in Montevideo and that the process can take well over a week.

On Friday morning Julio arrived promptly at 0830 with an assistant, and in forty minutes they were done and paid. Less prompt; however, was the fuel attendant. The appointed 0900 came and went without him, as did 1000, and with this came another day's moorage; check-out time is 1000. We continued to wait through 1100, 1200 and 1300, then at 1330 we were told the fuel man was coming at 1600.

While we were waiting for the fuel attendant, Edi and I had gone to the marina office to pay for our now eight days of moorage. Miss Dayglow's math was off; she counted our stay as seven days instead of eight. Even so, for the seven days we were charged 9047 Pesos, about $462, the most expensive moorage we had seen since leaving Vancouver. Also, in her ineptitude, she had insisted on taking Sequitur's length off the Ship Registry document, and we were charged for 13.82 metres, the tonnage length between the inside of her stem and the forward side of her rudder post. Sequitur actually measures 17.67 metres overall. Had she been sharper, we would have been charged over $700.

Shortly before 1700 the fuel attendant arrived. With less than a metre to spare, I stretched the hose across the inboard boat and took-on 687.5 litres for 23,650 Pesos, about $1206. At over $1.75 per litre, this was the most expensive diesel we had seen on our voyage. I then had to go with the fuel attendant three kilometres across town to the gas station to pay the bill. Fortunately, I had brought my camera with a photo of the tank gauge; the attendant was in the process of charging us for the 700 litres I had estimated we needed.

When I returned, we then took the paid and stamped marina invoice and our stamped passports to Aduana to get their stamps, and then we walked the kilometre to the Prefectura to get more stamps and a zarpe. The watchkeeper at the counter seemed uncertain of the procedure, and insisted that he needed our original Ship Registry document, which he needed to stamp. No amount of explaining could convince him of his error.

Frustrated, we walked back to the marina and I found an expired Ship Registry document, and in case the watchkeeper was observant, I also took out the current one. Fortunately, when I arrived back at the Prefectura, there was a more knowledgeable watchkeeper on duty, and as I suspected, the document was not needed. When he asked our destination, I told him we were heading along the coast of Brazil, but not necessarily intending on stopping there, because we had no visas. He suggested Canada as our destination, and I readily agreed.

We hadn't felt like backtracking to Uruguay's capitol, Montevideo to spend a week or more getting Brazilian visas. Our earlier research had told us that foreign cruisers are not very welcome in Montevideo and that Piriapolis is preferred. With our experience in Piriapolis, we thought that if it is considered the better place, then we definitely wanted to avoid Montevideo. We decided to head along the coast of Brazil with no visas and see what evolved. Politically, our exit papers had been issued for passage from Uruguay to Canada.

34. The South Coast of Brazil

At 1000 on Saturday the 10th of March we left Piriapolis, still unsure of our onward route. From Piriapolis it is about 3600 nautical miles to Cape Town, but we still needed repairs. Online I had found a Lewmar dealer listed in Rio de Janeiro, but my emails to them had bounced. It is a bit over 1000 miles to Rio, and we could put-in there without visas, claiming a need for repairs.

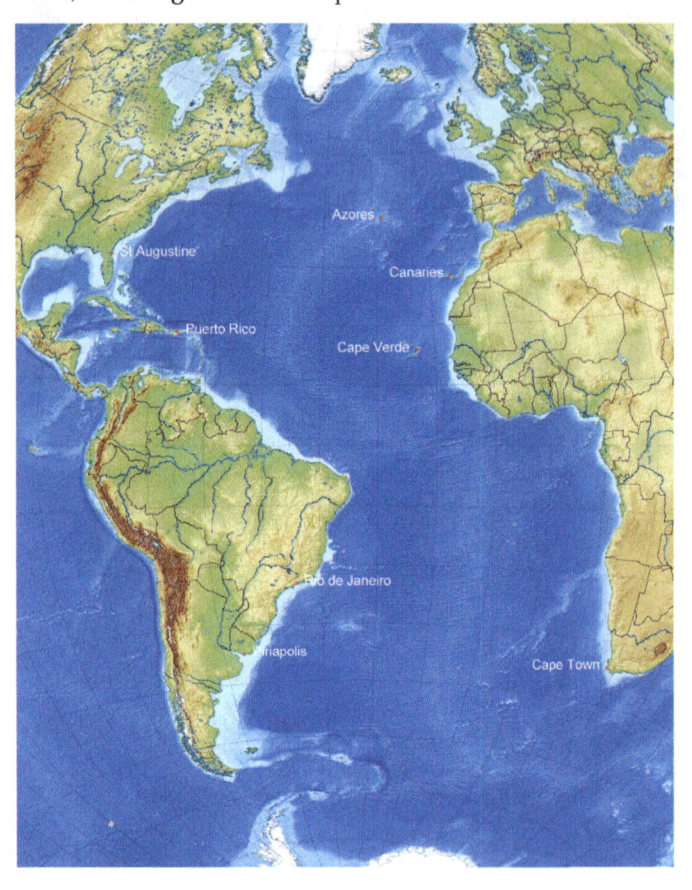

From Rio it is 3300 miles to Cape Town. Alternatively from Rio, it is 2600 to the Cape Verde Islands. From there we could head by the Canaries or the Azores 1600 or 2400 miles to Europe. Another thought was that if we couldn't get repairs in Rio, then 3600 miles around Brazil through the Windward Islands to Puerto Rico to find some First World service. Only another 1100 miles through the Bahamas to Saint Augustine, Florida, there is access to the Hunter factory.

It was blowing over 35 knots when we left the marina at 1000 on Saturday the 10th of March, but rather waiting for the squalls to pass we obeyed the moorage cutoff time so we wouldn't face paying an additional day's moorage and having to deal again with Miss Dayglow, the office manager.

We headed out with half the staysail and a third of the main, making near 8 knots. Within an hour the winds were a more reasonable 18 to 20 knots and we enjoyed a beam reach into the early afternoon, by which time the wind had backed to west and decreased to 12 knots. We continued into the night under various sail and motor-sail combinations as the winds dictated. On Sunday morning we set our clocks off Daylight Saving back to Standard Time, Zone -3.

For the next few days we rotated through all three sails out full and pulling, briskly moving with main and spinnaker, ghosting along under spinnaker alone, pounding along with deeply reefed main and staysail and motor-sailing with a blade of main for stability. We passed through everything from calms to 45-knot squalls, but mainly the winds were from the north-easterly sector and contrary to our track. We were; however, moved along by the northeast-setting Falklands Current.

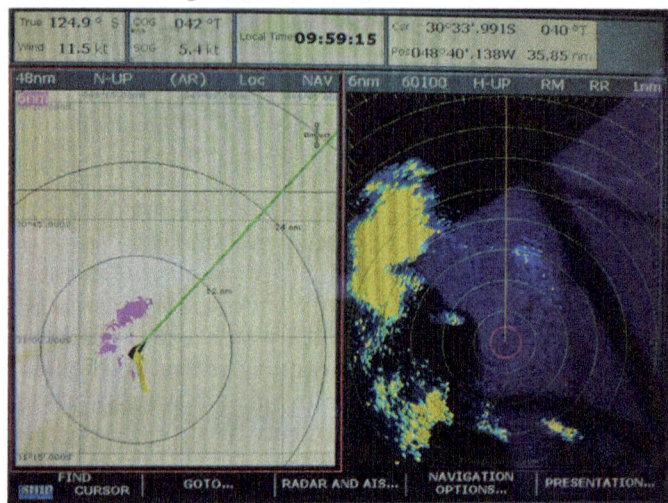

616

There was an almost daily series of squalls, which we could easily track on the radar and try to avoid. Many were impossible to escape, so for them we hunkered-down for their torrential downpours and their twisting gales.

On the 15th of March we lost the assistance of the northeast flowing Falklands Current and we began running against the southwest set of the Brazil Current and into very sloppy seas. The clew on the staysail parted as the sail luffed and flopped in the light winds and the very confused seas.

This appeared to be an identical failure to the one we suffered with the main on the south coast of Peru during our passage to Chile in December 2010. Again, it looked like the thread on the bobbin was rotten; each stitch of the bobbin thread was broken, while the upper thread remained intact. I rolled-up the staysail and put a running lash around it, deferring to later its restitching. We now had three very legitimate reasons to head into Rio: a broken windlass, a malfunctioning chart-plotter and a blown sail.

We passed through offshore oil fields in very deep water, in places over 1000 metres deep and over 100 miles offshore. It appears the Brazilians have mastered deep water oil extraction. Either that, or they accept the portion that is recovered and ignore that which is spilled.

When the seas allowed, we dined in style in the cockpit. We were still enjoying the farm-fresh eggs Sybie had gotten for us in the Falklands, as well as the wonderful back bacon, crumpets, roma tomatoes and basil we had bought there.

We continued to be plagued with squalls, and generally proceeded with shortened sails, in case one popped-up out of the blue. Though with nearly constant fully overcast skies, there was very little blue, and the downpours suddenly appeared from the jumble of nimbostratus above us.

Most of the squalls were predictable, showing darkly on the horizon and painting strongly on the radar screen as they tracked toward us, or occasionally past us without hitting.

With sunset, we were left to tracking the parade of storms by radar, aided by the rattle of wind and the rush of cold air that preceded a hit.

Between the squalls we were able to maintain our diet. I baked a spinach and cheese pie for dinner on our seventh day out.

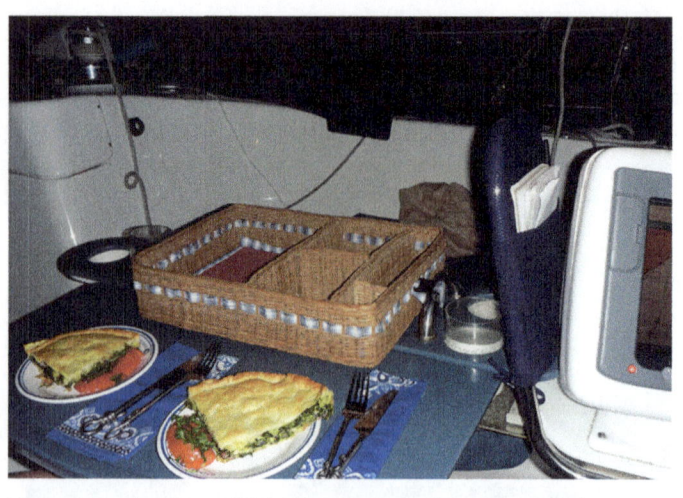

We enjoyed slices of it in the cockpit during a lull between squalls. We were averaging daily runs of near 100 miles, and we anticipated another three days to Rio.

We knew we were approaching the Tropics when we began finding flying fish on the decks.

Thankfully we didn't need to resort to eating deck pickings; our fridges, freezers and pantry were full of a wonderful selection of food. One morning, after her post-watch sleep, Edi prepared for brunch some delicious ham and egg quesadillas, which we enjoyed with our fresh-ground Starbucks in the cockpit.

Our sunrise on the tenth day illuminated the skyline above Ipanema and Copacabana Beaches as we approached the entrance to Rio de Janeiro's harbour. We looked forward to exploring this fabled area.

I awoke Edi early from her post-watch sleep, and she prepared a casual breakfast, which we enjoyed as we slowly motored past the beaches and made our way into the harbour in the warming sun.

As we went, the waters became increasingly polluted and we lost our appetite from the nauseous reek of spilled oil. The water had a sickly yellow-brown colour and it was full of floating garbage. Christ the Redeemer looked down on this from the peak.

We had been calling Rio Port Control on the VHF every 5 or 10 minutes for nearly two hours as we approached and entered the harbour, all without any response. Channel 16 was cluttered by chatter, catcalls, whistles and other nonsense of the local fishermen. It appeared to us that the Brazilian authorities had completely lost control of the radio frequency, and we concluded that they have ceased to monitored the channel. We headed to Marina Gloria, which is listed as the most convenient place to clear-in. However, the printed and online reports warn that it is not friendly to foreign cruisers.

We tried many times without success to raise Marina Gloria on VHF Channel 16 and then tried them on a number of other channels. We motored slowly into the marina's basin and circled for nearly half an hour trying to attract attention. We received no response to our radio, voice and hand signalling. Everyone seemed busy concentrating on ignoring us.

We saw no convenient place to moor, so we headed out and across the harbour to Niterói. There, at 0931 we came to 20 metres on the Delta in 5 metres of water a couple of cables off Clube Naval Charitas.

It was Tuesday the 20th of March, the last day of summer. In ten days we had covered 1026 nautical miles in mostly contrary conditions and we were finally back into the Tropics, having crossed Capricorn at 2121 the previous evening. We were weary, so we went below and slept.

On Wednesday morning after a hearty breakfast from our Falklands stores, we gathered our papers and launched the dinghy. It was a short distance to the marina, so we decided to row, rather than lowering and fitting the motor.

In the marina we tracked-down a guard, who directed us to the marina office. There we enquired about clearing-in, and we were given two sheets of paper. One was a description in English of the sequence of the three offices we needed to visit, with their addresses and transportation information. The other was an application for temporary moorage, which first needed our clearance completed.

We were fascinated by the moorage charges:
- first 3 days --- R21.79   = about $12 per day;
- days 4 to 15 -- R$43.58   = about $24 per day;
- days 16 to 30 - R$63.32   = about $36 per day;
- days 31 to 60 - R$84.92   = about $47 per day; and
- days 61 to 90 - R$118.54 = about $65 per day.

This definitely shows they do not want transients to stay very long. They had a similar sliding scale for anchoring fees, from R$12.74 to R$63.70 per day, so it seems they have somehow claimed anchoring rights in the large bay, though where the line was we couldn't tell. For financial considerations, we assumed that Sequitur was outside it.

We walked along waterfront to the fast ferry terminal, a kilometre or so from the marina. The gauge there told us it was 34º as we mined the ATM for some Brazilian Reais. Passage for the 20-minute ride across to downtown Rio is R$12 each on a rather modern, very fast catamaran with comfortably upholstered seating for, I would guess, some 300 passengers.

Off the ferry in downtown, we walked past some imposing old buildings, looking for directions to Praça Maua. It was lunchtime, and the sidewalks were alive with scurrying people. There was an upbeat vibrancy to the city. We asked directions and followed more the wagging hands than the nearly incomprehensible Portuguese, though with our truncated Spanish and my French we managed to unravel a few words.

620

We walked past many examples of throw-everything-into-it architecture. The traffic in the streets was near-gridlock, and the thoughts of a spinning meter in a crawling taxi put a ride out of mind. Besides, we enjoy walking.

With a round about detour caused by closures for construction for the 2016 Olympics, we arrived after 2.5 kilometres at the cruise-ship passenger terminal at Warehouse 1. Inside we were directed to a desk, where we were given visitor passes and escorted through to the Federal Police office.

We were shown to seats and asked to wait for an English-speaking officer to arrive. When half an hour later he arrived and we had explained to him our diversion to Rio to seek repairs, he was sympathetic. He began going through what appeared to be a procedures manual, but there seemed to be a conflict between him and a colleague, who kept his back to us. We sensed office politics, but eventually our side won, and our passports were stamped with 15-day visas to Brazil. One office down, two to go.

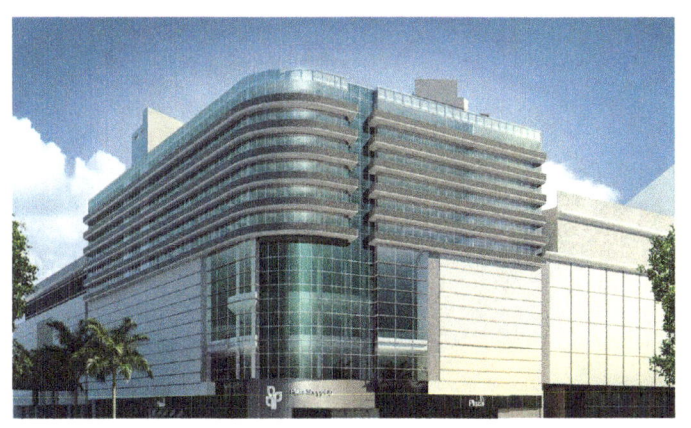

Outside we happened to spot a 100 Niterói bus stopped in a traffic snarl. I knocked on the door and we were admitted and paid our R$2.75 each for the ride across the harbour bridge to the bus loop in downtown Niterói. We followed wagging arms to Plaza Shopping, our clue to the location of Receita Federal, our office number two. A couple more requested directions and we zeroed-in on Rua Almirante Teffe and the office at 668.

Inside we added ourselves to the queue in front of the information counter. When our turn came, we were asked to wait for an English-speaking person, and when she arrived, she took our information to her "superior". She returned shortly and asked us to follow her to the sixth floor, but I was stopped by the guard because I was wearing Bermuda shorts; men are forbidden to wear them in federal offices. Edi's shorts were OK, so she went up.

On the sixth floor, Edi waited for 20 minutes for a woman to come out of the coffee room to meet her. She was then insulted and chastised for being in the wrong office; we should have checked-in in Rio. She said that she could confiscate our boat. Edi explained that we had attempted to get arrival instructions as we came into the harbour, but with repeated calls, received no response on the radio. The woman stated that they cannot be expected to respond to foreign yachts at night and on the weekend. Edi told her that this was during office hours on Tuesday morning. The woman fumed. Edi asked her how we could rectify the situation and then she watched as four people met in heated discussion. Finally after 20 minutes, a sympathetic employee apologized as he gave Edi the downtown address. It was late afternoon, the temperature was still in the mid 30s, so we caught a 33 bus back to Sequitur.

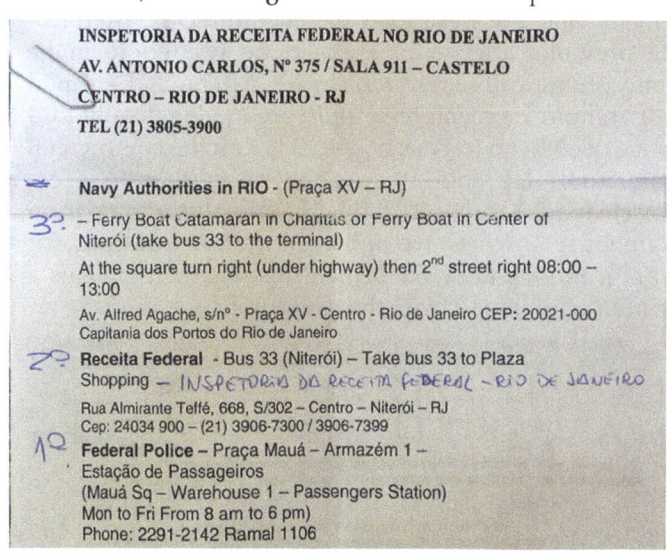

On Thursday morning, our third day in Rio we went ashore again for another attempt at being cleared by office two. As we walked through the gate at the ferry terminal, the display showed the temperature at 34° and the time 0942. It was going to be another hot day. It was still rush-hour; there were only a few open seats when we boarded, and the ferry soon filled to capacity.

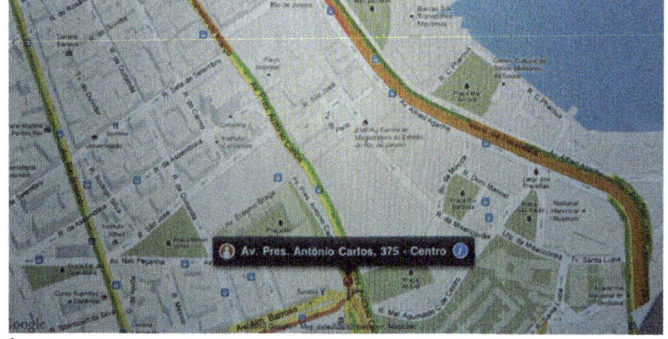

621

We had with us the new address, and also in my camera some photos of its location from the GoogleMaps application on my iPad. With its assistance, we walked the half kilometre or so to the building seeking what shade we could against the blazing sun. Inside we were issued visitor passes and directed to a guard-operated elevator to the ninth floor.

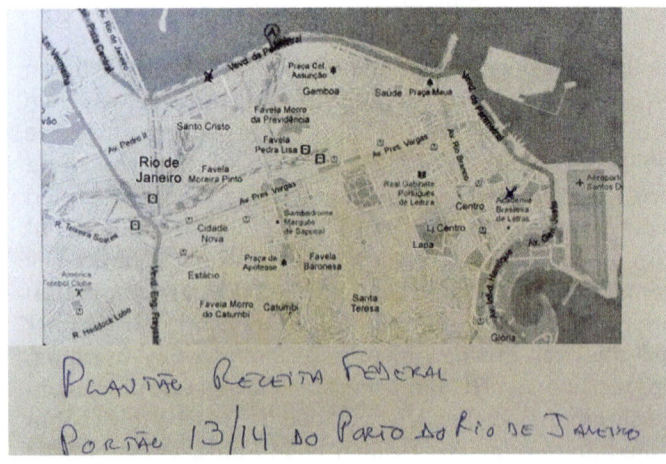

We waited in the air-conditioned comfort of Sala 911 for an English-speaking agent. He arrived and was puzzled why we had been sent to his office. He asked who had sent us, and Edi described the encounter in Niterói of the previous afternoon. He said he needed to make some phone calls and went away. After what seemed half an hour he reemerged and very apologetically told us we need to go to Warehouse 13/14 on the commercial waterfront. He said it was the only place cruisers can clear in. I suspected this was further along from Warehouse 1, where we had been the previous day for Immigration, and he confirmed this. He then gave us a printed map image from the computer.

We headed out into the upper-30s temperature and walked the familiar route through downtown to Praça Maua and Warehouse 1. We had attempted to go the short way past the construction by following the busy waterfront walkway, but because it passed in front of the naval base, I was refused admittance in my Bermuda shorts.

Once past the spiffied-up cruise-ship terminal, the waterfront decays rapidly into crumbling ruins, derelict buildings and derelict people living in nooks in the rubble. Compounding the decay is the noise and dust of six lanes of traffic roaring by beside us and six lanes on the elevated roadway above. It reminded us of what Seattle has made of its waterfront and it made us appreciate even more the superb evolution of Vancouver's.

After 5.7 kilometres through the sweltering heat, we arrived at our third office of Receita Federal. We explained our situation and showed our papers to a very sympathetic English-speaking officer and we were asked to wait. We sat outside in the heat, but fortunately in the shade for nearly an hour before they took pity on us and asked us to come inside their air-conditioned office.

As a heated discussion of our case took place in another office, we sat next to an array of stamps and stamp pads. We could use them to clear ourselves in, or we could even setup our own little Latin American bureaucracy.

Finally, after another half hour we were told they couldn't clear us in with our boat in Niterói. If we wanted them to clear us, we needed to bring Sequitur to Marina Gloria. We explained our attempts to contact Marina Gloria on Ch 16, and the agent went to his computer and printed a page from Gloria's website. He then said they monitor Channel 68. I pointed-out that it really read that they monitor Ch 16 and 68. He tried to phone the marina for us, but he received no answer. We thanked him for his assistance and we went out onto the road to flag-down a 100 bus to Niterói.

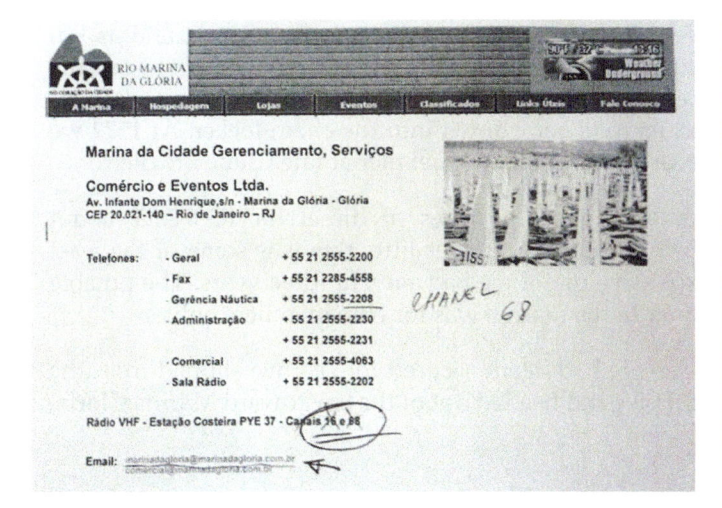

At the Niterói bus loop we caught a 33 bus toward Jurujuba, the one that goes past Clube Naval Charitas. We had been in a couple of disappointing supermarkets the previous day, but then on our ride from Niterói to Charitas, we had passed what looked like an upscale supermarket at the edge of Enseada de Icaraí. We had decided to stop on our way back from Rio, and had brought a cooler bag and assorted shopping bags in case it proved to be good.

The market is called Pao de Acucar and is part of the Sendas group. It is beautifully laid-out with broad diagonal aisles in the centre and very spacious produce, bakery, meats, deli and other focus areas around the periphery. It immediately reminded us of the wonderful Wong store in Miraflores, Peru. There appeared to be nearly every food item one might want if cost were no object. The shitaki mushrooms at $48 a kilo were not tempting, but the very fresh portobellos at $9 per kilo certainly were. We gave a pass to the asparagus at $36.50 per kilo, but bought some wonderfully inexpensive roma tomatoes, green peppers and zucchini, as well as a restock on great-looking onions, carrots and potatoes.

We saw very high prices on imported items, and rather reasonable prices on local products. However; one of the things that puzzled us was the pricing of Brazil nuts. They are R$95.99 per kilo, about $53 Canadian. We were not tempted to buy any; besides, we had already had our fill of the Brazil nuts who are staffing the bureaucracy.

We continued shopping, and from the meat department we bought a kilo of wonderfully trimmed beef tenderloin for $18, four nice pork tenderloins and six boneless and skinless chicken breasts all at $8.20 a kilo. We loaded our cart with all we thought we could comfortably juggle aboard the bus, and checked-out for just under $130.

We stopped in the office on our way through the yacht club and asked if they sold diesel fuel. The clerk asked us for our paperwork so that he could check us in and assign us a berth in the marina. We told him that we were heading into our fourth day of attempting to clear-in with only Immigration done thus far. He seemed impatient and agitated when he told us that they had no diesel, but that Iate Clube Brazileiro did.

Back onboard Sequitur, I found Iate Clube Brazileiro on the chart, directly across the bay, about 2 miles north of our anchorage. I emailed Marina Gloria asking for temporary berthing so we could head over to clear-in, but by the end of the business day I had received no response.

Our thinking was that if we needed to move to Gloria, we should refuel on the way. We decided to put the motor on the dinghy the next morning and head over to check-out the fuelling facilities at Brazileiro.

The motor went on easily; however, the motor end of the fuel line had lost its grab balls, and I could not get it to form a seal. We re-slung the motor on the stern mount and rowed ashore, from where we caught a 33 bus. Iate Club Brazileiro is on a point between Sao Francisco and Icarí, and the bus goes through a tunnel, rather than around the point. We missed getting off before the tunnel, so we continued through it and then through the maze of traffic-jammed streets out to the beach in Icarí, where we got off. From there we walked a little over a kilometre back to the club.

I had brought the faulty outboard fuel line with me in hope of finding a replacement or a repair. In a little shop inside the club compound we met Marcos Demetrio Rodrigues and his father Marcos Guilherme Rodrigues, Mercury outboard dealers. They had nothing for our Tohatsu, but Marcos G took the line to his workshop and modified it so it might work. They were both very helpful and wanted nothing for their service.

We thanked them, checked-out the fuelling dock and continued walking around the point to Sao Francisco, which was the shorter route to the bus. We caught a 33 to Pao de Acucar for another bout of produce meat and seafood shopping to top-off our fridges and freezers.

Back onboard with our purchases stowed, we began thinking seriously about our situation. We had not yet received any reply from Marina Gloria on our request for temporary moorage, it was already mid-afternoon on Friday and we were facing a weekend, which would further interfere with our already snail-paced clearing-in process.

We weighed using the cockpit power winch, and as Edi motored Sequitur slowly across the bay, I sorted-out the mess on deck, squared-away and secured the Delta and led its rode back down into the chain locker. At 1522 we secured alongside the fuel pier at Iate Clube Brazileiro.

We took on 442.1 litres of diesel for R$972.35, about $535. At about $1.21 per litre, this was some of the least expensive diesel we had seen in three years. The potable water in the marina was for club members only.

Once we had again secured for sea, we slipped from the fuel pier and headed out of the bay toward Marina Gloria.

35. The Long Brazilian Coast

However; when we had cleared Ponta Jurujuba and were out in Bahia de Guanabara, we turned to port and shaped course out of the harbour past the fortified Ponta de Santa Cruz. We hauled-down our quarantine flag, switched off the AIS transmitter and watched the walls for cannons pointed at us as we made our escape from the ridiculous Brazilian bureaucracy.

As we motor-sailed out through the entrance several naval warships made their way toward us from seaward. We were relieved to see them all continue past, returning to port for the weekend.

We headed between a pair of islands about ten miles from the harbour entrance, where we passed Etesco Takatsugu, a huge oil drilling ship, moored and apparently busy sinking another well. We wondered whether this was the source of the slick we were in.

The water reeked of petroleum, and had a sickly yellow-green colour. We assumed there had been an oil spill and that we were going through a chemical soup that had been added to the water as a coagulant or dispersant or whatever. Our water tanks were low, but we knew this was no place to flash-up the watermaker. We looked over our shoulders to see if we were being chased.

Through the evening there was a parade of cumulonimbus systems, some of which were unavoidable and hit us with torrential downpours and twisting winds into the upper 30s. We continued motor-sailing, about 20° off the wind with shortened sails, bucking the Brazil current.

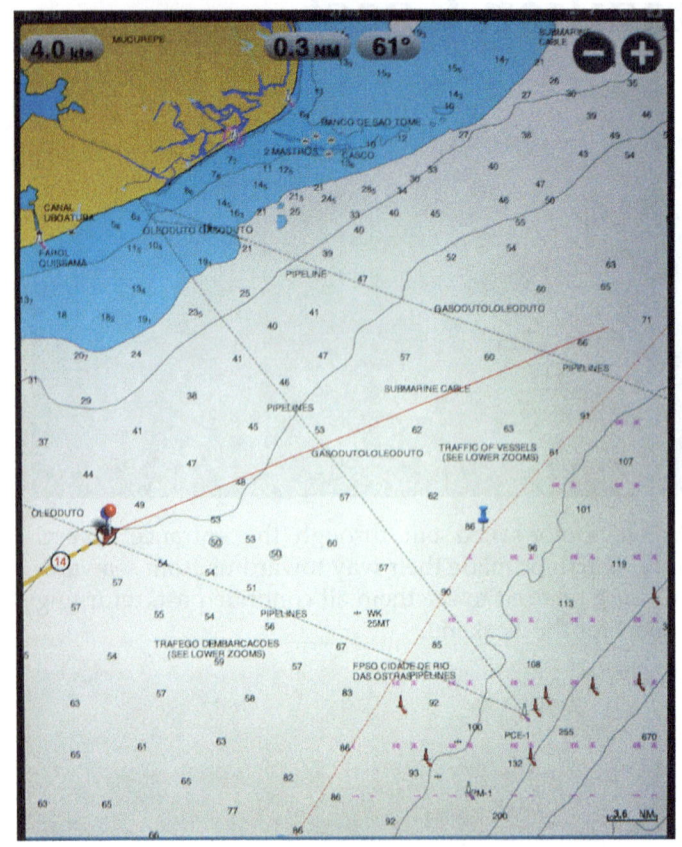

At 0700 we 6.6 miles south of Cabo Frio and more fully into the southwest stream of the current, making 4.8 knots with turns for 6. Noon on Saturday found us in outside the 12-mile limit east of Cabo Frio, and aiming for the gap between offshore oil fields and Cabo Sao Tome. As we motor-sailed into the now stronger current, we bashed into increasingly confused seas, which I resolved to be from an interference between the Brazil Current and the water flowing over Banco de Sao Tome.

In the evening our bumpy ride was compounded by the parade of squalls, several of which hit us with downpours and twisting gale-force winds. By sunrise on Sunday we were reduced to 3.5 knots at 2400 rpm, turns for 7 knots. I altered course to close the land around the end of Banco Sao Tome and seek some inshore relief from the Brazil Current.

When Edi arose from her post-watch kip, she prepared a wonderful ham and eggs brunch, which we enjoyed in the relatively calm waters we had entered north of the bank. We were then onto a broad continental shelf of 15 to 20 metres depth, which buffered the ocean swell and reduced the current.

North-northeast winds increased through the day, until by sunset they were above 20 knots, directly on the nose. We had lost the protection of the shoal water, and we were again into a stronger southwest-flowing current.

We decided to put into an anchorage to wait for more favourable winds, and we shaped our course toward Guarapari, a large city with, according to the charts, two bays that appeared to offer good anchorage.

At 0950 on Monday we came to 20 metres on the Delta in 5 metres of water in Enseada de Peroca, off the beach of Santa Monica. The bay is lined with upscale estates and houses above a broad, sandy beach, but the headland is very low and offered us no protection from the 20 to 25 knot winds which howled all day and into the night. Fortunately; however, our proximity to the land to windward meant there was very little fetch for any waves to build.

In the evening I prepared dry-seared beef tenderloin with béarnaise sauce, served with gnocchi in a portobello, shallot, garlic and cream sauce and a butter-sweat julienne of carrot, zucchini and poblano. With dinner we had a superb bottle of 2008 Araucano Humo Blanco Lolol Pinot Noir from Sequitur's cellar.

The wind continued to howl out of the northeast through the following day, so we decided to stay-put and relax.

We awoke with the dawn on Wednesday to find the winds down to north-northeast 10 to 12. With the assistance of the cockpit windlass, we weighed at 0616 and headed out under skies decorated with streaks of cirrus.

We encountered small wooden fishing boats, singly and in clusters. None of these had radar reflectors, and they began painting intermittently on radar at about 1.5 miles, and offered a rather trackable paint at a mile. This was no great problem during the day, but at night it really exercised our eyes, particularly since most of these boats, if they have navigation lights at all, have extremely weak ones, often not visible outside a mile. Compounding this is their habit of anchoring or simply drifting overnight and sleeping, with or without lights.

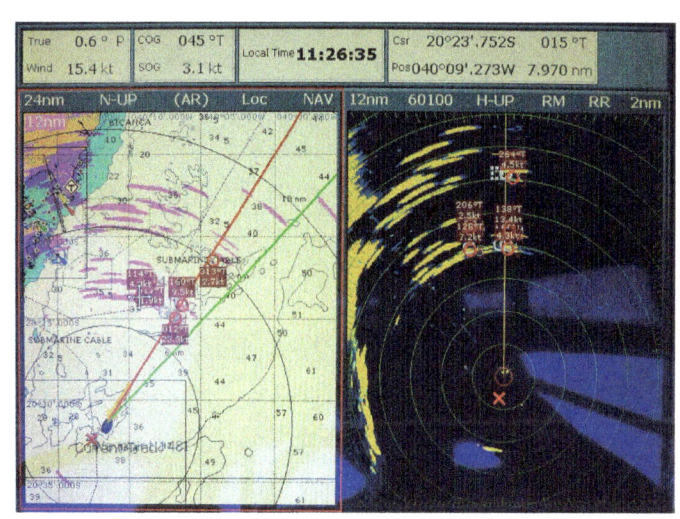

At 0945, as we motor-sailed within 10° of the wind, we were slowed to 1.5 knots with turns for 5, so I upped the revs to 2200 to make some better headway. Early afternoon as we approached the entrance to Puerto Vitoria the radar screen grew increasingly cluttered with contacts.

These strong paints were definitely not fishing smacks; they were huge oil tankers, apparently waiting to load. We weaved our way through some four dozen tankers. At one point we were able to count 27 above our horizon.

We were moving along generally in the middle of the 20 to 25-mile-wide continental shelf in 35 to 40 metres of water, trying to remain outside Brazil's 12-mile territorial limits. Frequently we passed through huge oil slicks, which are apparently the legacy Brazil is leaving the world in return for extracting deep-water oil.

Shoreward from us were several enormous columns of smoke. We were too far out to sea to see whether these were from land-based fires, but the smoke was too white to be from oil, so we assumed they were either from forest fires or from deforestation burns. Brazil has not painted for us a rosy picture, administratively nor environmentally.

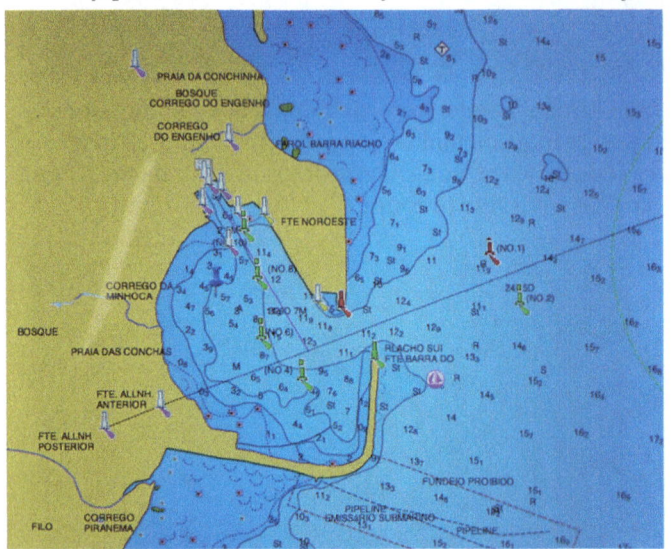

We continued motoring into the wind while fighting a strong opposing current. The seas were steeply choppy and confused, I assumed from the southwest flowing Brazil Current and the easterly swell fighting each other as they met the edge of the continental shelf. We decided to head closer in, and to find shelter and wait for better winds. On the chart was a port with an excellent set of aids to navigation, a lit channel and leading marks. This was good; we were not going to arrive at the entrance to the port until four hours after sunset.

At 2145 we lined-up on the entrance transit and entered the port. The waxing crescent moon was low on the horizon and added to the eeriness of the scene. There was an acrid odour in the cool, humid air and there was a large following swell in the basin. The green navigational beacons moved back and forth as we tried to orient ourselves, and then we realized the entire contents of the basin were surging back and forth, not the beacons. Our throats and nostrils were stinging from the pungent air. We decided to leave immediately.

I carefully turned, trying to get a sense of the rhythm of the surge and manoeuvring to avoid the beacons. We escaped without incident, quickly re-jigged our dinner, watch and sleep plans, and carried-on up the coast.

On Thursday morning Edi prepared another wonderful brunch after she arose from her post-watch snooze. We are still enjoying the delicious beef bangers we bought in the Falklands, as well as the farm eggs Sybie had gathered for us from her friends.

When I took-over the watch at 0600 on Friday morning, Edi had brought us to the southern edge of the Abrolhos Reefs. These are a complex of shoals, coral reefs and islets running 36 miles to seaward of Ponta de Baleia.

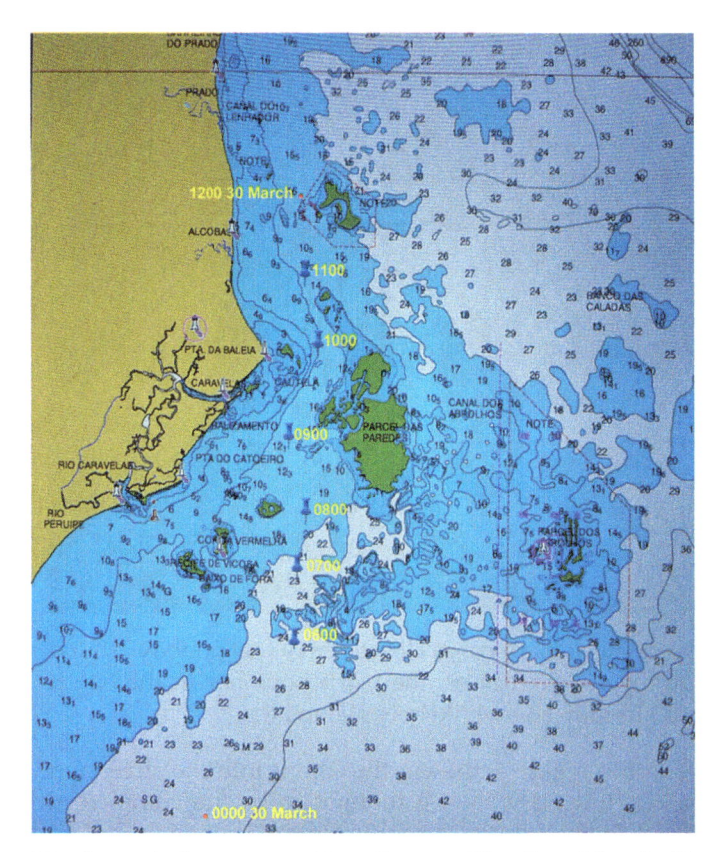

Northward for over 100 miles, a 25-mile-wide shelf, mostly 25 metres and shallower follows the coast. The eastern edge of this is charted as dropping sharply to 1000 metres and then continuing steadily to over 2000. I saw this shoal water as offering respite from the southbound current, I and eagerly began threading a course through the maze of charted, but unseen reefs lurking beneath the surface. My confidence was boosted by the two charted aids at the southern edge of the complex passages; they were both visually and by radar exactly where the chart indicated they were. Once we entered the shoal water, our speed over the ground more than doubled.

Saturday morning dawned glumly, with a sky full of nimbostratus and a radar screen full of rain cells parading toward us. What little wind there was came from astern and barely filled the sails, but at least we finally had winds with a southerly component. It alternately rained or drizzled or thickly misted, at times lowering visibility considerably. From this cloak of precipitation, little wooden fishing boats popped out without first announcing themselves on radar.

In the early afternoon the sky cleared, but as we approached sunset, we were again heading into a thickening and darkening northern horizon. Shortly after midnight it began drizzling again.

At 0222 in a steady light rain we came to 20 metres on the Delta in 5.9 metres of water in the basin in front of the Marina do Brazil in Ilheus. The tide was near its crest, with 0.8 of a metre to fall. There was a gentle easterly wind and the surge of the reef-filtered remains of the open ocean swell rolling into the open roadstead. We quickly shutdown, closed-up and went to bed. It was April Fool's Day, reminding us that in eight days we had bashed our way another 675 miles along a hostile coast.

After a very rolly sleep from the surge, we awoke midmorning to look at the scene the in daylight. The rig on a passing fishing boat made us think we were on the Nile, instead of in coastal Brazil. Because of the uncomfortable surge, we decided to weigh and look for a more protected anchorage, likely behind the breakwater in the southeast corner of the bay.

With the aid of the cockpit sheet winch we weighed and slowly motored over to take a look at what protection the breakwater afforded. Also we were in search of a fuelling facility, and we thought the most likely place would be inside the inner harbour. We were also looking for a wifi signal; we had seen none for over a week.

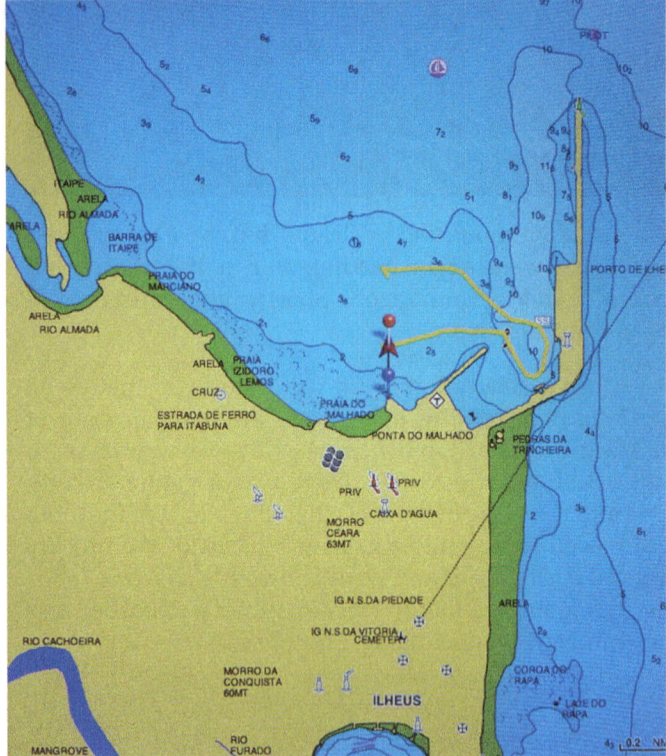

It took us a while to why we could not relate the chart with what we were seeing. The entrance to the inner harbour had been totally walled-off with a new breakwater. There was no entrance. The owners of the facility must have campaigned for the wrong side in the last election. We went back and anchored closer to the landing float in front of the yacht club.

We launched Non Sequitur and rowed in through the surge to the dinghy float. The surge was nearly half a metre up and down and washed about three metres back-and-forth, so landing was a tad tricky.

The yacht club appeared closed; there was nobody around in the yard, the offices, the workshops nor in the bar. It was Monday, so that likely explained it.

We found a gate and went through it into the street and walked toward what we thought to be the commercial area. At a Shell station a couple of blocks along, we asked about getting some diesel for the boat. We were motioned along up the street that led away from the water. I showed the fellow the fuel line from the Tohatsu outboard and asked about repair or replacement. This elicited the same set of arm waves.

A block and a half along we passed a very large supermarket, and then in another three blocks, we came to a second Shell station. Inside we met a young man with good English and a very helpful attitude. He told us he had worked at McDonald's in Southern California for two and a half years. He went out and called over three colleagues and they had a conference. One of the group also spoke English well, and he showed me a tank on a trailer that they regularly used to refuel boats. Diesel was R$2.00 per litre, CA$1.10 and there was a R$30 delivery charge.

I had brought my iPad, so on the Navionics chart of the basin, we located the fish pier, where they did the refuelling; it was in the crook, immediately east of the yacht club. He said at high tide there was sufficient water; I looked at the tide chart on the iPad and saw high at 1248. Knowing that we could easily take 300 litres, but likely not 350, I paid for 300 and arranged for it to be delivered at 1300, giving us sufficient time to stop at the supermarket on the way back. I also showed the fellow the Tohatsu fuel line and he made a phone call. He said the appropriate part would arrive at the pier with the fuel at 1300.

We walked back to the supermarket through the mid-30° midday, and were relieved to find a wonderfully stocked produce department. We bought a huge bag of green beans, three large cauliflower heads, six green peppers, a dozen roma tomatoes, a big bunch of bananas, four large mangoes and two huge avocados.

We bought a few other grocery items, but gave a pass to the salt cod, which was arrayed in aisle displays throughout the store. It must still be leftover from when the Portuguese depleted the cod on Newfoundland's Grand Banks.

We arrived back at the yacht club to find that the gate through which we had come out was closed. We continued around the peripheral wall looking for another entrance. The only other one was also closed, and there was no reply to our pushing the door buzzer.

By then we were close to the fish pier used for refuelling, so I walked over to look at it. A rickety narrow finger to a pair of crumbling concrete posts appears to be all the fishermen have left after the fill-in of the inner harbour. I spoke with the toothless guardian and indicated that we wanted to come in to take-on diesel. He told me to come in beside the yellow fish boat that was Med-moored there.

We walked back around to the club gate, and I managed to get it open. Back onboard, Edi stowed our produce while I re-rigged the anchor rode to the cockpit winch and prepared to weigh. As we were weighing a blue fishing boat came in and moored in the slot we were told to use. There was no more room on that side. The yellow boat on the other side had finished pumping its catch ashore, but showed no signs of leaving. Complicating the situation, its bow line was floating in a big arc from a mooring buoy and blocking our ability to back-in on our anchor, least we snag and cut it. The only alternative we saw was to head bow-in and raft on the yellow boat.

The surge was as big here as on the yacht club float, and the depth sounder showed we were bouncing to less than a metre under the keel. The yellow boat's skipper made it very apparent he didn't want us alongside. Eventually, he decided to leave, or was told to by the guardian, and he waved us off so he could pull his boat out on the mooring line. His mooring line was around our stern, nestled in the crook between the top of the transom and the davits uprights. This was a solid place, so I backed against the mooring line and allowed it to push our stern around to a proper orientation so that we could back-out clear. Properly turned and backing away, our a-cock-bill anchor snagged on the mooring line, so I stopped, went forward and hung over the side to clear it with my foot.

After the yellow fish boat had cleared the pier head, we turned and backed in, dropping the Delta on the way. As Edi paid-out the rode, I backed toward the finger, getting close enough to pass a line from the starboard stern cleat. With Sequitur balanced in the surge a couple of metres off the finger, we pulled a hose across and the operator turned on the pump on his trailer.

After about five minutes, a joint in the hose parted and our diesel was being pumped directly into the bay for nearly a minute before the operator could run back and switch-off the pump. Nobody ashore seemed the least bit concerned that ten or twenty litres of diesel had spilled. At home, a stray drop from the nozzle is enough to send boaters and fuel station attendants scrambling to get absorptive pads and dispersant.

There was enough length of hose remaining to pull it aboard and continue fuelling. Half an hour later the pump on the trailer ran dry, the attendant and the toothless guardian walked a hump of hose along out to the pier head, draining it of the last of the diesel.

Our main tank gauge was showing seven-eighths, about 500 litres, about 70 litres short of full. The auxiliary tank and four jerry cans were full, so we had about 850 litres aboard. With a knot or more of current behind us across much of the northern coast of Brazil all the way to the Windward Islands, and with the prevailing winds abaft the beam, we will not need anywhere near as much fuel as we have been using to this point.

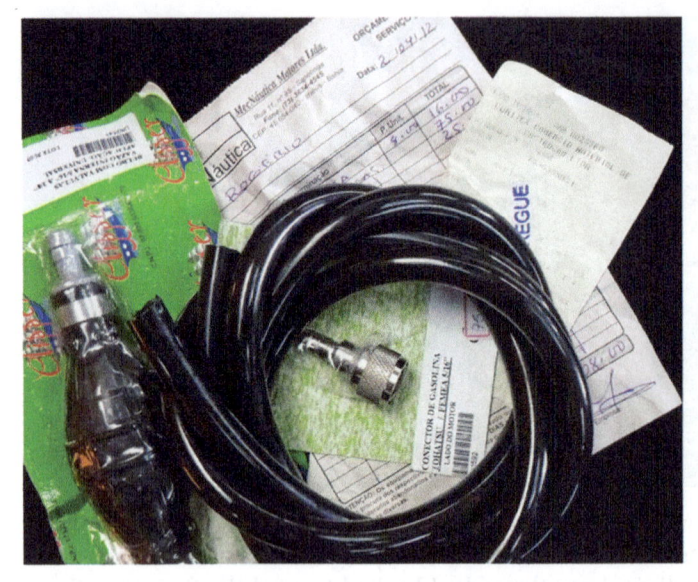

We passed the hose back across the gap, then pulled across a bag with our new Tohatsu fuel line fitting. They had bought bulb, line and fitting, rather than just the fitting, but we didn't mind paying the R$108 for the piece we needed. We sent R$110 plus the R$30 for the fuel delivery across on a jackline, plus a tetra-pack of Chilean wine for the helpful toothless guardian.

We had been fortunate in meeting a McDonald's customer-service trained young fellow and his cohorts at the Shell station. They were extremely helpful, as was the toothless guardian at the pier; however the remaining aspects of our fuelling stop were a real hassle.

Whenever we think of *"hassle"*, we are reminded of Edi's friend Isabelle, with whom she had sailed on three occasions in the Caribbean. Isabelle is Quebecoise, and her use of English is at times rather comical. Edi often heard her use the word *hassle* in describing people and events, pronouncing it with the French silent "H" as *"assle"*. It wasn't until Edi received an email from Isabelle with the term spelled *asshole* that she twigged to the crossover usage. Since then, *hassles* have taken-on new meaning for us.

Although we weren't fully ready to continue, and would have loved another day's break to catch-up on sleep, the surge in the anchorage made a restful sleep impossible. At 1406 we slipped the line from the rickety pier, weighed and continued north. The sky was crowded with nimbostratus and occasional cumulonimbus, and we couldn't avoid some rain showers. The winds though, were east-southeast at 9 to 12 knots, and we moved along on a beam reach under jib and main making 4.5 to 4.8 knots into the night.

As we sailed we baked the four loaves of no-knead bread that Edi had started the previous day, and while the oven was hot, two baguettes. For dinner we stuffed ourselves with fresh baguette slices and cream cheese.

To take advantage of a slight counter-current, and more gentle seas, we remained within six miles of the coast, just in from the drop-off at the edge of the continental shelf. Overnight we encountered very few fishing boats, assuming most were out at the drop-off. However on Tuesday morning as we crossed a canyon, we passed through a few dozen scattered little boats, most of which would be deemed unseaworthy at home.

The skyline of Salvador was already well above the horizon at 24 miles out. The wind was still near the beam, but it had eased to around 6 knots, so we motor-sailed, maintaining just under 5 knots. We ran the watermaker to bring our tanks to full.

632

At 12 miles south of Salvador the scale of the built-up area of the city could be more clearly seen. Many of the towers appear to be 40 or 50 stories tall, and they are densely packed.

At 6 miles we could see that many of the towers are residential, and those rising from what appeared to be seaside parkland along the southwest corner of the city look rather upscale.

At 1537 we came to 20 metres on the Delta in 6.8 metres of water in a small bay off the entrance to a huge marina filled mostly with powerboats.

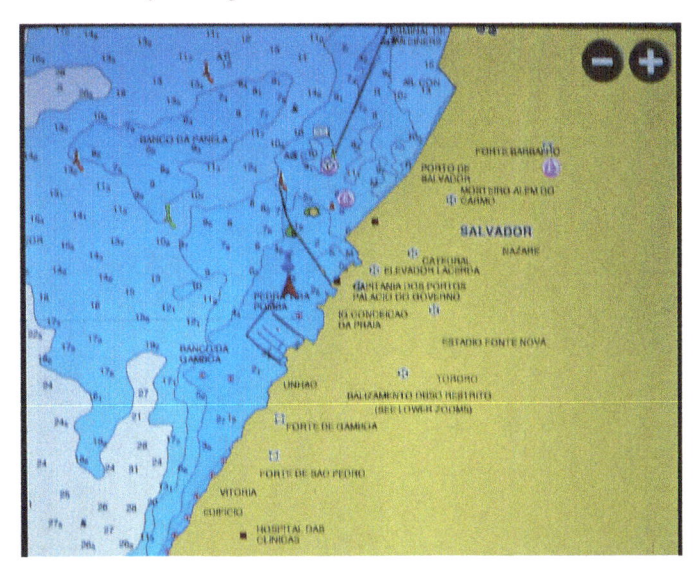

We were just below, and in full sight of the Palacio do Governo and the Capitania do Portos. We figured that if we were going to sneak in, we may as well do it through the front gate and sit on the front porch.

We relaxed for the remainder of the day, and in the evening I prepared skinless and boneless chicken breasts in a butter sauté of julienned red onion, shallot, garlic and cubed portobello mushrooms. We went to bed early and slept soundly for the first night since we had left Rio.

On Wednesday morning Edi prepared bacon and eggs with béchamel sauce and basil served with lightly toasted fresh baguette slices and sliced roma tomatoes.

After breakfast I assembled the new fuel line fitting and did a test attachment to the outboard. It fit. Mid-afternoon, after the temperature cooled to the mid-30s, we launched the dinghy, fitted the motor and went ashore to the marina. We walked along beside the freeway that had usurped the waterfront, much like in Seattle, Valparaiso and I am sure in many other cities with misguided planners. The very upscale marina and two restaurants intermingle with vacant and derelict buildings. Among these few respites from the waterfront slum is the headquarters of the 2nd Naval District. Otherwise the infrastructure is tired, decayed and crumbling.

We walked into the area around the old civic market to find broken sidewalks and broken people. We were accosted by aggressive beggars; we did not feel safe. We walked back through the square and followed the local example of forcing a way through the six lanes of unstopping traffic at the crosswalk. We continued through the crowd of beggars to the turnstiles, where for 8 Centavos, we bought passage up the elevator to the upper historic centre of the city.

We queued in a jostling crowd in a cramped, airless passage waiting for the lift, all the while very mindful of the wonderful opportunity the place provided for pickpockets. After a lift of a hundred-or-so metres, we emerged into another confining rabbit warren of airless passages that led to the outside. The elevator structure appears to be rather new; however, it suffers from very old design, with we suspect inputs from the pickpocket community.

We escaped with wallet, cameras and computers intact, and at the exit we went into a visitor information office to ask directions to a wifi signal we could use, and to a supermarket. All three young men at the counter spoke English well, and the one who served us showed us directions to Shopping Centre Lapa on his desk map.

One of the other fellows offered to give us a map, but the one serving us waved him off and instead, scribbled the name on a scrap of waste paper.

We took the scrap of paper and scraps of memory of the route to follow and headed out. When the sidewalk was wide enough to walk on, it was either broken and holed, or littered with storefront overflow. The area was very crowded, with an aggressive, jostling and rather unsavoury mix of people, most of whom walked in the street, challenging the rushing traffic and being challenged back. It was chaos. Making it even less comfortable was the upper 30° temperature. There were many street scenes we would love to have photographed, but we felt so unsafe that we dared not take out our cameras. Of the 150-or-so countries that Edi and I have together and separately visited, few have given us this degree of uneasiness.

By showing the name scrawled on the scrap of paper to a guard, a police officer and a helpful lady, we finally made it to Lapa. Inside we found Americanas, but it is not a supermarket, but a department store, and it was crammed with a frenzy of shoppers doing their last-minute Easter shopping. Easter shopping here appears more chaotic than last-minute Christmas, or early Boxing Day shopping at home. No one we asked knew of a Bom Preço in the area.

We carefully picked our way back out of the area, heading northward looking for signs of an escape back down to the harbour. Edi recognized a church or convent we had seen from our anchorage, and we followed a winding lane down past it. The lane appears to have once been a very fashionable address, before the divided highway along the waterfront below turned the neighbourhood to a collection of derelicts and slums.

There are signs of squatters or transients living in some of the ruins. A few of the more solid old buildings have been restored and have expensive-looking security walls, gates and hired guards.

Partway down the hill we had a wonderful overview of the marina, off which Sequitur was anchored. Powerboats predominate here, far outnumbering the sailboats, of which we counted fewer than two dozen among the hundreds of moored boats.

Back onboard Sequitur, we continued to be bothered by the wakes of the powerboats racing through the anchorage to get to the marina entrance, or accelerating to maximum speed immediately they had left the marina. It was the Wednesday before Easter, and we figured the boat traffic would increase significantly on Thursday as people slid-off early for an extended long weekend.

There were navy frogmen training in the anchorage around Sequitur, and we wondered if they also train their boarding parties by doing practice boardings of yachts at anchor. Thoughts like this came easily to mind with the tenuous nature of our presence in the anchorage.

We decided to head up-harbour on Thursday morning to see if there was a quieter and more secluded anchorage, hopefully one with a small community where we could find a supermarket and some wifi service. While the chart showed shoal water of one and two metres depth lying a mile and more off the entire 50-mile eastern shore of the bay, we were hoping to find a dredged channel through to a small suburb. What we found instead was no break in the urban-industrial sprawl and no signs of boat-friendliness.

After an hour and a half, we turned around and headed back out, having decided to continue up the coast another 280 miles to Maceio and try our luck there. By this time the tide had turned to flood, and we bucked it as we motor-sailed 20° off the wind out of the harbour. On our way out we met a 30-metre or so German-flagged ketch inbound from the north.

As we clawed our way into a 2.8-knot current and directly into the wind toward the race between Ponta de Santo Antonio and its off-laying reef, the engine temperature moved up from its normal range of 70° to 74°. When it reached 80°, I became concerned. I went below and removed a plastic bag and other bits of detritus from the raw water strainer. The temperature remained high, so I removed the cooling water intake hose from the seacock and after some resistance, managed to blow a wad of crud through it and out into the strainer bowl. The engine temperature came down a bit, but continued hotter than usual, and we attributed this to the high temperature of the dark brown sea, which the sun had warmed it to just over 40°.

Once we were past the cardinal buoy and out into less polluted water, the engine temperature came back to normal.

635

We continued for hours past a seemingly unending line of high-rise buildings ashore. When the sun set at 1733 we were still passing the sprawl of Salvador as we bucked directly into the wind and the current. At midnight we were abeam Ponta Acu da Torre and able to bend our course a few more degrees northward.

The wind continued from the northeast for the next two days, leaving us no option but to motor-sail a few degrees off it. A port tack would add too much southing to our track, a starboard tack would quickly put us on the beach. Early afternoon on Saturday we rounded Pontal da Barra and were able to bend our course another ten degrees northward.

At 0931 on Easter Sunday we came to 20 metres on the Delta in 3.5 metres of water in eastern side of the harbour in Maceio. The chaotic squalor of the fishing boats and the shoreside infrastructure reminded us of Paita, Peru, where we had had our dinghy and motor stolen and Sequitur's decks looted as we were ashore clearing-in. We had an uneasy feeling.

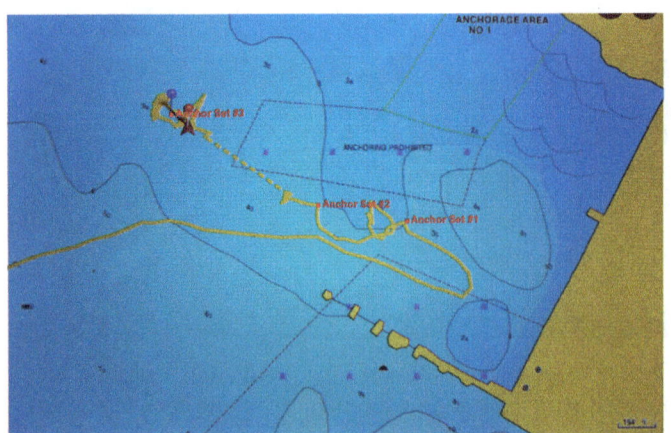

The tide was predicted to drop another half metre, then rise 2.5. We had a scope of over 3:1 for high tide and more than 1.5 metres under the keel at low. About an hour after we had anchored, we felt an occasional thudding. As it increased in frequency, we realized our keel was bottoming in the swells. We scrambled to rig the cockpit winch and within three minutes had weighed and motored off the shoal and dropped the anchor in 4.5 metres. An hour later in a wind gust, we dragged anchor 1.5 cables until it bit and held. We certainly miss having the Rocna easily available.

In port with us was the Brazilian Armada's tall ship, Cisne Branco, which had long lineups for an Easter open house. Because of the unsavoury aspect of the fishing boat culture next to us, and the tenuous hold of the anchor, we decided it was not wise to leave Sequitur, nor could we see a safe place to land ashore and leave our dinghy.

For Easter dinner I prepared tarragon chicken with green beans amandine, steamed baby potatoes and sliced roma tomatoes with shaved sea salt. With it we enjoyed another bottle of the 2008 Los Haroldos Cabernet Sauvignon we had bought in Ushuaia.

On Monday morning there was a low overcast of nimbus-whatever, out of which it variously drizzled, rained or downpoured. As we were having breakfast, I sensed movement outside, and went up to the cockpit to see a near toothless black in a ragged bathing suit stern-sculling a derelict wooden skiff a few feet from Sequitur. He had a beat-up ball cap embroidered with Capitan de Puerto, but the half dozen fish in the bottom of his boat convinced me further that this was not an official visit. He told me we should move closer in, onto one of the mooring buoys next to the fishing fleet; it was more protected from the wind there. I thanked him and said we would be moving within the hour. It certainly sounded like a ploy to make it easier for them to plunder Sequitur.

At 1040 we weighed and headed out to sea. When the anchor came up, the chain was wrapped around it and it was tangled in a piece of wire and some nylon line. No wonder it had dragged. We had very uneasy feelings about our security in the port, and even although the weather was unsettled and squally, we deemed it much safer at sea. Noon found us having rounded the buoy marking the southern extent of the reefs and heading up into the wind along the seemingly interminable Brazilian coast.

Through the day we dodged most of the squalls, being hit only a few times. The wind slowly veered until we could enjoy a broad reach, and by evening a beam reach. We remained on the shelf within six or eight miles of the coast, and out of the main current, the swell and the shipping lanes. A few large ships passed well to seaward and we met a few flimsy fishing rigs, which were more like two or three-man surfboards.

These little rigs were heading in toward the coast from to seaward of us, likely from eight or ten miles offshore at the edge of the continental shelf. It amazed us that the locals take these flimsy rigs so far to sea, and it was a delight to watch their skill in balancing them in the three metre swells, the blustery 12 to 20-knot winds and the wind-generated cross seas. We imagined that this is what some local windsurfers do for a living.

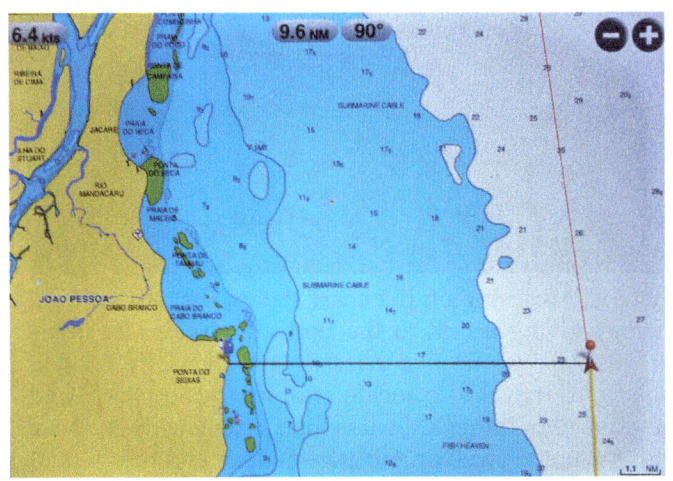

For weeks we have been beating against the wind and the current along the Brazilian coast. At 2034 on Tuesday the 10th of April, we rounded the nearly inconspicuous Ponta do Seixas, which is the easternmost point of the Brazilian coast, 4 cables south of the more prominent Cabo Branco. We were around the nose of Brazil and finally able to begin making some eastings. This would also, according to the guides and pilot, put both the wind and the current abaft our beam.

At noon on Wednesday we could see the new wire-stayed cross-harbour bridge, Ponte de Todos in Natal, which was shown on our iPad Navionics chart as having a vertical clearance of 55 metres. Our 2009 Navionics chip in the chart-plotter did not show the bridge. As we approached, we were joined by several fishing skiffs, windsurfing their way toward port with their catches.

There is a warning on the chart stating that the bar and channel giving access to the port are: *"subject to strong currents and vortices and demand local knowledge."* I had timed our arrival to coincide with low water slack, and we crabbed in through the less than a cable wide entrance with a 2-metre swell on our port quarter and the 20-knot southerly winds on the beam. With us sailed a two-man fishing surfboard.

We soon found the lee of the breakwater, rolled-in the sails and motored up-harbour in search of an appropriate anchorage. We were pleased to see a small collection of sailboats anchored off the yacht club, and we poked around among them trying to find sufficient swinging room.

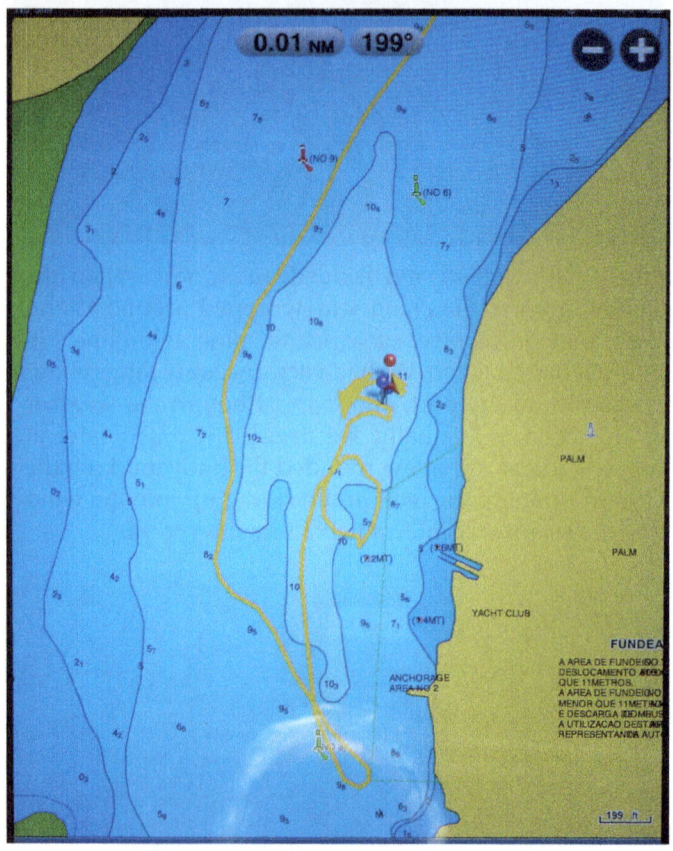

The water depth demanded too much scope for us to safely swing in the few empty spaces there were, so we turned and searched toward the other end.

638

Our aim was to be sufficiently close to the yacht club that we could pickup their wifi signal. Another loop through the moored and anchored boats left us with no option but to anchor at the northern end, beyond the last boats and the wifi. At 1440 we came to 40 metres on the Delta in 12 metres of water, and I backed-down at 2800 rpm to ensure the anchor was firmly set. There was another 1.5 metres of tide to rise, taking us to just shy of a 3:1 scope.

The place looked peaceful and we were well away from any potentially malfeasant fishing boat slum. The yacht club looked a bit upscale, but nobody seemed to take any great notice of our arrival. We were not bothered.

We opened the hatches and portlights and allowed the 15-knot breeze to blow through Sequitur and cool her interior. We variously napped and relaxed, and in the evening we had a celebratory bottle of Undurraga Brut Royale with dinner. We reflected on where we were and where we had been.

Since leaving Vancouver, we had covered 15,166 nautical miles, which is just over 70% of the distance around the earth. Almost a quarter of our travel, 3500 miles had been during the past seven weeks since we left the Falklands, and most of this through adverse and contrary conditions, both ashore and at sea. We needed a break.

Since we were rather inconspicuous among the comings and goings of anchored boats in front of the yacht club's marina, we remained onboard the remainder of the our arrival day. On Thursday because we were still not attracting attention and seemed to be a part of the normal scene, we decided to again remain onboard all day. We spent the time catching-up on sleep, doing maintenance and baking.

Edi made four fruit loaves, two carrot and candied ginger loaves and two banana and pecan loaves, and while we had a hot oven, we triple-baked several dozen biscotti in three variations of almond, pecan, dried cranberry and dried apricot.

Midmorning on Friday we launched Non Sequitur, fitted the motor and went in the short distance to the floats of Iate Club do Natal. We stopped at the admin office to ask about wifi, diesel fuel and supermarkets. From behind the counter, a very amiable young woman greeted us with fluent English.

She told us the wifi was open, with no password, that diesel was available, but was rather awkward, that there are several supermarkets, but at a distance and that the area around the club is unsafe and we needed to take taxis coming and going. She gave us a four-page document in English, which detailed the yacht club facilities as well as facilities and services in the area.

She then asked us our last port and our next port and for our passports and boat documents so she could fax our details to the Capitania do Portos. At this point Edi and I went into fast thinking mode. We told her our documents were on the boat, and we could bring them later, that our last port was Rio and we were thinking of Fortaleza as our next. She had us fill-out a page in the visiting boat log, and to complete a couple of forms with boat details, which I did without the passport numbers, Ship Registry number, call sign and so on. We then told her we hadn't had an internet connection for a couple of weeks, and needed to do banking and other administrative stuff, as well as catch-up on emails.

We found a table on the shaded patio, next to a scale model of the harbour area around the yacht club, and there we spent nearly two hours online, catching-up. About half an hour into this time, the woman from the office came by and asked for our passports and documents again. We told her we hadn't been back out to the boat yet, and that we wanted to take a trip to the supermarket while we were ashore.

When we had done everything we needed to online, we went back to the office to have a taxi called. The woman seemed unconcerned about our delinquent passports and papers. We went to the recommended supermarket and did a walk-through and then went out to find a restaurant; it was 1430 and we were hungry.

After many dozens of blocks of walking, the closest things we could find to a restaurant were the many grubby little dens offering a simple buffet by the kilogram. None looked appetizing, but finally as we saw them all closing after lunch, we ducked into one as the roll-down door was being lowered to half mast. Our first meal ashore since we arrived back in Puerto Montt in October was a solid reminder of why we love eating aboard Sequitur.

We went back to the supermarket and loaded-up on fresh fruit, vegetables, meat, fish and dairy in sufficient quantities to completely fill our fridges and freezers. We also picked-up grocery items to replenish our pantry shortages and then took a taxi back to the club, arriving shortly before 1700. The woman in the office acknowledged us as we juggled four loads from curb-side to the dinghy. We figured we didn't need to mention that it was too late in the day to bring in the documents.

Back onboard, after we had juggled and squeezed our purchases into place, I began a Bolognese with two kilos of ground beef and the last of our old tomatoes and onions. We took out four dinners' worth for pasta and froze them. I then added-in some diced carrots and potatoes, and when these were cooked, Edi made-up two dozen empanadas.

While the empanadas were baking, I prepared dinner, and as we baked and ate, I reconfirmed with the Navionics app on the iPad the tides and the time of sunrise. Low water slack over the bar at the harbour entrance was predicted for 0450 and sunrise would be at 0533.

The moment the woman in the office had mentioned passports and documents, we had independently, but in perfect harmony begun planning our Brazilian breakaway.

36. Escape From Brazil

At 0440 on Saturday the 14th we weighed using the cockpit power winch. At 0456 we passed under the bridge and ten minutes later we were through the narrows, over the bar and heading northeast.

As I looked back toward the harbour entrance, I saw a motorboat heading directly toward us through the predawn light. Above its windscreen I could make-out shapes that appeared to be police-type lights. As the boat grew, Edi thought it looked more like a sport fishing boat than a police launch. Then she saw the four trolling rods. Whew!

The sun was just beginning to add pink tinges to the horizon as I started securing the anchor in its chocks, untangling the anchor rode and stowing it back into the cable locker. The sun rose on schedule at 0533 as Edi brought up a thermos of freshly ground Starbucks. We began to relax.

Our 15-day emergency visas had long since expired, and we knew we had really pushed the limits of our undocumented stops in Brazil. Once clear of shoals, we headed directly toward the 12-mile limit, and even after rounding the nose of Brazil, we continued opening our distance from the Brazilian coast, heading toward the 200-mile limit. At noon on 15 April we were 98 miles off the coast in latitude 3°25′ South.

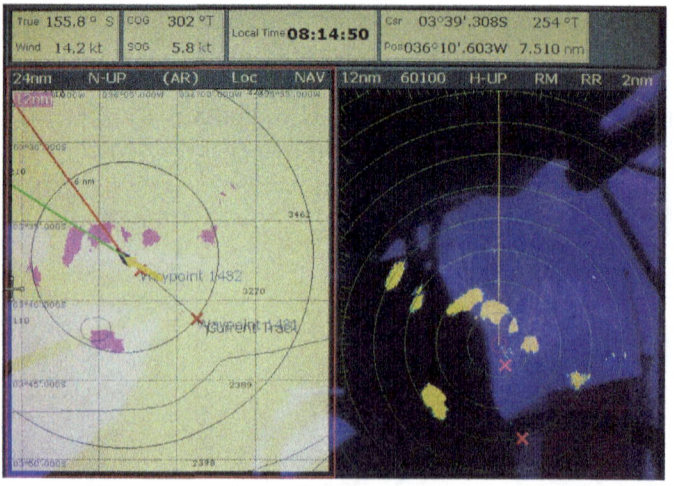

Overnight and into the early hours of daylight we had been hit by a series storm cells with 20 to 30-knot rotating winds and heavy to torrential downpours. These, I surmised were the result of all the moisture in the clouds that had built during the heat of the day cooling at sundown, reaching dew point and dumping the water back to the surface. I expected that we would be experiencing this daily cycle for much of our current passage.

Our routine continued with Edi preparing a nice brunch late morning after she had finished her post-watch sleep. After three years, our watch routine was still the same. A casual no-schedule during the day, spelling each other off for naps as required, then my cooking dinner around 1900 or 1930 and Edi going to bed until 0100 when she relieves me for the 0100 to 0600 watch. It has worked well for us.

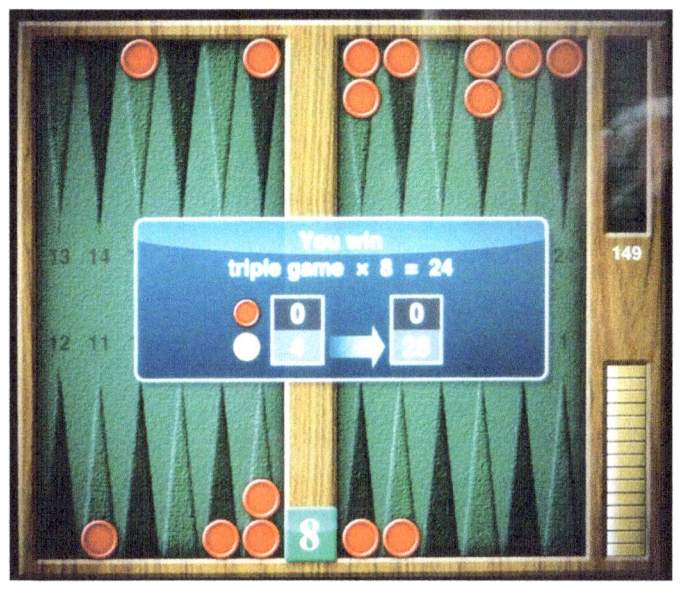

I finally got around to reattaching the clew cringle to the staysail. This took a little over six hours of very heavy going with my old stitching awl. I had first tried to do the job using a sailmaker's palm and needle, but there were too many layers of heavy material for this, and the awl was so much easier. Also, I prefer the lock-stitch that the awl gives.

Among the things we have to occupy our time on watch, and to keep us from getting bored and nodding-off, are our computer games, books and movies. Most days I play the fresh selection of thirteen games on Sudoku Daily, an iPad free download. I also play a few dozen matches of backgammon on iGamon, another free app. The games last just long enough to break the time between checking the horizon, the weather, the sails, the radar, the instruments and the gauges. As we headed north in the rainy gloom, I had my best game ever, double-skunking the computer expert in a re-re-doubled game.

We reattached the staysail and hoisted it. It was good to have it again; it offers a great degree of flexibility to our sail plan. With it out full and the main out about two-thirds, we can confidently head into a sunset filling with the squalls of the day's cumulonimbus buildup.

As I come off watch for my sleep, I normally start the generator to replenish the batteries and also the watermaker to keep the tanks at or near full. As we moved away from the Brazilian coast, the water cleared and took-on a wonderful blue colour, and our pre-filters were again lasting beyond a few hours before clogging.

643

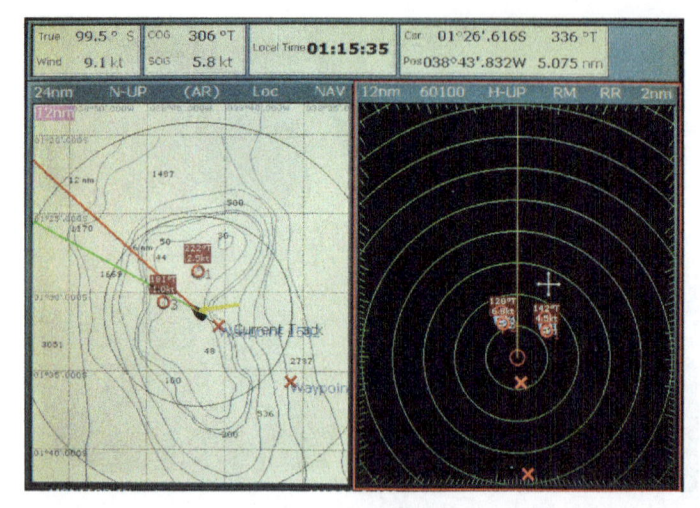

Late on Monday night we approached a seamount jutting abruptly from the sea floor over 4000 metres below to within 30 metres of the surface. The shallowest sounding on its summit is 26 metres. Even though this is 110 miles off the Brazilian coast, I had expected to see some boats fishing the area, so we were not surprised to pick-up two trackable radar contacts at about 3 miles. There were likely many more boats in the area, but since they do not show-up on radar outside 3 miles, and their navigation lights are too feeble to be seen beyond that, we will never know.

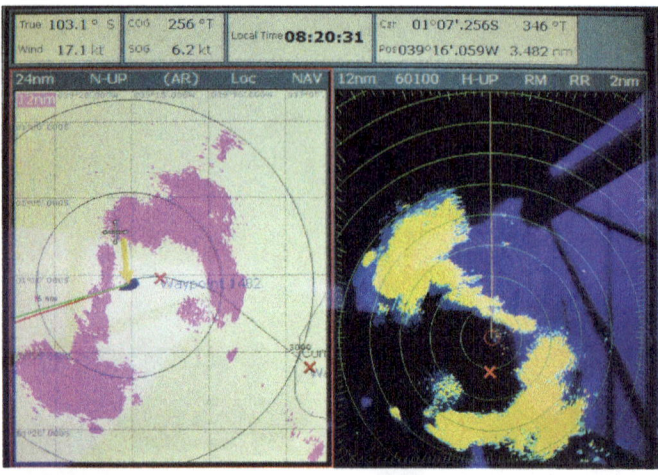

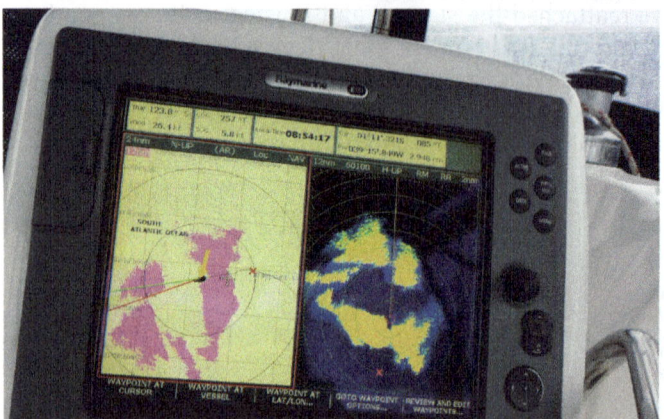

On Tuesday morning we were overtaken by a continuous series of storm cells. I altered to port in an attempt to remain on the better wind side of an approaching very large system. There was no way to avoid being hit, and soon we were in 25 to 30 knot winds and torrential downpours.

I noted that the weather systems were now moving westward, which could mean we had crossed the ITCZ, the inter-tropical convergence zone, otherwise known as the Doldrums. We were still south of 1° South. As the morning squalls dissipated, we found ourselves in northeasterly winds, which are the winds of the NE Trades, not of the SE Trades that theory told us we should still be in.

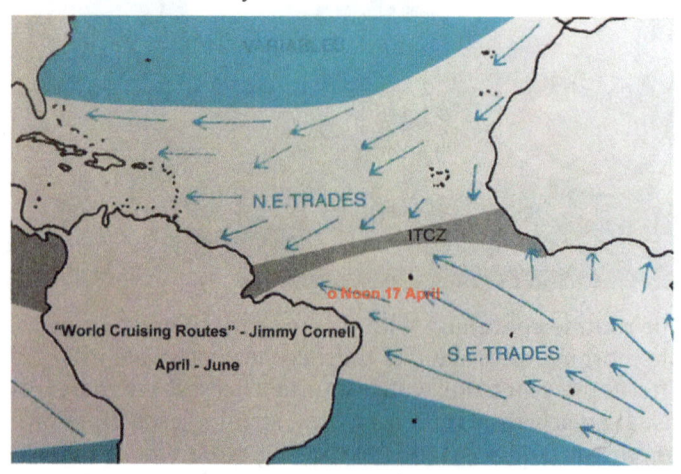

Jimmy Cornell's *World Cruising Routes* told us in this longitude, this time of year, the NE Trades began north of 4° North; we were still 5° south of that.

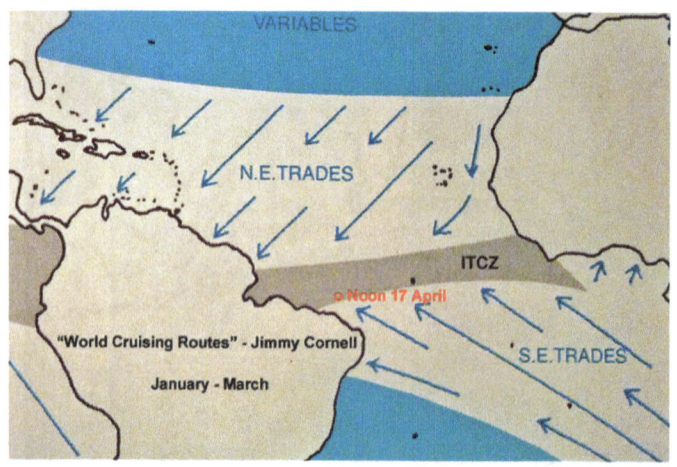

The January to March chart shows the NE Trades beginning at 2°30′ North, still over 3° north of us.

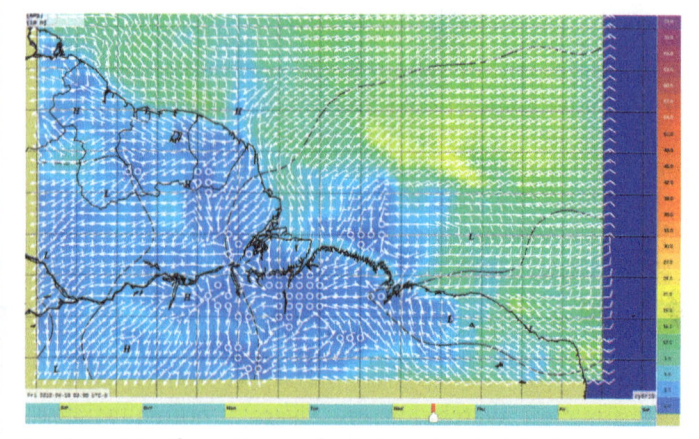

I referred to the gribs we had downloaded before we had left Natal and saw that the winds had been predicted to have a northerly component as we approached the Equator.

644

As the northeasterly winds continued and strengthened, we became increasingly convinced that the ITCZ had narrowed and dipped south for our easy crossing. We had crossed the Doldrums.

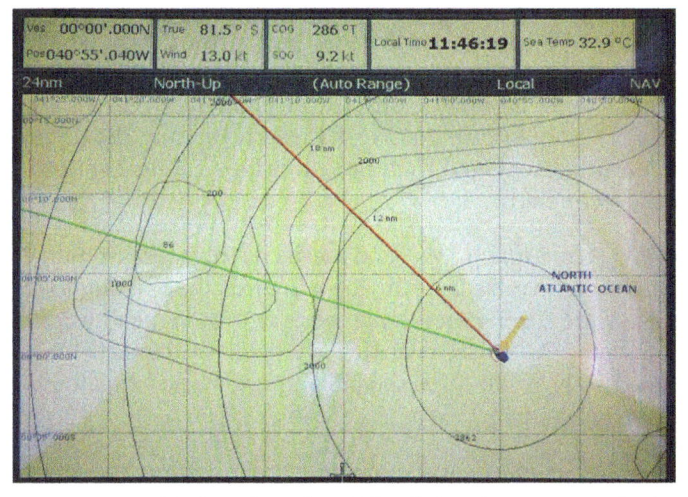

At 1146 on Wednesday the 18th of April we crossed the Equator into the North Atlantic; we were then over 3000 miles north of our most southerly point at Cape Horn. It had taken us over 4600 miles to do this south-north crossing of the South Atlantic. It is certainly not the typical direction for an ocean crossing, and our experience showed it to be much more onerous than had we taken the downwind sail in the Trades or the Westerlies of a typical crossing.

For the first day in many, we approached a rather friendly looking sunset. We sailed along on a beam reach at over six knots in a steady 12 to 14 knot northeasterly breeze. There were no evening and overnight squalls, and the only unpleasant aspect was the roll from beam seas.

The sloppy seas made cooking a tad more difficult and setting a proper table in the cockpit for dinner was impossible. These minor inconveniences, though, did not deter us from continuing to enjoy three good meals a day, including such dishes as frittata...

... and pangasius filets sautéed in butter and julienned garlic with potato coins and sliced roma tomatoes.

We began finding flying insects in the cockpit. Since we were about 150 miles off the coast, too far for them to have flown, we became quite concerned that we had somehow brought aboard some nits or larvae with our provisioning.

Then we began running into clumps, streaks and masses of amber-coloured floating seaweed. This sargassum is more closely associated with the Sargasso Sea to the north of us, and it is a well-known hatching place for insects, eels and other creatures.

We flew the spinnaker whenever there were no storm cells in the area and for several days enjoyed nice daily runs. At noon on the 24th we were 158 miles off the Brazilian coast and 39 miles from the boundary line of French Guyana. We had come 1225 miles from Natal and had 710 miles to go to Carlisle Bay, Barbados. We were satisfied with our progress and were looking forward to crossing the line on the ocean marking the end of Brazil.

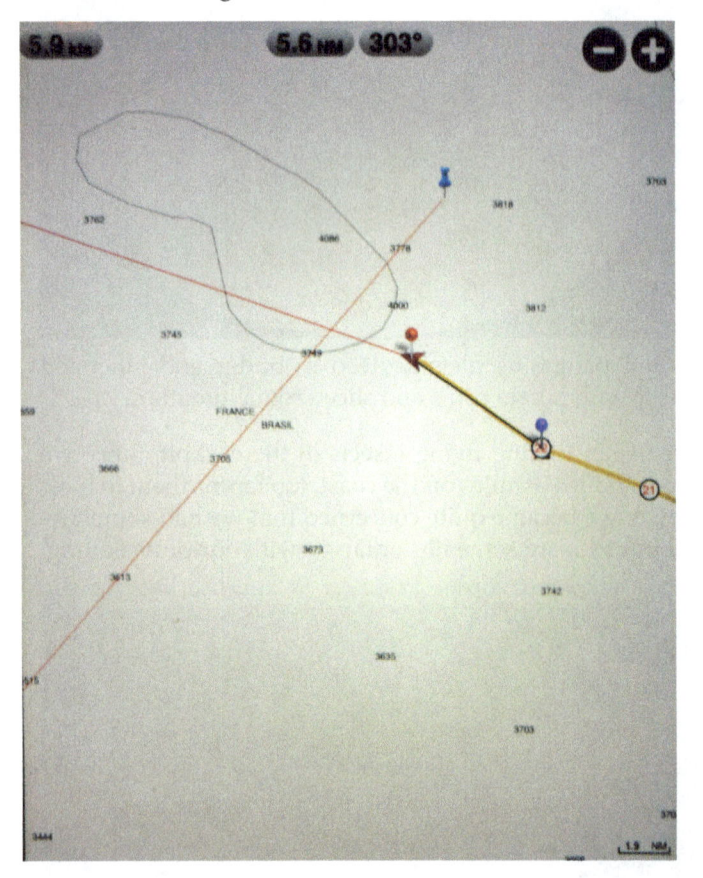

In the late afternoon we picked-up two radar contacts ahead of us, and we began tracking them. Since rounding Brazil's northeast point, besides the two fishing boats on the sea mount, we had seen only one other vessel, a huge tanker. We continued to close the radar contacts, which appeared to be within five miles of the line marking the boundary between Brazil and French Guiana and then picked them up visually.

As the sun was preparing to set, a clean, official-looking modern vessel approached our stern to within 50 metres and signalled us. There were what appeared to be uniformed men on the foredeck; they looked ready to board us.

We were still about seven miles from the French Guiana boundary and following the wind, we had slipped about five miles inside the Brazilian 200-mile zone. We were worried. We turned-up the volume on the VHF, which we had been keeping very low because of the catcalls, whistles and constant nonsensical chatter on Ch 16 by the Brazilian fishermen. We had early in our Brazilian adventure discovered that the authorities had lost control of the frequency.

I called *"Unidentified Ship"* and received a response from the larger vessel, a cable layer. In fluent English, the operator told us we were closing on a cable they were laying, and asked us to come 20° to starboard to avoid it. We thanked him, immediately came to starboard and we started breathing normally again.

It is a strange place for a submarine cable, and my thoughts are that it might be part of a detection grid to monitor ships entering Brazilian waters from the west, much like the submarine grids we laid off the Canadian east coast and monitored from Argentia, Newfoundland at the height of the Cold War.

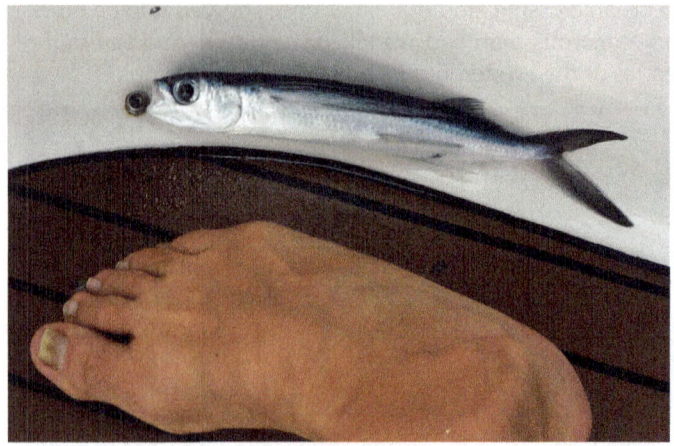

Every morning I checked the side decks for flying fish, which had flown their final night sortie. Most of these were in the 20 to 25 centimetre range, and if not discarded overboard, began to rot and smell rather quickly.

Our respite from storm cells and squalls was over, and we were again into a daily routine of clearing a couple of hours after sunrise, building cumulus and cumulonimbus through the afternoon and increasing rain squalls and twisting winds through the evening and overnight.

Most days it had calmed sufficiently by the time Edi had arisen from her kip that we could enjoy a relaxing brunch in the cockpit. We were still feasting on the wonderful back bacon and beef bangers we had stocked-up on in the Falklands, we had plenty of eggs, and our stock of tomatoes and other vegetables would last us well beyond Carlisle Bay, our immediate destination.

On the afternoon of 29 April, still 110 miles from Barbados, we spotted only the second flock of sea birds we had seen since leaving Uruguay in early March. In mid-March along the southern Brazil coast we had seen three brown boobies. Besides having seen only three sea birds along the thousands of miles of Brazilian coast, we frequently commented to each other that we had not seen a marine mammal since we had left the Falklands. There were no whales, no sea lions, no seals, no tortoises, no dolphins, no porpoises. Not at sea nor in the ports. None.

At 1128 on Monday the 30th we sighted the south coast of Barbados. At 1256 we spotted the first marine mammals since leaving the Falklands, as pods of dolphins frolicked with Sequitur's bow wake. At 1450 we came to 35 metres on the Delta in 8 metres of water off the beach in Carlisle Bay. The water was so clear we could watch the bottom in 15 metres of depth as we approached the anchorage.

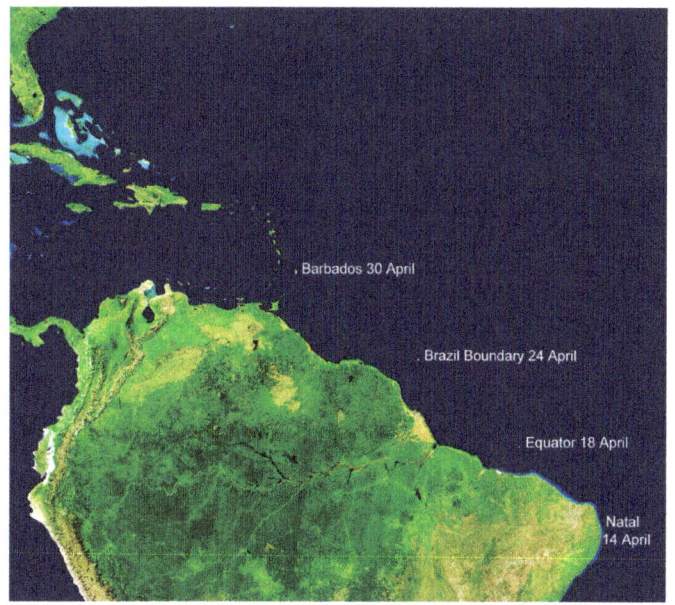

In a little over sixteen days we had come 1958 miles, much of it in rather sloppy beam seas. All but four days of the passage had been through long daily bouts of storm cells and squalls. We had finally escaped from Brazil and from its convoluted and disjointed bureaucracy and from a marine infrastructure that seems to us so unwelcoming to cruising boats.

647

It was the 30th of April, the 31st anniversary of my resigning my commission as a Canadian naval officer to buy a boat and sail off over the horizon. It was the 6th anniversary of my discussing with my wife (now ex-wife) that I still wanted to sail off. It was the 4th anniversary of Edi's response to my internet ad looking for a soul mate with whom to sail off. We remained onboard and relaxed through the afternoon.

In the evening we celebrated the 4th anniversary with Falklands beef tenderloin with gnocchi in a mushroom, shallot and garlic cream sauce, a butter-sweat of julienned carrots, white onions and green peppers and a garnish of sliced roma tomatoes with shaved sea salt. A bottle of J Lohr 2007 Los Osos Merlot from Sequitur's cellar complimented perfectly. Edi and I complement perfectly. We were content.

37. Through the Caribbean

We were laying to our anchor off the beach in Carlisle Bay, a small indentation in the southwestern corner of the island a few miles south of the capitol, Bridgetown. The anchorage provides little protection from the surge of the open Atlantic, and Sequitur rolled in beam swells as she weathercocked in the easterly wind.

Among our neighbours in the anchorage was a mega yacht complete with helicopter and assorted other toys. An odd assortment of day-trip boats paraded past us, including the Jolly Roger, a top-heavy double-decked pretend-to-be pirate ship with cut-down masts and a huge bar. It did daily runs for the tourists.

On Tuesday a huge cruise ship came in, and we sat in Sequitur's cockpit entertained by the capsizing rental jet-skis and plastic kayaks. We also watched large charter catamarans heading in and out with their decks seemingly standing room only with partying passengers. We remained onboard under our quarantine flag, relaxing and catching-up on sleep.

On Thursday we watched the mega yacht launch its workboat, a motor-yacht 15 metres or so in length. Then as we watched its helicopter take off and head ashore, we were reminded that we needed to head ashore ourselves. Resigning ourselves to having no helicopter, we would have to use our dinghy.

Unfortunately, Non Sequitur had sprung a leak in her starboard after tube. Friction from the constant motion in the beam seas had chafed through the airtight layers of the tube, and I needed to apply a patch. We lowered the dinghy on the davits, hauled it along the side and hoisted it to the foredeck with the spinnaker halyard. I began the repair.

As I worked on the dinghy, we watched as a young fisherman located a series of rather large shellfish traps using a hand-held GPS and a swim mask. He then grappled and raised each trap in turn, balanced it on the gunwales of the boat, checked it for catch, refreshed the bait and threw the trap back in. We could see no catch, and couldn't determine whether it was crab or crayfish, or both, or neither.

On Friday afternoon we launched the repaired dinghy and headed ashore. There is a narrow river mouth walled on both sides with wharves, along which are very tightly packed Med-moored tour boats and local yachts. Shortly before the low bridge, we found a place to secure the dinghy with chain and padlock, and then walked the short distance to Jordan's Supermarket.

We bought a wonderful selection of fresh produce, including broccoli, green peppers, bok choy, tomatoes, celery, onions, potatoes and carrots. Also we picked out 2 kilos of pork for the wok, a kilo each of chicken breasts and chicken thighs plus 2.5 kilos of peeled, cleaned and flash-frozen large raw prawns. We were nearly ready to head out again.

On our way back out the river mouth, we continued on into the fishermen's wharves to take a look at the fuelling facilities. We saw a solid third-world class fuel dock with easy access to modern Texaco pumps.

On Saturday morning we weighed using the cockpit winch and motored the half mile or so to the fuel dock.

We took on 487 litres of diesel for B$1189, which is $596, about $1.22 per litre, the second least expensive we have seen in the past couple of years. When I tried to pay with a credit card, the woman at the pump said cash only, so I headed ashore to an ATM.

To get out of the fishermen's wharves, I had to go through the fish processing area, and then through the public fish market. On the way back with the 1200 Barbadian dollars, I paused to buy some fresh mahi-mahi. I asked for B$11 worth, the change that would be leftover after paying for the diesel. The monger cut four thick steaks, trimmed and skinned them and took only one of the two tens I offered him, saying he didn't have time to make change. I gave the remaining $1190 to the woman at the pump, telling her to keep the change.

At 1101 we slipped and headed out, shaping our course toward Martinique, about 130 miles away to the northwest. We hauled down our quarantine flag, not having been bothered to check-in while in Carlisle Bay.

Shortly before sunset we sighted Saint Lucia, and watched the lights along its shores through the night. As we sailed, I ran the watermaker to bring our tanks back up to full. The south coast of Martinique was in sight at sunrise.

At 0859 we came to 25 metres on the Delta in Anse Mitan across harbour from the capitol, Fort de France. We hoisted the quarantine flag and scurried below just as the skies opened-up in a deluge. It rained heavily much of the remainder of the day, so we remained onboard, relaxing and fully content to be snug and dry.

In the evening I seared the mahi-mahi steaks and served them with steamed broccoli, sautéed potato coins and wedged tomatoes. With dinner we enjoyed another superb bottle of the Montes Leyda Vineyard 2010 Sauvignon Blanc, delighted we had stocked so much of it in Sequitur's cellars.

On Monday morning, after a British breakfast, we launched Non Sequitur and motored ashore to the village of Les 3 Ilets, where we secured the dinghy to a ladder on the side of the public pier.

We knew we were in French territory immediately we stepped ashore; there was a modern public toilette, exactly like the ones common in France.

We paused to smell the roses and the other wonderful flowers that lined the clean, well-maintained streets. We wandered the quaint village, poked into a bakery, examined the selection at the stalls in the village market, browsed the shelves in two small supermarkets, and then began working our way back, buying as we went.

Besides the mandatory baguettes, brie and chèvre, we bought a large mille-feuille au fondant and enjoyed it immediately we arrived back onboard. As we were devouring it in the cockpit, we noticed we had dragged anchor. We had also dragged in Carlisle Bay and we were increasingly disenchanted with the holding power of the Delta. We were in 3.2 metres of water and very close to the shoals, so we needed to move.

Rather than resetting the anchor, we decided to continue on north, so at 1318 we weighed and motored out of Petit Anse and past the downtown waterfront of Fort de France. It was raining lightly and there was just a slight southeasterly breeze, so we continued motoring through the afternoon until sufficiently clear of Martinique for the prevailing northeasterly wind to offer some assistance.

Off the west coast of Dominica and into Guadeloupe Passage we were hit by a succession of storm cells with torrential rains and 25 to 35 knot twisting winds as they passed over. As these were hitting us, we were fighting a strong counter-current, which slowed us to less than 3 knots over the ground, even though we were moving above 6 knots through the water. I could find no reference to this southerly current, only indications of northeast setting ones. The winds filled overnight to above 20 knots and there were very confused seas from the multi-directional winds of the storm cells.

An hour after sunrise we finally found some respite from the heavy seas as we reached Passe du Sud-Ouest between the islands of Iles des Saintes, Guadeloupe. The propellers of the wind generators on the south cliffs of Terre-de-Bas were spinning rapidly in the 25-knot winds as we passed, but the seas were dramatically calmer as we entered the lee of the rocks and islets.

This composite photo looking slightly south of west, shows the lay of the land of Les Saintes. We entered through the pass beyond the domed peak and continued through the large bay in the centre of the archipelago before turning southeastward to the anchorage off the village of Terre-de-Haut.

Since Edi was last here in 2007 and 2008, the community had installed a mooring field covering virtually all the anchorage off its waterfront. At 1001 we came to a mooring just off the public wharf at the centre of the downtown waterfront. It was the closest mooring buoy to the dinghy dock and to the possibility of wifi signals, and it had just been vacated.

On our passage I had made water to top-off the tanks, and the water in the anchorage looked clean enough to run the watermaker, so we took long showers and relaxed.

My hair had become rather wild, not having had it cut since February in the Falklands. There was a lovely breeze blowing, so Edi grabbed her scissors and set to work.

What emerged was a considerably more civilized-looking person, one much less likely to scare the people ashore.

After a brunch of baguettes, Brie and chèvre, we launched Non Sequitur and headed ashore. There were a dozen or more dinghies on the pier, all of them secured with chains or cables and padlocks. Whether this is for the general situation in the Caribbean, or for local reasons, we didn't question; we chained the motor and dinghy to the pier.

We were directed to Les Saintes MultiServices in an office above the retail shops along from the public wharf. Besides running an internet cafe, they also administer the mooring field fees and deliver fresh breakfast croissants, baguettes and so on to the boats.

When I enquired about moorage, I was shown to a computer where I completed our Customs and Immigration clearance online, printed a copy and took it to the counter. There were no fees, no government officials, no hassles; there was simply a polite young woman who took the form, stamped it and handed it back.

We walked along to the bakery where we bought four baguettes still warm from the oven. Further along at the public market, among the things we found were some very fresh ginger, some huge, juicy tomatoes and some small, almost mini courgettes. In the supermarket we picked-up some more brie and chèvre. In the freezer we spotted some huge coquilles St Jacques.

I have always wondered why North Americans throw away the roe when they shuck scallops. We bought a kilo bag, which contained 36 scallops, so I selected 18 of them and set them out to thaw.

As we waited for the scallops to thaw, we looked at where we were and thought of onward plans. We had come 6307 miles from Cape Horn and were sitting just shy of 16° North, in the middle of Hurricane Alley with just six weeks to go before the start of the Hurricane Season. Our insurers require that we be north of 31° North by the end of June, so we still had some voyaging to do.

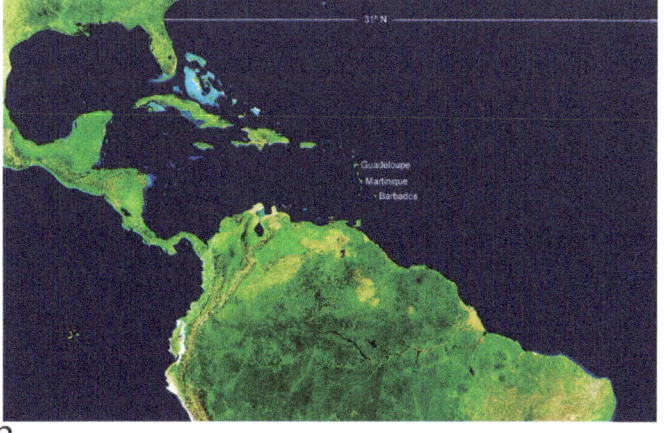

Our thoughts were to continue by way of the US Virgin Islands, Puerto Rico, Turks & Caicos and the Bahamas to Florida and then north to at least Brunswick, Georgia, which is just across the 31° line. We were hopeful that along this 1500-mile route we would find some decent weather, some proper sailing conditions, some pleasant anchorages and some repairs for our windlass.

As we mused, we watched a spectacular red and purple sunset. We had been in one storm after another for nearly three weeks, with hardly a break between them. We wondered whether the red sky portended better weather to follow.

I sautéed the scallops in butter with julienned garlic and shallots and served them with basmati rice, steamed cauliflower and sliced tomatoes. The Sancerre-like characteristics of the 2010 Montes Leyda Vineyard Sauvignon Blanc complemented perfectly.

Onboard we had a strong wifi signal from the internet service; their rate was US$10 per day or $30 per week. The mooring was €11 per night or €60 per week, so we had decided to stay a week.

There was a rather steady turnover of boats in the mooring field, with early morning departures and mid-to-late afternoon arrivals, and as the week progressed, the number of boats steadily decreased. It was nearing the end of the season; the rainy season had already begun. Some of our neighbours were end-of-season charters, but many appeared to be cruisers beginning to head out of the hurricane zone.

On one of the mornings that it wasn't raining, we took a walk up to Fort Napoleon on the summit of a 120 metre knob. The fort was constructed between 1844 and 1867 on the ruins of Fort Louis, which had been destroyed by the English in 1809. Iles des Saints had been discovered by Columbus on his second voyage in 1493. There are nine islands in the group totalling about 12.8 square kilometres, and they became a French colony in 1648. They were captured by the English in 1759, restored to France in 1763, captured again by the English in 1782 and restored a second time to France in 1816. The islands became a dependancy of Guadeloupe in 1946 as a French Overseas Department.

We reached the gates of the fort shortly after noon to read a fresh-looking notice taped to the wall by the admission desk indicating that the fort will close at 1230. We weighed the merits of, on the one hand, considering as exercise our climbing the hill in the 35° midday temperature, with on the other hand, spending €9 for admission for about 20 minutes of frantic dashing about. We saved the €9 and settled for the exercise.

We took a circuitous route back through town, stopping on the way for hot-from-the-oven croissants and baguettes at the little bakery by the church.

Back aboard Sequitur, we relaxed over a lunch of fresh croissants, chèvre, Brie and Stella Artois.

The quartered chicken pieces we had bought in Barbados had proved to be hen. We had greatly strengthened our jaw muscles with the forequarters, so I decided to do the hindquarters as coq-au-vin. While the flavour was delicious, and even if the meat did fall off the bones, the hour and a half in the Dutch oven did little to tenderize the old bird.

We spent much of a rainy day baking biscotti. Since the weather looked unsuitable for anything outside, we decided to dedicate most of the day to the project and to do six loaves. While the first three were in the oven for their first baking, Edi prepared a second trio using further combinations of chocolate, pecans, almonds, hazelnuts, raisins and dried apricots.

After baking the loaves, slicing them and then double baking the slices, over the course of about six hours we had made about twenty dozen biscotti.

After having seen no sea birds along the entire coast of Brazil, we were finally again being entertained by them here. We had pelicans, frigate birds and boobies diving for fish around the boat. Our good omen bird, a yellow-footed brown booby came and perched on the mooring buoy next to us, balancing itself with its tail feathers as the buoy bobbed and swayed in the chop. It reminded us of the boobies we have had ride our Rocna on several long passages.

Our week passed very pleasantly. We did a whole lot of very little, using the time to relax and catch-up on sleep. We also added some fresh stock to Sequitur's fridges and freezers, and Edi reorganized the food lockers. During this, she found the two huge jars of artichoke hearts that had been missing for over two years.

It was time to move on, so on Tuesday morning, the 15th of May we slipped from the buoy and continued northeast. We crossed from Iles des Saintes toward the coast of Guadeloupe motor-sailing in fickle winds, hoping once we cleared the influence of the islands the winds would fill and stabilize.

As we rounded the southwest cape of Guadeloupe, we thought we were back in Peru; the slopes looked the Inca terraces of Pisac, Ollantaytambo or Machu Picchu. On closer examination, we saw them as a mining operation.

We cut across the sea directly toward Saint Croix on a 200 mile crossing, rather than following the chain of the Antilles. The weather continued very unsettled, with frequent squalls and some longer deluges. Sunrise on Wednesday was red and angry looking and we experienced the reality of the old saw "Red sky in the morning, sailors take warning" with continuing storm cells.

On Thursday morning we entered the narrow zigzagging buoyed channel through the reefs into Christiansted, Saint Croix just as a squall hit with near-zero-visibility rain and 35-knot winds. Fortunately I had taken a good look at the route before the storm hit, and the Navionics chart on the chart-plotter was spot-on.

The rain was down to a drizzle as we secured at 1008 on the commercial wharf in Gallows Bay to clear with US Homeland Security. The processing was straightforward and professional, and it included Customs, Immigration and an agricultural inspection. Everything was quickly done in an office on the wharf side and onboard; there were no fees, there was no hassle.

Once we had cleared and hauled-down our quarantine flag, we went ashore to find a supermarket. The first people we saw to ask directions was an elderly couple, former Canadians who had moved to Saint Croix some thirty years previously. The man was just getting into their car, and said hop in; we're going there now. We found a wonderful selection in the supermarket, and among other things, bought fresh asparagus, crimini mushrooms, huge scallops and well-trimmed beef tenderloin.

We walked back and dropped off our purchases onboard, then headed into downtown to find an ATM and some US cash. We walked past crumbling infrastructure and derelict buildings reminiscent of what we had seen the past two years in South America.

There we came to the old Danish Customs House, built in 1844 and Fort Christiansvaern, dating from 1738 next to it, which have been preserved with three other nearby buildings as a US National Historic Site. These are the first well-maintained buildings that we had seen on our kilometre-or-so walk from the wharf.

While some noble old houses looked recently abandoned, other estates appeared to have been in decline for many years. This evidence of decay continued along both sides of the street, all the way into the edge of downtown.

Up King Street we passed Government House, a handsome, neoclassic structure built in 1747. Originally built as a private home, it was later acquired by the Danish to serve as one of the most elaborate Governor's Residences in the Lesser Antilles.

We found our bank machine and got our dollars, then we walked through nearly abandoned streets, past empty shops, bars, restaurants and other businesses, along a vacant waterfront boardwalk and then back through the decay lined streets to Sequitur on the Gallows Bay wharf. We asked the wharfinger about moorage alongside and were told it was $27 per day. This was rather inexpensive we thought, until we were told we had to pay for twelve hours of overnight security at $14 per hour; this took the daily fee to $195.

We were moored just inside the reef, less than half a cable from the last of the fourteen buoys and beacons that mark the route through it. Even though the wind blew strongly in the passing squalls, there was very little wave action, and we were able to relax. We decided to spend another day.

We then asked about anchoring or mooring and were told that the mooring buoys were a relatively recent addition, and they hadn't yet worked-out a price for them, so they were still free. We flashed-up and slipped from the wharf and motored out to the mooring field, where we came to a mooring in 3.8 metres of water in the calmest anchorage we have had in many weeks.

We enjoyed a leisurely breakfast in the cockpit: fresh toasted bagels from Saint Croix, delicious sharp cream cheese from Niterói, Brazil, capers from Martinique, smoked salmon from Puerto Montt, Chile and coffee from Mexico (we had finally run out of Starbucks beans). We then spent the remainder of the day relaxing and reading in the cockpit or hunkered-down below during the frequent squalls. The weather clearly showed us why the tourist season was over.

For dinner I dry seared the beef tenderloin rare and served it with gnocchi in a shallot, garlic and crimini cream sauce, a side of asparagus spears with mayonnaise and a garnish of sliced tomatoes with shaved sea salt. From Sequitur's cellar we enjoyed a superb bottle of 2006 Anakena Ona Syrah.

In the evening I seared the scallops in the pan still hot from a butter sauté of criminis, shallots and garlic and served them with asparagus with mayonnaise and sliced tomatoes. A bottle of the 2010 Montes Leyda Vineyard Sauvignon Blanc from Sequitur's cellar accompanied superbly.

We were up with the sun on Saturday morning. As we were preparing to slip from the buoy, a small wooden runabout motored by with three men and a large crayfish trap heading out for a morning set.

At 0626 we slipped and motored out through the buoyed channel in 6 to 7 knot easterly winds. The winds remained under 10 knots from near dead astern through the morning and into the afternoon, barely giving shape to the sails as we motor-sailed northeastward.

Mid-afternoon, as we were approaching Puerto Rico, a few storm cells came through from astern, but we were hit by only one squall, which dumped heavy rain for a quarter hour before scudding off.

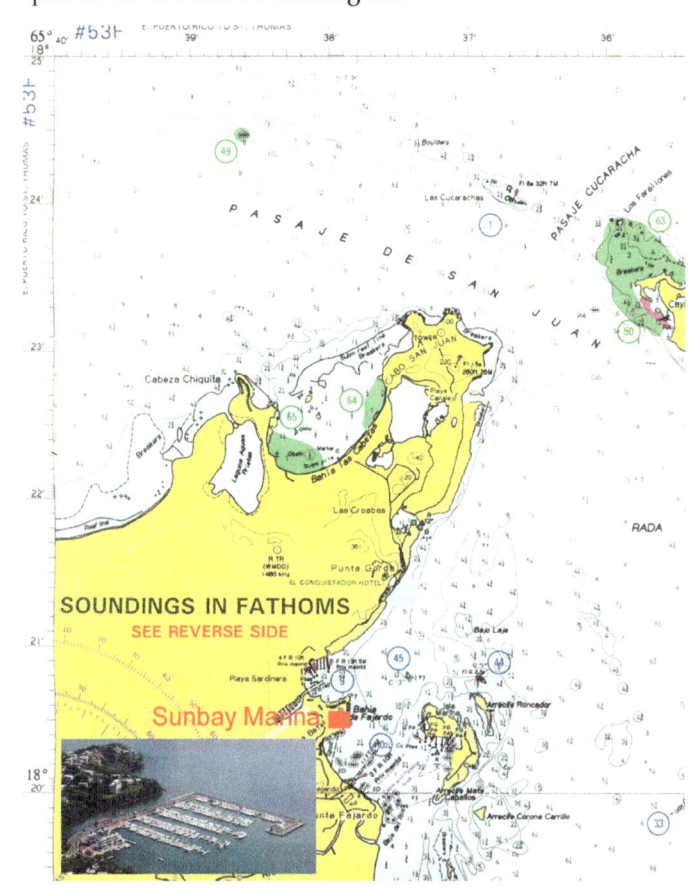

At 1718 we secured stern-to in a slip less than a metre wider than Sequitur's beam in Sun Bay Marina, Fajardo, Puerto Rico.

In the slip next to us was Ian in the Australian sloop, Misty Blue, and he took our lines and assisted us in. Once we had secured I headed up to the office to register and to have the manager contact US Homeland Security to initiate our clearing-in process.

Within half an hour, three security agents arrived onboard and went through a routine inspection and began filling-out forms. Among these was an application for a one-year US Cruising Permit at $37. I had nothing but $20s, and they scrambled for change, and I accompanied them back up the finger to their vehicle, where they issued me a cash receipt, before they drove off to their office. Shortly after 2000 one of the officers returned to Sequitur with the completed Cruising Permit and told us we could haul-down the quarantine flag. It is such a delight to again experience the ease and sanity of First-World bureaucracy.

It was very hot and humid, and we needed to keep some hatches open for ventilation. However, with the frequent rain showers and squalls, this meant rigging awnings. As a shortcut, I poked two golf umbrellas through the hatches and held them against the wind gusts with weights and bungee cords. Dewar's White Label and Moët et Chandon served well in the fore cabin.

One of the shortcomings of the US and Canada, is the lack of convenient public transit, at least compared to what we had experienced the past three years in Latin America. There is none here and we learned that taxis are very expensive. We hauled-out our folding bicycles for the first time on our voyage, pumped-up their tires, tuned them and after test rides, locked them on deck.

On Monday afternoon we pedalled up the steep hill from the marina and over a lower ridge then down to Skippers' Marine Supply, a rather large and well-stocked marine chandlery. We asked about the availability of Lewmar windlass parts. The agent quickly found what we were looking for *"on the mainland"*, the price was right, but shipping was expensive for anything quicker than a week or two. We figured we could make it to the mainland before any inexpensive package could arrive in Fajardo, so we passed.

We hopped back on our bikes and continued through a residential area filled with bland concrete bunkers, almost all of which are so grotesquely ornamented that we imagined each owner was trying to surpass their neighbours' bad taste.

After about three kilometres we came to Ralph's, a mega supermarket. Inside we found a good selection of fresh produce, including portobello mushrooms, fresh basil, green beans, roma and beefsteak tomatoes, and a full range of colours of bell peppers. We also bought turkey breast strips, boneless and skinless chicken breasts and mahi-mahi filets. Our purchases just made it into the bicycle baskets, and we slowly pedalled back, pausing for breathers on a couple of hill crests. It was early evening; the temperature was down to the low 30s, but the humidity was in the mid-90s.

We lazed and puttered onboard on Tuesday, and when it began to cool in the evening, we fired-up the oven and baked a quiche and three pizzas. One pizza we had for dinner, the other two were sliced and stowed in Lock-and-Locks in the fridge along with the quiche. They will do well for underway lunches and dinners on our three or four day passage to the Bahamas.

At 0910 on Wednesday the 23rd of May we left our slip and motored the short distance to the marina's fuel dock. There we filled our tanks, taking-on 125.02 US gallons of diesel at US$4.10 per gallon, which works out to 484.85 litres at CA$1.06 per litre. It is so good to again have the convenience of easy fuelling. At 0958 we slipped from the fuel dock and headed out.

There was a very light easterly breeze and we motor-sailed. Quickly we were in traffic as three large catamarans, each with at least two dozen partying deck passengers went motor-sailing by. One of them managed to squeak by ahead of us, while the other two took the more prudent route under our stern.

We had exchanged several emails with Eddie Breeden, Director of Customer Service at the Hunter Marine Group in Alachua, Florida. He had recommended we go to Saint Augustine Marine, which is owned by the Luhrs family, of the Luhrs Marine Group, which owns Hunter. Introductions and more emails had Sequitur scheduled for repairs and servicing beginning in early June.

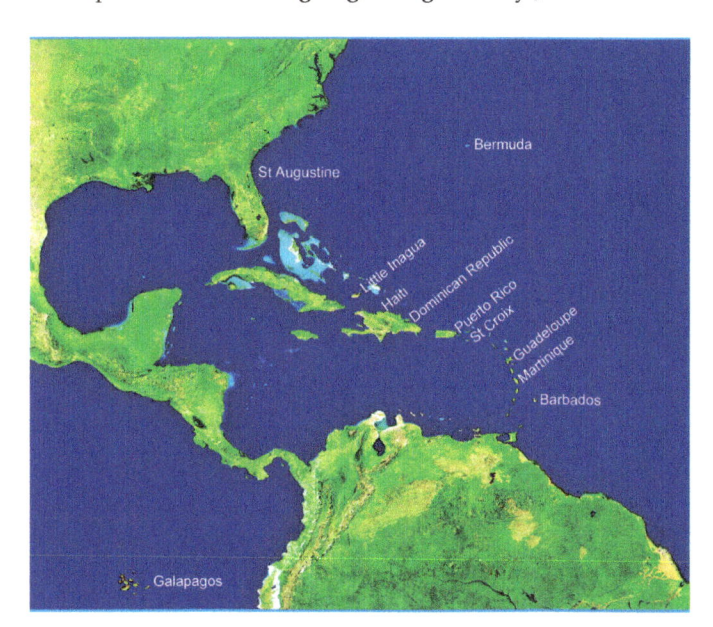

We figured the safest and least hassle-ridden route would be to avoid the Dominican Republic, Haiti, Cuba and the Turks & Caicos. The first three because of their politics and the reported rampant crime, the last because of the bureaucratic clearance hassle about which we had read. It is 470 miles to Little Inagua, the first anchorage in the Bahamas.

The wind remained either side of east through the day, mostly blowing 9 to 12 knots, so we motor-sailed. The engine at 1300 rpm aided the wind and the west-setting current in moving us along at 6 knots or slightly above. For dinner on Wednesday evening we had half of the shrimp quiche, garnished with sliced beefsteak tomatoes, sea salt and shredded fresh basil.

We had spent our first day without squalls in several weeks, nor were there any overnight. Sunrise on Thursday occurred behind a screen of cumulus, which offered a dramatic enhancement to the event. The cumulus soon dissipated and we enjoyed near cloudless skies much of the day.

After Edi had arisen from her post-watch sleep, she prepared a delicious brunch. She opened the last package of British back bacon we had bought in the Falklands and served some of it with basted eggs on toast lapped with sauce Béchamel and garnished by sliced beefsteak tomatoes and fresh basil.

Our first overnight had been crossing the Mona Passage between Puerto Rico and Hispaniola, our second overnight was past the shallows of Navidad Bank, preferring to be closer to the well-charted shoals than to the risk of unknown boats along the Dominican Republic coast. Our third overnight was well off the coast Haiti, again much rather being nearer the predictable shoal water than unpredictable coastal activity.

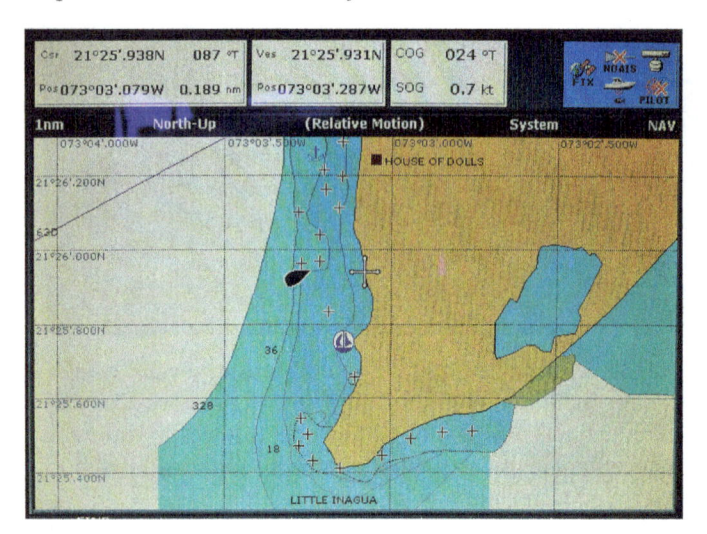

Shortly after midnight we crossed the declination of the sun as it made its way north for the solstice. At 1338 on Saturday we came to 35 metres on the Delta in 8.5 metres of water, tucked around the southwestern point of Little Inagua. We were a bit less than two cables off the beach in very clear water.

The anchorage is on a narrow band of sandy shoal less than two cables wide, with a steep drop-off into the abyss at its edge. With the clear water, we had easily seen the beginning of the shoal, and we had settled in with Sequitur's stern hanging over the edge. The anchorage provides shelter only in winds from north-northeast through south-southeast. Fortunately this is the prevailing direction and with the gentle easterly breeze, it was very comfortable. The island is very low, its highest point being lower than the top of Sequitur's mast, so it would afford only wave protection in a strong blow.

The entire island is a National Park, and it is apparently unpopulated. There is certainly no place to clear-in with the authorities, even if that had been our intention. This had been the prime factor in our choosing it for an en route break. We were claiming innocent passage through the islands with no intention of landing. We hoisted the quarantine flag and began to relax.

For dinner I sautéed mahi-mahi filets in butter with diced portobellos, shallots and garlic and served it with beans amandine, basmati rice and sliced roma tomatoes with shredded basil. We were pleased again with the quality of the 2011 Carmen Chardonnay, which continues to drink well above its price.

There was little wind, so we decided to spend another day. Sunday afternoon I prepared another quiche for en route dining, and while the oven was hot, Edi prepared three pizzas; one for dinner and two for lunches along the way.

At 0623 on Monday, with the assistance of the cockpit sheet winch, we weighed and then continued northwestward. There was a light easterly breeze, so we motor-sailed with mostly flaccid sails.

Our intention with the early departure was to sail overnight and arrive the following afternoon at the anchorage on the western side of Conception Island, about 200 miles distant. Before we had left Puerto Rico, I had marked on the iPad a selection of good anchorages along our proposed route, in case the weather turned adverse and we needed shelter.

We enjoyed a boost from the current and eventually from the wind, and we were making a consistent 6.5 knots as we rounded the Castle Island lighthouse at 1910. From there we headed northward past the west coasts of Acklins Island, Long Cay and Crooked Island.

At midnight we were abeam the southern end of Long Cay and through the night continued at or above 6 knots past the east coast of Long Island. At 0913 we crossed the Tropic of Cancer a little to the south of Rum Cay.

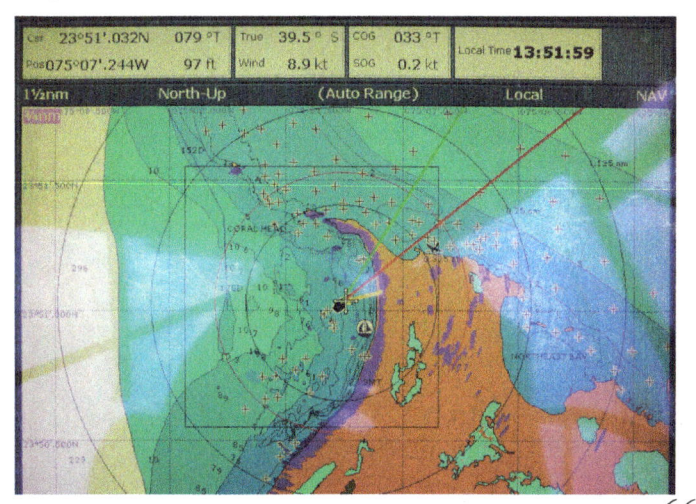

At 1343 on Tuesday the 29th of May we came to 20 metres on the Delta in 4.5 metres in the bay on the northwest side of Conception Island. We had come 198.5 miles, averaging just over 6.3 knots.

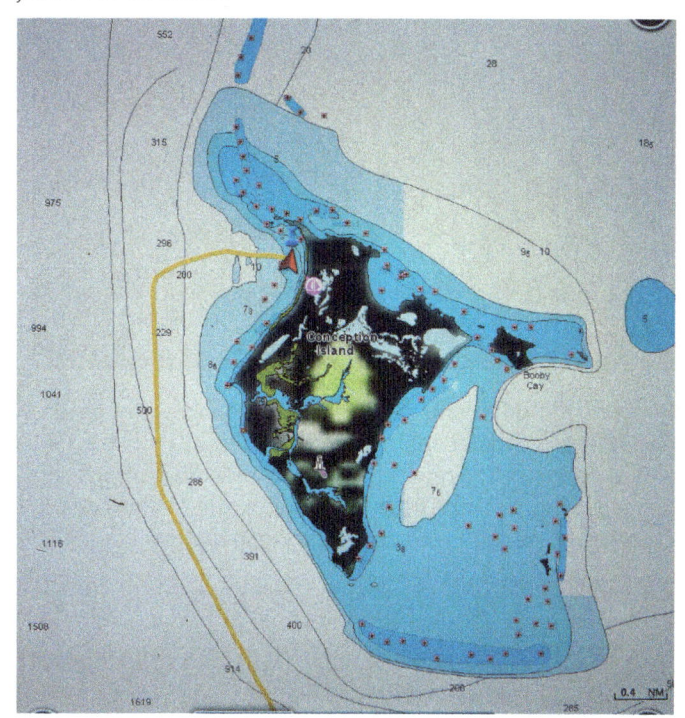

The anchorage has a rather extensive shoal area 3 to 10 metres deep, with sufficient room for several dozen boats. There are a few coral heads marked on the chart, but mostly the bay is clear of obstruction with a white sand bottom, and it appears to offer good protection from northerly, easterly and southerly winds. The island is another uninhabited National Park.

It was Edi's 65th birthday, and to help celebrate her becoming a senior, we had the last of our Puerto Eden king crab. I gently warmed it in a butter sauté of diced portobellos, shallots and garlic and served it with basmati rice and green beans amandine, garnished with beefsteak tomatoes and complemented by a bottle of Cava Segura Viudas.

663

We spent the following day relaxing aboard, enjoying the peacefulness of the anchorage and catching-up on sleep. In the evening we were rewarded with a splendid sunset; with our increasing distance from the equator, the twilights were becoming longer and the sunsets more slowly evolving.

It was glassy calm as we weighed at 0620 on Thursday morning to head out on another overnight passage. Among our potential destinations was another national park, this one on the southwest side of Great Abaco Island about 186 miles to the northwest. It remained calm through the day and overnight, with occasional ripples on the sea from a knot or two of gentle breeze. We motored with furled sails.

We continued in calm conditions through much of the day, with a gentle breeze growing in the late afternoon. This was insufficient to give shape to the sails, so we continued motoring into the sunset.

It was still calm on Friday afternoon as we passed Half Moon Bay on Little San Salvador Island. There we watched as a huge cruise ship shuttled passengers to and from their private day resort on the beach. The cruise lines use places such as this to work around the Jones Act, which prohibits foreign-flagged commercial vessels from carrying passengers or goods directly from one US port to another.

Late in the afternoon the southern and western sky began filling with taller and darker clouds, and a ripple appeared on the water.

By 1800, as we were picking our way between 1 and 2 metre patches and shoals approaching our anchorage off Cross Harbour Point, Great Abaco, a westerly wind had built to above 20 knots, with gusts into the 30s in squalls. We were hit by torrential rain and the seas began to heap. We didn't like the idea of anchoring in an open, shoal-dotted roadstead in 3 to 4 metres of water on a close lee shore in a building storm.

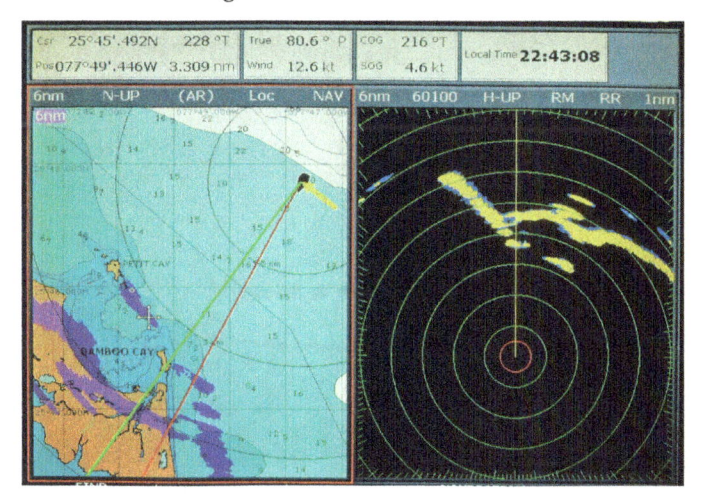

We turned and picked our way back out through the shoals and shallow patches. About 27 miles southwestward across North East Channel is a semicircular bay on Great Harbour Cay in the Berry Islands. We headed toward it and its appearance of affording protection from everything but northeasterly winds. At 2348 we came to 25 metres on the Delta in 3.1 metres of water in the southeastern quadrant of the bay.

We slept-in on Saturday morning. When we finally arose, Edi prepared a splendid international brunch with the last of our Falklands back bacon, basted eggs from Saint Croix lapped with Béchamel sauce and dotted with capers from Martinique, lightly toasted split baguette from the artisanal bakery in Les Saintes and roma tomatoes from Puerto Rico. With it we drank coffee we had bought in Callao, Peru.

At 1133 we weighed and headed out in a light breeze with just sufficient strength to fill the sails. We were bucking a slight current, which to my best guess was a branch split from the Gulf Stream by Grand Bahama. We motor-sailed, making between 5 and 6 knots into the current. Along the way we passed two cruise ships doing their passenger landings on non-US soil, so they can head to another US port.

We had a beautiful, but ominous sunset as a huge cumulonimbus cell moved in to engulf us in twisting winds and torrential rains. We continued through the evening with staysail and deeply reefed main, motor-sailing in westerly winds, mostly 10 to 12 knots, but well above 30 in the frequent squalls.

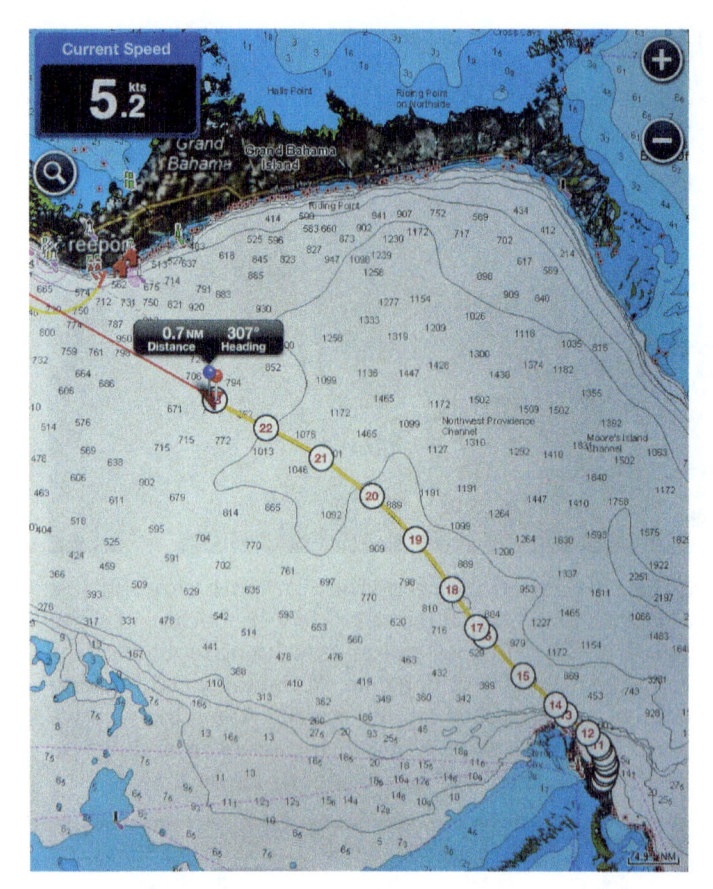

We motor-sailed as close to the wind as possible, but the current contrived to push us on a track east of our making the western edge of Grand Bahama. In the early evening the current finally allowed our course to begin bending more to the west, and by 2000, we were making good a track to clear the island. By midnight the current had increased to reduce our headway to under 4 knots, and then, even with turns for 7 knots and sails pulling, we were slowed to near 3 through the small hours.

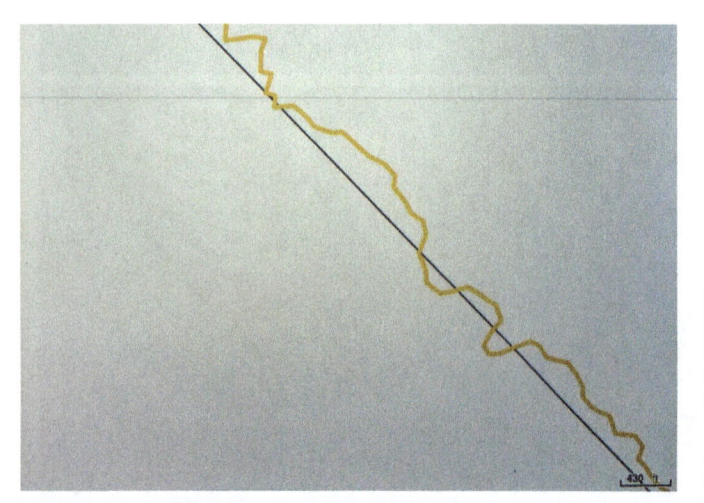

Throughout the day the plotted position from our GPS had been jumping 100 metres and more; the normal 5 or 6 metre accuracy on both our chartplotter and iPad was gone. Since it was happening on both of our systems, each from a separate GPS antenna, we ruled-out it being a local system problem. We suspected the United States, perceiving an increased security threat, had decided to reapply the Selective Availability function.

By sunrise our speed was under 4 knots in a counter-current, and our main fuel tank gauge was bouncing around one-eighth. At 0730 we were still under 4 knots and quickly burning fuel trying to make progress into the current. The Navionics chart on my iPad showed a fuel dock at the Old Bahama Bay Marina at West End, Grand Bahama, only 6 miles to our northeast. I headed in and at 0855 we secured to a wharf.

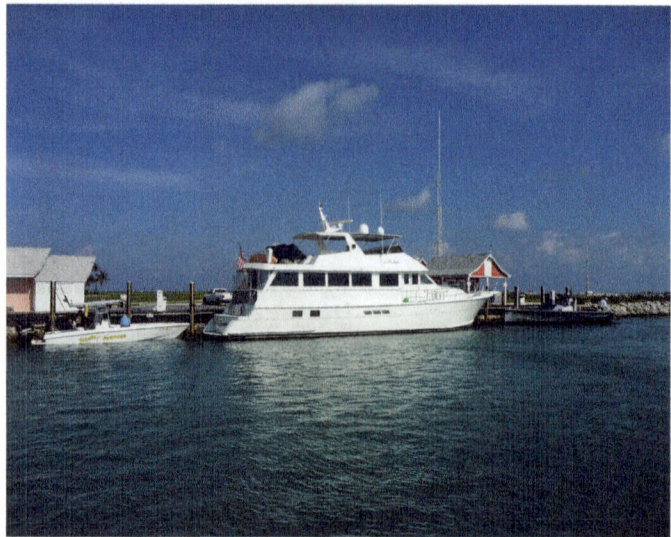

There was a line-up ahead of us waiting for the 0900 opening of the fuelling station. While we waited, I tried again to transfer fuel from the auxiliary tank. I had earlier attempted this, but although the pump made its whirring sound, there was no movement on either the auxiliary or the main fuel gauges. Again, I got the same results; it appeared the pump had clogged and needed cleaning, but this could wait.

Because we had touched land in the Bahamas, we had to clear Customs and Immigration, and we needed to do this before being allowed to fuel. Fortunately, there is a Customs office next to the fuel dock. Unfortunately, there is a $300 fee for a mandatory cruising permit. Fortunately, it is valid for a year from date of issue. The clearance process was quick and simple; one officer covering Customs, Immigration and Health. We then took on 113 US gallons (427.75 litres) at about $1.41 per litre. At 1025 we slipped and continued northward.

666

Because we had not planned cruising this area, I had no charts of the direction and rates of the currents, and instead, I had to try to figure-out their pattern. The wind was northwest, and the starboard tack gave us a southerly component. At 1300 I tacked, but the wind and current conspired to force us toward the shoals to our north. At 1500 I tacked again, and gradually as we made our way westward, the current began bending our course slightly northward. By 1800 we were making 7 knots, directly toward Saint Augustine just under 200 miles away. By 2000 we were touching 9 knots.

We had another spectacular sunset as we enjoyed more of the slices from the pizzas Edi had made in our anchorage at Little Inagua and frozen. She reheated them in a covered frying pan, which crisped the crust and steam-heated the toppings.

There was a steady parade of shipping as we progressed up the coast of Florida. Many were cruise ships parading slowly between ports to stretch the passengers' onboard experience. Among the other vessels we saw were bulk carriers, likely tankers carrying crude to a refinery or refined product to a market. Most passed visible on radar only or just peeking above the horizon, but some came within a few cables.

As we moved across the main axis of the Gulf Stream, our progress slowed, and by mid morning on Monday it became obvious that even with a strong push from the engine, we would not make Saint Augustine before sunset. I phoned Saint Augustine Marine on the satellite phone and asked about entering after dark, and they advised against it. There is ongoing dredging in the channel and there are temporary unlit buoys. I slowed the engine and calculated a course and speed to take us overnight to arrive at the entrance to the channel an hour before high water slack on Tuesday morning.

Overnight we were hit by a frontal system with thunderstorms and 25 to 30 knot winds. At 0830 we arrived at the entrance A buoy and tried to decipher a route in past the dredge and barge, which we assumed were in the channel. We had seen two sport-fishing skiffs come out between them, so I decided the channel lay there. Wrong! About a cable out we got 5 short blasts from the dredge: *"You are standing into danger"*. The dredge then came up on Ch 16 and advised that the channel lay close to the north of the small barge. Once we were past the dredge and barge we spotted small temporary red and green buoys nearly lost on the horizon among the background of the shoreline. We are glad we had chosen not to enter in the dark.

On the tail end of the flood tide we motored through the inlet and into the Intracoastal Waterway. Blocking our passage was the Bridge of Lions, which has a charted vertical clearance of 25 feet (7.6 metres). The centre span has a bascule opening, and with Sequitur's 21 metre mast height, I deemed it prudent to wait for the next scheduled opening of the bridge, due at 0930. During the ten minute wait for the bridge, we sculled in the current just off the anchorages that I had marked in case we had decided to come in overnight.

At 1014 on Monday the 4th of June we secured alongside the south float at Saint Augustine Marine. We had come 9375 miles from Puerto Montt, Chile in a little under six months with 47 anchorages and ports and 111 days at sea. Sequitur, our Hunter 49 had safely and comfortably brought us through one Force 12 storm, three Force 11s and several Force 10s and 9s. We had bucked adverse winds, currents and bureaucracies. In the three years since we left Vancouver on our shakedown cruise, we had made 20,044 miles. Both we and Sequitur were in need of a refit.

38. Refit and Reorganization

We were met on the float by Peter, the Customer Service Manager and Jim, the Yard Manager, and I quickly reviewed with them the list that I had emailed to them from Puerto Rico, which outlined the work we required. We were told it would be a few days before any work could begin, but that we would not be charged for moorage while we are waiting, nor during contracted work. What a refreshing idea!

The modern 9.3 Hectare waterfront site was established in 1993 by the Luhrs family to provide repair and maintenance for their own brands: Hunter, Luhrs, Mainship and Silverton, as well as other boats.

After we had settled-in, we walked ashore through the old town. The city was established in 1565, and is considered to be the oldest continuously occupied community in the continental United States of America. Even with all the modifiers to its title as the oldest, there are no surviving buildings from the early period. No wooden buildings survived the British burning of the city in 1702. The oldest remaining house is believed to have been built at the end of the sixteenth or early in the seventeenth century.

The oldest wooden school house in the US is here, and it first appears in the records in 1716. It sits nestled among other buildings of a similar age along St George Street, although many of these are reconstructions of destroyed structures.

We walked along to Castillo de San Marcos, which is titled as the oldest masonry fort in the United States of America. It was begun in 1672 and completed in 1695 using a locally quarried stone called coquina, which consists of ancient shells bonded together into a coarse limestone. One of the benefits of the coquina is that it is soft enough to absorb offensive cannonballs without shattering the structure. The fort was never taken by force despite multiple periods of attack. There are records of cannonballs being harvested for reuse from the exterior walls after attacks.

We saw many cannon ball holes in the walls along the seaward side.

A rather stagnant and pungent saltwater slew called Maria Sanchez Lake cuts into the southern part of the old city. We walked around it through an area of upscale houses, estates and mansions. From the grandeur of some of the estates, it appears that waterfront is waterfront regardless of its aroma.

We continued on to Sailor's Exchange, a wonderful big shop full of new and used, but mostly used boat parts. Almost immediately I spotted a used windlass that appeared complete and in good condition. It had Lewmar above-deck components, which looked to me to be identical to those installed in Sequitur.

The motor was different; a 1200w 12v Mako, instead of the Sequitur's 1000w 12v Cima. However; in my earlier research on replacing or repairing our windlass, I had determined that our existing wiring could easily handle a 1200w load. The price was $700, rather lower than quotes of $3023 plus shipping from the States to Uruguay, or the $3100 plus shipping to Puerto Rico. I took measurements and photos and gave the manager a $20 deposit to hold it for three days so I could make sure it was the way to go.

From Sailor's Exchange we continued on to the Winn-Dixie supermarket to buy some fresh produce and other essentials. Sequitur's fridges, freezers and pantry were rather depleted. We found a nice selection, including wonderful crimini mushrooms, roma tomatoes, fine green beans, asparagus, baby zucchini and shallots.

In the evening we enjoyed pangasius fillets sautéed in butter and slivered garlic served with grilled potato coins and steamed asparagus.

The following morning I priced a new gearbox and other parts needed to repair our existing windlass. With our discount through the Marine Centre's storeroom, I calculated the repair would be slightly more expensive than the used replacement, so I decided to go with the used windlass. The upgrade to 1200 Watts will better handle the 40 kilogram Rocna, and it is very likely that the used unit has been through many fewer anchorages than we put Sequitur's through. The replacement windlass fit perfectly and in post-installation trials, it worked flawlessly.

It was the rainy season, and we had daily humidity buildups culminating in heavy thunderstorms in the late afternoons and evenings. The daily temperatures remained very stable, hovering a few degrees either side of 30° and the humidity seemed always near saturation. It was well over a week before we had a rainless day.

Just over a week into our stay, Dave the electronics and electrical whiz came aboard to diagnose the problem with our Raymarine chartplotter. On 16 December, one week out of Puerto Montt, it had begun randomly shutting down and rebooting, and in the process resetting the system to factory defaults. This gave us chart soundings in feet rather than metres, time in AM/PM instead of a 24 hour clock and other similar US-centric units.

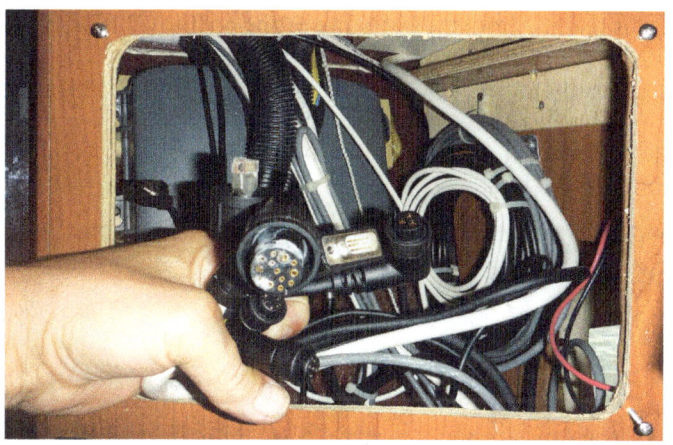

I had thought it was a software problem. Dave quickly found it to be hardware-related.

The radar input cable in the back of the master unit at the nav station was badly corroded. Everything else in the space was dry and dusty. On finding the corroded fitting, his first words were: *"It looks like this cable has been dropped into saltwater"*. The system had been installed by Specialty Yachts in Vancouver. Dave removed the chartplotter and had it sent to Raymarine to replace the corroded socket. At the same time he ordered a new radar cable.

Among the items I had authorized on the work-order was up to two hours to investigate a freshwater leak, which since our fit-out in Vancouver has been slowly draining our water tanks into the bilges. The service Manager at Specialty Yachts had dismissed this as condensation. The water flowed into the central bilge through the after limber hole, so my many sporadic and unsuccessful attempts to find the leak had concentrated on the plumbing aft of the bilge. This included the supplies to the galley sinks, the aft head toilet, sink and shower, the washer-dryer, the cockpit shower and the shore water connection.

However, before the work could be scheduled in St Augustine, while Edi was four layers down into the compartments below the salon seats cleaning and rearranging stowage spaces, she found water.

It was seeping from the hot water fitting on the water heater. The last two items of work done on the water heater were at Specialty Yachts in Vancouver during the installation of the water-heater feature of the Espar furnace and during the installation of the wind generator's overload power dump to the tank.

St Augustine Marine's mechanical whiz, Mark removed the fitting and we quickly saw that its threads had been damaged, and there was evidence of an attempt fix it with putty. Within minutes, Mark had replaced the faulty fitting with a new one, with its threads properly wrapped in Teflon tape. We no longer have a freshwater leak.

We continued to be amazed at the shoddy work that had been performed during Sequitur's fit-out in Vancouver. For three years its results had cramped our style, hampered our comfort and compromised our safety.

On Thursday the 21st of June we were hauled-out to inspect the hull, replace the zincs, repaint the bottom and clean, wax and polish the topsides.

We were pleased with how well the anti-fouling had held. Except for where the side of the keel had rubbed against the shoal during our grounding in Caleta Olla, the paint was nearly intact. Our grounding in January had been so gentle that my thought at the time was that the worst damage would be some paint being scraped off the side of Sequitur's keel. Our out of water examination proved this true.

The zincs had lasted well also, the one on the VariProp having about one-third remaining. This was better than I had expected with all the stray current that we suspected was alongside Micalvi in Puerto Williams and on the wharf at AFASyN in Ushuaia.

Among the accepted things in sailing is that sailboat hatches leak. We have been extremely fortunate in Sequitur not having any leaky hatches. Contributing to this is our diligence in servicing the gaskets and keeping the dogs properly adjusted. However, after many deep sluices of breaking waves over her decks in Force 12 and Force 11 storms, we noticed a small dribble from the port hatch in the fore cabin. We dug into the ceiling above our berth and found the area dry, but with evidence of some slight seepage through the hatch bedding. The starboard hatch looked fine, but we decided that while we were at it, we would have both hatches re-bedded.

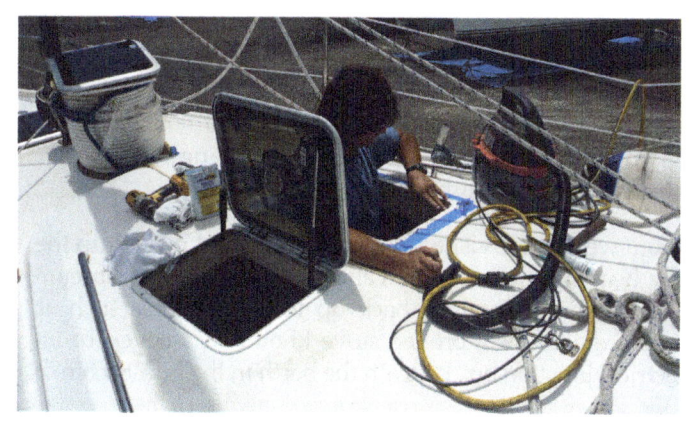

We had been getting up early because the workers start at 0700, but on Saturday morning, with no workers coming aboard, we slept-in. When we finally did get up, Edi prepared a delicious pain perdu slathered with Hollandaise and sprinkled with sautéed button mushrooms. With it we enjoyed coffee from the last of the stock we had laid-in before entering Mexico in 2009.

We spent the remainder of Saturday onboard, cleaning and doing some maintenance, but mostly relaxing and enjoying the wifi signal from the marina. It remained rather clear through the afternoon and into the evening with no thunderstorms and it was sufficiently clear at sunset to offer a rather pretty scene from the cockpit.

Edi had organized two loaner bicycles through Peggy at the reception desk in the Marine Centre. They were retro models: one-speed with balloon tires and pedal brakes. On Sunday afternoon we pedalled to Winn-Dixie for another round of grocery shopping. The cooler bags, held in place with bungee cords, balanced nicely on the rear carriers and a ten-pack of Stella Artois cans fit securely in one of the front baskets. We made it back to Sequitur with our stash just before the beginning of a heavy rainstorm and rapidly increasing winds.

Tropical Storm Debby was moving very slowly through the Gulf of Mexico some 275 miles southwest of us and we were likely feeling the effect of its spirals. Through Sunday evening the wind built to 40 knots and heavy rain continued.

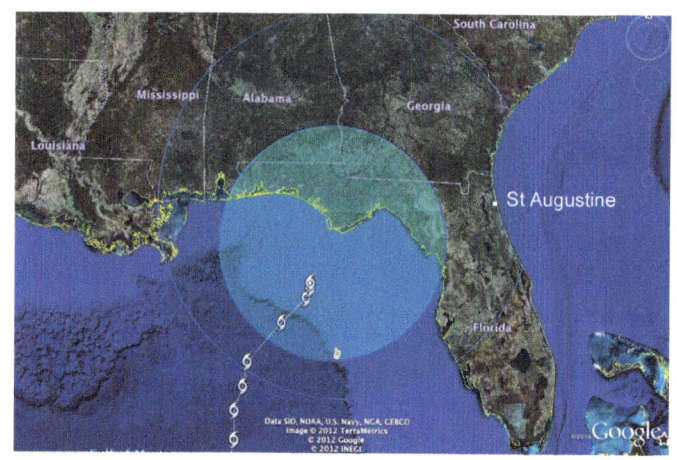

The winds had decreased and the rain slowed by the time we got up at 0650 for the workers at 0700. At 0800 on Monday NOAA showed Tropical Storm Debby near stationary 245 miles west-southwest of St Augustine. Its three-day and five-day cones of probability were nearly concentric circles centred on the current position, indicating that the storm could move in any direction.

During a lull in the rain on Monday afternoon, Jay and Bobby came and acid-washed the boat, removing stains and build-up and preparing it for polishing, waxing and buffing.

673

At 0700 on Tuesday, Burt from the Canvas & Upholstery Centre knocked on the hull and came aboard to remove our cockpit enclosure canvas. After five years and many storms it needed re-waterproofing and some minor restitching. Also we needed to replace two isinglass panels in the dodger. The sailmaker in La Punta, Peru had had only enough to do the central panel.

The Canvas & Upholstery Centre's loft is in a huge room above the offices of the Marine Centre. Hunt Bowman and his wife Judy own the company, and they also own SouthEast Sailing & Yachts, the Hunter dealer for the region. Hunt runs this and its associated used boat brokerage from offices in the canvas shop, and he had invited us to drive to Alachua with him to visit the Hunter factory.

At the Hunter factory I was able to put faces to the names of people with whom I had corresponded over the past few years. After numerous exchanged emails, I was delighted to finally meet Eddie Breeden, the Customer Service Manager, and we shared a lively banter before he was forced back to work. We did a casual tour of the facilities, with Hunt showing us around, and among other things, we examined a series of Hunter 33s being assembled on the line.

I had previously visited the factory in November 2006 when Sequitur was in the moulds, and again in January 2007 when she was nearing the end of the production line. We learned that 102 Hunter 49s were built before they renamed it the Hunter 50 in 2011. With a length of 49'-11", 50 is closer to the truth.

Before we left, we visited the stock room and picked-up the new headliner for our fore cabin, as well as a few obscure pieces to bring Sequitur back up to snuff, pieces such as a replacement for a broken stove knob and a cover for an electrical junction box beneath the berth in the guest cabin.

We arrived back at the yard in St Augustine mid-afternoon to find Jay and Bobby nearly finished polishing, waxing and buffing the topsides. The cockpit looked strange without the canvas, and I saw that during rains we would have to close the companionway and the four small hatches under awnings. Heat, high humidity and no ventilation are not good companions to comfort. Within minutes of our opening-up the boat, it began raining. Between the heavier downpours, I went out in the rain and blustery winds in my bathing suit and rigged a tarp over the boom so that we could keep at least the companionway and a couple of the small hatches open.

At 1800 on Tuesday, Tropical Storm Debby was 160 miles to the west-southwest and moving almost directly toward us in St Augustine. We could see the headlines: *"Debby Does St Augustine."* Through the remainder of the afternoon and the evening it rained heavily with winds in the mid-30 knot area with gusts into the 40s. We remained snug and dry, though with the added noise of the tarp rattling in the winds. It was raining heavily and blowing a gale when we went to bed at midnight.

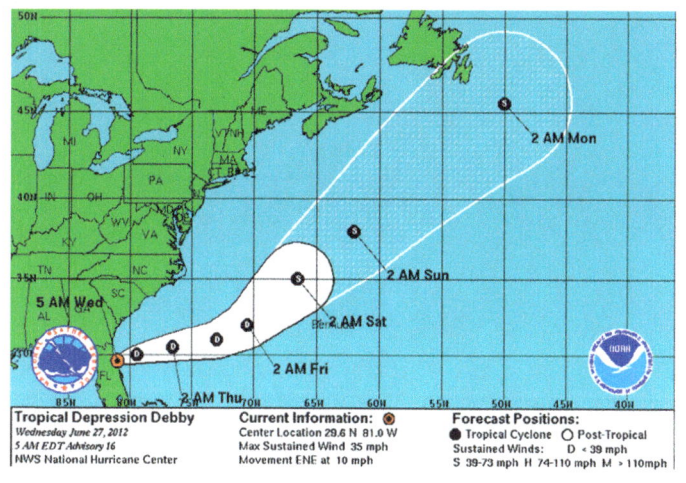

The 0500 Wednesday NOAA report showed Debby to be 22 nautical miles southeast of St Augustine and tracking directly toward us at 9 knots. This put the eye of the depression directly over us at 0730. We were pleased that the system had weakened and had been downgraded to a Tropical Depression.

During the lull as the eye passed over, Jay and Bobby finished cleaning, waxing and polishing the deck, and then began a thorough hosing-down and buffing. Items on the list of outstanding work were quickly scratched off, and at the end of June there were none left.

We were impressed by the expertise and efficiency of the workers and by the quality of the work they did. The boat was brought to the best condition she has ever been in. All the shoddy work, the errors and the glitches from her fit-out at Specialty Yachts in Vancouver had been resolved. Sequitur looked new again.

With the contracted work completed, Sequitur was moved by travel lift from the work yard to the dry storage area. After Tropical Storm Debbie had passed over, the weather had improved dramatically; it remained clear and hot for the remainder of our time in St Augustine. Too hot, in fact, with highs in the mid 30s and humidity well into the 90s.

I had arranged a hurricane stake-down procedure with the Marine Centre and had reorganized the insurance coverage from offshore cruising to dry storage at the edge of the hurricane zone.

Then Edi and I paused to think. It was exactly six years since I had ordered Sequitur, and within a week of five years since I had taken possession. For four years Edi and I had enjoyed many superb adventures in Sequitur as she safely and confidently took us in grand comfort and style to some very remote and wild corners of the planet.

I would be turning sixty-eight later in the summer and Edi's first old age security deposit had just arrived in her bank account. We thought that it was time for some more gentle boating. As a part of our change in direction, we listed Sequitur for sale.

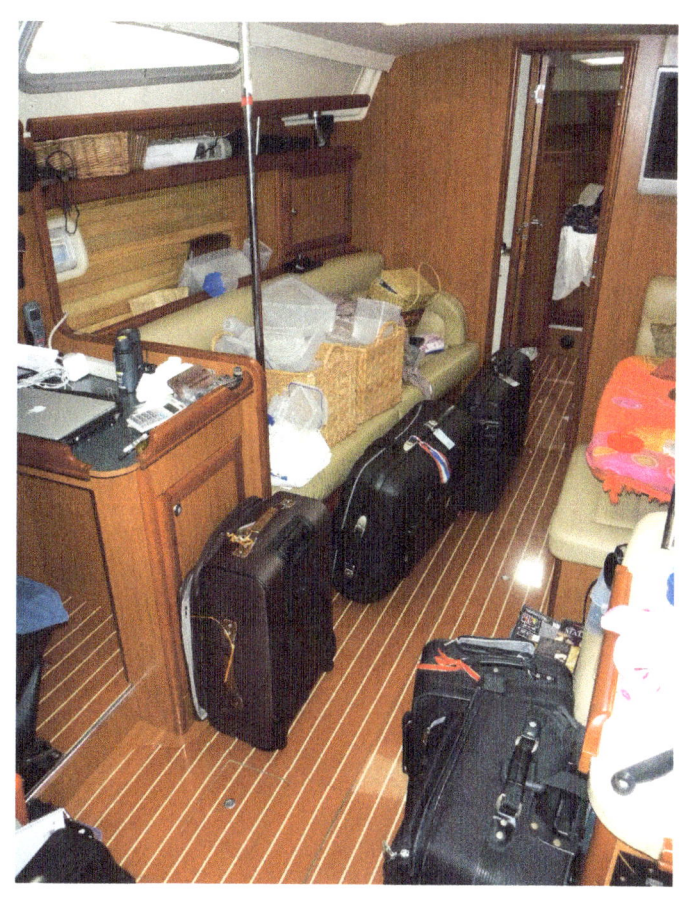

As the list of refit jobs had shrunk, Edi and I had begun the long process of packing-up from five years of living in Sequitur. Her interior became more chaotic and messy as we went, and we had to remind ourselves quite often that the chaos was a necessary step in the packing-up and cleaning-out process. We wanted her to be neat, clean and ready for her new owners to move in.

We packed our belongings into eight 23-kilo bags and four 10-kilo carry-ons, balancing and distributing the volume and weight, the tough and the fragile with the assistance of a brass 25-kilo fisherman's scale.

On Thursday the 5th of July, Hunt, our broker drove us and our twelve bags to the airport in Orlando, where we were relieved to see that our little fish scale had been very accurate. We caught a flight to Montreal and connected to Vancouver, where we arrived in the early evening, tired, beat-up and thoroughly drained emotionally from having left our dear Sequitur behind.

675

We rattled around in our loft in Vancouver, disoriented and restless. We were still addicted to boating. We were suffering from withdrawal symptoms. We spent a steadily increasing amount of time on the internet, searching, reading, researching and dreaming. We had realizing we were both approaching our best-before-dates for the type of cruising we had been doing and we had decided to look at a more sedate and gentle style of boating.

By Monday we knew we needed to take action, so we booked flights, rented a car and reserved an apartment. Shortly after sunrise on Thursday, after less than a week in Vancouver, we were rolling our carry-on bags toward the SkyTrain for a trip to the airport.

...but that's another story.

Sequitur by the Numbers

Length Overall - 15.21 metres
Hull Length - 14.58 metres
Waterline Length - 13.36 metres
Beam - 4.47 metres
Design Draft - 2.13 metres
Loaded Draft - 2.21 metres
Design Displacement - 14,884 kilograms
Loaded Displacement - 17,500 kilograms
Ballast - 5,087 kilograms
Mast Height - 20.9 metres
Sail Area - 131.3 square metres
Fuel Capacity - 840 litres
Water Tank Capacity - 485 litres
Holding Tank Capacity - 197 litres
Water Heater - 42 litres
Engine Yanmar 4JH4-HTE - 82.5 kilowatts
CE Category - A

Nautical Miles Logged - 20,044
Countries Visited - 16
Days at Sea - 253
Ports and Anchorages - 247
Strongest Williwaw Seen - 95 knots
Force 12 Hurricanes - 1
Force 11 Storms - 3
Force 10 Winds - too many to count
Tsunamis - 2

Loaves of Bread Baked - 120
Bagels Baked - 40 dozen
Biscotti Baked - 30 dozen
Bottles of Wine Consumed - 480
Crystal Stemware Breakage - 1 hollow-stem Champagne
Tableware Breakage - 3 dinner plates, 1 candle holder
Gourmet Meals Enjoyed - many hundreds
Superb Adventures - countless

CPSIA information can be obtained at www.ICGtesting.com
Printed in the USA
BVOW10s1313141013

333465BV00016B/11/P

9 780991 955602